# THE ECONOMICS OF TASTE

GERALD REITLINGER

# THE ECONOMICS OF TASTE

The Rise and Fall of
Picture Prices 1760–1960

Volume III

HACKER ART BOOKS
*New York*
1982

First published 1970 by
Barrie & Rockliff (Barrie Books Ltd.) London
© 1970 Gerald Reitlinger

Reissued 1982 by
Hacker Art Books, Inc. New York

Library of Congress Catalogue Card Number 82-80311
International Standard Book Numbers: Set 0-87817-288-2
Vol. 1 0-87817-292-0, vol. 2 0-87817-293-7
Vol. 3 0-87817-294-7

*Printed in the United States of America*

# CONTENTS

## PART I
### PAINTINGS AND DRAWINGS
arranged alphabetically under artists, with sections on the
following schools:

## PART II
### SALES ANALYSIS OF SCULPTURE

v

## PART III
### OBJETS D'ART

CONTENTS

# EXPLANATORY NOTE

In the narrative part of the first two volumes of *The Economics of Taste*
I attempted to record the movements of taste over the past two centuries as mirrored in the salerooms. Certain auction sales or private
transactions could then be treated in strict sequence as historical events
and their repercussions could be followed. But in a supplementary
volume, restricted to a period of ten years, the historical method is no
longer applicable. In fact Part One, the narrative section, has been
omitted altogether. An elementary acquaintance with the sales of the
1960s should show why this decision was necessary, for 'record-breaking' sales may provide exciting reading at the moment when they
occur, but as chronicles of the past they are of little permanent interest,
while in periods of continuing inflation they are of no interest at all. On
April 23rd, 1968, for instance, Sotheby's sold seven Picassos in succession
for £427,000. The evening was made the occasion for the first colour
television recording of an English art sale, moving the commentator to
the highest flights of oratory. 'Probably no artist in his lifetime has
acquired the eminence, the stature, the wealth. He has transcended the
need for money.' It sounded almost like *Adonais*

> He has outsoared the shadow of our night;
> Envy and calumny and hate and pain,
> And that unrest which men miscall delight
> Can touch him not nor torture him again.

And in the morning the newspapers responded faultlessly. And yet,
does anyone remember that evening at all, except for the very few who
are concerned in the buying and selling of Picasso? For no new movement of taste had been brought to the surface. The big drum had been
beating for Picasso for more than half a century, and no one expected
it to do otherwise.

Not that the salerooms in the 1960s were devoid of novelty. Almost
overnight one would find that model steam engines, Victorian Staffordshire figures, Russian ballet paraphernalia, Art Nouveau objects or
Chinese snuff bottles had become the sole subject of the most expensive
catalogues with the clearest indications of still more promotions to

commissioned rank yet to come; areas ripe for development, if one may borrow the passionate lyrical tongue of local government. But against the vast historical background of the art market these were but movements within movements and some of them hardly worthy of discussion, though they might provide amusement if accompanied with a strong dose of *Ecclesiastes*. To dovetail them into two centuries of the history of taste, together with an inordinate number of promotions of very minor painters, would involve a quite superfluous rewriting of much that was contained in the first two volumes.

In Volume One the chronological lists of prices for individual painters were preceded by short introductions. An expansion of this method seemed to me preferable to a long historical disquisition, while at the same time giving Volume Three the character of a work which could be consulted independently of its predecessors. In these introductions there will therefore be found a great many comparative prices from the past, and for this purpose use of the first two volumes has been made in order not to force on the reader the necessity of consulting them. To sum up the situation, the introductions to the chronological lists which supplemented the narrative section of Volume One, are no longer an appendix. In Volume Three they have become the main gist of the work.

The decision to follow this method has encountered a certain number of problems. Not the least has been that of the sometimes astonishing prices, paid for the work of painters, both of the past and the present day, who were quite obscure and even unknown in the previous decade. Manifestly not all are worthy of an individual introduction. In some cases they have achieved sudden fame from the sale of a single expensive picture. Such sudden explosions of enthusiasm can only be explained in terms of groups or schools. Lists embracing collective groups or schools were used in Volume One in the case of the lesser Italian, French, Flemish and German primitive painters, lesser painters of the 16th century Venetian and Flemish schools, and also in the case of English painters of sporting subjects. I have therefore added in Volume Three twelve new lists, but, wherever possible, individual painters have been separated, each in his sub-section. This method, however, is not feasible in the case of the multitude of named or designated painters of the primitive schools.

Following this method, the sales analysis of artists opens in Volume Three with two school-lists for the prices of abstract or half-abstract paintings, the one European, the other American. Here are 36 heroes of the saleroom, possibly ephemeral, but all of them capable of reaching the

£3,000 mark, corresponding to £600 in pre-war days. But Braque and Picasso, the only abstract painters in the sales analysis section of Volume One, continue to receive separate introductions, and these have also been accorded to several abstract or partly abstract painters who were not in Volume One at all, but who had entered the £3,000 – £50,000 class by the end of the decade. The painters are Juan Gris, Kandinsky, Paul Klee, Fernand Léger, Jean Miró and de Stael.

After abstract painters come American painters of the 19th–20th centuries, a patriotic market for wholly realistic pictures which reached quite unpredictable proportions during the decade. The next collective list, that of lesser Dutch painters of the 17th–18th centuries, is supplementary to the individual lists for Dutch painters as given in Volume One. They are only 'lesser' in the sense that their market rating was lower during the earlier period. In fact the 1960s saw several prices in the £50,000 to £100,000 region attached to somewhat unfamiliar names. But, in spite of promotions of this kind which took place almost overnight, the field by its very nature was not one that lent itself to *extravaganza*. The same cannot be said for three new collective lists which illustrate the market for English pictures. This has always been a more emotional affair. In a section of Volume One, entitled *The Return of the 18th Century*, I have attempted to analyse the extraordinary demand for English 18th century portraits which lasted from the 1850s to the collapse of the 'Duveen market' in the 1930s. This demand was restricted to a mere half dozen 'household names'. The new 18th century school-list of 14 artists includes five portraitists whom the Duveen market ignored almost completely, yet all of them in the 1960s could make the price of a moderately good Reynolds or even a Gainsborough. There are totally separate introductions in the case of Lely and Samuel Scott. Their new market status seemed to merit it.

The new list of lesser 19th century English painters supplements the list of painters of sporting pictures, which has been planned on a more generous scale in view of the much increased popularity of such works in the 1960s. The decidedly pedestrian works of Ladell, Shayer, Stark and Frederick William Watts are on a much lower plane than 19th century coaching and hunting pictures by Ansdell, Ferneley, Herring and Pollard at £20,000 to £35,000. But, though they counted for very little in their own day, they were dearer in the 1960s than those of such eminent Victorians as Landseer, Leighton and Alma Tadema. They could be dearer too than anything by Rossetti or Burne Jones. As to the list of the 20th century British school, it serves mainly to show that patriotic connoisseurship is much less reckless in this country, than it is in France, Germany, America and even Italy. The exception (discounting the dual nationality of Sargent) is the wholly inaesthetic Sir Alfred Munnings, the most expensive English painter of the century. He was not high enough rated in 1960 to merit a place in Volume One, but he gets a list and an introduction to himself in Volume Three.

A school-list of lesser French painters of the Louis XIV age and the 18th century owes its inception to the dramatic rise of Largillierre in 1963. This seemed to call for some further research into the *private* prices, paid when the *dix-huitième* fashion was at its height on the international Paris market. As a result, the whole picture of this market, as presented in Volume One mainly from the prices paid in the London salerooms, appeared much understated. I have therefore taken the prices of 18th century French pictures back to the region of 1900 in the case of David, Fragonard, Nattier, Pater, Hubert Robert and Watteau. Among the French painters, presented as a group, will be found the names of Boilly, Drouais, Largillierre, Oudry and St Aubin. Two lists on the same lines comprise 17th and 18th century Italian painters, and these include the names of Castiglione and Guercino, of Batoni, Joli, Longhi, Magnasco, Panini, Piazzetta and the Riccis. As an acknowledged painter of the English school now much in fashion, Zuccarelli seemed to merit an introduction on his own.

A further school-list of French painters embraces the minor Impressionists and Post-Impressionists, a market which only became worthy of notice in the later 1960s after the few remaining respectable works of the original Impressionists had soared beyond the reach of all save governments and multi-millionaires. Here will be found the absurdly overrated Henri Edmond Cross, but Mary Cassatt, Jongkind, Berthe Morisot and Odilon Redon receive the accolade of separate introductions. A fairly extensive school-list of the German-based *Expressionist* painters is something that should have featured in Volume One. It was omitted because in 1960 it was far less easy than in 1970 to perceive how far the Judgment of Paris had lost its dominion over buyers of modern art. Moreover, within the scope of Volume One all schools of patronage had to be viewed against the background of the history of taste. The fate of values which were already old and firmly established 200 years ago was of greater importance than new fashions which seemed to be bobbing up, left, right and centre, at the moment of going to press. But, of course, a volume devoted entirely to the price movements of the 1960s, must view these fashions differently. Thus the whole policy towards the Impressionist and later schools had to be reviewed. To take one instance, the list for Titian in Volume One covered

174 years and occupied three pages. The list for Picasso, covering forty years, occupied barely a page, only 8 entries exceeding the £20,000 mark. For the 1960s there are more than 50 such entries for Picasso among hundreds of lesser transactions. On the other hand the number of supposed Titians, sold in these ten years, comprises six paintings in all, two of which may be authentic.

This was typical of the art market as a whole. Except during the public holidays and the summer recess, there was probably at least one sale of old master paintings of a sort in one of the art centres of the world every day of the year. Of Impressionist and later paintings for the high class market, paintings costing £10,000 and more, there were at most a dozen to twenty sales in a year in Europe, America and Japan. Yet these sales produced enough modern pictures at this price-level to outnumber the old masters by perhaps five to one, so that to the newspaper reader modern picture sales and record-breaking sales became synonymous. Of course the situation existed already in 1960, but, viewed against the historical background of Volume One, it was only the symptom of a period and possibly a very brief one. In 1970 one has to consider that this period has lasted 18 years and that there is not the slightest indication of its ending. So in Volume Three the moderns get a bigger proportion of the space, while to repair some of the omissions of Volume One the price-history is taken back to the year 1900 or as far as one can go. Among the revisions of the lists in Volume One I have included such earlier 19th century French painters as Delacroix, Géricault, Théodore Rousseau, Courbet, Millet and Daumier.

In Volume One the post-Cézanne generation of painters was represented in the price analysis only by Braque, Chagall, Modigliani, Matisse, Picasso, Rouault and Soutine. As to Derain, van Dongen and Vlaminck, they appeared to make very little headway even in the 1950s against a market, apparently obsessed with abstract paintings, and were consequently omitted. During the next decade the situation changed so much that these painters now have their place in the sales analysis with separate introductions.

With the inclusion of so many new names there arises the question whether certain painters should not be dropped altogether because their names no longer mean anything at all to students and buyers, who have grown up in the post-war era. The difficulty lies in reconciling their interests with the need for continuity from Volume One. There are all but forgotten names among the 19th century English watercolour school, the successors of Turner, the Barbizon landscapists and the late 19th century realists. Yet these names created saleroom epics in their day, while their decline in the present century contains the ingredients of high drama. I cannot altogether abandon them in the 1960s. Their present situation is at least a reminder that not all art-hoarding has been an investment. The compromise which I offer is to include the painters of these schools whose work appeared on the market in the 1960s in sufficient quantities to indicate a movement upwards or downwards, and to omit the rest. Thus the names of Bastien-Lepage, Jules Breton, Ford Madox Brown, Copley Fielding, Leslie, Edwin Long, the Maris family, Mulready, Orchardson and Fred Walker have slipped out altogether. Those of Rosa Bonheur, William Collins, David Cox, Josef Israels, John Linnell Senr, Maclise, Meissonier, Clarkson Stanfield and Constantin Troyon are retained by a very narrow margin.

At the opposite pole there are the great masters, whose works reached the saleroom in the 19th century with sufficient frequency to make some sort of pattern possible. Today many of them are so rare, so preciously enshrined in museums, that only a plausible attribution finds its way to the saleroom once in many years. Individual treatment in separate lists is no longer possible. Belonging mainly to the Italian and Flemish primitive schools, the very few attributions which appeared on the market in the 1960s will be found in the school-lists. In Volume One they were listed separately under the following names, Antonello da Messina, Carpaccio, Cima di Conegliano, Piero della Francesca, Francia, Giorgione, Ghirlandajo, Filippo and Filippino Lippi, Lorenzo Lotto, Mabuse, Mantegna, Matsys, Memling, Antonis Mor, Moroni, Perugino, Sebastiano del Piombo, Pollaiuolo, Andrea del Sarto, Signorelli, Verrocchio and van der Weyden.

The sections concerning sculpture and portrait-miniatures have been re-arranged. They were included as *objets d'art* in Volume Two simply because Volume One had been restricted to pictures and drawings. Classification as *objets d'art* does in fact correspond with the practice of Sotheby's and Christie's who mix portrait-miniatures with watches and snuffboxes and only include the most modern forms of sculpture in their picture sales. But since pictures and *objets d'art* are now being treated in a single volume, there is no longer any justification for including sculpture and portrait miniatures among the latter. The miniaturists therefore form a group-list under the letter M in the picture section. European sculpture, extending from the Middle Ages till the present day, forms the second of the three main parts of the sales analysis, placed between pictures and *objets d'art*.

In dealing with *objets d'art* in the stricter interpretation one confronts the problem of the *new antiques*. Dislike them though one may, they demand the removal of some of the limitations of the material covered by Volume Two. In the *objets d'art* market of the 1960s there was nothing corresponding to the absolute domination of the moderns in the picture market. Nor was it possible since an *objet d'art* should be something, either made before the era of mass-production or which the methods of mass-production have by-passed. But the outlines of this distinction have certainly become blurred. It is one thing for fine modern watches, precision instruments and shot-guns to fetch four-figure prices, though something fairly new for them to be included in art sales. It is another thing altogether when £460 or £540 are paid for an *art nouveau* electric lampstand, cast by the hundred in some kind of base metal. Yet this is the high-art market of richly produced catalogues with numerous illustrations. Lower down the scale the definition, *antiques*, becomes still more blurred. In residential sectors of the rural scene there is an *antiques* sign to every 500 of the population. In the new pattern of gracious living a town of 3,000 inhabitants requires six at least, two of them repairing old china, in addition to four *boutiques*, a Cantonese and a Pakistani restaurant, a health-foods shop and a pets' corner. If they stick sensibly to the rules, the six antique shops should contain only what was made in my lifetime and by the well-tried methods of machine-belt production, though this is no machine cult like the market for real vintage cars and aeroplanes, pet traction engines, model puff-puffs and railway relics. It is indeed marginally aesthetic. Not long ago the same people would have bought works of art on the same outlay. But the promotion of non-art has now gone so far that silk cigarette cards, exchangeable at my preparatory school for four ordinary ones, reached Christie's catalogues by November, 1969. And at the upper end of the scale non-art in the 1960s included glass paper-weights at £6,800, Webb's cameo glass at nearer £8,000 and Edward Marshall Boehm's American birds in porcelain at $50,000 a pair.

It would be a grave error to review the *objets d'art* market of the 1960s without noticing the advance of non-art. It would have been wrong already in 1962 when Volume Two went to press, were it not the first purpose of the book to trace the fortunes of the same things over a period of two centuries. In Volume Three it is possible to study their further adventures and, at the same time, to view the kind of collecting that has no historical background at all. It has required some re-arrangement of the material without altering the framework. To each of the lists for arms, carpets, furniture, glass, pottery and porcelain, and silver there has been added a 19th century and modern section. Fabergé objects have an independent list while Japanese art includes subdivisions for *Inro* and *Netsuke*. There have also been some disappearances. Medici porcelain has vanished altogether while Palissy and Henri Deux ware, saleroom sagas of the last century, are reduced to four entries in the List 'pottery and faience, France'.

A review of prices over so short a period as ten years provides an opportunity for much closer classification than was possible within the space of a single volume covering 200 years. Most of the lists, retaining the headings of Volume Two, are now divided into sub-sections. In addition to new sub-sections for Italy and America, the furniture section includes a sub-section for reproductions, but clocks have been detached altogether and under this heading will be found sections dealing with Renaissance clocks, English clocks of the 17th–18th centuries and Breguet clocks of the early 19th century. Now that Asiatic flu' has been rechristened Asian flu' to avoid possible insult to its racial origins, the unfashionable title 'Negro sculpture' has been changed to 'Primitive art' and includes sections for America and Oceania, as well as Africa. Finally there are three entirely new lists, Icons, Indian sculpture and European watches.

# INTRODUCTION

## ART AND INFLATION

The notion of *Art as an investment* has created more press publicity for auction sales than has ever existed before. At the height of the sales season a record price is claimed for something or other almost every working day. One wonders whether the purpose of the writers is to show that very soon anything you buy will have become a gold mine, or whether it is to advise the Inland Revenue what to tax next. More than half of these records are not records at all. Obviously it is no part of a saleroom correspondent's business to point out that the so-called record price is expressed in pounds that are worth less than a fifth of a gold sovereign and one eighth of what a gold sovereign could buy when it was in general circulation. But, apart from the fall in purchasing power of *all* money, the pound has lost its relationship to the world's stable currencies, based on the price of gold. It means 2·40 dollars where it should mean 4·86 dollars, 10·26 Swiss francs where it should mean 25. Ought the pound to be regarded as an international medium of quotation at all? It has reached the point of idiocy when an object, sold in New York before November 18th, 1967, for $100,000, gets promoted to the status of a world's record in its kind because it is sold in London later for the equivalent of $90,000.

So perniciously misleading has this constant peddling of world records become that I have had to introduce a system which was not general in the first two volumes. Wherever a comparison is made with prices of the past—and these comparisons are the quintessence of the book—I have quoted the real price in terms of present day money in accordance with the time-scale which will be found, adjusted to a further decade of progressive inflation, at the end of the introduction. The real peak of the art market was somewhere about 1912. Works of art which became established in the course of the past century as the highest achievements of their kind, have often failed to maintain the level of 1912 in real money terms and sometimes they have failed to maintain it even in paper figures. Rembrandt himself with no less than 14 six-figure prices in the course of the 1960s will be seen to have done little more than stay abreast of inflation in the light of some of the prices which were paid before the depression of the 1930s. As to the many truly wild movements of prices in the 1960s, they had singularly little to do with long established taste. They were confined to certain limited categories of art which had either been rediscovered after long abeyance or quite newly promoted.

The choice of works for rediscovery or promotion has been exceedingly capricious and at times even perverse. Those who listen to the syren song of the brokers of *art as an investment*, should keep that in mind and cast an exceedingly wary look in the direction of the saleroom commentators whose enthusiasm grows ever more round-eyed as the price mounts. Theirs is the simple creed that, while the good need not be expensive, the expensive must always be good. They tell us of a *tremendously* rare and distinguished Italian Comedy figure of Isabella (Times-Sotheby index 15.11.69). So, a seascape looking exactly like a coloured picture postcard, becomes a *superb* clipper under full sail by Montague Dawson. There is an *exciting* Art Nouveau lamp in sandblasted gun metal and frosted glass mosaic, a *ravishing* set of table-mats, painted with titmice by Beatrix Potter, a *magical* Jackson Pollock and a *noble* Munnings. The real corruption of aesthetic values lies not, however, in the serenading of everything that is put on the table, but in that peculiar symptom of the later sixties, a proliferation of books which teach the tyro not how to acquire a discriminating taste, but how to get a return on his money. It does not really matter very much that some of the readers may live to regret the instruction they have received. The deliberate and indoctrinated confusion of artistic appreciation with self-interest means something far worse than that, namely the corrosion of what is left of civilized life.

That this confusion should be accepted almost universally denotes a sort of cultural revolution and a very recent one at that. It is wonderful how much the identification of art with money has taken root since 1961 when my first volume appeared. More than one reviewer in those days implied that it was presumptuous to dare to compare prices across the ages, as if these odd movements of money could have anything to do with matters so pure as currents of taste which just grow like daffodils. It was suspected that the chronological lists of prices were a form of stock exchange quotation, and I was sternly reminded that these were useless unless one knew precisely the condition of the work. Most reviewers, however, accepted the lists for what they were: illustrations of a particularly odd aspect of human behaviour or human folly as the case might be. But that is not what is wanted today. Within six years of the appearance of Volume One, graphs and indexes to help *the investor in art* had become an accepted feature of the financial press, led by Granny herself. I do not recollect having seen a single letter protesting at their basic fallacy, though one or two writers may have accused their bad taste. But indexes, it seems, have come to stay. *Index* is a good word, respectable, almost pontifical like the *index expurgatorius*.

The greatest fallacy in all these graphs and charts is the one that is least perceived. It is not just the fooling round with computers to produce an allegedly scientific averaging of a given painter's prices. After all, anyone can see that it is all knocked sideways in a matter of seconds when something special comes under the hammer. Nor is it the disarming concealment of falls from former splendour when some handsomely recommended artistic equity comes up for discussion. The greatest fallacy is none of these, but the total incomprehension of the nature of taste whose vagaries it is that still determine the relative advance of this or that.

It is quite easy under present conditions to fall into a state of *trauma* in which one loses sight of the existence of taste altogether in the compelling belief that organized publicity alone can promote anything on earth, and that, once promoted, the competition for anything on earth must continue till scarcity is followed by dearth and dearth by extinction. The belief may be compelling but the truth is never so simple. Who knows of the carefully engineered booms which failed to get off the ground; of the objects which became so scarce on the market that interest in them wilted altogether through the sheer impossibility of forming a collection? Who above all knows of the fine threads of which a boom is made, the long years of quiet, modest collecting by a few uncompetitive scholars or devotees, spending on their hobby no more than a few pounds a week? Knowing nothing whatever about such matters, the investor in art is not likely to know any more about the threads that are being woven even now, and which must one day change the whole balance of the market, a thing that has happened repeatedly. How, in the face of all that, can one watch the progress of the prices of works of art as if they had produced so many long tons of copper in the course of the past month?

It cannot be denied that enormous profits have been made in the past two decades by those who followed fashionable trends, regardless of cost, in order to sell-out a few years later, but these are not investors but speculators. The only investors are those who never meant to invest at all. Those who bought some twenty years ago, preferring such things as English 18th century drawings, the 'primitives' of English pottery and porcelain. Mughal miniatures, early Japanese porcelain and Chinese blue and white of the early Ming dynasty, may have seen their treasures multiply in value in some cases two or three hundred times over. But they will either have ceased to collect altogether or they will have joined the general rat-race, selling dear in order to buy even dearer. Those who bought from income or pin-money will compete with those who pledge their entire capital. That is the meaning of *art as an investment*, nothing less than the extinction of true collecting.

A million and a half's worth, two millions' worth of works of art sold in a single morning: at the height of the two sales seasons that banner with a proud device is hoisted somewhere almost every day. No one knows how much the frenzied passing to and fro of paper money is due to the various fiscal concessions, decreed by the governments of the world. But since these concessions are linked with the ultimate aim of public acquisition, one is beginning to accept the probability that very little of any importance will make a second appearance in the salerooms, unless it has failed to reach its reserve. As the good things vanish, sales get skimpier and catalogues bigger and more luxuriously illustrated. Non-art, the collector's substitute and second line of defence, is promoted with greater and greater assiduity. Everything portends the day when all that has been collected must become institutionalized. We are already within hailing distance of the State as the one and only patron, the bleakest possible substitute for the role of the Church in the early Middle Ages. No one seriously considers the consequences of such a situation, least of all the most obvious one, which is that this unique patron is unlikely to continue supporting the uncompromisingly intellectual trend of living art in the past sixty years (see page 21). Official art must become popular art. In the meantime museum directors absorb all the latest intellectual millinery, secure in the certainty that, when there is no longer an open market, there can be no visible slump of values. The *avant garde* collector shares that sense of security. His is the belief, in fact the death-wish of capitalism, that in the end there must always be a public buyer.

The last two years of the decade saw a *bouleversement* of the rates of exchange and a worldwide fall in equities in the region of 35 per cent, a 1929–31 slump in miniature. Yet these events left the art market in its more fashionable sectors advancing more rapidly than ever. After November, 1967, and the devaluation of the pound, works of art, suitable for millionaires and their State successors, doubled or trebled in value at the very least in terms of that currency, though its actual devaluation had been no more than 14·3 per cent. Patriotic as opposed to international tastes showed, however, that they could be vulnerable to the financial conditions prevailing in each country. In a country enslaved more than most to doctrinaire economic theorists, British art was exceptionally vulnerable, but vulnerability was tempered by the fact that this is also an Anglo-Saxon market, extending to the USA and the former Dominions. It was run-of-the-mill works, normally bought by dealers as stock in trade, which tended to reverse the upward movement of the past twenty years. The extension of the capital gains tax to works of art had created since 1965 a bias in favour of the lower reaches of the market, since it precluded works sold for less than £1,000. In 1968–69 a credit-squeeze with punishing rates for bank overdrafts and mortgages kept this bias somewhat in check. But taking the 1960s as a whole, it was the cheapest things that advanced much more than the great prizes of publicity; some of them in fact advanced so rapidly that by 1968 they had reached the international speculative category which made them immune to the shocks of small trading. Japanese *netsuke* and *inro*, for instance, the best of which had been barely in the £100–£200 class in 1960, reached £2,800 and £1,900 in 1969.

If one compares the 1960s, when everything went up, with the 1930s when everything went down, one is struck less by the difference in the financial climate than by the enormous psychological difference. Anyone who bought the humblest work of art in the former period must wonder how little conscious he then was of rarity and special quality, whereas today the whole world seems conscious of both. The subject cannot be avoided even in the lowest-browed form of conversation. Even if money becomes so short that no one can afford works of art, whether bought from pocket money or from capital, the indifference of the 1930s will have gone like the innocence that preceded the fall of man. Should the great slump of 1929–31 repeat itself on the same scale, one wonders whether there would be the same flight from art-buying. The lesser slump of 1968–69 produced a paradox which threatened to become an orthodoxy. It is that works of art go up in proportion as capital values, profits and dividends decline, that as substitutes for money, works of art are not liable to the same erosions as money itself.

Now, if this belief has indeed become an orthodoxy, it seems to me to ignore in the most singular fashion the basic cause of the erosion. In various degrees Western democracies are run on a system of *panem et circenses*. Political parties, parading under labels that become less and less significant, are voted to power through promising benefits to the majority at the expense of the property-owning minority. But in practice, as the huge litany of state benefactions extends, it is paid for by everybody and still not paid for enough. No one knows how much the printing of new money exceeds the amount which is scooped back by taxation. A Chancellor of the Exchequer who is chosen by a Ministry with a working parliamentary majority, wields an authority that no Roman emperor or *roi soleil* ever saw the tenth of. Not even the vaguest promise of retrenchment need pass his lips, so long as the property-owning minority are still there to be milked further. Private capital is nowhere *owned*, it is merely held on sufferance. Its ultimate destiny cannot seriously be doubted. Least of all would it seem to be doubted by investors in art who at heart hope or believe that their salvation lies in the things which in the last resort can be hidden from the Argus-eyed apparatus of State.

Art as an investment is a conception scarcely older than the early 1950s. In times of severe inflation the normal refuge of savings or capital is the hoarding of gold, diamonds or jewellery, also small objects of utility that can be stored easily in bulk. During the Central European inflation which followed the First World War works of art had little appeal, because a market which depended on the whims of taste in inflation-free countries was too uncertain. Obviously there is less of this uncertainty when inflation affects every country in the world. The much increased pace of the art market in 1968–69, impressive even when recorded in the currencies which did not suffer devaluation, derived from the fact that the same pressure on capital now existed absolutely everywhere. It was part of a world-wide recognition of a truth long apparent but, because of its indigestibility seldom admitted, namely that inflation was neither an unaccountable disease, nor a combination of bad luck, but essentially a political process with which no politician would dare interfere. Disinflation, meaning above all things an attack on the innumerable ways by which fictitious full employment was secured by State subsidy, had become in the later 1960s a word almost too frightful to be mentioned.

How then can investors in art hope to protect themselves from governments to which the whole structure of property is captive, governments which can requisition great enterprises or hamstring them as they please? The truth seems to be that political risks, even when most obvious, are seldom discounted. Investors in oil shares for instance are not deterred by the vulnerability of oil concessions, situated in the territory of hungry mushroom foreign governments, though this has been apparent for a whole generation. It is furthermore probable that the notion, 'art as an investment', is most popular with the least financially informed sort of property owner. It is doubtful whether investment is the real motive in the art purchases of 'big business'. The propagandists of art as an investment seem at least to direct their endeavours to a class that formerly bought stocks and shares out of savings. Most of those who spend upwards of £20,000 on a single object or picture, are not investors at all but buyers of prestige symbols and sometimes buyers of public honours as well through their ultimate benefactions, aided by various forms of tax relief. It needs repeating again that these high reaches of the market are not the fastest moving. In spite of an abrupt rise after November, 1967, in certain more recent painters such as Dufy, van Dongen, Derain and Vlaminck, a good deal of steam ran out of the market for the original Impressionists which had become the traditional millionaires' market. The proportion of bought-in pictures increased, the number of costly falls could be counted on rather more than ten fingers, while in 1969 colour-illustrations with a very familiar look began to appear in Tokyo auction catalogues, issued by the London houses. It seems that bought-in pictures find their way there much as old horses used to end up in Belgium and old passenger liners in the Greek islands. Their value does not increase in the process. In the meantime the cheapest things have grown so fast that some are no longer cheap by any standards. The dizziest movements of all are at any rate shared by that which is easiest to hoard or hide. The case of *netsuke* and *inro* has already been mentioned. A quarter of a million pounds can be buried in a trunk, filled with *netsuke* —and still more if it is filled with stamps or coins.

With the increased erosion of money, one may expect these symptoms to become more pronounced. Since 1960, when Volume One went to press, the erosion has exceeded 40 per cent, expressed in pounds, 34 per cent expressed in dollars or Swiss francs. What then *is* a pound? As the decade ended, its true situation was exhibited with an aptness of symbolism which could not have been bettered. The golden half sovereign of my boyhood became the fifty-new-pennies piece, a seven-sided bit of cupro-nickel which could well be mistaken for a discarded design for a French 50 centimes piece worth 9d. Archaeologists of a very distant future, searching among the mounds of steel rust that had once been cities, will recognize this object and shake their heads. 'Sometimes' wrote R. H. Hodgkin—and he was speaking of the inhabitants of Britain after the departure of the Romans—'they minted small barbarous copies of genuine Roman coins in base metal, sometimes they used minims or minimissimi, the smallest coin ever produced in this island. Since they are so small that fifty can be placed side by side on a halfpenny, we need not wonder that they have rarely been noticed by previous excavators.' History may not altogether repeat itself but it is not for lack of trying.

In Volume Two, published in 1963, I used the same yardstick to measure the depreciation of the pound as in Volume One, published in 1961. How peaceful life must have been! With inflation creeping at a rate of little more than 3 per cent each year, an adjustment after so short a passage of time seemed an unnecessary complication. The rate had not risen much in November, 1967, when the devaluation of the pound triggered off something like a 20 per cent fall in its purchasing power within the following 18 months. The pound of 1939, worth £3·7 in the money of 1961, now meant fully £5, while the pound of 1914 rose from £6 to at least £8. I repeat that in comparing prices with the past I have generally given the adjusted rate of exchange as well. But it must be emphasized that these estimates, based on a cross-section of the cost of living, are ultra-conservative. Works of art at four to six-figure prices are not bought by the lowest grade of wage-earners. Should not the rate of exchange be based entirely on the cost of *Luxurious* living?

'I believe that a single lady can get on very nicely upon an income of about £60,' remarked Sherlock Holmes in *A Case of Identity*, published in 1887. That minimal single lady might just scrape along with £480 in 1970 but in no sense of the word nicely. However, in the same year Sherlock Holmes noticed in *The Noble Bachelor* that Mr Moulton, the American, had settled his bill at one of the most select hotels in London. 'Eight shillings for a bed and eightpence for a glass of sherry pointed to one of the most expensive hotels. There are not many in London that charge at that rate.' Since the hotel was in Northumberland Avenue, it was either the Victoria, the Metropole or the Grand. Thirteen years later, in 1900, *Baedeker* listed these hotels without a star and as charging only five shillings for a room. The fashionable hotels were now in Mayfair, but at only one, the newly rebuilt Claridge's was it impossible to get a room for 7s. 6d., while the Savoy included a bath at this price. I suppose that in 1970 Mr Moulton could have his room, if it was a single-bedder, for ten guineas and that glass of sherry on his bill at 10s., and of course 15 per cent added-on for service. Conclusion: the minimal single lady of 1887 would have to spend 8 or 9 times as much in 1970, but Mr Moulton, the successful digger, more than 20 times.

Only five years after the appearance of *The Noble Bachelor*, M. Chauchard paid £44,000 for Millet's *Rentrée des moutons, la nuit*, a modern picture not twenty years old. Should we not call that £900,000 in terms of hotel bills? You see, you Picasso addicts, you just don't know what real picture prices are. A multiple of twenty times might work out equally well for any of the bare necessities of wealth in 1887–1900, salmon and grouse, the butler's wages, a Savile Row suit (or should not that be thirty times?), a pair of shot-guns and a hunter. On the other hand a passage across the Atlantic on the *Campania* (£15 first cabin) cost more than a tenth of a passage on the *Queen Elizabeth II*, while a trip to Paris cost nearly a third as much as in 1970. No doubt there are other discrepancies too. For that matter the minimal single lady would not have done so nicely on £60, if she had frequent occasion to use the sevenpenny omnibus from Ealing to Oxford Street. So reluctantly I return to a scale, based on the *general* cost of living, five times compared with 1939, eight times compared with 1914. These were the base-lines, chosen in the first two volumes, because each of these years was the termination of a long almost static period. It is only a rule of thumb, for nothing short of separate, elaborately charted graphs can produce the relative rate of exchange for each single year in 1970 terms.

*The Pound in terms of 1970 values*

| | |
|---|---|
| 1750–1795 | Multiply by 20 to 16 |
| 1795–1815 | Multiply by 16 to 12 |
| 1815–1850 | Multiply by 12 to 10 |
| 1850–1895 | Multiply by 10 to 8 |
| 1895–1914 | Static period; multiply by 8 |
| 1914–1921 | Multiply by 8 to 5 |
| 1921–1939 | Static period; multiply by 5 |
| 1939–1948 | Multiply by 5 to 2·5 |
| 1948–1960 | Multiply by 2·5 to 1·65 |
| 1960–1970 | Multiply by 1·65 to 1 |

# NOTE ON ABBREVIATIONS AND EXCHANGE RATES

As in Volumes One and Two, sales at Christie's are indicated by the letter C and sales at Sotheby's by the letter S. This is preceded by the name of the vendor when known. Present ownership, if known, is given at the end of the entry. Sales abroad are indicated by the name of the city, e.g. Paris, New York, preceded where possible by the name of the vendor. German, Swiss, Dutch, Italian and Scandinavian sales are preceded by the name of the auctioneer, e.g. Koller, Zurich, or Finarte, Milan. Prices are normally given in the original currency, as well as in Sterling, with taxes included where they are in force. The Sterling equivalents are based on the exchange-rate of the day of sale. The following approximations have been used, but there can be variations of as much as 1 per cent even when the pound is nominally stable.

*Before 18 November 1967*

| | |
|---|---|
| France | 13·78 francs to the pound (called FN) |
| Germany | 11·17 marks to the pound (called DM) |
| Holland | 10·15 florins to the pound (called Hfl) |
| Italy | 1,780 lire to the pound (called L) |
| Switzerland | 12·00 francs to the pound (called FS) |
| U.S.A. | 2·80 dollars to the pound |

*After 18 November 1967*

| | |
|---|---|
| France | 11·88 francs to the pound, but 13·36 after 9.8.69 |
| Germany | 9·56 marks to the pound, but about 8·83 after 26.11.69 |
| Holland | 8·63 florins to the pound |
| Italy | 1,500 lire to the pound |
| Switzerland | 10·38 francs to the pound |
| U.S.A. | 2·40 dollars to the pound |

## PART ONE

# PAINTINGS AND DRAWINGS

# ABSTRACT AND SEMI-ABSTRACT PAINTERS: EUROPEAN

(Excluding Braque, Max Ernst, Juan Gris, Kandinsky, Paul Klee, Fernand Léger, Joan Miró, Picasso and de Stael for whom see separate entries. See also Abstract Painters, American.)

This is of course the most daring and speculative of all art markets. It is based on the premise that because, fifty or sixty years ago, abstract painting was a revolutionary movement, derided and spurned by all official bodies, it must now remain enthroned, if not for ever, as long at least as any present day museum-curator can be expected to live. It is not merely such a simple matter as the dread of curators and their private benefactors lest they appear fuddy-duddies. Politics play their part as well. The State which sticks its nose into everything, must by no means be allowed to neglect the applied arts. But aid and subsidy must be for the *avant garde* alone. The state-subsidized pavilions at the *Bienniale*, the lumps of stone or bronze with a hole through the middle, placed for the cultural improvement of housing estates, these point the way for the hesitant benefactor. No danger now that Cézannes, van Goghs and Gauguins will wilt in obscurity, while public commissions are rained upon the high priests of supreme finish and absolute realism.

Awed by the example of governments and their experts, even the out and out speculator feels comparatively safe. He may not realize that posterity is un-likely to discover any van Goghs, Cézannes and Gauguins of the 1960s, but he knows that he has avoided possible Leightons and Alma Tademas. He cannot, he thinks, go wrong in buying what shocks the most. While cubist Braques and Picassos command £125,000, he may even find the painters in the following list underpriced. Sooner or later comes the glad news that the Tate Gallery or the Museum of Modern Art has paid more, much more, than he has paid himself. How wrong were all his friends!

It has not occurred to this happy mortal that he has been enrolled in the estab-lishment and that all establishment-taste looks silly a generation hence, what-ever the direction in which it has been navigated. The precedents of history are grim enough, but when the applied arts are as closely linked with State-aid as they are today, the revulsion must be even more radical. Big Brother is little likely to patronize the same taste when his is the one and only patronage in existence. Russia has shewn that *Admass* demands the crudest allegories and symbols, not the most obscure. When mindlessness is the sole objective, the shortest road is not via an enlarged doodle on a wall but via *Bubbles* or *Cherry Ripe*. But, to the speculator, or investor in art as he prefers to call himself, these are but academic questions. Long before 1984 he will have sold out.

Since this is an establishment-market like any other, it is advisable to get the price-scale into the right historic perspective. Half the painters in the foregoing list belong to the classical generation of abstract and semi-abstract painters who were heading this way at the time of the First World War, if not before. The most expensive item, the $100,000 *Arrosoir* of the short-lived Roger de la Fresnaye, belongs to this generation, though the painter was only 18 years old. On the other hand, extreme youth is by no means a characteristic of the more recent section of the expensive abstract picture market. Those of whom no one had heard till after the Second World War, had to be at least 42 years old to qualify for a market status of £3,000 and upwards in 1968. In the £10,000 to £20,000 class they had to be all of 65 if still alive, and preferably domiciled on the American continent. And that meant no more than £1,200 to £2,500 in the purchasing power of money at the turn of the century when there were any number of painters, now long forgotten, who could make at least as much— and earlier in life too.

JEAN (OR HANS) ARP. 1887–1966. *See also* Sculpture  £
1966  Thompson. N.Y.  Configuration, 1926, 23 × 26  3,240

GIACOMO BALLA. 1871–1958. Italy
1961  Brera, Milan.  Linea di velocita e cielo, 1914, 24 × 16
      L1 million+tax  about  645
1964  S.  Mercury passing before the Sun, 1914, 54–38  7,500
1966  Thompson. N.Y.  Linea di velocite vortice, 1913,
      27¾ × 30¾  5,400
1968  S.  I giocatrice di tennis, 1920, 14 × 19¼  2,800

ALBERTO BURRI. 1915–. Switzerland
1965  N.Y.  Sacco e rosso, 1954, old sacking on a stretcher
      measuring 59 × 98½, $9,400  3,355
1966  Thompson. N.Y.  Bianco, 1952, 33¾ × 39. Old sacking
      etc.  1,885

ROGER DE LA FRESNAYE. 1895–1925
1930  Bought for Toledo Museum.  Portrait of Mire the poet  400
1958  Paris.  Man drinking and singing, 1910, 80 × 46.  4 mil-
      lion old francs+tax  3,450
1959  Ney.  The Matador, 1907, 9½ × 7¼, $2,400  857
1965  Lefèvre, Paris.  Conquête de l'air, 1913, 20½ × 26  12,870
      Livres sur guéridon, oils, 1912, 32½ × 24  10,780
1966  Helena Rubinstein. N.Y.  L'Arrosoir, 1913, 34½ × 78¾,
      $100,000  35,975
1967  N.Y.  Les baigneurs, 1912, 63½ × 50½  25,000
      Nature morte à la botte de radis, 1912, 29 × 21½  4,250

| | | £ |
|---|---|---:|
| 1967 | Paris. Jeanne d'Arc, 1912, 80×40 | 5,580 |
| | La table Louis Philippe, 1922, 21½×26 | 6,090 |
| 1968 | C. Nature morte à la bouilloire, 1911, 22¼×28¼ | 6,825 |

ROBERT DELAUNEY. 1885–1941

| 1954 | Stuttgart. Les coureurs, wc, 7¼×13 | 230 |
|---|---|---:|
| 1962 | Paris. Portrait, Jean Metzinger, 22×17, FN20,000+tax | 1,725 |
| | Femme nue lisant, 18½×15¼, FN50,500+tax   About | 4,400 |
| 1963 | N.Y. Formes circulaires, 32×25½, $14,000 | 5,000 |
| 1964 | N.Y. Portrait of Jean Metzinger, 26½×17, $14,000 | 5,000 |
| 1965 | S. Les coureurs, 1930, 44×57 | 8,000 |
| | Ira Haupt. N.Y. Nature morte portuguaise, 1916 (see 1967), $8,200 | 2,930 |
| | N.Y. Jeune fille nue lisant, wc, 1915, oval 24×19¾, $7,000 | 2,500 |
| | Paysage de Paris, les tours, 65½×33, $18,000 | 6,430 |
| 1966 | Ault. C. Nature morte portuguaise, pastel, 28¾×40½ | 5,775 |
| | Thompson. N.Y. Relief-disque, 1936, 21¼×37¾ | 3,412 |
| | Motte, Geneva. Nature morte portuguaise, 38×30. FS100,000+tax | 9,583 |
| 1967 | From Moscow. S. Fenêtres ouvertes simultanément, 1912, 18×14¾. Tate Gallery | 14,500 |
| | Motte, Geneva. Nature morte portuguaise (see 1965) FS100,000+tax | 10,870 |
| | Paris. Le football, wc, 32×22¾. FN33,000+tax | 3,030 |
| 1968 | S. Rhythme Hélice, 63½×50½, 1936 | 5,000 |
| 1969 | Nature morte portuguaise, pen drawing, 8¼×10½ | 1,100 |
| | S. (after Delauney) Frontcloth for the ballet, Cléopatre, 1919, 28½×50 ft. | 5,500 |

JEAN DUBUFFET. 1901–

| 1960 | N.Y. Grand Jazz-band, 45×58, $27,000 | 9,740 |
|---|---|---:|
| | L'âme des sous-sols, $13,500 | 4,820 |
| 1961 | Stuttgart. Tête abondante, 1952, 24×20, DM42,000+tax | 4,480 |
| 1962 | S. Abstraction | 3,675 |
| 1963 | Aldrich. N.Y. Profile, genre aztec, 1945, 26×21½ | 3,400 |
| | Paysage grotesque, 35×46, $13,000 | 4,648 |
| | Olympia, corps de dame, 35×46, $17,000 | 6,075 |
| 1964 | S. Midi d'été, 1952, 32×36 | 2,500 |
| 1965 | S. Composition in mosaic pebbles, 1958, 44½×57 | 4,500 |
| | Zadok. S. Vue de Paris aux piétons furtives, 1944, 35×44 | 9,500 |
| | N.Y. Trotte la houle, 1964, 35×45½ | 3,170 |
| 1966 | Gustav Stein. S. Vaches au pré, 1954, 39½×32 | 7,200 |
| | Contemporary Arts. S. L'autobus, 1961, 35×45 | 6,800 |

| | | £ |
|---|---|---|
| 1966 | Thompson. N.Y. Le mur aux inscriptions, 1945, 39×32. | |
| | Museum Modern Art, N.Y. $26,000 | 9,312 |
| | 'Astravagale', 1956, collage, 28¾×16¾ | 8,270 |
| 1967 | S. Buste au bec, 1955, 25×19¼ | 5,000 |
| | N.Y. La violoniste, 1953, 59½×45 | 8,035 |
| | L'âne au travail, 1955, 28¾×36½ | 6,072 |
| | Motte, Geneva. Personnage, 46½×35½, FS43,000+tax | 4,750 |
| 1968 | Granz. S. Lippeur de vin clairet, 1945, 28¾×23¾ | 20,000 |
| | S. Le Majordome, 1954, 51¼×35 | 12,500 |
| | Chasse croisée, 1961, 32×39½ | 15,500 |
| | Hillman. N.Y. La Gitâne, 1954, 36¼×29, $36,000 | 15,000 |
| 1969 | S. Les rencontres, 1950, 35×45¾ | 20,000 |

ALBERT GLEIZES. 1881–1953

| 1962 | Stuttgart. Les Ponts de Paris, 24×29½, DM9,000+tax | 972 |
|---|---|---|
| 1965 | N.Y. Triptych, 1930, 63×78, $15,000 | 5,350 |
| 1966 | C. Paysage avec arbre, 1914, 39½×31½ | 6,090 |
| 1968 | Motte, Geneva. Nature morte à la guitare, 36¾×26, F535,000+tax | 3,800 |
| 1969 | S. Paysage rocheux et pont, 1910 | 4,600 |
| | Hutton. N.Y. Composition, Serrières, 1923, 86½×49¼, $8,500 | 3,620 |
| | Composition bleu et jaune, c. 1921, 79×43¼, $8,500 | 3,620 |
| | Composition à deux éléments etc., 1924, 52×35¼, $7,500 | 3,125 |

MARCEL GROMAIRE. 1892–

| 1952 | Girardin. Paris. Loterie foraine | 1,205 |
|---|---|---|
| 1961 | N.Y. La marchande de fruits, 31¾×39¼, $11,250 | 4,014 |
| 1962 | N.Y. L'ivrogne, 39½×31¼, $8,250 | 2,945 |
| 1963 | S. Boats, 1930, 18×21 | 3,000 |
| 1965 | Zadok. S. Nu sous un arbre, 1950, 31×38½ | 2,800 |
| 1966 | Thompson. N.Y. Trois baigneuses, 1932, 39×42, $17,000 | 6,070 |
| | Le repos de Midi, 31½×39, $13,500 | 4,855 |
| | S. Le Dimanche en banlieue, 1927, 63¼×51¼ (see 1968) | 4,000 |
| | Paris. La terre, FN39,000+tax | 4,530 |
| 1967 | C. Autour de la lampe, 1939, 31¾×39¾ | 3,780 |
| | Paris. Marché aux puces, 1927, 52×38, FN60,000+tax | 4,860 |
| | Intérieur au pot gris, 1955, 26×32½, FN36,000+tax | 2,916 |
| | La Seine à travers Paris, 32½×40, FN48,000+tax | 3,888 |
| 1969 | N.Y. La marchande de fruits, 1953, 31½×38½, $13,000 | 5,416 |
| | S. Le Dimanche en banlieue (see 1966) | 4,000 |

HANS HARTUNG. 1904–

| 1960 | N.Y. '756-12', $10,950 | 3,915 |
|---|---|---|

|  |  | £ |
|---|---|---|
| 1960 | Duveen.  S.  Noire et verte, 1955, 39×31¾ | 4,200 |
|  | Black, brown and yellow abstraction, 1950, 38×51 | 4,200 |
| 1963 | Aldrich.  N.Y.  Abstraction, 1955, 63×47½, $13,000 | 4,640 |
| 1965 | Zadok.  S.  Black circle on green ground, 38×52, 1948 | 3,200 |
|  | N.Y.  Peinture, 1950, 38×51, $6,250 | 2,225 |
| 1970 | Paris.  Composition, FN80,000+tax | 6,576 |

HENRI LAURENS.  1885–1954.  *See also* Sculpture

| 1962 | S.  Bouteilles de verre, collage, 23×15½ | 3,200 |
|---|---|---|
| 1965 | Lefèvre.  Paris.  Tête de femme, 1918, collage, 29¾×7¼ | 3,342 |
| 1966 | Thompson.  N.Y.  Femme assise, collage, 1918 | 3,420 |

RENÉ MAGRITTE.  1898–.  Belgium, *sur-réaliste, see* introduction
to Max Ernst

| 1959 | N.Y.  Hesitation waltz, 1950, 14×18, $2,000 | 714 |
|---|---|---|
| 1961 | N.Y.  Le point de vue, 21¼×28¾, $1,100 | 393 |
|  | S.  Le secret du cortège, 29¾×39½ | 1,350 |
| 1965 | N.Y.  Légende des siècles, 31½×23¾, $7,000 | 2,500 |
| 1966 | C.  La condition humaine, 1935, 21¼×28¾ | 2,730 |
|  | La belle captive II, 18×26½ | 3,150 |
|  | Thompson.  N.Y.  Le temps, 1935, 22×29, $7,250 | 2,590 |
| 1968 | S.  Le voix des airs, 10×7, 1928 | 3,400 |
| 1969 | S.  Le séducteur, 1950, 19×23 (conventional) | 13,500 |
|  | L'homme celèbre, 1926, 25½×31½ | 12,000 |
|  | L'avenir, 1934, 21×23 | 19,000 |
|  | Le prophète, *c.* 1947, 15½×22½ | 6,000 |
|  | Un simple histoire d'amour, 1959, 18×15 | 9,500 |
|  | Le palais d'une courtisane, *c.* 1929, 21¼×28¾ | 21,500 |
|  | Le plaisir, 1926, 29¼×28½ | 7,000 |
|  | l'Utopie, 1945, 23½×31¼ | 14,000 |
|  | Méditation, 1934, tempera, 12½×17¼ | 6,500 |

ALFRED MANESSIER.  1911–

| 1959 | Stuttgart.  Abstraction, 1953, 14½×18½, DM12,000+tax | 1,250 |
|---|---|---|
| 1961 | Paris.  Composition au masque, 29½×21½, FN30,000+tax | 2,450 |
| 1962 | Stuttgart.  Les Lavandes, 1959, 38¾×52, DM45,000+tax | 4,600 |
|  | Paris.  Le port endormi, 1951, 66×38¾, FN31,000+tax | 2,715 |
| 1963 | Aldrich.  N.Y.  Le torrent, 38×51, $12,000 | 4,288 |
|  | Pavane, 24×24, $6,500 | 2,325 |
| 1966 | Thompson.  N.Y.  Pour le fête de Christ, roi, 78×59 | 5,030 |

LOUIS CASIMIR MARCOUSSIS  1883–1941

| 1966 | Helena  Rubinstein.  N.Y.  Anvers,  1928,  56¾×37, $20,000 | 7,180 |
|---|---|---|

| | | £ |
|---|---|---|
| 1968 | Beddington Behrens. S. Intèrieur à contrebaisse et l'éscalier, 18×25½ | 1,800 |
| 1969 | C. Spectateurs, 25×31½ | 1,575 |

PIET MONDRIAN. 1872–1944. Holland

| 1962 | N.Y. Kerktoren, Zoutelande, 1910, 55¾×24½, $47,000 | 16,780 |
|---|---|---|
| 1964 | S. Composition with figures, 1912, 20×28 | 2,500 |
| 1965 | Haupt. N.Y. Composition of coloured squares, 23½×19½ | 15,000 |
| 1966 | N.Y. Similar production | 21,430 |
| 1968 | N.Y. 'Landscape', 10½×13½, $22,000 | 9,165 |
| 1969 | Composition 1, 1920, coloured squares, 29½×25½ | 27,000 |

BEN NICOLSON. 1894–. England

| 1958 | S. Composition, 1944, 35½×33½ | 880 |
|---|---|---|
| 1960 | Duveen. S. Rooftops, St Ives, 1948, 17½×27½ | 1,700 |
| | Verschoyle. S. Still life, 1946, 23½×22 | 1,300 |
| 1961 | Bowness. S. Gwithian, 1955, 41¾×41¾ (see 1965) | 2,800 |
| 1963 | Aldrich. N.Y. Pavane, 1955, 24×24 | 2,250 |
| 1965 | Ross. N.Y. April, 1957, 48×41½ | 5,000 |
| | N.Y. Gwithian (see 1961) ($15,000) | 5,414 |
| 1966 | Thompson. N.Y. White relief, 1939, 34½×38½ | 2,514 |
| | Lee Ault. C. Still life, 1945, 22½×21 | 2,761 |
| 1967 | Bennett. C. Geometrical abstraction, 1934, 27¼×39 | 1,785 |
| | S. Frostbound, Cumberland, 1927, 19½×23½ | 1,400 |
| | Clark (Dallas). S. Abstraction, 1937, 16×21½ | 1,800 |
| | Bannerson. S. Prince and Princess, pencil and oil on paper, 14½×21 | 2,600 |
| 1968 | Strauss. N.Y. Aegean landscape (squares) 1961, 28¾×69¾, $16,000 | 6,665 |
| 1969 | Russell. C. Brown and grey, oil and pencil, 1957, 8×7 | 2,310 |
| | Clarkson. C. Granite circle, cardboard mounted on panel dated 4.12.54, 16¾×24 | 1,995 |

SERGE POLIAKOFF 1906–1969. Russia

| 1960 | Motte, Geneva. Composition bleue, 46½×35½, FS19,600 +tax | 1,960 |
|---|---|---|
| 1966 | Bragaline. N.Y. Composition, 50½×37½ | 1,525 |
| | Thompson. N.Y. Composition no 28, 1952, 51×38 | 2,960 |
| 1969 | N.Y. Composition, 1954, 45¾×35, $3,000 | 1,250 |
| | Composition, undated, 35½×28, $3,000 | 1,250 |

LYUBOV POPOVA. –1923. Russia

| 1967 | S. (from Moscow). The traveller, 1915, 56×41½ | 9,000 |
|---|---|---|
| | Still life, untitled, 1916, 42×27½ | 5,000 |
| | Architectonic composition, 1917, 28×28 | 5,500 |

|  |  |  | £ |
|---|---|---|---|
| 1968 | S. | Architectonic composition, *c.* 1916, 28×28 | 2,800 |
|  |  | Constructivist composition, 1916, 14×12 | 2,300 |
|  |  | Architectonic composition, 1915, 28×55 | 7,500 |
| 1969 | | Houzer. C. Constructivist painting (on both sides) 1917 and 1920, 19×15¼ | 3,150 |

MARIA DE SILVA. 1908–. Portugal

| 1959 | Stuttgart. Town, seen from the South, 12½×20, DM5,400 +tax | 560 |
|---|---|---|
| 1962 | Stuttgart. Le Métro aërien, 1955, 63¼×88.  DM85,000+ tax | 8,630 |
| 1965 | S. Battle of reds and blues, 1953, 51×64 | 6,000 |
| 1967 | S. La ville, 1951, 25×20½ | 2,100 |
|  | Paris. Station, 1951, 30×24, FN14,500+tax | 1,188 |
| 1969 | N.Y. Jardins suspendus de Semiramis, 1958, 25¼×36½, $4,100 | 1,717 |

PIERRE SOULAGES. 1919–

| 1960 | S. Composition en noir, 36½×25½ | 1,700 |
|---|---|---|
|  | N.Y. Abstraction, $9,200 | 3,255 |
|  | Ernest Duveen. S. Composition, 1958 (£675 in 1958), 34½×45½ | 3,000 |
| 1963 | N.Y. '28 July, 1953 I.C.A.', 76½×51, $7,000 | 2,500 |
|  | Aldrich. N.Y. Composition, 1960, 63½×51½ | 2,104 |
| 1965 | Ira Haupt. N.Y. '7 Mai, 1958', 63×38 (see 1969) | 1,950 |
| 1966 | N.Y  7 Février, 1957, 17×61½ | 3,214 |
|  | S. Abstraction, 1957, 76½×51½ | 2,600 |
| 1968 | Hillman. N.Y. Untitled composition, 1954, 36¼×25½, $5,500 | 2,292 |
| 1969 | N.Y. Peinture—7 Mai 1958, 63×38 ($5,500 in 1965) $5,500 | 2,310 |
|  | '10 Octobre, 1952', 35×45½, $9,500 | 3,992 |

YVES TANGUY. 1900–1955. (sur-réaliste)

| 1954 | N.Y. Escarpe auditif, 9½×10½ | 304 |
|---|---|---|
| 1962 | S. Demain, 1936, 21½×18 | 3,000 |
| 1964 | S. Tître inconnu, 1928, 35×25 | 4,250 |
|  | Les transparents, 39×32, Tate Gallery | 8,000 |
| 1965 | S. Les survecants | 7,000 |
|  | Toilette de l'air, 1937, 39×31½ | 7,000 |
| 1966 | C. Le bonjour doré, 1929, 25½×35½ | 4,200 |
|  | Lonsdale. S. Je vous attends, 1934, 28¾×45 | 13,200 |
| 1968 | Lewis. N.Y. L'avenir des vois, 19¾×25½, $11,000 | 4,575 |

JACQUES VILLON.  1875–1963                                                              £

1960  Versailles.  Battage en Normandie, 12×25½, FN40,000+
      tax                                                                          3,180
1961  Versailles.  Composition avec nu, 1930, 10¾×7½, FN20,200
      +tax                                                                         1,730
1962  Finarte.  Milan.  Préhistoire, 1957, 26×36¾, L9 million+
      tax                                                                          5,190
      Les gens de la batterie, 1947, 39½×56½, L20 million+tax  13,080
      Motte.  Geneva.  Portrait d'homme, 36½×28¾, FS75,000
      +tax                                                                         7,500
1964  S.  La source, 1957, 21½×15                                                 2,800
      Sous la tente, 1929, 17½×23½                                               4,000
1965  Haupt.  N.Y.  Portrait, 1953, 32×24                                         8,214
      N.Y.  Du blé à la paille, 25×55                                            12,500
      Zadok.  S.  Chantilly, promenade de chevaux, 20×58                         11,500
1967  Paris.  Les cartes, 1903, coloured aquatint                                2,140
1968  S.  La vautour s'enfuit, 1956, 36×28¾                                       6,000
      N.Y.  Portrait.  Claude Mèran, 1923, 28½×23½, $15,000                       6,250
1969  Paris.  Le jardin, 26×36¾, FN100,000+tax                                   9,300

## ABSTRACT PAINTERS: AMERICAN

Although American abstract paintings differ no more from those of other
nations than one Hilton hotel differs from another, a tremendous effort has
been made to present the image of a national school with New York as the
successor of Paris. This is a status symbol market, centred in New York where
prices are generally higher than in Europe. However, the build-up of the 1950s
seems to have lost some of its momentum in the next decade. Jackson Pollock in
particular, despite the advantages of having been both native born and short-
lived, kept barely level with the prices of 1961. Empty panels of a single colour
(see Barnet Newman and Max Rothko) are still with us, and someone pays
money for them, but no longer 600 dollars a square foot. Is it possible that
*épater le bourgeois* is an exercise that can be overdone?

ALEXANDER CALDER.  1898–

1963  S.  Red Branch, 'mobile', 1949, painted steel and alumi-                    £
      nium                                                                         700
1965  Dotremont.  N.Y.  Verticale, hors de l'horizontale, wire
      and painted metal, 67 in. high, $10,000                                     3,570
      The red mobile, ditto, 78 in. high, $9,000                                  3,212
1966  Whitney Museum benefit.  N.Y.  The onion, black-
      painted steel structure, 72 in. square, $19,000                            6,785
1968  N.Y.  Zarabanda, painted on sheet metal with wire cord,
      60×28, $13,000                                                              5,418
1969  N.Y.  Standing mobile, sheet metal etc., 18¾ in., $7,500                   3,127

28

SAM FRANCIS. 1923–                                                                    £
1960   Ernest Duveen.   S.   Blue and yellow, 1956, 59×30½              2,800
       Kornfeld.    Berne.    Blue   painting,   1960,   46×35¼,
       FS25,000+tax                                                                     2,400
              Over Red, 1959, 74×38, FS28,000+tax                         2,685
1964   Kornfeld.   Berne.   Untitled, FS19,000+tax                       1,840
1965   Kornfeld.    Berne.    Untitled,   gouache,   40½×27¼,
       FS16,000+tax                                                                     1,535
       Ross.   N.Y.   'Red, No. 2', 76×45, 1954, $16,500              5,890
       C.   Red and blue painting, 25½×20½                               1,470
1970   N.Y.   Blue, 1951, 57½×35, $20,000                                8,333

LEE GATCH.   1902–
1969   N.Y.   The acrobats, 1960, 43½×35½, $5,500                     2,203
       The beach, 1959, 33×39¾, $6,000                                    2,500

ARSHILE GORKY.   1904–1948
1960   N.Y.   Composition, 27¼×25½, $6,350                              2,300
1965   Scull.   N.Y.   Terracotta, 1947, 44×56, $18,000              6,440
       N.Y.   'Dialogue of the edge', 1946, 32×41, $15,750           5,625

ADOLPH GOTTLIEB.   1903–
1965   Dotremont.   N.Y.   'Crimson spinning no. 1', 1959, 85×
       71, $11,900                                                                        4,250
1967   N.Y   Blast III, 1958, 69×40, $4,250                              1,520

PHILIP GUSTON.   1913–
1965   Dotremont.   N.Y.   'Urn', 1957, 68×60, $10,200              3,640
1968   N.Y.   Garden of M, 68×78, $5,000                                 2,083

FRANZ KLINE.   1910–
1961   N.Y.   Bar-room painting, 1940, 36×31, $4,500                   607
1965   Scull.   N.Y.   'Initial, 1959' (about a dozen gigantic brush-
       strokes occupying a white canvas), 100×77 in., $18,000       6,440
1966   Whitney Museum benefit.   N.Y.   Dahlia, 1951, 82×67,
       $21,000                                                                             7,300
1968   N.Y.   Black Sienna, 1960, 92×67, $28,000                      11,665

WILLIAM DE KOONING.   1904–
1963   Aldrich.   N.Y.   Two striding women, 29½×21½, $26,500     9,588
1964   N.Y.   Stenographer, 24×19½, $9,000                             3,214
1965   Haupt.   N.Y.   Merritt Parkway, 80×70½, $40,000            14,285
       Scull.   N.Y.   Spike's Folly, 1959, 79×68½, $23,000          8,214
              'Woman', 29×21, $24,000                                          8,570
              Police Gazette, 1955, 43×50, $37,000                        13,214

| | | £ |
|---|---|---|
| 1966 | N.Y. Grand Opening, newspaper collage, 36×30½, $12,000 | 4,285 |
| | Helena Rubinstein. N.Y. Elegy, 40½×47¾, $20,000 | 7,180 |
| 1967 | Epstein. N.Y. Composition on masonite, 1939, 28¼×22½, $17,500 | 6,250 |
| 1968 | N.Y. Composition, 22¼×28¾, $7,250 | 3,020 |
| 1969 | N.Y. 'Woman, study', 28½×22¾, $8,250 | 3,440 |
| 1970 | N.Y. Two striding women (see 1963) $40,500 | 18,750 |

ROBERT BURNS MOTHERWELL

| | | |
|---|---|---|
| 1965 | Dotremont. N.Y. Diary of a painter, 70×100, $11,000 | 3,930 |

BARNET NEWMAN. 1905–

| | | |
|---|---|---|
| 1965 | Scull. N.Y. 'Tundra, 1950', An orange oblong panel, 72 in. by 89, traversed by a single vertical line, $25,900 | 9,250 |

JACKSON POLLOCK. 1912–1956

According to Maurice Rheims, this painter's work reached the level of £464 in 1944, £720 in 1953, £3,500 to £10,000 in 1957 and £11,000 in 1959. In 1961 prices exceeding £25,000 were already rumoured. At the moment there may be a pause in the progress of this cult which is not altogether confined to the U.S.A. Nevertheless, on the market for purely post-war reputations the only rival to the founder of the drip-dry school is Jean Dubuffet and his gimmick is a very different one.

| | | £ |
|---|---|---|
| 1960 | S. Composition, 1951, 24¾×38½ | 2,900 |
| 1961 | Bought by Tate Gallery (Heinz fund), 'No. 23' About | 5,000 |
| | Freudman. S. Free form, 1946, 19½×14½ | 4,500 |
| 1962 | S. 'Number Three', 1949, 31¼×61¾ ($61,500) | 22,000 |
| 1963 | S. 'Comet', 1947, 37×18 | 5,000 |
| | 'Water figure' | 4,800 |
| 1964 | N.Y. 'White horizontal', 22×36½, $15,000 | 5,356 |
| | S. 'No. 19', 1948, 34×38 | 9,000 |
| 1965 | N.Y. Untitled, 1950, 22×39½, $6,000 | 2,500 |
| | Haupt. N.Y. Untitled, 1948, 22½×30½, $14,000 | 5,000 |
| | Dotremont. N.Y. 'Blue unconscious', 1946, 86×56, $45,000 | 16,060 |
| 1966 | Thompson. N.Y. Composition, 1941, 27×50, $24,000 | 8,630 |
| | Composition no. 16, 1949, 30¾×22¼, enamel splashes on paper, $32,000 | 11,450 |
| 1968 | Wolf. N.Y. 'Ritual', 1953, 90½×42¼, $44,000 | 18,330 |

MAX ROTHKO. 1913–1970

| | | |
|---|---|---|
| 1964 | C. Red on yellow, 1958, 29½×21¾ | 2,100 |
| 1965 | Dotremont. N.Y. Reds no. 22 (Plain oblong, slightly tinted), 80×70, $15,500 | 5,554 |

| ROBERT RAUSCHENBERG. 1925– | £ |
|---|---|
| 1965 Dotremont. N.Y. Gloria, 1956, 66×63½, $15,000 | 5,360 |
| Ira Haupt. N.Y. Summer storm, 'combine-painting', $12,950 | 4,625 |
| Scull. N.Y. Express, 1963, Montage of photographs 10 ft by 6 ft, $20,000 | 7,145 |
| 1966 Whitney Museum Benefit. N.Y. 'Yoicks', oils and collage, 96×72, $10,000 | 3,575 |

| JEAN RIOPELLE. 1923–. Canada | £ |
|---|---|
| 1960 S. Abstract Landscape, 1955, 34¾×45¼ | 800 |
| 1963 Aldrich. N.Y. Composition, 1952, 79×60 | 4,250 |
| 1966 C. Composition, 1949, 37½×50½ | 1,500 |
| 1968 Toronto. S. Composition, $13,500 Canadian | 5,280 |

| CLIFFORD STILL. 1904– | |
|---|---|
| 1960 Duveen. S. Blue and yellow, 1956, 59×30½ | 2,800 |
| 1965 Scull. N.Y. 'Painting', 1951, 93¼×75¼, $29,000 | 10,354 |
| 1968 N.Y. 'Painting' January 1951, 68×58, $26,000 | 10,833 |
| 1969 N.Y. Abstraction, 1948, Number H, 76×70, $43,200 | 17,916 |

| MARK TOBEY. 1890– | |
|---|---|
| 1961 Brera. Milan. Le dragon, tempera, L3 million+tax | 2,058 |
| 1962 Stuttgart. 'Encircled', tempera, 16×11½, DM25,500+tax | 2,760 |
| 1963 C. L'ange, 1956, tempera on paper, 24×32¾ | 1,575 |
| Composition, 1958, gouache on paper, 4×10½ | 378 |
| 1965 Ira Haupt. N.Y. Above the earth, VI, 1958, 44½×34¾ | 3,750 |
| Plane of poverty, 1960, 73×44, $15,000 | 5,354 |
| Scull. N.Y. Wild field, 1959, 29×27½, $14,000 | 5,000 |
| 1966 Institute of Contemporary Art benefit. S. Advance of history 1964, 25½×19½ | 2,500 |
| 1968 S. Earth rhythms, 25×18½ (indistinguishable from marbled linoleum) | 4,600 |

## HENRY ALKEN SENR AND JNR. (*See* Sporting Pictures)

## SIR LAWRENCE ALMA-TADEMA. 1836–1913

It would be premature to suggest that there are the beginnings of a cult for this most fallen of all fallen idols. The situation has, however, changed since 1960 when one of the most celebrated of Alma-Tadema's works failed to find a buyer at 250 guineas. Yet *The Finding of Moses* had been commissioned in 1905 for 5,000 guineas, the equivalent in 1960 of at least £30,000. Subsequently we have seen some very ingenious sales-promotion. Alma-Tadema, it seems, fore-shadowed—of all things—Hollywood. And so, in 1969, *A Farewell Kiss*, a very much less elaborate work, reached £4,600, a handsome tribute indeed to the picture's crass insensibility and its almost hilarious failure to convey the psychology of the Pagan world. The rise in Alma-Tadema can hardly be because these crowds of artists' models in togas or chitons, posed as in stage photographs under the same top-light, have been equated with the *Zeitgeist* of the age. Two factors have combined. The first is a handsome distribution of wealth which makes it impossible for anything whatsoever to be too vulgar. The second is the price of individual reputation—*any* individual reputation—which is now so inflated that £5,000 has become the price of contempt. To recover the astonishing relative standing which they possessed in the early 1900s some of these paintings would have to reach the £200,000 class.

| | | | £ |
|---|---|---|---|
| 1960 | Reeves. C. Roses of Elgabalus, $51\frac{1}{2} \times 84$ (commissioned 1888 £4,000, £483 in 1934) bought in at | | 105 |
| | The finding of Moses, commissioned 1904 £5,250, $53 \times 84$ (£861 in 1935) bought in at | | 252 |
| 1963 | Cargill. S. The Apodyterium, $20 \times 26$ | | 580 |
| | Ionides. S. Expiation (£2,047 in 1896, £52 10s. in 1940) | | 550 |
| | Martin. S. The Roman picture gallery, $24 \times 19$ | | 220 |
| | (Reduced version of the picture commissioned in 1874 at £10,000) | | |
| 1964 | Princess Labia. S. Anthony and Cleopatra, 1876, $25 \times 36\frac{1}{4}$ | | 2,000 |
| 1965 | C. Nude on a couch, $14\frac{3}{4} \times 8\frac{3}{4}$, 'painted at one sitting' | | 231 |
| 1966 | C. The Kiss, 1892, $17\frac{1}{2} \times 24$ | | 1,575 |
| 1968 | C. Water-pets, numbered CXXXIII, 1875, $25\frac{1}{2} \times 55$ | | 504 |
| 1969 | Glenn-Allen. S. A parting kiss, $43 \times 28\frac{1}{2}$, numbered CCXLI, 1887 | | 4,600 |
| | The oleander, numbered CCLXV, $35\frac{1}{2} \times 25\frac{1}{2}$ | | 3,000 |
| | N.Y. The sculpture gallery, 1867, $24 \times 18\frac{1}{2}$, $5,250 | | 2,188 |
| | Preparations in the Colosseum, numbered CCCVIII, $60\frac{1}{2} \times 30\frac{1}{2}$, $4,500 | | 1,875 |

## AMERICAN SCHOOL

(*See also Abstract Painters: American 19th–20th centuries*, Mary Cassatt, Sargent, Whistler)

This is of course a regional market, supported by a mixture of nostalgic and patriotic fervour like all regional markets, though more lavishly than most, our own for instance. English Impressionists like Wilson Steer and Sickert have not rivalled the five-figure prices of Childe Hassam, George Inness and Maurice Prendergast. What is significant is that these highly-priced American Impressionists are cheaper than completely realist painters like Frederick Remington and Charles Marion Russell, painters who flourished at the turn of the century and whose style was so dominated by action and incident as to relegate them to the category of magazine illustrators. Some of these works are actually painted in monochrome oils for reproduction in half-tone, the normal press-work procedure at that period. This seems a very peculiar preference, though perhaps no more peculiar than that which has put the race-course snapshot pictures of Sir Alfred Munnings in the £25,000 class.

Even more expensive than the magazine-cover realism of Remington and Russell are the belated strivings of the European romantic movement in the U.S.A. a generation earlier. In the 1850s and 1860s romantic America meant Red Indians and Mississippi side-wheelers and emigrants on the Western trail, the subjects of the Currier and Ives prints, skilfully lithographed after Palmer, Tait, Catlin and other artists. In 1969 a very average impression of the famous *Midnight race on the Mississippi* made £300. Subjects like these seem romantic today in the best sense and not a bit like crossing the St Gotthard in order to paint professional artists' peasants in the costume of *Cavalleria rusticana*. The masterpiece of the American romantic school was Albert Bierstadt's picture, *Emigrants crossing the plains at sunset*, painted just after the Civil War. It looks like a Currier and Ives print, blown out to eight feet. In 1868, before there was any American competition for old masters, for impressionists or even for Barbizon pictures, a patriotically inclined citizen of Cleveland bought this remarkable work for $15,000 which certainly had the purchasing power of $75,000 a hundred years later. In fact it was auctioned in New York in 1969 for the Cleveland Automobile Club at $120,000, the dearest American picture on the post-war market, not excluding Sargent.

In a sense the Canadian-domiciled German Swiss painter, Cornelius Krieghoff, belonged to the same school as Bierstadt (who later in life produced tepid echoes of Whistler and impressionism as a member of the Hudson River school), but Krieghoff retained his native roots in the romantic school of Northern Europe, painting in that tradition pine-trees and bad weather, combined with sentimental domesticity, a mixture well suited to pioneer life in the backwoods and vastly nostalgic in the Canada of today. But there are no $120,000 prices. For, alas, the poor man possessed only a modicum of competence, and scarcely a vestige of a personal style.

ALBERT BIERSTADT. 1830–1902            £

| | | £ |
|---|---|---|
| 1962 N.Y. Sunset, Grand Tetons, 1862, 18×29, $3,600 | | 1,285 |
| 1965 N.Y. Autumn landscape, 29×20½, $1,600 | | 572 |
| 1968 Schilling. N.Y. Emerald sea, 41¾×63¾, c. 1880, $22,000 | | 9,167 |
| 1969 N.Y. Coastal scene (1890x) 13½×18½, $13,000 | | 5,450 |
| Emigrants crossing the plains, 1867, 60×96, $120,000 at 2·38 | | 50,280 |
| Outlet of Lake Tahoe, 18¾×28, $7,000 | | 2,930 |
| Titus. S. Italian landscape, peasant woman carrying water, 24×29¾ | | 1,000 |

2*

WILLIAM M. HARNETT. 1851–1892           £

1967   N.Y.   Still life, 1877, 9×12, $5,750          2,054

1969   N.Y.   Mr Huling's rack picture, *trempe l'oeuil* of cards and
envelopes, 1888, 30×25, $75,000        31,250

CHILDE HASSAM. 1859–1935

1959   N.Y.   Britanny cottage-dwellers, 1897, 21½×18, $8,750    3,125

1962   N.Y.   The East window, 1913, $5,250        1,875

1964   N.Y.   Peach blooms, 21½×18½, $3,750       1,340
           Lady in a garden, 25×27½, $13,500     4,840

1966   N.Y.   Street scene, France, 18½×15¼, $7,500     2,675

1967   N.Y.   Rockport, 1919, wc, 15×22, $6,000      2,143

1968   N.Y.   Spring showers in Paris, *c.* 1896, 13×18, $32,000   13,333

WINSLOW HOMER. 1836–1910

1960   Cochrane.   S.   Fisherman's family awaiting boats, 1881,
           12¾×19          5,600

1962   N.Y.   Stormy sea and rocks, 1902, wc, 14×21, $13,000   4,607
           The Saguenay, Grande Décharge, 1902, wc, 13½×12¼,
           $24,000          8,570

1964   N.Y.   The country store, 1871, 11½×18, $26,000    9,285

1966   N.Y.   Farmhouse on a hill, 1878, 10×18½, $21,000    7,500

1967   N.Y.   Two zouaves, charcoal drawing, *c.* 1864, 13¾×9½,
           $6,500          2,321

1969   N.Y.   Milkmaid, wc, 9½×13¼, $12,000      5,000

1970   C.   (at Houston, Texas) Landscape, $46,000     19,166

GEORGE INNESS. 1825–1894

(In 1918 *Wood gatherers* made $30,000 or £6,183)

1962   N.Y.   Niagara Falls, 1885, 16×24, $3,800      1,355

1963   N.Y.   Late sunset, 1893, 40½×54, $7,000      2,500

1965   N.Y.   Snowy haystack, Montclair, 1889, 24×38, $9,250
           ($525, 1946)         3,300
           Virginian sunset, 1899, 30×45, $10,750    3,840

1966   N.Y.   Orchard, Montclair, 1894, 30×45, $9,500 ($800 in
           1948)          3,390

1968   N.Y.   The close of day, 27×22, $7,250      3,020

1969   Lyle Price.   N.Y.   After the shower, *c.* 1863–5, 12¼×18½,
           $23,000          9,538

CORNELIUS KRIEGHOFF. Canada. Floruit 1845–72

1951   C.   Canadian ice scene          262 10s.

1952   Robinson Fisher.   Another ditto       756

1955   C.   Landscape with Indian trappers      1,050

1958   S.   Return from market, 13½×20       2,310
           Rapids of the St Maurice, 1864, 13½×20    1,995

£

1959 S. Hudson bay Indians' portage, 1865, 13¾×21¾                2,100
    Waring. S. Three Indians round a fire, 13¾×21¼         1,700
    S. Indians lighting fire, 8¾×12½                              1,000
    Indians portaging canoe, 9½×12¼                               950
1960 S. Caribou shooting in winter, 1862, 13×18                    1,800
    Indians skinning stag, 13½×21½                               1,800
1962 S. Indian campment, 17¼×26½                                   2,000
1963 Connor. S. Crossing the ice, Quebec, 1860, 16¾×23¼           2,600
    Village scene in winter, 1950, 25¾×36¼                       5,000
    The horse-trader, 1871, 13¾×19¾                              4,000
    24 paintings made £51,100
1966 C. Trapper's family in horse and sledge, 1850, 17×26          6,825
    Williams. C. Six Krieghoffs made £28,875 between them
    Trappers and dead moose, 12¾×17¾                             6,300
    Trappers aiming at herd of deer, 12½×17½                     6,510
    Log cabin, horse and sledge, 12×17¼                          4,410
1967 S. Trappers' sledge race, 1856, 16×25                         5,600
1969 Coysh. S. Indian encampment by a river, 12½×21½              6,000
    S. Toronto. Two Indian trapper scenes, dated 1848, each
    $20,000 (Canadian)                                           7,693
    C. Montreal. Huron Indians at Lake Lagon, 21×33,
    $36,000 (Canadian)                                          14,060
    Lake Lagon, Autumn, 8¾×10¾, $8,000 (Canadian)              3,150


MAURICE PRENDERGAST. 1859–1924
1960 Nisenson. N.Y. Bathers, 9¾×8½, $2,750                          982
1965 Ross. N.Y. Beach at St Malo, 1907, 17½×21, $21,000            7,490
1969 Topstone. N.Y. Evening walk, 10¼×13¾, $31,000              12,917
    N.Y. Early beach, wc, 1897, 13¾×12¼, $20,000                 8,333
    Woman in a garden, wc, 11×6¾, $7,500                         3,125


FREDERICK REMINGTON. 1861–1909
1961 N.Y. On the San Juan road, monochrome oils, 27×40½,
    $7,500                                                       2,700
1964 C. Cowboy mounted, pen drawing, 11½×7¼                         735
1962 S. Mile after mile rushed the little column, monochrome
    oils, 27×40                                                  2,000
1967 Astor. C. The frozen shepherd, 1900, 26½×39                   9,135
    C. A cavalry officer of the buckskins, wc, 21×17              4,200
1968 N.Y. The search, 22×20, $8,000                                3,335
1969 N.Y. Trooper of the plains, *bronze equestrian figure* 26 in.
    high, $45,000                                               18,750

|      |      |   | £ |
|------|------|---|---|
| 1969 | The Cheyenne, equestrian bronze, numbered 63, 20 in. high, $22,000 | | 9,166 |
| | Cheyenne scouts, Oklahoma, monochrome oils for Harper's Magazine, 1889, 27½×17½, $31,000 | | 12,917 |

DIEGO RIVERA. 1886–1957. Mexico

| 1959 | N.Y. Young man with fountain pen, 32×25½, $17,000 | 6,071 |
|------|------|---|
| | White flowers, 32×25½, $10,250 | 3,662 |
| | Outskirts of Toledo, 83×73, $10,250 | 3,662 |
| 1960 | N.Y. The painter's daughter with an Indian nurse, 1928, 24¼×28¼, $6,250 | 2,232 |
| 1962 | Power. S. La bouteille d'anis, 1915 (cubist) 27½×25 | 1,050 |
| 1964 | S. Two Mexican peasants, 1925, 35×26½ | 1,050 |
| 1965 | N.Y. Nino con conjugetes, 1949, 30×39¾, $6,500 | 2,321 |
| | Portrait of Ilya Ehrenberg, 1915, 45¾×35¼ (cubist), $21,000 | 7,490 |
| 1966 | C. Nature morte à l'orange et deux verres, 1917, 28¾× 21¼ (cubist, see 1968, 1969) | 3,150 |
| | Ortiz. C. Portrait, Ramon Gomez de la Serna, 1915, 43×35½ | 5,250 |
| | N.Y. Nature morte, 1915, 31½×25¼ (cubist), $12,000 | 4,286 |
| | Female portrait, 1944, 48×60, $12,500 | 4,464 |
| 1968 | N.Y. Portrait, M. Best, 1913, 89×63½, $19,000 | 7,917 |
| | Portrait d'un Espagnol, 1912, 78½×65, $13,000 | 5,415 |
| | Nature morte à l'orange et deux verres (see 1966), $9,500 | 3,959 |
| 1969 | N.Y. Same picture, $8,000 | 3,333 |
| | Coseche de Heno, 1920, 18×21½, $19,000 | 7,917 |

CHARLES MARION RUSSELL. 1864–1926

| 1961 | S. Cowboys lassoing steer, 1902 | 2,300 |
|------|------|---|
| 1967 | Moncreiffe. S. The ambush, 18×29 | 14,400 |
| 1968 | C. Indians firing at a muleteer, wc, 20½×33¼ | 8,925 |
| | Indians herding horses, 1894, wc, 20½×33 | 11,550 |
| 1969 | N.Y. Counting coup, bronze group of fighting Indians, 11½ in. high, numbered 63, $32,000 | 13,333 |
| | Where the best of riders quit, Equestrian bronze, 14¼ in., $19,000 | 7,916 |
| | Indian courtship, wc, 9×7½, $8,000 | 3,333 |
| | Titus. S. A bar triangle bolter, wc, 1888, 9×11½ | 1,700 |

ROBERT SALMON. c. 1775–1842

| 1969 | N.Y. Boston harbour in 1839 (commissioned at $400), 40×60, $62,500 | 25,208 |
|------|------|---|
| | Rocks at Nahant, 1836, 48¾×76, $7,500 | 3,125 |

36

ANDREW WYETH.  1917–                                                £

1965  N.Y.  Worm fence, wc, $17\frac{1}{4} \times 21\frac{1}{2}$, $6,000                     2,140
             Berry baskets, wc, $12 \times 15$, $7,000                       2,500
1966  N.Y.  Iron age, wc, 1950, $21 \times 29$, $12,000                    4,286
             Marvel.  N.Y.  Winter fields, 1942, tempera on gesso,
             $17\frac{1}{2} \times 41$, $34,000                             12,140
1967  N.Y.  Ocean Inlet, Maine, $17\frac{3}{4} \times$   , $12,000          4,286
             Snellenburg.  N.Y.  'Due back', wc, 1965, $18\frac{1}{2} \times 23\frac{1}{2}$,
             $17,500                                         6,250
1968  N.Y.  Morning Light, $17\frac{1}{2} \times 21\frac{3}{4}$, $9,000                  3,750
             Teel's Island, $21\frac{1}{2} \times 29\frac{1}{2}$, $12,500                 5,200
1969  N.Y.  Barnacles, wc, $17\frac{1}{2} \times 21\frac{1}{2}$, $8,000
             Martinsville lobstermen, $c$. 1940, wc, $19 \times 29$, $18,000   7,500

OTHER PAINTERS

THOMAS HART BENTON.  1889–

1963  N.Y.  Missouri musicians, 1931, $29 \times 34\frac{3}{4}$                    3,572
1967  N.Y.  Weighing cotton, 1939, $31 \times 38$, $17,000                  6,072
1969  N.Y.  Gay Head, Martha's Vineyard, 1950,  $12 \times 16$,
             $10,000                                         4,166

WILLIAM MERRITT CHASE.  1849–1916

1969  N.Y.  Portrait, Mrs Howell, $16 \times 10\frac{1}{2}$, $9,000               3,750
             Moorish warrior examining sword, 1872, $57\frac{1}{2} \times 71\frac{1}{2}$,
             $9,000                                          3,750
             Self-portrait, $17 \times 13$, $16,500                        6,875

JASPER FRANCIS CROPSEY.  1823–1900

1969  N.Y.  Hastings on Hudson, 1886, $16 \times 30$, $5,250               2,182
             Autumn landscape, 1877, $12 \times 10$, $20,000               8,333
       N.Y.  New England landscape, 1867, $20 \times 33$, $20,000          8,333

EASTMAN JOHNSON.  1824–1906

1969  N.Y.  Interesting news, reclining girl, 1872, $17\frac{1}{2} \times 22$,
             $25,000                                        10,417

FRANK TENNEY JOHNSON.  1874–1939

1965  N.Y.  In the night, 1930, $16 \times 12$, $1,900                        679
1969  N.Y.  The harvest moon, 1923, $40 \times 30$, $15,000                6,250

ALFRED JACOB MILLER

1966  N.Y.  Indian procession, 1837, pen and wc, $7\frac{3}{4} \times 4\frac{1}{2}$,
             $15,000                                         5,360
             Captain Stewart's cavalcade, 1837, ditto, $8\frac{3}{4} \times 14\frac{1}{2}$,
             $10,000                                         3,570
1969  N.Y.  Trappers' camp, 1838, $45,000                              18,750

NEWELL CONYERS WYETH. 1882–1945     £

| | | |
|---|---|---|
| 1967 | McGraw. N.Y. Train robbery, 44×33, $7,750 | 2,768 |
| 1969 | N.Y. Mystery tree, 1908, 26×26, $6,250 | 2,604 |

## FRA ANGELICO. 1387–1455

These five little scraps of paintings, survivors from the predellas of dispersed altarpieces, will probably remain the last reputable Fra Angelico works to have reached the saleroom. These are the very bottom of the barrel. The Spencer Churchill panel is the most interesting because we know the price which the Earl of Northwick paid at the Duke of Lucca's sale in 1840. When this panel was sold for the majestic sum of £2 12s. 6d., there had already been a limited cult of the earlier Italian primitives, mainly a German cult, for nearly two generations, but it was not till 1846 that *Johann von Fiesole* became the subject of a learned monograph. By that time the *Last Judgement* of the present Staatliche Museum, Berlin, had already been sold at the Cardinal Fesch sale for £704 and resold to the future Earl of Dudley for £1,500. In 1885 the German government paid £10,500. The Spencer Churchill panel, eight inches long, is probably worth £20,000 by now in spite of its poor condition. How much then the Berlin altarpiece with its three crowded panels over 40 inches high? Even in an age when the *Quattrocento* is much less popular than it was in 1885, three quarters of a million might be an under-estimate.

| | | | |
|---|---|---|---|
| 1957 | Hawkins-Jones. S. St Nicolas and St Michael, a pair, 14½×5 | £<br>2 for | 7,800 |
| 1960 | Peregrine. S. St Benedict, fragment from the San Marco altarpiece, Florence, 15½×5½ | | 9,500 |
| 1961 | S. Nativity, predella panel, ex Sachsen-Meiningen Coll., 7¼×17 | | 9,000 |
| 1965 | Spencer Churchill. C. Miracle of Sts Cosmas and Damian, 3¾×8 (£2 12s. 6d. in 1840, £77 14s. 0d. in 1859) | | 14,125 |

RICHARD ANSDELL. (*See* Sporting Pictures)

ARCHIMBOLDO. (*See* Italian School, 16th–17th centuries)

ANTOINE ARLAUD. (*See* Miniatures)

JEAN ARP. (*See* Abstract Painters)

J. B. AUGUSTIN. (*See* Miniatures)

BAREND AND HENDRIK AVERCAMP.  (*See* Dutch School)

FRANCIS BACON.  (*See* English School: Modern)

HANS BALDUNG (Grien).  (*See* German School, 15th–16th centuries
(1969))

GIACOMO BALLA.  (*See* Abstract Painters: European)

JACOPO BASSANO.  (*See* Venetian School)

POMPEIO BATONI.  (*See* Italian School, 18th century)

MARY BEALE.  (*See* Miniatures)

### SIR WILLIAM BEECHEY.  1753–1839

Decidedly small beer. An immense number of portraits have survived, in-
fluenced successively by Reynolds, Hoppner and Lawrence in the course of a
working life of more than sixty years. The prices in this list are the best of their
respective years of sale. A hundred to two hundred pounds may be considered
normal. Yet in 1918 *Miss Harriet Stanhope* made £5,985, equivalent to £30,000
in the money of 1970. That however was mere chickenfood in the days when
Duveen was making the English 18th century portrait school, a millionaires'
market. The *Sarah Siddons*, sold in 1968 for £11,550, was not the beginning of
a new range of prices. A celebrity portrait always commands a special price,
though this is perhaps the least attractive of all the portraits of that formidable
woman.

|  |  |  | £ |
|---|---|---|---:|
| 1960 | N.Y. | Rear-Admiral Frederick Beechey, 30×24, $1,600 | 572 |
| 1961 | Whitmarch. N.Y. | The Sterling family (see 1967) $8,000 | 2,857 |
| 1962 | C. | The Raymond Symonds family, 101×70 | 1,365 |
| 1964 | S. | Miss Ellen Smith with parrot, 62×42 | 380 |
| 1964-7 | | Several authenticated portraits at less than £100 each | |
| 1967 | D. of Newcastle. C. | Thomas Hope of Deepdene in Turkish dress, 1799, 87×66 | 199 10s. |
| | N.Y. | The Sterling family, 44×56, $2,500 ($8,000 in 1961) | 893 |
| 1968 | Brooke. C. | Sarah Siddons with emblems of tragedy and Shakespeare monument, 93×56 (£67 in 1836) | 11,550 |
| | Shaftsbury Society. S. | Duke of Cambridge, 1808, 29½×24½ (commissioned for £84 to include a replica) | 850 |
| | Rathdonnell. C. | Thomas Bunbury, M.P., 25×20 | 525 |
| 1969 | Inchcape. S. | Mrs Waldron, ¾ length, 49×39 | 500 |
| | N.Y. | Miss Weatherborn, 29½×24½, $3,100 | 1,292 |

# GIOVANNI BELLINI. 1427–1516

Formerly this was a name used very recklessly. Since Morelli and Berenson attributions are made with much more caution. Yet it is by no means certain that any of the following works belong to the strict canon. To get an idea of the present value of a sound Giovanni Bellini, some of the prices paid in the present century for well-known gallery pictures may be considered. In 1920 René Gimpel sold the *St Francis in the desert* of the Frick Foundation for £51,450, while in 1936 Duveen sold the *Young Man in a Red Coat* of the Washington National Gallery for £57,530. Both these pictures should be worth several hundreds of thousands in devalued pounds. On the other hand, a Holy Family for which Jules Bache was reputed to have paid £31,000 or $150,000, was sold for £1,463 or $5,500 in New York in 1945 when it was no longer thought a Bellini.

|      |                                                                                       | £      |
|------|---------------------------------------------------------------------------------------|--------|
| 1958 | Gudrun Fischer.  S.  The Benediction of Jesus (sold as by Marco Basaiti), 23¼ × 18½  | 11,500 |
|      | S.  Nativity, 10¾ × 19                                                                 | 15,500 |
| 1963 | Cintas.  N.Y.  Madonna and child, 32 × 26½, possibly by Cima                          | 8,925  |
|      | Thyssen-Bornemizsa.  S.  St Sebastian, 25 × 21¾                                        | 2,800  |
|      | S.  Portrait of a Venetian Procurator, 11¾ × 13¾, bought in                           | 13,000 |

### DRAWINGS

|      |                                                                                                                      |        |
|------|--------------------------------------------------------------------------------------------------------------------|--------|
| 1958 | Holland-Martin.  C.  (Skippe collection) Christ at the column, Two pen studies on one sheet, 9½ × 5¼                | 15,750 |
| 1959 | C.  Three pen studies of an apostle on one sheet                                                                    | 15,540 |
| 1969 | C.  (School of Bellini) Sacrifice to Artemis, derived from arch of Constantine, architectural study on verso, pen, 10 × 8, Munich Print Room | 2,100  |

# BERNARDO BELLOTTO. 1720–1780

View-paintings are decidedly in and Venetian view-paintings more than any others. With the great Canaletto deservedly in the £100,000 class, the best works of his nephew seem underpriced. It is remarkable that not until 1946 could a first-class Bellotto make more than £2,000. A painting from the same series was sold in 1965 for £27,000, but works of the quality of the Dresden views are not likely to reach the saleroom except extremely rarely, and works comparable with the Warsaw views not at all. In Warsaw Bellotto focussed his eye with the unearthly space-time precision of an early Daguerrotype on an unforgettable mélange of French court life and half-nomadic savagery. Even in the days of *The Stonemason's Yard* Canaletto barely surpassed this achievement. The Warsaw views must certainly command Canaletto prices.

| | | £ |
|---|---|---|
| 1961 | Maxwell. S. View in Rome with Capitol, $28\frac{1}{2} \times 38\frac{1}{4}$ | 2,500 |
| | C. Venetian Capriccio, $19\frac{1}{2} \times 31\frac{1}{4}$ | 1,050 |
| 1962 | C. The Molo from the Vacino, Venice, $40\frac{1}{2} \times 48$ | 2,100 |
| | S. Piazza Navona, Rome, $62 \times 50$ | 1,300 |
| | Companion piece. The Capitol, $62 \times 50$ | 1,700 |
| | C. Veduta ideale, Padua, $24\frac{3}{4} \times 29\frac{1}{2}$ | 1,470 |
| 1963 | Fitzgerald. S. Campo San Gallo, Venice, $38\frac{1}{2} \times 58\frac{3}{4}$ | 4,200 |
| | S. Via di Ripetta, Rome, $57\frac{1}{2} \times 33\frac{1}{2}$ | 30,000 |
| | Quirinale Palace, Rome, same size | 17,000 |
| 1964 | Werthmueller. C. View on the Brenta with palace, $16\frac{1}{2} \times 26\frac{1}{4}$ | 3,150 |
| 1965 | Huntington Hertford. S. Dresden from the Elbe, $54 \times 37$. (In 1946 five larger views of Dresden made from £980 to £2,360) | 27,000 |
| | Williams. S. San Giovanni e Paolo, Rome, bought in Princess Amalie of Bavaria. C. Temple of Fortuna | 14,500 |
| | virilis, Rome, $29\frac{1}{2} \times 41\frac{1}{2}$ | 14,700 |
| 1967 | S. Royal gardens and park, Maritzburg, oval, $29\frac{1}{2} \times 40\frac{3}{4}$ | 1,800 |

## THOMAS HART BENTON. (*See* American School)

## NICOLAS BERCHEM. 1620–1683

Somewhat inexplicably 18th century collectors rated the works of this prolific Italianizing Dutchman as high as those of Rembrandt. Today they fetch at the best about as much as a few lines by Picasso, sketched on the back of a menu. Nor has there been any real appreciation in value in the 1960s. Some of the prices of the past, recorded in Volume One, are worth recalling in terms of present day purchasing power. Smith, for instance, who wrote the *Catalogue raisonné*, valued Lord Grosvenor's acquisition of 1806, *The Chateau de Bentheim*, at 3,000 guineas, equivalent perhaps to £45,000 in 1970. As late as 1882 a Berchem landscape could make £1,735, equivalent to £14,000. Seventy-five years were to elapse before another Berchem made as much as £900 in the London salerooms.

| | | £ |
|---|---|---|
| 1960 | Return from the hunt, $28 \times 24$ | 1,365 |
| 1961 | S. Mountainous landscape, $46 \times 50$ | 500 |
| 1962 | C. Extensive landscape, Tivoli, $42 \times 37$ | 1,155 |
| 1964 | C. Seaport with figures, $25 \times 30\frac{1}{2}$ | 2,100 |
| 1965 | Adda. Paris. Cattle in rocky landscape, $10\frac{1}{4} \times 12$, FN15,900+tax | 1,295 |
| | Strakosch. S. Landscape with cattle, nymph and satyr, dated 1642, $27\frac{1}{2} \times 23\frac{1}{4}$ | 1,050 |

| | | £ |
|---|---|---|
| 1966 | S.  Peasants at a ford, $16\frac{1}{4} \times 22\frac{1}{4}$ | 500 |
| 1967 | C.  Hawking party and ruined abbey, $25\frac{1}{2} \times 30$ | 315 |
| | Peasants and horses in marketplace, $37 \times 45\frac{1}{2}$ | 735 |
| | S.  Landscape with peasants, $32 \times 41$ | 850 |
| | Lunge.  S.  Italian peasants outside an inn, 1657, $15 \times 21\frac{1}{2}$ | 2,600 |
| 1968 | S.  Peasants and cattle in rocky landscape, dated 1670, $44\frac{1}{2} \times 39\frac{1}{2}$ | 2,200 |
| 1969 | C.  (Attributed as 'N. Berchem') *Capriccio*, harbour scene with ships etc., $39 \times 32$ | 3,675 |
| | S.  Landscape with sportsmen, $41 \times 54$ ($£152$ 5s. in 1876) | 5,200 |

## GERRITT BERCKHEYDE.  (*See* Dutch School)

## ABRAHAM VAN BEYEREN.  (*See* Dutch School)

## ALBERT BIERSTADT.  (*See* American School, 19th–20th centuries)

## WILLIAM BLAKE.  1757–1828

It is absolutely impossible to tell today what a first class example of William Blake's work would fetch on the open market. His paintings in watercolour or in tempera on paper reach the salerooms very rarely indeed, and since the Graham Robertson dispersal of 1949 there has been nothing outstanding. Blake has always been an artist for scholars and literary men and never a painter's painter, therefore the ideal of museum curators. It is probable that the great dispersals of 1918 and 1949 have been hived off almost entirely in museums and galleries, and that there is very little of equal importance that can find its way to the saleroom. It may also be the case that, while fashionable opinion continues to extol the tedious liberation of the unconscious mind, religious ecstasy is at a discount. In that case the works which made over £7,000 apiece in 1949 will not have followed the general trend of the market so that prices in the region of £30,000 to £40,000 are not to be expected.

| | | £ |
|---|---|---|
| 1957 | Gowe-Weston.  C.  Elijah in the chariot of fire | 4,200 |
| 1959 | S.  The good and evil angels, 1785, Cecil Higgins Museum, $11\frac{3}{4} \times 17\frac{3}{4}$ | 2,200 |
| | Mary Magdalene at the feet of Christ | 2,050 |
| 1961 | S.  The death of Ezekiel's wife ($£200$ in 1949), wc, $13\frac{1}{2} \times 18\frac{1}{4}$ | 2,500 |
| | C.  Miniature painting on copper, horse and two figures, 1805, $4 \times 2\frac{3}{4}$ | 3,360 |

| 1962 | S. | The raising of Lazarus, wc, $16\frac{3}{4} \times 11\frac{3}{4}$ | 3,500 |
| | | The humility of the saviour, wc, $12\frac{1}{2} \times 13\frac{1}{2}$ | 2,600 |
| 1966 | | Miracle of the loaves and fishes, tempera on copper, $13 \times 19\frac{1}{2}$ (sold with another in 1853 for 16s.) badly worn | 1,000 |
| 1967 | Mele. C. | Urizen, woodcut worked over in pen and wc | 735 |
| | Kearley. S. | St Luke, tempera, signed and dated 1799, $15\frac{1}{2} \times 10\frac{3}{4}$ | 1,600 |

## LOUIS LEOPOLD BOILLY. (*See* French School, 18th century)

## HENRY BONE. (*See* Miniatures)

## ROSA BONHEUR. 1822–1899

Of all the falls in value about which the press pundits are so discreetly silent this is perhaps the greatest. The dearest Rosa Bonheur painting in the past decade was sold in 1960 for 550 guineas, equivalent to about £70 in the late 1880s when, as a large completed picture, it may have been worth £4,000. In 1886 Junius Spencer Morgan paid $60,000 ($268,000 or £112,000 in 1970 money) for *The Horse Fair*, 16 feet long and now in the Metropolitan Museum, New York. In the following year a quite normal Rosa Bonheur in the Graham sale made £4,059. In 1949 it was sold for £199 10s. and might be worth £600 or £700 in 1970. It is called *A Highland Raid* and, as its title suggests, owes almost everything to Landseer. But it is quite certain that Landseer's most popular imitator no longer commands the prices of her master.

| | | | £ |
| 1960 | C. | Young bulls in a pasture, $51 \times 76$ | 577 10s. |
| 1965 | Dobiachowski. Berne. | Ploughing oxen, FS4,000+tax | 384 |
| 1966 | S. | Deer in a forest, winter, 1883, $17 \times 26$ | 170 |
| 1968 | Lord Belstead. S. | A sultry day, wc, 1872, $16 \times 29$ | 220 |
| | N.Y. | Cattle in hilly landscape, $19 \times 29$, $1,500 | 625 |
| 1969 | C. | Badger, 1874, $25 \times 31$ | 252 |
| | N.Y. | Horses in a stable, $31\frac{1}{2} \times 25$, $3,000 | 1,250 |

## RICHARD PARKES BONINGTON. 1801–1828

Inasmuch as he was the acknowledged inspiration of Delacroix and the absolute founder of the mid-19th century romantic school, both in England and in France, Bonington does not seem an overpriced painter. In 1878, when the merits of that school were not open to question, two of Bonington's full-sized oil paintings, of which he made very few, fetched 3,000 guineas each, equivalent to perhaps £30,000 in today's money. But even in 1970 it is not easy to envisage anything by Bonington making £30,000. The return of the romantic school to popularity has been slow and fitful even in the case of Delacroix himself.

| | | |
|---|---|---:|
| 1960 | Russell. S. Château de la duchesse de Berri (£325 10s. in 1922), 9½ × 15, oils | £ 6,800 |
| 1961 | S. Storm on the coast of Picardy, wc, 10 × 14 | 350 |
| 1965 | Turner. C. Street in Verona, oils, 23 × 17 (Sutherland Gower sale, 1911, £220 10s.) | 12,600 |
| 1966 | C. Oil sketch, young man in Tudor dress, 9½ × 5½ | 399 |
| | Lefold. S. Open landscape, sunset, wc, 5¾ × 7½ | 1,200 |
| | J de Rothschild. Paris. La gamme d'amour, after Watteau, wc, 2¾ × 4. With tax | 610 |
| 1967 | Ovenden. S. Interior with figures at a window, wc, 6 × 6½, Nottingham Museum | 700 |
| | Yates. S. The Tuileries, Paris, wc, 10 × 7½ | 3,200 |
| 1968 | S. View towards Sta Maria Maggiore, Venice, 1820, 5¾ × 7¼, wc | 1,000 |
| | Dawnay. C. In the forest of Fontainebleau, oils on board, 12¾ × 9½, c. 1826 (Evan Charteris sale, 1900, £30 9s.) | 8,925 |
| 1969 | Glenn Allen. S. Sailing brig and hulk at anchor, 15½ × 12½ | 8,600 |
| | C. An armourer's forge, oils, 12½ × 15½, bought in at | 2,100 |

## PIERRE BONNARD. 1867–1947

To fill in a serious gap which was left in Volume One the list has been brought back as far as 1906. Bonnard was then already a mature painter, but so far below the earlier Impressionists in public estimation that his works were barely in the £100 class. £500 was a most exceptional auction price even in 1939 and it remained high for Bonnard till 1951 when the era of inflation began. Bonnard was certainly not everyone's taste. The fact that he went a step further than the Impressionists in sometimes rejecting form altogether was particularly distasteful when the talk was all of *significant form* and when even abstract painting was obsessed with Cézanne's facets and planes. When this obsession gave way to wild and abandoned splashing of paint over a variety of surfaces, Bonnard's formlessness became a merit.

Have there been second thoughts on that question? In 1963 the Royal Academy invited the public to worship Bonnard at ten shillings a head at Burlington House, where forty years earlier he would not have stood a chance of showing a picture. He was then barely a £200 painter, whereas in 1963 propaganda for the exhibition claimed that some of the works shewn were worth over £100,000. It was even stated that Bonnard was the greatest painter of the century. In the introduction to the list in Volume One I had observed two years earlier, 'Bonnard rates higher than Sisley and Picasso and most of Monet'. But if that was true then, it was hardly so at the end of the decade. The Bonnards at £100,000 were not forthcoming and it was not till 1968 that £86,000 was paid in the saleroom for a large and important nude. By this time it looked at least as if Vlaminck's *Fauve* paintings, Cross's *pointilliste* acrobatics and even the slick and chic Raoul Dufy had caught up with Bonnard. However, after twenty years of booming Impressionist and Post-Impressionist paintings, one has learnt not to make any predictions about them.

|      |                                                                                          | £      |
|------|------------------------------------------------------------------------------------------|--------|
| 1906 | Blôt. Paris. Le dessert, 1,250 francs+tax                                                 | 123    |
| 1911 | Henri Bernstein. Paris. Nu à contre-jour, 2,800 francs+tax                                | 123    |
|      | Les petites faunes, 3,500 francs+tax                                                      | 154    |
| 1914 | Roger Marx. Paris. Orgue de Barbarie, 3,000 francs+tax                                    | 132    |
| 1918 | Sold by Léonce Rosenberg. La cascade, 4,600 francs                                        | 184    |
| 1924 | Leclenché. Paris. Nu au canapé                                                            | 145    |
| 1928 | Bought by Rees Jeffries. Lady at her toilette (see 1954)                                  | 154    |
| 1929 | Bought by John Boulton. Landscape (£6,510 in 1965)                                        | 280    |
| 1930 | Picture bought by Gimpel for the Toledo Museum                                            | 910    |
| 1936 | Bought for the Luxembourg. Paris. Le corset rouge, 35,000 francs at 125 to the £          | 280    |
| 1938 | Paris. La couturière, 51,000 francs+tax                                                   | 437    |
| 1939 | Canonne. Paris. Quai à Cannes, 75,000 francs at 175 to the £                              | 506    |
|      | Place Clichy, 46,000 francs+tax                                                           | 312    |
|      | Porte Molitor, 46,000 francs+tax                                                          | 312    |
|      | Echappée sur rivière, 45,000 francs+tax                                                   | 305    |
|      | Fleurs dans un vase, 36,000 francs+tax                                                    | 245    |
| 1948 | N.Y. Les boutiques, Boulevard de Battignoles, $3,850                                      | 960    |
| 1949 | Paris. La Seine à Vernon, 14½×18, 621,000 old francs+tax                                   | 550    |
| 1950 | Paris. Les mamans, 1894, 14×10½, 625,000 old francs+tax                                    | 560    |
| 1951 | Paris. Vernon, matinée d'automne, 42¾×50½, 2·8 million old francs+tax                       | 3,417  |
| 1953 | Paris. Femme nue, 1907, 2·8 million old francs+tax                                          | 3,470  |
|      | Fleurs sur table au tapis rouge, 22¾×24½, 7·2 million old francs+tax                        | 8,620  |
| 1954 | N.Y. The yellow screen, $14,000                                                            | 5,000  |
|      | C. Lady at her toilet                                                                     | 4,410  |
| 1955 | Paris. Femme aux mimeuses, 19×24½ (see 1963) 7·45 million old francs+tax                    | 7,350  |
|      | Bouquet de fleurs, 20×19½, 6·2 million old francs+tax                                       | 6,150  |
| 1956 | S. Vegetable stall                                                                        | 3,500  |
| 1957 | S. Nu au tub                                                                              | 5,500  |
|      | Fletcher. S. Le petit déjeûner, 17×21½                                                     | 5,040  |
|      | Lurcy. N.Y. Dining-room table with cat, 1948, 35½×29½, $70,000                             | 25,000 |
|      | Femme nue, 29×17¼, $50,000                                                                 | 17,860 |
|      | Murdoch. S. Buste de femme courbée, 17×26¼                                                 | 6,800  |

| | | £ |
|---|---|---|
| 1958 | Kirkeby. N.Y. Vendeuse de fruits, 23½×18, $40,000 | 14,250 |
| | At the stage door, 18×5, $17,000 | 6,075 |
| | Renée, portrait, 20×16, $17,000 | 6,075 |
| | Vernon. N.Y. Fenêtre ouverte, 40×28½, $94,000 | 33,555 |
| 1959 | Paris. Jeune Femme, 21½×14½, 10·15 million old francs+tax | 8,820 |
| | Les quais de Paris, 17½×26¾, 16·7 million old francs+tax | 13,620 |
| | S. Femme à la lampe, 1905, 17½×23½ | 13,500 |
| 1960 | C. Farmyard seen over a gate, Vernon, 24×29½ | 14,125 |
| | S. Femme nue, 54½×31½ | 18,000 |
| | Paris. Petite route au Cannet, 1924, FN225,000+tax, 30¼×25½ | 19,270 |
| | La table, 26×21½, FN250,000+tax | 21,780 |
| 1961 | Paris. Poppies in stoneware jug, 28½×21½, FN268,000+tax | 23,345 |
| | Juvilier. N.Y. La glace haute, 1914, 49×32½ (see 1965) $101,000 | 36,060 |
| | Somerset Maugham. S. Grandmother and child, 15×15 | 29,000 |
| | Metcalfe. S. The Terrasse family, 25½×32 | 10,000 |
| 1962 | Paris. La cuisine de Bonnard, 25¾×14½, FN151,000+tax | 13,255 |
| | Woolworth. N.Y. Après le déjeûner, 12¾×19, $28,000 | 10,000 |
| | N.Y. Nu à contre-jour, 48½×21½, $50,000 | 17,875 |
| 1963 | Versailles. Farm at Vernon, FN260,000+tax | 22,460 |
| | Paris. Femme au chien, 1891, 16½×13¼, FN190,000+tax | 16,550 |
| | Pot de fleurs avec figures, 36½×30½, FN350,000+tax | 30,450 |
| | Place Clichy, FN310,000+tax | 26,970 |
| | Femme en rouge devant un bouquet, FN252,000 +tax | 21,920 |
| | Aldrich. N.Y. Femme aux mimeuses, 19×24½, $55,000 (see 1955) | 19,643 |
| 1964 | Ross. N.Y. Paysage du Midi, 19×25½, $52,000 | 18,750 |
| | Glass. S. Still life with peaches, 12¼×10½ | 15,000 |
| | Lord Sandwich. C. Port de St Tropèz, 14½×26½ | 15,250 |
| | S. Peaches, 12¼×15½ | 17,000 |
| | La toilette, 1908, 30×18 | 21,000 |
| | Bloch. Paris. Coquelicôts au pot de grès, 28½×21½ | 22,357 |
| 1965 | S. Bridge of la Jatte, 1908, over 5 ft long | 19,000 |
| | La sortie, 1910, 23×26 | 18,000 |
| | Motte, Geneva. Paysage d'hiver a Vernon, FS178,000+tax (see 1968) | 17,000 |
| | N.Y. Le jardin inculte, 19¼×25¾, $60,000 | 21,425 |
| | Reisini. N.Y. La glace haute (see 1961), 49×32¼, $155,000 | 55,350 |
| | C. Golfe de St Tropèz | 11,025 |

| | | £ |
|---|---|---|
| 1965 | Versailles. Elegantes sur le Pont-Neuf, 14×20, FN96,000 +tax | 7,000 |
| | N.Y. La promenade, 18¼×25½, $50,000 | 17,875 |
| | Baigneuses de l'isle heureuse, oval, 26×38½, 1919, ditto | 17,875 |
| | S. La femme au chapeau, 26½×13¼ | 13,500 |
| 1966 | Capellières. S. Two decorative panels, 'à la campagne', 1927, 39½×12½ 2 for | 17,000 |
| | Helena Rubinstein. N.Y. Paysage animé, 51¼×86 (see 1967), $60,000 | 21,435 |
| | S. Les Puys, bords de mer, 28¼×21 | 18,500 |
| | C. Paysage en Provence, 13¼×16¾ | 11,550 |
| 1967 | Paris. Le grand jardin, 1900, 70×88, FN301,000+tax | 24,167 |
| | Cummings. S. Pannier de fruits en soleil, 23¾×17¼ | 23,000 |
| | S. Le parti de bal, 1905, 21×29 | 26,000 |
| | Paysage animé, 1913, 51½×86 (see 1966) | 31,000 |
| | S. Golfe de St Tropèz, 1936, 20×31 | 30,000 |
| | Femme dans un intèrieur, 32×25½, 1910 | 11,000 |
| | C. Street scene, 1902, 21¾×27½ | 24,150 |
| | Rubin. C. Jeune fille assise au lapin, 1891, 37¾×17 | 19,450 |
| | Paris. Au café, 12×18½, FN230,000 at 11·88+tax | 21,322 |
| | Motte, Geneva. Le gouter au jardin, 26×17½, FS136,000 +tax | 14,710 |
| | Portrait, Marthe Bonnard, 18×14¾, FS184,000+tax at 10·38 to the £ | 19,950 |
| | Paysage d'Hiver à Vernon, 1920, 15¾×24½ (see 1965) FS202,000+tax | 21,800 |
| | Paysage à Vernon, 17¾×20¾, FS182,000+tax | 19,740 |
| 1968 | N.Y. Mme Dupuy, bust portrait, 1916, 18½×15, $18,500 | 7,835 |
| | Malherbe. S. Promenade de jeunes ecolières, gouache study for a colour woodcut, 9½×14 | 19,000 |
| | S. Paysage animé de baigneuses, 1910, 22½×37½ | 12,400 |
| | Bluestein. N.Y. Femme nue à sa toilette, 1924, 18½×13½, $47,500 | 19,800 |
| | Paysage, le Cannet, 1935, 28¾×26, $82,500 | 34,375 |
| | Pleydell Bouverie. S. Vase de fleurs, 17½×12½ | 37,000 |
| | Mirisch. S. Nu au chien, 1940, 48½×19¾ | 52,000 |
| | C. Jeune fille en robe verte, 1910, 23¼×15¼ (bought in, see 1969) | 13,650 |
| | Lady Hay. S. Mimosas, lilas blancs et coquelicôts, 1917, 21×16½ | 15,000 |
| | Coode. S. Nu debout dans un intèrieur, 1921, 48×22 | 86,000 |
| | S. La rue, 1889, 21¾×15 | 41,000 |
| | Femme s'essuyant, 1909, 27½×13¾ | 40,000 |
| | Hadorn. C. Jeune fille enfilant une aiguille, 1905, 24×22 | 23,100 |
| | Herring. S. La maison au toit rouge, 8½×10¾ | 15,500 |

£

| | | | £ |
|---|---|---|---|
| 1968 | N.Y. Les fraises, 1910, 24¾×20, $115,000 (see 1969) | | 47,918 |
| 1969 | S. Nu au tub, *c.* 1917, 13¾×12 | | 19,000 |
| | Vase de fleurs, gouache, 14¾×22½ | | 12,000 |
| | Paysage classique, le Cannet, 1930, 23¼×18¾ | | 51,000 |
| | Magnin. N.Y. Femme accoudée avec chien et nature morte, 1917, 23½×19½, $190,000 | | 79,167 |
| | C. (Geneva). View across the bay at Cannes, 19×35, FS365,000+5% tax | | 36,750 |
| | Les pins, bord de la mer, *c.* 1923, 28½×21, FS340,000 +tax | | 34,327 |
| | C. (Tokyo). Landscape, 1903, 14¾×18¾, 29 million Yen | | 33,875 |
| | Jeune fille, robe verte, 1910, 23½×15¼ (see 1968), 20 million Yen | | 23,362 |
| | S. (Tokyo). Les fraises, 1910, 24¾×20 (see 1968) 30 million Yen | | 35,250 |
| | Au pied des montagnes, 1918, 21½×16½, 9 million Yen | | 10,600 |
| | S. La famille de Cipa Godebski, 34½×34¾, *c.* 1903 | | 28,000 |
| | Paysage classique Bord de Seine, *c.* 1915, 24½×15 | | 19,000 |
| | Vue de Grand Lemps, *c.* 1925, 19×23¼ | | 27,000 |
| 1970 | Bowers. S. Femme sortant du bain, 47×37 | | 82,000 |

## HIEROMYMUS BOSCH. 1450?–1516

The only painting by Bosch to appear in the saleroom in the 1960s was a small
fragment from a dispersed triptych. It made a price appropriate to a painter
who was not only a master of the weirdest of all phantasies but also among the
six greatest of the 15th century Flemish school. The possible value of a complete
work is anyone's guess. The exquisite roundel in the Boymans Museum, *The
Prodigal Son*, is 25 inches in diameter and was sold with the Figdor collection in
Berlin in 1931 for about £25,000, equivalent to at least £125,000 today.
Almost certainly it would be worth two or three times as much as that. It is interesting to observe that the National Gallery, which paid £150,000 merely to
stop a dull Italo-Byzantine Madonna by Duccio from going to Cleveland, did
not attempt to get the Bosch fragment, though they have only one example of
his work, and that none too certain.

£

| | | | £ |
|---|---|---|---|
| 1963 | S. The seven deadly sins, schoolpiece, 34×23 | | 3,400 |
| | Paris. Last Judgement (attributed) triptych, 28¾×18½ and 86, FN100,000+tax | | 8,030 |
| 1964 | S. Fragment from a Temptation of St Anthony, possibly from the Escurial, 10¼×7½ | | 35,000 |
| 1966 | Meyer. C. Temptation of St Anthony, 38×56 (now attributed to Peter Huys) | | 10,000 |

1967  S.  St Christopher with infant Christ, schoolpiece, 25¼ ×       £
      37½                                                          3,000
1968  Kadjar.  C.  Last Judgement, 33×37, schoolpiece              6,300

### DRAWINGS

1961  Randall.  S.  Two Pharisees disputing, pen, 6×4              6,500


## AMBROSIUS BOSSCHAERT.  (*See* Dutch School)


## SANDRO BOTTICELLI.  1444–1510

In 1931 Andrew Mellon bought the *Last Judgement* of the Hermitage Museum, Leningrad, for £173,600, the equivalent of £868,000 in 1970 money, thus close on a million of our devalued pounds for the least sympathetic of Botticelli's pictures. But so highly was Botticelli then esteemed that Mellon did not have to pay much more for the last of the truly authentic Raphael Madonnas. Very different was the climate in 1967 when the *Marriage Feast of Nastagio* returned to its first home, the Pucci Palace in Florence, after a century's wanderings. For the price was £105,000 and that in real money terms was less than its much inferior companion-panels had made in the Spiridon sale in Berlin in 1929.

The *Quattrocento* market is so wretchedly depleted that a Botticelli with so impeccable a pedigree and of such singular beauty might at least have made more than a Braque or Picasso of the cubist period. It is doubtful whether there will be any more Botticellis. But it is precisely the beauty of this long *cassone* panel that may provide the reason. Avoidance of beauty is a universal creed of long standing so that the perpetual insistence of the early Florentines on human perfection has become a source of irritation.

                                                                   £
1962  Elwes.  S.  Holy Family with angels, attributed, 29½×18   11,500
1963  Mackail.  S.  Annunciation, attributed roundel, 34 in.
      diam.                                                        4,500
      Cunninghame.  S.  Christ crowned with thorns, 26×19¾,
      attributed                                                  10,000
1966  Buller.  C.  Holy Family with St John, 35½×28 (1954
      £546, 1874 £1,680, 1893 £1,312 10s.) no longer accepted     5,250
1967  Watney.  C.  Marriage feast of Nastagio degli Oneste,
      *cassone* panel, 32×55. Now in the Pucci Palace, Florence,
      for which it was painted in 1483 (1874, bought in at
      £997 10s., 1879 £294, 1895 £1,365)                        105,000
      Ex Noack collection.  S.  Profile head of Simonetta
      Vespucci, 35¾×17½, one of four generally accepted versions 95,000

49

## FRANCOIS BOUCHER. 1704–1770

Those ten-foot panels at £42,000 to £71,000 seem dear for a décor which was *chic* and Parisian between the 1870s and 1920s but which now lingers chiefly in Latin America. But the true status of the Rosebery and Labia panels is shewn by the history of the two staircase-panels in the Michelham sale of 1926 which made £47,350 the pair—about £237,000 in the money of 1970. During the long supremacy of *grand manner* 18th century painting, the French school failed to rise to the astronomic heights of English portraiture. French paintings lacked the undivided attention of Lord Duveen. For the same reason their fall between the 1920s and 1940s was less dramatic. Particularly this applies to Boucher's decorative suites of panels, 8 to 12 feet high, but it is likely that after the Rosebery and Labia suites there are no more of these that can reach the open market. Most of the works in the following lists are small figured landscapes or highly finished chalk drawings which have kept pace with inflation even less.

| | | £ |
|---|---|---|
| 1960 | Ednam. C. The Mill and the Trout Stream, pair of ovals, 1766 (£9,800 in 1955), 16 × 13¼, compare also 1969  2 for | 10,500 |
| 1961 | Paris. Paysage bucolique, 19½ × 27½, FN41,000+tax | 3,550 |
| 1962 | Paris. An ancient tower, 17 × 13, FN120,000+tax | 10,635 |
| | La Fleuve Scamandre, 38 × 31½, FN80,000+tax  About | 7,000 |
| 1963 | Dunlap. N.Y. La belle villageoise, 16½ × 13, $22,500 | 8,035 |
| | Fribourg. S. Girl bathing her feet, 20¼ × 15¾ | 4,500 |
| | Fitzgerald. S. Mill near Charentan, 1739, 10½ × 13½ | 8,500 |
| 1964 | Paris. La petite fermière, 31 × 25½, FN146,000+tax | 11,600 |
| | Rosebury. S. Lovers in a park, 1758, 76 × 90 | 71,000 |
| | The fisherman, same dimensions, 1759 | 42,500 |
| | Three narrow panels en suite with the same  3 for | 23,000 |
| 1965 | S. Landscape with watermill | 15,000 |
| | Toilet of Venus, 38½ × 53 | 4,000 |
| | J de Rothschild. Paris. Le repos des fermiers, 34¾ × 54½ | 7,600 |
| 1967 | Labia. N.Y. Vertumnus and Pomona, 124 × 73, bought in at $160,000 | 57,145 |
| | Le billet doux, same size, bought in at $120,000 (see 1969) | 42,857 |
| | Both part of suite of 8 which made £6,052 in 1874. Five were sold for £23,415 in 1903 and bought in for £18,900 in 1923 | |
| | Gaekwar of Baroda. S. La Poésie, reclining nymph, 38 × 50½ | 22,500 |
| 1969 | Labia. S. Le billet doux, 124 × 73 (fell from $120,000 in 1967 to $110,400) | 46,000 |
| | Fribourg. S. Le moulin de Charenton and La Passerelle, dated 1755, ovals 16¼ × 13½  2 for | 39,000 |

| | | |
|---|---|---|
| 1969 | Talleyrand-Ruspoli, Florence. Reclining nymph (attributed), 9 million Lire+tax | £ 6,600 |
| | S. Standard nymph subject with pool and fountain, 24×29½ | 22,000 |

DRAWINGS

| | | |
|---|---|---|
| 1961 | Sala. N.Y. Reclining Venus with dolphin, black chalk, heightened, 9×13¼, $4,250 | 1,515 |
| 1962 | Havemeyer. S. Man kneeling on a rock, black and white chalk, 16×10¾ | 1,600 |
| 1963 | Rudolf. S. Woman in classical dress, black chalk heightened, 13¾×9 | 1,400 |
| 1964 | S. Water nymph, sanguine, 12¾×17 | 2,800 |
| 1966 | J de Rothschild. Paris. Reclining nude girl, crayon and pastel, dated 1760, 10¾×16¾, FN57,750+tax | 4,645 |
| 1967 | Pearson. S. Girls head in coloured chalks and wash, 8¾×6½ | 5,500 |
| 1968 | C. A cupid's hands, clasped, coloured chalks, 12¾×10 | 1,260 |
| | S. Three putti in clouds, coloured chalks, 8×7½ | 2,300 |
| | Cupids and rocococo shield, black and white chalks, 21×16½ | 1,700 |
| 1969 | Dufferin and Ava. S. Nude girl on bed, coloured chalks, 8×12 (£89 5*s*. in 1928) | 1,600 |
| | Kieffer. Paris. Deux enfants, black and white chalk, FN35,000+tax | 3,282 |
| | Benson. C. Child drinking from a bowl, black chalk and white on blue, 9½×7½ | 1,050 |

## EUGÈNE BOUDIN. 1824–1898

In 1961, when only one Boudin had passed the £10,000 mark, it seemed that these very pretty but incredibly stereotyped works had reached equilibrium. Such a thing, however, was impossible in a decade in which most art trebled in devalued money terms. So now we have Boudins in the £50,000 class, that is to say level with routine Pissarros and Sisleys or the more scrappy relics of Monet, Renoir and Degas, quite a promotion since 1945 when 18 Boudins in a single sale aggregated £4,735. Easy identification, a level standard, surprises and disappointments equally rare, these are virtues for the timid collector, who one would scarcely believe was capable of £50,000 purchases. But one has to alter one's mind about that.

Boudin's painstaking style and his good taste have never lacked admirers, except perhaps in the early 1940s when all art was neglected. In 1883, when he was at the height of his powers, a picture by Boudin made £240 at a Paris auction (6,000 francs). On his death in 1898 his executors were able to sell many works for more than this price, including one at 14,000 francs (about £616 including the tax or nearly £5,000 in 1970 terms). In 1929 a single beach scene was sold for £1,200 but during the long years of financial depression and wartime restrictions £900 remained a high price. Then in 1952, at the Gabriel Cognacq sale, a large regatta piece suddenly made £4,800. By 1957 a Trouville beach scene, full of crinolines, could reach £13,800. This was quite an exceptional Boudin, but in 1969 £10,000 to £15,000 was the routine price of average works, £30,000 to £52,000 the price of the unusual.

|      |                                                                                   | £      |
|------|-----------------------------------------------------------------------------------|--------|
| 1960 | Tozer. S. Raz de Seine, Bretagne, 1887, $24\frac{3}{4} \times 25$                 | 8,000  |
| 1961 | Buckner. S. Beaulieu, $22 \times 35\frac{1}{2}$                                   | 5,500  |
|      | Brisants, Antibes, 1893, $28\frac{1}{2} \times 19\frac{1}{2}$                     | 6,100  |
|      | C. Trouville, 1885, $14 \times 22\frac{1}{2}$                                     | 5,040  |
| 1962 | Woolworth. N.Y. Rouen, $18 \times 26$, $28,000                                    | 10,000 |
|      | Metcalfe. S. Father and child on beach, Deauville, 1892                            | 5,200  |
|      | Gaekwar of Baroda. Paris. Port de Havre, 1889, $26\frac{1}{2} \times$              |        |
|      | $36\frac{1}{4}$, FN106,000+tax                                                     | 9,220  |
|      | Port d'Anvers, $22\frac{1}{2} \times 35\frac{3}{4}$, FN155,000+tax                 | 13,400 |
| 1963 | S. Port de Trouville, $12\frac{1}{2} \times 16$                                   | 6,200  |
|      | C. Ships at Camaret, 1871, $18\frac{1}{2} \times 25$                              | 3,780  |
|      | N.Y. Port d'Honfleur, $18 \times 24\frac{1}{2}$, $10,000                          | 3,570  |
|      | Versailles. Snow scene, Dunkirk                                                    | 5,800  |
|      | Cargill. S. Etaples, $17\frac{3}{4} \times 25\frac{1}{2}$                         | 11,500 |
|      | Wilkins. S. Harbour scene, Bordeaux (1960, £2,500),                               |        |
|      | 1875, $19\frac{1}{2} \times 31\frac{1}{2}$                                        | 8,200  |
|      | C. Harbour, Trouville, 1882, $17\frac{1}{4} \times 25$                            | 6,825  |
|      | S. Coast scene                                                                     | 9,000  |
|      | Paris. Plage, $16 \times 25\frac{1}{2}$, FN122,000+tax                            | 10,520 |
| 1964 | S. Harbour scene, Fécamp, 1894, $18 \times 25\frac{1}{2}$                         | 5,400  |
|      | Hutton. S. On the beach, Trouville, wc 1865                                        | 4,700  |
|      | Inauguration of the Casino, Trouville, 1865, pencil                                |        |
|      | and wc, $9\frac{1}{2} \times 16\frac{1}{2}$                                       | 7,400  |
| 1965 | Paris. Les lavandiers, $9\frac{1}{2} \times 14\frac{1}{2}$, FN185,000+tax         | 14,825 |
|      | C. Beach at Berck Plage                                                            | 15,750 |
|      | S. Sailing brigs nearing port, $17\frac{1}{2} \times 25$, 1894                    | 7,500  |
| 1966 | Huntington Hartford. S. Raz de Seine, 1897, $23 \times 35\frac{1}{2}$             | 7,000  |
|      | S. Company on beach, Trouville, $5 \times 9$                                      | 8,500  |
|      | N.Y. Port de Dunkerque, 1891, $12\frac{3}{4} \times 16$, $14,550                  | 5,200  |
|      | Percy. S. Lavandières au bord d'une rivière, $8\frac{1}{4} \times 14\frac{1}{2}$  |        |
|      | (£54 12s., 1912, £68 5s., 1923)                                                    | 5,250  |
|      | Viscount Clifden. S. Yachts dans le bassin de Deauville,                           |        |
|      | 1896, $14\frac{3}{4} \times 18$                                                   | 9,000  |
|      | Paris. Crinolines sur la plage, $6\frac{3}{4} \times 12$, FN160,000+tax           | 12,780 |
| 1967 | Lord Sieff. S. La plage à Trouville, 1889, $21\frac{1}{2} \times 35$              | 30,000 |
|      | C. Bassin de commerce, Bruxelles, 1871, $18\frac{3}{4} \times 26\frac{3}{4}$      | 24,150 |

| | | |
|---|---|---|
| 1967 | Motte. C. Geneva. La plage à Trouville, 1890, 18½ × 30½, FS175,000+tax | £ 16,665 |
| | Paris. Les lavandiers, 5½ × 9½, FN93,000+tax | 7,412 |
| | Voiliers au port, 1869, 18½ × 26, FN88,000+tax | 7,058 |
| | Port de St Valèry, 18½ × 26, FN100,000+tax | 9,320 |
| | Lavandières au bord de la Touques, 1894, 9½ × 14¼, FN147,000 (post devaluation)+tax | 13,700 |
| 1968 | Domingo Edwards. N.Y. Bassin de Fécamp, 1894, 14 × 17¾, $16,000 | 6,650 |
| | Boise. S. Vue d'Antibes, 20 × 29½ | 15,000 |
| | Dunes à Etaples, 1890, 31¾ × 22½ | 9,000 |
| | Prestige. S. Chantier de construction, 1884, 15½ × 21 | 10,500 |
| | Widal. S. Port de Trouville, 1878, 11 × 16¼ | 10,800 |
| | C. Laveuses à Trouville, mer baisse, 1891, 13 × 17½ | 11,850 |
| | St Jean, Cap Ferrat, 1892, 19½ × 29½ | 9,450 |
| | Quai de la Douane, Venise, 1895, 10¼ × 13½ | 16,800 |
| | S. Bateau de pêche et lavandières, 10¾ × 8½ | 11,000 |
| | Entrée de port à marée haute, 9¼ × 12½ | 9,500 |
| | Venise, le Redentore, 1894, 14½ × 18 | 25,000 |
| | C. La plage, ciel chargé, 1885, 17½ × 25 | 30,450 |
| | Scoville. N.Y. Personnes sur la plage, Trouville, pencil and wc, 1870, 6¼ × 13, $17,500 | 6,795 |
| | Paris. Port de Dieppe, 18½ × 26, FN142,000+tax | 13,310 |
| 1969 | S. Venice, Campanile and Doge's Palace, 1895, 19½ × 29 (£330 in 1936) | 52,000 |
| | L'heure du bain sur la plage, wc and pencil, 6 × 9 | 4,800 |
| | Pêcheuses sur les sables à Berck, 11¾ × 19, 1875 | 22,000 |
| | La rade à Brest, c. 1870, 16½ × 25½ | 16,000 |
| | Fribourg. N.Y. Laveuses sur la Touques, 1895, 10½ × 16, $46,000 | 19,355 |
| | Paris. Femmes de pêcheurs sur la grève, 1870, FN330,000 +tax | 30,610 |
| | Camaret, 1872, 24 × 35½, FN190,000+tax | 17,635 |
| | Stephens. S. Vue de Dortdrecht, 1884, 17¾ × 25 | 14,500 |
| | S. La Canche à Etaples, 1886, 14¼ × 23 (£15 in 1888) | 14,000 |
| | Port de Trouville, 1881, 15¾ × 21½ | 10,000 |
| | Port de Bordeaux with sailing ship, 1874, 21 × 34¾ | 16,000 |
| | Eglise St Vulfran, Abbéville, 1884, 17½ × 14½ | 15,000 |
| | Pair to the above from another angle | 13,000 |
| | C (from Tokyo). Marché aux poissons, Trouville, 1884, 14½ × 18 | 13,125 |
| | S. Port de Honfleur, 1865, 11½ × 18¼ | 11,500 |
| | Coucher de soleil sur le port de Havre, 1882, 20¾ × 28¼ | 26,500 |
| | Personnages sur la plage de Trouville, 1869, 11½ × 18½ | 41,000 |
| | S. Bateaux à l'ancre à Camaret, 1873, 19¾ × 30 | 16,000 |

## ALBERTO BURRI. (*See* Abstract Painters)

## GEORGES BRAQUE. 1881–1963

In accordance with the general policy of Volume Three, where the modern school is concerned, the list extends back beyond 1960 as far as it can be traced, thus repairing some of the omissions of Volume One. There are really three quite distinct markets for Braque. Firstly there are the works of his cubist period. These share with the works of Picasso in the same style the distinction of being the most costly of the modern abstract school. There are very few pictures of this phase of Braque. The vast majority, painted between the First World War and the Second, are simplified realist paintings of still-life, small, tasteful and slight, and generally fetching from £10,000 to £30,000. Braque's third phase, dating from the 1940s, is very much more realistic as well as hotter in colour and apparently less esteemed. There may also remain in circulation paintings of Braque's *fauve* style, painted between 1905 and 1908. One of them was sold for £54,600, which was about the price of Derain's works of the same phase. The very high rating of *fauve* pictures is not difficult to understand. There is a vitality about them, a sense of youth and discovery that was never achieved again. It is much harder to see why the austere and sombre cubist works which followed, should be twice as dear as any other sort of modern painting. If it is the case that this very high market is buoyed up by financial speculators, it can hardly be through their personal taste. The sudden upsurge in the 1960s of Raoul Dufy and Kees van Dongen shows that the lure of slickness, superficiality and sheer vulgarity is as potent as ever. The very biggest speculation of all must, however, adapt itself to the tastes of gallery curators, and for them Braque's form of cubism with its air of monastic renunciation would have to be invented if it did not already exist.

| | | £ |
|---|---|---|
| 1918 | Still lifes at Paul Rosenberg's. Average price according to Maurice Rheims | 24 |
| 1921–3 | Séquestre Kahnweiler. Paris. 118 paintings made less than £800 between them (Maurice Rheims) | |
| 1932 | Georges Petit. Paris. Plage à Dieppe, 10 × 14 | 240 |
| 1934 | N.Y. Vase with anemones, 17½ × 21½ | 98 |
| 1935 | Still life, bought by Rees Jeffreys (see 1954) | 43 10s. |
| 1937 | 'L'oeil clair'. Paris. Joueuse de mandolin (cubist phase see 1965) | 110 |
| | Hollander and Bernheimer. C. Nu dans un paysage (Maynard Keynes collection) | 220 10s. |
| | Corbeille de fruits | 220 10s. |
| | Nature morte | 183 15s. |
| 1944 | Barbée. N.Y. Nature morte, 18 × 27, $3,200 | 796 |
| 1945 | Chrysler. N.Y. Grapes, $2,700 | 672 |
| | Still life with fruit, ditto | 672 |

| | | £ |
|---|---|---|
| 1946 | N.Y. Vase d'anémones, 1927, $4,000 | 995 |
| 1950 | Chrysler. N.Y. Grandes baigneuses, $52\frac{3}{4} \times 80$, $3,500 | 1,250 |
| | N.Y. Apples, $1,200 | 428 |
| 1951 | Paris. Paysage à l'Estaque, $18\frac{1}{2} \times 15\frac{1}{4}$, Fauve phase | 685 |
| 1954 | Paris. La toilette jaune, $14\frac{1}{2} \times 22$ | 1,680 |
| | Rees Jeffries. S. Still life (£43 15s. in 1935) | 4,035 |
| | Bradley Campbell. N.Y. Fruit, $11,350 | 4,055 |
| 1955 | C. Nature morte | 2,310 |
| 1957 | S. Abstract composition, cubist period | 7,800 |
| | Lurcy. N.Y. Sausages on plate, $12,000, $9\frac{1}{2} \times 14$ | 4,286 |
| 1959 | S. L'entonnoir, $16\frac{1}{2} \times 28\frac{1}{4}$ | 9,100 |
| | Les citrons, $13\frac{1}{2} \times 17\frac{3}{4}$ | 8,500 |
| | Fruit on dish, 1930, $14\frac{1}{2} \times 21$ | 15,000 |
| | Chrysler. S. Femme à la mandoline, cubist, 1910, $36 \times 28\frac{1}{4}$ | 36,000 |
| | Foght. S. Le Ciotat, semi-Fauve style, 1907, $18\frac{1}{2} \times 22\frac{1}{2}$ | 12,000 |
| 1960 | Museum of Modern Art. N.Y. The violin, 1912, cubist phase, $31\frac{3}{4} \times 21\frac{1}{4}$, $144,000 | 51,400 |
| | Dudensing. S. Gemme au miroir, 1946, $45\frac{3}{4} \times 35$ | 42,000 |
| 1961 | S. Bottle and newspaper, cubist, 1911, $18\frac{1}{2} \times 23\frac{1}{2}$ | 32,000 |
| | Le banc, 1952, $29\frac{1}{2} \times 45\frac{3}{4}$ | 22,500 |
| | Oysters on plate, 1939, $15 \times 18$ | 10,500 |
| | Frank. S. Paysage à l'Estaque, 1907, semi-Fauve phase, $24\frac{1}{2} \times 31$ (compare similar landscapes of this year, 1959 and 1969) | 16,500 |
| | Juvilier. New York. La Calanque (Fauve style), 1907, $23\frac{1}{2} \times 28\frac{3}{4}$, $47,000 | 16,785 |
| 1962 | Bought by Tate Gallery, London. Still life with fish, cubist | 35,000 |
| | Sarlie. S. Still life, 1938, $19\frac{3}{4} \times 25\frac{1}{2}$ | 20,000 |
| | S. Glass and newspapers, oval, cubist, $14\frac{1}{4} \times 21$ | 27,000 |
| | Aldrich. N.Y. Dahlias rouges, 1952, $16 \times 18$, $25,000 | 8,750 |
| 1964 | S. Still life with lobster, 1942, $12\frac{1}{4} \times 25\frac{1}{4}$ | 10,000 |
| | Glass. S. La cuvette bleue, 1942, $23\frac{1}{2} \times 31\frac{1}{2}$ | 23,000 |
| | Marguerites, 1946 | 24,600 |
| | Motte, Geneva. Nature morte, $20 \times 26$, FS272,000+tax | 26,240 |
| 1965 | S. Raisins et citrons, 1921, $8 \times 25$ | 15,000 |
| | Lefèvre. Paris. L'homme à la guitare, 1914, cubist phase, $52 \times 19$, FN1,560,000+tax | 125,256 |
| | Le quotidien, collage, 1914, $29 \times 42$ | 13,258 |
| | Femme à la mandoline (£110 in 1937) FN330,000+tax | 23,497 |
| | Bragaline. N.Y. Balustre et crâne, 1939, $18 \times 21$ | 16,120 |
| | Kornfeld, Berne. Allée d'oliviers, Fauve period, 1907, $15 \times 18\frac{1}{2}$, FS160,000+tax | 15,430 |

| | | £ |
|---|---|---|
| 1965 | de Zayas. N.Y. Barques de pêche (cubist), 1909, $36\times28\frac{3}{4}$ (see 1968), $67,500 | 24,100 |
| 1966 | Thompson. N.Y. Bouteille de rum, 1918, oval, $38\times26\frac{3}{4}$, $120,000 (cubist phase) | 41,400 |
| | Institute Contemporary Arts. S. La mandore, cubist work of 1909, $28\frac{1}{2}\times23\frac{1}{2}$ | 34,000 |
| | Aldrich foundation. C. Le bouquet jaune. Realist work of 1952, $25\frac{1}{2}\times12$ | 14,700 |
| | Fordyce. N.Y. Nature morte, 1920, $28\frac{1}{4}\times35\frac{1}{4}$ | 19,650 |
| | Rainer. C. Face et profile, 1942, $19\frac{3}{4}\times18\frac{3}{4}$, bought in | 10,500 |
| 1967 | Motte, Geneva. Lobster on tablecloth, 1943, $16\frac{3}{4}\times37$, FS345,000+tax | 38,690 |
| | The billiard table, $20\times26$, FS240,000+tax | 26,100 |
| | S. Le bougeoir, cubist phase, 1911, $18\frac{1}{4}\times15$ | 29,000 |
| 1968 | Bluestein. N.Y. Fishing boats, 1909, cubist, $36\times28\frac{3}{4}$, $132,000 (£24,450 in 1965) | 55,000 |
| | Elmer Rice. N.Y. Pêcheuse, head, 1928, $18\times15$, $35,000 | 14,585 |
| | Verre et carte, 1918, $14\times18\frac{1}{2}$, $40,000 | 16,665 |
| | Granz. S. Papier collé, cubist, 1912, $24\times18\frac{1}{2}$ | 17,000 |
| | Fruit dans un plat, 1924, $12\times20\frac{1}{2}$ | 17,000 |
| | S. Hommage à Bach, cubist phase almost monochrome, 1912, $21\times28\frac{1}{2}$ | 115,000 |
| | Pichet et pommes, 1933–4, $11\times28\frac{1}{2}$ | 29,500 |
| | C. Canal St Martin, 1906 (Fauve period) $19\frac{3}{4}\times24$ | 54,600 |
| | Les soleils (realist) 1943, $12\frac{1}{4}\times10\frac{1}{4}$ | 14,700 |
| | La couverte verte, 1942, $25\frac{3}{4}\times32$ | 21,000 |
| 1969 | S. Nature morte aux pichets, fauve style, 1906, $20\frac{3}{4}\times25$, bought in | 50,000 |
| | Le Bas. C. (Geneva). Nature morte avec citron et corbeille de fruits, 1920, $7\times25$, FS230,000+5% tax | 23,220 |
| | De Zayas. C. (Geneva). Maisons à l'Estaque, 1907 (semi-Fauve style), $21\frac{1}{4}\times18$, FS200,000+5% tax, compare 1961 | 20,197 |
| | Paris. Paysage au clocher, cubist, 1908–9, $22\times18\frac{1}{2}$, FN270,000+tax | 25,000 |

## JAN BREUGHEL THE ELDER. 1558–1625

A useful general-purposes painter, whose works tend to be easy to recognize, pretty and in good preservation, for which qualities they command the appropriate price. Average works which fetched £30 to £40 in the 1920s, now make as many hundreds. Those that were worth as much as £100, make from £10,000 to £16,000, in one instance £43,700. This is remarkable for pictures that have no special appeal to the modern *Zeitgeist* to make them voguish, but Jan Breughel had fallen unnaturally low before the present inflation-era, together with the entire Flemish school of the slightly pre-Rubens period. Such works did considerably better in early and mid-Victorian times when Jan Breughel's figured landscapes were worth £150 to £400, equivalent to a range of £1,500 to £4,000 in the money of 1970. On the whole the flowerpieces tend to fetch more than the figured landscapes. They are painted in a style so distinct that they seem almost the work of another painter and I have found it convenient to list them separately, if only to enable the reader to compare the prices with those of the flower-paintings by Jan Breughel's followers, which will be found under the heading, 'Flemish school after 1550'. It will be seen that some of Jan Breughel's flower-painting followers, such as Verandael, run him very close indeed. Imitators of his landscapes, crowded with figures, have even surpassed him, one by Maerten van Cleve having made close on £20,000 in 1967 (see page 143).

### FLOWERPIECES

(a good example was sold for £290 in 1944)

| | | £ |
|---|---|---|
| 1959 | S.  Summer flowers, porcelain bowl, 15¼×25¼ | 4,500 |
| | Flowers and stone urn, 15¼×23½ | 5,200 |
| 1960 | Topic.  S.  Elaborate flowerpiece, 28¾×12¼ | 15,000 |
| 1961 | C.  Flowerpiece, 38½×27¾ | 10,500 |
| | S.  Flowers, porcelain bowl, 18½×25½ | 6,200 |
| 1962 | Paris.  Flowerpiece, 16×13, FN150,000+tax | 11,980 |
| 1965 | O'Brien.  S.  Mixed flowers and vase | 15,800 |
| 1967 | Paris.  (attributed) Flowers in copper vase with miniature painting, 30¼×22½, FN100,000+tax, about | 8,000 |
| | Wingfield Castle.  C.  Flowers and Chinese blue and white *kende* bottle, 17½×12 | 12,600 |
| | Brandt, Amsterdam.   Flowers in a glass *Roemer* and flowers in a basket, long panel, 22×36, dated 1615, Hfl340,000+tax | 43,700 |
| 1968 | S.  Flowers in a stone vase, including fritillaries, 23¼×18 | 13,500 |

### LANDSCAPES AND FIGURE-SUBJECTS

| | | |
|---|---|---|
| 1959 | Dooyes.  S.  Landscape with revellers, 1622, seven-inch roundel | 4,400 |
| 1961 | S.  Jonah and the whale, 16½×28½ | 3,500 |
| | S.  (with van Balen).  Allegories of Air and Water (a similar pair made £40 19s. in 1823, £304 10s. in 1882) 2 for | 4,000 |
| | Populous landscape, dated 1611, on copper, 16×15½ | 9,200 |
| 1962 | S.  Landscape, numerous peasant figures, 14×17¼ | 4,700 |
| 1964 | Bruce Ingram.  S.  River landscape, dated 1610, 16×23½ | 10,000 |
| | A second ditto on copper, 7½×10 | 4,200 |

| | | £ |
|---|---|---|
| 1965 | Spencer Churchill.  C.  Landscape with Flight into Egypt, $20 \times 25\frac{3}{4}$ | 12,600 |
| | Harewood.  C.  Garden of Eden, $19\frac{1}{4} \times 14\frac{1}{2}$ | 8,925 |
| | C.  Bacchanal, $25 \times 32$ | 4,200 |
| | Venus at the forge of Vulcan (see 1967) $25 \times 42$ | 4,200 |
| 1966 | S.  Cottages by a river, $4\frac{3}{4} \times 6\frac{3}{4}$, on copper | 2,600 |
| | Village activities, $9\frac{1}{2} \times 12\frac{1}{2}$ | 4,900 |
| | Lord Swansea.  S.  Country road near Antwerp, 1606, $11 \times 16\frac{1}{2}$ | 12,800 |
| 1967 | C.  Venus at the forge of Vulcan (see 1965) | 2,940 |
| | C. (with Joos de Momper).  Mountainous landscape, figures and carts, $18\frac{1}{2} \times 26$ | 4,200 |
| | Holy family with wooded landscape, $25 \times 36$ | 4,200 |
| | Riders by a river, peasants with cattle, a pair, $13 \times 18$ (2) | 5,725 |
| 1968 | Campbell.  S.  The garden of Eden, $22\frac{3}{4} \times 34$ | 4,700 |
| | Phillips, Son and Neale.  Landscape dated 1638, $9\frac{3}{4} \times 14\frac{1}{4}$ (Jan Breughel the Younger, a son) | 11,000 |
| | C. (with Jan van Kessel).  Holy family in floral landscape, $20 \times 25$ | 4,200 |
| 1969 | Berry.  C.  Village and boats on an estuary, copper, $7\frac{1}{2} \times 9\frac{3}{4}$ | 6,300 |
| | C.  Estuary with ferry, figures etc., copper, $6\frac{1}{4} \times 10\frac{1}{2}$ | 5,250 |
| | S. (with Hendrik van Balen).  Offering to Cybele, surrounded with garland and flowers, $40\frac{1}{2} \times 27$ | 12,000 |
| | Raphael's dream, inscribed 1595, $13\frac{3}{4} \times 20$ | 5,200 |
| | Wagons and village by an estuary, $10 \times 13\frac{1}{4}$ | 7,500 |

## PIETER BREUGHEL THE ELDER.  1525–1569

Works by the later members of the Breughel family have often been confused with the first Pieter Breughel, genuine examples of whose work are rarely seen in the saleroom. There has been only one full-scale picture on the market since the Second World War, but the *Peasant Wedding* of the Spencer Churchill sale seemed a rather deadened thing after the stupendous Vienna series. In 1918 the Munich Pinakothek bid £15,250 in Berlin for the entrancing *Land of Cocagne*. This should be at least a quarter-million picture today, while some of the Vienna Pieter Breughels should be worth even more.

| | | £ |
|---|---|---|
| 1959 | C.  Head of a peasant, $9\frac{1}{2} \times 7$ | 2,730 |
| 1960 | C.  Wedding feast with bagpipers, $14 \times 21$ | 3,990 |
| 1963 | S.  St John preaching in the wilderness, $45 \times 65\frac{1}{2}$ with signature (?) and date, 1564 | 6,200 |
| 1964 | C.  Flute player and drummer, fragment, $8 \times 7$ | 24,150 |
| 1965 | Spencer Churchill.  C.  Peasant wedding, $23\frac{1}{2} \times 44\frac{1}{2}$ | 81,900 |

## DRAWINGS AND ETCHINGS

| | | £ |
|---|---|---|
| 1952 | Probert. S. Rhine landscape, pen. Pierpont Morgan Library | 6,510 |
| 1958 | Huggill. Alpine scenery, pen, dated 1547, $9\frac{3}{4} \times 17$ | 7,000 |
| 1964 | S. Landscape with rabbit, etching | 10,000 |
| 1966 | S. Another state of the same | 10,500 |
| 1969 | S. (School piece) Bee-keepers, pen, copied signature, $8 \times 12\frac{1}{2}$ | 1,200 |

# PIETER BREUGHEL THE YOUNGER
## or 'Hell Breughel'. 1564–1638

The younger brother of Jan Breughel had more in common with the work of his father, Pieter Breughel the Elder. Though an even less original painter than his brother, he was a better executant, more brilliant in colour and finer in detail. His figured landscapes are considerably dearer than Jan Breughel's, three of them having reached the £20,000–£30,000 class, but with the latter's flower-pieces he did not compete.

| | | £ |
|---|---|---|
| 1963 | S. Garden scene, $16\frac{3}{4} \times 22\frac{3}{4}$ | 8,000 |
| 1964 | C. Kermesse with many figures, $16 \times 17\frac{1}{2}$ | 16,800 |
| | Fischer, Lucerne. The tax receiver, $23 \times 34\frac{1}{2}$, FS55,000+tax | 5,400 |
| 1965 | S. Kermesse, $20 \times 31\frac{1}{2}$ | 9,000 |
| | Spencer Churchill. C. Gardeners as emblem of Spring, $9\frac{1}{2} \times 14\frac{1}{2}$ (see 1966) | 4,725 |
| | Middleton. C. Village by a river, $15\frac{1}{4} \times 24\frac{1}{4}$ | 6,300 |
| | Houses in a flooded river, $4\frac{3}{4} \times 7\frac{1}{4}$ | 3,900 |
| | Bird. Paris, Wedding breakfast, FN95,000+tax, $27 \times 41\frac{1}{2}$ | 7,327 |
| | S. Peasant wedding, $20 \times 31$ | 7,000 |
| 1966 | Mueller-Stinnes. S. Spring, larger version (see 1965) | 14,000 |
| 1967 | Ackerman. S. (with Frans Francken II). A picture gallery 1612, $35 \times 43\frac{1}{2}$ | 7,000 |
| | N.Y. The seven works of Mercy, $16 \times 23\frac{1}{2}$, $10,000 | 3,571 |
| | Colville. C. Four roundels with single figures, illustrating familiar proverbs, each 3 in. diam. 4 for | 5,040 |
| | S. The blind leading the blind, $22 \times 33$ | 6,800 |
| | Village Kermesse, dated 1609, $20\frac{1}{2} \times 26\frac{1}{2}$ | 13,800 |
| 1968 | S. Peasants brawling in village street, $28\frac{3}{4} \times 42$ | 8,000 |
| | Lord Woolton. C. Village with skating on frozen river, $15 \times 22$, bought in at | 13,650 |
| | C. Collecting the tithes, $28 \times 49$ | 7,350 |
| | Peasants' round dance in a village after Pieter Breughel the elder, $21\frac{1}{4} \times 29\frac{1}{4}$ | 25,200 |

| | | £ |
|---|---|---|
| 1969 | C. (attributed Breughel school).   The feeding of the five thousand, on copper, 12×16 | 5,250 |
| | Kermesse, 17½×28½ | 25,200 |
| | Ditto with tent and maypole, 20×29 | 21,550 |
| | Gough.  S.  Village kermesse, signed, 18½×26 | 17,200 |

## ANGELO BRONZINO.  1502–1572

At the great Taylor sale of 1912 two male portraits by Bronzino made £11,340 and £6,090, that is to say about £90,000 and £48,000 in our money. What then has happened to this very rare painter? There seems to have been a strong vogue for painters of the post-Holbein generation between the Hamilton Palace sale of 1882 and the Holford sale of 1928. The high prices for Bronzino were a little exceptional because Bronzino worked in Italy, whereas the prizes of this market were portraits of the English nobility. After the great financial depression which began in 1929, when a Bronzino portrait was sold in Berlin for £4,800, portraits of every school fell severely, but Continental portraits had not been boosted as much as portraits of the English 18th century school. Thus they have had less ground to recover, but they have not completed their journey.

| | | £ |
|---|---|---|
| 1962 | Paris.  Eleonore of Toledo, 29½×24, FN60,000+tax | 5,100 |
| | Stukker, Berne.   Unknown lady's head, 24×18½, FS65,000 +tax | 6,220 |
| 1963 | Cintas.  N.Y.  Unknown lady's head, 27×35, $5,000 | 1,586 |
| 1964 | Martins.  C.  Holy family with SS John and Elizabeth (several other versions), 40½×33 | 4,200 |
| 1965 | Margadale.  C.  Bianca Capella, 34×27 (£51 in 1855, £24 3s. in 1859) | 1,575 |
| 1968 | C.  Cosimo III, Duke of Tuscany, ¾ length, 32½×18 | 3,150 |
| 1969 | S.  Miniature portrait of boy and girl, painted on both sides, 3½ in. diam. (school of Bronzino) | 2,100 |

## CHARLES BROOKING.  (See English School, 18th century)

## SIR EDWARD BURNE-JONES.  1833–1898

To appreciate the significance of this list it must be recalled that in the year 1900 a body of subscribers collected no less than £6,500, equivalent to £52,000 of our money, in order to present the huge *King Cophetua and the beggar maid* to the Tate Gallery. The picture was even dearer than *Love and the Pilgrim*, which had made £5,775 two years earlier, and which was destined to be bought in at £21 during the bombing raids of 1940. But in 1957, after years of prices in the low hundreds at the best, another of these famous large pictures, the *Laus Veneris*, actually made £3,400. It looked as if a boom was on the way. In Volume One, however, I wrote that, though Burne-Jones had fallen slower and risen quicker than his contemporaries, Millais, Leighton and Alma-Tadema, it would be unwise to predict the future of this market. After ten years it still seems that this caution was justified. Though the craving for escapist art spreads wider, buyers are still forced into a state of shame at giving it too visible an expression. Few are the flats that display the Quest of the Holy Grail upon their walls.

|  |  | £ |
|---|---|---|
| 1957 | Agnew. S. Laus Veneris, 48×72 (£2,677 10s. in 1886) | 3,400 |
| 1958 | Potten. S. Love among the ruins, 38¾×60½ (£5,040 in 1913) | 480 |
|  | Psyche's wedding (£2,730 in 1913, see 1963, 1966), 46½×82 | 630 |
| 1959 | S. The briar rose, three panels (£609 in 1952), 23½×52¾ 3 for | 1,000 |
| 1961 | C. St Matthew writing the gospel, grisaille, 56×27½ | 525 |
| 1963 | Munck. S. The sleep of King Arthur, 111×254 | 1,680 |
|  | C. Psyche's wedding (see 1958, 1966), 46½×82 | 2,205 |
| 1965 | S. The fall of the angels, 97×46½, monochrome cartoon | 800 |
|  | Cassavetti. C. Chanson d'amour, preliminary oil sketch | 787 10s. |
|  | Beatrice, pastel, 1870, 26×19 | 735 |
|  | Figures in a landscape, 1884, 13½×7½ | 472 10s. |
|  | C. The romance of the rose, 10 ft×5 ft | 630 |
| 1966 | Huntington Hertford. S. Psyche's wedding, 46½×82, bought by the Brussels Museum (£680 in 1958, £2,205 in 1963) | 1,900 |
| 1967 | Watney. C. 2 pastel cartoons for tapestry, the departure of the Holy Grail, 29×54 (£1,260 in 1898) £630 and | 735 |
|  | S. Allegorical portrait, Maria Zambaco, 1870, wc bodycolour, 31×22 | 850 |
|  | Yates. S. Pygmalion and the image, suite of four, each 25½×19 2 for | 1,400 |
|  | 2 for | 1,700 |
|  | Robinson. C. The madness of Sir Tristram, wc bodycolour, 1862, 23½×22¼ | 1,575 |
| 1968 | S. Annunciation, wc bodycolour, 12×10¾ | 500 |
| 1969 | Paris. Portrait of a girl, black crayon drawing, FN7,500+ tax | 625 |
|  | Hinton East. C. Ceres, wc, 38×26 | 1,995 |
|  | Grosvenor. S. Flamma Vestalis, 1886, 42½×14¾ | 3,200 |

ALBERTO BURRI. (*See* Abstract Painters, Europe)

GUSTAVE CAILLEBOTTE. (*See* French School, Minor Impressionists)

ALEXANDER CALDER. (*See* Abstract Painters, American)

## ANTONIO CANALETTO. 1697–1768

At the time of the publication of Volume One, even the best of Canaletto had barely overtaken the market rating of Francesco Guardi's theatrical and super-ficial productions. It was only in 1960 that £10,000 was first paid at auction for any Canaletto picture, though the thousand guineas which the Duke of Buccleuch paid in 1838 for the famous view of Whitehall was equivalent to quite as much as that in the money of 1960, while the £3,360 which the Earl of Dudley bid in 1873 for a Venetian subject meant £23,000. There was actually a time between the 1890s and 1920s when no Canaletto could make £1,000. This was because there had been an insatiable demand for *vedute* of Venice in the artist's own lifetime, which Canaletto met by employing workshop assistants who made abundant use of the ruler and compass. Collectors who paid the high prices of the 19th century, often failed to distinguish between the holograph paintings of Canaletto's earlier years and his subsequent studio productions. Final disillusionment took the form of patronizing Victorian painters who tried to provide the same article, painters such as Holland, Roberts and Muller, who may be said to have killed the Canaletto market. Its recovery has taken the form of two very widely separated levels. On the one hand a few thousands will buy a view of Venice that may have been touched by Canaletto's hand in places, on the other, the noble *Prato della Valle* of the Brownlow sale makes £105,000. But a Canaletto masterpiece such as the *Stonemason's Yard* which Sir George Beaumont gave to the infant National Gallery in 1826, should be worth two or three times as much as that, seeing that £154,000 can be paid for a pair of *vedute* even in Canaletto's later and highly standardized style. In 1920 they cost less than £2,000.

As to the lower tier of prices for workshop Canalettos, it is worth noting that they sell as well or better under other names, three canal scenes which were attributed to Marieschi making about £18,000 apiece. Even such humble disciples as Joli and William James are in the £3,000–£6,000 region, while as much or more can be paid for the early Victorian painters of *vedute* who replaced Canaletto, a Muller for instance at £9,200.

| | | £ |
|---|---|---|
| 1960 | Gibson Fleming. S. View from S. Giorgio Maggiore, 23 × 36¼ | 32,000 |
| | View towards the Redentore, 23 × 36¼ | 20,000 |
| 1961 | Snapper. S. Doge's palace with regatta, 22½ × 36 | 18,000 |
| | S. San Giovanni e Paolo and canal, 46¼ × 58¼ | 16,000 |
| | Countess of Craven. C. Grand Canal and Salute, 53½ × 91½ | 40,000 |
| | Paris. Piazza and Chiesa san Zobenigo, 19½ × 33¼, FN150,000 + tax | 13,020 |
| 1965 | Harcourt Powell. C. Two views of London from the Thames, looking N and S from Somerset House terrace, 15 × 28 (small replicas of the views in the Royal collection) 2 for | 58,800 |
| | Smith. S. Four school-paintings of Venetian subjects, attributed to Marieschi, 21¼ × 32½, £15,000, £17,500, £18,000, | 18,500 |
| | Harewood. C. Capriccio with sluice-gate, dated 1734, 42¾ × 14½ (£1,470 in 1937) | 15,225 |
| | Fonda. S. Oval church by a canal, capriccio, 23 × 36½ | 8,000 |
| 1966 | Dunkals. S. Padua, the Portello from the Brenta, 24½ × 42½ (£3,600 in 1954, a better version £9,450 in 1955) | 6,500 |
| | Patrick Hall. S. Pair of Capriccios, lagoons from the Venetian mainland, 19½ × 26¼ 2 for | 28,000 |
| | S. The Molo from the Dogana, 17 × 23 | 9,000 |
| 1967 | S. Regatta on the Grand Canal, painted for D. of Buccleuch, 1748–52, 45¾ × 58½ | 100,000 |
| | Campo Santa Margherita, painted for Consul Smith, 1742, 18 × 30 | 60,000 |
| | Sta Maria della Salute with barge, 18¼ × 15 | 38,000 |
| 1968 | S. The Molo from the Bacino, a capriccio, 51¼ × 41¼, bought in at | 11,000 |
| | Oppenheimer. C. Grand Canal from the Rialto, 23½ × 36 | 18,900 |
| | C. Colosseum and arch of Constantine, 23½ × 37½, bought in at | 13,650 |
| | S. Grand canal from Campo San Vio, 20¼ × 27 | 22,000 |
| 1969 | Brownlow. S. The Prato della Valle, Padua, 16 × 34½ | 105,000 |
| | The Colleoni monument, Venice, with gondola, 16 × 13½ | 17,000 |
| | Duff. S. Rialto bridge from the North, 29 × 43½ | 86,000 |
| | Grand Canal from Rialto, companion-piece | 68,000 |
| | (D. of Leeds sale, 1920, the pair £1,995) | |
| | Hardie. S. (ex Hillingdon). Piazza San Marco, a fairly late work, 17¾ × 29½ | 28,000 |

DRAWINGS

| | | £ |
|---|---|---|
| 1957 | Blofield. S. View in Padua, 7×10 | 1,550 |
| | Capriccio with coach and monastery, 7½×10¾ | 1,100 |
| | View on the lagoons, 7¾×11 | 700 |
| 1959 | Ten Cate. S. Capriccio in the lagoons, pen and wash, 8¾×14 | 1,300 |
| 1963 | Tomalin. S. Warwick Castle with priory gardens, 14×36¼ | 4,200 |
| | S. Grand Canal, Venice, 8½×15 | 2,400 |

## JAN VAN DE CAPELLE. (*See* Dutch School)

## CARLO CARLONE. (*See* Italian School, 18th century)

## VITTORE CARPACCIO. (*See* Venetian School)

## ANNIBALE CARRACCI. 1560–1609

This is a ghost market, for there is so little that can be attributed safely to this favourite painter of late 18th century collections. Scholarly propaganda has not yet created a very striking demand for the Roman and Bolognese electic school. The sum of 20,000 *livres* which the Regent Duke of Orleans paid in 1717 for the *Vision of St Roche*, had the purchasing power of £15,000 to £20,000 in the money of 1970. At the Consul Weber sale in Berlin in 1911 *The Vision* made no more than £215, equivalent to £1,720. The well known *Descent from the Cross* or *Three Maries*, which reached the National Gallery in 1913, was valued in 1798 for the Earl of Carlisle at 4,000 guineas, in 1970 the equivalent of £67,200, a sum that it might not greatly exceed.

| | | £ |
|---|---|---|
| 1960 | Myron Taylor. N.Y. Triumphs of Bacchus, 24×13½ | |
| | 4 for | 507 |
| 1961 | Allendale. C. Portrait of a sculptor, 44×40 | 1,785 |
| 1962 | Fischer, Lucerne. Portrait of young man (by Agostino Carracci), 20¼×33, FS25,000+tax | 2,500 |
| 1965 | Spencer Churchill. C. Pietá, 20¾×25¾ | 4,200 |
| | (by Agostino Carracci) Adoration of the shepherds, 38½×30 | 630 |
| 1968 | Warwick Castle. C. Pietá, on metal, 16×20½ | 1,575 |
| 1969 | Bompas. C. Supposed self-portrait in ruff, 17×13 | 5,040 |

£

### DRAWINGS

| | | £ |
|---|---|---|
| 1958 | Holland Martin.  C.  Nude youth, red chalk, $10\frac{1}{2} \times 6\frac{1}{2}$ | 336 |
| 1969 | O'Brien.  S.  Head of young man in profile, red chalk, $8\frac{3}{4} \times 7\frac{1}{2}$ | 3,300 |
| | Fenwick-Owen.  S. (by Agostino Carracci) Resting male nude, red chalk, $15 \times 9\frac{1}{2}$ | 1,700 |

## MARY CASSATT.  1845–1926

Of the two women painters among the original Impressionists Berthe Morisot was the higher priced till the end of the decade, when the Impressionist market went *comprehensive* and a slight preference for sensitivity was ironed out. Mary Cassatt was the one member of the group who could fairly be accused of being smart and slick. In her later years René Gimpel recollected Degas remarking that Mary Cassatt was engaged in painting the Infant Jesus and his English Nanny— and that seems to sum up the case pretty well. But of course American patriotism plays a huge part in this market and the lady is now in the £60,000 class.

| | | | £ |
|---|---|---|---|
| 1950 | Paris. | Repos dans l'herbe, gouache on canvas, $25\frac{1}{4} \times 23\frac{1}{4}$ | 505 |
| 1953 | N.Y. | Child's head, $13 \times 10$, $585 | 209 |
| 1954 | N.Y. | Spanish dancer, $25\frac{1}{2} \times 19\frac{1}{2}$, $1,400 | 500 |
| | Paris. | Maternité, $18\frac{1}{2} \times 14\frac{1}{2}$, 400,000 old francs+tax About | 500 |
| | | Bought by Ernest Duveen (see 1960) Girl in green hat | 2,500 |
| 1957 | S. | Le lecteur au parc, $45 \times 35$ | 6,000 |
| 1958 | Paris. | Girl knitting, pastel, 9 million old francs+tax | 7,840 |
| 1959 | N.Y. | Alexander Cassatt and his family, 1884, $39\frac{1}{2} \times 32$, $39,000 | 13,928 |
| 1960 | Duveen.  S. | Girl in green hat, $24 \times 19\frac{1}{2}$ (see 1954) | 7,500 |
| | N.Y. | The sisters, pastel, $29 \times 23\frac{3}{4}$, $26,000 | 9,285 |
| 1961 | N.Y. | Mother and child, pastel, $29\frac{1}{2} \times 24\frac{1}{2}$, $30,000 | 10,714 |
| 1962 | Hines.  S. | La liseuse, 1877, $31 \times 25\frac{1}{2}$ | 9,000 |
| | Paris. | Female portrait in profile, $29 \times 24$, FN70,000+tax | 6,000 |
| | | Les deux soeurs, $26 \times 32\frac{1}{2}$, FN106,000+tax About | 9,000 |
| 1963 | S. | Portrait of Suzanne, pastel, $16\frac{3}{4} \times 11\frac{3}{4}$ | 5,200 |
| | | Dame aux gants, pastel, $13\frac{3}{4} \times 10\frac{3}{4}$ | 5,800 |
| 1964 | Hutton.  S. | Buste d'enfant, $13\frac{1}{4} \times 10\frac{1}{4}$ | 3,800 |
| | S. | La Lecture, pastel, $18 \times 25$, 1896 | 7,500 |
| 1965 | S. | Mother and child, pastel, $18\frac{1}{2} \times 22$ | 14,000 |
| | | Ditto, $27\frac{1}{2} \times 24$ | 6,000 |
| | | Maternité, pastel, $18 \times 21\frac{3}{4}$ | 12,500 |
| | Jarvis.  N.Y. | Fillette au chapeau blanc, $20\frac{3}{4} \times 17$ | 6,070 |
| | S. | Petite fille sortant du bain, oils, $25\frac{1}{2} \times 20$ | 5,000 |

|      |                                                                                                              | £      |
|------|--------------------------------------------------------------------------------------------------------------|--------|
| 1966 | S.   Girl with straight fringe, pastel, 19¾ × 19                                                              | 3,500  |
|      | C.   Lady in straw hat with little girl, bought in at                                                         | 17,850 |
|      | Princess Labia.   N.Y.   Portrait de Suzanne, 1891, 11¾ × 11¾                                                 | 5,200  |
|      | N.Y.   Jeune femme, corsage bleue, avec fillette, robe rouge, 30 × 25, $21,000                                | 9,642  |
| 1967 | C.   Vase de lilas, 1889, 23½ × 18¼                                                                           | 4,725  |
|      | N.Y.   Jeune fille au chapeau blanc, 1908, 24 × 19¾, $32,500                                                  | 11,632 |
| 1968 | Portalés.   N.Y.   Maternité, pastel, 1889, 23½ × 18, $84,000                                                 | 35,000 |
|      | S.   Mère et bébé, pastel, 26 × 20½, 1899                                                                     | 23,000 |
|      | Petite fille assise dans une bergère jaune, 23¼ × 20                                                          | 9,000  |
|      | N.Y.   Mère et enfant, 1908, 27½ × 23½, $42,000                                                               | 17,708 |
|      | Fillette, 1909, 18 × 15, $16,000                                                                              | 6,665  |
| 1969 | S.   Mère et enfant, pencil drawing, 8¼ × 6                                                                   | 3,200  |
|      | N.Y.   Mère et enfant, pastel, 1902, $140,000                                                                 | 58,333 |

PIETER CASTEELS.   (*See* Flemish School, after 1550, landscapes etc.)

GIOVANNI BENEDETTO CASTIGLIONE.   (*See* Italian School, 16th–17th centuries)

## PAUL CÉZANNE.   1839–1906

Only four nineteenth century paintings have passed the half million mark, Renoir's *Pont des Arts*, Monet's *Terrasse à Ste Adresse*, Van Gogh's *Cypress and Flowering Tree* and Cézanne's *Baigneuses*, the least happy work among them. These are purchases on the national level where almost anything can be paid for what are regarded as landmarks in the history of art. Thus Cézanne's several pyramidical compositions of nudes are considered a breakthrough in the new vision, even though the subject was beyond his competence. No more of these huge *baigneuses* are to be expected in the salerooms and possibly no more Cézannes of the first importance, but there are small land-scapes and still-lifes in oils which have not been frozen off in public collections and which can make anything from £25,000 to £300,000.

Roger Fry at one of the London Group dinners forty to fifty years ago pro-posed a toast to the memory of Cézanne, 'the Columbus of modern painting'. To this Walter Sickert replied that Columbus was the man who knew how to make an egg stand up straight—but Cézanne! The fact is that as long as painters are not required to stand their egg up straight, the works of the pioneer must go up.

| | | £ |
|---|---|---|
| 1874 | Durand Ruel exhibition. Paris. Maison du pendu, bought by Count Doria, 300 francs | 12 |
| 1894 | Tanguy. Paris. Le petit port, bought by Chocquet (see 1899), 150 francs+tax | 6 15s. |
| | Duret. Paris. Three paintings made from £20 to £35 | |
| 1897 | Chocquet. Paris. 32 paintings by Cézanne | |
| | Mardi Gras (Hermitage Museum), 4,600 francs+10% tax | 203 |
| | Maison du pendu, bought Camondo, now in Louvre, 6,000 francs+tax | 272 16s. |
| | Anvers, 2,626 francs+tax | 115 10s. |
| | Le petit port (see 1894), 2,200 francs+tax | 96 10s. |
| 1900 | Paris. Nature morte, 6,750 francs+tax | 298 |
| | Maison à la campagne, 5,500 francs+tax | 242 |
| 1903 | Emile Zola. Paris. L'enlèvement (see 1930), 4,200 francs +tax | 184 16s. |
| 1907 | Vien. Paris. Nature morte, 1877 (see 1913), 19,000 francs +tax | 836 |
| 1910 | Paris. Portrait of M. L'empéraire (£32 in 1892), 35,000 francs+tax | 1,540 |
| 1911 | Henri Bernstein. Paris. Le paysan (see 1960), 24,000 francs+tax | 1,056 |
| | Maison en Provence, 23,000 francs+tax | 1,012 |
| 1912 | Rouart. Paris. Baigneuses (Barnes foundation), 18,000 francs+tax | 792 |
| | Nature morte, 7,000 francs+tax | 308 |
| 1913 | Mariczell de Nemés. Paris. Nature morte, 1877, 50,000 francs+tax | 2,180 |
| | Baigneuses, 46,000 francs+tax | 2,025 |
| | Apples and Buffet, each at 45,000 francs+tax | 1,980 |
| | Garçon au gilet rouge (see 1958), 90,000 francs+tax | 3,960 |
| 1916 | Julius Stern. Berlin. Tulips, 40,000 marks | 2,000 |
| 1918 | Degas. Paris. Self-portrait, 30,500 francs+tax | 1,342 |
| 1919 | Octave Mirbeau. Paris. Au fond du ravin | 1,640 |
| 1922 | Kelekian. N.Y. Apples on a plate, bought Lilian Bliss, $21,000 at 4·50 to the £ | 4,665 |
| 1924 | Sold by Georges Bernheim to Alphonse Kann. Little girl with doll (according to R. Gimpel) About | 6,000 |
| 1925 | Gangnat. Paris. Le grand arbre à Montbriand, bought by Pellerin who left it to the Louvre | 6,500 |
| 1927 | Wildenstein. N.Y. Asking price according to R. Gimpel for 'Still life with blue carpet', $50,000 | 10,325 |
| | 'No Cézanne can make 400,000 francs (£3,200) in France.' | |
| 1928 | Soubées. Paris. Jeune homme au petit chapeau 250,000 francs (£2,000)+tax | 2,400 |

| 1929 | First Cézanne in London salerooms: | £ |
| | Bernard d'Hendecourt. S. Mont St Victoire, wc | 400 |
| 1930 | Havemeyer. N.Y. L'enlèvement (see 1903), $25,000 | 4,860 |
| 1932 | Georges Petit. Paris. Apples on a plate, 250,000 francs + tax | 4,500 |
| | Pacquemont. Paris (70 francs to £+tax), l'Estaque | 1,250 |
| | Bol de fleurs, bought Chester Dale | 1,950 |
| 1934 | Paris. L'enlèvement (see 1903, 1930), 186,000 francs+tax | 3,100 |
| 1939 | S. Mont St Victoire | 4,200 |
| | National Gallery, Melbourne, buys *Route montante* | 9,735 |
| | Canonne. Paris. Le pilon du roi, landscape | 3,420 |
| 1940 | N.Y. Mme Cézanne, portrait bought by Walter Chrysler (see 1959), $27,700 | 6,925 |
| 1942 | Bought by Albert Barnes. Les baigneuses, one of four large versions (compare 1964), $70,000 | 17,500 |
| 1946 | van Horne. N.Y. Portrait, Mme Cézanne, $25,000 | 6,200 |
| 1948 | Reber, Lausanne. Private sale to Emil Buehrle of a third version of the Boy in a red waistcoat | 37,500 |
| 1951 | Kemde salerooms. N.Y. Landscape, $5,750 | 2,054 |
| 1952 | Cognacq. Paris. Apples and biscuits, 33 million francs+tax | 39,780 |
| | Landscape, 24 million francs+tax | 28,940 |
| | C. Two bathers, oil sketch | 2,940 |
| 1953 | Portrait of an old peasant woman, bought by National Gallery | 32,000 |
| 1954 | Bradley Campbell. N.Y. The watercan, $10\frac{1}{2} \times 13\frac{1}{2}$ | 6,750 |
| 1955 | Stuttgart. Table de banquet, $11 \times 16$ | 6,450 |
| 1956 | Second version of the Boy in the red waistcoat, bought by David Rockefeller, allegedly for $180,000 | 64,280 |
| | Paris. Cinq baigneurs | 16,000 |
| | Louveciennes, landscape | 10,600 |
| | Au jas de Bouffon | 15,500 |
| 1957 | Sold by Edward G. Robinson, N.Y. to Stavros Nearchos. The black rock | 71,400 |
| | Paris. La clairière, small landscape | 8,600 |
| | Weinberg. S. Mme Cézanne, small sketch, $18 \times 14\frac{3}{4}$ | 14,000 |
| 1958 | Goldschmidt. S. Les grosses pommes, $18 \times 21\frac{1}{4}$ | 90,000 |
| | Boy in red waistcoat, first version, $36\frac{1}{2} \times 28\frac{3}{4}$ (see 1913), National Gallery, Washington per Paul Mellon | 220,000 |
| | Kirkeby. N.Y. Garçon couché sur l'herbe, $21\frac{1}{4} \times 25\frac{3}{4}$, $125,000 | 44,500 |
| 1959 | Janssen. S. Blue dish with peaches, $10\frac{1}{4} \times 8\frac{1}{2}$ | 17,000 |
| | Self-portrait, 1883, $13 \times 10$ | 32,000 |
| | Sair. N.Y. Vénus et l'amour, $8\frac{1}{4} \times 8\frac{1}{2}$, $32,000 | 11,430 |
| | Chrysler. Mme Cézanne, head, $21\frac{1}{4} \times 17\frac{1}{4}$ | 40,000 |

|      |                                                                                                                  | £       |
|------|------------------------------------------------------------------------------------------------------------------|---------|
| 1959 | Kenefick. S. Le paysan (see 1911), $31\frac{1}{2} \times 25$                                                      | 145,000 |
|      | Head of Victor Chocquet, $18\frac{1}{4} \times 15$                                                               | 24,000  |
| 1960 | Burden. N.Y. Les pommes, $19\frac{1}{4} \times 23\frac{3}{4}$, \$200,000                                          | 72,000  |
|      | Coe. S. Deserted house at Thelonnet, 1892, $19\frac{1}{4} \times 23$                                             | 38,000  |
| 1961 | Juvilier. N.Y. Bathers, $13\frac{3}{4} \times 8\frac{1}{2}$, \$44,000                                             | 15,714  |
|      | S. Nature morte, assiette de poires, $15 \times 18$                                                              | 67,500  |
| 1962 | Woolworth. N.Y. Apples and a glass, $10\frac{1}{4} \times 14$, \$65,000                                          | 23,214  |
|      | Metcalfe. S. Bathsabée, 1875, $12\frac{1}{4} \times 9\frac{1}{4}$                                                | 10,500  |
|      | S. Wooded landscape, 1894, $18\frac{1}{4} \times 22$                                                             | 26,500  |
| 1963 | Cargill. S. Auvers sur l'Oise, 1873, $27\frac{3}{4} \times 22\frac{1}{2}$                                        | 38,000  |
|      | Goldfiel. S. Les baigneurs en repos, $15 \times 18\frac{1}{4}$                                                   | 41,500  |
| 1964 | Bought by National Gallery from the Pelerin family, *Les Baigneuses*, $91 \times 88$, begun 1898 but not completed  About | 500,000 |
| 1965 | de Zayas. N.Y. Maisons à l'Estaque, 1882, $25\frac{1}{2} \times 32$, \$800,000                                   | 285,000 |
| 1966 | N.Y. Le jas de Bouffon, landscape, $29 \times 21\frac{1}{2}$, \$350,000                                          | 126,100 |
| 1967 | S. Sous bois, $32 \times 25\frac{1}{2}$, unfinished landscape                                                     | 90,000  |
|      | Pitcairn. N.Y. Cézanne's father reading a newspaper, *c.* 1860, very early work, $66\frac{1}{2} \times 45$, National Gallery, London, \$250,000 | 89,285  |
|      | Weekes. N.Y. Five apples, $5 \times 10$, \$40,000                                                                 | 14,250  |
|      | N.Y. Head of Cézanne's son, 1880, $8\frac{1}{2} \times 5\frac{1}{4}$, \$55,000                                    | 19,642  |
|      | Unknown head in academic style (Salon, 1882), $18 \times 14\frac{3}{4}$, \$20,000                                 | 7,125   |
| 1968 | N.Y. La faience italienne, 1873, $16\frac{1}{2} \times 21\frac{1}{2}$, \$96,000                                   | 40,000  |
|      | Boise. S. Le jas de Bouffon, preliminary sketch, 1885, $17\frac{3}{4} \times 21$                                  | 41,000  |
|      | Le moulin à l'huile, 1870, $14\frac{1}{2} \times 17\frac{3}{4}$                                                   | 35,000  |
|      | C. Le jas de Bouffon, 1875, $14 \times 21\frac{1}{2}$, bought in at                                               | 27,300  |
|      | The same, sold a few months later in Tokyo, 24 million yen                                                        | 28,200  |
|      | Cassirer. S. Maison de Bellevue near Aix, $21 \times 25\frac{1}{4}$                                               | 155,000 |
|      | N.Y. Apples, $5 \times 10$, \$40,000                                                                              | 16,665  |
| 1969 | N.Y. Chaumière dans les arbres, Auvers, 1873, $23\frac{1}{2} \times 19\frac{1}{4}$, \$220,000                     | 92,370  |
| 1970 | C. La Faïence italienne (see 1968)                                                                                | 68,250  |

## WATERCOLOURS AND DRAWINGS

|      |                                                                        |          |
|------|------------------------------------------------------------------------|----------|
| 1929 | Hendecourt. S. Mont St Victoire                                        | 400      |
| 1944 | Barbée. N.Y. Landscape with aqueduct, 18 in. long                     | 276      |
| 1946 | S. Mountainous landscape                                               | 450      |
| 1947 | C. V-shaped trees                                                      | 304 10s. |
|      | Pommes et poires                                                       | 325 10s. |
| 1949 | Kornfeld. Berne. Foliage, $7\frac{3}{4} \times 4\frac{1}{2}$, FS2,100+tax | 190      |
| 1954 | N.Y. Fontaine à Aix, \$5,150                                           | 1,833    |
|      | Mont St Victoire, \$3,200                                              | 1,167    |

| | | | £ |
|---|---|---|---|
| 1956 | Paris.  Landscape near Aix, 7 million old francs+tax | | 5,800 |
| 1957 | Weinberg.  S.  L'entrée du jardin, $18 \times 11\frac{3}{4}$ (see 1964) | | 7,500 |
| 1958 | S.  La carrière de Bibemus, $12 \times 18\frac{1}{4}$ | | 2,800 |
| | Koenigs.  S.  Mont St Victoire, $18 \times 11\frac{3}{4}$ | | 7,800 |
| | Euler.  S.  Le jardinier Vallier, $19 \times 11\frac{3}{4}$ | | 20,500 |
| | Pot de geraniums, $12\frac{3}{4} \times 18\frac{3}{4}$ | | 5,500 |
| 1960 | Barbara Church.  N.Y.  Basket of flowers,  $12 \times 18\frac{1}{2}$, $16,000 | | 5,710 |
| | S.  Two studies of trees | 2 for | 5,600 |
| | Teltsch.  S.  Mill by a river, $12 \times 19\frac{1}{2}$ | | 7,500 |
| 1961 | Paris.  Chateau de Montgerault, 1889, $18\frac{1}{2} \times 22$, FN121,000 +tax | | 10,500 |
| 1963 | Paris.  Paysage d'Aix, FN68,000+tax, $16\frac{1}{2} \times 11\frac{3}{4}$, 1897 | | 5,800 |
| 1964 | N.Y.  L'entrée du jardin, $18\frac{1}{4} \times 11$ (see 1957), $37,000 | | 13,214 |
| 1965 | C.  Study of trees, black chalk | | 7,350 |
| | Bragaline, N.Y.  Bateau, Lac d'Annecy, $8\frac{1}{2} \times 18\frac{1}{2}$, $19,000 | | 6,800 |
| 1967 | Lord Sieff.  S.  Still life with coffee pot etc., seven apples, $18\frac{1}{4} \times 24\frac{1}{4}$ | | 145,000 |
| 1968 | S.  La hutte dans le bois, wc and pencil, $17\frac{1}{4} \times 11\frac{1}{2}$ | | 22,000 |
| | La chêne, wc and pencil, $15\frac{1}{2} \times 11\frac{3}{4}$ | | 5,000 |
| | Gangnat.  S.  Pot de geraniums, $18\frac{1}{4} \times 11\frac{3}{4}$ | | 67,000 |
| 1969 | Carl Pissarro.  S.  Charcoal study for *la moisson*, touched with watercolour, 1875–6, $4\frac{3}{4} \times 8\frac{1}{2}$, figure on verso | | 12,900 |

## MARC CHAGALL.  1887–

Though born and brought up in Russia, Chagall worked in Paris in 1912–14 and largely in Paris after 1922, in spite of which his style owes nothing at all to Cubism, abstract painting and other manifestations of the Parisian *avant-garde*. His links are with the consciously peasant-like style of the Munich Russians and the Russian ballet decor. This link with German-centred internationalism made him a German rather than a French taste, a taste which through being banned under Hitler has now become 'establishment'. The fact that he is a Jewish painter, who painted Jewish themes, has given him a market in New York as well as in Germany where his present rating was built up. In my 1960 list Chagall's highest priced picture was a flowerpiece at £12,400. In 1969 it was still *Les Fiancés* at £73,000. These top-prices for Chagall meant rather more than the normal advance of modern paintings in the 1960s, but in the 1950s his work had multiplied in value ten times over. Thus a lesser work, which was sold in New York in 1950 for $1,000, made $25,000 in 1967. But Chagall's prices are very uneven. In his later work his obsession with violins and roses, brides and Christmas-cracker colours became excessively tedious and his execution very slipshod.

£

| 1927 | Paris.   La réflexion, 9,375 francs+tax | 90 |
|---|---|---|
| 1933 | N.Y.   Nuit sur le village, 29×37, $150 | 36 |
| 1939 | C.   The dream, gouache | 10 10s. |
| 1943 | C.   The cloud | 94 10s. |
| 1948 | N.Y.   Le concert bleu, $3,700 | 925 |
| 1949 | Sternberg.   N.Y.   Village street, 21×25¾, $1,500 | 535 |
| | Les amoureux dans les fleurs, 50½×43¾, $3,250 | 1,178 |
| 1950 | N.Y.   La mariée à double face (see 1967) $1,000 | 357 |
| 1952 | N.Y.   Flowers, 26×21½, $2,400 | 860 |
| 1954 | N.Y.   Midsummer night's dream, 17½×28½, $3,500 | 1,250 |
| | Paris.   Les amoureux au bouquet, gouache, 19×17½ | 730 |
| | Stuttgart.   Men building a bridge, tempera and wc, 1903, 12½×19¼, DM11,500+tax | 1,150 |
| 1955 | Stuttgart.   The drunkard                    About | 3,000 |
| 1957 | S.   Paysage à Peira Cava | 3,800 |
| | Lurcy.   N.Y.   Violinist and roses, 24½×19½, $12,500 | 4,465 |
| | L'ésprit des roses, 36×28½, $12,000 | 4,286 |
| 1958 | Regnault.   Amsterdam.   Violincellist, 1939, 40×29, Hfl118,000+tax | 13,560 |
| | Danseuse, 25½×19½, same price | 13,560 |
| 1959 | S.   La pendule, 26×16 | 4,500 |
| | Paris.   L'Isba, gouache, 6¾×7½, 4,050,000 old francs+tax | 3,400 |
| | Le promeneur par le temps de neige, Witebsk, 13¼×12¾, FN66,000+tax | 5,615 |
| 1960 | S.   Les amoureux au bouquet de fleurs, 19×18 | 4,200 |
| | Ernest Duveen.   S.   Bouquet de fleurs, 1926, 38¾×31½ | 12,800 |
| | Paris.   Jeunes filles aux fleurs, 1927, 40×24¾, FN145,000+tax | 12,490 |
| | Les mariés de la Tour Eiffel, 26½×20, FN81,000+tax | 6,850 |
| 1961 | Paris.   L'acrobâte au cheval rouge, 26½×20, FN70,000+tax | 5,850 |
| | Juvilier.   N.Y.   Lovers, 53¼×40, $82,500 | 27,679 |
| | N.Y.   Fiancés au bouquet blanc, 1944, 26½×24¾, $37,000 | 13,215 |
| | Chrysanthèmes, 1922, 36¾×28¾, £43,000 | 15,375 |
| | Kornfeld, Berne.   L'ecuyère, 1927, gouache, 20½×26½, FS69,000+tax | 6,855 |
| | Motte, Geneva.   Le Christ, la Vierge et L'Enfant, 1959, gouache, 17½×14½, FS48,000+tax | 4,900 |
| 1962 | S.   Les amoureux, 20½×25½ | 8,500 |
| | N.Y.   Barque à St Jean, gouache etc. (see 1965), 30¼×22¼, $32,500 | 11,607 |
| | In the country, wc, $16,200 | 5,775 |
| 1963 | Wolf.   S.   Flowerpiece, 1937, 39×28 | 15,000 |
| | Zimet.   S.   The blue violinist, gouache, 23¾×19¼ | 5,950 |

£

| 1963 | Aldrich.  N.Y.  Hommage à Paris, 1954, 30×39, $52,500 | 18,142 |
|---|---|---|
| 1964 | Glass.  S.  La belle rousse, 44½×55¾, 1949 | 25,500 |
| | S.  Paysan russe à l'eventail | 13,000 |
| 1965 | N.Y.  La madonne du village, 40×30, 1942 | 29,460 |
| | Paris.  La noce, 20×24 in. (FN155,000+tax), see 1962 | 12,400 |

N.Y.  La barque à St Jean, gouache, 30½×22¼, $43,500
(see 1962)                                                    15,155
      La mariée sous le baldaquin, 1949, 45¼×37, $82,500    29,460
Reisini.  N.Y.  Les pommes du pin de Piera Cava, 28¾×
24, $42,000                                                   14,650

1966 Rubinstein.  N.Y.  Scène de cirque, gouache, 24×28½,
$29,000                                                       10,420
      Le meunier, son fils et l'âne, 19¾×15¾, gouache,
$23,000                                                       8,270
      L'acrobate à cheval, gouache, 24×18, $42,300    15,100

1967 N.Y.  La marchande de pain, 25¾×29½, $70,000    25,000
      La mariée a double face (see 1950), $25,000    8,930
S.  La maison brulée, 1917, 22½×24, Contemporary Art
Foundation, Switzerland                                       30,000
Paris.  Self-portrait, FN200,000+tax (see 1968), 31½×25¾    17,067
N.Y.  Fiddler on the roof, gouache and pastel, 1925, 21×
25½                                                           11,071
Hayman.  S.  Golgotha, 1912, 18¾×23¼    10,500
Museum of Modern Art.  S.  La sainte chapelle, 1953,
39½×32                                                       33,000
S.  The bride, gouache, 1950, 25¼×20    14,500
Zagayski.  N.Y.  Violinist in the snow, gouache and
pastel, 1930, 19¾×25½                                        13,392
Menzel.  N.Y.  Nez et échelle, 1926, gouache, 25¼×18
(see 1968)                                                   10,714
N.Y.  L'acrobate au cheval rouge, 1927, 35×26½    10,714
Paris, Self-portrait, 1940, oils, 31½×25¾, FN218,000+tax    17,375

1968 N.Y.  Violinist, gouache, 31×20¾, 1943, $42,000    17,500
      Flowers, c. 1920, 31½×23¼, $27,500 (at 2·40)    11,460
S.  Bella avec livre et vase de fleurs, 1926, 18¼×25½    19,000
Bluestein.  N.Y.  Scène de village avec pendule, 1952,
25¼×21, $52,500                                              21,875
S.  Nature morte sur les toits, 18×21½, 1923    25,000
      Nez et échelle, gouache, 1926, 25¼×18 (see 1967)    10,000
      Les fiancés, 1927–30, 57¾×35¼    73,000
N.Y.  Cheval de cirque, 1926, wc gouache, 25¾×19½,
$22,500                                                       9,325
Wright.  N.Y.  Clown musicien, gouache, c. 1937–8,
26×18½, $31,000                                              12,918

£

| 1969 | Bankhead. N.Y. L'atelier de l'artiste, 32 × 23½, $62,500 | 26,255 |

1969 Bankhead. N.Y. L'atelier de l'artiste, 32 × 23½, $62,500  26,255
  S. Le mariage juif, outline gouache, 19 in. square  11,600
  C. (Tokyo). The shepherd, coloured chalks, 1958, 26 × 21¾  15,185
  Lincoln Harris. S. (Tokyo). Les fiancés et l'ange rouge,
  1935, 29 × 19¾, 24 million yen  28,000
  C. (Geneva). Couple, ville, fleurs, 1958, 21½ × 25½,
  FS280,000+tax  28,264
  S. Vase de fleurs et personnages, 1928, 46 × 34¼  59,000
    Vase de fleurs, 1949, gouache, 25 × 19½  12,000

PHILIPPE CHAMPAGNE. (*See* French School, 17th–18th centuries)

## JEAN BAPTISTE CHARDIN. 1699–1779

In this very short list of saleroom prices for the works of a painter who has now become exceedingly rare, there are only two that denote absolute authenticity, coupled with high quality. Nor does the higher price necessarily define the top of the scale, since the Louvre which bought this self-portrait, already owns two others in which the painter figures likewise in *pince-nez* spectacles and what seems to be one of Mme Chardin's bonnets. Moreover a Chardin *genre* subject should be dearer than a still life or a pastel. There are some indications from the past. At the Doucet sale of 1912 the Metropolitan Museum paid £13,225 (equivalent to £106,000) for *Les Boulles de Savon*. The *House of Cards* of the National Gallery, Washington, is believed to have cost Andrew Mellon $150,000 (£30,860; now equivalent to £154,300) in 1931. On the other hand, the price paid to Prince Liechtenstein in 1951 by the Kress Foundation for *La Gouvernante* and *La Garde Attentive* did not apparently exceed £50,000, equivalent to £100,000 in 1970 terms for the two pictures. In 1951 all French painting of the 18th century was still well below the levels of the great Doucet sale of 1912. But many have since become so weary of the unsolicited *Sturm und Drang* of modern painting as to increase the appeal of a man who spent his whole life tranquilly translating form and light into his own language.

1962 Woolworth. N.Y. Salmon, copper kettle, etc. 10½ × 14½,  £
  $50,000  18,142
1963 Dunlap. N.Y. Boy drawing, 15 × 18, $20,000  7,145
  Fribourg. S. La charmeuse or la leçon de serinette,
  25¾ × 21¾  4,000
1964 S. The same picture  5,200
1965 S. Dead rabbit and two small birds, 14½ × 17¼  4,000
1966 J. de Rothschild. Paris. Self-portrait, pastel, 16 × 12½,
  taken over by the Louvre (the spectacles worn by Chardin
  in the picture, were sold for £355) FN 750,000  54,608
    Hare and partridge with orange, 27½ × 24  46,568
1968 Kaplan. S. Still life with pots, table cloth, etc., 35¾ × 53½  4,000

THOMAS MERRITT CHASE. (*See* American School, 19th century)


CIMA DI CONEGLIANO. (*See* Venetian School)


PIETER CLAESZ. (*See* Dutch School, 17th–18th centuries)


## CLAUDE LE LORRAIN
### or Claude Gellée. 1600–1682

In 1966 two figured landscapes by Claude were sold in London. Both had the best of pedigrees, the original drawings having been preserved and numbered in Claude's *Liber Veritatis*. The first made £175,000, three times as much as the price of any other Claude, the second, looking only a little more browned and flattened, £25,200. The one price was the result of American museum competition with no holds barred, the other the normal market value of the commodity. And where was that American museum competition in 1934 when the National Gallery, Melbourne secured a *Flight into Egypt* for £577 10s.? Well, they had not got round to Claude at all. These were just English country house pictures, cured and kippered for a century or two by a smoking drawing-room chimney that nothing could put right. The return of Claude, as described in Volume One, did not begin till the early months of 1940, the 'phoney war' months when *Sacrifice to Apollo* made £1,785. It was the highest price for Claude since 1884, when this same picture had reached £6,090. It must also be recalled that in 1808, when all men of good will needed a well-behaved Italian landscape to go with the Etruscan urns and the bust of Cicero, Hart Davis, the Bristol merchant, had paid £12,600 for the *Sacrifice to Apollo*, together with its inferior companion, the *Landing of Aeneas*, which meant about £190,000 in the money of 1970. In that light £175,000 does not even look expensive.

It will be noticed that in 1968 a Claude drawing made close on £20,000, being one of the fourteen dearest old master drawings sold in the course of the decade. In fact Claude's drawings never suffered the same decline as his pictures. Even in 1935, when a *Liber Veritatis* painting was sold for £220 10s., having fallen to less than a third its price in 1929, a drawing of ships could still make £735.


| | | £ |
|---|---|---|
| 1959 | D. of Westminster. S. Worship of the golden calf, 56×98 | 36,000 |
| | Sermon on the Mount, ditto | 35,000 |
| | (bought 1806 for £525 and £2,100) | |
| 1960 | Holker Estates, private sale to National Gallery, Edinburgh. Apollo and the Muses, 9½ ft×6 | 47,000 |
| 1961 | S. Landscape with flight into Egypt, 82×60 | 10,000 |

| | | £ |
|---|---|---|
| 1962 | Norman Crompton. Private sale to Birmingham City Museum. Embarcation of St Paul, small painting on copper, 1655 | 4,400 |
| | Heywood-Lonsdale. C. Aeneas and Dido leaving for the hunt, dated 1676 (£840 in 1801), 46×67 | 54,600 |
| 1963 | Bought by Fitzwilliam Museum. Small octagonal panel, Lake Albano and Castelgandolfo | 17,000 |
| | Sterling of Keir. S. Christ on the road to Emmaus, 13¾×15¾ | 7,500 |
| 1964 | Cust. C. Wooded landscape, river and temple, 14½×20½ | 3,675 |
| 1965 | Williams. S. Landscape with *riposo*, dated 1662 | 10,500 |
| | S. Oval landscape with shepherds and dancing dog, 15¾×20 (Lord Radstock, 1826, £733, country auction, 1941, £50) | 20,000 |
| 1966 | Miss V. Price. C. Landscape with judgement of Paris, *Liber Veritatis* No. 103, 48¾×58¾, Metropolitan Museum | 175,000 |
| | C. Landscape with cattle, *Liber Veritatis* No. 105, ex Reynolds, Desenfans, etc., 39½×51 | 25,200 |
| 1968 | Haddington. C. Octagonal landscape on copper with piping herdsman, dated 1641, *Liber Veritatis* No. 11, 11×13½ | 37,800 |

### DRAWINGS

| | | |
|---|---|---|
| 1963 | Norman. C. Study of trees, pen and wash on blue paper, 9½×6½ | 2,000 |
| | Basilica of Constantine, pen and ink, 5×7¾ | 650 |
| 1968 | Harewood. C. Tivoli from the East, 8½×12¼, black chalk, coloured washes | 19,950 |
| | Wooded landscape, Jacob and Laban, pen and wash, 8×12, signed and dated 1661 | 6,300 |

JOOS VAN CLEEF, the younger. (*See* Flemish School, before 1550)

JOHN CLEVELY JUNR. (*See* English School, 18th century)

## WILLIAM COLLINS. 1788–1847

Only a continuity with Volume One justifies the inclusion of such a meagre list under a separate heading. Until 1900 this second-rater, following first in the footsteps of Morland and then of Constable and Bonington, was well in the £2,000 class. In 1872 his *Cromer Sands* had made £3,780 at Christies, equivalent to about £35,000 in 1970 money. The modest speculation, revealed in the list, may be based simply on the premise that all names are worth something and that all art is going up.

£

| 1964 | C. | Donkeys and figures on a beach, 9×12 | | 157 10s. |
| 1966 | C. | Beach scene, 19½×24 | | 199 10s. |
| | C. | Beach scene, 19½×24 | | 199 |
| | | Fishermen and boats, a pair, 7×9¼ | 2 for | 178 10s. |
| | S. | Low tide, 1820, 34×37½ | | 900 |
| | | Frost scene at Richmond, 33×43 | | 1,500 |
| 1969 | S. | Figures outside a cottage, 24½×29½ | | 380 |

## JOHN CONSTABLE.  1776–1837

This short list raises a number of questions. There has not been a single work of Constable's in the salerooms in the 1960s which can fairly be described as a completed picture. The last such were a small group, sold in 1959 and not at all expensive, a two-foot *Vale of Dedham* at £9,450, and a *Stratford Mill*, over four feet long, at £4,620. Since 1959 we have seen oil sketches and preliminary studies make as much. As to his big Royal Academy landscapes with figures, Constable painted very few of them and it may be that there are no more to come. The last under the hammer was *The Young Waltonians*, sold to a private collector in 1951 for £44,100. According to the general movement of the art market it ought to be worth several times as much, but is it? In the field of landscape the Impressionists and Cézanne have stolen everyone's thunder. Not even Turner, Corot and Courbet are in the £100,000 class of landscape paintings. Furthermore the elaborately constructed studio landscape, distasteful to Constable himself, is out of favour. Constable's oil sketches are relatively expensive, just because they are oil sketches. The bottom of the barrel seems close at hand. Since the few things that reach the saleroom are rather scrappy, they do not get dearer.

£

| 1960 | Constable. S. | Portrait, the painter's sisters, 15×11½ | 5,200 |
| | C. | Open landscape with clouds, 7×10½ | 2,520 |
| | S. | Old barn, 9¾×15¼ | 4,000 |
| | | Landscape near Dedham, 8¼×13¼ | 3,200 |
| | | Rainbow near Flatford, 11¾×20½ | 2,200 |
| 1961 | Buzzard. S. | Cloud study, 1822, 11×19 | 6,800 |
| | | Another ditto, 8×5 | 1,600 |
| 1962 | N.Y. | Dedham vale, oil sketch, 22×27, $10,500 | 3,570 |
| 1963 | Fitzgerald. S. | Windmills near Brighton, 1822, 13×19½ | 9,200 |
| 1964 | Morhange. S. | Somerset House, study, 8×6, c. 1820 | 5,200 |
| | C. | Netley Abbey, 11½×16½ | 6,300 |
| | Colquhoun. S. | Hampstead Heath, sunset, 11¾×19 | 9,500 |

| | | £ |
|---|---|---|
| 1965 | S. Portrait, Mrs Constable asleep, 1827, 18½×13½ | 3,800 |
| | Harewood. C. Castle-Acre Priory, 9½×13½ | 3,675 |
| | Fisher. S. Osmington, Dorset, 5¾×9¾ | 2,900 |
| | Humphrey Brooke. C. Fête champêtre after Watteau, 16×14 | 1,995 |
| | C. Extensive landscape, 7×10¼ | 2,940 |
| | S. By the Stour with white horse, study for Frick Library version, 9½×12 | 3,600 |
| 1967 | Peel. S. The painter's son John, head, c. 1828, 15¾×12 | 1,800 |
| 1968 | Burton. S. Golding Constable's house, East Bergholt, 1813, 19¼×29¼ | 2,800 |
| | S. View in the park at Arundel, oil on paper, 9½×13 | 1,200 |
| 1969 | Village scene, on millboard, 5½×8½ | 1,600 |
| | Griffin. S. Donkey and foal in stable, 8×10¼ | 1,575 |
| | Peel. C. Houses in Hampstead, stormy sky, 12×16 | 1,995 |
| | Norris. S. River scene, figures and lock, pencil, 8×12 | 1,300 |
| | C. Study of trees with a house, 8×10. Bought in at | 6,510 |
| | Half length child-portrait, presumed painter's daughter, 29×24½ | 3,360 |

## SAMUEL COOPER. (*See* Miniatures)

## JOHN SINGLETON COPLEY. (*See* English School, 18th century)

## JEAN BAPTISTE COROT. 1796–1875

During the years 1910–18 ten paintings by Corot made from £10,500 to £17,000 at public auction. The 1970 equivalent would be £84,000 to £135,000, a rating higher than Sisley or Pissarro and very nearly up to Renoir and Monet. The great posthumous cults of Millet, Meissonier and Corot had however been buried and forgotten long before the post-war era, otherwise the sudden rise of the Impressionists in the 1950s might have been less of a surprise.

During the 1960s too there were prices for Corot which compared favourably with the Impressionists on some occasions, Corots at over £50,000 and one at over £100,000. But comparison with the list in Volume One will show that the Corots which made as much in the money of 1910–18, were something quite different. These dancing nymphs among willow groves, which Corot's agents could sell in the U.S.A. even in his own lifetime, were regarded by the painter as commercial propositions in which it was sufficient for him to repeat himself. One of these, which was sold in New York in 1913 for $75,000, made precisely half as much in 1963. On the same principle in 1946 a portrait, formerly the least popular sort of Corot, was the first to make over £4,000 since the beginnings of the great depression. In 1967 a portrait reached $310,000, seven times as much as any standard 'nymphs and groves' Corot, sold during the decade. The illusion that Corot painted well only when young must however be abandoned. The magnificent nude, *Vénus au bain*, which made £57,550 in 1961, was finished in the last year of his life.

| | | £ |
|---|---|---|
| 1958 | Sold by Edward G. Robinson to Stavros Niarchos, l'Italienne, portrait figure, reputed price $200,000 | 71,400 |
| 1959 | Valued by National Gallery for Lane Bequest. Small early view of Avignon (about £300 in 1912) | 30,000 |
| | Gould. S. Flesselles, village street, 13×15 | 6,800 |
| 1960 | C. Souvenir d'Italie, 17×23½ | 5,775 |
| | Biblis (£3,360 in 1889), bought in at | 5,250 |
| 1961 | N.Y. Le soir, 29×24, $25,000 | 8,930 |
| | S. La solitude, souvenir de Vigens, 1866, 38½×51 | 6,500 |
| | Paris. Souvenir d'Albano, 1872, 17½×32, FN75,000+tax | 6,580 |
| | Maharanee of Baroda. Paris. Vénus au bain (£6,750 in 1920, £27,090 in 1956), 46½×36, FN690,000+tax | 57,550 |
| 1962 | Woolworth. N.Y. Epernon, 14×18¾, $25,000 | 8,930 |
| | N.Y. Girl playing a mandoline, 17¼×13¼, $35,000 | 12,500 |
| | Guggenheim. S. Eurydice, 1870, 29×20 | 8,000 |
| 1963 | S. View of Naples, 69×33 | 7,000 |
| | Cargill. S. Méditation, 1840, 18½×13½ | 18,500 |
| | Souvenir de l'Ecluze, 1868, 15½×21½ (£3,570 in 1927) | 8,800 |
| | Wiman. S. Woodland landscape, 1870, 38×51 | 9,000 |
| | N.Y. Orpheus and Eurydice, 45×55 (£804 in 1886, £15,520 in 1913) (fall from $75,000 to $37,000) | 13,212 |
| 1965 | S. Canal bank at Vimoutiers, 15¾×21¾ | 8,500 |
| | Landscape, dated 1860, saules et chaumières, 14×10½ | 9,000 |
| | Haft, Palm Beach. Poplar and walnut by the water, $32,000 | 11,540 |
| | S. Le dortoir communal, le soir, 29×23¾ | 9,000 |
| 1966 | Eliot Hodgkin. S. Quarry near St Lô (£20 in 1874), 19¼×22¾ | 18,000 |
| 1967 | S. Chemin dans les monts boisés, c. 1830–5, 12×18 | 11,000 |
| | Chester Beatty. S. La ferme normande aux trois commères 1872 (£80), 18×24 | 27,000 |
| | Pero. S. Jeune baigneuse, couchée sur l'herbe, 15¼×22¾ | 10,500 |
| | C. Chemin creux au Printemps, 14¾×11 | 5,250 |
| | Danse des trois bergères, 25¼×19½ | 5,250 |
| | Weeks Bros. N.Y. Girl, in red with mandoline, 18½×14½, Norton Simon Foundation, $310,000 | 110,715 |
| | C. Le dortoir communal, le soir, 28×22¾, bought in at | 12,600 |
| | Ravin du Morvan, c. 1845, 18×18¾ | 14,175 |

|      |                                                                                              | £      |
|------|----------------------------------------------------------------------------------------------|--------|
| 1968 | Boise. S. Mantes with cathedral from river, $21\frac{1}{2} \times 17\frac{3}{4}$              | 15,000 |
|      | Phillips, Washington. S. La grande metairie, 1860–5, $21\frac{1}{2} \times 31\frac{1}{2}$     | 52,000 |
|      | C. Cour de ferme, environs de Fontainebleau, *c.* 1830, $16 \times 19\frac{1}{4}$             | 31,500 |
|      | Pleydell-Bouverie. S. Quai des pêcheurs, Trouville, 1930–40, $10 \times 15\frac{1}{2}$        | 18,500 |
|      | S. Danse des nymphes, *c.* 1860, $23\frac{1}{2} \times 21\frac{1}{2}$                         | 19,500 |
|      | Alise Ste Reine, la fontaine Jacob, $13\frac{3}{4} \times 8\frac{1}{4}$                       | 12,000 |
|      | N.Y. Les pêcheurs, 1874, $19 \times 28\frac{3}{4}$, $30,000                                   | 12,500 |
| 1969 | N.Y. Le joueur de flute, 1850, $52\frac{1}{2} \times 42\frac{1}{2}$, $45,000                  | 18,950 |
|      | van Waay, Amsterdam. Italian landscape with shepherd, Hfl115,000+tax                          | 14,820 |
| 1970 | C. (at Houston, Texas). Danse des nymphes, $75,000                                            | 31,250 |

## ANTONIO ALLEGRI, called CORREGGIO. 1494–1534

Attributions to this painter which have appeared in the salerooms, have proved a pretty dubious collection. With the exception of drawings, there has been no certain Correggio since the early 19th century.

### DRAWINGS

|      |                                                                                        | £     |
|------|----------------------------------------------------------------------------------------|-------|
| 1893 | Holford. C. Three children, red chalk                                                   | 831   |
| 1917 | Earl of Pembroke. S. Infant Christ in the manger                                        | 750   |
| 1954 | Henry Reitlinger. S. Sheet of studies                                                   | 550   |
| 1965 | Lord David Cecil. S. Figure of Christ, part of ceiling, S. Giovanni Evangelista, Parma, red chalk | 3,500 |

## FRANCIS COTES. 1725–1770

The portrait of John Simpson of Esslington, later presented by subscribers to the National Gallery, cost £4,200 at the great Holford sale of 1928, the equivalent of £21,000 in the money of 1970. There are no signs as yet of such prices repeating themselves for one of the more attractive of 18th century portraitists. Compared with the prices paid for portraitists such as Arthur Devis or even Gilbert Stewart, Cotes seems undervalued.

|      |                                                                                    | £     |
|------|------------------------------------------------------------------------------------|-------|
| 1961 | Whitmarsh. N.Y. Concert champêtre                                                   | 983   |
| 1964 | Kemsley. S. Thomas Craithorne and wife, 1767, $52\frac{1}{2} \times 59\frac{1}{2}$ | 3,200 |

| | | £ |
|---|---|---|
| 1965 | S. Self-portrait, sketching under a tree, 44×34 | 900 |
| | Clive. C. Mary Colmore, 1764, 48×39 | 787 10s. |
| 1968 | Menzies. S. Eleanor Grant of Arndilly, ¾ length, 49×39½ | 5,500 |
| 1969 | Bruguière. C. Elizabeth Sedley, 1767, 50×40 (£450 in 1953) | 3,150 |
| | Francis Burdett in green suit, half length, 50×40 (£240 in 1953), bought in at | 2,940 |
| | Francis Burdett in red suit, 50×40 (£480 in 1953) | 7,872 10s. |

## JOHN SELL COTMAN. 1782–1842

The sale of a Cotman watercolour for £4,800 in 1960 opened prospects of a re-valuation which has not altogether materialized. There are too few completed works available. The kind that cost £300 to £500 in the 1920s and which might now make £5,000 to £9,000, reach the salerooms very seldom. Having something of the 18th century about him, Cotman is nevertheless dearer than the romantic watercolour painters who worked in his time, Bonington, Copley Fielding, de Wint and David Cox.

(ALL WATERCOLOURS OR DRAWINGS)

| | | £ |
|---|---|---|
| 1960 | Russell. S. Blasting St Vincent's rocks, Clifton, 1825, 13¼×22¼ | 4,800 |
| 1962 | S. Roman aqueduct, Normandy, 9×14 | 750 |
| 1965 | Bruce Ingram. S. River scene, tinted drawing, 7×14½ | 320 |
| | Portrait drawing of a young man, 11×8 | 190 |
| | S. River landscape with white cloud, 1832, 12½×18½ | 5,600 |
| 1966 | C. Church at Lyndhurst, 8×10¾ | 231 |
| | River at Lakenham, 9¾×13 | 231 |
| 1968 | Bridge and ruined church, 1835, 10½×13½ | 750 |
| | Sedgwick. S. Kirby Lane Hall, Norfolk, pencil and sepia wash, signed 1818, 6½×9½ | 700 |
| | Walsingham Priory, companion piece, same date | 450 |
| | Pierce. S. The devil's tower, Norwich, 13¾×19¾ | 440 |
| 1969 | Edmison, Glasgow. Pass of Lauterbrunnen, 1831 | 9,000 |
| | C. Gravel pit and two workmen, 7¼×10½ | 1,365 |
| | Graham. C. Interior, Norwich Cathedral, pencil and wash, 9¾×6¾ | 682 10s. |
| 1970 | C. Chepstow Castle, *c.* 1801, 11¾×9¼ | 630 |
| | Ely Cathedral (pencil with wc), 10¼×16¾ | 682 10s. |

## GUSTAVE COURBET. 1819–1877

The list has been brought back to the beginning of the century in order to correct the very inadequate all-over picture presented in Volume One. The new list emphasizes even more how much these rather swarthy paintings gave way to the Impressionists in the period, 1919–52. Two important subject pictures were sold in Paris during these years, but they made no more than £2,250 and £1,152. As with other French 19th century painters, the Cognacq sale of 1952 marked the beginning of a new market, but a very uneven one in Courbet's case. Only one work can be said to have made the price of a moderately good Impressionist picture, but the *Two Girls by the Seine*, which the National Gallery acquired for £62,000 is in many respects superior to the completed version in the Luxembourg. In general Courbet's favourite subjects, deer in forests, poachers, broken down coaches in the snow, and forbidding quarries, are not very popular. Courbet's market is none the less much higher than that of the Barbizon painters of his generation, with whom he had much in common.

| | | £ |
|---|---|---:|
| 1902 | Desfosses. Paris. Femme couchée (le repos) see 1952, 20×25½ | 295 |
| 1904 | Binant. Paris. Casseurs de pierres. Dresden gallery | 1,800 |
| 1912 | Rouart. Paris. La femme des ponçets | 1,452 |
| 1913 | Mariczell de Nemés. Paris. Venus and Psyche | 3,800 |
| 1918 | Curel. Paris. La remise aux chevreuils | 1,840 |
| 1920 | Bought by the Louvre from Mme Desfosses. L'atelier du peintre (£4,000 in 1892, £2,400 in 1899, £14,800 in 1919) | 19,000 |
| | Also La Source | 4,300 |
| 1923 | Small painting, the wave, bought for National Gallery, Melbourne | 345 |
| 1925 | C. Villa of the Duc de Morny at Deauville, 1865 | 525 |
| | L'orage, bought by subscribers for the Tate Gallery | 338 |
| 1927 | Sir James Ross. C. Seascape, 1872 | 398 |
| | De Beer. C. Deer-hunting | 441 |
| 1932 | Georges Petit. Paris. La liseuse d'Ornans, 26×32 | 2,250 |
| 1937 | Leonard Gow. C. Les enfants du choeur | 420 |
| 1938 | Paris. La grandmère (125 fr to £+tax) | 1,152 |
| 1945 | N.Y. Wintry landscape | 472 |
| 1949 | Paris. A doe in the snow, 1866 | 416 |
| 1952 | Cognacq. Paris. Femme couchée, le repos (see 1902) 20×25½ | 6,874 |
| 1954 | Bessoneau. Paris. Grotte de source de la Loue | 2,350 |
| | Combat des cerfs, 23½×32½ | 1,720 |
| 1957 | Weinberg. S. Hiver au Jura, 19×23½ | 1,900 |
| | Apples on a plate (see 1962), 18½×22½ | 5,500 |
| 1959 | N.Y. Château de Chillon, 34×45, $19,000 | 6,785 |

| | | £ |
|---|---|---|
| 1959 | S. Les fils du sculpteur Leboeuf, 13×13¾ | 3,800 |
| | Valuations for National Gallery, Lane bequest: | |
| | Self portrait of the painter | 10,000 |
| | The snowbound coach | 15,000 |
| 1960 | C. Chalet on the cliffs, 13×21 | 262 10*s.* |
| | N.Y. Portrait, Tony Marlet, 18¼×15, $12,900 | 4,600 |
| 1961 | Paris. Les braconniers, 40¾×49, FN200,000+tax (see 1967) | 17,085 |
| | C. Le torrent, 22½×28 | 3,150 |
| 1962 | Woolworth. N.Y. Sous bois, 21¼×25¾, $10,000 | 3,572 |
| | MacKean. S. Apples on a plate, 18½×22½, painted in prison, 1871 (see 1957) | 11,000 |
| 1963 | Le casseur de pierres, 1850, 19×21¾ | 6,000 |
| | S. Portrait, Countess Karolyi, 32×25½, 1865 (see 1969) | 20,000 |
| 1964 | S. Portrait, Mlle Jacquet, 31½×24½, 1857 | 10,500 |
| | Unfinished version, two girls by the Seine (Luxembourg), bought for National Gallery, 37½×49½ | 62,000 |
| | C. Roebuck by a stream, 38×51, bought in | 27,358 |
| | Paris. Child-portrait, Beatrice Bouvet, 37×29½ | 7,900 |
| 1966 | S. Tethered riding horse, 12¾×16 | 2,300 |
| | Double portrait, unfinished, 21×17 | 1,700 |
| | Lot and his daughters after Guido Reni, 35×45½ | 6,800 |
| 1967 | Geiger. C. Portrait d'un peintre belge, 18¼×15 | 2,310 |
| | Kienleichner. C. Le puits noir, 25½×31½ | 8,925 |
| | C. Le bois sous la neige, 25×21 | 10,500 |
| | Motte, Geneva. Les braconniers, FS235,000+tax (see 1961) | 22,520 |
| 1968 | Boise. S. La vague, 17¾×23½ | 2,900 |
| | Le petit cavalier à St Aubin sur mer, 21×25½ | 11,500 |
| | La voile blanche, 1877, 26½×46½ | 7,000 |
| | Maillefeu. S. Biche forcée a la neige, 1856, 35¼×57¾ | 37,000 |
| | C. Study for Chevreuils à la rivière, 1868, 27¾×22 | 3,990 |
| | Coucher de soleil, 1865, 15×21¼ | 6,825 |
| | Environs d'Ornans à la fin du jour, 1872, 25×30½ | 3,380 |
| | Paysage d'hiver, effet de neige, *c.* 1860, 23¾×28¾ | 9,450 |
| | Scarabello. N.Y. Le cerf dans la neige, 1856, 36½×58¼, $40,000 | 16,660 |
| 1969 | S. Le brame, 1859 (deer in forest), 33×43, bought in at | 2,800 |
| | S. (Tokyo). Countess Karolyi, 1865 (see 1963), 36 million yen | 42,250 |
| | C. (Geneva). La rèveuse, nude bust-portrait, *c.* 1860, 18½×22, FS180,000+5% tax | 18,172 |
| | Seascape viewed from a beach, *c.* 1866, 19¾×24, FS105,000+tax | 10,600 |

# DAVID COX. 1783–1859

Another ghost market. In 1960 I noticed that there were no symptoms of a comeback for David Cox, once the coveted prize of Midland industrialists. After ten more years of creeping inflation there are still no symptoms—or rather the prospects have become even worse. A famous work, *Ulverston Sands*, made as much as 750 guineas in 1955, but there has been nothing as dear since. The picture might indeed go for less than that in 1970. Watercolours have got to be 18th century, even if there is more water than colour in them, so a bundle of the pedestrian works of Francis Towne is good for £1,600 to £2,600 a drawing. The vogue for all these prim topographies shows how the romantic taste has declined.

It is all the more worth recalling how much David Cox could make in the past. In 1872, for instance, one of his oil paintings, which are now rarely seen but which the present age would undoubtedly find even less congenial than his watercolours, made £3,601. Entitled *Peace and War*, it had been thought worthy of £32,000 in 1970 money. In 1892 another oil painting by Cox, *The Vale of Clwyd*, made £4,725 (£42,500). As late as 1926 a big watercolour, *Counting the Flock*, could be good for £4,830, though the popularity of the romantic English watercolour was already waning. This was still equivalent to £25,000 in 1970 terms, but, three years later, prices for David Cox were slashed to a tenth. No doubt his turn will come, but this painter's work was ludicrously overrated and it seems to be a feature of artists' posthumous biographies that this cannot happen to them twice.

(All are watercolours)

| | | £ |
|---|---|---|
| 1961 | S. Gathering heather, Carrington Moss, 1852, 23 × 33 | 300 |
| | C. Amiens and the Tuileries, a pair, 10¼ × 7¼.    2 for | 252 |
| 1962 | S. Crossing the moor, 1852, 13¾ × 7¾ | 550 |
| 1964 | Ingram. S. Fort Rouge, Calais | 400 |
| | Phillips, son and Neale. Buckingham Palace with troop of Life Guards | 370 |
| 1966 | British Printing Corporation. C. The Hayfield, 1838, 21¾ × 32½ | 78 10s. |
| | Going to market, 13½ × 19½ | 115 10s. |
| | S. Interior at Haddon Hall, 1833, 10 × 7½ | 220 |
| 1968 | Koch Settlement. C. Wooded landscape and travellers, 1856, 20¾ × 29 | 68 8s. |
| | Clarke. C. The Conway river near Betws y Coed, 8 × 10¾ | 157 |
| | C. Highland lake landscape, 1829, 5¼ × 8 | 420 |
| | S. Aldeborough Sands, 10¼ × 14 | 480 |
| | Lake Windermere, 10¾ × 16 | 480 |
| 1969 | C. Castle Rising near King's Lynn, 12 × 19 | 420 |
| | Molyneux Makin. S. Sand dunes, Calais, 1832, 7 × 10¼ | 520 |

JOHN ROBERT COZENS. (*See* English School, 18th century)

## LUCAS CRANACH THE ELDER. 1472–1553

Popular German art-histories continue to talk about the age of Raphael, Michelangelo, Dürer and Cranach as if they were all one happy family, a relic of the days when *Gott* was still *mit uns*. German gallery-curators, on the other hand, do not appear to lose their heads when works by Lucas Cranach, even very good ones, reach the saleroom. There can be few left that are more enticing than the allegory, called *Charity*, which found no buyer at £16,000 in 1968. It has been suggested that many curators in Germany despair of making even a beginning towards replacing the losses of the war, and so they fill-up with Paul Klee and Kandinsky.

In reality Cranach has never been a very high-priced painter. In 1928 one of his many *Lucretia* pictures was sold in Paris for rather more than £4,000, at that time the highest auction price and equivalent to £20,000 in 1970. The *Sibylla von Cleve* of the Erickson sale of 1961 was sold for the equivalent of £53,500 in 1970 money.

| | | £ |
|---|---|---|
| 1960 | S. Portrait, Johann Bugenhagen, 1532, 20½ × 14¼, now in Kunsthalle, Hamburg | 10,000 |
| 1961 | Makower. S. Girl in scarlet dress, 22¼ × 15 | 1,900 |
| | S. Samson and Delilah, 22¼ × 14¼ | 10,000 |
| | Erickson. N.Y. Sibylla von Cleve (about £525 in 1938), 20¾ × 15, $107,500 | 38,400 |
| 1962 | S. Madonna and child, dated 1516, 19¾ × 13¼ | 8,800 |
| | Mme B de B, Paris. Adam and Eve (£6,510 in 1959), FN200,000+tax, 23½ × 19¼ | 16,680 |
| | Judith with head of Holofernes, 36 × 23¼, FN82,000+tax | 6,860 |
| | Portrait of a bridal couple (Lucas Cranach the younger) | 6,700 |
| | Male portrait, ditto | 6,030 |
| 1964 | C. Virgin, Magdalen and St John at the Cross, 24½ × 15¼ | 21,000 |
| 1965 | S. Venus in a hat and nothing else, oval miniature, 4 in. high | 16,000 |
| 1966 | Wright. S. Electress Sibylla of Saxony, 8 × 5½ | 2,800 |
| | C. Portrait, inscribed Bleihard Sindringer, 1532, 19½ × 13¾ | 3,780 |
| | Lempertz, Cologne. Hercules and Omphale, 32 × 47, dated 1531, DM75,000+tax (see 1967) | 7,830 |
| | Fischer, Lucerne. Lucretia, dated 1548, FS53,000+tax | 5,050 |
| 1967 | Fischer, Lucerne. A second Lucretia, 30¼ × 23, FS92,000+tax | 8,805 |
| | Hercules and Omphale (see 1966), FS63,000+tax | 5,700 |

| | | £ |
|---|---|---|
| 1967 | S. Frederick the Wise, Elector of Saxony, dated 1532, $5\frac{1}{2} \times 5\frac{1}{2}$ | 4,000 |
| | Paris. Portrait of the same, dated 1533, $5 \times 5\frac{1}{2}$, FN42,000 +tax | 3,960 |
| | Unknown half-length portrait, dated 1536, $21 \times 13\frac{1}{2}$ | 2,800 |
| | Randall. S. Brush-drawing in brown wash of a stag, $5\frac{1}{2} \times 6\frac{3}{4}$ | 10,500 |
| | S. Frederick the Magnanimous, Elector of Saxony | 2,800 |
| | C. Silenus with tankard, beer-vat and sleeping nymph, $23 \times 15$ | 15,750 |
| 1968 | Lempertz, Cologne. Holy Family, DM155,000+tax | 17,770 |
| | S. Charity, nude reclining figure with infant children, $19 \times 29\frac{1}{2}$, bought in at | 16,000 |
| 1969 | S. Deposition (ascribed), $11\frac{1}{4} \times 6\frac{3}{4}$ | 4,500 |
| | C. Cupid, the honey-thief, complaining to Venus, 1532, $20 \times 13\frac{1}{2}$ | 21,550 |
| | Head of Martin Luther, dated 1532, $14\frac{1}{4} \times 9\frac{1}{4}$ | 3,990 |
| | *Riposo* with orange tree and walled town, $34 \times 22\frac{1}{2}$ | 31,500 |
| | Korber. S. Hercules and the boar of Erymanthus, $43 \times 36$, bought in | 6,500 |

## LORENZO DI CREDI. (*See* Italian School, central, 15th–16th centuries)

## CARLO CRIVELLI. 1435–1491

One of the rare and fine Italian primitive painters whose work may never more be seen in the saleroom. In fact the Erickson Madonna was the only true Crivelli to come under the hammer since 1905. As an epitome of the more recent history of the *quattrocento* taste, the record of this picture is worth a section on its own. It is now in the Metropolitan Museum.

| | | £ |
|---|---|---|
| 1961 | Erickson. N.Y. Madonna and child, signed and dated 1472, in carved gilt tabernacle, forming centre of a dispersed polypitch, $41 \times 17\frac{1}{4}$ in. high. Cardinal Fesch sale, 1845, £40, Morland sale, 1863, £53 11s., Graham sale, 1886, £151 5s.; bought by Colnaghi who sold it to Robert Benson who sold it to Duveen, who sold it in 1929 to Erickson for $350,000 or | 72,050 |
| | Price $220,000 in 1961 or | 73,500 |

The 1929 transaction is recorded by René Gimpel. It will be noticed that while, expressed in pounds, the 1961 price remained about the same, it had dropped to two-thirds in dollars and to a quarter in real purchasing power. To judge from the history of the Botticelli *cassone* panel in 1967, the Crivelli Madonna may not have recovered appreciably in 1970.

# JOHN CROME. 1769–1821

The market for Crome was actually higher than the market for Constable until the end of the 19th century. In the 1960s it was once again fairly comparable but only because of the lack of completed works in either case. It is in fact very difficult to judge the value of such a picture as the *Porringland Oak* in 1970. While schoolpieces by so humble a follower as James Stark (see English School, 19th century) can make nearly £6,000, one can expect something more impressive of Crome. The *Willow Tree* of the Billings sale in New York in 1913, made the equivalent of £93,500, but it is doubtful whether anything by Crome can be worth as much as that. There is a revival in Hobbema, while cool-headed East Anglians who followed the Dutch landscape school, are preferred to Turneresque romantics—only they are a little too provincial.

|      |                                                          | £      |
|------|----------------------------------------------------------|--------|
| 1961 | Atkinson. S. A Norwich backwater, 14½ × 19               | 8,800  |
| 1962 | N.Y. Burgh church, Suffolk, 21 × 34, $2,900             | 1,040  |
| 1965 | S. Back of the Gibraltar Inn, Norwich, 1812, 21 × 15½   | 600    |
| 1967 | Bonham, auctioneer. View of Norwich                      | 900    |
|      | S. Path through a wood, 16 × 13¾                         | 700    |
| 1969 | S. Castle Acre Priory, 35 × 27½, bought in              | 11,000 |

# JASPER FRANCIS CROPSEY. (*See* American School, 19th century)

# HENRI EDMOND CROSS. (*See* French School, Minor Impressionists)

# AELBERT CUYP. 1620–1691

Cuyp in 1970 typifies the peculiar taste of the market for the Dutch school. High prices are paid each season for works by painters whose names have very little resonance to the general public, van de Capelle, Michael Sweerts, Emanuel de Witte, Pieter Saanredam. It is impossible to predict who will be the next Dutch painter to reach the £60,000 class. At the same time several classical masters who became an international taste in the early 18th century are in decline, some like van der Werff, Berchem, Jan Both and Wouverman quite catastrophically. Others survived the romantic period to become much in demand during the late 19th century realist reaction. Static and respectable even after the First World War, they might have been expected at least to keep step with inflation, but that is not the case. Cuyp may seem a relatively dear painter, inasmuch as there are six works in this list which have made from £17,000 to £52,500 since 1959. But £21,000 was paid for one of Cuyp's splendid river views of Dortdrecht as far back as 1928, and that would be equivalent to £105,000 in 1970.

| | | £ |
|---|---|---:|
| 1959 | D. of Westminster. S. View of Dortdrecht, 18½×26 | 25,500 |
| 1960 | van Aalst. C. Cattlepiece, 23×28½ | 3,780 |
| 1961 | C. Philip baptizing the eunuch (attributed), 41½×58 | 5,250 |
| 1963 | S. View of Dortdrecht | 5,000 |
| | Howard. S. Uebingen Castle, 16¾×20¼ | 20,000 |
| | S. William of Orange, whole-length child portrait, 60×35½ | 1,890 |
| | S. View of Dortdrecht, pen and ink drawing | 1,400 |
| 1964 | S. Yacht off the Guard house, Dortdrecht, 42×78 | 18,000 |
| 1965 | Adda. Paris. Rider, grey mare and sheep, 37×39 (£84 in 1914, £435 15s. in 1886), FN90,000+tax | 7,175 |
| 1966 | Spencer Churchill. C. Boy holding three horses, 14×19½ (£114 in 1834, £64 1s. in 1846, £152 5s. in 1859) | 1,890 |
| 1967 | Mayhew. C. Fishing boats in an estuary, 34×48 | 4,410 |
| | C. Landscape with the walk to Emmaus, 43½×59 | 4,200 |
| 1968 | S. Figures in woody landscape with painter sketching, 38¾×53½ | 7,200 |
| | Pearson. S. Girl in sheepskin coat with golf club, 15×10 | 3,570 |
| | Bridson (at Aldwick Court). Little girl carrying basket (Jacob Cuyp, 1598–1651) | 4,400 |
| 1969 | C. Two men with cow in stable (£23 10s. in 1785), 12½×17 | 2,520 |
| | Bruguière. C. Shepherds in a wide landscape, 15½×21½ | 52,500 |
| | Looking over the Maas at sunset, 19×28¾ | 11,550 |
| | Beit. C. Riders by a ruined castle, 58½×73½ | 5,775 |

RICHARD DADD. (*See* English School, 19th century)

SALVADOR DALI. (*See* introductory note to MAX ERNST)

SIR NATHANIEL DANCE. (*See* English School, 18th century)

## CHARLES DAUBIGNY. 1817–1878

Daubigny is the least sombre and heavy of the Barbizon painters and the dearest. But the market for Daubigny, Théodore Rousseau, Constantin Troyon, Henri Harpignies and Narcisse Diaz is still very weak, despite signs of recovery at the beginning of the decade. Ten years after his death, Daubigny's *Retour du troupeau* made £1,680 at the famous Secrètan sale, the equivalent of about £15,000. By 1919 this picture had reached 7,800 guineas in the Drummond sale, equivalent to £41,000. The fall in the Barbizon school began with the great crash of 1929. Daubigny's *La sauloire*, sold for $12,500 in New York in 1926, was down to $2,100 in 1934. Between 1935 and 1955 it was very difficult for anything by Daubigny to reach £500. Nor has there been much follow-through for the rise in the Barbizons which began in 1955. But the wonder of the present public is not that the Barbizon school was recently so cheap, but that these rather unenterprising works ever attracted so much attention.

| | | £ |
|---|---|---|
| 1959 | D. of Westminster.  S.  Le point du jour, 1869, 31½×56½ | 1,850 |
| 1964 | Fischer, Lucerne.  Départ pour la pêche à Villerville, 10½×20¼, FS28,000+tax | 2,800 |
| | Abrahams.  S.  Pond with storks, 1874, 15×26 | 1,900 |
| 1965 | S.  Au bord de l'Oise, 15×26 | 3,900 |
| | Sunset on the river, 12½×22 | 1,785 |
| | Cascade de Mahoura, 1872, 38×51 | 1,200 |
| 1966 | S.  Le verger, 1872, 19¾×29½ | 5,200 |
| | Kerity la Plaine, 11¾×21½ | 1,680 |
| 1968 | C.  Bonnières, crépuscule, 1861, 32½×57½ (Salon picture) | 3,990 |
| 1969 | Scott.  C.  Maison au bord de la rivière, 9×17¾ | 1,680 |
| | C. (Tokyo).  Landscape, 1877, 8,800 yen, 15¾×27½ | 10,337 |
| | S.  Ferme au bord de la rivière, 1875, 13¼×22½ | 3,200 |

## HONORÉ DAUMIER.  1808–1879

To fill some of the gaps left in Volume One, the list has been taken back to the beginning of the century. The most astonishing additional item is the price of one of the many variations on the Don Quixote theme at the Bureau sale of 1927, namely £12,100. The astonishment is due, not because this sum meant the equivalent of more than £60,000 in the money of 1970, but because in the Paris salerooms of 1927 no Monet or Renoir could have made half as much, no Cézanne could have made a third and no Sisley or Pissarro much more than a tenth. In 1927 conservative taste still rated Millet and Degas as the two greatest modern painters, and Daumier was a more concise and more sombre Millet who, moreover, possessed that scholarly preciousness which appeals to curators of national collections. The Louvre in fact bought Daumier's *La blanchisseuse* at the same sale.

In the list of prices for Daumier in the past decade, one wonders whether the *Don Quixote* of the Lane bequest was over-valued in 1960, when £50,000 meant the equivalent of £70,000 in 1970. Probably not. More almost than any other modern painter, Daumier tended to be scrappy. In fact there has been nothing first class since 1961, apart from a collection of drawings and plaster sculptures sold in Paris in 1966 (see also sculpture, 19th century).

| | | £ |
|---|---|---|
| 1902 | Strauss. Paris. Le curieux d'étampes | 1,030 |
| 1907 | Vien. Paris. Le drame | 1,124 |
| 1910 | Alexander Young. C. View over a river | 157 10*s.* |
| 1912 | Rouart. Paris. Les avocats | 1,102 |
| | L'atelier | 888 |
| | Crispin et Scapin, bought for the Louvre | 2,400 |
| 1913 | Borden. N.Y. Voiture du troisième (Havemeyer Coll.), $40,000 | 8,250 |
| 922 | Bought by National Gallery, Melbourne, Don Quixote reading | 1,450 |
| | Les pièces de conviction | 1,200 |
| 923 | Bought by National Gallery, Edinburgh. Self-portrait | 700 |
| 927 | Bureau. Paris. La Blanchisseuse, bought for the Louvre | 5,600 |
| | Don Quixote and Sancho Panza | 12,100 |
| 932 | Georges Petit. Paris. Oedipus and the shepherd | 2,100 |
| 944 | Barbée. N.Y. Don Quixote, 10×8 | 1,368 |
| | Charles Deburan, 14½×9½ | 1,493 |
| 946 | van Horne. N.Y. Le premier bain | 3,793 |
| 952 | Cognacq. Paris. Baigneuses, 13×9½, 5·7 million francs +tax | 5,820 |
| 956 | Goldschmidt. S. Les baigneurs, 13×10 | 9,000 |
| 958 | Ten Cate. S. Children coming out of school, 10½×8½ | 4,800 |
| | S. Girl with child, 21½×23¾ | 5,000 |
| 959 | Chrysler. S. Small male head, 8¼×6¼ | 5,500 |
| 960 | Davies. S. Tête de sonneur, 1860, 13¾×10¾ | 7,000 |
| | Une baignade, 11×15½ | 6,500 |
| | Valued for National Gallery, Lane bequest, Don Quixote | 50,000 |
| 961 | Beard. S. The third class carriage, earliest version, 10¼×13¾ (compare 1913) | 37,000 |
| 964 | C. Deux passants, 8½×12½ | 7,875 |
| | La confidence, 10½×13½ | 15,225 |
| 965 | Avnet. N.Y. Le boucher, Montmartre, 8¼×9 | 13,570 |
| | S. Un coup de vent, 8×5½ | 4,200 |
| 967 | S. Le fardeau, replica, 17¼×14 | 3,200 |
| 968 | Lewis. N.Y. Réunion d'avocats, 7×8¾, $50,000 | 20,830 |
| | N.Y. Enfants jouant, 13¼×17¼, $15,000 | 6,250 |
| 969 | S. Le trio (les chanteurs), 8½×6¼ | 18,000 |

DRAWINGS

| | | |
|---|---|---|
| 927 | Bureau. Paris. Drawings at £3,000 and £4,000 | |
| 929 | Hendecourt. S. Actor declaiming | 940 |
| 952 | Cognacq. Paris. Deux confrères (£80 in 1903) | 2,348 |
| | N.Y. 'Vous aviez faim! Ce n'est pas un raison' | 250 |

| | | £ |
|---|---|---|
| 1956 | Goldschmidt. S. Le forgeron, $15 \times 10$ | 8,500 |
| 1958 | Ten Cate. S. Avant l'audience, crayon, $8 \times 8\frac{1}{2}$ | 1,100 |
| 1963 | N.Y. Defender of the widow and orphan, $18 \times 15$, pen and wash, $14,000 | 5,000 |
| | S. Le chasseur buvant, $14 \times 18\frac{1}{2}$ | 7,500 |
| | Man's head, $8\frac{1}{4} \times 6\frac{1}{4}$ | 2,800 |
| 1964 | S. Don Quixote descending mountain, pen and wash, $10\frac{3}{4} \times 7\frac{1}{2}$ | 1,200 |
| | C. Sheet of two figure studies on both sides, charcoal, $13\frac{1}{4} \times 10\frac{1}{4}$ | 895 5s. |
| 1965 | Kornfeld, Berne. Au tribunal, charcoal, $8\frac{1}{2} \times 9$ | 3,950 |
| 1966 | G.D. Paris. Two drinkers, pencil and wash, $13 \times 9\frac{1}{2}$, FN84,000+tax | 6,790 |
| | Advocate, standing figure, charcoal, $13\frac{1}{2} \times 8\frac{1}{4}$, FN75,000+tax | 6,040 |
| | Advocate pleading, pen and wash, $7\frac{1}{4} \times 5\frac{3}{4}$, FN60,000 +tax | 4,838 |
| | G.D. 2nd sale. Quatre hommes en buste, $6\frac{1}{2} \times 10\frac{1}{2}$, FN65,000+tax | 5,236 |
| | Advocate pleading, $6\frac{1}{4} \times 7\frac{1}{2}$, FN49,000+tax | 3,948 |
| 1969 | S. Cavalier, pen and ink, $15 \times 18\frac{1}{2}$ | 5,800 |

## GERARD DAVID. 1460–1523

There have been sufficient reasonably attributed works of this great Fleming i the salerooms in the present century to justify a separate entry. Two work sold in the 1960s at £20,000 and £27,300, are no true indication of the value c first class examples. There are for instance the two miniature paintings whic were formerly attributed to Gerard David, and which were sold in 1967 as th work of Juan de Flandes at £57,750 and £87,150 (see Flemish school befor 1550). The *Pietà*, which cost the Louvre £4,000 in 1902, might be worth mo than these.

| | | £ |
|---|---|---|
| 1902 | Bought for the Louvre, Pietà, 100,000 francs | 4,000 |
| 1912 | Dollfuss. Paris. Holy Family and four saints, 50,000 francs+tax | 2,200 |
| 1913 | Mariczell de Nemés, Paris. Madonna feeding child, 120,000 francs+tax | 5,280 |
| 1918 | Oppenheim. Berlin. Holy Family | 4,125 |
| | von Kaufmann. Berlin. Nativity. About | 10,000 |
| 1940 | Northbrook. C. Small Madonna (£23 2s. in 1880) | 892 10s. |
| 1959 | C. The Risen Christ, $17\frac{1}{2} \times 13\frac{1}{2}$ | 4,725 |

| 1963 | Jeandebien. S. Adoration of the Kings, attributed, 60×46 | £ 8,000 |
|---|---|---|
| 1964 | S. St Jerome and St Augustine, panels, 20¼×7 2 for | 20,000 |
| 1965 | Spencer Churchill. C. Adoration of the Kings (1859 as van Eyck, £519 15s.), 26½×28¼ | 27,300 |
| 1967 | Paris. School triptych, marriage of St Catherine, 35×50, FN86,000+tax | 6,830 |
| 1968 | C. Crucifixion, attributed, 38×29¾ | 5,250 |

## JACQUES LOUIS DAVID. 1748–1825

The list has been taken back to the beginning of the century in order to show the enormous prices paid for David's big portrait groups in the days when the French school followed in the wake of the Duveen boom in the 18th and early 19th century portraiture. These prices were omitted from Volume One. *Jeanne de Richemont and her Son* made the equivalent of nearly £250,000, *M and Mme Lavoisier* close on £200,000. Both are splendid portraits, but one wonders whether these frigid uncharming works would really command as much in 1970. David, the highest feed painter in the world in his day, has had more than one period of unpopularity. Just after his death, in 1826, the Louvre bought the *Reclining Mme Recamier*, that most famous of schoolroom pictures, for £247 4s., much less than David's commission fee for *M and Mme Lavoisier*. There are certainly no other works like these to come.

| 1902 | Bought for the Louvre. Portraits of M and Mme Seriziat 2 for 140,000 francs | £ 5,600 |
|---|---|---|
| 1908 | Cheramet. Paris. Portrait of Marquise de Pastoret | 1,640 |
| 1914 | Bought by Comtesse de Fitzjames. Portrait of Marquise d'Ovilliers, 1790, in Louvre since 1923, 200,000 francs | 8,000 |
| 1918 | Sold to E. J. Berwind by Gimpel, N.Y. Jeanne de Richemont and her son (Metropolitan Museum) | 45,700 |
| 1922 | Marquise de Ganay. Paris. Pius VII and Cardinal Caprera (£252 in 1834, £712 in 1865, £535 10s. in 1892) | 2,600 |
| 1919 | Curel. Paris. Jeune fille tenant un chien | 3,256 |
| 1924 | Wildenstein sells to J. D. Rockefeller Jnr. M. et Mme Lavoisier (£317, 1788), 113×89, Metropolitan Museum | 38,000 |
| 1926 | Highly finished drawing for the *sacre de l'Empereur*, bought by the Louvre | 1,200 |
| 1930 | Havemeyer. N.Y. Portrait of a Girl. Coll. Chester Dale | 5,370 |
| 1936 | de la Riboisière. Paris. Portrait, Caffieri Jeune | 1,132 |
| 1943 | Rogers. N.Y. La citoyenne Crouzet | 3,750 |
| 1950 | Stein. N.Y. Telemachus and Eucharis, 1818 | 1,412 |

| | | £ |
|---|---|---|
| 1951 | N.Y.  Lally Tollendal, portrait | 5,160 |
| | Rochefoucauld.  N.Y.  Mme de St Sernin | 2,860 |
| 1954 | Cassel von Doorn.  Paris.  M et Mme Pecoul, 1784 | |
| | 2 for | 1,125 |
| 1959 | C.  Two drawings of the Roman campagna  2 for | 840 |
| 1961 | Paris.  Cupid and Psyche, 1817 | 20,420 |
| 1964 | C.  Barère de Vieuzac, $13 \times 37\frac{1}{2}$ (replica) | 1,365 |
| 1965 | Finarte.  Milan.  Female portrait dated 1791, $10\frac{1}{4} \times 12\frac{3}{4}$, | |
| | 4·5 million lire+tax  About | 2,850 |
| 1967 | C.  Self-portrait, $28\frac{1}{4} \times 22\frac{3}{4}$, a school replica of the portrait | |
| | in the Louvre  Bought in at | 4,000 |
| 1969 | Kieffer.  Paris.  La mort de Senèque, early work, | |
| | FN115,000+tax, $16\frac{3}{4} \times 20\frac{3}{4}$ | 10,700 |

## EDGAR HILAIRE DEGAS.  1839–1917

In the 1960s there were six Degas pictures in the £100,000–£230,000 range and fifteen more which exceeded £40,000 each, though in the 1950s Degas had barely passed the £20,000 mark. Good examples showed a three-fold or four-fold advance in 10 years, but there was no question in the 1960s of paintings by Degas at half a million or more as there was in the case of Renoir, Monet and Cézanne. The ratios were very different at the time of the Rouart sale of 1912 Monet, Cézanne, van Gogh and Gauguin were then in the £1,000 region at the best, whereas Renoir and Manet rose suddenly beyond £5,000, while Mrs Montgomery Sears had to pay £21,000, including commission, for Degas' *Danseuses à la barre*. Since this had the purchasing power of about £170,000 in 1970 money, the price can still be reckoned the second highest to be paid for a Degas. Probably *Danseuses à la barre* was worth more than this in 1970 but not as much as double.

This relative decline in the status of Degas was the logical sequel to the acceptance of Impressionism and Post-Impressionism by the 'establishment' Both in 1912 and at his executors' sale in 1918 Degas was the most expensive of the whole school because his work was the least Impressionist. To the destruction of this disparity in the 1930s the numbing repetitiousness of the Degas ballet subjects must have contributed much. It was, however, perceived that they were less monotonous when executed in pastel, a medium which forced Degas to use a fresher palette. In 1928 William Cargill paid £12,800 for a ballet scene in oils and only £4,200 for one in pastel. But in 1963 the pastel made £105,000 as against £55,000 for the oil-painting, a 25-fold rise as against a four-fold rise.

In order to make these comparisons clearer, the list has been brought back to 1900 and expanded to include much that was omitted in Volume One.

|  |  | £ |
|---|---|---|
| 900 | Tavernier. Paris. Le ballet, pastel, 12,800 francs+tax | 564 |
| 902 | Milliken. N.Y. Les coulisses, $6,000 | 1,236 |
| 905 | Galloway. C. The ballet, fan-painting, gouache | 273 |
| 907 | Vian. Paris. La famille Mante, 21,000 francs+tax | 900 |
| 908 | Milliken. C. Race-horses awaiting the signal | 682 10s. |
| 912 | Rouart. Paris. Danseuses à la barre, 435,000 francs+ tax | 19,140 |
|  | sold with commission to Mrs Montgomery Sears £21,000 and then presented to the Louvre |  |
|  | On the beach, bought Hugh Lane (see 1959), 82,500 francs and tax | 3,640 |
|  | Rape of the Sabine women, 54,000 francs+tax | 2,497 |
|  | Répétition de danse, 150,000 francs+tax | 6,600 |
|  | Café concert, 52,000 francs and tax | 2,274 |
| 913 | 2nd Rouart sale, Paris. Avant le course, 105,000 francs+ tax | 4,604 |
|  | Mariczell de Nemés. Paris. Danseuses saluantes (see 1952), 28,500 francs+tax | 1,254 |
| 914 | Roger Marx. C. La toilette, pastel (see 1918) | 4,410 |
|  | Atelier de modiste | 525 |
| 918 | Eden. C. La toilette, pastel (see 1914) | 4,620 |
|  | Bought for Tate Gallery, London, portrait, Princess Metternich | 562 10s. |
|  | Degas. Paris. La famille Bellotti, bought by the Louvre, 322,500 francs | 13,300 |
|  | Semiramis, bought by the Luxembourg, 67,500 francs | 2,970 |
|  | Malheurs de la ville d'Orleans, bought by Louvre, 55,000 francs | 2,200 |
|  | Quatre danseuses, 145,000 francs+tax | 6,380 |
|  | Au foyer, exercises de danse, 110,000 francs+tax | 4,840 |
|  | Portrait of Duranty, 80,000 francs+tax | 3,520 |
|  | Répétant en duo, 100,000 francs+tax | 4,400 |
|  | Danseuses aux bouquets, 70,000 francs+tax | 3,080 |
|  | 43 pictures exceeded £1,000 each, 335 lots made £243,600. Prints and drawings made £72,000 and the private collection of Degas £87,000 (10% tax included). |  |
| 919 | Drummond. C. Self-portrait | 2,205 |
| 924 | Tate Gallery (Courtauld fund) buys. Les jeunes Spartiates | 1,200 |
| 925 | Tate Gallery (Courtauld fund) buys. Miss Lola au cirque Fernando | 3,350 |
| 926 | Tate Gallery (Courtauld fund) buys. Femme assise, pastel | 3,700 |
| 927 | Murray. C. Deux danseuses, oils | 7,560 |
| 928 | Bought by William Cargill (see 1963). Five dancers, oils | 12,800 |
|  | Danseuse basculante, pastel, 26×14½ (see 1963) | 4,200 |

| | | |
|---|---|---|
| 1933 | Lederlin. Paris. Woman before a mirror, 24×30, oils, 18,000 francs+tax, a slump price | £ 285 |
| 1934 | Durand Ruel. N.Y. Femme assise, 27½×19½ | 226 |
| 1937 | Leonard Gow. C. Jockeys sous pluie, pastel | 3,885 |
| | Portrait in oils, bought by National Gallery, Melbourne | 2,275 |
| 1938 | Tate Gallery buys Woman combing her hair, oils | 4,083 4s. |
| | Paris. Danseuse en bleu, pastel, 210,000 francs+tax | 2,000 |
| | Woman washing herself, pastel | 1,240 |
| | Jockey mounted, oils (see 1963) | 1,450 |
| 1940 | Durand-Ruel's price for ballet subjects in pastel | 6,200 |
| 1944 | Barbée. N.Y. Trois danseuses, pastel, 23×28 | 2,363 |
| 1947 | Durand-Ruel's price for a ballet subject in pastel (according to Maurice Rheims) $50,000 | 12,500 |
| 1949 | Paris. Degas père et son sécrétaire, oils, 32½×33½ (2·8 million francs+tax) | 2,250 |
| 1951 | N.Y. Trois jockeys (£900 in 1942) | 2,130 |
| 1952 | Felix Wildenstein. N.Y. Blanchisseuse, pastel | 3,750 |
| | Cognacq. Paris. Danseuses saluantes, pastel (see 1913), 10·5 million old francs+tax | 13,056 |
| 1953 | N.Y. Three dancers, yellow skirts (see 1958), pastel, $32,175 | 11,370 |
| | Large nude (bought Alexander Korda, see 1962) oils, $36,400 | 13,000 |
| 1954 | Paris. Danseuses russes, 24½×25, pastel | 8,460 |
| 1956 | Paris. Ballet scene, oils | 19,000 |
| 1957 | Paris. Small self-portrait | 7,500 |
| | Weinberg, S. Self-portrait, oils on paper, 1854, 15×11¾ | 6,500 |
| | Le jockey blessé, oil sketch, 10×15¾ | 5,800 |
| | Lurcy. N.Y. Four dancers, $53,120 | 17,900 |
| | Russian dancers (see 1963), pastel, 1895, 19×26¾, $35,000 | 12,500 |
| 1958 | S. Three dancers, yellow skirts (see 1953), pastel, 32×25½ | 11,000 |
| | Kirkeby. N.Y. Dancers on landscape stage, oils, 55×33½, $66,300 | 23,680 |
| 1959 | N.Y. Danseuses, jupes saumon, 38¼×25½, pastel, $65,000 (see 1969) | 23,240 |
| | Rubin. S. Three dancers, pastel, 1890, 20×24½ | 22,000 |
| | Valued for National Gallery, (see 1912). On the Beach | 50,000 |
| | N.Y. Danseuses sur la scène | 64,288 |
| 1960 | Robinson. N.Y. Trois jockeys (£1,100 Kerrigan sale, New York, 1942) then $4,400, now $65,000 | 23,230 |
| | Gimpel. S. Helène Rouart, whole-length, 63½×47½. Bought in | 44,000 |
| | Sold by Chester Beatty to Birmingham City Gallery. The Roman beggar woman, academic work, 1857 (aged 18) | 35,000 |

| | | $£$ |
|---|---|---|
| 1961 | S. (from Finland). Danseuse rajustant sa sandale, pastel, 21×14 | 9,000 |
| | Blanchisseuse portant pannier, 1888, 21×27 Bought in at | 38,000 |
| | C. Four dancers, pastel, 18×22½ | 9,975 |
| | N.Y. Danseuses, jupes saumon, pastel, 35×25¾, $75,000 | 26,650 |
| | Paris. Danseuse en rose, pastel, 31×28, FN360,000+tax | 30,820 |
| 1962 | Metcalfe (Korda). S. Conversation, pastel, 24¾×22 | 24,000 |
| | Large nude, 1896, oils, 30¾×32¾ (£13,000 in 1953) | 72,000 |
| | Woolworth. N.Y. L'étoile, pastel, 16½×16, $85,000 | 32,150 |
| 1963 | Cargill. S. Danseuse basculante, pastel, 26×14¼ (£4,200 in 1928) | 105,000 |
| | Five dancers, oils, 29¾×31½ (£12,800 in 1928) | 55,000 |
| | Jockey mounted, oils, 10×8 (£1,450 in 1938) | 37,000 |
| | Portrait, Paul Valpinçon, oils, 12½×9½ | 16,000 |
| | Hatvany. S. Russian dancers, pastel, 1895, 19×26¾ (£12,500 in 1957) | 46,000 |
| 1964 | S. Three dancers, pastel, 18¼×24½ | 15,000 |
| 1965 | Freilinghausen. N.Y. Rehearsal for the ballet, pastel, 21¾×26¾, $410,000 (comparable piece Magnin sale, 1969) | 146,370 |
| | Haft (at Palm Beach). Danseuse fatiguée, pastel, 24×17½, $130,000 | 46,500 |
| 1966 | Helena Rubinstein. N.Y. Deux danseuses, bras levés, pastel, 1900, 28×15, $31,200 | 11,140 |
| | Mercier. S. Jockey mounted, preliminary outline in oils, 12¾×9¼ | 24,000 |
| | S. Baigneuse au bord de l'eau, unfinished pastel, 41¾×36 | 18,000 |
| 1967 | Paris. Trois danseuses avant l'exercice, 1880, unfixed pastel, 24½×18½, FN310,000+tax | 24,890 |
| | Kydd. C. Femme nue couchée, pastel, 12½×16 | 12,600 |
| | N.Y. Female nude, unfinished, pastel, 32½×20¼, $32,500 | 11,607 |
| | Motte, Geneva. Woman with two children in park, 46×50, FS375,000+tax | 40,750 |
| 1968 | S. Danseuse en rouge, 1897, pastel, 25×19¾ | 15,000 |
| | Bluestein. N.Y. La sortie du bain, charcoal and pastel, 19×25¾, $72,500 | 30,210 |
| | Pleydell Bouverie. S. Repasseuse à contrejour, 1883, oils, 31½×25. Bought in | 145,000 |
| | (Later acquired by Walker Art Gallery, Liverpool at £140,000 including remitted death duties.) | |
| | C. Jephthah's daughter, outline oil sketch for mural, 14×10½ | 8,400 |
| | Femme se coiffant, pastel and charcoal, 33½×34½ | 24,150 |
| | Trois danseuses, pastel, 18¼×21 | 18,400 |

Hillman. N.Y. Quatre danseuses, pastel, 1903, $28\frac{1}{2} \times 33$, $185,000     £ 77,080

S. Deux danseuses à mi-corps, rajustant leurs épaulettes, 1897, pastel, $22\frac{1}{2} \times 16\frac{1}{2}$    65,000

     Jeune femme et ibis, with phantasy Arab town, $38\frac{3}{4} \times 29\frac{1}{2}$    25,000

Etude de nu pour une danseuse, rough pastel sketch, 1902, $36\frac{3}{4} \times 19\frac{1}{4}$    24,000

Paris. Portrait, Alfred Niaudet, 1877, $18\frac{1}{2} \times 12\frac{3}{4}$, FN700,000+tax    63,300

1969   S. Avant la classe, trois danseuses, pastel, $21\frac{1}{4} \times 19\frac{3}{4}$    100,000

Montague. S. Trois danseuses rouges, pastel, 1896, $25\frac{3}{4} \times 20\frac{3}{4}$    56,000

C. Danseuses, jupes saumon, pastel, $38\frac{1}{4} \times 25\frac{1}{2}$ ($65,000, New York, 1959)    71,400

Blaine. S. Deux danseuses au foyer, pastel and gouache, c. 1876, $11\frac{3}{4} \times 8\frac{1}{4}$    62,000

S. Femmes nues, pastel over a monotype, $5\frac{1}{2} \times 8$    17,800

Magnin. N.Y. Danseuse sur la pointe, premier sujet, pastel and gouache c. 1898, $21\frac{1}{2} \times 29$, $550,000    229,167

Erwin Swann. S. Trois danseuses, jupes jaunes, 1891, oil, $32 \times 25\frac{3}{4}$    120,000

S. Danseuse a l'éventail, charcoal and pastel, c. 1895–1900, $26 \times 18\frac{3}{4}$    70,000

## CHARCOAL DRAWINGS

1960   S. Girl with fan, pencil and coloured chalk, 1872, $12 \times 9\frac{1}{2}$    3,800

1962   S. Study for la petite danseuse de quatorze ans, $18 \times 22\frac{1}{2}$    7,200

1965   Harvey of Tasburgh. S. Après le bain    9,000

1966   S. Quatre danseuses, $26\frac{1}{2} \times 39$    8,400

1968   S. Groupe de danseuses, touches of pastel, $26\frac{3}{4} \times 24$    26,000

S. Deux danseuses nues au repos, $31\frac{1}{2} \times 42$    9,800

1969   S. Trois danseuses évoluant, $24 \times 34\frac{1}{2}$ (sold in Tokyo later in the year, £13,050)    12,500

     Scène de ballet, $14\frac{1}{2} \times 20\frac{1}{2}$    12,500

     Danseuse, red chalk, $12\frac{1}{4} \times 8\frac{3}{4}$    18,500

     Danseuse, pas de bourrée, brown chalk, touches of pastel, $13\frac{1}{4} \times 9$    6,500

     Quatre danseuses, $12\frac{1}{4} \times 19\frac{1}{4}$    12,500

     Danseuse, charcoal touched with pastel, $12\frac{1}{4} \times 9\frac{3}{4}$    20,000

     Deux danseuses, c. 1897, charcoal, $18\frac{3}{4} \times 14$    10,200

## EUGENE DELACROIX. 1798–1863

I suspect that Delacroix has always been much more unpopular than his trend-setters supposed. He carried the banner of the Romantic Movement against the petrified neo-classicism of the David school. He won—but only to enthrone the *Salon* costume subject picture for two generations, and to see such fancy-dress manipulators as Delaroche and the Baron Leys make more money than himself. The Impressionists thought they were doing Delacroix justice, and those who backed the Impressionists decided that he was a forerunner of all that was good. So in 1921 the Louvre paid 700,000 francs for *Sardanapalus*, equivalent then to £14,700—and now £93,500. Delacroix was a *grand maître*. You had to swallow him whole, his tiresome literary obsessions with Byron and Scott, his pilferings from everywhere, cavorting steeds and pink bottoms from Rubens, bearded doges from Tintoretto, pseudo-medievalism from the German *Nazarener* and smudgy brushwork from the English.

The list in Volume One failed to show this revival of interest in Delacroix when the Impressionists established themselves. The new list shows that the high tide was in 1912. There was already some recession eight years before the Louvre bought *Sardanapalus*. In the 1950s there were still some lesser completed works which could reach the salerooms, making no more than £4,500 to £9,000. In the 1960s there were only studies, the two most important suffering a notable fall. So we just don't know what *Marino Faliero* would be worth in 1970.

|  |  | £ |
|---|---|---:|
| 1898 | Musée Kums. Antwerp. Le passage du gué, 76,300 francs+tax | 3,360 |
| 1904 | Binant. Paris. Small version of the Murder of the Archbishop of Liège. Lyons Museum, 20,000 francs | 800 |
| 1907 | Henry. N.Y. Portrait, Princess Olga, $10,800 | 2,220 |
|  | Cavalier arabe, $7,000 | 1,440 |
| 1912 | Landolphe Carcano. Paris. Murder of the Archbishop of Liège, bought by Louvre, 205,000 francs | 8,204 |
|  | The riding school, 125,000 francs+tax | 5,604 |
|  | Moroccan courtyard, 77,500 francs+tax | 3,400 |
| 1913 | Jean Balli. Paris. The entombment, (£392 in 1878) | 1,218 |
|  | Paris. Hercules and Alcestis (£1,470 in 1908) | 1,138 |
|  | Magdalen in prayer (£700 in 1908) | 148 |
| 1918 | Degas. Paris. National Gallery buys full-length portrait of Baron Schwiter, 1830 | 3,520 |
| 1919 | Hamilton Palace. C. Tiger and lion | 483 |
|  | Erlanger. C. Lion devouring horse (see 1937) | 550 |
|  | A tiger | 700 |
| 1920 | Bought by the Copenhagen Royal Gallery, the Battle of Poitiers, price according to R. Gimpel | 12,000 |

| | | |
|---|---|---|
| 1921 | Bought by the Louvre from Baron Vita, Sardanapalus, (£3,840 in 1873) 700,000 francs at 47 to £ (over 16ft long) | £ 14,800 |
| 1929 | Bernard d'Hendecourt. S. Young man in dark blue coat | 740 |
| 1932 | Strauss. Paris. Mlle Rose, 1824, 13 × 18, 95,000 francs + tax | 1,600 |
| | Oil sketch, Crucifixion (sold by the painter in 1853 for 1,200 francs or £48) 115,000 francs + tax at 70 to the £ | 1,930 |
| | Georges Petit. Paris. Odalisque, 80,000 francs + tax at 70 | 1,350 |
| 1933 | Camdano. Paris. Tasso in the madhouse, 46,000 francs + tax at 70 to the £ | 780 |
| 1934 | Paris. Horses watering, 29 × 37, 200,000 francs + tax at 70 to the £ | 3,365 |
| 1937 | Leonard Gow. C. Lion devouring horse (£550 in 1919) | 237 12s. |
| 1946 | van Horne. N.Y. Christ on the Sea of Galilee, $12,400 | 3,110 |
| | The dying Moor, oil sketch, $7,200 | 1,800 |
| 1948 | N.Y. Tiger and turtle, 18 × 24, $6,700 | 1,680 |
| | Verniniac. Paris. Portrait, Charles de Verniniac, 24½ × 20, 2 million francs + tax | 1,700 |
| | N.Y. Caesar before the body of Pompey, oil sketch, 13¾ × 16¼ | 357 |
| 1951 | Rochefoucauld. N.Y. Academic nude, 32 × 25, $12,000 | 3,750 |
| 1954 | Bessoneau. Paris. Les Natchez, 1824, 35½ × 46¾, 4·45 million old francs + tax | 4,580 |
| | La leçon de lecture, 37 × 48½, 3·6 million old francs + tax | 3,590 |
| 1956 | Goldschmidt. S. l'Arabe blessé, 18 × 22 | 9,000 |
| | Portrait, Bernay d'Orville, 1830, 24½ × 19¾ | 8,500 |
| 1957 | S. Tobias and the angel, 15½ × 13½ | 700 |
| 1958 | S. Death of Actaeon, oil sketch, 1862, 17½ × 13¼ | 500 |
| | Paris. Andromache rescued by Perseus, oil sketch, 16¾ × 13¼, 3·3 million old francs + tax | 2,850 |
| 1959 | S. Le naufrage, oil sketch, 14¼ × 17½ | 2,600 |
| | Goodyear. S. Ophelia (£420 in 1870) 20½ × 25½ | 6,500 |
| 1960 | C. Seated Arab, pencil and wc | 420 |
| | Paris. Academic nude, oils, FN21,500 + tax | 1,896 |
| 1961 | Melbye. S. Evzone grec, pen and ink drawing, 11½ × 9 | 3,700 |
| 1962 | S. Death of Marcus Aurelius, 13¾ × 16 | 6,700 |
| | N.Y. Portrait, Julie de la Boutraye, oval, 28¾ × 23½, $30,000 | 10,700 |
| 1963 | Mattieson. S. La chasse au tigre, gouache, 1833, 9½ × 12½ | 6,000 |
| 1965 | Havemeyer. S. Studies for the ceiling of the Palais Bourbon, oil on paper, 20 × 35 (see 1968), bought in 2 for | 35,000 |
| | Hahnloser. S. Lelia kneeling by the dead Stenio, 1847, 8½ × 6¼ | 2,800 |
| | Susanne Fourment after Rubens, oils, 25¾ × 20¾ | 3,500 |

| | | £ |
|---|---|---:|
| 1965 | Warner. C. Adoration of the Magi after Rubens, oils, 25¾×21 | 5,250 |
| 1966 | Warburg. S. Tiger and serpent, 1847, 9½×12½ | 6,800 |
| 1967 | C. Indian, armed with Ghurka *kris*, wc, 9×8¾ | 1,470 |
| | Faust and Mephisto, study in oils for one of a set of lithographs (£146 in 1892) | 5,775 |
| 1968 | Prince de Ligne. S. Charles II of Spain after Juan Carreno, 1850, 45½×35 | 13,000 |
| | C. Etude de sangliers, 14×19¼ | 3,780 |
| | Havemeyer. C. Studies for the ceiling of the Palais Bourbon, oil on paper, 20×35 (see 1965)   2 for | 16,925 |
| | S. Lion devouring a crocodile, 9¾×13 | 6,500 |
| 1969 | Paris. The humanity of Trajan, oil sketch, FN180,000+ tax, 20¼×18 | 16,890 |
| 1970 | S. Hamlet and the grave-diggers, 1835, 39½×32 | 11,000 |

## ROGER DE LA FRESNAYE. (*See* Abstract Painters)

## ROBERT DELAUNAY. (*See* Abstract Painters)

## PAUL DELVAUX. (*See* Introductory Note to MAX ERNST)

## ANDRE DERAIN. 1880–1954

Derain was excluded from Volume One because in 1960 there was only a modest market for his works. He turned out an enormous number of almost brown monochromes which used to command themselves exceedingly to the Bloomsbury wing of British connoisseurship—much more than Picasso who sometimes excited suspicions of a sense of humour. Even in the 1920s Derain was already a painter in the four-figure class, but in 1960 a brown Derain made £8,000 with difficulty. And the same could be said even of 1969. A high price for a post-1914 Derain would be £7,000 to £9,000 and an average price £1,000 to £2,000. But in 1965 there appeared a second-tier market with the saleroom discovery of Derain's works of the *Fauve* period (1904–9). For of all the young men in their twenties, practising this gay and dashing style, he seems to have been the best, possessing a quality which can only be described as *vibrant*. How Derain came to lose it—and lose it so desperately—I do not profess to know.

£

| | | |
|---|---|---:|
| 1921 | Descaves. Paris. Landscape | 865 |
| 1926 | Paris. Landscape | 1,025 |
| 1936 | Landscape, bought for Tate Gallery, London | 475 |
| 1948 | Paris. Nature morte, 306,000 francs and tax | 275 |
| 1950 | Paris. Sous bois, $16\frac{3}{4} \times 29\frac{1}{2}$ | 373 |
| | N.Y. The Pool of London, 1905, *Fauve* style $3,700 | 1,322 |
| 1953 | Paris. Femme au bouquet, $36\frac{1}{2} \times 29\frac{1}{4}$, 830,000 old francs + tax | 1,005 |
| | Portrait de jeune fille, $24\frac{1}{2} \times 20$ | 925 |
| 1954 | Bradley Campbell. N.Y. Still life, $21\frac{3}{4} \times 18$ | 1,464 |
| 1957 | N.Y. Vase de fleurs, $21\frac{3}{4} \times 18\frac{1}{2}$, $5,500 | 1,964 |
| | Arbre dans le chemin creux, $16 \times 13$, $22,000 | 7,857 |
| 1958 | S. River landscape, $30\frac{1}{2} \times 70$ | 3,400 |
| | St Paul de Vence, $25 \times 31\frac{1}{2}$ | 2,200 |
| 1961 | S. Spanish landscape, $34\frac{1}{2} \times 28\frac{1}{4}$ | 4,800 |
| 1963 | S. La table garnie, 1921, $38\frac{1}{4} \times 64\frac{1}{4}$ | 7,000 |
| | Paris. Basilique St Maximin, $24\frac{3}{4} \times 29\frac{1}{4}$, FN105,000+tax | 9,120 |
| | C. Pool of London, 1905, $20\frac{1}{4} \times 24\frac{3}{4}$, Fauve style, wc bodycolour | 4,725 |
| 1964 | S. Rue de Cadaqués, 1927, $15 \times 18$ | 2,600 |
| | Vase aux dahlias, $18 \times 21$ | 4,000 |
| | Port de Douarnanez, $17\frac{1}{2} \times 21$ | 6,000 |
| 1965 | Zadok. S. La Tamise, 1905, $25\frac{1}{2} \times 29\frac{1}{2}$, Fauve style | 30,000 |
| | Echeverria. N.Y. La danse, 1905, $72\frac{1}{2} \times 90\frac{1}{2}$, Fauve style | 25,000 |
| 1966 | Lefèvre. Paris. Faubourg à Colioure, 1905, $24 \times 29$, Fauve style, FN500,000+tax | 40,640 |
| | Heber-Percy. C. Près de Sanary, $17\frac{1}{2} \times 21$ | 4,830 |
| 1968 | S. Houses of Parliament and Westminster Bridge, 1906, $29 \times 36\frac{1}{4}$, Fauve style | 60,000 |
| | Grand nu, 1923, $35\frac{1}{2} \times 28\frac{3}{4}$ | 5,000 |
| | Paysage de l'île de France, Fauve style, 1904, $15\frac{1}{2} \times 21$ | 26,000 |
| | Thames embankment, 1906, $26 \times 39$, Fauve style | 60,000 |
| | S. Forêt de St Cyr les Lecques, 1921, $28\frac{3}{4} \times 36\frac{1}{4}$ | 16,500 |
| | Le verger, 1907 (semi-Fauve), $21\frac{1}{4} \times 25\frac{1}{2}$ | 18,000 |
| 1969 | S. Arbres, l'Estaque. Slight sketch in Fauve style, 1906, $18\frac{1}{4} \times 15$ | 33,500 |
| | Sieff. S. Le Mappemonde, 1914, $41 \times 29$ | 9,500 |
| | N.Y. Le pont à Châtou (semi-fauve style), 1906, $15\frac{1}{2} \times 12\frac{1}{2}$, $18,000 | 7,562 |
| | C. (Geneva). Paysage environ de Châtou, *c.* 1905, Fauve style, $19\frac{3}{4} \times 25\frac{3}{4}$, FS200,000+5% tax | 20,191 |
| | S. Le camp romain, *c.* 1920-5, $24 \times 19\frac{3}{4}$ | 11,500 |

# ARTHUR DEVIS THE ELDER. (1708–1787)

The unpretentiousness, one might almost say the naiveté of the pre-Reynolds generation has come to be appreciated so that here is an 18th century portraitist who has improved his rating when that of his fashionable successors has declined. A Devis conversation piece made £2,415 in 1932, equivalent in 1970 money to £12,000. In the 1960s there were conversation pieces at £46,000 and £48,000, but the condition of many of Devis's works is poor and there are subjects to be had for less than £1,000.

|  |  | £ |
|---|---|---|
| 1961 | Craigie-Lucas. C. Robert Frith, 28×17 | 2,310 |
|  | Earl of Dundonald. C. Young man, 1755, 30×24 | 5,460 |
|  | Bowes. S. The Buckley-Bore family, 38½×43½ | 5,200 |
| 1963 | Lawton. C. Mr and Mrs Charles Crewe, small full-lengths, 18½×13½, each | 1,995 |
|  | Dunlap. N.Y. Mr and Mrs Purvis, 30×25, $3,750 | 1,338 |
|  | Ionides. S. D. of Newcastle and family at Clumber, 48×66 | 5,200 |
| 1964 | S. Three gentlemen in a park, c. 1745 | 5,000 |
|  | C. Lord Lyttleton with wife and brother, 1748, 49½×39½, Huntington Library. Cal. | 18,900 |
|  | Ireland. S. Louis Combrune, 1745, 23½×16 | 1,700 |
|  | The Gardnor family, 21½×29½ | 5,000 |
| 1965 | C. Anne Streatfield, 1756, 23½×16 | 3,360 |
|  | Desmond O'Brien. S. John Arden of Harden Hall, 1746, 29×24¼ | 3,000 |
|  | William Chaworth, 1747, 29×24 | 5,000 |
|  | Portrait, William Trollop, 29×24 (bought in, see 1967 and 1968) | 4,700 |
|  | Mr Munday of Osbaston, 1749, 29×23½ | 5,200 |
|  | Maxwell Clark. C. Sir Charles Sedley, 1752 | 4,410 |
|  | Sir Robert Burdett with gun and retriever | 6,825 |
|  | Mr Rightson Munday holding a letter | 6,300 |
| 1966 | Griffith. S. The Clavey family at Hampstead, 1754, 49×39 | 21,000 |
|  | Frankland. C. Viscount Curzon, whole length in room, 23½×16 | 1,680 |
| 1967 | Desmond O'Brien. C. William Trollop (see 1965), 29×24 | 1,890 |
|  | Portrait, Rev Sir William Bunbury, Bart, 28¾×23¾, bought in (see 1968) | 1,050 |
| 1967 | Heber Percy. C. John, 3rd Duke of Rutland in landscape, 30×24 | 7,870 |
| 1968 | Mitchell. Unknown gentleman leaning on fence, 23¼×16 | 850 |

£

| 1968 | S. William Trollop, 29×24 (see 1965 and 1967) | 1,600 |
| | Sir William Bunbury (see 1967) | 1,700 |
| 1969 | Clapham. S. Unknown family with five children and go-cart on a garden terrace with canal, dated 1749, 39¾×48½ | 46,000 |
| | C. Mr and Mrs Thomas Player in landscapes, 19½×13½ 2 for | 4,410 |
| | Strickland. S. Sir George and Lady Strickland in the grounds at Boynton Hall, 1751, 35×44 | 48,000 |
| | Tyssen. S. Mrs Sarah Tyssen in garden, 1743 | 3,800 |
| | Clifton. S. Viscount Molyneux and Mary Clifton, his grand-daughter, interior scene, 29×24½ | 3,000 |
| | C. Sir John Vanhatton leaning on a gate, 29×24½ | 5,250 |
| 1970 | C. Edward Parker and daughter in garden of Dallam Hall, 1757, 49½×39½ | 19,950 |

## PETER DE WINT. 1784–1849
### (all watercolours)

In the heyday of the English watercolour market de Wint was not quite as expensive as David Cox, but dear enough. One of his three-foot watercolours that are now seldom seen, a view of Southall in Lincolnshire, was painted for 35 guineas and sold in 1875, a generation after de Wint's death, for 1,650 guineas. By 1965 these golden guineas meant a purchasing power little short of £16,000, but in that year a view of Lincoln, the same size, was sold for 2,400 guineas, and this was the first four-figure price for de Wint in the past fifty years. There are some signs of recovery in his smaller works. It is no longer a size market. A 55-inch watercolour may make no more than a 10½-inch watercolour.

£

| 1959 | MacLennan. S. The boulder stone, 14×25½ | 320 |
| 1960 | S. Bolton Abbey, 18½×33 | 260 |
| 1961 | C. Open landscape | 168 |
| | S. On the Witham, Lincolnshire, 11¼×17½ | 200 |
| 1962 | C. View of Whitby, 35½ in. long (£840 in 1922) | 845 |
| 1965 | Russell Johnson. C. Distant view of Lincoln, 16¾×34½ | 2,520 |
| 1966 | C. Archway at Kenilworth, 11×12¼ | 420 |
| | Italian landscape, 8×10½ | 147 |
| | S. Wynstay Park, Denbigh, 31½×54½ | 820 |
| | C. Saltwood Castle, 11×27 (wrongly called Sandgate) | 315 |
| 1967 | Raphael. C. Clare College, Cambridge, 11½×17½ | 504 |
| | Hughes. C. Stacking barley, 21½×34½ | 273 |

|  |  |  | £ |
|---|---|---|---|
| 968 | C. Herdsman, cattle and stream, $6\frac{1}{2} \times 10$ | | 420 |
| | Extensive landscape with farm buildings, $9 \times 17\frac{1}{2}$ | | 441 |
| | Besterman. C. Windsor Castle from the park, $6 \times 10\frac{1}{2}$ | | 840 |
| | S. Rustics on a road, $13 \times 19\frac{1}{4}$ | | 320 |
| 969 | Brian Hamilton. C. Landscape with windmill and wagon, $11\frac{1}{4} \times 18$ | | 3,150 |
| | Tewkesbury Abbey, $12\frac{1}{4} \times 18\frac{1}{2}$ | | 1,785 |
| | Windsor, old lock, $18 \times 35\frac{1}{2}$ | | 1,207 10s. |
| | Brotherton. S. Extensive landscape, $12 \times 19\frac{1}{2}$ | | 1,500 |
| | C. Goodrich Castle on the Wye, before 1834, $10\frac{1}{2} \times 14\frac{1}{2}$ | | 1,575 |
| | Clough. C. Warwick Castle, $15 \times 23$ | | 630 |
| | Kenrick. C. Beverstone Castle, $17 \times 23\frac{1}{4}$ | | 945 |
| | C. Vale of Llangollen, $13 \times 37\frac{1}{2}$ | | 840 |

## CARLO DOLCI. 1616–1686

The price, paid by Sir Charles Duncombe in 1762 for *St Andrew Praying*, was equivalent to something like £7,500 in the money of 1970. But 360 guineas in 1762 was a very big price for a picture and as much as any contemporary painter could earn from the most elaborate composition. It was very much like paying £60,000 for a hundred-year-old Impressionist picture today. Yet in 1962 *St Andrew Praying* cost the Birmingham City Gallery no more than £5,000. This posthumous adventure reveals the small market reaction to all that scholarly propaganda in favour of the Italian 17th century. It is no longer possible to buy an altarpiece at four shillings a foot, as it was a generation ago, but for the price of one early Picasso you can fill a gallery. And Carlo Dolci's *Madonna con stelle*, for which in the 1870s the Earl of Dudley offered £20,000 (about £180,000, 1970 scale), remains at Blenheim.

|  |  | £ |
|---|---|---|
| 960 | S. Charity, $31 \times 37$ | 315 |
| | Leslie. S. Magdalen washing the feet of Christ, $70\frac{1}{4} \times 87\frac{1}{2}$ | 400 |
| 962 | Bought by Birmingham City Gallery from Lord Faversham, St Andrew Praying (£378 in 1762) | 5,000 |
| 963 | S. The painter's wife, chalk drawing, $7\frac{1}{2} \times 5\frac{5}{8}$ | 400 |
| 964 | de Knayth. S. Holy family, $49\frac{1}{2} \times 39\frac{3}{4}$ | 2,000 |

## Domenico Zampieri, called
## DOMENICHINO. 1581–1641

The same observations apply. *The vision of St John*, for which Hart Davis was reputed to have paid 12,000 guineas in 1810, was sold at Christies in 1889 for a hundred guineas. What would its value be in 1970?

| 1965 | Spencer Churchill. C. Mountainous river landscape, 51×71 (£51 9s. in 1832) | £ 399 |
| 1967 | C. Landscape with Tobias and the Angel, 37½×50½ | 1,260 |
| 1968 | S. Figures under trees, brown ink drawing, 6¾×5 | 680 |
| 1969 | S. Landscape with Tobias and the angel, 12¼×19 | 2,500 |
| | St John the Evangelist, 36¼×26¾ (Orleans coll., valued 1798 for Earl of Carlisle £630; at Castle Howard till 1945) | 8,200 |

## KEES VAN DONGEN. 1877–1968

It is no common destiny to have had one's drawings lithographed in *Gil Blas* at the turn of the 19th century in the company of Steinlen, and to have lived into 1968 to see one's paintings, which made a hundred pounds or so in the 1920s, sold for £33,300, the equivalent of £7,000 in that glorious prime. Of all present-day cults of the pioneer moderns, that of Kees van Dongen was perhaps the least predictable. To patronize the moderns in the 1920s was a serious business of brown Derains, gas-lit Vlamincks and ash-coloured cubist compositions. Van Dongen's pictures like their subjects seemed painted in lipstick and talcum powder. He was *vulgar*. He had none of the subtle undertones with which Toulouse Lautrec, another magazine illustrator, had depicted the same sort of livestock. The proper thing was to ignore him.

At this distance of time it is the glaring obviousness of van Dongen's work that gives it a special charm, like the obviousness of Frith's Derby Day, for these paintings look very like the 1920s—and the 1920s have become romantic *et voila tout*.

| 1939 | Canonne. Paris. Venice, grand canal, 11,500 francs+tax | £ 72 |
| 1949 | Tzanck. Paris. Femme à la toilette, 40×23½, 100,000 old francs+tax | 145 |
| 1950 | Paris. Les deux baigneuses, 40×32½, 90,000 old francs+tax | 126 |
| 1951 | Paris. Le Havre, le bateau d'Honfleur, 20×24½, 240,000 old francs+tax | 292 |
| 1953 | Girardin. Paris. La guitare, 36½×28¼, 800,000 old francs+tax | 898 |
| | N.Y. Femme nue, 25×35½, $1,750 | 625 |
| 1954 | Paris. Scène de plage, 14½×24 | 670 |
| 1956 | S. Soutiers noirs au Havre, 1909, 21½×18 | 480 |
| 1958 | S. The Sacré Coeur, Montmartre, 17¾×19¾ | 200 |
| | Paris. Music Hall, 1904, 29¼×34, 2·7 million francs+tax | 2,350 |
| 1959 | S. La Goulue en dompteuse, pastel, 17×12 | 350 |
| | N.Y. Street scene in Tangiers, 22×19, $3,250 | 1,162 |

| | | £ |
|---|---|---|
| 1960 | N.Y. Mille baisers, 39½×32, $6,000 | 2,145 |
| | Paris. Le Matchiche, 26×21½, FN86,000+tax | 7,285 |
| | Abreu. S. Les danseuses, 36×28½ | 9,200 |
| 1962 | Paris. Nu assis, 20×26, FN110,000+tax | 9,420 |
| | Motte, Geneva. Portrait, Mme Utrillo-Valore, 72½×45½, FS120,000+tax | 12,000 |
| | Ida Rubinstein and Anna Pavlova, 1909, 21½×26, FS88,000+tax | 8,800 |
| 1963 | Motte, Geneva. La tranchée, 32½×40, FS156,000+tax | 15,580 |
| | Paris. La maison rouge, 32½×40, FN110,000+tax | 9,420 |
| | S. L'acrobate, 8×19½ | 7,400 |
| | S. Danseuses, 36×28½ | 9,200 |
| 1964 | Bloch. Paris. Le hussard, 40×32½, FN150,000+tax | 13,950 |
| | Femme accoudée, 22½×20, FN130,000+tax | 11,545 |
| | Le lit, 40×32¼, FN115,000+tax | 10,160 |
| | S. L'acrobate, 28×19¼ | 7,400 |
| | Le chapeau bleu, Kiki de Montparnasse, 39½×32 | 7,200 |
| | Le pont Alexandre, 1922, 31×39 | 6,500 |
| 1965 | S. Le coquelicot, 22×18, 1906 | 14,000 |
| | Bar au Caire, 25½×21½ | 9,800 |
| | Restaurant à Venise, 1920, 35½×28 | 7,400 |
| | Chevaux sur la plage, 13×15¾ | 3,600 |
| | Lucie, la mulatresse, 39½×32 | 6,500 |
| | Lempertz, Cologne. Woman with Siamese cat | 8,700 |
| 1966 | Helena Rubinstein. N.Y. Femme au collier, fond rouge, 1905, 39×31, $47,000 | 16,930 |
| | S. L'atelier, 1917, 25½×21 | 6,200 |
| | Caille sur canapé, 1922, 31¼×50½ | 6,000 |
| | Nu allongé, 1908, 22×26, 'Mika' (see 1967) | 6,800 |
| | Paris. Seated nude | 7,126 |
| 1967 | N.Y. The Spanish dancer, $55,000, 39½×32½ | 19,643 |
| | S. La moisson, 20½×25¼ | 7,400 |
| | De Diehl. S. Danseuse, 25×20¾ | 7,500 |
| | Paris. 'Mika', nue sur un divan, 21½×26 (see 1966) | 9,570 |
| | S. Amazone et baigneuse, 1925, 25½×21¼ | 6,500 |
| | Murdoch. S. Le lion, 1904, 57½×32½ | 5,000 |
| | Motte. Geneva. La Parisienne, 22×18½, FS83,000+tax | 9,052 |
| | L'acrobate, 1904, 31½×28¾ | 8,862 |
| | Paris. Arabes en haute Egypte, 32×36, FN98,000+tax | 10,550 |
| | Deauville races, 26×40, FN200,000+tax | 15,940 |
| 1968 | Paris. Jardins botaniques, Monte Carlo, FN165,000+tax | 15,375 |
| | Rainy day, Monte Carlo | 15,375 |
| | N.Y. Autobus Battignoles-Odéon, 1903–5, 18×26 | 18,335 |
| | Au Bois de Boulogne, 1920, 21½×26 | 12,500 |

| | | £ |
|---|---|---|
| | S. Portrait, Maude Lotti, *c.* 1906, $32\times39\frac{1}{4}$ | 23,000 |
| | Girl's head, 1903–5, $18\times14\frac{3}{4}$ | 9,000 |
| | Roudinesco. N.Y. Portrait, Anatole France, *c.* 1922, $72\times45\frac{1}{2}$, $80,000 | 33,300 |
| | Femme au grand chapeau, 1912, $28\frac{1}{2}\times23\frac{1}{2}$, $40,000 | 16,655 |
| | Grand nu (Zita) 1911, $51\times38\frac{1}{2}$, $55,000 | 27,500 |
| | Le piquenique au Louvard, $32\times29\frac{1}{2}$, 1924, $65,000 | 27,083 |
| | Champ de courses à Deauville, 1920, $36\frac{3}{4}\times29$, $49,000 | 20,416 |
| | Cocoline, $28\frac{3}{4}\times23\frac{3}{4}$, *c.* 1925, $40,000 | 16,665 |
| | Au Restaurant Shepherds, Cairo, 1928, $39\frac{1}{2}\times32$, $49,000 | 16,665 |
| | Comoedia Montparnasse Blues, 1920–3, $39\frac{1}{2}\times32$, $78,000 | 32,500 |
| | L'habit Deauville, 1920, $28\frac{3}{4}\times23\frac{3}{4}$, $33,000 | 13,750 |
| | C. Fête de nuit, Venise, 1921, $28\frac{3}{4}\times36\frac{1}{4}$ | 10,500 |
| 1969 | C. La chanteuse, 1920, $27\frac{3}{4}\times19\frac{3}{4}$ | 14,700 |
| | Roudinesco. N.Y. La clownesse, *c.* 1907, $25\frac{1}{2}\times18$, $30,000 | 12,604 |
| | Paris. Portrait, Eve Francis, 1923, FN150,000+tax | 13,940 |
| | S. Vase de chrysanthèmes, van Gogh style, $51\frac{1}{2}\times35$ | 15,000 |
| | Versailles, la Cour d'Honneur, 1930, $31\frac{1}{2}\times39\frac{1}{2}$ | 8,000 |
| 1970 | N.Y. Portrait, Mme Malpelaux bras levés, 1909, $92,500 | 38,450 |

## GERARD DOU or DOW. 1613–1675

Beckford's 'greatest Flemish painter in the world' has not fared much better in the 1960s than in the previous decade. The *Young Mother* made £8,000, one of those prices that the press likes to describe as an all-time record. But in 1771, when it was sold for 30,000 livres, it was not only the dearest painting by Dou, but one of the three or four dearest pictures that had ever been sold at auction. In fact it had the same status as a half-million picture in 1970. It should be added that this quite attractive painter had a higher rating before the First World War than at the present moment. In 1894 *The Flute Player* made £3,675, equivalent to nearly £33,000.

| | | £ |
|---|---|---|
| 1960 | S. Interior, woman spinning, $19\frac{1}{4}\times20\frac{1}{2}$ | 1,500 |
| | Paris. Le petit musicien, FN11,500+tax | 984 |
| 1961 | Makower. S. Girl at a well, $12\frac{1}{4}\times8$ | 1,400 |
| 1963 | Bowlby. S. Physician at a window, $19\frac{1}{4}\times14\frac{1}{2}$ | 1,000 |
| | Girl at a window, $22\frac{1}{4}\times17\frac{1}{4}$ | 950 |
| 1965 | Turner. C. Rembrandt's father, half-length, $15\frac{1}{4}\times12\frac{1}{4}$ | 1,365 |
| | Gatacre. C. Two skulls on a table, $21\frac{1}{2}\times18$ (£10 in 1875) | 840 |
| 1966 | Vernon. S. (ex Grosvenor family). The young mother, $19\frac{1}{2}\times14\frac{1}{2}$ (£1,184 in 1771, £1,340 in 1793) | 8,000 |

FRANÇOIS DROUAIS. (*See* French School, 18th century)

JEAN DUBUFFET. (*See* Abstract Painters)

## RAOUL DUFY. 1880–1953
(Gouache paintings unless otherwise stated)

Despite the enormous quantity of gouache paintings by Raoul Dufy which still reach the salerooms, their value went up during the decade by five times. They do not have quite that period feeling which is to be got from van Dongen and they are even more superficial. Nevertheless they sometimes achieve higher prices than van Dongen, though the highest of all are paid for Dufy's *Fauve* pictures which are quite untypical. It seems that all who painted in that style can command £50,000 to £60,000.

The list in Volume One has been revised. It will be noticed how very harshly the great depression of the 1930s dealt with him. In the late 1920s few of Dufy's gouaches were to be had under £100, but at the outbreak of the war £25 to £40 would have bought almost any of them. Dufy's style has been a Godsend to commercial artists, but I do not think that explains why some of these slaphappy trifles cost as much as a good Canaletto.

| | | | £ |
|---|---|---|---|
| 1930 | Canonne. Paris. 4 typical gouache paintings | 4 for | 318 |
| 1939 | 2nd Canonne sale, Paris. Bassin à Marseille | About | 25 |
| | Hotel Soubées, 13,000 francs+tax | | 86 |
| | Walter Taylor. C. The boat-house, 19×15 | | 35 15s. |
| 1940 | Eumorphopoulos. S. Falaises | | 110 |
| 1944 | S. Séchage de voiles | | 200 |
| | Barbee. N.Y. Fenêtre ouverte | | 423 |
| | Ascoli | | 199 |
| 1949 | Astor. S. View of Langres | | 350 |
| | N.Y. Ste Adresse | | 400 |
| | Paris. Table before a window | | 470 |
| 1951 | Paris. Orchestre | | 612 |
| 1952 | Paris. Les canotiers, 1922 | | 622 |
| 1953 | Paris. Les courses, 20×29 | | 4,200 |
| 1954 | Paris. Avenue du bois de Boulogne | | 2,065 |
| 1955 | Paris. Fête de gymnastique, 22×18½ | | 3,600 |
| 1957 | Lurcy. N.Y. Imaginary view of Paris, 76×61, $26,000 | | 9,300 |
| | Paris. Deauville races | | 8,000 |
| | Antwerp | | 6,000 |
| | Moulin de la Galette | | 4,500 |

| | | £ |
|---|---|---|
| 1959 | S. Landscape | 3,400 |
| | Ascot Paddock, 1935, $19\frac{1}{4}\times25\frac{1}{2}$ | 2,400 |
| | Paris. Stands at Havre regatta, $24\times28$, FN150,000+tax | 12,500 |
| 1960 | Motte. Geneva. L'orchestre, 1951, $20\frac{1}{2}\times27$, FS80,000+tax | 7,735 |
| | S. Set of 14 wc designs for a frieze for the liner *Normandie* made £19,000 (£28,000 in 1970), average price | 1,475 |
| | Willert. S. Le bassin de Deauville, *c.* 1930, $25\frac{3}{4}\times32$ | 4,800 |
| | C. Paddock at Ascot, $19\frac{1}{4}\times25\frac{1}{4}$ | 1,995 |
| | Hughes. S. Le départ des huit-mètres, 1934, $17\frac{1}{2}\times42\frac{3}{4}$ | 4,800 |
| | C. Riviera promenade scene, $15\times18$ | 2,310 |
| 1962 | N.Y. Bois de Boulogne, $23\frac{3}{4}\times29$, \$19,000 | 6,786 |
| 1963 | Jowitt. S. Casino, Nice, $18\frac{1}{4}\times21\frac{3}{4}$ | 4,100 |
| | Paris. Henley Regatta, 1931, $29\frac{1}{4}\times24$, FN83,000+tax | 7,275 |
| | Orphée, oils, $24\frac{1}{2}\times16\frac{1}{2}$, FN60,100+tax | 5,310 |
| 1964 | Hutton. S. Beach at le Havre, Fauve phase, 1906, $25\times31\frac{1}{2}$ | 17,000 |
| | S. Church of St Vincent, le Havre, 1907, $32\times23\frac{1}{2}$ | 5,500 |
| | S. L'orchestre noire, $18\times24$ | 7,000 |
| | Bloch. Paris. Plage de Ste Adresse, 1904, oils, $26\times32\frac{1}{2}$, FN92,000+tax | 7,320 |
| 1965 | Zadok. S. Regatta at Cowes, 1927, $52\times34$ | 25,000 |
| | C. Fishers among rocks | 8,400 |
| | La rivière, 1908 (Fauve style), oil, $35\frac{1}{2}\times32$ | 8,610 |
| | N.Y. Le piano méchanique, $18\times22$, \$17,000 | 6,070 |
| | Benenson. N.Y. Le bassin de Deauville, $25\frac{1}{2}\times31\frac{3}{4}$ | 10,000 |
| | Tishman. N.Y. Studio with carpet and easel, $14\frac{3}{4}\times18$, \$125,000 | 44,650 |
| | Boulton. C. L'atelier, 1909, $32\times25\frac{1}{2}$ | 5,040 |
| 1966 | S. Amphitrite, 1936, $74\times63$ | 22,000 |
| | Helena Rubinstein. N.Y. Marine, $28\frac{1}{4}\times34\frac{3}{4}$ | 7,900 |
| | Heber Percy. C. Aux courses, Goodwood, $19\frac{1}{2}\times25\frac{1}{2}$ | 3,832 |
| 1967 | C. Promenade à Trouville, $24\frac{3}{4}\times31\frac{1}{4}$ | 4,410 |
| | Romero. C. Ascot, avant la course, 1928, $15\times19\frac{1}{2}$ | 6,300 |
| | C. Le jardinier, 1915, $31\frac{3}{4}\times71\frac{3}{4}$ (Cubist) | 6,825 |
| | Régate à Cowes, $25\frac{1}{4}\times31\frac{1}{2}$, $25\frac{1}{4}\times31\frac{1}{2}$ | 8,925 |
| | Hills. N.Y. Three people having tea, Perpignan, $14\frac{1}{2}\times17\frac{3}{4}$, \$15,000 | 5,358 |
| | Motte. Geneva. Sur la jetée (oils), $20\times24\frac{1}{2}$, FS58,500+tax | 6,400 |
| | Les courses, $17\frac{1}{2}\times25\frac{1}{4}$, FS60,000+tax | 6,650 |
| | La coupe de fruits, 1909, oils, $18\frac{1}{2}\times22\frac{1}{2}$, FS72,000+tax | 7,872 |

| | | £ |
|---|---|---|
| 1968 | Elmer Rice. N.Y. Eiffel Tower from the Seine, 1925, 21½×25¾, $15,000 | 6,250 |
| | S. Port de Caudebec, 23×28½ | 9,000 |
| | Gros temps, le Havre, 1907, 20½×24½ (Fauve style) | 7,000 |
| | Bluestein. N.Y. Le bassin de Deauville, 25¾×32, $29,000 | 12,820 |
| | Roudinesco. N.Y. Les trois ombrelles, Fauve style, oil, 1906, 23½×29, $140,000 | 58,000 |
| | Vieilles maisons sur le bassin, Honfleur, Fauve style, oil, 1905–6, 23¾×29¾, $100,000 | 41,670 |
| | Le canal, Marseille, academic work, 1902, oil, 21½×25½, $14,000 | 5,800 |
| | Le quatorze juillet à Antibes, 1910, 21½×25, $40,000 | 16,665 |
| | Régate à Henley, c. 1933, 25¾×32, $26,000 | 10,417 |
| | Aux courses, Ascot, 1930, 21×25¾, $45,000 | 18,750 |
| | Le paddock, Deauville, 1933, 23¾×29, $50,000 | 20,825 |
| | Courses à Deauville, 25¾×32, 1931, $52,000 | 21,665 |
| | Course à Ascot. l'enclos royal, 1930, 21½×51½, $62,000 | 25,840 |
| | Yachts dans le port de Deauville, 23¾×28¾, 1938, $42,000 | 17,506 |
| | Au cirque, 1934, 25¾×32, $37,000 | 15,415 |
| | Le yacht, Trouville, 1927, 18×21¾, $28,000 | 11,660 |
| | Paris. Au paddock, FN300,000+tax | 27,940 |
| | S. Mme Dufy en rose, 1908, 45¾×35 | 24,000 |
| 1969 | Roudinesco. N.Y. Ascot, les courses, 1932, 15×18 | 10,000 |
| | Black. S. Fenêtre aux barreaux de couleurs, oils, 1906, 30×25½ | 30,000 |
| | S. (Tokyo). Port de Deauville, c. 1930, 20×29¼, 19 million yen | 21,250 |
| 1970 | S. Auto-portrait aux Fleurs, 1908, 31¾×25½ | 20,000 |
| | Yul Brynner. C. Le 14 Juilliet, Fauve style, 1906, 21¾×18 | 25,200 |

## ALBRECHT DÜRER.   1471–1528

So far as paintings go, the market is at an end, apart from the very remote possibility of sales by museums and galleries. This brief list contains the record for Dürer since the beginning of the century, revised from Volume One. With drawings it is otherwise. Two drawings from the Lubomirski album in Lwow have reached the salerooms, having emerged from the clutches of Hermann Goering. Three drawings have neared the £30,000 mark, while the famous *Stag Beetle* at £58,000 has proved itself the dearest drawing ever sold even in terms of real money, £58,000 being equivalent to more than £7,000 in 1914.

| | | £ |
|---|---|---:|
| 1904 | Marquess of Northampton. Private sale to National Gallery. Portrait, Dürer's father, 1497, now considered a late copy | 5,000 |
| 1914 | J. Fairfax Murray. C. Salvator Mundi (attributed) | 2,835 |
| 1931 | Figdor. Berlin. Bust-portrait, man with curly hair | 7,500 |
| 1936 | Sold by Duveen to Andrew Mellon, same picture, now National Gallery, Washington | 41,200 |
| 1944 | Sir Francis Cook. Private sale to National Gallery, The Madonna of the Iris | 12,000 |
| 1951 | Czernin, Vienna, private sale to Kress Foundation of Head of unknown young man, oil on paper, 1516, 16½×13¼ | 88,000 |
| 1965 | Brenda Cook. C. Via crucis. grisaille panel, one of several copies                   Bought in at | 15,540 |

### DRAWINGS

| | | |
|---|---|---:|
| 1958 | Holland-Martin (Skippe coll.) C. Two horsemen, pen, 5×4¾ | 4,200 |
| 1964 | Victor Bloch. S. Nude man with lion, pen (the Lubomirski album), 10⅛×5⅝ | 8,000 |
| 1966 | London Library. S. Shepherds piping and fiddling, pen and watercolour on title page of an Aldine printed Theocritus, 1496 (1883 £15; 1894 £295; 1919 £260) | 26,000 |
| 1967 | Paris. Woman reading a book, pen drawing, 340,000 francs+tax | 27,298 |
| | Randall. S. Holy family, slight pen sketch (Lubomirski album), 4¾×3¼ | 5,000 |
| 1968 | S. Melancholia, first state of the engraving | 4,800 |
| 1969 | Tyser. S. Stag beetle, wc bodycolour, signed and dated 1505, 5·68×4·6 in. (Sackville-Bale, 1881, £79, see Volume One). Bought by Alain Delon, Paris | 58,000 |
| | Boerlage-Koenigs. S. Half-length Virgin Mary, pen, signed and dated 1521, 6×4·16 in. | 30,000 |

## DUTCH SCHOOL
### 17th–18th centuries
(Painters not listed in Volume One)

See separate headings for Berchem, Cuyp, Dou, Goyen, Hals, Hobbema, Hooch, Huysum, Maes, Metsu, Mieris, Ostade, Potter, Rembrandt, Ruysdael, Steen, Terborch, van de Velde, Vermeer, Wouverman.

Apart from Sweerts and Terbruggen, the painters in this list may fairly be described as formularist. They stick to the same kind of subject, their standard of craftsmanship is very even and, until the post-war period, they have been in relatively inexpensive class. Some, however, such as de Witte, Kalf, van de Capelle and Saanredam have become costly painters, measured by almost any yardstick. Apart from Rembrandt, Vermeer, Frans Hals, Hobbema, de Hooch, Cuyp and Salomon Ruysdael, they rate higher than any of the painters of the more traditional choice of the Dutch school. This school has become a regional market rather than an international market since the disappearance of Vermeer and the best of Pieter de Hooch. It is not easy to see why this should have created such a complete reversal of preference, but one may perhaps detect a shadow of rational impulse in it.

The reasoning seems to be that there are only four or five truly great Dutch painters, the rest being no more than good professionals; that, since the Ostades, van de Veldes and Mierises are no longer great masters in international estimation, there are other Dutch professionals who are just as good and whose choice of subject is more attractive. Hence the impressive sums paid for Saanredam's whitewashed church-interiors, van de Capelle's brown-sailed fishing boats and Bosschaert's glasses of flowers. The fishing-boat picture which made £54,600 at the Spencer Churchill sale of 1965, had cost Lord Northwick £184 16s. in 1846, therefore a fairly expensive picture in the days when gloomy seascapes by Clarkson Stanfield, very wet and brown, were the latest thing. Though it is hard to see what message these brown sails have for our satiated age, another van de Capelle made £125,000 in 1969. One can only conclude that regional pride means more, now that nationalism has become a dirty word.

Yet, seeing that sums of £60,000 and more are paid at least twenty times a year for perfunctory Impressionist works and ice-cold abstractions, these Dutch paintings do not appear overvalued, however rapidly they may have advanced. One is still a little surprised at meticulous flowerpieces which make £30,000 to £40,000. The most derivative of them, those of Jan van Os who lived into the 19th century, are not even the cheapest at £22,000 and more. This need surprise no one. Virtuosity and *trompe l'oeil* effects have always counted more than rarity and originality in this market. At £54,000 a Fantin-Latour has cost half as much again as any Dutch or Flemish flower painting of the classic period.

BEREND AVERCAMP. 1612–1679

|  |  |  | £ |
|---|---|---|---|
| 1956 | S. | Skating scene, $11\frac{1}{2} \times 20\frac{1}{2}$ | 14,000 |
| 1957 | S. | Winter scene with skating, $16 \times 25\frac{1}{2}$ | 17,000 |
| 1962 | Paris. | Skating scene, $16 \times 25\frac{1}{2}$, FN124,000+tax | 10,515 |
| 1963 | Heldring. S. | Skating scene, $18\frac{3}{4} \times 35\frac{1}{4}$ | 19,500 |
|  | S. | Skating scene, $12\frac{1}{2} \times 21\frac{1}{2}$ | 10,000 |
| 1965 | C. | Skating scene, $14\frac{1}{2} \times 20\frac{1}{2}$ | 8,400 |
| 1967 | C. | (Hendrick Avercamp) Crowded skating scene, $14 \times 17\frac{1}{4}$ | 18,900 |
|  | Paris. | (Hendrick Avercamp) Skating scene, $15\frac{1}{2} \times 35\frac{1}{4}$, FN330,000+tax | 30,790 |
| 1969 | Gough. S. | Skating scene, $17\frac{1}{2} \times 34$ | 5,000 |

GERRITT BERCKHEYDE. 1638–1698
(in the Beresford Hope sale, 1917. C, twelve of Berckheyde's best wor
made from £315 to £787 10*s*. each)

| | | £ |
|---|---|---|
| 1959 | S. Lutheran church, Amsterdam, $20\frac{1}{2}\times24\frac{1}{2}$ | 3,500 |
| | Flower market, Amsterdam, 1686, $20\frac{1}{2}\times24\frac{1}{2}$ | 5,700 |
| 1961 | D. of Leeds. S. The Binnenhof and the Gevangenpoort, the Hague, a pair $15\frac{3}{4}\times18\frac{3}{4}$ 2 for | 28,500 |
| 1965 | Spencer Churchill. C. The Binnenhof, the Hague, $20\times24$ | 10,500 |
| | The Groote Markt, the Hague, $15\times21\frac{1}{2}$ | 13,650 |

ABRAHAM VAN BEYEREN. 1620–1675

| | | |
|---|---|---|
| 1959 | D. of Westminster. S. Still life, fruit etc., $14\times18$ | 1,150 |
| | Fishing boats, rough sea, $25\frac{3}{4}\times34\frac{3}{4}$ | 1,300 |
| 1962 | S. View of Dortdrecht, $28\times37\frac{1}{2}$ | 2,000 |
| 1964 | C. Still life, peaches, grapes, etc., $37\times48$ | 10,500 |
| 1967 | Paris. Still life with shell-fish, $16\times22\frac{1}{2}$, FB33,000+tax | 3,112 |
| 1968 | C. Fishing boats in breeze, $23\times28\frac{1}{2}$ | 2,940 |
| 1969 | S. Pair of fruitpieces with wine glasses and *roemer* 2 for | 10,200 |

AMBROSIUS BOSSCHAERT. And Family

| | | |
|---|---|---|
| 1961 | Phillips, son and Neale. Flowers in a basket | 2,100 |
| | C. Still-life with grapes, $23\frac{1}{2}\times35$ | 5,250 |
| 1963 | Maude. S. Two flowerpieces on copper, $9\frac{1}{4}\times6\frac{3}{4}$ 2 for | 14,000 |
| | Hutton. S. Flowers in glass vase, $8\times6\frac{1}{2}$ | 12,500 |
| 1964 | S. Flowers in vase, dated 1606, $9\times6\frac{1}{2}$ on copper | 12,500 |
| 1965 | Lady Berlin. S. Flowers, brown glass vase, $22\frac{3}{4}\times16\frac{3}{4}$ | 2,900 |
| 1967 | Abbey. S. Flowers, brown glass vase, undated, $32\frac{1}{4}\times24\frac{3}{4}$ | 3,800 |
| | S. Flowers in glass beaker, $16\frac{1}{4}\times13$ | 6,500 |
| 1968 | S. Flowers in carved stone vase, $24\times19$ | 3,150 |
| 1969 | S. Flowers in a glass *roemer* on window ledge, $9\frac{1}{2}\times6\frac{3}{4}$ (on copper) | 32,000 |
| | C. (Abraham Bosschaert) *Omnia vanitas*, silver, globe etc., $26\frac{1}{2}\times35$ | 4,040 |
| | Belot. S. Tulips etc., studded glass beaker, on copper, $9\frac{1}{2}\times7$ | 30,000 |
| | C. Roses and columbines, same glass beaker, $7\frac{1}{2}\times5$ | 11,550 |
| 1969 | van Waay, Amsterdam. (Ambrosius Bosschaert Jnr) Flowerpiece, Hfl28,000+16% tax | 3,738 |
| | Vandervell. S. Overturned basket, fruit and flowers (Johannes Bosschaert) 1627, $20\frac{1}{4}\times30\frac{1}{2}$ | 5,500 |

JAN VAN DE CAPELLE. 1624–1679    £

1958  S.  Estuary and barges, 16×21½                4,800
1959  Austen Harris.  S.  Fishing boats at anchor, 21×24½   6,500
1963  S.  Winter scene, 24½×31½                      2,000
1965  Spencer Churchill.  C.  Ships in harbour, 33½×52   42,000
        Fishing boats at anchor, 22¾×25½             54,600
1969  Elwes.  S.  Fishing boats with State yacht firing salute,
        30½×42½                                      125,000
        S.  Yacht with numerous shipping in estuary, 19¼×24½   15,000

PIETER CLAESZ. 1597–1661

1958  Woods.  S.  Breakfast still life, 22½×32           750
1961  Paris.      Wineglass, overturned jug etc., 18¾ × 25¼,
        FN25,000+tax                                  2,180
1962  S.  Breakfast still life, 1643, 17×23½          4,000
        Paris.  Elaborate *Vanitas*, 32×44½, FN20,000+tax   1,740
1963  S.  Still life with oysters, 16¼×22½           3,800
        Breakfast still life, 15½×21¾                 2,300
1965  S.  Still life, bowl of fruit, 24×33           1,400
1967  Crawshaw.  S.  Still life with crab and peaches, 1644,
        34×27½                                        7,400
1968  Lemons, grapes, glass and knife, 1627, 7¾×9¾   10,500
        S.  Grapes and wine glasses, overturned nautilus cup,
        20¾×26¼, bought in                            4,000
1969  Delmege.  S.  *Roemer*, bread rolls, pewter plate etc.,
        20¼×15½                                       11,000
1970  N.Y.  Herrings, beer glass, stoneware jug etc., 14¼×22½,
        $29,000                                       12,083

CAREL FABRITIUS. 1624–1654

1960  van Aalst.  C.  Portrait, Rembrandt, 14¾×12    14,700
1965  C.  Portrait, unknown man                       7,350
        Young man holding goblet, 31×27               3,700
1968  Kaplan.  S.  Joseph and the baker's dream, 42×45   2,600

JAN VAN DER HEYDEN. 1637–1717

1958  Fisher.  S.  Market town with Catholic procession,
        13×17¾                                        5,800
1959  S. (with Adriaen v.d. Velde).  Toll House at Maarsen,
        18½×23½                                       7,800
1965  Wenner-Gren.  S.  Avenue of trees and country house,
        19×23½                                        6,800
1968  S.  Square in Dutch town with ruined church, 16¼×23¼  23,000
        C.  Library interior, open copy of Blaeuw's atlas, dated
        1711–12, 26×22                                7,870

| Willem Kalf. 1621–1693 | | £ |
|---|---|---|
| 1958 | S. Still life, blue and white bowl, silver cup etc., 15×19 | 380 |
| 1963 | Lempertz, Cologne, Still life, 23×21¼, DM22,000+tax | 2,255 |
| 1966 | Still life with silver objects, 39×31 | 3,000 |
| 1968 | C. Still life, orange, glass goblets and carpet, 28×25¼ | 32,550 |

| Aert van der Neer. 1635–1703 | | |
|---|---|---|
| 1960 | Charles Russell. C. Winter landscape, 18¾×25 | 7,600 |
| | Dreeseman, Amsterdam. The *Oude Schans* and *Montelbaanstoren*, Amsterdam, 16¾×22¾, Hfl85,000+tax About | 10,230 |
| 1961 | Paris. Pleasures of winter, 25½×30, FN245,000+tax | 21,000 |
| | S. Winter scene, 9¾×15½ | 8,800 |
| 1962 | S. Winter scene, 29½×41¾ | 11,500 |
| 1963 | Heldring. S. Moonlit river, 24¾×30¼ | 18,000 |
| 1966 | C. Winter landscape, 26½×39 | 4,410 |
| | Guthrie. C. Moonlit river scene, 28×35½ | 1,890 |
| 1967 | Robertson. S. Winter landscape, 1644, 21½×32½ | 11,000 |
| | Gesink. S. Moonlit river scene, 20½×28½ | 6,500 |
| | C. Skating scene, 1643, 33¼×44½ | 14,500 |
| | River with fishing boats and nets, 25½×37½ | 3,570 |
| 1968 | van Haegen. C. Skating scene with view of Dort, 17×24½ | 5,775 |
| | Stratford. C. Skating scene, dated 1641, 19½×36 | 3,360 |
| 1969 | Bruguière. C. Coastal scene with windmill, 11½×16½ | 2,520 |
| | Burning house by a moonlit river, 10½×13 (£162 15*s*., 1876) | 19,950 |

| Jan van Os. 1744–1808 | | |
|---|---|---|
| 1947 | C. A pair of flowerpieces, dated 1773 2 for | 3,045 |
| 1961 | S. Fruit and flowers, sculptured vase, 32½×24 | 3,600 |
| 1965 | C. Roses, fruit etc., 34×27 | 19,950 |
| | Another, less sumptuous, same dimensions | 6,300 |
| | Whitehead. S. Another, 37¾×28½ | 2,900 |
| 1966 | C. Fruit and flowers with birds' nest, 24½×19 | 4,620 |
| | Fruit and flowers, same dimensions | 4,830 |
| | Warner. C. Flowerpiece with birds' nest, 27×22 (see 1967) | 3,990 |
| 1967 | S. Fruit and flowers, 31¼×23½ | 2,450 |
| | C. Fruit and flowers, with birds' nest, 27×22 (see 1966) | 4,200 |
| 1968 | C. (attributed). Fruit and overturned basket, 23×19½ | 3,360 |
| | Anthony Asquith. S. Fruit and flowers, stone ledge, 34×28 | 22,000 |
| 1969 | S. Fruit and flowers, vase on stone ledge 16½×13¼ | 4,200 |
| | Rey. S. Flowers, fruit and fish, marble ledge, 26¾×20 | 9,200 |
| | Godfrey-Faussett. S. Mixed flowers, sculptured urn etc., 23×18¼ | 4,800 |

| | | £ |
|---|---|---|
| **Bonaventura Pieters.** 1614–1652 | | |
| 1959 | C. Estuary and small craft, 1640, 20×38 | 2,205 |
| 1963 | S. Shipping off Amsterdam, 35½×51½ | 6,800 |
| 1965 | S. Sailing vessels in light breeze, 14¾×19¾ | 1,200 |
| **Pieter Saanredam.** 1597–1665 | | |
| 1962 | Brandt, Amsterdam. Church interior, 1641, 43½×41¼, Hfl65,000+tax | 6,870 |
| 1963 | Heldring. S. Interior, St Bavin, Haarlem, 1628, 14½×18 | 36,000 |
| | Town Hall, Haarlem | 12,000 |
| **Jan Siberechts.** 1627–1703 | | |
| 1959 | S. Herdswoman and girl, 1667, 49×48½ | 5,500 |
| 1960 | C. Flooded road, 27×34 | 6,810 |
| 1962 | S. View of Wollaton Park, 1697, 74×53 | 3,200 |
| 1967 | S. Peasants crossing a ford, 1662, 51½×77¼ | 8,000 |
| **Michael Sweerts.** 1615–after 1656 | | |
| 1966 | Cook Trust. C. The little copyist, 12½×15½ | 28,350 |
| 1967 | S. Pilgrims visiting a monastery, 16¼×13 | 6,200 |
| | C. Portrait head of a boy, 8¾×6½ | 1,260 |
| 1968 | S. Young man in grey coat, white collar, 12×9½ | 4,000 |
| | S. Boy in turban with bunch of flowers, 29½×23¾, bought in | 12,000 |
| 1970 | C. Head of a girl, brown dress, pearl earrings, 22½×20 | 22,050 |
| **Hendrik Terbruggen.** d. 1629 | | |
| 1957 | Foxwell. S. Crucifixion (bought for £60), 61×40¼, Metropolitan Museum | 15,000 |
| 1958 | C. St Jerome at prayer, 43½×34 | 1,155 |
| 1965 | Wenner Gren. S. Boy musician singing, 28¾×24¾ | 5,800 |
| 1968 | S. Adoration of the kings, 74×63¼, bought in | 40,000 |
| 1969 | S. Man in feathered hat, playing lute, 39¾×33 | 5,000 |
| | C. Shepherd and sleeping nymph with dog and goat, 44×62 (has also been attributed to van Everdingen), bought in at | 5,775 |
| **Jan ten Compe** | | |
| 1961 | C. View of the Mint, Amsterdam, 21×88½ | 4,200 |
| 1964 | C. Timberyards, Amsterdam, 1756, 18×24 | 3,990 |
| 1967 | C. Pair of Amsterdam canal views, 1739, 14×19  2 for | 2,915 |
| **Emanuel de Witte.** 1618–1692 | | |
| 1960 | Dreeseman, Amsterdam. The Bourse, Amsterdam, 1653, 19½×19, Hfl125,000+tax | 14,765 |
| | Brandt, Amsterdam. Street in Amsterdam, Hfl100,000+tax | 11,814 |

1963    Heldring.   S.   Interior, Oude Kerk, Amsterdam, 1662,    £

      $23\frac{1}{4} \times 18$                                                 11,200

1965    C.   Interior of a kitchen with maids, $37\frac{1}{2} \times 51$       1,470

1968    Fry.   C.   Family group, maid offering fruit, dated 1678,

      $26 \times 33\frac{1}{2}$                                                 63,000

1969    Montmolin.   C.   Interior, the Neuwe Kerk, Amsterdam,

      1657, $34 \times 40$                                            19,950

      S.   Church interior (Oude Kerk, Amsterdam?) 1672,

      $31 \times 27\frac{1}{2}$                                               3,600


## GEORGE ENGLEHEART.   (*See* Miniatures)


## ENGLISH SCHOOL

### 18th century

(See separate headings for Beechey, Cotes, Devis, Gainsborough, Hogarth, Hoppner, Lawrence, Raeburn, Reynolds, Romney, Samuel Scott, Sporting pictures, Stubbs, James Ward, Benjamin West, Richard Wilson, Zoffany.)

This is not merely a miscellany of minor painters. The selection illustrates a very definite and interesting trend of the post-war market. Only one portrait, Copley's *Lord Eglinton* is in the Grand Manner. Most are of the *warts-and-all* school and some of them a bit wooden. The landscapes are not romantic but well behaved topographies, apart from *capriccios* in the picturesque taste. The dearest things in the list are conversation-pieces and architectural views which evoke the intimacy rather than the pomp of a vanished past. It is the same trend that has sent Seymour up to £63,800, Devis to £48,000 and Samuel Scott's Thames-side views to £33,000. The present list is more modest, since only Copley, Rowlandson and Charles Brooking pass the £10,000 mark. But the interesting thing is this. In 1925 when the great Duveen could get £80,000 and more for the most blue-blooded of his whole-length portraits by Gainsborough, Reynolds, Romney, Hoppner and Lawrence, not one of the portraits in my list could have made more than £200, some of them maybe not more than £40. Yet in the 1960s even Gainsborough seldom fetched more than these Copleys, Dances, Ramsays and Stuarts. And in 1925, when Reynolds and Gainsborough seemed the culmination of all the painting of the ages, some of the list had not been heard of except by such specialists as the incredibly learned Colonel Grant. Even today, nothing whatever is known of William James, a generic name for any moderately competent English imitation of Canaletto, based on a few ex-hibition-catalogue entries. But something very curious can be learnt about William Marlow, a competitor in the same field. In 1771, when two supposed Canaletto views of Verona were auctioned in London for the unusually high m of 550 guineas, Horace Walpole wrote as follows to Horace Mann. 'It is ome about that they are copied by Marlow, a disciple of Scott. Both master nd scholar are indeed better than the Venetian; but the purchasers did not mean o be so well cheated.'

It will be noticed that the watercolours of Sandby and the Cozens family, ainted in the days when the technique was extremely restricted, fetch more an any watercolours of the subsequent classic generation, except for those of urner. As to the marine paintings which have sale catalogues all to themselves, is interesting to observe the failure of Charles Brooking's works to maintain e prices of the Bruce Ingram sale, when they were dearer than the Van de elde paintings which Brooking imitated. The list also includes a few of those rim and dreary sea-battles which used to grace the walls of country hotels, om one of which an example emerged to make £3,500. Not in the list are wo even stuffier sea-battles by Philip Loutherbourg, 7 feet wide, which were ainlessly disgorged by the Junior Carlton Club to make no less than £30,450 etween them in 1968.

A market that depends so much on local colour and the social landscape, aturally favours Rowlandson, who till very recently was quite definitely a oor man's artist. In the 1930s and most of the 1940s the sum of £10 bought ery good Rowlandsons and £50 superlative ones. Even in the 1950s the best ould be had for £150 with the exception of that *tour de force*, Vauxhall Gardens. There are still plenty of cheap Rowlandsons on the market, works fflicted by old age and debauch, or outright botcheries by imitators.

| CHARLES BROOKING.   1723–1759 | £ |
|---|---|
| 957   C.   Men of war becalmed, 24½×29½ | 997 10s. |
| 958   Akroyd.   C.   Men of war and small craft, 14½×22 | 892 |
| 963   Bernard.   C.   Men of war and fishing boats becalmed, 14×21½ | 5,460 |
| 964   Ingram.   S.   A yacht firing a salute, 15×22½ | 15,500 |
| French ship, captured by English privateers, 23×23 | 10,500 |
| Vessels in a calm with English yacht, 14¾×22½ | 14,500 |
| Seven paintings made a total of £45,620 | |
| 965   Mavroleon.   C.   Royal yacht firing salute, 14½×21¾ | 10,500 |
| Dutch fishing boats in estuary, 14½×8½ | 5,250 |
| Thompson.   C.   Fishing boats in open sea, 26½×34½ | 3,150 |
| Spencer Churchill.   C.   Fishing boats in bay, 17½×24½ | 3,990 |
| 966   C. (attributed).   Men of war at anchor, 19½×14½ | 2,415 |
| 967   Walter Thompson & Co.   C.   Two cutters and man of war, 42×66 | 9,450 |
| S.   Man of war firing salute in harbour, 12½×20½ | 3,900 |
| Whitaker.   C.   Squadron in a gale, 33×42½ | 2,520 |
| Man of war and cutters in breeze, 41×65 | 7,350 |

1968    C. (attributed as 'Monamy').    Man of War at anchor in    £
harbour, $31 \times 45$          5,250

Vernon.   S.   Dutch barges in calm, $14\frac{1}{2} \times 22\frac{1}{4}$      3,500

N.Y.   Men of war off Dover, $30\frac{3}{4} \times 41\frac{3}{4}$, \$12,000      5,000

De la Rue.   C.   Fishing boats in a calm and yacht firing a
salute, a pair, $14\frac{1}{2} \times 22\frac{1}{2}$             2 for   8,400

C.   Men of war firing salute, $18\frac{1}{4} \times 22\frac{3}{4}$      3,675

### JOHN CLEVELY JNR.   d. 1786

1960    Rice.   C.   Launching man of war at Deptford, $42 \times 72$    1,155

1964    C.   Hurst Castle and Isle of Wight, $10\frac{1}{2} \times 15$      210

1965    S.   HMS *Duke of Grafton* and other men of war, 1774,
$34\frac{1}{2} \times 35\frac{1}{4}$          920

1968    C.   Shipyard with numerous vessels, 1762, $21\frac{1}{2} \times 37\frac{1}{2}$    6,510

1969    C.   Shipping off the Needles, pen and wash, $17\frac{1}{2} \times 24\frac{1}{2}$    1,155

Thames and St Paul's from Limehouse, pen and wc,
$13\frac{3}{4} \times 20$          2,940

London Bridge and Southwark cathedral, companion
piece          2,310

### JOHN SINGLETON COPLEY.   1737–1815

The Earl of Eglinton, doing battle in Highland dress, seems an intruder in thi
list both as to price and subject, for it is the only *grand manner* work in the selec
tion. Several factors made it expensive for the Mellon Foundation. Firstly i
rarity, for Copley, who spent his working life on monster exhibition works lik
the *Death of the Earl of Chatham* and *The Siege of Gibraltar*, had little time fo
whole-lengths. Then there is the combined Scottish and American interest an
the fact that the picture would make a splendid whiskey advertisement. In fac
it has much in common with Raeburn's whole length of *The McNab* whicl
became one.

1967    Hamilton.   C.   The Earl of Eglinton leading his men    £
against the Cherokees, 1780, $93 \times 57$      57,750

1968    Simmons.    C.    Study for the Death of Chatham,
heightened chalk drawing, $10\frac{1}{4} \times 12\frac{1}{2}$      2,310

Two drawings for the Siege of Gibraltar, $13 \times 9$   2 for   1,365

Dawnay.   C.   Oil study of heads for the Death of
Chatham, $17\frac{1}{4} \times 26\frac{1}{2}$      7,875

1969    Hector MacNeal.   C.   Thomas Loring, RN, 1761, half
length, $29\frac{1}{2} \times 24\frac{1}{2}$.        Bought in at   11,550

Companion piece, John Loring, RN      25,200

Mary Winslow, pastel, $22\frac{1}{2} \times 17\frac{1}{2}$      7,875

Companion piece, Mr Winslow      7,875

S.   Colonel George Lewis, directing the artillery, detail
from the Siege of Gibraltar, $29\frac{1}{2} \times 24\frac{1}{2}$ (£31 10s. in 1794)    7,200

## ALEXANDER COZENS. –1786 and       £

## JOHN ROBERT COZENS. 1752–1799

(J. R. Cozens unless otherwise stated. All wc or pen and wash.)

| | | |
|---|---|---|
| 1948 | C.  Two Swiss views      2 for | 1,890 |
| 1960 | Russell.  S.  Waterfall at Lodore, $14 \times 14\frac{3}{4}$ | 2,200 |
| 1961 | Dyson Perrins.  S.  Lake Nemi, $14\frac{3}{4} \times 21$ | |
| |    Lake Albano, 1780, $14 \times 20\frac{3}{4}$ | |
| 1962 | S.  Lake Albano, $17 \times 24\frac{1}{2}$ | 2,950 |
| |    Park at Astroni, 1782, $10\frac{1}{4} \times 14$ | 2,300 |
| 1963 | S.  View from the inn at Terracina, $10 \times 14\frac{1}{2}$ | 1,000 |
| 1965 | Gray.  S.  Isola Bella, 1790, blue and grey wash, $12 \times 18$ | 3,200 |
| | Girtin.  S.  Tomb of the Plautii, Tivoli, 1789, $10 \times 14\frac{3}{4}$ | 800 |
| | S.  Lake Nemi, $14\frac{1}{2} \times 21$ | 550 |
| 1966 | Twidell.  S.  Villa Lante, Rome, blue and grey wash, $10 \times 14\frac{3}{4}$ | 2,400 |
| |    Convent on the walls of Naples, blue and grey wash, $10 \times 14\frac{3}{4}$ | 1,400 |
| 1967 | Carlingford.  S.  Coast near Rimini, $10 \times 15$ | 350 |
| 1968 | Sedwick.  S. (Alexander Cozens).  Wooded landscape with eagle, sepia wash, $17\frac{3}{4} \times 24\frac{1}{4}$ | 3,800 |
| | S.  Grotto in the Campagna, sepia wash, 1778, $14\frac{3}{4} \times 21$ | 4,200 |
| | (Alexander Cozens).  Lake among rocky cliffs, $14\frac{1}{2} \times 10\frac{3}{4}$ | 1,800 |

## SIR NATHANIEL DANCE.  1734–1811

| | | |
|---|---|---|
| 1965 | C.  (Unattributed but almost certainly by Dance.)  Young man seated at a table, $28 \times 24$ | 1,200 |
| 1967 | Jessel.  S.  Mr and Mrs de Mowbry in a garden, $21 \times 29\frac{1}{4}$ | 1,900 |
| 1968 | S.  Unknown lady 1763, oval, $23 \times 20\frac{1}{2}$ | 3,800 |
| 1969 | C.  James Grant and other gentlemen in Rome, 1766, $37\frac{1}{2} \times 48$ (formerly attributed to Pompeio Batoni) | 9.450 |
| 1970 | Telfer Smollett.  C.  English *milords* and their *Cicerone* in Rome, 1763, $38 \times 28\frac{1}{2}$ | 10,500 |

## FRANCIS HAYMAN.  1708–1776

| | | |
|---|---|---|
| 1962 | S.  Figures in landscape, $42\frac{1}{2} \times 39$ | 4,200 |
| 1963 | S.  The Grant Family, $39 \times 41\frac{1}{2}$ | 6,500 |
| 1964 | S.  Robert Lovelace abducting Clarissa Harlowe, $24\frac{1}{4} \times 29\frac{1}{2}$ | 1,800 |
| 1966 | S.  Jonathan Tyers and family at Vauxhall gardens, $38 \times 33$ | 2,400 |
| 1968 | St John.  S.  Two half-length portraits of members of the St John family, $30 \times 22$ | £1,600; £1,800 |
| | Simmons.  C.  The lawyer's visit, pencil and wash, $5\frac{3}{4} \times 7\frac{1}{2}$ | 735 |

FRANCIS HOLMAN. Floruit 1770–1800 £

1965 C. Men of war off the North Foreland, 28×50 840

S. Men of war in action, 35¼×42½ 360

Men of war in rough weather, 23½×34½ 380

1966 S. British and American ships in action, dated 1799, a pair, each 23½×36 2 for 1,500

1967 S. Man of war and lighthouse, 38×49½ 3,200

1968 S. Beach scene with fleet and elegant figures, 38×50, Tate Gallery 8,500

WILLIAM JAMES. Floruit 1760–1771

1959 S. Riva degli Schiavone and Piazetta, Venice, 29½×49½ 2 for 1,750

1965 Edana Romney. S. Venice, the Bacino and Salute, each 31×49 2 for 7,000

C. Thames from Lambeth Palace, 27×35 1,155

1966 De Chair. C. Canal in Venice, 31×51¼ (see 1968) 1,995

1967 C. Canal in Venice, 31×51½ 2,100

1968 S. Venice, the Molo and Sta Geremia, each 29¾×49½ 2 for 6,000

Alan Brown. S. Venice, Riva degli Schiavone, 31½×50 5,500

Phillimore. C. Canal in Venice, 31×51½ (see 1966) 1,575

Prince Littler. N.Y. Regatta, Grand Canal, 36½×50¾, $10,500 4,375

Sta Maria della Salute, 30½×51¼, $8,000 3,335

Winslow Hulse. C. Grand Canal and the Caritá, 28×36 1,365

SS Giovanni e Paolo, 22×41 2,940

1969 Kemsley. S. (at Dropmore). London Bridge etc., from Somerset House terrace (called *Francis Smith*), 22×42½ 5,500

Green. S. Salute and Bacino from Riva degli Schiavone, 29½×49½ 1,800

S. Salute from the Piazzetta, 30½×51¼ 4,000

Regatta off the Doge's palace, 36½×59¾ 4,000

WILLIAM MARLOW. 1740–1814

1960 C. Shipping on the Rhine, wc, 10½×14½ 105

1964 Wasserman. S. Kennington toll-gate, 25½×44 500

Storer Trust. S. Westminster and Blackfriars bridges, oval, each 28×36 2 for 3,900

Whitehall, looking NE, 27½×35½ 3,900

C. View of Netley Abbey, 38½×56½ 945

1965 Russell Johnson. C. Lake in St James's Park, pen and wc, 12¼×20¼ 1,260

Wyndham. S. Château de Pierre Encise, Lyon, 35½×49 4,400

| | | £ |
|---|---|---|
| 1965 | Hardwicke. S. Two paired views of Naples and Florence, 34×46 | {2,100 / 4,800 |
| 1966 | S. Thames at Blackfriars Bridge, 27¾×39½ | 1,500 |
| | Castel San Angelo and Ponte Rotto, Rome, a pair, 28¾×49¼ (2) | 3,500 |
| 1967 | C. Rhône at Lyon, 43×53½ | 2,310 |
| | Thames ferry at Greenhithe, 46½×71 | 1,470 |
| | Hughes Stanton. S. (attributed) Bay of Naples below Posilippo, 26×40 | 1,800 |
| 1969 | Kemsley. S. (at Dropmore). The Arno, Florence, and the Ponte Sta Trinita in sumptuous Chippendale giltwood frames, 44×38 overall 2 for | 16,000 |

JOHN HAMILTON MORTIMER. 1740–1779

| | | |
|---|---|---|
| 1959 | Lady Lovat. S. Interior with Sergeant Beaufoy and John Clementson, 39×49½ | 3,300 |
| 1967 | McAlpine. C. Fight between Jack Broughton and George Stevenson, 1741, 27×34½ | 315 |
| 1968 | N.Y. Captain Herbert Taylor, 30×22½, $1,750 | 730 |
| 1969 | Libbis. S. Self-portrait in Vandyck dress, pen drawing, oval, 18½×16¼ | 1,900 |
| | Companion piece, back view writing, 19×16¾ | 2,100 |
| | C. Self-portrait in cloak and turban, 24×19½, pen drawing | 1,260 |

ALLAN RAMSAY. 1713–1784

| | | |
|---|---|---|
| 1964 | Palmer. S. Earl Temple, 1762, whole-length, 88×57½ | 2,800 |
| 1965 | Boswell-Elliot. S. Lord Auchinleck, 49½×39½ | 4,500 |
| 1967 | Hardwicke. C. Hon Mrs Charles Yorke, 43½×35 | 1,785 |
| | Hon Charles Yorke, 50×40 | 1,470 |
| | Wingfield Castle. C. Robert Adam, half-length, 1764, 34×26 | 3,675 |
| 1968 | Boswell-Elliot. S. Lord Auchinlech, head, 1754, 29×23¾ | 3,000 |
| | Barton. N.Y. Henry Fox, 25×21½, $3,500 | 1,456 |
| 1969 | Nairn. S. Sir Henry Erskine Bt, oval, 1750, 29½×24½ | 1,700 |
| | The same in red coat, 1765, 28½×23½ | 9,500 |

THOMAS ROWLANDSON. 1756–1827

(all are in pen and ink and watercolour washes)

| | | |
|---|---|---|
| 1959 | S. Mealtime in the kitchen, 11×17 | 150 |
| 1960 | Dyson Perrins. S. Portsmouth Point, 9×12½, Portsmouth Library | 800 |
| 1963 | Versailles. Vauxhall Gardens, 17×13½, FN11,000+tax | 947 |
| 1964 | Miller. S. Canterbury–Dover coach, 11½×17½ | 800 |
| | S. York Races, 5½×9¼ | 190 |
| | C. Horse resting with hounds, 1806, 6×8¾ | 420 |

£

| | | |
|---|---|---|
| 1964 | S. Celebrating Lord Howe's victory, 1794, $10\frac{3}{4} \times 17\frac{1}{2}$ | 220 |
| 1965 | Leon Jones. S. Thames with boats and figures at low tide, $9\frac{1}{2} \times 12\frac{1}{2}$ | 520 |
| | Russell Johnson. C. French prisoners on parole at Bodmin, $9\frac{3}{4} \times 15\frac{1}{4}$ | 735 |
| | Arrival of stage coach at Bodmin, $9\frac{1}{4} \times 15$ | 840 |
| | C. Four deer under an oak tree, $6 \times 9$ | 273 |
| | Achenbach Foundation. S. Horses under a tree, $7 \times 11\frac{1}{2}$ | 440 |
| 1966 | C. Going to market, $7\frac{1}{4} \times 10\frac{1}{2}$ | 525 |
| | S. Company at the Pavilion, Brighton, $9 \times 12$ | 892 10s. |
| | Hemphill. C. Market Square at Juliers, Westphalia, inscribed and dated 1791, $12\frac{1}{2} \times 21\frac{1}{4}$ | 1,680 |
| | Snowdon from Llanberis lake, $5\frac{1}{2} \times 16\frac{1}{2}$ | 577 10s. |
| | S. The Tuileries Gardens during the peace, 1801–3, $10\frac{3}{4} \times 16\frac{3}{4}$ | 1,500 |
| | MacDonald-Hastings. S. The fencing lesson, $7 \times 11$ | 850 |
| 1967 | Bernard Penrose. C. 9 drawings illustrating Matthew Bramble's trip to Bath from Smollett's *Humphrey Clinker* Total for the 9 drawings | 8,011 5s. |
| | among them, The concert, $4\frac{3}{4} \times 7\frac{3}{4}$ | 1,155 |
| | The breakfast, $4\frac{3}{4} \times 7\frac{3}{4}$ | 1,155 |
| | C. French family *en voyage*, $7\frac{3}{4} \times 12$ | 577 10s. |
| | Pearson. S. Concert at Vauxhall Gardens, 1784. Rowlandson's reputed masterpiece with numerous portraits of notables, $19 \times 29\frac{1}{2}$ (£2,730 in 1945) | 11,000 |
| | The *Brilliants*, debauch in a London club, $11\frac{1}{4} \times 18\frac{3}{4}$ | 1,600 |
| | Courtship and Matrimony, a pair, $14 \times 11\frac{1}{2}$ 2 for | 3,000 |
| | A duel at Highgate or Islington, $11 \times 15\frac{1}{2}$ | 1,000 |
| 1968 | C. Travellers crossing a stream, dated 1795, $15\frac{1}{2} \times 20\frac{3}{4}$ | 682 10s |
| | Workman. S. Haymakers resting by a wagon, $9\frac{3}{4} \times 14\frac{3}{4}$ | 880 |
| | Market day, $14\frac{1}{2} \times 21\frac{1}{2}$ | 950 |
| | Simmons. C. Wagon going to a fair, $5\frac{3}{4} \times 9\frac{1}{4}$ | 1,365 |
| | Coach at Bermondsey Abbey, $5\frac{3}{4} \times 9\frac{1}{4}$ | 997 10s |
| | N.Y. Horse-racing, 1790, $13\frac{1}{2} \times 23\frac{1}{2}$, \$2,250 | 938 |
| 1969 | Hunter. C. Passengers on a Dutch packet in a breeze, dated 1791, $7\frac{3}{4} \times 10\frac{3}{4}$ | 1,995 |
| | Sweet. C. Review of the militia at Brackley, 1807, $10 \times 15$ | 1,365 |
| | The Salutation Inn, Greenwich, $14 \times 21$ | 1,155 |
| | Horne. S. Promenade at Richmond Bridge, $11\frac{1}{4} \times 18\frac{1}{2}$ | 3,200 |

PAUL SANDBY. 1725–1809 (wc or gouache)

| | | |
|---|---|---|
| 1942 | C. Morning, noon, evening and night, set of four highly finished gouache views 4 for | 241 10s |

£

| | |
|---|---|
| 059 C. Ascent to the round tower, Windsor, $14\frac{1}{2} \times 17\frac{1}{4}$ | 441 |
| William Sandby. C. Self-portrait | 420 |
| Ranger's lodge, Windsor Park, $20 \times 16$ | 399 |
| Lady Maynard. C. Female portrait in miniature style, $7 \times 4\frac{1}{2}$ | 599 |
| Two academic male studies 2 for | 567 |
| Stonemasons working | 430 10s. |
| Soames House (Knight, Frank) Virginia Water, $27\frac{1}{2} \times 43\frac{1}{2}$ | 500 |
| 060 C. River landscape, polite company, $22 \times 35$ | 2,100 |
| 062 Carbonell. S. Eton College, bodycolour, 1768, $15 \times 21\frac{1}{2}$ | 2,800 |
| 064 S. Horsemen at a well with view of Windsor, 1763, $23\frac{1}{2} \times 17$ | 280 |
| 65 Russell Johnson. C. Caernarvon Castle, pen and wc, $15\frac{1}{4} \times 20$ | 231 |
| Harewood. C. After the Gordon riots; the Guards in St James' Park, 1780, $12 \times 18$ | 5,250 |
| Norman Gate at Windsor, bodycolour, $14\frac{3}{4} \times 21$ | 6,300 |
| St Georges Chapel, Windsor, ,, ,, | 6,825 |
| North Terrace, Windsor ,, ,, | 8,820 |
| Same view looking West ,, ,, | 8,925 |
| 66 Coldstream Guards. C. Military encampment, Hyde Park, 1780, $18\frac{1}{2} \times 11\frac{1}{2}$ | 1,575 |
| C. Caernarvon Castle, moonlight, 1794, $14 \times 21\frac{1}{2}$ | 630 |
| 67 Hopkinson. C. Anglers at Dartmouth, pen and wash, 1785, $13\frac{1}{2} \times 20\frac{1}{2}$ | 367 10s. |
| 68 de la Warr. C. View of Knole, pen and wc, $16\frac{3}{4} \times 29\frac{3}{4}$ | 6,300 |
| Simmons. C. Clapham Common, wc, $9\frac{3}{4} \times 12\frac{1}{4}$ | 1,680 |
| 69 Brian Hamilton. C. Welsh Bridge, Shrewsbury, wc, $14\frac{1}{2} \times 19\frac{1}{2}$ | 1,470 |
| Graham. C. Distant view of Roche Abbey, pen and wc, $11\frac{1}{2} \times 18\frac{3}{4}$ | 630 |

OMINIC SERRES. 1722–1793

| | |
|---|---|
| 58 S. Taking of Belle Isle, 1761, a suite, $13\frac{1}{2} \times 19\frac{1}{4}$ 3 for | 700 |
| 65 Dunbar. C. Fishing boats and man of war in breeze, $24\frac{1}{2} \times 29\frac{1}{2}$ | 367 10s. |
| C. Dutch squadron, rough sea, 1771, $36 \times 55\frac{1}{2}$ | 367 10s. |
| Compton. S. Keppel's fleet at Havana, 1767, $19\frac{1}{2} \times 29\frac{1}{2}$ | 900 |
| 56 S. Dutch shipping becalmed, 1771, $15\frac{1}{4} \times 20\frac{1}{2}$ | 1,000 |
| 57 C. Valetta Harbour, $27 \times 42$ | 682 10s. |
| Baring. C. Men of war offshore in breeze, 1768, $24 \times 36$ | 1,365 |
| N.Y. Men of war in rough sea, 1750, $25\frac{1}{2} \times 45\frac{1}{2}$, $2,000 | 714 |

| 1968 | Dolphin Hotel, Southampton. S. Hood's fleet at Gibraltar, 1793, $34\frac{1}{2}\times57\frac{1}{2}$ | £ 3,500 |
|---|---|---|
| | C. Sicilian royal family, escorted into Leghorn, 1788, $44\times71\frac{3}{4}$ | 2,520 |
| | Shipbuilding at Blackwall Reach, $41\times65$ | 6,825 |
| | Stucley. S. Men of war off Cape of Good Hope, 1786, pair, $14\times19\frac{1}{4}$ 2 for | 3,200 |
| 1970 | C. Same subject, 1795, $28\times39$ | 7,875 |

GILBERT STUART. 1755–1828

There may be objections to the inclusion of Gilbert Stuart and Singleton Copley under the heading, *English School*. But there was no American tradition at this time. The two American-born painters worked in England, the former for half his painting life, the latter for almost the whole of it, and nothing could be more English than their style. It is rather strange that the patriotic impulse which stimulates the American market into paying $120,000 for a romantic Wild West picture by Albert Bierstadt, should ignore Gilbert Stuart except when he painted the national hero. In the 1960s Stuart was not even in the $25,000 class. This would suggest that he is considered an English painter even when painting American sitters. However, at the end of the First World War Henry Clay Frick paid $75,000, then equivalent to £15,420 and in 1970 to £123,400, for a portrait of George Washington.

| 1963 | Cintas. N.Y. John Shaw, New York, 1793, $26\times28\frac{1}{2}$, $19,500 | £ 6,964 |
|---|---|---|
| | C. George Washington, head, $27\times21$ | 3,570 |
| 1964 | Kingsmill. S. Captain MacBride in naval uniform, 1788, oval, $29\frac{1}{2}\times24\frac{1}{2}$ | 3,000 |
| | Captain Ludwidge, pair to the above | 2,600 |
| 1965 | S. William Pitt, 2nd Earl of Chatham, 1783, $49\frac{3}{4}\times39\frac{1}{4}$ | 1,200 |
| | Farr. S. 1st Earl of Clonmel, oval, $28\times23$ | 1,400 |
| | Countess of Clonmel, pair to the above | 1,400 |
| | Sir Charles Malet, half length, $29\times24\frac{1}{2}$ | 3,600 |
| | General Sir Richard Grenville, $26\times21$ | 1,400 |
| | N.Y. Captain William Locker, oval, 1785, $28\times23\frac{1}{2}$ | 1,700 |
| | Ozias Humphrey, half length, $30\times25$, $9,000 | 3,210 |
| 1967 | Flesh. C. Bernard Shaw, oval (great-uncle of the dramatist), $28\times23$ | 1,470 |
| 1968 | S. Miss Eleanor Stewart, three-quarter length, $50\times40$ | 9,500 |
| 1969 | Lyle-Price. S. Lord Edward Fitzgerald, *c.* 1790, $37\frac{3}{4}\times29\frac{1}{2}$ | 4,800 |

## ENGLISH SCHOOL
### 19th century
### (Painters, not listed in Volume One)

With the exception of Richard Dadd who spent most of his working life in a lunatic asylum and was like nobody on earth, this little group of English 19th century painters who arrived in the four-figure class in the 1960s, are a pretty humdrum lot. William Shayer Snr went on copying George Morland almost into the era of the telephone and the bicycle. Stark belonged to the Norwich school and carried on the tradition of Crome. Watts's only mission in life was to produce something that looked like a Constable for more than a generation after Constable's death. Ladell, like several other humble practitioners as unrecorded as himself, made very competent imitations of the still-life and flower pictures of van Huysum. Nothing is known of him, except that the best of his works are dated in the 1860s.

Quite late in life William Shayer Snr sold one of his more elaborate works for £50. Before the 1950s almost any painting in the ensuing lists could be bought for that sum. Yet with the exception of the pre-Raphaelite period of Sir John Millais, none of the great Victorians whose works were still making thousands in the 1920s, could come anywhere near the top prices for Shayer and Watts in the late 1960s, certainly not Rossetti, Burne Jones or the other Watts. Above all, nobody wants the Holy Grail. The fact is that Shayer's apple-cheeked England (which was even more phoney) is better suited to the escapism of today from television aerials, pylons and petrol pumps.

| | | £ |
|---|---|---:|
| **RICHARD DADD.** 1817–1886 | | |
| 1960 | S. Titania sleeping, wc, 25½×30½ | 290 |
| 1961 | C. The Packet Delayed and Members of the Yacht club, a pair, wc, 1858, 14×10                2 for | 315 |
| | S. '12th May, 1854', wc, 14½×10¼ | 340 |
| 1964 | Laughton. S. The gardener at Binfield, c. 1860, 8×12 | 2,400 |
| | Oberon and Titania, 1854–8, oval, 24×29¾ | 7,000 |
| | Simpson. S. Melancholy, 1854, pen and wc, 14½×10 | 240 |
| | S. Greek shepherds, 22¾×19¾ | 550 |
| | Caravan halted by the sea, 1843, 35½×59½ | 400 |
| 1966 | Clayton-Stamm. C. Wandering musicians, 1878, 24×20 | 2,205 |
| 1967 | S. Juvenile members of the yacht club, drawing, 1853, 18×10 | 460 |
| | | |
| **EDWARD LADELL.** 1840–1866 | | |
| 1959 | S. Fruit etc. with Delft vase, 13¼×11½ | 220 |
| 1960 | S. Fruit etc., stone ledge, 16½×13½ | 420 |
| 1962 | C. Still life, fruit etc., 16½×12½ | 1,050 |
| 1965 | S. Fruit and wineglass with landscape, 20¼×16½ | 1,800 |
| 1966 | S. Fruit and birds' nest, 17×14 | 1,750 |

| | | | £ |
|---|---|---|---|
| 1966 | Bateman. C. Grapes and flowers on marble ledge, 1862, 6½×13½ | | 1,680 |
| | Similar subject with ivory casket, 16½×13½ | | 1,890 |
| 1967 | S. Fruit, glass vase and casket, 13½×11½ | | 1,380 |
| | Grapes, peach and pear, 9½×11¾ | | 650 |
| | Roses, carnations and birds' nest, 19½×15½ | | 2,300 |
| | Newsome. C. Grapes and plums with wineglass and casket, 16×13½ | | 1,785 |
| | C. Similar subject, 13½×11½ | | 997 10s. |
| 1968 | C. Pair of fruit pieces, 13×11½ | For | 2,730 |
| | S. (Gleneagles Hotel). Rose, birds' nest and fruit with silver tazza, 16½×13¼ | | 2,900 |
| | S. Goblet of wine with fruit, 1864, 16¾×13½ | | 2,400 |
| 1969 | S. Fruit, flowers and stoneware jug, 20½×16½ | | 2,800 |
| | Fruit and wine glass on table, 17×14¼ | | 1,900 |
| | (by *William Duffield* in a similar style) | | |
| | Fruit, stoneware tankard and white cockatoo, 1858, 42½×33 | | 2,700 |

## WILLIAM SHAYER SNR. 1788–1879

| | | | |
|---|---|---|---|
| 1958 | S. (with E. C. Williams). The Plough Inn, Eltham, 1864, 29×24½ | | 500 |
| 1959 | C. Fishermen on the Yare, 30×44 | | 2,310 |
| 1960 | S. The fruit-seller, 1835, 27½×35½ | | 950 |
| 1964 | S. A tinker family, 17¾×24 | | 480 |
| 1965 | C. Peasants resting beneath trees, 33×43 | | 2,100 |
| | Wooded scene with peasants and white pony, 27×35 | | 1,470 |
| 1966 | C. (with E. C. Williams). Carrying the hay, and Wayside Talk, a pair, each 35×55½, 1955 | 2 for | 1,785 |
| 1967 | (with E. C. Williams) C. Village in Kent with wagon and sheep, 1856, 29×50 | | 2,100 |
| 1968 | S. Cornish fishermen unloading catch, 1843, 19¼×39¼ | | 1,150 |
| | Clarke. C. (with E. C. Williams). Peasants outside an inn, 28½×46½ | | 3,150 |
| | Barlow. S. Outside the Red Lion, 39½×51½ | | 6,800 |
| | Cattle. S. Tinker family, 17½×23½ | | 3,100 |
| | Selwyn-Smith. S. Gardener's cottage, Alverstoke, 28×36 (sold by the painter in the 1840s for £50) | | 2,700 |
| | Brooke-Davison. S. Village festival, 29¼×39½ | | 7,500 |
| | S. Gipsy encampment, 32¼×39½ | | 1,900 |
| 1969 | S. (with Sidney Richard Percy). Near Ambleside, 32¼×46 | | 1,200 |
| | Eriksen. C. Wooded landscape with cattle, 29½×24½ | | 1,470 |
| | C. The village inn, 1860, 29½×24½ | | 2,730 |
| | Andrews. C. Near Appledore, Devon, figures and cart, 28×41 | | 2,415 |

| | | £ |
|---|---|---|
| James Stark. 1794–1859 | | |
| 1962 | C.  On the Gipping, Suffolk, $25\frac{1}{2}\times51\frac{1}{2}$ | 1,365 |
| 1964 | Balfour.  S.  Beach near Cromer, 1834, $29\frac{3}{4}\times39\frac{3}{4}$ | 3,000 |
| 1965 | Spencer Churchill.  C.  View near Trowse, Norwich, $22\times30\frac{1}{2}$ | 3,990 |
| 1966 | S.  Wooded landscape and cottage, $16\times12\frac{1}{2}$ | 1,250 |
| | C.  Watering place in a wood, $19\frac{3}{4}\times27\frac{1}{4}$ | 2,205 |
| | and two more wooded landscapes at £1,680 each (see 1968) | |
| 1967 | Yates.  S.  Deer in a park, $17\frac{1}{4}\times23\frac{1}{2}$ | 1,600 |
| 1968 | Cotton.  C.  Wooded landscape (see 1966), $15\times19\frac{1}{4}$ | 1,575 |
| | C.  Wooded landscape, cattle and driver, $17\frac{1}{2}\times23\frac{1}{2}$ | 1,050 |
| | S.  View on the Yare with barges, $16\frac{3}{4}\times29$ | 3,200 |
| | C.  Landscape with horsemen riding under trees, $17\times21\frac{3}{4}$ | 1,260 |
| 1969 | S.  Cottage, wooded landscape, $15\frac{1}{4}\times19\frac{1}{2}$ | 1,400 |
| | Cottage by a stream, $17\frac{3}{4}\times23\frac{3}{4}$ | 4,200 |
| | C.  Figures and sheep on wooded road, $24\frac{3}{4}\times39$ | 3,990 |
| | Beausire.  S.  Woodland landscape in Hobbema style, $12\frac{1}{2}\times16\frac{1}{2}$ | 5,400 |
| | | |
| Frederick William Watts. 1800–1870 | | |
| 1958 | C.  View at Dedham, cart and stream, $47\times71$ | 945 |
| 1960 | C.  Dedham Lock, 1951, $38\times50$ | 1,260 |
| 1961 | Shock.  C.  Woodland road, 1840, $23\times18\frac{1}{2}$ | 367 10s. |
| 1964 | Bostwick.  S.  Old Locken, Bucks, $40\times55$ | 1,950 |
| 1965 | S.  Cottages near Aylesford, Kent (see 1968), $16\frac{1}{2}\times20$ | 472 10s. |
| 1966 | British Printing Corp.  C.  Barges on the upper Thames, $38\frac{1}{2}\times50\frac{1}{2}$ | 2,520 |
| | Bland.  C.  Thames near Windsor with man in punt, 1842, $19\frac{1}{2}\times27$ | 2,100 |
| 1968 | S.  Cottages near Aylesford (see 1965), $16\frac{1}{2}\times20$ | 1,100 |
| | C.  Windmill, barge and anglers, $36\times52$ | 9,975 |
| | S.  Dedham Lock, $39\frac{1}{2}\times49$ | 6,500 |
| | Cattle fording with wagon on stone bridge, $25\times30$ | 2,500 |
| | C.  Cottage and ferryboat, $20\times29$ | 2,730 |
| 1969 | Buxton.  C.  Hilly river landscape with church, $25\frac{1}{2}\times35$ | 3,990 |
| | Deen.  S.  Arundel Castle and town from the Arun, $25\frac{1}{2}\times39\frac{1}{2}$ | 3,000 |
| | Heald.  S.  Summer landscape with horse and cart, $36\times50\frac{1}{4}$ | 3,200 |
| | C.  Tintern Abbey, $13\times19\frac{1}{4}$ | 1,155 |
| | S.  Totnes, Devon, $34\frac{1}{2}\times29\frac{3}{4}$ | 1,900 |

# ENGLISH SCHOOL
## 20th century

(See separate headings for John, Munnings and Sargent. For Henry Moore *see also* Sculpture, Modern. For Ben Nicholson, *see* Abstract Painters.)

I wonder how many people seriously believe that, in strict order of rotation, the following are the greatest English painters of the past 110 years; Sargent, Sir Alfred Munnings, Francis Bacon, Sir Winston Churchill. Maybe, those who pay the appropriate prices, do not give the matter a thought. Yet this is what the saleroom figures seem to reveal. As against £30,000 for Sargent and £25,000 for Munnings, and even £14,000 for Sir Winston Churchill, Walter Sickert, the most original painter of his age in this country, barely passed the £2,000 mark in the 1960s. Most of the public believe that enormous advances in value have something to do with good taste and sound judgment. The remainder who believe the exact opposite, may care to look for an underlying philosophy behind these prices, for there is one. It is based on the assumption that for the past hundred years Paris has been the only metropolitan school, and that Impressionism and post-Impressionism, which made it so, can only be practised successfully in Paris. Hence the relatively low rating of the English Impressionist Sickert, or the German Impressionist, Liebermann. Artists who work in their own countries and who are not 'metropolitan', must according to this law, be as provincial as possible and as blatantly obvious in order to achieve success.

Partially this law is already becoming obsolete, the conditions that produced it having ceased to exist. The most successful living practitioners in England and America produce abstractions which have no national characteristics at all. They belong to an international school without possessing any metropolitan centre such as Paris was in the past. It is therefore not surprising that, immediately below the four names I have already mentioned, the most expensive English painting, sold in the 1960s, was a semi-abstract work by Victor Passmore at £11,600.

Apart from the preference, either for photographic realism or for abstract painting rather than the Impressionistic strivings of the early part of the present century, there is no clear market pattern for the modern English school. The octogenarian Lawrence Lowry, for instance, fits into none of these categories. He can be regarded as a successor to David Cox and Birket Foster as a Midland taste. An easily perceived quaintness, a not too strident proletarian emphasis and absolutely no surprises whatsoever, these are all the right qualities for a provincial public—and enough to lift this painter in the course of the decade from the £300 region to the £8,000 region. There was much the same degree of progression for the large mixed-media drawings of Henry Moore, which reached 8,000 guineas in 1969. Here also a certain proletarian cosiness lurks beneath some of the mannerisms of Picasso. The *blütezeit* which commands such prices, is the air-raid shelter period of the 1940s, the home front, redolent of *spam, snoek* and powdered egg.

## FRANCIS BACON

| | | £ |
|---|---|---:|
| 1957 | S. Performing dog, $78\frac{1}{2} \times 54\frac{1}{2}$ | 110 |
| 1958 | Grigg. S. Study for a portrait, 1949, $56\frac{1}{2} \times 50\frac{1}{2}$ | 450 |
| 1961 | Finarte, Milan. Bearded man, $20\frac{1}{2} \times 24\frac{1}{2}$, 3·2 million lire + tax | 1,978 |
| 1963 | N.Y. 'Sphinx, I.C.A.', $60 \times 46$, $10,000 | 3,572 |
| 1964 | C. Study for a Pope, 1955, $60 \times 46$ | 5,775 |
| | Man in blue II, $60 \times 40$ | 3,570 |
| 1965 | S. Study for 'Figure V', $59\frac{1}{2} \times 46\frac{1}{2}$ | 4,200 |
| | 'Pope with owls,' $60 \times 46$ | 5,200 |
| 1966 | Institute Contemporary Arts. S. Three heads of Henrietta Moraes, 1966, each $13\frac{3}{4} \times 11\frac{3}{4}$      3 for | 6,000 |
| | Farson. S. Head, 1962, $16 \times 16\frac{3}{4}$ | 2,400 |
| 1967 | S. Seated figure, 1960, $59 \times 46$ | 7,500 |
| | Head of a man, 1948, $31\frac{1}{2} \times 25$ | 1,600 |
| 1968 | Lullin. N.Y. Two figures, 1961, $78\frac{1}{4} \times 56$, $32,500 | 13,540 |
| 1969 | Erwin Swann. S. Dog, 1952, $78 \times 54\frac{1}{2}$. Galleria Internazionale, Milan (compare 1957) | 18,500 |

## L. S. LOWRY. 1888–

| | | |
|---|---|---:|
| 1959 | S. Front gardens, 1944, $13\frac{3}{4} \times 29\frac{1}{2}$ | 200 |
| | Fish shop, 1949, $15\frac{3}{4} \times 19\frac{3}{4}$ | 290 |
| 1965 | S. Election news, 1945, $20 \times 16$ | 750 |
| | Scott-Stevenson. C. In Salford, 1928, $15\frac{1}{4} \times 21\frac{1}{2}$ | 1,260 |
| 1966 | Brierley. C. Street scene, 1948, $11 \times 20$ | 1,680 |
| | Siddeley. C. Narrow street, 1962, $20 \times 16$ | 2,730 |
| | Fleming. C. Estuary, 1955, $15\frac{1}{2} \times 21$ | 1,470 |
| | Foulks. S. Open space, 1950, $29\frac{1}{2} \times 39\frac{1}{2}$ | 3,000 |
| | Abrahams. S. The meeting, 1949, $19\frac{1}{2} \times 23\frac{1}{4}$ | 3,200 |
| 1967 | Foy. C. Sunday afternoon, 1957, $45 \times 60$ | 7,875 |
| | Dunsmuir. C. Industrial street scene, 1949, $11\frac{1}{2} \times 15\frac{3}{4}$ | 3,150 |
| | Frisby. C. Beach scene, 1948, $17\frac{3}{4} \times 25\frac{1}{2}$ | 3,885 |
| | Rowse. C. Old Berwick, 1936, $20\frac{1}{2} \times 13$ | 3,255 |
| | Boase. C. Returning from work, 1929, $17 \times 24\frac{1}{2}$ | 3,990 |
| 1968 | Nash. C. People standing about, 1935, $15\frac{1}{2} \times 19\frac{1}{2}$ | 5,775 |
| | C. The Bridge, 1931, $19 \times 15\frac{1}{2}$ | 3,675 |
| | Liddell. S. Lytham pier, 1945, $17\frac{1}{4} \times 23\frac{1}{4}$ | 5,200 |
| | The estuary, 1944, $15\frac{3}{4} \times 19\frac{3}{4}$ | 3,800 |
| | William Wallace. C. Manufacturing town, 1922, $17 \times 20\frac{3}{4}$ | 4,620 |
| | Alison. C. On the Sands, 1957, $19\frac{3}{4} \times 23\frac{3}{4}$ | 3,045 |
| | Yoxall. S. Garden Place, Ancoats, 1944, $15\frac{1}{2} \times 19\frac{1}{2}$ | 4,000 |
| | S. Horse and cart outside house, 1944, $16\frac{1}{2} \times 20\frac{1}{2}$ | 3,600 |
| 1969 | C. The day shift, 1952, $14 \times 18$ | 6,825 |
| | S. Oldham, 1957, $19\frac{1}{2} \times 29\frac{1}{2}$ | 5,500 |

£

| | | | £ |
|---|---|---|---|
| 1969 | Bury. C. Harbour scene, 1957, 18×24 | | 7,350 |
| | Tillotson. C. Sandsend near Whitby, 1953, 13½×20½ | | 3,150 |
| | Brodie. C. (Hopetoun). Steps at Wick, 1937, 16¼×20¼ | | 4,725 |
| | C. Open space, Market Street, Manchester, 1950, 16¼× 20¼ | | 7,825 |
| | British American Tobacco Co. S. Queen's Dock, Glasgow, 1947, 17¾×24 | | 3,500 |
| | C. Wilson's Terrace, 1953, 20×16 | | 5,250 |
| | S. Street going up hill, 1960, 19½×23½ | | 4,500 |

HENRY MOORE. 1898–

Drawings only. (*See also* Sculpture, modern)

| | | | |
|---|---|---|---|
| 1959 | Weinmüller, Munich. Children playing, gouache, 11½×9, DM2,550+tax | | 262 |
| 1960 | C. Ideas for sculpture, pen, chalk, etc., 10×17 | | 714 |
| 1961 | S. Sheet of studies for a Madonna for Northampton, 7½×6¾ | | 900 |
| 1964 | S. Reclining figures, pen, chalks etc., 1944, 15×22 | | 1,500 |
| 1966 | Flag. S. Ideas for sculpture, 1939, pen, chalks etc., 11×14¾ | | 1,050 |
| | Roberts. S. Sleeping figures, pen, chalks, 1941, 12×18 | | 4,000 |
| | Studies for sculpture. Sleeping figures, pen, chalks, 1942, 9×6¾ | | 1,000 |
| | Rienitz. S. Two women with a child in a shelter, 13×15½ | | 2,500 |
| 1967 | Ballard. C. Ideas for sculpture, 1938, 14½×21½ | | 1,470 |
| | S. Reclining figures for sculpture, same media, 10×16½ | | 2,100 |
| 1968 | N.Y. Family group, pen and wash, 1944, 12¼×11¾, $10,500 | | 4,370 |
| 1969 | Rhodes. S. Three women with a child, pen and ink, chalks and wash, 1943, 13×21¾ | | 5,600 |
| | C. Studies of mother and child, mixed media, 9×6½ | | 2,730 |
| | S. Studies of lyre-birds, mixed media, about 7×7 2 for | | 2,300 |
| | C. Standing figures, rock background, 1945, 15½×22 | | 8,400 |
| | Family group, 1944, 14¼×11¼, both in mixed media | | 5,250 |
| | Erwin Swann. S. Studies for sculpture, 1952, 11½×9¼ | | 3,400 |
| | S. Tube shelter, mixed media, 1940, 11×15 | | 4,700 |
| | Two, shelter, mixed media, on one sheet, 13¼×9½ | | 4,400 |

WALTER SICKERT. 1860–1942

| | | | |
|---|---|---|---|
| 1959 | C. Portrait, Christine Sickert, 20×16 | | 1,050 |
| 1961 | S. Pulteney Bridge, Bath, 1917, 27½×44½ | | 2,200 |
| | The objection, 1912, 32½×19½ | | 950 |
| 1963 | Joyce. C. Edward VIII in uniform of Welsh Guards, 72×36 | | 840 |

| | | £ |
|---|---|---|
| 1964 | Silley.  S.  The iron bedstead, $15\frac{3}{4} \times 19\frac{3}{4}$ | 1,200 |
| 1965 | Odo Cross.  S.  Seated nude, 1905, $17\frac{3}{4} \times 14\frac{3}{4}$ | 980 |
| | Cottisloe.  S.  Venetian girl, 1901, $19 \times 14\frac{1}{2}$ | 1,400 |
| | Eglise St Jacques, Dieppe, $17 \times 14$, 1902 | 1,450 |
| 1966 | S.  Woman in red dress, $15\frac{1}{2} \times 19\frac{1}{4}$ | 1,000 |
| | St Mark's Venice, 1901, $23\frac{3}{4} \times 19\frac{1}{4}$ | 1,200 |
| | Eglise St Jacques, 1905, $21 \times 18$ | 1,500 |
| 1967 | C.  Street scene, Dieppe, $18 \times 15$ | 1,260 |
| | De Pass.  C.  The horses of St Mark's, $21 \times 17\frac{1}{2}$ | 2,310 |
| 1968 | Bennet.  S.  St Jacques, Dieppe, sunset, 1905, $21\frac{1}{2} \times 18$ | 1,300 |
| | Eastman.  S.  The Eldorado, Paris, 1906, $19 \times 23\frac{1}{2}$ | 2,200 |
| | S.  Casino, Dieppe, 1917, $17\frac{1}{2} \times 21$ | 1,500 |
| | The yellow skirt, 1901, $10\frac{3}{4} \times 14$ | 840 |
| 1969 | Hosking.  S.  Quai Duquesne, Dieppe, 1900, $21\frac{1}{2} \times 18$ | 2,000 |
| | Partridge.  S.  Dieppe, 1900, $10\frac{1}{4} \times 14\frac{1}{4}$ | 800 |
| | S.  Sally, interior with nude, c. 1908, $19\frac{1}{2} \times 15\frac{1}{2}$ | 2,100 |
| | Robert Smith.  S.  San Barnabà, Venice, c. 1901, $24 \times 17\frac{1}{2}$ | 2,300 |

## GRAHAM SUTHERLAND.  1903–

| | | |
|---|---|---|
| 1961 | Somerset Maugham.  S.  Thorn forms, 1946, $26 \times 20$ | 4,000 |
| 1964 | Lardington.  S.  Standing form, red background, $58 \times 26\frac{1}{2}$ | 1,500 |
| 1967 | Juda.  S.  Gorse on sea wall, 1939, $24\frac{1}{2} \times 19$ | 2,600 |
| | Palm palisade, 1947, $19\frac{1}{2} \times 15\frac{1}{2}$ | 2,000 |
| | Estuary shore, 1946, $15 \times 29\frac{1}{2}$ | 950 |
| | Seekers.  C.  Palm tree, 1959, $51 \times 38$ | 3,990 |
| | Rankine.  S.  Hydrant II, 1954, $43\frac{3}{4} \times 35\frac{1}{2}$ | 2,100 |
| | Somerset Maugham.  S.  His portrait head, drawing, mixed media, $12 \times 10\frac{1}{2}$ | 3,300 |
| 1968 | N.Y.  Christ seated, oil study for the Coventry Cathedral tapestry, 1954, $54\frac{1}{2} \times 19$, $13,000 | 5,415 |
| 1969 | Gernsheim.  S.  Hommage à Picasso, 1952, $20\frac{3}{4} \times 17$ | 1,470 |
| | C.  Machine, dated 2.4.59, $52 \times 38\frac{1}{2}$ | 3,990 |

## MAX ERNST.  1891–

As a painter still living, Max Ernst is highly priced mainly on account of a style which he has long abandoned, the *sur-réalisme* of the later 1920s and the 1930s. This has now become little more than an historic incident, but for the best part of 20 years *sur-réalisme* threatened to banish the cult of the abstraction by substituting the assembly of conventionally defined but apparently unrelated images. Its best known exponent, Salvador Dali, favoured an almost pre-Raphaelite imitation of nature to bring out the incongruity and the shock of his associations. Max Ernst's visions were very much less concrete and in the end he became a completely abstract painter. The remarkable ten foot *arbre de la vie* of 1928 is really an abstract picture. Its high price of £28,000 was exceeded in 1969 by a truly sur-réaliste work, conceived in conventional images, the *Ville endormie*, painted in 1938 by the little publicized Paul Delvaux. The price, £32,000, was the more surprising because a Delvaux picture, very like it and even bigger, was sold in 1967 for $9,250. Salvador Dali himself had not much exceeded £6,000 at auction in March, 1969 when his *Ossification matinale du Cyprès* made a sudden 410,000 francs in Paris (equivalent with tax to £38,269). With another typical *sur-réaliste* work, the *Palais d'une courtisane* of René Magritte at £21,500, a new threshold of prices seemed to have been entered by this somewhat forgotten school.

|  |  | £ |
|---|---|---:|
| 1952 | Brussels.  Fleur étrange | 240 |
| 1959 | N.Y.  Sea forms, 21½×25½, $4,500 | 1,607 |
|  | S.  Desert landscape, 1925, 21¼×14½ | 1,600 |
| 1961 | Stuttgart.  La parole est au corbeau, 1957, 44×37¼, DM62,000+tax | 6,360 |
| 1962 | Stuttgart.  Oiseaux et océans, 54×61½, DM152,000+tax | 15,610 |
|  | Chant de la grenouille, 1953, 26×38, DM78,000+tax | 8,035 |
|  | Finarte, Milan.  Galapagos, 1955, 32½×40.  L8·5 million +tax | 5,750 |
| 1963 | Aldrich.  N.Y.  Clairière, 24×19¾, $6,250 | 2,235 |
|  | S.  Jardin gobe-avions, 1934, 23×28 | 3,000 |
|  | Arbre solitaire et arbres conjugaux, 1942, 31×39 | 11,000 |
|  | Paris.  Les trois cyprès, 1951, 40¾×40¾, FN70,000+tax | 6,090 |
| 1964 | S.  Pendant que la terre dort, 35¼×45¾ | 7,000 |
|  | Forêt, oiseau et soleil, 31×39 | 5,000 |
|  | La mariée du vent II, 32×39½ | 9,000 |
| 1965 | C.  Personnages dans un sans tête, 63½×51 | 11,550 |
|  | A l'intèrieur de la vue, l'oeil, 31½×24 | 6,825 |
|  | N.Y.  Enfant Minerve, 1956, 51×35 | 8,035 |
| 1966 | S.  Coquillages, 25×31½ | 7,400 |
|  | Institute Contemporary Arts.  S.  The moon was full, 1966, 28¾×36¼ | 4,000 |
|  | N.Y.  Der Hausengel, 15×18, $7,500 | 2,320 |
| 1967 | Finarte, Milan.  Figure in landscape, 25½×19½, 1·9 million lire+tax | 1,176 |
|  | Composition monochrome, 49½×37, 13 million lire+tax | 7,920 |
|  | S.  Fleurs et oiseaux dans un paysage, 1928, 19¼×23¾ | 5,200 |
|  | C.  Les prunes, 12¾×19 | 2,520 |
| 1968 | S.  L'enfant qui rit, 1954, 11¼×15¼ | 3,000 |
|  | Le soleil couchant, 1929, 39½×32 | 8,200 |
|  | Fleur coquille, 1927, 7½×9½ | 3,600 |

|  |  | £ |
|---|---|---|
| 1968 | S.  La mer, geometric abstraction, 1927–9, $17\frac{3}{4} \times 14\frac{1}{4}$ | 4,800 |
|  | Motte, Geneva.   Composition au cheval, 1913, $14\frac{1}{2} \times 20$, FS117,000+tax | 12,680 |
|  | Composition, 1913, FS100,000+tax | 10,679 |
| 1969 | Hayward Weir.  N.Y.  Sleeping Eskimo, abstract, 1948, $28 \times 24$, \$27,000 | 11,342 |
|  | S.  La poulpe, c. 1925, $25 \times 31\frac{1}{2}$ | 18,000 |
|  | La ville, abstract, 1955–6, $8\frac{3}{4} \times 11\frac{1}{4}$ | 3,000 |
|  | S.  L'arbre de la vie, 1928, $118 \times 82\frac{1}{2}$ | 28,000 |
|  | Flocons, c. 1927, $19\frac{1}{2} \times 14$ | 10,300 |

## WILLIAM ETTY.  1787–1849

Since my introductory note, written in 1960 when no Etty had got much beyond £500 in forty years, there has been some change. There is now even a demand for Etty's completed Royal Academy pictures, enough at least to push them up to the £4,000 region. But there can hardly be a more unpopular school than the 'history painting' of the late 1830s and 1840s, when the Romantic Movement turned into treacle even in the person of Samuel Palmer, and only Turner remained great. Etty's completed pictures have in fact barely caught up with inflation. The history of that lavish but inept composition, *Pluto and Proserpine*, illustrates the process. In 1839 Etty sold it for £350, quite a high fee when £1,000 was about as much as even the most fashionable painter could make. In 1877 when the romantic style, though no longer practised, had become the most admired of all, the picture was auctioned for 750 guineas, less than the thousand guineas which its late owner, the amazing Baron Grant, had paid quite recently. In 1918 the situation was very different. Since no one wanted anything except realism or Impressionism, *Pluto and Proserpine* had dropped down to 10 guineas, less than the value of the frame. By 1934 almost every painter in Chelsea owned one of those Etty studies of the nude that now make from £300 to £3,000. Even so, no one was prepared to pay more than £90 for a monster 76 inches wide. In 1967 *Pluto and Proserpine* was again under the hammer and, this time it made £2,500. Yet in actual purchasing power this was little more than two-thirds of the price which Etty received in 1839.

|  |  |  | £ |
|---|---|---|---|
| 1962 | Lindsay Smith.  C.  Portrait, Matilda Bicknell, $18\frac{1}{2} \times 15\frac{1}{2}$ |  | 420 |
| 1963 | C.  The lute player (£60, 1927; £140, 1954), $17 \times 19$ |  | 504 |
| 1964 | Gabriel.  S.  Children's heads, $9\frac{3}{4} \times 13\frac{1}{2}$ |  | 420 |
|  | Fruit and tumbler, $12\frac{1}{2} \times 16\frac{1}{4}$ |  | 1,000 |
|  | Psyche delivers the casket to Venus, $17 \times 21$ |  | 680 |
|  | Oil studies of nudes | 12 (total) | 2,095 |

|      |                                                                                                      | £     |
|------|------------------------------------------------------------------------------------------------------|-------|
| 1965 | Devas.  C.  Venus and her satellites (£315 in 1834)                                                   | 3,255 |
|      | Portrait of Jenny Lind, 35×27                                                                         | 1,680 |
|      | Resold to Milwaukee Museum                                                                            | 2,500 |
|      | Earl of Sandwich.  C.  Leda, unfinished study in Michelangelo pose, 17×21                             | 3,675 |
| 1966 | Earl of Normanton.  C.  Venus and cupid, oil sketch, 10½×6¾                                           | 420   |
| 1967 | S.  Pluto and Proserpine, 50×76½ (£350 in 1839; £1,050 in 1872; £745 10s. in 1877; £10 10s. in 1918; £90 in 1934) | 2,500 |
|      | C.  Nude study, 16½×13½, signed and inscribed, 1830                                                   | 398   |
| 1968 | C.  Leda and the swan, study, 24½×34                                                                  | 315   |
|      | Caswell.  S.  Danae reclining, oil study, 19¾×26¾                                                     | 700   |
|      | Another reclining nude, 17×26                                                                         | 600   |
| 1969 | S.  Seated Bacchante, nude study, 23×19                                                               | 700   |
|      | C.  Portrait, Catherine Etty, the artist's niece, 23¾×19                                              | 525   |

## JAN VAN EYCK.  1385–1441

The last unquestioned van Eyck to change hands was *The Three Maries* from Doughty House, a fair-sized work, nearly three feet wide, for which in 194 J. D. van Beuningen paid £225,000. In 1970 terms that sum meant more than million, but the picture which is in the Beuningen-Boymans Museum, Rotter dam, may be worth twice as much. In 1872 it cost Francis Cook £336, havin been for years in Middleton's English hotel in Brussels.

In the past thirty years two other pictures have changed hands, having at on time or another passed as the work of van Eyck.

| 1954 | Bought from the Rothschild family by the Frick Foundation, *The Sibyl*, now attributed to Jan van Eyck and Petrus Christus (Nieuwenhuys sale, Brussels, 1883, £800, sold later to Adolphe de Rothschild for £4,000) $750,000 | £ 267,000 |
|------|------|------|
| 1966 | Impey.  S.  St George and the dragon, 5⅝×4⅛, formerly in Plaoutine collection, Petersburg, attributed to Hubert van Eyck and also to the Master of Flémalle. Now in Metropolitan Museum | 220,000 |

## KAREL FABRITIUS.  (*See* Dutch School)

## HENRI FANTIN-LATOUR.  1836–1904

In 1960 the highest price for a Fantin-Latour flowerpiece was £15,000. I 1969 it was £54,000. This meant no more than the general response of a works of art to a decade of inflation and less than the rise in the more popula modern painters. But Fantin-Latour was not a modern painter at all, though he belonged to the generation of the Impressionists and figured in the 1960s only in sales of modern paintings. He had in fact become an old master of a kind moderately fashionable. If Fantin-Latour had painted not flowerpieces but landscapes, he would have ranked in the 1960s no higher than the painters of the Barbizon school, whose market fortunes he had shared in the past. Thus between 1914 and the slump of 1929 quite a number of Fantin-Latour flower-pieces were sold at prices between £1,200 and £2,800, the latter already a ceiling of about £14,000 in 1970 terms.

| | | £ |
|---|---|---:|
| 1960 | S. White and yellow roses in a glass, 10¼×14 | 5,000 |
| | C. Pair of flowerpieces, dated 1863, 19×16½    2 for | 5,880 |
| 1961 | S. Pieds d'alouettes, glass vase, 1891, 28¾×23½ | 21,000 |
| | Geraniums dans un verre droit, 1888, 16¾×13½ | 12,000 |
| 1962 | Beattie. S. Pivoines, 1891, 22×20 | 12,500 |
| 1963 | Cargill. S. White and pink mallows, 20½×18¾ (£1,200 in 1919) | 25,000 |
| | Spray of rhododendrons, 21½×22½, 1874 (£1,200 in 1919) | 18,800 |
| | Fitzgerald. S. Roses in a vase, 17½×14½ | 20,500 |
| | Robert French Trust, Glasgow sale. Roses in vase, 1884 | 17,000 |
| | Zinnias in basket, 1891 | 15,000 |
| 1964 | Combemarle. C. Flowerpiece | 13,650 |
| 1966 | S. Roses in vase, 16½×14 | 14,000 |
| | C. Narcissuses, jacinths and tulips, 1864, 21¼×17¾ (Buckler, C. 1906, £215 5s.) | 22,050 |
| | Bateman. C. Fleurs diverses, 1878, 10×13 | 8,925 |
| | Zinnias, 1891, 13½×17¾ (Barnes. c. 1894 £22 1s.) | 13,650 |
| | Fordyce. N.Y. Roses in a bowl, 1889, 19½×24 ($77,500) | 27,300 |
| 1967 | Boise. S. Toutes les roses du jardin, 1884, 25×21½ | 23,000 |
| | Honeyman. C. Roses, 1882, 12×19 | 16,275 |
| | Downer. C. Oeillets d'Inde, 1893, 18×19¾ | 18,900 |
| 1968 | S. Vase de pivoines, 1881, 22½×26¾ | 54,000 |
| | Gros vase de dahlias et fleurs variées, 1875, 18¾×23¾ | 36,000 |
| | Roses blanches et jaunes, 1876, 17¾×12¾ | 19,000 |
| 1969 | Oliphant. S. Les brodeuses, conversation piece, 12×15¼ | 7,800 |
| | Astor. S. Azalées et bruyères, 1874, 15¾×8¾ | 14,000 |
| 1970 | S. Red and white roses in glass, 1890, 15¼×13¾ | 27,000 |

## LYONEL FEININGER. (*See* German School, modern)

## JOHN FERNELEY SNR. 1781–1861

For half John Ferneley's long working life Sir Thomas Lawrence was the un-disputed head-boy of English painting. While Ferneley was getting twenty or thirty guineas for a gentleman's likeness with his hunters, grooms and pack of foxhounds thrown in, Lawrence was knocking off whole-lengths at 700 guineas each and with the minimum of sittings. In the 1920s, when both painters were much in demand, Ferneley rose from the two or three hundred level to as much as £3,000, but Duveen could sell Lawrence at £40,000 to £80,000. Having never been made a Royal Academician, Ferneley's very existence had been ignored by most 19th century English writers on painting. In the 1960s that had become an advantage which made him a more expensive painter than Lawrence. In 1961 I observed that Ferneley continued, as in the 1920s, to make £2,000 or £3,000. So strong was the appeal of nostalgia in the next few years that by 1969 a family group had made £29,400. For all that, Ferneley remains little more than a pretty journeyman painter.

| | | £ |
|---|---|---|
| 1961 | C. Frank Hall Standish, mounted on his horse, 1819, 33 × 39½ | 2,205 |
| 1963 | S. Horse-fair in a country town, 24½ × 42½ | 1,700 |
| 1965 | Harewood. C. Grey hunter, 1827 | 1,260 |
| | Smith. C. Two hunters with dog and deer, 1832 | 6,510 |
| | Groom with two horses in London street, 1833 | 7,560 |
| | C. Two horses with Shetland pony in landscape | 4,725 |
| 1966 | Chisholm. C. *Spaniel*, winner of the Derby, 1831, 33 × 41½ | 8,400 |
| | Aykroyd. S. Hounds in full cry, Melton Mowbray, 1825, 23 × 62 | 8,000 |
| | Companion piece, The end of a Long Run | 6,500 |
| | Earl Howe. C. Groom with Lord Howe's grey hunter, 43½ × 49½ | 9,975 |
| | Earl of Ernle. S. *Pilot* and *Sambo* taking a ditch, 1850, 17½ × 23½ | 2,800 |
| 1967 | Des Graz. S. Lady Lindsey and bay hunter, 1853, 33½ × 41¼ | 4,800 |
| | Sir Montague Welby and chestnut hunter, 1843, 33½ × 41¼ | 3,200 |
| | Bartlett. C. Brood mares grazing, 1832, 40 × 49 | 13,125 |
| | Gordon. S. Two hunters, *Longford Lass* and *the Jew* at Belvoir Castle, 1853, 39 × 51 (commissioned 20 guineas) | 17,000 |
| 1968 | Woodhouse. S. Bay mare and foal in landscape, 1840, 27 × 35 | 1,500 |
| | Westenra. C. Two race horses, wide landscape with view of Melton Mowbray, 1831, 14¾ × 19½ (3 guineas in 1883) | 11,550 |
| | Floyd. C. A memorable run with the Quorn, 1835, 36 × 59 (£33 12s. in 1895, £94 10s. in 1910) | 9,975 |
| | Cunard. C. York and Ainsteys foxhounds, 1842, 32 × 60½ | 5,040 |
| | Alexander. C. John Morant on dark grey hunter, 41 × 33½ | 13,650 |

| 1968 | Middleton. N.Y. Mr Biddulph's three hunters, 1830, | £ |
|---|---|---|
| | 43½×62 (commissioned for 30 guineas) $44,000 | 18,335 |
| | D'Arcy Irvine. N.Y. *Rudolph*, bay hunter, 1842, | |
| | 27½×35½, $7,000 | 2,932 |
| 1969 | Gascoigne. S. Grey hunter and mansion (Dale Park, | |
| | Arundel), 23½×37½ | 4,600 |
| | C. Two racehorses with view of Melton Mowbray, 1831, | |
| | 30×33½ | 7,875 |
| | Grey hunter and dog in landscape, 33½×41½ | 3,150 |
| | Wiley. S. Four greyhounds in landscape, 1833, 30×33½ | 13,000 |
| | C. *General Chasse*, chestnut colt, 1838, 31×42 | 13,125 |
| | The Ferneley children and ponies, 1830, 56½×43½ | 29,400 |
| | N.Y. (John Ferneley Jnr) Meet of Sir Tatton Sykes's | |
| | Hounds, $11,500 | 4,792 |
| | S. Dappled grey hunter with small dog, 1838, 26½×34½ | 3,000 |
| | *Rockingham*, dark bay, St Leger 1833, 34½×42¼ | 3,200 |
| | Fenwick. C. Four hunters, romantic wooded landscape, | |
| | 14½×19½ Bought in at | 5,250 |

## FLEMISH SCHOOL
### before 1550

(Excluding Jerome Bosch, Jan van Eyck and Gerard David, for whom see separate entries.)

The great Flemish masters of the 15th century have now almost certainly vanished from the market. In fact Flemish paintings of that age are seldom seen in the salerooms in any shape or form, and, when they are seen, their shape is poor. A few fine primitives stand out in these lists, such as the anonymous early triptych, sold in Paris in 1961, and the two quite enchanting miniature panels by Juan de Flandés, sold by Christies in 1967. The majority of the paintings belong, however, to the 16th century, and many of them are in that singularly unattractive style which seems to be Late Gothic and High Baroque at the same time. Between the two wars and before the advent of an inflation which made *all* old master paintings a speculation, Flemish pictures, painted in the technique if not in the spirit of the great primitive masters, could often be bought for £100 and even £40. Such works will have gone up in terms of depreciated pounds from 50 to 200 times over. Even so ugly a painter as Cornelius van Oostsanen can make £37,000, a truly pretty painter such as Patinir £74,000. Museum curators, obsessed with Italians either very early or very late, do not seem to find this a significant school, but there is much patriotic support from Belgium, a wealthy country.

Names in the following lists may have been used somewhat freely. Joos van Cleve has become a denomination for competent portraits that suggest no one in particular. Herri met de Bles is believed not to have existed. Like Boston, he is a state of mind.

JOOS VAN CLEEF or CLEVE the Younger.   Floruit 1530–1550                      £

| | | |
|---|---|---:|
| 1956 | Verney.  C.  Portrait of Burgomaster and wife | 1,720 |
| | N.Y.  Girl's portrait, $11,000, 21½ × 17¼ | 3,928 |
| 1959 | Strazza.  C.  Weeping virgin | 5,460 |
| 1961 | Makower.  S.  Portrait of a young man, 20½ × 14¾ | 5,200 |
| 1962 | Berwind.  N.Y.  Small Madonna, formerly attributed to Mabuse, 29 × 21½, $40,000 | 14,280 |
| 1965 | Spencer Churchill.  C.  A lady as Mary Magdalen, 13¼ × 10½ (£54 12s. in 1859) | 4,725 |
| | A young prince, formerly considered Edward VI by Holbein, 21½ × 14¾ (see 1969) | 12,600 |
| 1966 | Francis Cook.  C.  Replica of the Madonna of the Cherries (Napier sale, 1877, £54 12s) 28 × 20 | 14,700 |
| | Peto.  S.  Man in a furred robe, 14½ × 10¾ | 7,200 |
| 1967 | Watney.  C.  Portrait, unknown gentleman, 22 × 17 | 4,725 |
| 1969 | C.  A young prince, once called Edward VI (see 1965), bought in | 12,600 |

JAN GOSSAERT DE MABUSE.   1470–1532

| | | |
|---|---|---:|
| 1959 | Paris.  Mars, Venus and Cupid, 21½ × 16¾, 3·9 million old francs + tax | 3,408 |
| 1962 | Mme B. de B.  Paris.  Portrait, young, girl, 20¾ × 16, FN170,000 + tax | 14,800 |
| 1964 | S.  Portrait of a young woman, 16½ × 12¾ | 6,500 |
| | C.  Adoration (school of Mabuse, c. 1530) | 4,200 |
| 1968 | Lempertz.  Cologne.  Holy Family, DM275,000 + tax | 31,510 |

QUENTIN MATSYS.   1466–1530

| | | |
|---|---|---:|
| 1962 | Paris.  Landscape with St Christopher, 12 × 16, FN58,000 + tax | 5,120 |
| 1965 | S.  Holy Family, attributed | 2,600 |
| 1966 | C.  Head of an old woman, 16 × 13½ | 1,155 |
| 1968 | Shuttleworth.  C.  Holy Family and Cherubs, 7 × 5½ | 1,995 |
| 1969 | Kieffer.  Paris.  Susannah and the elders (by Jan Matsys), 43½ × 80, FN160,000 + tax | 14,520 |

HERRI MET DE BLES.   1480–1550

| | | |
|---|---|---:|
| 1961 | S. (Possibly Cornelis Cornelissen).  Temptation of St Anthony | 5,000 |

| | | | |
|---|---|---|---:|
| 1964 | S. | Rocky landscape, Temptation of St Anthony, 12½ × 21¾ (see 1969) | £ 5,500 |
| 1965 | S. | Mountainous landscape and buildings, 20 × 30 | 10,000 |
| 1968 | van Waay, Amsterdam. Biblical scene, round panel, 14 in. diam., Hfl35,000+tax | | 4,570 |
| | | Landscape with travellers, 21¼ × 34, Hfl25,000+tax | 3,208 |
| 1969 | S. | Temptation of St Anthony, 12½ × 21¾ (see 1964, now ascribed to *Jan Mandyn*) | 22,500 |
| | C. | St Christopher bearing the infant Christ, roundel 12½ in. diam., bought in | 11,025 |

BERNARD VAN ORLEY. 1493–1542

| | | | |
|---|---|---|---:|
| 1953 | Ashburnham. S. David and Bathsheba | | 4,200 |
| 1962 | C. | St Catherine and St Mary Magdalen, 32 × 21¼ | 8,400 |
| 1966 | S. | Holy Family in landscape, 24½ × 21¼ | 7,200 |
| 1967 | Watney. C. Adoration of the Magi, triptych, 46 × 68 | | 3,150 |
| | Marie zu Wied. S. Conversion of Constantine, 48½ × 33½ | | 3,500 |
| 1968 | Delamere. C. St Jérôme and St Denys, 31¼ × 16 2 for | | 3,150 |
| 1969 | Poulett. S. Christ, presented to the people (ascribed), 37 × 30¾ | | 6,200 |

JOACHIM PATINIR. 1485–1524

| | | | |
|---|---|---|---:|
| 1953 | Ashburnham. S. Landscape with Riposo | | 3,600 |
| 1964 | Bruce Ingram. S. Landscape with martyrdom of St Catherine, 15 × 19¼ | | 18,000 |
| | C. | Flight into Egypt, 18 × 31 | 5,460 |
| 1968 | S. | Populous and wooded landscape, *c.* 1520, 17¼ × 21¾ | 74,000 |
| 1969 | Delmege. S. Seascape, Jonah and the whale, ships etc., 9 × 13 | | 13,500 |
| | C. | St Jérôme in landscape, adoring crucifix, 15 × 19, bought in | 9,975 |

JAN PREVOST. 1462–1529

| | | | |
|---|---|---|---:|
| 1956 | C. | Adoration of the Magi, triptych | 4,200 |
| 1960 | S. | Franciscan monk, 10 × 8 | 2,700 |
| 1962 | Max von Hohenlohe. C. Adoration of the Magi, 18¾ × 16¼ | | 18,500 |
| 1963 | Lempertz. Cologne. Holy Family, 14 × 10, DM60,000+tax | | 6,150 |
| 1968 | C. | Nativity with St Joseph, 9¾ × 51, bought in at | 7,350 |
| | | Adoration of the Magi, Presentation and Annunciation, triptych, 38½ × 61 | 5,040 |
| 1969 | S. | Adoration of the Kings (ascribed), 21½ × 16 | 3,200 |

JAN SCOREL. 1495–1562                                    £
1952  S.  Triptych, scenes from Passion                 2,400
1960  Holy Family                                       2,100
1966  Cowley.  S.  Portraits of man and wife, 16¾×11¾  2 for  6,000

ROGIER VAN DER WEYDEN.  1400–1464
1966  Francis Cook.  C.  Madonna and Saints standing before
      an altar, 18×12                                   12,600
1967  C.  Young man in red doublet, schoolpiece, 14½×10½  3,780
      Paris.  Holy Family, 17½×12¾, schoolpiece, FN105,000+
      tax                                               8,900

ADRIAEN YSENBRANDT.    –1551
1956  C.  Holy Family                                   8,925
1957  Baerwald.  S.  Holy Family in landscape           4,200
1963  S.  Holy Family in landscape                      3,400
1964  S.  Adoration of the Kings, 18×14                 19,000
1966  Newray.  C.  Adoration of the Magi, 18×14         10,500
1967  C.  Lady in fur sleeves in landscape, 9¾×7        6,775

ANONYMOUS PAINTERS
1959  Paris.  MASTER OF THE FEMALE HALF-FIGURES, the Mag-
      dalen writing, 17×12¾                             2,608
1960  C.  MASTER OF THE EMBROIDERED LEAF.  Holy Family in
      landscape, 29×24½                                 8,400
      S.  MASTER OF THE ST LUCY LEGEND.  Holy Family    2,400
1961  Makower.  S.  MASTER OF ST GUDULE.  St Catherine
      disputing with theologians, 14×11½ (see 1967)     6,200
      Erickson.  N.Y.  MASTER OF ST AUGUSTINE.  Life of St
      Augustine, centre-panel from altarpiece, 54×59¾, c. 1490
      (£315 in 1888 as Gerard David), $110,000, Metropolitan
      Museum                                            39,285
      Mme B. de B.  Paris.  UNKNOWN PAINTER, early 15th
      century, Life of St Hypolitus, triptych, FN1 million+tax,
      41¾×117, Boston Fine Arts Museum                  85,400
1962  UNKNOWN BRUGES PAINTER of 1473.  Triptych, Adora-
      tion etc., 86¼×14½ over-all, extended             26,000
      MASTER OF ALKMAAR.  Pair of saints, landscape back-
      ground, each 14¼×9½                        2 for  28,500
      Max von Hohenlohe.  C.  SCHOOL OF MASTER OF
      FLÉMALLE, Holy Family, 17½×12                     6,825
      N.Y.  MASTER OF THE HOLY BLOOD.  Holy Family, 25¼×
      17¾, $4,500                                       1,607
      Paris.  HISPANO-FLEMISH SCHOOL, late 15th century,
      Golgotha, 37×19½, FN200,000+tax                   17,080

£

| | | |
|---|---|---|
| 1963 | Lempertz, Cologne. MASTER OF THE MAGDALEN LEGEND, Holy Family, 14½ × 11, DM50,000+tax | 5,420 |
| | HELDRING. S. MASTER OF THE FEMALE HALF FIGURES, *c.* 1525–40, The Magdalen playing the lute | 14,000 |
| | Sterling of Keir. S. UNKNOWN MASTER, *c.* 1520, Holy Family in landscape, 25 × 18 | 10,000 |
| 1964 | Bruce Ingram. S. MASTER OF THE LIFE OF THE VIRGIN, Last Judgement, 22 × 16 | 15,000 |
| | S. MASTER OF THE HOLY BLOOD. Holy Family with saints, triptych, 25 × 38 | 8,400 |
| | C. MASTER OF THE ST URSULA LEGEND. The Pietá, triptych | 5,775 |
| 1965 | Spencer Churchill. S. MASTER OF ST SEVERIN, Mass of St Gregory (£84 in 1838) | 8,925 |
| | MASTER OF 1518. Adoration of the Magi | 7,875 |
| 1966 | Aurora Trust. S. MASTER OF ST BARTHOLOMEW ALTAR. Fragmentary head of St James in van Eyck style, 6¼ × 5 | 6,000 |
| 1967 | C. UNKNOWN PAINTER. Portrait of a prelate dated 1545, 18 × 12½ | 2,730 |
| | C. UNKNOWN PAINTER. St Veronica holding a sudary, 11½ × 7¾ | 4,200 |
| | Maria zu Wied. S. MASTER OF 1518, Adoration of the Kings dated 1525, pointed top, 43 × 28¾ | 6,500 |
| | C. MASTER OF THE VIEW OF ST GUDULE. St Catherine and the theologians, 14 × 11½ (see 1961) | 9,450 |
| 1968 | C. MASTER OF THE ST CATHERINE LEGEND. Descent from the Cross, triptych, wings painted both sides, 45 × 19½, bought in | 36,750 |
| | S. UNKNOWN PAINTER, *c.* 1520. Presentation in the temple, 32¾ × 23½ | 9,000 |
| | MASTER OF THE VIEW OF ST GUDULE. Marriage of the Virgin, 16½ × 10¾, showing view of Brussels and bought by Brussels Museum | 8,000 |
| | C. MASTER OF THE MAGDALEN LEGEND. Crucifixion, triptych, 16½ × 20 | 3,990 |
| | Lempertz, Cologne, MASTER OF HOOGSTRAETEN, the Jesse tree, 46¾ × 34½, DM100,000+tax | 11,900 |
| | MASTER OF DELFT. Virgin, St Anne and donors, triptych, 37½ × 30, DM140,000+tax | 16,600 |
| 1969 | S. MASTER OF THE MAGDALEN LEGEND. Holy Family in walled garden, 34¾ × 26½ | 3,200 |
| | Westminster Diocesan Trust. S. MASTER OF THE LIFE OF THE VIRGIN. SS Sebastian, Nicholas and Anthony, gold ground, 70 × 35 | 3,400 |

OTHER PAINTERS                            £

1960   Stuyck, Brussels. CORNELIS MASSYS. Calvary, 26×22½,
360,000BFr.+tax                    About   3,120

1961   Craven. S. HANS MEMLING, retable wing with saints    17,000
S. JOEST VAN KALKAR. Holy Family, 24×19      12,000

1962   C. CORNELIS ENGLEBRECHTSEN (1468–1533). Holy
Family with St Anne, 45×34                 9,500
ditto   Calvary                            2,940

1964   S. LUCAS GASSEL. Landscape with St Jérôme      3,000
       AELBERT BOUTS. Nativity              12,500
       St Jérôme in landscape             15,000

1965   Spencer Churchill. C. DIRCK BOUTS. Holy Family,
11×9½                              15,750

1966   Mouton. C. COECKE VAN AELST. Triptych. Annunciation and *Riposo*, 47½×64             8,925
Scarfe. S. COLIN DE COETER, St Michael and St Agnes,
62½×32¾                       30,000

1967   Farrow. S. COECKE VAN AELST. Triptych. Adora-
tion of the Kings, 35¾×51½             3,000
S. Attributed HANS MEMLING. Madonna and Child,
10×8½                             6,800
WATNEY. C. JUAN DE FLANDES. Christ tempted by
Satan, 8×6, National Gallery, Washington      57,750
ditto   Marriage feast of Cana, 8×6, Coll. Linskey, New
York, both in Bardini sale, 1899, as Gerard David   87,150
CORNELIS VAN OOSTSANEN. Portrait of unknown man,
11½×8½                         4,200
Maria zu Wied. CORNELIS VAN OOSTSANEN. Adoration
with Saints. Triptych dated 1517, 33×40¾     37,000
Dundas. JAN DE COCK. St Christopher and Holy Child,
21½×18                         6,825

1968   de la Pasture. C. GOOSSEN VAN DER WEYDEN. Triptych
comprising the Pietà, Calvary and Flagellation, 43×54
(£400 in 1947, £2,100 in 1949)          6,825
Kaplan. S. CORNELIS ENGELBRECHTSEN. Triptych.
Adoration, 16¼×20¼                5,000
S. JAN DE BEER. Presentation and Visitation, panel
painted on both sides, 28½×22¾         4,500
C. GWILLIM STRETES. Half-length portrait, Catherine
Parr, c. 1543, 25×20 (Hamilton Palace sale, 1882 as Holbein
£840) National Portrait Gallery          7,350
       Attributed JUAN DE FLANDÉS. Annunciation, 18×13½   3,360
S. JACOB CORNELIS. The Passion. Triptych, 18 in.
high                              14,000

| | | | £ |
|---|---|---|---:|
| 1968 | S. | JEAN BELLEGAMBE. Conversion of St Paul (transferred to canvas) 39×45¾, bought in | 28,000 |
| | | GOOSSEN VAN DER WEYDEN. The circumcision, c. 1520, 53½×40½, bought in | 5,000 |
| 1969 | C. | SCHOOL OF DIRCK BOUTS. St Augustine, half-length, 8×7 | 5,040 |
| | S. | CORNELIS MASSYS. Sacrifice of Isaac, 11¼×15½ | 1,900 |
| | | Dashwood. C. BRUNSWICK MONOGRAMMIST. Preaching of the Baptist, mountainous landscape, 33×44, bought in | 7,350 |
| | C. | JAN MANDYN. St Christopher and the infant Christ, 11½×16½, bought in | 4,410 |

## DRAWINGS

| | | | |
|---|---|---|---:|
| 1960 | Kornfeld, Berne. AELBERT BOUTS. Study of two angels, pen, 8×8½, FS23,000+tax | | 2,300 |
| 1961 | Randall. S. HUGO VAN DER GOES. Female figure (St Barbara?) seated on the ground, fine pen work on green ground with whitened lights, 9×7½ | | 30,000 |
| 1969 | Boerlag-Koenigs. PIETER CORNELISZ KUNST (Att.) St Dominic, another saint on reverse, 8¼×5½, pen | | 2,400 |
| | ditto St Agatha, pen, 8½×5¼ | | 950 |

# FLEMISH SCHOOL

## after 1550

(See separate entries for the Breughel family, Rubens, Teniers, Vandyck.)

The lists comprise several very distinct groups. The flower-painter list should be consulted in connection with Jan Breughel, the founder of this school. The painters of figure compositions, landscapes and animals include Jordaens, Snyders and Casteels who belong to the Rubens generation, but most of them are contemporary with the younger Breughels and show the influence of that family. Of this group Joos de Momper stands out as a fairly original person by reason of his fantastic mountains. He has reached the £12,000 class, but before the last war could be bought for £20–£40. This is not in the least uncommon among the Flemish mannerists of the late 16th and early 17th centuries. Particularly to be noticed is the Lambert Lombard picture, a transitional work, retaining some traces of Gothic art, which rose from £84 in 1929 to £11,550 in 1965. And still more, perhaps, the Maerten van Cleve, a Breughelesque performance which rose from £38 18s. in 1923 (at which it had to be bought in) to £19,950 in 1967. These pictures in fact share the fortunes of the works of the two younger Breughels, having been very much more costly in the late

19th century before the older heirlooms of English country houses were entirely rejected by the market in favour of 18th century portraits in the Grand Manner.

The same holds good, though in a less striking degree, for English country-house ancestor paintings, made by visiting Flemings in the early Stuart age. It is claimed that a strong recovery is on the way, but before 1970 and the sale of the *Family of Lord Capell*, the market was hardly sensational. Of the Earl of Craven's 38 portraits by Gerrit van Honthorst (a Dutchman by birth, but Flemish by training) the three most important hovered below £5,000. Yet at the Hamilton Palace sale of 1882 *Mary Stuart, Duchess of Orleans*, made £462, equivalent in 1970 money to fully £4,000; hence no significant advance in 75 years, though the break-up of a famous collection meant an occasional stronger market. Thus at the Holford sale of 1928 a whole-length by Suster-mans made £13,125, equivalent to £65,000. But between 1934 and 1959 the sum of £1,000 could probably have bought any Flemish portrait of this school however grand its pedigree.

The very sudden rise of Jacob Jordaens in 1965 is less dramatic than it looks. Both the portrait of *Arnold de Pret*, bought by the Antwerp Museum in 1883 for £2,080, and *The Artist and his Wife* which made £3,980 at the Darnley sale of 1925, were £20,000 purchases in 1970 terms.

| JACOB JORDAENS. 1593–1678 | | £ |
|---|---|---|
| 1960 C. The miraculous draught of fishes, 46×77 | | 1,785 |
| 1961 S. Fruit-vendors, 20¾×22 | | 2,500 |
| 1965 S. The artist's wife, 36×28¼ | | 2,500 |
| Countess of Suffolk. S. St Paul at Lystra, 51¼×69 | | 3,500 |
| Spencer Churchill. C. The education of a prince (£10 10s. in 1833), 37½×59 | | 68,250 |
| 1966 C. Equestrian young man with pages, 28×22 | | 2,100 |
| 1968 Kaplan. S. Temptation of the Magdalen, 50×38¾ | | 14,000 |
| Reedtz-Thott. S. The Betrayal of Christ, 88¾×97, bought in at | | 25,000 |
| Vienna, Dorotheum. Ripe apples, 46¾×42½, 380,000 sch. +tax | | 7,000 |
| 1969 Earl of Wemyss. S. 'As the old sing, the young pipe,' 1638 or soon after, 57×85¾ | | 79,000 |
| Church of St Francis Xavier, Amsterdam. C. Road to Calvary, 94½×68½, bought in at | | 13,650 |

| JUDOCUS or JOOS DE MOMPER. –1634 | | |
|---|---|---|
| 1952 D. of Northumberland. S. Mountainous landscape | | 1,300 |
| 1958 C. River scene, travellers on road, 14×20 | | 577 10s. |
| 1959 S. Landscape with travellers | | 1,000 |
| 1963 S. Mountainous landscape | | 3,600 |
| 1965 Bird, Paris. Winter scene, FN125,000+tax | | 10,035 |
| Spencer Churchill. C. Pontefract Castle, 1630, 41½×72 | | 1,155 |

| | | | £ |
|---|---|---|---|
| 1967 | C. (with Jan Breughel). Hilly landscape with carts, 18½×26 | | 4,200 |
| | S. Village in winter, 19¼×25¼ | | 4,000 |
| 1968 | S. Mountainous landscape, 28×46 | | 2,500 |
| | River landscape, peasants in a cart, 27½×37¼ | | 4,300 |
| | (With Sebastian Vrancx). Landscape with village and château, 24×41 | | 11,500 |
| 1969 | C. Landscape with ice and skaters, 19¾×26 | | 5,040 |
| | Castle and broad valley with horsemen on road, 19¼×33½ | | 12,600 |
| | Broad hilly landscape with waggons, 17¾×29¾ | | 3,360 |
| | S. Mountainous landscape, unframed, 15×29 | | 4,300 |

ANTONIS MOR (Sir Anthony More). 1512–1572

| | | £ |
|---|---|---|
| 1960 | C. Portrait, Nicolas Granvella, 43×29½ | 1,890 |
| 1963 | S. Male portrait, dated 1547 | 1,800 |
| 1965 | Margadale of Islay. C. Elizabeth of Valois, 41×37 | 1,575 |
| | Winston Guest. S. Half-length, Mary Tudor, 29½×22½ (£4,410 in 1925) | 11,000 |
| 1968 | Warwick Castle. C. Unknown gentleman, 20½×16 | 2,940 |

FRANS POURBUS THE YOUNGER. 1570–1622

| | | £ |
|---|---|---|
| 1967 | Parker. C. Head of unknown man, dated 1589, age 48, 19×13 | 2,520 |
| | S. (attributed). Whole-length, Sir Thomas Winne, 83×51½ | 2,400 |
| | Wingfield Castle. C. (by F. Pourbus the elder). Garden of Eden with animals, dated 1565, 5½×9 | 1,785 |
| 1968 | S. Louis XIII as a boy, 1614, 22¾×18¾ | 2,000 |

FRANS SNYDERS. 1579–1657

| | | £ |
|---|---|---|
| 1911 | C. Dead game and lobster | 546 |
| 1959 | Duke of Westminster. S. Landscape, fox and herons | 1,600 |
| 1960 | S. A larder | 7,600 |
| 1961 | C. Parrots and other birds, 49×38 | 2,730 |
| 1962 | S. Still life with fruit and glass tumblers, 26½×36½ | 3,200 |
| | Earl of Bradford. S. Still life with dogs, 68×97 | 4,800 |
| 1967 | Watney. C. Concert of birds, 65½×96 | 2,310 |
| | Billy Rose Foundation. S. Similar subject, 72×59 | 1,500 |

CORNELIS DE VOS. 1585–1651

| | | £ |
|---|---|---|
| 1904 | Paris. Family group | 2,240 |
| 1911 | C. Portrait, said to be of Spinoza | 165 5s. |
| 1913 | Fischhof, Paris. Portrait, young woman and child | 2,892 |

£

| | | |
|---|---|---|
| 1934 | Sulley. C. Lady and her children | 1,050 |
| 1959 | Christie. C. Female portrait, 1619 | 997 10s. |
| 1964 | Fischer, Lucerne. (by Simon de Vos) courtezan and gallant, 67×58, FS30,000+tax | 3,000 |
| 1968 | Werner. S. Full-length, boy carrying big hat, 48×31, bought in | 3,100 |

FRUIT AND FLOWER PAINTERS

(*See also* Jan Breughel, Dutch School, Jan van Huysum)

| | | |
|---|---|---|
| 1955 | C. NICOLAS VERANDAEL. Flowers in a glass vase, $18\frac{1}{2}\times13$ | 1,312 10s. |
| 1958 | C. BALTAZAR VAN DER AST. Flowerpiece | 6,825 |
| 1960 | C. BALTAZAR VAN DER AST. Still life of peaches, $14\frac{1}{2}\times24$ | 2,205 |
| 1961 | Stuart-Heaton. S. MARIA VAN OOSTERWYCK, summer flowers, $32\frac{3}{4}\times26\frac{1}{4}$ (glass vase) | 3,400 |
| | S. LOUISE MOILLON. S. Grapes and peaches, 1634, $24\frac{1}{4}\times28$ | 5,700 |
| 1963 | C. BALTAZAR VAN DER AST. Still life with shells, $21\frac{1}{2}\times26$ | 16,800 |
| | S. ABRAHAM MIGNON. Flowerpiece | 5,200 |
| 1964 | S. BAPTIST VAN FORNENBURGH. Flowers in vase, $15\frac{1}{4}\times9\frac{1}{4}$ | 9,000 |
| | JOHANNES VAN DER AST. Flowers in a vase, $9\frac{3}{4}\times6\frac{1}{2}$ | 6,000 |
| 1965 | C. ABRAHAM MIGNON. Flowerpiece, $35\times26\frac{1}{2}$ | 4,725 |
| | NICOLAS VERANDAEL. Mixed flowers, $22\frac{3}{4}\times15\frac{1}{2}$ (compare 1955) | 14,700 |
| 1966 | S. NICOLAS VERANDAEL. Pair of flowerpieces, $15\frac{3}{4}\times12\frac{1}{2}$, 2 for | 6,000 |
| 1967 | Wingfield Castle. C. NICOLAS VERANDAEL. Flowers in glass vase, $22\times16\frac{1}{4}$ | 5,040 |
| | JACOB VAN HOULSDONCK Basket with fruits, $23\times35$ | 9,660 |
| | S. SIMON VERELST. Flowers in glass vase, $23\frac{3}{4}\times18\frac{1}{2}$ | 3,150 |
| 1968 | Prestige. S. BALTAZAR VAN DER AST. Flowers including striped tulips, glass vase, $15\frac{3}{4}\times11\frac{1}{4}$ | 8,500 |
| | S. BALTAZAR VAN DER AST. Flowerpiece on copper, $11\times8\frac{1}{4}$ | 8,200 |
| | NICOLAS VERANDAEL. Flowers in glass vase, $20\frac{1}{2}\times13$ | 3,800 |
| | BALTAZAR VAN DER AST. Flowers in tigerware vase, $13\frac{1}{2}\times10\frac{1}{2}$ | 3,800 |
| | JACOB MARELL. Still life with vase of flowers, 1637, $36\times30\frac{1}{2}$ | 4,400 |
| | C. DANIEL SEGHERS. Flowers in a glass vase, $19\times13$ | 3,675 |
| | S. MARIA VAN OOSTERWYCK. Rich vase of flowers, dated 1667, $37\frac{1}{2}\times29\frac{3}{4}$ | 5,200 |
| | JEAN BAPTISTE MONNOYER. Summer flowers, stone ledge by a window, $39\frac{1}{4}\times35\frac{1}{4}$ | 3,500 |
| | Bearns, Torquay. ABRAHAM MIGNON. Still life of flowers | 6,600 |

968   Lempertz, Cologne. JAN BAERS. Flowers, fruit and shells,   £
dated 1624, 14×24, DM110,000+tax         About  13,060

969   C. JACOB VAN HOULSDONCK. Strawberries and carnations in Ming blue and white bowl on table; on copper, 11½×15      7,800

      PETER HARDIME. Summer flowers in glass vase, 35¼×27¼      3,600

      S. CORNELIS VAN SPAENDONCK. Mixed flowers, stone vase etc., dated 1793, 31½×25      9,000

      C. JEAN BAPTISTE MONNOYER, 29¼×24½, flowers in sculptured urn      2,730

      Brandt, Amsterdam. PIETER BINOIT, fruit, nuts, etc., with squirrel, Hfl37,000+tax      4,898

      Dunraven Limerick. C. JACOB VAN HOULSDONCK. Basket with plums and grapes, 17½×25      11,550

      van Waay, Amsterdam. ABRAHAM BLOEMERS. Flowerpiece, Hfl44,000+16% tax      5,874

970   C. ABRAHAM MIGNON. Hollyhocks etc., with birds and insects in grotto      13,650


PORTRAITS (mainly painted in England)

921   Willoughby de Broke. C. MARK GEERAETS. Queen Elizabeth      2,950

928   Grey. C. MARK GEERAETS. Lady in yellow      1,995

928   Holford. C. JUSTUS SUSTERMANS, whole-length, unknown lady      7,350

      Holford. C. JUSTUS SUSTERMANS. Whole-length boy with a red hat      13,125

929   C. MARK GEERAETS. Wife of a yeoman of the jewel house, c. 1610 (sold with the actual dress in which she sat)      4,200

933   Eden. C. GERARD SOEST. The 2nd Lord Baltimore. Baltimore Museum      4,200

952   BROCKETT. S. MARK GEERAETS. Sir Henry Lee, 1600      1,000

965   Moussali. S. GERRIT VAN HONTHORST. Charles 1st, 30¼×20¼, National Portrait Gallery      4,000

      Spencer Churchill. C. UNKNOWN PAINTER, c. 1950, Mary, Countess Rivers      2,940

967   Watney. C. SCHOOL OF DE HEERE. Unknown English girl, aged 15, dated 1573, 31×25      2,310

      Spencer Nairn. C. GERARD SOEST. Two children of the Hay family, 48½×40      3,990

968   C. CORNELIS JONSON. Oval portrait, Lady Anne Clifford, 1631, 30×24½      1,995

      Lullin. C. JAN MYTTENS. The artist and his family in landscape, dated 1641, 34×46      2,100

1968 Craven. S. Attributed DANIEL MYTTENS, Equestrian  £
portrait, John, Lord Craven of Ryton, 104×96½      6,400
  C. UNKNOWN. Bust portrait of Anne of Austria, c. 1616,
  22¾×19                2,625
  Lord Craven. S. PAUL VAN SOMMER, James I, 1618,
  81×56½                1,800
    ditto. Anne of Denmark, 77×55      2,400
  GERRIT VAN HONTHORST. Frederick, King of Bohe-
  mia, 84½×57½             4,600
  Elizabeth, the 'Winter Queen' en suite     5,200
  Princess Hohenzollern-Hechingen as a child, 58½×43,
  1649                4,800
  38 portraits by Honthorst made £36,620
1969 Poulett. S. (Attributed) PAUL VAN SOMMER. Head of
girl in jewelled dress, dated 1616, 31×25     3,500
  S. School of GUILLIM STRETES. Edward VI, half-length,
  inscribed, but probably posthumous, 21½×16½   4,500
  S. GERRIT VAN HONTHORST. Laughing man with violin,
  31¼×24¼              3,500
  C. (Attributed) GEERAETS. Lady Montague of Bough-
  ton, oval, 29×23 (or possibly GILBERT PEAKE), £378 in 1930 1,890
    Called ENGLISH SCHOOL, early 17th century. Un-
  known lady with three children, oval, 95½×64½  3,570
  Bruguière. C. MARK GEERAETS. Lady Tanfield, whole-
  length, 110×60             1,995
1970 C. CORNELIS JONSON, Arthur Lord Capell with extensive
family. c. 1640, 63×102 (£120 in 1939)     28,350

LANDSCAPES, FIGURE COMPOSITIONS BY OTHER PAINTERS

1953 Henry Reitlinger. S. LAMBAERT LOMBARD (1506–1566).
Miracle of the loaves and fishes (see 1965), £84 in 1929,
40½×44              1,520
  BARTOLOMAEUS SPRANGER. Venus and Adonis, 51¾×
  43¾ (£126, 1923)           850
1959 Vienna. GERRIT VAN HONTHORST. Girl lighting a candle,
30¾×14, Sch.18,000+tax        2,750
1963 Heldring. S. ABEL GRIMMER. The 4 seasons, 1596,
round, 10½ in. (4)           23,000
1964 C. PAUL BRILL. River landscape on copper, 8½×11½ 3,990
  S. CORNELIS VROOM. Combat of the San Martin and
  Ark Royal. Greenwich Maritime Museum   4,000
1965 Spencer Churchill. S. LAMBAERT LOMBARD. Miracle of
the loaves and fishes (see 1953)      11,550
  C. SEBASTIAN VRANCX. Ploughing and sowing, a pair,
  10¾×14¼             4,410

966   S.  Jan van Kessel.  The four elements, copper, 27 × 34   £
                                       4 for  6,800

967   Murray Usher.  S.  Jacob van de Gheyn.  II.  Mountainous landscape, pen and wash drawing, 11½ × 15¼    6,500

      C.  Maerten van Cleve.  Village with dancing peasants in manner of Jan Breughel, 22 × 39 (£39 18s., bought in, 1923)  19,950

      S.  (Attributed) Abel Grimmer.  Woody landscape and river, 30 × 41    4,100

      C.  Adam Willaerts.  The Dutch fleet at Amboyna, 1623, 37 × 47½    3,990

968   C.  Pieter Casteels.  Birds in a park, 1725, 59 × 46½    3,150

      Lord Ilford.  C.  Tobias Verhaecht.  Winter landscape with travellers, 19½ × 25½    3,990

      S.  Jan de Bisschop.  Panorama of Rome, pen and wash drawing, 28½ × 40    3,100

      Pieter Casteels.  Birds in a park, 60½ × 65¾    5,400

      Phillips, son and Neale.  Lucas Gassel.  Roundel landscape, 8¼ in. diam.    5,800

      S.  Sebastian Vrancx (with Joost de Momper).  Landscape, with village and chateau, 24 × 41    11,500

      Craven.  S.  Pieter Casteels.  Ducks, birds and rabbits, a pair, 29 × 46½           2 for  10,000

      Spaniel and poultry en suite with above    4,200

      Adam Willaerts.  Arrival of Elector Palatine at Flushing, 1623, 35 × 61¼    8,000

      C.  Hendrik Vroom.  Ships of the Spanish Netherlands, c. 1600, 18 × 32½    2,730

      Vansittart.  S.  Anon (called 'Danckerts').  Perspective view of Denham Palace, c. 1700, 39½ × 48½    3,800

      Lempertz, Cologne.  Roelant Savery,  mountainous landscape, 18 × 36, DM70,000+tax    8,350

969   Berhman.  S.  Abel Grimmer.  The months of the year, series of roundel panels, dated 1599, 5 in. diam.,   12 for  35,000

      S.  Adam van Breen.  Breughelesque winter landscape with numerous skaters, dated 1602, 15 × 19¼    8,500

      Paul Brill.  Landscape with St Jérôme praying, copper, 10 × 12¼    6,600

      Granville.  S.  Sebastian Vrancx.  Set of small landscapes with figures, 10¼ × 14¼           4 for  8,200

      S.  Willem van Haecht.  Royal visit to the van der Geest gallery, dated 1628, 40¾ × 54¾    24,000

      C.  Abraham Govaerts.  Landscape with river, waggon etc., in the Breughel style, 19 × 28¾    4,200

      Gillis van Coninxloo.  Wooded landscape with shepherd, 20 × 27    4,410

# MYLES BIRKET FOSTER. 1825–1899

The end of the Second World War was celebrated by Midland industrialists like the end of the First—with an orgy of Birket Foster buying. The *Weald of Surrey* made £2,152 10s. in somewhat battered pounds, a reminder of 1918–24 when at least five Birket Foster watercolours achieved four-figure prices. But in 1961 the *Weald of Surrey* fell to £577 10s. Eight years passed before there was another four-figure Birket Foster, but the highest price now meant no more than £240 in 1920 terms. What had happened to the king of the nostalgia market? Sentimentalized rural England was clearly still in demand in 1968 when Shayer's village merriments sold for close on £8,000.

The trouble is that these highly finished watercolours are *too* pretty. *Victoriana* are more admired when they are so hideous that they must surely hide a deeper significance than a drawer-full of lavender-scented memories. The contents of the drawer are not to be transferred to the wall because there are no Joneses they could live up to. There are mobiles at the bottom of my garden.

| | | £ |
|---|---|---|
| 1961 | C.   The Weald of Surrey (£2,152 10s. in 1945), 24×48 | 577 10s. |
| 1962 | Brackett, Tunbridge Wells.   Large landscape | 640 |
| | Kaye.   C.   Holmwood Common, 13×28 | 178 10s. |
| 1965 | S.   Bass's cottage at Whitley, 11×13½ | 29 |
| | Farmyard scene | 200 |
| 1966 | Beharrell.   C.   Eton Chapel from the river, 13×27½ | 577 10s. |
| | British Printing Corp.   C.   40 lots £8,487 3s. | |
| | Church of S. Giorgio Maggiore, Venice, 23×35¾ | 682 10s. |
| | Dolphin Bridge, Grand Canal, 8¼×12 | 525 |
| | Hop-pickers, Farnham, 28×41 | 525 |
| | Spring Time, 11¾×21½ | 472 10s. |
| | Expectation, 13¼×27½ | 462 |
| | British Printing Corporation 2nd sale, 57 lots made £6,381 18s. | |
| | Summer landscape, 1860, 11¼×25 | 504 |
| | Henley on Thames, 13½×28 | 325 10s. |
| 1968 | S.   Dairymaid driving cattle in landscape, 14×23½ | 320 |
| | C.   The timber waggon, 29½×25½ (£577 5s. in 1917, £787 10s. in 1918).   First 4-figure price for Birket Foster since 1945 | 1,155 |
| | Hall Place Estates.   S.   Set of Thames side scenes, each 4×5½, mounted on a screen                        20 for | 5,400 |
| 1969 | Kenrick.   C.   Children angling from a punt, 14×24 | 997 10s. |

# JEAN HONORÉ FRAGONARD.  1732–1806

'he Erickson Rembrandt at $2,300,000 in 1961 was less of a shock to accepted alues than the Erickson Fragonard, *La Liseuse* at $875,000. Such prices were for aphael and Rembrandt, perhaps for Cézanne, but not for this slight, too conciously elegant thing. Of course the price was artificial, one of those meaningss boat-races between the benefactors of the two national collections of the J.S.A., in which anything can happen. Yet historically there was plenty of recedent. In 1961 the memoirs of the art dealer, René Gimpel, had not yet ppeared. If they had been available, the price might have surprised a great deal ss. So completely do Gimpel's accounts of the *ultimate* prices of the French 8th century school alter the balance that I have taken the list back to the eginning of the century in order to get the record straight. Fragonard, it must e realized, was the Gainsborough of the French 18th century school. Perhaps e should be counted the better painter of the two, but his work was never oosted so much as the famous *Blue Boy*, nor was his subsequent market-fall as reat as Gainsborough's. All the same, some of Gimpel's recorded prices are evealing. An oval portrait, *Mlle Guimard*, was sold to John W. Simpson in 1906 or the equivalent of £250,000 in 1970 money. *Le billet doux* was sold to Jules Bache in 1919 for the equivalent even of a little more. As late as 1927, when 'arisian taste was already beginning to wobble, Joseph Bardac paid a sum to be quated with £102,000 for *La Femme à la Charette*.

There was no sequel to *La Liseuse* at $875,000. Small and light works, the best he salerooms could offer in 1962–9, varied between £22,000 and £36,000. As o Fragonard's dashing rococo pen-and-wash drawings which the Goncourt rothers had helped to make fashionable a century earlier, £7,000 does not eem much for the year 1961. But there is no reason to suppose that *Le Taureau :nragé* would make much more in 1970, whereas the price, made by *La danse* in 929, was equivalent to £24,000.

| | | £ |
|---|---|---|
| 898 | Bought by J. Pierpont Morgan from Agnew, the ten panels —called *L'amour de la jeunesse*, for £64,000 (see 1915); cost per panel works out at | 6,400 |
| 899 | Bought by Ernest Crosnier from R. Gimpel, *La Liseuse*, 32 × 25½ (see 1912, 1961), 85,000 francs at 25 to the £ | 3,400 |
| 904 | Bought by Crosnier from Gimpel, the Duc de Fezensac's pair of decorative panels          2 for | 26,000 |
| 905 | Crosnier.  Paris.  Le billet doux (see 1919), 420,000 francs +tax | 18,500 |
| | Resold by Gimpel to Joseph Bardac, 700,000 francs | 28,000 |
| 906 | Bought by John W. Simpson from Gimpel, Paris, two oval portraits | |
| | Mlle Guimard, $145,000 | 29,040 |
| | Mlle Colombe, $82,250 | 16,920 |

| | | | £ |
|---|---|---|---|
| 1907 | Sedelmeier. Paris. Le réveil de Venus, 125,000 francs+ tax | | 5,520 |
| 1912 | Roussel. Paris. La Liseuse (see 1899, 1961) 165,000 francs +tax | | 7,280 |
| | L'éducation tout fait (see 1924), 230,000 francs+tax | | 10,000 |
| | Doucet. Paris. Sacrifice au Minotaure (£212 in 1880), 360,000 francs+tax | | 15,830 |
| | Berwind. N.Y., buys from Gimpel la mère vertueuse, $85,000 | | 17,500 |
| 1915 | Bought by H. C. Frick from Duveen 10 panels, L'amour de la jeunesse (see 1898) for 1 million dollars. Price per panel | | 20,550 |
| 1918 | Bought by Berwind, N.Y. from R. Gimpel. *Les deux soeurs* | | 40,000 |
| 1919 | Bought by Jules Bache from R. Gimpel, *Le billet doux* (see 1905), $250,000 at 4·86 to £. Metropolitan Museum, N.Y. | | 51,500 |
| 1920 | Beurdeley. Paris. Venus and Cupid | About | 5,000 |
| 1923 | Salomon. N.Y. Mlle Colombe as Venus, $35,000 | | 8,700 |
| 1924 | Wildenstein, Paris, asking for *l'éducation tout fait* (see 1912) according to R. Gimpel, 1·5 million francs then at 80 to the £ | | 19,400 |
| 1927 | Bardac. Paris. The regions of the world, 615,000 francs +tax at 125 to the £ | 4 for | 6,170 |
| | Le songe du mendiant, 500,000 francs+tax | About | 5,000 |
| | Bought by Bardac. La femme à la charette (from Gimpel) 2½ million francs | | 20,400 |
| 1933 | Lederlin. Paris. Le lever, 120,000 francs at 84 to the £+ tax | | 1,800 |
| 1937 | Burat. Paris. Rosalie Fragonard. Fr150,000 at 115 to the £+tax | | 1,585 |
| | Boecke. C. Portrait, Mlle Gerard | | 4,095 |
| 1938 | Faucher-Magnan. Paris. Le verrou (see 1964) Fr340,000 +tax | | 3,210 |
| 1952 | Potocki. S. L'homme a l'epée | | 7,500 |
| | Cognacq. Paris. Jeune fille aux chiens, 10·6 million old francs+tax at 980 to the £ | | 12,954 |
| | Jeune fille lisant, 3·7 million old francs+tax | | 4,600 |
| 1955 | Sotheby. S. La folie and l'amour, oval, 17×13 | 2 for | 4,500 |
| 1959 | Chanter. S. Le philosophe, oval, 22×28¼ | | 13,000 |
| | Oil study for la fontaine d'amour | | 3,200 |
| 1960 | Gould. S. L écurie de l'âne, 14×17½ | | 3,500 |
| | Penard y Fernandez. Paris. L'heureux ménage, roundel, 14 in. diam., FN160,000+tax | | 11,663 |
| | Paris. Hide and seek, 19¼×24½, FN150,000+tax | | 13,145 |
| 1961 | Erickson. N.Y. La liseuse, 32×25½ (£3,400 in 1899, £7,280 in 1912) $875,000. National Gallery, Washington | | 312,500 |

£

| | | |
|---|---|---|
| )62 | Paris. Venus enlevée par les amours, FN59,000+tax | 5,150 |
| | N.Y. Jeune fille au collier de perles (£400 in 1872) $100,000 | 35,700 |
| )63 | Gimpel Exors. C. Le repas de l'enfant, 24×29 | 8,190 |
| | S. La jardinière, 34×39 | 36,000 |
| )64 | S. La verrou, 10¼×12¾ (£3,210 in 1938) | 27,000 |
| | La sultane, 17¾×14½ | 25,000 |
| )65 | Hahnloser. S. Girl reading a letter, incomplete sketch, 13×10½ | 4,000 |
| )66 | Hyer. S. L'amour vainqueur, oval cupid panel, 24½×16 | 5,500 |
| )67 | Hugh Rose. S. Venus binding Cupid's wings, 7¾×12 | 34,500 |
| )68 | Kaplan. S. (with Francois Vincent). The drawing lesson, 22½×28 | 3,800 |
| | Paris. (Attributed) Le berger souriant, 36¾×29¼, FN260,000+tax | 24,260 |
| )69 | James. S. La liseuse, 12¼×8¾ | 33,000 |
| | Fribourg. S. Head, Mlle Griois, 21¾×18¾, bought in at | 22,000 |
| | C. Le repos de Diane, 33×48½, bought in | 27,300 |

### DRAWINGS

| | | |
|---|---|---|
| )94 | De Goncourt. Paris. La culbute, 16,500 francs+tax | 724 |
| | Les cascatelles, 17,500 francs+tax | 770 |
| '96 | Josse. Paris. The dancing lesson | 436 |
| | La verrou (£180 in 1880, £960 in 1905) | 324 |
| 05 | Beurdeley. Paris. La verrou (see 1880, 1894) | 960 |
| | La rêveuse (£3,165 in 1952) | 880 |
| | Crosnier. Paris. Le taureau echappé, pen and wc, 32,500 francs+tax | 1,420 |
| 08 | Knowles. C. Entrance to a park, sepia wash | 693 |
| 09 | Doisteau. Paris. Jupiter and Danae, sepia wash (£4,000 1959) | 1,604 |
| 12 | Carcano. Paris. Le sacrifice au minotaure (£2 10s. in 1814, see 1914), 47,500 francs+tax | 1,904 |
| | La renvenue, sepia wash, 64,750 francs+tax | 2,840 |
| | Le songe du mendiant, sepia wash | 1,280 |
| | La femme à la fontaine | 1,300 |
| 14 | Hodgkins. Paris. Le sacrifice au Minotaure, 12½×15¾ (see 1912, 1961) | 1,760 |
| 25 | Lehmann. Paris. Le terrasse | 3,600 |
| 29 | Straus. Paris. La danse, sepia wash | 4,830 |
| 35 | Faucher Magnan. S. Le taureau | 1,100 |
| | La sultane | 780 |

£

| | | £ |
|---|---|---|
| 1937 | Greffulhe. S. Tivoli gardens, sepia wash | 2,900 |
| 1938 | Mortimer Schiff. C. Tivoli gardens, sanguine | 398 |
| 1952 | Cognacq. Paris. La rêveuse (£880 in 1905), 3·1 million old francs+tax | 3,860 |
| 1956 | S. Le taureau enragé (£7,000 in 1961) | 1,600 |
| 1959 | Chanter. S. La resistance inutile, pen and sepia wash, 9×13¾ | 4,500 |
| | Danae and Jupiter (£1,604 in 1909) | 4,000 |
| | Les pétards | 2,400 |
| | Sketch book, 141 pages | 16,500 |
| | Others at £1,000 to £2,400 | |
| | Paris. Le repos dans le foret, sanguine | 2,152 |
| 1960 | S. The kiss in the smoke | 1,700 |
| | Paris. Le galant surpris | 1,756 |
| 1961 | Paris. The artist's servant, sanguine | 4,350 |
| | S. Sacrifice au minotaure, wc and chalks (£2 10s. in 1814, £1,940 in 1912) | 5,500 |
| | Murat. S. Le taureau enragé (£1,600 in 1956) pencil and wash, 14½×19¼ | 7,000 |
| | Temple of Venus at Tivoli, chalk and wash, 13½×17½ | 4,800 |
| 1963 | Paris. 'Dites donc s'il vous plait', wc, FN76,000+tax | 6,120 |
| | C. The reading lesson | 1,890 |
| | Fribourg. S. Boucher d'Argis in prison, pen | 3,200 |
| | Unknown man holding book, pen | 2,600 |
| 1964 | Tattevin. S. Jupiter and Danae, sepia wash | 1,800 |
| 1965 | S. Park of the villa d'Este, sanguine | 2,300 |
| 1966 | Paris. L'éducation d'un chien, 10×14¼, sepia wash | 4,080 |
| 1967 | Paris. Essaim d'amours, pen and wash, 9½×14½ (FN30,000 +tax) | 2,382 |
| 1968 | C. Cavalry officer in action, pen and wash with pencil, 10¾×7½ Bought in at | 1,890 |
| | S. La bonne mère, elaborate gouache, oval, 16½×13½ | 5,000 |
| 1969 | Kieffer. Paris. Arch of Titus, Rome, red chalk, FN23,000 +tax | 2,170 |
| 1970 | Auctions A.G. Basel. 'S'il n'était pas Fidèle,' sanguine, FS65,000+10% tax | 6,875 |

PIERO DELLA FRANCESCA (attributed). (*See* Italian School, Cent
15th–16th centuries)

FRANCESCO FRANCIA. (*See* Italian School, Northern)

SAM FRANCIS. (*See* Abstract Painters, American)

# FRENCH SCHOOL
## 15th and 16th centuries

)60 Paris. LUDOLPHE DE CHARTREUX. Baptism of Christ, £ altar panel, *c.* 1480, FN320,000+tax — 27,400

Tibor de Budai. C. FRANÇOIS CLOUET. Portrait of Jacques de St André, 9½×7¾ — 4,890

)63 Cintas. N.Y. FRANÇOIS CLOUET. Duc d'Alençon, 12¼×9½, $13,000 — 4,645

Thyssen-Bornemisza. S. AVIGNON SCHOOL. Pietà — 10,500

)65 Wildenstein. N.Y. Private sale to National Gallery, Dublin. AVIGNON SCHOOL, *c.* 1400. Annunciation with St Stephen and two donors — 220,000

Spencer Churchill. C. CORNEILLE DE LYON. Male portrait, 6½×5 (£4 4s. in 1832) — 13,360

Reichmann. S. AVIGNON SCHOOL. St Hubert, 64½× 47½ — 3,500

Guggenheim Foundation. S. MASTER OF MOULINS. Head of a girl in a veil holding a pansy, 11½×8¾ — 14,000

)66 Mountain. C. UNKNOWN. Bishop and two kneeling donors, part of triptych, *c.* 1450, 21×12 — 3,150

)67 C. Attributed NICOLAS FROMENT. Portraits of man and wife, much restored, 15×9 — 2 for 7,350

Watney. C. CORNEILLE DE LYON. Portrait of the chancellor Henart, 6¼×5 — 11,550

)68 C. FRANÇOIS CLOUET. French nobleman, *c.* 1550, miniature, 1¼ in. — 630

Lempertz. Cologne. LUDOVICO BREA (Avignon School). Praying monk, triptych panel, DM167,000+tax — 19,135

### DRAWINGS

)56 S. MASTER OF MOULINS. Portrait head in leadpoint (Louvre) — 4,800

)63 S. FOUCQUET SCHOOL. Donkey attacked by lions, pen, 5×7 — 1,300

)66 S. Coronation of Charles VIII, pen drawing of *c.* 1500, 8½×5¾ — 3,000

# FRENCH SCHOOL
## 17th and 18th centuries

(See separate entries for Boucher, Chardin, Claude, David, Fragonard, Greuze Lancret, Nattier, Pater, Poussin, Quentin-Latour, Robert, Vigée-Lebrun Watteau.)

Some earlier prices for the paintings of François Drouais suggest that most o these painters have not yet recovered their early 20th century market status One exception, however, is Largillierre. In 1959 M. Maurice Rheims con sidered that the portraits of Rigaud and Largillierre had fallen since 1920 be cause they mated badly with the painting styles of the last eighty years. 'On to of that, add their size, their frames, the severity of their faces.' That was befor the sale of *La belle Strasbourgeoise*. Rheims in 1959 reckoned the value o Largillierre's portraits at no more than £350 to £1,500. But such was the im pact of the sale of *La belle Strasbourgeoise* in 1963 that in the following yea three of the Throckmorton family portraits had to be bought in, because th first of them had already cleared as much money as the trustees were entitled t raise.

There is something remarkable in a painter whose 'ceiling' price rises fron £1,470 to £145,000 in two years. Nor is there anything about Largillierre fruity style which commends itself so much to the spirit of this age that th City of Strasbourg has to pay such a price in order to secure this townswoma in a very large hat. Saleroom rivalries have their own mysteries, but a greate mystery remains, inasmuch as the new prices for Largillierre continue to hold whereas there is no sign of the same thing happening to Rigaud who was on of the highest feed portrait painters that ever lived. Possibly the sudden rise o portraits by Sir Peter Lely in 1968 may be a precedent for Rigaud.

| | | £ |
|---|---|---|
| LOUIS LÉOPOLD BOILLY. 1761–1847 | | |
| 1948 | C.   Lady at a table | 2,730 |
| 1952 | Cognacq.   Paris.   La crainte enfantine (1902 £585, 1907 £568), 1·1 million old francs+tax | 1,372 |
| 1960 | C.   Portrait, Mlle Gérard, $15\frac{1}{4} \times 12\frac{1}{2}$ (see 1968) | 1,995 |
| | Lady Juliet Duff.   C.   Girl in a grey satin dress, $16 \times 13$ | 1,575 |
| | Gould.   S.   Le deux soeurs, $17\frac{3}{4} \times 14\frac{1}{2}$ | 1,800 |
| 1961 | Paris.   Réunion dans un parc, $32 \times 22\frac{3}{4}$, FN41,000+tax | 3,590 |
| 1963 | Fribourg.   S.   La dame aux roses, $28\frac{1}{4} \times 22\frac{3}{4}$ | 8,000 |
| 1965 | Warde.   C.   The interrupted supper, a pair, $13\frac{3}{4} \times 17\frac{1}{2}$ | |
| | 2 for | 3,900 |
| | Spencer Churchill.   C.   Ivory crucifix on a wall, $24\frac{3}{4} \times 18\frac{1}{4}$ | 12,600 |
| 1966 | Sarah Young.   C.   Self-portrait at an easel, $19\frac{1}{2} \times 14$ | 1,260 |
| 1968 | Eliot Hodgkin.   S.   Chalk study for 'la partie de billard', $9\frac{1}{2}$ in. square, 1807 | 1,250 |

£

| | | |
|---|---|---|
| 1968 | C. Mlle Gérard and two children (see 1960) | 5,250 |
| | S. Little girl in turban with Empire tabouret, 28 × 23 | 6,200 |
| 1970 | Paris. La lettre or le petit messager, FN170,000+tax | 14,800 |

## PHILIPPE DE CHAMPAGNE. 1602–1674

| | | |
|---|---|---|
| 1963 | Ryle. S. Portrait of Colbert, 29½ × 22¾ | 7,500 |
| | Hasson. C. The Presentation, 43 × 34 | 7,875 |
| | Sterling of Keir. S. St Theresa, 18¾ × 15¼ | 9,000 |
| 1965 | Williams. C. Adoration of the shepherds, 42 × 33½ | 6,300 |
| 1968 | Werner. S. The Abbess Marie-Jacqueline Arnaud, 1654, 21¼ × 17½ | 4,800 |
| | Kaplan. S. Cardinal Mazarin, whole-length in room, 21¼ × 15 | 3,000 |

## FRANÇOIS DROUAIS. 1727–1775

| | | |
|---|---|---|
| 1882 | Arbuthnot. C. Princess Clotilde of Sardinia as a child | 162 15s. |
| 1903 | Vaile. C. Portrait, Mme Du Barry | 2,100 |
| 1919 | Sold to E. J. Berwind by René Gimpel. The scholar, and the Little Girl with a cat, $200,000     2 for | 41,250 |
| 1923 | Sold to Jules Bache by Wildenstein. Child holding a flower, $60,000 at 4·40 to the £ | 13,365 |
| 1926 | Bischoffsheim. C. The house of cards, and Blowing bubbles, a pair of ovals, bought by Gimpel     2 for | 13,650 |
| 1927 | Harcourt. C. The children of Count Bethune | 8,825 |
| 1952 | Cognacq. Paris. Enfant à la pêche, 3·2 million old francs +tax at 980 to the £ | 4,575 |
| 1960 | Paris. Le jeune élève, 22½ × 19½, FN37,000+tax | 3,225 |
| | C. The birds' nest, oval, 1770, 36 × 43 | 2,100 |
| 1961 | Duke of Leeds. S. Amelia, Baroness Conyers, 27½ × 23 | 1,600 |
| 1962 | Harcourt. C. Oval portrait, Mme Du Barry in male dress, 27 × 23 | 17,850 |
| 1965 | Margadale. C. Duc de Maine, 93 × 62 | 1,155 |
| 1968 | Paris. Girl in a straw hat, 1760, 24½ × 20½, FN55,000+tax | 5,160 |

## GEORGES DE LA TOUR. –1652

| | | |
|---|---|---|
| 1968 | S. Girl with brazier, nocturne, 25¾ × 21 | 25,000 |
| | Bought in Paris by National Gallery, Dublin, the Image of St Alexis, variant on the picture at Nancy     About | 100,000 |

## NICOLAS DE LARGILLIERRE 1656–1746

| | | |
|---|---|---|
| 1958 | Urquhart. S. Portrait of a lady, dated 1740, 35½ × 28 | 1,100 |
| 1961 | C. Duchesse de Rohan, 30½ × 24½ | 1,470 |
| 1962 | Bellairs. S. Bouquet of summer flowers, 1677, 41 × 35 | 5,600 |

| 1963 | Paris. Alloys de Theys d'Herculais, 45½×49, FN54,000+ tax | £ 4,490 |
|---|---|---|

Fitzgerald. S. La Belle Strasbourgeoise, 1703, 55¾×41. Bought by Strasbourg Museum (£42 in 1770, 1,510,000 francs or about £12,000 at the Côty sale, 1936)  145,000

| 1964 | Throckmorton. C. Elizabeth Throckmorton as an abbess, 1729, 31¾×25½ | 65,100 |
|---|---|---|
| | Anne Throckmorton as a nun, 31¾×25½, bought in | 39,900 |
| | Sir R. Throckmorton in armour ,53¾×41½, bought in | 57,750 |
| | Another English nun, 31¾×25½, bought in | 8,400 |
| 1965 | Inglis. C. Self-portrait, half-length, 36×28½ | 7,350 |
| 1968 | C. Mme de Jussaud and two daughters, 54×40½ | 15,750 |

MATHIEU LE NAIN. 1607–1677. LOUIS LE NAIN. 1593–1648

| 1952 | Cognacq. Paris. Petits danseurs (£790 in 1913) 3·7 million old francs and tax | 4,480 |
|---|---|---|
| 1959 | N.Y. (Mathieu) Peasants at a well, 20×24, $6,000 | 2,140 |
| 1960 | Rhodes. C. (Mathieu) Pietà | 66,090 |
| 1964 | C. Peasant group, attributed | 3,045 |
| 1966 | C. (Louis) Holy Family, 52×44 (Vienna, 1906, £70) | 47,250 |

NICOLAS LEPICIÉ. 1735–1784

| 1961 | Paris. La politesse interessée, 1772, 16½×12¾, FN33,500+ tax | 2,925 |
|---|---|---|
| | Les accords à la promesse approuvée, 18¾×22¾, FN36,000 +tax | 3,136 |
| 1963 | Fribourg. S. Young girl drawing, 17¼×14¼, oval | 2,000 |
| 1968 | J. de Rothschild. Paris. Interior of a douane, 39½×64¾ | 11,970 |
| | Pen and wash study for the same | 1,200 |
| | L'heureuse famille, 24×29½ | 3,855 |
| 1969 | Kieffer. Paris. La jeune mère, pen and wash, FN23,000+ tax | 2,170 |

JEAN BAPTISTE LE PRINCE. 1734–1781

| 1962 | Versailles. L'amant surpris, a pair, 12×9½, pen and wc FN35,000+tax | 2 for 3,050 |
|---|---|---|
| 1968 | Prince de Ligne. S. Le concert russe, 1766, 28×22½ | 11,000 |
| | La chiromancienne, 1766, 28×22½, both painted for Catherine the Great of Russia | 8,000 |

JEAN MICHEL MOREAU OR MOREAU LE JEUNE. 1741–1814

| 1959 | Chanter. S. N'ayez pas peur, drawing for the well known engraving, pen and wash, 16½×8¾, 1775 | 7,000 |
|---|---|---|

£

| | | |
|---|---|---|
| 1965 | Fribourg. S. La soirée de St Cloud, pen and wash, 9¼×13 | 2,250 |
| 1967 | C. Les adieux, pen and wash drawing *after* the engraving, 10½×7½ | 787 10s. |

JEAN BAPTISTE OUDRY. 1686–1755

| | | |
|---|---|---|
| 1960 | Paris. Nature morte, 52×38, FN55,000+tax | 4,685 |
| | Motion. S. Gazelle, baited by three hounds, 1745, 70½×81¼ | 8,800 |
| 1961 | Paris. l'hallali du cerf, 1725, 43¼×64½, FN24,000+tax | 2,092 |
| 1963 | Paris. Comédiens italiens, 26×34, FN90,000+tax | 7,860 |

GABRIEL DE ST AUBIN. 1724–1780

| | | |
|---|---|---|
| 1923 | S. Le parade chez Nicolet, pen and wash, numerous figures | 1,700 |
| 1959 | S. Femme lisant, mixed-media drawing, 8¾×6¾, Rikjs- museum | 1,100 |
| 1963 | Fribourg. S. L'academie particulière, oils, 7×10¾ | 5,000 |
| | Guingette auz environs, pen and wash, 10×7¾ | 1,800 |
| 1967 | Rothschild. S. Printed catalogue of Julienne sale, 1767, with numerous marginal drawings (£4,000 in 1959) | 5,000 |
| 1969 | Boerlag-Koenigs. S. Young lady watching a procession, standing on a calèche, pencil touched with other media, 6¾×9 | 2,800 |

LOUIS TOCQUÉ. 1696–1772

| | | |
|---|---|---|
| 1961 | Erickson. N.Y. Mlle Suzanne le Mercier, 32×25½, $20,000 | 7,140 |

# FRENCH SCHOOL

## Minor Impressionist and Post-Impressionist painters

Of the many contemporary followers of the Impressionists a few became decidedly fashionable in the later 1960s. The selection is not easily explicable. Some who had quite a respectable standing in the first quarter of the present century, for instance Cazin, Caillebotte, Lebourg, Lepine, Loiseaux, Maufra, Serusier and le Sidaner, barely reached the £6,000 level at the end of the 1960s, not even the equivalent of £700 in their own day. On the other hand, Henri Edmond Cross, whose name meant little a few years ago, quite suddenly became as dear as Bonnard and dearer than Signac, the second generation Impressionists. At the same time, Guillaumin, Maximilien Luce and the Belgian painter, Theo van Rysselberghe, reached the £15,000–£40,000 class. It must be said of all four painters that their works only made high prices when they

imitated the *pointilliste* style. Guillaumin's Monet-like rocks and Luce's indus-
trial subjects made very much less. It seems that the public of the 1960s liked
nothing so much as an overworked gimmick, and this was something these
painters had made full use of. Thus Cross's *Pointe de la Galère* made more in the
saleroom than anything by Bonnard, Vuilliard or Signac. Cross carried Seurat's
highly laborious technique beyond the mathematical formularism of the
original without any of its monumental quality. This banale decoration, for it
is nothing more, recalls those knowing colour-printed paper screens which
could once be found in the 'arts and crafts' section of the leading department
stores. As an historical aberration, the purchase should rank high, seeing that it
cost only a little less than Botticelli's *Marriage feast of Nastagio*.

Valtat and Marquet belong to a later generation, both having survived the
Second World War. The former painted in a style half-way between Bonnard
and *les Fauves*. The latter owed very little to the *avant-garde*, but his fresh
looking and enticing harbour scenes have little depth to them, for all that they
can make from £10,000 to £18,500 on occasion.

GUSTAVE CAILLEBOTTE. 1848–1894         £

| | | | | £ |
|---|---|---|---|---|
| 1958 | S. | Lady in black on sofa, 1882, $31\frac{1}{2}\times25\frac{1}{2}$ (see 1965) | | 60 |
| 1963 | C. | Tree-lined river bank, $16\frac{1}{4}\times25$ | | 472 10s. |
| 1965 | N.Y. | Lady in black on sofa, 1882, $31\frac{1}{2}\times25\frac{1}{2}$ (see 1958), $8,250 | | 2,945 |
| 1966 | C. | L'homme au chapeau haut de forme, $21\frac{1}{2}\times15$ | | 1,890 |
| | | Le peintre Morot dans son atelier, $17\frac{1}{4}\times21\frac{1}{4}$ | | 2,100 |
| 1967 | S. | Vase de lilas, $25\frac{1}{2}\times21\frac{1}{4}$ | | 3,600 |
| 1968 | N.Y. | Peintre dans son atelier, $19\times21\frac{3}{4}$, $10,000 | | 4,160 |
| 1969 | Josefowitz. | S. Vue d'une rivière, $28\frac{3}{4}\times23\frac{1}{2}$ | | 5,200 |
| | Paris. | L'allée du parc, 1886, FN30,000+tax | About | 2,800 |
| | S. | Jardin à la campagne, *c.* 1882, $25\frac{1}{2}\times21\frac{1}{2}$ | | 5,500 |
| | | Bord de rivière, $41\frac{1}{2}\times59$ | | 6,500 |

HENRI EDMOND CROSS. 1856–1910

| 1960 | Paris. | La cueillette des fleurs, $13\frac{1}{4}\times9\frac{1}{2}$, FN8,500+tax | 730 |
|---|---|---|---|
| 1962 | Paris. | Lac du Bois de Boulogne, $23\frac{1}{2}\times32\frac{1}{2}$, FN82,000+tax | 7,140 |
| | S. | Canal à Venise, $21\frac{1}{2}\times17\frac{3}{4}$ | 1,600 |
| 1964 | Versailles. | Grand canal de Venise, $14\frac{3}{4}\times24$, FN90,000 | 7,235 |
| | S. | Portrait du paysan, $15\frac{1}{2}\times12\frac{1}{4}$ | 500 |
| | | Paysage de forêt, wc and charcoal, $14\frac{3}{4}\times22\frac{3}{4}$ | 1,300 |
| 1965 | N.Y. | Village en Hollande, gouache, $8\frac{3}{4}\times13$, $2,500 | 886 |
| | S. | Le verger, $25\frac{1}{2}\times31\frac{3}{4}$ | 2,350 |
| 1968 | Roudinesco. | N.Y. Antibes, matin, 1908, $32\times25\frac{1}{2}$, $70,000 | 29,165 |
| | | Femme en violet, 1896, $24\times21\frac{1}{2}$, $24,000 (bought in, 1970 at £8,000) | 10,000 |

| | | £ |
|---|---|---|
| 1968 | N.Y. Haleurs de filets de pêche, 1899, 23×32, $40,000 | 16,665 |
| | Bluestein. N.Y. La route sur la côte, 1907, 28¾×26¾, $56,000 | 23,335 |
| 1969 | S. La pointe de la Galère, 1892, 25×36 | 91,000 |
| | Le faux-poivrier, 29×36¼ | 38,000 |
| | C. Falaises à St Palais, 22¼×27½ | 5,775 |
| | N.Y. Paysage et baie, *c.* 1885, 29½×39½, $13,500 | 5,660 |
| | Fribourg. N.Y. Venice, sailing boats at the Dogana, 14½×23¾, *c.* 1903, $26,000 | 10,825 |
| | S. Mediterranée, vent d'Est, 23×32 | 16,500 |

Jean-Baptiste Armand Guillaumin. 1841–1927

| | | |
|---|---|---|
| 1957 | S. Au bord de la mer, 20¾×28¼ | 280 |
| | Farmyard and chestnut trees, 23×28 | 520 |
| 1958 | S. Forest clearing, 14½×20¼ | 230 |
| | Damienne, près d'Orsay, 1884, 11×23, pastel | 340 |
| 1959 | S. Chemin dans la Campagne, 17¾×21¼ | 1,400 |
| 1960 | N.Y. Rochers sur mer, 23½×28¾, $4,500 | 1,607 |
| 1963 | C. Stream in wooded landscape, 22¼×28¼ | 399 |
| 1964 | Mledek. S. Laboureur dans un paysage, 21¾×27¾ | 2,200 |
| 1965 | C. Boigneville, les Carneaux, 31×25¼ | 997 10*s.* |
| | La rivière tranquille, 25½×31¾ (see 1969) | 2,940 |
| | N.Y. Portrait de Martinez dans l'atelier, 1878, 35½×29½, $45,000 | 16,060 |
| 1966 | S. Paysans semant des haricots, 1888, 16½×22¾ | 3,400 |
| | C. Jeune fille à la robe rose, 32×25¾ | 2,310 |
| 1967 | C. Pruniers en fleur, 1895, 23½×28½ | 2,990 |
| 1968 | Hoentschel. S. Le point du jour, 1874, 21×25 | 19,000 |
| | Roudinesco. N.Y. Rochers au bord de la mer, 1906, 23¾×29, $18,000 (£5,200 in 1970) | 7,500 |
| | Rochers sur la plage, 29×36½, $18,000 | 7,500 |
| | Femme lisant, 25½×31¾, $37,000 | 15,415 |
| | C. Rochers oranges, 28½×23½ | 4,725 |
| 1969 | S. Crozant en Automne, 21×28½ | 5,000 |
| | Gelée blanche à Crozant, 29×39 | 9,500 |
| | Fribourg. N.Y. Windmills and canal, Villeneuve, 1902, 15×18½, $22,000 | 9,240 |
| | Paris. La Seine à Paris, FN450,000+tax | 41,997 |
| | S. La rivière tranquille, 25½×31¾ (see 1965) | 9,000 |
| | Pêcheur et voilier, Ivry, 1891, 18×21½ | 9,000 |
| | La lecture, portrait Mme Guillaumin, 32×25½ | 9,000 |
| | L'aqueduc à Arceuil, 1874, 19½×25 | 15,500 |
| | Déchargeurs, bord de la Seine, *c.* 1880, 22¾×28¼ | 9,500 |

| | Maximilien Luce. 1861–1918 | £ |
|---|---|---|
| 1960 | Paris. Bridge at Rouen, 29¼×36¾, FN12,200+tax | 1,062 |
| 1963 | N.Y. The Leuvehaven, Rotterdam (see 1969), 21½×31¾, $8,000 | 2,855 |
| 1965 | N.Y. Hautes fourneaux, Charleroi, 1896, 39½×31¾, $3,000 | 1,072 |
| 1966 | Motte. Geneva. Rue Réaumur, 18½×15¼, FS20,000+tax | 2,084 |
| 1967 | C. Rouen, 35½×31 | 1,680 |
| 1968 | S. Rue Réaumur, 1896, 18×15 | 3,000 |
| | Roudinesco. N.Y. La rue Mouffetard, 1896, 25½×31¾, $35,000 (bought in at £11,500, 1970) | 14,582 |
| | Port de Rouen, 1913, 32×39½, $19,000 | 7,915 |
| | S. Eglise de Gisors, 1898, 28¾×36 | 10,500 |
| | Port de Rouen, 1905, 28×35½ | 4,300 |
| 1969 | S. Vue de Merèville, 1903, 19½×29½ | 8,000 |
| | The Leuvehaven, Rotterdam, 21½×31¾ (see 1963) | 8,000 |
| | La Seine à Billancourt, 1910, 25×35½ | 4,000 |
| | Paysage, 1907, 19½×25 | 5,500 |
| | Mer et rochers, Agay, 21×25½ | 6,500 |
| | Village au bord d'un fleuve, 1896, 19×25 | 3,500 |
| | Près de Lavandou, Var, *c.* 1905, 25×35¾ | 10,500 |
| | Moulineux près d'Etampes, 1897, 15½×18½ | 4,500 |
| | La baignade, *c.* 1895, 25×31 | 3,600 |

| | Albert Marquet. 1875–1947 | |
|---|---|---|
| 1957 | S. La Rochelle, 24½×29¼ (£2,200 in 1965) | 1,300 |
| 1958 | S. Au Sable d'Olonne, 12¾×15¾ | 600 |
| | Place des Ternes, 24½×29½ | 1,200 |
| | Quai de la Rue Neuve, Marseille, 1918, 12½×15¾ | 800 |
| | Seine à Argenteuil, 1917, 19½×23½ | 750 |
| 1959 | Paris. Honfleur, le port, 3·05 million old francs+tax | 2,675 |
| | S. Porquerolles, 13¼×16½ | 1,900 |
| 1960 | Paris. Fuentarabia, 26×32½, FN37,100+tax | 3,240 |
| | Duveen. S. Nôtre Dame, 1918, 21×25 | 3,200 |
| | Paris. Marché aux pommes, 26×32½, FN55,000+tax | 4,840 |
| 1964 | C. Port de Marseille, 23½×28¾ | 4,725 |
| | S. Pont St Louis, 23×28¼ | 8,000 |
| | Les tentes, 1933, 19½×24 | 8,700 |
| | Au bord de la mer, Algérie, 25×31 | 10,000 |
| 1965 | Haft. Palm Beach. Jardin d'Algérie, 13¼×16¼, $9,500 | 3,400 |
| | N.Y. Docks à Hambourg, 25½×31¾, $21,000 | 7,500 |
| | Phillips. N.Y. Ile St Louis, 25×31½, $18,000 | 6,430 |
| | C. Port de Marseille, 29×36, 1916 | 7,350 |

| | | £ |
|---|---|---|
| 966 | Motte. Geneva. Port d'Alger, $8\frac{3}{4}\times10\frac{1}{2}$, FS22,000+tax | 2,105 |
| | Rue à Bougie, $20\times24\frac{1}{2}$, FS29,500+tax | 2,820 |
| | S. Alger, 1941, $14\frac{3}{4}\times21\frac{1}{2}$ | 2,800 |
| | C. Port d'Alger, 1921, $13\times16$ | 3,500 |
| 967 | S. Sidi Bou Said, 1923, $19\frac{3}{4}\times24$ | 5,600 |
| | Paris. St Jean de Luz, $26\times32\frac{1}{2}$, FN93,000+tax | 7,450 |
| 968 | Roudinesco. N.Y. Port d'Alger, 1925, $25\frac{3}{4}\times32$, $35,000 | 14,584 |
| | N.Y. Port du Havre, 1934, $19\frac{1}{2}\times24$, $17,000 | 7,060 |
| | S. Les meules, $30\frac{3}{4}\times43\frac{1}{2}$ | 6,200 |
| 969 | S. Port de la Rochelle, 1920, $19\frac{3}{4}\times24$ | 12,500 |
| | Guibert. C. Pont St Michel, neige, $25\frac{1}{2}\times31\frac{1}{2}$ (£44 in 1909) | 16,800 |
| | Fribourg. N.Y. Le balcon, *c.* 1945, $25\frac{1}{2}\times19\frac{3}{4}$, $26,000 | 10,925 |
| | Hayward Weir, N.Y. Le Pont-Neuf, Paris, $21\frac{1}{2}\times28\frac{3}{4}$, $24,000 | 10,082 |
| | Fribourg. Paris. Seine with Nôtre Dame, FN65,000+tax | 6,063 |
| | Paris. Le Pont-Neuf, Paris. FN162,000+tax | 15,040 |
| | Paris. Quai des Grands-Augustins, $24\times29\frac{1}{2}$, FN170,000 +tax | 15,730 |
| | La Seine à Paris, $26\times32\frac{1}{2}$, FN200,000+tax | 18,517 |
| | C. (Tokyo). Transporter bridge, Rouen, 1912, $26\times32$, 8·2 million yen | 9,780 |
| | S. (Tokyo). Le port d'Alger, $21\times26$, 7·7 million yen | 9,300 |
| | C. (Geneva). Route l'Apertier, Alger, 1924, $21\frac{1}{4}\times32$, FS100,000+tax | 10,045 |
| | S. Le remorqueur sur la Seine au Pec, *c.* 1930, $24\frac{3}{4}\times31$ | 18,500 |
| | Grand Canal, Venice, 1936, $23\frac{1}{2}\times28\frac{1}{2}$ | 13,500 |

THEO VAN RYSSELBERGHE (Belgium). 1862–1926

| | | |
|---|---|---|
| 962 | Paris. Jeune femme au buste nu, 1906, Pointillist style, $13\frac{1}{4}\times16\frac{1}{2}$, FN5,100+tax | 448 |
| 964 | N.Y. Elizabeth van Rysselberghe, lisant sur le balcon, $24\times19\frac{3}{4}$, $7,000 | 2,500 |
| 965 | N.Y. Trois fillettes, 1901, $21\times25$, $3,500 | 1,250 |
| 966 | Motte. Geneva. Paysage, 1906, $16\frac{3}{4}\times22\frac{1}{2}$, FS17,500+ tax | 1,665 |
| | N.Y. Jardin et arcades, $31\frac{3}{4}\times33$, $5,750 | 2,060 |
| | C. La mère du peintre, 1900, $45\frac{1}{4}\times34\frac{1}{2}$ | 2,940 |
| 969 | S. Whole-length portrait, Mme Dubois, 1888, $75\frac{1}{2}\times37\frac{1}{4}$ | 20,000 |
| | Les rochers, Belle Isle, 1888–90, $19\frac{1}{4}\times23\frac{1}{2}$ | 7,000 |
| | Paysage aux cyprès, Côte des Maures, $63\frac{1}{2}\times44\frac{1}{2}$ | 2,800 |
| | Girl reading with azalea on table, $23\times28$ | 5,500 |
| | Hutton. N.Y. Femme au collier rose, $37\frac{1}{2}\times32\frac{1}{2}$, $3,000 | 1,250 |
| | S. L'église sur le canal, 1906, $23\frac{1}{2}\times28$ | 5,600 |

| Louis Valtat. 1869–1952 | | £ |
|---|---|---|
| 1959 | Paris. Vase de fleurs, 24½×20, FN18,000+tax | 1,575 |
| 1964 | S. Vent de l'Est, 23×31¼ | 1,500 |
| | Bloch. Paris. Cargo à Ouistreham, 15½×22½, FN20,100 +tax | 1,648 |
| 1965 | N.Y. Danseuses des Folies Bergères, 39½×32, $7,250 | 2,580 |
| | Haft. Palm Beach. Paysage en Provence, 25×32, $5,750 | 2,060 |
| | Woman in red, 1906, 29×36½, $28,000 | 10,000 |
| | S. Grand vase de fleurs, 36×28½ | 1,700 |
| 1966 | Motte. Geneva. Jardin, 13¾×10, FS13,800+tax | 1,324 |
| 1967 | Paris. Le jardin à Choisel, 21½×29¼, FN27,000+tax | 2,160 |
| | N.Y. La pinède méditerranée, 1903, 38¼×51, $20,000 | 7,140 |
| 1968 | N.Y. Cagnes, double-sided painting, 17½×21, $6,500 | 2,293 |
| | Rochers au bord de la mer, 25½×32, $11,500 | 4,793 |
| | S. Les ecayères, Arcachon, 1896, 21×25 | 7,000 |
| | Le bateau-mouche, 1895, 20¾×25¼ | 8,500 |
| 1969 | S. Bol de pêches, 1906, 14¾×18 | 6,200 |
| | N.Y. Moulin rouge, *c.* 1900, 12¼×16¾ | 4,200 |
| | S. Le pommier sauvage, 23×28 | 4,800 |
| | La Parisienne, 1893, 86¾×67¾ | 12,500 |
| | Atelier, 1890, 67¾×86¾ | 7,800 |
| | Le vase bleu, *c.* 1928, 23¼×28¼ | 6,000 |
| 1970 | N.Y. Paysage, 1905, 24¾×32, $28,000 | 11,668 |

## ROGER DE LA FRESNAYE. (*See* Abstract Painters, Europe)

## WILLIAM FRITH. 1824–1909

On the proceeds of the famous *Railway Station*, commissioned in 1862, Frith earned 5,000 guineas including the exhibition and engraving rights, a feat that had only been surpassed by Holman Hunt's *Finding of Christ in the Temple*. It would be equivalent to close on £50,000 in 1970 and that might very easily be the present value of the picture. But Frith painted nothing else to equal *Derby Day*, *Ramsgate Sands* and the *Railway Station*. His habitual output took the form of costume-pieces, incredibly out of sentiment with their period, or anecdotes of painful banality, indifferently painted. The sudden rise (still far short of Frith's Victorian prime) which occurred in 1967, should not perhaps be taken too seriously. Those red cardinals that embellish the windows of Duke Street are much dearer than any of Frith's story-telling pictures, which look almost sensitive by comparison.

| | | |
|---|---|---|
| 1962 | Newton. S. The Road to Ruin, set of four, each 27½×32 | £ |
| | (£6,300 in 1878, £460 in 1919) | 4 for 7,200 |
| | C. Merry making in the olden time, 20×34 | 472 10s. |
| | Claude Duval, 1860, 28½×40 (£2,047 in 1873, £655 in 1910, £160 in 1946) | 450 |
| | S. The flower-seller, 30×24¾ | 300 |
| | The shooting party, 39×54 | 330 |
| 1964 | S. The crossing sweeper, 1893, 16½×13¾ (see 1967) | 320 |
| | Bonham's rooms. Five o'clock tea, 1893 | 250 |
| 1966 | C. The letter, 16×12¾ | 252 |
| | Nell Gwynn at Drury Lane, 1869, 23½×19¼ | 210 |
| | Sidelong glances and laughing eyes, oval, 12¾×10½ | |
| | | 2 for 199 10s. |
| | S. Village merrymaking, 1905, 20½×33½ | 250 |
| 1967 | C. The new recruit, 20×22 | 609 |
| | The crossing sweeper (£320 in 1964), 16½×13¾ | 336 |
| | Dearden. S. Charles II's last Sunday, 1867, 67×100 (£1,732 10s. in 1891) | 1,600 |
| 1968 | Alan Brown. S. A lesson in etiquette, 1876, 35×56 | 1,400 |
| | S. The sick doll, 1886, 27¾×35¾ | 750 |
| | Sordoni. N.Y. For better, for worse, 60¼×49, $5,250 | 2,188 |

## THOMAS GAINSBOROUGH. 1727–1788

The following transactions through Lord Duveen, corrected and augmented from Volume One, should be considered before examining the list for the 1960s.

| | | |
|---|---|---|
| 1913 | Bought by H. C. Frick, *Portrait of the Hon. Miss Frances Duncombe*, a replica of the Longford Castle picture. Reputedly $400,000 at 4·86 to the £ | £ 82,450 |
| 1921 | Bought by Henry Huntington, *The Blue Boy*, formerly in the Duke of Westminster's collection, $620,000 at 4·20 to the £ | 148,000 |
| | Also, The Cottage Door, $300,000 at 4·10 to £ | 73,000 |
| 1928 | Bought back by Duveen at the Gary Sale, New York, *The Market Cart*, $350,000 at 4·86 to the £ | 74,400 |
| 1936 | Bought from Duveen by Andrew Mellon, portrait of *The Duchess of Devonshire*, formerly at Althorp | 84,400 |
| | Portrait, *Mrs Sheridan*, ex Victor Rothschild Collection | 80,000 |

Frick's purchase of 1913 was recalled in the obituary notices of his death in 1919, when René Gimpel wrote in his diary that the figure was correct to his certain knowledge. It meant £658,600 in 1970. Huntington's purchase of *The Blue Boy* in 1921 meant £740,000. By the same scale, the remaining pictures range between £365,000 and £420,000. These are not Gainsborough prices but Rembrandt prices. Whatever its prestige rating might be in 1970, *The Blue Boy* would certainly not be worth three quarters of a million. But, as an equity, the *Hon. Miss Frances Duncombe* will have failed very much more. Instead of £658,000, she might not even reach £50,000. And the same could also apply to *The Cottage Door* and *The Market Cart*.

There is, however, no comparison to be made between normal saleroom competition and the prices commanded by a genius like Duveen who possessed the confidence of the richest men in the world. In the saleroom there was far less disparity in terms of real values between the markets of the 1920s and 1960s. Among the English 18th century portraitists, Gainsborough was the one painter to show true recovery powers—and for once price had some relation to merit. *Mr and Mrs Andrews* is one of the great masterpieces of all time. Now that a not very lyrical early Renoir can be sold for about £650,000, it seems to have been a cheap national purchase at £130,000 plus commission. But this picture is the very reverse of Gainsborough's *grand manner* and would have made only a few thousands in the Duveen era.

It is no credit to this age that three magnificent Gainsborough landscapes were sold in the 1960s for less than some of the productions of Dufy and van Dongen.

| | | | £ |
|---|---|---|---:|
| 1959 | Leigh.  S.  Earl of Chesterfield Countess of Chesterfield} 86×61 | | 14,000 34,000 |
| | (£6,825 and £17,860 in the Carnarvon sale, 1925). Now in Paul Getty collection | | |
| 1960 | Andrews.  S.  Mr and Mrs Andrews in a park, very early work 1749, bought Agnew, now National Gallery, 27½× 47 | | 130,000 |
| | Sandy Lodge (Knight Frank).  The painter's daughter | | 5,500 |
| | Benson.  S.  Landscape, the midday rest, 1786, 21½×27½ (see 1969) | | 6,200 |
| 1961 | Sonia Henie.  S.  Mr and Mrs Chad, pair of heads  2 for | | 2,500 |
| | Bruce Neame.  C.  Mrs Robert Hingleston (sold with the scarf in which she was painted) | | 1,470 |
| 1962 | Sold to the National Gallery, Edinburgh, by the D. of Sutherland.  Fanciful landscape with mountains | | 55,000 |
| 1963 | Cintas.  S.  Lady Gideon, 1766, whole-length, 82½×72¼. Beaverbrook gallery, Fredericton | | 54,000 |
| 1965 | Williams Wynn.  S.  Landscape with Hagar and Ishmael, 30×36½ | | 10,000 |
| | C.  Wooded landscape with sheep, 11½×13¼ (£168 in 1882) | | 18,900 |

|  | | £ |
|---|---|---|
| 966 | Earl Howe.  C.  Wooded landscape with cattle, 28 × 53. | |
| | Bought in at | 19,950 |
| 967 | D. of Sutherland.  C.  Miniature self-portrait, 3 × 2½ | 2,730 |
| | Billy Rose Foundation.  S.  Hon Mrs Charles Yorke, oval, 30 × 24 | 4,500 |
| | Duke of Newcastle.  C.  The beggar boys, 1785, 62½ × 70 (Gainsborough sale 1789, £84) | 13,650 |
| | S. (Toronto).  1st Marquess of Donegal, 91½ × 60, $65,000. Ulster Museum, Belfast | 21,700 |
| 968 | Constable-Curtis.  S.  Upland valley and shepherd, dated 1784, 46¼ × 58½ (£651 in 1841, £210 in 1851, £399 in 1863) | 36,000 |
| | Palmer-Morewood.  C.  Cattle returning at evening, 40 × 50 | 29,400 |
| 969 | May.  S.  Mrs Wilkes, oval half-length, 27½ × 22½ | 1,200 |
| | Lyle-Price.  S.  Countess of Dundonald, painted oval, 29½ × 24½ | 6,200 |
| | Hardie.  S.  The midday Rest, 1786, 21½ × 27½ (see 1960) | 15,000 |
| | Bruguière.  C.  Dr Richard Warren, half-length, 50 × 40 (£1,050 in 1949) | 12,600 |

## DRAWINGS

| 960 | S.  River landscape, black chalk and oil, 8¾ × 12 | 400 |
|---|---|---|
| 961 | Smythe.  C.  Diana and Actaeon, chalks, 11 × 14½ | 861 |
| 965 | Bruce Ingram.  S.  Wooded stream and driven cattle, chalks, 12 × 12½ | 1,400 |
| | Denny.  S.  Riders approaching village, black chalk and washes, 8¼ × 12 | 900 |
| 966 | Higginson.  S.  Wooded landscape, figures, sepia wash, 9¾ × 13¼ | 420 |
| 967 | S.  Wooded path and country house, wc and chalks, 9¼ × 11½ | 1,000 |
| 968 | Koch settlement.  S.  Duchess of Buccleuch, charcoal and chalks, whole-length, 11½ × 9½ | 1,155 |
| | Huntington.  S.  Study of a lady walking, chalk and body colour, 19¼ × 12¼ (£310 in 1936, £380 in 1950) | 4,200 |
| | C.  Wooded landscape with pool, 10¼ × 12, black chalk and white | 1,470 |
| | Hilly river landscape | 1,155 |
| 969 | Toppin.  S.  Cattle driven on wooded road, 10 × 13½ | 1,300 |

LEE GATCH.  (*See* Abstract painters, American)

# PAUL GAUGUIN. 1848–1903

Only four Gauguins of the Tahiti period were sold in the 1960s, counting completed works alone, and of these two were of minor importance. In the absence of Tahiti pictures, works of the Breton period rose in their place. In paper pounds the highest price was that of a smaller version of the well-known *Bonjour, Monsieur Gauguin*, sold for close on £140,000 in Geneva in 1969. But this precedence for a Breton Gauguin was entirely ocular. The price of £130,000 in 1959 money for *J'attends ta réponse* was already equivalent to £185,000 and the picture's real value in 1969 at least double that. As to a monumental Tahiti work such as the *Que sommes nous* of 1898, its value might be nearer a million than half a million. Gauguin's more typical works of the Breton period, betraying the influence of the Impressionists and even of Millet, ended the decade on a much lower plane. *Bonjour, Monsieur Gauguin* was in fact more like a Tahitian work in its personal independence.

The list has been revised as far back as the Gauguin sale of 1895 in order to correct the inadequacies of Volume One.

| | | £ |
|---|---|---:|
| 1895 | Gauguin. **Paris.** (49 lots): | |
| | Manao Tapapao. Coll. Conger Goodyear. 900 francs +tax | 39 6s. |
| | Mao Taporo (see 1957), 360 francs+tax | 15 16s. |
| | Hina Maruru (see 1965), 350 francs+tax | 15 8s. |
| | J'attends ta réponse (see 1959), 375 francs+tax | 16 8s. |
| 1896 | Bought by the composer Delius. 'Nevermore'. Courtauld Gallery | 20 |
| 1903 | Bought by Ignace Fayet from Daniel de Manfreid. *Te Reriora.* Courtauld Gallery | 44 |
| 1906 | Blôt. Paris. Fleurs de Tahiti, 2,630 francs+tax | 116 |
| 1907 | Vian. Paris. Britanny landscape | 78 |
| 1912 | Hoogendijk, The Hague. Young Tahitian girl | 442 |
| | Rouart. Paris. Papeete, 29,500 francs+tax | 1,302 |
| 1923 | Goodfriend. N.Y. *Bonjour, Monsieur Gauguin* (see 1969), $1,500 About | 390 |
| 1924 | S. First Gauguin in London salerooms; small self-portrait wearing spectacles | 95 |
| 1926 | D. of Rutland. C. *Te fare maorié*, 1890 | 798 |
| | Bought by Whitworth Gallery, Manchester, gouache landscape, Brittany | 260 |
| 1930 | N.Y. River landscape, Brittany | 405 |
| 1937 | N.Y. Tahiti landscape, 28×17½ | 350 |
| 1938 | Bought by W. A. Cargill. Three dancing Breton girls (see 1963) | 3,200 |
| 1939 | German State Galleries, Lucerne (sale ordered by Hitler): | |
| | 'From Tahiti' | 2,400 |
| | Self-portrait | 8,000 |

| | | £ |
|---|---|---|
| 1940 | Eumorphopoulos. S. Apples in a bowl | 170 |
| 1943 | Leopold Sutro. C. Jean, child-portrait in pastel | 126 |
| 1944 | Barbée. N.Y. Small Tahiti landscape | 945 |
| 1949 | N.Y. Près de la ferme, 28×39 | 1,500 |
| 1952 | Brussels. Vahiné à la fleur, 1902, 20¾×14½ | 2,400 |
| 1953 | Paris. Contes barbares, 14×11½ | 7,060 |
| | Lousada. C. Apples and flowers on a newspaper | 420 |
| 1957 | Weinberg. S. Jeunes baigneurs bretons, 1888, 36×28½ | 17,000 |
| | Thompson Biddle. Paris. Apples, 1901. Coll. Nearchos | 104,630 |
| | Apples and grapes (see 1961) | 36,200 |
| | Pont Aven, landscape | 14,300 |
| | Edward Robinson, private sale to Stavros Nearchos. Horsemen on the beach | 71,400 |
| 1958 | Heinz. N.Y. Small basket of flowers | 19,300 |
| 1959 | Goodyear. S. J'attends ta réponse (see 1895), 29×37½ | 130,000 |
| | S. Landscape near Rouen, 1884, 22×33¾ | 8,500 |
| 1960 | Coe. S. Tahiti, landscape with figures, 1891, 35½×27¾ | 38,000 |
| | Paris. La fiancée, 1888, 16×13 | 9,892 |
| | Maxime Blum. C. Place d'Elseneur, 21½×23¾ | 1,470 |
| | S. Coast of Britanny, 1886, 29×43½ | 9,000 |
| | C. Beach-scene, 1876 | 3,990 |
| | N.Y. Jeune Bretonne, 1883, 12×18¾, $22,000 | 7,857 |
| 1961 | Adeane. S. Apples and grapes (see 1957) 1889, 19¼×21¾ | 45,000 |
| | Paris. L'homme au *pareo* rouge et chapeau, 16½×13¼, FN205,000+tax | 17,835 |
| 1962 | Woolworth. N.Y. Landscape near Rouen, 23¾×28¾, $47,500 | 16,965 |
| | Somerset Maugham. S. Panel, painted on a glass door, Tahiti, 39½×21½ | 13,000 |
| | Metcalfe (Korda). S. Flowerpiece | 7,000 |
| | S. Portrait, Mme Gauguin | 18,000 |
| 1963 | Porter. C. Paysan à Pont-Aven, 30×24 | 8,400 |
| | Wolf. S. Le petit Laveur, Martinique | 11,000 |
| | Cargill. S. Three dancing Breton girls, 1888, 27¾×34 (see 1938) | 75,000 |
| | Aldrich. N.Y. Breton washerwomen, 35×29, $110,000 | 39,313 |
| 1964 | Mardon. S. Two Tahitians, 1899, 36½×23 | 90,000 |
| | Bloch. Paris. L'entrée du village, 1889, 21½×13¼ | 6,000 |
| 1965 | Rattner. N.Y. Jeanne d'Arc, mural, 1889, 52×22¾, $65,000 | 23,214 |
| | S. Paysage à Viroflay, 1875, 18¼×12¾ | 4,000 |
| | La maison du Pan Du, 19½×23½ | 28,000 |
| | Graetzer. S. Jardin à Vaugirard, 22×18 | 14,000 |

£

1965   de Zayas.   N.Y.   Hina Maruru, 1893, 36½ × 27½ (see 1895),
$275,000     98,214

1966   S.   Two Tahitians, crayon drawing, doubled by monotype, 24¾ × 20¼     11,000

Brookes   Veren.   N.Y.   La   vague,   1888,   23½ × 28½,
$150,000     53,850

Carewe.   C.   Nuit de Noël, 28 × 32, snow-scene.

Bought in at 50,400

Sieff.   S.   La baignade, Pont Aven, 1886, 23½ × 28¾     34,500

Maresco Pearce.   La maison au bord de la mer.   National
Gallery (price inclusive of death duty remission)     47,000

1967   S.   Aline et Pola, Copenhagen, 1885, early pastel, 27¾ ×
20½     25,500

Dallas Museum.   N.Y.   L'abreuvoir, 1885, 17¾ × 21¾     10,714

1968   Kawasaki.   S.   La barque, Tahiti, 1896, 19¾ × 14½     22,000

Saville.   N.Y.   *Clovis*, child of the painter, Copenhagen,
1882, pastel, 10¾ × 10, $18,000     6,575

N.Y.   Fillette, couchée dans une prairie, 1884, 28¾ × 23½,
$57,500     23,960

1969   C. (Tokyo).   Portrait, la fiancée, 1888, 12¾ × 15, 26 million
yen     30,371

Ermolaev.   C. (Geneva).   Bonjour, Monsieur Gauguin,
1889, 29½ × 21½, smaller version of the Prague picture
($1,500 1923), FS1,370,000 + 5% tax     138,292

Oliphant.   S.   Vache dans un pré, 1884, 21¼ × 17¾     33,500


MARK GEERAETS.   (*See* Flemish School, after 1550, portraits)


## JEAN LOUIS GÉRICAULT.   1791–1824

*Le radeau de la Méduse* was sold in 1824 after Géricault's early death for £240. In that year Wilkie received £1,260 for his newly completed *Chelsea pensioners*, John Martin got 800 guineas for *The Destruction of Herculaneum*, Turner refused 750 guineas for *Dido building Carthage*, while the British Institution awarded a thousand guineas each to two thoroughly flabby performances, Hilton's *Christ crowned with thorns* and James Ward's *Allegory of Waterloo*. Private enterprise did even better, for in 1823 Graves, the printseller, paid 2,000 guineas for the *Stephen Langton and the Barons* of the younger Devis. So the fancy dress and froth of the early romantics were already dear in 1823–4, whereas Géricault, who possessed the true Renaissance quality of *terribilità*, was cheap—and still is. Presumably *Le radeau de la Méduse* ought to be worth at least £150,000 in 1970 as an historic work, known to everybody, but the few scraps of Géricault that have remained in private ownership, could barely buy a postcard from van Gogh.

| | | £ |
|---|---|---|
| 1899 | Holbrooke. C. L'attélage | 997 10s. |
| 1901 | Bought by the Louvre. Self-portrait | 420 |
| 1906 | Cheramy. Paris. Officier de la Garde. Rouen Museum | 760 |
| 1912 | Dollfuss. Paris. Race in the Corso (£253 in 1876) bought by the Louvre | 1,440 |
| 1935 | Coats. C. Prancing grey horse | 283 10s. |
| 1944 | S. A dappled horse, small oil painting | 220 |
| 1950 | Paris. Le berger nu, $36\frac{3}{4} \times 29\frac{1}{4}$ | 644 |
| 1951 | S. Coronation of Marie de Medici, oil sketch | 280 |
| 1952 | Cognacq. Paris. Jupiter and Alcmene, $9\frac{1}{2} \times 12\frac{3}{4}$ | 2,962 |
| 1954 | Paris. General le Tellier on his deathbed, 1818, $9\frac{1}{4} \times 12\frac{1}{2}$ | 508 |
| 1959 | Paris. Paysage d'Italie, $101\frac{1}{2} \times 88$, 3·8 million old francs + tax | 3,302 |
| 1960 | Paris. St Peter Martyr, after Titian, $26 \times 21\frac{1}{4}$, FN14,000 + tax | 1,480 |
| 1963 | Paris. Le chat blanc, $14 \times 18$ | 8,650 |
| | Horse's head, $22 \times 18\frac{1}{2}$ | 8,650 |
| | Matthiesen. S. Le Baiser, sepia chalk and flake white, $8 \times 10\frac{1}{2}$ | 7,200 |
| 1965 | Motte. Geneva. Horse in stable, wc, $5 \times 9$, FS24,000 + tax | 2,300 |
| | S. Academic study, male nude, oil on paper, $11\frac{3}{4} \times 9$ | 4,500 |
| | Horse's head after Carle Vernet, $23\frac{3}{4} \times 19\frac{1}{2}$ | 3,600 |
| | C. Academic study, male nude, $31\frac{1}{2} \times 24\frac{1}{2}$ | 3,150 |
| | Paris. L'enseigne du forgeron, 4 ft $\times 3\frac{1}{2}$, FN250,000 + tax | 19,753 |
| 1966 | C. Chien de mante, allongé sur le sol, after Oudry, $8\frac{1}{4} \times 11\frac{1}{2}$ | 1,260 |
| | Stoclet. S. Flagellation of Christ after Annibale Carracci, $20 \times 26\frac{1}{2}$ | 3,800 |
| 1967 | S. Le coureur de Marathon, oil on paper, $17 \times 22\frac{1}{4}$ | 1,200 |
| | Paris. Supposed portrait of the composer Boieldieu, $26 \times 21\frac{1}{4}$, FN68,000 + tax | 6,340 |
| 1968 | Kaplan. S. The vagabond, half-length, $24\frac{3}{4} \times 20\frac{1}{4}$ | 4,000 |
| | C. Head, oval, study for *le radeau de la Méduse*, 1818, $17\frac{3}{4} \times 21\frac{1}{2}$ | 1,575 |
| | Le gladiateur, academic nude study, $29\frac{3}{4} \times 22\frac{3}{4}$ | 1,995 |
| | S. Les catacombes, $6\frac{1}{4} \times 8\frac{1}{4}$ | 2,100 |
| | Motte, Geneva. Deux chevaux au trot, $11\frac{1}{4} \times 8$, FS63,000 + tax | 7,000 |

# GERMAN SCHOOL
15th–16th centuries

(Excluding Dürer, Cranach, Holbein, for whom see separate entries.)

Compared with the unimpressive list of the 1960s, it appears that the earl German school received a stronger market-support before the First Worl War. At the Dollfuss sale of 1912 the Louvre had to pay £6,230 (equivalent t £50,000) for a primitive of the Cologne school. It was also in Paris in the follow ing year that a Renaissance *Venus and Cupid* by Baldung Grien made £5,06 (£43,000). Prices exceeding £2,000 were quite common just before the Firs World War, and these meant £16,000 and upwards, something which wa almost unknown in the 1960s.

This market has suffered more than any other from wars. After the Firs World War there was an international prejudice against the German school This had disappeared by the late 1920s, for in 1927 an anonymous portrait head of about the year 1500 made £8,000, equivalent to £40,000 in 1970, at th resplendent Figdor sale. The nationalistic taste of Hitler's Third Reich should have raised prices even further, but instead it depressed them. Dealers who con trived to get their threatened stocks out of Germany, found that there was n international market, while the German government would not provide th foreign currency to buy them back. After the Second World War the officia traditional taste for the German middle ages and Renaissance was no longe popular. German speculators had apparently more faith in Chagall, Kandinsk and Paul Klee. The sale of a Hans Baldung panel for nearly a quarter-million a the very end of the decade changed the whole picture. Baldung may have bee the only disciple of Dürer who was liable to be confused with his master, yet i is still astonishing that this ugly and by no means unique panel should have cos as much as one of the most exquisite products of the van Eyck circle, th Plaoutine *St George*. But the inference to be drawn is that the latter is already worth a million, and that it is not so much love of the early German schoo which has made the Baldung so dear as a new threshold of prices for the entir old-master market.

| | | | £ |
|---|---|---|---|
| 1961 | Makower. S. **Bartold Bruyn**, Portrait, Princesse de Chaulnes | | 1,400 |
| | Weinmüller, Munich. **Master of the Leitmeritz altar**, two panels, legend of St Ursula, 1510 | 2 for | 5,000 |
| | **Master of 1468.** Two altar panels from Tegernsee | 2 for | 4,800 |
| 1962 | Guggenheim Foundation. S. **Hans Maler.** Portrait, Queen Anne of Hungary, 1520, 20×14¾ | | 5,700 |
| | **Bernard Strigel.** Male portrait, 14½×11¼ | | 4,500 |
| | **Hans Kulmbach**, portrait | | 3,800 |
| | Lempertz, Cologne. **Master of Freisach**, c. 1450, Crucifixion, gold background | | 7,165 |

£

962   COLOGNE SCHOOL, c. 1490, Martyrdom of St Ursula, 56×
33½, DM42,000+tax    4,310
  Paris. UNKNOWN, c. 1500, Christ and the moneylenders,
38×65    14,080

963   Bass, N.Y. HEINRICH FÜNHOF, Hamburg, c. 1480, Miracle
of the loaves and fishes, 33×39, $22,000    7,855
  Lempertz, Cologne, CHRISTOFF AMBERGER, Portrait, Cosimo
de' Medici, 39½×30, DM52,000+tax    5,335
  C. HIERONYMUS HÖPFER. Portrait of a bishop, 1520,
13½×10¼    7,350

964   C. MICHAEL PACHER, abbot and abbess, 20×14½    7,875
    HANS MIELICH, female portrait    11,550
    MASTER OF THE MANSI MAGDALENE, Pietà    5,040
    ANONYMOUS, portrait of a man, 1542    5,250
    COLOGNE SCHOOL, John the Baptist, fragment, 6¾×4¾    6,090
  Thyssen-Bornemisza. S. COLOGNE SCHOOL, 15th century, St Anne in landscape    4,500

965   Spencer Churchill. S. CHRISTOPHER AMBERGER, female
portrait, 1530    3,570
  Timken. S. ANONYMOUS PAINTER, c. 1530, Lady Jane
Gray, 72×37. National Portrait Gallery    4,000
  Blackett. C. GEORG RAPHON. Pair of side panels,
Nativity and Death of the Virgin    2 for   7,770
  Frazer. C. ANONYMOUS PAINTER, c. 1510 (Lower Rhine-
land school). Panel with 12 scenes from the Passion,
44×31    10,500
  Weinmüller, Munich. JACOB SEISENEGGER. Portrait,
Anne of Cleves, c. 1545, 16¾×13½    6,580

966   Vernon Harcourt. C. CONRAD FABER, male portrait
dated 1534, 16¼×12½    7,350
  S. BERNARD STRIGEL, portrait of a lady, 16×23    6,500
  Lempertz, Cologne. MASTER OF THE STRACHE ALTARPIECE,
Crucifixion, 33¼×24, DM150,000+tax    About   16,000
    LOWER RHINE SCHOOL, dated 1481, St Anne with read-
ing companions, DM60,000+tax    6,270

967   C. MASTER OF FRANKFURT. Adoration of the shepherds,
40×27½    3,360
  Watney. C. HANS EWORTH. Portrait of Joan
Wakeman, 1566, 36×27    12,600
  Rex Beaumont. C. BARTOLD BRUYN, portraits of a lady
and gentleman, 1560 and 1565, each 17×11½    2 for   7,665

968   Paris. RHINELAND SCHOOL, triptych, Holy Family, St
Christopher and St Sebastian, 51¼×35½    2,380
  Paris. RHINELAND SCHOOL, 15th century. Virgin and the
Holy Spirit, 16½×11½, with tax    5,870

1968 Lempertz, Cologne.  RHINELAND SCHOOL, 2 altar wings of £
two panels each, 36×44                                                              4,795
MASTER OF ILSUNG MADONNA.   Two altar wings, *c.* 1480,
Presentation and Nativity, 33½×13¾, DM55,000+tax
2 for  6,550
C. MARTIN SCHAFFNER.   Christ appearing to the 3
Maries, 43½×34                                                                      8,400
S. BOHEMIAN SCHOOL, late 14th century.   Pietá on gold
ground, 31×25                                                                        3,900
1969 Winkler. S.  MASTER OF KAUFBEUREN.   Virgin adoring
Holy Child, 30¾×28½                                                              5,800
Lempertz, Cologne.   Triptych, Crucifixion,  62×88,
RHINELAND SCHOOL, *c.* 1410, DM600,000.  Bought by
Münster Landesmuseum                                                           62,500
Cattrell. S.  HANS BALDUNG GRIEN (1480–1545).  The
temptation of Eve, on panel, 25¼×12¾                                  224,000

### DRAWINGS AND PRINTS

1961 Randall. S.  PIETER VISCHER THE ELDER, Scylla (recto)
and Orpheus and Eurydice (verso) pen and black chalk,
1514, 11½×8½                                                                    13,500
NICOLAS GERHAERT.   Angel with two shields, black
chalk, 6¾×8½                                                                       2,500
HANS BURGKMAIR.   Dancing bear, pen, 9¾×5½             4,600
1966 Evelyn. S.  MELCHIOR LORCK.   Three ladies of Ham-
burg, pen, 1571                                                                       3,200
Other drawings by Lorck, £1,300 to £1,800
Schorcken. S.  MASTER P.M.   The women's bath, 1490,
unique engraving in finished state                                          32,000
MASTER E.S.   Three figures forming a letter M, en-
graving of *c.* 1450                                                              13,000
1967 E. V. Randall. S.  MAIR VON LANDSHUT.   Angel, pen
touched with white, 4½×3¾                                                   800
MASTER OF ST CATHERINE's wheel.   One of the Wise
Virgins, pen, 8¼×4¾                                                              3,800
1968 S.   School of WOLGEMUT.   The Virgin reading in a study,
pen, brush and body colour on blue paper, 7×6               1,800
1969 S.   School of MARTIN SCHÖNGAUER.   Woman in coif
praying, pen, 5½×3¾                                                               820
Boerlag-Koenigs. S.  SOUTH GERMAN, *c.* 1480, betrayal of
Christ, pen and wash, 12¼×8                                                 2,000
WOLF HUBER.   Standing labourer, red chalk, *c.* 1535,
11¼×6½                                                                                9,000

# GERMAN SCHOOL
## Modern

ome high prices in these lists are interesting in that they denote a change in the olitics of taste rather than a change in taste itself. One remembers those umerous popular German books on modern art of pre-war days, in which a ost of German names rubbed shoulders with Matisse, Picasso and the rest. arely were works by these German painters exhibited in London, Paris or Jew York. In reproduction they did not look inviting. Somehow they seemed o lack style. There was also the feeling that, because the painters did not reside i Paris, they belonged to a provincial school, sustained by patriotism. Though Munich was an international centre where painters from Eastern Europe ractised, it was regarded as a backwater outside the main current.

This situation changed so much in the 1950s and 1960s that several works by German-based painters, who developed their style outside the Parisian orbit, ntered the £25,000 to £50,000 range (see separate titles, *Paul Klee* and *andinsky*). Among 20th century British or American painters who practised i their own countries, only certain realist and Royal Academy pictures could each such heights, nor was there any truly international market for them, vhereas German 'expressionism' attracted both American and Continental ompetition.

The change of course was an outcome of the Nazi régime. Before the war a reat many painters, dealers, critics and gallery-directors were forced to flee heir country. They tended to settle in the U.S.A., where a clientèle of German rigin existed. When London came to be the clearing house of the inter-ational art market, 'expressionist' works began to appear on the saleroom valls, and now one cannot imagine a modern-paintings sale without them. Expressionism' is a blanket term covering a number of styles. Some derive ery clearly from Paris. Nölde, Munch, Kirchner and von Jawlensky seem to ave links with the short-lived *fauve* school, Feininger derives from the cubist hase of Braque and Picasso. With all that, modern German painting looks trikingly un-French. Its ruggedness and violence lacks the restraining discipline f the French art-school training. I doubt whether Expressionism is popular ither in France or England, but it is clearly a school that has attracted specu-ators, since, even in the 1940s, it had very little market value. I have included iebermann in the lists, though quite outside the more recent current, because e was regarded in his days as the leading German exponent of French Impres-ionism, but in the 1960s he no longer rated very high.

| | | £ |
|---|---|---|
| YONEL FEININGER. 1871–1956 | | |
| 960 Bordersen. C. Scharenkreuzer, 1930, 17×30 | | 3,360 |
| Stuttgart. Schwarze Welle, 1937, 19½×28¾, DM85,000+ tax | | 8,550 |
| 961 Lempertz, Cologne. Die grosse Kutterklasse (yacht race) 1929, 14¾×28, DM95,000+tax | | 9,725 |

£

| | | |
|---|---|---|
| 1961 | Stuttgart. Landungssteg, 1912, DM102,000+tax | 10,500 |
| 1962 | Stuttgart. Ship of stars, 1957, 20×30, DM91,000+tax | 9,365 |
| | Finarte, Milan. Architektur. II. 15 million lire+tax | 9,640 |
| | Barque at sea, 1953, 11·5 million lire+tax        About | 7,800 |
| 1964 | Kornfeld, Berne. Rathaus in Treptow, 19×31 | 8,620 |
| | Lempertz, Cologne. Gaberndorf, 1921, 39½×40 | 12,400 |
| 1965 | Kornfeld, Berne. Burning house, wc, 9½×9¼ | 862 |
| 1966 | S. Häuser und Menschen, 1909, 21½×18 | 7,200 |
| | Ruine am Meer, 1930, 26½×19¾ | 12,600 |
| 1967 | Usiskin. N.Y. Cammin, 23½×19¾, $10,000 | 3,575 |
| 1969 | N.Y. Das gestrandete Schiff, 1924, 12×18¾, $17,000 | 7,140 |
| | Tibbe. S. The sailing ship, 1939, pen and wc, 7¼×10¼ | 3,000 |
| | N.Y. Skyline at night, wc, design for mural frieze, 9¼×50, $10,500 | 4,375 |

## ALEXANDER VON JAWLENSKY. 1867–1941

| | | |
|---|---|---|
| 1958 | S. Tête de pierrot, 15½×12½ | 480 |
| 1960 | Stuttgart. Garten in Caranto, 19½×21, DM41,500+tax | 4,270 |
| | Gesänkter Kopf, 23×21½, DM65,000+tax | 6,700 |
| | Five others at £2,000 to £3,000 | |
| | N.Y. Japanische Blümen, 1913, 21×19¼, $7,500 | 2,680 |
| | Sizilianisches Mädchen, 1913, 27½×19¾, $6,250 | 2,235 |
| 1961 | Stuttgart. Prerow, 1911, landscape, 19½×21½, DM33,000+tax | 3,390 |
| 1962 | Stuttgart. Girl with black hair, 21¼×19½, DM46,000+tax | 4,735 |
| 1965 | N.Y. Frauenkopf, 20¾×17½, $7,000 | 2,500 |
| 1967 | S. Haus in Bergen, 1912, 19¾×21¼ | 4,200 |
| | Bunte Blümen, 1916, 20½×21¼ | 2,400 |
| | Palms in Ascona, 1915, 19×21 | 3,000 |
| | Portrait, 1906, 21×19 | 5,000 |
| | Arpels. S. Sinnende, Portrait, 1912, 21¼×19 | 8,000 |
| | Kornfeld. Berne. Mit rundem Tisch, FS36,000+tax | 4,430 |
| | Lempertz. Cologne. Sizilianerin, 1913, 26½×22, DM80,000+tax | 9,560 |
| 1968 | Mayer. S. Damenbildnisse and Mädchen als Matrose, double portrait on both sides canvas, 1911, 28¼×19½ | 25,500 |
| | Head, Fräulein Kimmel, 1910, 21×19½ | 15,500 |
| | Sakharoff. S. Haus in Bäumen, St Prex, 1915, 13×16 | 8,500 |
| | N.Y. Kreuzritter, 1933, 17½×13¾, $10,500 | 4,375 |
| 1969 | S. Frauenkopf, 1912, 27¾×19¾ | 10,000 |
| | N.Y. Apple still-life and cornfield, double sided painting, c. 1904–7, 20¾×19¼, $14,500 | 6,092 |

LUDWIG KIRCHNER. 1880–1958         £
*ee also under sculpture, modern.*

| | | |
|---|---|---:|
| 1958 | N.Y.  Houses in Sertigsthal, 36×47, $4,500 | 1,607 |
| 1959 | S.  River boatmen near Dresden, 1905, 25×35½ | 2,500 |
| | Davos, landscape, 29×39½ | 2,400 |
| | Stuttgart.  Dodo mit grossem Federhut, 32×27½, DM90,000 | 9,255 |
| 1960 | Stuttgart.  Grosse Landschaft mit blühenden Bäumen, 28×30, DM65,000+tax | 6,695 |
| | Aus dem Wald schreitende Akt, 50¼×36, DM43,000+tax | 4,435 |
| | and five others at upwards of £2,500 | |
| 1961 | Stuttgart.  Fehmarnbucht, landscape, 48×36, DM61,000 +tax | 6,280 |
| 1963 | Aldrich.  N.Y.  Negro dancer, 1905, 67×37, $26,000 | 9,285 |
| | Couple under Japanese sunshade, 1912, 39¼×29, $15,500 | 5,535 |
| 1964 | Kornfeld.  Berne.  Der Galgenberg in Jena, 27¾×26¼, 1915, FS36,000+tax | 3,450 |
| | Lempertz.  Cologne.  Strasse mit Passanten, 36×28, DM35,000+tax | 3,650 |
| | Sanatorium in Davos, 30¾×45¾, DM14,500+tax | 1,500 |
| 1967 | Ala Story.  N.Y.  Davoser Häuser im winter, 1927, 47¾×35½, $15,000 | 5,360 |
| | Lempertz.  Cologne.  Paar am Tisch, 1912–14, 40×30, DM92,000+tax | 9,400 |
| 1968 | Durst.  C.  Sertigsberge, Davos, 1924, 47½ in. sq. | 16,800 |
| | Guler.  C.  Bernheuer, 1920, 35½×30½ | 12,600 |
| 1969 | Leonard Hutton.  N.Y.  Gut Staberhof II, 1912, 35×46½, $50,000 | 20,833 |
| | S.  Zwei nakte Frauen im Walde, 34¼×47¼, 1909 | 21,000 |
| | Gernsheim.  C. (Geneva).  Vier badende zwischen Steinen und Meer, *c.* 1913, 29×38½, FS140,000+5% tax | 14,086 |
| | Einraderfahrer, 1911, 33½×37½, FS180,000+tax | 18,168 |
| | Rusch.  C. (Geneva).  Berglandschaft, 1921, 23¾×27¾, FS180,000+tax | 18,168 |

OSKAR KOKOSCHKA. 1886–

| | | |
|---|---|---:|
| 1958 | Countess Strafford.  S.  Flowers in glass, 27½×39½ | 2,200 |
| 1959 | S.  Capriccio, ladies in a forest, 1943 | 3,000 |
| 1960 | Finlay.  S.  Algérienne au tonneau, 31½×39 (see 1969) | 3,000 |
| | Fischer.  Lucerne.  Arab woman, 1928, 35½×52, FS91,000 +tax | 8,960 |
| | Weinmüller.  Munich.  View of Prague, 1935, 36×48, DM100,000+tax | 10,300 |

£

| 1960 | Landschaft bei Grinzing, $28\frac{1}{2}\times40$, DM55,000+tax | 5,665 |
| 1961 | Kornfeld, Berne. View of Prague, 1937, $33\frac{1}{2}\times46$ FS104,000 +tax | 10,400 |
| 1962 | Stuttgart. Grosser Blümenstrasse, $26\times28$, DM119,000+ tax | 12,270 |
| | S. Child in the hands of its parents, $28\frac{1}{2}\times20\frac{1}{2}$ | 4,800 |
| 1963 | N.Y. Still life, $28\frac{3}{4}\times39\frac{1}{4}$, $26,500 | 9,465 |
| | S. Clown with dog, $35\frac{3}{4}\times23\frac{3}{4}$ | 9,500 |
| 1964 | Lion. S. Roses, 1925, $29\times22\frac{3}{4}$ | 4,000 |
| | Maslon. S. Portrait, Herwarth Walden, 1910, $40\times27\frac{1}{2}$ | 23,000 |
| 1965 | Kornfeld, Berne. Girl at a table, wc, $27\frac{3}{4}\times20\frac{1}{2}$, FS20,000 +tax | 1,915 |
| 1967 | S. Portrait, Robert Freund, 1909, $23\times18\frac{1}{2}$ | 7,000 |
| | N.Y. Portrait, Kathleen, Countess of Drogheda, $40\times30$, $72,500 at 2·80 | 25,895 |
| 1968 | Elmer Rice. N.Y. Vernet les bains, 1925, $32\frac{1}{4}\times45\frac{1}{4}$, $40,000 at 2·40 | 16,675 |
| | Silberman. N.Y. Italienische Bauers Frau, $25\times31\frac{1}{2}$, $42,500 | 17,707 |
| 1969 | C. Portrait, Marthe Hirsch, 1935, $32\times39\frac{1}{2}$ | 15,225 |
| | N.Y. L'Algérienne au tonneau (see 1960), $31\frac{1}{2}\times39$ (£3,000 in 1960), $72,500 | 30,208 |

## MAX LIEBERMANN. 1847–1933

| 1957 | S. Peasant girl and hay rick, 1905, $20\times27$ | 400 |
| 1960 | Lempertz, Cologne. Portrait, Otto Braun, $48\times38\frac{3}{4}$, DM36,000+tax | 3,705 |
| 1962 | Weinmüller, Munich. Sonntag Nachmittag in Laren, 1897, $26\frac{1}{2}\times32$, DM40,000 | 4,120 |
| 1964 | Fischer, Lucerne. Terrasse mit Ausfluglern, $16\times20$, DM28,000+tax | 2,920 |
| | Badende Knabe, Amsterdam 1878, $72\frac{1}{2}\times90$, DM50,000 +tax | 5,200 |
| | Lempertz, Cologne. Haus Oppenheim in Wannsee, 1922, $22\times30\frac{1}{4}$ | 3,430 |
| 1965 | Lempertz, Cologne. Garten in Wannsee, $21\frac{3}{4}\times30$, DM31,000+tax | 3,300 |
| 1967 | Hauswedel, Hamburg. Reiter am Strand, 1928, $21\frac{3}{4}\times30\frac{3}{4}$, DM62,000+tax | 7,380 |
| 1969 | S. Haus und Garten, $23\frac{1}{4}\times28$ | 3,000 |
| | Reiter am Meer, 1908, $27\frac{1}{2}\times39$ | 2,000 |
| | Lempertz, Cologne. The painter's garden in Wannsee, 1918, $29\frac{1}{2}\times37\frac{1}{4}$, DM60,000+tax      About | 7,000 |
| | Der Witwer, 1873, $24\frac{3}{4}\times18\frac{1}{2}$, DM64,000+tax | 7,400 |

AUGUST MACKE. 1887–1914                 £

959   Lempertz, Cologne.   Im Garten, 39½ × 31½, DM54,000+
       tax                                                    5,565

       Stuttgart.   Kleiner zoologischer Garten, 16¾ × 27¼, 1912,
       DM63,000+tax                                        6,485

960   Stuttgart.   Helle Strasse mit Menschen, 24 × 18, DM70,000
       +tax                                                7,207

962   Stuttgart.   Begonias, apples and pears, 1914, DM50,500+
       tax                                                 5,175

964   Lempertz, Cologne.   Indischer Brautzug, 1913, fresco
       cartoon on paper, 58 × 124, DM10,000+tax       1,030

965   Kornfeld, Berne.   Red tulips in vase, 27¾ × 30¾, FS54,000+
       tax                                              5,175

968   C.   Parklandschaft, 1906, 29¼ × 22½           1,995

969   S.   Lesende Frau, 1913, 20¾ × 16¾           6,500

       Ketterer, Munich.   Drei nakte Mädchen, 52 × 36½,
       DM78,000+tax                                        9,200


FRANZ MARC. 1880–1916

960   N.Y.   Spherical forms, 20 × 25, $10,000        3,572

961   Stuttgart.   Abstract forms, 1914, 32 × 45, DM50,000+tax   5,155

       Kornfeld, Berne.   Fabeltier, 1913, wc, 18½ × 15½, FS80,000
       +tax                                               8,000

969   Vier Kuhe, wc and pencil, c. 1913, 6¾ × 8¾      2,050


EDUARD MUNCH (Norway). 1863–1941

959   N.Y.   Kernacker, 1917, 29¾ × 39, $14,000        5,000

960   Stuttgart.   Mädchen auf rotem Tuch, 32½ × 26, DM164,000
       +tax                                              17,000

962   Stuttgart.   Bewachsenes Haus, 1902, 37 × 44, DM210,000
       +tax                                             21,630

       Herbstlandschaft, 16¾ × 26½, DM153,000+tax    15,770

964   Kornfeld, Berne.   Zwei Mädchen, wc, 22¾ × 28¼, FS42,000
       +tax                                             4,025

965   Kornfeld, Berne.   Badender junger Mann, 80 × 39½, 1908,
       FS100,000                                         9,580

       S.   Portrait, Georg Stang, 1889, 35½ × 23½     7,000

       Inspiration, double portrait, 1914, 26¾ × 35½     6,200

       Landscape, Jelloy Moss, 1916, 25¾ × 31½ (see 1967)   6,000

967   S.   Three early landscape sketches, 1880, 5¾ × 7
                                        £4,000, £3,500, 4,500

       Landscape, Jelloy Moss (see 1965)          9,800

968   Boman.   C.   Eva Mudocci, first state lithograph   5,040

       S.   Das kranke Mädchen, first state lithograph   4,200

1968 N.Y.  Girl's head against shore, woodcut in colour, $18\frac{1}{2}\times$  £
16½, $15,000                                                    6,250
     Kornfeld, Berne.  Badende Kinder, 1908, $23\times27$,
     FS98,000+tax                                                   10,600
1969 Leonard Hutton.  N.Y.  Frau im Grünen, $36\times28\frac{3}{4}$, 1929,
     $57,000                                                     23,750
     Thimig.  S.  Scene from Ibsen's *Ghosts*, wc design made
     for Max Reinhardt, $17\frac{1}{4}\times27\frac{1}{4}$                                    17,500


EMIL NÖLDE.  1863–1956

1959 Stuttgart.  Meer und helle Wolken, $30\times40$, DM82,000+
     tax                                                             8,450
     Kornfeld, Berne.  Christus und die Sünderin, 1926, $36\times$
     $42\frac{3}{4}$, FS112,000+tax                                              11,200
1960 Stuttgart.  Family group, $38\frac{3}{4}\times26$, DM110,000+tax          11,280
     Asters, $29\times35\frac{1}{2}$, DM50,000+tax                             5,140
     Brodersen.  C.  Sommerwolken, $28\times34\frac{1}{2}$                         2,940
     Stuttgart.  Meerbild, $22\frac{1}{2}\times28$, DM47,000+tax                   4,880
1961 S.  Still life with horse and mask, $28\frac{1}{2}\times34\frac{1}{2}$                  2,500
     Kornfeld, Berne.  Die drei Russen, 1915, $29\frac{1}{2}\times40$,
     FS144,000+tax                                                  14,400
     Stuttgart.  Verspottung, 1909, $34\frac{1}{2}\times42\frac{1}{2}$, DM82,000+tax  8,450
1962 Stuttgart.  Blümengarten, 1926, $29\frac{1}{4}\times35\frac{1}{4}$, DM101,000
     +tax                                                           10,400
1963 Larry Aldrich.  N.Y.  Russian peasant head, $27\times24$, 1913,
     $18,000                                                      6,425
1964 Kornfeld, Berne.  Two cossack headmen, 1914, $29\frac{1}{2}\times35\frac{1}{2}$  9,200
     Portrait, Gustav Schiefler, $35\frac{1}{2}\times29\frac{1}{2}$, FS66,000+tax   6,325
1965 Kornfeld, Berne.  Frau am kleinen Tisch, $22\frac{1}{4}\times22\frac{1}{4}$          5,175
     Lempertz, Cologne.  View of Etna, $16\times22$, DM24,000+
     tax                                                             2,500
1966 S.  Bei der Schleuse, 1910, $27\frac{3}{4}\times33\frac{1}{2}$                      4,200
     Ritzerfeld.  S.  'Meer D', seascape, 1930, $28\frac{1}{2}\times39\frac{1}{4}$         6,500
1967 S.  Clouds, 1918, $24\times18$                                      4,000
     Hauswedel, Hamburg.  Bei der Schleuse, $29\times34$,
     DM56,000+tax                                                   6,220
1968 S.  Alchymisten, bearded head, 1911–13, $24\times16\frac{3}{4}$             15,200
1969 Leonard Hutton.  N.Y.  Tropenglut, 1915, $29\times34\frac{1}{2}$,
     $45,000                                                      18,750
     Still life 'E', 1914, $28\frac{3}{4}\times31\frac{3}{4}$, $32,500                      13,541
     Die drei Königen, 1911, $20\frac{1}{4}\times16\frac{3}{4}$, $30,000                12,500
     Thimig.  S.  Zwei Schauspielerinen, wc 1911, $9\times11\frac{3}{4}$      2,600
     N.Y.  The artist's wife, wc, 1920, $18\frac{3}{4}\times14$, $16,000         6,665
     S.  Sommerwolken, 1913, $28\frac{3}{4}\times34\frac{1}{2}$                        15,000

MAX PECHSTEIN. 1881–1945                                           £

958  S.  Reclining nude on couch, 30½×39½                         100
960  Stuttgart.  Girl in sailor dress, DM18,000+tax              1,835
961  N.Y.  Fishing fleet, 1919, 36×45¾, $5,000                   1,785
962  Fischer, Lucerne.  Stilleben, 1923, 32½×28½, FS26,000+
     tax                                                          2,600
964  Kornfeld, Berne.  Dunes at Nidden, girl's portrait on other
     side, 32¾×40½, FS16,500+tax                                  1,585
965  Weining, N.Y.  Frühling, 27¾×31½, $5,500                     1,965
966  N.Y.  Dorfstrasse mit Bäumen, 1932, 21×36, $3,250           1,160
     S.  Stilleben, 1913, 58×41                                   1,700
         Sunflower in vase, 1912, 31½×28                          2,000
967  Hauswedel, Hamburg.  Am Meer, 1919–21, 40½×32¼,
     DM40,000+tax                                                 4,765
968  C.  Reifendes Korn, 1922, 19½×22½                            2,730
     Motte, Geneva.  Meererzahlung, 1920, 48×36¼, FS70,000
     +tax                                                         8,300
969  Hutton, N.Y.  Nach dem Bade, 1921, 30½×39, $12,000          5,040
     C.  Gewitter, 1922, 31×39¼                                   4,200
     N.Y.  Intermezzo, still life with flowers, 1921, 39¾×32,
     $11,000                                                      4,583


DOMENICO DEL GHIRLANDAJO.  (*See* Italian School, Central [1969])


## THOMAS GIRTIN.  1775–1802
### All are watercolours or drawings

It may be a mistake to assume that the upward trend in the value of Girtin's
watercolours was halted in the 1960s, since in general the 18th century picturesque topographical school, to which Girtin belonged, rose steeply. It would be
truer to say that there has been a dearth in the salerooms of works of importance
by this very rare and short-lived painter. At his best, Girtin ought to rival the
two Cozenses who reached the £4,000 class, or even Paul Sandby at £9,000.

                                                                  £
959  S.  Laverthorpe bridge and postern, York, 12½×19½            480
960  Russell.  S.  Fishing village and estuary, 11½×20¾          2,100
     C.  Kirkstall Abbey                                          472 10s.
965  C.  Watermill, pencil and wc, 4½×7¾                          120 15s.
968  S.  Old house near Richmond, Yorks, 1796, 12×15¾            500
         Bala lake and Cader Idris, 12½×18¼                       450
970  S.  Lake Windermere and Wray Castle, 14×19½                  320

ALBERT GLEIZES.  (*See* Abstract Painters, Europe)


VINCENT VAN GOGH.  1853–1890

The difference in value between a completed painting of van Gogh's Dutc▌
period and one of his Arles period is even greater than that which separates ▌
Breton Gauguin from a Tahiti Gauguin. Much of the work which van Gog▌
did in Holland was so immature and derivative that the prices mean nothin▌
more than a costly form of autograph collecting—and very much more costl▌
in the case of drawings. To spend 11,000 guineas on an imitation of a book
illustration by Walter Crane seems to me to be carrying autograph-collectin▌
to excess. Till 1969 the magical drawings which van Gogh did at Arles wer▌
actually cheaper than his dreary pastiches of Millet, though the latter don'▌
seem to be nearly as rare. I have not succeeded in discovering whether there ▌
anyone who thinks they are actually *better*.

Mlle de Ravoux at £157,500 ($437,000 in 1966) was till 1970 the deares▌
painting by van Gogh. Yet it is not one of his more famous and popular pic▌
tures. A much less distinguished work, the most conventional of van Gogh'▌
flowerpieces, ran it quite close in New York at $310,000 in 1969, already a▌
much in paper terms as the outstanding *Gardens at Arles*, sold in 1958 fo▌
£132,000. To those who wondered what such a work was worth after th▌
passage of 11 or 12 years, the answer was provided within a few months by th▌
sale of a second and not inferior version of the Tate Gallery's *Cypresstrees* for $1▌
million or £541,000. There must be van Gogh pictures that are worth a millior

|      |                                                                                 | £      |
|------|---------------------------------------------------------------------------------|--------|
| 1890 | Sold by Theo van Gogh to Mlle Bock, Brussels, la Vigne Rouge, 400 francs         | 16     |
| 1895 | 'Père Tanguy'. Paris. Usines à Clichy (£31,000 in 1957), 21¼×28¼, 100 francs+auction tax | 4 8s.  |
| 1900 | Tavernier. Paris. Le déjêuner                                                    | 36 8s. |
|      | Maison à la campagne                                                             | 40     |
|      | Blôt. Paris. Roses tremières                                                     | 44     |
| 1906 | Blôt. Paris. 2nd sale. Sunflowers (see 1924)                                     | 160    |
| 1912 | Hoogendijk, The Hague. The swingbridge at Arles. Rijksmuseum (see 1932)          | 1,280  |
|      | The postman                                                                      | 440    |
| 1913 | Mariczell de Nemès. Paris. Still life                                            | 1,450  |
| 1914 | Kelekian. N.Y. Self-portrait. Detroit Art Museum                                 | 1,300  |
| 1921 | Price paid by Theodore Pitcairn for the portrait of Mlle Ravoux (£157,500 in 1966) said to have been | 4,000  |
| 1924 | Tate Gallery, Courtauld fund purchases. Cypress trees (compare 1970)             | 3,300  |
|      | The yellow straw chair                                                           | 696    |
|      | Sunflowers (see 1906)                                                            | 1,304  |

£

| | | |
|---|---|---|
| 1926 | ditto. View of Arles | 2,100 |
| 1927 | Murray. C. Vase of flowers | 1,260 |
| 1928 | Prince de Wagram. Paris. Public gardens at Arles (see 1958) | 3,100 |
| 1932 | Pacquement. Paris. La méridienne, 29×37　About | 4,000 |
| | Georges Petit, Paris. Bridge at Arles (see 1912) 270,000 francs+tax at 70 to £. Rijksmuseum | 4,620 |
| 1935 | Newman. N.Y. Printemps près d'Arles | 3,100 |
| 1939 | S. Olive trees at St Rémy | 4,000 |
| 1940 | N.Y. Portrait | 3,920 |
| | Male portrait, bought by National Gallery, Melbourne | 2,196 |
| 1943 | Sutro. S. Park at Arles | 1,550 |
| 1948 | Regendanz. C. Les fortifs, large watercolour (Cassirer, Berlin, 1926, £300) | 1,155 |
| 1951 | Paris. Pont de Châtou, 10 million old francs+tax | 11,950 |
| 1952 | Cognacq. Paris. Les chardons (thistles), 16½ million old francs and tax (see 1968)　About | 19,600 |
| 1953 | Paris. Eglise sous neige, Dutch period, 1885, 12×16½ | 4,950 |
| 1955 | N.Y. Flowers in a glass vase | 12,700 |
| 1957 | Weinberg. S. Usines à Clichy, 1887, 21¼×28¼, (see 1895) | 31,000 |
| | Angel's head after Rembrandt, 1889, 21¼×25¾ | 26,000 |
| | Paysan bêchant, 1885, 12½×12 (see 1964) | 6,500 |
| 1958 | Goldschmidt. S. Public Gardens at Arles (see 1928), 28¾×36½, Coll. Henry Ford II | 132,000 |
| | S. Field with yellow flowers | 17,000 |
| | Kirkeby. N.Y. Moored barge, 18½×21½, $67,500 | 24,107 |
| 1959 | Hopkins. S. Coal barges, Arles, or *les déchargeurs* (see 1963, 1965), 21¼×25¼ | 30,000 |
| | Bridge at Asnières (see 1966) bought in, 20¾×28¼ | 45,000 |
| 1962 | Metcalfe (Korda). S. Still life, 1889, 18¾×24½, citrons et gants blancs | 80,000 |
| | Woolworth. N.Y. Wasteland on edge of Paris, 18¼× 21½, $90,000 (see 1967) | 32,140 |
| 1963 | Wolf. S. Asylum at St Rémy, 1889, 17½×23¼ | 92,000 |
| | S. Les déchargeurs (see 1959, 1965), 21¼×25¼ | 45,000 |
| | Zimet. S. Les glâneurs, 1881, early pastiche of Millet | 14,000 |
| 1964 | Bloch. Paris. Paysan bêchant, 1885 (see 1957) | 10,350 |
| | Hutton. S. Auvers, 1890, small landscape | 48,000 |
| | Phillips. S. Peasant woman after Millet, 1890, 26×32 | 25,000 |
| 1965 | C. Woman peeling potatoes, early work, 17×12¼ | 8,925 |
| | Maurice Haft, Palm Beach. Le sémeur after Millet, 1890, 26×32 | 89,650 |
| | N.Y. Les déchargeurs, $625,000 (see 1959, 1963) | 85,705 |

| | | £ |
|---|---|---|
| 1965 | Cooper. C. Dutch peasant woman, early oil painting, 1884 | 8,400 |
| | Fayet. S. Pietà after Delacroix, smaller version, $16\frac{1}{2}\times 13\frac{1}{2}$ | 40,000 |
| | De Schlepper. S. Watermill at Nuenen, early work, 1884, $17\times 22\frac{1}{2}$ | 7,500 |
| | Alley of trees, Nuenen, 1885, $25\frac{1}{2}\times 34$ | 9,500 |
| 1966 | S. Study in oils, light on foliage, 1890, $12\frac{3}{4}\times 9\frac{1}{2}$, bought by Stockholm National Gallery | 14,200 |
| | Landscape at dusk, Nuenen, 1885, $13\frac{3}{4}\times 17$ | 11,000 |
| | Pitcairn. C. Mlle Ravoux in blue, 1890, $29\frac{1}{2}\times 21\frac{1}{2}$ (bought in 1921 for about £4,000) | 157,500 |
| | de Mesnil. N.Y. Pont sur la Seine à Asnières, 1886, $20\frac{3}{4}\times 28\frac{1}{4}$ (£45,000 in 1959) $142,500 | 50,900 |
| | Motte, Geneva. Paysanne moissonant, $15\frac{1}{2}\times 9\frac{1}{2}$, FS546,000 +tax | 51,950 |
| 1967 | Tetsch. S. Vase de pivoines, 1889, $21\frac{1}{2}\times 17\frac{3}{4}$ | 18,000 |
| | C. Wasteland on edge of Paris, $18\frac{1}{4}\times 21\frac{1}{2}$ (see 1962). Bought in at | 54,600 |
| | N.Y. Moulin à l'eau, 1884, $23\frac{3}{4}\times 31\frac{1}{2}$, $30,150 | 11,686 |
| 1968 | S. Après l'orage, 1884, after J. F. Millet, $26\frac{1}{2}\times 49\frac{1}{2}$ | 19,000 |
| | Pitcairn. C. The artist's mother, $15\frac{1}{2}\times 12\frac{1}{4}$ | 115,500 |
| | C. Les chardons, 1888, $21\frac{3}{4}\times 17\frac{3}{4}$ (see 1952) | 35,700 |
| | Paysage de Brabant, 1885, $8\frac{3}{4}\times 14\frac{1}{2}$ | 23,100 |
| | de Bruyn. C. Tête de paysanne, Dutch period, 1885, $15\times 12$ | 25,200 |
| | S. Nature morte, Nuenen, 1884, $12\times 15\frac{3}{4}$ | 13,000 |
| | N.Y. Presbyter's garden at Nuenen, 1885, $20\frac{1}{4}\times 30\frac{1}{4}$, $45,000 (£29,000 in 1970) | 18,786 |
| 1969 | Pitcairn. C. Le semeur, c. 1888, $13\frac{1}{4}\times 16$ | 78,750 |
| | Magnin. N.Y. Zinnias dans un vase, 1887, $23\frac{1}{2}\times 17\frac{3}{4}$, $310,000 | 131,250 |
| | S. La vieille tour dans les champs, $13\frac{3}{4}\times 18\frac{1}{2}$, painted at Nuenen, 1884 | 12,500 |
| 1970 | Crocker. New York. Le cyprès et l'arbre en fleur, Arles 1888, $20\frac{1}{2}\times 25\frac{1}{2}$, a 2nd version of the Tate Gallery picture (£3,300 in 1924) $1,300,000 | 541,000 |
| | Le laboureur, Arles 1889, $19\frac{1}{4}\times 24\frac{1}{2}$, $875,000 | 364,580 |

DRAWINGS

| | | |
|---|---|---|
| 1922 | S. Woman spinning (Dutch period) | 52 |
| 1957 | Weinberg. S. Derrière le Schenkweg, wc, $14\frac{3}{4}\times 21\frac{3}{4}$ | 2,200 |
| | Le tisserand, wc, 1884 (see 1965), $12\times 17$ | 3,200 |
| | Homme portant un fagot, wc, 1884, $13\times 12$ | 3,200 |
| | Travaux de champs, wc, 1882, $12\times 19\frac{1}{2}$ | 3,200 |

| | | £ |
|---|---|---|
| 1957 | S. Lever de soleil, pen, 1883, $12\times15\frac{1}{4}$ | 3,200 |
| | Mère et enfant, pencil and wash, 1883, $14\times9\frac{1}{4}$ | 2,800 |
| | Le charpentier, pencil, 1882, $18\frac{3}{4}\times9\frac{1}{4}$ | 2,800 |
| 1959 | S. Man with a hoe, Dutch period (see 1963) $23\frac{1}{4}\times17\frac{1}{2}$ | 6,500 |
| 1960 | S. Roofs, 1888, pen, $10\times13\frac{1}{4}$ | 5,000 |
| | Rewald. S. Old man with umbrella, 1882, $19\times10\frac{3}{4}$ | 3,800 |
| | S. Landscape at Arles, pen | 2,200 |
| | Paysanne bêchante, chalk and wash, $20\frac{1}{2}\times16$ | 5,000 |
| 1961 | S. Le semeur, pastiche of Millet, 1881, $24\times15\frac{3}{4}$, bought in at | 4,500 |
| 1963 | S. Two peasants hoeing, sketched on a postcard | 2,550 |
| | Man with a hoe, Dutch period (see 1959) $23\frac{1}{4}\times17\frac{1}{2}$ | 10,500 |
| | Earl of Sandwich. C. Chalk study, willows, $17\times11\frac{3}{4}$ | 4,830 |
| 1965 | Streuber. S. The weaver, wc, 1884 (see 1957) | 5,000 |
| 1966 | Pitcairn. C. Sorrow, pencil and charcoal, $17\frac{3}{4}\times10\frac{3}{4}$ 'in the English style', (after Walter Crane?) | 11,550 |
| 1967 | Kornfeld, Berne. Paysanne bêchante, wc and charcoal, $10\frac{1}{2}\times18\frac{3}{4}$, FS90,000+tax | 8,620 |
| 1968 | S. Le semeur, version of a Millet theme, 1882, $19\frac{1}{2}\times9\frac{1}{2}$ | 6,800 |
| 1969 | Lempertz, Cologne. Park at the Institut St Pol, Saint Rémy, $18\frac{3}{4}\times24\frac{1}{2}$, pen and sepia, DM160,000+tax About | 19,000 |
| | Timmermans. S. Moulin à Gennep, Dutch period 1884, wc, $12\times18\frac{1}{2}$ | 7,000 |
| 1970 | Auctions A.G. Basel. Jardin publique. Arles, 1889, pen, FS280,000+15% tax | 30,952 |

## ARSHILE GORKY. (*See* Abstract Painters, America)

## ADOLPH GOTTLIEB. (*See* Abstract Painters, American)

Francesco Goya y Lucientes

## GOYA. 1746–1828

here have been very few Goya paintings sold in London. When they were ill available, Paris was the market. On this account I have gone back to the ırn of the century, considerably augmenting the list in Volume One. From ıis an interesting point emerges. Though seldom, if ever, has so much been aid for so ill-attributed a picture, the state purchase of the Wellington porait in 1961 for over £140,000 was no true record for Goya. Both Jules Bache's *Iiguel Osorio da Suniga* and Andrew Mellon's *Marquesa de Pontejos* cost their owners as much or nearly so in terms of the purchasing power of money in 1925 and 1936. No portraits of this importance have reached the salerooms since the war. In 1949 the Spanish Government was said to have offered 3¼ million pesetas or about £40,000 for the truly magnificent whole-length portrait of *The Countess of Chinchón*. The owners expected to obtain $400,000, then equivalent to £142,000, in the U.S.A., but such masterpieces are no longer suffered to depart with equanimity and their value in 1970 can only be conjectural. Something equivalent to the *Maja desnuda* might well be worth a million. In the absence of that kind of Goya, an etching costs over £20,000 and the slightest scrap of a brush drawing £6,000.

|  |  |  | £ |
|---|---|---|---:|
| 1896 | Bought by National Gallery, London from the Duke of Osuna, Madrid, portrait, Dona Isabel Cobos de Porcel | | 405 |
| | The Bewitched and the Picnic, oil sketches | 2 for | 262 10s |
| | Sold elsewhere in same sale, L'escarpolette | | 600 |
| 1898 | Musée Kums, Antwerp. The Louvre buys the lady with a fan | | 1,160 |
| 1900 | Paris. The little shepherd | | 1,180 |
| 1905-7 | Havemeyer purchases: M. and Mme Sureda | 2 for | 1,750 |
| | The Duke of Wellington (for a worked-up version see 1961) | | 700 |
| 1908 | Chêramy. Paris. Portrait of Lola Ximenes | | 2,920 |
| | Earl of Clarendon. C. Pepe Illeno, the bullfighter (see 1919) | | 546 |
| 1911 | Consul Weber, Berlin. Portrait, Don Perez Estala. Hamburg, Kunsthalle | | 3,600 |
| | Sold by Gimpel, N.Y. The bullfighter (£300 in 1867) $24,000. Metropolitan Museum | | 4,940 |
| 1912 | Rouart. Paris. Spanish peasant girl | | 6,248 |
| | Doucet. Paris. Duke and Duchess of Alba | 2 for | 5,240 |
| 1916 | C. A lady in black | | 3,465 |
| 1919 | Drummond. C. Pepe Illeno the bullfighter (see 1908) | | 2,628 |
| 1920 | Paris. Bought by René Gimpel, la Princesse de Bourbon | About | 9,500 |
| 1922 | Marquise de Ganay. Paris. Portrait, Countess of Monte Hermosa | | 3,520 |
| 1925 | Sale by Henri Bernstein, Paris. Miguel Osorio da Zuniga (the little red boy) see 1928, $50,000 | | 10,500 |
| | Bought by National Gallery, Melbourne, a fat court lady | | 5,600 |
| 1928 | Bought from Duveen by Jules Bache, the little red boy (see 1925) National Gallery, Washington. Price according to Behrman, $160,000 | | 32,940 |
| 1929 | Walter Burns. C. The sermon, small oil | | 2,940 |
| 1930 | Havemeyer. N.Y. Lady with guitar (doubted). Ringling Museum, Sarasota, Fla. | | 4,340 |

|      |                                                                                                                                     |         | £ |
|------|-------------------------------------------------------------------------------------------------------------------------------------|---------|---|
| 936  | Bought from Duveen by Andrew Mellon. Portrait, Marquesa de Pontejos. National Gallery, Washington, $212,500                          | 43,750  |   |
|      | Winterfield. S. Gasparini, the court *tapissier*                                                                                     | 1,300   |   |
| 938  | N.Y. La joven, figure of a young girl, 29×23                                                                                         | 1,200   |   |
| 939  | St George. S. Dona Antonia Zarate. Field Coll. Chicago                                                                               | 6,800   |   |
| 941  | Harding. N.Y. The child, Victor Guye                                                                                                 | 8,500   |   |
| 951  | Paris. Two pendant portraits                                      2 for                                                              | 23,650  |   |
| 952  | S. Las pobrecitas, small oil sketch                                                                                                  | 3,800   |   |
|      | Bachstitz, Paris. Woman with a fan, 41×30½                                                                                           | 6,720   |   |
|      | Groult. Paris. Un refugié de la fortune, 16¾×6½                                                                                      | 4,750   |   |
| 953  | Paris. Girl's portrait                                                                                                               | 8,060   |   |
| 954  | Paris. The heroine of Saragossa, 33×25¾                                                                                              | 3,320   |   |
|      | Dona Basilia de Solero de Pig, 44×34, 8 million old francs+tax                                                                       | 9,650   |   |
| 957  | S. Las pobrecitas, 2nd version                                                                                                       | 1,800   |   |
|      | Paris. Don Manuel Godoy                                                                                                              | 2,860   |   |
| 958  | S. Lady in mantilla                                                                                                                  | 2,200   |   |
| 961  | D. of Leeds. S. Duke of Wellington. National Gallery, whence it was stolen but returned in 1965, 25¼×20½                            | 140,000 |   |
| 963  | Sterling of Keir. S. Two gouache fantasies on ivory, 3¼×3⅛                                    2 for                                 | 12,000  |   |
|      | Hirsch. S. Three princes of the Spanish royal house, sketch, 27×40                                                                   | 3,000   |   |
| 964  | S. Another gouache miniature on ivory                                                                                                | 4,800   |   |
| 969  | Delmege. S. Oil sketch, study for the Agony in the Garden, 1819, 17×13½                                                              | 8,000   |   |
|      | C. Ideal portrait of Ignatius Loyola holding a book; excessively doubtful, 32×22½, bought in at                                      | 2,730   |   |
|      | C. Bandits maltreating a woman with a child, probably a schoolpiece, 12×16½, bought in at                                            | 3,360   |   |
|      | Stafford. S. Caravan leaving town in a storm, roughly sketched, 42½×33½, bought in at                                               | 32,000  |   |
|      | Bought from Kocherthaler collection by the Nationa Gallery of Ireland, the Dreamer, reclining female half length                     | 145,000 |   |

### DRAWINGS

|      |                                                                            |        |
|------|----------------------------------------------------------------------------|--------|
| 960  | S. Bearded woman with a child                                              | 1,400  |
| 961  | Girl playing with puppies, 9¾×6½, 1805                                      | 6,000  |
| 964  | S. The giant, etching (one of 6 known copies) Boston Museum               | 20,500 |
| 966  | Bercovici. S. Unholy union, brush-drawing, 7×5¾                            | 5,000  |

# JAN JOSEFSZ VAN GOYEN. 1596–1673

One of the more abrupt rises of that unpredictable year, 1969, was the price c a van Goyen, close on £40,000 and this at the end of a decade in which th level of his frequently appearing works scarcely moved at all. There were half dozen pictures at £22,400 to £27,000 but £24,000 had been paid for the Duk of Westminster's View of Emmerich as far back as 1959. It was therefore te years before these exceedingly subtle little landscapes caught up with inflatior In the meantime Dutch landscapes by painters of less artistic significance, suc as Berckheyde and Avercamp, had multiplied in value several times over. Th market for the Dutch school in the 1960s tended to favour painters who ha been cheap in the past (see preliminary remarks under *Dutch School*).

| | | | £ |
|---|---|---|---|
| 1959 | S. Castle of Montfoort, 1646 | | 6,000 |
| | D. of Westminster. S. View of Emmerich, 26×37½ | | 24,000 |
| 1960 | van Aalst. C. View over a town, 1647, 12¼×15 | | 9,425 |
| | Pair of river scenes | 2 for | 15,750 |
| | S. River scene with fishermen, 25¾×36, 1646 | | 6,000 |
| | C. Beach at Scheveningen, 1644, 15½×23½ | | 7,350 |
| 1961 | D. of Sutherland. C. Wooded landscape with tower, 1648, 37½×50 | | 13,650 |
| | C. River scene, 1651, 21½×35½ | | 6,825 |
| | S. Rudge. S. River scene, 1647, 14¾×21½ | | 11,000 |
| | Russell. S. Estuary and fishermen, 1641, 19×30 | | 7,500 |
| 1963 | Heldring. S. Landscape with monastery, 1650, 22½×35¾ | | 7,500 |
| | Estuary scene, 1646 | | 5,800 |
| | S. Horsefair at Ruyswick | | 8,800 |
| | C. Sailing boats, 9×11 | | 5,560 |
| 1965 | C. Coast scene, 1655 (£84 in 1888), 14×23½ | | 12,075 |
| | Neville. S. Riverbank and château, 1645, 28×38 | | 8,000 |
| | Bellew. C. Ferry at Dortdrecht, 9¼×13¼ (200 guineas in 1879) | | 8,085 |
| | Adda. Paris. Fishing port, 18×23 | | 4,390 |
| | Lord Bruce. S. Open landscape with town, 18½×33, (Bought in, see 1966) | | 6,000 |
| 1966 | Blackwood. S. Boats near Dortdrecht, 1648, 14½×13¼ | | 14,000 |
| | C. River landscape with fishing boats, 1641, 14×13 | | 7,350 |
| | S. Fishing boats in a river, 7½×13 | | 5,700 |
| | Lord Bruce. S. Open landscape with town, 18¾×33 (see 1965) | | 3,990 |
| 1967 | Bowyer Smith. S. Winter landscape, 1625, 15×25½ | | 15,000 |
| | C. View on the Waal river, 1652, 25½×38 | | 10,500 |
| | Shipping in a breeze, 15×23½, dated 1644 | | 14,700 |
| | River scene with ruins, dated 1634, 29½×38½ | | 5,250 |

| | | £ |
|---|---|---|
| 1967 | Paris. Pigeon house, oval, 1641, 14½×19½, FN60,000+tax | 5,642 |
| | Banks of the Maas, 1639, 24½×18, FN90,000+tax | 8,395 |
| | Iris Micklem. S. Pilot's house near Dortdrecht, 1645, 9½×12¾ | 4,000 |
| 1968 | At Bonhams. View of Haarlem, 40½×56¾ | 3,500 |
| | Colman. C. View of Rhenen, 1639, 37×51½ | 2,940 |
| | C. View with church near Egmont, 12½×20¾, 1633 | 5,460 |
| | Penton. C. Tower by an estuary with fishing boats, 19×26½ | 5,040 |
| | Wrottesley. S. Estuary scene, 1636, 12¾×16¾ | 27,000 |
| | River and windmill, 1647, 15¼×23¼ | 8,000 |
| | Brandt, Amsterdam. River landscape, 1636, numerous figures, 14½×29¼, Hfl60,000+tax | 7,900 |
| | Paris. Shipping becalmed in estuary, 1648, 15½×22½, FN221,000+tax | 20,770 |
| 1969 | S. View of Overschie from river with church and ferry dated 1642, 12¼×15¼ | 23,500 |
| | Blijdenstein. S. Estuary, numerous boats, dated 1641, 10¼×15¾ | 12,000 |
| | Kieffer. Paris. River landscape, FN240,000+tax (6,500 francs+tax in 1922, about £120) | 22,260 |
| | Finch. S. Guardhouse with view of Dortdrecht, 1652, 20¼×30 | 13,000 |
| | Thomas. S. View in Amsterdam, grisaille on paper, 9¾×16½ | 11,500 |
| | S. Coast scene with fishermen, 1644, 10¼×12¾, bought in | 5,000 |
| | Paris. River landscape, FN240,000+tax | 22,421 |
| | S. Water-gate by an estuary, dated 1644, 14¾×22¼ | 25,000 |
| | Bruguière. C. Estuary landscape, sailing boats unloading 1655, 14×20 | 38,850 |
| | Boats on a river, dated 1651, 9½×15¾ | 10,500 |
| | Boats in an estuary, dated 1652, 12½×15½ | 14,700 |

BENOZZO GOZZOLI (attributed). (*See* Italian School, Central (1962))

## Domenico Theotocopuli, called EL GRECO. 1548–1614

The great vogue for El Greco in the first quarter of the century was inadequately illustrated in Volume One. The list has therefore been brought back to 1901. Sales during the 1960s may convey the false impression that interest in El Greco is flagging. But, as is the case with so many old masters, it is the quality available which is declining and not the demand. The paintings from the former

Herzog collection, for instance, now in the Budapest museum, will probably have multiplied in value at least fifty times since the eve of the First World War. Of all the truly *baroque* painters El Greco is still the dearest. It was certainly the Cézanne cult which made him so. Sixteenth century prismatic paint surfaces are no longer the surprise that they were, but, since we have Cézannes at half a million pounds, there could equally be half-million El Grecos.

|  |  | £ |
|---|---|---|
| 1901 | Bought in Spain by Mrs O. Havemeyer. Cardinal Guevara in spectacles, $14,000 | 2,880 |
| | View of Toledo. Metropolitan Museum | 2,880 |
| 1906 | Bought by Durand-Ruel, the Assumption of the Virgin | 3,500 |
| | Resold to Chicago Art Institute | 10,950 |
| 1907 | Don Abreu. C. Christ at Calvary | 1,995 |
| 1908 | Chêramy. Paris. Crucifixion. Lyons Museum, | 1,100 |
| | St. Domenica | 1,276 |
| 1912 | Bought from Knoedler by H. C. Frick, the Man in Armour | 31,000 |
| | Rouart. Paris. An apostle | 2,540 |
| 1913–15 | Bought from Mariczell de Nemès by Baron Herzog (since 1950 Budapest Museum of Fine Arts) | |
| | St Andrew, 28×21 | 1,460 |
| | Holy Family with St Elizabeth, 54×41 | 2,880 |
| | Christ on the Mount of Olives, 68×45 | 4,000 |
| | Annunciation, 43×28½ | 1,600 |
| | Christ mocked, 51×66 | 3,600 |
| | Head of an apostle, 22×18½ | 2,420 |
| 1913 | Mariczell de Nemès. Paris. Agony in the garden | 4,950 |
| | Holy Family, 180,000 francs+tax | 7,900 |
| 1918 | Degas. Paris. St Ildefonso (£17 in 1878, Millet sale) see 1936 | 3,805 |
| 1921 | Bought by J. Quinn. Moneylenders driven from the Temple, $18,000 | 4,500 |
| 1923 | Sandeman. C. Christ led to Calvary. Cardiff Museum | 3,360 |
| 1926 | C. St Martin dividing his cloak (see 1936) | 1,365 |
| 1930 | Havemeyer. N.Y. Small head of St Peter | 3,200 |
| 1931 | Berlin. Supper in the house of Simon | 6,850 |
| 1933 | N.Y. St Thomas, 21×43, $12,000 at 5·01 to £ | 2,480 |
| 1936 | Purchases by Andrew Mellon from Duveen, now National Gallery, Washington: St Ildefonso (see 1918) | 7,220 |
| | St Martin and the beggar (see 1926) | 24,700 |
| 1939 | St George. S. St Catherine | 3,800 |
| 1953 | Lord Greene. S. Small figure of St Paul (see 1960) | 2,050 |
| 1956 | Sold by Wildenstein to Stavros Nearchos. The Pietà of the Beraudière collection. 120 million old francs | 100,000 |
| | Goldschmidt. S. Small head of the Virgin | 14,000 |

| | | |
|---|---|---|
| 1958 | C. Christ healing the blind, replica of early work at Parma, sold as Veronese (see 1960) | 37,800 |
| | S. Small half-length, St Philip | 7,000 |
| 1959 | Del Monte. S. St James, 27×21. New College Chapel | 72,000 |
| 1960 | Polak. S. Half-length St Paul (£2,050 in 1953), 24×19¼ | 5,000 |
| | Sale to Charles Wrightsman of Christ healing the blind (£37,800 in 1958) | Over 100,000 |
| 1961 | Brieva. Paris. The martyrs of the Thebaid legion, 60×65 | 7,100 |
| 1963 | Cintas. N.Y. Annunciation, 27×40 | 9,825 |
| 1964 | Bought from Agnew by Staatliche Museen, Berlin. Mater dolorosa, half-length, dated 1585 | 109,000 |
| 1966 | S. The Holy Face on the kerchief of St Veronica, 24×19¾ (see 1967). Bought in at | 5,500 |
| | Pitcairn. C. Crucifixion, background view of Toledo (no pedigree beyond 1931), 40½×44 | 42,000 |
| | St John the Baptist, 19½×15½ | 24,150 |
| | Unknown family group, 36½×66 | 29,400 |
| 1967 | N.Y. The Holy Face on the kerchief of St Veronica (see 1966), 24×19¾, $16,000 | 5,715 |

## JEAN BAPTISTE GREUZE. 1725–1805

The highest price in terms of real money for a painting by Greuze is still that paid by the Earl of Dudley at the Foster sale of 1876 for *A Girl carrying a Puppy*, namely £6,720. In 1970 this would mean £70,000 for a picture worth perhaps a quarter as much. Greuze's dewy-eyed maidens, virtuous peasants and smug moralities have been out of fashion since at least the 1920s, but there survives some recognition of his technical capacity in the moderate prices paid for Greuze drawings. There might also be some recognition of his fine sense of portraiture, should any of Greuze's rare straightforward portraits reach the market. They have been dear before. According to René Gimpel's diary, Wildenstein was asking 1,650,000 francs in 1924 for the *Countess de X, playing a mandolin*, now at Baltimore. In 1924 this meant about £20,000, in 1970 about £100,000. That however was before the collapse of the great boom in French 18th century painting.

| | | £ |
|---|---|---|
| 1952 | Cognacq. Paris. Enfant à la pomme, 2·85 million francs + tax | 3,425 |
| 1953 | N.Y. Portrait of a boy | 2,232 |
| 1957 | Ambatielos. S. Small boy in white coat | 2,100 |
| 1961 | C. Peasant family in kitchen, 1778 | 3,990 |

£

| | | |
|---|---|---|
| 1963 | Stukker, Berne. Head of a small boy (+tax) 14½×18½ | 2,550 |
| | S. L'enfant aux perroquets, 25×21 | 700 |
| 1965 | Fitzgerald. S. La rêveuse, girl's head, 17½×14½ | 3,800 |
| 1967 | S. Head of a little girl, 15½×11¾ | 3,000 |
| 1968 | S. Girl with bird and cage, 1775, oval, 27½×23¼, bought in at | 15,000 |
| 1969 | Kieffer. Paris. La fausse innocente, 16×12¾, FN219,000 +tax | 20,115 |
| | (59,000 francs+tax in 1934, about £600) | |

### DRAWINGS

| | | |
|---|---|---|
| 1963 | Fribourg. S. Woman sewing, red chalk, ex Hermitage Mus. Leningrad | 1,000 |
| 1965 | C. La philosophe endormie, red chalk (portrait of Mme Greuze) | 4,410 |
| 1968 | C. Study for *le paralytique*, black and red chalk, 20×11½ | 1,312 10s. |
| | S. Self-portrait, pastel, 18×15 | 1,200 |

## JUAN GRIS. 1880–1927

Juan Gris, Fernand Léger and Jean Miró belong to the semi-abstract generation of painters who were already past their best in the 1920s. By dying in
1927 Juan Gris was saved from parodying his own style and is therefore in a
moderate degree the dearest of the three. These painters were sometimes
attracted to the objects of daily life, as displayed on hoardings, and with rather
less crudity were the forerunners of the movement maladroitly described as
'pop Art'. Needless to say, theirs is one of the most rapidly advancing of
markets and many moves ahead of currency inflation. Works by Juan Gris,
which might not have reached £1,000 in the 1950s, were in the £30,000 to
£50,000 region before 1970.

£

| | | |
|---|---|---|
| 1937 | Hollender and Bernheimer. C. Figure grise | 170 5s. |
| | Homme tenant *le jour*, 1918 | 110 5s. |
| | Nature morte avec mandoline, 1919 | 122 10s. |
| 1945 | Chrysler, N.Y. Two still lifes, $925 and $1,100 | 231 and 275 |
| 1949 | N.Y. Jerez de la Frontera, 25½×32 | 1,214 |
| | Paris. Le pacquet de café, 1914, 18×31½ | 497 |
| 1952 | Brussels. Nature morte au verre, 1916, 11¼×20¾ | 580 |
| 1954 | Rees Jeffries. C. The open book | 1,260 |
| 1959 | S. Arlequin attablé, 35½×25¾ | 8,500 |

| | | £ |
|---|---|---|
| 960 | Rewald. S. Still life, wc | 2,000 |
| | Museum of Modern Art, N.Y. In the lamplight, 15 × 18, $23,000 | 8,214 |
| | S. Harlequin with guitar, 1925, 30½ × 34½ | 16,000 |
| 961 | Laughlin. S. Le pacquet de café, collage, 25½ × 18½ | 9,200 |
| 962 | Wardell-Power. S. Glass bottle and newspaper, 28 × 21 | 10,500 |
| 963 | Zimet. S. Paysage, 1917, 45½ × 28½ | 6,500 |
| 964 | S. Abstraction, 1927 | 13,000 |
| | Hecht. S. The two pierrots, 1922, 39 × 45 | 10,000 |
| | C. Le fûmeur, crayon, 27½ × 23 | 3,360 |
| 965 | Lefèvre. Paris. Nature morte à la lampe, 1914, collage, 22 × 18½ | 15,600 |
| | Nature morte aux raisins, collage, 22 × 18 | 22,482 |
| | Arlequin, joueur de guitare, oils, 40 × 27 | 16,418 |
| | Le tapis rouge, compôtier et carafe, 26 × 33½, oils | 12,378 |
| | Nature morte au journal, 1916, oils, 32 × 18 | 25,428 |
| | Compôtier et journal, 1918, oils, 87 × 26 | 19,320 |
| | Le moulin à café, 1920, oils, 24 × 32½ | 16,200 |
| | S. Nature morte, 1918, oils, 18¼ × 21½ | 7,000 |
| 966 | Thompson. N.Y. Le table du musicien, oils, 1914, 31½ × 23¼ | 16,125 |
| | Helena Rubinstein. N.Y. Femmes et oiseaux dans la nuit, mixed media, 15½ × 14¼ | 10,070 |
| | Lefèvre. Paris. 2nd sale. La crûche, 1920 | 10,450 |
| | l'Ecossaise, 1918 | 9,225 |
| 967 | S. Still life, 1919, oils, 18 × 10½ | 14,000 |
| | Lefèvre. Paris. Compôtier, flacon, 1920 (11·82 francs to the £) 24 × 29 | 11,100 |
| | S. Nature morte avec tasse, 18¾ × 10¾, 1913 | 12,000 |
| 968 | Granz. S. Bouteille de Bordeaux, 1914, 21½ × 12¾ | 36,000 |
| | L'Intransigeant, 1915, 25¼ × 17¾ | 32,500 |
| | La bouteille de vin rosé, oil and collage, 1914, 17½ × 10½ | 17,000 |
| | S. Paysage, Loches, 1916, 21¾ × 15, oil on panel | 12,000 |
| | Bluestein. N.Y. Nature morte au poème, 1915, 31¾ × 25½, $120,000 | 50,000 |
| | S. Bol et compôtier, 1925, 18 × 21¾ | 16,500 |

## MARCEL GROMAIRE. (*See* Abstract Painters, Europe)

## FRANCESCO GUARDI. 1712–1793

An old master, whose paintings are by no means rare on the market and to whom prevailing fashions have been almost continuously kind since the 1890s, could not be expected in the 1960s to advance with the speed of some pioneer of cubism and abstraction. Some old masters, to whom the same description might apply, did not advance at all. In the case of Guardi, the larger *capriccio* (seldom more than two feet wide) rose from £14,500 in 1959 to £54,600 in 1965. They would not seem to be dearer in 1970, even on paper. But it must be noticed that the common run of Guardi *capriccios* are very small and that even a three-foot Guardi must now be hard to find. On the other hand there has been a belated recognition that these are but journeyman works, compared with the earliest Venetian *vedute* of Canaletto. This is not the first time that the vogue for Guardi has been overplayed, since a Guardi regatta scene was sold at Christies in 1919 for 6,200 guineas, equivalent in 1970 to £32,500. But if one may trust René Gimpel, a regatta scene, six feet long, was sold in 1912 to Charles B. Alexander for $55,000, equivalent in 1970 to about £90,000. It is seldom realized how completely Francesco Guardi's little-varying style covers the span of the 18th century. He was born when there was still a *roi soleil* on the throne of France, and he died in the year that Louis XVI had his head cut off.

|  |  |  | £ |
|---|---|---|---|
| 1959 | S.   Lagoon scene, 12½ × 20½ |  | 14,500 |
| 1961 | Andraee.   C.   Flowerpiece with parrot, 58 × 80, tentative attribution |  | 11,550 |
|  | Navarro.   S.   Piazza san Marco, 11½ × 19 |  | 6,500 |
|  | Makower.   S.   Venice from the islands, 15 × 20½ |  | 17,000 |
|  | Adeane.   S.   Torre dell'orologio |  | 7,500 |
|  | Lees.   S.   Two postcard-size capriccios | 2 for | 4,200 |
| 1962 | S.   View over the Grand Canal |  | 15,000 |
|  | C.   Seaport capriccio |  | 4,520 |
|  | Paris.   Flowerpiece, attributed, FN175,000+tax |  | 15,322 |
| 1963 | Paris.   Capriccio, 7¾ × 6 |  | 6,570 |
|  | Marten.   S.   Water fête on the lagoon, 16 × 26 |  | 14,000 |
|  | Three decorative panels from Bantry House, episodes from *Gerusalemme Liberata*, 98½ × 43 each (eight panels sold in 1956, £12,000) see also 1964.   Bought in at (3 for) |  | 15,000 |
|  | Fribourg.   S.   View towards the Redentore, 10 × 17½ |  | 12,500 |
|  | View towards the Dogana, slightly smaller |  | 9,000 |
| 1964 | S.   Flowerpiece |  | 6,825 |
|  | Bootle-Wilbraham.   S.   Piazza san Marco, 19 × 33 |  | 34,000 |
|  | Bought from Geoffrey Merton for Washington National Gallery two further panels, 98½ × 43, from Bantry House (see 1956 and 1963) | 2 for | 150,000 |
| 1965 | S.   Capriccio, Roman ruins, 9¼ × 11¾ |  | 19,500 |
|  | Spencer Churchill.   C.   Entrance to Grand Canal, 16 × 21 |  | 54,600 |
|  | Grand Canal, companion-piece, same size |  | 35,700 |

£

| | | |
|---|---|---|
| 1965 | Storer. S. Capriccio with ruins, $37 \times 45\frac{1}{2}$ | 18,000 |
| | Adda. Paris. Piazza San Marco, $16 \times 25$ | 21,280 |
| 1966 | S. Doge's Palace from the Bacino, $24 \times 29$, bought in at | 20,000 |
| | James de Rothschild. Paris. Grand Canal, FN570,000+tax, $18\frac{1}{2} \times 30\frac{1}{2}$ | 45,766 |
| | Piazza San Marco, $16\frac{1}{2} \times 21\frac{1}{2}$, FN450,000+tax | 36,189 |
| | Grand Canal, $6\frac{3}{4} \times 12\frac{1}{2}$, FN335,000+tax | 26,897 |
| | S. Two capriccios with ruins, $33 \times 26$ 2 for | 16,000 |
| 1967 | S. Three capriccios, each $8 \times 6\frac{1}{2}$ 6,000, 6,800 and 8,000 | |
| 1968 | Harewood. C. Two views of the Piazza San Marco, $11\frac{3}{4} \times 20$ 2 for | 10,500 |
| | Prince de Ligne. S. Capriccio with tower and bridge, $3\frac{1}{4} \times 4\frac{3}{4}$ | 6,200 |
| | S. Piazza San Marco, $20\frac{1}{2} \times 33\frac{1}{4}$ | 20,000 |
| | Paris. Piazza San Marco, $16 \times 24\frac{3}{4}$, FN240,000+tax | 22,400 |
| | S. Figures among ruins, signed, $40\frac{1}{2} \times 47\frac{1}{2}$ | 50,000 |
| 1969 | C. Bridge over Venetian canal, $22\frac{1}{2} \times 28\frac{1}{2}$ | 9,450 |
| | S. Venice from the Bacino, $17 \times 26\frac{1}{4}$ | 16,000 |
| | Capriccio, lagoon scene, $7\frac{3}{4} \times 12\frac{1}{2}$ | 6,500 |

### DRAWINGS

| | | |
|---|---|---|
| 1960 | Motte, Geneva. Gallery in Piazza San Severo, Venice, sepia on blue, FS41,000+tax | 4,080 |
| 1963 | S. Venetian courtyard, pen and ink, $7 \times 8$ | 4,500 |
| | Study for a Pietà | 1,550 |
| 1964 | S. Piazza san Marco | 1,700 |
| 1967 | Paris. Wolf-hunt, pen and wash, $18\frac{1}{2} \times 25\frac{1}{2}$, FN44,000+ tax | 3,490 |
| 1969 | S. Capriccio, mixed media, a Palladian design for the Rialto Bridge | 8,000 |

GUERCINO. (*See* Italian School, 16th–17th centuries)

PHILIP GUSTON. (*See* Abstract Painters, America)

JEAN BAPTISTE GUILLAUMIN. (*See* French School, Minor Impressionists)

PIERRE ADOLPHE HALL. (*See* Miniatures)

HARRY HALL. (*See* Sporting Pictures)

# FRANS HALS. 1584–1666

Before the war, the Munich Alter Pinakothek owned only one Frans Hals. For a more important specimen they paid in 1969 the price of a Raphael or a Leonardo, since the unprepossessing likeness of *Willem van Heythuysen* cost the Bavarian state government not less than £1,355,000. For the sale of a single picture the price was surpassed only by the purchase from the same Liechtenstein collection of Leonardo's portrait of *Ginevra di Benci*. This cost the National Gallery, Washington 5 million dollars two years earlier.

The market for Frans Hals in the 1960s was very far from leading up to this astonishing climax. In fact the appeal of Hals's swashbuckling vulgarity had dwindled from its heyday in the early years of the century, despite two recent sales at £182,000 and £214,000. Thus in 1907 *The Artist's Family*, now in the Thyssen collection, cost Duveen £30,000. Duveen himself sold Henry Clay Frick a portrait of an old woman in 1910 for $150,000. In terms of purchasing power, both these prices exceed £250,000 in the money of 1970. Andrew Mellon in the 1930s gave even more, for the *Young Men in a Red Sash* of the Hermitage collection cost him £52,000 in 1931. The portrait of *Baltazar Coymans* was sold him by Duveen in 1936 for $350,000 or £72,000. In 1970 terms the first can be called £260,000, the second £360,000. Presumably the *Burgomaster's family* of the National Gallery and the *Laughing Cavalier* of the Wallace collection should be valued at least as high as *Willem van Heythuysen*. Nothing of this sort however is to be expected in the salerooms. The enormous prices of the past have swept up the best into the laps of millionaires and thence into public galleries.

|  |  | £ |
|---|---|---:|
| 1959 | Oliven. S. Portrait, Frans Post, 16½×13 (£15,000, 1928) | 48,000 |
| 1960 | Warde-Aldam. S. Unknown cavalier, 29×24 (£15, 1885) | 182,000 |
| 1961 | Fisher. S. Unknown gentleman, 30×25 | 16,000 |
|  | Erickson, N.Y. Pieter van der Mirsch, the man with the herring, 34½×27½ | 51,785 |
|  | Wyndham. C. Head of an unknown girl, 22½×21. Bought in at | 84,000 |
|  | S. Head of unknown woman, bought in | 18,000 |
| 1962 | Same picture, bought for Ferens Art Gallery, Hull | 35,000 |
| 1963 | Cintas. N.Y. Young man with a lute, drinking, 35½×29½ | 214,000 |
|  | Portrait head, Aerhout van Dravestein, 24×28 | 25,000 |
|  | French. S. Young man with ruffled hair, 13×26 | 11,000 |
| 1965 | Kempendieck. C. Unknown male portrait, 25×34½, Bought in Arnhem in 1963 for £2 10s. | 73,500 |
| 1967 | Count de Bendern. The fluteplayer, circular bust portrait, 14 in. diam., stolen in Geneva and valued for insurance at | 125,000 |

£

967 Watney. C. Jacobsz Olycan, bust portrait, $26\frac{1}{2}\times22\frac{3}{4}$ 52,500
   Wife of Jacobsz Olycan, very plain, $26\frac{1}{2}\times23$ 10,500
  N.Y. Adrianus Tegularius, preacher of Haarlem, oil
  sketch, $11\frac{1}{4}\times9\frac{1}{4}$, $32,500 11,600
969 Countess Rey. S. Unknown man in lace collar, half-
  length, $31\frac{1}{4}\times23$ 8,000
  S. 'Junker Ramp and his girl', $10\frac{3}{4}\times8\frac{3}{4}$, oil sketch,
  bought in at 7,500
  Bruguière. C. Called 'Hals'. Head of laughing boy
  with a flute in painted circle, $13\frac{1}{2}\times12$ 6,825
  Sale by Prince Liechtenstein, Vaduz, to Bavarian Government, whole-length portrait, Willem van Heythuysen,
  $82\times54$, FS14 million 1,355,000

WILLIAM M. HARNETT. (*See* American School, 19th and 20th centuries

HANS HARTUNG. (*See* Abstract Painters, Europe)

CHILDE HASSAM. (*See* American School)

FRANCIS HAYMAN. (*See* English School, 18th century)

JOHN HERRING SENR. (*See* Sporting Pictures)

JAN VAN DER HEYDEN. (*See* Dutch School)

NICOLAS HILLIARD. (See Miniature Painters)

MEINDERT HOBBEMA. 1638–1709

f Frans Hals seems an unlikely painter to excite the idolatry of the mid-
twentieth century, Hobbema should be still more so. Daring, which is the
only quality a modish person is permitted to require from a work of art, is
plainly lacking here. Even Gainsborough and Constable were at their dullest
when they came nearest to imitating Hobbema. And, if it is true that Crome
died with the word Hobbema on his lips, one is not surprised. Why then

£125,000 in 1966 for another of those painstaking worthy woods? I suspect that it is all on account of precedent, for Hobbema was even dearer in the days before the Dutch inspiration of the Barbizon school had given way to the Impressionists; the days when collectors were protected from over-exciting themselves and when absence of strain was charged for on the bill. Thus in 1900 James Pierpont Morgan, who was never *experimental*, bought one of the coveted woody landscapes from Sir George Holford for £20,000 (£160,000 on the 1970 scale). In 1912 King Leopold II of Belgium sold *The Farm in the Sun* for £28,000 (£224,000) and, next year, E. D. Libbey of Toledo gave £26,000 (£208,000) for *The Path through the Wood*. Even more was paid for a *House in the Wood* at the Six sale of 1928, namely £33,000, but owing to the higher cost of living this meant no more than £165,000 in 1970 terms. We may again see Hobbemas as dear as these, bought by museum directors bidding against each other from sheer force of habit.

|      |                                                                                                 | £       |
|------|-------------------------------------------------------------------------------------------------|---------|
| 1960 | van Aalst. C. Wooded river landscape, 12¾ × 14¾                                                  | 14,700  |
| 1963 | Paris. Wooded landscape, 23¾ × 33½, FN285,000+tax                                                | 24,540  |
|      | S. Wooded landscape                                                                              | 6,500   |
| 1965 | Edgar. S. Wooded landscape, 23¾ × 33                                                             | 4,000   |
| 1966 | Lady Mary Grosvenor. S. Wooded landscape, 34½ × 47½, figures by Lingelback. (Bought by Lord Grosvenor with the Agar collection in 1806, when John Smith valued it at 300 guineas.) | 125,000 |
|      | S. Ruin by a river, 14¾ × 20                                                                     | 5,200   |
| 1969 | S. Wooded landscape with cottages dated 1665, 37¼ × 48 (Lord Malmsbury sale, 1876, £1,102 10s. Bought in at £16,800 in 1956) | 34,500  |

## WILLIAM HOGARTH. 1697–1764

In 1965, when the somewhat homely physiognomy of Daniel Lock made 50,000 guineas at the Spencer Churchill sale, Hogarth became by almost any standards an expensive painter. It meant that the paintings which Hogarth had designed for his famous suites of engravings, *The Rake's Progress*, *The Harlot's Progress*, *Marriage à la Mode* were worth at the very least £150,000 for each canvas. In this there is nothing surprising except the time table. In 1921 when Gainsborough's *Blue Boy* was sold by Duveen for £148,000, one of the better versions of Hogarth's *Beggar's Opera* was sold for a thousand guineas the price it had made in 1905. That was during the long market dominance of the Grand Manner portrait, when Hogarth had nothing to offer in the way of adding pomposity to a millionaire interior. In fact his works were treated precisely as they had been in the 18th century. But now when the search is all for conversation pieces and local colour, when hunting subjects by Seymour and Ben Marshall can make about £60,000 each, what can be more desirable than a story-telling picture by Hogarth himself? But since 1963 it has become probable that there are none left that can reach the market.

| | | £ |
|---|---|---|
| 1959 | Tennant. S. Peg Woffington, oval portrait, $29\frac{1}{2} \times 24\frac{1}{2}$ | 3,000 |
| 1961 | Duke of Leeds. S. Polly Peachum in *the Beggar's Opera*, painted for John Rich, one of several versions. (Rich sale, 1762, £35 14s.) $23\frac{3}{4} \times 29$ | 30,000 |
| 1963 | Private sale by Lord St Oswald to Sheffield Corporation. Garrick in *the Tempest*, $75 \times 98\frac{1}{2}$ | 30,000 |
| | Young. C. The Stafford family, $38 \times 54$, poor condition | 1,155 |
| | Ionides. S. The brothers Clark taking wine (Formerly attributed to Gavin Hamilton) | 3,200 |
| | S. Portrait head of unknown woman, dated 1745 | 1,700 |
| 1965 | Brenda Cook. C. Unidentified family conversation, $21 \times 29\frac{1}{2}$ | 39,900 |
| | Spencer Churchill. C. Portrait of Daniel Lock, $36 \times 27\frac{3}{4}$ (£45 3s. in 1845) | 52,500 |
| | Croft. S. Ashley Cooper with wife, child and greyhound 1731, bought by Tate Gallery, $24\frac{3}{4} \times 29\frac{1}{4}$ | 18,900 |
| 1967 | C. The angel of Mercy, design for an altarpiece, $23\frac{1}{2} \times 19$ | 4,410 |
| | Holland Martin. C. Thomas Herring, Archbishop of York, 1744, $49 \times 30$ | 19,950 |
| | Long. C. Oil sketch for the Modern Midnight Conversation, 1733, $25 \times 30$ | 4,725 |
| 1968 | Bonham's Rooms. Head of unknown man, $30 \times 20$, unattributed | 4,400 |
| | Bearns, auctioneer, Torquay. William James of Ightham Court, 1744, $29\frac{1}{2} \times 24\frac{1}{2}$ | 24,000 |
| 1969 | Bonham's Rooms. Conversation piece in a garden, attributed $18 \times 32$ | 4,800 |

## HANS HOLBEIN THE YOUNGER. 1497–1543

The only certain Holbein painting to come on the market in the 1960s was a miniature, no more than $1\frac{1}{2}$ inches across. The price, £21,000, was not equal to the more optimistic predictions. The last Holbein miniature to be sold, the locket-portrait of *Mrs Pemberton*, which Duveen gave to the Victoria and Albert Museum in 1935, cost him £6,195, the equivalent in November, 1969, of £31,000. But there is no comparison between that unforgettable work and the plainly painted likeness of a plain unknown woman, somewhat rubbed, which faced the saleroom in 1969. That it had no recorded history and that it had eluded all who had written about Holbein, were adverse factors, though it was hardly disputed that this was truly a thirteenth Holbein miniature to be added to the known canon of twelve.

What then might be the value of a full-sized Holbein portrait? The last to be sold, the head of Anthony Butts, was acquired in 1934 by the Boston Fine Arts Museum at the slump-price of £12,000, but in 1936 Andrew Mellon paid Duveen a reputed half million dollars for an infant-portrait of Edward VI which is no longer accepted—and that in 1969 meant as many pounds. The whole-length Duchess of Milan, for which the nation had to find £72,000 in 1910, will presumably be a million and a half pound picture or something very near it. With drawings the situation is analogous. The last was a design for a stained glass window, sold in 1955 for £3,400. The last portrait-drawing was sold in 1947 for £900, but the inscribed historical portrait drawings at Windsor should be worth more than £50,000 each.

| | | £ |
|---|---|---|
| 1961 | Erickson. N.Y. Lord Abergavenny, 1533, 16×11½, head, much restored, $35,000 | 12,500 |
| 1965 | Minken. S. Lady Jane Grey, 72×37, schoolpiece. National Portrait Gallery | 4,000 |
| 1966 | Bought by National Portrait Gallery. Sir Thomas More, 1527, replica of Frick foundation portrait | 15,000 |
| 1969 | S. Unknown woman's head, miniature, 1½ in. diam. probably painted in England, c. 1540 | 21,000 |

FRANCIS HOLMAN. (*See* English School, 18th century)

WINSLOW HOMER. (*See* American School)

GERRIT VAN HONTHORST. (*See* Flemish School after 1550, portraits)

## PIETER DE HOOCH. 1629–1683

Since an interior by Emanuel de Witte, not a name to conjure with, could achieve £63,000 in 1968, there are surely surprises to be expected from Pieter de Hooch. Or maybe there are not. His later and darker works have made no response to inflation. His brilliant courtyard paintings have not been seen in the saleroom for 33 years. The one in the Fattorini Collection, U.S.A., made £17,500 at the Victor Rothschild sale of 1937, equivalent to £87,500. A year earlier, Andrew Mellon had bought the example in the National Gallery, Washington, for $200,000, equivalent in 1970 to £206,000. Six-figure prices are certain if such pictures return to the market. On the other hand the interiors with figures will undoubtedly have fallen. The price of a by no means first-rate example in the Secrétan sale of 1889, £11,040, was the equivalent of quite £100,000. Another made £12,500 at the Six sale of 1928, equivalent to £62,500. But in the 1960s nothing of this kind made as much as £20,000.

| | | £ |
|---|---|---|
| 954 | Butterworth. N.Y. Woman nursing a sick child, 26½×21¾, $34,000 | 12,150 |
| 957 | C. Soldiers drinking in a barn | 4,095 |
| 958 | Kaplan. N.Y. Interior with figures (£27 15s. in 1777) | 8,925 |
| 960 | Dreesman, Amsterdam. Interior of the town hall, Amsterdam, 45×39½, HFL185,000+tax        About | 20,900 |
| 963 | Princess Labia. S. Interior with noble company | 11,000 |
| 966 | Canaday Trust, Toledo. S. Interior with music party, 24×28 (£152 in 1863, £127 in 1874) now attributed to Van den Burch | 5,400 |
| 968 | Kaplan. S. A musical party, 25¼×29, a late work | 8,500 |
| | C. Interior with smoking gentleman and maidservant, 27×20½ | 7,350 |
| 969 | N.Y. (attributed) Girl with a wineglass, 16½×13, $32,000 | 13,335 |

## JOHN HOPPNER. 1759–1820

Hoppner surely holds the title of the most overrated old master ever known to the art market. Even the formidable competition of some 20th century practitioners doesn't get near him. In 1914 E. T. Stotesbury paid the 1970 equivalent of £614,500 for *The Tambourine Girl*, whose subsequent tumble will be found in Volume One. In 1926 Andrew Mellon gave $200,000 for the Frankland sisters, equivalent to just over £200,000 on the 1970 scale. Even in slump-ridden 1935 the great Duveen had to give £12,075 (£60,375) to get back the portrait of *Phoebe Hoppner*. And all this for no better reason than the lack of any other 'grand manner' practitioners between the deaths of Reynolds and Romney and the rise of Sir Thomas Lawrence.

It will be noticed that even in the 1960s Hoppner's price could shoot up when it was a question of a noble duke recovering an ancestor.

| | | £ |
|---|---|---|
| 959 | Lloyd. C. Countess of Oxford and daughter, whole-length | 1,470 |
| 962 | S. Lady Elizabeth Bligh as a child | 2,800 |
| 963 | Cintas. S. 6th Duchess of Bedford (bought by present Duke), 85×56½ | 9,000 |
| | Paris. Miss Jordan, half-length | 3,515 |
| 964 | C. Brother and sister, oval, 22×27 | 3,570 |
| 965 | S. Lady Elizabeth Whitbread | 1,300 |
| 967 | Flesh. C. Miss Maria Bover, 28½×24½ | 2,310 |
| 968 | Craven. S. Two sons of 6th Lord Craven, whole-length in Vandyke costume, 92½×56 | 3,400 |
| 969 | Bruguière. C. Lady Coote of Donnybrooke, 50×40 | 1,890 |
| 970 | C. (Catalogued as 'Hoppner') Pair of half-lengths, boy and girl, 29½×24½                    2 for | 11,025 |

JOHN HOSKINS. (*See* Miniature Painters)


## WILLIAM HOLMAN HUNT. 1827–1910

A great deal of Holman Hunt's working life was absorbed by half a dozen famous works which took years to complete, and which are now enshrined in the public galleries of Manchester, Liverpool and Birmingham. Hunt also painted studies and potboiler pictures which sometimes reach the salerooms. These have made more than an average response to the impact of inflation. Can one, for instance, think of a single watercolour view-painting, made after the death of Turner, which could rival the 3,200 guineas, paid for Holman Hunt's study of the Great Pyramid in 1968? After that, one must consider *The Scapegoat* as at least a £50,000 picture.

|      |                                                                                                      | £         |
|------|------------------------------------------------------------------------------------------------------|-----------|
| 1961 | Joseph. C. Dolce fa niente, 1866, 40×32 (£745 10s. in 1871, £241 10s. in 1938, see also 1966)       | 472 10s.  |
|      | Burt. C. The lady of Shallott (3,360 in 1919), 74×57, completed in 1909                              | 9,975     |
| 1962 | Sydney Cockerell. S. Amaryllis, 25×20                                                                 | 400       |
|      | S. Sorrow, 1889, 25×20                                                                                | 400       |
| 1966 | C. Dolce fa niente (472 10s. in 1961)                                                                 | 2,940     |
| 1967 | S. The haunted manor, oils, 1849, 9¼×13¼. Tate Gallery                                               | 1,800     |
| 1968 | C. The great Pyramid, wc bodycolour, 1854, 6×9¾ (£63 in 1897)                                        | 3,360     |
| 1969 | C. Head in coloured chalks, Mrs Holman Hunt, 1880, 18×13                                             | 525       |
|      | S. Ross, Toronto. S. Doctor Rochecliffe at Woodstock, RA picture, 1847, 27½×35½                      | 950       |


## JAN VAN HUYSUM. 1682–1749

It will be recalled from Volume One that the reputation of this painter stood very high a generation after his death, when a pair of flowerpieces were sold in London for 1,000 guineas which was more than anyone would have paid for two first rate Rembrandts. Huysum's fame rested on his light transparent colours, so different from the flowerpieces of his predecessors. In the 1960s however, the predecessors fetched very much more, for instance Baltazar van der Ast at £16,800, while later imitators of Huysum like Jan van Os fetched more too (£19,950 in 1965 and £22,000 in 1968). Even a mid-Victorian pasticheur like Edward Ladell could fetch almost as much as the originals whose value had risen little since the 1920s.

|  |  |  | £ |
|---|---|---|---|
| 960 | C. Flowerpiece and stone urn | | 5,800 |
| 961 | C. Flowerpiece | | 4,410 |
| 963 | S. Flowerpiece, 33×27 | | 1,800 |
| 965 | Flowerpiece, 29½×23 | | 4,000 |
| | C. Roses, irises and poppies, 21½×18 | | 3,675 |
| 966 | Flowerpiece, signed, 25×19½ | | 2,520 |
| 967 | van Waay, Amsterdam. Fruit and flowers, 21¼×17¾, Hfl56,000 | | 6,080 |
| 968 | Flowerpiece, signed, 29½×21¾ | | 4,800 |
| | C. Landscape with nymphs etc., 21½×33½ | | 5,250 |
| | Flowers, glass vase, 16×12½ | | 2,940 |

## JEAN DOMINIQUE INGRES. 1780–1867

The list has been taken back to the beginning of the century to rectify the somewhat inadequate picture, presented in Volume One. It will be perceived that the frozen neo-classicism and tight brushwork of the greatest of academic painters declined in popularity with the dominance of Impressionism, in the 1950s, though the portrait of *Madeleine Ingres* in 1928 had made the equivalent of £34,500. The price, paid by the National Gallery in 1936 for the famous portrait of *Mme Moitessier*, meant something like £73,500. A work of this importance would certainly be a six-figure picture in 1970, but notice should be taken of the fate in 1966 of two of Ingres's charming small exercises in the Italian Renaissance manner, one of which failed to reach its reserve, while the other showed only a moderate advance since 1957.

With drawings it is another matter. Ingres was the greatest portrait draughtsman since Holbein, and the market has recognized the fact almost since his death.

|  |  | £ |
|---|---|---|
| 1896 | Paris (bought by Degas). Portrait, M. Leblanc | 140 |
| | Mme Leblanc (see 1918) | 300 |
| 1897 | Bought by the Louvre. Portrait of M. Bertin aîné, 1832 | 3,200 |
| 1899 | Bought by the Louvre. La grande odalisque, 1814 | 2,400 |
| 1918 | Degas. Paris. M et Mme Pastouret. The Louvre | 3,960 |
| | M et Mme Leblanc (see 1896) Metropolitan Museum 2 for | 11,880 |
| | M. de Norvins, 1813, 38¾×31. National Gallery | 3,388 |
| | Roger and Angelica, 18¾×15½, 1816, National Gallery | 330 |
| | Oedipus and the Sphinx, 1808, 7×5¾. National Gallery | 330 |
| 1919 | C. Lady in white satin, 1814 | 1,427 10s. |

| 1924 | Brâme. Paris. Asking price for oil study for the Triumph of Homer according to R. Gimpel | £ 2,600 |
|---|---|---|
| 1927 | Empress Eugènie. C. Louis XIV and Molière (bought in 1863 from the painter for £1,000) | 304 10s. |
| 1928 | S. Portrait, lady in pale blue | 620 |
| 1929 | Lapauze. Paris. Portrait of Madeleine Ingres | 6,900 |
| 1933 | Camdano. Paris. Angelica chained to the rock | 4,645 |
| 1935 | Baron Vitta. Paris. Portrait of M. Nogent | 3,170 |
| 1936 | Bought by the National Gallery. Portrait, Mme Moitessier, 1858 | 14,676 |
| 1948 | N.Y. Raphael and la Fornarina (£380 in 1865) | 1,430 |
| 1949 | Paris. Francesca da Rimini and Paolo Malatesta, 14×11½, 400,000 francs+tax (compare 1966) | 560 |
| 1950 | Paris. Stratonice, reduced replica, 33½×25½ | 860 |
| 1954 | Bessoneau. Paris. La vierge couronnée, 1859, 28×20½ | 6,940 |
| | L'entrée de Charles V à Paris, 19¾×22½, 1821 | 5,430 |
| 1957 | Brussels. L'Aretin et l'envoyé de Charles V, also L'Aretin chez le Tintoret, pair, 15×13¼ (see 1966) with tax, 2 for | 6,200 |
| 1959 | Valued for the National Gallery, Lane Bequest: Portrait, Duc d'Orleans | 7,500 |
| 1966 | S. L'Aretin chez le Tintoret, 15×13¼ (see 1957) | 4,700 |
| | Paolo et Francesca, 11½×9. Bought in at | 16,000 |
| 1967 | C. (formerly attributed to Ingres) Portrait of Mme de Stäel, before 1810, 23×28½ | 2,940 |
| 1969 | Sieff. S. Le mort de Leonardo de Vinci, 1851, replica of 1818 picture in Bonington style, 18¾×17¾ | 10,000 |

### DRAWINGS

| 1914 | de Biron. Paris. Mme Verbeckhoven, pencil | 660 |
|---|---|---|
| | M et Mme Lavergne, pencil | 660 |
| 1918 | Degas. Paris. La famille Forestier | 796 |
| 1919 | Montgermont. Paris. Mme Lescot (£252 in 1888) | 900 |
| 1926 | Greffulhe. S. A lady seated | 440 |
| 1928 | S. Portrait of Mrs Margaret Badham | 820 |
| 1929 | d'Hendecourt. S. Mme Reiset and daughter | 940 |
| | Lapauze. Paris. Comtesse de Ségur-Lamoignon, pencil | 1,350 |
| | La naissance des Muses (pen and wash) | 1,530 |
| 1936 | Duc de Trevise. Paris. Dr de France, pencil | 400 |
| | François Côty. Mlle de Sennones, pencil, 72,000 francs at 125 to the £+tax | 690 |
| 1947 | S. Mrs Woodhead and Rev Henry Carter, bought by Fitzwilliam Museum | 1,200 |
| 1951 | Stern. N.Y. M. Charles Dupaty | 732 |
| 1959 | Paris. Mme Gallois, pencil | 6,650 |

| | | £ |
|---|---|---|
| 1960 | S. Sheet of studies of a child | 1,000 |
| | N.Y. Seated nude, pencil | 1,250 |
| 1962 | S. Nude study, pencil, Rome 1819, $8\frac{3}{4}\times 11\frac{1}{2}$ | 1,200 |
| 1963 | Kornfeld, Berne. Augustin Caristie, 1819, pencil | 3,660 |
| | C. Single figure, study for Apotheosis of Homer, black chalk (N.Y. 1960, £679) | 3,150 |
| 1964 | Hutton. S. A young architect, 1810 | 2,600 |
| | Sitwell. S. Lord Glenbervie, 1816, $8\times 6\frac{1}{2}$ | 5,200 |
| | Lady Glenbervie, 1816, $8\frac{1}{8}\times 6\frac{1}{2}$ | 5,100 |
| | Hon Frederick North-Douglas, $8\frac{1}{4}\times 6\frac{3}{8}$ | 8,500 |
| | Hon Frederick North, $8\frac{1}{2}\times 6\frac{1}{2}$ | 5,200 |
| 1965 | Karl & Faber, Munich. Franz List, 1839, DM105,000+ tax | 10,340 |
| 1966 | Bernadough. S. Portrait of Louis Haudebourt, $9\frac{1}{4}\times 6\frac{3}{4}$ | 6,000 |
| | Wilson. S. Thomas Church in Rome, 1816, $18\frac{1}{2}\times 6\frac{1}{2}$ | 10,500 |
| | Rev Joseph Church in Rome, $8\times 6\frac{1}{2}$ | 9,000 |
| 1968 | C. M. Brochard, highly finished pencil drawing made in 1796 at the age of 16, circular, $3\frac{1}{4}$ in. diam. | 945 |
| 1969 | C. Mme de Lauréal, 1814, pencil, $4\frac{3}{4}\times 3\frac{3}{4}$. Bought in | 3,360 |
| | The infant Orestes presented to Strophius, early work, pen and wash, $9\frac{1}{2}\times 14\frac{1}{2}$ | 735 |
| | S. Comtesse de Castellane, 1834, fine graphite pencil, $11\frac{1}{4}\times 9$, Bought in at | 4,000 |
| 1970 | Auctions A.G. Basel. Pencil portrait, unknown man, Rome, 1817, FS78,000+15% tax | 8,625 |

## GEORGE INNES. (*See* American School)

## EUGÈNE ISABEY. (*See* Miniatures)

## JOSEPH ISRAELS. 1824–1911

*The drowned fisherman*, now transferred from the Tate Gallery to the National Gallery, cost £4,830 at Christies in 1910, the equivalent of £38,640 in 1970. Yet an exceptionally attractive Israels made only £2,400 in 1969 and that was nearly three times as much as any of his works, sold since 1924. In 1918 a large characteristic subject picture, *Grace before meat* had reached £3,675 at the Westmacott sale—to descend to 75 guineas in the same rooms in 1957. This tremendous *débâcle* was characteristic of the whole late-19th century Dutch

school. The merit of Israels, van Marcke, Mauve and the Maris family, all o
them capable of making £3,500 to £7,000 at the time of the First World War
lay in the fact that they had brought the Barbizon style of landscape and th
'social realism' of Courbet, Millet, Breton, l'Hermitte and Bastien-Lepag
from Paris to Northern Europe. With the Barbizon school and the socia
realist painters still in abeyance in 1970, their Dutch imitators can hardly b
expected to do any better.

The market of these painters had been truly international, whereas their pre
decessors of the 'Dutch revival' were a provincial school, little better than a
offshoot of the German romantic movement which produced Corneliu
Krieghoff, the Raphael of Canada (see American School). Mysteriously th
Dutch patriotic market appears to rate these leaden formularized works
great deal higher than Israels and the three Maris brothers to whom one ma
at least concede the merit of an individual style. In 1960 no 'Dutch revival
picture had got anywhere near the £1,000 mark, but in 1969 ice-bound an
doom-sodden early Victorian pastiches of Avercamp, knocked off by the yard
were priced at £7,875 for Andreas Schelfout, £3,990 for Charles Leickert
£3,300 for Johann Bernard Klombeek and £2,730 for Frederick Marianu
Kruseman. Dutch town views in a Wardour street version of Berckheyd
included one by William Koekkoek (three other painters in the family) a
£5,040, and several Cornelius Springers in the £3,000 region. These painters
and Israels too, are to be found in that saleroom Limbo which is called 'narrativ
paintings' or '19th and 20th century paintings', and which includes Duke Stree
cardinals and other works which impose no strain on the intelligence and ver
little on the nervous system. For all that, Israels and his aspirations to Geniu
may yet have their day. There are straws in the wind. The Drowned Fisherma
is *on view*.

| | | £ |
|---|---|---|
| 1961 | van Waay, Amsterdam. Dressing room at a dancing school, 26×20, Hfl8,500+tax          About | 1,000 |
| | Beach at Scheveningen, 48½×59½, Hfl3,300+tax          About | 400 |
| 1963 | C. Kitchen interior, 1860 | 210 |
| 1964 | S. The net-mender | 420 |
| | Beach-scene | 580 |
| 1966 | Reid. C. The soldier and the sailor, wc, 24½×28 | 262 10s |
| | The old woman, 36×25 | 299 |
| 1967 | Honeyman. C. Flower-pickers returning, wc, 17×28 | 198 10s |
| | Potato-pickers returning, companion piece | 78 15s. |
| | van Waay, Amsterdam. Female portrait, 18¼×13½, Ffr5,300+tax | 608 |
| | Brandt, Amsterdam. Children on the Beach, 24½×36½, Hfl5,000+tax | 565 |
| 1969 | Bjerke. S. Young girl crocheting in a doorway, 1865, 25×19 | 2,400 |

# ITALIAN SCHOOL

## 13th–14th centuries

The following list ought to put the affair of the National Gallery's Duccio panel into its right perspective. It is pretty incredible that expert valuers and auctioneers in these days of easily accessible popular illustrated books should allow a work, obviously of the age of Giotto, to be catalogued as 15th century. But there is no reason why it should have been seen that this was a potential £150,000 picture. The fact is that a picture can cost anything, when galleries, backed by the treasuries of the great powers, compete against each other. In 1965, for instance, the National Gallery acquired a three-foot painted cross of the 13th century at the Stoclet sale. It is a work from the crude perimeter of Byzantine civilization, such as one sees in small-town museums in Italy, displayed in quantity and treated with scant respect. But the snobbery of *the early* has long been with us, so the painted cross cost the Nation £100,000 plus commission. Ordinarily such prices were out of the question in the 1960s for the *Docento* and *Trecento*. The maximum was £35,000 and in the 1950s £10,000, Duccio himself not excluded. A complete Duccio triptych Crucixion made £5,070 in 1943, a Holy Family panel £1,600 in 1957, while another crucifixion, part of a triptych, made £16,000 at the same Stoclet sale of 1965 where that ugly cross was sold for £100,000. So there is no real competition between Duccio and Picasso. Italian primitives remain a learned taste, even though that taste can no longer be indulged at less than half the cost of a good riding hack—as at the Fuller Russell sale of 1885 where the National Gallery bought two panels by Ugolino da Siena for 25 guineas. They would be worth at least £50,000 in 1970.

|  |  | £ |
|---|---|---|
| 1959 | Sold to Agnew by Prince Liechtenstein, LORENZO MONACO, Annunciation (refused by Toronto Museum) | 35,000 |
|  | Del Monte. S. MASTER OF THE OSSERVANZA ALTARPIECE, Resurrection, predella panel | 31,000 |
|  | Marquess Northampton. C. PARRI SPINELLI, drawing, pen on vellum after a Giotto fresco | 6,090 |
|  | Loeser. S. BERNARDO DADDI, St Dominic | 2,800 |
|  | Loeser. S. Head of Christ under 10 in. | 2,940 |
|  | BARNA DA SIENA, small crucifixion | 2,100 |
| 1961 | Fischer, Lucerne. GIOVANNI DEL BIONDO, Madonna enthroned 42 in. high, 35,000 francs+tax | 3,208 |
| 1962 | Guggenheim Foundation. S. LORENZO MONACO, King David playing the harp 21½ × 14½, Metropolitan Museum | 24,000 |
|  | Lempertz, Cologne. DUCCIO SCHOOL, Holy Family with angels, 13½ × 9¼, DM44,000+tax | 4,515 |
|  | Springell. S. UNKNOWN N. ITALIAN artist, drawing in wc on vellum of lovers and a castle, 5¾ × 4 | 2,000 |

| | | |
|---|---|---:|
| 1962 | S. STEFANO DI ZEVIO, drawing, allegory of Charity, bought by Berlin Print Room | 4,000 |
| 1963 | S. MASTER OF THE FABRIANO ALTARPIECE, Holy family | 6,700 |
| 1965 | Stoclet. S. MASTER OF ST FRANCIS, 13th century painted cross, 36×28. National Gallery | 100,000 |
| | GIOTTO SCHOOL deposition, 14½×10 | 17,000 |
| | DUCCIO DI BUONINSEGNA, Triangular crucifixion, 15×13½ | 16,000 |
| | MASTER OF THE MAGDALEN, 13th century, Holy Family 36½×25 | 16,000 |
| | S. LORENZO MONACO. Holy Family. National Gallery, Edinburgh | 32,000 |
| | Spencer Churchill. C. LORENZO MONACO, Presentation to the temple, predella panel, 12¼×15½ (£11 11s. in 1864) | 8,925 |
| | 2nd Stoclet sale. S. BERLINGHIERO BERLINGHIERI, 13th century. Holy family, triptych, 16½×20 | 18,000 |
| | BERNARDO DADDI, Debarkment of St Ursula, 23¼×25 | 14,000 |
| | Wenner-Gren. S. PAOLO DI GIOVANNI, Holy family with saints, 21×10 | 16,000 |
| | S. MASTER OF BAMBINO VISPO, Holy Family, 27½×20 | 4,800 |
| 1966 | C. RIMINI SCHOOL, passion of Christ, triptych of numerous small panels, 25½×27. Bought in | 7,875 |
| | ROSELLO DI JACOPO, Madonna, part of tabernacle, 51×19 | 3,360 |
| | Attributed ORCAGNA. Presentation to the temple, 14¼×25¼ | 9,450 |
| | Lee of Fareham. C. MASTER OF MONTE OLIVETO Madonna and two wing panels, 20×14½ | 4,725 |
| | Francis Cook. C. NALDO CECCARELLI, gold ground Madonna dated 1347, 22×13½ | 35,700 |
| 1967 | Burns. S. BERNARDO DADDI, St Catherine, 70½×32 | 22,000 |
| | Farrow. S. BERNARDO DADDI, figures from crucifixion triptych, 13¼×16¼ | 9,000 |
| | ALLEGRETTO NUZI, Simon Magus and the demons, 13½×10 | 3,800 |
| | C. TORINO VANNI, St Barbara, half-length, 24½×15 | 6,300 |
| | LORENZO DI NICCOLO, Birth of the Virgin, 9¼×14¾ | 9,925 |
| | Tayleur. S. BARNA DA SIENA, The Man of Sorrows, Gothic arch, 10½×5 | 6,000 |
| | Hyland. C. UGOLINO DI NERI, Bearded saint, arcaded, 20×18. Bought in | 21,000 |
| | ANGELO PULCINELLI, St Catherine with St Moses of Egypt, 31½×20, bought in at | 14,700 |

| | | | £ |
|---|---|---|---|
| 1967 | C. N. ITALIAN, c 1350, Six scenes from the passion, each 10 in. square | 6 for | 6,300 |
| | S. VITALE DI BOLOGNA, Madonna and child, altar fragment, $15\frac{1}{2} \times 13\frac{1}{2}$ | | 4,300 |
| | Paris. School of BERNARDO DADDI. Holy family with goldfinch, $45\frac{3}{4} \times 21\frac{3}{4}$ (NF200,000+tax) | | 16,070 |
| | C. ATTRIBUTED SPINELLO ARETINO. Holy family, Gothic panel, $38 \times 20$ (see 1969) bought in at | | 5,250 |
| | RIMINI SCHOOL, Holy family with passion of Christ, triptych, $25\frac{1}{2} \times 37$ | | 5,775 |
| | ATTRIBUTED, ORCAGNA. Presentation in the temple, predella panel, 10 figures, $14\frac{1}{4} \times 25\frac{1}{4}$ | | 7,875 |
| 1968 | S. GIOTTO SCHOOL, c 1330, Crucifixion, $16 \times 13$ | | 14,000 |
| | NARDO DI CIONE, Holy family, round top, $27\frac{3}{4} \times 17$. Bought in at | | 18,000 |
| | de Chair. S. NICCOLO DI TOMASO. Holy family with saints, c 1400, $19 \times 18$, bought in | | 3,800 |
| | Bridson, Bruton, Knowles, Auctioneers (at Aldwick Court). DUCCIO DA BUONINSEGNA, Holy family, late 13th century retable panel, $16 \times 11$ | | 2,700 |
| | Resold to the National Gallery | | 150,000 |
| 1969 | S. BERNARDO DADDI, St Peter, half-length, round top gold background (ascribed), $24\frac{1}{2} \times 14$, bought in at | | 10,000 |
| | C. Attributed SPINELLO ARETINO, Holy family, saints and angels in Gothic arch, $38 \times 20$ (see 1967) | | 7,350 |
| | ROSELLO DI JACOPO FRANCHI, Holy family, Sts Jerome and Stephen. Gothic tabernacle, $28 \times 15$ | | 6,300 |
| | Leuchter. S. COLA PETRUCCIOLI. Complete Gothic triptych from Orvieto, Holy Family with life of the Virgin, whole width, $79\frac{3}{4}$ in. | | 17,000 |
| | Meynell Church Trustees. C. MASTER OF OSSERVANZA ALTARPIECE, Assumption of the Virgin, Gothic altar panel, c. 1400, $21\frac{1}{2} \times 14$ | | 28,350 |
| | School of GIOVANNI DA MILANO, Annunciation, diptych, $12 \times 7\frac{1}{2}$ | | 5,775 |
| | Stafford. S. MARIOTTO DI NARDO, Crucifixion, arched panel, $14\frac{3}{4} \times 5\frac{3}{4}$ | | 6,500 |

## ITALIAN SCHOOL

### Florence, Central Italy, 15th–early 16th centuries

Excluding only Botticelli, Raphael, Michelangelo, for whom see separate entries.)

In 1964 a pair of long panels of saints by Filippino Lippi made £84,000, a tribute to the rare occurrence of well-known 15th century names in the salerooms. The sale of two highly reputable Botticellis three years later hardly confirmed this degree of estimation. In its present state, the QUATTROCENTO is not a well-supported market. There are few things left to interest the museums of the world, while those individuals who are rich enough to be interested, no longer crave for the pious simplicity of the Age of Faith. They prefer it displayed on Christmas cards. Moreover such Italian primitives as could still find their way to the salerooms in the 1960s, had been treated with little consideration during most of a lifetime of five hundred years and, therefore, tended to be rubbed down and overpainted. Otherwise so rare and significant a painter as Pesellino would not have been available at the price of a Degas charcoal drawing.

|      |                                                                                                                                                           | £      |
|------|-----------------------------------------------------------------------------------------------------------------------------------------------------------|--------|
| 1960 | Tibor de Budai. C. FRANCESCO BOTTICINI. Holy Family, Gothic top, 45½×26                                                                                  | 3,360  |
|      | Powell. S. NERI DI BICCI. Baptism and crucifixion, pair of predellas, 10½×19    2 for                                                                    | 2,200  |
| 1961 | C. FILIPPINO LIPPI. Holy Family, 43½ in. roundel                                                                                                         | 7,350  |
|      | Christensen. S. NEROCCIO DE' LANDI. St Catherine, 15¾×11½                                                                                                | 10,000 |
|      | Erickson. N.Y. PIETRO PERUGINO. St Augustine with other saints, 35×25 (£617 in 1850) $130,000                                                            | 44,640 |
| 1962 | Mme de B. Paris. ANDREA MANTEGNA (attributed) Massacre of the innocents, predella panel, 8½×10, FN120,000+tax                                            | 10,100 |
|      | UNKNOWN, LATE 15TH CENTURY. St Peter of Verona and the devil, FN114,500+tax                                                                              | 9,600  |
|      | SCHOOL OF BENOZZO GOZZOLI. Sacrifice of Lucretia, 16×23½, FN121,000+tax                                                                                  | 10,100 |
|      | SCHOOL OF GENTILE DI FABRIANO. Procession before a town wall, cassone end-panel, 16×23, FN165,000+tax                                                    | 13,900 |
|      | Brandt, Amsterdam. GIACOMO PACCHIAROTTO, Holy Family with St Joseph, 16×11¼                                                                              | 4,185  |
| 1963 | Hasson. S. PIETRO PERUGINO. Sts Celestinus and Jerome, 17×17 each    2 for                                                                               | 8,925  |
|      | Scrope. C. Attributed to BOTTICINI, roundel, Holy Family and St John                                                                                     | 2,625  |
|      | Sterling of Keir. S. JACOPO CARUCCI. Portrait, Bartolommeo Campagni, dated 1549                                                                          | 11,000 |
|      | Cintas. N.Y. COSIMO ROSSELLI, Pietà, 24×35                                                                                                               | 8,035  |
|      | Hasson. C. LORENZO CREDI. Coronation of the Virgin, bought in (£315 in 1856, £1,350 in 1945) 36×17                                                       | 7,350  |
|      | Finarte, Milan. BENVENUTO DI GIROLAMO (Siena) Holy Family, Sts Catherine and John, 26¾×18, L6·9 million.+tax                                             | 4,655  |

£

964   C. Francesco Bacchiacca, Via crucis, fragment, $27\frac{1}{2} \times 37$ (see 1965)    4,200

       Sano di Pietro. Birth of the Virgin    11,550

Lady Melchett. S. Lo Spagna. Three figures of saints
on 15 in. panels (see 1968)    3 for  7,500

S. Filippino Lippi. Two groups of saints, each $61 \times 23$  84,000

965   Drury Lowe. S. Bacchiacca, via crucis, $18\frac{1}{4} \times 22\frac{3}{4}$ (for
another version, see 1963)    5,200

S. School of Piero della Francesca. Two fresco fragments, angels' heads, $25 \times 19$    £2,400 and 4,000

       Bacchiacca, Baptism of Christ    16,000

Lord Bruce. C. Att. Andrea del Sarto, Holy family,
$55 \times 41$    1,575

Brackley. C. Fra Bartolommeo, Nativity, $5\frac{1}{2} \times 3\frac{1}{2}$,
bought in at    23,100

Spencer Churchill. C. Garofalo. Martyrdom of St
Stephen, dated 1530, $104 \times 76$ (£1,606 5s. in 1866)    15,750

S. Andrea di Bartolo. St Michael    7,000

Drury Lowe. S. Raffaellino del Garbo, deposition,
78 in. high    5,400

Fostoria. S. Neroccio de' Landi. Mystic marriage of
St Catherine, $15\frac{3}{4} \times 11\frac{3}{4}$    7,500

       C. Mariotto Albertinelli, Noli me tangere, $22 \times 19\frac{1}{2}$  9,450

N.Y. Master of san Miniato. Sts Nicolas and Apol-
lonia, $11 \times 32$, $10,000    3,585

966   C. Bernardo Pinturicchio. Holy Family, rabbit and
swan, $11\frac{1}{2} \times 8\frac{1}{2}$    3,360

       C. Bacchiacca, God naming the beasts, $19\frac{3}{4} \times 14\frac{1}{2}$  3,150

Lee of Fareham. C. Master of stratonice, Holy family
with angels, $70 \times 37$    3,570

Dudley Sherwood. S. Domenico Beccafumi, half-
length Madonna with saints in roundel, $25\frac{3}{4}$ in. diam.  3,800

Joseph. S. Pseudo-Pier Francesco Fiorentino. Mado-
nna, round-topped panel, $31\frac{3}{4} \times 19\frac{3}{4}$    4,200

967   Farrow. S. Vincenzo Foppa. St Jerome, gold ground,
$13 \times 7\frac{3}{4}$    5,000

       Jacopo de del Sellaio, Esther before Ahasueras,
roundel, 21 in. diam.    22,000

Burns. S. Master of the Adinari cassone, two cassone
panels illustrating *Trionfe*, each $16\frac{3}{4} \times 69\frac{1}{4}$    2 for  15,300

S. Francesco Salviati. Holy family, c. 1530, 43 in.
roundel    7,500

Watney. C. Bacchiacca. Unknown lady in helio-
trope dress with music score, $40\frac{1}{2} \times 31\frac{1}{2}$    38,850

£

1967 Hyland.  C.  SANO DI PIETRO.  St Donatus with dragon, predella, 8¾×14¼, bought in at    14,275

Watney.  C.  LORENZO DI CREDI.  Virgin nursing child Christ, 27½×17½    3,990

Hyland.  C.  NERI DI BICCI.  Tobias and angel, Gothic panel, 67½×28    6,825

C.  RAFFAELLINO DEL GARBO.  Holy family, tondo, 43½ diam.    3,675

(Sold as GHIRLANDAJO, 1886, £535 10s.)

S.  MASTER OF PRATOVECCHIO.  Holy family with Sts Bridget and Michael, triptych, 59×54 & 74½. Coll. Paul Getty    14,000

C.  Attributed POLLAIUOLO.  Knight and footman in landscape, 19×17    9,450

Southesk.  S.  LORENZO DI CREDI, Virgin adoring Holy Child, roundel, 34 in. diam.    2,000

Marshall.  S.  PESELLINO.  Madonna and child enthroned, 20½×12¾    25,500

1968 Warner.  S.  School of PIERO DI COSIMO.  Allegory of rejected love, cassone panel, 36½×82    6,000

Barry.  S.  LO SPAGNA.  Three saints in panels, each 15½×5½ (see 1964). Bought in    3 for  6,000

Watney.  C.  ANDREA DEL SARTO.  Self-portrait, 34× 26½ (£934 10s. in 1899)    38,850

Warwick Castle.  C.  BARTOLOMMEO DI GIOVANNI, Two saints in roundels, 8×8    2 for  4,935

Leggett.  S.  PIER FRANCESCO FIORENTINO.  Holy family with St John, 26½×16½    2,900

Norberg.  S.  ANTONIAZZO ROMANO.  Holy family with St John, gold ground, 27×19½    3,600

C.  JACOPO PONTORMO.  Sts Zenobius and Bartholomew, kneeling figures on panels, 7¾×6¾,    2 for  6,615

Killearn.  S.  BARTOLOMMEO DI GIOVANNI.  Christ walking on the water and appearing to the disciples, 2 predella panels, 18×67    2 for  6,600

Craven.  S.  NERI DI BICCI.  Angel of the annunciation (cut down) 28¼×21¾    3,500

C.  FLORENTINE SCHOOL c. 1500.  Holy family with St John, arched top, 27×17    2,100

1969 S.  GAROFALO.  Lady with jewels and mirror, 37¾×32½    6,500

BERNARDO PINTURICCHIO.  Holy family, gold ground, 17½×13¼    15,000

MASTER OF THE DOMINICAN EFFIGIES.  St Margaret (£2,900 in 1966)    5,000

£

969 Talleyrand-Ruspoli Florence. DOMENICO DEL GHIRLAND-
AJO. St Peter. 100 million Lire+tax | 73,700
Arrowsmith. S. SCHOOL OF SANO DI PIETRO, Holy
family and saints, 30½×22½ | 3,000
Bompas. C. NERI DI BICCI. St Jerome with Tobias
and the Angel in Gothic tabernacle, 14×8¾ | 3,990
C. GIROLAMO DA SANTA CROCE. Annunciation, 18½×23
(£2,520 at Spencer Churchill sale, 1965) | 4,200
Prinknash Abbey. C. SCHOOL OF MASOLINO. Madonna
head on tooled gold background, 9¼ in. square (1879 as
Orcagna, £11 11s.) c. 1420 | 9,450
C. GIOVANNI BOCCATI DA CAMERINO. St Savinus in
conversation, part of altarpiece at Orvieto, 1473, 10½×14½ | 7,350
BACCHIACCA, Holy family with infant St John,
30×21 | 1,995
GIAN FRANCESCO MAINERI. Adoration of the shep-
herds, 12×9½, bought in at | 6,825
S. LORENZO DI S. SEVERINO (yngr) St George and dragon,
arched panel in Uccello style | 4,800

### DRAWINGS

962 Springell. S. PIETRO PERUGINO. Baptism of Christ,
pen | 1,100
LORENZO DI CREDI, Holy Family | 1,600
FRA BARTOLOMMEO. Madonna crowned with two
angels, 8¾×6 | 4,000
Landscape with Siena cathedral, pen | 2,800
963 Rudolf. S. ATT. PINTURICCHIO, St Catherine of Alex-
andria | 1,050
S. SIENESE SCHOOL, 15th century. A jaguar, pen and wc,
7½×5¼ | 800
964 Burt. C. FRANCESCO DI GIORGIO. Adam and Eve, pen
on vellum, 13×10, bought by Holman Hunt in Florence | 9,450
Hutton. S. LUCA SIGNORELLI. Man in cloak, black and
white chalk | 7,500
965 Harewood. C. LUCA SIGNORELLI. A group of devils,
pen study for the Orvieto Last Judgement fresco | 6,825
Wrangham. S. FOLLOWER OF MANTEGNA, sheet of pen
and wash figure studies | 2,400
966 S. FRA BARTOLOMMEO. C. Annunciation, pen, 4¾×6¼,
landscape on reverse side | 4,900
968 Fairfax-Cartwright. C. RAFFAELLINO DEL GARBO. Holy
family with angels, pen and wash, 7×8¾ | 8,925

# NORTH ITALIAN SCHOOL
15th and early 16th centuries

(Excluding Correggio, Crivelli, Leonardo and the Venetian painters for whom
see separate entries.)

Some North Italian paintings of the Bolognese and Leonardesque school
were sold before the war at prices which seem enormous, compared with the
ensuing list, but it has to be realized that the survivors which can still reach the
market are generally in bad condition. Where the condition is good, even the
work of a second-rate painter like Niccolo di Maestro Antonio can make
£60,900. Even allowing for condition, Leonardesque paintings are probably
not as popular as they were. René Gimpel records the sale of an alleged portrait
of Cesare Borghia by Solario in 1905 for £4,545, equivalent to £36,400 in
1970. Two other Solario paintings were sold in London in 1911 and 1914 for
£4,200, equivalent to £33,600, while an unattributed Leonardesque Annunciation made 140,000 francs in Paris in 1914, equivalent with tax to £6,204 or
£49,600 in the money of 1970. In 1936 Andrew Mellon paid Duveen £59,600
for a portrait of a lady by Bernardino Luini, now in the National Gallery
Washington. This was the equivalent of close on £300,000 almost the price of
a Leonardo—as it was once thought to be.

| | | £ |
|---|---|---:|
| 1959 | Brandt, Amsterdam. VITALE DA BOLOGNA, St George and dragon, 34×28, Hfl48,000+tax | 5,675 |
| 1960 | Tibor de Budai. C. VITTORIO CRIVELLI. Holy family and saints, triptych, 57×56 | 3,150 |
| 1963 | S. ANDREA SOLARIO. Holy family | 1,650 |
| | School of FRANCESCO COSSA. Birth of St John Baptist | 2,600 |
| 1964 | Fischer, Lucerne. GIOVANNI BOLTRAFFIO. Holy family, 16×12½, FS30,000+tax | 3,000 |
| 1965 | Harewood. C. CRISTOFERO SCACCO. John the Baptist, 62×26 | 10,500 |
| | Margadale of Islay. C. BERNARDINO DEI CONTI. Leo-nardesque head of a lady | 30,450 |
| | Spencer Churchill. C. FRANCESCO FRANCIA. Madonna of the rose garden, 44½×36 | 1,317 10s |
| | Harewood. C. UNKNOWN c. 1500. A priest holding a book, 27¼×20¾ | 4,725 |
| 1966 | C. LORENZO COSTA. Lady of the Este family as a female saint, 17½×13½ | 2,940 |
| | Westminster diocesan trustees. S. BARTOLOMMEO MON-TAGNA. Pair of organ shutters from Vicenza, depicting St Bartholomew and St Augustine, 112×54, bought in at | 12,000 |
| | Subsequently sold to Walker gallery Liverpool for | 9,000 |

£

966 Baer Severin. S. Master of Turin adoration. The
Judas kiss and Christ before Pilate, each 45½ × 19　　2 for　6,500
C. Ercole de' Roberti. Holy family with Sts Jerome
and Dominic, 25½ × 33. Bought in　　　　　　　　3,360
Ortolano. Adoration of the Magi, 19¼ × 28¼
(£52 10s. in 1857)　　　　　　　　　　　　　　2,730
Fitzwilliam Museum. S. Attributed Boltraffio, Holy
family, 24 × 18　　　　　　　　　　　　　　　　2,000
C. Bartolommeo Montagna. Mystic marriage of St
Catherine, 21½ × 23½　　　　　　　　　　　　　6,825
Bernardino Luini. Holy family, 23 × 18　　　　1,985
967 Watney. C. Niccolo di Maestro Antonio (Ancona).
Holy Family and saints, signed and dated 1472, 62 ×
80　　　　　　　　　　　　　　　　　　　　60,900
Pier Matteo d'Amelia. Bishop-saint trampling on
Arian heretics, 46½ × 16　　　　　　　　　　　7,350
Verona school c. 1460. Jonathan and the Philistine
host, cassone panel, 16½ × 21¼　　　　　　　13,650
Princess Labia. S. Niccolo di Maestro Antonio.
Holy Family enthroned, narrow arched panel, 56 × 19　6,500
968 C. Lorenzo Costa. Adoration of the shepherds,
9 × 11½　　　　　　　　　　　　　　　　　　5,355
Kaplan. S. Battista Dossi Ferrarese. Holy Family,
23 × 15¾　　　　　　　　　　　　　　　　　4,800
S. Giovanni Mansueti. Coronation of the Virgin with
God the Father and angels, 65 × 57. Bought in　3,500
C. Bernardino Zaganelli. Holy family, St Sebastian
and St Roche, 19 × 15¼　　　　　　　　　　　5,775
Unknown painter c. 1490. Retable-panel with 14
scenes from the Passion of Christ, 11½ × 25　　4,410
Batting. S. Niccolo Giolfino, Verona c. 1480. Marcus
Scaevola and the brand, 10½ × 12½　　　　　9,200
969 Tucher. S. School of Cossa. Holy family with
angels and cherubs, Gothic arched top, 49 × 23　9,000
S. Pasqualino di Niccolo. Holy family, 20½ × 16¾　4,600
C. Michele Giambono. A bishop-saint enthroned,
32 × 18　　　　　　　　　　　　　　　　　　5,250
Francesco Melzi. Holy family with St Anne and infant
St John, after Leonardo, 63 × 45　　　　　　　3,675
Gaudenzio Ferrari. Holy Family, 20½ × 14½　2,625
S. Zanobi Macchiavelli. Holy Family and saints, altar
panel transferred to canvas, 53¾ × 62½　　　5,000
Vincenzo Campi. Fruit and vegetable sellers,
57½ × 85¼　　　　　　　　　　　　　　　4,000

DRAWINGS

| | | £ |
|---|---|---|
| 1958 | Holland-Martin (Skippe Coll.). C. FRANCESCO COSSA. Venus embracing Cupid at the forge of Vulcan, 11×16, c. 1470 | 8,400 |
| 1961 | Randall. S. ANONYMOUS, watercolour fragment c. 1470, a sailing ship | 3,000 |
| 1961 | Springell. S. STEFANO DI ZEVIO. Charity, pen, 10½×8¼ | 4,000 |
| 1963 | Rudolf. S. LORENZO COSTA. Sheet of studies, 7½×11 | 2,600 |
| | S. ATT. ALTICHIERO. Surrender of a town, pen | 1,000 |
| | FRANCESCO COSSA. Page holding a lance, pen, 9½×4¼ | 1,700 |
| 1964 | Matthiesen. S. VERONA SCHOOL before 1450, half-length bearded man, pen, 4½×5 | 1,200 |
| | GIOVANNI DA UDINE, wc study, lapwing and teal, 7×5¾ | 1,300 |
| 1968 | C. LORENZO COSTA, studies of triumphal procession, pen, 6½×10¼ | 3,675 |

## ITALIAN SCHOOL
### 16th–17th centuries

(See separate entries for the Carraccis, Carlo Dolci, Domenichino, Parm gianino, Guido Reni, Salvator Rosa, Venetian School.)

GUISEPPE ARCHIMBOLDO  £

| | | | |
|---|---|---|---|
| 1963 | S. The four seasons, a set of fantasies, 28½×23½ | 4 for | 10,500 |
| 1965 | Wenner-Gren. S. Fantastic female head, 31¾×24 | | 8,500 |
| | Others at £5,100 and £4,000 the pair | | |

GIOVANNI BENEDETTO CASTIGLIONE.    –1670

| | | |
|---|---|---|
| 1958 | C. The angel appearing to the shepherds. Birmingham City Gallery | 3,360 |
| 1962 | Springell. S. Apollo and Marsyas, pen drawing touched with oils, 16×21. Metropolitan Museum | 2,800 |
| 1967 | Clark. S. Roman sacrifice, oils on paper, 28×17 | 2,800 |
| 1968 | C. Young Oriental with horse, brush drawing, 13×8¾ | 1,470 |
| 1969 | Allegri. S. St John Baptist and St Augustine, oils on paper, 22×15 | 2,600 |
| | C. Finding of the infant Cyrus, 38×52, on canvas | 5,040 |

LUCA GIORDANO. 1632–1705

| | | |
|---|---|---|
| 1969 | C. Beheading of St John the Baptist (unframed, un-illustrated) 69×90 | 12,600 |

RAZIO GENTILESCHI. 1562–1647

| | | |
|---|---|---:|
| 65 | Spencer Churchill. C. Lot and his daughters, 61×75 (£147 in 1859 as Velazquez) | 39,900 |
| 69 | C. Girl in turban as a Sybil, 25½ in. square | 3,150 |
| 70 | S. Madonna adoring infant Christ, 54½×38¼ | 13,000 |

OVANNI FRANCESCO BARBIERI, called IL GUERCINO. 1591–1666

| | | |
|---|---|---:|
| 53 | Ashburnham. S. Presentation to the temple (Denis Mahon) | 1,900 |
| 65 | Spencer Churchill. C. Christ and the woman of Samaria, 44×60 (£325 10s. in 1840, £378 in 1873) | 15,700 |
| | Samson and the honeycomb, 39¾×45¾ (£472 10s. in 1838, £404 10s in 1859) | 7,750 |
| 67 | C. (Attributed) Samson and Delilah, 66×87 | 1,155 |
| 69 | S. St John Baptist, half-length in landscape, 29¾×24 | 1,800 |

### DRAWINGS

| | | |
|---|---|---:|
| 63 | S. Ganymede, red chalk, 10½×7¼. Metropolitan Museum | 560 |
| | Man wearing turban, pen and wash, 10¼×6½ | 650 |
| 66 | S. Saul pointing to a harp, pen and wash, 9×11¼ | 780 |
| 68 | Davin. C. A banker and his wife, pen and wash, 9¼×13¼ | 735 |
| | Bauer. S. Virgin, kneeling and reading a book, pen and wash, 7×6½ | 650 |
| | O'Brien. S. Patron Saints of Modena and Holy Child, black chalk, 9¼×18 | 1,750 |
| | Green. S. Red chalk half-length, St Peter, 7×8 | 550 |
| 69 | S. Head of girl reading book, pen, 5½×8¼ | 900 |
| | Beeke. C. Head of bearded old man, pen and wash, 7¼×6¾ | 735 |

# ITALIAN SCHOOL
## 18th century

xcluding Bellotto, Canaletto, Guardi, the Tiepolos, Zucharelli, for whom see arate entries.)

This is a mixed bag. Batoni, Joli, Panini and the Riccis produced English untry house pictures, mementos brought home from the Grand Tour, or, in the case of Joli, often painted in England. Joli is a very recent promotion the progression of prices in the 1960s shows. Batoni, fifteen years older than ynolds, was his master in Rome and largely accountable for his style, a good portraitist whose work makes about as much. Panini's classical capriccios an architectural views had some influence on Canaletto. He was probably unde rated in the 1930s, when his work made £200 with difficulty, but seems hard worthy of the £40,000 class if Hubert Robert is to be excluded from it.

Of the other painters Magnasco was a sort of rococo continuator of Salvat Rosa, a discovery of the present century, already becoming a knowing tas at the time of the First World War but, nevertheless, available within the £10 range till the early 1950s. Piazzetta and Longhi, excellent painters both, paint mainly for their own Venetian clientèle, and are not normally English count house embellishments.

POMPEIO BATONI.   1708–1787

| | | | £ |
|---|---|---|---|
| 1960 | Earl of Shrewsbury.  S.  John Chetwynd, 3rd Earl Talbot, 1773, 108×71¾ | | 4,800 |
| 1963 | Ionides.  S.  Lord Eardly and his tutor, 107×73 | | 18,000 |
| 1964 | Bonde.  C.  James Adam in Rome, 67×47 | | 4,410 |
| | Throckmorton.  C.  Peter Giffard, 52½×38 | | 3,675 |
| 1965 | Hill.  C.  Mozart at the age of 14, 21½×17½ | | 4,725 |
| 1967 | Benson.  S.  Frances Lyle Brown, 29×24 | | 1,470 |
| 1968 | Headfort.  C.  Thomas, 1st Marquis of Headfort, Rome, 1782, 70×58 | | 5,775 |
| | Lady Headfort and infant child, pair to above | | 4,200 |
| 1969 | San Marco, Florence.  Judgement of Solomon, L11 million+tax | | 8,066 |

CARLO CARLONE.   1686–1775

| 1962 | S.  Adoration of the Magi, 27½×16 | 8,000 |
|---|---|---|
| 1965 | C.  The arts triumphant over barbarism, 55×49½ | 36,700 |
| 1967 | C.  Allegory of sculpture, ceiling study, 19×27 | 3,990 |
| 1969 | C.  Beheading of San Felice, altarpiece modello, 26×45½ | 4,410 |

ANTONIO JOLI.   Floruit 1740–1760

| 1957 | C.  Thames side at Richmond, 29×38 | | 1,470 |
|---|---|---|---|
| 1959 | S.  Pair of views of Naples, 30½×51½ | 2 for | 2,400 |
| 1960 | S.  St Paul's and Westminster Abbey, each 40×50 | 2 for | 6,000 |
| | Horse Guards Parade, 29×46¾ | 2 for | 6,000 |
| | S.  Pair of Italian coastal views, 29×39½ | 2 for | 1,300 |
| | C.  Vatican and Castello San Angelo, 34×46 | | 2,310 |
| 1961 | D. of Leeds.  Pair of Naples views, 38½×52¾ | 2 for | 1,800 |
| | S.  San Giorgio Maggiore, Venice, 31×38 | | 2,100 |
| 1964 | S.  Piazza Navona.  Rome, 21×34¾ | | 950 |
| | Piazza san Marco, Venice, 21×34¾ | | 980 |
| 1965 | Harewood.  C.  Colosseum and arch of Constantine, 45½×48½ | | 1,995 |
| | S.  Ponte san Angelo and St Peter's, 44½×43½ | | 6,300 |

£

1966 Renshaw.  C.   St Peter's from the Lungo Tevere, 38 × 38    1,995
View of the Arno, Florence, 38 × 38    1,890
Newton.   S.   Embarcation of Charles III at Naples, 1759,
29 × 50    4,200
1967 C.   Thames view with unfinished Westminster Bridge,
1745, 14¾ × 27½    12,600
View from the river with Saint Paul's, 1746, 42 × 68   10,500
Companion view with Westminster Abbey, 1747,
42 × 68    9,925
1968 S.   Thames from Richmond and view from Richmond
Hill, each 24 × 27                                         2 for    12,000

PIETRO LONGHI.   1702–1762
1948 James.  C.   Taking coffee: artist's studio, pair 23½ × 20  2 for    3,360
1958 C.   The mountebank, 23½ × 20    3,150
1963 Sterling of Keir.   S.   An artist's studio, 15 × 20¾    41,000
1964 Pereira.   S.   The visit, 25¾ × 19    24,000
Artist sketching in elegant company, companion-
piece, 23¾ × 19    24,000
C.   The rehearsal, 23 × 18½    11,550
Companion-piece, same size    7,350
1967 Pereira.   S.   The quack doctor, 23½ × 19    5,500
Girl dancing at a picnic, 23¼ × 18¼    3,500
1968 Bridson (at Aldwick Court).   Artist painting a lady's
portrait    2,400
1969 C.   A pair (attributed) Imperial embassy in Istanbul, 1732,
41½ × 50½    4,410
Man playing bagpipes, drawing, black chalk and
wash, 10½ × 8¼    1,050
Peasant kneeling, companion-piece    682 10s.

ALESSANDRO MAGNASCO.   1667–1749
1958 S.   Stormy shore with smugglers, 45½ × 34½    450
1960 C.   Wooded landscape with figures, 87 × 67    10,500
1965 Spencer Churchill.   C.   Mountainous scene, 47 × 67    2,835
1967 Altmann.   S.   Monks in a landscape, 36½ × 28    3,000
C.   Similar subject, 28½ × 22¼    2,310
S.   Monks and shrine in rocky landscape, 29½ × 22¾    2,200
Landscape with monks in procession, signed and dated
1699, 92 × 114    23,000
1966 Finarte, Milan.   Pair of landscapes with figures, 51½ × 39½,
15 million lire+tax                                      2 for    9,800
1968 C.   Mountainous coastal scene, 45 × 35    3,675
1969 S.   River landscape with figures, 36¼ × 51¼    5,000
Phillips, son and Neale.   Pair of figured landscapes   2 for   9,500

GIOVANNI PAOLO PANINI. 1695–1768                                    £
1958  S.  Classical ruins, St Peter working a miracle, 45¾×48      1,350
1959  Lempertz, Cologne.  2 capriccios with Roman ruins,
      48¾×71½, DM10,500+tax                                        1,080
1961  D. of Leeds.  S.  Interior of San Paolo, Rome, 30×42        25,000
      Companion piece, interior of St Peter's                      26,000
1964  C.  The Colosseum, Rome, 44×57                                4,200
1965  Spencer Churchill.  C.  Pair of classical capriccios,
      24¾×18½                                                       5,250
1967  S.  Pope Benedict in procession at the Fontana di Trevi,
      45¾×67¾, unframed                                            10,000
      Ingleby.  S.  Pilgrims outside a palace, 35×45                5,400
      Astor Settlement.  C.  Two capriccios of classical ruins,
      37×52½                                               2 for   12,600
1968  Thesiger.  S.  Roman ruins, Belisarius begging, 46×48½       3,800
      Astor.  C.  Classical ruins, dated 1737, 29×41½              3,675
      C.  Classical ruins, return of the prodigal son, 37½×52      21,000
1969  S.  Forum and Campidoglio from Arch of Constantine,
      dated 1751, 22¾×37                                           27,000
      Haddo.  S.  Interior of the Pantheon, dated 1735, 50½×40     38,000
      S.  Theatre of Marcellus etc., capriccio, 1759, 57½×77¼      13,000
1970  N.Y.  Pair of Roman Capriccios, 1738, 37½×52½,
      $50,000                                               2 for   20,833

GIAMBATTISTA PIAZZETTA.  1682–1754
1960  Beckford.  S.  Man in turban, chalk drawing                   1,100
1966  Pascal.  S.  The paintress Guilia Lamia, 27×21¾              17,500
1967  S.  Portrait, Pope Nicholas IV, 37×33                         1,900
1970  S.  Self-portrait, black and white chalk, 15½+12½             3,500

GIOVANNI BATTISTA PITTONE.  1686–1755
1958  Earl of Ancaster.  S.  Riposo in landscape, 87½×61½           7,200
1960  S.  Apotheosis of St Jerome, 87½×61½                          8,200
1961  S.  The sacrifice of Polyxena, 50×36                          3,500
1962  S.  The sacrifice of Polyxena, 29½×21¾                        2,400
1963  Finarte, Milan.  A third version, 22¾×38¾, L2·5 million+
      tax                                                           1,685
1969  Paris.  The continence of Scipio and the sacrifice of
      Jephthah, 54×64½, FN82,000+tax                       2 for    7,600

SEBASTIANO RICCI.  1659–1729
1958  D. of Devonshire.  C.  Marriage feast of Cana, 65×53          8,400
      Holy family in landscape, 23½×31½                             6,825
      St Paul preaching in Athens, 74×63                            3,990
1965  Harewood.  C.  (With Marco Ricci) Apotheosis of the
      Duke of Devonshire, 23½×28¾                                   1,575

| | | | £ |
|---|---|---|---|
| 1966 | Inchcape. C. Holy family in landscape, 23½ × 31½ | | 7,140 |
| 1968 | Viva King. C. Neptune and Amphitrite, 24 × 29½ | | 1,995 |
| | S. Pan and Syrinx and Apollo and Daphne, ovals, 58 × 40 | 2 for | 2,600 |
| 1970 | C. The Rape of Proserpine, 32 × 29 | | 3,990 |

MARCO RICCI. 1679–1734

| | | | |
|---|---|---|---|
| 1960 | Leslie Estates. S. Baptism of Christ, 26 × 40 | | 3,800 |
| 1964 | Lord St Oswald. C. Pair of river landscapes, 14½ × 28, | 2 for | 3,780 |
| 1965 | Williams Wynn. S. Opera rehearsal, 18½ × 22 | | 12,000 |
| | S. Pair of landscapes, 23¾ × 28¾ | 2 for | 4,500 |
| 1968 | Dorotheum, Vienna. Landscape with sacrifice of Isaac, 54½ × 74¾, 140,000 schillings + tax | | 2,590 |
| 1969 | C. Jacob's dream, gouache, 11¼ × 17 | | 945 |
| | Landscape in Gaspard Poussin style, cattle and figures, 40 × 47 | | 6,300 |
| | S. Capriccio, classical ruins and sea, 35 × 44½ | | 7,800 |

WILLIAM JAMES. (*See* English School, 18th century)

ALEXANDER VON JAWLENSKY. (*See* German School, Modern)

AUGUSTUS JOHN. 1879–1961

The sales which took place in 1962, shortly after his death, showed that Augustus John was the most expensive modern English painter by a considerable lead. The self-portrait of 1938 was sold at a price which not even Munnings and Sargent had achieved. Almost immediately after the executor sales the prices fell and for the next seven years no John picture could make £800. Prices recovered in 1969, but in money that had lost 30 per cent of its purchasing power. Furthermore, John's paintings no longer led the market for the modern English school. It seems that in this market the highest prices are paid either for abstract and semi-abstract works or for the flashier forms of realism. The half-way modernity of the pre-war English school is relatively in small demand. This, however, does not apply to John's drawings. It is recognized that for a considerable part of his life he drew like an old master. There was only a temporary fall after the executor sales and then the finest of these drawings, which could have been bought in the 1920s for £20 each, were once again worth over £2,000.

| | | £ |
|---|---|---|
| 1962 | Augustus John, Exors.  C.  Self-portrait, 1938 | 8,925 |
| | Dorelia at Alderley Manor, 1911, 80×39½.   National Museum of Wales, Cardiff | 8,400 |
| | Portrait, Wyndham Lewis, 1911, 24×31½ | 5,460 |
| | Portrait, Robin John, 1915 | 3,360 |
| | Five other portraits at £2,000 to £3,000 | |
| | O'Malley.  S.  Portrait, W. B. Yeats, 24×18 | 6,500 |
| | Hesslein.  S.  Gypsy encampment, 1906, 35×32 | 5,000 |
| | Girl on seashore | 2,600 |
| | Woman, child and beetle, 29½×27½ | 2,600 |
| 1964 | Cornelius.  S.  The serving-maid, 20¾×14 | 600 |
| 1965 | Vaughan Morgan.  C.  Mrs Florence Clifton, 23½×20 | 231 |
| 1966 | Fattorini.  S.  Château en Provence, 14½×21 | 600 |
| | Blanche.  S.  A coloured girl, 15½×13 | 350 |
| | S.  Marchionness of Winchester, 23½×20 | 300 |
| | C.  Girl in red flowered dress, 30×22 | 299 |
| | Arran Isles, 12×19¾ | 472 10s. |
| 1967 | Hicks.  C.  Renvyle, Galway, 12¾×18 | 472 10s. |
| | Pink magnolias, 23½×17½ | 367 10s. |
| | Samuels.  S.  Dorelia in landscape, S. France, 14½×17½ | 750 |
| 1968 | C.  Camellia in glass, 19½×15½ | 787 10s. |
| 1969 | Bankhead.  N.Y.  Portrait, Tallulah Bankhead, 1930, 48×24½, $19,000 | 7,916 |
| | Portrait, Gerald du Maurier, 36×28, $5,000 | 2,100 |
| | Fison.  S.  Portrait, Iris Tree, 33½×24½ | 2,400 |
| | C.  Blaenau Ffestiniog, N. Wales, 11×20 | 997 10s. |

### DRAWINGS

| | | |
|---|---|---|
| 1961 | Makower.  S.  Girl in a hat, sanguine, 11×9¾ | 3,800 |
| | Two women, whole-length, pencil and wash, 19¾×13 | 1,600 |
| 1962 | Lady Dodds.  S.  Dorelia, pencil and wash, 19×8½ | 1,600 |
| | S.  Another version, pencil and wash, 15¾×9¾ | 1,300 |
| | Hesslein.  Dorelia and companion, pencil wash, 20×14 | 2,500 |
| | Head of Dorelia, red chalk, 14×10 | 1,700 |
| | John Exors.  C.  Dorelia and Euphemia, pencil and wash, 1905, 15½×10¼ | 2,520 |
| 1965 | S.  Dolores, red chalk, 18¾×13¼ | 180 |
| | Mrs McEvoy, red chalk, 17½×11 (see 1969) | 700 |
| | Lady Rothenstein, 1899, pen and wash, 9¾×6¼ | 320 |
| 1966 | Humphries.  S.  Woman in red turban, pencil and wc, 15¾×7¼ | 280 |
| 1967 | S.  Dorelia in a long dress, chalk and wash, 16½×8¾ | 520 |
| | Samuels.  S.  Self-portrait, black chalk, 1901, 10¼×7 | 1,100 |
| | Portrait, Jacob Epstein, pencil, 1906, 8×6¼ | 1,150 |

| | £ |
|---|---|
| 968 Lady Lamb. C. Ida Nettleship and Dorelia, red chalk, 11½×9¾ | 966 |
| Slade. C. Two heads of a child, pencil, 12½×9 | 1,890 |
| 969 Cottesloe. C. Mrs Ambrose McEvoy, red chalk, 17½×11 (see 1965) | 945 |
| Foster Fairey. Portrait, James Joyce, pencil, 18×12 | 1,600 |

EASTMAN JOHNSON. (*See* American School, 19th–20th centuries)

FRANK TENNEY JOHNSON. (*See* American School, 19th–20th centuries)

ANTONIO JOLI. (*See* Italian School, 18th century)

## JOHAN BARTOLD JONGKIND. 1819–1891

This Dutch painter arrived in Paris in the 1840s as a disciple of Andreas Schel-out, who was one of a group of imitators of Avercamp's frozen landscapes, painted in the leaden and gloomy idiom of their day. Jongkind soon abandoned this idiom, which achieved an unpredictable saleroom popularity in the later 1960s. Instead he fell into the Bonington seascape tradition which he imbibed from Isabey much as Boudin imbibed it. Both painters had an influence on Monet and shared in the evolution of the Impressionist style. Jongkind in the 1860s had actually got a great deal nearer to Impressionism than Boudin ever did, but without Boudin's high degree of skill. In fact Jongkind achieved no success at all, living solitary and most of the time mentally deranged. After his death, his works began to appeal to those who found out-and-out Impressionism a little too disturbing. The two prices, quoted from the year 1901, ten years after Jongkind's death, were actually rather higher than those of the landscapes of Sisley and Pissarro at this date. When Impressionism secured universal acceptance, Jongkind's popularity declined. In the 1930s almost any Jongkind could be bought for £35 to £40. The prices of the turn of the century were not reached again till that landmark in the evolution of the Impressionist market, the Cognacq sale of 1952. Jongkind's prices have not risen again to the level of Sisley and Pissarro, yet a picture of his, bought thirty years ago for £30 or £40, can show a profit of £20,000 in devaluation terms or £4,000 in real money.

| | £ |
|---|---|
| 1901 Bériot. Paris. Nevers, 8,000 francs+tax (see 1952) | 352 |
| Weiller. Paris. Rue des Francs-Bourgeois (see 1952) 6,000 francs+tax | 264 |

223

| | | |
|---|---|---|
| 1912 | Rouart. Paris. Seven paintings made a total of 33,750 francs with tax or £1,350. Average price | £ 193 |
| 1929 | 'E.S.' Paris. Skating scene, 9,300 francs+tax | 99 |
| 1939 | Canonne. Paris. Honfleur, voiliers, 9,000 francs+tax About | 60 |
| | 12 others at £14 to £34 | |
| 1947 | Kent. S. Moonlight at Dortdrecht | 360 |
| 1949 | Paris. Bateaux de pêche échoués, 12½×16½, 25,000 francs +tax | 296 |
| 1950 | Pairs. Canal hollandais au clair du lune, 1853, 17×24 | 205 |
| | Rue de village en Hollande, 1853, 16×22 | 410 |
| 1952 | Cognacq. Paris. Rue des Francs-Bourgeois, 13½×16¾, 1·52 million old francs+tax (£264 in 1901) | 1,880 |
| | Rue à Nevers, 24×16¾, 1·40 million old francs+tax (£352, 1901) | 1,740 |
| | Port de l'entrepôt a Bruxelles, 13¼×18½, 1·42 million old francs+tax (see 1954) | 1,766 |
| | Patineurs près de Rotterdam, 10¾×16¾, 1·05 million old francs+tax | 1,302 |
| 1954 | Paris. Port de l'entrepôt, Bruxelles (see 1952) 1·6 million old francs+tax | 1,503 |
| | Henry Reitlinger. S. Skating scene in Holland | 780 |
| | C. Harbour scene, 9¼×12¾ | 1,102 10s. |
| 1955 | Stuttgart. Le port du chemin de fer, Honfleur, 1866 | 2,800 |
| | Paris. Skaters on a Dutch canal, 35×46 About | 2,600 |
| 1959 | Gould. S. Grenoble, 1885, 12¼×21¼ | 7,200 |
| | Notre Dame from Pont-Neuf (see 1964) | 1,500 |
| | S. Les patineurs, 1865, 9×13½ | 1,200 |
| 1960 | Thatcher. S. Sailing ships at Antwerp, 1866, wc, 9×13 | 1,400 |
| | C. Skating scene | 2,100 |
| | S. View of Dort, 1864, 11×17¾ | 2,000 |
| 1961 | S. View of Havre, 1865, 9¼×16½ | 1,700 |
| | Brinkmann. S. Road by a canal, wc, 9×14½ | 1,300 |
| 1962 | Bloch, Paris. Patineurs en Hollande, 1866, 13¼×20 | 10,200 |
| 1962 | S. Skaters at Overschie, 1876, 22×32½ | 13,500 |
| 1963 | C. Harbour scene, earliest style, 1846, 14½×9 | 2,310 |
| 1964 | Esnault Pelterie. S. Chemin de halage, 1864, 13½×18 | 17,800 |
| | S. L'estuaire, 1867, 12½×17½ | 4,400 |
| | C. Les grands voiliers à Honfleur, 1865, 13×19 (see 1939) | 5,250 |
| | Notre Dame from Pont-Neuf, 20¾×31½ (see 1959) | 3,150 |
| 1965 | S. Bas-Meudon, 1865, 13×18¼ (see 1967) | 6,000 |
| | Village d'Overschie, 1875, 9½×12¾ | 2,000 |
| | Vue d'un coin de la Seine à Paris, 1851, 13½×21 | 14,000 |
| 1966 | S. Barge on Dutch canal, 1862, 16×21½ | 3,200 |
| | Sailing barge or Kof on the Scheldt, 1871, 13×18 | 3,200 |

| | | | £ |
|---|---|---|---|
| 1966 | C. | Seine at Rouen, 1865, 17×21½ | 13,125 |
| | S. | Street in Paris, 1870, 9×12¼ | 4,000 |
| 1967 | S. | Paysage à Bas Meudon, 13×18½, 1865 (see 1965) | 21,000 |
| | Chester Beatty. S. | Patineurs en Hollande, 1864, 16×21½ | 6,000 |
| | | Les balayeurs de neige, 1879, 12½×9½ | 5,600 |
| 1968 | C. | Embouchure de la Meuse, 1868, 12½×17½ | 7,350 |
| | S. | Plage en Normandie, 1866, 13¼×22 | 19,500 |
| 1969 | S. | Plage de Ste Adresse, 1862, 9¾×18 | 9,800 |

## JACOB JORDAENS. (*See* Flemish School, after 1550)

## WILLEM KALF. (*See* Dutch School)

## VASSILY KANDINSKY. 1866–1944

He was born in Moscow in a year when Ingres was still alive but he only began to paint in 1900. By the outbreak of the First World War he had become one of the forefathers of abstract painting. Whether posterity will continue to regard that as a matter of admiration is pure conjecture, but the build-up of the present homage of the market is interesting. In the climate of the 1940s Kandinsky's work shared the Nadir of all German-based manifestations of modernism. A return to favour after the war was concerned less with his explosive abstractions than with his easily grasped *Expressionist* pictures, mostly small landscapes, poetic in feeling and looking like the work of a totally different person. By 1959 this situation had changed. A typical Kandinsky abstraction was sold for about £12,500 in Stuttgart. Five years later, when a group of no less than 50 abstract Kandinskys appeared at the Guggenheim Foundation sale, six made over £20,000 each, and one of them achieved £50,000, putting Kandinsky momentarily on the same plane as Braque and Picasso. The bidding had been heavily stimulated by the belief that, outside the Samuel Guggenheim Foundation, there were very few abstract Kandiskys left. In fact only a few appeared in the salerooms in the next five years and one of these had been in the 1964 sale. (It fell.)

The buying at the 1964 sale was international rather than Germanic. The Boymans-Beuningen Museum of Rotterdam, renowned for a discriminating taste in Vermeers, acquired eleven abstract Kandinskys (or was it eleven yards?). But those who inherit a copy of Sotheby's solidly bound catalogue among other happy memories of this age, should realize that the originals do not look nearly so much like Christmas-crackers as the coloured illustrations suggest.

In the later 1960s Kandinsky's Expressionist landscapes of his Munich period, painted between 1903 and 1910, almost caught up with his abstract works. In 1960 the highest price was £7,400, in 1968 £27,000 for an exceptionally large and attractive work. Almost as much was paid in the following year for a small abstract Kandinsky, in fact rather more than the 1964 scale of prices, but over a period of five years representational works had clearly advanced faster. Another release from the Guggenheim Foundation might alter the balance again.

|  |  | £ |
|---|---|---:|
| 1951 | Archbald. N.Y. Dream, 11½ × 19¾ (abstract) | 125 |
| 1954 | Stuttgart. Composition, red with blue stripes, 14 × 15¾ | 670 |
|  | Bessoneau, Paris. La route, 13 × 12½ | 595 |
| 1955 | Kornfeld, Berne. Kallmunz bei Regensburg, 9½ × 13½ (see 1964) | 192 |
|  | Stuttgart. Abstraction | 4,420 |
| 1959 | S. Winter landscape in the mountains, 13 × 17½ | 5,000 |
|  | Street in Munich, 1901 | 1,500 |
|  | Benziger, Stuttgart. Doppelte Aufstieg, abstraction 27½ × 19½ | 12,500 |
| 1960 | Motte, Geneva. Poids monté, abstract 1935, 23½ × 29½ FS74,000+tax | 7,400 |
| 1963 | Aldrich. N.Y. Bavarian mountains, 1908, 13 × 17½, $20,000 | 7,150 |
|  | Kornfeld, Berne. Four form-elements, abstract FS35,000 +tax | 3,400 |
|  | N.Y. Kirche in Froschhäusen, $22,500 | 8,000 |
| 1964 | Kornfeld, Berne. Geometric abstraction, 1942, 15½ × 15 | 4,408 |
|  | S. Ludwigstrasse, Munich, 1908, 26½ × 38 | 12,000 |
|  | Solomon Guggenheim Foundation. S. Fifty abstract compositions made £536,500 | |
|  | Large study, 1914, 39½ × 31, Boymans-Beuningen Museum | 40,000 |
|  | Improvisation, 1914, 43¾ × 43½, Contemporary Arts Establishment, Switzerland | 50,000 |
|  | Betönte Ecken, 1923, 51 × 51 | 22,000 |
|  | Rift No. 362, 1926, 39¾ × 38 | 20,000 |
|  | Rigide et courbe, No. 625, 1935, 45 × 63¾ | 24,000 |
|  | Der gute Kontakt, 1938, 35 × 48¾ | 20,000 |
|  | 14 others exceeded £10,000 each | |
|  | S. Kallmunz, landscape, 1903, 9½ × 13 (see 1955) | 3,600 |
|  | Rapallo, 1906, 9½ × 13 | 3,800 |
| 1965 | S. Summer in Murnau, 1908, 12½ × 16 | 5,000 |
|  | Corn stooks, 1908, 12½ × 17½ | 2,600 |
|  | Kornfeld, Berne. The Princess and the magic horse, tempera on board, 1906, 19¼ in. square, FS27,000+tax | 2,580 |

|      |                                                                                                      | £      |
|------|------------------------------------------------------------------------------------------------------|--------|
| 1966 | S. Starnberger See, 1908, 12 × 15½                                                                    | 5,100  |
|      | Hart. S. Dorfstrasse mit Burg, 1909, 19 × 25                                                          | 14,000 |
|      | C. Einige Spitze, abstract, 1925, 27½ × 19¾                                                           | 12,075 |
|      | Dorsky. C. Oberpfalztal, 1903, 9½ × 12¾                                                               | 4,410  |
| 1967 | C. Leichter Gegendruck, 1929 (abstract) 19¼ × 19½                                                     | 5,250  |
|      | Die Klippen von Rapallo, 9½ × 13, 1906                                                                | 4,725  |
|      | Hills. N.Y. Risse, gouache 1928 (abstraction) 19 × 12½ (£3,800 in 1964)                               | 3,925  |
|      | N.Y. Street in Starnberg, 1905, 9½ × 13                                                               | 5,355  |
| 1968 | N.Y. Dorfstrasse, 1905, 10½ × 16½, $16,000                                                            | 6,650  |
|      | Kallmunz mit Burg, 1904, 13 × 9½, $15,000                                                             | 6,250  |
|      | Ahrenberg. S. Frühe Stunde, 1906–7, 37½ × 50¼                                                         | 27,000 |
|      | S. Blauer Reiter auf Tunisischem Markt, 28¾ × 36                                                      | 7,000  |
| 1969 | Essvoll. C. Landschaft mit Hügeln, 16¼ × 19¼                                                          | 14,700 |
|      | C. Bauernhof im Sommer, 9¼ × 12¾                                                                      | 7,350  |
|      | Hutton, N.Y. Dorfstrasse in Kochel, c. 1906, 9 × 13, $25,000                                          | 10,417 |
|      | Street in Lana, 1908, 13 × 16, $26,000                                                                | 10,834 |
|      | Rapallo, Boot am Meer, c 1906, 9½ × 13, $26,000                                                       | 10,834 |
|      | S. Kuhle, Abstraction in oil and lacquer on board, 19¼ × 27½, 1941                                    | 26,000 |
|      | Faisceaux des gerbes, 1908, 13 × 17½                                                                  | 7,500  |
|      | C. Belastung, abstraction in pen and tempera, 18½ × 12¾                                               | 5,145  |

## LUDWIG KIRCHNER. (*See* German School, 20th century)


## PAUL KLEE. 1879–1940

Next to Kandinsky, the Swiss-born Paul Klee is the highest prized painter of the international school who were trained in Munich. The appeal of these enlarged doodles, elegantly tinted in a wide range of mixed media, seems fairly universal, though Swiss patriotism, as much as American and German museum competition, plays its part in the truly extraordinary prices. It will be noticed that the real momentum in this market hardly began before 1955 and that the prices vary enormously even now.

|      |                                                                       |       | £   |
|------|-----------------------------------------------------------------------|-------|-----|
| 1948 | Stuttgart. Stadtkomposition, 12½ × 9                                   | About | 140 |
| 1949 | Sternberg. N.Y. Côte meridionale, 1925, 14½ × 18¾, $2,000            |       | 500 |
| 1951 | Motte, Geneva. Zerstörter Ort, 1920, 10 × 8¾, FS2,250+ tax            |       | 220 |

£

| | | £ |
|---|---|---|
| 1953 | Kornfeld, Berne. Omega, oil and tempera, $15\frac{1}{2} \times 21\frac{1}{2}$, FS6,000+tax | 575 |
| 1954 | Stuttgart. Häuser mit Fahnen, wc, 1915, DM5,800+tax | 655 |
| 1955 | Stuttgart. Am Nil, $30 \times 49$, tempera on paper, 1939, DM3,600+tax | 3,560 |
| | Die Künstlerin, wc, $17 \times 11\frac{1}{2}$ | 1,322 |
| 1959 | N.Y. Haus an der See, tempera, 1924, $12 \times 10\frac{3}{4}$, $6,250 | 2,232 |
| 1960 | Rewald. S. Indischer Blümengarten, gouache, $9 \times 14$ | 4,200 |
| | Kornfeld, Berne. Villen für Marionetten, on lino, $12 \times 9\frac{3}{4}$, FS92,000+tax | 9,200 |
| | Benziger, Stuttgart. Spiralblüten, $16\frac{1}{2} \times 12\frac{1}{2}$, DM100,000 +tax | 10,360 |
| | Kreuz und Spiralblüten, tempera and wc, $6\frac{1}{4} \times 12\frac{3}{4}$, DM95,000+tax | 9,775 |
| | and six others at £3,000 to £7,500 | |
| 1961 | Church. N.Y. 'Hall C' 1920, $7\frac{3}{4} \times 17\frac{1}{2}$, $25,000 | 8,930 |
| 1962 | Lempertz, Cologne. Sumpflegende, 1919, $18\frac{3}{4} \times 16\frac{1}{2}$, DM88,000+tax | 9,055 |
| 1963 | Aldrich. N.Y. Häusentreppe, oil on paper, $13\frac{1}{2} \times 9\frac{3}{4}$ | 5,380 |
| | S. Brutaler Pierrot, 1927, wc, $12\frac{1}{2}$ square | 3,000 |
| 1964 | Kornfeld, Berne. Freundliches Spiel, tempera on stucco, $11 \times 12$ | 12,650 |
| 1965 | Lefèvre. Paris. Le clown à l'enfant, 1931, $27\frac{1}{4} \times 20$, with tax | 5,970 |
| | Dynamique d'un tête, oils, $26 \times 20$, with tax | 9,580 |
| 1965 | S. Abfahrt der Schiffe, 1927, oils $18 \times 22$ | 22,000 |
| | C. See gespenst. Oils, $18 \times 22$ | 3,360 |
| | Kornfeld, Berne. Stadt und Tempel gekrönt, wc, $7 \times 9\frac{1}{2}$, FS60,000+tax | 5,870 |
| | Street scene in Tunis, wc, $9\frac{3}{4} \times 10\frac{1}{2}$, FS50,000+tax | 5,048 |
| 1966 | C. Fantastische Göttin, 1916, wc, $9\frac{3}{4} \times 16\frac{3}{4}$ | 2,520 |
| | Woolworth. N.Y. Löwengruppe, ink and wash, $8\frac{1}{4} \times 15$ | 5,200 |
| | Thompson. N.Y. Dreimal drei Kreuze, pen on paper, $10 \times 10$ | 3,235 |
| | Artissenbildnis, 1927, oils on board, $24\frac{3}{4} \times 16$ | 18,350 |
| | Dampfer und Seegelboote, 1931, gouache, $17\frac{1}{4} \times 28\frac{3}{4}$, $80,000 | 28,775 |
| | Draussen, buntes Leben, gouache, 1931, $18\frac{3}{4} \times 12\frac{3}{4}$ | 6,840 |
| 1967 | N.Y. Bote und Klippen, oil etc., $18\frac{1}{4} \times 26\frac{1}{4}$, $26,000 | 9,286 |
| | Olsen Foundation, N.Y. Ein Kind mit gelbe Blüme, 1939, oil on paper, $25 \times 23$, $21,000 | 7,500 |
| | Mister Zeit, 1934, wc on paper, $25\frac{1}{2} \times 19$, $20,000 | 7,145 |
| | Pannisch, süsser Morgen, gouache, $12\frac{1}{4} \times 19\frac{1}{4}$ | 3,580 |

£

968   S.  Gebärde eines Antlitzes, II, 1939, gouache, 24½ × 8¼    8,500
Elmer Rice.  N.Y.  Florentinisches Villenviertel, $82,500 at
2·40 to £                              34,380
     Reiter mit Lanze, 1929, 21 × 17, oils, $34,000     14,165
Was alles hängt, wc, 1930, 19 × 12½, $19,200      8,000
Flögplatz, tinted drawing, 1925, 3 × 13½, $10,500    4,375
Granz.  S.  Südische Garten, thin oils on board, 1936,
10½ × 12½                                 36,000
    Büste, oil and wc on paper, 1922, 19½ × 12¼     10,500
    Vögel im November, 1923, oil and wc on paper,
    14¾ × 17½                           11,000
    Côte de Provence, wc 1927, 10 × 12½       9,500
    Aquarium, oil on gesso, 1927, 14¾ × 20½     16,000
    Tragoedie, oil and tempera on gauze, 22¾ × 17¼  13,000
Cushing.  N.Y.  Abstraction, 1919, wc, 9½ × 12½   5,000
S.  Bote und Klippen, 1927, 18¼ × 26¼, mixed Media (see
1967)                                    13,000
    Sixtet der Genien, pastel on cloth, 1937, 14 × 19½  16,000
    Winterschlaf.  Tempera on paper, 12¼ × 19    11,500
    Alter Friedhof, 1925, mixed media, 14½ × 19    11,000
Kornfeld, Berne.  Feuer Abends, 1929, oils on board,
14¾ × 14½, FS133,000+tax                14,420
969   C.  Bühnenprobe, 1925, mixed media, 19 × 11¾   11,025
N.Y.  Pflanziches Wesen, 1917, pen and wc, 8 × 7¼,
$17,000                                  7,084
    Blümenstocke II, overpainted Lithograph, 1923,
    10 × 6¾                             4,360
C. (Geneva.)  Starker Traum, gouache, 1929, 19¼ × 8¼,
FS85,000+5% tax                      8,582
S.  Schlafende Tiere, pen and gouache, 1939, 13½ × 20½  6,500


FRANZ KLINE.  (*See* Abstract Painters, America)


OSKAR KOKOSCHKA.  (*See* German School, modern)


WILLIAM DE KOONING.  (*See* Abstract Painters, America)


CORNELIUS KRIEGHOFF.  (*See* American School,
19th–20th centuries)


EDWARD LADELL.  (*See* English School, 19th century)

# NICOLAS LANCRET. 1690–1743

Apart from Fragonard, the French followers of Watteau have not recovered the rather overrated status which they held on the international market in the first quarter of the century. The two leading painters of *fêtes champêtres* were no exception, though Lancret and Pater may appear at first glance well enough priced even in terms of inflation money. Take for instance the Henry Say sale of 1908 in Paris, where a *fête champêtre* by Lancret made 280,000 francs. With tax this meant £12,320 and in 1970 money £98,500. We are nowhere near this. The post-war recovery from the prices of the great depression got off to a good start, but this was not maintained during the 1960s. There was nothing to equal the price of *Le tasse de chocolat* which was sold at Sotheby's in 1945 for £12,500, equivalent in 1970 to £31,250.

| | | £ |
|---|---|---:|
| 1959 | Chrysler. N.Y. L'escarpolette, 45 × 36, $28,000 | 10,000 |
| 1965 | Bird. Paris. The St Martin family (see 1966). Bought in at | 7,386 |
| | Schmeidler. S. Lovers in a landscape, 18¼ × 20¾ | 3,500 |
| 1966 | S. The St Martin family, 27½ × 33½ (see 1965) | 3,000 |
| 1967 | Paris. The Minuet and the Bourbon Conti family, 20 × 26¾ | 2 for 24,860 |
| 1968 | S. Le turc amoureux, 23½ × 15¼ | 11,000 |
| 1969 | C. Fête champêtre with table and tent, 23 × 19 | 5,775 |

# SIR EDWARD LANDSEER. 1802–1873

The 'mild and selective revival', noticed in Volume One, has gathered speed to the extent that one picture in the 1960s made a five-figure price. In general the highest prices are paid for oil-sketches which avoid Landseer's gloomy and leaden Victorian pomposity. They are rated as lively and spirited in spite of an insensibility that it would be very difficult to match. The painting of a royal review in 1838, which was bought for the Queen in 1966 for £13,650, comes well into this category. Devoid of dogs in spectacles, tearful crofters, or mauled and tortured game, it is not the kind of Landseer picture which the mid-Victorians liked, since it remained in the painter's studio and made only £168 in 1874, following his death.

Landseer's completed Royal Academy pictures, made famous by steel engravings, were fairly shy visitors to the saleroom in the 1960s with the prospect of less than four-figure prices. One of the best known of his dog pictures in its day, *A Distinguished Member of the Humane Society*, made only £350 in 1967. Painted in the last year of Landseer's life, the picture brought him 2,500 guineas or £23,600 in the money of a century later. But there have been far worse falls from grace for this prince of artisan painters. *The Fatal Duel* was sold in 1933 for £39 8s. Its price at Christie's in 1880 had been £5,250, the equivalent in 1933 of £9,450 and in 1970 of £47,250.

| | | £ |
|---|---|---|
| 1959 | C. Old grey mare in stable, $48\times60$. The first to exceed £1,000 in 36 years | 2,260 |
| 1960 | C. Scene of the Olden Time at Bolton Abbey (£400 in 1834, £105 in 1944) | 63 |
| 1961 | C. Partridge and black cock, surprised by sportsmen | 231 |
| | Ptarmigan in the snow (both oil sketches) | 682 10*s.* |
| 1962 | Lindsay Smith. C. Rachel, a dog portrait, 1835, $13\frac{1}{2}\times9\frac{1}{2}$ | 1,050 |
| | C. Good Friends, horse and dog in stable | 945 |
| | S. 'There's life in the old dog yet', finished subject picture, 1838, 8 ft 8 in. × 6 ft 10 in. | 900 |
| | S. Wellington visiting the field of Waterloo, oil sketch | 1,200 |
| | Two stags under a tree, charcoal drawing | 320 |
| 1965 | Lord Brunton. C. Otter hounds in the water, $23\times60$ | 787 10*s.* |
| | Four paintings of dead game, each $19\frac{1}{2}\times25\frac{1}{2}$ 4 for | 1,113 |
| 1966 | C. Black horse and trooper, large oil sketch, $38\frac{1}{2}\times48\frac{1}{2}$ | 1,102 10*s.* |
| | S. Page of sketches of Ireland, 1851 (oils). Bought by National Gallery, Dublin | 320 |
| | C. Queen Victoria and the Duke of Wellington, reviewing the Life Guards, 1838, $22\times34\frac{1}{2}$ (£163 in 1874, £825 in 1959) | 13,650 |
| | Head of a deerhound, oil sketch, $17\times23\frac{1}{2}$ | 1,050 |
| 1967 | C. Gentleman with hounds, half-length, $30\times25$ | 399 |
| | S. Oil sketch for Bolton Abbey in the Olden Time, $13\times16\frac{1}{2}$ (see 1960, £99 10*s.* in 1874) | 640 |
| | Attachment, completed picture, 1829, $39\times31\frac{1}{4}$ (see 1968) | 300 |
| | A Distinguished Member of the Humane Society (well-known doggy picture), $43\frac{3}{4}\times56$, 1872 | 350 |
| | Terrier and puppies, 1861, sheet of oil studies, $19\frac{1}{4}\times24\frac{1}{2}$ | 2,500 |
| 1968 | C. Highland river landscape, $10\times13\frac{1}{2}$ | 1,575 |
| | S. Attachment, 1829 (see 1967) | 280 |
| 1969 | S. Highland lassies, 1852, oval, $31\times29$ | 950 |
| | King Charles spaniel, oval on board, $12\frac{1}{2}\times14$ | 1,900 |
| | Chisholm. C. (Glasgow.) Dead fawn, 1829, on panel, $11\frac{3}{4}\times15\frac{1}{2}$ | 336 |
| | C. Grey Arab horse and Oriental groom, 1824, $27\frac{1}{2}\times35\frac{1}{2}$ | 2,520 |
| | C. (At Hopetoun.) Greyhound and stone urn, pencil and wc, 1822, $4\frac{1}{4}\times5\frac{3}{4}$ | 472 10*s.* |

NICOLAS LARGILLIERRE. (*See* French School, 18th century)

GEORGES DE LA TOUR. (*See* French School, 17th century)

## MAURICE QUENTIN DE LATOUR. 1704–1788

The selection that has reached the salerooms in the 1960s is clearly not of the best, with the exception of the self-portrait which was sold in 1967 for £20,000. This was rather less in terms of real money than its price in 1903. One would have thought that rarity alone would have commanded a better price. At the famous Jacques Doucet sale of 1912 seven of these portrait pastels made from £3,000 to £4,700 (equivalent to £24,000–£27,500). At the same sale the portrait of *Duval d'Epinoy* was bought by Henri de Rothschild for 620,000 francs and tax, then equivalent to £27,300 and now to £218,400, but Quentin de Latour's masterpiece went to Calouste Gulbenkian for much under cost price in 1943. What would it be worth in 1970? The French 18th century has not hitherto shewn itself the most flourishing of markets.

|      |                                                                                        | £          |
|------|----------------------------------------------------------------------------------------|------------|
| 1959 | S.  Mme Savalette de Lange, pastel, 22½ × 19½                                           | 8,500      |
|      | Chrysler-Foy. N.Y.  Masque of the painter, 12 × 9, pastel                              | 3,928 10s. |
|      | Head of a smiling girl, pastel                                                          | 2,500      |
| 1966 | Paris.  Mme de la Condamine, 22 × 18, pastel                                            | 3,100      |
| 1967 | N.Y.  Unfinished self-portrait on vellum, 15½ × 12, $8,250                              | 2,946      |
|      | du Rels.  S.  Self-portrait, 1754, 17½ × 14½ (£3,000 in 1903)                           | 20,000     |
| 1969 | C.  Supposed head of Mlle Fel, preliminary pastel sketch 11½ × 9½                       | 1,785      |

## HENRI LAURENS.  (*See* Abstract Painters, Europe)

## HENRI DE TOULOUSE-LAUTREC. 1864–1901

It is curious that in the 1960s, when all the original Impressionists showed that their works could make six-figure prices, the best of Toulouse-Lautrec remained below £40,000. The prices in my list are not, however, an indication of lack of interest but simply of rarity. Even the dearest works are scarcely more than studies. An extremely perfunctory *ébauche* for the famous *au salon* made £20,000 in 1962. The original picture in the Museum at Albi could well be worth half a million.

|      |                                                                             | £      |
|------|-----------------------------------------------------------------------------|--------|
| 1959 | N.Y.  Femme rousse dans un jardin                                           | 64,288 |
|      | Chrysler.  S.  Retour de chasse, oils, academic style, 1883, 37 × 54       | 15,000 |
|      | Marcel Lender, sketch for colour lithograph                                 | 13,000 |
|      | Medallion, girl's head, for mural decoration                                | 6,000  |
| 1960 | Paris.  Bettine, portrait                                                    | 25,450 |
|      | Le coucher, 1899                                                             | 25,565 |

|   |   |   | £ |
|---|---|---|---|
| 1962 | Somerset Maugham. S. Le polisseur, 1887, academic nude study, $25\frac{1}{2} \times 32$ (see 1966) | | 27,000 |
| | S. Oil sketch for two figures in the picture, *au salon*, at Albi, 1894, $23\frac{1}{2} \times 15\frac{3}{4}$ | | 20,000 |
| | Paris. Clownesse, gouache on board, $18\frac{3}{4} \times 12\frac{3}{4}$, FN290,000+tax | | 25,280 |
| | Melby. S. Le dernier salut, wash drawing, 1887, $23\frac{3}{4} \times 17\frac{3}{4}$ | | 6,000 |
| 1963 | Cargill. S. Ballet dancers, gouache | | 35,000 |
| 1964 | Bloch. Paris. Au bal de l'opéra, gouache on board, $26 \times 20\frac{3}{4}$ (see 1966) | | 32,000 |
| | Hutton. S. Moulin de la Galette, charcoal drawing, outlined for magazine reproduction | | 25,000 |
| 1965 | Maurice Haft (at Palm Beach). ·Man in straw hat, oils $19\frac{1}{2} \times 10\frac{1}{2}$ ($90,000) | | 32,200 |
| | S. Drawing touched with gouache, Femme nue se coiffant | | 8,000 |
| | Avnet, N.Y. Danseuse dans sa loge, mural, 1885, $45 \times 39\frac{1}{2}$, $105,000 | | 37,500 |
| 1966 | Huntington Hertford. S. Academic study, male nude, 1883, $31 \times 25$ | | 9,500 |
| | S. La vache enragée, charcoal and wash for a poster, $30\frac{1}{2} \times 22\frac{3}{4}$ | | 7,800 |
| | N.Y. Au bal de l'opéra, 1894, charcoal and gouache on board, $25\frac{1}{2} \times 21$ (see 1964) $98,000 | | 35,100 |
| | Huntington Hertford, N.Y. Le polisseur (£27,000, 1962) $25\frac{1}{2} \times 32$, $30,000 | | 10,780 |
| 1967 | S. Escalier de la Rue des Moulins, slight oil sketch on millboard, 1893, $26 \times 21$ | | 20,000 |
| | Paris. Rolande de la Rue des Moulins, gouache sketch on millboard, $19 \times 13\frac{3}{4}$, FN80,000+tax | | 6,380 |
| 1968 | de Bruin. C. Escalier de la Rue des Moulins, preliminaries in pastel, $27 \times 16\frac{3}{4}$ | | 4,725 |

## SIR THOMAS LAWRENCE. 1769–1830

The list which follows is of such a humdrum kind that it may be useful to give some idea how the works of this painter have fallen without having recourse to Volume One. The high tide of Lawrence's truly extravagant market, as built up by Lord Duveen, was at the Michelham sale of 1926. The price paid by Duveen under the hammer for *Miss Mary Moulton Barrett*, a child portrait better known as *Pinkie*, was £77,700, at that time the highest auction-bid for a picture that had ever been known. If it is true that the price paid by Henry Huntington was £90,000, we get the equivalent in 1970 of £450,000. On a slightly less exalted plane the price paid by the Metropolitan Museum in 193 (when the market was already falling hard) for *Nelly Farren* was 200,000 dollars or £41,200 (equivalent to £206,000).

A better idea of what happened to 'the Duveen market' can be obtained by following the fortunes of pictures by Lawrence which have been resold. A the Roussel sale in Paris in 1912 a whole-length portrait of *The Countess o Pembroke* was sold for 400,000 francs and tax. This meant £17,600, more than twice as much as any Lawrence portrait had fetched at auction at that date In 1932 the picture was sold for almost the same number of francs, plus a much increased tax, but the franc had fallen so much that this meant only £6,450 In 1914 E. T. Stotesbury had paid Duveen $50,000 (£10,350) for the *Hon Miss Caroline Upton*. In 1944 the picture was sold at auction in New York for $9,000 then worth £2,250. The biggest falls occurred on the eve of the Second World War. A Lawrence of the less costly kind, a head of *Lord Castlereagh* which was sold in 1928 for £4,410, made only £567 ten years later.

It is interesting to reflect that most of the whole-length portraits, for which Lawrence charged 700 guineas in the 1820s, would not make more than £4,000 to £5,000 in 1970, not even half the purchasing power of Lawrence's original fee. And yet Lawrence was unquestionably among the world's greater portrait painters. One could cite for instance an unfinished girl's head which was sold in 1965 for £3,000.

| | | £ |
|---|---|---|
| 1961 | Whitmarsh. N.Y. Mrs John Williams, head, 1804 | 2,679 |
| | Mrs Falconer Atlee, half-length, 1810 | 3,215 |
| | Paris. Unknown dark-haired girl, head, 24 × 22, FN61,000 +tax | 5,280 |
| 1962 | S. Lord Amherst, whole-length, 93 × 57¼ | 4,200 |
| 1963 | Dunlap. N.Y. Charles, Earl Gray, head, 12¼ × 9¼ | 3,750 |
| | Cintas. S. Duke of Newcastle, whole-length, 93 × 56½ | 8,200 |
| | George IV in garter robes, half-length | 4,000 |
| 1965 | Craigmyle. S. Miss Thayer, 29½ × 24½ | 4,200 |
| | 2nd Lord Ribblesdale, unfinished oval, 22 × 19 | 2,200 |
| | S. Head of unknown girl, unfinished, 23½ × 21½ | 3,000 |
| | Springold. S. Duchess of Cleveland, 1813, whole-length, 90 in. high (bought in, see 1968) | 2,100 |
| 1966 | Avnet. S. Countess of Charlmont and her infant son, 48½ × 38½ | 750 |
| | Hodgkins. C. Lady Charlotte Owen, half-length, 50 × 40 | 1,050 |
| 1967 | Carew-Pole. S. Children of John Angerstein, 1807, 76 × 65¾, (first five-figure price in 32 years) | 23,000 |
| | Oliphant. S. Julia Angerstein, chalk drawing, 9¾ × 8¾ | 1,900 |
| | Gerry. N.Y. Benjamin West, half-length, 1810, 60½ × 70½ | 3,571 |

| | | | £ |
|---|---|---|---|
| 968 | Smith. C. Charles and Henry Arbuthnot, pencil and wc, $8\frac{1}{2}\times 7$ | | 1,155 |
| | C. Boy in green and brown coat, $29\times 24$ | | 5,775 |
| | Springold. N.Y. Duchess of Cleveland, whole-length, 1813 (see 1965) $10,000 | | 4,157 |
| | Craven. S. William, Earl of Craven, whole-length, 1802, $92\frac{3}{4}\times 56\frac{3}{4}$ | | 5,000 |
| | Bruguière. C. Lucy Sotheron, half-length, $50\times 40$ | | 7,825 |

## FERNAND LÉGER. 1881–1955

éger, though his works are much less costly than those of Picasso or Braque,
one of the most popular painters of the Cubist generation. He had been
ained originally as an architectural draughtsman and his paintings, when not
wholly abstract, tend to be based on mechanical or architectural forms, rendered
s highly solid cylindrical shapes, a style which was at one time called *tubisme*.
Iotly coloured and forceful, these somewhat blatant works played their part
a inspiring the mindless 'pop art' of the fifties and sixties. Léger is often
ssociated with Juan Gris, who was less obsessed with solidity and perhaps a
ttle less blatant. A Léger has been sold for £36,000 and a Gris for £50,000.
will be noticed that a small gouache by Fernand Léger which made £3,800
t Sotheby's in 1969, cost only £2 in 1934. This was by no means exceptional.
he early thirties were a difficult time for painters in Paris. Even the falling franc
iled to stimulate the limited international market for what was then ultra-
iodern painting. Large works by Léger, Gris and Miró, for which at least
,200 would have been asked normally, were going for a fifth as much or less.

| | | | £ |
|---|---|---|---|
| 949 | Moos, Geneva. Les soeurs, $26\times 21\frac{1}{2}$, FS1,800+tax | | 178 |
| 953 | Paris. La disque rouge, 1919, $36\frac{3}{4}\times 26$, 1·25 million francs +tax | | 1,520 |
| 960 | Baroness Gourgaud. N.Y. The smoker, 1917, $82,500 | | 29,464 |
| | Paris. Baigneuse, FN28,000+tax | | 2,435 |
| 963 | Aldrich. N.Y. Elements méchaniques, $15\times 10\frac{1}{2}$, $13,275 | | 4,742 |
| 964 | Glass. S. Le compôtier, 1948, $23\times 26$ | | 5,500 |
| 965 | N.Y. Le fumeur, contraste des formes, wc, $11\frac{1}{4}\times 9\frac{1}{4}$, $14,050 | | 5,025 |
| | Lefèvre, Paris. Contraste des formes, gouache, $25\times 19$, FN110,500+tax | | 8,780 |
| | Landscape, 1914, oils, $29\times 40$, FN240,000+tax | | 19,430 |
| | L'échafaudage, oils, $32\frac{1}{2}\times 24$, FN185,000+tax | | 14,854 |
| | Fleurs et poupées, 1937, $35\frac{1}{2}\times 52$, FN135,000+tax | | 10,880 |
| | Esquisse pour la ville, oils, 1914, $26\times 21\frac{1}{2}$, FN185,000+tax | | 14,854 |
| | Nature morte, feuille jaune, 1927, oils, $29\times 36\frac{1}{2}$, FN95,000+tax | | 7,590 |

| | | £ |
|---|---|---|
| 1965 | Ira Haupt. N.Y. Le campeur, $35,000 | 14,642 |
| | S. Still life for a dining room, 1930, 33×47 | 6,800 |
| | N.Y. La morte à trois feuilles, 38½×51¼, $28,000 | 10,000 |
| 1966 | Thompson. N.Y. | |
| | L'escalier, 1914, 34½×49, $100,000 | 35,960 |
| | The compass, 1925, 35½×28¼, $30,000 | 10,790 |
| | Fragment méchanique, 1943, 49¾×44, $30,000 | 10,790 |
| | Les trois soeurs, 1951, oils, 50×37, $50,000 (see 1967) | 20,140 |
| 1967 | C. Nature morte à l'as de carreaux, 1929, 35½×25¼ | 5,775 |
| | Ervin. C. Les trois soeurs, 1951, (see 1966) bought in at | 14,700 |
| | Lefèvre, 3rd sale. Paris. L'arraignée bleue, 1938, 36½×26 (FN11·88 to the £+tax) | 7,300 |
| | Composition au Roi de Coeur, 1948, 36¾×26 | 6,190 |
| | Mabille. S. Nature morte, semi-abstract, 1918, 25½×32 | 17,000 |
| | N.Y. Deux femmes à la toilette, 1920, 25×19½ | 12,500 |
| | Paris. Architecture, 1923, 26×36¾. FN110,000+tax | 8,930 |
| | Les quatre personnages, 21½×26. FN85,000+tax | 6,750 |
| 1968 | N.Y. Femme au perroquet, 37¼×26½, $18,500 | 7,710 |
| | Granz. S. Le fumeur, pen and wc, 1911, 16×12½ | 7,500 |
| | Le clown, 1918, 13×9½ | 12,500 |
| | S. Deux femmes couchées, ink and gouache, 1913, 19¼×25 | 10,200 |
| | Bluestein. N.Y. Elements méchaniques, 1920, 25½×21¼, $34,000 | 14,164 |
| 1969 | Ringsted. C. La couverture dans le paysage 1949, 19¾×25½ | 6,825 |
| | Silberman. N.Y. Figure, contraste des formes, 1912, 25×18½, monochrome, ink, etc., $35,000 | 14,584 |
| | S. Personnage, couché dans un paysage, gouache, 1921, 10×14 (£2 in 1934) | 3,800 |
| | N.Y. Femme nue devant un fenêtre, 1921, pencil, 15×12, $7,750 | 3,229 |
| | S. Les acrobates, 1940, 21¼×25¼ | 13,000 |
| | Hadorn. C. Une journée d'été, 25¾×36¾, bought in | 32,000 |
| | S. Abstract composition, pen and ink, 8¾×11 | 4,400 |

## FREDERICK, LORD LEIGHTON. 1830–1896

The interesting detritus of a once flourishing market. It cannot be said precisely that there is a growing demand for classical nudes and semi-nudes in the texture and colours of bath-soap, but anything with a name to it becomes a rarity—and sometimes almost overnight. In 1960 the 10 ft *Sargonsian bride* was sold for £200. Its price in 1874 was equivalent to something like £24,000. *Cupid and syche* did scarcely any better in 1966, but in 1968 the less celebrated *Hercules ld Alcestis* suddenly made £2,000. Thus Leighton became equal again with e other gods of Mr William Gaunt's Victorian Olympus.

|  |  | £ |
|---|---|---|
| ɔ58 | Lever Art Gallery. C. Oil sketch for *Cimabue*, 1855 | 115 10s. |
| ɔ60 | Knight, Frank and Rutley. The Sargonsian Bride, 144 × 60 (£1,200 in 1866, £2,677 10s. in 1874) | 200 |
| ɔ61 | Stanley of Alderley. C. Two Venetian noblemen, 39 × 28½ | 35 15s. |
| ɔ63 | C. Return of Proserpine, small oil sketch | 241 10s. |
|  | Solitude, 6¾ × 3 | 178 10s. |
|  | Motcomb, auctioneers. Portrait of unknown man | 550 |
| ɔ65 | S. 'Letty', Miss Dene in black hat, trimmed with fur, 17½ × 14¾ | 350 |
| ɔ66 | S. The bath of Psyche (£1,050 in 1890) replica of Tate Gallery picture, 73½ × 23½ | 220 |
| ɔ68 | S. Rubiniella, black and white chalk drawing, 8 × 6 | 130 |
|  | Phoebe, R.A. picture, 1885, 23½ × 20½ | 520 |
|  | Knight, Frank and Rutley. Hercules struggling with Death for the body of Alcestis. R.A. picture 1871, 55 × 65½ | 2,000 |
|  | C. Bacchante, R.A. picture 1892, 50 × 37 | 840 |
| ɔ69 | Knight, Frank and Rutley. Cymon and Iphigeneia, 1884, (£2,310 in 1909, £493 in 1938) | 1,200 |
|  | Parkinson. C. Dancing nymph and amorino, gold ground, 42 × 66½ (£57 15s. in 1951) | 682 10s. |
|  | S. Contemplation, 21¾ × 16¾ | 800 |

## SIR PETER LELY. 1617–1680

has been the habit ever since Duveen built up the market for English portraits the 18th century to decry Lely as a journeyman-painter, though he was no ore so than Reynolds. In late Victorian times he was rated relatively much gher, a portrait in the great Hamilton Palace sale of 1882 making the equiva- nt of £3,600 in 1970 money. In the 1930s, when the English 18th century ɔrtrait market collapsed, Lely fared even worse. The sum of £40 would have ɔne quite a long way, and even at the end of the last war Lely's beauties of harles II's court could have been bought for under £100. It is never apparent ɔw a boom in a painter's work begins, but few rises have been more sudden an that of Lely's portraits in 1968. Doubtless, anxious eyes are now watching e portraits of Sir Godfrey Kneller.

|  |  | £ |
|---|---|---|
| ɜ64 | Cathcart. C. Nell Gwyn with orange tree and statue | 220 10s. |
| ɜ82 | Hamilton Palace. C. Lord Newark, 49 × 40 | 388 10s. |
| ɜ86 | Lord Cholmondely. C. Mrs Deering | 435 15s. |

£

| 1919 | 2nd Hamilton Palace sale.  C.  Portrait | 2,730 |
| 1958 | C.  Nell Gwyn holding a wreath, 49×40 | 157 |
| 1966 | Brewis.  S.  Sir John Cotton and family, 1660, 60½×80 | 3,800 |
| | Carritt.  C.  Anne, Countess of Suffolk, 49½×39½ | 399 |
| 1967 | Watney.  C.  Earl and Countess of Clarendon, 65½×49 | 735 |
| | Anne Hyde, later Duchess of York, 49×39 | 231 |
| | Spencer Nairn.  C.  John, Duke of Lauderdale, 48½×39, National Gallery, Edinburgh | 4,725 |
| 1968 | C.  Henry and Amabel Grey as children, 1680, 67½×50 | 525 |
| | Earl of Craven.  C.  Girl playing a lute, 56×36¾ | 29,000 |
| | Man playing a violin, companion-piece | 18,000 |
| | Man playing a lute, 43½×35 | 5,800 |
| 1969 | Malcolm Macdonald.  S.  Marjory, Lady Lovelace, half-length, 49×39½ | 800 |

## THE BROTHERS LE NAIN.  (*See* French School, 17th and 18th centuries)

## NICOLAS LEPICIÉ.  (*See* French School, 17th and 18th centuries)

## JEAN BAPTISTE LE PRINCE.  (*See* French School, 17th and 18th centuries)

## LEONARDO DA VINCI.  1452–1519

The market for the paintings of Leonardo was restricted in the 1960s to two transactions only. This is the cost of the greatest and rarest of names and the price of *Ginevra di Benci* need surprise no one. Calculated on the time-scale which I have adopted throughout this book, the *Benois Madonna*, a much less attractive work, cost the Tsar of Russia as much or more in 1914 ($1½ million or £310,400).

Of the list of drawings only the very slight sketch, sold in 1963 for £19,000 inspires all-round confidence. One can assume in the year 1970 that such drawing as the *Man on a Rearing Horse* of the Oppenheimer sale of 1937 (£4,305) would command at least £60,000.

| 1956 | Prince Liechtenstein, said to have refused an offer from the Canadian government for the portrait of Ginevra di Benci (see 1967) $3,000,000 | £ 714,000 |
| 1962 | Bought by the National Gallery from the Royal Academy, the Virgin and child with John the Baptist and St Anne, cartoon on brown paper in charcoal and white, much damaged, 54¾×39¾ | 800,000 |

67  Bought by the National Gallery, Washington, from Prince        £
    Liechtenstein, the portrait of Ginevra di Benci. Price
    reported to be $5,000,000, equivalent in 1967 to £1,784,000
    and in 1970                                                2,083,355

### DRAWINGS

62  D. of Saxe-Coburg Weimar.  S.  Alleged set of studies for
    the heads in the *Last Supper* (1830, £536 14s.; 1850, £666).
    Now attributed to Solario, very much restored, 25 × 18½
                                                      8 for    8,000
63  Del Judice.  S.  Head of Leda, cartoon fragment (attri-
    buted) (1927, £1,785; 1954, £3,400)                        6,800
    Noel.  C.  Grotesque head of a man, leadpoint, 4 × 3,
    attributed (£5 in 1859)                                   14,700
    Pollen.  S.  Holy Family with cat, 3¼ × 2¾               19,000
67  Griffiths.  S.  The 8 Last Supper heads (see 1962)  8 for  4,900

## JOHN FREDERICK LEWIS.  1805–1876

ie three early-Victorian romantic painters of the Oriental scene seem to be
a the road to recovery, and Lewis as much as David Roberts or William
uller. But there is still a very long way to go, and it is impossible to imagine
y of these painters as among the highest-priced in the London salerooms—
they were in the late 19th century. In 1893 Lewis's *Koran commentator* was
ld at Christie's for 2,550 guineas, something not far short of £24,000 in the
oney of 1970. In reality Lewis rated even higher than that in 1893, a year
hen £7,000 was thought a lot for a specially good Rembrandt portrait.

|  |  | £ |
|---|---|---|
| 60 | S.  The mendicant, wc (£241 10s. in 1894) | 150 |
|  | C.  Indoor gossip, oils | 525 |
|  | The reception, oils (see 1967), £892 10s. in 1891, £110 5s. in 1937, 24½ × 29½, painted 1873 | 840 |
| 61 | S.  The court of the lions, Granada, tinted drawing | 100 |
| 64 | S.  The bull ring, Seville, 1835, wc, 25¼ × 33½ | 170 |
|  | Interior, Sta Sophia, pen and wc, 14½ × 20¾ | 140 |
| 65 | Russell Johnson.  C.  Roman pilgrims resting in a church, wc, 10½ × 16 | 294 |
| 67 | Farrow.  S.  The reception (see 1960) | 5,200 |
|  | Lewinson.  S.  Cairo bazaar, the Della'l, 1875, 29½ × 20½, oil | 1,850 |
|  | C.  Cairo Bazaar, the Gourich, 29 × 40, oil | 315 |
|  | Yates.  S.  Religious procession, Seville, 33 × 25, wc | 380 |

£

| | | |
|---|---|---|
| 1968 | N.Y.  The Circassian, oils, *c.* 1850, 18×24, $2,700 | 1,125 |
| | Edwards.  C.  Two women in a harem, unfinished wc, 14×17½ | 472 10 |
| | Bowring.  C.  Mass in the cathedral, Cordoba, 1833, wc bodycolour, 19½×26 | 525 |
| | Campbell-Blair.  S.  The Frank encampment, wc, 1856, 25½×53 (£607 in 1860, £260 in 1952) | 5,200 |
| | Pope.  C.  Arab horsemen, wc, 13×14½ | 441 |
| | C.  Ferreting, wc, 10½×7½, 1828 (early work) | 525 |
| | Stretford Corporation.  C.  Street and mosque of Ghooleya, Cairo, oils, 1876, 44½×34.  Bought in (see 1969) | 1,050 |
| | Hewitt.  S.  In the harem, wc, 12×18¼ | 900 |
| | Sacking the convent, wc, bodycolour, 1838, 20½×28¾ | 380 |
| 1969 | S.  The prayer of the faith, wc bodycolour, 1872, 23×17½ (£1,176 in 1875, £483 in 1916, £68 5s. in 1935) | 3,200 |
| | La Sevillana, 1835, wc, 14½×10½ | 850 |
| | C (Glasgow).  Street and mosque of Ghooleya (see 1968) | 1,785 |
| | Lord Milford.  S.  The prayer of the faith, oil version, 1872, 36×28 | 3,200 |
| | Fitzpatrick.  S.  The boy-prince Hassan with slave attendant, Cairo, wc, heightened, 20×14½ | 900 |

## MAX LIEBERMANN.  (*See* German School, modern)

## JOHN LINNELL SNR.  1792–1882

I have included Linnell in Volume Three simply because of the high prices his works in the past. This is in fact a ghost market which, since its lowe depths in the 1930s, barely kept pace with thirty years of inflation, though more positive movement could be detected in 1969. Linnell lived 90 years a painted for at least 70 of them. As a young man he was adventurous enou to imitate William Blake, while in middle age he inflicted his own niggli fussy style on his son-in-law, Samuel Palmer. In the 1870s, when the cult of t Romantic generation was in full swing, Linnell remained alive to see pictures fetch enormous prices, among them two cumbersome landscapes 2,500 guineas each, the equivalent in 1970 of £23,500.

£

| | | |
|---|---|---|
| 1963 | S.  Welsh hill scene, 1863 (dearest in 43 years) oil | 700 |
| | C.  The game of cricket, 1854, oil | 861 |
| 1964 | S.  Eve tempting Adam, 1825, wc in style of Blake | 125 |

|  |  |  | £ |
|---|---|---|---|
| 1965 | S. | Driving home the flock, 1863, 38½×53½, oil | 320 |
|  | C. | Isle of Wight from Lymington quay, 1828, oil, 11×15 | 630 |
| 1966 | C. | Extensive landscape, 1858, 18½×30½, oil | 399 |
| 1967 | C. | The sheepfold, 1859, oil, 39×49 | 157 |
| 1969 | Coleman Dunn, C. | Wooded hillside, wc, 19×27 | 1,995 |
|  |  | Portrait, the artist's wife, coloured chalks, 19¼×15¾ | 420 |
|  |  | Doorway in an ancient building, oil, 6½×12½ | 630 |
|  |  | Brotherton. S. Sheep washing, 3¼×7½, oil in the style of William Blake | 780 |
|  |  | S. Noon, the Haymakers' rest, 1871, 27½×38½, oil | 850 |
|  |  | Porritt. C. Surrey woodlands, 1868, 39×54, oil | 892 10s. |

FILIPPINO LIPPI. (*See* Italian School, Central (1961 and 1964))

PIETRO LONGHI. (*See* Italian School, 18th century)

LORENZO LOTTO. (*See* Venetian School)

PHILIP LOUTHERBOURG. (*See* Introductory note, English School, 18th century)

LAWRENCE LOWRY. (*See* English School, 20th century)

MAXIMILIEN LUCE. (*See* French School, minor Impressionists)

JEAN GOSSAERT DE MABUSE. (*See* Flemish School, 15th–16th centuries)

AUGUST MACKE. (*See* German School, modern)

DANIEL MACLISE. 1811–1870

Maclise is included for the same reason as Linnell. At the Spencer Churchill ..le of 1965 *Robin Hood and his men* figured among the many pictures, bought ..ack for Northwick Hall after the sale of 1859. The great collecting Earl of ..orthwick had bought this picture from Maclise together with a sixteen-feet picture now in the National Gallery, Dublin, *The marriage of Strongbow*. For the latter we have Redford's authority that the price paid at the Royal Academy exhibition of 1854, was £4,000—and that would be certainly not much short of £40,000 in the money of 1970. Maclise, who painted murals for the House of Lords, seldom produced anything less than ten feet long, and one of these medievalist monsters was sold in 1937 for £2 10s. framed.

|      |                                                                              | £        |
|------|------------------------------------------------------------------------------|----------|
| 1965 | C. The choice of Heracles, 40×49                                              | 441      |
|      | Spencer Churchill. C. Robin Hood entertains the king, 1939, 72×144 (£1,370 5s. in 1859) | 682 5s.  |
|      | S. A Stall on the Ice with skaters, 32¾×49½                                   | 1,155    |
| 1966 | C. The tryst, 1859, 47½×34                                                    | 199 10s. |
| 1967 | Wright. C. The marriage of Eva and Strongbow, wc version, 20×31¾             | 336      |
| 1970 | C. Girl on a terrace with parrot, oval, 29×22½                                | 441      |

## NICOLAS MAES. 1632–1698

A picture by Maes, *Woman Standing at a Pump* made £3,000 in 1894, having multiplied in value four times in 48 years. There were not many pictures of any school which made more than that in 1894, except what were then considered the moderns. Yet £3,000, or a little more, remained the top price for Nicolas Maes for another 73 years—till 1967 when all of a sudden *The Eavesdropping Servant* made 37,000 guineas. Why this tribute to a most excellent Dutch painter of the second rank could not have been paid before I cannot attempt to explain. The fact remains that at the end of the 1960s this was the school most liable to create market surprises.

|      |                                                                              | £      |
|------|------------------------------------------------------------------------------|--------|
| 1960 | Agnew Somerville. S. Family group, 48½×66½                                    | 3,200  |
|      | N.Y. Vertumnus and Pomona (£420 in 1950)                                      | 425    |
| 1963 | S. Lady sewing, 15½×12                                                        | 800    |
| 1964 | C. A bough of peaches against a wall, 21×17                                   | 3,360  |
| 1965 | Spencer Churchill. C. The Lacemaker, 22½×28½ (£35 3s. 6d. in 1832)            | 2,155  |
| 1966 | Bjorklund. S. Occupations of peasant family, pen and wash drawing in Rembrandt style, 6½×7¾ | 560    |
| 1967 | Sandford. S. Family at home with view of Dortdrecht, 43½×47¼ (Bought in at £3,150 in 1921) | 5,000  |
|      | Lord Clinton. C. The Eavesdropping Maid, 1655, 18×28                          | 38,850 |
| 1968 | C. Maidservant scouring copper pan, 15¾×18½                                   | 1,575  |

| | | £ |
|---|---|---|
| 1969 C. | Small boy in plumed hat with lemon branch, 27×24 | 13,650 |
| Austin. C. | Old woman at spinning wheel, sketch in red chalk, 7¾×7¼ | 2,940 |
| C. | Gentleman in brown wig, leaning on a plinth, 27×21½ | 1,785 |
| | Gentleman and lady, ¾-length, a pair, 20×16        2 for | 3,990 |
| | Portrait of John Locke, 1680, 48×39. Bought in at | 3,360 |
| | Two children and an eagle, allegory, 32½×39½ | 3,150 |
| S. | Josias Ingelbrechts and his wife, 21¾×17        2 for | 3,200 |

## ALESSANDRO MAGNASCO. (*See* Italian School, 18th century)

## RENÉ MAGRITTE. (*See* Abstract Painters, Europe)

## ALFRED MANESSIER. (*See* Abstract Painters, Europe)

## EDOUARD MANET. 1832–1883

Very few paintings by Manet were sold in the 1960s, and only one of them was a work of importance, *Le Fumeur*, which made a fairly predictable $450,000 in New York in 1965. The scarcity was partly due to the painter's short life of 50 years. But it owed more to the fact that Manet had been older than the other members of the Impressionist circle, that most of his works were painted in a pre-Impressionist style and that, as a consequence, the hiving off into public collections had been going on longer. That Manet was appreciated much earlier is shewn by a comparison of top-prices. The Luxembourg Museum paid 9,000 francs (about £775) as long ago as 1890 for *Olympia*. Eight years later Durand-Ruel sold *La femme à la Guitare* to Mrs Montgomery Sears for £2,800. In 1910 the Stadtgallerie, Mannheim, bought the *Execution of the Emperor Maximilian* for £4,500. These prices were much higher than anything achieved by Degas, Monet or Renoir at this period. Whether a Manet can compete in 1970 with Renoirs and Monets at £646,000 and £588,000 is probably an unanswerable question because by all indications there are no more first-class Manets that can reach the market.

The list has been taken back to the end of the last century in order to repair some serious omissions in Volume One.

| | | £ |
|---|---|---|
| 1898 | Sold by Durand-Ruel to Mrs Montgomery Sears, La Femme à la Guitare (£18 in 1868) 70,000 francs | 2,800 |
| 1899 | Chocquet. Paris. Paveurs de la Rue de Berne, 25¼×31½ (see 1913, 1924) | 462 |
| | Manet dans son atelier | 440 |

| | | £ |
|---|---|---|
| 1902 | Milliken. N.Y. Le fumeur (see 1965), $3,100, 39×31 | 638 |
| 1903 | C. Jetée a Boulogne | 504 |
| 1906 | Lord Grimthorpe. C. Jeune femme à la cravate blanche | 257 15 |
| 1910 | Bought by Stadtgallerie, Mannheim. The Execution of the Emperor Maximilian, 93×120 | 4,500 |
| 1912 | Rouart. Paris. Le leçon de musique (£176 in 1884), 120,000 francs+tax | 5,280 |
| | Buste de femme, bought in at 90,000 francs | 3,600 |
| 1913 | Mariczell de Nemès. Paris. Paveurs de la Rue de Berne, (see 1899, 1924) 25¼×31, 72,500 francs+tax | 3,190 |
| 1918 | Degas. Paris. Bought by Louvre, pastel portrait, Mme Edouard Manet, 39½×24, 62,000 francs | 2,480 |
| | Sold by Georges Bernheim, portrait, Manet's mother, 40×30½ | 6,000 |
| 1919 | Cochin. Paris. La serveuse de bocks (£100 in 1884, see 1924), 75,000 francs+tax | 3,292 |
| | According to R. Gimpel, Paul Rosenberg asked 500,000 francs for Girl in pink at a café table (32·5 francs to £) | 15,000 |
| 1922 | Sold by Durand-Ruel. La Promenade, 36½×27½ (£60 in 1884, see 1958) 100,000 francs        About | 2,000 |
| 1923 | Price paid by Paul Rosenberg for Le bon bock, 37½×33¼ according to R. Gimpel, 800,000 francs at 75 to £ | 10,640 |
| 1924 | Sold by Hoentschel to Georges Bernheim. Les Paveurs de la Rue de Berne (see 1899, 1913) 850,000 francs at 70 to £ | 12,140 |
| | Bought by Courtauld Fund for Tate Gallery. La Serveuse de Bocks (£100 in 1884, £3,292 in 1919) 38½×52 | 10,000 |
| 1925 | Bought by the National Gallery, Melbourne. Maison à Reuil | 4,600 |
| 1926 | Cowan. C. The ship's deck, oil sketch | 997 10 |
| 1930 | Havemeyer. N.Y. Marguerite de Conflans, portrait | 2,170 |
| 1931 | Bought by Jacob Goldschmidt. Rue Mosnier aux drapeax (£25 in 1879, £480 in 1898, see also 1958) $65,000 | 13,170 |
| 1932 | Strauss. Paris. Portrait, Berthe Morisot, 24×29, 1868. 360,000 francs+tax at 72 to £ | 5,980 |
| 1933 | Lederlin. Paris. La chanteuse au café concert, 26×32, 43,500 francs+tax at 68 to £ | 724 |
| | Bought by Jacob Goldschmidt. La Promenade (£60 in 1884, see also 1958) 36½×27½, $35,000 | 7,220 |
| 1937 | Gow. C. Two roses in a glass | 1,050 |
| 1938 | Paris. Les moissonneurs, 1873 (125 francs to £) | 1,900 |
| 1943 | N.Y. White lilacs in vase $19,000 | 4,725 |
| 1944 | N.Y. Le petit Lange, 46×28, $19,500 | 4,850 |
| 1945 | N.Y. Jeune femme aux cheveux, 24×20, $4,800 | 1,192 |
| 1949 | Versailles. Still life, two pears, 11¼×12¾ | 1,795 |

£

951 Sacha Guitry. Paris. Emile Faure, portrait, 18½×15¼   1,488
952 Cognacq. Paris. Portrait of a young girl, 11·6 million old
    francs+tax (£22 in 1884, £316 in 1889)     about 14,000
        Pelouse à Longchamps, 8·65 million old francs+tax
        (£250 in 1889)     10,650
        Wildenstein. N.Y. Jeannine Martin, Pastel portrait
        $28,000     10,000
955 N.Y. Beach at low tide, $13,500     4,820
        Four oranges, 7½×9½, $14,500     5,200
957 Weinberg. S. Bullock in a meadow, 36×27½     11,000
958 Goldschmidt. S. La Promenade, 36½×27½ (see 1933)     89,000
        Self-portrait with palette, 1879, 32¾×26¼     65,000
        Rue Mosnier aux drapeaux (£13,170 in 1931) 24½×31¾ 113,000
        Kirkeby. N.Y. Girl in a garden, 45×37, $39,200     14,000
959 Valued for the Lane bequest by National Gallery:
        Eva Gonzalés at an easel, 80×54     150,000
        Musique aux Tuileries, 30½×47     200,000
        (Bought for less than £1,000 each in 1909–12)
960 N.Y. Jeune fille, appuyée sur un vase de jardin, 1880,
    24½×28¼, $29,000     10,357
        Paris. Femme au bord de la mer, 29×20, FN430,000+
        tax     38,400
962 S. Mme Guillemet reading, 36½×29, 1878     23,000
        Alice Lacouvée, oil sketch (see 1966) 28×22½, Bought
        in at     12,500
963 S. Landscape. Oloron Ste Marie, 24½×18     8,000
964 C. Mme Manet dans la serre, 31½×39½     3,990
        The Matadors, wash drawing     2,735
965 Miller, N.Y. Le fumeur, 39×31, 1866 (£638 in 1902)
    $450,000     160,714
966 C. Repas chez Simon after Veronese, 11½×24     2,100
        S. Alice Lacouvée (see 1963) 28×22½     16,100
967 Weekes, N.Y. Chapeau au bords rabattus, 1882, un-
    finished pastel, 21½×18¼, $75,000     26,786
968 Paris. Fishing boat on beach, c. 1873, FN510,000+tax     47,835


ANDREA MANTEGNA. (*See* Italian School, Central (1962))


FRANZ MARC. (*See* German School, modern)


LOUIS MARCOUSSIS. (*See* Abstract painters, Europe)

WILLIAM MARLOW.  (*See* English School, 18th century)

ALBERT MARQUET.  (*See* French School, minor Impressionists and
post-Impressionists)

## BEN MARSHALL.  1766–1835

In 1968 a picture by Ben Marshall was sold for £58,000, which was far mo
than anything by Reynolds, Romney or Lawrence could have made and
much as a Gainsborough of the very best quality. Yet Marshall is not eve
mentioned by the brothers Redgrave in their survey of British painting i
1866, or by George Redford in his *Art Sales* of 1888. From the meagre inform
tion of Walter Shaw-Sparrow it appears that Marshall had no academic trai
ing, that he began as an apprentice to a minor portraitist and was never ma
an associate of the Royal Academy. The only public notice Marshall receive
in his own life-time was from *The Sporting Magazine*—and that not alway
favourable. His fee for a lovingly painted equestrian group at the height of h
activity was 50 guineas—when Sir Thomas Lawrence was getting 600 or 7c
for rapidly produced whole-length portraits of uneven quality.

It was sporting men who rediscovered him, cautiously in the 1890s, vorac
ously in the 1920s when *Mr Fermor's Hounds* made the equivalent of £21,0c
in 1970 money. Marshall's golden simplicity which endears him to the preser
*Zeitgeist*, was a still later discovery.

|  |  | £ |
|---|---|---|
| 1961 | Breadalbane.  C.  Horse and groom, unidentified (£94 10s. in 1910) | 6,300 |
| 1963 | S.  Sir Robert Frankland Russell and horse, 1810, $27\frac{1}{2} \times 35\frac{1}{2}$ | 6,200 |
| 1965 | Charrington.  C.  Setter, standing by gateway | 819 |
| 1966 | Aykroyd.  S.  Hunters in a paddock, startled by a dog, 1810, $39 \times 49$ | 18,500 |
|  | J. V. Grinsted on chestnut cob, $38\frac{1}{2} \times 49$ | 8,500 |
|  | Gamecock and two hens in farmyard, $33\frac{3}{4} \times 40$ | 9,000 |
|  | Brown and white setter in landscape,1801, $24\frac{1}{4} \times 29\frac{3}{4}$ | 3,400 |
| 1966 | Stephenson.  C.  *Babel* in loose box, 1827, $20 \times 23\frac{3}{4}$ | 1,785 |
|  | Mayhew.  C.  Col. H. F. Mellish, whole length, $92 \times 56\frac{1}{2}$ | 4,200 |
| 1967 | C.  Chestnut horse in open landscape, 1799, $27 \times 35$ | 3,150 |
| 1968 | Astor.  C.  Light bay hunter, 1808, $29\frac{1}{2} \times 39\frac{1}{2}$ | 7,350 |
|  | N.Y.  *Butcher's boy*, a bay hunter in an open landscape, 1803, $33\frac{1}{4} \times 38\frac{3}{4}$, $19,500 | 8,125 |
|  | de Baulny.  S.  Monsieur le Pelletier de Monamide, hounds, groom and spare mounts, 1808, $38\frac{1}{4} \times 48$ | 58,000 |
| 1969 | S.  *Euclid* held by groom with trainer and boy, 1820, $39\frac{1}{4} \times 49\frac{1}{4}$ | 30,000 |
|  | Wiley.  S.  *Berry brown*, cob in estuary landscape, 1816, $24 \times 31$ | 6,000 |

| | | £ |
|---|---|---|
| )69 | Shafto-Hilton. S. Three worthies of the turf, unfinished, 1835,19×15 | 12,000 |
| | Boston. S. Self-portrait, 1811, with favourite Newfoundland dog, 27¼×34 | 3,000 |

## JOHN MARTIN. 1789–1854

ι spite of a certain amount of literary propaganda, this is no more than a ghost ιarket. The prices of the 1960s give no indication that Martin was almost the ιost idolized British painter of his day. The British Institution paid 1,200 ιuineas for *Belshazzar's feast* in 1821, the Duke of Buckingham 800 guineas for *'he Destruction of Herculaneum* in 1823. To get the time-scale for 1970 one may ιultiply by 12. Neither romantic *grandezza* nor apocalyptic visions of woe are ιited to a permissive society.

| | | £ |
|---|---|---|
| )63 | S. Reduced replica of Belshazzar's Feast | 700 |
| )64 | Laughton. S. 24 oil-sketches for the engravings for Paradise Lost (£2,000 in 1823) 24 for | 8,420 |
| )66 | S. Archers stalking a stag, sepia wash drawing after Claude, 1821, 7¾×10½ | 100 |
| | C. Joshua commanding the sun to stand still (£205 in 1816 £472 10s. in 1861) | 304 10s. |
| )67 | Dixon. S. Solitude, oils, 1843, 19½×35 | 400 |
| )69 | C. View over Richmond Park, 1847, wc, 11¾×21 | 787 10s. |

## MASTERS, ANONYMOUS

ιaster of Alkmaar, Master of 1518, Master of the embroidered leaf, Master f the Female half-figures, Master of Flémalle, Master of the Holy Blood, ιaster of the Life of the Virgin, Master of the View of St Gudule, Master of the t Lucy Legend, Master of the Magdalen legend, Master of St Severin, Master f the St Ursula Legend.
ιee *Flemish School* before 1550

ιaster of 1468, Master of Frankfurt, Master of Freisach, Master of Kaufeuren, Master of the Manzi Magdalene, Master of the Strache Altar-piece.
ιee *German school,* 15th and 16th centuries.
ιaster of the Magdalen, Master of Monte Oliveto, Master of the Osservanza ιltar-piece, Master of St Francis.
ιee *Italian School,* 14th century.

ιaster of the Adinari cassone, Master of Pratovecchio, Master of S. Miniato, ιaster of Stratonice
ιee *Italian school,* 15th century.

## HENRI MATISSE. 1869–1954

In 1927 Matisse was far and away the most expensive of the modern painter René Gimpel records in his diary that Bernheim Fréres were asking $20,00 (more than £4,000) for a single painting in New York. Whether they receive their price or not, it is certain that two Matisses were sold in Paris at auctio that year for over £2,000 each, almost twice as much as any Picasso and sever times as much as any Braque, Derain, Léger, Juan Gris, Miro or Modiglian Yet in the 1960s Matisse was at the bottom of this list. It is not easy to accoun for the change in preferences. Matisse may have painted more important work than appear in this section, but it cannot be said that the highest priced Matiss in the saleroom towards the end of the decade were scrappy or untypical of h best. Perhaps this is the true clue to the apparent fall in his relative positio Like Whistler, he gave too little of himself. Matisse's oil paintings tend to loo like enlarged outline drawings in colour. But without the vulgarity of a Duf or van Dongen to sustain it, this apparently light-hearted approach may hav failed to satisfy the fashions of the saleroom, at any rate to the extent that n television cameras were switched on to record the sale of a Matisse picture a over £100,000. It seems, however, that others noticed this too so that ver early in 1970 a *Fête de fleurs*, sold in New York, narrowly missed the £100,00 sound barrier—and, as a finished work, it was even more reticent than mos Matisses.

| | | £ |
|---|---|---|
| 1911 | Henri Bernstein. Paris. La Jetée a Colioure, 1,600 francs +tax | 70 |
| 1926 | Quinn. N.Y. Bowl of apples, $1,200 | 254 |
| 1927 | Waubert. Paris. Les crevettes roses, 150,000 francs+ tax at 125 | 1,470 |
| | Soubées. Paris. La robe jaune 225,000 francs+tax at 125 to £ | 2,170 |
| | Odalisque, 210,000 francs+tax | 2,045 |
| | N.Y. Bernheim asking $20,000 for a single painting, according to R. Gimpel | 4,120 |
| 1930 | Canonne. Paris. Le concert, 170,000 francs+tax at 125 to £ | 1,600 |
| 1932 | Pacquemont. Paris. L'ananas, 75,000 francs+tax at 70 to £ | 1,270 |
| | Le coffret chinois, 60,000 francs+tax | 1,004 |
| 1937 | Hollender & Bernheimer. C. Ruisseau au village | 273 |
| | Femme nue devant une fenêtre | 96 12s. |
| 1939 | Canonne, 2nd sale. Paris. Femme à sa coiffeuse, 66,000 francs+tax at 180 to £ | 440 |
| | Femme devant un bouquet, 44,000 francs+tax | 293 |
| 1940 | Eumorphopoulos. S. Landscape | 105 |
| | N.Y. Still life after de Heem, 7 ft long, $12,750 at 4·00 to £ | 3,190 |

|  | | £ |
|---|---|---|

941 Horace Harding. N.Y. Nature morte, $12,750     3,190

947 N.Y. Bouquet of anemones, $4,900 at 4·00 to £     1,225

949 von Sternberg. N.Y. Cucumbers, $15\times18$, $2,550 at 2·80 to £     912

Chrysler. N.Y. Olga, $38\frac{1}{2}\times32$, $5,500     1,965

954 Paris. La fenêtre ouverte, 4·8 million francs+tax     4,795

Bradley Campbell, N.Y. Au fauteuil, $13,775     4,920

Rees Jeffreys. S. Portrait of Derain (£280 in 1928)     7,035

955 N.Y. Gorges du Loup, $18\times22$ (£22,140 in 1965), $8,765     3,130

956 S. Plate of fruit     4,200

957 Paris. Le jabot bleu, 5·2 million old francs+tax     5,200

Bought by Stavros Niarchos from Edward Robinson: The Dinner Table, $75,000     26,800

Georges Lurcy. N.Y. Dans le boudoir, $13\times21$, $25,200     9,000

958 Arnold Kirkeby. N.Y. Fleurs et céramique, $65,000     23,215

960 S. Girl seated at a window, 1921     18,750

C. The painting lesson. National Gallery, Edinburgh     21,000

Bought by the Tate Gallery, nude woman, nearly 10 ft high     16,000

N.Y. Bolero violet, 1941, $28\frac{1}{2}\times21$, $42,500     15,140

961 S. Woman in chaise longue, 1921, $17\frac{1}{2}\times21\frac{1}{2}$     12,000

962 Somerset Maugham, S. Woman with green umbrella, $27\frac{1}{2}\times22\frac{1}{4}$     32,000

Interior with seated woman, 1940, $21\frac{1}{4}\times25\frac{1}{2}$     38,000

S. Coupe d'oranges, 1916, $21\frac{1}{4}\times25\frac{3}{4}$     12,000

964 Morhange. S. A dancer, pastel, $17\frac{3}{4}\times23\frac{3}{4}$, 1925     15,200

Still life, 1949     22,000

965 Berne. N.Y. Gorges du Loup, 1922, $18\times22$ (see 1955)     22,140

S. Citrons et mimosas, 1944, $21\times28\frac{3}{4}$     22,000

966 S. Woman, half-draped, in armchair, $20\frac{3}{4}\times14\frac{1}{4}$     15,000

Berez. S. La perruche et la sirène, 1953, mural decoration in cut-out paper, 11 ft by $25\frac{1}{4}$ ft     32,000

Thompson. N.Y. La femme à la fontaine, 1917, $31\frac{3}{4}\times25\frac{1}{2}$, $70,000     25,140

Algue blanche, abstract collage, 1953, $20\frac{1}{2}\times15\frac{3}{4}$     5,925

966 Helena Rubinstein, N.Y. Paysage à Colioure, 1911, $35\frac{3}{4}\times24\frac{3}{4}$, $45,000     15,100

Henry Ford II. C. Le vase de Chine, 1922, $13\frac{1}{4}\times22$     28,350

S. Les filets à Etretat, $12\frac{3}{4}\times16$, 1920     10,000

967 Paris. Femme assise en bleu, oils, 1937, $25\frac{1}{4}\times24$, FN310,000+tax (post devaluation) at 11·88 to £     28,770

968 Bluestein. N.Y. La Seine à Paris, 1911, $10\frac{1}{4}\times13\frac{3}{4}$, $30,000     12,500

Dordat. S. Les Fleurs jaunes, 1902, $18\times21\frac{1}{2}$     22,000

| 1968 | Ahrenberg. S. Apollon, tile-mosaic, made from a paper collage, 1953, 128×168 | £ 34,000 |
|---|---|---|
| | S. Notre Dame, seen from a window, 1902, 18¼×21¾ | 25,500 |
| 1969 | Silberman. N.Y. Entrée de cabaret breton, early work dated 1896, 14¾×18, $27,000 | 11,326 |
| | C. (Geneva.) La France, seated figure, 18×15, 1939, FS464,000+5% tax | 46,360 |
| | Le Bas. C. (Geneva.) Peaches, pewter plate, spotted table cloth, before 1927. 18×25½, FS405,000+5% tax | 40,930 |
| | La Persane, pencil drawing, 1929, 22×15, FS140,000+ tax | 14,135 |
| 1970 | N.Y. Fête des Fleurs à Nice, C. 1921, 29×39½, $230,000 | 95,830 |
| | Bennett. S. Les concombres, Fauve style, 1907, ($3,600, 1949) | 56,000 |

## QUENTIN MATSYS. (*See* Flemish School, before 1550)

## ERNEST MEISSONIER. 1815–1891

The interest of these few entries is purely historical. To look at Meissonier little pictures on the saleroom walls is to be reminded of the red cardinals of Duke Street, of Croegaert and Brunery, of silly and arch anecdotes, posed by professional models and painted with the same scrupulous accuracy of detail all through. For Meissonier did nothing more nor less than that, and was hailed throughout the last third of the 19th century as the greatest genius of the age—and of any other age too. In fact one of Meissonier's most famous masterpieces, the 8½ ft battlepiece *Friedland* was sold in 1964 for a price that would not have been at all high for a red cardinal picture. The history of this picture, though totally forgotten, is a morality play in itself. The first version was painted at the height of the neo-Napoleonic cult of the 2nd Empire. In 1867 Meissonier was reported to have refused £6,000—and never had so much money been refused by any painter in the world. In 1875, when it was finally completed, *Friedland* was sold at the Vienna Universal Exhibition to F. A. Stewart of New York for $80,000 or £16,500. Next to Murillo's *Immaculate Conception*, bought by Napoleon III in 1852 for £24,600 *Friedland* was the second most expensive picture ever sold, the price being equivalent to all £150,000 in 1970. It seems likely that the version, sold in 1964, changed hands privately in 1892 at £20,700 (about £185,000 in **1970**). But that was not the limit for Meissonier. Another huge battle picture which he painted twice over *1814*, was sold to M. Chauchard in 1890 for 850,000 francs or £34,000—the equivalent of £305,000 in 1970. Since Meissonier was still alive, it will be perceived that the Picasso wonder is not all that it seems. Chauchard's *18* is protected from the winds of change by the massive walls of the Louvre, b the second version was resold in 1927 for 1,400 guineas.

Apart from *Friedland*, the few Meissoniers that reached the salerooms in the 1960s were generally single figures in various historical fancy dress. For them the market is still going down.

| | | £ |
|---|---|---|
| 1960 | Muller, Amsterdam.  Le fumeur rouge, $7\frac{3}{4} \times 5\frac{1}{2}$, Hfl11,000 +tax | 1,265 |
| 1963 | S.  Le liseur, $8\frac{1}{2} \times 6\frac{1}{2}$ (£448 in 1945) | 300 |
| 1964 | Paris.  Friedland, 1888, 60×102, FN55,000+tax (probably the version sold in 1892 for £20,700 and in 1913 for £6,300) | 4,340 |
| 1965 | van Waay, Amsterdam.  Le fumeur rouge (see 1960) | 685 |
| 1966 | S.  Two views of a cavalier, $7\frac{3}{4} \times 5\frac{1}{2}$                    2 for | 85 |
| | A bagpiper, $9 \times 5\frac{3}{4}$ | 50 |
| 1968 | S.  On guard, wc bodycolour, $11\frac{1}{2} \times 6\frac{3}{4}$ | 170 |
| | C.  The musketeer, $12\frac{1}{2} \times 9\frac{1}{2}$ | 336 |
| 1970 | S.  Charles 1st, riding, $7 \times 4\frac{3}{4}$ | 420 |

## HANS MEMLING.  (*See* Flemish School before 1550 (other painters))


## HERRI MET DE BLES.  (*See* Flemish School before 1550)


## GABRIEL METSU.  1615–1661

There were no very interesting prices for this painter in the 1960s. One has to go back in time. At the great Steengracht sale of 1913 *The Sick Child* made £4,530, equivalent to £116,000. In 1936 Duveen sold Andrew Mellon *The Intruder*, now in the National Gallery, Washington, for $225,000, equivalent 1970 money to £231,500. We have seen a de Witte interior at £63,000. A six-figure price for a first-rate Metsu, if there is such a thing left, should not be impossible.

| | | £ |
|---|---|---|
| 1960 | S.  Lady with a spaniel, 1667, $22\frac{3}{4} \times 17$ (£1350 in 1937) | 5,000 |
| 1965 | Gatacre.  C.  Still life with Delft pitcher, 29×17 | 3,990 |
| | The Drinker, $7 \times 5$ (£3 12s. in 1895) | 997 10s. |
| 1966 | de Biro.  C.  Expulsion of Hagar, 44×34 | 2,520 |
| | Brenda Cook.  C.  Card players, signed, $18\frac{1}{2} \times 19\frac{1}{2}$ | 3,360 |
| 1967 | C.  Alleged portraits of the artist and his wife, sold as Frans van Mieris, $8\frac{1}{2} \times 6\frac{3}{4}$                    2 for | 8,925 |
| 1968 | S.  Smoker in brown coat outside an inn, 1753, $12\frac{3}{4} \times 10$ | 1,575 |
| 1969 | C.  Smoker with other figures in a room, $16 \times 14\frac{1}{2}$ | 3,360 |

## JEREMIAH MEYER.  (*See* Miniatures)

# MICHELANGELO BUONAROTTI. 1475-1564

The catalogue of the collection of the late Sir Joshua Reynolds, dated Marc 1795, lists forty-four paintings by Michelangelo in a sale where the lo averaged less than £25 a picture. However, the view of the most up-to-dat pontificators seems to be that Michelangelo left behind him no portable paint ings at all, though one exceedingly bizarre attribution did appear on the al market of the 1960s. There was also a sheet of drawings, one side of whic gained the correct acceptance at £26,000. What would be the value in 197 of the British Museum's study for *The Creation of Adam*, bought in 1926 fe £600? Ought one to multiply by a hundred?

|      |                                                                                                                              | £      |
|------|------------------------------------------------------------------------------------------------------------------------------|--------|
| 1960 | S.  Temptation of St Anthony, said to have been painted at the age of 13 from an engraving by Martin Schongauer | 13,000 |

### DRAWINGS

|      |                                                                                                                         | £      |
|------|-------------------------------------------------------------------------------------------------------------------------|--------|
| 1962 | Springell.  S.  Study of heads, $8\frac{3}{4} \times 11$; on the back a disputed sketch, Christ before Pilate (about £1,000 in 1930) | 26,000 |
| 1964 | Victor Bloch.  S.  Ascanius dragging Aeneas from the bed of Dido, black chalk, under 3 in. square                      | 12,500 |

# THE MIERIS FAMILY

The Mierises, father and son, continued the tradition of Gerard Dou, the mo admired painter among fashionable Parisians of the 18th century. High detailed shop interiors and *trompe l'oeuil* figures, leaning out of the frame, we then all that a man of taste most desired. This is now a completely inert marke Yet, close on a hundred years ago, the old standards still prevailed, for in 18; the great collecting Earl of Dudley paid £4,300 (equivalent to £38,700 1970) for *The Enamoured Cavalier*. After the Earl's death, in 1892, the pictu fell only slightly. It was still almost as dear as any Rembrandt.

FRANS MIERIS THE ELDER.  1635-1681

|      |                                                                                 | £     |
|------|---------------------------------------------------------------------------------|-------|
| 1960 | Pairs.  La coquette                                                              | 805   |
| 1963 | S.  Soldier seated at a window                                                   | 1,100 |
|      | Earl of Feversham.  S.  Boy blowing bubbles from a window, $10\frac{3}{4} \times 7$ | 900   |
| 1965 | C.  Lady with sculptured urn at a window                                         | 504   |
| 1966 | S.  Self-portrait with wine glass, 1670, $7 \times 5\frac{1}{4}$                 | 2,200 |

| | | |
|---|---|---|
| 67 | Schlesinger. S. Gentleman offering fruit to lady, $14\frac{1}{4}\times$ $11\frac{1}{2}$ | 1,200 |
| | Viscount Astor. C. Sportsman, dead game and dogs, $52\times43$ | 1,785 |
| | Paris. Man smoking pipe, $6\frac{1}{2}\times5\frac{1}{4}$, FN10,000+tax | 984 |
| 69 | Bruguière. C. Lady at her toilette with maid and gallant $12\frac{1}{4}\times9\frac{1}{2}$ | 2,520 |

VILLEM MIERIS. 1662–1747

| | |
|---|---|
| 65 | Spencer Churchill. C. Self portrait with glass of wine, dated 1701, $8\frac{3}{4}\times7\frac{3}{4}$ |

1,155

## SIR JOHN MILLAIS. 1827–1896

his is a fairly typical case of a nineteenth century painter of the 'establishment', whose very high market rating was prolonged into the early 1920s, whose fall then became precipitate, but whose works have since gone up rather more rapidly than the pace of inflation. There is, however, this peculiarity, namely that the high prices of the early 1920s and the recovery prices of the 1960s apply mainly to the seven or eight years of his life when Millais practised the Pre-raphaelite style. The drawings of Millais have gone up even more when they belong to this period. Drawings, such as seldom made more than £20 in the 1930s, could be worth over £2,000 in 1967.

A special case is the *portrait of Ruskin in a landscape*, because the price of 4,000 guineas was created by its quite unique literary and romantic associations. A five-figure price invites the question of the possible value in 1970 of *Christ in the House of his Parents*, for which 10,000 guineas were raised in 1922 in order to present it to the Tate Gallery. Possibly it would be somewhere between £70,000 and £100,000, a lot for a painting of 1849 which was quite outside the main current of Corot, Courbet and Millet. Yet it seems very little one considers that the far inferior potboiling works which Millais churned out between the 1860s and the 1890s earned him the equivalent of £10,000 £45,000 each in 1970 terms.

| | | £ |
|---|---|---|
| 62 | C. The Raven and the Monk, small painting, 1852 | 2,100 |
| 63 | C. The Ransom, 1862, $51\times46$ | 441 |
| 65 | Houldsworth. S. Escape of a Heretic, $42\times30\frac{1}{2}$, 1857, (£673 in 1862) | 1,000 |
| | Dyke Ackland. C. Portrait of Ruskin, 1854, $28\frac{1}{2}\times24$, (£350 in 1854) | 25,200 |
| 66 | Huntington Hertford. C. Sweet Emma Morland, fancy portrait, 1892, $47\frac{3}{4}\times35\frac{3}{4}$ | 399 |
| | C. Portrait of unknown lady, $31\frac{1}{2}\times21\frac{1}{2}$, bought in at | 1,785 |
| | S. The Huzzar's Farewell, oil sketch, $5\frac{3}{4}\times4\frac{3}{4}$ | 340 |
| 67 | Murray. S. Rachel Ray, seated on a style, wc, $5\frac{3}{4}\times3\frac{1}{4}$ | 399 |
| | C. The artist's wife, 1873, $39\times33$ | 5,250 |

£

| | | |
|---|---|---:|
| 1967 | Gribble.  C.  Clarissa, recollection of Gainsborough, 1887, 56×34½ | 525 |
| | C.  Autumn leaves, 1856, 43×50, replica of picture in Manchester City Gallery | 2,310 |
| | Browze.  C.  Effie Millais as a child, 1867, oval wc, 6½×5½ | 1,785 |
| | S.  Girl in embroidered silk at a piano, 1886, 47½×38 (see 1969) | 950 |
| 1968 | George S.  Peace concluded, 1856, arched top, 45×36, (£945 in 1856, £462 in 1946) | 11,500 |
| | S.  (at Gleneagles Hotel.)  The Empty Cage, 35×27, child portrait, c. 1890 | 1,150 |
| | N.Y.  'Yes' or 'accepted', 1877, 59×46, $4,750 (£1,050 in 1898, £42 in 1944) see 1969 | 1,980 |
| 1969 | Cottell.  S.  The Farmer's Daughter, c. 1869, 16¾×12¾ | 1,200 |
| | E. G. Millais.  C.  'Sleeping', the artist's four-year-old child, 1866, 35½×27½ (£1,470 in 1890, £845 in 1926) | 9,450 |
| 1969 | Huntly.  C.  Amy, Marchioness of Huntly, Whole length, 1870, 86×50 | 7,350 |
| | C.  Reduced replica, Christ in the House of his Parents (with Rebecca Solomon) £40 in 1863, £44 10s. in 1886, 15×24 | 1,260 |
| | The deserted garden, 49×73, 1875 (Hermon sale, 1882, £945) bought in | 1,365 |
| | Resold a few months later at Hopetoun for | 1,890 |
| | S.  Girl in flowered dress at piano, dated 1886, 47½×38 (£950 in 1967) | 1,200 |
| | 'Yes' or 'accepted', 1877, 59×46 (£1,980 in 1968) | 1,400 |
| | The gambler's wife, 1869, 34×15 (£924 in 1874) | 500 |
| | The Somnambulist, 1871, 59½×35½ | 400 |
| 1979 | Tweedale.  C.  Marchioness of Tweedale, half-length, 1896, 60×40 bought in at | 1,150 |

### DRAWINGS

| | | |
|---|---|---:|
| 1964 | S.  The dove returning to the ark, pen, 1853 | 560 |
| 1967 | Millais.  C.  Accepted, 1853, pen, 9¾×6¾ | 1,995 |
| | Rejected, companion drawing | 1,260 |
| | Millais and Effie Gray fishing from a boat, 1853, pen 7¼×9 | 2,100 |
| | Wayside refreshment, pen, 1853, 7½×8 | 1,365 |
| | Effie Gray cutting Millais's hair, 1853, 7¾×9 | 997 10s. |
| 1969 | C.  Little boy on swing, wc, 1862, 5¼×3¼ | 577 10s |
| | Little Miss Bountiful, wc bodycolour, finished late work, 18×12½ | 504 |

ALFRED JACOB MILLER.  (*See* American School, 19th century)


## JEAN FRANCOIS MILLET.  1814–1875

Millet shared with Meissonier the most extravagant of the market booms of the past, but it is not fair that he should be relegated to this company. While Meissonier's *Friedland* was the world's second dearest picture in 1875, Millet's *rentrée des Moutons* was the second dearest in 1892 after Raphael's *Ansidei Madonna*. But, unlike Meissonier the tailor's painter, Millet was in some degree worthy of his laurels. His prices remained fairly stable till the 1920s, when the modern picture market became dominated by the bright colours of the impressionists. A time came when good Impressionist works were almost unprocurable at any price. Thus Millet's sombre but thoroughly painter-like works were re-appraised. The price of £42,000, paid for the portrait of *M. de Vitt* in 1968, was certainly no more than was due to its merits.

In this exceptional instance I have taken the list back as far as 1889. This is because the picture, as presented in Volume One, was neither complete nor altogether correct. The exceedingly important reference in *Chronique des Arts*, 1909, was a subsequent discovery. It will be appreciated that the prices of 1892, which must be multiplied by 8½ to get the present day co-efficient, leave those of Picasso well behind. Yet while Picasso's saleroom victories are relayed round the world in colour television, M. Chauchard's purchases of 1892 were made in secret and only rumours leaked out at the time.

| | | £ |
|---|---|---|
| 1889 | Bought from Mrs Bischoffsheim by Mme veuve Pomery, Les glaneuses.  The Louvre | 16,000 |
| | Secrétan.  Paris.  l'Angélus, bought for the Louvre. | 22,120 |
| | Sale disowned.  Sold later to Brandus and thence to Chauchard who left it to the Louvre in 1909    Price | 32,000 |
| 1890 | Senéz.  N.Y.  l'Attente | 8,000 |
| 1892 | van Pract.  Brussels.  Private sales to Chauchard.  All were left to the Louvre in 1909.  (According to Chronique des Arts, 19 June, 1909) | |
| | La bergère, (incorrectly given by Maurice Rheims as 1·2 million francs) 1 million francs | 40,000 |
| | La rentrée des moutons la nuit, 1·1 million francs | 44,000 |
| | Le vanneur ⎫ | |
| | La fileuse ⎪ probably about £20,000 each | |
| | La fermière ⎬ | |
| | La petite bergère ⎭ | |
| 1894 | Garnier.  Paris.  La herse.  75,000 francs+tax | 3,300 |
| 1898 | Dana.  N.Y.  The turkey-keeper, $20,000 | 4,120 |
| 1909 | Sir J. Day.  C.  The goose-maiden, 12×9 | 5,250 |
| | Graves.  N.Y.  La tonte des moutons, $27,500 | 5,680 |

£

| | |
|---|---|
| 1910 Butler. N.Y. La bergère, pastel (see 1945, 1956) $30,250 | 6,020 |
| Henry. N.Y. Travailleurs au point du jour | 10,980 |
| Yerkes. N.Y. Killing the pig (£960 in 1876) $40,000 | 8,130 |
| 1911 Bought in Holland for H. C. Frick, La Femme à La Lampe $100,000 | 20,600 |
| 1912 Rouart. Paris. L'homme à la veste, 115,000 francs+tax | 5,060 |
| Stephens. C. Oedipus, taken from the tree (£441 in 1910) | 2,450 |
| 1914 The same picture, sold to Sir James Ross, Montreal | 12,000 |
| Coates. C. Gardienne du troupeau (£965 in 1949) | 5,880 |
| 1923 Ruffer. C. Le coup de vent | 1,890 |
| 1927 According to R. Gimpel, John Levy, N.Y., was 'asking $40,000 for a fine Millet' | 8,230 |
| Coates. C. Sleeping nymph and faun | 651 |
| 1929 Hollingsworth. C. L'amour vainqueur, early work | 651 |
| 1934 N.Y. The knitting lesson (see 1945) $15,000 | 3,200 |
| 1935 Blumenthal. Paris. La glaneuse, 75,000 francs +tax at 75 to the £ | 1,180 |
| N.Y. Wooded landscape, 16×13, $2,480 | 510 |
| 1937 Leonard Gow. C. Le briquet, pastel | 283 10s. |
| 1945 Thanhauser. N.Y. La fileuse, 15×11½, $6,800 | 1,695 |
| Vanderbilt. Return from the well, 1862, $30,000 (dearest in the saleroom in 35 years) | 7,500 |
| The sower, 1850, $26,000 | 6,500 |
| The knitting lesson (£3,200 in 1934), $12,500 | 3,125 |
| La bergère, pastel (see 1910 and 1956), $11,000 | 2,750 |
| 1949 N.Y. Gardienne du troupeau (£5,880 in 1914), $2,500 | 965 |
| 1956 N.Y. La bergère, pastel (see 1910 and 1945), $3,000 | 1,071 |
| 1958 Ten Cate. S. Hanging the washing in the orchard, 10×13 | 650 |
| 1962 S. The donkey, 31×39 | 1,450 |
| 1963 N.Y. La fin de la journée, 24×29, $30,000 | 10,715 |
| Moutons après la tonte, 23½×28½, $21,000 | 7,500 |
| 1964 Paris. Female portrait, 1840s | 5,300 |
| Male portrait, companion-piece | 2,570 |
| 1966 Rohan-Chabot. C. Les pêcheurs, 32×25¾ | 3,570 |
| 1968 S. A l'abri de l'orage, pencil, charcoal and pastel, 14½×19½ | 2,600 |
| Portrait de M. de Witt, 1847, 39×31¾ | 42,000 |
| Forrestier-Paton. C. L'anxiété, fisherman's wife, 17¾×12 | 3,780 |
| 1969 S. La Bergère, small version, 1871-2, 16¾×14. Bought in | 4,000 |
| Resold in Tokyo in following season, 7 million yen | 8,200 |

# MINIATURE PAINTERS

## (mainly portraits)

With the exception of Palissy ware and Limoges enamels, there is probably no section of the art market which has fallen more from the glories of the past than portrait miniatures. It may be thought that £600 to £700 is a lot of money or three inches of simpering looks and fluffy millinery by Engleheart, Meyer, Plimer or Smart. But these treasured tokens cost 25 guineas before the locket had been bought—and that in the late 18th century was equivalent to more than £400 in the money of 1970. And even in those days old miniature portraits of historic personages had a value sometimes greater than today. Thus in 1775 Horace Walpole paid 3,200 livres for a miniature by the first Petitot of the notorious Mme d'Olonne, the heroine of the scabrous *Histoire amoureuse des Gaules*. At the rate of exchange of the day this meant £145, in modern terms £2,320—and it is not certain that the best of Petitot's miniatures can make as much in 1970. Horace Walpole's veneration for portraits from the past was by no means generally shared in 1842 when his miniatures came up for sale at Strawberry Hill. Even so, some of them were dear by present standards, for instance Isaac Oliver's *Lady Lucy Percy* at 100 guineas, the equivalent in 1970 of £1,260.

The best instance of the prejudice against miniatures, as such, is Nicolas Hilliard, who was not only a worthy follower of Holbein but the only great English painter before Hogarth. About a dozen of his miniatures were sold in the 1960s and none of them at more than £5,500. At the Hamilton Palace sale of 1882 a miniature portrait of James I in a jewelled case made £2,835, equivalent to £25,500. In 1902 Pierpont Morgan bought the Armada jewel, containing Hilliard's portrait of Queen Elizabeth, for 5,000 guineas equivalent to £42,000. By 1935, this famous object had dropped to £2,835 which meant no more than £14,200 in 1970 money. When one comes to the run-of-the-mill miniaturists of the late 18th century the fall is even more pronounced. Thus four family portraits by Andrew Plimer were sold in 1900 for £3,045, yet in the 1960s the best of Andrew Plimer was worth no more than 400 to 800 guineas in devalued money. It may be thought that the portrait of *Sir Barry Close* at £2,520 in 1968 was remarkable, because here was a miniature by John Smart at a Hilliard price. Yet in 1900 three miniatures by John Smart made £2,300, equivalent to £18,400, while in 1902 another miniature of the extreme end of the 18th century Cosway's *Mme du Barry* made 1,000 guineas on its own, equivalent to £8,400.

The prejudice is not easy to account for. Miniatures are often catalogued with snuffboxes, watches, automata and objects in precious materials, markets that can hardly be called depressed. I suppose that those who should be buying portrait miniatures are 'investing' in Fabergé and glass paperweights. Or maybe it is just that portrait miniatures are neither fish, flesh nor fowl. They are paintings, but they are sold as *objets d'art* or jewelry.

J. B. Augustin    £
1963 Fribourg. S. Unknown girl, 1820    360
1968 C. Louis XVIII, 2½ in. diam.    609
     de la Hey. C. Duchess of Angoulême, 1815, 3½ in.    600
1969 S. Unknown officer, 2¾ in.    460
     Another unknown officer, jewelled frame, 3 in.    520

Samuel Cooper. 1609–1672
1960 C. Charles II, 3½ in.    525
     Samuelson. C. Bridget Cromwell    399
1961 S. Young man, jewelled frame    850
     C. Duke of Lauderdale, 1664. National Portrait Gallery    2,100
1966 C. Lady Frances Cooper    787 10s.
1968 Broughton. S. Sir Brian Broughton, 2¾ in.    500
     de la Hey. S. General Fleetwood, dated 1650    850
     Anne, Countess Morton, 2¾ in.    950
     S. Elizabeth Claypole, daughter of Oliver Cromwell, 2¾ in.    980
1969 Hickson. S. Unknown gentleman, lawn collar, 2½ in.    950
     S. Unknown young man, 2½ in.    900
     Nyburg. S. Charles II in profile, 1⅛ in. diam.    1,000

Richard Cosway. 1740–1821
1962 C. 2-sided pendant, Lady d'Eresby and Lady Georgiana Bertie    682 10s.
1964 C. Princess Augusta Sophia, 3¼ in.    199 10s.
1968 de la Hey. S. Lady Conyngham, 3½ in.    1,000
1969 C. Earl and Countess of Hopetoun, 1789. Oval, 3 in.    2 for 2,100
     Two sisters as Ceres and Persephone, oval, 3 in.    651
     Joshua Smith, 2½ in., inscribed and dated 1789    840
     Hickson. S. Unknown girl, yellow sash, 2½ in.    520
     Nyburg. S. Mrs Brownlow North and her son, 1791, 3½ in.    1,300
     C. Self-portrait, pencil and wash, 4¼ in. diam.    682 10s.

Nicolas Dixon
1961 C. Charles II (£96 12s. in 1882)    1,155
1967 C. Earl of Sutherland, 1670, 3 in.    1,102 10s.

George Engleheart. 1752–1829
1966 Oakes. C. Lady Ward. 2 in. high    630
     Digby. C. Mrs Mills, 1783, 2 in.    399
     C. Mrs William Hayley, 1809, 3 in.    409 10s.

| | £ |
|---|---|
| 1967 Astor. C. Elizabeth Young, 1784, 2½ in. jewelled frame | 682 10s. |
| Hutchinson. C. A midshipman, 1809, 3¼ in. diam. | 525 |
| 1968 C. Captain Peter Halkett, 1803, 3¼ in. | 609 |
| Mrs Madan and child, 3¼ in. | 577 5s. |
| Gloucester. C. Marquess of Downshire, 3 in. | 630 |
| de la Hey. S. Mrs Catherine Green, 2¾ in. | 620 |
| Girl in pink bonnet, 2¼ in. | 620 |
| 1969 C. Unknown gentleman, 1810, 3¼ in. diam. | 682 5s. |
| Unknown old lady, inscribed and dated 1810, 3¼ in. | 630 |

### PIERRE ADOLPHE HALL

| | |
|---|---|
| 1963 Gilbert. C. Marquis de St Yver | 1,312 10s. |
| 1964 C. Unknown lady, box pendant | 325 10s. |
| 1968 de la Hey. S. Unknown girl, 2¼ in. | 550 |

### NICOLAS HILLIARD. 1537–1609

| | |
|---|---|
| 1960 Samuelson. C. Anne of Denmark | 399 |
| 1961 C. Robert Dudley, Earl of Leicester, 1576, National Portrait Gallery | 3,675 |
| James 1st | 1,050 |
| 1962 Reeves Bulkely. S. Mr and Mrs Mole, double-sided pendant | 2,000 |
| 1963 Gilbert. C. Unknown woman | 714 |
| 1964 Hickson. S. Unknown lady, signed, 1602 | 5,000 |
| (School-piece) Unknown gentleman, c. 1605 | 1,000 |
| 1966 Steele. S. Unknown girl in Jewelled dress | 1,100 |
| C. Queen Elizabeth, jewelled and enamelled frame, 2½ in. | 924 |
| 1967 S. Unknown man, aged 52, dated 1577 (£620 in 1955) | 2,500 |
| Watney. C. Unknown man, 2 in. diam. (by Lawrence Hilliard) | 840 |
| 1969 Montague Cholmeley. S. James 1st, inscribed, 1610, 2¾ in. | 5,500 |
| Hickson. S. Unknown gentleman, 2 in. oval, faded | 700 |

### JOHN HOSKINS. 1600–1664

| | |
|---|---|
| 1961 D. of Leeds. S. Charles II as a boy, gold frame, 3⅝ in. | 1,080 |
| 1966 S. Elizabeth of Bohemia, 2 in. | 460 |
| 1968 de la Hey. S. Henrietta Maria, 3½ in. square (£52 in 1925) H.M. the Queen | 7,500 |
| Unknown gentleman, 2⅛ in. | 700 |
| John Gauden, bishop of Worcester, 1655, oval 2 in. (£48 in 1934, £110 in 1961) | 1,000 |
| Unknown lady, 2¾ in. | 750 |
| 1969 Lord Dickinson. S. Unknown lady, oval, 1656 | 1,300 |
| Unknown long-haired man in armour, 1654, oval | 1,300 |

EUGÈNE ISABEY.  1803–1886                                              £
1962  C.  Duchess of Montebello                                      525
1963  Fribourg.  S.  Napoleon, half-length                           420
      Gilbert.  C.  Marquise de Grammont (£84 in 1949, £651
      in 1962)                                                   892 10s
1967  C.  Mme Boucher, 1827. 5¼ in.                                  504
1969  S.  Empress Marie Louise, 2 in.                                320


JEREMIAH MEYER.  1735–1789
1961  C.  Master George Meyer                                        630
1964  C.  Unknown lady, 2 in.                                    325 10s
1966  C.  Mrs Thomas Hayley, 2¾ in.                                  336
      Thomas Hayley as a child, 3 in.                                441
1968  S.  Unknown gentleman, 2½ in.                                  680
      de la Hey.  S.  Unknown young woman, 3¾ in.               1,000
      Another, apparently a companion-piece                         850


ISAAC OLIVER.  1556–1617
1960  C.  James 1st                                                  294
1965  Meyers.  S.  3rd Earl of Southampton, c. 1600                  500
1967  Dundas.  C.  Supposed Sir Walter Raleigh, dated 1610,
      1¾ in.                                                         735
1968  de la Hey.  S.  Anne of Denmark, 2¾ in.                       650
1969  Webb.  S.  Unknown girl, brush, brown ink and gold,
      2¼ × 2                                                         400
      Westmorland.  C.  Elizabeth, Queen of Bohemia, 2 in.      1,050


PETER OLIVER.  1594–1647
1965  Steininger.  S.  Lady Arabella Stewart, 2¼ in.                700
      C.  Holy family, 1630, on vellum after Correggio, 4½ × 3½     861
1966  C.  Lady Arabella Stewart, 2¼ in.                             819
1968  de la Hey.  S.  Charles 1st as a youth, 2 in.             1,800
      C.  Venus and Cupid, 1645, 4 in.                              630
      de la Hey.  S.  Lord Vere of Tilbury, 2½ in. (£80 in 1925)   900
1969  Barker.  S.  Venus and Adonis after Titian, grisaille,
      1631, 7½ × 9                                                   700


JEAN PETITOT THE YOUNGER
1964  Hankey.  C.  Unknown lady, 1 in. high                     262 10s
1967  C.  (Schoolpieces.)  The Young Pretender, the Old
      Pretender, Maria Sobieska and Cardinal York, dated 1743,
      each 4 in. high                                 4 for     1,680
1969  Nyburg.  S.  Unknown lady with hand on her bosom,
      3 in.                                                          750

## ANDREW PLIMER. 1763–1837        £

| | | |
|---|---|---|
| 1966 | Oakes. C. Two sisters, 3¾ in. Diamond frame | 819 |
| | C. The Misses Rushout as the Three Graces, 4¼ in. | 483 |
| 1969 | de la Hey. S. Young man, dark blue coat, oval, 3 in. | 650 |
| | Fosbery. S. Selina Plimer, the artist's daughter, 3½ in. | 800 |
| | Nyburg. Unknown lady, jewelled frame, 3 in. diam. | 600 |
| | York. C. Unknown child, 3¾ in. | 630 |

## JOHN SMART. 1740–1807

| | | |
|---|---|---|
| 1960 | S. His grandson, oil on paper | 300 |
| 1961 | C. Miss Mary Bathurst, 1792 | 735 |
| 1966 | C. Miss Young | 1,060 10s. |
| 1966 | Sir Robert Sloper, 1787, 2 in. high | 892 10s. |
| | Lady Emily Young, 1796, 3¼ in. | 1,050 |
| | S. Robert Monzy, 1800 | 650 |
| 1967 | N.Y. William Betty, 3 in., $2,200 | 786 |
| 1968 | S. Unknown gentleman, 1783, 1¾ in. | 500 |
| | Lanesborough. S. Unknown lady, 1774, 2 in. | 600 |
| | C. Unknown gentleman, 1798, 3 in. | 682 10s. |
| | Captain Marriott, 1777, 1½ in. | 682 10s. |
| | Ward. C. Sir Barry Close, 1794, 3 in. | 2,520 |
| | de la Hey. S. Eurasian young woman, painted in Madras, 1788 | 850 |
| | Young man, 1779, under 2 in. (£160 in 1961) | 900 |
| | Brotherton. S. Augustus Floyer, landscape background, 1793, oval, 3½ in. | 1,700 |
| 1969 | Gilbert. S. Miss Frances Gore, 1783, oval, 1¾ in. | 850 |
| | C. Unknown man in blue coat, 1782, oval, 2 in. | 1,207 10s. |
| | Hon. Basil Cochrane, 1789, 2½ in. | 997 10s. |
| | de Lautour. S. Comte de Lautour, painted in India, 1793, half length, 2¾ in. high | 1,350 |
| | S. Mary Fraser, dated 1800, 3 in. oval | 1,200 |
| | Unknown young man painted in Madras, 1794, 2¾ in. | 800 |
| | Unknown officer and wife, dated 1790, pair, oval 2¾ in.       2 for | 2,500 |
| 1970 | Soothborough. S. Lord Clive (after Dance) 1776, 1¾ in. | 2,300 |

### OTHER PAINTERS

## ANTOINE ARLAUD

| | | |
|---|---|---|
| 1968 | S. Robert Cecil, 1698, 3½ in. | 1,100 |
| 1969 | S. The old Pretender as a young man in armour, 1710, 3½ in. | 780 |

## HANS JAKOB BESSERER

| | | |
|---|---|---|
| 1968 | Martin. C. The temptation of Christ, landscape on vellum, 4½ in. wide, dated 1641 | 997 10s. |

HENRY BONE. 1755–1834, *enamels*                                                £
1968   Reford.   C.   George III after Beechey and Ward, 12¾ in.   1,281
           Earls of Bristol and Bedford after Vandyck, 14 in.        861
           Four other enamel copies at £500 to £650
1969   C.   Five oval enamel miniatures of Louis XIV beauties
           after Mignard                                         5 for  3,255

MARY BEALE. 1632–1697
1968   de la Hey.   S.   Unknown young woman, late 17th
           century, 2¾ in.                                              700

FRANCOIS CLOUET. 1500–1572
1968   C.   French nobleman, *c.* 1550, 1¼ in.                          630

RICHARD CROSSE
1969   de Lautour.   S.   Three children of the Comte de Lautour
           (£50 8s. in 1793) half-lengths, 3½ in. high         3 for  4,000

FRANCOIS DUMONT
1968   Martin.   C.   General Jacques Gobert, 'l'an 3me' (1795),
           2¾ in.                                                       651

THOMAS FLATMAN. 1637–1688
1968   de la Hey.   S.   Unknown Cromwellian gentleman, 2½ in.   1,500

LUKE HEREMBOUT or HORENBOUT
1967   Watney.   C.   Jane Seymour, style of Holbein, 1½ in. diam.   3,990
1969   S.   Katherine of Aragon on vellum (attributed) circular,
           1½ in. diam., much restored                                 420
1970   Hutton.   S.   Unknown English couple *c.* 1530, 1⅞ in.,
           bought in                                          2 for     760

OZIAS HUMPHREY. 1742–1810
1968   S.   Unknown gentleman, 1772, 1¾ in.                            460

EDWARD NORGATE
1965   Hickson.   S.   Unknown man, 1603                             1,000
1969   Hickson.   S.   Unknown Lady, *c.* 1610, 2⅛ in.              1,600

JEAN BAPTISTE SINGRY
1967   C.   Antoine Michot, 1819, 11 in.                               357

FRANCISZEK SMIADECKI
1969   Gilbert.   S.   Unknown gentleman, *c.* 1665, oval 3 in.      1,000
           C.   Alleged John Hampden, 2¾ in. oval               1,207 10s.

NATHANIEL THATCH                                                          £
1968   de la Hey.   S.   Princess Palatine, 1649, 2½ in.                1,750

SIR JAMES PALMER
1969   S.   Alleged 3rd Earl of Southampton, signed and dated
          1623, 1½ in.                                                  4,400


## JEAN MIRÓ. 1893–

Miró was born a good twelve years later than Picasso, Braque, Léger, Gris or
Paul Klee, but he was exhibiting before the first world war and, though a
living painter, ranks with them among the forefathers of abstract painting.
The period 1905–1920 has now become a heroic age, a time of yearning for
experiment which has provided the justification for the subsequent half-century
of gimmicks, churned out to suit the *bon ton*, decreed by a sort of intellectual
establishment. Veneration for that heroic age accounts, among other things,
for the somewhat incredible prices paid for the sparse and frigid patternizing
of the Catalan-Parisian Jean Miró—and for its emulation. But devotees, both
artists and patrons, would do well to consider the words of William Hazlitt,
written in 1814.

'The arts hold immediate communication with nature and are only derived
from that source. When that original impulse no longer exists, when the inspiration of genius is fled, all the attempts to recall it are no better than the tricks
of galvanism to restore the dead to life. The arts may be said to resemble
Antaeus in his struggle with Hercules who was strangled when he was raised
above the ground and only revived and recovered his strength when he touched
his mother earth.'

|  |  |  | £ |
|---|---|---|---:|
| 1945 | Chrysler. N.Y.  Peinture, 1935, $500 | | 125 |
| 1950 | Paris.  Ville d'Espagne, 1916, 24¼ × 27 | | 112 |
| 1954 | N.Y.  Promenade, 1936, 31 × 23½ | | 570 |
| 1955 | S.  Brazil, 1936 | | 480 |
| 1959 | S.  Sans titre, 1927, 45 × 57½ | | 3,800 |
| 1962 | S.  La lampe à petrole, white chalk and gouache 31½ × 35½ | | 11,000 |
| 1963 | Aldrich.  N.Y.  Composition sur fond bleu, 14½ × 10¼, $6,500 | | 2,320 |
| | Semi-abstract figure subject, 76½ × 38, $35,000 | | 12,500 |
| 1964 | S.  L'oiseau comète et l'ombrelle fleurie, 23½ × 31½ | | 13,000 |
| | La chevelure défaite, 1951, 50¼ × 70¼ | | 18,000 |
| 1965 | Lefèvre. Paris.  Fou du roi, oils, 1926, 46½ × 58, FN99,500+tax | | 7,985 |
| | Composition, 1933, oils, 50 × 38½, FN187,000+tax | | 13,650 |
| | Blue star, 1927, oils, 45 × 35½, FN142,000+tax | | 10,370 |
| | Le Catalan, 1925, oils, 40 × 32½, FN 131,000+tax | | 9,580 |

£

| 1965 | Zadok. S. Les porrides, Pradès, 1917, 20×24½ | 10,000 |
|---|---|---|
| | Dotremont. N.Y. Cheval de cirque, 1927, oils, 76×110, $57,500 | 20,535 |
| 1966 | S. Vase de fleurs et papillon, 1922, 32×25½ | 12,400 |
| | Thompson. N.Y. Self-portrait II, abstraction, 1938, 50½×76¾, $85,000 | 30,575 |
| | Paysage poétique, 47½×35½, 1937 | 11,750 |
| | Three mural panels, 22×99½, $113,250 3 for | 40,450 |
| | Halloween, 1953, 42×22¾, $57,500 | 20,675 |
| | Institute of Contemporary Arts. S. La chanteuse de l'opéra, abstract 1966, 32×21½ | 6,700 |
| | Helena Rubinstein. N.Y. Femme nue avec oiseau, 31×25, $37,250 | 13,300 |
| | Portrait (!) 1927, 51¼×45 | 7,910 |
| | Thompson. N.Y. '1953', 42×22¾, $57,500 | 20,670 |
| 1967 | Juda. S. Signes et symboles, 1938, chalk and gouache, 27¼×41¼ | 2,800 |
| | Lefèvre. Paris, 3rd sale. The bird, 1926, 29×36¾, FN70,000+tax | 7,207 |
| | Painting on a black ground, FN48,000+tax, 31½×43½ | 4,552 |
| 1968 | N.Y. 'Peinture, 1933', 51×64, $13,000 | 5,415 |
| 1969 | S. Groupe de personnages, 1938, 28¾×36¼ | 30,000 |
| | Peinture, 1927, 38¼×51¼ | 24,000 |
| 1969 | Thimig. S. Abstract design for the ballet, 'Jeux d'en-fants', mixed media, 19×30¼ | 3,800 |
| | Swann. S. Femmes, oiseaux, étoiles, charcoal, pastel and wash, 1942, 25¼×19 | 9,500 |
| | S. Oiseaux dans l'éspace, 1960, 45½×35 | 18,000 |

## AMADEO MODIGLIANI.  1884–1920

Between 1946 and 1954 the highest price for a Modigliani painting rose nearly sevenfold, between 1954 and 1960 nearly sevenfold again. In the 1960s, how-ever, prices for average portraits barely doubled. The highest price was still under £100,000 and not more than 150 per cent above that of 1960. This in-dicates no prejudice against Modigliani, who died so soon that he never lost the poetic quality which was occasionally to be found among modern painters before 1920. One of his *odalisques*, something that has not been seen in the salerooms for a generation, might well command more than £150,000. The simple explanation is that in the 1960s abstract and semi-abstract works tended to advance faster than representational works. Among representational paint-ings of Modigliani's generation only those of Picasso are capable of a higher rating. As judges so often permit themselves to observe, 'rightly or wrongly'

| | | £ |
|---|---|---|
| 925 | Francis Carco. Paris. La modèle | 165 |
| | Nu couché | 235 |
| 927 | Waubert. Paris. Female bust-portrait | 700 |
| 933 | Lederlin. Paris. Half-length nude, 25,000 francs+tax | 445 |
| 934 | Chester Johnson. N.Y. Self-portrait, 18×15 | 242 |
| 939 | Druet. Paris. Nu blond | 560 |
| 940 | Eumorphopoulos. S. Female Portrait | 530 |
| 946 | Paris. Mme Zborowski, half-length | 480 |
| | N.Y. Female portrait, $3,320 | 829 |
| 947 | N.Y. Elena, small head, 1917, $2,250 | 560 |
| 949 | N.Y. Le grand nu (nearly 4 ft) $18,000 | 4,460 |
| 951 | Kemde. N.Y. Same picture, $1,485 | 530 |
| 952 | Brussels. Girl's head, 16½×12 | 680 |
| 954 | Girardin. Paris. Portrait d'homme, 5·5 million old francs+tax | 5,550 |
| | Arthur Campbell. N.Y. Raimondo, small head | 5,450 |
| 956 | N.Y. Mme Hébuterne, small head (see 1959) | 3,750 |
| 958 | N.Y. Another portrait of Mme Hébuterne | 4,100 |
| | Half-length male portrait, bought Edward G. Robinson | 23,600 |
| | Portrait of Mme Aynaud-Vaillant | 23,250 |
| | Amsterdam. Mme Czekowska, half-length | 22,000 |
| 959 | S. Mme Hébuterne (see 1956) | 11,000 |
| | Head of Beatrice Hastings | 12,000 |
| 960 | S. Head of Leopold Zborowski | 8,500 |
| | Sarlie. S. Sculptor in blue shirt, 32×25½ | 38,000 |
| | Duveen. S. Girl's head, 23¾×14¾ (under £100 in 1926) | 24,000 |
| | Coe. S. Boy with red hair, 1919, 38½×25 | 21,000 |
| | C. Small portrait, bought in | 4,410 |
| | Girl's head | 10,500 |
| | N.Y. Boy in green shirt, $57,250 | 20,450 |
| 961 | Versailles. Head of Stravinsky, FN120,000+tax | 10,020 |
| 962 | S. Man with a waxed moustache, 1918, 36¼×21½ | 37,000 |
| | L'Italienne, head, 1918, 23¾×17½ | 18,000 |
| 963 | S. The red boy, 1916, 35¼×23 | 24,000 |
| | Sellin. N.Y. Half-length male portrait, 29×21½ | 9,820 |
| | C. Head of Jeanne Hébuterne (see 1966) | 7,350 |
| | Head of Rouveyre, 25×16 (see 1965) | 7,870 |
| 964 | N.Y. Half-length, the young farmer (see 1969) 29×19, oil on paper, $62,500 | 22,320 |
| | C. Marthe, portrait head, 1918 | 9,925 |
| | Woman in blue, half-length, bought in | 15,750 |
| | Evatt. S. Half-length, Morgan Russell | 31,500 |

£

| 1965 | Maurice Haft (at Palm Beach). Girl in white collar, $19\frac{1}{2} \times 27\frac{3}{4}$, $65,000 | 23,550 |
| | S. Head of a red-haired girl | 7,000 |
| | Woman in blue | 15,000 |
| | Paris. Female half-length, 1918, NF380,000+tax | 29,950 |
| | André Lefèvre. Paris. La fille du peuple, 1918, $40\frac{3}{4} \times 26$, FN1,200,000+tax | 96,360 |
| | Portrait of Max Jacob, 1916, $29\frac{1}{2} \times 24$, FN500,000+ tax | 40,145 |
| | Louise, head and shoulders, $22 \times 18$. FN400,000+tax | 32,116 |
| | Paris. La servante, unfinished, half-length, $32\frac{1}{2} \times 18$ | 21,450 |
| | N.Y. Portrait of André Rouveyre, 1915, $25\frac{1}{2} \times 16\frac{1}{2}$ (see 1963) | 14,250 |
| | La cantatrice de Nice, $17 \times 13$ | 10,000 |
| 1966 | C. Head of Jeanne Hébuterne (see 1961) | 8,400 |
| | Fordyce. N.Y. Jeune fille de Montmartre, 1917, $25 \times 17\frac{1}{2}$ | 21,500 |
| | Helena Rubinstein. N.Y. Femme au chapeau neuf, $24 \times 18$ | 14,370 |
| 1967 | Zagayski. N.Y. Portrait of Marie Wasilieff, 1915, $28\frac{1}{2} \times 20\frac{3}{4}$, $40,000 | 14,276 |
| 1968 | Timoner. N.Y. Femme de la bourgeoisie, Mme C, $23\frac{3}{4} \times 18$, $55,000 | 22,180 |
| | Bluestein. N.Y. La blonde aux boucles d'oreille, $18 \times 11$, $87,000 | 36,250 |
| | Portrait, Mme C. D. 1918, $31\frac{1}{2} \times 19\frac{1}{4}$, $92,000 | 38,670 |
| | S. Head, Beatrice Hastings, c. 1916, $18\frac{1}{4} \times 11\frac{1}{4}$ | 18,000 |
| | N.Y. Fille du peuple, $32 \times 21\frac{1}{4}$, c. 1917, $80,000 | 33,330 |
| 1969 | C. Tokyo. Portrait of a young farmer, 1918, oil on paper (see 1964), $29\frac{1}{2} \times 19$, 51 million yen | 59,754 |

DRAWINGS

| 1945 | Chrysler. N.Y. The sculptor Lipschitz, pencil $160 | 40 |
| 1954 | Gerald Reitlinger. S. Sculptural figure, coloured chalks | 350 |
| 1956 | O'Connor. Paris. Cariatide rose, gouache | 2,084 |
| 1957 | N.Y. Cariatide, tempera and gouache | 1,486 |
| 1960 | Rewald. S. Portrait head, pencil | 1,000 |
| | S. Cariatid figure, green gouache | 2,200 |
| 1959 | S. Cariatid figure touched with watercolour | 3,606 |
| 1961 | Finarte, Milan. Reclining nude, 24 in. drawing, touched with oils, lire 1·8 million+tax | 12,000 |
| 1965 | Lefèvre. Paris. Girl's head, oil on paper, FN210,000+ tax | 16,860 |

| | | |
|---|---|---:|
| 967 | Lefèvre. Paris. 3rd sale. Cariatide, pastel and sanguine, FN80,000+tax, $21\frac{1}{2} \times 17$ | £ 7,395 |
| | Cariatide, pencil, $17 \times 10\frac{1}{2}$, FN26,000+tax | 2,390 |
| 968 | Bluestein. N.Y. Cariatide, 1914, pencil, $24\frac{1}{2} \times 19$ | 5,830 |
| | C. Cariatide à gauche, pencil and wc, $25 \times 19\frac{1}{4}$ | 13,125 |
| 969 | S. Cariatide, pencil and red crayon, $21 \times 17$ | 6,500 |
| | Jeune homme au chapeau, pencil outline, $18\frac{3}{4} \times 11\frac{3}{4}$ | 3,800 |

## JOOS DE MOMPER. (*See* Flemish School, after 1550)

## PIET MONDRIAN. (*See* Abstract Painters, Europe)

## CLAUDE MONET. 1840–1926

With a record even more formidable, Monet and Renoir vie with Picasso as the favourite painters of the 1960s. At least 17 of Monet's works were sold for upwards of £50,000 each, seven of them exceeded £100,000 while one of them made £588,000, a strange fate for a man who painted swiftly and often, and whose working life exceeded 60 years. There seemed never to be any lack of Monets of some sort, but by the end of the decade £20,000 hardly bought the preliminaries of a study for a study.

Monet lived long enough to see something of the tremendous speculation which raised his works to this level. By 1898 the pictures for which he had asked £10 to £20 in the early seventies were being bid up to £800 at auction. Twenty years later René Gimpel recorded in his diary that Rosenberg had bought a Monet for £6,000 for which he was asking £12,000. This was at the end of the first world war. The painter was then 78 years old and could hardly ask such prices for what he was still capable of producing. In 1920 Gimpel observed that Monet expected 30,000 francs (then £800) for moderate-sized landscapes for which he had asked 10,000 francs (then £400) in 1914. However, in the same year Monet sold one of his octogenarian works, the huge almost abstract Giverny lily ponds, to Japan for £4,000.

The fall in even the best Monets had already begun in 1926, the year of his death, when Gimpel bought both versions of *the Monet sisters in a punt* for only £1,250. These large pictures could well have made eight times as much just after the First World War. To some extent such falls are inevitable when a painter works too long and parodies his own style, but in fact all Impressionist paintings began to fall at this time. In terms of the real value of money they did not recover till the 1950s. The death of the last of the founder-painters relegated Impressionism to the basest form of antiquity, the penultimate. It had thriven on its boldness and freshness and now there were so many other varieties of freshness and boldness to be had. The recovery of the 1950s must be understood for what it was. The Impressionists were being bought as the last of the old masters—and still are. Soon the question must be faced whether, looked at as old masters, the leavings of this market are realistically valued. At the end of the decade a Monet of any significance could hardly be had for under £120,000. Monets at £25,000 to £30,000 were still available, but only typical of the painter at his worst—and that was a singularly bad worst.

| | | £ |
|---|---|---:|
| 1902 | Strauss. N.Y. Le débâcle (see 1938) | 996 |
| | Milliken. N.Y. Sortie du port de Boulogne | 1,410 |
| 1905 | Bought by Hugh Lane from Durand-Ruel. Vetheuil, effet de neige. National Gallery (see 1959) | 700 |
| 1906 | Lord Grimthorpe. C. Le phare de l'hospice | 204 15s. |
| 1910 | Andrew Maxwell C. Effet de neige | 504 |
| 1913 | Bought by Durand Ruel from Mme Prat. La Terrasse à St Adresse, 38½ × 51, 1867 (see 1926, 1967), 42,400 francs | 1,700 |
| 1917 | Sutton. N.Y. The Seine at Vetheuil | 2,920 |
| | Bordighera | 3,180 |
| 1918 | Price paid by Rosenberg for 'Woman with Japanese kimono and fans' | 6,000 |
| | Price demanded for ditto (according to R. Gimpel) | 12,000 |
| 1919 | N.Y. Houses of parliament and Thames | 4,250 |
| | Débâcle à Vetheuil | 3,350 |
| | Drummond. C. Poppy field | 1,312 |
| 1920 | American Art Association. N.Y. La Tamise à Londres | 2,900 |
| | Mrs Charles Hunter. C. Island of San Giorgio, Venice | 630 |
| | Bought for the Luxembourg. Femme dans un jardin | 4,250 |
| | Bought for the Louvre. Le promenade en campagne | 3,300 |
| | Bought by Matsutaka, one of the recent water-lily pictures, painted at Giverny | 4,000 |
| | For moderate-sized landscapes Monet asks 30,000 francs (as against 10,000 francs or £400 in 1914—R. Gimpel) | 800 |
| 1923 | N.Y. Railway bridge at Argenteuil (see 1927, 1963) | 960 |
| 1924 | Bought by Courtauld fund for the Tate gallery. Plage à Trouville | 650 |
| 1925 | John Singer Sargent. C. Bordighera | 882 |
| 1926 | Bought by R. Gimpel from Monet. The Monet sisters in a punt. Two versions (see 1946, 1962), 200,000 francs at 160 to £ | 2 for 1,250 |
| | Bought by subscribers for Tate Gallery. Les peupliers | 900 |
| | Dame, assise dans un parc | 525 |
| | Bought by Theodore Pitcairn. La Terrasse à St Adresse, (see 1913, 1967), 38½ × 51, $11,000 | 2,268 |
| 1927 | Bought by W. A. Cargill. Railway bridge at Argenteuil, 1873-4, 23 × 28½, (£960 in 1923, see 1963) | 1,200 |
| | Murray. C. Falaises à Fécamp | 1,522 10s. |

£

| | | |
|---|---|---|
| 1929 | Bought by John Boulton.   Stream at Giverny (£10,500 in 1965) | |
| 1932 | Newman.  N.Y.  Printemps à Vetheuil, 23×31 | 530 |
| 1932 | N.Y.  Falaises à Dieppe, $1,500 at 3·48 to £ | 432 |
| | Jules Strauss.  Paris.  Antibes.   205,000 francs+tax at 70 to £ | 432 |
| 1933 | N.Y.  Flower piece, 1878 | 3,420 |
| 1936 | Paris.  La grande rue d'Argenteuil | 845 |
| | Bought by National gallery, Melbourne.   Vetheuil, 1878 | 1,140 |
| 1938 | Albert Pra.  Paris.  Le débâcle (£996 in 1902) | 1,546 |
| | La neige, 140,000 francs at 125 to the £+tax | 755 |
| 1939 | Canonne.  Paris.  La Cathédrale rose, 172,000 francs+ tax at 180 to the £ | 1,322 |
| 1940 | Harcourt Johnstone.  S.  View in Hyde Park | 1,140 |
| 1944 | S.  Cliffs at Pourville | 640 |
| | N.Y.  Landscape, $8,000 | 340 |
| 1946 | Bought by Alexander Korda.   The Monet sisters in a punt, 43×56¾ (see 1926, 1962) | 1,992 |
| | van Horne.  N.Y.  The Seine at Bougival, $7,750 | 5,000 |
| 1948 | N.Y.  Islot à Port Villiers, $8,250 | 2,763 |
| 1950 | Paris.  Thames with bridge, oil sketch | 2,070 |
| 1952 | Cognacq.  Paris.  Trois-mâts à Rouen, 4·6 million francs +tax | 684 |
| | Seine à Argenteuil 4·1 million francs+tax | 5,300 |
| | Clocher de Bethancourt 4·5 million francs+tax | 4,720 |
| 1954 | Bessoneau.  Paris.  La Seine à Lavacourt, 1883, 24×40 | 5,200 |
| 1957 | Georges Lurcy.  N.Y.  Woman in a garden.  Bought Douglas Dillon, $93,250 | 3,235 |
| | Weinberg.  S.  Blue house at Zaandam, 17¾×24 | 33,300 |
| | Rochers de Belle Isle, 25×31½ | 22,000 |
| | Paris.  Giverny, 1894 | 6,000 |
| | Antibes, 1887, 1·8 million old francs+tax | 8,200 |
| | Inondation | 17,500 |
| 1958 | N.Y.  Monet's child in cradle, $84,700 | 8,300 |
| | Paris.  Fishing boats, Etretat | 30,250 |
| 1959 | S.  Bassin de Nymphéas à Giverny | 12,120 |
| | Church at Pourville under snow | 13,000 |
| | Venice, 1908 (see 1962) | 14,000 |
| | National Gallery values Hugh Lane's snow landscape (£700 in 1905) | 12,000 |
| 1960 | Viles.  S.  Nymphéas à Giverny, 1906, 35¼×34½ | 15,000 |
| | Davies.  S.  Grand canal, Venice, 1908, 28¼×35¾ | 18,000 |
| | C.  Water garden, Giverny | 19,500 |
| | N.Y.  Houses of Parliament, 1904 | 19,950 |
| | | 15,000 |

£

| 1961 | Paris.  Pont d'Argenteuil (£860 in 1897) | 122,360 |

1962 Somerset Maugham.  S.  Zaandam, 1871, $15\frac{3}{4} \times 28\frac{1}{2}$  40,000
Metcalf (Korda).  S.  The Monet sisters in a punt (see
1926, 1946), $43 \times 56\frac{3}{4}$, Coll. Baron Thyssen  56,000
Power.  S.  Venice, 1908 (see 1959)  18,500
C.  Garden at Giverny, $51 \times 78\frac{1}{2}$.  Bought in  29,400
Woolworth.  N.Y.  Le débâcle aux glaces, $45,000  16,965

1963 Aldrich.  N.Y.  Water-lilies, Giverny, 1918, $60 \times 79$,
$110,000 (*compare* 1966)  39,107
Galerie Bayeler.  Basel.  Sold to National Gallery, a still
larger version, $97 \times 168$.  Special Treasury grant of  35,000
Wolf.  S.  Fishing boats, Pourville, 1882, $21\frac{1}{4} \times 26$  30,000
Cargill.  S.  Railway bridge, Argenteuil, 1873–4, $23 \times 28\frac{1}{2}$
(see 1927)  77,000
Zimet.  S.  Bateaux echoués, 1881, $23 \times 32$  30,000
S.  Le chemin d'Epinay, 1874, $21\frac{1}{2} \times 29$  34,000
Canonne.  S.  Wooden bridge, Argenteuil, 1873, $21\frac{1}{4} \times$
$28\frac{3}{4}$  48,000
Woolworth.  C.  Honfleur, 1864, $15\frac{1}{2} \times 28\frac{1}{2}$, Monet's first
exhibited picture.  21,000
C.  Argenteuil  39,900

1965 Fitzgerald.  S.  Spring at Argenteuil  24,000
Cliffs at Pourville, 1882  25,000
Paris.  On the cliffs, Mme Monet and her son, 1876, 2·4
million francs+tax  181,800
C.  Cornfield, 1887  21,550
Haft, Palm Beach.  Juan les Pins, 1888, $28\frac{3}{4} \times 36\frac{1}{2}$, $190,000  67,800

1965 Rickson.  N.Y.  Les peupliers, 1891, $36 \times 32$, $105,000  33,925
Aequus Corporation.  C.  Waterloo Bridge, 1901  19,950
C.  Nymphéas, $39\frac{1}{2} \times 79\frac{1}{2}$ (compare 1966)  40,140
Channing.  N.Y.  Church of San Giorgio Maggiore,
$25\frac{1}{2} \times 36$  22,500

1966 S.  Falaises à Pourville, 1882, $22\frac{1}{2} \times 31$  32,500
N.Y.  Grotte à Port Dormois, Belle Isle, 1886, $25\frac{1}{4} \times 32$  25,950
Grant Pick.  N.Y.  Nymphéas, 1924, $51\frac{1}{2} \times 78\frac{1}{4}$ (com-
pare price of a similar work in 1963)  19,720
Helena Rubinstein.  N.Y.  Falaises à Etretat, $23 \times 31\frac{1}{2}$,
$40,000  14,350
C.  Rouen Cathedral, 1894, $42 \times 29$.  The worst of more
than 30 versions.  60,900
S.  Meule au coucher du soleil, 1891, $25\frac{1}{2} \times 36\frac{3}{4}$  24,000

1967 N.Y.  Scène de canal, Amsterdam, 1873, $24 \times 40$, $95,000  33,929
Chester Beatty.  S.  La plage à Ste Adresse, 1867, $23\frac{1}{4} \times 31\frac{1}{2}$
Perhaps his earliest impressionist work  41,000

| | | £ |
|---|---|---|
| 1967 | S. Hiver à Argenteuil, 1875, 24¼×40 | 116,000 |
| | Pitcairn. C. La terrasse à Ste Adresse, 1867, 38½×51 (sold by Monet for £16, see also 1913, 1926) | 588,000 |
| | Nearchos. C. Le quatorze Juillet, 1872, 23½×32 | 36,750 |
| | C. The garden at Giverny, 1919–20, 28¾×35¾ | 23,100 |
| | Paris. La Seine à Argenteuil, 1872, 18¾×38½, FN950,000 +tax | 75,670 |
| | Motte, Geneva. La Seine à Andelys, 32½×37, FS232,000 +tax | 24,922 |
| 1968 | Paris. Landscape with white frost. FN380,000+tax | 34,928 |
| | Fitzhugh. N.Y. La Seine à Lavacourt, 1878, 18×24 | 19,600 |
| | S. Printemps à Giverny, 1886, 25½×21¼ | 30,000 |
| | Falaises à Pourville, marée baisse, 1882, 23×31½ | 19,000 |
| | Pleydell-Bouverie. S. Portrait of the child Jean Monet in 1871, 16×12¾ | 52,000 |
| | Kawasaki. S. Le val de Falaise, 1885, 25×31 | 50,000 |
| | C. La Seine près de Vernon, 1883, 28¾×35¼ | 44,100 |
| | Charing Cross Bridge, 1899, 25½×32 | 29,925 |
| | Prairie à Giverny, 32×35¾ | 24,150 |
| | La côte de Normandie, 1882, 23×31 | 28,350 |
| | S. Vallée de la Scie, Pourville, 1882, 23¼×31 | 32,000 |
| | Brandeis University. N.Y. Mme Camille Monet, half-length, 1875–6, 46×35. Bought in at $500,000 | 208,333 |
| | Louveciennes, effet de neige, 1874, 22×25¾, $250,000 | 104,166 |
| | La route de Vetheuil, 1878, 19½×24, $180,000 | 75,000 |
| | Paris. Saules aux bords de l'Epte, FN650,000+tax | 61,000 |
| | Furholmen. S. Mont Kolsaas, preliminaries of an oil sketch, 24½×35½ | 25,200 |
| | Motte, Geneva. Paysage à Moret, FS170,000+tax | 19,950 |
| | S. Falaises près de Dieppe, 1897, 25×38¾ | 24,000 |
| | Vue de la Creuse, 28¾×36, 1889 | 24,000 |
| | Ginsberg. N.Y. Falaise de Villers, mer agitée, 25½×32, $62,500 | 26,040 |
| | Hersloff. N.Y. Route à Giverny, 1885, 23¾×32, $60,000 | 25,130 |
| | Bought-in and resold in Tokyo (S) in October for 17 million yen or | 20,000 |
| 1969 | S. Les eaux de la Somme, effet de soleil, 1889, 28¼×35¾ | 25,000 |
| | Schulthess. N.Y. Mont Kolsaas, oil sketch, 1895 25¾×29½, $40,000 | 16,750 |
| | C. (Tokyo). Cliffs at Dieppe, 26 million yen, 26×40 | 30,371 |
| | C. (Geneva). Matin sur la Seine, 1897, 28×35, FS426,000+tax | 42,034 |

| | | |
|---|---|---|
| 1969 | Paris. Three painters working in a garden, 1888, FN1·5 million+tax | 135,740 |
| | Landscape, 1874, FN490,000+tax | 44,820 |
| | Lafont. C. Jetée du port de Havre par mauvais temps, probably 1867, $19\frac{3}{4} \times 24$ | 75,600 |
| | Paris. Les Glaçons, 1888, $24 \times 40$, FN340,000+tax | 31,700 |

## HENRY MOORE. (*See* English School, modern)

## ANTONIS MOR. (*See* Flemish School after 1550)

## JEAN MICHEL MOREAU (Moreau le jeune). (*See* French School, 18th century)

## BERTHE MORISOT. 1841–1895

Manet's *bien elevée* pupil was scarcely regarded as a professional painter in her own right, rather than a gifted amateur, till the 1950s. And she imitated Manet so closely that high prices were not risked till the 1960s. The market has been kept alive by the relative scarcity of her works, but the big jump in prices in 1968 was no more than typical of that year of devaluation fears. The market rating of Berthe Morisot is scarcely higher than that of Mary Cassatt, even though the latter's works are far more numerous and show much less sensibility. Berthe Morisot's *Port de Fécamp* was quite as slight a thing as the Whistler nocturne, painted a few years later, which caused all that hou-ha. But the *Nocturne* would certainly not make £57,800.

| | | £ |
|---|---|---|
| 1951 | Paris. Mother and child in garden, $26\frac{1}{2} \times 21\frac{1}{2}$ | 1,928 |
| | Archibald, N.Y. Landscape, $23 \times 27\frac{1}{2}$ | 575 |
| 1953 | Paris. La couturière, $22\frac{3}{4} \times 28\frac{1}{2}$ | 3,480 |
| 1954 | Paris. Les deux enfants, $18\frac{1}{2} \times 23$ | 2,358 |
| 1956 | S. Jeune fille au chapeau, $23 \times 21\frac{1}{2}$ | 3,400 |
| 1958 | Kirkeby. N.Y. La mère aux oies, $25\frac{1}{2} \times 21$, \$31,000 | 11,070 |
| 1959 | N.Y. Portrait, Jeanne Foumanoir with dog, $25\frac{3}{4} \times 32$, \$25,000 | 8,935 |
| | Treves. S. Girl on a sofa, $18\frac{1}{2} \times 25\frac{3}{4}$ | 4,500 |
| | Valued for National Gallery, Lane bequest. l'Eté | 7,000 |
| 1963 | Paris. Julie Manet with her nurse | 10,000 |
| 1963 | Cargill. S. Sur la falaise de Portrieux, $15 \times 22$ | 6,200 |
| 1964 | Hutton. S. Jeune fille mettant son patin, $13\frac{1}{4} \times 10\frac{3}{4}$ | 3,500 |
| | La petite Marcelle en pied, $15\frac{3}{4} \times 12\frac{1}{2}$ | 3,200 |
| | S. Miss Reynolds and Julie Manet, $27\frac{1}{4} \times 22\frac{3}{4}$ | 12,000 |

| | | £ |
|---|---|---|
| 65 | S.  Young woman with veil, 1872 | 20,000 |
| | Jeune femme au manteau vert, 1894, 43 × 28¾ | 6,500 |
| | Daniels.  S.  Fillettes au jardin, 23½ × 28¾ | 14,500 |
| | S.  Bougival, landscape, 1882, 14 × 17 | 5,200 |
| 68 | Pleydell-Bouverie.  S.  Sur la plage, Petites Dalles 1873, | |
| | 9½ × 19¾ | 46,000 |
| | S.  La jetée, 1875, 9½ × 20¼ | 20,000 |
| | Paris.  Port de Fécamp, 1874, 46½ × 22, FN620,000+tax | 57,800 |
| 69 | Silberman.  N.Y.  Forêt de Compiègne, 20¾ × 25, c. 1885, | |
| | $26,000 | 10,925 |
| | S.  Marine à Cowes, 1875, 17 × 25½.  Bought in at | 16,000 |
| | Enfant au lit, pastel sketch, 12 × 16, c. 1885 | 4,200 |
| | Fillette dans un jardin, 1887, 21¼ × 25½.  Bought in | 14,000 |
| | La cage, 1885, 19½ × 14¾ | 8,900 |
| | Paris.  La petite barque, 11¼ × 14, FN183,000+tax | 17,600 |

## GEORGE MORLAND.  1763–1804

he picture, *Dancing Dogs*, was sold in 1905 for £4,200 and in 1929 for £9,040,
ie modern equivalents being £33,600 and £45,200. Yet, since the dispersal
f the oddly named *National Gallery of British Sports and Pastimes* in 1951, no
lorland picture has exceeded £3,300. The fall can be explained in several
·ays. In the first place the collapse of the Duveen market carried with it not
nly portraits but the whole of the English 18th century school, including the
olour prints after Morland subjects which had been so grotesquely overrated
·the 1920s. On top of that, there are too many Morland pictures, they are
·o dark, their sentiment is too forced, there is something yokelish about them.
lowever there is something else less easily accountable. The imitations of
lorland in an even more yokelish style which William Shayer Senior pro-
iced as late as the 1870s, could fetch more than double as much as any Morland,
·ld in the 1960s. The trouble seems to be that at times Morland painted really
·ell, whereas for those who devoutly love boring pictures, Shayer must be
·rfection.

| | | £ |
|---|---|---|
| 60 | Gibson  Fleming.  S.  Coast  scene  with  smugglers, | |
| | 29½ × 53½ | 1,800 |
| | Another coast scene | 1,800 |
| | Farmyard scene | 1,300 |
| 61 | Whitmarsh.  N.Y.  Grandfather and grandmother, two | |
| | children's portrait heads | 2 for  2,500 |
| | Small farmyard subject | 1,680 |
| 63 | Craigmyle.  S.  Self-portrait, 20½ × 16 | 1,700 |

£

| | | | £ |
|---|---|---|---|
| 1964 | Knight. S. The Return from Market, Kilburn, $44\frac{1}{2} \times 54\frac{1}{2}$ | | 3,200 |
| 1965 | Cunnynghame. C. Landscape with farming figures, 1792, $29\frac{1}{2} \times 24\frac{1}{2}$ | | 1,050 |
| 1966 | Fletcher. S. Leaving for the shoot, $27\frac{1}{4} \times 35$ | | 3,300 |

1966    Fletcher. S. Leaving for the shoot, $27\frac{1}{4} \times 35$    3,300

         The dearest in 15 years but 19 paintings by Morland made only £10,300 between them.

1968    Trowell. S. Beach scene at Shanklin, Isle of Wight, $16\frac{1}{2} \times 22$    620

         Prestige. S. (with J. C. Ibbetson). Hampstead Heath, figures and donkeys, $17\frac{1}{2} \times 23\frac{1}{2}$    1,400

         C. (Attributed) Pair of shooting scenes, $12 \times 17$    2 for    2,310

1969    S. Effects of extravagance and idleness, 1794, $29\frac{1}{4} \times 24\frac{3}{4}$    800

         Parkinson. C. Pegwell Bay with cart and figures, $32 \times 52$    787 10s

         (19 paintings by Morland from one collection made only £11,200 in all)

         Hardie. S. Fishermen on beach, stormy sky, 1793, $39\frac{3}{4} \times 35\frac{1}{2}$    1,200


# GIAMBATTISTA MORONI. (*See* Venetian School)


# JOHN HAMILTON MORTIMER. (*See* English School, 18th century)


# ROBERT BURNS MOTHERWELL. (*See* Abstract painters, American)


# WILLIAM MULLER OF BRISTOL. 1812–1845

There were three English painters of the romantic Near East who followed in the footsteps of Byron; Lewis, David Roberts and Muller, the last of whom was perhaps the most overrated. All three landslided in the 1920s. Muller *Chess players*, sold in 1874 for £4,052, the equivalent of £36,500 on the 197 scale, was acquired by the Bristol City Gallery at a sale in 1931 where it made £78 15s. But, as late as the Second World War, large Muller landscapes in very useful frames could be bought for £15 to £20. Since 1968 there has been a rush of enthusiasm, but the peculiar price of £9,200 owes most to the rising popularity of view-paintings of Venice which has raised Marieschi to £18,000 Joli to £12,600, James and Holland to £6,000.

|      |    |                                                                                              | £ |
|------|----|----------------------------------------------------------------------------------------------|---|
| 1961 | S. | Xanthus, 1845, wc, 21×14                                                                       | 130 |
| 1963 | S. | Water-mills, 1842, oil, 39×50                                                                  | 200 |
| 1966 | C. | Falls of Tivoli, 20½×16½, wc                                                                  | 78 15s. |
|      | S. | Via Mala pass, 1838, 21×33                                                                     | 60 |
|      |    | Doge's Palace, 1839, oil, 23½×42¼                                                             | 260 |
| 1967 | C. | Castellamare, Lake Maggiore, 1843, 18½×28¾                                                    | 178 10s. |
|      |    | Album of 26 finished wcs of the Near East, each 12×17, £2,940. Average price                 | 113 |
| 1968 | S. | Bay of Naples, looking towards Vesuvius, 1834, 36×48                                          | 280 |
|      |    | Mowbray. S. Grand Canal towards the Salute, 1837, 52¼×90                                     | 9,200 |
| 1969 |    | Bristol Club. S. Tombs of Lycia, Asia minor, 41×76 (£129 3s. in 1846, £3,937 5s. in 1887)    | 2,200 |
|      |    | Mediterranean port, style of Claude, 1838, 41×69                                              | 2,800 |
|      | S. | View near Bristol, 1840, 17¼×29                                                               | 800 |
|      | C. | Grand Canal with Salute and Dogana, 29×50                                                     | 4,725 |

## EDUARD MUNCH. (*See* German School, modern)

## SIR ALFRED MUNNINGS. 1877–1963

The market for Munnings is linked with the painters of hunting, racing and coaching pictures who worked in the early and middle 19th century. But it is linked only to the extent that horsy men buy horsy pictures. Some glimmer of aesthetic perception is to be detected even in such potboiling painters as Cooper Henderson and the younger Henry Alken, but it would require the finest of lenses to discover any in Sir Alfred Munnings, the highest-priced English painter of the present century. Munnings sells partly in America and the prices for his works are governed by those of the American Sargent, whose sloshing brush strokes Munnings reproduced in the oily colours, associated with children's boxes of plasticine.

|      |                |                                                        | £ |
|------|----------------|--------------------------------------------------------|---|
| 1951 | Hutchinson. C. | After the race, 40¾×60 (see 1967)                     | 1,575 |
|      |                | In the saddling paddock, Cheltenham, 43×64            | 1,575 |
|      |                | The start, Newmarket, 36×78                           | 1,417 10s. |
|      |                | 'Why weren't you out yesterday?', 44×56               | 1,102 |
|      |                | Four others at £420 to £840                            | |
| 1958 | Hammond. S.    | Early morning, Newmarket, 24¾×72½                     | 2,000 |
|      |                | The start at Newmarket, 36½×72                        | 3,500 |
|      |                | Going out at Epsom, 34½×49½                           | 3,600 |
|      |                | Going out at Kempton, 24¾×30                          | 1,500 |
|      |                | Autumn tapestries, 28×36                              | 2,000 |

£

| | | £ |
|---|---|---|
| 1959 | S. *Bahram*, held by a groom, 24½ × 29½ | 2,400 |
| 1960 | S. A winner at Epsom, bought in | 2,400 |
| | Hanbury. C. Passing the number-board, 19½ × 23½ | 1,050 |
| 1965 | Marsh. S. Epsom paddock, *Mahmoud* being saddled, 25 × 30 | 8,700 |
| | Saddling, 11½ × 16 | 1,700 |
| | Moss. S. On the Downs at Epsom, 29½ × 35½ | 10,200 |
| | Lady Diana Cooper. S. The Belvoir hunt, 19½ × 24 | 2,200 |
| | Combemarle. C. Gordon Richards on *High Stakes*, 1954, 19¾ × 26½ | 7,350 |
| 1966 | C. Morning ride, the artist's wife, 1913, 28 × 36 | 6,825 |
| | Lord Ivor Spencer Churchill with the Quorn, 1924, 20 × 28 | 3,675 |
| | Hop-picker's fires, 1920, 22 × 24 | 2,940 |
| | Union club, Birmingham. S. The grey cob, 19½ × 23½ | 4,200 |
| | Bunting. S. The vagabonds, 1902, 49½ × 80½ | 2,700 |
| | S. Newmarket start, 21 × 24 | 6,000 |
| 1967 | David Astor. C. Lord Astor's horses at Manton, 30 × 40 | 12,600 |
| | C. Start of a steeplechase, 20 × 24 | 7,560 |
| | Merry. S. After the race, Cheltenham saddling paddock, 40½ × 60 (£1,575 in 1951) | 8,500 |
| | S. A shepherd on a white pony driving sheep, 28½ × 38½ | 6,700 |
| | Keith. S. At Hethersett races, 1904, 13½ × 17½ | 5,200 |
| | Starkie. S. Country horse-fair, 13¾ × 20½ | 4,400 |
| | S. Point to point steeplechase, 19½ × 23¼ | 7,000 |
| 1968 | C. W. W. Astor on *Geoffrey Austin* with hounds at Cliveden, 1931, 30 × 36 | 11,550 |
| | S. Oil sketch for the same, 14 × 18 | 2,400 |
| | Lonsdale-Fell. N.Y. Horses at grass, 24½ × 30½, $38,000 | 15,833 |
| | S. A summer hack on Exmoor, 25½ × 35½ | 3,000 |
| | Huntsman on grey horse with hounds in wood, 19½ × 23¾ | 3,600 |
| 1969 | Combemarle. C. The whip, 25½ × 32 | 17,850 |
| | Start of the Cambridgeshire, 1952–3, 11½ × 23½ | 17,220 |
| | Royal Caledonian Schools. C. Marjorie, girl on dappled horse, *c.* 1913, 36 × 40 | 6,825 |
| | Myers. C. Who's the lady?, 44 × 70. Bought in at £17,325, sold afterwards for | 16,800 |
| 1969 | S. *Mackwiller*, bay mare ridden by Jennings, with Chantilly race-course, *c.* 1926, 31¾ × 34½ | 25,000 |
| | Newmarket start, study No. 4, 19¾ × 23¾ | 15,000 |
| | C. Gypsies outside their tent, 1920, 20 × 24 | 4,725 |

## ESTABAN MURILLO. 1617–1682

early Victorian times Murillo was the favourite painter of the world, the eator of a work that became in the year 1852 the dearest ever sold—at 24,600, the equivalent of close on a quarter million in 1970 money. Since 52 the saleroom record has been that of changing fashion and only feeble wers of recovery, and above all the realization that there was little left but orkshop products. The sale—if such a thing is possible—of one of Murillo's agnificant realist paintings of peasant and vagabond life, would alter the hole picture. The *Gypsy Girl*, sold in 1956 for £25,000, would be a six-figure fair.

|  |  | £ |
|---|---|---|
| 61 | S. Nativity, school picture | 4,500 |
| 63 | Sterling of Keir. S. Portrait head of a girl, 25×20 | 9,000 |
| 66 | Earl of Normanton. C. Moses striking water from the rock, oil study, 13×29½ | 1,470 |
| 67 | S. Holy Family, 40×30 | 7,500 |
| 68 | C. Alleged self-portrait with sketchbook and lace collar, 40×33¼ | 3,150 |

## ALEXANDER NASMYTH. 1758–1840
### and
## PATRICK NASMYTH. 1786–1831

espectable Scottish landscape painters, the value of whose best works has rely trebled in a century—which is another way of saying that a hundred ears ago they were worth more than three times as much as in 1970 in real oney terms. The somewhat ludicrous prices, paid for such derivative land-ape painters as Frederick William Watts, suggest that the two Nasmyths may : undervalued.

LEXANDER NASMYTH

|  |  | £ |
|---|---|---|
| 63 | Martineau. S. Patrick Miller and family in landscape, 37¼×47 | 5,200 |
| 64 | S. Edinburgh, 1822 | 2,100 |
| 65 | C. Pass of Achray | 1,470 |
|  | Windermere | 840 |
| 67 | Culme-Seymour. S. Edinburgh from the West, 24½×36¼ | 4,700 |
| 68 | Clarke. C. Falls of the Tummel, 1807, 21×33 | 1,890 |
|  | N.Y. Edinburgh from the South West (£515 15s. in 1932), 18×24, $2,250 | 937 |

277

PATRICK NASMYTH                                                    £

| 1960 | S. Near Clifton, 1828 | 2,100 |
| 1962 | Martineau. S. Distant view of Edinburgh, 1812, 26¾×34½ | 2,700 |
| 1964 | S. Near Godstone, 1828, 28×36 | 2,200 |
| 1965 | S. Near Tunbridge Wells, 1829, 27½×38 | 2,400 |
| 1966 | Hull. C. Extensive wooded landscape, 1817, 22×33 | 1,417 10s |
| | C. Teviotdale with castle and cattle, 1813, 23×33½ | 1,260 |
| | Lambton. C. Wooded landscape with watermill, 23×32 | 1,470 |
| 1968 | Ednam. C. Douglas Bridge, Inverary, 1818, 22×33 | 2,625 |
| | Hotham. C. Kilchurn Castle and view from Murchiston, pair, 8½×11½ 2 for | 630 |
| 1969 | Duchess of Argyll. C. (in Glasgow). Inverary from the Loch, 41½×65 | 6,300 |
| 1970. | S. Alva, Stirlingshire, 33×45¾ | 3,600 |

## JEAN MARC NATTIER. 1685–1766

It is impossible to follow the very high prices, paid for painters of the post Watteau school in the first quarter of this century, without reference to price paid privately on the Paris market. For this reason I have carried the list bac. to 1895, thereby correcting the inadequate impression, created in Volume One It will at once be seen that the apparently enormous price, paid for the *Marquis de Baglione* in 1961, was no wonder at all. On the 1970 scale Henry Huntingto. paid for a Nattier portrait in 1909 the equivalent of £186,700. In 1919 Ambatie los paid very nearly as much for another portrait. Even an open auction pric in 1926 was as high as £60,000 in present day money, while at the Lione Philips sale of 1913 Christies sold a portrait for £4,830. This was equivalent t £33,500 in 1966 when the same picture made no more than £1,890.

|  |  | £ |
|---|---|---|
| 1895 | Lyne Stephens. C. Lady on clouds with doves | 4,095 |
| 1898 | Sold by Durand-Ruel to Ambatielos. *The Marquise de Baglione as Flora* (see 1961). According to R. Gimpel | 6,400 |
| | Sold by Durand-Ruel to the Marquis de Chaponay, a female portrait at 200,000 francs (see 1919). R. Gimpel | 8,000 |
| 1899 | Paris. Mme de Chateauroux and Mme de Flaves, a pair (£700 each, Taleyrand sale, 1817) 2 for | 1,400 |
| 1903 | Reginald Vaile. C. Comtesse de Neuberg | 4,725 |
| | Lady with blue scarf | 3,255 |
| 1905 | Brandus. N.Y. Comtesse d'Argenson | 3,500 |
| 1908 | C. Marquise de Romilly | 2,940 |
| 1909 | Henry Huntington buys a female portrait from Knoedler (According to Gimpel) for $90,000 | 18,350 |

| | | £ |
|---|---|---|
| 12 | Mme Roussel. Paris. Marquise de Ventimille as Flora (see 1936 and 1963) | 4,800 |
| 13 | Lionel Philips. C. Marquise de Tournelle (see 1942) | 4,055 |
| | Marquise de Flavacourt (see 1966) | 4,820 |
| | Lord Brooke, 1741 (see 1920) | 3,360 |
| | Murray Scott. C. Mme Victoire (£409 10s. in 1887) | 2,205 |
| 18 | Curel. Paris. Portrait of Courvoisier | 4,400 |
| | Princesse de Bourbon-Conti | 5,500 |
| 19 | Sold by Wildenstein to Ambatielos, a portrait of a lady (see 1898). According to R. Gimpel | 34,000 |
| 20 | Asher Wertheimer. C. Lord Brooke (see 1913) | 3,675 |
| | Mme Victoire (see 1913) | 997 10s. |
| 26 | Bischoffsheim. C. Duc de Ponthièvre, bought Duveen | 12,075 |
| 29 | Princess Paley. C. Lady in blue and white | 3,675 |
| 32 | Milliken. N.Y. Comtesse de Clermont, $7,500 at 3·42 to £ | 2,230 |
| 35 | Blumenthal Paris. Mme Bouret, 270,000 francs at 75 to £+tax | 4,250 |
| 36 | Greffulhe. S. Marquise de Ventimille, bought in (see 1912, 1963) | 5,200 |
| 37 | Louis Burat. Paris. Head of a young girl | 1,720 |
| 42 | Lockett. C. Mme de Tournelle (£4,055 in 1913) | 585 |
| 51 | Stehli. N.Y. Marquise de Ligneris | 3,925 |
| 54 | N.Y. Mlle Adelaide, daughter of Louis XV, 32×25¾ | 2,538 |
| 57 | Mae Rovensky. N.Y. Oval portrait of a lady | 5,350 |
| 59 | S. Portrait of Mme Tocqué, 1741 | 6,500 |
| 60 | Paris. Louis XV, bust portrait, 32×26½, FN58,000+tax | 5,052 |
| 61 | Erickson. N.Y. Marquise de Baglione as Flora, 1746, 54×41¾, $175,000 (see 1898) | 62,500 |
| 62 | N.Y. A lady as Diana, oval, 29×23½ | 5,355 |
| 63 | Kavanagh. S. Marquise de Ventimille as Flora, 39×31, (see 1912, 1936) | 7,500 |
| 64 | S. Male portrait | 2,200 |
| 65 | S. Duchesse de Montmorency, 31½×21¼ | 800 |
| 66 | S. Hodgkins. C. Marquise de Flavacourt as Diana 40×55 (£4,830 in 1913, £997 10s. in 1926) | 1,890 |
| 67 | S. Mme Henriette, daughter of Louis XV as a Vestal, 1749, 32¼×37½ | 3,000 |
| 68 | S. Comtesse de Beaujeu, 40×31½ | 3,500 |

## AERT VAN DER NEER. (*See* Dutch School)

## BARNET NEWMAN. (*See* Abstract Painters, America)

BEN NICHOLSON. (*See* Abstract Painters, Europe)


EMIL NOLDE. (*See* German School, modern)


ISAAC AND PETER OLIVER. (*See* Miniatures)


BERNARD VAN ORLEY. (*See* Flemish School before 1550)


JAN VAN OS. (*See* Dutch School)


## THE OSTADE FAMILY

It is difficult to account for the movements in the market for the classic Dut school. Town views, church interiors, shipping scenes and the more prospero sort of *genre* subject seem the most likely to advance suddenly and briskl Much less likely are scenes of low life with someone being sick in a corner, tradition which can be traced back to Pieter Breughel the elder in the midd sixteenth century, and which remained deliriously popular everywhere and all times during the 18th, but these are just the kind of pictures that are mo likely to fail in their response to inflation. *Passe pour* the Breughel family, b not their later Flemish and Dutch followers. David Teniers the Elder, th favourite painter in the last years of the court of Louis XIV, has fared the wor of them all. Among the Dutchmen Isaac van Ostade is better esteemed than h brother Adriaen, having lived a short life and produced much less. But bot brothers made a poor market showing in the 1960s. A hundred years earli the 18th century affection for all this picturesque squalor could still assert itse In 1861 the Earl of Dudley paid the equivalent of £41,000 for a kitchen interi by Adriaen van Ostade.

ADRIAEN VAN OSTADE. 1610–1685

|  |  | £ |
|---|---|---|
| 1961 | S. Village scene, peasants playing bowls, $16\frac{3}{4} \times 20$ | 6,800 |
| 1962 | Lempertz. Cologne. Peasants beside an inn, 1665, $15\frac{3}{4} \times 17\frac{1}{4}$, DM26,000+tax | 2,665 |
| 1963 | Heldring. S. Landscape with oaktree, $13\frac{3}{4} \times 19$ | 8,500 |
| 1965 | C. An old peasant | 3,150 |
|  | Spencer Churchill. C. Boors merrymaking, $10 \times 12\frac{1}{4}$ | 1,365 |
| 1966 | Cook Trust. C. Three musicians, roundel, $8\frac{3}{4}$ diam. | 1,890 |
| 1968 | C. Three boors playing backgammon at an inn, $9\frac{1}{2} \times 8\frac{3}{4}$ | 3,675 |

AAC VAN OSTADE. 1621–1649 £

63 S. Peasants outside a cottage, 1649, 19×15½. Bought by Baron Thyssen 13,000

65 Adda, Paris. Winter landscape, 1644, 20×28½ 7,180

66 Dunkels. S. Women selling fruit by a cottage, 24×18¾ 4,200

Mangold. S. White horse drawing sledge, 1644, 25¼×34¾ (ex Munich Pinakotek) 16,000

67 Kingham Hill Trust. S. Landscape with barn, 39×51½ 3,400

68 Paris. Scène de patinage, 16×24, FN95,000+tax 8,380

## JEAN BAPTISTE OUDRY. (*See* French School, 18th century)

## SAMUEL PALMER. 1805–1881

e rediscovery of the early works of Samuel Palmer as a kind of William ake without tears dates from the early 1920s. As a literary man's market lmer's work rose only mildly and then slumped badly during the thirties and rties. The 1960s introduced a new order of values but mainly for Palmer's ort 'first Shoreham period', 1828–31, of which only seven completed works ched the salerooms in the course of the decade.

£

60 Eardley Knolles. S. The weald of Kent, monochrome gouache, 7½×10½, *c.* 1830 6,000

61 S. The evening star, 1825, oils, 9×11 (see 1964) 5,200

Monastery near Naples, wc, 1849 1,300

Llyn Gwynned, 1843, wc 1,700

62 S. Bridge at Shoreham, 1881, pen and wash, 8¾×10¾ 1,000

62 The bellman, monochrome gouache, 1828, 6¾×9½ 3,800

Tintern Abbey, pencil (£6 16*s.* 6*d.* in 1928) 1,600

63 Pardoe. S. Cow lodge and mossy roof, pen and wc, *c.* 1828, 10×14½ 7,200

64 S. Landscape, North Wales, 1835, pen and wash, 17×20½ 2,500

Hewitt. S. The evening star, oils, *c.* 1825, 9×11 (see 1961) 4,800

S. Opening the sheepfold, wc, 5⅝×8¼ 1,000

65 S. The rescued fisherman, 1861, 12¾×17¼, wc 600

Valancourt and Emile at the chateau le Blanc, wc, 19×27½ 1,050

7 Bell. S. The corn at twilight, Shoreham, 1831, 5¾×6½, sepia gouache 5,800

Pardoe. S. View over Shoreham, pen and wash, 2¾×4¼ 880

Three studies of the rising moon on one sheet, 7½×4½ 750

| | | £ |
|---|---|---|
| 1967 | Westwood. S. Waterfall near Dolgelly, wc, 1835, 18½×14¾ | 1,300 |
| | S. Rugged landscape, 1835, wc bodycolour, 14¾×18½ | 320 |
| 1968 | S. Head of George Richmond, pencil and wash, 1827, 5×4 | 1,300 |
| 1969 | Edmiston, Glasgow. The golden valley, watercolour gouache, 1831, 5×6½ | 14,000 |
| | The deserted villa, evening, Italy, 1845 | 2,600 |
| | Russell. S. Tintern Abbey at sunset, wc bodycolour, 1861, 12¾×27¼ | 4,600 |
| | de Poix. S. 'Will o' the wisp', cattle crossing stream, wc heightened with white, very late work, 4½×8½ | 1,400 |
| | S. Emily and Valancourt at the Chateau le Blanc (not the 1965 version), wc heightened, 19¾×27¾ | 2,400 |
| | Beausire. S. View from Rook's Hill, Kent, 1835, wc, heightened with white, 20×16 | 3,200 |
| | Coast scene, N. Devon, c. 1835, wc and pencil, 10×14½ | 1,300 |
| | Trees at Reigate, wc bodycolour, 10¼×14¾ | 1,300 |
| 1970 | At Church Hall, Woodbridge. Shepherds with flock, full moon, monochrome gouache, 1831 | 9,400 |

## FRANCESCO MAZZOLA
### called Il Parmigianino. 1504–1540

A collectors' substitute for Correggio at the beginning of the 19th centu and now on the way to recovery in common with the mannerist generation Italian painters. The prices give no indication of the extreme rarity of Parm gianino's work.

| | | £ |
|---|---|---|
| 1965 | Spencer Churchill. C. Holy family, 9¾×11½ (bought for same price at D. of Devonshire's sale, 1958) | 2,205 |
| | Cook Trust. C. Riposo, 14×17 (£112 7s. in 1830) | 19,950 |
| 1969 | C. (Unattributed but possibly Parmigianino school), Holy Family with three figures, 66½×30½ | 6,300 |

### DRAWINGS

| | | |
|---|---|---|
| 1959 | Earl of Northampton. S. Ganymede at the feast of the Gods, pen and wash | 2,625 |
| 1967 | Burnett. S. Sheet of drapery studies, pen, 7¼×5½ | 1,650 |
| | Holy family, red chalk, 7¼×4½ | 1,150 |
| 1969 | S. Lion, red chalk, 3×4¼ | 2,000 |
| | Crayfish, grey-wash, heightened with white, 3×5½ | 3,800 |
| | Death of Dido, red chalk, 4×6 | 5,600 |

## JEAN BAPTISTE PATER. 1696–1736

he list has been taken back to 1900 for reasons already explained under the ading, *Nattier*. It seems pretty incredible that Jules Bache should have paid e present equivalent of £165,000 for a *Fête champêtre* in 1926, but I think that the Gimpel's journal is to be relied on. Some return of homage to Lancret d Pater may now be discerned, but one could not have found a quieter and s crowded spot than the room where all these *Fêtes champêtres* were displayed Burlington House in the winter of 1967.

| | | | £ |
|---|---|---|---|
| 01 | Bought by Ernest Crosnier, Paris, from R. Gimpel, a pair of fêtes champêtres, Rustic Pleasures and the Bath, | 2 for | 8,000 |
| 03 | Reginald Vaile. C. Pleasures of the country | | 2,100 |
| 08 | Henri Saye. Paris. Conversation galante | | 3,960 |
| 06 | Bought by Benjamin Altman, N.Y. from R. Gimpel, a large pair of fêtes champêtres | 2 for | 9,250 |
| 07 | Sedelmeyer. Paris. Fiançailles dans le parc | | 3,200 |
| 10 | C. A pair of fêtes champêtres | 2 for | 2,782 10s. |
| 13 | Murray Scott. C. Fête champêtre | | 2,415 |
| 19 | C. Fête champêtre | | 3,835 |
| | Crowning of a shepherd (sold by R. Gimpel) | | 3,250 |
| 23 | Sold to Berwind, N.Y. by Wildenstein, a pair of large fêtes champêtres | | 13,000 |
| 26 | Bought by Jules Bache, the Earl of Carnarvon's fête champêtre, according to R. Gimpel, $160,000, then worth | | 32,940 |
| 33 | Goldschmidt-Rothschild, Berlin. Company in a park | | 846 |
| | Réunion champêtre | | 1,068 |
| 43 | Sir Berkeley Sheffield. C. Pair of fêtes | 2 for | 2,730 |
| 51 | Digby. S. The same pair | 2 for | 4,200 |
| 50 | Stehli. N.Y. L'escarpolette | | 3,570 |
| 55 | Paris. Two pairs of military encampments, each pair | | 7,400 |
| | Vagliano. C. The Swing and the Dance (£808 10s., 1895) | 2 for | 14,700 |
| 59 | Llangattock. C. Bathing nymphs | | 5,040 |
| 61 | Snapper. S. Le bain (ex Rodolfe Kann) | | 16,500 |
| 52 | S. Elegant company in a park (ex Thyssen coll.) | | 7,800 |
| 56 | Pauncefort Duncombe. C. Fête champêtre, 50×38½ | | 14,700 |
| | Companion-piece, nymphs in landscape, same size | | 7,350 |
| 67 | S. La chasse chinoise, 21¾×17¾ | | 11,000 |
| | Pair of fêtes champêtres, 16¼×21½ | 2 for | 7,000 |
| | Glidden. N.Y. Seated man, drawing in red chalk, 6¾×5, $2,950 | | 1,025 |
| 68 | Paris. La bonne aventure and le chemin au bord de la rivière, each 13¾×17¾, FN240,000+tax | 2 for | 22,220 |
| | S. Fête champêtre, (ex Maurice de Rothschild and Lord Rosebery), 28½×35 | | 52,000 |

JOACHIM PATINIR.  (*See* Flemish School, before 1550)


MAX PECHSTEIN.  (*See* German School, 20th century)


PIETRO PERUGINO.  (*See* Italian School, central)


### PABLO PICASSO.  1881–

In the following list there are 60 works at £20,000 and over. Betweeen the years 1958 and 1969, 17 of them exceeded £50,000 and three of them £100,000. No other painter, belonging exclusively to this century, stands comparison and only Cézanne, Degas, Monet and Renoir in the last century. But the list conveys nothing like the whole picture. Early in 1969 it was reported that the Museum of Modern Art, New York, had acquired the Gertrude Stein collection. The price was 6 million dollars (2½ million Sterling). There were 47 pictures, of which 38 were by Picasso. Thus the average price of each single work was £53,000. Reduced to life-size, namely £6,625 in the gold sovereigns of 1914, it meant that every item in this modish assembly was valued as high as a lesser Titian or Rembrandt and several times as much as the average valuation in 1914 of all the old masters in the Louvre or National Gallery.

In the face of figures that are quite vertiginous it is essential to keep one head. In the first place it has to be realized that among the small band of pioneers of the modern movement in painting before the First World War Picasso alone succeeded in working as well as living into the 1960s. In the 1920s, when Picasso was a middle-aged and already highly esteemed painter, £800 to £1,000 for a single canvas was still the high water mark of success. But in the 1960s, when Picasso was a vigorous octogenarian, the world thought nothing of Pop singers who became millionaires before they were twenty, of millions of dollars paid for film rights on a single trivial work of fiction. It was obvious that some figure in the painting world must attract some of the enormous rewards of personal publicity which were to be got from this horrifying new era of telecommunication. Who else could it be but Picasso?

In the second place it has to be realized that within the extremely wide range of his prices in the 1960s Picasso offered almost every kind of commodity and that the highest prices of all were paid for two completely representational pictures, *Maternité au bord de la mer* at £190,000 and *Paysage à Gozol* at about £180,000, pictures painted at the ages of 21 and 25. The first is so little a work of the present age that its inspiration seems to have been one of Daumier's last and worst lithographs, *Epouvantée de l'héritage*, published at the beginning of 1871 before the capitulation of Paris. It must, however, be admitted that prices of £125,000, £98,000 and £94,000 have been paid for Picasso work which are almost completely abstract. All three were pioneer exercises

Cubism, for which museum directors feel highly compulsive urges, so much so that an early Cubist Braque, very like the £125,000 *Point de la Cité*, made almost as much a good three years earlier. Cubism is very much a special case.

At public auction no other abstract Picasso got beyond £60,000 before 1970. As to Picassos, painted in the 1950s and 1960s, the period of monsters, one, dated 1960, cost the Fort Worth Museum £37,500. In general they made from £12,000 to £40,385, hardly more than the coloured pen drawings of Picasso's adolescence. The preference may have been determined by Picasso himself, when he advised the public that as a boy he could draw like Raphael. So, at £20,000 to £32,000 the boyhood drawings made Raphael prices.

The question abides; can these values stand up to all the changes in aesthetic fashion which even a quite short passage of time may bring about. The whole experience of the past suggests that there is no reason under heaven why a collection of 50 Picassos, which is sold for two millions, should not fall in value (though not of course in actual prices) to the equivalent of two thousands. But even if this should happen, not much in the way of the punishment for *hubris* will be seen falling on the heads of the publicity-maniacs, for the ultimate destination of almost everything in the following list is a public institution. Only the scraps that are left may prove vulnerable.

| | | £ |
|---|---|---|
| 1923 | Séquestre Kahnweiler. Paris. 132 paintings and drawings, sold over the previous two years, made a total according to Maurice Rheims of £1,400 | |
| | Séquestre Uhde. Paris. Joueuse de mandoline (Cubist), 24,500 francs+tax | 422 |
| | Buste de femme | 180 |
| 1924 | Exhibition at Paul Rosenberg's. 12 pictures priced at £1,250 each (Gimpel) | |
| 1926 | Paris. Femme en chemise, 87,500 francs+tax at 152 to £ | 840 |
| 1930 | Bought by Toledo Museum. The blind man (gouache) $4,250 | 880 |
| | 'It is hard to find $20,000 (£4,000) even for the most beautiful Picasso in New York'—René Gimpel | |
| 1933 | Lederlin. Paris. Longchamps, 21×27, 27,500 francs+tax | 473 |
| 1934 | Flowerpiece, 1901, bought by Tate Gallery | 700 |
| 1937 | Hollender and Bernheimer. C. Portrait of a woman | 157 10s. |
| | Still life, semi-abstract, bought in | 105 |
| 1945 | Thanhauser. N.Y. Les amants, 1900, $4,250 | 1,060 |
| | Chrysler. N.Y. Buste de femme, pre-cubist, 1906, $3,000 | 750 |
| 1946 | N.Y. Verre d'absinthe, oils, 15×12, 1912, $2,310 | 578 |
| 1947 | N.Y. Bottles, semi-abstract, $1,275 | 319 |
| | Abstract composition, $1,600 | 400 |

£

| | | | £ |
|---|---|---|---|
| 1948 | N.Y. Les fugitifs, $4,425 | | 1,107 |
| 1949 | N.Y. La gommeuse, $31 \times 20\frac{3}{4}$ (see 1960), $5,000 | | 1,260 |
| | Chrysler, N.Y. L'homme à la sucette, $26\frac{1}{2} \times 17\frac{1}{2}$ | | 1,825 |
| | Nu gris, $42 \times 29$, $4,500 (at 2·80 to the £) | | 1,607 |
| 1950 | Bock, Paris. La loge, gouache, 1902, $12\frac{1}{2} \times 16$, 1·48 million francs+tax | | 1,816 |
| 1952 | de Harme, Paris. Guitare, 1912, $26\frac{1}{2} \times 19\frac{1}{4}$, 1·6 million francs+tax | | 1,917 |
| 1953 | Girardin. Paris. Sur la plage, $11\frac{1}{2} \times 14\frac{3}{4}$, 2·35 million francs+tax | | 2,375 |
| | Turner. S. La Niçoise, portrait de Mme Helluard | | 1,250 |
| 1954 | Rees Jeffreys. S. The bull fight | | 2,835 |
| 1956 | Alleged price paid by Nelson Rockefeller for an early Cubist girl with mandoline | | (35,000) |
| 1957 | Lurcy. N.Y. Interior, semi-abstract | | 3,215 |
| 1958 | Cronyn. N.Y. Woman with blue stockings, 1907 | | 7,500 |
| | Josephine Stein. S. Woman in armchair (see 1960) | | 9,500 |
| | Regnault, Amsterdam. Interior, semi-abstract, 1934 | | 13,000 |
| | Kirkeby. N.Y. Madonna and child, early realistic work, $152,000 | | 54,285 |
| 1959 | Val Rubin. S. La belle Hollandaise, 1905 (bought since 1945 for £6,000), $30\frac{3}{4} \times 26\frac{1}{2}$. Queensland Gallery | | 55,000 |
| | S. Bal de Mardi Gras, 10 ft stage design | | 6,500 |
| 1960 | Sarlie. S. Crouching woman, $25\frac{1}{4} \times 19\frac{3}{4}$ | | 48,000 |
| | La Gommeuse (£1,260 in 1949), 1901, $32 \times 21\frac{1}{2}$ | | 30,000 |
| | Woman in armchair (£9,500 in 1958), 1909, $32 \times 25$ | | 30,000 |
| | Man with red glove, 1938, $26 \times 17\frac{1}{4}$ | | 26,000 |
| | Still life with candle, 1944, $25\frac{3}{4} \times 36\frac{1}{4}$ | | 17,000 |
| 1961 | Church. N.Y. Fernand, cubist work, 1912, $75,000 | | 26,780 |
| 1961 | Somerset Maugham. S. La Grecque, 1924, $71\frac{3}{4} \times 29$ | | 30,000 |
| | Death of Harlequin, 1905, painted both sides, $23 \times 37\frac{1}{2}$ | | 80,000 |
| | Power. S. Bathers, 1907 | | 29,000 |
| 1963 | Wolf. S. Three women, outline painting, classicist style | | 14,000 |
| | S. Still life with candle, 1944 | | 14,000 |
| | Tishman. S. Cubist still life, le compôtier, 1910, $21 \times 17\frac{3}{4}$ | | 18,500 |
| | Zimet. S. Girl's head, 1901, student work | | 32,000 |
| | La toilette, $8 \times 5$, 1922 | | 13,000 |
| | N.Y. Nu assis, 1908, $28\frac{1}{2} \times 23\frac{1}{2}$, $100,000 | | 35,714 |
| 1964 | Bloch. Paris. Lemon and tumbler, 1944, $10\frac{3}{4} \times 8\frac{3}{4}$ | | 34,775 |
| | Walter Ross, N.Y. Glass, bouquet, guitar and bottles, $117,500 | | 41,960 |
| | S. Woman in a chair, 1960 | | 19,000 |
| | Abstraction dated 1960 | | 23,000 |

| | | £ |
|---|---|---|
| 965 | Thanhauser Gallery, N.Y. Private sale to Bavarian state government, portrait of Mme Chamier, 1903 | 90,000 |
| | Bought from the painter by the Tate Gallery, London, Three Dancers, 1925, over 7 ft | 60,000 |
| 965 | Zadok. S. Woman in an armchair, 1937 | 50,000 |
| | Lefèvre. Paris. Demoiselle d'Avignon, 1907, 26×23 FN350,000+tax | 28,100 |
| | Femme dormant, 1908, 32½×26, FN620,000+tax | 49,780 |
| | Nature morte au crâne de boeuf, 52×38, FN650,000+ tax | 52,200 |
| | Ma Jolie, 1914, 18×16, FN400,000+tax | 32,117 |
| | Dotremont. N.Y. Femme au corsage bleu, 1941, 46×35 | 41,020 |
| | Compôtier et guitare, 1927, 38×51 | 25,100 |
| | N.Y. Grande tête de femme, 1962, 39½×32 | 16,070 |
| | Nu accroupi, 1959, 57×44½ | 15,175 |
| 966 | Thompson. N.Y. Femme à la mandoline, 1908, 39× 31½, $100,000 | 35,850 |
| | Trois baigneuses, 1923, 31½×39, $115,000 | 41,360 |
| | Portrait with two noses, 1939, 23½×17½, $52,500 | 18,750 |
| | Woman with a flower, 1932, 63¾×51¼, $92,000 | 33,600 |
| | Still life, 1943, 31½×50¾, $75,000 | 26,965 |
| | Sykes. S. Flowers in a pitcher, 1901, oils, 19¼×15½ | 15,900 |
| | Helena Rubinstein. N.Y. Inspiration (Tapestry), 76×66 | 7,000 |
| | Dorsky. C. Femme assise, Vallauris, 1953, 39½×32, bought in | 13,650 |
| 967 | S. Maternité au bord de la mer (période bleue) Barcelona, 1902, 32¾×23½, $532,000 | 190,000 |
| | Les soles, 1940, semi-abstract, 23½×36¼ | 15,500 |
| | Chester Beatty. S. Course de taureaux, Barcelona, pastel, 1900 (aged 19), 13¾×15½ | 42,000 |
| | Municipality of Florence. N.Y. Femme couchée lisant, 1960, 51×76¾, $105,000. Fort Worth Museum | 37,500 |
| | Lefèvre. Paris. Playing card, glass and bottle, 1916, 10¾×14, FN185,000+tax | 17,000 |
| | C. Au café, pastel, c. 1900, 18×11½. Bought in at | 28,350 |
| | Geller. C. Homme à la lampe, 1898 (aged 17), 39½×25½ | 21,000 |
| | N.Y. Le marin, 1956, 53×51, $42,500 | 15,160 |
| 967 | N.Y. La commode chinoise, 1953, 58×45, $37,500 | 13,393 |
| | Paris. Nature morte, 1919, 14×10¾, FN132,000+tax | 12,325 |
| 968 | N.Y. Woman in armchair playing guitar, abstract, 6×5, $23,000 | 9,600 |
| | Papazoff. N.Y. Femme nue sur un lit, 14¼×14¼ | 30,214 |
| | Verre et dos de carte-à-jouer, 1914, 9¾×6¼, $40,000 | 16,500 |
| | L'oiseau blessé, 1912, 18¼×11, $57,000 | 23,750 |
| | Paris. L'étreinte, lovers embracing, 1905, dedicated to | |

£

| 1968 | Guillaume Apollinaire, FN1,000,000+tax | 93,220 |

1968  Guillaume Apollinaire, FN1,000,000+tax  93,220
       L'homme à la guitare, cubist, 1918, FN512,000+tax 47,845
       Granz.  S.  Le point de la cité, cubist abstraction, almost
       monochrome, 1912, oval, 35½×28  125,000
       Ma jolie, abstraction, 1914, oils, sand, saw-dust, glass beads,
           etc., 20¼×26½  98,000
           Nature morte dans un paysage, 24×29½  58,000
           Nature morte au crâne de mouton, 1939, 19½×23½  13,000
           La lampe et les cerises, 1945, 28¾×29¼  30,500
       25 Picassos made £546,500
       Stralem.  S.  L'Arlésienne, 1912, 30×21¾, semi-abstract  45,000
       S.  Femme couchée au chat, 1964, 44½×76, semi-abstract  28,000
           Le nu au bas, 1901, 26¼×20½  79,000
       Diaghilev-de Basil Foundation.  S.  Curtain after Picasso
       for The Three Cornered Hat, 1924, painted area 22 ft 3 in.×
       27 ft 8 in.  69,000
       Brandeis University.  N.Y.  Paysage de Gozol, fauve
       style, 1906, 27½×39, $430,000  159,167
1969  S. (Tokyo).  Tête d'homme, 1964, 18½×14½, 10 million
       yen  11,650
           Verre et compôtier, 1922, 10¾×14, 14 million yen  15,330
       C. (Geneva).  Guéridon devant une fenêtre ouverte, 1919
       13¾×9½, FS280,000+5% tax  28,340
           L'artiste et sa modèle, 38¼×51¾, 1963, FS400,000+
           tax  40,385
       Finarte.  Milan.  La dame en noir, 26×18½, L32 million+
       tax  24,530
       Painter and model, 36¾×29¼, L26 million+tax  about  20,000
       Paris.  Nature morte aux fleurs, 1941, 36¾×29, FN280,000
       +tax  26,000
1969  Paris.  La bouteille de rhum, cubist, 1911, FN1,113,000+
       tax  about  94,000
       C.  Tête d'homme barbu, 1965, 24×19¾.  Bought in  12,075

### DRAWINGS, WATERCOLOURS AND PRINTS

1936  Hollender and Bernheimer.  C.  Dancers, pen and ink  60 16s
1940  Eumorphopoulos.  S.  Children, wc  210
1941  Red Cross sale.  C.  Three Graces, pen and ink  73 10s
1950  Bock.  Paris.  La loge, wc gouache, 1902, 12½×16,
       750,000 old francs+tax  1,816
1954  Rees Jeffreys.  S.  The Sibyl, pen and wash  4,410
1956  Paris.  The dove, pen and wash, nearly 30 in. wide,
       FN150,000+tax  1,700

| | | £ |
|---|---|---|
| 1959 | S. L'arlequin du Cirque Medrano, pen and wc gouache, 11¾×3¼ | 12,000 |
| 1960 | Paris. Café group, Barcelona, 1899, carcoal (at age of 18) FN52,000+tax | 4,607 |
| 1962 | Woolworth. N.Y. Drawing signed P. Ruiz, 1900, $19,000 | 6,850 |
| 1963 | Aldrich. N.Y. The pipes of Pan, pencil and chalk, $18,000 | 6,425 |
| 1965 | Lefèvre. Paris. Tête de femme rouge, pen and ink, touched with gouache, 1906, 25×19, FN280,000+tax | 22,700 |
| 1966 | Rubinstein. N.Y. Boy's head, 1906, 14×8½, wc gouache, $40,200 | 14,360 |
| | Els Quatre Gats, Barcelona, 1897, charcoal, 16¼×11 (aged 16) | 14,360 |
| 1967 | Lefèvre. Paris. Le compôtier, 1909, charcoal, 24¾×18½, FN104,000+tax | 9,672 |
| 1968 | Granz S. Homme et femme, charcoal and pastel, 1921, 40½×28 | 30,000 |
| 1969 | S. 'Chambre 22', pen and wc, 1904, 21½×17¾ £(303 in 1950) | 32,000 |
| | Paris. The Catalan poet, Maséras, Barcelona, 1899 (aged 18), FN 295,000+tax. Charcoal drawing | 27,000 |
| 1969 | S. Verre, as de tréfles et poire coupée, c. 1914, collage and gouache, 13×7¾ | 21,000 |
| | N.Y. Suite of 100 etchings made for Ambroise Vollard 1930–37, on large paper including several proofs, $140,000 | 100 for 58,333 |
| | Suite of 45 coloured lino-cuts made since 1945, $100,000 | 45 for 41,670 |
| | Les saltimbanques, suite of 12 drypoints and etchings pre-1912, $63,000 | 12 for 26,250 |
| | S. Femme assise dans un fauteuil, pen and wc, 1914, 10½×7½ | 8,500 |
| | C. (Geneva). Groupe de saltimbanques, pen and wc, 1904, 14¾×10¼, FS260,000+tax of 5% | 26,250 |

## BONAVENTURA PIETERS. (*See* Dutch School)


## CAMILLE PISSARRO. 1831–1903

From the ensuing list it will be seen that Pissarro's paintings did not achieve four-figure prices before the middle 1920s, when Degas, Manet, Monet and Renoir had already reached five figure prices on occasion. A Pissarro which passed the £100,000 mark in 1968 suggested that the disparity had been levelled off till it was seen what an important Monet and a less important Renoir could be worth. Even at $260,000 Pissarro had barely exceeded his relative status. However, the history of a medium quality Pissarro should help to dispel the illusion that Impressionist pictures, bought in the 1920s, have advanced much more than old masters. *Le ruisseau à Osny*, bought in 1922 for £560, was sold in 1964 for £27,300 and in 1968 for £38,542. It sounds formidable but in 1922 one could have bought Flemish paintings of the Breughel school or Italian paintings by some of the eclectic baroque masters for £20 to £30, which today could be worth 500 to 700 times as much—and all this without being the least bit adventurous.

|      |                                                                                                   | £          |
|------|---------------------------------------------------------------------------------------------------|------------|
| 1874 | Paris.  Barrage sur l'Oise                                                                         | 38         |
| 1888 | Laroux.  Paris.  Village sous neige                                                                | 24         |
| 1890 | May.  Paris.  Route à Roquancourt                                                                  | 56         |
| 1894 | Nunés.  Paris.  Hiver                                                                              | 174        |
| 1899 | Alfred Sisley.  Paris.  Tuileries in winter                                                        | 192        |
| 1900 | Guasco.  Paris.  River bank                                                                        | 328        |
| 1912 | Rouart.  Paris.  Five landscapes made a total of 23,600 francs+tax, equivalent to £1,038      average | 207        |
| 1922 | Bought by J. Boulton.  La berge à St Mammès, 1884 (£13,360, 1965)                                  | 500        |
|      | Brook at Osny,1883 (£27,300, in 1965, £38,542 in 1968)                                             | 560        |
| 1924 | B. C. Smith.  C.  Le Pont-Neuf, 1901                                                               | 141 15s.   |
| 1925 | Bought by Tate Gallery, Courtauld Fund.  Boulevard des Italiens                                    | 1,575      |
| 1927 | Murray.  C.  Bords de la Vionne.  National Gallery, Melbourne                                      | 1,102 10s. |
| 1933 | Bought by Tate Gallery, Courtauld fund.  The Louvre under snow                                     | 1,000      |
| 1937 | Bought by W. A. Cargill.  The Thames at Charing Cross Bridge (£47,000 in 1963)                     | 2,600      |
| 1938 | Albert Pra.  Paris.  La causette, 77,000 francs at 125 to the £+tax                                | 748        |
| 1946 | Van Horne.  N.Y.  Old Chelsea Bridge, 1890                                                         | 1,578      |
| 1947 | Lady Kent.  S.  Village Street                                                                     | 1,250      |
| 1950 | N.Y.  Paysan à la Chesne                                                                           | 1,322      |
|      | La Seine à Paris                                                                                   | 1,322      |
| 1951 | C.  Winter scene                                                                                   | 567        |
| 1952 | N.Y.  La vigne                                                                                     | 2,500      |
|      | Poirier en fleurs                                                                                  | 2,637      |
| 1953 | Paris.  Le jardin de l'hotel, 26×32                                                                | 6,070      |
|      | N.Y.  Jardins du Louvre, 1899, 28½×35½ (see 1962)                                                  | 5,000      |
| 1954 | Rees Jeffreys.  S.  Montfoucault                                                                   | 2,940      |
| 1955 | Sir E. Cripps.  C.  Orchard                                                                        | 3,990      |

|      |                                                                                                  | £      |
|------|--------------------------------------------------------------------------------------------------|--------|
| 1957 | S. Bassin des Tuileries                                                                           | 5,500  |
|      | Weinberg. S. Bank Holiday at Kew, $17\frac{3}{4} \times 21\frac{1}{4}$                            | 9,000  |
|      | Orovida Pissarro. S. Jardin à Pontoise, $17\frac{3}{4} \times 21\frac{1}{2}$                      | 5,600  |
|      | Lurcy. N.Y. Pont-Neuf (compare very similar picture, 1968)                                        | 20,360 |
|      | Country road                                                                                      | 6,430  |
| 1958 | N.Y. Route d'Auvers                                                                               | 23,325 |
|      | Henry Heinz, N.Y. Après-midi, Rouen                                                               | 13,650 |
| 1959 | S. Village à travers les arbres, 1868, $21\frac{1}{4} \times 17\frac{1}{4}$                       | 12,000 |
|      | Soleil couchant à Moret                                                                           | 10,500 |
|      | Quarry at Pontoise                                                                                | 4,200  |
|      | Hugh Lane Bequest. Marly, 1873 (bought before 1912 for about £300). Valued for insurance at       | 14,000 |
| 1960 | Gladys Robinson. N.Y. Avant-port de Dieppe                                                        | 12,500 |
| 1961 | Paris. Sunset landscape                                                                           | 6,850  |
| 1962 | Woolworth. N.Y. The Louvre, winter sunshine                                                       | 25,000 |
|      | Somerset Maugham. S. Snow at Louveciennes, 1871, $21\frac{1}{4} \times 17\frac{1}{2}$             | 26,000 |
|      | Quai St Sever, Rouen, 1896, $28\frac{3}{4} \times 39$                                             | 28,000 |
|      | Metcalfe. S. Gardens at the Louvre (see 1953)                                                     | 18,000 |
| 1963 | Cargill. S. The Thames at Charing Cross bridge, (£2,600 in 1937) $23 \times 36$                   | 47,000 |
|      | St Stephens Church, lower Norwood, 1870, $16\frac{3}{4} \times 20\frac{3}{4}$                     | 27,000 |
|      | Zimet. S. Poplars at Eragny, 1899, $28\frac{3}{4} \times 36$                                      | 25,000 |
| 1964 | S. Road and level crossing, Pontoise, 1873, $25 \times 32$                                        | 32,000 |
|      | Varangeville, 1899, $25 \times 21$                                                                | 20,000 |
|      | Combemarle. C. La route d'Osny à Pontoise, 1872                                                   | 36,750 |
|      | River landscape                                                                                   | 25,200 |
|      | Flowerpiece                                                                                       | 35,700 |
| 1965 | S. June Morning, 1873                                                                             | 28,000 |
| 1965 | Motte, Geneva. Les Laveuses à Eragny, FS400,000+tax                                               | 38,350 |
|      | Paris. Rocky landscape, Montfoucault, $26 \times 36\frac{3}{4}$, FN385,000+tax                    | 30,560 |
|      | Boulton. C. Brook at Osny, 1883 (£560 in 1922), $25\frac{1}{2} \times 21$ (see also 1968)         | 27,300 |
|      | C. La sente des poilleux, Pontoise, 1878, $23\frac{3}{4} \times 23\frac{3}{4}$                    | 17,850 |
| 1966 | S. Snow scene, Louveciennes, 1872, $18 \times 21\frac{3}{4}$                                      | 28,000 |
|      | Pool at Montfoucault, 1875, $23\frac{1}{2} \times 28\frac{3}{4}$                                  | 21,000 |
|      | Rousing. S. Route de Versailles, snowscape, 1872, $12\frac{1}{2} \times 18$                       | 84,000 |
|      | S. Le Loing à Moret, 1902, $21\frac{1}{4} \times 25\frac{1}{2}$                                   | 20,000 |
|      | La récolte des poix, gouache, 1887 (£12), $20\frac{1}{2} \times 25\frac{1}{2}$                    | 14,500 |
|      | Deux femmes cousant, 1902, $14\frac{1}{2} \times 17\frac{1}{4}$                                   | 16,800 |
|      | C. Coin de Louveciennes, 1870, $18\frac{1}{2} \times 15\frac{3}{4}$                               | 17,850 |

| | | £ |
|---|---|---|
| 1966 | Mercier. S. L'hermitage, environs de Pontoise, 1877, 26×21½ | 29,000 |
| | Hyer. S. L'hiver à Montfoucault, 1875, 45×43¼ | 37,000 |
| 1967 | Cummings. S. Inondation, Eragny, 1892, 21¼×26 | 18,500 |
| | Chester Beatty. S. La mare à Ennery, 1874, 21×25¼ | 32,000 |
| | La prairie de Moret, 1901, 21×25¼ | 19,000 |
| | S. Vue de Berneval, 1900, 28½×35 | 24,000 |
| | Les côteaux de Gisors, 1885, 17¾×21½ | 10,500 |
| | Echague. N.Y. Coin de village, 1863, 15¼×20½, $60,000 | 21,428 |
| | Route à Pontoise, 23¾×21½ | 20,535 |
| | Zagayski, N.Y. Statue d'Henri IV, 1901, 18×15¼ (see 1969), $32,500 | 11,614 |
| | Paris. Paysage sous bois à Pontoise, 1865, 21½×26, FN210,000+tax | 16,800 |
| | Motte, Geneva. Bassin des Tuileries, 1900, 21½×26, FS223,000+tax | 21,500 |
| 1968 | Boise. S. La mare aux canards à Montfoucault, 1875, 18×21½ | 28,000 |
| | Bluestein. N.Y. La côte de Chou à Pontoise, 1882, 32×25½, $92,500 | 38,542 |
| | C. Lever de soleil à Rouen, 1898, 25½×32 | 68,250 |
| | Kawasaki. S. Bords de l'Oise à Auvers, 1878, 21×25 | 24,000 |
| | Brandeis University. N.Y. Paysage à l'Hermitage, Pontoise, 1874, 23¾×28¾, $145,000 | 60,416 |
| | Jardin des Tuileries, matinée de Printemps, 1899, 28¾×36½, $260,000 | 108,333 |
| | Portail de l'église St Jacques, Dieppe, 1901, 30½×25½, $7,200 | 57,167 |
| | N.Y. Bouquet de fleurs, 1877, 28×23, $95,000 | 39,583 |
| | Le Pont-Neuf, Paris, 19½×25¾, $210,000 | 87,500 |
| | S. Fenaison à Eragny, 1901, 18¼×23 | 21,000 |
| | Thomas Pissarro. S. Marché au blé, 1884, 18½×22¾ | 23,000 |
| | S. Poilaille, Pontoise, and Laveuses, Pontoise, canvas painted on both sides, 12½×15¾ | 26,000 |
| | N.Y. Le roisseau à Osny, 1883, 25½×21¼, (£560 in 1922, £27,300 in 1965), $92,500 | 38,542 |
| | N.Y. Vue d'Eragny, 1895, 21¾×25¾, unfinished oil sketch, $33,000 | 13,784 |
| | Paris. Sunset at Eragny, FN260,000+tax | 24,286 |
| | Motte, Geneva, La route d'Ennery, 21½×26, FS406,000 +tax | 45,300 |
| 1969 | S. Paysans et meules de foin, 1878, 21¼×25½ | 46,000 |
| | C. Vue de Pontoise, 1873, 20¾×31¾ | 89,250 |

£

| | | | |
|---|---|---|---|
| 1969 | S. | Paysage à Valeremeil, *c.* 1878, 14½×21 | 20,000 |
| | Kaplan. N.Y. Statue d'Henri IV, 1901, 18×15¾ ($32,500 in 1967), $41,000 | | 17,230 |
| | S. | La recolte des pommes de terre, 1893, 18¼×21¾ | 50,000 |
| | | La moisson, 1892, 18½×20½ | 38,000 |
| | | Jeanne et Paul-Emile Pissarro jouant, 1890, 8¾×10¾ | 10,800 |
| | N.Y. | Le jardin de Pontoise, 1878, $130,000 | 54,167 |
| | Le Bas. C. (Geneva). Printemps à Pontoise, 13×18¼, FS360,000+tax | | 36,376 |
| | S. | Woman mending a stocking, gouache, 1881, 12¼×9½ | 15,500 |
| | | Remorqueurs et péniches au bord de l'Oise, 1876, 17×22, bought in | 35,000 |
| | | Le pré à Eragny, 1885, 18×21¾, bought in | 26,000 |
| | | Route de St Germain, Louveciennes, wc, 1871, 12×19¼ | 6,500 |
| 1970 | Crocker. N.Y. Place du vieux cimetière, Pontoise, 1872, 21¼×25½, $190,000 | | 79,160 |

GIOVANNI BATTISTA PITTONE.   (*See* Italian School, 18th century)

ANDREW PLIMER.   (*See* Miniature Painters)

ANTONIO POLLAIUOLO (attributed).   (*See* Italian School, central (1967))

SERGE POLIAKOFF.   (*See* Abstract Painters, Europe)

JAMES POLLARD.   (*See* Sporting Pictures)

JACKSON POLLOCK.   (See Abstract Painters, America)

LYUBOV POPOVA.   (*See* Abstract Painters, Europe)

PAUL POTTER.   1625–1659

The price of the Duke of Somerset's *Dairy farm* in 1890 was 5,800 guineas, the equivalent in 1970 of little short of £55,000. Perhaps a really good example of Paul Potter's cattle paintings would fetch more than that. The painter, for whose work Louis XVI paid more than any Rembrandt was then worth, lived only 34 years and has been rare at all times. Only three Potters were sold in the 1950s, only two in the 1960s, and even then not without murmurs of doubt.

| | | £ |
|---|---|---|
| 1963 | Paris (attributed). Horses watering by a bridge, 18×30, FN51,000+tax | 4,445 |
| 1969 | Paris. Group of dogs in a room, dated 1649, 46×59, FN200,000+tax | 18,000 |

# NICOLAS POUSSIN. 1594–1665

It is less than half a century since the best work of Poussin was barely able to reach £500. The great favourite of the early 19th century shared in the general decline of the Roman and Bolognese eclectic schools of the 17th century Guido Reni, for instance, declined even more. It is open to question whether Poussin's somewhat rigid methods of painting are so much more popular in 1970 than they were in 1920, but for many years collectors and curators alike have fallen for a form of stamp-collecting, by which the virtues of a school are less important than its rarity. In 1920 the rarity of an unpopular school was of no consequence at all, and few painters could be rarer than Poussin. No painting by Poussin reached the salerooms in the 1960s beyond a small pair of landscapes. The *Nativity*, bought by the National Gallery in 1956, seems in retrospect to have been a very low-priced picture. Its possible value in 1970 can perhaps be gauged from the last transaction in this list.

|      |                                                                                       | £       |
|------|---------------------------------------------------------------------------------------|---------|
| 1956 | Jocelyn Beauchamp. S. Nativity, National Gallery                                       | 29,000  |
| 1962 | Heathcote Amery. S. Two landscapes with figures, 25 × 31                               | 2 for 25,000 |
| 1967 | Barres. S. Antique Roman reliefs, sheet of pen and wash studies                        | 1,500   |
| 1968 | Bought by Charles Wrightsman. The companions of Rinaldo. Price reported to have been about $700,000 | 291,655 |

## MAURICE PRENDERGAST. (*See* American School, 19th–20th centuries)

## JAN PREVOST. (*See* Flemish School, before 1550

# SIR HENRY RAEBURN. 1756–1823

The market for Scottish lairdry is not what it was, though Raeburn has fallen no more than Reynolds, Romney or Lawrence from the eminence to which Duveen contrived to exalt them. The prices of the 1960s must be considered in relation to the epic transactions of the past, recorded in Volume One. The portrait of Mrs Hart, for instance, was sold in the U.S.A. in 1913 for the equivalent of £250,000. In the 1920s Duveen was prepared to give as much for the portrait of the McNab, famous as a whiskey advertisement (£50,000 in the money of the period). A hint of its present value is provided by the price in 1967 of Singleton Copley's *Earl of Eglinton in Highland dress* namely £57,750 for a picture looking still more like a whiskey advertisement. If this sounds too exalted for the list which follows, it must be explained that Raeburn had a very plain lot of sitters and was not as a rule disposed to paint them any less so.

| | | £ |
|---|---|---|
| 961 | Erickson. N.Y. Quintin McAdam as a boy, 1817, 61 × 47¼ (Highest auction price for Raeburn since 1926) | 21,428 |
| | Captain David Kinloch, R.N., 30 × 24¾ | 2,590 |
| | C. John Cunningham of Craigends, 25 × 30 | 1,785 |
| 964 | Ross Todd. S. Robert Allen of Kirkleston, 48¾ × 38¼ | 2,800 |
| | Kemsley. S. Earl of Fife, 92 × 58½ | 2,500 |
| | Marquess of Hastings and his ADC, 93 × 58½ | 2,800 |
| 965 | Colin Smith. C. Helen Duff, half-length | 4,200 |
| 967 | C. Matthew Fortescue, 50 × 40 | 2,205 |
| | Billy Rose Foundation. S. Lady Don and her grand-daughter, 48¾ × 38 | 3,000 |
| | S (at Gleneagles Hotel). Robert Hodson Gay, 49¼ × 38¾ | 1,800 |
| 968 | Menzies. S. David MacDowall-Grant, standing with bay hunter, whole length, 94 × 58½ | 7,500 |
| 969 | S (in Glasgow). Margaretta, Lady Hepburn, half-length, 48 × 40 (bought Knoedler., N.Y., 1929, $75,000 or £15,450, Harding sale, N.Y., 1941, $11,000 or £2,750). Bought in at | 7,350 |
| | Hardie. S. Mrs William Forsyth, half-length, 29 × 24 | 3,800 |
| 970 | C. Margaretta, Lady Hepburn (see 1969) bought in again at | 5,775 |

## ALLAN RAMSAY. (*See* English School, 18th century)

## RAPHAEL (RAFFAELLO SANTI). 1483–1520

The value of a firmly established Raphael Madonna today is anyone's guess. A million pounds can only be a basic figure. As to a full-sized altarpiece, a minor sovereign state, possessing such a thing, could pay off its national debt. Only one authenticated painting reached the salerooms in the 1960s, a much restored 16-inch predella panel from the *Citta di Castello Crucifixion*. It made £95,000 in 1968. Three companion-panels have been on the market in the present century, the Fenway Court *Pietà* in 1900 at £4,000, the National Gallery *Via crucis* in 1913 at the same price, and the Metropolitan Museum's *Agony in the garden* in 1922 at £7,350, all of them being in better condition than *St Jerome and Sabinianus*.

The price of the drawings is interesting because the previous highest price for Raphael was only £2,000 and paid no longer ago than 1956. But the Metropolitan Museum's *Holy Family* has ceased to be the dearest drawing ever sold. In 1968 a Rembrandt drawing made £35,000, while in 1969 Durer's *Stag Beetle* cost a private buyer £58,000.

| | | £ |
|---|---|---|
| 1963 | Fitzgerald. S. St Jerome punishing Sabinianus the heretic, predella panel, 9¾×16, formerly part of the Citta di Castello Crucifixion (National Gallery), much over-painted | 95,000 |
| | Princess Labia. S. Portrait of a papal secretary, 21×26½ (£3,255 in 1927), bought in at | 42,000 |
| 1966 | Lee of Fareham. C. Holy Family with lamb, dated 1504, 12×8½, attributed in 18th century | 4,200 |
| 1969 | Bought by Boston Fine Arts Museum, alleged portrait of Eleonora Gonzaga, *c.* 1505, 10½ in. high, said to have belonged to the Fischi family, Genoa. Authenticity hotly disputed. Reputed price 1 million dollars | 416,665 |

### DRAWINGS

| | | |
|---|---|---|
| 1960 | Rauch, Geneva. Cartoon (fragment) for the Vatican *Disputa*, bistre and gouache, 9½×17 | 2,800 |
| 1963 | Rothwell. S. Pen and ink study for the Borghese *pietà*, ex Samuel Rogers and Thomas Lawrence, bought for British Museum (with commission, £28,350) | 27,000 |
| 1964 | Rothwell. S. Madonna, Child and St John, pen and ink, 8¾×6¼ (£27 6s. in 1833, £146 in 1856), bought by Metro-politan Museum, N.Y. | 32,000 |

## ROBERT RAUSCHENBERG. (*See* Abstract Painters, American)

## ODILON REDON. 1840–1916

Rather less is paid for Odilon Redon's *symboliste* pictures, decidedly literary and crammed with poetic images, than for his flowerpieces and occasional portraits which have close links with the original impressionists, but a lower market rating. The flowerpieces multiplied in value about twenty times between 1954 and 1964.

| | | £ |
|---|---|---|
| 1942 | Reid. C. Le vase bleu (see 1964), 15½×15½ | 336 |
| 1948 | Paris. La barque, pastel, 22×18½, 120,000 francs+tax | 295 |
| 1949 | Zoubalof. Paris. Fall of Phaeton, 15×18 | 374 |
| 1951 | Archibald. N.Y. Head of Violette Heymans | 250 |
| 1952 | Amsterdam. Flowers, 29½×24 | 265 |
| 1954 | N.Y. Femme dans les fleurs, 1904, 16×12½ | 357 |
| | Bonnard, Paris. Flowers, 25½×20½ | 1,220 |
| 1955 | Stuttgart. Winged genius bearing a severed head, pastel, 21¾×10½ | 400 |
| 1957 | Weinberg. S. Flowers in stoneware jug, 1910, 19¾×23¼ | 12,000 |
| 1958 | S. Bowl of nasturtiums, 11×9 | 900 |
| | N.Y. Le vitrail, 36½×29, $4,000 | 1,408 |

£

| | | |
|---|---|---|
| 1959 | Kaplerer.  S.  Ophelia, pastel, $22\frac{3}{4} \times 19$ | 7,500 |
| | S.  Cavalier aux deux barques, $18\frac{1}{4} \times 17\frac{1}{2}$ | 3,800 |
| 1960 | Rewald.  S.  Fish, wc study | 1,700 |
| | N.Y.  Pot of geraniums, $25\frac{1}{2} \times 19\frac{3}{4}$, $15,000 | 5,354 |
| | Van Waay, Amsterdam.  Prometheus, $18\frac{1}{2} \times 11$, Hfl25,000 +tax | 2,900 |
| 1962 | N.Y.  Au Fond de la mer, $23 \times 19$, $22,000 | 7,857 |
| 1964 | Nachman.  S.  Pot of geraniums, $19\frac{3}{4} \times 12\frac{3}{4}$, 1905 | 20,500 |
| | Hutton.  S.  Pavots dans un vase bleu, $15\frac{1}{2} \times 15\frac{1}{2}$ (see 1942) | 15,500 |
| | S.  Les saintes femmes, pastel, $24 \times 20$ (see 1968) | 5,600 |
| 1965 | S.  Study of butterflies, wc, $10\frac{1}{2} \times 8$ | 2,100 |
| | Pot de geraniums, $25 \times 19$ | 16,500 |
| | La pêcheuse, pastel, $23\frac{1}{2} \times 18$ | 4,200 |
| | Cain and Abel, pastel, $23\frac{1}{2} \times 18$ | 2,500 |
| | Avnet.  N.Y.  Fleurs, fond rouge, 1905, $21\frac{3}{4} \times 18\frac{1}{4}$ | 17,860 |
| | Phillipps.  N.Y.  Fenêtre gothique, 1900, $25 \times 19$ | 14,250 |
| 1966 | S.  La morte d'Ophélie, on board, $27\frac{1}{2} \times 21$ | 5,500 |
| | Havemeyer.  C.  Chanson de Roland, pen drawing after Doré, 1865, $13\frac{1}{4} \times 10$ | 2,100 |
| 1967 | S.  Portrait, Mme Sabouraud, 1907, $30\frac{3}{4} \times 36$ | 20,500 |
| | Erickson.  C.  Fleurs mêlées, $32 \times 25\frac{1}{2}$, bought in at | 19,950 |
| | N.Y.  La voile jaune, $23 \times 18\frac{1}{4}$, $22,000 | 7,856 |
| | Motte, Geneva.  Allégorie en rouge, $12\frac{1}{2} \times 9\frac{1}{2}$, FS30,000+ tax | 3,340 |
| | Silberman.  N.Y.  Le saintes femmes, pastel, $24\frac{1}{2} \times 20$ (£5,600 in 1964), $30,000 | 12,500 |
| 1968 | Paris.  Vase de fleurs, $22 \times 15\frac{1}{2}$, FN510,000+tax | 47,240 |
| 1969 | S.  Portrait, Mme Violette Heymans, 1909 (unfinished study) $11\frac{1}{2} \times 8\frac{1}{4}$ | 6,800 |
| | Harris.  N.Y.  Fleurs et papillon, fond bleu, $11 \times 9\frac{1}{2}$, c. 1905, $22,500 | 8,950 |
| | Silberman.  N.Y.  Christ and the serpent, 1910, $26\frac{1}{2} \times 20\frac{1}{2}$, $26,000 | 10,925 |
| | Paris.  Butterflies, FN150,000+tax | 13,940 |
| | S.  Le couple, tempera on board, $12\frac{3}{4} \times 14\frac{3}{4}$, Bought in | 10,000 |

## REMBRANDT VAN RYN.  1606–1669

It is an improbable combination to have been one of the most prolific painters who ever lived and yet to remain the highest priced painter whose works are likely to reach the salerooms. Titian lived all but a hundred years, yet only two of his paintings, damaged and disputed at that, reached the salerooms in the

1960s. Rembrandt lived only 63 years, yet there were at least 18 of his paintings, sold in the 1960s, and four more in private transactions, besides 21 drawings. Some were only oil sketches of heads, but the list also includes the saleroom 'records' of the decade, the *Aristotle* and the *Titus Rembrandt in Childhood*.
Let it be said at once that, in spite of all the press histeria, these were not records
at all. Rembrandt had become almost the dearest money could buy before the
end of the 19th century. In the days of sound finance and real currency they
esteemed him more than in the inflationary 1960s.

The price, paid by P. A. B. Widener for *The Mill* in 1911 was equivalent to
£625,000 on the 1961 scale, not so much less than the Erickson *Aristotle* made
in that year. Since then we have seen an allegedly important early Renoir at
£645,800. But Widener's Rembrandt would have paid for the twenty best
works of the four great Impressionists combined. That was what they thought
of Rembrandt in 1911. Incidentally the price which Erickson paid Duveen for
*Aristotle* in 1928 was reported to have been $750,000, then worth £154,330.
The 1961 equivalent was little short of £600,000. Why then all the gasps at
£821,000? One may ask whether an age, in which the arbiters of taste can spend
6 million dollars on a collection of Picassos, is worthy of Rembrandt at all.
Even the bidding for different Rembrandts shows a remarkable lack of dis-
crimination. The child-portrait of Titus, a much scraped work, gets run up to
£798,000 on account of its sentimental appeal, and in the same week a magnificent portrait of Titus's mother makes only £125,000 because she had lost
her looks and her figure when she sat for it—two thirds the price of Picasso's
pretentious *Maternité au bord de la mer.* 'Give me an ounce of civet, good apothe-
cary, to sweeten my imagination.'

| | | £ |
|---|---|---|
| 1960 | Moore. S. (Ex coll. Lord Beauchamp) Young man, 1633, oval, 27½×21½ | 40,100 |
| | Companion-piece, young woman, dated 1634 | 22,000 |
| | Van Aalst. C. Saskia as Juno (discovered in Bonn, 1936), 49×52, bought in at | 52,500 |
| | Bought by National Gallery from Lord Cowper, the Panshanger equestrian portrait (Treasury contribution £128,000) | 170,000 |
| 1961 | Erickson. N.Y. Aristotle contemplating the bust of Homer (bought from Duveen in 1928 for $750,000), 56½×53¾. Metropolitan Museum, $2,300,000 | 821,400 |
| | Head of an old man, dated 1659, 15×10½, $180,000 | 64,286 |
| | Portrait, Prince Frederick Henry of Orange, 32×28 | 39,300 |
| | Bought in England by the Stadtgallerie, Stuttgart, Self-portrait in red cap and fur collar (£11,500 in 1937) | 321,500 |
| 1962 | Kincaid Lennox. S. St Bartholomew or the man with the knife, 1661, 34½×29½ | 190,000 |
| 1963 | Cintas. N.Y. Supposed head of Hendrickje Stoffels, 23½×19½, $260,000 | 92,855 |

| | | £ |
|---|---|---|
| 1964 | Earl of Derby. Private sale to National Gallery. Belshazzar's Feast, £170,000. With remission of death duties | 375,000 |
| | S. An apostle reading, 1661, 34×28 | 168,000 |
| | Still life, partridges and teal (bought recently £60), 28×22 | 110,000 |
| 1965 | Boughton Knight. Bought by Rijks Museum per Agnew, *The Cradle* (Nativity, £1,050 per Payne Knight, 1800) Reputed price | 250,000 |
| | Adda. Paris. Self-portrait, 8×6¾, FN500,000+tax about | 40,000 |
| | Old man's head, 10¼×8¼ (uncertain), FN240,000+tax | 19,340 |
| | Wenner-Gren. S. Saskia as Minerva, 1635, 53½×45½ | 125,000 |
| | William. B. Leeds. S. Unknown old man, 1635, 26¼×20¾ | 140,000 |
| 1965 | Cook (Doughty House). C. Titus the painter's son in childhood (bought from Lord Spencer, 1915, £60,000), 24½×20½, Norton Simon Foundation | 798,000 |
| 1968 | S. Bearded man, cap and gold chain, 1643, 8¼×6½ | 46,000 |
| 1969 | Heywood-Lonsdale. C. Self portrait in dark blue beret and gold necklace, dated 163..., 25×20 (£1,312 10s. in 1879, £1,890 in 1884) Norton Simon Foundation | 483,000 |
| | Mountain. C. Head of an old man, perhaps Rembrandt's father in feathered hat and steel gorget, 26×20 (£100 in 1877, £7,350 in 1938) | 315,000 |

## DRAWINGS

| | | |
|---|---|---|
| 1960 | Mensing, Amsterdam. Kostverloeren Castle, pen and wash | 7,636 |
| | Koenigs. S. Balaam and the Angel, 6¼×9, pen | 4,800 |
| 1961 | Symonds. S. Shah Jehan and his falconer, after an Indian miniature, 8½×7 | 13,500 |
| | Paris. Solomon and the Queen of Sheba, pen and wash, 8×11½, FN100,000+tax (see 1969) | 8,720 |
| 1963 | S. Blind man leaning on a stick | 3,200 |
| | Rudolf. S. Sketch of an old man with a small boy, 6×6½ | 12,000 |
| 1964 | C. A lion, crayon | 6,925 |
| 1965 | S. The old Pesthuis, Amsterdam, much damaged, bought in | 7,500 |
| | Lord Harewood. C. Head of an actor declaiming | 3,415 |
| | Brackley. S. Two heads on one sheet | 3,150 |
| | A lion | 2,940 |
| | S. Farmhouse amid sand dunes, 14×8 | 6,500 |
| 964 | Kornfeld, Berne. An execution of prisoners by beheading, pen and wash, FS66,500+tax | 6,670 |

| 1966 | S. Christ healing the sick (the hundred guldern plate), unique second state of this etching | £ 26,000 |
|---|---|---|
| | Lot and his daughters, pen and wash, $4 \times 6\frac{1}{2}$ | 16,000 |
| | Expulsion of Hagar, pen and wash, $6 \times 4\frac{3}{4}$ | 14,000 |
| 1967 | Rosenwald. S. Seated actor in plumed hat, pen, $7\frac{1}{2} \times 5\frac{3}{4}$ | 23,000 |
| | Randall. S. The geographer, pen and wash, $5 \times 4\frac{1}{4}$ | 5,000 |
| 1968 | Widal. S. The mocking of Christ, pen and brown ink, $7\frac{3}{4}$ in. | 35,000 |
| 1969 | Wells. S. Solomon and the Queen of Sheba, pen and slight wash, $8 \times 11\frac{1}{2}$ (see 1961) | 31,500 |
| | Widal. S. Standing man in broad brimmed hat, pen, $4\frac{3}{4} \times 3$ | 6,500 |
| | Morritt. S. Christ and the woman of Canaan, pen, $7\frac{3}{4} \times 11\frac{1}{4}$ | 30,000 |
| 1970 | Methven. C. Sheet of heads, pen and wash, $5 \times 6\frac{1}{2}$ (Sackville-Bale sale, 1881, 14 guineas) | 22,050 |

## FREDERICK REMINGTON. (*See* American School, 19th–20th century)

## GUIDO RENI. 1575–1642

In 1845 Ruskin delivered a diatribe against the National Gallery for spending nearly £3,000 on two Guido Renis. They never bought another till 1959, when no Guido Reni had made a thousand guineas for more than a century. The price of the Spencer Churchill Guido Reni in 1965 suggests that some of the painstaking scholarly propaganda in favour of Guido Reni and the Italian baroque painters has borne fruit. Speculators are doubtless interested. The only trouble is the absence of Guido Renis. Even in the days before the proliferation of museums, the commodity was rarer than was supposed.

| | | £ |
|---|---|---|
| 1954 | C. Vision of St Francis, $82 \times 59$ | 183 15s. |
| 1960 | Bukowski, Stockholm. Artemisia, half-length figure, $31\frac{1}{2} \times 24\frac{3}{4}$, Skr.12,500+tax | 1,040 |
| 1965 | Spencer Churchill. C. Angel appearing to St Jerome (£640 10s. in 1810, £273 in 1846, £367 10s. in 1859), $78 \times 58\frac{1}{2}$ | 23,100 |
| | Czernin. C. A lady as Cleopatra, $21\frac{1}{2} \times 17\frac{1}{2}$ | 3,150 |
| 1964 | Fischer, Lucerne. Seated Venus and running Cupid, a pair, $38\frac{1}{2} \times 26$, FS28,000+tax | 2,800 |
| 1970 | S. Europa and the bull, $61 \times 44$ | 3,000 |

## PIERRE AUGUSTE RENOIR. 1841–1919

There are nearly eighty paintings in this list which made upwards of £20,000 in the saleroom, and among them the most expensive modern picture sold in the 1960s. Yet the supremacy of Renoir in the salerooms was by no means assured. Relative to the other Impressionist painters, there has been this uncertainty concerning Renoir since the beginning. Thus the picture which has perhaps the best claim to be regarded as his masterpiece, the *Déjeuner des canotiers*, was sold in 1895, when Renoir was past the prime of life, for 7,500 francs or £300. In 1895 both Manet and Monet had fetched much higher prices than this. Seventeen years later, at the famous Rouart sale of 1912, when for the first time a Renoir made over £4,000, it was Degas and Manet who were in the lead, the former enormously so. However, if we may trust René Simpel's journal, Maurice de Rothschild bought a Renoir in the following year for half a million francs or £20,000, equivalent to £160,000 in 1970. It is certain at least that from 1913 Renoir became appreciably dearer than Monet and comparable with Manet and Degas. On the whole, the Impressionists had incurred less hostility when they stuck to landscape, for it seems to have taken forty years to reconcile the public to those plump strawberry-coloured nudes. Renoir's position was now so assured that at the lowest depth of the international financial depression of 1932 his *Child with a hoop* could still make over £6,000 at auction.

The depressed markets of the 1940s ended with the Cognacq sale of 1952, where Renoir headed the list with *Les deux sœurs* at 19 million francs and *Jeune fille au chapeau* at 22½ million, equivalent with taxes to £23,420 and £27,170 with close on double the purchasing power of 1970. Such prices for Renoir had been heard of before in transactions with millionaires, but they were something quite new at public auction. Within seven years of the Cognacq sale, *La serre* had been sold for £71,300, *La pensée* for £72,000 and *Les filles de Durand-Ruel* for £91,000. On the basis of these prices the National Gallery in 1959 put a valuation of a quarter of a million on the picture, *Les parapluies*, of the Lane bequest. Yet, till the sale of the *Pont des Arts* in 1968 for £645,834 these prices remained the highest paid for Renoir. Four Monets had been sold in the meantime at six figure prices. It looked as if Renoir had dropped back in the affection of millionaires. But if one examined the pictures themselves rather than the list of prices, it was obvious that nothing of the kind had happened. It was simply that there had been a continuous flow of Renoir's potboiling pictures or studies and nothing first-class. The prices for *L'enfance* (£60,000 in 1960) and *Girl combing her hair* (£65,000 in 1964) were disproportionately high for what they were. On this scale *Les canotiers de Charentan* or *Les enfants de Mme Charpentier* or *Les parapluies* should have been worth at least two million pounds apiece. It was hardly surprising that in 1967 the £60,000 picture, *L'enfance*, had to be bought in for a nominal £55,000. But whether there is still a first-class Renoir that has survived, free of the fetters of public ownership, is more than doubtful. A clothed figure subject, which just missed the £200,000 mark in 1969, was honest and worthy rather than compelling.

|      |                                                                                                                                      | £      |
|------|--------------------------------------------------------------------------------------------------------------------------------------|--------|
| 1900 | La femme au chat, now in National Gallery, Washington, said to have been sold for 50,000 francs                                       | 2,000  |
| 1907 | Vian. Paris. La tonnelle, 26,000 francs+tax                                                                                           | 1,140  |
|      | L'ingénue                                                                                                                             | 1,004  |
|      | Bought by Metropolitan Museum, Mme Charpentier et ses enfants                                                                         | 3,500  |
| 1911 | Bernstein. Paris. Baigneuse couchée, 32,000 francs+tax                                                                               | 1,400  |
| 1912 | Rouart. Paris. La Parisienne, 52,500 francs+tax                                                                                       | 2,312  |
|      | Allée cavalière au bois de Boulogne, 95,000 francs+ tax                                                                               | 4,180  |
| 1913 | Bought from Durand-Ruel by Maurice de Rothschild, life-sized *Danseuse*, according to R. Gimpel for half a million francs            | 20,000 |
| 1914 | C. (First Renoir to be sold there) Femme à la rose                                                                                    | 630    |
| 1919 | La loge, sold by Durand-Ruel for 100,000 francs                                                                                       | 4,000  |
|      | In December four Renoirs were sold in Paris for £7,000 in all.                                                                        |        |
| 1920 | N.Y. Canotiers à Châtou, $28,000, then 3·38 to £                                                                                      | 8,370  |
|      | Dans la prairie, $28,600 .                                                                                                            | 8,550  |
| 1922 | Sale of Renoir's studio, 103 studies and paintings bought by Galerie Barbezanges for 1½ million francs or £20,000.                    |        |
| 1923 | Bought from Durand-Ruel by Duncan Philips, Washington.                                                                                |        |
|      | Les canotiers de Charentan. Price according to Maurice Rheims, $200,000. No other confirmation.                                       | 50,000 |
| 1924 | Bought by Courtauld fund for Tate Gallery. La première sortie                                                                         | 7,500  |
| 1925 | Gangnat. Paris. Baigneuse blessée, bought in, 600,000 francs+tax                                                                     | 6,600  |
|      | Two lifesize panels of dancers, National Gallery (see 1960), bought in                             2 for                             | 8,530  |
| 1927 | Gallerie Barbezanges. Les blanchisseuses, price asked according to R. Gimpel (£400, asked by Renoir in 1918)                          | 6,400  |
| 1932 | Georges Petit. Paris. Child with a hoop, 361,000 francs +tax at 70 to the £                                                          | 6,150  |
|      | Jules Strauss. Paris. Portrait, Richard Wagner, 257,000 francs+tax                                                                    | 4,320  |
|      | Jardin d'essai à Alger, 21×26                                     about                                                               | 3,000  |
| 1932-4 | Albert. C. Barnes buys la famille Henriot and Jeanne Durand-Ruel for $50,000                          2 for                         | 10,280 |
| 1933 | Danthon. Paris. La femme à la sourire, 232,000 francs+ tax                                                                           | 3,890  |

| | | £ |
|---|---|---|
| 1935 | Newman.  N.Y.  Jeune fille à sa toilette, 16½ × 13 | 596 |
| | La jeune mère, $5,200 | 848 |
| 1938 | Albert Pra.  Paris.  Les fruits, 465,000 francs+tax at 180 to £ | 3,038 |
| | Têtes d'enfants, 512,000 francs+tax | 3,462 |
| 1939 | Canonne.  Paris.  Les deux sœurs (£387 in 1909, see also 1952) | 2,180 |
| | Bought by W. A. Cargill, Head of a girl in black (see 1963) | 4,600 |
| 1942 | Bought in U.S.A. by Albert C. Barnes.  Mussel fishers of Berneval, $185,000 at 4·00 to the £ | 46,250 |
| 1944 | Barbée.  N.Y.  Gabrielle au collier vert, 22 × 18 | 2,300 |
| 1946 | Hugo Moser.  N.Y.  Girl in a sailor suit, 1895, 23 × 27 | 1,742 |
| 1948 | S.  Gabrielle en rouge | 2,200 |
| | N.Y.  Baigneuse | 3,750 |
| 1951 | S.  Small half-length of a girl | 2,300 |
| 1952 | Cognacq.  Paris.  Les deux sœurs (£2,180 in 1939), 19 million francs at 987 to the £+tax | 23,420 |
| | Jeune fille au chapeau garni de fleurs, 22½ million francs+tax | 27,170 |
| 1956 | Paris.  The rose-trimmed hat | 16,200 |
| | S.  La ferme, small landscape | 6,000 |
| 1957 | Bought by Stavros Nearchos from Edward Robinson.  Après le bain, $60,000 | 21,450 |
| | S.  Small baigneuse | 9,500 |
| | Weinberg.  S.  Girl in red blouse, 24¾ × 20½ | 22,000 |
| | Paris.  Mosquée d'Alger | 22,000 |
| | Lurcy.  N.Y.  La serre, $200,000 | 71,300 |
| 1958 | Bernard.  S.  La fête de Pan | 14,000 |
| | Goldschmidt.  S.  La pensée (£884 in 1899) 25½ × 21½ | 72,000 |
| | Kirkeby.  N.Y.  La couseuse | 31,070 |
| | Jardin à Sorrente | 37,500 |
| 1959 | N.Y.  Les filles de Durand-Ruel, 32 × 26, $257,000 | 91,075 |
| | Lady with parasol, 21½ × 25½ | 55,000 |
| | Jeune fille au chapeau blanc | 33,070 |
| | S.  Portrait, Misia Serte, National Gallery | 12,600 |
| | Chrysler.  S.  Dead pheasant in snow, 19¼ × 25½ | 19,000 |
| | S.  Ambroise Vollard en Torrero | 22,000 |
| | Les Parapluies, valued for National Gallery (bought by Hugh Lane for £1,000 before 1910) | 250,000 |
| 1960 | Schonmann.  S.  Femme nue dans l'eau, 1888, 31 × 25 | 38,000 |
| | Les deux laveuses, 1900, 25¼ × 23¾ | 38,000 |
| | C.  Mme Georges Vallière (bought in), 1913, 35½ × 28½ | 12,600 |
| 1961 | S.  Young girl walking in a field, 1900, 18 × 22 | 33,000 |

| | | £ |
|---|---|---|
| 1961 | Critchley. S. Jean Renoir at five years, 1891, 25½×19¾ (*L'enfance*, see 1967) | 60,000 |
| | Bought by National Gallery. Two life-size dancers, 1909 (1925, £8,530, bought in) | 2 for 163,000 |
| 1962 | Somerset Maugham. S. River scene at Argenteuil, 21¼×25½ | 48,000 |
| | Three girls, walking out, 25¼×21 | 48,000 |
| | S. Nude girl, bust-portrait, *c.* 1888, 17×31½ | 36,000 |
| | Nude girl (Andrée assise, 17¼×14½ (see 1969) | 9,000 |
| | Metcalfe. S. Two girls by the water (see 1965), 12¾×16¼ | 42,000 |
| | S. Portrait, Christine Lerolle (see 1968) | 25,000 |
| | N.Y. La fête de Pan, 1879, 24½×19 | 35,700 |
| 1963 | Wolf. S. Baigneuses, pastel, 1889, 24½×19 | 29,000 |
| | Cargill. S. Head of girl in black, 1875, 12½×9¼ (£4,600, 1939) | 46,000 |
| | M. et Mme Godard, 13½×16¼ (£2,400 in 1937) | 24,000 |
| | Heads of two little girls, 21½×18 | 61,000 |
| | S. Unfinished girl's head, 1882, 21×17½ | 26,000 |
| 1964 | S. Girl combing her hair, 1886, 25½×21¼ | 65,000 |
| | The young soldier, 1877, 21×12½ | 46,000 |
| | Chrysanthema in vase, 1880, 31½×25 | 56,000 |
| 1965 | Motte, Geneva. Girl with arms crossed, 22½×18¾ | 35,700 |
| | S. Jeune fille dans les champs, 1900, 22×18 | 28,000 |
| | Still life with pomegranates, 14×18 | 21,000 |
| | Haft. Palm Beach. Enfant en bleu, 1885, $150,000 | 53,600 |
| | Moser. N.Y. Flowers in vase, 1878, 18¾×30, $125,000 | 44,640 |
| | S. Rough oil sketch, people in landscape, 23½×28½ | 24,000 |
| | N.Y. Jeune fille au bord de l'eau, 12¾×16¼, $43,000 (£42,000 in 1962, Metcalfe. S.) | 15,360 |
| 1966 | S. Portrait, Henri Bernstein, 1910, 31½×25 | 16,000 |
| | Trois perdrix, 12¼×15¼ | 18,375 |
| | Paris. Oliviers de Cagnes, 1909, 12¾×21¼ | 28,375 |
| | Femme accroupie, 1913, 12×13¼ | 24,700 |
| 1967 | Silver. N.Y. Flowers in vase, 1881, 26×21½, $100,000 | 35,714 |
| | Cummings. S. L'enfance (Jean Renoir) 1891, 25½×19¾ (£60,000 in 1961), bought in at | 55,000 |
| | Paris. Profile of a little girl, 11¼×7½, FN615,000+tax | 48,015 |
| | N.Y. Femme au chapeau, 26½×21½ | 25,357 |
| | Mother and child, 1900, 25¾×21½, $105,000 | 37,500 |
| | S. La fontaine, 1895, 18×11½ | 17,000 |
| | La source, single nude, 1895, 25×17½ | 20,000 |
| | C. (from Austria). Vase de lilas, *c.* 1873, 21¼×25½, bought in | 29,400 |

| | | £ |
|---|---|---|
| 67 | N.Y. Femme au corsage bleu, 24×18 | 12,500 |
| | Paris. Femme nue se coiffant, 14½×9½, FN155,000+tax | 12,360 |
| | La partie de croquet, 18½×22, FN250,000+tax | 19,980 |
| 67 | Motte, Geneva. Church and cliffs, Varengeville, *c.* 1880, 21½×28, FS134,000+tax | 14,490 |
| | Femme à la rose, 22½×18½, FS380,000+tax | 41,250 |
| | N.Y. Mère et enfant, 25¾×21½, $105,000 | 43,780 |
| 68 | Papazoff. N.Y. Baigneuse, 13¾×10¼, 1916–18, $37,500 | 15,625 |
| | Paris. Jeune fille à la rose, 20½×16, FN560,000+tax | 52,350 |
| | Les collettes, 18½×20½, FN420,000+tax | 39,160 |
| | Femme à la blouse bleu, FN260,000+tax | 32,216 |
| | Reclining nude, 1888, FN720,000+tax | 67,161 |
| | Boise. S. Nu couché, vu de dos, 1897, 9¾×18 | 21,000 |
| | Les laveuses au Beal, Cagnes, 1912, 17½×21 | 22,000 |
| | Lavandières et baigneurs à Essoyes, 1900, 17×21 | 27,000 |
| | Schwarzschild. S. Jeune femme assise dans un intèrieur, pastel, 1879–80, 24¼×18 | 56,000 |
| | C. Baigneuse au crabe, pastel, 1897, 17¾×24 | 17,850 |
| | Portrait Mme Rouart, née Christine Lerolle, 1897, 26½×21, (see 1962) | 37,800 |
| | C. Study in oils for 'la danse à la campagne', 17¾×9¾ | 38,850 |
| | Brandeis University, N.Y. Le Pont des Arts, 1868, 24½×40½, Norton Simon Foundation, $1,550,000 | 645,834 |
| | S. La femme au chat, sketch (for final version see 1900), 1876–8, 13×9¾ | 60,000 |
| | C. Pierre, fils d'Alfred Sisley, child's head, 10¼×8¼ | 19,950 |
| | Paris. Jeune fille de profile, 1888, 9×8, FN970,000+tax | 89,915 |
| | Jeune fille portant une corbeille de fleurs, 31¾×24¾ (see 1969), bought in at FN700,000 | 59,750 |
| | S. Jeune fille coiffée d'un fichu d'orange, 21¾×17½ | 38,000 |
| | Blow, N.Y. Femmes nues dans une niche, 1890, 51½×16¼, $90,000 | 37,500 |
| | Stratton. N.Y. La femme à la draperie, *c.* 1908, 18½×15, $40,000 | 16,665 |
| 69 | Fribourg. N.Y. Le liseuse, head, 15½×12½, $215,000 | 89,583 |
| | C. Jeune fille portant une corbeille de fleurs, 31¾×24¼ (see 1968), bought in at £42,000, sold privately | 40,000 |
| | Fribourg. N.Y. Le poirier, 17¼×14½, $85,000 | 35,715 |
| | C. (Tokyo). Portrait, Mme Henriot, 1916 (1962. S. £5,500), 29 million yen, 19¾×15½ | 33,875 |
| | Paris. Portrait, Mlle Rivière, 1907, FN550,000+tax | 50,960 |
| | C. (Tokyo). La blanchisseuse, crude sketch, 10×6, 15 million yen | 16,703 |
| | S. Anémones, 1901, 13×15¼ | 37,000 |

£

| 1969 | S.  La ferme, 1892, $23\frac{1}{4} \times 30\frac{3}{4}$ | 14,000 |

1969   S.  La ferme, 1892, $23\frac{1}{4} \times 30\frac{3}{4}$     14,000

S. (Tokyo).  Nude, Andrée assise, $17\frac{1}{4} \times 14\frac{1}{2}$ (£9,000 in 1962) 35 million yen    39,900

Magnin.  N.Y.  Femme en jupe rouge, s'essuyant les pieds, *c.* 1888, $26 \times 20$, \$470,000    195,833

    L'escalier, Algiers, *c.* 1882, $28\frac{1}{2} \times 23\frac{1}{2}$, \$230,000    95,833

    Landscape, \$70,000    29,167

C. (Geneva).  Head of Jean Renoir at five years, 1899, $12\frac{1}{4} \times 12\frac{1}{4}$, FS270,000+tax of 5%    27,269

    Paysage normand, 1895, $16\frac{1}{2} \times 22\frac{1}{4}$, FS360,000+tax    36,345

Paris.  Femme au chapeau, 1914, FN484,000+tax    43,725

S.  Portrait de jeune fille, *c.* 1870, $19\frac{1}{2} \times 16\frac{1}{2}$    13,000

    Jeunes arbres dans le forêt, 1865, $28\frac{3}{4} \times 23\frac{1}{2}$ (pre-Impressionist)    28,500

    Pommes et raisins, $11\frac{3}{4} \times 14\frac{1}{2}$    14,000

    Nature morte, objets diverses, *c.* 1880, $13 \times 16\frac{1}{4}$    15,000

1970 Crocker.  N.Y.  Nature morte aux fleurs, 1884, $23\frac{1}{2} \times 29\frac{1}{4}$, \$280,000    116,660

### DRAWINGS

1960 Paris.  Woman with a muff, red chalk    4,750

1962 Mme Renoir and child, red chalk, $29 \times 21\frac{1}{2}$    10,000

    Metcalfe.  S.  Mlles Lerolle au piano, charcoal, $19 \times 24\frac{3}{4}$    11,500

1964 Hutton.  S.  Two girls walking out, red chalk    14,200

1968 S.  Gabrielle, poitrine nue, red chalk, 1890, $16 \times 13\frac{1}{2}$    8,000

1969 S.  Claude Renoir as a child, *c.* 1909, $15\frac{1}{2} \times 15$, charcoal    10,200

    Mère et enfant, *c.* 1885, red chalk, $28 \times 23$    10,000

## SIR JOSHUA REYNOLDS.  1723–1792

The prices in the 1960s compared exceedingly closely with those of Romne and Lawrence, though not with Gainsborough's. They were the burnt-o embers of the famous Duveen market. The Spencer Churchill sale of 196 contained the one portrait in this list which had been, in its day, considere important enough for Duveen who had offered 60,000 guineas for it in th 1920s, equivalent to £256,000 in 1965 when this swaggering pretentious wo seemed dear at £9,450. Several Reynolds portraits did actually change han in the 1920s at the absurd price of 60,000 guineas and two of them made ev more. In 1921 Henry Huntington paid £73,500 for *Mrs Siddons as the Tra Muse*. According to Mr R. H. Rush, the portrait of Lady Compton in th National Gallery, Washington, cost Andrew Mellon half a million dollars

1936. Translatable at that time as £103,000, the price would be equal to £516,500 in the money of 1970.

There are Reynolds portraits which deservedly make no more than a few hundreds among the thousands that he ground out in his forty years and more of arduous practice. There are others that are masterpieces, like the unfinished head of Omai. It seems wholly ridiculous that it made less than any discarded scrap of a thing by Renoir.

|  |  | £ |
|---|---|---|
| 1961 | Lilian S. Whitmarsh, N.Y. Anne Popham, small half-length | 2,235 |
| | Lady Hague. S. 2nd Earl of Shannon, half-length | 1,300 |
| | Duke of Sutherland. C. Lord Ligonier at the battle of Dettingen, replica of Tate Gallery picture, $67 \times 59$ | 9,450 |
| 1962 | Heathcote-Amory. S. Portrait of Wang-Y-Tong, $24 \times 18$ | 4,800 |
| 1963 | Fitzgerald. S. Unfinished head, Omai the Tahitian (£4,080, Coty sale, Paris, 1936) | 22,000 |
| 1964 | S. Unfinished head, Wang-Y-Tong, the Chinese boy (£750 in 1954) | 2,800 |
| | C. Richard Barwell with son, $98 \times 61$ (£4,270 in 1956), bought in | 1,890 |
| | Eliot-Hodgkin. S. Tan-Chitqua, the Chinese face modeller, oil sketch | 2,800 |
| 1965 | Spencer Churchill. C. Elizabeth, Duchess of Hamilton, $94 \times 58$ (Gwydyr sale, 1829, £69 9s.), an offer of 60,000 guineas from Duveen was refused in the 1920s | 9,450 |
| | Boswell Elliott. S. James Boswell, half-length, 1787, bought for National Portrait Gallery | 25,000 |
| | Adda. Paris. Unidentified reclining girl, $21 \times 15\frac{3}{4}$ | 320 |
| 1966 | C. Richard Crofts, three-quarter length, $51 \times 45$ | 1,470 |
| | Spencer auctioneer, Wilmslow. Richard Burke, head | 3,000 |
| | Scaife. S. Thomas Henry Rumbold, $49 \times 39\frac{1}{2}$ (£8,000 in 1927) | 7,200 |
| | Harrington. S. 3rd Earl of Harrington, $93 \times 56\frac{1}{2}$ | 9,500 |
| 1968 | Aron. S. Lady Mary Coke, half-length, 1758, $29\frac{1}{2} \times 24\frac{1}{2}$ | 18,000 |
| | Winston Guest, N.Y. General Sir William Fawcett, 1784, $54 \times 49\frac{1}{2}$, $15,000 | 6,250 |
| 1969 | C. Miss Harriet Powell as Leonora in *The Padlock*, 1769, half-length, $29 \times 24$ | 1,995 |
| | S. Lady Mary Grenville, whole length, $88 \times 57$ (£1,400 in 1964) | 4,700 |
| | Westmorland. S. Sir John Lade with dog, seated half-length, 1778, $39 \times 35\frac{1}{2}$ | 12,000 |
| | Stout. C. Theodosia Magill (Countess Clanwilliam), 1764, half-length, $50 \times 40$ | 14,700 |

RICCI, MARCO AND SEBASTIANO. (*See* Italian School, 18th century)

JEAN RIOPELLE (Canada). (*See* Abstract Painters, America)

DIEGO RIVERA (Mexico). (*See* American School, 19th–20th century)

## HUBERT ROBERT. 1733–1808

These extremely pretty though somewhat repetitious *capriccios* have multiplied in value eight to ten times over since the end of the war. I have, however, revised the list as given in Volume One, and from this it will at once be seen that Hubert Robert has shared in no small degree in the fall of the French *dix-huitième* market since the first quarter of the century. The price of 65,000 dollars, paid by Jules Bache for a large *capriccio* in 1927, was equivalent to £67,000 in 1970 terms. Two auction sales in Paris in 1919 and 1920 show prices for single *capriccios* equivalent to £64,500 and £31,400. Yet £12,000 was the highest price in the 1960s. A theatrical and superficial Guardi could make more than four times as much. That Hubert Robert's subtle sense of values and impeccable mastery of his medium should be so under-appreciated is as much as one need expect of a market which rates Picasso with Rembrandt.

|      |                                                                                                 | £        |      |
|------|-------------------------------------------------------------------------------------------------|----------|------|
| 1910 | C.  Building, seen through an archway                                                            | 220      | 10s. |
| 1912 | Doucet.  Paris.  Parc de St. Cloud, 10 × 8                                                       | 4,300    |      |
|      | Le jet d'eau, 10 × 8                                                                             | 3,400    |      |
|      | Others at £1,000 to £2,000                                                                       |          |      |
| 1919 | La Beraudière.  Paris.  (According to Gimpel.)  A pair of capriccios with classical ruins etc. at 800,000 francs+tax (34 to the £)                          2 for | 25,800 |      |
| 1920 | Sigismund Bardac.  Paris.  A ruined bridge (47 francs to £)                                      | 6,280    |      |
| 1921 | Georges Petit.  Paris.  Forêt de Caprarola                                                       | 5,560    |      |
|      | 3 others exceeded £4,000 each                                                                    |          |      |
| 1926 | C.  Paysage avec cascade (see 1961)                                                              | 1,522    | 10s. |
|      | Cascade (see 1961)                                                                               | 1,443    | 15s. |
| 1927 | Bought by Jules Bache (according to Gimpel) a large *capriccio* for $65,000                      | 13,400   |      |
| 1928 | U.S.S.R. government (Stroganoff coll.).  Berlin.  Park with ruins and figures, 10¾ × 8           | 740      |      |
| 1929 | Princess Paley.  C.  Roman buildings, a pair            2 for                                    | 5,880    |      |
| 1933 | Hermenonville.  Paris.  Parks of Hermenonville and Meréville, 50,000 francs+tax      2 for       | 825      |      |

|  |  | £ |
|---|---|---|
| 1935 | Faucher-Magnan. S. Les blanchisseuses | 2,500 |
|  | Orangerie à Versailles | 1,150 |
| 1937 | Greffulhe. S. Small pair of *capriccios* 2 for | 2,900 |
|  | Glatigny. Paris. Cascatelles de Tivoli (112 francs to £) | 795 |
| 1941 | Harcourt-Johnstone. S. Pêche à la ligne | 270 |
| 1951 | Paris. Terraces, Villa d'Este | 3,940 |
| 1956 | N.Y. Les lavandières and colonnades antiques 2 for | 6,785 |
| 1957 | Ambatielos. S. Ruined temple | 4,500 |
|  | Landscape with temple, drawing, red chalk | 980 |
|  | Fountain and aqueduct, drawing, red chalk | 800 |
| 1960 | Paris. The lawn-dressers | 3,620 |
|  | Timken. N.Y. Classical ruins, $29\frac{1}{2} \times 39$ | 1,963 |
| 1961 | Jules Strauss. Paris. Houdon working on a statue | 2,530 |
|  | Alvin Fuller. C. Paysage avec cascade (see 1926) | 1,995 |
|  | Another cascade landscape (see 1926) | 3,625 |
|  | Mediterranean coast scene, $39 \times 24$ | 6,300 |
|  | Guggenheim. S. Cascade at Tivoli, $28\frac{1}{2} \times 35\frac{1}{4}$ | 6,000 |
|  | Erickson. N.Y. Pont de pierre and Au bois, two oval *capriccios* (from Stroganoff collection, U.S.S.R.) 2 for | 10,714 |
| 1963 | Fribourg. S. The same two pictures now down to (2) | 8,200 |
| 1965 | Paris. The Marne at Charentan and the mill at Charentan, each, $14 \times 18$, FN300,000+tax 2 for | 23,750 |
|  | Paget. C. Set of four six-foot landscape panels 4 for | 4,357 10s. |
|  | Bull. C. Capriccio with classical archway | 4,200 |
|  | S. Wine cellar at Caprarola, 1765 | 3,600 |
| 1966 | S. Artists sketching at Tivoli, $21\frac{1}{4} \times 17\frac{3}{4}$ | 3,500 |
|  | Lord Sackville. S. Mediterranean coast scene (see 1961) $39\frac{1}{2} \times 55\frac{1}{4}$ (down from £6,300) | 5,000 |
|  | S. Pair of landscapes with pyramid and temples, 1748, $37\frac{3}{4} \times 46\frac{3}{4}$ 2 for | 5,000 |
|  | Paris. Le miroir d'eau, $50\frac{3}{4} \times 44$, FN104,000+tax | 8,250 |
| 1967 | Goelet. S. Avenue in a park, red chalk, $16 \times 20$ | 2,800 |
|  | Paris. Canal in a park and dungeon, $138 \times 69\frac{1}{4}$, FN60,000 +tax 2 for | 4,783 |
| 1968 | Kaplan. S. Le matin, 1790, $15\frac{1}{2} \times 12\frac{1}{4}$ | 2,000 |
|  | C. Roman arcade with figures and statues, wc, 1789, $25\frac{1}{2} \times 20\frac{3}{4}$ | 1,260 |
| 1969 | C. Discovery of the artist's gravestone, fanciful composition, dated 1788, black chalk, $13 \times 18\frac{3}{4}$ | 1,575 |

## DAVID ROBERTS. 1796–1864

One of those crowded church interiors with that peculiar gloomy leaden Early Victorian look was sold in 1933 for 10 guineas, having made 1,400 guineas in

1891. It was chosen in Volume One as an extreme case of the decline of the romantic taste. Yet of all the Early Victorian romantics Roberts has perhaps recovered the most. There are indeed five four-figure pictures in this list, but it will be noticed that four are views of Venice and one is a Thames-side view, and it seems that in the 1960s no one who painted such things in the nostalgic past could go far wrong. Roberts, the Orientalist, a sort of Richard Burton of the paint brush, is far less esteemed. A few hundreds will buy any of these painstaking topographies. As to Roberts, the visionary, the painter of huge brown biblical scenes of doom and destruction in the fashion of John Martin, there is the sad little transaction, recorded for 1961.

|      |                                                                                                                                                                                                            | £        |
|------|------------------------------------------------------------------------------------------------------------------------------------------------------------------------------------------------------------|----------|
| 1960 | S.  Jacob's well at Shechem, wc., $13\frac{1}{2}\times19\frac{1}{2}$                                                                                                                                        | 40       |
| 1961 | Army and Navy Club.  C.  The destruction of Jerusalem by the Romans, 12 ft×7 ft (a companion-piece was bought by Sir Robert Peel from the Earl of Northwick in 1838 for 215 guineas)                       | 26 5s.   |
| 1963 | Phillips, son and Neale. Doge's Palace and Grand Canal, 1853, 48×72.  First four-figure price for Roberts in 70 years (see 1965)                                                                           | 1,500    |
|      | S.  St Peter's, Rome, and Castel San Angelo, 1860, (£315, 1881)                                                                                                                                           | 420      |
|      | C.  San Giovanni e Paolo, Venice, oil on paper (£178 10s., 1881)                                                                                                                                          | 367 10s. |
| 1964 | S.  Mont St Michel, 1848, 10×16, wc                                                                                                                                                                       | 450      |
|      | Salute and Dogana, 1859, $17\frac{1}{2}\times13\frac{1}{2}$, wc                                                                                                                                           | 520      |
|      | Bruce Ingram.  S.  Four views of Egyptian temples, wc, 13×19, £300, £400, £420 and                                                                                                                        | 440      |
| 1965 | C.  Tower of London, 1964, wc, $9\frac{3}{4}\times13\frac{1}{2}$ (see 1968)                                                                                                                               | 472 10s. |
|      | Spencer Churchill.  C.  View over Granada, 1836, wc                                                                                                                                                       | 735      |
|      | Lord Burton.  C.  Palace of the Doges, Venice, oils, 1853, 48×72 (see 1963)                                                                                                                               | 3,675    |
|      | S.  Church interior, 1848, wc                                                                                                                                                                             | 300      |
| 1966 | C.  Temple of Philae, wc, $13\times20\frac{3}{4}$                                                                                                                                                         | 273      |
| 1967 | C.  Desert landscape, 1850, $11\frac{1}{2}\times15$                                                                                                                                                       | 273      |
|      | Interior, Malines cathedral, 1835, $36\times26\frac{1}{2}$                                                                                                                                                | 231      |
|      | Buchanan Jardine.  S.  St Paul's from Ludgate Hill, $29\frac{1}{2}\times24\frac{1}{2}$                                                                                                                    | 600      |
|      | C.  Interior, St Anne's church, Bruges, 1850, 20×23                                                                                                                                                       | 735      |
|      | Houldsworth.  S.  Chapel of St Helena, Bethlehem, wc, 1839                                                                                                                                                | 380      |
| 1968 | Neville Berry.  S.  The Salute from the Grand Canal, 1859, $35\frac{1}{2}\times49$                                                                                                                        | 2,200    |
|      | Tennant.  N.Y.  The Gesuati, Venice, 1854, $21\frac{1}{4}\times50\frac{1}{4}$                                                                                                                             | 2,500    |

| | | |
|---|---|---:|
| 968 | C. St Paul's from the Thames, wc, $9\frac{3}{4} \times 13\frac{1}{2}$ (for companion-piece, see 1965) | £ 1,680 |
| | Jaffa, pencil and wc, 1839, $12\frac{1}{4} \times 19\frac{1}{2}$ (£42 in 1917, £46 4s. in 1921) | 945 |
| 968 | Tetuan, 1833, pencil and wc, $9 \times 26\frac{1}{4}$ | 525 |
| 969 | C. The Bacino with the Dogana and Salute, $40\frac{1}{2} \times 76$, bought in | 6,300 |

## GEORGE ROMNEY. 1734–1802

the 1960s Romney shared the depressed market fortunes of Reynolds and awrence, but not of Gainsborough. Even the whole-length portrait of heridan made no more than £12,000. It should be remembered that, before ne First World War and some years before the sale of *The Blue Boy* and the *ragic Muse*, Romney led them all. At the Oppenheim sale of 1913 Duveen aid £41,370 for the portrait of *Anne de la Pole*, while in the following year Iuntington paid Duveen £45,000 for *Penelope Lee Acton*. These prices would be quivalent in 1970 terms to £331,000 and £360,000. Furthermore, though iainsborough had overtaken them, they continued into the 1920s. Thus in 926 Andrew Mellon paid Knoedler £70,000 for *Mrs Davenport*, for which ;60,900 had been paid at Christies. Mellon therefore gave the 1970 equivalent f £350,000 for a picture that might conceivably be worth £15,000.

| | | £ |
|---|---|---:|
| 960 | S. Sir Edward Every, whole length, 1780 (£5,040, 1925) | 2,800 |
| 961 | Curwen. C. Isabella Corwen of Workington Hall, $96 \times 59$ | 6,825 |
| | Whole length, Earl Delamere | 3,990 |
| | Alvin Fuller. C. Master Thomas Wallace | 5,460 |
| | Elizabeth Wallace | 4,410 |
| | Erickson. N.Y. Mrs James Lowther, $30 \times 25$, $32,000 | 11,428 |
| 963 | C. Sir George Prescott, half-length | 1,575 |
| | Cintas. S. Richard Brinsley Sheridan, $86\frac{1}{2} \times 52$ | 12,000 |
| 964 | C. Unknown little girl, head. Beaverbrook Gallery | 2,730 |
| | S. Mrs Robertson, 1786, $49 \times 39\frac{1}{2}$ (£42 in 1786) | 7,200 |
| | Storer Trust. S. 5th Earl of Carlisle, $29\frac{1}{4} \times 24\frac{1}{4}$ | 3,400 |
| | Craigmyle. S. Lady Hamilton in a Welsh hat, $49 \times 39$ | 2,000 |
| 966 | Ward-Thomas. C. Serena in the boat of apathy, $47\frac{1}{2} \times 60\frac{1}{2}$ (£787 10s. in 1961) | 1,575 |
| | Douglas. S. Miss Duncombe, $31\frac{1}{4} \times 27\frac{3}{4}$ | 2,000 |
| | S. Miss Vernon as Hebe, 1777, $38\frac{3}{4} \times 40$ | 2,400 |
| 967 | Astor. C. Mrs Charles Chaplin, $49\frac{1}{2} \times 39$ | 3,360 |
| | N.Y. Lady Wedderburn, $30 \times 25$, $5,000 | 1,860 |
| 968 | Aron. S. Marquise de Tréville, oval, $32 \times 26$ | 4,200 |

| | | £ |
|---|---|---|
| 1969 | Lord Bolton. C. L'Allegro and Il Penseroso, pair of whole length female portraits, 1770, 93 × 56½ 2 for | 2,777 10. |
| | Kimball. S. Lady Hamilton as *Ariadne* overlooking the sea, 55¼ × 44 (Neeld sale, 1944, £4,785) | 2,900 |
| | Bruguière. C. Captain Francis North, half-length, 1780, 50 × 40 | 5,250 |
| | William Hayley, half-length, 25 × 30 | 2,730 |

## SALVATOR ROSA.  1615–1673

In the early 1800s Salvator Rosa was a favourite among English collector *Mercury and the Woodman* was sold in 1824 for the equivalent of about £26,00 In spite of an intellectual cult for the later Italians, no such price was paid in th 1960s. In 1953, when the two Salvator Rosas from Ashburnham House wer sold for £6,100, there had not been a picture at £500 for more than a century But the market which got off to such a bold start, has been patchy and il supplied. It is not too far-fetched to suppose that a first-class work by this mo individual painter would make well over £50,000 in the present state of ol master prices.

| | | £ |
|---|---|---|
| 1960 | Paris. The sleeping soldier, 12 × 9 | 1,536 |
| 1962 | Vincent. S. Tempestuous coast scene, 36 × 46 | 2,400 |
| 1965 | Spencer Churchill. C. Vision of Aeneas (27 guineas in 1832), 76½ × 46½ | 17,850 |
| | C. The prodigal son, pen and wash drawing, 15 × 11 | 682 10s |
| 1966 | Danby. C. Satan tempting Christ in a wild landscape, 30 × 39 | 4,410 |
| | Earl of Shaftesbury. C. A pair of rocky landscapes, 85½ × 57½ | 3,980 |
| 1968. | S. Knife-grinder and tinker, a pair, 48 × 33½ 2 for | 2,000 |

## DANTE GABRIEL ROSSETTI.  1828–1882

Possibly because they are less formidable in bulk, the works of Rossetti hav recovered rather more than those of Burne-Jones, but the escapist passion fo *Victoriana* fights shy of the Holy Grail. The mid-19th century has become agree able only when it does not aspire to high art. Shayer's apple-cheeked peasant and even the potboiling sets of hunting scenes of the younger Henry Alken ca do better than these works. The only surprise is the price of Rossetti's drawing

| | | £ |
|---|---|---|
| 1959 | Dyson Perrins. S. Pandora (see 1965, £577 10s. in 1887) | 220 |
| | The blue bower, 1865. First four-figure price since 1909 | 1,900 |

| | | £ |
|---|---|---|
| )62 | Aylwin. S. Last meeting of Launcelot and Guenevere, wc, $9\frac{1}{4} \times 14\frac{1}{2}$ (£100 in 1858) | 400 |
| | Elizabeth Siddall, pencil drawing, $10 \times 7\frac{1}{2}$ | 950 |
| )65 | C. Vision of Fiametta, $57\frac{1}{2} \times 35$ (£1,207 in 1888, £400 in 1956) | 3,990 |
| | Pandora, $50\frac{1}{2} \times 30\frac{1}{2}$ (see 1959 and 1966), bought in Cassavetti. C. Charcoal portrait, Maria Zambaco, $39 \times 28$ | 840 |
| | | 441 |
| | Leyland. S. Mona Rosa, oil-portrait, 1867, $26 \times 21$ (£105 in 1877) | 1,800 |
| | The return of Tibullus to Delia, wc, 1867, $19 \times 22\frac{3}{4}$ | 800 |
| | C. Proserpina, oils, 1877, $46 \times 22$ (£357 in 1926, £252 in 1884) | 5,250 |
| )66 | C. Pandora (see 1959, 1965) | 1,260 |
| )67 | Kerrison Preston. Paolo and Francesca, heightened wc, $12\frac{1}{2} \times 23\frac{1}{2}$, 1862 (£420 in 1939) | 2,500 |
| | Chidell. S. Jane Morris, study in chalks for *The Day Dream*, 1880, $17\frac{1}{2} \times 14$ | 900 |
| )68 | Hamilton. C. Jane Morris, 1873, pen and ink, $8\frac{1}{2} \times 6\frac{1}{2}$ (£16 16s. in 1883) | 1,680 |
| )70 | Brocklebank. C. 'Sweet tooth', half length portrait of a girl, wc, 1864, $15\frac{1}{2} \times 12$ (£40 8s. in 1904) | 5,775 |

## MAX ROTHKO. (*See* Abstract Painters, America)


## GEORGES ROUAULT. 1871–1958

ough they do not compare with those of his contemporaries, Braque and casso, the prices of Rouault's deliberately unattractive works are fairly remark-le. Rouault owed his heavily outlined style to his early training as a painter of ined glass windows. Few people are probably aware that Rouault's idiot-:ed clowns, whores and judges were meant as a puritanical Roman Catholic otest against the corruption of his age. Inspired by Goya and Daumier, he ly abandoned academic religious pictures when he was 32. Rouault had no nnection with the much-publicized rebel art of his day and was for long un-own. In 1917, when he sold two paintings to Dr Girardin for £4, he was eady 46 years old, having been born, it was said, in a cellar during the battles ainst the Paris Commune in 1871. In the 1920s Rouault began to be written-, and his work advanced to the £200 region. The real boom started after : Girardin's sale in 1953 and with such rapidity that in 1958, the year of )uault's death, a picture was sold for more than £22,000. Another ten years ere to pass before such a price was reached again.

|      |                                                                                   |        | £      |
|------|-----------------------------------------------------------------------------------|--------|--------|
| 1917 | Purchased by Dr Girardin                                                           |        |        |
|      | Le Clown and Le pitre                                                              | 2 for  | 4      |
|      | Femme couchée                                                                      |        | 8      |
|      | Femme aux bas                                                                      |        | 16     |
| 1927 | Paris.  Roland lutteur (gouache), (see 1966)                                       |        | 192    |
| 1934 | Anderson's.  N.Y.  Head of a clown                                                 |        | 82     |
| 1935 | Roger Fry.  S.  Head of a clown                                                    |        | 20     |
| 1944 | Barbée.  N.Y.  Fille de cirque (see 1949)                                          |        | 920    |
| 1946 | S.  Head of judge                                                                  |        | 880    |
|      | N.Y.  Clown à la rose                                                              |        | 1,070  |
|      | Fille de cirque (see 1944)                                                         |        | 824    |
| 1950 | S.  Three clowns                                                                   |        | 240    |
| 1951 | N.Y.  The clown                                                                    |        | 930    |
|      | Christ before Pilate                                                               |        | 855    |
| 1953 | Girardin.  Paris.  Les Poulot, wc, $28 \times 21$                                  |        | 6,150  |
| 1954 | Bessoneau.  Paris.  Benito, le clown, $21\frac{1}{2} \times 26\frac{3}{4}$         |        | 5,940  |
|      | N.Y.  Head of Christ, $23\frac{1}{2} \times 20\frac{1}{2}$                         |        | 1,730  |
| 1955 | N.Y.  Christ et le pauvre                                                          |        | 4,017  |
| 1956 | S.  Head of Christ                                                                 |        | 2,400  |
| 1958 | S.  Paysage biblique                                                               |        | 5,000  |
|      | N.Y.  Crépuscule, paysage légendaire, $62,200                                      |        | 22,215 |
| 1959 | S.  A clown                                                                        |        | 9,500  |
|      | Flowerpiece                                                                        |        | 4,200  |
| 1960 | Sarlie.  S.  Fille du cirque, $24 \times 19\frac{3}{4}$                            |        | 9,000  |
|      | Duveen.  S.  The three judges                                                      |        | 20,000 |
|      | Robinson.  N.Y.  Potentat Pierrot, $35,000                                         |        | 12,500 |
|      | Coe.  S.  Palais d'Ubu Roi, $41\frac{3}{4} \times 29\frac{1}{2}$                   |        | 14,000 |
| 1962 | Versailles.  L'Oriental, FN135,000+tax                                             |        | 11,680 |
|      | Somerset Maugham.  S.  Crucifixion                                                 |        | 6,500  |
|      | S.  Nude, 1909, $16\frac{1}{2} \times 19\frac{1}{2}$                               |        | 13,000 |
|      | Two clowns, 1930, $18\frac{1}{2} \times 11\frac{1}{2}$                             |        | 12,000 |
| 1963 | S.  Nu avec roses dans ses cheveux, 1909, $16\frac{1}{2} \times 19\frac{1}{2}$     |        | 15,000 |
|      | Wolf.  S.  Maternity                                                               |        | 7,800  |
|      | The king, 1937, $17\frac{1}{2} \times 13$                                          |        | 7,500  |
| 1964 | Bloch.  Paris.  Vase de fleurs, $21 \times 20$, FN185,000+ tax                     |        | 18,380 |
|      | Glass.  S.  Tête de Pierrot, 1937, $23\frac{3}{4} \times 17\frac{1}{2}$            |        | 15,000 |
|      | Echeverria.  C.  Femme au chapeau vert, $25 \times 19$ (see 1969)                  |        | 6,825  |
|      | Ross.  N.Y.  Fleurs décoratives, $28 \times 23$                                    |        | 16,425 |
| 1965 | Zadok.  S.  Femme au chapeau fleuri, 1938, $22 \times 16$                          |        | 12,700 |
|      | S.  Christ and the fishermen                                                       |        | 10,500 |
|      | Tête de pierrot                                                                    |        | 9,000  |
|      | Motte, Geneva.  Matutina, $29\frac{1}{4} \times 21\frac{1}{4}$, FS170,000+tax      |        | 15,600 |
|      | Bragaline.  N.Y.  Tête de Clown, $15\frac{3}{4} \times 10\frac{1}{2}$             |        | 8,930  |

| | | | £ |
|---|---|---|---|
| 1966 | S. Marriage breton, 1937, $27\frac{1}{4}\times47$ | | 14,000 |
| | Lefèvre, Paris. Roland lutteur, gouache, 1906 (see 1927) | | 9,795 |
| 1967 | S. *Miserere*, 1939, $28\times19\frac{3}{4}$ | | 7,500 |
| | La sainte Face, $24\times21$ | | 11,000 |
| | C. Les Augurs, $20\frac{3}{4}\times20$ | | 3,850 |
| | Dugdale. C. La sainte face, $9\frac{1}{2}\times8$ | | 3,150 |
| | Higgins. N.Y. Le saint suaire, $28\frac{1}{2}\times23\frac{1}{2}$, $32,500 | | 11,607 |
| | Block. C. Baigneuses, $17\frac{1}{2}\times24\frac{1}{4}$, 1910 | | 10,500 |
| | MacWelson. N.Y. Le saint suaire, $26\times20\frac{1}{4}$, 1937, $20,000 | | 7,014 |
| | Paris. Les fleurs du mal, $29\times22\frac{3}{4}$, FN190,000+tax | | 15,140 |
| 1968 | N.Y. L'homme du cirque, 1936, $23\frac{1}{2}\times15\frac{3}{4}$, $45,000 | | 18,750 |
| | Bluestein. N.Y. Le Chinois, 1937, $41\times28\frac{1}{2}$, $92,500 | | 38,535 |
| | Rosenberg. N.Y. Clown à la grosse caisse, $26\frac{3}{4}\times19\frac{3}{4}$, $37,500 | | 15,620 |
| | Paris. Clown à la rose, wc gouache, 1908, $40\times26$, FN435,000+tax | | 40,500 |
| | S. Reine de cirque, 1952, $23\frac{1}{4}\times16\frac{1}{4}$ | | 15,000 |
| | Le saint suaire, 1937, $23\times16\frac{1}{2}$ | | 11,000 |
| | Solange, $18\frac{1}{2}\times14$ | | 17,000 |
| | Paysage biblique, c. 1955, $19\times24\frac{1}{2}$ | | 15,000 |
| 1969 | Juvilier. N.Y. Femme au chapeau vert, $25\times19$ (see 1964), $56,000 | | 23,525 |
| | C. (Tokyo). Head of Christ, c. 1939, $20\times17$, 15 million Yen | | 17,522 |
| | The lovers, 1932, oil on paper, $17\times12\frac{1}{2}$, 11 million Yen | | 13,362 |
| | S. (Tokyo). Paysage biblique, $10\frac{3}{4}\times7\frac{3}{4}$, 13·5 million Yen | | 15,750 |
| | Tete d'ecuyère en profil, 1934, $25\frac{1}{4}\times16\frac{1}{4}$, 18 million Yen | | 21,150 |
| | S. L'Accusé, 1908, $38\frac{3}{4}\times28\frac{1}{4}$ | | 35,000 |
| | Swann. S. Nous croyant Roi, pastel, pen and wash, $23\times16$ | | 5,000 |

## HENRI ROUSSEAU (le douanier). 1849–1910

ꞁe first of the officially recognized modern primitives. Heaven knows what
is simple man would have made of all these prices, yet there appears to be
ꞁe limit to what can be paid for the child-mind. In fact there has been no
vance in these fairly scarce products in the course of the decade. I fancy,
vertheless, *The Sleeping Gypsy* would now be a six-figure picture.

| 1926 | Quinn. Paris. Sleeping gypsy and lion, Museum of Modern Art, N.Y., 350,000 francs+tax | £ 3,205 |
|---|---|---|
| 1928 | Bought by Ferdinand Howald. The tiger hunt. Columbus Art Institute, $5,000 | 1,030 |
| 1950 | Moos, Geneva. Pêcheur a la ligne, $7 \times 10$ | 350 |
| | Stuttgart. Lac Daumesnil, $15 \times 9\frac{3}{4}$ | 780 |
| 1954 | Paris. Flowers and book, $16 \times 12\frac{1}{2}$ | 1,250 |
| 1959 | S. Statue of Diana, $9 \times 4$ | 2,000 |
| | N.Y. View of St Cloud, $13\frac{1}{4} \times 10$, $25,000 | 8,930 |
| | Paris. Vue de Paris, oil on paper, $9 \times 6\frac{1}{2}$ | 1,250 |
| 1961 | S. Les joueurs de football, 1908, $39\frac{1}{2} \times 31\frac{1}{2}$. Guggenheim Foundation | 37,000 |
| | S. Un coin du chateau de Bellevue, $23\frac{1}{2} \times 19$ | 8,000 |
| | View of Paris fortifications, 1906, $18 \times 21\frac{1}{2}$ | 14,000 |
| 1963 | Hyde Bonner. S. La sainte famille, $35 \times 25$ (see 1965) | 7,000 |
| 1964 | Bloch. Paris. Le maréchal de logis, Frumence Biche, 1893, $36\frac{3}{4} \times 29\frac{1}{4}$, FN70,000+tax | 5,620 |
| 1965 | N.Y. Vue des fortifications, $18 \times 24$, $44,000 | 15,714 |
| | La sainte famille, $35 \times 25$, $19,600 | 7,000 |
| | Lefèvre. Paris. Paysage avec une vache, 1909, $13\frac{1}{4} \times 18\frac{1}{2}$ | 9,960 |
| | S. Route de village, 1886, $14\frac{1}{4} \times 18$ | 10,000 |
| 1966 | S. Landscape with fisherman in punt, 1886, $9\frac{1}{4} \times 14\frac{1}{2}$ | 11,000 |
| | Paris. Chemin de fer de la ceinture, $14\frac{1}{2} \times 18\frac{1}{2}$ | 5,200 |
| | La baignade à Alfortville, $14\frac{1}{2} \times 18\frac{1}{2}$ | 5,580 |
| 1968 | Paris. Parc Montsouris, $26 \times 21\frac{1}{2}$, FN50,000+tax | 4,705 |

## THÉODORE ROUSSEAU. 1812–1867

No one is surprised that the paintings of the Barbizon school are cheap. T
surprise is that they should ever have been dear. No one in terms of real mor
paid as much for a Picasso as the long forgotten Senator Clark of Idaho paid
Rousseau's *Fisherman* in 1913 (see Vol. I, p. 174). But prices, equivalent
£40,000 in 1970 money, had been paid as far back as 1878. What qualities w
they paying for? Théodore Rousseau's short painting life was contempor:
with the romantic style as practised by the followers of Turner and Delacro
when a landscape was absolutely obliged to contain brightly coloured figu:
Rousseau and the Barbizon school in general left out the figures and refused
dramatize their landscapes. Their pictures were earthy, realist and, despit
breadth and freedom of brush work that foretold Impressionism, rather Dut
That did not make them rich, and the boom which began towards 1880, fou
most of them dead. It lasted well into the 1920s. Some speculation in
Barbizons may now be expected. In 1969 a Daubigny was sold—in Tokyo
all places—for more than £10,000. However, an age, so captivated with

hibitionism as the present, is unlikely to accept the Barbizons as anything more than an incident in art-history, accessible to students on written application a fortnight in advance.

| 1898 | Fuller-Dana. N.Y. The charcoal burner's hut (£4,000 in 1878, £3,050 in 1889) | £ 7,300 |
|---|---|---|
| 1907 | Henry. N.Y. Le rayon de soleil | 4,320 |
| 1909 | Cuthbertson. C. Winding road | 4,830 |
| 1910 | Butler. N.Y. Bosquet d'arbres (see 1926), $27,250 | 5,610 |
| | Yerkes. N.Y. Paysage | 5,220 |
| 1912 | Carcano. Paris. L'allée des châtaigniers (£1,080 in 1868), bought by the Louvre, 270,000 francs | 10,800 |
| 1913 | Bought by Senator Clark of Idaho. The fisherman, $164,000 | 33,000 |
| | MacMillin. N.Y. Plaine en Berry, $42,300 | 8,730 |
| 1918 | Curel. Paris. Maison de Garde, 135,000 francs+tax | 5,940 |
| 1926 | Billings. N.Y. Bosquet d'arbres (see 1910), $25,000 | 5,140 |
| 1934 | Eli Springs. N.Y. Same picture falls to $5,000 | 1,028 |
| 1945 | Cornelius Vanderbilt. N.Y. Gorges d'Apremont, $2,700 | 673 |
| | Farm on the Oise, $2,700 | 673 |
| | River landscape, $3,200 | 798 |
| 1951 | S. Woods at Fontainebleau, 25×39 | 200 |
| 1952 | Nuttall. N.Y Impending storm | 464 |
| 1956 | Metropolitan Museum. N.Y. Evening, $1,800 | 643 |
| 1958 | Lehman. N.Y. Small landscape with cows | 1,150 |
| | S. Marais dans les Landes | 2,100 |
| 1960 | Ionides. C. Landscape | 387 10s. |
| 1963 | C. Lisière d'un bois coupé, Fontainebleau, 19½×28 | 1,890 |
| 1964 | C. Pond in a wood, 13×23¾ | 1,890 |
| 1965 | C. Sunset landscape | 367 10s. |
| | Valley in Auvergne | 1,312 10s. |
| 1967 | S. Clairière dans la forêt, 1850, 34×35¾ (the dearest in more than 40 years) | 3,400 |
| 1968 | Scott. C. Village dans l'Auvergne, 7¾×12½ | 3,570 |

## THOMAS ROWLANDSON. (*See* English School, 18th century)

## PETER PAUL RUBENS. 1577–1640

In terms of the true purchasing power of money the most famous names in the history of painting have advanced very little since the beginning of the century. Even in the era of inflation the few works that have reached the market have barely kept pace with devaluation. Paintings that have been very expensive for a very long time, cannot be expected to share in the adventurous speculations which take place when an artist is rediscovered overnight like James Seymour or Antonio Joli. Rubens provides the occasional exception, for the simple reason that his market was unnaturally depressed in the first half of the century. In the year 1885 the Duke of Marlborough sold three works to the Rothschild family for prices equivalent to £204,000, £236,000 and £305,000 in 1970 terms (actually £22,750, £26,250, and £35,000). Such sales were no longer possible when buying on this scale passed to the first-generation millionaires of the New World, who could not accommodate themselves to all this fleshiness. In the course of the next 70 years only three works by Rubens reached £50,000, and all were portraits. The moral prejudice against the pagan subjects of Rubens, which had been strong once before in early Victorian times, did not end till the Cleveland Museum's purchase of one of the versions of *Diana and the Nymphs* in 1956 at £100,000.

In the ensuing list, which has been taken back to the beginning of the century and amplified from Volume One, it will be noticed that a number of works have been demoted to the rank of school-pieces or workshop copies. Realization in the early years of the century of the bad commercial practices, which were tolerated in Rubens's day, provided a further and perhaps even stronger factor in depressing the market. There were, however, two purchases in 1965 and 1966 by the Metropolitan Museum and the National Gallery which suggested that directors and trustees were finding the critics of the past too critical. Despite these two hilariously incredible revisions of judgement, Rubens's oil sketches, which are at any rate the work of a single hand, tended in the 1960s to advance more rapidly than the alleged final versions. One of these, *Constantine and Maxentius* was sold at Christies in 1939 for 1,500 guineas. Its companion made 50,000 guineas on the same spot in 1968. The pair of brilliant oil sketches (an unworthy description for works so complete) which were sold a year later for £350,000, would certainly not have made as much as £5,000 in 1939, and perhaps no more than £3,000. This is more like the progression of an Impressionist picture than that of an old master.

|      |                                                                                                                          | £      |
|------|--------------------------------------------------------------------------------------------------------------------------|--------|
| 1901 | Alfred Buckley.   Descent from the Cross, oil sketch                                                                      | 3,360  |
| 1902 | Mathiesson.   N.Y.   Holy family (£3,715 in 1899)                                                                         | 10,000 |
| 1910 | de Mesnil.   Paris.   Holy Family (£4,480 in Crabbe sale 1890)                                                            | 3,200  |
|      | Yerkes.   N.Y.   Ixion deceived by Juno.   Louvre (valued £3,200 in 1806), $30,000                                        | 6,160  |
| 1911 | Butler.   C.   Lot and his daughters (£1,942 10s. in 1886, see also 1927)                                                 | 6,825  |
| 1915 | Blakeslee Galleries.   N.Y.   The Bourg St Vinox adoration, (£1,248 in 1768, £1,260 in 1853), School-piece, $13,000       | 2,689  |
| 1918 | Albert Oppenheim, Berlin.   Triumph of Good Government                                                                    | 8,100  |

| | | £ |
|---|---|---|
| 1919 | 2nd Hamilton Palace sale.   C.   Daniel in the lions' den, 80×130, bought by Lord Cowdray (£5,145 in 1882, see also 1963, 1965) | 2,520 |
| | Bought by H. C. Frick.   Portrait, Marquess Spinola, Frick Foundation, $90,000 according to R. Gimpel | 18,500 |
| 1923 | Brownlow.   C.   Flight into Egypt, nocturne oil sketch | 2,625 |
| 1924 | Duke of Westminster.   C.   Three of the four Loeches cartoons for a tapestry (which were bought in 1818 for £10,000).   Ringling Museum, Sarasota   3 bought in at | 2,415 |
| 1925 | Earl of Darnley.   C.   Head of an old woman.   National Gallery, Toronto | 2,100 |
| 1926 | C.   Holy family, ex Blenheim Palace (£1,428, in 1886, £3,759 in 1946).   School-piece, 41×30 | 1,732 10s. |
| 1927 | Ross.   C.   Lot and his daughters (£6,825 in 1911, £1,942 10s. in 1886).   School-piece, 85×96 | 2,205 |
| 1928 | U.S.S.R. Government.   Berlin.   Head of an old man with long white hair, 26¾×21 | 1,495 |
| | Holford.   C.   Erection of the Cross, oil sketch, National Gallery, Toronto | 5,460 |
| | Mrs Leverton Harris.   C.   Anton Triest, archbishop of Ghent, head | 9,660 |
| 1929 | U.S.S.R. Government, sale to Calouste Gulbenkian, whole-length portrait of Helena Fourment (ex Hermitage Museum), now in Gulbenkian Foundation, Lisbon | 55,000 |
| 1933 | Barrymore.   S.   Set of oil sketches for a tapestry suite, the life of Achilles.   Boymans Museum, Rotterdam.   Bought by J. D. Beuningen   6 for | 9,200 |
| 1935 | Bought from J. P. Morgan, Jnr by the Metropolitan Museum.   Portrait, Anne of Austria (£3,885 in 1886) | 51,500 |
| 1936 | Bought from Duveen by Andrew Mellon.   Portrait of Isabella Brandt.   National Gallery, Washington, $250,000 | 50,425 |
| | Bought by National Gallery from D. of Buccleuch.   The Watering Place, landscape | 20,000 |
| | Currie.   C.   Portrait, Princess Doria | 2,835 |
| 1939 | D. of Newcastle.   C.   Constantine and Maxentius, oil sketch (£273 in 1856), compare 1968 | 1,575 |
| 1944 | Neeld.   C.   Portrait, Peter Pecquius | 16,800 |
| 1946 | N.Y.   Holy Family (£1,428 in 1886, £1,732 10s. in 1926) School-piece, $15,000 | 3,750 |
| | Earl of Halifax.   C.   Holy family and infant St John, small oil sketch | 6,930 |
| 1949 | S.   Suicide of Dido, oil sketch (recently bought at a country auction for £2 10s.) | 3,200 |
| 1951 | Lord Belper.   S.   Via crucis, grisaille painting (see 1961) | 5,000 |
| 1955 | Vanderbilt-Twembly.   N.Y.   Philip IV, portrait head | 5,750 |

£

1956   Bought by Cleveland Museum.   Diana and Nymphs
       (compare 1962)                                          100,000
1957   Christopher Norris.   S.   Adoration of the Magi, oil
       sketch                                                   14,000
1958   Guttman.   S.   Coronation of the Virgin, oil sketch      7,500
       Barchard.   S.   Abraham and Melchizedek, oil sketch for
       the *Loeches tapestries* (see Vol. 1, p. 54)             33,000
1959   Duke of Westminster.   S.   Adoration of the Kings,
       altarpiece of the White Sisters, Louvain, $129\frac{1}{4}\times97\frac{1}{4}$ (£700
       in 1783, £800 in 1806).   New College chapel per Major
       Allnatt                                                 275,000
       Kingston Hall Estates.   S.   Portrait head, bearded man,
       $27\times21$                                             35,000
1960   Bought by Walker Gallery, Liverpool, from D. of Devon-
       shire estate, Holy Family, oil sketch                    50,000
       Bergander.   C.   Portrait, Dr Garnerius, $43\frac{3}{4}\times29\frac{1}{4}$, bought
       in                                                       11,550
       Tibor de Buday.   C.   Proxy marriage of Henri IV, oil
       sketch for Triumphs of Marie de Medici, $23\frac{1}{2}\times19$    4,751 5s.
1961   Makower.   S. (with Jan Breughel).   Pan and Syrinx,
       $15\times24$                                             14,200
       S.   Via crucis, grisaille oil sketch, $25\frac{3}{4}\times18$ (see 1951 and
       1965)                                                    21,000
1962   Bought by Paul Getty, 2nd version of Diana and the
       Nymphs (see 1956)      said to have been approximately 200,000
1963   Cintas.   N.Y.   Woman taken in adultery, $40\times54$, replica
       of the Brussels picture (£2,100 in 1816)                 8,929
       Sold by Whitehall Estates.   Daniel in the lions' den, over
       10 ft long (£5,145 in 1882, £2,520 in 1919, see also 1965),
       then attributed to Jordaens                                500
       Bass.   N.Y.   Holy family with St Anne, $60\times46$ (£183 15s.
       in 1878), $75,000                                        26,785
1965   Roose.   S.   Conversion of St Paul, $28\times40$         24,000
       Francis.   S.   Woman and boy by candlelight, attributed
       oil sketch, $29\frac{1}{2}\times23\frac{3}{4}$           19,000
       Williams-Wynne.   S.   The Latin fathers of the church,
       oil sketch for tapestry cartoon, $26\frac{1}{2}\times18\frac{1}{2}$    17,500
       Lyndall-Alesbury.   S.   Via crucis, $25\frac{3}{4}\times18$, grisaille (see
       1961)                                                    18,000
       Margadale of Islay.   C.   Eleonora de Bourbon, early por-
       trait in Pourbus style                                   30,450
       Spencer Churchill.   C.   Lion hunt, 10 ft school-piece
       (£157 10s. in 1859, £300 in 1847)                         5,775
       C.   Oil sketch of the same much repeated subject, $22\times41$    7,875

1965   Stonor.   S.   Oil sketch for the lost painting, Neptune and   £
Amphitrite, $13\frac{3}{4} \times 20\frac{1}{2}$                                        12,000

Sold by Knoedler, N.Y., to Metropolitan Museum, Daniel in the lions' den (£5,150 in 1882, £2,520 in 1919, £500 in 1963), $500,000                          178,600

1966   S.   Nymphs and satyrs, $29\frac{1}{4} \times 39$, possibly a school-piece     9,500

Eva Savage.   C.   Judgment of Paris, $52\frac{3}{4} \times 68\frac{1}{2}$, no pedigree.   Bought in, 1965 (when offered as a Lankrink) at £1,575.   Bought in again and subsequently acquired by the National Gallery (!)                        25,250

C.   Samson and Delilah, oil sketch for a picture now in Cologne, $21 \times 23\frac{1}{2}$                                25,250

1967   Wyatt.   S.   The triumph of Hope, oil sketch, $6\frac{1}{2} \times 8$     9,000

1968   Bernard de Chatenet.   S.   David and Abigail, oil sketch $17\frac{1}{4} \times 27$, very dubious                   bought in at   14,000

C.   Wooded landscape at sunset, $11 \times 15$          21,000

C.   Holy Family with Sts Elizabeth and Joseph, $45\frac{1}{2} \times 34$ (£483 in Blenheim sale, 1886).   School-piece       4,620

Kaplan.   S.   Head of bearded man, $28 \times 21\frac{1}{2}$         13,000

Half-length, Sir Theodore de Mayerne, $44\frac{1}{4} \times 35$     4,200

C.   Marriage of Constantine, $18\frac{1}{2} \times 25\frac{1}{2}$, oil sketch for panel in tapestry suite (compare 1939) (£37 16s. in 1819)     51,450

S.   Head of bearded man, curling locks, $27\frac{3}{4} \times 21\frac{1}{4}$, bought in                                    36,000

1969   Mertens.   Grisaille oil sketch, the Last Supper, $24\frac{1}{4} \times 19$   15,000

S. (Ex Edmond de Rothschild).   The Rape of the Sabines and the Conciliation of the Romans and Sabines, pair of oil sketches, $22 \times 34\frac{1}{2}$                   2 for   350,000

Bruguière.   C.   Half-length portrait of a Dominican friar in prayer, $25\frac{1}{2} \times 30\frac{1}{2}$                        7,875

S.   Head, bearded old man, attributed, $18 \times 12\frac{1}{2}$       5,000

## DRAWINGS

1902   Sir J. C. Robinson.   C.   Study for the Garden of Hesperides                                      861

1914   Biron.   Paris.   Portrait of a lady, sanguine and crayon   642

1918   Sir E. Poynter.   S.   Double portrait, Rubens and his wife   490

1920   Marquess of Lansdowne.   C.   Girl's head, charcoal     330

1928   Holford.   C.   Portrait, Helena Fourment, crayon and sanguine                                     6,825

Bancroft.   S.   Susanne Fourment, crayon and sanguine   2,650

1936   Henry Oppenheimer.   C.   Two studies of a faun.   Cleveland Museum                               1,102 10s.

Landscape study                                    892 10s.

| | | £ |
|---|---|---|
| 1940 | Ellis.   S.   Nymphs bathing | 430 |
| 1954 | Henry Reitlinger.   S.   Angel blowing trumpet, crayon | 510 |
| 1959 | Holland Martin (Skippe Coll.).   C.   Martyrdom of St Ursula | 787 10s. |
| | Cain cursed by God, red chalk | 777 |
| 1963 | C.   Battle scene, pen and ink, attributed, $7\frac{3}{4} \times 10\frac{1}{4}$ | 840 |
| | Sterling of Keir.   S.   Head of Susanne Fourment | 4,200 |
| 1965 | S.   St Francis receiving the infant Christ | 3,150 |
| | Samson (after Tobias Stimmer) | 1,100 |
| | Jaffe.   S.   Soldier with halberd, chalk and wash | 5,000 |
| | von Masch.   S.   Thomyris and Cyrus, wash and body colour, $16 \times 24$ | 8,000 |
| 1969 | Fenwick-Owen.   S.   Lion, black chalk heightened white, study for Daniel in the lions' den, $10 \times 11\frac{1}{2}$ | 20,000 |
| 1970 | Burchard.   S.   Recumbent Pan, red and black chalk, body colour and wash $12\frac{1}{2} \times 19\frac{1}{2}$ | 18,500 |

## CHARLES MARION RUSSELL.   (*See* American School, 19th–20th centuries)

## JACOB VAN RUYSDAEL.   1628–1682

Waterfalls and ruins are not what are wanted of the Dutch school in 1970. Town views, domestic interiors, flowerpieces and fishing boats—yes, but not Jacob van Ruysdael though the National Gallery accepted twelve of his works in the last century and would doubtless have taken more, had they been offered. 20,000 guineas may seem a high price for an unpopular style, but not when compared with those of 2 or 3 generations ago, for instance 4,200 guineas in 1895 and 12,000 guineas in 1919, equivalent in 1970 to £35,000 and £63,000 respectively.

| | | £ |
|---|---|---|
| 1960 | Russell.   S.   Wooded landscape with shepherds, $19\frac{3}{4} \times 20\frac{3}{4}$ | 8,500 |
| | Edge of the Zuyder Zee | 4,500 |
| 1961 | S.   Wooded landscape, attributed | 5,300 |
| 1962 | S.   Wooded landscape | 3,000 |
| | Bonham's.   Open wooded landscape, $16 \times 16$ | 9,450 |
| 1963 | Heldring.   S.   Wooded landscape, 1648 | 5,500 |
| | View of a town in winter | 8,500 |
| | S.   Road by a wood, ex Hermitage Museum | 3,900 |
| | Wooded landscape (see 1969) | 4,500 |
| | D. of Leeds.   S.   Hilly landscape with trees, $38\frac{3}{4} \times 49$ | 12,000 |

| | | | £ |
|---|---|---|---|
| 1966 | Zetland. S. Wooded landscape, $24 \times 33\frac{1}{2}$ | | 7,800 |
| | Cook Trust. C. Landscape with mill, sold as the work of a follower, $19 \times 27\frac{1}{2}$ | | 8,950 |
| | Boomkamp. S. Landscape with a silver birch, $38\frac{1}{2} \times 51$ | | 9,500 |
| | Paris. Landscape with tall trees | | 8,650 |
| 1967 | S. Coastal scene with paddlers, $21 \times 26\frac{1}{2}$ | | 3,800 |
| 1968 | Wooded landscape with cornfield, signed, $16 \times 17$ | | 13,000 |
| 1969 | Ford at the edge of a wood, $23\frac{1}{4} \times 19\frac{3}{4}$ | | 7,000 |
| | Hardie. S. Wooded landscape with torrent, $17 \times 20$ (see 1963) | | 20,500 |
| | Bruguière. C. Waterfall with house, $26\frac{3}{4} \times 20\frac{1}{2}$ | | 5,040 |
| | Hardie. S. Wooded landscape, waterfall, $17 \times 20\frac{3}{4}$ | | 14,000 |

## SALOMON VAN RUYSDAEL. 1600–1670

The uncle's work is sometimes much higher priced than the nephew's. This occurs when he painted in a less artificial convention and with something of Van Goyen's observation of tone and atmosphere which has appealed to the last three generations of collectors. The sudden leap to 50,000 guineas in 1969 was the more remarkable because the subject of this bid was not outstanding.

| | | £ |
|---|---|---|
| 1960 | van Aalst. C. The ferry | 15,750 |
| | Milligan. C. Estuary scene dated 1651 | 9,450 |
| | Benn. S. River landscape, 1647, $28 \times 36\frac{3}{4}$ | 7,000 |
| 1962 | S. Estuary scene, $7\frac{1}{2} \times 10\frac{1}{2}$ | 7,200 |
| 1963 | Heldring. S. River landscape, 1663 | 10,800 |
| 1964 | Werner. S. River scene, 1644, $24\frac{1}{2} \times 36$ | 19,500 |
| 1965 | C. Wooded landscape, cattle and ferry, 1661, $42 \times 60$ (see 1969) | 7,875 |
| 1966 | Mangold. S. The edge of the wood, $21\frac{1}{4} \times 31\frac{1}{2}$ | 4,000 |
| | Vivian. C. Ferry and cart horses, 1637, $38 \times 54$ | 6,300 |
| 1967 | Boomkamp. S. Distant view of the Hague, 1647, $29\frac{1}{2} \times 43\frac{1}{2}$ | 8,500 |
| 1968 | Kaplan. S. Skating scene with church, 1659, $29\frac{1}{2} \times 39\frac{3}{4}$ | 11,500 |
| | Wrottesley. S. Wooded landscape with church, 1657, $14 \times 20\frac{3}{4}$ | 16,000 |
| | C. Town with river and fishing boats, $25 \times 40\frac{1}{2}$ | 8,190 |
| 1969 | C. Wooded landscape, cattle and ferry, $42 \times 60$ (see 1965) | 12,600 |
| | S. Fishing boats in estuary, $9\frac{1}{2} \times 11\frac{3}{4}$ | 4,200 |
| | Bruguière. C. Ferryboat and village, 1655, $33\frac{3}{4} \times 44\frac{3}{4}$ | 52,500 |

THEO VAN RYSSELBERGHE. (*See* French School, Minor Impressionists)

PIETER SAANREDAM. (*See* Dutch School)

PAUL SANDBY. (*See* English School, 18th century)

GABRIEL DE SAINT AUBIN. (*See* French School, 17th and 18th centuries)

ROBERT SALMON. (*See* American School, 19th century)

## JOHN SINGÉR SARGENT. 1856–1925

This is one of the most interesting market recoveries of the 1960s. The fall of the Sargent market was not due to the slump of the 1930s. It had started earlier, having been triggered off by the growing American preference for true Impressionism in the 1920s. The high watermark for Sargent was reached soon after his executors' sale in 1925. In 1928 the most famous of his huge swash-buckling whole-length groups was sold to the Metropolitan Museum for £18,000, the equivalent of £90,000 in 1970. In 1929 there came the first tremors. By the time that the Second World War had broken out, a two-foot landscape in oils could be had for under £50, while £5 to £10 would have bought any of the once so fashionable charcoal portrait-drawings. The recovery went so far that in 1970 £7,000 for the former and £1,000 for the latter would be average prices. The interesting thing is that this recovery began in the middle 1950s just when the new mania for the Impressionists dominated American buyers. Sargent's position was no longer prejudiced by his rejection of Impressionism. The cultural tyranny of Paris had collapsed, the U.S.A. had become a world power, and patriotic connoisseurship could flourish, unabashed, except for the fact that patriotic markets are always in some degree subordinate to truly international markets. Even in 1969 when about £30,000 was paid for a very unemotional portrait group which might just have reached £1,000 four years earlier, Sargent did not become a market rival of the Impressionists.

£

959 N.Y. Monet's garden at Giverny, oil — 1,555
961 Valence. C. Don Baltazar Carlos after Velazquez, 24½ × 17½ (£6,300 in 1925) — 1,995
Alvan Fuller. C. Javanese dancer, oil, 68 × 31½ (£2,310 in 1925) — 6,825
San Vigilio, Corfu, oil, 22 × 28 (£7,350 in 1925) — 4,200
Baltazar Carlos on horseback after Velazquez (£1,940 in 1925), 18 × 14½ — 2,940
962 Parsons. S. Study for 'Carnation, lily, lily, rose', 23½ × 19½ (the final version was sold in 1887 for £700) — 2,700
963 Valdes. C. Boy's head reclining, wc — 735
C. Venice, small wc — 441
964 S. Garden of Gethsemane, wc — 1,600
C. Ornamental temple in garden, oil, 19 × 23 — 1,155
965 C. Tyrolese crucifix, 1913, oil, 28½ × 21½ — 1,260
S. Miss Gould, whole length — 850
Lady Huntingdon, whole length, 92 × 50½ — 1,250
N.Y. Still-life of a salmon, wc, 12¼ × 18½, $1,600 — 575
Mme Errazuris, charcoal portrait — 1,000
966 C. The Salute, Venice, pavement view, wc, 9¾ × 12¼ — 441
Whitney Museum Benefit. N.Y. Bowls at Ightham Moat, 1889, 56 × 90 — 4,525
967 C. Pencil study for 'gassed', 1918, 18 × 23½ — 231
Vlasto. C. Caterina Vlasto, 1897, 59 × 33½ — 997 10s.
Harker. S. Scuola di san Rocco, Venice, oil, 25 × 25 — 7,000
968 Howard Johnston. N.Y. Claude Monet painting in his *bateau-atelier*, 23½ × 19¼, $37,500 — 15,625
Lewis. N.Y. Valdemosa, Majorca, girls gathering blossom, 1910, oil, 28 × 22, $13,500 — 5,625
C. Head of an Arab, wc, 1905, 12½ × 10¼ — 1,575
Dilke. N.Y. Mrs Ashton Dilke, 34¾ × 27¼, $14,500 — 6,042
969 N.Y. Mrs Edward L. Davis and her son, whole-length group, $72,500, 1890, 86 × 48 — 30,215
C. Study for detail from Carnation, lily, lily, rose, 1886, 28½ × 18½ (1942 with another, £40) — 5,775


ANDREA DEL SARTO. (*See* Italian School, central, 15th–16th centuries)


JAMES NOTT SARTORIUS. (*See* Sporting Pictures)

JAN SCOREL. (*See* Flemish School, before 1550)

## SAMUEL SCOTT. 1710–1772

The sudden growth of this market is linked with the build-up of the Pau
Mellon foundation and dates from 1958. Previously paintings by Samuel Sco
had been a standard commodity for seventy years, varying according to siz
from £100 to £500, the London and Thames-side views being preferred to h
ship-paintings. It is astonishing that a painter who did little but copy Canalettc
should rate in the 1960s above Reynolds and Romney, but there was one c
Scott's contemporaries and admirers who would not have quarrelled with tha
judgement. Horace Walpole decided in 1763 that Scott was 'the first painter c
his age'. In 1771 he went even further, pronouncing Scott's disciple, Willia
Marlow to be 'a better painter than the Venetian,' two works of his having ju
made Canaletto prices (see English school, 18th century). In the 1960s Scott
larger Thames-side views twice exceeded £30,000, but Canaletto's versions o
the same majestic scale would certainly have made at least four times as mucl

|      |                                                                                       |       | £        |
|------|---------------------------------------------------------------------------------------|-------|----------|
| 1754 | Dundas.   View through the arches of Westminster Bridge                                |       | 15 4s.   |
| 1757 | Scott's charges for Thames-side pictures:                                              |       |          |
|      | Kitcat size, 26 × 50                                                                   |       | 26 5s.   |
|      | Half-length size, 39 × 75                                                              |       | 42       |
| 1853 | Bought by the Earl of Northwick, two views of London                                  |       |          |
|      | including Westminster Bridge (see 1965 and 1968)                                       | 2 for | 44 2s.   |
| 1883 | C.   A similar pair of views                                                           | 2 for | 75 12s   |
| 1888 | Hardwicke.   C.   Pool of London below London Bridge, 124 × 42                         |       | 441      |
| 1941 | Rothermere.   C.   Westminster Bridge from South Bank (sold as Canaletto)             |       | 4,620    |
| 1945 | Lord Moyne.   C.   Thames with unfinished Westminster Bridge, 14¾ × 27¾, now attributed to Joli (see 1967) |       | 231      |
| 1950 | S.   Horse Guards Parade, 29½ × 49½                                                    |       | 500      |
| 1951 | S.   Thames-side view, 17 × 22¾                                                        |       | 155      |
| 1958 | C.   London below Westminster Bridge, 43 × 58                                          |       | 2,100    |
| 1960 | C.   Old Westminster Bridge, 31 × 48                                                   |       | 2,835    |
| 1961 | C.   Building of Westminster Bridge, 1742, 33 × 61                                     |       | 7,350    |
| 1963 | C.   St James' Park, 25 × 57                                                           |       | 11,550   |
| 1964 | Jervoise.   S.   Building Westminster Bridge, 1750, 39 × 75                            |       | 32,000   |
| 1965 | Peake.   S.   Two views of the Thames-side from Somerset House, 29 × 39½               | 2 for | 14,000   |
|      | S.   Pool of London with Tower, 38¾ × 75¾                                              |       | 20,000   |
|      | Spencer Churchill, C.   Two views including Westminster Bridge, 27 × 46 (see 1853 and 1968) | 2 for | 21,000   |
|      | Wanstead House and river, 39¼ × 49                                                     |       | 2,520    |

| | | £ |
|---|---|---|
| 965 | Lord Braybrook. S. Pool of London and Tower, 1746, 39×75 | 33,000 |
| | Thames at Westminster, 1746, 39×75 | 21,000 |
| 966 | C. Men of war off rocky coast, school picture, 1738, 25×51 | 1,575 |
| | Lady Diana Cooper. S. Launch of a 60-gunner, 1745, 24×34 | 2,000 |
| | S. Harwich from the sea, 19½×35 | 7,200 |
| | Zouche. C. Charing Cross and Northumberland House, school picture, 33½×49 | 2,520 |
| | S. Thames at Lambeth, 23½×44½, 1758 | 2,900 |
| 967 | C. Thames with unfinished Westminster Bridge, 14¾×17¼ (see 1945, now attributed to Antonio Joli) | 12,600 |
| | The Paper Buildings in the Temple, 33¼×48½ | 5,775 |
| | Landing of William III at Torbay, painted 1726, 36½×42½ | 6,825 |
| 968 | C. Thames-side, downstream from Westminster Bridge, 26×47 (see 1853 and 1965) | 10,500 |
| | Anthony Asquith. S. Horse Guards' parade and Rosamond's Pond, 15×29 | 28,000 |
| 969 | C. School-piece ascribed 'Scott', London Bridge from Tower, 13½×50½ | 2,730 |
| | Solly. S. St Saviour's dock, charcoal and wc drawing, inscribed and dated 1753, 11¼×17½ | 2,500 |
| | Lloyd. S. (ascribed S. Scott). Horse Guards Parade, 35½×53 | 3,800 |
| | Sold by United Services Club. Lord Anson's victory off Cape Finisterre | 26,000 |

## DOMINIC SERRES. (*See* English School, 18th century)

## GEORGES PIERRE SEURAT. 1859–1891

Less than a dozen works by Seurat reached the salerooms in the 1960s, studies not more than seven inches wide at the price of completed works by any of the Impressionists and their successors. Seurat lived only 32 years, and almost all that he produced were stages in the construction of a few large works of a laboriously fine texture. Whether these prices express the present popularity of Seurat's peculiar obsessive style or only its rarity it would be very hard to say. In 1926 Albert C. Barnes paid more for *Les poseuses* than anyone had given for a Cézanne. The price expected in 1970 for a small replica of this work suggests that Seurat has retained his status.

| | | £ |
|---|---|---|
| 1921 | Kelekian. N.Y. La poudreuse (bought by J. Quinn), $5,200 | 1,300 |
| 1922 | de Zayas. N.Y. Les poseuses, small replica, $15\frac{1}{2} \times 19\frac{1}{4}$, (see 1970) Bt. J. Quinn, $5,500                           about | 1,375 |
| 1923 | La cirque, bought by J. Quinn. The Louvre (1924) | 1,900 |
| 1924 | Bought by Tate Gallery, Courtauld Fund. Une baignade | 3,917 |
| | Bought by F. C. Bartlett. La grande jatte, Chicago Museum, modern Art. $24,000 | 6,000 |
| 1926 | Bought by Albert C. Barnes. Les poseuses. Barnes Foundation (allegedly $50,000) $79 \times 99$ | 10,285 |
| 1932 | S. Landscape, oil sketch, $6\frac{1}{2} \times 10$ (compare 1963–6) | 160 |
| 1944 | Barbée. N.Y. L'Isle de la grande jatte, first study in oils, $6 \times 10$ | 1,592 |
| 1947 | N.Y. Seascape, small oil sketch | 350 |
| 1950 | Paris. Paysage au tas-bois, oil sketch, $6\frac{3}{4} \times 6\frac{1}{4}$ | 562 |
| 1954 | N.Y. Parade des danseuses, coloured crayons | 2,320 |
| 1957 | Edward Robinson. N.Y. Private sale to Stavros Nearchos (according to R. H. Rush), Le Crôtoy, 1889 | 66,800 |
| | Weinberg. S. Le Faucheur, $15 \times 19$ | 22,000 |
| | Study for la grande jatte, $6\frac{1}{2} \times 9\frac{3}{4}$ | 7,000 |
| | Street scene, study, $6 \times 9\frac{3}{4}$ | 5,500 |
| | La crepuscule, charcoal drawing, $9 \times 12$ | 3,000 |
| 1958 | Sutherland. S. Study for *Une baignade*, $6\frac{1}{4} \times 10$ | 12,000 |
| 1960 | Rewald. S. Honfleur, charcoal drawing, $9\frac{1}{2} \times 12$ | 5,000 |
| 1962 | Woolworth. N.Y. Au bord d'une rivière, 1884, $6\frac{1}{4} \times 10$ | 8,570 |
| 1963 | Cargill. S. Study for *une baignade*, $6\frac{3}{4} \times 10\frac{1}{2}$ | 28,000 |
| | Personnages dans un pré, $6 \times 9\frac{3}{4}$ (compare 1958) | 34,000 |
| 1965 | Boulton. S. Two landscape oil sketches, $6\frac{1}{2} \times 10$ | ⎰ 37,000 ⎱ 33,000 |
| 1966 | S. Paysannes à Montfermeuil, $6\frac{1}{4} \times 9\frac{3}{4}$, 1882 | 36,000 |
| | C. Vers le Bourg, oil sketch, 1883, $6\frac{3}{4} \times 10$. Bought in at | 21,000 |
| 1969 | S. Estacade de Port en Bessin, $8\frac{3}{4} \times 11\frac{3}{4}$, charcoal sketch | 5,000 |
| 1970 | C. Les poseuses, replica of the Barnes picture (see 1926), $15\frac{1}{2} \times 19\frac{1}{4}$ (de Zayas sale, N.Y. 1922, $5,500) | 430,500 |

### JAMES SEYMOUR. (*See* Sporting Pictures)

### WILLIAM SHAYER SENR. (*See* English School, 19th century)

### JAN SIBERECHTS. (*See* Dutch School)

### WALTER SICKERT. (*See* English School, 20th century)

## PAUL SIGNAC. 1863–1935

The second *pointillist* painter was Seurat's junior by four years, but he lived a normal span of time, produced many more pictures and was less scrupulously painstaking. Both painters evolved a sort of succession style to Impressionism, but popularity was even slower in coming to them than to the Impressionists. In 1930, when even an important sale could not raise the price of three Signac landscapes beyond £540, the painter was already 67 years old. Substantial prices were not paid before the late 1950s. As in the case of most modern painters, Signac's prices were more than doubled in 1968–9, when eight of his works which hardly surpassed the average, made from £36,000 to £52,000 each.

|      |                                                                                                        | £      |
|------|--------------------------------------------------------------------------------------------------------|--------|
| 1930 | Canonne.  Paris.  Three landscapes made a total of                                                     | 540    |
| 1939 | Canonne, 2nd sale.  Paris.  Les bouées, 16,000 francs at 185 to £+tax                                  | 100    |
| 1952 | N.Y.  Quai St Bernard, 18×32, $4,500                                                                   | 1,606  |
| 1954 | N.Y.  Faubourg de Paris, 1883, 28¾×36¼, $2,760 (see 1968)                                              | 986    |
|      | S.  Antibes at dawn, 10×13½                                                                             | 530    |
| 1957 | Lurcy.  N.Y.  Beach scene, St Brieuc, $31,000                                                          | 11,070 |
|      | Riverside landscape, $17,000                                                                            | 6,075  |
| 1958 | S.  Le rayon vert à St Tropez, 28¾×36¼                                                                  | 6,200  |
|      | Le Gallais.  N.Y.  The mill                                                                             | 8,930  |
|      | Kirkeby.  N.Y.  Bateaux et pêcheurs                                                                     | 12,140 |
| 1959 | Paris.  Marseille, Fort St Jean, 26×32½, 11·5 old francs+ tax                                           | 10,050 |
| 1960 | Rewald.  S.  Salle à manger, coloured drawing, 1886, 7×9                                               | 2,000  |
|      | Paris.  L'Odet à Quimper, 1923, 29½×37¼, FN105,000+ tax                                                | 8,715  |
|      | Les Andelys, 29½×36¾, FN105,000+tax                                                                     | 8,715  |
| 1961 | Paris.  Port de Saint Tropez                                                                            | 17,675 |
|      | Paris.  View of Constantinople                                                                          | 9,800  |
|      | S.  Grand Canal and Salute, 1908, 29×36                                                                 | 11,700 |
|      | Constantinople, 1907, 25¾×21¾                                                                           | 11,500 |
| 1962 | Paris.  Bateaux pavoisés au phare de Groix                                                             | 10,850 |
|      | Wolf.  S.  Asnières et Quai de Tournelle, canvas painted on both sides, 23½×36 (bought in at £34,000, 1970) | 12,000 |
|      | Aldrich.  N.Y.  Garden at St Tropez, 26×32, $43,000                                                    | 15,350 |
|      | S.  La jetée de Flessingue, 23×32¼ (see 1968)                                                          | 12,000 |
| 1964 | Logan.  S.  Portrait of Félix Fénéon (mathematically formularized) 1890, 28¾×36¼ (see 1968)            | 21,000 |
| 1965 | S.  Paris, suburban street, 28¾×36                                                                      | 11,000 |
|      | The rainbow, 1893, 16×19¾                                                                               | 9,500  |
| 1966 | Henry Ford II.  C.  Jardin à St Tropez (see 1962), bought in                                           | 14,700 |

£

| 1967 | C.  Jardin de Banlieue à Asnières, 1883, 18×24 | 5,040 |
|---|---|---|
| | S.  Port de Cannes, 1902, 10½×13 | 6,000 |
| 1968 | Paris.  Faubourg de Paris, FN165,000 untaxed.  Bought by the Louvre ($2,760, 1954) | 13,980 |
| | Arc en ciel à Venise, 1905, 29×39½, FN520,000+tax | 48,160 |
| | S.  La jetée de Flessingue, 1896, 23×32¼ (see 1962) | 26,000 |
| | Venise, le matin, 1908, 28¾×36 | 39,000 |
| | Roudinesco.  N.Y.  Mouillage à la Giudecca, 29×36½, 1908, $125,000 | 52,072 |
| | Le pont des Arts, 1925, 35×45½, $125,000 | 52,072 |
| | Notre Dame de la Garde, Marseille, 1931, 29×36½, $92,500 | 38,540 |
| | La Salis, Antibes, 1916, 36½×29½, $95,000 | 39,583 |
| | Josefowitz.  N.Y.  Portrait, Félix Fénon (see 1964), $110,000 | 45,584 |
| 1969 | Paris.  Antibes, FN395,000+tax | 36,640 |
| | S.  St Briac, la croix des marins, 1885, 13×18½ | 9,000 |
| | Paris.  Le Port de Pontrieux, 18×22, 1888, FN550,000+tax | 51,413 |

LUCA SIGNORELLI.  (*See* Italian School, Central (drawings))


MARIA DE SILVA.  (*See* Abstract Painters, Europe)


ALFRED SISLEY.  1840–1899

Sisley's paintings are sometimes confusable with those of Camille Pissarro who was nine years his senior. On the whole his works are less monotonous and there are certainly much fewer of them. Till the middle 1920s Sisley's work was considerably dearer than Pissarro's. In the 1960s the situation seemed to be reversed. In 1968, when five pictures by Pissarro were sold at £57,000 to £108,000, only two by Sisley had passed £50,000. That, however, was a situation which could change from one moment to another—and in June, 1969 it did.

£

| 1880 | Sold to Durand-Ruel.  Inondation (see 1969), 300 francs | 12 |
|---|---|---|
| 1899 | Count Doria.  Paris.  Early frost, 9,000 francs+tax | 396 |
| | Dachery.  Paris.  Noisy le Roi | 374 |
| | Marly | 396 |
| | Soleil couchant (see 1903) | 266 |
| | Sisley Exors.  Paris.  25 pictures at £110 to £385 | |

| | | £ |
|---|---|---|
| 900 | Tavernier. Paris. Inondation | 614 |
| 901 | Feydeau. Paris. Pont de Morêt (see 1961), 25,500 francs +tax | 120 |
| | Weiller. Paris. La route de Choisy, 5,300 francs+tax (see 1952) | 234 |
| | Barrage de St Mammès, 6,100 francs+tax (see 1952) | 268 |
| 903 | Zygamalas. Paris. Soleil couchant (see 1899) | 440 |
| 906 | Depeaux. Paris. Inondation, 24,000 francs+tax | 1,056 |
| | Lord Grimthorpe. C. View on the Seine | 168 |
| 925 | Bought by Tate Gallery, Courtauld fund. Pont de Morêt | 1,200 |
| 927 | Murray. C. Bought by Tate Gallery, bridge at Sèvres | 840 |
| 932 | S. Small landscape | 110 |
| 937 | Bought by W. A. Cargill (see 1963) Bougival | 1,050 |
| 939 | Canonne. Paris. Pont de Morêt (200 francs to £+tax) About | 900 |
| 941 | Goldschmidt. C. Landscape | 315 |
| 942 | A. T. Reid. C. Bords de la rivière | 504 |
| 944 | S. On the Seine | 370 |
| | Barbee. N.Y. Junction of the Loing and Seine | 1,020 |
| 945 | Thanhauser. N.Y. Chemin des fontaines | 1,250 |
| 947 | N.Y. La route de St Germain | 1,125 |
| 952 | Wildenstein. N.Y. La Seine au point du jour | 3,400 |
| | Cognacq. Paris. Route de Choisy, 4·4 million old francs +tax (£234 in 1901) | 5,180 |
| | Bords du Loing, 4·8 million old francs+tax | 5,670 |
| | Barrage de St Mammès, 4·15 million old francs (£268, 1901) | 4,830 |
| | Peupliers a Morêt, 4 million old francs+tax | 4,680 |
| 953 | N.Y. St Mammès | 4,328 |
| 954 | Paris. Entrée des Sablons, 21½×29 | 4,250 |
| 956 | Sir E. Cripps. S. Country street | 5,460 |
| 957 | Weinberg. S. Le Seine à Paris, 1870, 14½×21½ | 9,000 |
| | Lurcy. N.Y. Entrée du village, $35,000 | 12,500 |
| | Le Loing à Morêt, $37,500 | 13,400 |
| | Riverside landscape, $31,000 | 11,070 |
| 960 | Cassirer. S. Environs de Marly, 1873, 14¾×21 | 12,500 |
| | S. Riverside landscape | 8,000 |
| 961 | Paris. Spring, near Morêt | 19,175 |
| | Inondation, Port Marly, 1873, FN785,000+tax | 67,085 |
| | S. Mills on the Loing, 1888, 21¼×28½ | 20,800 |
| | Morhange. S. Snow landscape, 1873, 20×26 | 22,000 |
| | Lady Esher. S. Thames at Hampton Court, 1874, 18×21½ | 26,500 |

| | | £ |
|---|---|---|
| 1961 | Maharanee of Baroda. Paris. Bridge at Morêt (see 1901), FN630,000+tax | 54,355 |
| | S. Morêt, le Matin, 1888, $14\frac{3}{4} \times 21\frac{3}{4}$ | 20,000 |
| 1962 | Somerset Maugham. River banks near Morêt, 1880, $25\frac{1}{2} \times 35\frac{3}{4}$ | 30,000 |
| | S. Le Loing à Morêt, 1883, $19\frac{3}{4} \times 25\frac{1}{2}$ | 29,000 |
| | Woolworth. N.Y. Le chemin des grés a Bellevue | 18,750 |
| 1963 | S. Chantiers à St Mammès, 1880, $25\frac{1}{2} \times 36$ | 23,000 |
| | Peniches au barrage du Loing, 1885, $18 \times 21\frac{3}{4}$ | 22,000 |
| | Bords du Loing vers Morêt, 1883, $19\frac{3}{4} \times 28\frac{3}{4}$ | 21,000 |
| | Cargill. S. Bougival, 1873, $20\frac{1}{4} \times 27\frac{3}{4}$ | 26,000 |
| | Bougival (see 1937) | 24,500 |
| | Zimet. S. Langland Bay, 1897, $31\frac{1}{2} \times 25\frac{1}{2}$ | 19,000 |
| | S. Effet de neige, 1873, $17\frac{1}{2} \times 21$ | 20,000 |
| 1964 | S. Bridge at Morêt, 1888, $30\frac{3}{4} \times 28$ | 30,000 |
| | Fischer, Lucerne. Factory chimneys in the banlieue, $13 \times 16\frac{1}{4}$, FS120,000+tax | 12,000 |
| | Combemarle. C. River landscape, 1885 | 28,350 |
| 1965 | Biggins. S. On the Loing, 1884 | 20,000 |
| | Clover field, 1874 | 22,500 |
| | Haft, Palm Beach. Bords du Loing, 1885, $90,000 | 32,200 |
| | Boulton. C. The Loing at Morêt, 1891, $28\frac{3}{4} \times 36\frac{1}{2}$ | 33,600 |
| | Avnet. N.Y. Hampton Court, 1874, $13\frac{3}{4} \times 23\frac{1}{2}$ | 17,860 |
| | Motte, Geneva. Le Loing à Morêt, $14\frac{3}{4} \times 24$, FS282,000+tax | 25,850 |
| 1966 | Chaplin. N.Y. Ladies' Cove, 1897, $25\frac{1}{4} \times 32$ (see 1969) | 17,180 |
| | S. Les chasseurs, 1873, $18 \times 25\frac{1}{2}$ | 33,000 |
| 1967 | Chester Beatty. S. Hiver à Véneux-Nadon, 1881, $20\frac{3}{4} \times 28$ | 37,000 |
| | En aval du pont de Morêt, 1891, $21 \times 25\frac{1}{2}$ | 26,000 |
| | Skinner. C. Route a l'entrée du village, $12\frac{1}{2} \times 18$ | 25,200 |
| | S. Chantier à St Mammès, 1880, $21\frac{1}{4} \times 28\frac{3}{4}$, ex Cassirer | 26,000 |
| | Paris. Chemin de Versailles à Chaville, $20 \times 25\frac{1}{2}$ | 23,980 |
| | C. Le chemin des près, le matin, 1890, $15 \times 18$ (see 1968), Bought in at | 15,700 |
| | Echagué. N.Y. Coin de village (Corot style) 1863, $15\frac{3}{4} \times 20\frac{1}{2}$, $80,000 | 28,393 |
| | Paysage à St Mammès, 1881, $13\frac{1}{2} \times 19$, $50,000 | 17,807 |
| 1968 | Paris. Rue de Louveciennes, 1875, $18\frac{1}{2} \times 12\frac{3}{4}$, FN220,000 | 17,470 |
| | Motte, Geneva. La plaine de Véneux, $15\frac{1}{2} \times 21$, FS230,000 | 24,710 |
| | Le barrage de St Mammès, $14 \times 22$, FS350,000+tax | 37,460 |
| | Paris. Le chemin des près, le matin (see 1967), FN230,000 +tax | 18,300 |
| | S. Bords de la Seine, St Cloud, 1879, $15 \times 18$ | 30,000 |

£

| | |
|---|---|
| 9 Fribourg. N.Y. Le sentier aux Sablons, 1883, $18\frac{1}{2}\times22$, $77,500 | 32,558 |
| S. Inondation, route de St Germain, $17\frac{1}{2}\times23\frac{1}{2}$ (see 1880) | 60,000 |
| Péniches sur le Loing, 1896, $21\times25\frac{3}{4}$ (see infra) | 49,000 |
| Paris. Bords de Seine à Port-Marly, 1875, FN1 million+ tax | 93,550 |
| Auberge à Hampton Court, 1874, FN700,000+tax | 64,900 |
| S. La lisière du bois, Sablons, 1884, $23\times28$ | 55,000 |
| Ladies' Cove, Langland Bay, 1897, $25\frac{1}{2}\times32$ (see 1966) | 32,000 |
| Paysage de Printemps, effet de matin, 1890, $11\times18$ | 18,000 |
| Paysage à Louveciennes, 1873, $20\frac{3}{4}\times28\frac{1}{2}$ | 39,000 |
| Motte, Geneva. Péniches sur le Loing (see *supra*), FS580,000+tax | 61,490 |
| S. (Tokyo). Cabane dans la forêt, 1896, $26\frac{1}{4}\times32\frac{3}{4}$, 19 million Yen | 22,350 |
| C. (Geneva). Vue de Morêt au Printemps, *c.* 1880, $23\frac{1}{2}\times28\frac{3}{4}$, FS400,000+5% tax | 40,384 |
| S. Le talus du chemin de fer à Sèvres, *c.* 1879, $14\frac{1}{2}\times17\frac{3}{4}$ | 22,000 |
| Paysage d'Hiver, pastel, $14\frac{3}{4}\times18$ | 9,200 |

## JOHN SMART. (*See* Miniatures)

## FRANS SNYDERS. (*See* Flemish School after 1550)

## PIERRE SOULAGES. (*See* Abstract painters, Europe)

## CHAIM SOUTINE. 1894–1944

painter who did not long outlive his discovery by the dealers in the 1930s. e enormous prices of 1961 and 1962 were not maintained throughout the cade. I don't know whether this was due to the singularly bleak effect, pro-ced by a mass of these savage and rather messy works when exhibited at the te Gallery in 1964. But there are plenty of enthusiasts for Soutine.

£

| | |
|---|---|
| 30 Bought by Toledo Museum. The turkey | 320 |
| 37 'Vente P.W.'. Paris. La jeune servante (115 francs to £) | 115 |
| Le canard | 124 |
| Les peupliers | 248 |
| Enfant en pied | 206 |
| 38 Bought by Tate Gallery. Prêtre en soutane | 393 15s. |

£

| 1947 | N.Y.   Boy in blue, half-length | 500 |
| 1948 | C.   Tulips (see 1952) | 210 |
| 1949 | S.   Skinned rabbit | 400 |
|  | Adolphe Schloss.   Paris.   Les poissons, $26 \times 20$ | 195 |
| 1952 | Paris.   La route rouge | 1,972 |
|  | C.   Tulips (see 1948) | 651 |
| 1954 | Bessoneau.   Paris.   Le valet de chambre, $26 \times 21$ (see 1961) | 4,712 |
|  | Rees-Jeffreys.   S.   La tricoteuse (see 1957) | 4,725 |
| 1955 | Paris.   Femme au fauteuil rouge, $32 \times 18$ About | 3,000 |
| 1956 | S.   Flowers in vase, $21 \times 14\frac{1}{2}$ | 2,800 |
|  | N.Y.   Woman with dog | 4,400 |
| 1957 | S.   La tricoteuse (see 1954) | 7,500 |
|  | Lurcy.   N.Y.   Paysage aux vaches | 6,785 |
| 1958 | Regnault, Amsterdam.   Portrait head | 12,000 |
| 1960 | Paris.   Girl with ducks, FN185,000+tax, about | 16,000 |
|  | S.   L'étudiant, $28\frac{3}{4} \times 24$ | 8,000 |
|  | Jacques Sarlie.   S.   L'homme aux rubans, 1926, $31\frac{1}{2} \times 23\frac{1}{2}$ | 14,000 |
| 1961 | Juvilier.   N.Y.   Le valet de chambre (see 1954) | 27,143 |
|  | Motte, Geneva.   Le boeuf écorché.   FS163,000+tax | 15,000 |
| 1962 | Metcalfe.   S.   The pastry cook, $25 \times 19\frac{3}{4}$, 1927 | 28,000 |
| 1964 | S.   Girl with doll, 1932 | 13,000 |
|  | Female portrait | 12,500 |
|  | Le château rouge à Cherêt, $121 \times 30$ | 8,000 |
|  | Bought by Tate Gallery, landscape | 17,000 |
| 1965 | Boulton.   C.   Girl's head, $18\frac{1}{2} \times 16\frac{1}{2}$ | 7,560 |
|  | N.Y.   Paysage de banlieue, $35\frac{1}{2} \times 24$ (see 1966) | 5,750 |
| 1966 | C.   The red beef carcase, $31\frac{1}{2} \times 18\frac{3}{4}$ | 5,670 |
|  | Thompson.   N.Y.   Garçon en bleu, 1926, $32 \times 23\frac{1}{2}$ | 17,860 |
|  | S.   Paysage de banlieue (see 1965) | 8,500 |
|  | Le jeune valet, $25\frac{1}{2} \times 21\frac{1}{2}$, bought in | 7,500 |
|  | Ben Uri Society.   S.   Trees at Cherêt, bought in | 8,500 |
|  | S.   Femme à la chaise, 1930, $31\frac{1}{2} \times 17\frac{1}{2}$ | 10,100 |
|  | Fordyce.   N.Y.   Jeune fille en rouge, $31 \times 23\frac{1}{2}$ | 17,060 |
| 1967 | Escayrac.   N.Y.   Paysage tourmenté, 1919, $21\frac{1}{2} \times 28\frac{1}{2}$ | 9,820 |
|  | Motte, Geneva.   Girl's head, $25\frac{1}{2} \times 19\frac{3}{4}$, FS170,000+tax | 18,330 |
|  | Femme à la robe noire, $26 \times 20$, FS173,000+tax | 18,650 |
| 1968 | Silberman.   N.Y.   Paysage arbreux, $18 \times 24$, $24,000 | 10,000 |
|  | N.Y.   Veau devant rideau rouge, c. 1924, $32 \times 19\frac{1}{2}$, $20,000 | 8,335 |
| 1969 | Alden Brooks.   N.Y.   Femme sur un divan rouge, c. 1918, $21\frac{1}{4} \times 32$, $46,000 | 19,335 |
|  | N.Y.   Poulets à la nappe blanche, c. 1930, $19\frac{3}{4} \times 24$, $17,000 | 7,140 |
|  | Le Bas.   C. (Geneva).   Le faisan mort, c. 1926, $22 \times 31$, FS180,000+5% tax | 19,037 |

## SPORTING PICTURES
18th and 19th century

eparate entries for Ferneley, Landseer, Ben Marshall, Stubbs and James Ward.)

The first boom in English sporting pictures was in the 1920s when at least one
' these painters made higher prices in terms of real money than in the 1960s.
ne present revival owes much to the competition of Mr Paul Mellon with
r J. Dick and other American collectors who are nostalgically interested in
intings of English country life of the past. While one would hesitate to de-
ribe this market as more than remotely bordering on the aesthetic, it does
em to depend rather less than it did in the 1920s on the merits of horses,
dged on points, or on the annals of hunting and racing. Nevertheless the
ndard work is still the *British Sporting Artists* of Walter Shaw Sparrow,
blished in 1922 when the boom had scarcely begun and when the author
uld still complain of 'super dealers' who in the shadow of the sale of
ainsborough's *Blue Boy* would observe, 'Sporting pictures? No, I never touch
em.'

It is amusing to find that James Pollard, now almost the most expensive
inter of them all, gets only a short paragraph in this huge book, and that
thing but contempt is bestowed on the younger Henry Alken as a plagiarizer
' his father, though now there is very little market distinction between them.
mes Seymour who rocketed to posthumous fame in 1968, receives more
tention, but is constantly referred to as a primitive, 'quaintly immature',
ainly because in common with most of his successors, he observed the conven-
on of the 'rocking horse gallop'. To be a primitive was not yet a merit in
22, and yet the notion that popular sporting prints, lithographed in colour,
d something in common with Italian primitive paintings of the *quattrocento*
d been aired forty years earlier by Samuel Butler in *Alps and Sanctuaries*.
tler professed not to know who Mr Pollard was, but he had seen a lithograph
' the *Funeral of Tom Moody the Huntsman* which was in the spirit of the painters
' the Camp Santo at Pisa. Butler, who must have seen Pollard's prints con-
ntly, was clearly trying to annoy intellectual snobs who raved about Benozzo
ozzoli, whereas Shaw Sparrow noticed quite rightly that Pollard's flat style
as more suited to colour prints than oil paintings.

There is something not easily explicable about the present cult. It has made
ubbs, Ben Marshall and even Seymour dearer than Gainsborough. The same
omaly continues nearer our own time. A set of four highly stereotyped
nting scenes by the younger Henry Alken made £16,000 in 1967. This
inter died in 1892, having prolonged a Regency tradition into the period of
urne-Jones and Whistler, almost till the *fin du siècle*. Yet he can be dearer than
ther. A hunting portrait by Harry Hall, painted as late as 1867, made £6,000
hile the dearest of all 19th century hunting pictures, the ten-foot *Caledonian
oursing Meeting* of 1844, achieved no less a price in 1969 than £35,700. This was
very peculiar case because Richard Ansdell who painted it, was the only artist
my list to be made a Royal Academician, apart from Sir Francis Grant who

was normally a studio-portraitist. This meant that Ansdell was considered in l
own time a creator of *high art*, the reward of half a century's devotion to imit
ing 'Spanish' Phillip (a £4,000 seller in the 1880s) Wilkie and above
Landseer. But in the 1960s no Landseer made even half as much as Ansdell's *Cor
sing Meeting*, which contained as many portraits and fragments of local colour
Frith's *Derby Day*. In fact one cannot imagine any English painting of the a
succeeding Constable and Turner which could match this price except a tru
pre-Raphaelite Holman Hunt or Millais and these are no longer obtainable.

It must be observed that this solitary sale created no boom at all in the othe
wise forgotten Ansdell. In the following season his much more typical *Go*
*herds, Gibraltar*, a six-footer, came up at Sotheby's. It had been bought by t
financier, Baron Grant, at the Royal Academy exhibition of 1874 f
1,200 guineas, the equivalent in October, 1969, of more than £11,000. In 187
after Grant's picturesque failure, his art speculations, all recent, came under t
hammer; yet even now *The Goatherds* were good for 720 guineas. But in 19
they departed at £380, the equivalent of barely £50 at the time of Gran
purchase. An even more typical Ansdell, one of his interminable six-fo
Highland drover subjects was sold for £336. The *Caledonian coursing meeti*
would seem, therefore, to have been an accident both as to execution and pri

| | | | £ |
|---|---|---|---|
| **HENRY ALKEN, SENR.  1772–1851** | | | |
| 1951 | Hutchinson.  S.  Leicestershire steeplechase, set of eight | | 1,050 |
| 1963 | S.  Set of four small foxhunting scenes (see 1966) | 4 for | 3,200 |
| 1964 | Bostwick.  S.  The Derby, 1844, start and finish, $13\frac{3}{4} \times 19\frac{3}{4}$ | | |
| | | 2 for | 2,800 |
| 1966 | Tilney.  S.  Set of 4 foxhunting scenes (see 1963) | 4 for | 6,600 |
| | Aykroyd.  S.  Similar sequence, $9\frac{1}{2} \times 13$ | 4 for | 7,600 |
| 1968 | C.  The Forest Stakes, 1847, $9\frac{3}{4} \times 13\frac{3}{4}$ | 4 for | 9,975 |
| | Dudley Ward.  S.  Pair of coaching scenes, 1840, $10 \times 16\frac{1}{2}$ | | |
| | | 2 for | 8,800 |
| 1969 | Gocher.  S.  Going to covert and the Return, $11 \times 17$ | 2 for | 4,200 |
| 1970 | Hardy-Roberts.  S.  Set of 4 Foxhunting scenes, $16 \times 22$ | | |
| | | 4 for | 11,000 |
| **HENRY ALKEN, JUNR.  1812–1892** | | | |
| 1967 | Mountjoy Fane.  C.  Set of coaching scenes, painted in the | | |
| | 60s or 70s, $7\frac{1}{2} \times 10$ each | 8 for | 7,350 |
| | S.  Set of 4 hunting scenes, $10\frac{1}{4} \times 14\frac{1}{2}$ | 4 for | 16,000 |
| 1969 | Wright.  S.  Tandem and mail coach at speed, a pair, | | |
| | $9\frac{1}{2} \times 18\frac{1}{2}$ | 2 for | 1,000 |
| | C.  Set of 4 hunting scenes, $11\frac{1}{2} \times 15\frac{1}{4}$ | 4 for | 2,730 |
| 1970 | S.  Driving to the meet and to the races, $11\frac{1}{2} \times 17\frac{3}{4}$ | 2 for | 3,800 |
| **JOHN HERRING, SENR.  1795–1865** | | | |
| 1959 | C.  Start of the Derby | | 3,255 |
| | Start of the Oaks | | 3,045 |

£

| | | |
|---|---|---|
| 51 | S. The Leamington Hunt, $35 \times 50$ | 2,800 |
| 52 | C. Hunters in landscape, 1847, $27\frac{1}{2} \times 42$ | 2,730 |
| 55 | C. Stable yard, 1852 | 2,310 |
| | Harewood. C. Stable yard, 1848 | 997 10s. |
| 56 | Akroyd. S. Landscape with hunt in full cry, 1838, $41\frac{1}{4} \times 59$ | 16,000 |
| | Phillimore. C. Finish of the St. Leger, 1840 (£441 in 1955) | 6,300 |
| | Houston. S. Cotswold Hunt, $24\frac{1}{2} \times 39\frac{1}{4}$ | 3,400 |
| 57 | Pearson. C. Two favourite hunters of John Scott, 1838, $27\frac{1}{2} \times 35$ | 6,825 |
| | S. Sir W. Earle's chestnut hunter, $24\frac{1}{2} \times 29\frac{1}{2}$ | 5,800 |
| | C. *Attila* in loose box, 1842, $27\frac{1}{2} \times 35\frac{1}{2}$ | 3,045 |
| 68 | Parkinson. C. *Sautern* with Fred Archer up, 1828, $18 \times 28\frac{3}{4}$ | 13,650 |
| | C. The baron's charger, costume picture, 1853, $39\frac{1}{2} \times 49\frac{1}{2}$ | 6,300 |
| | Coach-horses at a posting inn, 1841, $27\frac{1}{2} \times 35$ | 23,100 |
| | *Flying Dutchman*, winner of the Derby and St Leger, 1849 (Commissioned in 1853 at 35 guineas), $17\frac{1}{4} \times 23\frac{1}{4}$ | 12,600 |
| 69 | S. *Charles XII* in stable, 1843, $27\frac{1}{2} \times 35\frac{1}{2}$ | 3,800 |
| | Family of Thomas Dawson of Middleham with pony, 1842, $19 \times 24$ | 6,000 |
| | C. Sunrise; team of plough-horses going out to work, 1840, $27\frac{1}{2} \times 35$ | 3,570 |
| | Seven portraits of racehorse with or without their riders made from 1,300 to 2,000 guineas each. | |
| | de Mahler. S. *St Giles* with Scott up, 1832, $27\frac{1}{4} \times 35\frac{1}{4}$ (unillustrated) | 14,500 |
| | Grooms dressing hunter outside a stable, 1849, $27 \times 36$ | 2,800 |
| | C. *Constantine*, bay gelding, 1839, $27 \times 35$ | 3,675 |
| | Summer, horses in farmyard, 1847, $27 \times 26$ | 2,310 |
| | Houldsworth. C. (Hopetown). *Vanish*, chestnut colt with Sam Darling up, 1830, $21 \times 29\frac{1}{2}$ | 10,500 |
| | Holford. S. Old Friends, grey hunter in stable with dog and ducks, 1851, $39\frac{1}{4} \times 49\frac{1}{2}$ | 7,200 |
| | *Touchstone* and three others galloping on the downs, 1841, $23 \times 41$ | 12,000 |
| | *Brunette*, *Discount* and *Lottery*, racing, unfinished, $27\frac{1}{4} \times 35$ | 9,800 |
| | Beaumont. C. Bay hunter and grey in open landscape, 1839, $27 \times 35$. Both bought in | 5,250 |
| 70 | Leader. S. The Goodwood cup with three runners, $27 \times 41\frac{1}{4}$ | 24,500 |
| | MacRae. S. Leeds coach, Swan Inn, Bottisham $27 \times 33$ (£315 in 1903) | 21,000 |

JAMES POLLARD.  1782–1860          £

| | | £ |
|---|---|---|
| 1956 | N.Y.  Hyde Park Corner with coaches | 1,033 |
| 1960 | Wormald.  S.  North Country mails at the Peacock, Islington, 1821 (£168 in 1927), $32 \times 60\frac{3}{4}$ | 19,000 |
| | Carriage and horses of Smith Barry, Esq. | 4,800 |
| 1961 | S.  Last run of the Royal Mail, 1847 | 1,300 |
| 1964 | S.  Mailcoach in a flood, 1825, $19\frac{1}{2} \times 29\frac{1}{2}$ | 6,300 |
| | Mailcoach in a snow drift, matching piece | 5,250 |
| 1965 | C.  Norwich–London mail. | 3,360 |
| | Approach to Christmas, $16\frac{1}{2} \times 20\frac{1}{2}$ | 7,875 |
| 1966 | Chisholm.  C.  Trafalgar Square with coach, curricles, etc. 1836, $29\frac{1}{2} \times 30$ | 12,600 |
| | The *Norwich Times* in the Mile End Road, $16\frac{1}{2} \times 20\frac{1}{2}$ | 7,875 |
| | (Attributed as 'Pollard'), White Horse cellars, Piccadilly, $17\frac{1}{2} \times 25\frac{1}{2}$ | 10,500 |
| 1967 | S.  Norwich and London coach, 1824, $20 \times 30$ | 3,000 |
| | Donahue, N.Y.  London and Edinburgh Royal Mail, 1821, $30 \times 39\frac{3}{4}$, \$55,000 | 19,643 |
| 1968 | Prestige.  S.  The London–Shrewsbury Wonder, $8\frac{3}{4} \times 13\frac{1}{2}$ | 4,500 |
| | C.  Last of the mail coaches at Newcastle, July 5, 1847, $8\frac{1}{2} \times 11\frac{3}{4}$ (lately acquired for 25s.) | 1,995 |
| 1969 | Finch.  S.  Barouche and 4 greys with Jacobean mansion, dated 1830, $16\frac{1}{2} \times 21$ | 13,000 |
| | C.  Falcon Inn and coach etc., Waltham Cross, $13 \times 17$ | 1,890 |
| | Angus.  S.  London to Manchester Royal Mail, $19\frac{1}{2} \times 30$ | 18,500 |
| | Necarsulmer.  S.  Norwich mail at Ilford, 1830, $13\frac{1}{2} \times 17$ | 7,000 |
| | S.  Mail coach under Highgate archway, c. 1830, $16\frac{1}{2} \times 20\frac{1}{2}$ | 1,600 |
| | Louth Mail, passenger descending, 1846, $9\frac{1}{4} \times 13\frac{3}{4}$ | 1,500 |
| 1970 | S.  Suite of 4 hunting scenes, 1839, $15\frac{1}{2} \times 21\frac{1}{2}$  4 for | 19,000 |

JOHN NOTT SARTORIUS.  1755–1828

See numerous entries in Volume One. In 1928 *Thomas Oldacre on Brush* made £4,925, equivalent to £24,700.

| | | |
|---|---|---|
| 1959 | Theriot.  S.  Lord Chesterfield's *Don Juan* | 2,200 |
| 1963 | S.  Three fox-hunting scenes, 1819, $20\frac{1}{2} \times 27$  3 for | 3,500 |
| 1967 | Alison.  C.  Mr Bowes with groom and bay horses, 1784, $28\frac{1}{2} \times 40\frac{1}{2}$ | 3,360 |
| | Baillie.  C.  Race at Newmarket, 1786, $27\frac{1}{2} \times 35\frac{1}{2}$ | 2,310 |
| 1969 | Partridge.  S.  Set of four hunting scenes, dated 1787, $13\frac{3}{4} \times 18\frac{3}{4}$ (compare 1963)  4 for | 21,000 |
| | S.  Teeing the fox, 1795, $27 \times 35\frac{1}{2}$ | 1,700 |
| | Gold.  C. (by *John Francis Sartorius*).  Sportsman and three dogs at Queen's Elm, Chelsea (not a house in sight), 1827, $21 \times 29\frac{1}{2}$ | 6,300 |

£

59　C.　*Hambletonian* and *Diamond*, racing, 29½ × 42, 1807　2,730

Three huntsmen with hounds in landscape, 1774, 46 × 71, bought in　5,250

Chestnut hunter in landscape with groom, 1799, 24 × 29, bought in　2,940

## MES SEYMOUR.　1702–1752

51　C.　Ladies and gentlemen hunting　4,200

56　Kidd.　S.　Mr Russell on his chestnut, 34 × 43　3,600

Vernon.　S.　Training at Newmarket, 35 × 43　2,600

58　Harris St John.　S.　Mr and Mrs St John following hunt in six-horse carriage, 49½ × 106　12,000

View of Dogmersfield Park, the detached upper part of the same picture, 45 × 105　5,500

Lord Craven.　S.　Coursing at Ashdown Park, 24 × 29　6,800

A kill at Ashdown Park, 1743, 71 × 94 (with commission £63,800, Tate Gallery)　58,000

59　Gage-Brown.　C.　Gentleman on roan horse with black spaniel, 1743, 40 × 41　13,650

Jeremy Tree.　C.　*Caelia* and groom, 1748, 24½ × 29½
Bought in at　2,100

Wintour.　S.　Hunting party with ladies and gentlemen in woodland clearing, 38¾ × 49　9,000

C.　*Flying Childers* at gallop with jockey in blue, before 1741, 34½ × 53　Bought in at　6,825

## IN WOTTON.　1686–1765

51　Duke of Leeds.　S.　George II at Newmarket, 49½ × 66　5,500

Other racing pictures by Wootton at £1,000 to £4,000

S.　George II at Dettingen　4,000

Three portraits of Arab thoroughbreds at £1,000 to £1,500

53　S.　The meet, 36 × 57　6,400

55　S.　George III at Newbury races　4,800

56　Houston.　S.　Duke of Beaufort and horses, 1740, 38½ × 43¾　2,800

58　York Minster Fund.　S.　Starting point, Newmarket, 1716, 35¾ × 57½ (commissioned for £16 2s. 6d.)　7,000

Guest.　C.　The Hampton Court Arabian with Turkish groom, *c.* 1740, 44 × 64　4,200

Lord Craven.　S.　George I at Newmarket with horses, jockeys etc., 39 × 48½　3,800

59　Peck.　S.　George I's chestnut Arabian, *Horn*, with Turkish groom and greyhound, 48 × 67½　2,400

N.Y.　The Hampton Court chestnut Arabian, $4,750　1,979

OTHER PAINTERS

£

1961   C.   James Barenger (1781–1831)   Moving off, 1819    3,150

1965   S.   William Barlow (1626–1702)   Charles II at Windsor
races, 1684, 43¼×73½.   Much restored    2,600
C.   Sir Francis Grant (1813–1878)   Equestrian portrait    2,730
Capone.   C.   Richard Barrett Davis (1782–1854) Richard
Simpson and the Puckeridge hounds, 1841    Bought in at    5,775

1966   Graham.   C.   George Garrard (1760–1826)   Grey geld-
ing and stable boy, 37×39    2,520
Askew.   C.   William Barraud (1810–1850) and Henry
Barraud (1812–1874)   The Old Surrey foxhounds, 1838,
33×44½    1,840
C.   Ramsay Reinagle (1785–1862)   Set of 4 shooting
scenes, 1849, 14½×20                   4 for    4,725
K. F. Bombled.   Races at Chantilly, 1866, 35½×72    1,575

1967   Donohue.   N.Y.   Unknown, c. 1820.   Duke of Argyll
as a boy, riding pony, 21½×27¾, $12,000    4,286
Gordon.   S.   H. B. Chalon (1770–1849)   *Sir David*
with Sam Chifney at Newmarket, 1807, 33×44½    4,500

1968   Chester Beatty.   S.   Eugène Lami.   Diligence arriving at
Chantilly, 22×34, 1848    6,000

1969   Clapham.   C.   James Ross.   The Kill, set in fanciful
mountain landscape in Berchem style, dated 1732, 39½×49    6,000
Trotman-Dickinson.   S.   James Ross.   A   hunt   near
Bucknell, 45½×68½    3,800
S.   Harry Hall, *Pretender*, winner of the Derby, 1858,
45½×55    1,700
Earl Poulett.   S.   Harry Hall. Lord Poulett and Hamble-
don hounds, 1867, 43×56    6,000
*The Lamb*, Liverpool, 1868, George Cole up, 43×56    2,400
Alston.   C.   By S. J. E. Jones.   Duck shooting and part-
ridge shooting, a pair, 13½×17½           2 for    5,775
ditto.   Shooting woodcock, second pair, 13½×17   2 for    4,410
Brocklebank.   C.   Richard Ansdell (1818–1887)   The
Caledonian coursing meeting, Ardrossan, 1844, 60×119    35,700
C.   J. L. Agasse.   Lord Bingley's hunter, wooded lands-
cape, 27×35½    2,940
Cooper Henderson.   Dover–London mail passing
gig at night, 20½×29½    2,940
C. B. Spalding.   Hambledon hounds at Preshaw with
mansion, 1844, 39½×67    1,785

## NICOLAS DE STAËL. 1913–1955

De Staël belongs essentially to the post-war generation. Had he lived, he would now be at the height of his powers. He is easily the most expensive painter of his time. Jackson Pollock, for instance, who was born two years earlier and also died young, has not reached this level, still less Dubuffet and de Kooning who were born thirteen and nine years earlier. The popularity of de Staël rests largely on a single gimmick, that of choosing the simplest of shapes such as bottles and jam-jars and making them simpler still against a background of nothing at all. Although this painter's end was tragic, saleroom success came to him in his own time, for in 1954 the sum of £1,000 was still quite a lot for the work of a painter who was only beginning to achieve recognition.

|  |  | £ |
|---|---|---|
| 944 | Highest price according to Maurice Rheims | 464 |
| 953 | Highest price according to Maurice Rheims | 720 |
| 954 | Paris. Still life, 25 × 32 (see 1960), 800,000 old francs+tax | 800 |
|  | Another still life composition, 1,150,000 old francs+ tax | 1,150 |
| 1957 | S. Composition, 1947, 28 × 36 | 1,800 |
| 1959 | S. Composition en bleu, 1946, 31¾ × 25½ | 3,000 |
| 1960 | Duveen. S. Bottles, 1952 | 13,000 |
|  | Still life, 25 × 32 (see 1954) | 9,200 |
|  | Motte, Geneva. Marseille à la neige, 1954, 24 × 32½, FS118,000+tax | 11,670 |
|  | S. La route d'Uzès, 1953, 23 × 31¾ | 6,200 |
| 1961 | Paris. Les footballeurs, 24½ × 30, FN102,000+tax | 8,655 |
|  | S. Poire et couteau, 1954, 21 × 29 | 8,000 |
|  | Hirshorn. S. Compôtier et bougie, 1954, 24 × 32 | 8,000 |
|  | Newman. S. Composition, 1948, 41 × 79½ (see 1968) | 11,400 |
| 1962 | S. Le phare de Gravelines, 59 × 80 | 7,200 |
| 1963 | Aldrich. N.Y. The storm, 51¼ × 35¼ | 8,430 |
|  | S. Composition grise, 1948, 58½ × 27 | 10,600 |
|  | Paris. Sous la neige | 8,950 |
| 1964 | Glass. S. Paysage, 1952, 19¼ × 23½ | 8,000 |
| 1965 | Weintraub. N.Y. Volume de choses, 72½ × 39 | 16,075 |
|  | Haupt. N.Y. Paysage, Honfleur | 10,715 |
|  | Paysage, le Ciotat | 12,142 |
|  | Fleurs, 1951, 58 × 28½ | 24,285 |
|  | Zadok. S. Musique en tête, 1948, 32 × 24 | 8,000 |
| 1966 | N.Y. Sicile, 1954, 25 × 36½, $26,000 | 9,284 |
|  | Thompson. N.Y. Rectangles vertes et jaunes, 51 × 38, 1950 | 15,270 |
|  | Nature morte aux poires, 31¾ × 35½, 1953 | 9,310 |
|  | Clark. S. Composition, 1951, 10¼ × 16¼ | 6,000 |

£

| 1967 | Bendon.  S.  Composition, 1951, 28½×36¼ | 7,500 |
| 1968 | N.Y.  Abstract composition, 1948, 41×79¼ (see 1961), | |
| | $46,000 | 19,125 |
| | S.  Les Indes galantes, semi-realist, 1953, 64×44½ | 38,000 |
| | Composition, 1950, 18×25 | 10,000 |
| | Motte, Geneva.  Abstraction, 1954, FS220,000+tax | 23,496 |

## CLARKSON STANFIELD.  1793–1867

Included as a *ghost market* on account of the high 19th century prices, discusse
in Volume One. *St Michael's Mount*, one of Stanfield's gloomy romantic eigh
footers, was sold in 1892 for 3,000 guineas, over £25,000 in 1970 terms. In 192
it made £150, equivalent to £750 on the 1970 scale, but in the 1950s £30 t
£40 could have bought oil paintings of a fair size. Clarkson Stanfield ha
descended to those miscellaneous sales which are catalogued as '19th and 20t
century pictures'. One of the last entries in the list is a Christie sale of Octobe
1969, showing a modest advance on previous prices for Clarkson Stanfield, bu
the reticent catalogue made no mention of the price which this work fetched i
1865—the equivalent of fully £20,000.

£

| 1958 | Lever Art Gallery.  C.  Coast scene with fishermen | 504 |
| 1964 | C.  View on the river Bidassoa, 1853 | 630 |
| 1965 | C.  Harbour and fishing boats, 43×66 | 399 |
| 1966 | S.  St. Thomas's Hospital and South Bank, 28¾×49 | 280 |
| | C.  Dutch boats leaving harbour, 1856, 32×47 | 210 |
| 1967 | Eckman.  S.  Tilbury Fort, 1853, 23¼×35¾ | 320 |
| | Rudloff.  C.  Heidelberg with castle, 1841, 23×35½ | 787 10s |
| | C.  Ennverick on the lower Rhine, 1835, 19×29¼ | 787 10s |
| 1969 | C.  Scene on the Maas near Dort, R.A. picture, 1850, | |
| | 33×59 (£2,215 10s. in 1865) | 840 |
| 1970 | Bonham's Rooms.  Dutch river scene, dated 1844 | 925 |

## JAMES STARK.  (*See* English School, 19th century)

## JAN STEEN.  1626–1679

By no means the cheapest of the Dutch *genre* painters, but very much falle
since the height of this market before and after the First World War, Jan Stee
did not always paint low company, but he was never very far away from it
Anything less attractive than the scene, depicted in *Wine is a mocker*, could hardl
be imagined. Yet it was just this sort of thing that the rich *fermiers* and *intendant*

of 18th century Paris enjoyed living with. One of these scenes of merriment cost the Rijksmuseum £18,370 in 1913, the equivalent of £147,000.

| | | £ |
|---|---|---|
| 1959 | S. The Physician's visit | 2,610 |
| 1960 | Dreeseman, Amsterdam. Samson and Delilah, 1668, 28 × 13¾, Hfl65,000+tax | 7,450 |
| | Wedding scene, 44 × 34, Hfl102,000+tax | 11,680 |
| | The anger of Ahasueras, 28½ × 37½, HFl40,000+tax | 4,650 |
| 1961 | S. Village wedding | 4,800 |
| | Paris. The marriage contract, 42 × 50¾, FN150,000+tax | 12,910 |
| 1963 | S. Cincinatus and the Roman envoys | 1,800 |
| | A country wedding | 2,800 |
| 1964 | S. The rich family and the poor family, a pair    2 for | 4,200 |
| | Strater. C. St Nicolas's day, 26 × 23 | 4,410 |
| 1965 | S. Wine is a mocker, 35 × 42 (£2,000 in 1954) | 14,000 |
| | Spencer Churchill. C. Company in a garden (£39 18s. in 1832), 24 × 18½ | 4,200 |
| | S. The physician's visit, 19 × 15 (Pâtureau sale, Paris, 1857, £320) | 2,000 |
| 1967 | Earl of Derby. C. A quack doctor at a village fair, 42 × 36 | 5,775 |
| | Glyn. S. Village wedding, 26½ × 33 | 24,000 |
| | C. Tavern group, 21 × 19 | 3,150 |
| 1969 | Ongering-Schwarte. S. Bowl-players at dusk, 19½ × 26¼ | 20,000 |
| | Bruguière. C. Children in a game-dealer's shop, 22½ × 17¾ | 18,900 |

CLIFFORD STILL. (*See* Abstract Painters, America)

GILBERT STUART. (*See* English School, 18th century)

GEORGE STUBBS. 1724–1806

The position of Stubbs in 1970 was not merely that of the highest priced English painter of horses and sporting scenes. He was also the highest priced English painter of *any* school. It is odd that Stubbs's *Goldfinger, Mare and foal* and Seymour's *Kill at Ashdown Park* should each have been dearer than any Gainsborough picture, sold in the 1960s-odd in terms of the art market for the last hundred years, but apparently not at all odd in Gainsborough's own life-time or shortly after. Some of the prices which were paid when Stubbs was over 70 and even over 80 years old and, one would have supposed, becoming a

bit *vieux jeu*, are exceedingly revealing. In 1797 Wedgwood's executors paid
£236 17s. 6d. for the famous Wedgwood family group in the Etruria Museum
and £189 for the painting on Wedgwood's creamware, *The labourers*. In 1801
Stubbs won a lawsuit against Sir Vane Tempest who was obliged to pay him
300 guineas for the portrait of a single horse, much to the disapproval of the
official portraitist of the day, John Hoppner. Even after Stubbs's death the
wealthy banker, Thomas Hope, failed to obtain a picture at his executors' sale
for £200—and executors' sales were generally a *débâcle* at this period. Yet in
the amazing 1920s Stubbs never became a 'Duveen painter'. His best price in
the saleroom was 4,200 guineas. Herring and Sartorius could fetch as much,
and this at a time when a Gainsborough portrait could make anything up to
£150,000. One may contrast the year 1969 when Mr Jack Dick paid £200,000
for a famous big frieze of mares and foals, after which it was confidently predicted that the *Hunting cheetah* picture of the Pigot family would fetch £150,000
at auction. In fact it reached £220,000 and yet remained in England. Thus the
singularly clumsy composition of one of Stubbs's least attractive works was
rated higher than any Gainsborough or Turner on the post-war market. It must
be left to other ages to decide whether this was any crazier than ranking Stubbs
with Sartorius and Herring—or with ignoring him altogether as George Redford
did in his *Art Sales* of 1888.

|  |  | £ |
|---|---|---|
| 1960 | Earl of Shrewsbury. S. Poodle, 49 × 39 | 17,000 |
|  | Matthew. S. A white spaniel | 2,800 |
|  | At Harrods'. Princess Charlotte's zebra (£220 10s. in 1923) | 20,000 |
|  | de Robeck. S. Baron de Robeck riding, 1791, 39¾ × 50 | 20,000 |
|  | Wyatt. S. Mr and Mrs Wilson hunting, 1752 | 4,000 |
| 1961 | Lady Elliott of Harwood. S. Gyrfalcon, 32 × 39 (£304 10s. in 1905) | 11,500 |
| 1963 | S. Family of Rev. Carter Thelwell with pony carriage, oval gouache, 11 × 13½ | 6,000 |
| 1964 | S. A bay hunter, 23¾ × 28 | 5,000 |
|  | de Rhos. S. Bulls fighting, 1786 | 10,500 |
| 1965 | Bonham's Rooms. Hunter in landscape, 40 × 50 | 24,000 |
| 1966 | Adair Trust C. *Goldfinder* with mare and foal, 1774, 31½ × 39½ | 75,600 |
|  | *Snap*, thoroughbred stallion, 1771, 39½ × 49½ | 47,250 |
|  | Two mares and a foal, 1774, 31½ × 39½ | 14,700 |
|  | Raoul Millais. C. Grey cob by a stream, 23¾ × 27½ (£700 in 1959, see also 1969) | 5,040 |
|  | Vyner. C. Lady Coningsby mounted, 25 × 29½ | 17,350 |
| 1967 | Heely. S. Self-portrait, 1781, enamelled on oval Wedgwood creamware plaque, 26¾ × 20 | 8,000 |
|  | Watney. C. Riders coursing a hare, 31 × 39, re-ascribed to Wilhelm van Kobell | 6,825 |

£

968 Leader. S. Horse, attacked by lion, 27×40 (£126, 1915) 8,000
  Brymer. S. Chestnut hunter by a river, huntsman in
  green coat, 23½×27½ 37,000
  N.Y. Lion and lioness, 1774, 30×28, $18,500 7,700
  C. Fox-hound, pencil drawing, 3¾×4 1,155
969 Bought from Earl Fitzwilliam by J. Dick, long frieze of
  broodmares, two foals and filly, painted for Marquess of
  Rockingham in 1760s 200,000
  C. Grey cob by stream (£5,040 in 1966) 3,990
  Crewe. S. John Crewe with two bay hunters in landscape, 31½×37¼ 36,000
970 Pigot. S. George III's cheetah with Indian handlers and
  stag, c. 1765, 71×107. Manchester City Gallery 220,000
  McRae. S. Captain O'Kelly's *Eclipse*, c. 1770, 39½×49½
  (£693 in 1902, £735 in 1915, £7,350 in 1929) 28,000

## GRAHAM SUTHERLAND. (*See* English School, 20th century)

## MICHIEL SWEERTS. (*See* Dutch School)

## YVES TANGUY. (*See* Abstract Painters, Europe)

## JAN TEN COMPE. (*See* Dutch School)

## DAVID TENIERS THE YOUNGER. 1610–1674

Volume One I observed that a graph, showing the market for paintings by
eniers since the 18th century, would be a 'mildly oscillating horizontal line'.
hat at least was the situation in 1961. In the course of the next decade there was
tendency to catch up with the pace of devaluation. Instead of a top limit of
ss than £3,500, a half-dozen paintings made from £5,000 to £7,000 each. The
w valuation is almost as difficult to account for as the very high valuation
vo hundred years ago. Teniers was in the direct descent artistically from
eter Breughel the Elder, but a much more original painter than either of
reughel's sons, whose works make two or three times as much. Teniers
inted far too many pictures and they are far too much alike. Had he been a
agiarizing Impressionist painter of the second generation, this would still
ave him in the £30,000 class at the very least. But, alas, these are the browned
d blackened works of a 17th century Fleming. In Volume One will be found
e record of two Teniers pictures of village fairs, bought in 1811 and 1815 by

the Prince Regent for £1,732 10s. and £1,680. In the money of 1970 th
would mean £23,200 and £22,400, but the sum of £5,000, which was paid i
1867 by the Royal Gallery, Brussels for another *Kermesse*, would be equivale
to £50,000.

| | | £ |
|---|---|---|
| 1962 | S. The three towers at Perck, $17\frac{1}{2}\times20\frac{1}{2}$ | 4,200 |
| 1963 | Princess Labia. S. Skittle-players outside an inn, $19\times23$ | 7,000 |
| | Figures at an inn | 3,000 |
| | Figures in a guardroom | 2,500 |
| 1965 | Wenner-Gren. S. Le fendeur du bois, 1654, $22\times33$, ex | |
| | Hermitage Museum, Leningrad | 5,000 |
| | Spencer Churchill. C. Mountain landscape with hermits, | |
| | (with J. Momper), $52\times48\frac{1}{2}$ | 6,300 |
| | Rudkin. S. From the Teniers Gallery (117 miniature | |
| | copies for £2,031 11s. in 1886). Three of the Four Seasons | |
| | after Bassano, $8\frac{3}{4}\times6\frac{1}{2}$                    3 for | 4,100 |
| 1966 | S. St Clare before the Cross after Bassano (Teniers | |
| | Gallery), $8\frac{3}{4}\times6\frac{1}{2}$ | 1,100 |
| 1968 | Paris. Smokers in a tavern, $16\frac{1}{2}\times15\frac{3}{4}$, FN57,000+tax | 5,410 |
| 1969 | S. Village wedding, $21\times32$ | 6,500 |
| | Peasants with cattle on a farm, $24\frac{3}{4}\times33$, bought in | 3,800 |
| | Bowls-players outside an inn, $17\times25\frac{1}{4}$ | 4,000 |
| | Fishermen unloading catch on the beach, $32\frac{3}{4}\times22\frac{3}{4}$ | 4,500 |

## GERARD TERBORCH. 1617–1681

Another Dutch *genre* painter, whose works, despite their rarity, proved a ver
flat market in the 1960s. The price paid by Richard Wallace for the *Peace
Münster* in 1868 was equivalent to £72,000 in 1970 money. That of the S
family's *Lady with Gallants*, bought by Andrew Mellon from Duveen in 19.
for £36,100, was equivalent to £180,500. It is almost impossible to assess t
present value of two such pictures in a market which became so moody a
unsettled as the Dutch school in the course of the 1960s.

| | | £ |
|---|---|---|
| 1961 | C. Portrait head, Pieter de Graaf, $14\times11$ | 1,155 |
| | Erickson. N.Y. Portrait, Albert Nylant, $28\times30$ | 7,860 |
| | Matching portrait, Julian Pannier, $22,000 | 7,860 |
| 1963 | Bowlby. S. The sleeping gallant (£8,750, Berlin, 1918) | |
| | $30\times29\frac{1}{4}$ | 5,000 |
| | Thyssen-Bornemisza. S. Sportsmen resting, $32\frac{1}{2}\times40$ | 1,600 |
| | Arvelo. C. Male portrait, $25\frac{3}{4}\times19$ | 3,675 |
| 1968 | Paris. Unknown man, $6\frac{1}{4}\times7\frac{1}{4}$, FN42,000+tax | 3,930 |

| | | £ |
|---|---|---|
| 1969 | S.   Officer in armour, arms of van Reede, $15\frac{1}{2}\times12\frac{1}{2}$ | 2,000 |
| | C.   Portrait, supposed Andries de Graeff, $15\times11$ | 3,990 |

## HENDRIK TERBRUGGEN. (*See* Dutch School)

## GIAMBATTISTA TIEPOLO. 1693–1770

The market for Tiepolo was surprisingly low throughout most of the 1960s. In 1933 the Melbourne Gallery paid £25,000 for *The Banquet of Cleopatra*, equivalent to £125,000 in 1970, but there was nothing like a six-figure price till the end of the decade when the fortunes of Tiepolo became different indeed. In 1965 an oval ceiling panel nearly 10 feet wide, cost the National Gallery £409,500. Why a ceiling panel which certainly entails the removal of two or three pictures to the morgue-like crypt known as the Reserve Collection Rooms, should be so necessary I do not profess to know. On this occasion *The Times* no longer referred to 'that facile decorator of the later Venetian school'. Such was the verdict of 1885 when the gallery won its first Tiepolos, the two oil sketches for the *Emperor Henry IV at Canossa*, in a public bid of 156 guineas. £409,500 is another thing. When money speaks, all else keeps silent—an odd phenomenon for an age which has generated more humbug about the profit motive than any other age since the first encounter of the camel with the eye of the needle.

In 1960 a good Tiepolo, of fair size, was worth £25,000, in 1970 perhaps eight times as much. That was by no means the case with drawings. The mania for the drawings of Giandomenicho, the younger Tiepolo, an illustrator of less than moderate competence and dead-right for present standards of taste, seems to have depressed the market for one of the greatest draughtsmen who ever lived.

| | | £ |
|---|---|---|
| 1960 | Pollnitz.   S.   Christ and the woman of Samaria, $33\frac{1}{2}\times41\frac{3}{4}$ | 7,500 |
| | Washer.   S.   Head of Diogenes (bought in San Francisco, 1939, for about £50), $21\times17$ | 2,800 |
| | Robinson.   N.Y.   Triumph of the Church, grisaille, $30\times43$, $9,000 | 3,214 |
| | Paris.   Beauty, abducted by Time, over 7 ft long (£3,160 in 1925), FN310,000+tax | 25,360 |
| 1962 | N.Y.   Head of an old man, $24\times20$, $9,000 | 3,214 |
| | Paris.   Satyr family and amorini, FN215,000+tax | 18,365 |
| 1965 | Wenner-Gren.   S.   Six grisaille panels, 9 ft high, from the Porto Palace, Vicenza (with Giandomenicho Tiepolo), £7,300 in 1929.   On offer in 1967 at £150,000        6 for | 70,000 |
| | Allegory of the wealth of Venice, ceiling painting, oval, $207\times119$ | 11,000 |

£

| 1966 | Adler. C. Bearded Oriental, 23 × 19 | 1,630 |
|---|---|---|
| | S. A similar head, 23¼ × 18¼ | 1,800 |
| | Boar Hunt, 12¼ × 26 | 5,000 |
| 1967 | C. River goddess with pitcher, grisaille on gold, 31¾ × 25 | 5,775 |
| 1968 | S. The agony in the garden, 30¼ × 34¼, bought in | 5,500 |

(Ex Philippe de Rothschild). The meeting of Antony and Cleopatra, sold in N.Y. to Charles Wrightsman, $350,000 146,000
Finarte, Milan. Christ, crowned and mocked, a pair, 40½ × 25¾, 12 million lire+tax      2 for    9,260

1969 Mertens. S. Rough oil sketch for a frieze, the brazen serpent, 6½ × 26¼      9,500

United Arab Republic. C. Venus entrusting Eros to Chronos, oval ceiling painting, 115 × 75. National Gallery      409,500

    Suite of allegorical groups, grisaille on gold, oval 33 × 26. Bought in      4 for    68,250

James. S. Time discovering truth, oval ceiling design, 16¼ × 24 in.      20,000

Montague. S. Neptune and Ceunis, 19 × 12¾, damaged. Bought in      13,000

S. Alexander and Archimedes in architectural settings by Mengozzi-Colonna, 83 × 57½. Bought in      2 for    17,000

### DRAWINGS

| 1963 | S. Three figure studies, pen and wash | 1,300 |
|---|---|---|
| | C. Study for a ceiling at Wurzburg | 787 10s. |
| | Rudolf. S. Head of an old man | 1,450 |
| | Bloch. S. Sacrifice of Iphigeneia, study for fresco | 1,000 |
| 1964 | S. Satyr and satyress, pen and wash study for fresco | 2,800 |
| 1965 | Harris. S. Three pen and wash studies for a fresco £2,800, £3,000 | 3,800 |
| | S. Monks adoring Holy Family | 2,200 |
| 1966 | Paris. Head of bearded Oriental, pen and wash, 12½ × 9 | 2,260 |
| | Vincent. S. Adoration of the shepherds, pen and wash, 16½ × 11¾ | 2,300 |
| | S. Oriental swordsman, pen, wash and chalk, 11 × 7¾ | 2,100 |
| 1968 | Lord David Cecil. S. Bearded head, pen and wash, 8 × 6½ | 1,300 |
| 1969 | Tussenbroek. S. Circe and companions of Ulysses, pen and wash, 9¼ × 15 | 1,500 |
| | van Berg. S. Sheet with reclining figure, seen from below; on both sides, pen and chalk, 4½ × 6¾ | 1,500 |

## GIANDOMENICHO TIEPOLO.   1727–1804

£

| | | | |
|---|---|---|---|
| 963 | S. | Reinhold Merck.   Carnival in Venice, 29¾ × 47¼ | 72,000 |
| 965 | C. | Girl's head, symbolizing music | 8,400 |
| 966 | C. | A musician, half-length, 30 × 22½    Bought in at | 9,660 |
| 968 | | Pair of round landscapes, each containing two *pulcinelli*, 38 in. diam    2 for | 2,310 |

### DRAWINGS

Most of these are pen and wash drawings on the broad scale of 11 × 16 inches, originally forming picture-books or albums. The *Pulcinello* album contained 50 drawings which were on offer in the early 1920s, complete for £500. Individual drawings from this album rose to 250 guineas in 1936, £640 in 1953, £920 in 1956, £1,700 in 1959 and £5,785 in 1966, since which the market has remained fairly static.

£

| | | | |
|---|---|---|---|
| 963 | C. | White horse, pen and wash, 12 × 17 | 5,880 |
| 964 | C. | Six pen and wash drawings from a scrap-book   6 for | 4,809 |
| 965 | | Lord Beauchamp.   C.   Bernini's statue of Neptune, pen and wash study | 1,575 |
| | | C.   Horace Walpole's album.   166 drawings totalled £87,260. | |
| | | Six exceeded £1,000         The dearest made | 1,470 |
| | | S.   Twelve drawings from the Beurdeley album, illustrating Venetian social life, pen and wash, 11 × 16.   The total was £43,100 | |
| | | Bull-baiting | 3,500 |
| | | Bourgeois dinner-party | 4,200 |
| | | Minuet without masks | 5,600 |
| | | Street poultry-seller | 3,600 |
| | | Women's causerie | 3,400 |
| | | Bird-fanciers | 5,200 |
| | | Going to church | 3,400 |
| | | Promenade in the garden of a palace | 4,000 |
| | | Visit to a pregnant friend | 3,500 |
| | | Three others at £1,900 to £2,600 | |
| 966 | | Paris.   Death of Pulcinello, 11 × 16, FN72,000+tax | 5,785 |
| | | Two more Pulcinello drawings       £2,650 and | 3,290 |
| | | 2nd sale.   Two others at          £2,650 and | 3,290 |
| 967 | | 3rd sale.   Four drawings from the Beurdeley album, Venetian street life      Average price | 3,795 |

| | | £ |
|---|---|---|
| 1967 | Goelet. S. Four drawings from the Pulcinello album made £18,800. | |
| | Pulcinello as a portrait painter | 5,800 |
| | Pulcinello at the zoo | 5,000 |
| | Pulcinello at the circus | 4,000 |
| | S. 18 drawings from the Beurdeley album made | 53,300 |
| | Family party in a villa garden, $11\frac{1}{2} \times 16\frac{3}{4}$ | 4,800 |
| | Paris. Faunes et faunesses, pen and wash, $7 \times 11$ | 1,252 |
| | Four more drawings from the Beurdeley album, $11\frac{1}{2} \times 16\frac{3}{4}$ | |
| | Street picture-seller, FN34,000+tax | 2,710 |
| | Spectators at a peepshow, FN42,000+tax | 3,340 |
| | Acrobats, FN55,000+tax | 4,384 |
| | Watching the lions, FN57,000+tax | 4,528 |
| 1969 | Fonda. S. Dromedary resting, pen and wash, $6 \times 5$ | 2,400 |
| | S. From the Beurdeley album, the Quack Dentist, $11\frac{1}{2} \times 16\frac{3}{4}$ | 3,700 |

## Jacopo Robusti called
## IL TINTORETTO. 1518–1599

In the saleroom Tintoretto has never been a high-priced painter. Virtually the whole of his well attested work consists of altar-pieces or suites of wall panels. There are few documented easel-pictures. Bad condition and pupil-copying have both weighed heavily against Tintoretto. An altarpiece would be another matter, but in 1853 when the British government had a chance to acquire the *Salute* and *San Cassiano* altarpieces for £12,000, not all the propaganda of Ruskin could move them. In 1963 one well-attested easel picture, *The Pool of Bethesda*, returned to the market. On paper it had multiplied its value ten times in 16 years. Yet £47,250, the price of a Baroque masterpiece, was just enough to buy the smallest of small misses in pinafores by Renoir. There had been better prices, paid for Tintoretto before the end of the First World War, three since 1910 at £10,000 to £11,500 equivalent to £80,000–£89,500. Two portraits, bought by The National Gallery, Melbourne, in the 1920s at £14,000 each, work out at £70,000 in 1970. Portraits, attributable to Tintoretto, continue to reach the market and, if they are as good as these, they might make as much. The utterly unpredictable price of a Bassano at the end of 1969 suggests that the *Pool of Bethesda* may have multiplied in value several times since 1963. This is unlikely to bring other Tintoretto subject pictures to the surface. There just aren't any.

| | | £ |
|---|---|---|
| 1960 | Gladys Robinson. N.Y. Small head of a prelate | 5,000 |
| 1961 | C. Profile head, so called Alessandro Farnese | 3,150 |

| | | | £ |
|---|---|---|---|
| :963 | Hasson. C. Raising of Lazarus (now called Christ at the pool of Bethesda (£168 in 1795, £3,360 in 1927, £4,830 in 1947) | | 47,250 |
| | S. Pietà, attributed | | 3,600 |
| :964 | C. Flagellation of Christ, 58×49. Bought in | | 7,875 |
| :965 | Farr. S. The three graces with Mercury, 64½×45 | | 4,500 |
| :966 | S. Martyrdom of SS Nazarius and Celsus, 61½×29½, bought in | | 3,200 |
| | Robilant. S. Paradise with Christ in Glory, 15 ft long, innumerable figures *after* the mural painting in the Doge's palace | | 3,500 |
| | Cook Trust. C. Susanna and the elders, 16×17½ | | 4,410 |
| :967 | Lord Wharton. S. The resurrection of Christ, 75¾×57 | | 5,000 |
| | Heber Percy. C. Nicola Doria as a youth, 1545, 75×43½ | | 16,800 |
| :968 | C. Portrait, a procurator of St Mark's, 45×37½ | | 2,520 |
| | Kaplan. S. Resurrection, oil study, 17¾×13¾ | | 5,000 |
| :969 | Delmege. S. Holy family, alleged early work, 36×26½ | | 4,500 |
| | C. Martyrdom of Nazarius and Celsus, 61½×29½. Bought in | | 3,150 |
| | Batthyany. S. Portrait, Venetian senator, 25×19 | | 9,000 |

### DRAWINGS

| | | |
|---|---|---|
| :962 | Springell. S. Seated man, chalk, heightened with white, 10¾×7¼ | 2,200 |
| :964 | S. A dead man, chalks | 1,000 |
| :965 | Victor Bloch. S. Two studies of a male nude on one sheet | 900 |
| :968 | Morritt. S. Study, drawn from the head of Michelangelo's Giuliano de' Medici, black and white chalk, 14¾×11 | 3,300 |

## JAMES TISSOT. 1836–1902

A market recovery which began towards 1930 but which has failed to get off the ground—a little inexplicably. At a time, when such an inordinate fuss is being made about minor mid or late Victorians, surely Tissot is a more worthy subject than Atkinson Grimshaw or Sidney Richard Percy or Edward Ladell.

| | | £ |
|---|---|---|
| :963 | S. Hide and seek, 30×22 (£892 10s. in 1957) | 2,200 |
| | Ionides. S. The letter, 39¾×22 | 1,900 |
| :964 | S. On the river, 1871 | 420 |
| | Victoria station platform, 1895, 23×12 | 850 |
| | Picnic by the river, 1870 | 1,700 |

|      |                                                          | £     |
|------|----------------------------------------------------------|-------|
| 1965 | C.  Large girl's head (27 guineas in 1900)               | 1,785 |
|      | The milliner's shop                                      | 3,150 |
| 1966 | Vallombreuse.  S.  Study for *the ball on shipboard* (completed version, £600 in 1937), 38×27 | 1,400 |
| 1967 | Chagrin d'amour, 19½×14¾                                 | 1,500 |
| 1969 | S.  Les adieux, monochrome gouache, 1871, 39×24 (in Tokyo).  Lady with kimono and vases, 14¾×18½, 2 million Yen | 1,800 |
|      |                                                          | 2,825 |
| 1970 | Wilson.  S.  Terrace, the Trafalgar Tavern, Greenwich, 10¼×14½ | 4,100 |

Tiziano Vecellio, called
### TITIAN.  1480 [?]–1576

In this very short list there is no indication of the price which an important Titian—a Venus for instance—would fetch in 1970. Were it not for that most enigmatic sale of a Jacopo Bassano in 1969 for £273,000, one would be inclined to believe that neither Titian nor any other 16th century Venetian painter appealed to the taste of this age in the least. Probably in Titian's case rarity and the accumulated esteem of past ages take the place of universal pleasure. *The Allegory of Prudence* is small, hideous, and quite unintelligible. While it once had a message, dramatic and easily perceived, it now has none, except for art experts. Yet nothing can be more certain than that the National Gallery, Washington, would have paid half a million dollars for it.

Strange to say, there have been only two periods during the whole time that important Titians were available, in which they shared the highest price-rating. These were the first quarter of the 19th century and the years 1918–35. The *Man in a Red Cap* (£50,000 to H. C. Frick in 1915), the *Portrait of Philip I* (£60,000 in 1913) and the *Venus with Organ Player* (£50,000 in 1917) were all in present money-terms in the £400,000 class. The Cornaro family (£122,000 in 1929) the *Venus with Mirror* (£112,250 in 1931) the *Venus with Luteplayer* (£100,000 in 1932) and a female portrait, bought by Andrew Mellon (£113,300 in 1936) were in the £500,000–£600,000 class.

|      |                                                          | £       |
|------|----------------------------------------------------------|---------|
| 1959 | Duke of Westminster.  S.  Group, Duke of Urbino and his son (£700 in 1870) | 24,000  |
| 1961 | C.  Portrait of Suleiman II of Turkey, made after an engraving, 28½×24 | 7,350   |
| 1964 | Fischer, Lucerne.  Holy family with saints, 59½×100, FS120,000+tax | 12,000  |
| 1966 | Offered by National Gallery, Washington, for the Allegory of Prudence, 29×26 (£11,550 in 1959), given to National Gallery, London | 170,000 |
|      | Abbott.  S.  The painter's daughter Lavinia with a casket, 46×37 (Orleans sale, 1798, £420).  Schoolpiece | 4,500   |

| | | | |
|---|---|---|---|
| 1968 | Filipinetti. C. Much damaged bust-portrait of unknown man, attributed by Morassi in 1957, 32×25½ | £ | 37,800 |

DRAWINGS

| | | | |
|---|---|---|---|
| 1966 | Holland-Martin. C. Horse's head, black chalk, 12×7 | | 1,260 |

## MARK TOBEY. (*See* Abstract Painters, America)

## LOUIS TOCQUÉ. (*See* French School, 18th century)

## CONSTANTIN TROYON. 1810–1865

A large and famous Troyon picture, *Les hauteurs de Suresnes*, was sold in 1944 for 120 guineas. What the great Pierpont Morgan had paid for it is unknown, but in 1895 the vendor, M. Thomy-Thierry, was believed to have refused half a million francs or £20,000, equivalent in 1970 to £170,000 at least. This misadventure has been sufficient to exclude from the market of the 1960s important Troyons, which used to fetch £6,000 to £13,000 before the end of the First World War. Troyon, who was nearly always a cattle painter, was the dullest of the Barbizon school as well as the dearest. There is no sign of any upward movement.

| | | £ |
|---|---|---|
| 1962 | Hornby. C. Le chasseur, 10½×18 | 367 10s. |
| 1967 | S. Vaches dans un pré, 9½×13½ | 50 |
| | Vaches dans les ruines, 39½×53 | 40 |
| | S. Portrait of Georges Sand, playing a guitar, 35¾×28¼ | 500 |
| 1968 | Fischer, Lucerne. Landscape with cattle, FS10,600+tax | 1,155 |
| 1970 | Tweeddale. C. Vaches au pâturage, 32×46, bought in at | 1,050 |

## JOSEPH MALLORD WILLIAM TURNER. 1775–1851

It is instructive to look up Turner in the three splendid volumes of Algernon Graves's *Art Sales*. Beginning within a few years of his death and continuing to the eve of the First World War, there seems to be a continuous rise in prices, from 2,000 guineas in 1854 to 7,000 guineas in 1875, to 8,500 guineas in 1899 and 12,500 in 1908, and finally £21,700 at the Borden sale in New York in 1913. And for much of the time Turner's followers keep him company. Romantic landscape painters who worked on into the 1860s, profited in their own lifetime from Turner's posthumous boom. In Graves's volumes they occupy far more space than the old masters and, on the whole, they seem to be higher-priced. The effect is very much that of the lists of prices for the Impressionists in the present volume. It should dispel the fallacy that a lack of balance between the old masters and the moderns is something abnormal, or confined to the present age.

The very meagre list which follows, shows what happens to the favourite of two generations or three after scarcity and the absence of the best has combined with a loss of freshness to create the less coveted status of a dingy old master. In the entire 1960s there were only five completed Turner oil-paintings, three by fours or bigger. The dearest, *Ehrenbreitstein*, was far from creating any true record, though it was the second dearest English picture to be sold, since the sum of £88,000 in 1965 meant no more than £13,000 in 1913. *Ehrenbreitstein* is not the most satisfactory of Turner's major works. It has lost the 18th century balance of the young Turner without acquiring the almost abstract quality of his last years. Should one expect higher prices for better Turners? There are a few interesting precedents. The *Queen of the Adriatic* is believed to have cost Frick $300,000 in 1923, the equivalent of at least as many pounds in 1970. The most sumptuous of the Venice Turners cost Sir James Ross £30,450 in 1927 at open auction (£152,250). A Turner of this kind might very well be worth a quarter million to judge from the price of £62,000 paid in 1969 for *Helvoetsluys*, a grey oily seascape of the most mortal dullness, which had multiplied its paper-money price 6½ times over in 15 years. But there is little likelihood of anything as good as the *Queen of the Adriatic* or Sir James Ross's Venetian picture ever reaching the saleroom.

In the 1960s Turner's watercolours were more plentiful than his oil paintings with at least twenty completed examples in the saleroom, but they told a different story. In 1919 the famous Swiss series reached their apogee, when *Zurich* made £6,510, the equivalent of £32,500. In 1959 two from this series made over £11,000 each, but in the 1960s a nineteen-inch Turner watercolour was worth £5,000 to £7,000, much less than a scribble, made by the seventeen-year-old Picasso in a Barcelona café.

| | | £ |
|---|---|---:|
| 1960 | N.Y. 'Port Ruysdael', 1827, 36×48 (£1,995 in 1863, £6,720 in 1919) | 11,072 |
| 1961 | N.Y. Warwick Castle, 23×32, $44,000 | 15,750 |
| 1962 | Swaythling. C. Mercury and Herse, 75×63 (£577 10s. in 1813, £7,875 in 1897, £2,625, bought in, 1946) | 8,190 |
| 1965 | Brenda Cook. C. Grand Junction Canal, 1810, 36×48 (£1,837 10s. in 1874) | 9,950 |
| | Lord Allendale. S. Ehrenbreitstein and the tomb of Marceau, 1835, 35¼×47½ (£1,890 in 1863) | 88,000 |
| 1967 | Shenley. C. Mountains and cattle, 9½×11½ (£8,925 in 1959) | 5,040 |
| 1969 | C. Boyhood self-portrait, c. 1790, inscribed, 20½×15½ | 1,260 |
| | S. Helvoetsluys, the City of Utrecht going to sea, 35¼×47¼, 1832 (Bicknell, 1863, £1,680. Price, 1895, £6,720, Ross, 1927, £9,925, Coats, 1954, £9,240) | 62,000 |

## WATERCOLOURS

|      |                                                                                              | £       |
|------|----------------------------------------------------------------------------------------------|---------|
| 1959 | Mirrieless. C. Lake Zug (£1,155 in 1895)                                                     | 11,028  |
|      | Lake Lucerne (£2,310 in 1890)                                                                | 11,550  |
| 1960 | S. Bedford, 13½×19½ (£504 in 1878)                                                           | 5,500   |
|      | Pugliese. S. Llanthony Abbey, 11¾×16¾                                                        | 5,000   |
|      | S. Bellinzona                                                                                 | 3,500   |
| 1961 | Sullivan. S. Yarmouth Sands, 9½×14                                                           | 6,400   |
|      | S. Llangollen, 10½×16                                                                         | 3,000   |
| 1962 | S. Vesuvius in eruption, 1817, 11×15½                                                        | 3,800   |
| 1964 | Craigmyle. S. Venice, 1818, 11¼×16¼                                                          | 6,000   |
|      | Temple of Aegina, wash drawing                                                                | 2,400   |
| 1965 | S. Tours, 4¾×7¼                                                                              | 2,900   |
|      | Andernach, 9½×11¾                                                                            | 2,800   |
|      | Allendale. S. Interior of St. Peter's, 1821                                                  | 2,900   |
| 1966 | Wargrave Manor (Knight, Frank). Stamford                                                     | 7,500   |
| 1967 | O'Gordon. C. Sunset on a lake, 1842, 8½×10½                                                  | 3,150   |
|      | Neame. C. Temple at Farnley Hall, 12½×17                                                     | 4,200   |
|      | C. Falls at Lauterbrünnen, 10½×15                                                            | 1,680   |
|      | Yates. S. West Cowes at Sunset, 1828, 11¼×16¼                                                | 5,200   |
|      | Nahum. S. Sunrise off Margate, 1830, 8¾×10¾                                                  | 1,900   |
| 1968 | Parkinson. C. Two views of Hornby Castle, 1800, 27×40, bought in at                  2 for   | 2,450   |
| 1969 | Gillington. C. Mainz, 1819, 7¾×12½ (£84 in 1890)                                            | 4,200   |
|      | Doggett. S. The valley of Cluses from the Aiguillette (ex John Ruskin), 15½×11               | 3,800   |
| 1970 | Auctions A. G. Basel. Moselle valley with bridge at Coblenz, undated, unknown provenance, FS75,000+tax | 8,292 |
|      | C. Lake Nemi. 1818, 5×8¼ (£388 10s. in 1869)                                                | 8,925   |
|      | Rye from Rye Harbour, 7¼×10¾ (£346 10s. in 1920)                                            | 1,365   |
|      | Robert Smith. S. Distant view of Oxford, boyhood work, c. 1794, 9×13                         | 2,000   |

## MAURICE UTRILLO. 1883–1955

What's in a name? Would anyone pay £30,000 for an Utrillo of the 1930s, if the signature was not that of the same man who found a new poetry in the lime-washed walls of the Paris *banlieue* in the early 1900s? Would anyone for that matter pay £100? There lurks, however, behind the sprawling signature of the later Utrillo a perverse logic of the saleroom. It works like this. An Utrillo of 1911 has made close on £30,000, but there are neither enough works of this quality nor enough buyers who can spend £30,000, so a third or a quarter of this price is spent on a parody. It is well known that Utrillo's later work was produced under tragic conditions, but it seems that even this shipwreck of a talent has a dramatic interest which must be paid for. In the last twenty years of his life he ceased to paint at all.

| | | £ |
|---|---|---|
| 1922 | Bought in Paris by J. Boulton.  Rue de banlieue, 1912 (see 1965) | 100 |
| 1925 | Francis Carco.  Paris.  Eglise à Clichy | 218 |
| 1928 | C.  La rue Boyer, 1913 | 525 |
| 1932 | Pacquement.  Paris.  Place du Tertre | 137 |
| 1933 | Lederlin.  Paris.  Vieux château à la Ferté-Millon | 330 |
| | Moulin de la galette under snow (see 1959) | 420 |
| 1934 | Johnson.  N.Y.  Church at Montmagny, 15×21 | 98 |
| 1937 | N.Y.  Corte, Corsica, 23¼×32 | 93 |
| 1939 | C.  Tour St Jacques | 54 12s. |
| | Canonne.  Paris.  Rue de Sannois, 28,000 francs+tax | 125 |
| 1940 | Biron.  S.  Village church | 72 |
| 1942 | Reid.  C.  Village church, 1914 | 504 |
| 1944 | Pincus-Brennen.  N.Y.  Paysage de banlieue, $4,150 | 1,040 |
| 1946 | N.Y.  Presbytery in Corsica | 678 |
| 1947 | N.Y.  Rue Mont Cenis (see 1963) | 525 |
| 1949 | Gregory.  S.  The barracks | 950 |
| 1950 | Paris.  Derrière la maison | 1,130 |
| 1951 | N.Y.  Suburban street | 768 |
| 1952 | N.Y.  Moulin à Montmagny | 1,175 |
| 1953 | Paris.  Le Lapin Agile, Montmartre (see 1958) | 2,050 |
| 1954 | Paris.  Rue St Vincent | 2,860 |
| 1956 | N.Y.  Small town in Paris banlieue | 5,175 |
| 1957 | Paris.  Rue Sancelles | 9,350 |
| 1958 | N.Y.  Le Lapin Agile (see 1953) | 10,000 |
| 1959 | Paris.  Restaurant in the valley, 1906 | 10,200 |
| | Montmartre, snow scene | 12,500 |
| | | 6,000 |
| | S.  A château | 4,500 |
| | Church under snow | 6,500 |
| | Street scene | 7,350 |
| 1960 | C.  Eglise Sacré Cœur, Montmartre, 1910, 19×28 | 6,300 |
| | Street in Montmartre (£9,200 in 1957), 22¼×28¾ | |
| | S.  Escalier de la Reine Berthe, Chartres, 1908, 29¼×21½ | 7,800 |
| 1961 | Barbara Church.  N.Y.  Rue de Crimée, 1910 | 18,570 |
| | S.  Street in Montmartre | 10,500 |
| 1962 | Somerset Maugham.  S.  Street at Conquet, Brittany, 1911, 24×32 | 11,000 |
| 1963 | Paris.  Rue Mont Cenis, 30×42 (£525 in 1947) | 12,500 |
| | Zimet.  S.  Rue de Stains, 1909, 19½×28¾ | 15,000 |
| 1964 | Hutton.  S.  Rooftops, Montmartre, 1908, 19¼×17¾ | 10,200 |

| | | £ |
|---|---|---|
| 1965 | S. Eglise de Grosley, 1914 | 7,500 |
| | Rue Norvins, 1913 | 6,500 |
| | Boulton. C. Rue de banlieue, 1912, 23¾×22 (see 1922) | 13,650 |
| | Church at Aubonne, 23¾×32¾ | 12,600 |
| 1966 | Cummings. S. Le Lapin Agile, 1914, 22×30½ | 14,000 |
| | C. Le moulin rouge, 1925, 21×17¾ | 13,500 |
| | C. Eglise et château, Pont à Mousson, 1928, 38½×28¾, bought in | 9,925 |
| | Reinach. N.Y. Château de l'Arbresle, 1928, 23½×28¾, $19,000 | 7,926 |
| | Motte, Geneva. Paris street scene, FS72,000+tax | 7,515 |
| | Tour du philosophe, Moulin de la Galette, 20¾×29¾, FS120,000+tax | 13,020 |
| 1968 | N.Y. L'abside de Chauconin, 1916, 20¼×29, $15,000 | 6,250 |
| | S. La rue St Vincent, 24½×30¾, 1930 | 9,000 |
| | C. Place du Tertre, Montmartre, 21×28½, 1911 | 29,400 |
| | S. Château de Montguichet, 1911, 23½×31½ | 13,000 |
| | Rue de Mont Cenis, *c.* 1915, 25¼×31¼ | 13,000 |
| | Eglise de Grosley, 1912, 22×30 | 10,000 |
| | Roudinesco. N.Y. Au sacré cœur de Montmartre, 1926, 39½×32, $60,000 | 25,000 |
| | Rue à Ivry, 1924, 21×27½, $30,000 | 12,500 |
| | Ermitage de Mont Cindre, 1934, 18½×27, $27,500 | 11,416 |
| | C. Paysage de neige, 1917, 19¾×25¼ | 12,600 |
| | Hadorn. C. Rue de Mont Cenis, 24¾×32¾ | 27,300 |
| | Godick. N.Y. Montmartre, 18×21½, $30,000 | 12,500 |
| | Paris. Château de Ganay, 1933, gouache, 12¾×20¾, FN332,500+tax | 30,850 |
| 1969 | C. Dourdan, château et église, 28¾×23¾ | 8,925 |
| | Le café Briard, Paris, 24×19½ | 9,450 |
| | Rue de Limas, Rhone, 1929, 25×36 | 12,075 |
| | N.Y. Rue à Bourg la Reine, *c.* 1923, 19¾×25½, $32,500 | 13,652 |
| | Rue de banlieue, Paris, 19¾×24, $25,000 | 10,416 |
| | Hayward Weir. N.Y. Le pont de l'avenue de St Ouen, *c.* 1914, 21½×28¾, $51,000 | 21,250 |
| 1969 | S. Rue St Rustique, 22×18 | 10,500 |
| | Le chantier des Gobelins, 1922, 17¾×22¾ | 12,000 |
| | Eglise en Provence, *c.* 1925, 19¾×25½ | 15,000 |
| | St Bernard, Ain (after Utrillo) Backcloth for the ballet, *Barabau*, 1925, 33 ft, 10×40 ft 4 | 6,500 |
| | Auvers sur Oise, 23×29 | 9,000 |
| | Eglise de banlieue, Lyon, *c.* 1920, 25½×31¾, bought in | 9,500 |
| | Eglise de St Germain, 31¾×23¼, bought in | 17,000 |

|      |    |                                                                           | £      |
|------|----|---------------------------------------------------------------------------|--------|
| 1969 | S. | Rue de Mont Cenis, *c.* 1936, $22 \times 30\frac{1}{4}$                    | 18,500 |
|      |    | La barraque, Nangis, 1931, $23\frac{1}{2} \times 28\frac{3}{4}$, bought in | 15,000 |
|      | C. | Rue à Montmartre, 1914, $29 \times 22$, bought in                          | 13,125 |
|      |    | Dome of the Sacré Cœur, Montmartre, $21\frac{3}{4} \times 18\frac{1}{4}$, 1911, bought in | 14,175 |

## LOUIS VALTAT.  (*See* French School, minor Impressionist painters)

## ADRIAEN VAN DE VELDE.  1635–1672

'The once brisk market is practically extinct'—thus the verdict of Volume One in 1961. In fact there were two transactions in 1963 and 1965 which altered the picture of the 1950s. But these works in the style of Potter and Wouvermans are more in the taste of the 18th century than the mid-20th and are still cheap as the classic Dutch school goes. In 1875 a small cattlepiece by Adriaen van de Velde made £4,515 at Christie's, the equivalent in 1970 of more than £40,000.

|      |                                                                                                     | £     |
|------|-----------------------------------------------------------------------------------------------------|-------|
| 1959 | S. (with J. van der Heyden).  Toll-house at Maarsen, $18\frac{1}{2} \times 23\frac{1}{2}$            | 7,800 |
| 1963 | Heldring.  S.  Landscape, 1661, $14\frac{1}{4} \times 18\frac{3}{4}$                                 | 6,200 |
| 1965 | Jackson.  C.  Two sporting dogs, $32 \times 40$                                                      | 3,150 |
| 1968 | van Waay, Amsterdam.  Landscape with figures, $42\frac{1}{2} \times 53\frac{1}{2}$, Hfl40,000+tax   | 5,260 |

## WILLEM VAN DE VELDE, the Younger.  1633–1707

In the 1960s the work of this painter shared the growing popularity of sea paintings. Six works made from 13,000 to 26,000 guineas each. It must, however, be noticed that a late pastiche of van de Velde's style by Charles Brooking (see English school, 18th century) made £15,500, and that both in 1876 and 1927 there were van de Velde shipping pictures at the 1970 equivalent of £22,000.

|      |                                                                           | £      |
|------|---------------------------------------------------------------------------|--------|
| 1958 | Cassel van Doorn.  N.Y.  Fleet at anchor, $23 \times 39$, $42,500         | 15,175 |
|      | S.  Fishing boats                                                         | 5,500  |
| 1960 | S.  Fleet at anchor                                                       | 13,000 |
| 1963 | S.  Fleet at anchor                                                       | 9,000  |
|      | Men of war and coastal shipping                                          | 2,300  |
| 1964 | Bruce Ingram.  S.  Fleet in a calm, $20\frac{1}{2} \times 26$             | 14,000 |

| | | £ |
|---|---|---|
| 965 | Williams. C. Fleet with boats in a calm | 13,125 |
| | C. De Reuter's flagship, pen and wash drawing, 3 ft long | 1,050 |
| | Wakelin. S. Three men of war, grisaille painting, dated 1949, 23¾ × 32½ | 4,800 |
| | Adda. Paris. Le coup de canon, 9 × 8¾ (Hamilton Palace sale, 1882, £304, 10*s*.) | 2,635 |
| 967 | Noordtzij. S. Crowded shipping in a calm, 26 × 39 | 6,000 |
| 968 | C. Men of war and fishing boats in a calm, 31 × 45 | 15,750 |
| | S. Men of war in a calm, grisaille, 24½ × 29¼ | 2,400 |
| | Harman Hunt. C. Battle of the Texel, 1673, 31 × 56¼ | 2,940 |
| | Cussins. S. Black chalk drawings, ship's stern, 8¼ × 11½, | 480 |
| | English frigate from port quarter, 7¼ × 6 | 650 |
| 969 | Massey. S. The Dutch war-fleet under sail, 1672, pen and wash, 10 × 16¾ | 800 |
| | C. British men of war in calm, 18 × 14 | 4,410 |
| | Bruguière. C. Fishing boats and a larger vessel in a calm, 20 × 25 | 27,300 |
| 969 | Lord Dickinson. S. Men of war landing troops on rocky coast, grisaille, 25¾ × 38¾ | 5,000 |

## ANTHONY VAN DYCK. 1599–1641

n 1906 Vandyck was not merely considered one of the six greatest painters of he world. He was actually the dearest. The portrait of *Elena Grimaldi-Cattaneo* ad just been bought by P. A. B. Widener for half a million dollars. The only ther picture that had made as much was Raphael's Colonna altarpiece, bought y Pierpont Morgan in 1901. It would be hard to imagine a Vandyck portrait n 1969 at £825,000. Since Andrew Mellon's purchase of *Philip, Lord Wharton* rom the Hermitage Museum in 1931, there had not been a Vandyck portrait in he salerooms even at £25,000. Of course there has been nothing on the market omparable with the Cattaneo portraits which were smuggled out of Italy in 906. Even so, Vandyck is the only one of 'the six great masters of the world' who has actually declined in value in the 20th century. It has to be realized that Vandyck was bought by Duveen's multi-millionaires because he was the ounder-painter of the English portrait school. Within a fairly short time, the ighest prices for Vandyck were matched by the prices paid for Gainsborough nd Reynolds, who had not been regarded previously as rivals to the 'six great ainters of the world'. As a result of this assimilation, the enormous fall of Gainsborough and Reynolds in the 1930s brought down Vandyck with them. The sale of a royal portrait to a multi-millionaire in 1969 brought back something of Vandyck's former status, but he was no longer preferred to Rubens nd Rembrandt. In the salerooms of the 1960s the highest price paid for a Vandyck, was actually given for a drawing—but a drawing of the purest magic, a landscape, rival to the one in the British Museum, with a strong smell of having been made from nature in England.

| 1960 | Heywood Lonsdale. C. Unknown lady with chain girdle, $41 \times 29$ | £ 6,300 |
|---|---|---|
| | C. Jan Malderus, Bishop of Antwerp | 2,520 |
| 1961 | Hart. S. Unknown nobleman, $52 \times 40$, the first Vandyck portrait to reach a five-figure price in 34 years | 19,000 |
| | Erickson. N.Y. Genoese officer, 1626, $45\frac{1}{2} \times 38\frac{1}{2}$, $27,000 | 9,650 |
| 1963 | Cintas. N.Y. Earl of Newport and Lord Goring, $48 \times 57$ | 9,825 |
| | Lucy, Countess of Carlisle, 1637, $85 \times 50$ (see 1967) | 14,000 |
| | C. Female portrait, attributed as an early work | 6,300 |
| | Bass. N.Y. Bishop Antoon Triest, schoolpiece, $50 \times 41$ (see 1965) | 3,930 |
| 1964 | Fischer, Lucerne. Head of a praying Magdalen, $25\frac{1}{2} \times 20\frac{1}{2}$, FS30,000+tax About | 3,000 |
| 1965 | S. Bishop Antoon Triest (see 1963) Bought in at | 3,500 |
| 1966 | Finarte, Milan. Portrait of a lady with a dwarf, $80 \times 50\frac{1}{2}$, 18 million lire+tax | 11,800 |
| 1967 | S. Lucy Countess of Carlisle (see 1963) | 7,000 |
| | Wegmann, Amsterdam. Apostle's head, $16\frac{1}{4} \times 13\frac{1}{2}$, Hfl18,000+tax | 2,030 |
| 1968 | Paris. Isabella Waerbeke (replica of Wallace Collection picture), $27\frac{1}{2} \times 22\frac{1}{4}$, FN58,000+tax | 4,625 |
| | Kaplan. S. Madonna and child with St. Anne, $27 \times 21\frac{3}{4}$ | 21,000 |
| 1969 | S. Head, unknown bearded man in wide collar, $16\frac{1}{4} \times 12\frac{1}{2}$ | 8,600 |
| | Bought by Charles Wrightsman from Colnaghi, signed portrait of Queen Henrietta Maria, ex Corsini Palace. Price believed to have exceeded | 100,000 |
| | S. Half-length apostle (St Simon), $43 \times 35$, bought in | 5,800 |
| | Thomaso Raggi, three-quarter length in armour, $49\frac{1}{2} \times 39$ | 7,000 |

### DRAWINGS

| 1963 | C. Adoration of the shepherds, crayon | 1,890 |
|---|---|---|
| 1967 | Paris. Head of Isabella Waerbeke, charcoal and crayon, FN50,000+tax | 4,249 |
| 1969 | Loch. C. Edge of a wood, pure landscape, pen and brown wash, $8 \times 10\frac{3}{4}$ | 25,200 |

## DIEGO VELAZQUEZ. 1599–1660

There was a memorable outcry in 1906 when the nation was required to raise £45,000 to prevent the *Rokeby Venus* going to the U.S.A. It was the first of the reat rescue operations of the century. But, within seven years, at least three elazquez portraits, far from comparable with the Venus, left Europe for the U.S.A. at prices in excess of £80,000 (equivalent to £640,000). There is not much doubt that this would be the value of a well authenticated Velazquez in 1970. *Calabazas* was one of those excellent portraits which never gained the acceptance of the pontifical Beruete, yet it made £178,500 in 1965.

|  |  | £ |
|---|---|---|
| 1965 | Brenda Cook. C. Calabazas, the court jester, whole-length (not universally accepted), 64×42 | 178,500 |
| | Francis. S. Count of Olivarez, whole length schoolpiece, 81¼×43 (Louis Philippe sale, 1853, £325 10s.) | 50,000 |
| | Lord Bruce. C. Restored fragment, dog and cactuses | 3,990 |
| | C. School-portrait of an unknown Italian, 1620 | 14,700 |

## VENETIAN SCHOOL
### late 15th and 16th centuries
(*See* separate entries for Bellini, Tintoretto, Titian, Veronese)

Until December, 1969, the contemporaries of Titian were one of the least saleable of schools. There is no suggestion of an era of inflation in the lists which follow. Some of these works may have come to England in the early 17th century, when they filled a role similar to that of the French Impressionists in the present century. But in the next two centuries they gave way to the taste for the Roman and Bolognese schools, and then to the Florentine primitives. It was only during the relatively brief period when Berenson was associated with Duveen that some attempt was made to build up the lesser Venetians as a rich man's market. Thus in 1911 René Gimpel paid £16,500 for Bartolommeo Veneziano's portrait of *Gabriella Sforza*, now in the Huntington Library. This meant the equivalent of £132,000 in 1970 money. Other portraits by this painter were sold in London in 1927 for £11,025, and in Paris in 1913 for £7,000, the equivalents of £55,000 and £35,000.

It would be difficult to imagine Venetian sixteenth century portraits which could realize such prices in the 1960s. But in those days it would have been even more difficult to predict a price, worthy of Rembrandt or Rubens, for—of all people—Jacopo Bassano before the end of the decade. In 1968 a particularly attractive Bassano was thought very dear at £8,500. Nor was size any merit. I recall a Bassano, even bigger than the *Flight into Egypt*, which cost 80 guineas towards the end of World War I and was sold for the same price 36 years later. Jacopo Bassano was, after all, little more than a very competent eclectic painter who strung together stock figures from the repertory of Veronese and Tintoretto, and who clearly employed many assistants. So one cannot tell whether a quarter-million-pound Bassano means a break-through in the

Venetian *cinquecento* market or merely an irrational saleroom duel. But afte
Tiepolo ceiling-panels at over £400,000 one can expect *anything*.

£

| | |
|---|---|
| 1959 Tibor de Budai. C. LORENZO LOTTO, half-length male portrait | 3,570 |
| Loeser. S. BARTOLOMMEO VENEZIANO. Holy family, dated 1502 | 4,600 |
| S. JACOPO BELLINI. Small nativity, bought in | 15,500 |
| Duke of Westminster. S. JACOPO BASSANO. Holy family | 1,800 |
| 1960 S. FRANCESCO SAVOLDO. Temptation of St Anthony, 26¾×47 | 12,000 |
| Robinson. N.Y. DOSSO DOSSI, Allegory of Love, 60×50 | 6,070 |
| PARIS. ANDREA SCHIAVONE, Annunciation | 3,437 |
| 1961 C. LEANDRO BASSANO. The flood | 1,260 |
| N.Y. GIAMBATTISTA MORONI. Portrait, Vincenzo Garignani | 2,857 |
| 1963 C. ANTONIO VIVARINI. St Francis and reading monk | 2,520 |
| Sterling of Keir. S. ANDREA PREVITALI. Lady playing a lute, 44×67 | 6,100 |
| Cintas. N.Y. GIAMBATTISTA MORONI. Portrait, young girl, $22,000 | 7,865 |
| GIOVANNI BUTINONE. Baptism of Christ | 6,000 |
| 1964 C. MARCO BASAITI. Portrait of a young man | 8,820 |
| 1965 Spencer Churchill. C. ANDREA SCHIAVONE. Venus and Adonis, 31×45 | 1,890 |
| LORENZO LOTTO. Portrait, bearded man, 37×27½ (52. 10s. in 1859) | 2,520 |
| BONVICINO MORETTO. The visitation, 28×36 | 4,410 |
| PARIS BORDONE, Riposo, 61×92½ | 2,520 |
| S. DOSSO DOSSI. Death of St Peter Martyr, 38×43½ | 1,890 |
| Finarte, Milan. GIAMBATTISTA MORONI. Portrait, Antonio Bertindas, 38¾×30½ About | 2,500 |
| Harewood. C. PARIS BORDONE. Venetian general, armed by two pages, 45×61½ | 16,800 |
| PAOLO MORANDO. Portrait, ill-tempered young man, 28½×22 | 5,040 |
| ANON. Portrait of an ecclesiastic, 27×20 | 4,725 |
| 1966 Lady Melchett. S. GIROLAMO DAI LIBRI, St Peter and St John, each 32½×15½ 2 for | 2,800 |
| C. BARTOLOMMEO VENEZIANO. Salome with head of John the Baptist, 16½×20¾ | 1,155 |
| S. MARCO BASAITI. Portrait of a young man, signed and dated 1496, 11¼×9½ | 3,800 |

1966 Lee of Fareham. C. PALMA VECCHIO. Venus reclining £

in Landscape, 44½ × 66     3,570

Brocklebank. S. VITTORE CARPACCIO. Holy family

with saints, 20½ × 30, bought in     9,000

Cook Trust. C. CIMA DI CONEGLIANO. Holy family,

signed, 28 × 22     3,990

1967 Watney. C. DOSSO DOSSI. Half-length portrait, dated

1525 and inscribed Laura Pisani, 37½ × 31½     3,675

GIROLAMO ROMANINO. Apollo and Marsyas, 15½ × 20¼   2,855

PARIS BORDONE. Portrait of a courtesan, 45 × 35, Coll.

Paul Getty     2,940

Schloss Neuwied. S. GIULIO CAMPI. Young man in

black doublet (Clement Marot?), 48 × 55½     3,000

1968 Werner. S. PALMA VECCHIO. A young lady as St

Catherine, 16½ × 12     6,000

JACOPO BASSANO. Holy family with infant St John,

29 × 33     8,500

Kaplan. S. BATTISTA DOSSI. Holy family, arched panel,

23 × 15½     4,800

Warwick Castle. C. GIROLAMO SAVOLDO, hooded

Magdalen, variant of Berlin Staatliche Museen version,

39 × 31½     8,400

C. BONIFAZIO DE' PITATI, Adoration of the Kings, 43½ × 78   3,675

CIMA DI CONEGLIANO. The dead Christ, supported by

two angels in the tomb, 4¾ × 4¼     1,890

Finarte, Milan. PARIS BORDONE. Death of Adonis,

12½ × 44, 11 million lire + tax     8,432

1969 C. Attributed CIMA. Adoration of the Magi, 19¼ × 23½,

bought in     3,360

Poulett. S. PALMA GIOVANE. Christ's entry into Jeru-

salem, 65 × 94     1,400

Prinknash Abbey Trustees. C. JACOPO BASSANO. Flight

into Egypt, led by an angel, 47 × 78. Norton Simon

Foundation     273,000

C. PORDENONE. Portrait, man in black with gold chain,

22½ × 21     2,520

Harvey. C. SCARSELLINO. Virgin and child, adored by

four saints, 22½ × 29     840

C. BONVICINO MORETTO. St Peter leaning on a plinth,

66 × 39     3,360

Inchcape. S. MARCO ZOPPO. Pietà after Giovanni

Bellini, 17¼ × 13     3,700

DRAWINGS

1958 Holland-Martin. C. LORENZO LOTTO. Chalk study of £
drapery, 16 × 11, bought British Museum     8,925
         Miracle of St Lucia, 9 × 14¾, ditto     1,575
       C. DOMENICO CAMPAGNOLA. Landscape, pen and wash     1,427 10s.
       SCHOOL OF GIOVANNI BELLINI. Christ's descent into
limbo, pen     1,527 5s.
       GIOVANNI PORDENONE. St Christopher, pen and wash     2,205
1962 Springell. S. VITTORE CARPACCIO. Standing youth,
pen, 9¾ × 7½     7,800
1963 S. GIOVANNI DA UDINE. Two birds, wc     1,300
       C. ANON, c. 1500. Landscape, pen     3,360
1965 Harewood. C. VITTORE CARPACCIO. Group of ecclesi-
astics, pen     13,650
1968 C. LORENZO LOTTO. Martyrdom of a saint, pen and
chalk, 10¾ × 7¼     1,890


## NICOLAS VERANDAEL. (See Flemish School, after 1550, fruit and flower painters)


## JAN VERMEER OF DELFT. 1632–1675

This is like that whole chapter which Dr Johnson could repeat, 'There are no snakes to be met throughout the whole island'; for there have been no true Vermeers on the market since 1932, apart from the private sale in 1955 of the Arenburg girl's head, the true price of which, I now understand, was $350,000 or £125,000. In 1932 *The Little Street in Delft* cost Sir Henri Deterding £75,000. Two very uncertain Vermeers in the National Gallery, Washington, cost Andrew Mellon about as much in 1936, while some of the downright forgeries of H. A. van Meegeren were sold during the war for £85,000 to £123,000 in equivalent English money of the time. It is therefore anyone's guess what an authentic Vermeer would be worth in 1970—and a purely academic problem since by all indications there are none that can reach the market. In the 1960s one would have assumed a half-million to a million according to quality. But since Prince Liechtenstein sold his swinging Frans Hals portrait for nearly a million and a half, one must think in higher terms unless pure sensitivity has ceased to command a special price.

£

1963 Bass. N.Y. Self portrait, apparently a derivation from
the Meysens engraved portrait of 1670, $90,000     32,415

## PAOLO CAGLIARI called
## IL VERONESE.  1528–1588

*The Family of Darius*, bought by the National Gallery from Count Vittore Pisani in 1857 for £13,650 (equivalent to £135,000) was then the second dearest picture in the world, exceeded only by Murillo's *Immaculate Conception*, bought by the French government in 1852 for £24,600. Since there is no other Veronese painting, fifteen and a half feet long, which is likely to come on the market, we shall never know the present value of *The Family of Darius*. The list which follows cannot offer much assistance. It is not even certain that any one of these pictures is by the hand of Veronese himself. The last certain Veronese on the market was sold in 1947 to the National Gallery, Melbourne, for £30,000, the equivalent in 1970 of £65,000, but this picture, the *Rewards of Philosophy*, would certainly be worth more than £65,000. After the sale of that highly derivative Bassano for £273,000 in December, 1969, one would say five times at the very least.

And yet Veronese has generally been a cheap painter. The price of the gigantic *Family of Darius* was a freak. As one instance, *Venus and Mars, United* which was sold for 300 guineas at the exhibition of the Orleans collection in 1798, made 6,000 guineas in 1903 and cost the Metropolitan Museum £8,000 in 1910.

| | | £ |
|---|---|---:|
| 1966 | S.  A concert, alleged study for the fresco at Maser, 15½ × 25¾, bought in | 3,000 |
| | Susanna and the elders, attributed, 18 × 12 | 4,500 |
| | Earl of Haddo.  C.  Adoration of the shepherds, 41 × 50 | 42,000 |
| 1967 | S.  Annunciation, attributed, 11¼ × 17¾ | 5,000 |
| 1968 | S.  Half-length portrait, bearded man in armour, 42½ × 32 | 5,775 |

### DRAWINGS

| | | |
|---|---|---:|
| 1962 | Springell.  S.  Female head, chalk | 2,600 |
| 1963 | Rudolf.  S.  A man, seated, chalk | 1,400 |
| 1965 | Harewood.  C.  Sheet of studies, pen and wash | 3,780 |
| 1969 | S.  Moderation, study for a Series of the Virtues, black and white chalk on blue paper, 8 × 9 | 1,900 |
| | Death of Adonis, pen and wash, sheet of studies on reverse, 12¼ × 8½ | 9,800 |
| | Boerlag-Koenigs.  S.  Sheet of studies, pen and wash, 8½ × 5¼ | 4,000 |
| | S.  Sheet of studies, Baptism of Christ, pen and wash, 8¾ × 3¾ | 3,800 |
| | St George and dragon, pen 3½ × 2¼ | 4,000 |

# MARIE LOUISE VIGÉE-LEBRUN. 1755–1842

The portrait of the Princess Tufialkin was no doubt thought dear enough i 1963 when it made $24,000 or £8,516 at the Cintas sale. For in the 1960s ther was not much appreciation for the hard and tight French painting of the nec classic age. It was rather different after the First World War when there was flight of French portraits to the U.S.A. The picture had then been bought b Barton Jacobs of Baltimore for $50,000, equivalent to as many pounds in 196; But that was not even dear for a Vigée-Lebrun. Ten years earlier, at the Douce sale of 1912, Henri de Rothschild had paid £17,600 for the *Princesse a Talleyrand*. In 1918, J. R. Berwind paid $120,000 or £24,700 for *Mari Antoinette in red*, while in 1919 Wildenstein paid 440,000 francs for *Mlle d Gazon as Nina*, then equivalent to £12,600. On the 1970 scale these three pric represent about £140,000, £125,000 and £63,000. Mme Vigée-Lebrun was tiresome millinery-minded painter who could charge 500 guineas, whe Romney and Hoppner asked 120 or 150. The prices of millinery paintings in th Duveen age are unimaginable in 1970, but many other things which make a much in 1970 would have been unimaginable then.

|  |  |  | £ |
|---|---|---|---|
| 1959 | N.Y. | Princess Poniatowska, $6,500 | 2,321 |
|  |  | Comtesse de Châtenay, 1785, 25½×21½, $9,000 | 3,214 |
| 1963 | Paris. | Head of unknown girl, 37×28½ | 3,320 |
|  | Cintas. N.Y. Princess Tufialkin, 22×25, $24,000 ($50,000 in 1923), Columbus Art Gallery |  | 8,516 |
| 1964 | Sanderson. C. Lady Mornington (Gabrielle Rolland), 38½×29 |  | 6,300 |
| 1966 | James Rothschild. Paris. La jeune musicienne, 36×28, FN22,000+tax |  | 1,740 |
| 1967 | Paris. Princess Galitzine as Flora, Petersburg, 1799, 54½×39¼, FN50,000+tax |  | 4,268 |
| 1968 | Weinmüller, Munich. Unknown girl's head, 1797, 19¼×14, DM32,000+tax |  | 3,800 |
| 1969 | C. Marie Antoinette (attributed), 24×21 |  | 1,785 |
|  |  | Young man in open necked shirt, presumed to be Robert Byron in 1805, 21×18 | 2,628 |

# JACQUES VILLON. (*See* Abstract Painters, Europe)

# MAURICE DE VLAMINCK. 1876–1958

Having been lightly touched by the *fauve* movement towards the age of thirty Vlaminck settled down to a long life of routine landscapes, all apparentl painted in the same blueish gas-light. Soon after the First World War they wer aking several hundred pounds apiece. In 1958, at the time of his death, they ade as many thousands. In the 1960s the regular appearance of at least twenty ꞌ his works every year in the salerooms was no obstacle to Vlaminck being bitually a five-figure painter. For instance, in 1968–9, M. Roudinesco's rteen annual purchases of the 1920s and 1930s, all of them standard Vlamincks, ade from £11,000 to £22,000.

Anti-moral: Go on doing what you know you can do and don't stop.

|  |  |  | £ |
|---|---|---|---|
| 19 | Descaves. Paris. Landscape |  | 180 |
| 25 | Poret. Paris. Large landscape |  | 430 |
| 49 | Paris. Pont sous la neige, $32\frac{1}{2} \times 40$ | About | 300 |
| 51 | Paris. Route de village, $26 \times 37$ |  | 352 |
| 52 | Stuttgart. Village street, $21\frac{1}{2} \times 26$ |  | 680 |
| 53 | Girardin. Paris. Bougival sous la neige, $21\frac{1}{2} \times 36$ |  | 880 |
|  | Derain. Paris. Portrait of Derain, $10\frac{3}{4} \times 9$ |  | 3,360 |
| 54 | Bonnard. Paris. Femme au chien, $44\frac{1}{2} \times 35\frac{1}{2}$ |  | 3,025 |
|  | Bouquet de sauges, $24\frac{1}{2} \times 18\frac{1}{4}$ |  | 1,020 |
| 55 | Derain. Paris. Landscape |  | 3,712 |
|  | N.Y. La chaumière, $28\frac{1}{2} \times 36$, $13,000 |  | 4,607 |
| 57 | Clive Bell. S. Village in Provence, $21\frac{1}{2} \times 25\frac{1}{2}$ (bought for £14) |  | 2,600 |
|  | N.Y. Vase with peonies etc., $30 \times 25$, $8,000 |  | 2,500 |
| 58 | S. Poissy, le pont, $23\frac{1}{2} \times 32$ |  | 5,400 |
|  | Flowers in a bowl, $21 \times 18$ |  | 3,400 |
|  | N.Y. River scene, c. 1906 (Fauve style), $25\frac{1}{4} \times 31\frac{1}{2}$ $60,000 (compare 1969). |  | 21,430 |
| 59 | Paris. Le lavoir sous neige |  | 6,080 |
|  | Foght. S. La cruche blanche, 1908, $30\frac{3}{4} \times 25$ |  | 5,000 |
| 60 | S. Mont Valérien |  | 5,200 |
|  | C. Stormy landscape, $27\frac{1}{2} \times 36$ |  | 6,300 |
|  | S. Yacht in harbour |  | 6,000 |
|  | Paris. River landscape |  | 5,890 |
|  | N.Y. Paysage d'Hiver, $20 \times 25\frac{3}{4}$, $13,500 |  | 4,828 |
| 61 | S. Landscape |  | 6,500 |
| 62 | S. (from Austria). Nature morte, 1904, $28\frac{3}{4} \times 36\frac{1}{4}$, Fauve phase |  | 12,000 |
|  | S. (from U.S.A.). Mont Valérien (Fauve phase), 1908, $25 \times 32$ |  | 18,000 |
|  | Port de Cassis |  | 8,000 |
| 63 | S. Landscape, 1905 (Fauve phase) $31\frac{1}{4} \times 61\frac{3}{4}$ |  | 20,000 |
|  | Tishman. S. Les bassins du Havre, 1906, $32 \times 39$, ditto |  | 20,500 |
|  | S. Bords de la Seine, 1911, $25\frac{1}{2} \times 31\frac{1}{2}$ |  | 9,000 |
|  | S. Still life, apples etc., $28\frac{3}{4} \times 36\frac{1}{4}$ |  | 10,500 |

£

| | | £ |
|---|---|---|
| 1964 | S.  Fishing boats and lighthouse, 35×45 | 8,000 |
| | Bloch.  Paris.  Barge on the Seine, 24×29 | 7,348 |
| 1965 | Osulsky.  S.  Nature morte, 1908, 28×35½ | 10,500 |
| | Nielsen.  N.Y.  La maison de mon père, 1904 (Fauve phase), 21×25½ | 16,075 |
| | Boulton.  C.  Bords de la Rhône, 1914, 28×35 | 9,450 |
| | N.Y.  L'orage, 21¼×25¾ | 7,500 |
| 1966 | S.  Le moulin, 28½×36 | 7,500 |
| 1967 | C.  Village street under snow, 34×45¾ | 10,500 |
| | Higgins.  N.Y.  Village au bord d'une rivière, 1909, 25¼×31½, $32,500 | 11,607 |
| | S.  Nature morte with fruit and wine bottle, 1908, 28×35½ | 12,500 |
| | Evatt.  S.  Paysage au pont, 1910, 27½×35 | 9,000 |
| | C.  View over a town, 1909, 28¼×23¾ | 15,225 |
| | N.Y.  L'entrée du village, 24¾×26 | 7,500 |
| | Hotel du Laboureur, 35½×43¼, $30,000 | 10,715 |
| | Motte, Geneva.  Compôtier, 24×29, FS75,000+tax | 8,210 |
| | Poissy, 1902, 24×12½, FS144,000+tax | 15,850 |
| | Village, Ile de France, 20¾×32½, FS120,000+tax | 13,050 |
| | Bouquet au vase blanc, 21½×18, FS100,000+tax | 10,980 |
| 1968 | S.  Péniches à Châtou, 1908, 25×31½ | 11,500 |
| | Papazoff.  N.Y.  Village street, 21½×25¾, $19,000 | 7,915 |
| | S.  Bouquet de chrysanthèmes, 1912, 28½×23 | 9,500 |
| | Inondation, bords de la Seine, 1910, 35½×28 | 14,100 |
| | Bluestein.  N.Y.  L'Oise à Auvers, 1910, 25×31¾, $44,000 | 18,460 |
| | S.  Voiliers au port de Honfleur, 1918, 23×28½ | 15,000 |
| | Sentier au bord d'une rivière, c. 1914, 25×31¾ | 15,000 |
| | Petits voiliers et péniche sur la Seine, 1908, 28¾×36 | 23,000 |
| | Un pont et trois pêcheurs, 1911–12, 21×25½ | 12,000 |
| | Péniche sur la Seine à Châtou | 25,000 |
| | Vue de Bougival, 1911, 31×25 | 9,500 |
| | Roudinesco.  N.Y.  Paysage Valmondois, 25¾×32 (post-Fauve style), 1917, $40,000 | 16,665 |
| | Nature morte aux artichauts, 32½×46, 1926–8, $27,000 | 11,250 |
| | La Bauche, Savoie, 29×36¼, 1926, $27,000 | 11,650 |
| | Village sous la neige, 1927, 29×36½, $43,000 | 17,915 |
| | Village sous la neige, Epernon, 32×39½, 1923–4, $45,000 | 18,750 |
| | Vase de fleurs variées, 25¾×19¾, 1923, $30,000 | 12,500 |
| | Eglise et champ de blé, 32×29½, 1928, $52,000 | 21,670 |
| | Barque de pêche, 25½×36½, 1926, $33,000 | 13,750 |

| | | £ |
|---|---|---|
| 1968 | Maisons sous la neige, 32×39½, 1929, $37,500 | 15,625 |
| | Le petit pont, 23¾×29, 1923, $31,000 | 12,928 |
| | Grand bouquet de fleurs, 1933, 32×23½, $36,000 | 15,000 |
| | N.Y. Réflexions, semi-fauve landscape, 1910–11, 25½×31¾, $63,000 | 26,200 |
| | Hussey. C. Le Carouge, Valmondois, 29×36 | 22,050 |
| | Refsum. C. Village aux toits rouges, 23×28 | 14,700 |
| | S. Compôtier de pommes, 1908, 23¾×28¾ | 13,000 |
| | Godick. N.Y. Vase of flowers, 21¾×15, $17,000 | 7,082 |
| | Roche. N.Y. Les toits, 32×39½, c. 1920, $63,000 | 26,082 |
| | Wright. N.Y. Maisons au bord de l'eau, 23½×35, c. 1911, $35,000 | 14,584 |
| | N.Y. Meules dans un champ, 24×29, $29,000 | 12,082 |
| 1969 | S. Bateau-lavoir sur la Seine, 1908, 28¾×21¼ | 19,000 |
| | Village en neige, c. 1930, 21×25¼ | 16,000 |
| | Vase de fleurs, 18×15 | 9,500 |
| | C. Bateaux à pêche au port, 23¼×28¼ | 7,750 |
| | Roudinesco. N.Y. Vase de fleurs, 1925, 24×19½, $29,000 | 12,515 |
| | Auvers sur Oise, gate, 1923, 18½×22, $17,000 | 7,140 |
| | La route de Mantes, 1923, 29×36½, $35,000 | 14,705 |
| | N.Y. Le viaduc, 25½×31½, c. 1914, $32,500 | 13,654 |
| | S. Pont sur la Seine à Châtou, Fauve style, 1906, 26½×37¼ $87,000 | 87,000 |
| | Vieux pont de Mantes, 1909, 21¼×25¾ | 20,000 |
| | Vase de fleurs, 1914, 31×25 | 15,000 |
| | Kirk Douglas. S. La ferme aux peupliers, c. 1910, 25×31 | 15,000 |
| | Champ de blé et village, 21×25½ | 12,000 |
| | C. (Geneva). La Seine à Châtou, c. 1912, 23×28¾, FS220,000+tax | 23,253 |
| | S. Viaduc de St Germain, Fauve style, 1907–8, 35½×31½, bought in | 34,000 |
| | L'allée sous les arbres, c. 1909, 28¾×23½, bought in | 11,000 |
| | Vue de village, c. 1912, 25×31½ | 10,000 |
| | Same title, c. 1912, 21×25¼ | 11,800 |
| | La rivière au vallon, c. 1912, 25½×31¾, bought in | 12,000 |
| | Paysage sous la neige, 27½×39½ | 11,800 |
| | C. London Bridge, 1911, 19×23½, bought in | 14,125 |
| | Paysage à Courbevoie, 29×36½ | 9,450 |
| | S. Paysage à Châtou, c. 1911, 21½×25½, bought in | 10,000 |

CORNELIS DE VOS. (*See* Flemish School after 1550)

## EDOUARD VUILLARD. 1868–1940

As a second generation Impressionist, Vuillard tended, like Bonnard, to reject form altogether, but with less daring and less reliance on colour. His works are therefore less highly priced than Bonnard's. There was a steep rise in the prices for Vuillard in 1957 and, up to this point, Vuillard and Bonnard shared the same rating. In the 1960s Vuillard's prices scarcely kept level with the pace of inflation, though this may have been due to the absence of important examples. He could at times be very scrappy, while, towards the end of his life, he painted works of a more conventional and less subtle character, the proliferation of which has depressed the market.

|  |  | £ |
|---|---|---|
| 1914 | Roger Marx. Paris. Breakfast | 162 |
| 1925 | Gangnat. Paris. Interior | 523 |
| 1929 | Natanson. Paris. Three paintings, bought for the Louvre 3 for | 1,700 |
| 1932 | Pacquemont. Paris. Vase de fleurs, bought for Luxembourg | 785 |
| 1933 | Bought for Tate Gallery by the Courtauld fund. Le toit rouge | 236 15s. |
| 1935 | C. Une femme lisant (gouache) | 107 2s. |
| 1938 | Albert Pra. Paris. Entrée de la ville, 94,100 francs+tax | 896 |
|  | Chambre aux cretonnes, 50,100 francs (125 to the £)+tax | 472 |
| 1939 | Canonne. Paris. La conversation (resold, Christies, 1940, £189), 39,000 francs+tax at 180 to £ | 259 |
| 1944 | Barbée. N.Y. L'intimité, 25×24½, $4,900 | 1,219 |
|  | Still life, $1,500 | 375 |
| 1947 | C. La fenêtre ouverte | 924 |
| 1950 | S. Beach scene | 300 |
| 1954 | Paris. Femme au chien | 2,940 |
| 1956 | S. Small interior | 1,200 |
| 1957 | N.Y. Chez les Hessels | 4,800 |
|  | Lurcy. N.Y. Les Tuileries | 25,000 |
| 1958 | Kirkeby. N.Y. Au bord de la Seine | 8,000 |
| 1959 | N.Y. Le salon, $27,600 | 9,859 |
|  | Paris. Visitors to the artist's studio, 1900, FN104,000+ tax | 9,035 |
|  | Valued for National Gallery, Lane bequest, the Mantelpiece (bought before 1912 for about £300) | 8,000 |
| 1960 | Rewald. S. Jeune fille assise, brush drawing | 4,400 |
|  | Robinson. N.Y. La loge, pastel, $31,200 | 11,142 |
|  | C. Portrait, René Blum, 1912, 28½×39½ | 4,410 |
| 1962 | Metcalfe. S. At the piano, Cipa Godebski and Misia, 25×22 | 23,500 |
|  | Portrait, Mme Bonnard, 15¼×12 | 17,000 |

£

1962 Woolworth. N.Y. Self-portrait in mirror, $17\frac{3}{4} \times 21\frac{1}{4}$   16,072
C. Head, Cipa Godebski   4,725
Aldrich. N.Y. Self-portrait, $30\frac{1}{2} \times 19$, \$47,500   20,530
1964 Fischer, Lucerne. Banks of the Seine, Paris banlieue, $20\frac{3}{4} \times 25$, FS120,000+tax   12,000
S. Lamplit interior, 1908, $28 \times 27$   20,000
Santamara. S. Rue St Florentin, interior, $19\frac{1}{2} \times 20\frac{3}{4}$ (see 1969)   16,000
1965 S. Large pastel interior, 1905   8,500
Maurice Haft (at Palm Beach). Le salon vert des Hessels (\$83,000)   29,600
Weintraub. N.Y. Comtesse de Noailles in bed, $44 \times 50\frac{1}{2}$ (\$74,000)   26,425
Sussman. N.Y. A la fenêtre, $13\frac{3}{4} \times 11\frac{3}{4}$   11,650
N.Y. Femme nue debout, $15\frac{3}{4} \times 11\frac{1}{2}$   8,930
1966 C. La cuisinière, $15\frac{1}{4} \times 12\frac{1}{2}$   8,400
Byron Foy. N.Y. Interior with two women, $19\frac{3}{4} \times 28\frac{1}{2}$   16,800
N.Y. La poële à la petrole, gouache on paper, $36 \times 26\frac{1}{2}$   7,960
Henry Ford II. C. Salon de Mme Hessel, $18\frac{3}{4} \times 29$, bought in   12,600
1967 Paris. Femme lisant devant un bureau, $40 \times 32\frac{3}{4}$   22,300
Motte, Geneva. Interior, $24\frac{1}{2} \times 20$, FS88,000+tax   9,750
Femme accoudée, oil on board, $10\frac{3}{4} \times 14$   6,810
Mme Hessel in her garden at Ouistreham, pastel on paper, $24\frac{1}{2} \times 46\frac{1}{2}$, FS100,000+tax   10,868
1968 N.Y. Portrait en bleu, $27 \times 21\frac{3}{4}$, \$20,000   8,335
Mme Hessel et ses amies, c. 1918, $38\frac{1}{4} \times 51\frac{1}{4}$, \$30,000   12,500
Pleydell-Bouverie. S. Mme Vuillard sur le balcon, 1899, $15 \times 13\frac{1}{4}$   15,500
Malherbe. S. Mme Vuillard cousant, 1895, $12\frac{1}{2} \times 14\frac{1}{2}$   27,000
S. Henri Vacqués, operating at the hospital, $25\frac{1}{2} \times 19\frac{1}{4}$   9,200
Paris. Femme se coiffant, $23\frac{1}{4} \times 18$, FN82,000+tax   7,640
1969 C. Intèrieur avec Mme Vuillard, 1897, $17 \times 25$   17,850
S. Interior, Rue St Florentin, Misia and Thadée Nathanson, (see 1964), $19\frac{1}{2} \times 20\frac{3}{4}$   34,000
Nu assis sur un canapé, $32 \times 25\frac{3}{4}$   10,000
S. (Tokyo). Mélisane, figure in landscape, $9\frac{1}{4} \times 12\frac{1}{2}$, 7 million Yen   8,250
Le Bas. C. (Geneva). Intérieur, c. 1910, $20\frac{1}{2} \times 15\frac{1}{4}$, FS135,000+tax   14,278
Motte, Geneva. Le Square, Ventimille, $30 \times 40$, FS115,000 +tax   12,740
S. Carafe de vin et quatre pêches, c. 1888, $9 \times 11$   15,500
Aldridge Museum. S. Femme sous une lanterne, $9\frac{1}{4} \times 12\frac{1}{2}$   7,800

# JAMES WARD. 1769–1859

Ward's important part in the evolution of the romantic landscape has little to do with present prices. These reflect the growing popularity of horse and dog portraits and other sporting subjects, to which he devoted the latter half of his long working life. In fact this short list should be considered in relation to the section, *Sporting Pictures*. It will be seen that Ward does not rate as high as Ferneley, Herring, Pollard or Seymour, yet in 1919 a portrait, not an outdoor subject, made £7,140. This in real purchasing power meant more than three times the price of any of Ward's works that were sold in the 1960s. From a market angle, the demand for the paintings of this interesting man is reduced by the vast length of his painting life and the disparity of his many styles.

|      |   |                                                                                                                              | £      |
|------|---|------------------------------------------------------------------------------------------------------------------------------|--------|
| 1960 | S. | Snow-scene with shooting party, $39\frac{3}{4}\times51\frac{3}{4}$, 1826                                                    | 5,800  |
| 1964 | S. | Sir Charles Blunt, boar-hunting in India, a suite, $27\frac{3}{4}\times41\frac{3}{4}$, 1816                       4 for    | 4,750  |
| 1965 |   | Spencer Churchill. C. Napoleon's charger, *Marengo*, $28\frac{1}{2}\times35\frac{1}{2}$ (£33 12s. in 1829)                  | 6,300  |
|      |   | Arab stallion in wooded landscape (£9 9s. in 1829)                                                                          | 6,825  |
|      |   | Battle of Marston Moor, costume-piece in the manner of Maclise (£89 5s. in 1859, see 1969), 1825, $31\frac{1}{2}\times44$   | 735    |
|      |   | Bonham's Rooms.  Hunter and dog in a stable, $25\times30$                                                                    | 3,000  |
| 1966 | S. | Start and finish of a race, $19\frac{3}{4}\times37\frac{3}{4}$                                              2 for          | 4,000  |
| 1968 | S. | A black poodle, 1812, $27\frac{1}{2}\times35$                                                                               | 4,400  |
|      | C. | A drink at the spring, 1838, $17\times21$                                                                                   | 1,365  |
|      | S. | King Charles spaniel on cushion, 1809, $25\times29\frac{1}{2}$                                                              | 1,900  |
|      | C. | 'Two extraordinary oxen,' $35\times53\frac{1}{4}$                                                                           | 1,050  |
| 1969 |   | Levett.  S.  Rev. T. Levett with dogs, shooting, $27\frac{1}{2}\times36$                                                    | 11,000 |
|      | S. | Battle of Marston Moor (see 1965)                                                                                           | 1,200  |
|      | C. | Cliffs at Dovedale, pen and wc, $11\times17\frac{3}{4}$                                                                     | 735    |
|      |   | Lloyd.  S.  Unknown country house and lake with family group, *c.* 1800, $51\times77$                                       | 2,800  |
|      | C. | Grey mare and chestnut foal in barn, 1829, $24\times29\frac{1}{4}$, bought in at                                            | 2,100  |
| 1970 |   | Flying Horse Hotel, Nottingham.  S.  Stallions fighting, 1808, $39\frac{1}{2}\times53\frac{1}{2}$                           | 6,500  |

# ANTOINE WATTEAU. 1684–1721

The publication in 1963 of René Gimpel's *Journal d'un collectionneur* proved mine of information on the prices paid for the French *dix-huitième* during th Duveen era. It has made it necessary to revise some of the lists for Fren painters in Volume One. For Watteau in particular the over-all picture w extremely inadequate, since saleroom prices in the early part of the century ga no indication of the scale of the final transactions. It will be noticed in the new list that a Watteau panel could cost the present equivalent of at least £80,000 in 1898, that *l'Accordée du village* made the equivalent of £134,000 in 1919, while the price which the Soviet Government received in 1934 for *Le Mezzetin* meant £157,500. As compared with this special transaction between two governments at a time when private buying was very depressed, the price which *L'île enchantée* reached two years later at the famous Côty sale was only £4,850 or £24,200 in 1970 money. The price of £150,000, which was probably paid for the *Lute-player* in 1959, suggests that the present value of a soundly attributed Watteau of this quality should be at least half a million, but the habitually bad condition of almost all Watteau's work might militate against this. As to drawings, nothing of importance has come under the hammer since *The Savoyard Beggar* in 1964. For quite eighty years Watteau's drawings have justly rated little below Raphael, Leonardo, Dürer and Rembrandt. There must be some that are worth more than £50,000.

|  |  | £ |
|---|---|---:|
| 1898 | Sold by Durand-Ruel to Marquis de Chaponay, Harpsichord-lid, figures on gold ground (according to R. Gimpel) | 10,000 |
| 1899 | C. La musette | 1,434 |
|  | Broadwood. C. L'accordée du village (see 1904) | 1,365 |
|  | Sold by R. Gimpel to Crosnier. Le conçert Italien | 4,780 |
| 1900 | Sold by R. Gimpel. Le songe du poète (bought in London, 1890, £400) | 6,000 |
| 1901 | Sold by R. Gimpel to Crosnier. L'accordée du village (see 1919), 191,000 francs | 7,640 |
| 1902 | Sold by R. Gimpel to Crosnier. Plaisirs rustiques, 195,000 francs | 7,800 |
|  | Le repos or the sleeping lovers (see 1905), 140,000 francs | 5,600 |
| 1903 | Sold by Gimpel to Berwind. N.Y. Les comédiens (with a small Boucher) (see 1924)    2 for | 10,000 |
| 1904 | C. Guitar player surprised | 2,520 |
|  | Bourgeois, Cologne. L'accordée du village (see 1899) | 5,000 |
| 1905 | Crosnier. Paris. The sleeping lovers (see 1902) | 6,080 |
| 1907 | Gabbitas. C. La contredanse | 2,625 |
| 1910 | Bought for Melbourne National Gallery. Les jaloux | 3,000 |
| 1913 | Murray Scott. C. Fête champêtre (see 1951) | 6,510 |
| 1918 | C. La mariée du village | 2,940 |
| 1919 | Wildenstein and Gimpel asking for L'accordée du village (see 1901), $130,000 | 26,750 |
| 1924 | Les comédiens, valued for Lord Iveagh by Wildenstein | 30,000 |
|  | Scott. C. Two miniature masquerade figures (£63 in 1828, £535 10s. in 1875)    2 for | 3,265 |

| | | £ |
|---|---|---|
| 1925 | Michel Levy. Paris. L'enseigne de Gersaint (£350 in 1886), *schoolpiece version*, bought in at | 6,400 |
| 1934 | Hermitage Museum, sale by U.S.S.R. government to Metropolitan Museum, Le Mezzetin (£28 7s. in 1761), $150,000 | 31,500 |
| 1936 | François Côty. Paris. L'île enchantée, 560,000 francs+ tax | 4,850 |
| 1945 | Neeld. C. L'île de Cythère (see 1957) | 2,625 |
| 1951 | Stehli. N.Y. Fête du dieu Pan (see 1913), 26×32 | 4,465 |
| 1957 | Mae Rovensky. N.Y. L'île de Cythère (see 1945) | 6,250 |
| 1959 | S. Formerly coll. D. of Cambridge. La rêve de l'artiste (said to have been completed by Schall) | 2,800 |
| | Bought by Stockholm Gallery from Henry Stehli, N.Y. The Luteplayer or music lesson Reputed price | 150,000 |
| 1962 | Paris. Mlle Julienne as the Nymph of the Fountain, 29×30, FN200,000+tax | 17,280 |
| 1969 | Sir John Soane Museum. Valuation of *Les Noces*, 36×25, at the time of its theft (£42 in 1802) | 150,000 |

DRAWINGS

| 1894 | Josse. Paris. Sheet of 8 heads in sanguine, 30,000 francs+ tax | 1,310 |
|---|---|---|
| | Sheet of 3 girl's heads, in sanguine, 24,000 francs+tax | 1,056 |
| 1896 | E. de Goncourt. Paris. Printemps, single figure, 22,000 francs+tax | 1,062 |
| | Mezzetin dansant, 17,500 francs+tax | 858 |
| | Sheet of 7 heads in sanguine and white (see 1914, 1963) | 770 |
| 1905 | Beurdeley. Paris. Sheet of heads, sanguine touched with white, 25,000 francs+tax | 1,100 |
| 1908 | Knowles. S. Lady with fan, charcoal | 350 |
| 1911 | C. Two ladies, sanguine and white | 1,648 10s. |
| | Three negro heads on one sheet (see 1922) | 1,213 10s. |
| 1912 | Landolphe Carcano. Paris. Three women, sanguine and crayon | 1,932 |
| | Standing and seated woman, sanguine and crayon | 3,124 |
| | Study of an arm and head | 1,684 |
| | The pilgrim, sanguine and chalk | 1,320 |
| | Sheet of 7 heads, sanguine (see 1896, 1914, 1963) | 3,124 |
| | 2 children in sanguine touched with white | 1,754 |
| | Three others exceeded £1,000 each. | |
| 1914 | Hodgkins. Paris. Sheet of seven heads, ex de Goncourt and Carcano, 1896 and 1912 (see also 1963) | 2,640 |
| 1922 | Max Bonn. S. Study of three negro heads (see 1911) | 3,200 |
| 1926 | Behague. S. Study of head and two hands | 760 |
| 1931 | Ferrers. S. Sheet of three figures, sanguine | 1,550 |

| | | £ |
|---|---|---|
| 35 | Faucher-Magnan. S. Three sheets of figure studies, sanguine Each | 1,300 |
| | Study of hands | 620 |
| 36 | François Côty. Paris. Two chalk studies of a girl on one sheet, 320,000 francs+tax at 125 to £ | 3,025 |
| 37 | Greffulhe. S. Sheet of studies | 5,800 |
| 38 | Mortimer Schiff. C. A Moor's head, sanguine | 945 |
| | Three ladies, red and black chalk, $10\frac{1}{4} \times 13\frac{3}{4}$ | 756 |
| 48 | S. Savoyard peep-show man, sanguine (see 1964), $13\frac{1}{8} \times 7\frac{3}{4}$ | 1,300 |
| 54 | Andrew d'Antal. S. Three children, chalk | 2,700 |
| 56 | Paris. Study of two girls, sanguine | 2,000 |
| 59 | S. Two reclining figures, chalk | 900 |
| 62 | Paris. Triumph of Ceres, cartoon design, $24 \times 30$ | 7,320 |
| | Standing male figure, chalks, $10 \cdot 8 \times 8 \cdot 4$ | 6,570 |
| 63 | Paris. Les guitaristes, two figures, red and black chalk, FN189,000+tax, $10\frac{1}{2} \times 8\frac{1}{4}$ | 15,650 |
| | Single seated figure, red chalk | 13,675 |
| | Sheet of male heads (£700 in 1896, £3,124 in 1912), FN180,000+tax, $9 \times 13\frac{1}{4}$ | 15,565 |
| 64 | S. Savoyard beggar, red chalk (see 1948), $13\frac{1}{8} \times 7\frac{3}{4}$, Chicago Art Institute | 18,000 |
| 69 | C. Landscape sketch, red chalk, the Ponte Rotto and temple, $7\frac{1}{2} \times 9\frac{1}{4}$ | 1,785 |

## FREDERICK WILLIAM WATTS. (*See* English School, 19th century)

## GEORGE FREDERICK WATTS. 1817–1904

The portrait of Ellen Terry in armour was sold in 1968 for £980, the dearest work by Watts since 1913 in paper terms. The boom in Watts, so confidently predicted in the 1950s, can hardly be said to have materialized in the 1960s. One of the six versions of *Love and Death* was sold in 1890 for the equivalent of more than £12,000 in 1970 money. The version, sold in 1967, made £483. Despite the enthusiasm of young intellectuals, it is hard to see what message these pompous allegories in a pseudo-Venetian style, much emasculated, have for the present age. Something, perhaps, may be expected of Watt's earlier portraits which are at least moderately competent.

| | | £ |
|---|---|---|
| 65 | Spencer Churchill. C. Portrait of Tennyson, $25\frac{1}{2} \times 25\frac{1}{2}$ | 840 |
| | Cassavetti. C. Maria Cassavetti as a child, $49 \times 39$ | 735 |
| | S. Adam and Eve, expelled from Paradise, $14 \times 10$ | 160 |
| 66 | Foulkes. C. Adam and Eve, 1896, $25 \times 14\frac{1}{2}$ | 94 10s. |

|      |                                                                                                                    | £ |
|------|--------------------------------------------------------------------------------------------------------------------|------|
| 1966 | C. Portrait sketch of Holman Hunt, 19×15                                                                            | 94 10 |
|      | Reid. C. Time, death and judgement, 42×32                                                                           | 651 |
|      | Love and death, 45½×23½ (one of six versions, £1,381 10s. in 1890, £1,050 in 1913, see also 1967)                  | 231 |
|      | Spring, child portrait, 46×20½                                                                                      | 294 |
|      | S. Portrait, Dorothy Dene, 1888, 23½×19½ (see 1968)                                                                 | 280 |
| 1967 | C. Sunset on the Nile, 1887 (commissioned for £630) 24×41                                                           | 577 10 |
|      | Love and death, 1899, 45½×23½ (compare 1966)                                                                        | 483 |
|      | Newman. C. The good Samaritan, 1850, 39½×47½                                                                        | 199 10 |
|      | C. Justice, allegorical riding figure, 1872, 26×20                                                                  | 199 10 |
| 1968 | Kerrison Preston. S. Watchman, what of the night? Ellen Terry in armour, 1880, 25½×20½                             | 980 |
|      | Clive. S. Girl's head, 1875, 18½×14½                                                                                | 200 |
|      | Portrait of Dorothy Dene, 1888, 23½×19½ (see 1966)                                                                  | 320 |

## BENJAMIN WEST. 1738–1820

Since 1959 there has been some recognition that Benjamin West was a tru
remarkable all-purposes painter. Previously he had been in the wilderness f
more than thirty years—since the Metropolitan Museum's purchase of t
portrait of Benjamin Franklin in 1926 for £3,300. That was at the height of t
Duveen 18th century portrait cult and the price was equivalent to £16,500
1970. The present market which is extremely selective, comprises three differe
sorts of picture. In the huge biblical and classical subject pictures, painted eith
in pseudo-Raphaelesque style or in the neo-classic manner of David, we ha
West at his worst. Yet these frigid works, now almost worthless, were t
foundations of West's vast fortune, and eventually earned him what were the
the highest fees ever to have been bestowed on a living painter. In the extren
contradiction of his battle pictures, either in modern dress or reasonably corre
historical costume, we have West the innovator of a style that was to influen
generations. Finally in *The Age of Innocence* (£7,000 in 1967) and *Kosciusko
London* (£210 in 1945) we have West practising a style of primitive simplici
which seems to anticipate the pre-Raphaelites by more than two generations.

|      |                                                                               | £ |
|------|-------------------------------------------------------------------------------|------|
| 1961 | S. Mr and Mrs John Williams, half-length portraits 2 for                      | 440 |
|      | Countess of Craven. C. Sacrifice of a bull, 4 ft × 5 ft, 1775                 | 420 |
| 1962 | Neeld. C. First sermon of St Peter, 12 ft×10 ft                               | 126 |
|      | Cicero finding the tomb of Archimedes, 49×72                                  | 525 |
| 1963 | C. The death of Caesar                                                        | 399 |
| 1964 | S. Ramsgate sands, 1780, 13½×17                                               | 3,800 |
| 1967 | Francis. C. Composite design for the paintings in the Chapel Royal, Windsor, pen and wc, 11½×18½ | 735 |

|  |  |  | £ |
|---|---|---|---|
| 67 | C. | Pen and sepia landscape, Windsor Great Park, $19 \times 26$ | 441 |
| | | The angel releasing St Peter, pen and sepia, 1783, $15\frac{3}{4} \times 11\frac{3}{4}$ | 399 |
| | Eckman. | S. The Age of Innocence, 1776, oval, $24\frac{3}{4} \times 29\frac{1}{2}$, Tate Gallery | 7,000 |
| 68 | Francis. | C. Log cabin in a forest, ink and wc, boyhood study made in America in the 1750s, $9 \times 13$ | 367 10s. |
| | N.Y. | Hannah presenting Samuel to Eli, 1801, $19 \times 25\frac{1}{2}$, $10,000 | 4,156 |
| | Emrys Evans. | C. Diana and Actaeon and the Calydonian boar, pair, $29\frac{1}{2} \times 20$ (imitations of Claude)  2 for | 3,255 |

## ROGIER VAN DER WEYDEN. (*See* Flemish School before 1550)

## JAMES ABBOTT McNEILL WHISTLER. 1834–1903

ne would scarcely credit from this scrappy little list that in 1919 Henry Clay ick paid Duveen for *Lady Meux, harmony in pink and grey*, together with other large portrait, the sum of $200,000, then worth £41,300 and equi-lent to more than £200,000 in 1970. René Gimpel mentions in the same year at Edmund Davies had been offered a similar price, £20,000 for *At the Piano*, very early work of 1860 for which Whistler had received £30. This is a par-ularly interesting detail, because *At the Piano* is still the last completed histler oil painting to have reached the salerooms. It was sold, twenty years er Gimpel's entry, at Christies in 1939 when it made £6,405 at the Davis e. While this was equal to £32,000 in the money of 1970, it is by no means rtain that *At the Piano* is worth as much. The tremendous American support the Whistler market was killed by the Impressionist cult. It might take more an *At the Piano* to bring it back. There are too many little slips of pastel on own paper, while the very laborious large pictures are all in public institu-ns. The slips of brown paper were meant to irritate, but the public of the 60s did not want to be irritated. It wanted to be shocked.

|  |  |  | £ |
|---|---|---|---|
| 62 | S. | The green umbrella, oils | 945 |
| | Benedict. | S. Venice, pastel, $11\frac{1}{4} \times 7\frac{1}{2}$ | 1,901 |
| | | Girl's head, 1903, oil, $19\frac{1}{4} \times 11\frac{3}{4}$ | 2,600 |
| | | On the Normandy coast, oil, $5\frac{3}{4} \times 9\frac{1}{4}$ | 1,100 |
| 65 | Wards. | C. The sea at Pourville, oil, $5\frac{1}{2} \times 9\frac{1}{2}$ | 2,835 |
| | Fellowes. | S. The gold girl, gouache study for a mosaic, $10 \times 7$ | 2,600 |
| | Waller. | C. The little nude, pastel on brown paper | 918 15s. |
| | | Suite of 29 drawings of blue and white porcelain,  29 for | 2,625 |

|      |                                                                                                         | £        |
|------|---------------------------------------------------------------------------------------------------------|----------|
| 1966 | Blanch.   S.   Venice, pastel, $5\frac{1}{2} \times 10\frac{1}{2}$                                       | 800      |
|      | Waller.   C.   7 pen and wash studies of blue and white porcelain     The dearest of them at            | 294      |
| 1967 | S.   Rose et or, Napolitaine, a portrait of Carmen Rossi, oils, $19\frac{1}{4} \times 11\frac{1}{2}$    | 700      |
| 1968 | Swift-Newton.   S.   La mère Gérard, oil on board, c. 1855, $12 \times 8\frac{1}{2}$                     | 1,100    |
|      | Waller.   C.   Harmony in gold and brown, c. 1890, pastel on brown paper, $5\frac{3}{4} \times 10\frac{1}{4}$ | 1,050    |
| 1969 | Stansfeld.   S.   Snowy landscape, pastel on brown paper, $4\frac{3}{4} \times 11\frac{1}{2}$           | 680      |
|      | Nocturne, pastel on brown paper, $5\frac{1}{2} \times 11\frac{1}{2}$                                     | 580      |
|      | C.   Boats in an estuary, wc, $8\frac{1}{4} \times 4\frac{3}{4}$                                         | 1,207 10s |

## SIR DAVID WILKIE.   1785–1841

*Distraining for Rent* was sold in 1890 for £2,310, the equivalent of rather mor than £20,000 in 1970, but this was not a high price for English painters of th last generation or two in 1890. In fact Wilkie is one of those painters who hav had an enormous influence on art, but were only really popular in their ow lifetime. Another of Wilkie's famous anecdotal pictures, *The Irish Whiskey-sti* made £840 at the King of Holland's sale in 1850, but only £483 in 1950. Ther has not been another Wilkie picture of this importance on the market sinc then, but it is doubtful whether the over-elaborated subject pictures, now ver brown in tone, are worth so much more than Wilkie's oil sketches and studic for which there is a modest demand.

|      |                                                                                               | £         |
|------|-----------------------------------------------------------------------------------------------|-----------|
| 1959 | C.   The pedlar (£420 in 1913)                                                                 | 1,732 10s |
|      | Smith Cunningham.   C.   The Turkish letter writer (£446 5s. in 1842, £420 in 1895)            | 525       |
| 1963 | C.   Queen Victoria, riding into Holyrood, 1840, oil sketch                                    | 504       |
| 1965 | C.   Wooded landscape, oil, $10 \times 12\frac{1}{2}$                                          | 1,050     |
| 1967 | Lady Wilson.   C.   Joseph Wilson and grandson, 1839, $31 \times 27$                           | 997 10s   |
| 1968 | C.   Landscape with two goats (on board), $7\frac{1}{2} \times 9\frac{3}{4}$                   | 1,785     |
|      | Lawley.   C.   Oil sketch for 'the cut finger', 1809, $9\frac{1}{2} \times 11\frac{1}{2}$      | 682 10s   |
|      | Colnin Tennant.   N.Y.   The village festival, oil sketch, 1809, $13\frac{1}{2} \times 18\frac{1}{4}$, $7,000 | 2,917     |
| 1969 | C. (in Glasgow).   Duke of Wellington and *Copenhagen*, study for whole length picture, $24 \times 18\frac{1}{2}$ | 1,995     |
|      | C.   Oil sketch for *the village festival* (not the 1968 version), $16\frac{1}{2} \times 13\frac{1}{4}$ | 577 10s   |

1969 Egerton Cooper. C. Another ditto in wc bodycolour, £
probably made after the completed picture of 1811,
$11\frac{1}{2} \times 15\frac{3}{4}$ 399
C. (at Hopetoun). Portrait, Lady Mary Fitzgerald, 1808,
$11\frac{1}{2} \times 8\frac{1}{2}$ 1,050
Edmiston, Glasgow. Interior with lady, nurse, child and
dog, 1836, $12\frac{1}{2} \times 9\frac{1}{2}$ 3,400

## RICHARD WILSON. 1714–1782

Like the leading portraitists of his day but for other reasons, the landscape-painter, Richard Wilson, failed to share in the boom in the English 18th century school in the 1960s. To be sure of saleroom success, 18th century landscapes have to be meticulously topographical, 'documentary' as it were, or else full of human activity and local colour. Wilson remained too much an Italianist all his life, never far from the conventions of Claude or Gaspard Poussin. Thus the saleroom successes of the 1920s have not repeated themselves. For instance in 1929 *The Thames at Twickenham* made £6,720, equivalent to £33,600 in 1970.

£

1961 At Bonham's rooms. The children of Niobe (£840 in
1806, £451 10s. in 1876) 2,100
S. Extensive landscape with lakes, $32 \times 49$ Bought in at 4,800
1962 S. The Tiber near Rome, $38\frac{1}{2} \times 53\frac{3}{4}$ 6,000
1963 Extensive landscape, attributed 3,675
S. River scene 1,400
1965 Spencer Stanhope (at Retford). Lake Albano 16,800
1966 Gardner. S. Rome from the Ponte Molle, $37 \times 52$
(£1,050 in 1882) 3,000
Sharpe. S. Kilgarran Castle, $26 \times 34$ 1,100
1967 C. Solitude, 1768, $34\frac{1}{2} \times 49\frac{1}{2}$ (£367 10s. in 1909) 630
S. (at Gleneagles Hotel). Rome from the Ponte Molle
(£1,050 in 1882, £3,000 in 1966) 1,800
C. Lake Avernus and Temple of Apollo, $16 \times 21\frac{3}{4}$ 787 10s.
1968 Prestige. S. River landscape at evening, $18\frac{1}{4} \times 24$ 3,400
Seven paintings, attributed to Richard Wilson
Made a total of 9,020

## EMANUEL DE WITTE. (*See* Dutch School)

## JOHN WOOTTON. (*See* Sporting Pictures)

# PHILIPS WOUVERMAN (or WOUWERMANS) (1614–1688)

Wouverman has had a considerable impact on English painting. The appeal of his picturesque horsemen can be followed through Loutherbourg, Ibbetson, Morland and Rowlandson as far as Landseer. Consequently he was a high-priced painter in the early 19th century. The *Horse Fair* of the Wallace collection cost the Marquess of Hertford in 1854 the equivalent of £33,600. In the present century Wouverman has shared in the general decline of the Italianizing Dutch painters. In the 1930s and 40s these pictures were barely in the £1,000 class, while in the 1960s only one price showed the impact of inflation. This is one of several instances—Wilkie is another—of a much imitated style proving a market handicap.

|      |                                                                           | £      |
|------|---------------------------------------------------------------------------|--------|
| 1959 | Rolfe.  S.  Hawking-party, taking leave of hostess                         | 4,200  |
| 1960 | Paris.  Landscape                                                          | 2,600  |
| 1961 | Makower.  S.  The sand hill, 1652, 14×17                                   | 7,200  |
|      | S.  Harvest festival                                                       | 3,500  |
| 1962 | S.  Wooded landscape                                                       | 2,600  |
|      | Solders at a farrier's booth, 13¾×16                                       | 2,600  |
|      | At Bonham's.  Hawking party                                                | 2,300  |
| 1963 | Sterling of Keir.  S.  Landscape with horsemen                             | 6,000  |
|      | Princess Labia.  S.  Infantry attacking cavalry                           | 2,200  |
| 1965 | C.  Cavalry encamping                                                      | 1,365  |
|      | Horsemen at a farrier's booth                                              | 2,730  |
|      | Adda, Paris.  Departure for the hunt, 30×40½                               | 2,870  |
|      | Romanoff.  S.  Soldiers carrying off cattle, 11¾×14½                       | 3,800  |
| 1966 | Dunkels.  S.  A hunting party resting, 25×19¾                              | 4,200  |
| 1967 | Earl of Feversham.  C.  Hawking party in extensive landscape, 29½×44½      | 15,750 |
|      | Ahlstrom.  S.  Landscape, travellers resting, 23¼×33                       | 5,200  |
| 1968 | Campbell.  S.  Landscape with hawking party, 7½×10                         | 6,500  |
|      | Kaplan.  S.  Huntsmen at an inn, 13×16¼                                    | 3,200  |
| 1969 | Disney.  S.  Peasants outside a cottage, 14½×18                            | 4,000  |
|      | May.  S.  Peasants at a ford at twilight, 14½×17½                          | 8,000  |

ANDREW WYETH.  (*See* American School, 19th–20th century)

NEWELL CONYERS WYETH.  (*See* American School, 19th–20th century)

ADRIAEN YSENBRANDT.  (*See* Flemish School before 1550)

# JOHANN ZOFFANY. 1733–1810

With Stubbs at £220,000 and even Ben Marshall and Seymour at £60,000, one would expect that Zoffany's big family groups would at least do as well, having that richness of local colour and directness of statement which lovers of the English 18th century now require. The failure to reach these levels may owe something to the overcrowding of so many of Zoffany's canvases. It is also possible that a picture of the importance of *The Townely Gallery* in the Burnley Museum (£1,312 10s. in 1939) might in fact make as much as £60,000.

|  |  | £ |
|---|---|---|
| 960 | Lady Lister. S. Unknown family group, 35¾ × 27¼ | 5,000 |
|  | Lewis. S. The Laurie family, 1771 | 7,000 |
| 962 | Whitehead & Whitehead, Chichester. Third Duke of Richmond with Negro attendant | 7,900 |
|  | Fitzgerald. S. The Sumner children playing with see-saw, 39¼ × 49½ | 21,500 |
| 964 | Kemsley. S. Betty Farren as Hermione (in Reynolds's manner), 94½ × 63 | 1,100 |
|  | Phillips, son and Neale. Captain John Polhill with horse | 4,200 |
| 965 | Clerke-Browne. C. The Wilson family at Binfield | 3,150 |
| 966 | O'Brien. S. James Blew and family, 29¼ × 31¼ |  |
|  | bought in at | 17,000 |
| 967 | Wilkinson. S. The Husey family, 48 × 39 | 4,500 |
| 969 | Davidson. S. William Powell as Posthumus in *Cymbeline*, 35 × 27½ | 2,200 |

# FRANCESCO ZUCCARELLI. 1702–1788

The Sienese Zuccarelli came to England in 1752 and painted there for rather more than twenty years, becoming a founder-member of the Royal Academy and enjoying the patronage of the Royal Family. He turned out endless pairs of chimneypiece landscapes with figures in a style owing much to Gaspard Poussin. They are what were formerly called furnishing pictures, when £100 could still buy something. £100 to £500 remained the standard price for a pair of Zuccarellis for about eighty years. Then, in the early 1950s, the first signs of movement appeared, partly a response to inflation, partly a realization that even respectable furnishing pictures were getting scarce. It has come to the point that for a respectable furnishing picture two or three thousands are no more than an average price. But Zuccarelli's pictures can sometimes make three times as much as that. In the saleroom this slick operator is the equal of Hubert Robert and more than the equal of Richard Wilson.

|  |  |  | £ |
|---|---|---|---|
| 882 | Sudeley. C. Macbeth and the witches (£69 5s. in 1761) |  | 152 5s. |
| 883 | Walker. C. A pair of figured landscapes | 2 for | 367 10s. |

£

| | | | £ |
|---|---|---|---|
| 1899 | C. A pair of landscapes (see 1953) | 2 for | 6 6s. |
| 1923 | Lockett Agnew. C. Several pairs at 150 to 300 guineas | | |
| 1928 | U.S.S.R. government, Berlin. Pair of landscapes, 40×29, | 2 for | 240 |
| | C. Pair of figured landscapes | 2 for | 588 |
| 1937 | Earl of Lincoln. C. Pair of landscapes (see 1953) | 2 for | 372 10s |
| 1953 | C. Pair of landscapes (£6 6s. in 1899) | 2 for | 1,050 |
| | Zetland. C. Pair of landscapes (£372 10s. in 1937) | 2 for | 4,200 |
| | S. Pair of landscapes | 2 for | 3,670 |
| 1954 | C. Single landscape | | 3,675 |
| 1955 | S. Single landscape | | 2,000 |
| 1956 | N.Y. Pair of landscapes, $10,000 | 2 for | 2,800 |
| 1959 | S. Pair of mythological landscapes, 43½×58 | 2 for | 6,500 |
| 1961 | Ionides. S. Thames at Richmond, 31×48¾ | | 3,100 |
| 1963 | Wright. C. Landscape, dance of the four seasons, 19×26 | | 2,940 |
| 1964 | Single mountainous landscape, 20½×29 | | 7,875 |
| 1965 | C. Another single mountainous landscape, same size | | 7,875 |
| | Williams. S. Pair of landscapes with shepherds, 20½×37¾ | 2 for | 6,000 |
| | Bevan. S. Landscape with infant Bacchus, 39½×49½ | | 3,600 |
| 1966 | Renshaw. C. Horseman in a landscape, 1742, 28×44 | | 8,925 |
| | Dunkels. S. Two views of Verona, 19¾×39¼ | 2 for | 6,400 |
| | C. Figures in wooded landscape, 27×21 | | 3,150 |
| | (With Antonio Visentini), Pair of Venice Capriccios, 16×22 | 2 for | 4,200 |
| 1968 | S. Landscape, figures by a river, 19¾×36½ | | 6,600 |
| 1969 | C. Extensive wooded landscape, 40×54 | | 3,150 |
| | Travellers and peasants by a stream, 15×21 | | 4,200 |
| | S. Landscape with miracle of the Virgin, 24½×33 | | 2,500 |
| | Two drawings en grisaille (attributed), 10×12½ | 2 for | 4,200 |
| | Stout. C. View of Tivoli with goats and figures, 41½×50 | Bought in at | 5,250 |
| | Pair of landscapes with figures, 26×19½, bought in | 2 for | 7,875 |

## PART TWO

# SALES ANALYSIS OF SCULPTURE

Northern Europe, Gothic and Renaissance
Italian Renaissance, marble, terracotta, plaster
Italian Renaissance, bronze
Late 17th and 18th centuries, mainly French
Neo-Classic, first half of the 19th century
Second half of the 19th century, sculptors arranged alphabetically
20th century, sculptors arranged alphabetically.

# NORTHERN EUROPE
before 1650

Who is it who buys Gothic sculpture? In the 1830s and 1840s, when the most elaborate reliefs or chimneypieces could be bought for a few pounds, it was quite fashionable to smother whole rooms with Gothic and Renaissance sculpture, cut down to fit the space. In the 1880s, when attributions to 15th and 16th century names were discussed with great solemnity, the same objects could cost thousands. In fact Northern sculptures of the High Renaissance were sometimes worth more than they are today in terms of our devalued pounds, for instance a pair of German wooden roundel portrait heads in 1886 at £2,400, a relief by Hans Dollinger in 1887 at £2,600. £20,000 to £23,000 seems an unlikely range of prices for such things in 1970, even for the bronze statue of Peter Visscher from the Spitzer sale of 1893.

The decade preceding the First World War proved dearer still. The market for medieval and Renaissance art was convulsed by the collecting adventures of James Pierpont Morgan. In 1911 the Emperor Maximilian stone relief of the von Lanna sale made £3,625. René Gimpel sold Benjamin Altman a French 16th century marble bust by Germain Pilon for $55,000 or £11,350 in the same year, while in 1913 the Berlin Kunstgewerbe Museum paid £3,500 for a painted limewood Madonna of the 15th century. All these prices must be multiplied by eight.

In the 1931–45 depression, prices at the very best tended to be in three figures rather than four. One recalls very attractive wooden Gothic reliefs at less than £100, things that have since made several thousands. But if £4,000 had become a rockbottom price for the rather better than average piece, the market is neither very exciting nor very well supplied. Museum buying is paramount and it is noticeable that the rare appearance of sculpture from earlier periods means much higher prices, for instance two Madonnas in the round, sold by Lempertz of Cologne. The first, a French sandstone figure of the 14th century, made £13,500 in 1962. The second, a Rhineland wooden figure of the same age, made £34,375 in 1968.

| FRANCE AND FLANDERS | £ |
|---|---|
| 1960 Myron. C. Taylor, N.Y. Portrait bust of a lady, painted wood, *c.* 1450, $3,000 | 1,072 |
| Limestone statue of St Catherine, *c.* 1420–40, $3,500 | 1,250 |
| 1962 Lempertz, Cologne. Sandstone Madonna and Child from Crécy, 14th century, DM125,000+tax | about 13,500 |
| Paris. Flemish 15th century retable, painted and gilded, 93 in. high | 4,650 |
| Lady Powis. S. Life-sized bronze bust of Lord Herbert of Cherbury by Hubert le Sueur, 1631 | 6,200 |
| 1963 S. Stone relief, abbot holding model of church, Burgundian, 15th century | 980 |
| Crucifixion, black oak, Flemish, *c.* 1410 | 1,900 |

£

1965 C. Retable, Holy Family and saints, carved wood,
Flemish, *c.* 1500, 73 in. wide over-all                                                          2,940
Stoclet. S. Painted wood Virgin and child, N. French,
13th century, 26 in. high                                                                              3,500
Early Gothic stone head of a king in the Chartres style,
*c.* 1200                                                                                                   1,600

1966 Stuker, Berne. Pietà, wood, part gilded, Flemish late 15th
century, 45 in. high                                                                                  3,830
Musée Hulin, Sarlat. Paris. Painted wood Virgin by
Pierre de Bruey, *c.* 1500, FN105,000+tax                                                     8,425
Limestone Romanesque Virgin from Aurillac                                         2,168
French Late Gothic female saint, calcareous stone                                2,088
N.Y. Cross-legged Venus, Flemish late 16th century,
bronze, 7½ in. high, $7,750                                                                      2,765

1967 Jaffe. S. Wrestling women, bronze group, 'Italo-
Flemish', late 16th century, 8¾ in.                                                             4,800
S. Seated female nude, 'Italo-Flemish' bronze, mid-16th
century                                                                                                     2,425
S. Pair of oak equestrian figures, signed by Hendric Roose,
early 16th century                                                          2 for       1,900

1968 Oezle, Amsterdam. Bronze group, woman milking cow,
N. Netherlands, *c.* 1570, 5½×8¼, Hfl66,000+tax                                    8,650

1969 S. Jupiter, Mercury, Centaur and Amorini, Fontainebleau
school, marble relief, late 16th century, 14×18½                                    3,200
Guinness. S. Burgundian walnut relief, George and
dragon, *c.* 1480, much overpainted, 39×22                                          2,000
Château de Laarne. S. The Three Graces, gilt-bronze by
Georg Petel after Rubens, *c.* 1630, 12 in. high                                     12,000
Hercules and the Nemean lion, S. German, 1550           4,800
S. Four giltbronze apostles, style of Susini, S. German,
*c.* 1650, 11 in. high                                                          4 for       2,800

## GERMANY

1960 S. Wood relief of three saints by Tilman Riemenschneider        6,200
10 in. wooden head of Christ, 12th century                                     1,200
Painted wood group, *c.* 1460                                                          1,200

1962 S. Pair of bronze aquamanile figures of does, late 15th
century (£22 in 1952)                                                          2 for       1,100
Samson with lion's head, S. German, *c.* 1520, bronze       2,800
C. Pair of pearwood plaques by Pieter Flötner, dated 1543       504
Guggenheim Foundation. S. Limewood Madonna, 49
in. high, late 15th century                                                                 2,100

1963 Mayer. S. Suabian 15th century wood relief, death of
the Virgin                                                                                          850

£

| | | | |
|---|---|---|---|
| 1963 | Weinmüller, Munich. Painted wooden, relief, Adoration, *c.* 1520 | | 3,530 |
| | At Scarisbricke Hall (Jackson Stopes). Pair of 15th century wooden equestrian figures | 2 for | 1,950 |
| | Pair of bronze figures, stag and boar, *c.* 1600 | 2 for | 1,700 |
| | Bass. N.Y. Virgin, painted wood, Rhineland, 13th century | | 1,165 |
| 1964 | St Barnabas, Nottingham. C. Crucifixion, oak relief group, *c.* 1520, 55 × 38 in. | | 3,390 |
| | Lempertz, Cologne. Suabian pinewood Pietà, c. 1430, DM90,000+tax | | 9,100 |
| 1965 | C. Iron casket, 1565, with scenes in relief from Ovid | | 1,995 |
| | Spencer Churchill. C. Hercules, 13 in. boxwood figure by Christoff Weidlitz, *c.* 1540 | | 8,810 |
| | Limewood Holy Family, style of Riemenschneider, 37½ in. | | 1,050 |
| | Iron casket, classical reliefs by Jorg Sigman, Nuremberg, 1565 | | 1,995 |
| | Adda. Paris. Gilt-bronze engraved casket, scenes from the Passion by Michael Man of Nuremberg, *c.* 1560, under 5 in. long | | 2,630 |
| 1966 | Lempertz, Cologne. Wooden Madonna, *c.* 1420, 69 in. high, DM55,000+tax | | 5,626 |
| | James de Rothschild. Paris. Coffer with silver and gilt-bronze reliefs, Nuremberg, 15½ in. high | | 2,960 |
| 1968 | Lempertz, Cologne. Wooden Virgin and child, Cologne school, *c.* 1300, DM300,000+tax | | 34,375 |
| | Limewood painted relief, George and dragon, Bohemian school, *c.* 1380, DM50,000+tax | | 5,727 |
| | Limewood painted relief, Via crucis, S. German school, late 15th century, DM63,000+tax | | 7,220 |
| | Weinmüller, Munich. School of Konrad Meit, Worms, *c.* 1544, Adam and Eve, limewood figures, 21 in. high, DM55,000+tax | | 6,550 |
| | Koller, Zurich. Virgin and child, limewood, *c.* 1500, 37½ in. high, FS40,500+tax | about | 4,400 |
| | Virgin and St Anne, school of Erasmus Graesser, *c.* 1516, limewood, 42½ in. high, FS42,000+tax | | 4,575 |
| 969 | Guinness. S. Pietà, Suabian school, painted limewood, *c.* 1510, 31 in. wide, 23½ in. high | | 4,000 |

 NGLAND, SPAIN

| | | |
|---|---|---|
| 960 | N.Y. Stone altar retable, part-gilt, from Poblet, Hispano-Flemish, *c.* 1440, $16,000 | 5,713 |

| | | £ |
|---|---|---|
| 1966 | S. Three 14th century Nottingham alabaster reliefs | 1,500 |
| | 800 and | 1,400 |
| 1967 | Kevorkian. S. Spanish wooden Madonna, painted and gilded, 26 in. high, 13th century | 1,050 |
| 1968 | S. Nottingham painted alabaster relief, the Last Supper, 15½ in. high, late 14th century | 2,100 |
| | Lawson. C. Deposition, Nottingham alabaster, c. 1420, 16×11 in. | 3,255 |
| 1970 | S. Spanish stone-relief, Holy Family with musician angels, late 15th century, 31×23½ | 4,800 |

## ITALIAN RENAISSANCE
### before 1650

There were a fair number of bronzes on the market in the 1960s, but surprisingly few examples of carved stone or original modelling in terracotta or stucco. Surprising too was the level of prices. The white glazed tympanum by Andrea della Robbia, which made $40,000 at the Myron Taylor sale of 1960, ranks among the masterpieces of *Quattrocento* sculpture. Yet one doubts whether it would make $70,000 or £30,000 even in 1970, not enough to buy an enlarged brass motor-car mascot, one of many casts from a model by Brancusi. On the one hand, the National Gallery thought fit to spend £409,500 on a Tiepolo ceiling panel which adds nothing, absolutely nothing, to what the Gallery can already teach on this subject. On the other hand, the Walker Gallery, Liverpool, obtained its *Trecento* marble caryatid figure, a work of great rarity and importance, for £2,835. Blessed indeed is the museum which does not command all the money it wants.

What the market for the sculpture of the Italian primitives used to be may be gauged from the grotesque incident of the recent re-appearance of *The Lady with the Primroses*. If, on the one hand, her history recalls how many have been the errors of *expertise* on the tricky subject of *Quattrocento* modelling, it also recalled how high have been the stakes. $300,000 for a stucco bust had not been unusual at the height of Duveen's millionaire market. As late as 1934, when this market was already becoming shaky, Duveen sold J. D. Rockefeller II five stucco busts, attributed to Verrocchio, Donatello, Desiderio and Laurana, at half a million dollars each, the equivalent in 1970 of as many pounds. Confidence has been too much undermined for any repetition of these prices. Thus a good example of the Verrocchio style in stucco made £10,000 in the devalued paper of 1964.

Italian bronzes in the 1960s were relatively dearer than the surviving examples of direct carving or modelling. But in terms of real money the alleged buoyant state of this market does not stand up to the records of the past. A reference to Volume Two will show the fatuity of the claim that the alleged Cellini *Diana* established an all-time record for an Italian Renaissance bronze in 1968, when it made £32,000. The sum meant no more than £4,000 in the money of 1914 when at least half a dozen bronzes had exceeded this price in the open saleroom. But the *Diana* could not be welcomed in 1968 as more than a *possible* trial-piece from a first modello, whereas it would have been accepted as a unique Cellini bronze in those less disillusioned days. In Duveen's hands it would have been a £100,000 affair.

No other Italian bronze figure on the market of the 1960s came near the top levels of the pre-1914 period. There was nothing of the 15th century and singularly little with any real claim to have been cast in the early 16th. In fact the half dozen dearest pieces at £7,000 to £8,500 of devaluation-money were 17th century rather than 16th, an indication of the growing respect for high Baroque. And the dearest bronze of this type at £12,000 was not even Italian but Flemish.

## MARBLE, TERRACOTTA, PLASTER

|  |  | £ |
|---|---|---|
| 1962 | Lempertz, Cologne. North Italian marble pietà, late 15th century, 12½ in. by 15 in., traces of gilding, DM16,500+tax | 1,650 |
|  | Venetian Gothic retable, *c.* 1430, painted and gilded, 86×80 in., numerous saints in niches, DM80,000+tax | 8,340 |
| 1964 | Earl of Pembroke. C. Venus, 16 in. relief plaque in marble, ascribed ANTONIO LOMBARDO, *c.* 1507 | 5,775 |
|  | Diblee. C. 33 in. relief in hard plaster. Holy Family, school of VERROCCHIO, bought in at £9,975, but subsequently sold privately | 10,000 |
| 1965 | Mrs Hamilton Rice. N.Y. The Lady with the Primroses, stucco bust after VERROCCHIO, bought by Metropolitan Museum, $225 | 80 |
|  | (In 1920 it was bought by Duveen in Rome for £17,000 and allegedly sold to Mrs Hamilton Rice for £71,000, see *Daily Telegraph*, 27.10.65) |  |
|  | S. Detached marble figure, St Francis, 28 in. high, style of TINO DI CAMAINO, *c.* 1320 | 1,150 |
|  | Dorotheum, Vienna. Painted stucco relief, the Holy Family, 31×24, attributed to ROSELLINO | 3,360 |
| 1967 | N.Y. Two marble reliefs, Venus and Cupid in the style of MOSCA, *c.* 1530, 13½ in. high                2 for | 558 |
|  | Marble relief, Holy Family, 25 in. high, attributed to GIOVANNI DALMATA, *c.* 1520 | 642 |
| 1968 | S. BERNINI, modello for the face of Proserpina in the Borghese; fragment, 6 in. high | 3,500 |
|  | Three marble pulpit reliefs, Venice, *c.* 1300, 29×30¼                                   3 for | 3,800 |
|  | 51½ in. marble relief, Holy family and angels, Venice, *c.* 1450 | 3,500 |

| | | £ |
|---|---|---|
| 1968 | S. Terracotta madonna and child, style of DESIDERIO, 54 in. high | 2,900 |
| | Terracotta head, Cosimo II of Tuscany by PIETRO TACCA, 10 in. high, c. 1620 | 3,400 |
| | Lanckoronska. C. Caryatid angel for a marble pulpit, school of ARNOLFO DI CAMBIO, 36×15, late 14th century, Walker Gallery, Liverpool | 2,835 |
| | Marble cupid, Florentine, c. 1550, 22 in., Victoria and Albert Museum | 1,575 |
| 1969 | Villa Demidoff. S. (Florence). Terracotta modello by ALESSANDRO ALGARDI, Attila and Pope Leo I, 1646, 43¼× 25½, 12 million lire+tax | 8,000 |
| | S. Half-length marble relief of a female saint, 14¾×10½, style of TINO DI CAMAINO, c. 1350 | 2,000 |
| | Marble tabernacle with risen Christ and two angels, style of VERROCCHIO | 2,000 |
| | Marble relief, Holy Family, 28×22, style of FRANCESCO DI SIMONE FERRUCCI, c. 1480 | 5,200 |
| | Attributed GREGORIO DA FERRARA. Painted stucco head of mourning Virgin, c. 1470, 18 in. high | 950 |
| | N.Y. Marble tondo, Holy Family, attributed BENEDETTO DA MAJANO, $12,000 | 5,000 |

### DELLA ROBBIA WARE, SCULPTURE IN COLOURED CERAMICS

| | | |
|---|---|---|
| 1960 | Myron C. Taylor, N.Y. Archangel Michael holding the scales, tympanum relief by the master-hand of ANDREA DELLA ROBBIA, (£4,400, Berlin, 1930) | 14,280 |
| 1963 | Berwind. N.Y. Holy Family, arcade panel, 27½ in. high, after ANDREA DELLA ROBBIA | 1,072 |
| 1964 | Finarte, Milan. Two modelled fruit baskets by GIOVANNI DELLA ROBBIA, c. 1520                                          2 for | 1,500 |
| 1965 | C. Holy family, bas-relief, 25×16½ in. after ANDREA DELLA ROBBIA | 2,205 |
| 1966 | Christie. C. Arched relief, 16½ in. high, Madonna adoring child | 336 |
| 1967 | Kaufman Keller. C. Madonna adoring child, arched relief, 27½ in. high, style of LUCA DELLA ROBBIA | 2,625 |
| 1968 | Dighirian. S. Holy family with infant St John, arched relief, 6 ft. 10½×4 ft. 10½, dated 1523 and attributed to GIOVANNI DELLA ROBBIA, bought by the Italian government for the town of Vinci whence it came | 15,000 |
| | Killearn. S. Roundel Holy Family, 21 in. diam., style of ANDREA DELLA ROBBIA | 1,700 |
| | N.Y. Holy Family, roundel in wreath, 32 in., $4,000 | 1,666 |

## ITALIAN RENAISSANCE—BRONZE

| | | | £ |
|---|---|---|---|
| 1960 | S. | School of RICCIO, Padua, goat, 3 in. high | 1,450 |
| | | Silver gilt figure of Meleager by ANTICO, bought by Victoria and Albert Museum | 4,000 |
| 1961 | S. | RICCIO, kneeling satyr | 2,300 |
| | | GIROLAMO CAMPAGNA, kneeling man supporting salt (compare 1969) | 1,550 |
| | | Hercules and the bull, 9½ in., possibly AUGSBURG, c. 1560 | 3,500 |
| 1962 | Gilou. S. | Panther, PADUAN SCHOOL, 5½ in. long | 620 |
| | S. | Pair of Venetian andirons, early 17th century  2 for | 950 |
| | | School of RICCIO, Venus holding mirror | 2,700 |
| | | Lion attacking centaur, Florence, late 16th century | 900 |
| | | Panther, N. Italian, c. 1500 | 4,000 |
| | | VITTORE CAMELIO, Hercules and Antaeus, early 16th century | 3,800 |
| | C. | Door-knocker, Neptune and Tritons, by ALESSANDRO VITTORIA, late 16th century | 630 |
| | | TIZIANO ASPETTI, Mercury and Argus, c. 1590, bought by Fitzwilliam Museum | 475 |
| 1963 | C. | Rape of the Sabine women, after GIOVANNI BOLOGNA (£367, 1931; £325, 1952) | 1,217 10s. |
| | S. | Kneeling woman, 9¾ in. high, Bologna school | 2,400 |
| | | Berwind. N.Y. ALESSANDRO VITTORIA, four gilt-bronze disciple figures, c. 1600, 11½ in.  4 for | 2,850 |
| | | Narcissus, 18 in., after SANSOVINO | 1,375 |
| | | BACCIO BANDINELLI, Hercules slaying Lichas, 20 in. | 1,250 |
| | | Rasmussen, Copenhagen. GIROLAMO CAMPAGNA, youth supporting cockle shell, late 16th century (compare 1961, 1968, 1969) | 2,360 |
| | | GIOVANNI BOLOGNA, Hercules and Antaeus, 18·4 in. (similar in 1929, £1522 10s.) | 2,980 |
| | | Hercules and Nessus, same series, 16 in. | 5,348 |
| | | Fitzgerald. S. After GIOVANNI BOLOGNA, small Venus | 2,100 |
| | | Fribourg. N.Y. After GIULIANO FINELLI, pair of leaping horses, 9¼ in. long, on Louis XV gilt-bronze pedestals  2 for | 9,200 |
| 1964 | | Stuker, Berne. FRANCESCO SUSINI, Venus reproving Love, 22 in. dated 1583  about | 3,000 |
| | | School of RICCIO, equestrian figure, 9½ in. high | 4,260 |
| | | Mrs Gaby Solomon. S. Two small replicas of the Horses of St Mark's, marble plinths, late 16th century  2 for | 5,200 |

£

1965  Mowbray Buller. S. Pair of 17th century horsemen on
Boulle mounts, 12½ in. high    1,850

      Virgin, child and St Anne after SANSOVINO, 12¼ in.    1,600

      RICCIO SCHOOL, Venus pudica, 9¾, in. (under £300,
Paget sale, 1949)    4,160

      BELLANO SCHOOL, c. 1480, Sleeping Hercules, 5½ in.    1,575

      Padua, c. 1520, 8½ in., Hercules and Nemean lion    3,500

    School of OLIVIERI, Nude woman supporting a bowl,
10 in.    2,085

  Adda. Paris. School of VITTORIA, c. 1550, Two Tritons
riding tortoises, 4½ in.    2,405

      PIETRO DA BARGA, c. 1550, Silenus nursing the infant
Dionysus, 12 in. high    2,550

      Venice, late 16th century. Boy riding a dolphin,
6 in.    2,550

    School of LEONE LEONI, late 16th century, gilt-bronze
casket-inkstand, surmounted by herm, 10 in. long    2,550

    School of GIOVANNI BOLOGNA, c. 1600, a fowler on
plinth    2,000

      ditto Venus at the bath, c. 1570, 9¾ in.    7,150

      GIROLAMO CAMPAGNA (signed) Venus Marina, 17½ in.
high    7,020

      ROCCATAGLIATA, c. 1600, Meleager, 9¾ in. high    2,860

    School of ROCCATAGLIATA, elaborate inkstand, c. 1600,
15 in. high    1,496

    Pair of Venetian andirons, Mars and Venus, signed
GIROLAMO CAMPAGNA, c. 1620, 19 in. high    2 for  2,080

    Another pair, Venus and Meleager, 34 in. high
                                 2 for  2,275

    Peace and War, pair of andirons after TIZIANO
ASPETTI, 17th century, 21½ in. high    2 for  3,832

1966  Gaby Solomon. S. GIOVANNI BOLOGNA school, c. 1600,
Hercules and Hydra, 18½ in high    2,100

      SANSOVINO school, allegorical figure of poetry,
c. 1550, 19 in. high    1,650

    Mellon-Scaife. N.Y. SANSOVINO, reclining athlete, 16 in.
long, $17,000    6,070

1967  Burns. C. Pair of kneeling angels, gilt-bronze, late 17th
century, 23 in. high    2 for  2,990

    Dundas. C. Donatellesque head of St Francis of Assisi,
late 15th century    1,995

    S. BARTOLOMMEO AMMANATI, standing Neptune, gilt-
bronze, c. 1550, 9¼ in. high    3,400

£

1967    S.   BACCIO BANDINELLI, crouching Hercules, *c.* 1530–50, 6¼ in.       2,800

GIOVANNI BOLOGNA school. Lion attacking horse, 2 castings on single plinth, 14½ in. high       7,600

Adda.   C.   Panther, 11½ in. long, Padua, *c.* 1520       2,310

S.   Astronomy, allegorical figure after GIOVANNI BOLOGNA, early 17th century, 15 in. high       4,000

ROMAN SCHOOL, late 16th century, Apollo with lyre, 14 in.       3,300

N.Y.   Earth, portrayed as old man with globe and plough, ROMAN SCHOOL, late 16th century, 9¾ in. high, $21,000       7,580

Spinario, style of RICCIO, 8¼ in. (£440 in 1888, £1,680 in 1912)       2,500

David with Goliath's head, Padua, *c.* 1500, 9¾ in.       2,855

1968    Holton.   S.   Two evangelists in the style of ALESSANDRO VITTORIA, dated 1611, height 13 in.      2 for    2,600

Erard.   S.   Pacing horse after the St Mark's horses, Venice, *c.* 1500, height 10¼ in.       2,900

C.   Stallion, 9 in. high, Florence, *c.* 1520       3,360

S.   10-in. figure of Diana, purporting on little evidence to have been cast from a modello by CELLINI       32,000

Apollo and Daphne, manner of FOGGINI, late 17th century, 18 in. high, bought by the Louvre       6,800

S.   Pacing horse, 11 in. long, BOLOGNA-SUSINI workshop, Florence, *c.* 1600       8,500

Mervyn-Williams.   S.   Tiber and Arno, Florentine relief, 6½ × 24 in., intended for base of a statue, *c.* 1570       8,000

S.   Standing Neptune, school of TIZIANO ASPETTI, 28½ in. high       5,800

Gilt-bronze salt, supported by kneeling youth, 7½ in. high, by GIROLAMO CAMPAGNA, late 16th century (compare 1961, 1963, 1969)       5,400

Set of four Evangelists, Venice, *c.* 1600, 11½ in. high      4 for    8,500

Kneeling satyr, ANDREA RICCIO style, c. 1520, 8 in. high       4,800

CIGOLI, anatomical figure of man with bow, 19½ in. high, *c.* 1580, Hfl64,000+tax       8,375

Galloping horse, Florence, *c.* 1600, 8½ × 10, Hfl57,000+ tax       7,485

1969    von Bergen.   S.   Style of ALESSANDRO VITTORIA, Neptune, 15¾ in.       2,500

Style of CAMELIO, *c.* 1550, gilt-bronze Hercules, 8½ in.    4,700

Carey.   S.   GIROLAMO CAMPAGNA, kneeling nude youth

£

1969  supporting gilt-bronze salt, 8 in. high (compare 1961, 1963,
      1968)                                                        3,400
      Gubbay.  C.  Rape of the Sabines, 17th century copy
      after GIOVANNI BOLOGNA, 20 in. high                          2,100

## SCULPTURE
### LATE 17TH AND 18TH CENTURIES
(mainly French)

A considerable part of this list consists of drawing room sculpture in marb
or tinted terracotta by the masters of the second half of the 18th centur
Clodion, Houdon, Falconet, Marin and Pajou, a school very little esteem
between the French Revolution and the later 1850s, but thereafter advanci
steadily till the eve of the great depression, when prices had become part o
world of phantasy. A marble bust by Houdon, sold in 1967 for £16,300, m
sound an expensive item for a school so little in the taste of today. It was inde
as dear as anything by Houdon on the post-war market. But examine t
small selection of prices paid in the second and third decades of the centur
some of which will not be found in Volume II.

1912  Doucet sale, Paris. SABINA HOUDON at ten months,
      marble, 450,000 francs+tax, £19,800 (£158,400 on 1970
      scale)
1915  Sold by Gimpel to Henry Clay Frick. HOUDON, marble
      bust of Mme Cayla as a Bacchante, $200,000 or £41,200
      (£330,000 on 1970 scale)
1917  Sold to Henry P. Davison by Jacques Seligman in N.Y.,
      HOUDON, bronze bust, La frileuse. About £35,000 or
      £245,000 on the 1970 scale.
1919  Sold by Gimpel to Ledyard Blair. HOUDON, marble bust
      of Hue de Miromesnil, $120,000 (£24,760) or £123,800 on
      the 1970 scale
      Sold by Gimpel to Jules Bache. PIGALLE, marble bust of
      Mme Pompadour, $160,000 (£32,860) or £164,240 on the
      1970 scale
1928  Gary sale, N.Y. The baby SABINA HOUDON (see 1912)
      bought by Knoedler for Edward Harkness, $245,000 or
      £50,650, £253,250 on 1970 scale
1929  Sold by Duveen to Andrew Mellon. HOUDON's marble
      bust of Washington, £52,500 or £262,000 on the 1970
      scale.

So far as 1970 goes, busts by Houdon at a quarter of a million and more a
definitely not in. Is that very expensive baby, one wonders, worth ev

£20,000? The present market seems to have reverted to the early 19th century preference for Baroque over Rococo, since the dearest item in the list is a marble bust in the fruity Louis XIV style of Guillaume Coustou. Even if £20,000 in 1969 money meant no more than £4,000 in the 1920s, it is doubtful whether such a bust would then have made a fifth as much.

|  |  | £ |
|---|---|---|
| 1961 | N.Y. PAJOU, terracotta bust of Mme Vigée-Lebrun, 1783, $16,500 (according to Gimpel, Wildenstein paid 225,000 francs, then worth £6,328 in December, 1919) | 5,880 |
|  | PAJOU, Birth of the Dauphin, tinted terracotta group, 17 in. | 3,580 |
| 1962 | Paris. CLODION, two wax reliefs of nymphs and satyrs 2 for Lady Bailey. S. Pair of marble sphinxes, c. 1760, English | 2,250 |
|  | gilt-wood stands 2 for | 950 |
|  | S. LEMOYNE, bronze bust, Louis XV, 1750 | 1,000 |
| 1963 | Paris. GIRARDON, Equestrian bronze figure of Louis XIV, 22 in. high, damescened with gold, FN132,000+tax | 10,550 |
|  | HOUDON, marble bust, Jean de la Fontaine, FN70,000+ tax | 5,620 |
|  | Fribourg. S. *Vénus accroupie* after the statue, dated 1688, by COYSEVOX, Louis XIV gilt-bronze mounts | 2,100 |
|  | Pair of galloping horses in bronze after FINELLI, Louis XV mounts 2 for | 9,200 |
|  | PAJOU, terracotta bust of the sculptor Lemoyne | 1,600 |
|  | HOUDON, marble bust, Marquis de Miromesnil | 2,000 |
|  | S. PIGALLE, boy's head, terracotta, 1771 | 1,900 |
|  | LEMOYNE, head of unknown lady, terracotta | 2,600 |
|  | Dunlap. N.Y. CLODION, Silenus and nymphs, terracotta on drum | 2,500 |
| 1964 | Mrs Gaby Solomon. S. Terracotta bust of Nicolas Coypel by LEMOYNE, signed | 2,900 |
| 1965 | Nurk. S. HOUDON, marble bust of Mme Marie Adelaide of France (£2,400 in 1933) | 8,000 |
|  | Hamilton Rice, N.Y. HOUDON, half-length marble portrait, Comte de Gibert, 1791, 33 in. high | 1,340 |
| 1966 | Lockhart Ross. S. ROUBILLAC, marble bust of Sir Peter Warren | 1,150 |
|  | Hasson. C. HOUDON, marble bust of his infant child, Anne | 2,625 |
|  | CLODION, terracotta figure, Flora, 20½ in. high | 1,575 |
| 1967 | Paris. HOUDON, commemorative marble bust of Molière, signed and dated, 1782, 33 in. high, FN205,000+tax | 16,300 |
| 1968 | Cl Terracotta *modello* for RYSBRACK's monument to Nicolas Rowe, 1740, 18 × 14 | 5,250 |

£

1968  Lawson. C. Lucas Faydherbe, Madonna and child,
27 in. high, marble, *c.* 1675                                              3,780
S.  Marble busts of Isaac Newton and Alexander Pope,
19½ in. high, after François Roubilllac, *c.* 1750      2 for   2,600
S.  La petite Lise, marble bust signed by Houdon, 1774,
15 in.                                                                        8,500
      Louis XIV bronze group after Giovanni Bologna,
      Rape of Europa, 13½ in. wide, Fitzwilliam Museum   2,400
      Massacre of innocents, bronze relief by Giuseppe
      Piamontini, *c.* 1690–1700, 26½ × 33                  5,200
      Ditto, fall of the Titans, 24 × 31½                      5,500
Paris.  Girardon, equestrian bronze statue of Louis XIV,
nearly 4 ft high, FN134,500+tax                                     12,585
Viguier, Paris.  By Coysevox, marble portrait relief,
Louis XIV, framed, 38½ × 33½, FN30,000+tax                    2,820
      By Chinard of Lyon.  Bust portrait, Camille Jordan,
      dated 1803, terracotta, 13¼ in. high, FN13,500+tax   1,280
Oezle, Amsterdam.  By Andreas Schluter, *c.* 1700.
Two bronze leaping horses, 14½ × 16, Hfl85,000+tax
2 for  11,150
Willoughby.  S.  The Four elements, Louis XIV bronze,
15½–17 in. high                                                       2,800
Pleydell-Bouverie.  Pair of terracotta busts of Bacchanteas
by Joseph Marin, *c.* 1780–90, 12¾ in. high        2 for   2,900
N.Y.  Maternité, terracotta group by Marin, 17 in. high,
$5,000                                                                      2,083
      Marble Venus on high plinth, 18½ in. high, attributed
      to Falconet, $8,000                                        3,333
Harrie.  S.  Terracotta angel, maquette for the Admiral
Vernon monument by Michael Rysbrack, 17½ in.         3,400
1969  S.  School of Coysevox, terracotta bust of Louis XIV,
*c.* 1680   28½ in. high                                               4,000
N.Y.  Pair of terracotta satyr groups, attributed Clodion,
18 in. high, $9,200                                        2 for   3,833
      Marble bust of the infant Sabina, Houdon, *c.* 1791,
      24 in. high, $11,000                                       4,583
Church.  S.  Pair of reclining marble figures of Cleopatra
and Ariadne by Delvaux and Scheemakers, signed, 24½ in.
long, *c.* 1720–30                                          2 for   3,000
Fribourg, N.Y.  Marble sleeping Bacchante, ascribed to
Falconet (Walters sale, 1941, $11,000) 12½ in. high,
$3,200                                                                      1,333
      Pair of tinted wax reliefs of classic acrobatic scenes,
      ascribed Clodion, each 15¾ × 6¼, $10,000    2 for   4,160

|  |  | £ |
|---|---|---|
| 69 | N.Y. Terracotta Bacchante, signed Marin and dated 1781, 13½ in. high, $7,750 | 3,228 |
| | C. Pair of Louis XIV bronze reclining figures, Nile and Tiber, by Jacques Buirette, 17½ in. wide    2 for | 3,465 |
| | Proctor-Beauchamp. S. Equestrian bronze figure of Louis XIV on heavily sculptured plinth by Nicolas de la Colonge, 1726, after the statue by Desjardins, 1688, formerly at Lyon, 29½ in. high, Lyon Museum | 1,500 |
| | Bought by Walker Gallery, Liverpool. Marble bust of the sculptor Nicolas Coustou (1658–1733) by his brother Guillaume Coustou (1678–1746) c. 1700 | 20,000 |

## SCULPTURE
### NEO-CLASSIC, FIRST HALF OF THE 19TH CENTURY

ntonio Canova (1757–1822) was possibly the highest feed sculptor who ever ved. When he was in London in 1816, he received 2,500 guineas from the uke of Wellington for a life-sized statue of Napoleon in the nude. The 70 equivalent would be more than £30,000. Canova rated as high in 1843, hen a life-sized Magdalen made £2,380 at the Aguado sale and this might : considered £24,000. Yet in 1969 the *Demidoff Venus* made no more than 2,380, in real terms only 8 per cent of Canova's fee for the Napoleon. nd yet neo-classicism is not altogether unpopular, witness the rapidly ad- ncing market for plaques and medallions in the purest neo-classic style, ade in jasper ware or basalt ware by the firm of Wedgwood and Bentley. ıt there are other factors in the case of sculpture which diminish the popularity ˙ the neo-classic school. In the first place a life-sized marble, once essential every great English country house, has now become a thorough nuisance. nd then again the product is suspect. It is doubtful whether Canova's followers ˙er touched the marble at all, though Canova himself may have chiselled a tle. A bronze, cast direct from the *modello*, preserves the features of the iginal faithfully. Consequently, a pair of 18 inch bronzes by Canova cost in 68 as much as a pair of life-sized marble Venuses.

|  |  | £ |
|---|---|---|
| 61 | S. Thorwaldsen. Ganymede and the eagle, marble, 1817 | 1,150 |
| 62 | Bought for the Victoria and Albert Museum. Canova, Theseus and the Minotaur, marble | 3,000 |
| | Lord Londonderry. S. Dancing girl in tunic, 70 inch marble figure by Canova | 1,250 |
| | Reclining nymph awake, 65 in., marble, Canova | 1,050 |
| 63 | Lord Londonderry. S. Venus leaving the bath by Canova, marble, 69 in. | 1,900 |

£

| | | £ |
|---|---|---|
| 1966 | Grittleton marbles.  C. RAFAELLE MONTI,  Eve after the Fall, 52 in. marble, 1851 | 840 |
| | TADOLINI.  Pair of 62 in. marbles, *Pescatrice* and Venus and Cupid (£215 5s. each in 1854)        2 for | 630 |
| | ROBERT WYATT, Ino and Bacchus (£378 in 1854) | 525 |
| | JOHN GIBSON.  Venus verticordia, 1833, 69 in. marble. The original version of the *Tinted Venus* which made £630 in 1916 and £165 in 1929) | 630 |
| 1967 | C.  Pair of African watercarriers in mixed marbles and metals by CORDIER, 1862, 76 in. high        2 for | 1,575 |
| | Paris.  Marble bust of Napoleon by CANOVA, 31¾ in. high | 418 |
| 1968 | Koller, Zurich.  CANOVA.  Pair of bronze putti on marble plinths, 18½ in. high FS41,000+tax        2 for | 4,460 |
| 1969 | Villa Demidoff.  S. (Florence).  CANOVA, Marble Venus made for Prince of Canino, lire 3·8 million+tax, 68 in. high | 2,566 |
| | HIRAM POWERS, marble bust, Princess Mathilde Demidoff, 1840, 23½ in. high, lire 2·2 million+tax | 1,614 |

## SCULPTURE
### SECOND HALF OF THE 19TH CENTURY

The three most famous sculptors of the official and academic school, Carpeaux Barye and Dalou, are no longer the great names of this period Carpeaux alone has been included in the list, and his relatively modest prices are very much lower than those that were paid in his own lifetime and by the next generation In 1913 the terracotta figure *La danse* was sold among the contents of Carpeaux' studio for 230,000 francs or about £10,100 with tax. The 1970 equivalent would be over £80,000, but in 1957 *La danse* was sold for $3,500 or £1,250 It might be optimistic to expect more than £3,000 to £4,000 in 1970. The fate of Rodin, who invented a style which shared in the success of Impressionism has been rather different. At the MacCulloch sale of 1913 a bronze cast of *Le Baiser* made 2,900 guineas, equivalent to £24,200, a remarkable price since the last example sold (1968) did not soar beyond £13,500. The enormous vogue for Rodin barely suvived his death. In the 1920s it was practically impossible to obtain £1,000 for his most important work. The cult of *significant form* exalted the massive solidity of Maillol and Bourdelle at the expense of Rodin' Impressionism in the round. Thus the recovery, which lifted the price of the life-sized *Age d'airain* to $85,000 in 1969, did not begin till, 1960.

It is curious that the only 19th century sculptors who rival or surpass Rodin in the salerooms, were painters who practised sculpture as amateurs, Renoir whose models were much over-reproduced, rates fairly low, whereas Degas whose bronzes were even more repetitious than his paintings of the same subjects, rates riduculously high. There is something oddly innocent about this market. Can anyone be certain how many copies there are of *La petite danseuse de quatorze ans*, of which one example, cast by a commercial firm, made £53,000 in 1967? In hardly any case among modern bronzes is the ownership of the original *modello* disclosed or its destruction certified. Quite often high prices are paid for posthumous casts. Daumier who died in 1879, made a series of plaster models of his political lampoon, *Le ratapoil*. From the largest of these a series of 26 casts was made nearly half a century after his death. Whether this operation cost as much as £30 a figure in 1925 is more than doubtful, yet in 1968 the figures were selling at £8,500 to £14,000 apiece, having advanced from £1,250 in 1960. Bronze casts were made from some of Gauguin's wooden fictitious South Seas idols as late as 1959. Ten years later a set of five was worth $33,000. Provided that a bronze has been cast from the original model, the possibility of others to come seems no deterrent. It is only when a mould has been made round a cast bronze in order that it may beget children in its turn that there are sounds of protest. In December, 1969 seven Rodin bronzes were withdrawn from a sale after the firm who had normally cast for Rodin, disowned them.

## JEAN BAPTISTE CARPEAUX. 1827–1875

| | | £ |
|---|---|---:|
| 1957 | Lurcy. N.Y. La Danse, terracotta, 1874, 32 in. high (£10,100, Paris, 1913) | 1,250 |
| 1966 | S. Marble bust, Mlle Anna Foucart, 1866, 20 in. high | 500 |
| 1968 | S. L'amour désarmé, bronze, 31 in. high, 1870 | 1,400 |
| | N.Y. La Chinoise, bronze bust, 1866, 22 in. high, $4,250 | 1,770 |
| 1969 | N.Y. La négresse, bust in same series, 25 in. high, $5,750 | 2,400 |

## HONORÉ DAUMIER. 1808–1879

| | | £ |
|---|---|---:|
| 1960 | S. Ratapoil, bronze, posthumous series (see 1965, 1968), 17¼ in. | 1,250 |
| 1961 | Paris. Les émigrés, original plaster model of the bronze relief, bought by the Louvre | 10,200 |
| 1963 | S. L'important malicieux, smaller version, 8¼ in. high, one of 25 | 1,200 |
| 1965 | N.Y. Le Ratapoil, bronze, 17¼ in. (see 1960, 1968) | 8,640 |
| | Berne. Le Ratapoil, bronze, smaller version, 13¼ in. high | 4,150 |
| 1966 | 'G.D.' Paris. Le Ratapoil, original plaster modello | 26,540 |
| | Self-portrait, plaster modello, FN295,000+tax | 23,250 |
| | The same cast in bronze | 9,600 |
| | Ten other bronzes from £1,500 to £3,200 | |
| 1968 | Lewis. N.Y. L'important malicieux, bronze bust, 17 in., $9,000 | 3,784 |
| | S. Le Ratapoil, 17¼ in. One of 26 casts made in 1925 (see 1960, 1965) | 8,500 |

£

| 1968 | S.   A second, sold a few months later | 14,000 |
|---|---|---|
| | N.Y.   A third, sold a few months later | 10,000 |
| | Lempertz, Cologne.   A fourth, sold a few months later, numbered 7, DM56,000+tax | 6,700 |
| | Kornfeld, Berne.   Self-portrait, 1885, bronze, 29 in. high, FS116,000+tax | 12,900 |
| 1969 | S.   L'amoureux and le lecteur, posthumous bronze casts by Valsuani, about 7 in. high                                        each | 3,200 |
| | Five others at £1,600 to £3,000 | |

EDGAR HILAIRE DEGAS.   1839–1917

| 1952 | Bought for Tate Gallery.   La petite danseuse, bronze, 34 in. high, cast posthumously in 1922 | 9,076 |
|---|---|---|
| 1957 | S.   La masseuse, bronze | 1,245 |
| | Ballet dancer, 4th position (compare 1968) | 1,900 |
| 1960 | C.   Woman wiping her neck, bronze, 12½ in. high | 1,680 |
| | S.   Cheval au galop, bronze, 12¼ in. high | 5,100 |
| 1961 | Adam.   S.   Pacing horse, bronze, 11½ in. high, one of 22 cast | 4,000 |
| 1963 | Sellin.   N.Y.   Woman examining her foot, bronze, $11,500 | 4,106 |
| | Aldrich.   N.Y.   La révérence, bronze, 13 in. (see 1968) | 2,857 |
| 1964 | S.   Woman drying her hair, bronze, 18¾ in. high, numbered 50 | 4,800 |
| 1965 | S.   Galloping horse, bronze, 12 in. high | 8,750 |
| | N.Y.   Femme se coiffant, bronze, 18¼ in., $14,000 | 5,000 |
| 1966 | S.   Woman wiping her neck, bronze, 12½ in. high, numbered 44, (see 1960, £1,680) | 4,000 |
| | Gaubier.   S.   Danse espagnole, bronze, 16¼ in. numbered 20 | 6,500 |
| | Horse and rider, bronze, 11¼ in. high | 11,000 |
| | Sykes.   S.   Head supported on a hand, bronze, 4½ in. high, numbered 62, 1882–7 | 7,000 |
| 1967 | S.   Cheval se cabrant, bronze, 12¼ in. high | 18,500 |
| | Boyd.   S.   Petite danseuse de quatorze ans, bronze, 28½ in., one of a series cast by Hébrard | 53,000 |
| | Heldring.   S.   Cheval au pas, bronze, 9 in. high | 16,000 |
| 1968 | S.   Cheval sautant un obstacle, bronze, 11½ in., one of 50 | 19,000 |
| | Grande arabesque premier temps, bronze, 19 in., one of 22 | 12,000 |
| | Danseuse habillée au repos, bronze numbered 51, 16½ in. | 14,500 |
| | Danseuse, quatrième position, one of 22, bronze, 23½ in. | 18,000 |

| | | £ |
|---|---|---|
| 1968 | S. Femme s'étirant, bronze numbered 54, 14½ in. | 9,000 |
| | Bluestein. N.Y. La révérence, bronze, 13 in. (see 1963) | 5,835 |
| | C. Danseuse mettant son bas, bronze numbered 29, 19 in. | 16,275 |
| | S. Jockey à cheval, bronze, 12½ in., one of 22 | 16,000 |
| | Danseuse saluant, 9 in. bronze numbered 31 | 9,500 |
| 1969 | C. Cheval faisant une descente de main, 7¼ in., bronze, numbered 22 | 18,900 |
| | N.Y. L'écolière, 10½ in. high, one of 20 bronzes cast in 1956, $15,000 | 6,250 |

PAUL GAUGUIN. 1848–1903

| | | |
|---|---|---|
| 1961 | S. Painted wooden head of a Tahitian with coral necklace, 10 in. high | 11,500 |
| 1964 | Medley. C. Oviri, bronze, self-portrait in relief | 7,875 |
| 1965 | S. Bronze bust, Mme Schuffnecker, 1889, one of 10, 60 in. | 2,500 |
| | N.Y. Six fictitious South Sea idols, 12 to 21 in. high, wood (see 1969) 6 for | 12,750 |
| 1966 | S. La petite Parisienne, bronze, 1881, 10¾ in. | 1,100 |
| 1967 | Shelton, N.Y. Self-portrait, bronze bas-relief, 14 × 13½ in., $15,000 | 5,353 |
| 1968 | Lewis, N.Y. Self-portrait, masque cast in terracotta, 11½ in. high, $4,000 | 1,665 |
| 1969 | N.Y. Five fictitious South Sea idols, cast in bronze from the wood carvings in 1959 (see 1965), $32,000 | 13,440 |
| | S. Oviri, posthumous cast from ceramic figure, 29¼ in. | 3,800 |

PIERRE AUGUSTE RENOIR. 1841–1919

| | | |
|---|---|---|
| 1957 | S. Bronze portrait-medallion, 'Coco', one of 30 casts, 1907, 8½ in. high | 550 |
| 1964 | S. Hymne à la vie, bronze with clock, 1916, 28 in. high (see 1969) | 1,200 |
| 1965 | N.Y. Danseuse à la voile, bronze, 25½ in. high, $7,500 (see 1969) | 2,680 |
| | Goldsmith. S. Petite Vénus debout, bronze, 23½ in., 1913 | 3,800 |
| | S. Laveuse et forgeron (eau et feu) two crouching figures, bronze, 10¼ in., 1916 each | 1,600 |
| 1966 | S. Bust of Mme Renoir in a bucket-shaped hat, one of 20 bronze casts, 1916, 23½ in. high | 3,100 |
| | La petite laveuse acroupie (larger version of la laveuse, see 1965), 14½ in. Two copies at £2,800 and | 3,300 |
| 1967 | Josten. N.Y. Pair of terracotta cast reliefs of dancers, 23 × 15¾, $6,250 2 for | 2,232 |
| | C. Head of Venus, bronze, 10 in. high | 1,417 10s. |

£

| | | £ |
|---|---|---|
| 1968 | Lewis. N.Y. The same $10,000 | 4,165 |
| | N.Y. Joueur de fluteau, 24 in. bronze, 1918, numbered 13, $13,000 | 4,584 |
| 1969 | N.Y. Danseuse à la viole, 25½ in. high, bronze cast in 1964, $16,500 | 5,935 |
| | S. (Tokyo). Danseuse à la viole. Posthumous bronze cast in 1964, 26¾ in. high, 5·1 million yen about | 6,000 |
| | Hymne à la vie (with clock) one of 8 cast in 1914, 29 in. (compare 1964), 3·4 million yen about | 4,000 |
| | Variante de la petite Vénus debout, c. 1913, bronze, 23½ in. (differs very slightly from example sold in 1965) | 6,500 |

AUGUSTE RODIN. 1840–1917

| | | |
|---|---|---|
| 1957 | McGillivray. S. Portrait-bust, Victor Hugo, 22 in., 1887 | 160 |
| | Caryatide tombée, bronze, 17½ in. | 230 |
| 1958 | N.Y. Man with a broken nose, bronze, $3,250 | 1,160 |
| | Death of Adonis, bronze, $3,000 | 1,070 |
| 1960 | Lempertz, Cologne. Bronze head of Balzac | 1,550 |
| | Duveen. S. Romeo and Juliet, marble | 5,500 |
| 1961 | S. Bronze bust, Bernard Shaw | 1,350 |
| 1964 | N.Y. Christ and Magdalen, marble | 3,840 |
| | S. Christ and Magdalen, second version, marble, 44½ in. | 1,800 |
| | Eve, marble, 30 in. high (£725 in 1923; £650 in 1924) | 12,500 |
| 1965 | S. Brother and sister, 17 in., marble | 5,000 |
| | Avnet, N.Y. Maternité, marble, 18 in. high, 1885, $18,500 | 5,900 |
| 1966 | Thompson. N.Y. Bronze version of the Balzac monument, 50½ in. high, 1893, Rhode Island school of Design, $70,000 | 25,180 |
| | S. Balzac, nude figure, bronze, 30½ in. high | 7,000 |
| | S. La méditation, bronze, 1886, 22½ in. | 3,000 |
| | Mère et Enfant, bronze, unnumbered and undated, 16 in. | 3,400 |
| 1967 | N.Y. Le penseur, bronze, 28 in., one of 10 casts, $40,000 | 14,286 |
| | Paris. L'âge d'airain, bronze, 71¼ in. high (compare 1969) FN180,000+tax | 14,470 |
| | Boyd. S. Jean d'Aire, citizen of Calais, bronze, 18¾ in. | 4,400 |
| | Bronze bust of Balzac, 11½ in. | 4,500 |
| | Le penseur, smaller bronze version, 15½ in. high | 7,500 |
| | Doxrud. N.Y. Bronze head of Balzac, 15 in., $9,000 | 3,214 |
| | de Kay. N.Y. Brother and sister in a grotto, marble, 1890, 24½ in. high, $19,000 | 7,786 |
| 1968 | Lewis. N.Y. Le penseur, bronze version, 1889, 14¾ in., $16,500 | 6,665 |

£

1968  N.Y.  Another example of the same, sold a few months
later, $13,000         4,584

      Bronze portrait bust, Hon. George Wyndham, 1903,
19½ in., $11,500 (£250 in 1959)    4,718

Josefowitz.  N.Y.  Eve, bronze version, 29½ in., $29,000  20,415

      Jean d'Aire, citizen of Calais, bronze, 1884 (see 1967),
18¾ in., $15,000 (another at Sothebys £4,400)    6,250

S.  Eve, bronze version, 29½ in., 1881 (see above and 1969)  8,500

      Le baiser, bronze, 29 in.  (At the McCulloch sale, 1913
one of this series made £3,045 equivalent to £22,800
in 1968)    13,500

Bluestein.  N.Y.  Girl's torso, bronze, 19¾ in., $15,000,
one of 12 casts, 1889, also called Cybele    6,250

N.Y.  Severed head of John the Baptist, marble, 1887,
length 15 in., $18,500    3,540

Hersh.  N.Y.  Titan, marble, 20 in. high, $10,000    4,165

S.  Balzac nu, plaster, 1893, 30 in. high    4,500

S.  Eustache de St. Pierre, bronze, 1907, 19 in. high    4,200

Beddington Behrens.  S.  Jean de Fiennes, 1884, one of
12 posthumous casts made in 1925, 18¼ in. high    3,000

Williamson.  C.  Frère et soeur, bronze, 1891, 15¼ in.
high    4,200

C.  Iris, messager des dieux, bronze, 1890, 37½ in. high  11,550

N.Y.  St John the Baptist, bronze, 1878, 19¾ in. high,
$22,000    9,172

      Eustache de St Pierre, 1886, bronze, 1 of 12 cast,
18½ in.    6,665

      Centauresse, bronze, 1890, 18 in. high, $10,000    4,155

1969  N.Y.  Désespoir, stone 37 in. high, $37,500    15,626

S.  La méditation, bronze, 1885, 29 in. high (for smaller
1886 version, see 1966)    16,500

N.Y.  L'âge d'airain, modelled 1877, bronze version,
71 in. high (£14,470 in 1967), $85,000    35,700

S. (Tokyo).  Eve, bronze, one of 12, 29½ in. (compare 1968),
7·5 million yen    8,520

S.  Le baiser de l'aïeule, bronze, c. 1894, 20 in. high    5,800

Garrick Club.  C.  Bellona, bronze bust after a modello
of 1878, 32 in. high    7,350

MEDARDO ROSSO.  1858–1928

1964  St Mary's Priory.  S.  Malato all'ospedale, bronze, 1889,
7¾ in.    1,500

      Bimbo Ebreo, head in wax and plaster, 1892, 9 in. high  1,500

1965  S.  The same    2,100

£

| 1966 | S. | Donna ridente, plaster, 1890, 14 in. high | 1,800 |
| | | Another version, 21¾ in. | 2,000 |
| | | Bimba ridente, 1890, bronze, 10½ in. | 1,400 |
| 1968 | Josefowitz. N.Y. Omnibus; frieze of three heads, plaster | | |
| | | and wax, 32½ in. long, $15,000 | 6,750 |

## SCULPTURE
### 20TH CENTURY

In the 1930s the inducements to become a sculptor were few indeed. For t academically trained sculptor there were far less public commissions availal than in the glyptomaniac late 19th century or in the aftermath of the Fi World War. For the modernist sculptor there was practically no pub patronage at all. Merely to continue working was very expensive and one h to live as well. The taste for drawing-room bronzes was receding rapidly it became as good as extinct. By the late 1930s Epstein's portrait bronzes we mostly down to £30 each, perhaps no more than the cost of casting. Eve modern sculptor was affected in the same way. Then in 1952 the Tate Galle paid £9,000 for one of Degas' bronze *danseuses*, but it was not till the 190 that *modern* bronzes, which were not strictly representational, could make much. In the ensuing lists there are some works in experimental materials su as chromed steel, aluminium and ply-wood, but bronze predominates ev among works of the severest abstract character. A bronze is only a reproducti of an original work and generally one of a series at that. Yet there are seve sculptors who can get thousands of pounds for each of these reproductions one new work. The clue to the considerable change in the status of the livi sculptor resides in the fact the modern sculpture in the right setting makes : less severe demands on the eye than modern painting.

There are several interesting peculiarities in these lists. It will be noticed tl painter-sculptors still rate very high. The company includes Braque, Chaga Kirchner, Matisse, Modigliani and Picasso. On the other hand, Maillol, t founder of modern sculpture and for long the supplanter of Rodin, is not high up in the list as one would expect. Three of the sculptors are British, b Epstein whose market is Anglo–American, rates well below Henry Moore, t favourite of international exhibition juries. Of all the works listed Henry Moor 90-inch reclining bronze figure is the dearest, though at $160,000 it cost lit more than Giacometti's elongated and gimmicky *femme de Venise* which is no means on the monumental scale. But even Henry Moore's figure was n as was asserted in 1968, the dearest piece of modern sculpture sold in tl century. At £10,100 in 1913 the academic figure, *La danse* by Jean Bapti Carpeaux, was considerably dearer in real money terms.

Here then are some handsome tributes to the popularity of sculpture at most emancipated, yet the list prompts one very sobering reflection. I ha restricted it to sculptors who have on occasion reached the £5,000 region on the market of the 1960s. Since £5,000 in 1970 means no more than £625 meant in 1914, the restriction is not very severe. Yet out of 27 sculptors listed only 8 are still alive and the youngest of them is 57 years old.

| | | | £ |
|---|---|---|---|
| ALEXANDER ARCHIPENKO. 1887–1964 | | | |
| 1964 | D. | Green bronze torso, 18¾ in., 1921 | 1,900 |
| 1967 | S. | Another copy of the same | 4,000 |
| 1968 | N.Y. | Boxers, bronze abstraction, 1914, 23 in. high, $25,000 | 10,400 |
| | | Bluestein. N.Y. White torso, patined bronze, 1916, 18¾ in. high, $8,000 | 3,335 |
| | | Black seated torso, bronze, 1909, 15¼ in., $7,000 | 2,916 |
| | | Seated figure, bronze, 1913, 18 in. high, $9,000 | 3,640 |
| 1969 | S. | Book and vase on table, bronze relief, 1918, 18 × 13½ | 4,100 |

| | | | |
|---|---|---|---|
| JEAN ARP. 1887–1966 | | | |
| 1963 | S. | Abstraction in polychrome wood, 22½ in. high | 1,100 |
| 1965 | N.Y. | Torse chorée, polished bronze, 34 in. high, 1956, $9,000 | 3,216 |
| | | Evocation of a human form, marble, 1950, 33 in. high, $26,000 | 9,285 |
| | | Abstract composition in bronze, 1959, 36 in., $19,500 | 4,107 |
| 1966 | Thompson. N.Y. Sculpture mythique, stone, 1949, 25½ in., $8,500 | | 3,035 |
| 1967 | Epstein. N.Y. Outrance d'un outre, abstract bronze, 17½ in. high, $8,000 | | 2,820 |
| 1968 | N.Y. | Torso, polished bronze, 14 in. high, $8,000 | 3,335 |
| | | Torse-vase, 1963, bronze, 30 in. one of five, $15,000 | 5,416 |
| 1969 | S. | Vu et entendu, bronze (5 cast) 1942, 13½ in. | 4,500 |

| | | |
|---|---|---|
| ERNST BARLACH. 1870–1938 | | |
| 1963 | Hauswedel, Hamburg. The blind man, bronze | 2,750 |
| | S. Der singender Mann, bronze, 19½ in. high (see 1966) | 3,600 |
| 1965 | Cohn. N.Y. Der Einsame, 23-inch bronze, 1911, $10,000 | 3,572 |
| 1966 | Thompson. N.Y. Der singender Mann, bronze (see 1963), $15,000 | 5,365 |
| 1967 | N.Y. Moses with the tables of the Law, bronze, 1918, 20 in. high, $10,000 | 3,572 |

| | |
|---|---|
| CONSTANTIN BRANCUSI. 1876–1957 | |
| 1960 N.Y. The blonde negress, polished bronze, 15½ in., $40,000 | 14,270 |

£

| | | |
|---|---|---|
| 1960 | Lloyd Robinson. N.Y. Two penguins, marble group, $32,000 | 11,602 |
| 1961 | Brache. S. Abstract bronze, 1914 | 8,000 |
| 1965 | S. Cariatide, abstract in oak, 1915, 65½ in. high | 8,000 |
| 1966 | Helena Rubinstein. New York. Bird in space, brass, 20th casting out of 30, $140,000 | 50,000 |
| | The blonde negress, marble version, 1928, 30 in., $92,000 | 32,800 |
| 1967 | Farquhar. N.Y. Le baiser, plaster, 1908–10, 11 in. high | 8,214 |

GEORGES BRAQUE. 1882–1963

| | | |
|---|---|---|
| 1969 | N.Y. Hymen, 30½ in. high, one of six cast, stone, 1953, $27,500 | 11,680 |

REG BUTLER. 1913–

| | | |
|---|---|---|
| 1964 | Kloman. S. The unknown political prisoner, wire and metal, stone base, 17¼ in. high | 1,200 |
| 1966 | Thompson. N.Y. Girl with a vest, bronze 1953, 35 in. $7,750 | 2,765 |
| | 'Manipulator', bronze 1954, 67 in. high, $15,000 | 5,358 |
| 1967 | S. Girl tying her hair, one of 8 bronze casts, 18½ in. | 880 |
| 1969 | N.Y. Figure in space, 1954, bronze, 15½ in. high, $3,000 | 1,250 |
| | Man machine, bronze, 30½ in. long, $3,250 | 1,362 |
| | Roland. S. Girl taking off her shirt, bronze, 20 in. | 1,250 |

MARC CHAGALL. 1887–

| | | |
|---|---|---|
| 1963 | S. Les amoureux, marble, 22½ in. high | 5,200 |
| 1967 | S. Vase sans titre, coloured ceramic, 1962, 15¼ in. | 2,000 |

RAYMOND DUCHAMP-VILLON. 1876–1918

| | | |
|---|---|---|
| 1967 | Spingarn. N.Y. Femme assise, gilded bronze, 1915, 28 in., $25,000 | 8,928 |
| | Clarke. S. Horse and rider, semi-abstract, 1914, one of 8 bronze casts, 11 in. high | 1,800 |

JACOB EPSTEIN. 1880–1959

| | | |
|---|---|---|
| 1957 | S. Bronze head of Bernard Shaw (see 1963, 1968), 21¾ in. | 300 |
| 1958 | S. Genesis, original marble, 64 in. high | 4,200 |
| 1960 | Dolin. S. Head of Anthony, bronze, 16½ in. | 850 |
| | S. Lead modello for the Llandaff Christ | 800 |
| | Bronze bust, 'Mona' | 800 |

| | | £ |
|---|---|---:|
| 0 | C. Bronze head, Sholem Asch (see 1968) | 819 |
| | S. Bronze head, 'Kathleen' | 1,250 |
| 1 | S. Lead modello for Madonna and Child, 13¾ in. (see 1969) | 850 |
| | S. Bronze bust, Field Marshal Smuts | 1,100 |
| 3 | S. Bronze head of Bernard Shaw (see 1957, 1968) | 1,000 |
| | C. Bronze head of Churchill, 1946, one of 11 casts | 2,730 |
| | N.Y. Another cast of the same (see also 1966–8) | 3,840 |
| 4 | S. Clasped arms, marble, 1923, 36½ in. long | 1,800 |
| | Half-length bronze, Haile Selassie, 1936, 45 in. high | 2,300 |
| | Group of two doves, marble, 1914, 13¾ in. long | 2,000 |
| | Goodman. S. Bronze head, Albert Einstein, one of 10, 1933 (see also 1966, 1967), 20 in. | 2,100 |
| 5 | N.Y. Chaim Weitzmann, bronze bust, 1933, 18 in. | 1,518 |
| 6 | C. Bronze head of Churchill, 1946 (see 1963) | 5,040 |
| | S. Another copy of the same | 6,000 |
| | Albert Einstein (see 1964, 1967) | 4,800 |
| | (37 busts and heads made £28,310) | |
| 7 | Rosenthal. C. Albert Einstein, smaller version, 17 in. (see 1968) | 6,300 |
| | Leeds. N.Y. Churchill, bronze 1946 (see 1963, 1966) | 7,500 |
| 8 | Lewis. N.Y. ditto | 5,000 |
| | S. Another ditto | 5,500 |
| | C. Another ditto | 5,460 |
| | C. Albert Einstein, 17 in. 1933 (see 1967, 1969) | 5,460 |
| | Bernard Shaw, 1934, 17½ in. (£1,000 in 1963, £3,360 in 1967) | 3,150 |
| | N.Y. Joseph Conrad, 1924, 20 in. $9,500 | 3,958 |
| | N.Y. Sholem Asch, 1953, 15 in. head (£819 in 1960) | 1,458 |
| | Bronze half-length, 'Kathleen', 1948, 27½ in. high | 2,292 |
| | Arnold Brown. C. Haile Selassie, smaller version, 13¾ in. One of 6 casts, 1936 | 1,575 |
| 9 | N.Y. Bernard Shaw, bronze, 1934, 18½ in. high, $15,000 | 6,250 |
| | Lead modello for the Cavendish Square Madonna and child, 13½ in. high (see 1961, £850), $4,400 | 1,848 |
| | S. Esther with long hair, bronze, 1944, 19 in. | 3,000 |
| | Self-portrait, 1920, 15 in. bronze | 1,900 |
| | Rabinadrath Tagore, 1926, bronze, 19½ in. | 2,700 |
| | Ralph Vaughan Williams, 1950, bronze, 19½ in. | 1,500 |
| | Albert Einstein, 1933, bronze 21 in. (see 1964, 1966, 1967) | 5,000 |

PERICLE FAZZINI. 1913–

| | | |
|---|---|---:|
| 8 | Lewis. N.Y. La bagnate, bronze, 36 in. $15,500 | 7,455 |

£

**ALBERTO GIACOMETTI.  1901–1966**

| | | |
|---|---|---|
| 1962 | S.  Bronze head | 2,500 |
| 1964 | S.  La femme qui marche, one of 6 casts, 1933, 59 in. | 9,400 |
| 1965 | Zadok.  S.  Diego, l'homme au blouson, one of 6; 1954, 22 in. | 6,500 |
| | La demoiselle de Venise, bronze, 1956, 44 in. | 8,500 |
| | N.Y.  Two exceedingly elongated bronze figures, each $22,000 | 7,860 |
| 1967 | Epstein.  N.Y.  Head of Diego, bronze, 1961, 15½ in. | 8,928 |
| | C.  Another version, one of 6 casts, 16½ in. high | 8,610 |
| 1969 | C. (Geneva).  Le chien, one of 8 bronze casts, 1951, 36¼ in. long, FS380,000+5%tax | 38,364 |
| | N.Y.  Groupe de trois hommes 35 in., painted bronze, $100,000 | 42,333 |
| 1970 | N.Y.  Another version of the same, $90,000 | 37,500 |
| | Femme de Venise (1), painted bronze, 1956, 41¼ in. high, $150,000 | 62,500 |
| | Sylvester.  S.  Femme debout, bronze, 1960, 23½ in high | 17,000 |

**JULIO GONZALÉS.  1876–1942**

| | | |
|---|---|---|
| 1965 | Zadok.  S.  Montserrat II, mediaevalist bronze head, 1942, 13 in. | 4,800 |
| | N.Y.  Pointed head, bronze abstraction, 1930, 14¼ in. | 1,072 |
| 1967 | Lefèvre.  Paris.  Arlequin, iron construction, FN100,000 +tax | 9,248 |

**LUDWIG KIRCHNER.  1881–1958**

| | | |
|---|---|---|
| 1968 | Kornfeld, Berne.  Double bed, sculptured inlaid woods, FS35,000+tax | 3,900 |
| | Door, sculptured gesso reliefs on both sides, one of 7, cast posthumously in 1968, 70 in. high, FS108,000+tax | About  12,000 |

**HENRI LAURENS.  1885–1954**

| | | |
|---|---|---|
| 1963 | Aldrich.  N.Y.  Seated figure, bronze, 18 in. $4,500 | 1,607 |
| 1965 | Zadok.  S.  Luna, bronze figure, 13 in. 1948 | 2,600 |
| | N.Y.  Nature morte, painted stucco relief, 1923, 20×25¾, $7,000 | 2,500 |
| 1966 | Thompson.  N.Y.  Femme assise, bronze, 27½ in. | 5,500 |
| 1967 | Epstein.  N.Y.  Kneeling woman, one of 6 bronze casts, 1929, 14 in. high, $5,500 | 1,962 |
| | S.  Petite cariatide, one of 6 casts, 1930, 17¾ in. | 2,900 |
| 1968 | N.Y.  Le jour and la nuit, pair of bronze reliefs, 1937, numbered 2–6, 32×24½, $16,000 | 2 for  5,835 |

£

969  S.  Le grand adieu, bronze group, one of 5 casts, 1941,
28 in. high                                                    19,000

√ILHELM LEHMBRUCH.  1881–1919

962  C.  Terracotta female bust                                   3,675
965  Lempertz, Cologne.  Female bust in cast stone               7,370
968  Olsen.  N.Y.  Drei Dame, cast stone relief, 36×24 in.
1914, $10,000                                                 4,165
Ketterer, Munich.  Junglingskopf, 1913, red cement,
21½ in., 1913, DM43,000+tax                                   5,120
969  N.Y.  Geneigter Frauentorso, cast stone, 1913, 35½ in. high,
$13,500                                                       5,625

CQUES LIPSCHITZ.  1891–

965  Zadok.  S.  L'accordéoniste, bronze, 1918, 25½ in. high     5,800
966  S.  Femme assise, bronze, 1925, 18 in.                      2,400
968  Bluestein.  N.Y.  Mother and child, 1914, bronze, 23 in.
$22,000                                                       9,165
The meeting, 1914, bronze, 31½ in. high, $25,000            10,400
Seated man with guitar, bronze, 1922, 15¾ in. high,
$11,000                                                       4,560
Zacks.  N.Y.  Mother and child, semi-abstract bronze,
1941–5, 51½ in. high, $47,500                                19,790
C.  Femme à l'éventail, marked 2–7, bronze 26½ in. high       6,300
S.  Thesée, bronze, one of 3 casts, 1967, 26½ in.            6,500
969  N.Y.  Pierrot assis, unique lead casting, 12½ in. $14,000   5,870

RISTIDE MAILLOL.  1861–1944

957  S.  Portrait head of Renoir, bronze, 16 in.                   550
960  N.Y.  La jeunesse, bronze, $15,000                          5,380
963  Catzennstein.  S.  Baigneuse debout, bronze, 21¾ in.        1,500
965  Ira Haupt.  N.Y.  Etude pour la Montagne, terracotta
cast, 9¾ in. high, $7,500                                     2,675
N.Y.  Bronze nymph, 61½ in. high, $31,000                   11,080
La baigneuse, 1906, one of 6 bronze casts, 48½ in.
$20,000                                                       7,145
966  Helena Rubinstein.  N.Y.  Torso of a girl walking in
water, bronze, 44 in. high, $37,000                          13,250
967  Boyd.  S.  Baigneuse debout, bronze, 26½ in. (see 1968)     4,200
Paris.  Ile de France, academic nude, bronze, 33½ in. high,
FN69,000+tax                                                  5,510
968  N.Y.  Tête de Vénus, one of 5 bronze casts, 16 in. $7,000   2,918
Kingsley.  N.Y.  Victoire, bronze relief, 10×10½, numbered 10, $10,000                                             4,200

£

| | | |
|---|---|---|
| 1968 | Bluestein. N.Y. L'action enchainée, bronze, 1906, 12½ in. | 2,918 |
| | S. Eve à la pomme, one of 6 casts, 1899, 22¾ in. | 5,200 |
| | Leda, seated bronze figure, 1900, 11½ in. | 2,500 |
| | Danseuse saluant, bronze numbered 31, 9 in. | 9,000 |
| | Baigneuse a l'écharpe, bronze numbered 1–16, 1930, 13¾ in. | 9,000 |
| 1969 | N.Y. La Mediterranée, bronze, 6½ in. high, $12,000 | 5,040 |
| | Pomona vêtue, whole-length bronze, 35 in., 1922, $16,000 | 6,750 |
| | S. (Tokyo). Jeune Catalonienne, armless bronze figure, 1925, 2·95 million yen, 18½ in. high | 3,460 |
| | S. Study for monument at Port Vendres, bronze, 17 in. | 3,000 |
| | Standing figure, La France, bronze 19¾ in. high | 5,200 |
| | Kneeling girl, bronze 8 in. high | 9,500 |
| | Pomona vetue, bronze, c. 1922, numbered 7, 35 in., see above | 6,000 |
| 1970 | N.Y. Torse de jeune fille, marble, 1911, 28½ in., $30,000 | 12,500 |

GIACOMO MANZU. 1908–

| | | |
|---|---|---|
| 1962 | S. Giant female figure, ebonized wood | 2,800 |
| 1964 | S. Self-portrait with model, 1946, bronze, 18½ in. | 2,050 |
| 1967 | N.Y. Madre e Bambino, bronze bas-relief, 14×17½, $5,250 | 1,875 |
| 1968 | Lewis. N.Y. Cardinale seduto, bronze, 22 in., $20,000 | 8,332 |
| | S. Standing cardinal, 1956, unique bronze cast, 12¼ in. | 5,200 |
| | MacLennan Morse. N.Y. Il fauno e la nymfa, unique bronze cast, 1965, 31½×15¾×8¼, $15,500 | 5,542 |
| 1969 | S. Crucified Christ, supposed unique cast, bronze, 15½ in. | 2,800 |
| | Striptease, unique bronze, 1965, 21¾ in. high | 5,000 |

GERHARD MARCKS. 1889–

| | | |
|---|---|---|
| 1965 | N.Y. African queen, 45-inch bronze, 1953 | 4,620 |
| 1968 | N.Y. Mutter und Kind, bronze, 52¼ in. 1957, $21,000 | 8,750 |
| 1967 | Gildea. N.Y. Halbbekleidete Maja, 43¾ in. bronze, 1952, $6,500 | 2,285 |
| 1968 | N.Y. Drei Grazien, bronze, 1956, 22½ in. high, $5,250 | 2,170 |
| | Venus binding her hair, bronze 1960, 56¼ in. high, $10,000 | 4,168 |
| 1969 | N.Y. Seraphine, die liebliche Giraffe, 1955, bronze 41 in. high, $9,500 | 3,992 |
| | Hirero Konigin, bronze 1955, 45 in. high, $15,500 | 6,512 |
| | Afrikanischer Ram, bronze 48 in. long, 1963, $15,000 | 6,300 |
| | Gefesselter Prometheus II, bronze 1948, 31 in. high, $11,000 | 4,620 |

| ARINO MARINI.  1901– | £ |
|---|---|
| •64 S.  Pomona, bronze, 11 in. high | 1,400 |
| •65 Zadok.  S.  Bronze horseman, 35 in. 1946–7 | 7,200 |
| •67 Olsen.  N.Y.  Horse and rider, bronze, 59½ in. | 8,214 |
| •68 Lewis. N.Y.  Horse and rider, bronze, 39 in. $39,000 | 16,250 |
| S.  Miracolo, bronze, 55¾, one of 6, painted red | 6,600 |
| 69 N.Y.  Another example of the same, $18,000 | 7,560 |

| ENRI MATISSE.  1869–1954 | |
|---|---|
| •60 Ahrenberg.  S.  Seated nude, bronze, 31½ in. 1922–5 | 11,000 |
| Figure décorative, bronze, 1908, 28¾ in. | 8,000 |
| Les deux négresses, bronze (see 1965), 1908, 18½ in. high | 5,200 |
| 49 Bronzes were sold for £109,600 | |
| •63 S.  Nu assis, Olga, bronze, 1910, one of 10, 17 in. high | 2,800 |
| Tête de Jeanette, bronze, 1910–13, 24½ in. high | 2,600 |
| Aldrich.  N.Y.  Nu assis, bronze, 17 in. $13,000 | 4,644 |
| •65 S.  Les deux négresses, bronze, 18½ in. (see 1960) | 6,000 |
| N.Y.  Le Serf, bronze, 1900, 36 in. high, one of 9, $29,000 | 10,360 |
| •66 Thompson.  N.Y.  Figure décorative, one of 10 bronze casts, 28 in. high, $45,000 | 16,070 |
| S.  Jaguar dévorant un lièvre, one of 10 bronze casts in the style of Barye, c. 1900, 22½ in. long | 2,200 |

| MADEO MODIGLIANI.  1884–1920 | |
|---|---|
| •62 Paris.  Head in stone, FN100,000+tax | 8,085 |
| •66 C.  Girl's head, one of 10 bronze casts, 9¾ in. high | 1,260 |
| •68 Paris.  Another girl's head, one of 10 bronze casts, 9¾ in. high, FN70,000+tax | 6,500 |

| ENRY MOORE.  1898– | |
|---|---|
| •60 Gregory.  S.  Seated girl, stone, 1931, 17¾ in. high | 2,800 |
| N.Y.  Reclining nude, bronze, 28 in. | 3,380 |
| Mother and child, stone, 34 in. high | 2,400 |
| C.  Reclining female figure, alabaster, 8½×18½ | 5,775 |
| S.  Mother and child, bronze, 1956, 7½ in. high | 1,500 |
| •61 Juvilier.  N.Y.  Reclining figure, stone | 6,430 |
| •62 S.  Bronze seated high-relief figure, 1957 | 2,200 |
| Pleydell-Bouverie.  S.  Bronze group of two women seated with child, 1945 | 2,700 |
| •63 S.  Girl seated against a square wall, bronze, 1958 (see 1965) | 2,800 |
| Goodman.  S.  Family group, bronze (see 1964 and 1968) | 6,500 |

£

| 1964 | C. The same, one of 7 cast, 15¼ in. high, 1947 (see 1968) | 7,350 |
| | N.Y. Girl seated against a square wall, bronze, 1958 (see 1963, 1965), $8,750 | 3,125 |
| 1965 | N.Y. The same, $23,000 | 8,214 |
| | Avnet. N.Y. The ladderback rocking chair, 8½ in. bronze, one of edition of 9 (see 1967) | 5,000 |
| | Seated nude, 1957, bronze, 58½ in. $41,000 | 14,643 |
| | Seated woman, bronze, 41½ in. $33,000 | 11,786 |
| 1966 | Thompson. N.Y. Bird and egg, alabaster, 22 in. | 6,114 |
| | Seated woman, bronze, 41 in. high, $47,000 | 17,000 |
| | Whitney Museum benefit. N.Y. Mother and child against an open wall one of 12, 9 in. high, $22,150 | 7,910 |
| | S. Upright interior form, bronze, 1951, 30½ in. high | 7,000 |
| 1967 | S. Three motives against a wall, no. 2, bronze. One of 10 casts, 1959, 43 in. long | 4,300 |
| | Levee. S. Reclining figure, 1957, one of 12, length 27½ in. | 7,000 |
| | Seated torso, 1956, one of 9, height 16 in. | 6,500 |
| | Benenson. N.Y. The Ladderback rocking chair, bronze, 8½ in. (see 1965), $13,000 | 4,642 |
| | Clarke. N.Y. Figure against a curved wall, 9 in. One of 12 bronze casts. $15,000 | 5,353 |
| | Olsen Foundation. N.Y. Reclining figure, 36 in. high, one of 7, cast in 1953, $34,000 | 12,145 |
| | Lempertz, Cologne. Three standing figures, single bronze casting, 1953, 29 × 12, DM90,000 + tax    About | 11,000 |
| 1968 | Lewis. N.Y. Two seated girls against a wall, one of 10 bronze casts, 1960, 19½ in. high, $21,000 | 8,796 |
| | Raxlen. N.Y. Reclining figure, 90 in. long, one of 3 cast in 1951, $160,000 | 67,150 |
| | Olsen. N.Y. Mother and child, bronze, 20¼ in., one of 7 cast in 1953, $17,000 | 7,085 |
| | N.Y. Family group, bronze, 15¼ in., 1947, $38,000 (see 1964) | 16,165 |
| | C. Reclining figure, 1938, lead, 2¾ in. high, 5¼ in. long | 3,990 |
| | N.Y. 'Two piece no 10' newly cast, 1968, 36 in. long, $31,000 | 8,700 |
| 1969 | C. Seated figure, one of 7 bronzes cast in 1949, 9 in. | 10,500 |
| | Family group, one of 7 bronzes cast in 1944, 7 in. | 10,500 |
| 1970 | N.Y. Reclining figure, No. 4, black-patined bronze, 1954, 23 in., $52,500 | 21,875 |
| | Maquette for reclining figure, 6½ in., $14,500 | 6,042 |

## ELIE NADELMANN.   1882–1946

£

1966 Helena Rubinstein.   N.Y.   Plaster horse, 32 in., 1911       6,280
     Plaster bas-relief, two nudes, 1911, 37½ × 49½, $9,000    3,215
1967 S.   Hermaphrodite, bronze, 1905, 15 in.                    1,600
1969 N.Y.   Femme debout, bronze, 1906, 15 in. $8,000            3,333

## PABLO PICASSO.   1881–

1957 Weinberg.   N.Y.   Head of a man, semi-abstract bronze     1,050
1959 S.   Bronze head of a woman                                 2,550
1966 Thompson.   N.Y.   Le coq, one of 6 bronze casts, 1932,
     26 in. high, $49,500                                        17,678
     S.   Figure in Polynesian style, one of 12 bronze casts, 1907   1,200
1968 N.Y.   Head of a man, bronze, 1905, 6¾ in., $7,250          3,020
     S.   Le taureau, bronze, 1962, 4½ in. long, one of 12       2,800
1969 S.   Figurine, wood, Polynesian style, 1907                 5,100
     Head of Max Jacob as a clown, realistic bronze, 1905,
     16 in.                                                      23,000

## GERMAINE RICHIER.   1904–1959

1966 S.   Sablier au soleil, grand couple, enamelled bronze, 55 in.
     high                                                        11,500
1967 S.   Don Quixote, bronze, 21 in. high                       5,000
     Epstein.   N.Y.   La sauterelle, bronze, 23¾ in. $8,000     2,855
     S.   Don Quixote and the windmill, bronze, one of 11
     casts, 1949, 21 in.                                         5,000
     Le pentacle, one of 6 casts, 1954, 32 in. high              3,000
1968 S.   Don Quixote and the windmill, another version, one of
     8 casts, 1949, 20¼ in.                                      2,200

## OSSIP ZADKINE.   1890–1967

1963 S.   Portrait head of a man, ebony, 13 in.                  150
1965 N.Y.   Seated female musician, bronze, 19 in. $6,000        2,170
1966 N.Y.   Femme à la colombe, bronze, 1928, 31 in. $5,500     1,964
1968 N.Y.   Il Penseroso, painted wood, length 80 in. $18,000    7,915
     Miami Museum.   N.Y.   Musicians, 1924, bronze, 22½ in.,
     $7,500                                                      3,125
     S.   Woman with a lute, bronze, 16½ in.                     2,500
1969 S.   Adam and Eve, bronze, 24¼ in. high                     2,500
     Femme a l'éventail, 1914, cast in 1920, 34¼ in. high        4,000
     Retour de la fille prodigue, bronze group, 1950, 30¼ in.    4,400

**PART III**

# OBJETS D'ART

# ARMS AND ARMOUR
## ARMOUR

Till the late 1920s armour was an essential part of every rich man's collection. So long as the high Renaissance meant the supreme achievement of the European tradition, armour was Europe's greatest contribution to the art of working in metal. Completeness was the highest prize, however it might be achieved. Thus at the Earl of Pembroke's sale in 1921 Duveen paid £25,000 for a 16th century Greenwich suit, *Cap à pie*, which he was able to sell to Clarence McKay of New York. The buying price was equivalent to £125,000, the selling price only to be conjectured, but in any case something that could not have been repeated in the 1960s. There has been, however, since the mid-19th century an essentially learned market for the bits and pieces which have survived from the genuine combattant armour of the 15th century. This market, now restricted to a much smaller band of enthusiasts, retains its splendid medieval vocabulary which sprinkles the sale-catalogues with bascinets, burgonets and salets, with couters, vambraces and chanfrons. This is still a live market, whereas 16th century parade armour has fallen on evil days, following the general comprehension that a *Cap à pie* suit or even a half-suit must invariably have been cannibalized or restored. As to the bits and pieces which are capable of a moderate response to the impact of inflation, the greatest prize remains, today, as in the mid-Victorian period, those rare survivors of late 14th century battle armour, the *hounskulls* or pig-faced bascinets of the Tyrol. To trace their progress briefly, the example in the Metropolitan Museum cost £425 in 1888, the equivalent of £3,800. In 1939 the Tower Armories paid £2,730, the equivalent of £13,700. In 1965 Sotheby's sold an example, lacking the pig-face vizor, for £9,000, an inadequate advance, since it is improbable that another will ever be sold.

The subtle curves of plain steel battle-armour have not escaped the amateurs of 'significant form'. It is far otherwise with armour designed as ornament. At the dispersal of the Pierpont Morgan armour in 1916 Duveen was said to have paid $100,000 for the *Negroli casque*, a most Leonardesque affair in the form of a monster. The price can be equated with £164,000, though one cannot imagine the casque making more than a sixth as much in 1970. The amateurs of chased steel have concentrated on pistols rather than hats.

|  |  | £ |
|---|---|---|
| 1961 | Dunraven Limerick.  S.  Fluted and etched half-suit, Greenwich, *c.* 1570 | 850 |
|  | S.  Milanese barbute or gladiator helmet, late 15th century | 1,100 |
| 1962 | S.  *Armet à rondelle*, Milanese helmet, late 15th century (£490 in 1929, £65 in 1946) | 620 |
| 1964 | Earl of Harrington.  S.  Half-suit, Milan, *c.* 1590, style of Pompeio della Chiesa | 1,250 |
|  | *Cap à pie* suit by Pfeffenhauser, Augsburg, *c.* 1580 | 5,900 |

£

| | | |
|---|---|---|
| 1964 | Fischer. Lucerne. *Cap à pie* suit with tilted vizor, Milan, *c.* 1570 | 2,665 |
| | Countess Craven. S. Breast and burgonet of Maximilian II by Frauenpreis and Sorg, *c.* 1550 | 2,400 |
| 1965 | Barnett (ex Ockwells Manor). S. Couter and vambrace for the left arm, Italian, 15th century | 2,200 |
| | Early 16th century Italian chanfron | 800 |
| | Armet à rondelle by Giovanni di Salimbene, *c.* 1490 | 2,800 |
| | *Hounskull* bascinet, Tyrolese, *c.* 1380, lacks its pig-faced vizor (others at £2,730 in 1939, £1,005 in 1904, £425 in 1888) | 9,000 |
| | Pair of Milanese sablons, 15th century (Tower Armories) | 3,500 |
| | Milanese vizored salet, *c.* 1450 (Tower Armories) | 4,000 |
| | Armet a rondelle, German, *c.* 1515 | 1,900 |
| | German composed *Cap à pie* suit, *c.* 1520 | 1,900 |
| | S. Tilting helmet, Daniel Hopfer, Augsburg, 1530 | 2,000 |
| | Fischer. Lucerne. Tilting suit of the Duke of Pless, German, late 15th century, with complete helmet, FS240,000+tax | 23,000 |
| 1966 | Fischer. Lucerne. Part horse-armour by Pompeio della Chiesa, Milan, *c.* 1570, FS45,000+tax | 4,300 |
| | Haldane. C. German *Cap à pie* suit, *c.* 1630, much restored | 650 |
| | Lord Bossom. C. Maximilian half-suit, *c.* 1530 | 1,365 |
| 1967 | S. Two 15-inch embossed plaques from the 'snake armour' of Henri II by Etienne Delaune, *c.* 1556–9 | 1,650 |
| 1968 | Kevorkian. S. Mamluq silver damascened spiked helmet, mark of St Irene Arsenal, Istanbul, 16th century | 2,100 |
| | Another Mamluq silver damascened spiked helmet, with same mark | 850 |
| | S. Salet, Milanese, 2nd half 15th century | 2,200 |
| 1969 | C. Composite fluted Maximilian suit, *Cap à pie* but largely restored, *c.* 1520 | 1,417 |
| | Chanfron, style of Negroli, Milan, *c.* 1580 | 546 |
| | Lord Waleran. C. Italian *Cap à pie* suit, bright steel, some restorations, *c.* 1560, on dummy | 1,417 |

### SWORDS AND OTHER HAND ARMS

Early in 1970 the Dresden Historisches Museum sold one of the most richly mounted swords ever to reach the open market and the price at Sotheby's, £21,000, was worthy of the occasion. But in the 1960s swords, unless they were Japanese, and reputed medieval, did not command a lively market. For instance, the presentation dress-swords of the Napoleonic wars must rank among the finest metal chasing produced in this country, those presented by the Lloyd's Patriotic Fund in particular. The cheaper type, gilded and enamelled but not jewelled, cost the donors £50, the equivalent in 1970 of at least £650. So their value has hardly increased at all despite rarity and great historical importance.

| | | £ |
|---|---|---|
| 1960 | Carrington-Pierce. S. Presentation sword, 1781, by James Shrapnell | 500 |
| | C. Plain 13th century sword (excavated) | 441 |
| 1962 | C. Presentation enamelled sword, 1805, Trafalgar £100 model | 441 |
| 1963 | Hamilton. S. Presentation enamelled sword, 1800 | 1,000 |
| 1964 | S. Indian presentation sword, early 19th century, jewelled gold fittings | 1,100 |
| | Harrington. S. Flemish swept-hilt rapier, c. 1600 | 800 |
| 1966 | S. Ceremonial arrow-head, Bohemia, late 15th century, 12 in. long, Metropolitan Museum | 950 |
| | Stirling. C. Presentation sword, jewelled and enamelled, Ray and Montague, 1807 | 1,312 |
| | Redmill. S. Presentation enamelled and gilt sword, 1805 | 1,100 |
| 1968 | S. Presentation gold-mounted dress sword, c. 1800 | 650 |
| | S. Presentation sword, 1809, Lloyd's Patriotic Fund, £50 type | 800 |
| | Dresher. D. Neapolitan left-hand dagger, 22 in. c. 1650 | 1,100 |
| | Christie. N.Y. Silver-mounted plain sword by I. Clark, Boston, c. 1750, 37½ in., $4,000 | 1,625 |
| 1969 | S. Venetian *schiavona*, silver-studded hilt, 18th century | 640 |
| | C. Presentation sword, 1806, Lloyd's Patriotic Fund, £50 type | 945 |
| | Debenham Storr. Presentation sword, given to Viscount French in 1920, jewelled gold hilt | 1,700 |
| | S. Presentation sword, 1800 (capture of the *Hermione*) richly chased and enamelled gold hilt by Rundell, Bridge (cost 300 guineas) | 2,900 |
| | Presentation small sword, 1821, restored gold hilt | 580 |
| | C. German crossbow, elaborately inlaid, early 17th century | 693 |
| | Swept-hilt rapier, N. Europe, c. 1630 | 609 |
| | Presentation militia sword by Thomas Hamlet, c. 1808 | 462 |
| | S. Swept-hilt sword, numerous mythological figures in chiselled steel, ex Royal Armoury, Madrid, mid-16th century | 3,000 |
| 1970 | Historisches Museum, Dresden. S. Swept-hilt rapier, hilt in chased and jewelled gilt-bronze by Israel Schuech, | |

|      |                                                                                 | £       |
|------|---------------------------------------------------------------------------------|---------|
| 1970 | blade by Martinez, Toledo, 1606                                                  | 21,000  |
|      | Rapier, blade signed Andrea Ferraro, hilt by Wolf Paller, Dresden, d. 1583       | 7,000   |
|      | Estoc sword, cross-hilt of blackened iron, silver etched pommel, late 16th century | 6,000 |
|      | Owens-Thurston. C. Naval presentation sword, 1814                                | 378     |

### FLINT-LOCK AND WHEEL-LOCK PISTOLS, 16TH–17TH CENTURIES

As long ago as 1884 Count Basilevsky was believed to have paid 60,000 francs or £2,400 for a 16th century musket *à pied de biche*. It may be that so rare an item might make its 1970 equivalent, namely £20,500, but ancient firearms of fine workmanship or special rarity have been a relatively expensive taste for more than a hundred years. It cannot be said that they partook of the wilder market movements of the 1960s. Yet more people collected old firearms than ever before. As in the case of all classes of *objets d'art* that are still within the reach of the small collector, the more modest relics of the past went up much more in proportion than the show-pieces.

|      |                                                                                          |       | £         |
|------|------------------------------------------------------------------------------------------|-------|-----------|
| 1961 | S. German wheel-lock petronel, 1581                                                      |       | 2,100     |
|      | Milan wheel-lock pistol, c. 1530 (both bought by Tower Armories)                         |       | 360       |
| 1962 | Howard Vyse. S. Wheel-lock petronel fowling piece, 1612                                  |       | 2,600     |
| 1963 | S. Pair of wheel-lock pistols, Brescia, 1640                                             | 2 for | 2,550     |
| 1964 | Dagobert Runes. S. German wheel-lock pistol, c. 1570                                     |       | 2,300     |
|      | Pair of Dutch wheel-lock pistols, c. 1650                                                | 2 for | 3,800     |
|      | Wheel-lock pistol, carved horn reliefs, Nuremberg, c. 1570                               |       | 2,300     |
|      | Pair of wheel-lock pistols, Hans Stockmann, Dresden, c. 1610 (£42 in 1929)              | 2 for | 3,600     |
|      | Double-barrelled wheel-lock pistol, Christian Platz of Lignitz, c. 1570                 |       | 2,000     |
|      | Double-barrelled wheel-lock pistol, Dresden, c. 1610, 31 in. long                        |       | 5,000     |
|      | Augsburg wheel-lock pistol, c. 1580, 19¼ in.                                             |       | 2,300     |
| 1965 | Fischer, Lucerne. Pair of wheel-lock pistols by Comminazzo of Brescia, 1670, FS26,000+tax | 2 for | 2,500   |
| 1966 | Fischer, Lucerne. Pair of wheel-lock pistols by Felix Werder, Zurich, c. 1640, 22 in. long, FS26,000+tax | 2 for | 2,500 |
|      | Paris. Pair of wheel-lock pistols, Nicolas Vincent, Toul, c. 1650                        | 2 for | 3,713     |
|      | Chapman. C. Scottish heart-butt belt-pistol, 1710                                        |       | 1,207 10s. |

| | | £ |
|---|---|---|
| 67 | Rosenbach Foundation. S. German sword-stick, combining a wheel-lock pistol, late 16th century | 3,200 |
| 68 | C. Pair of flint-lock belt-pistols, 16 in. long, by Jacques Lesconnet, *c.* 1650       2 for | 1,470 |
| | Phillips, son and Neale. *Snap-haunce* pistol with lemon-shaped butt of Scottish type, incomplete | 4,000 |
| | Combined wheel-lock pistol and war-hammer, mid-16th century, S. Germany | 2,000 |
| | C. Wheel-lock hose pistol, 21½ in. marked CH 1591. S. German | 2,310 |
| | Wheel-lock hunting rifle, 1st quarter 17th century, 34 in. | 1,217 10s. |
| | Knight, Frank. Wheel-lock breech-loader sporting rifle, South German, 1702 | 1,750 |
| 69 | S. Double wheel-lock gun, superimposed load, German, *c.* 1600, length 40 in. | 7,000 |
| | S. (at Gleneagles Hotel). French wheel-lock carbine, richly inlaid, late 16th century, 32 in. long | 1,200 |
| | S. South German wheel-lock carbine, 32 in., *c.* 1590 | 1,000 |
| | Pair of S. German wheel-lock holster pistols, 23 in. long, chased the length of the barrels, *c.* 1570     2 for | 6,000 |
| | Paris. Flint-lock pistol, Lyons, 1636–40, superimposed barrels, 25¼ in., FN50,500+tax | 4,715 |
| 70 | Historisches Museum, Dresden. S. Ball-butt pistol by Klaus Hirt of Wasungen, octagonal barrel, 23 in. Late 16th century | 5,800 |
| | Another ditto 22 in. | 4,800 |

## DUELLING PISTOLS, REVOLVERS AND SHOTGUNS, 18TH–19TH CENTURIES

Colt revolver of 1847 can make as much as so rare an object as a late 16th century double-barrelled wheel-lock. This scale of values which would have seemed crazy in the 1930s, is part of the fairly recent cult of romantic machinery which includes model locomotives, vintage cars and aeroplanes, and even traction engines and agricultural machines. Most of the objects in this list have, however, some aesthetic appeal. The early 19th century duelling pistols with their cases and accessories are miracles of craftsmanship and even the Colt of the Wild West had perforce to be a thoroughly workmanlike job, free of the cumbrous fussiness of that age. As to shotguns, made later in the 19th century, their value, if still serviceable and impeccably maintained, is determined by their replacement cost. A pair of Purdeys, made to order with minimal decoration, cost in 1969 not less than £2,600.

| | | £ |
|---|---|---|
| 60 | Greener. S. Colt 'second model' revolver and pocket revolver. New York, 1849     2 for | 2,100 |

1960   C.   Pair of early 19th century duelling pistols by J.   £
Murdoch, arms of Clinton    2 for   2,155

1961   C.   Pair of Collier percussion revolvers, unrecorded design
   2 for   787 10s
     Pair of Colt presentation dragoon revolvers, case and
accessories    1,785

1962   Lynedoch.   S.   Pair of duelling pistols, Nicolas Boutet,
Versailles, 1818    2 for   500

1964   Astor.   C.   Pair of flint-lock target pistols by the same,
fitted case, 16½ in. long (see 1968)    2 for   2,310
     Routledge.   S.   Pair of flint-lock target-pistols by
Manufre, Versailles, early 19th century    2 for   1,600
     S.   Dragoon-revolver by Samuel Colt, New York, no. 134   850
       Colt revolving rifle by Paterson, New Jersey, no. 154   960
       Belt revolver by Paterson    1,300

1965   S.   Pair of 18th century Scottish flint-lock pistols    1,500
     C.   Pair of duelling pistols, Joseph Manton, c. 1830   2 for   1,470

1966   Rougement.   C.   Pair of flint-lock holster pistols by
Boutet, Versailles, c. 1800, fitted case    1,940 10s
     Paris.   Rifle made in Brazil, 1817, for Jaime VI of Portugal,
with tax    3,372

1967   Philips, son and Neale.   Pair of flint-lock breech-loader
pistols by Jouvet, Paris, 1780    2 for   4,000
     C.   Pair of Scottish all-steel flint-lock pistols by Thomas
Cadell, c. 1750    2 for   3,360
     S.   Pair of holster flint-lock pistols, by Griffin, mid 18th
century    2 for   1,500
     C.   Pair of proto-revolvers, 'seven-shot single action flint-
lock pepperbox', by Mairet, Artiste aux Ponts, Paris,
c. 1760, 11½ in. long    2 for   4,830
       Pair of 16-bore shotguns, percussion back-action by
Dickson of Edinburgh, case and accessories, unused,
late 19th century    2 for   1,102 10s
     S.   Colt Whitneyville dragoon revolver, 1847, no. 1024   4,200
       Pair of flint-lock presentation pistols by Bennett and
Lacy, 1811, in Oriental style    2 for   3,000
       Pair of flint-lock pocket pistols, 6½ in., Mahay, Paris,
1740    2 for   3,200
     Roy Cole.   C.   Pair of flint-lock target pistols by Boutet,
Versailles, c. 1789–1809, 16½ in. long (see 1964)    2 for   7,140

1969   S.   Pair of flint-locks by Griffin and Tow, London, 1774,
with case and accessories    2 for   1,200
     C.   Flint-lock target pistol, octagonal barrel, heavily
chased by Nicolas Boutet, Versailles, and Le Page, Paris,
c. 1815    1,890

| 1969 | | £ |
|---|---|---|
| Flint-lock double-barrelled over and under pistol by Joseph Egg, Piccadilly, no. 2169, 1820 | | 1,417 |
| Pair of flint-lock duelling pistols, case and fittings by Manton, c. 1815 | 2 for | 1,680 |
| Hartford Colt dragoon revolver, no. 123, London, fittings and case, c. 1850 (compare Colt revolvers, sold in 1964) | | 2,205 |
| Mauser automatic pistol, presentation model, richly chased, New York, 1896 | | 945 |
| S. Pair of miniature holster pistols, 10 in. long, by la Roche, Paris, 1750 | 2 for | 1,700 |
| Pair of holster pistols by Heylin, Cornhill, 14 in. long, c. 1780, incomplete | 2 for | 1,200 |
| Knight, Frank. Pair of sidelock ejector shotguns by Purdey, late 19th century | 2 for | 1,900 |
| S. Pair of flint-lock dress pistols, hexagonal chased barrels, Marshall, Edinburgh, c. 1820, 10½ in. long | 2 for | 1,500 |
| Pair of German flint-lock pistols, hunting scenes etc., c. 1760–80, 17 in. long, Metropolitan Museum | 2 for | 1,000 |
| C. Pair of modern 12-bore hammerless ejectors by Holland and Holland (bought by the makers) | 2 for | 1,155 |
| Pair of flint-lock hunting rifles, etched octagonal barrels, 18th century, believed Austrian | 2 for | 966 |
| Marquess of Tweeddale. C. Flint-lock fowling piece, French, early 18th century, heavily chased, 41 in. | | 2,415 |
| Eccles. C. 7-barrelled box-lock pepperbox revolver, signed Twigg, London, 1790s, 9¾ in. long | | 1,837 10s. |
| S. Pair of presentation flint-lock pistols in case with fittings, Gregory, London, 1830, 18 in. long | 2 for | 4,000 |

# CARPETS
### EUROPEAN

The most expensive carpets on the market in the 1960s were not Oriental at all but French. Three large 18th century French carpets in the coarse but highly durable weave of the Savonnerie factory made prices in the £25,000 region, six times as much as any Persian carpet of the classic period. Possibly the market will see no more of this size and quality but the advance was largely optical. Like the French furniture that matched them, carpets of this kind had been almost as dear in real money terms in the early years of the century. For instance in 1912 Christie's sold a 25-foot Savonnerie carpet of the reign of Louis XIV for £2,730, equivalent in 1970 to £21,800. There was nothing that added more magnificence to an 18th century décor than these carpets, yet they had become worthless as soon as they were out of fashion. At the Gwydyr sale of 1829 a big Savonnerie carpet with a 'chiaroscuro' centre made 20 guineas at Christie's.

|      |                                                                                                              | £      |
|------|--------------------------------------------------------------------------------------------------------------|--------|
| 1960 | C.  18th century Spanish needlework carpet, 32 ft × 20 ft                                                     | 3,045  |
|      | Chrysler.  N.Y.  Aubusson armorial carpet, much repaired, 19½ × 26½ ft (Stowe sale, 1848, £21)               | 715    |
|      | Penard y Fernandez, Paris.  Louis XVI Beauvais carpet                                                        | 10,640 |
|      | Elton.  S.  Green-ground Axminster, c. 1820, 21 × 13½ ft. Bought Francis Dupont Museum                       | 2,100  |
| 1961 | Sala.  N.Y.  Savonnerie, c. 1760, $32,500                                                                     | 11,600 |
|      | Berberyan.  N.Y.  Bessarabian Aubusson, c. 1840, 20¼ × 13 ft                                                 | 3,570  |
|      | Savonnerie, early 18th century, 17¼ × 14 ft                                                                   | 3,215  |
|      | Axminster, c. 1790, 28¾ × 18¾ ft                                                                              | 3,400  |
| 1963 | Ionides,  S.  Axminster, c. 1790, 21¼ × 17 ft                                                                 | 3,300  |
|      | ditto, 17 × 11¾ ft                                                                                            | 2,700  |
|      | Mrs Derek Fitzgerald.  Axminster, c. 1790, 30¾ × 19¼ ft                                                       | 1,700  |
|      | Fribourg.  S.  Aubusson, c. 1790, 21¼ × 19 ft                                                                 | 4,100  |
|      | S.  Circular Aubusson, c. 1820–30, 21 ft 10 in. diam.                                                         | 1,150  |
| 1964 | Paris.  Savonnerie, Régence period, 1715–23, 17 ft 6 in. × 10 ft 4 in., FN350,000+tax                        | 27,965 |
|      | Berberyan.  N.Y.  Moorfields, c. 1780, 28 × 21 ft, $20,000                                                    | 7,140  |
|      | Paris.  Black ground Savonnerie, Louis XVI, 16 × 9¾ ft. FN305,000+tax                                        | 24,370 |
|      | Philips, son and Neale.  Savonnerie, mid-19th century, 23 ft 9 in. × 13 ft 9 in.                              | 1,850  |
| 1965 | Earl of Shrewsbury.  C.  The Ingestre Moorfields carpet, 34 ft 8 in. × 14 ft 2 in. (bought-in, 1959, £12,500)| 5,250  |
|      | Mrs Hamilton Rice.  Paris.  Savonnerie, Louis XV, (FN370,200 including tax)                                   | 26,890 |
| 1966 | N.Y.  Savonnerie, Louis XVI, 14 × 10 ft 7 in. ($32,500)                                                       | 11,600 |

| | | | |
|---|---|---|---|
| 1966 | S. | Spanish in Moorish tradition, 16th century, 13 ft 10 in. ×9 ft 9 in. | £ 4,200 |
| 1967 | C. | Savonnerie, Directoire period, 24×15 ft | 3,990 |
| | | Watney. C. (at Cornbury Park). Axminster, *c.* 1860, 26×16½ ft (2 square cut out) | 1,365 |
| | | Viscount Clifden. S. Axminster, late 18th century in Savonnerie style, *tête de nègre* ground, 15 ft 11 in.× 11 ft 2 in. | 3,200 |
| | | S. Spanish corridor carpet, late 17th century, 12×7½ ft. (repaired) | 1,700 |
| | | Portugese needlework carpet, 17th century, 27 ft 2in.× 17 ft 1 in. | 5,400 |
| | | N.Y. Savonnerie, late 18th century, 35×15 ft | 2,500 |
| 1968 | C. | Tufted English carpet, *c.* 1840, 26¼×14¼ ft | 1,680 |
| | | Springfield. C. English heraldic carpet, perhaps Norwich, dated 1571, 7 ft 5 in.×7 ft 3 in. | 2,940 |
| 1969 | S. | Modern Savonnerie, *tête de nègre* ground, 27 ft×21 ft | 3,000 |
| | | Modern Savonnerie, ivory ground, 16 ft×13 ft 2 in. | 1,200 |
| | | Late 19th century Bessarabia, brown ground, 21×8½ ft | 3,400 |
| | | Fribourg. N.Y. Savonnerie, Louis XVI, 16×12½ ft, $4,750 | 1,980 |
| | | Another 15 ft×12 ft 5 in., $7,000 | 2,916 |
| | | C. Axminster in Savonnerie style, early 19th century, 22 ft 3 in×17 ft | 2,730 |
| | | Designed by the firm of William Morris, late 19th century, 18 ft×15 ft | 598 10s. |

## ORIENTAL, ANTIQUE: 15TH–19TH CENTURIES

Till the very end of the decade this remained a mere shadow of a market. There was little scholarly predilection for carpets hundreds of years old, patched, rewoven or worn to a ghost as inevitably they must be. Even museums were shy of objects that presented such awkward problems of space and conservation. Small rugs in reasonable condition and capable of use, showed some response to the impact of inflation. Ghiordes prayer-rugs for instance, worth from £40 to £80 in the 1920s, could cost £400 to £900 in 1965–70. But the Ispahans, Kirmans and Indo-Persians, more than a century older and awkward in size, showed no such increase. In 1927–8 three 16th century carpets passed through the salerooms at prices over £20,000. There was nothing of equal importance in the 1960s but it is unlikely that such carpets would make equivalent prices in 1970, that is to say, from £103,000 to £115,500 each. They might not greatly exceed that £22,000 carpet in the Kevorkian sale of 1969, which was by no means a 16th–17th century object, though it seemed to herald a new range of prices.

| | | | |
|---|---|---|---|
| 1960 | S. | Azerbaijan silk rug with verses in praise of Nadir Shah, dated 1745 | £ 800 |

| | | £ |
|---|---|---|
| 1960 | C. Needlework carpet, 18th century made at Goa for Lord Clive | 2,995 |
| | Myron Taylor. N.Y. Hispano-Mauresque, 17th century, over 23 ft long | 1,606 |
| | 14 ft Persian hunting carpet, 16th century | 3,213 |
| 1961 | S. Ispahan, c. 1600 (ex Austrian imperial family), 23 × 8 ft | 3,000 |
| 1963 | Maharajah of Jaipore. S. Lahore, 17th century, 36 ft 9 in. × 12 ft 11 in. | 3,200 |
| | S. Kula rug with dragon pattern, 17th century (compare 1969) | 2,000 |
| | Anatolian 'Holbein' carpet, 16th–17th century | 880 |
| | Indo–Persian hunting carpet, 24 ft 10 in. × 13 ft, 17th century | 1,600 |
| 1965 | Fribourg. S. Chinese 18th century carpet, yellow ground, 18 ft 4 in. × 15 ft 8 in. | 950 |
| | S. Indo–Persian hunting carpet, 17th century, 23 ft × 13¾ ft | 1,900 |
| | 'Siebenbürgen' rug, c. 1700, 5 × 4 ft | 700 |
| | Konia (Anatolia) runner 16 × 7 ft, 18th century | 1,250 |
| | Other Anatolian rugs, £550 to £750, Ghiordes, Ladik, Kula etc. | |
| | Adda. Paris. Spanish 17th century runner, 13 ft 9 in. × 6 ft 8 in. | 4,795 |
| | Indo–Persian, 17th century runner, 13 ft 9 in. × 6 ft 8 in. | 4,795 |
| | Indo–Persian fragment, 17th century, 6 ft 6 in × 6 ft 3 in. | 1,530 |
| | 16th century Ardabil prayer rug, 61 × 44 in. | 2,397 |
| 1967 | Alexandrine de Rothschild. S. 16th century Ispahan velvet, gold and silver threads, 4 ft 6 in. × 6 ft 8 in. | 2,500 |
| | Russell. S. 16th century Indo–Persian corridor runner, very worn, 24 ft 8 in. × 9 ft 10 in. | 1,500 |
| | Farrow. S. Lahore floral rug, 17th century, 6 ft 11 in. × 4 ft 9 in. | 5,000 |
| 1968 | Paris. 'Polonaise' rug, 17th century, 78 × 69 in. (FN63,000 + tax) | 5,950 |
| | Another ditto 108 × 69¼ in., FN67,000 + tax | 6,253 |
| | Another ditto 110 × 61½ in., FN51,500 + tax | 4,805 |
| | Another ditto 78½ × 56½ in., FN40,000 + tax | 4,745 |
| | N.Y. Tabriz prayer rug with Mihrab and trees, 5 ft 5 in. × 3 ft, $10,000 | 4,140 |
| | S. Ushak, c. 1600, 9 ft 10 in. × 6 ft 7 in. | 950 |
| 1969 | S. So-called dragon carpet, Kula, 17th century, 17 ft × 8 ft 4 in. | 3,800 |
| | Kula prayer rug, 9 ft × 5¼ ft, 17th century | 1,500 |

| | | | £ |
|---|---|---|---|
| 1969 | S. | Seven Kula and Ghiordes prayer rugs 5 ft to 6½ ft long, 17th–18th centuries, made from £400 to | 720 |
| | | Ghiordes prayer rug, c. 1700, 5 ft 9 in. × 4 ft 3 in. | 900 |
| | | Holroyd-Reece. S. Indian in Ispahan style, called 18th century, 14 ft × 11 ft 5 in. | 2,600 |
| | | Kevorkian. S. 'Shah Abbas' Persian carpet, c. 1600, wine red field, 25 ft 10 in. × 10 ft 3 in., so described | 22,000 |
| | | Another 'Shah Abbas' Persian carpet, c. 1600, wine red field, 15 ft 9 in. × 6 ft 11 in., Metropolitan Museum, N.Y. | 5,600 |
| | | So called Kurdish carpet, 19th century Persian with traditional Herati design, 29 ft × 9 ft 7 in. Islamic Museum, Berlin | 4,000 |
| | | 'Polonaise', early 17th century, 8 ft × 4 ft 4 in. | 7,900 |
| | | Another 'Polonaise', early 17th century, 6 ft 9 in. × 4 ft 9 in. | 6,600 |
| | | Mughal shaped carpets, a pair, 14 ft 8 in. × 8 ft 8 in. 2 for | 7,400 |
| | | N.W. Persian, animals and medallions, c. 1700, 15 ft 6 in. × 8 ft 5 in. | 7,500 |
| | | Mughal flower carpet, mid-17th century 15 ft × 9 ft 10 in. | 4,800 |
| | | 19th century trellis-and-cypress Yoshagan, 15 ft 8 in. × 8 ft 4 in. | 4,200 |
| | | 22 carpets made £90,000. | |

## LATE 19TH CENTURY AND MODERN

A large part of this list consists of reproductions of the classic Persian styles of the 16th–17th century, and it will at once be perceived that they can cost as much or more than the originals. Condition is everything and no notice is taken of the utter lifelessness of the imitation. The Koun Kapou copies in particular, quite a small example of which made £3,400, look as if the patterns have been repeated by some sort of machine, though in fact they represent hand-craftsmanship at its most laborious. They were made in small numbers at an Armenian factory in the suburbs of Istanbul in the early 1900s and cost over £100 on the local market even then. The metal threads seem to be the attraction, whereas in the slightly older establishment at Hereke the speciality was something peculiarly horrible, namely designs shorn in relief.

| | | £ |
|---|---|---|
| 1961 | Tabriz silk carpet, over 14 ft long | 1,400 |
| 1963 | Tabriz, 30½ ft × 18½ ft | 1,450 |

| | | £ |
|---|---|---|
| 1963 | Berwind. N.Y. 19th century silk Tabriz, 25 ft 4 in. × 17 ft 6 in. | 3,125 |
| 1965 | S. Herez silk tile-pattern carpet, 11 ft 10 in. × 8 ft 10 in. | 2,500 |
| | C. Kashan silk carpet, 10 ft 3 in. × 6 ft 8 in. | 1,417 10s. |
| | Philips son and Neale. Sarouk carpet, 16 ft 8 in. × 10 ft | 1,450 |
| | S. Three embossed silk Kashan carpets, 70 to 100 sq ft., each of them | 1,200 |
| | Hamilton Rice. N.Y. Tabriz carpet, 40 ft long | 4,250 |
| | Tabriz, 10 ft 1 in. × 7 ft 7 in. | 2,800 |
| 1966 | S. Herez silk carpet, 11 ft 7 in. × 7 ft 3 in. | 1,800 |
| 1967 | S. Koun Kapou silk and metal thread, 7 ft 7 in. × 4 ft 9 in. | 1,800 |
| | Hereke silk and metal thread, 6 ft 9 in. × 4 ft 5 in. | 1,200 |
| | Farrow. S. Koun Kapou silk and metal thread, 5 ft 3 in. × 3 ft 7 in. 2 for | 3,600 |
| | Single Koun Kapou silk and metal thread, 5 ft 10 in. × 3 ft 11 in. | 1,700 |
| | Koun Kapou tile carpet, 9 ft 8 in. × 6 ft 11 in. | 3,400 |
| | C. Herez silk carpet, 9 ft 6 in. × 6 ft 8 in. | 1,890 |
| | Ian Anderson. C. Hereke silk carpet, Ispahan style, 6 ft × 3 ft 3 in. | 1,680 |
| | N.Y. Tabriz silk carpet, 24½ ft × 15 ft | 2,500 |
| 1968 | C. Tabriz silk carpet, 16th century style, 14 ft 9 in. × 10 ft 2 in. | 2,520 |
| | de Mendos. N.Y. Silk Tabriz rug with inscriptions in 17th century style, 5 ft 5 in. × 3 ft 10 in., $10,500 | 4,333 |
| 1969 | S. Hereke silk and metal thread, 6 ft 6 in. × 4 ft 4 in. | 1,150 |
| | Ghiordes silk prayer rug, 5 ft 7 in. × 4 ft 1 in. | 1,200 |
| | Kemsley. S. (at Dropmore). Agra in Shah Abbas style, 23 ft × 15 ft | 5,600 |
| | Agra in Shah Abbas style, 25 ft 5 in. × 15 ft 8 in. | 4,200 |
| | Agra in Shah Abbas style, 18 ft 6 in. × 10 ft 8 in. | 4,600 |
| | C. Silk Tabriz, 11 ft 4 in. × 8 ft 1 in. | 1,680 |
| | Silk Herez pole-medallion carpet, 15 ft 10 in. × 10 ft | 3,990 |
| | Silk Tabriz, 12 ft × 9 ft 3 in. | 2,940 |
| | Glen-Allen. S. Tabriz, 21 ft 3 in. × 15 ft 6 in. | 2,900 |
| | Norris. S. Agra, 16 ft 3 in. × 12 ft 11 in. | 1,500 |
| | C. Agra, Indo–Persian style, 23 ft × 12 ft | 3,990 |

# CHINESE ART
## POTTERY, T'ANG DYNASTY AND EARLIER
### (i.e. not later than 10th century A.D.)

A set of six T'ang dynasty dancing maidens, one of the best ever sold, made £58 at the Burnett sale of 1941. In 1966 three musician figures of the same size reached 2,630 guineas at Christie's. This is no more than an average increase for T'ang pottery. An enormous saddle horse, $32,000 in 1969, might have made $200 with difficulty in the depressed 1930s. A cream glazed amphora, which cost £5,040 in the same year, might not have exceeded £20.

This startling recovery of T'ang burial pottery, which surpasses even in real money terms the enthusiastic prices of the early 1920s, has not been very critical. It ignores the high probability that there are other areas in Honan where standard grave furniture still awaits the spade in unknown quantities. Equally it ignores the ease with which moulded objects may be copied and elementary glazes reproduced. A mass-exportation by a Chinese government, hungry for foreign currency, might burn some fingers—and deservedly. The matricidal process of denigrating the European heritage had long over-reached itself. A glance at the list of Italian Renaissance sculpture sales (page 389) will show what treasures of original modelling in plaster or terracotta by disciples of the greatest masters of the *Quattrocento* could be bought in the 1960s for far less than the cost of some of these mass-produced funeral dolls. In November, 1969, the entire press appeared to accept one of the silliest handouts ever produced, a new world's record for a piece of pottery (as opposed to porcelain) because a T'ang horse had been sold for £16,000. The price of the *flambeau* of Henri Deux ware or St Porchaire in the Fountaine sale of 1884 was rather more than double, when expressed in *that* sort of money. But artistically and historically, its interest was about tenfold, compared with this steed among tens of thousands of stable-companions.

|  |  |  | £ |
|---|---|---|---|
| 1960 | S. | Glazed galloping horse with female rider | 380 |
| 1961 | S. | Two small light-glazed T'ang horses | 620 and 600 |
|  | C. | Light-glazed pawing horse | 2,200 |
| 1962 | S. | Horse in mottled glaze. Prinzessehof, Leewarden | 600 |
|  |  | Horse and rider, lightly glazed | 600 |
|  |  | Porter and pack, lightly glazed | 580 |
|  |  | Large glazed Bactrian camel. Aberdeen University Museum | 580 |
|  |  | Horse and rider with drum, lightly glazed | 660 |
|  |  | Han dynasty wine vase, irridescent green glaze | 580 |
|  | C. | Pair of unglazed lady musicians 2 for | 1,260 |
|  |  | Pair of polo players, 12½ in. 2 for | 1,260 |
| 1963 | Shriro. S. | Mottled glaze alms-bowl | 1,300 |
| 1964 | Lady Mitchell. S. | Polo player, unglazed, mounted at a flying gallop | 3,500 |

| | | | £ |
|---|---|---|---|
| 1965 | S. Cream-glazed horse, 14 in. | | 1,300 |
| | Randon-Bennett. S. Unglazed figure, described as an Armenian (Schoenlicht sale, 1955, £100) | | 560 |
| | S. Pair of glazed equestrian figures, 16½ in. high | 2 for | 1,600 |
| 1966 | Lempertz, Cologne. Saddled horse, straw-coloured glaze, 33 in. high, DM21,000+tax (compare 30 in. example, 1969) | | 2,180 |
| | Adgey-Edgar. S. Pair of glazed equestrian figures, 15½ in. high | 2 for | 2,300 |
| | C. Three kneeling girl musicians, unglazed, 6½ in. | 3 for | 2,761 10*s.* |
| | S. Standing horse, 19 in. mottled glaze | | 1,500 |
| 1967 | S. Standing horse, cream-glazed, 18 in. high | | 1,700 |
| | Standing horse, brown-glazed, 20 in. high | | 1,700 |
| | Chow. C. Horse with foreign rider, 14 in., bought in | | 840 |
| | N.Y. Painted unglazed figure, Wei dynasty, 29½ in. | | 1,570 |
| | C. Begging bowl, mottled glaze, 8 in. diam., bought in | | 1,895 |
| | S. Pair of mottle-glazed male figures, 34 in. high | 2 for | 850 |
| 1968 | S. 'Hsing ware' ewer, 8½ in. | | 800 |
| | Larson. S. Mottle-glazed camel, 22¼ in. high | | 900 |
| | S. Recumbent horse, Wei dynasty, 7¾ in. long, unglazed | | 1,100 |
| | Potiche jar and cover, mottled glaze, 8½ in. high | | 3,800 |
| | C. Squatting lion, white glaze, 8½ in. high | | 525 |
| | Pair of mottle-glazed standing T'ang mourners, hands folded, 41½ in. high (£700 in 1962) | 2 for | 2,940 |
| | S. Standard 11 in. unglazed saddle-horse | | 600 |
| | Delawarr. C. T'ang saddle-horse, glazed, splashed brown, 11½ in. | | 2,310 |
| 1969 | S. Bactrian camel, brown and straw-coloured, 20¼ in. high | | 1,700 |
| | Saddle-horse, brown and yellow glaze, 19 in. high | | 1,850 |
| | C. Amphora with dragon handles, cream glaze, 22½ in. high | | 5,040 |
| | Adgey-Edgar. S. Pair of unglazed kneeling girl musicians, 7¾ in. high (compare 1966) | 2 for | 1,700 |
| | S. Straw-coloured T'ang horse, 13¼ in. high | | 1,600 |
| | Samuel. S. Mottled T'ang horse, 18¼ in. high | | 1,600 |
| | Unglazed saddle horse, traces of paint, 11 in. called Sui dynasty | | 1,029 |
| | S. 15 in. olive green jar, 'proto-porcelain' Han dynasty | | 1,500 |
| | Lady Dodds. Unglazed red camel, T'ang dynasty, with a dubious rider, 19 in high | | 3,400 |
| | Wilson. S. Pair of green glazed ducks, alleged T'ang dynasty, 5½ in. high | 2 for | 1,850 |
| | N.Y. Saddle horse, 30½ in. high, cream glaze, mottled saddle and trappings, $32,000 | | 13,333 |
| | S. A similar beast, 23 in. high | | 16,000 |

| | | | £ |
|---|---|---|---|
| 969 | S. | Ewer in cobalt blue lead-glaze with cut down spout, 8½ in. | 6,000 |
| | | White *Hsing* ware ewer, T'ang dynasty, ovoid body, lion's head handle and short spout (compare 1968), 7½ in. high | 3,200 |
| | | Tripod globular jar, standard T'ang mottled glaze, 6¾ in. high | 4,800 |
| | C. | Unglazed pacing horse, 20½ in. high | 3,360 |
| | | Pair of straw-coloured mourning figures, 23½ in. high 2 for | 1,680 |
| 970 | Backhaus. C. | Standing female glazed figure, 24 in. | 7,500 |

# CHINESE ART

## POTTERY AND PORCELAIN, SUNG AND YÜAN DYNASTIES, A.D. 960–1368

Before the discovery of 'early Ming' in the 1930s the enlightened collecto
escaping from *famille verte* and *famille rose* in export styles, was expected
collect Sung wares. The prizes of this market were the 'numbered Chu
pieces and, in a lesser degree, Tzu Chow painted pottery, incised white T'i
bowls and the celadon jars with moulded dragons, called Kinuta in Japan. A
else was within reach of the unambitious collector of modest means. Mo
recently the stampede for *objets d'art* as an investment has promoted sever
types, formerly quite cheap, into the millionaire class. Numbered Chun, bes
with doubts, has lost its supremacy. Carved white T'ing ware now vies, le
understandably, with moulded Northern celadon of sombre olive-green con
plexion. The Northern celadon bowl which made £8,190 in 1965, might n
have reached £100 fifteen years earlier. The little narcissus bowl of lavender
ware which staggered everyone in 1970 at £46,000, might then have been r
dearer. Common burial-pottery may remain in fair supply for some time
come, but the Sung wares of realy beauty and quality are clearly a rapid
advancing market and must remain so, unless the produce of new excavatio
reaches the West. That, however, is a very real possibility in a country so mu
at odds with its own traditions as the new China.

|      |                                                                                                                  | £     |
|------|------------------------------------------------------------------------------------------------------------------|-------|
| 1959 | S. *Ju* ware narcissus bowl on four feet, 8¾ in. wide (see 1970)                                                  | 2,100 |
| 1960 | Charles Russell. S. *Kinuta* celadon vase with solid dragons                                                     | 1,750 |
|      | Pair of moulded and combed Northern celadon bowls, 6¼ in. diam.                               2 for             | 2,300 |
| 1962 | C. *Mei P'ing* shaped vase, *Ching p'ai* ware, 13th century                                                      | 2,310 |
| 1963 | Shriro. S. Similar vase, 9½ in. high                                                                             | 2,100 |
|      | Pair of moulded *shu fu* bowls, red glaze, late 13th century                                   2 for             | 1,750 |
|      | *Kuan* ware square-shaped bowl, 3¾ in. diam.                                                                     | 1,200 |
|      | Moulded Northern celadon bowl                                                                                    | 850   |
|      | Norton. S. Saucer dish, lavender *Chun* ware, 8 in. diam.                                                        | 900   |
|      | *Kuan* ware bowl, 3¾ in. diam.                                                                                   | 1,200 |
| 1965 | Pollen. S. Moulded T'ing saucer dish, 12 in. diam. (£225 in 1948)                                                | 1,900 |
|      | Fuller. C. Northern celadon moulded shallow bowl with peony, 7¼ in. diam., J. D. Rockefeller III collection      | 8,190 |
|      | *T'ing* ware dish, incised with flowering branch, 8 in.                                                          | 1,155 |
|      | Randon-Bennet. S. *T'ing* ware saucer dish with single peony (£200 in 1955)                                      | 500   |
| 1966 | S. *T'ing* ware carved white bowl, 13 in. diam.                                                                  | 2,300 |
|      | Desmond Gure. C. Pair of moulded Northern celadon bowls, 5½ in. diam.                          2 for             | 4,830 |

| | | | | |
|---|---|---|---|---|
| 1966 | Aykroyd. S. *T'ing* ware white carved bowl, 8½ in. diam. (£340 in 1955) | | £ | 1,600 |
| 1967 | C. Pair of Northern celadon moulded bowls, 5½ in. | 2 for | | 2,310 |
| | Chow. C. *Tzu Chow* white incised *mei p'ing* vase, 17 in. high | Bought in at | | 1,575 |
| | *Tzu Chow* carved and inscribed vase, uncertain age, 30½ in. high (£1,050 in 1970) | Bought in at | | 3,150 |
| | Plain *Chun* bowl, 8¾ in. diam. | | | 1,417 10s. |
| | Funerary urn jar, alleged *Yueh* ware | | | 966 |
| | N.Y. Purple *Chun* ware bowl, 7¾ in. diam. $5,000 | | | 2,085 |
| 1968 | S. Pair of moulded Northern celadon shallow bowls, 7 in. diam. | 2 for | | 1,600 |
| | C. Figure of Kuan Yin, 11½ in. high, *Ching p'ai* ware of the Yüan dynasty. Victoria and Albert Museum | | | 892 10s. |
| | S. Carved *T'ing* bowl, 8¾ in. diam. (Ezekiel sale, 1946, £235) | | | 4,000 |
| | Sedgwick. Carved white *T'ing* bowl, 8¾ in. diam. (Traugott sale, 1957, £450) | | | 6,500 |
| | Northern celadon incense burner on squatting figures heavily repaired, 7¼ in. × 7¼ in. | | | 3,000 |
| | Carved *T'ing* white bowl, 8 in. diam. | | | 1,500 |
| | *Shu fu* bowl, greenish glaze, Yüan dynasty, 8 in. diam. | | | 1,100 |
| | S. *Lung Chuan* celadon dish, relief dragon, Yüan dynasty, 14½ in. diam. | | | 560 |
| 1969 | Ephrussi. S. Grooved cylindrical tripod jar, green glaze, 7¾ in. high | | | 1,500 |
| | S. *T'ing* dish, incised dragon, 7¾ in. | | | 1,200 |
| | Filliol. C. Alleged *Ch'ing p'ai* group, Yüan dynasty, Putai and companion, 7 in. high | | | 787 10s. |
| | N.Y. Korean *mei p'ing* vase, inlaid celadon, 12th–13th century, 15½ in. high, $4,100 | | | 1,738 |
| | Tokyo. C. Pair of incised Northern celadon bowls, 5½ in. diam. 3 million yen | 2 for | | 3,504 |
| | S. 'Kinuta' celadon vase with coiled dragon and lid, 10½ in. high (compare 1960) | | | 4,400 |
| | Hobart. N.Y. Korean celadon lotus-shaped incense burner, 8 in. high, $9,000 | | | 3,750 |
| | Southern *Kuan* incense bowl, flattened shape, 4¾ in. diam., $5,000 | | | 2,082 |
| | Korean inlaid celadon winepot, Koryo dynasty, 6½ in. high, $19,000 | | | 7,917 |
| | Bowl in same style, 7¼ in. diam., $3,000 | | | 1,250 |
| | S. Pair of incredibly hideous vases with appliqué figures in Ch'ing pai glaze, 33 in. high, possibly Yüan dynasty | 2 for | | 1,600 |

433

£

1969  C.  Celadon trumpet-necked vase, 24½ in. Yüan dynasty  1,417 10s.
Hobart.  N.Y.  Pair of combed and moulded Northern
celadon bowls, 5½ in. diam., $7,000    2 for  2,917

1970  Plesch.  S.  Narcissus bowl, lavender *Ju* ware on four feet,
damaged, 8¾ in. wide (£2,100 in 1959)    46,000
C.  Northern celadon moulded and combed dish, 11¾ in.  5,250

# CHINESE ART
## PORCELAIN, MING DYNASTY, 1368–1644

arly Ming' was one of the most exciting sections of the art market in the
60s. Yet most of the objects in the ensuing lists represent the very opposite of
tzy taste, as manifested in Kaendler figures at £13,000 or Augustus the Strong
ses at £16,000 the pair. Richness and colour play very little part in determin-
g the prices in this market which is dominated by blue and white. On the
her hand there is nothing very wild about early Ming, nothing *outré* to
ivate the intellectual *avant garde* like Kava bowls and wooden idols from the
.cific islands. Early Ming is learned and analytical in its appeal, certainly not
rer than European ceramics of the same age and very much more repetitious.
et the eight most expensive ceramic objects, sold in the 1960s, were all of them
rly Ming porcelain. At £16,500 to £27,300, nothing European, either of the
me age or of the period of the great porcelain factories, could approach any-
here near them.

In the course of the 1960s Chinese porcelain of the 14th, 15th and early
th centuries was capable of multiplying its paper-money value ten times
er, but in reality the movements, recorded in this list, are much smaller than
ose of the previous decade. In 1950 early Ming porcelain had scarcely ad-
nced since the 1930s, when collectors first began to compete seriously for it.
150 in 1950 could have bought practically anything, whereas late Ming por-
lain had sometimes fetched very much more. No one could have predicted in
50 that early Ming blue and white would approach the £3,000 mark in a
atter of seven years, still less that it would reach £25,000 in fifteen years. The
eed with which the normal pace of the art market was overtaken remains
en now partially a mystery. No one knows what proportion of the ensuing
ts went straight into museums, but some of the dearest items were certainly
ught for private individuals. It is nevertheless the requirements of museum
rectors that have called the tune. Before the First World War, in the heyday
' the incredibly priced *famille noire* and *famille jaune*, it was the brash taste of
illionaires which determined what the American museums would get from
em. Since the new U.S. fiscal laws it is the museums which determine what
e millionaires shall buy. This largely accounts for the unexpected predomin-
ce of an essentially learned and highly specialized taste. It does not, however,
plain why so many things of immeasurably greater artistic importance
ould be less sought by museum directors. A great deal of the bidding for early
ing porcelain has been pure stamp-collecting. A six-inch bowl, sparsely de-
rated in under-glaze blue, rose from £36 in 1940 to £16,500 in 1967. A
h'eng Hua mark on a blue and white piece, which can be trusted as an authen-
: 15th century original, has turned out to be rarer than was supposed, and this
least was the prettiest example of its kind. But there is no reason at all why it
ould be worth more than an important white glazed sculpture by Andrea
lla Robbia.

It is true that comparable aberrations took place during the First World War

in the dispersal of Pierpont Morgan's porcelain, when *famille noire* vases of o
moderate aesthetic merit were bought at the price of Rembrandts. This was
hang-over of a tradition, as old as individual wealth, which valued lavish
above genius. That tradition is now all but dead, but it is pedantry rather tl
taste that seems destined to fill the void.

More even than in the case of the purchasers of T'ang burial pottery, on
struck by the optimism of the purchasers of early Ming porcelain. Writing
the *Burlington Magazine* in 1948, the late Mr Edgar Bluett denied that the s
vivors were unusually numerous. He suggested that the number of thi
pieces, identified with the period 1402–35 at a recent exhibition of the Orie
Ceramic Society, might be multiplied by three to obtain the number
genuine pieces in the entire world. Most of the thirty pieces in the 1946 exh
tion must by now be frozen off the market, while specimens from the Chir
national collections, which should account for a large part of this authori
estimate, have certainly not been released since 1946. Yet what was the situat
in the 1960s? My list (by no means complete) includes 26 examples which b
the mark of the nine-year reign of Hsüan-Tê (1426–35), and 47 more, whi
though unmarked, are identical in style with the marked pieces, and wh
were sold at 'Hsüan Tê prices'. In fact every year could be relied on to prod
seven or eight in the saleroom, pieces of imperial or mandarin quality, q
exclusive of peasant or export wares—and all this from a period of nine ye
half a millennium ago.

It has been suggested that the mark of Hsüan Tê continued to be used a
the emperor's death, that furthermore an analysis of glaze bubbles has reve
several blood-groups among a seemingly homogeneous selection. But
bubbleologists do not postulate a span of years beyond the middle-15th c
tury. So, even in view of these second thoughts (by no means univers:
shared) the annual number of saleroom offerings from the nine-year reign c
tinues to be a lively miracle.

### MONOCHROME PIECES

| | | £ |
|---|---|---|
| 1960 | Peter Boode. S. White stem-cup with unique mark of T'ien Shun (1457–64), 4½ in. diam., Rijksmuseum, Amsterdam | 2,600 |
| 1962 | Nathan. S. Underglaze red 14th century saucer (see 1967) | 2,100 |
| | S. Plain white 15th century dish, 15½ in. diam. | 900 |
| 1963 | Norton. S. Engraved white bottle, 12½ in. high, attributed to reign of Yung Lo (1404–25) | 3,800 |
| | Plain yellow saucer, attributed late 15th century | 2,200 |
| | Plain yellow bowl, mark of Chia Ching (1522–66) | 1,600 |
| | White bowl, slight relief, believed early 15th century | 4,000 |
| | White dish, incised dragon, 6½ in. diam. Hung Chih (1488–1505) | 2,000 |
| | Yellow bowl, 8 in. diam. Hung Chih mark | 2,100 |

£

| 1963 | S. Yellow bowl, 8 in. diam. Chia Ching mark (1522–66) | 1,900 |
| 1965 | Evill. S. Yellow bowl, mark of Wan Li (1573–1619), 7 in. diam. | 1,400 |
| 1966 | S. White saucer, incised dragon, 6¼ in. diam. Hung Chih mark | 1,800 |
| 1967 | S. White bowl, 8¼ in. diam. ascribed Yung Lo (1404–25) | 1,800 |
| | 14th century saucer, relief under copper red (see 1962) | 2,600 |
| | Heavy bowl, mottled blue, 10¼ in. diam. Hsüan Tê mark (1426–35) | 4,200 |
| 1968 | S. Turquoise dish, 6 in. diam. Hsüan Tê mark (£380 in 1963) | 3,800 |
| | Palmer. S. 15th century dish, 'sacrificial red,' 6¾ in. diam. | 2,900 |
| | 15th century dish, 'sacrificial red,' 8½ in. diam. Hsüan Tê mark | 4,200 |
| | 16th century yellow dish, mark of Chia Ching, 7 in. | 950 |
| | Blue dish, mark of Wan Li (1573–1619), 10 in. diam. | 1,400 |
| | Sedgwick. S. White dish, flanged rim, traces of gilding 15th century, 14 in. diam. | 1,500 |
| | S. Sacrificial red dish, Hsüan Tê mark, under 6 in. diam., fissured | 700 |
| 1969 | S. Yellow saucer dish, mark Hung Chih, 8½ in. diam. (1488–1505) | 1,995 |
| | Yellow saucer dish, mark Chêng Té, 8¾ in. diam. (1506–21) | 1,785 |
| | Hobart. N.Y. White scalloped dish, 14th century, lobed rim, 11½ in. diam. $3,750 | 1,562 |
| | C. Another ditto but much superior, 7¾ in. diam. attributed Yung Lo (1403–24) | 3,360 |
| | S. Pair of yellow saucer dishes, 7 in. diam. mark of Chêng Té (1506–22) 2 for | 1,700 |
| 1970 | S. White bowl with incised decoration, 6½ in. high, attributed Yung Lo (1403–24) | 5,200 |
| | C. (Tokyo) 15th century ewer, unmarked, bluish white with slight engraving, 13½ in. high, 13 million yen | 15,046 |

### DECORATED IN UNDERGLAZE RED ON WHITE
#### 14th–15th centuries

| 1961 | Decroos. C. 18 in. dish, 14th century | 2,730 |
| | S. 14th century platter, 7¾ in. diam. (see 1965) | 780 |
| | Garner. S. Cut-down 14th century bottle | 520 |
| 1962 | Palmer. S. Ewer, 14th century, 13 in. high | 8,800 |
| | Platter, 14th century, 7¾ in. diam. | 1,300 |
| 1963 | Norton. S. Stem cup, early 15th century, white dragons on red | 4,400 |

| | | |
|---|---|---:|
| 1965 | Fuller. C. Platter, lobed rim, 7½ in. diam., 14th century (see 1961) | 2,100 |
| 1967 | C. Baluster vase, 21½ in. high, damaged, 14th century, Bought in | 6,090 |
| 1968 | Sedgwick. S. Cut-down bottle, 14th century, 12 in. high (compare 1961) | 1,900 |
| | S. Dish, 18 in. diam., 14th century with plantain centre, half effaced | 1,800 |
| | David Foundation. S. Tub-shaped bowl with two dragons, both underglaze red and blue. Hsüan Tê mark, 6¾ in. diam. | 3,500 |
| 1969 | Hobart. N.Y. 14th century platter, lobed rim, 7¾ in. diam. (compare 1961, 1962, 1965), $7,500 | 3,125 |

### BLUE AND WHITE, LARGE DISHES
#### 14th–15th centuries

| | | |
|---|---|---:|
| 1960 | S. Palace dish, stylized lotuses, 15¼ in. | 580 |
| 1961 | Mackenzie. C. Palace dish, bunch of grapes, 15 in. | 1,155 |
| 1962 | David. S. Palace dish, tree and plant combinations, 25 in. | 2,700 |
| | Palmer. S. Palace dish, stylized lotuses, 17 in. | 2,600 |
| 1963 | Norton. S. Palace dish, water-plants, and ribbons, 10¾ in. (see 1967) | 1,450 |
| | Philips son and Neale. Pair of palace dishes with bunch of grapes pattern (£136 in 1936) 2 for | 3,800 |
| | 2nd Norton sale. Palace dish, stylized lotuses, 16 in. | 1,800 |
| | Scott Taggart. S. 14th century dish, 18 in. (£680 in 1958) | 3,200 |
| | S. Palace dish, two peonies in scrolls, 17½ in. diam. | 2,500 |
| 1964 | Wistrand. S. Palace dish, waterplants and ribbons, 15½ in. | 1,900 |
| | Stylized lotuses, 16½ in. diam. | 1,250 |
| | Evill. S. Palace dish, grapes pattern, rim reduced, 14¾ in. | 1,200 |
| | David. S. With Hsüan Tê mark, loquats and other fruits, 18 in. | 3,100 |
| 1965 | Evill. S. Palace dish, waterplants and ribbons, 13 in. | 2,600 |
| 1966 | S. Palace dish, bunch of grapes pattern, 15 in. | 3,200 |
| 1967 | S. 14th century dish, 18½ in. diam., 17th century incised ownership mark of Mughal Emperor Jehangir | 7,000 |
| | Hoskyns. S. Palace dish, bunch of grapes pattern, 17¼ in. | 3,200 |
| | C. Palace dish, stylized lotuses, 15 in. (compare 1960) | 3,150 |
| | Wakefield. S. Palace dish, stylized lotuses, 13½ in. unusual border | 3,200 |
| | Chow. C. Palace dish, waterplants and ribbons, 15¾ in. | 5,040 |

| | | £ |
|---|---|---|
| 1968 | Burnett. C. Palace dish, stylized lotuses and ribbons, 17 in., badly damaged | 787 10s. |
| | Sedgwick. S. 14th century dish with cock-pheasants, 18 in. diam., damaged (£330 in 1958), Victoria and Albert Museum | 4,500 |
| | Palace dish, 14¾ in., stylized crysanthema, damaged | 900 |
| | C. Palace dish, waterplants and ribbons, 17½ in. diam., bought in | 3,360 |
| | David Foundation. S. Palace dish, grapes pattern, 15 in. | 4,500 |
| | Palace dish, petalled rim, stylized lotuses, 13¼ in. | 4,000 |
| | S. 14th century dish, 18 in. diam., broken in two Bought in at | 1,200 |
| 1969 | Modynos. S. Palace dish, bunch of grapes pattern, petalled rim, 16½ in. diam., weak colour | 4,400 |
| | S. (Tokyo). Palace dish, waterplants and ribbons, 16 in. diam., 5·3 million yen | 6,222 |
| 1970 | S. Palace dish, stylized lotuses, 15¼ in. diam. (similar 1960, £580) | 6,800 |

### BLUE AND WHITE, OTHER SHAPES

| | | |
|---|---|---|
| 1960 | C. Massive 14th century jar (*kuan*), British Museum (compare 1969) | 2,520 |
| 1961 | S. Bowl with Portuguese emblems, c. 1520 | 1,800 |
| | Much damaged ewer, arms of Portugal upside down, c. 1520 | 500 |
| | 15th century *Mei p'ing* vase (£95 in 1954) | 880 |
| 1962 | S. Stem cup, 2½ in. high, mark of Hsüan Tê (compare 1966) | 310 |
| | Nathan. S. 14th century saucer dish with spout, under 7 in. diam. | 2,700 |
| | S. 15th century jardinière, octagonal | 1,100 |
| | 14th century platter, 7¾ in. diam | 1,400 |
| | Dish with Arabic inscriptions, mark of Chêng Tê (1506–22), see 1968 | 2,200 |
| 963 | Norton. S. Early 15th century *mei p'ing* vase and cover with tree motifs | 8,000 |
| | *Lien tzu* bowl, late 15th century (£16 in 1937) | 2,700 |
| | 15th century water sprinkler (see 1967, 1968) | 1,350 |
| | Shriro. S. Potiche jar, 7¾ in. high, early 15th century | 2,100 |
| | Norton. 2nd sale. S. *Mei p'ing* vase, c. 1500, scroll pattern (£75 in 1953) | 2,100 |
| | 2nd sale. S. *Mei p'ing* vase, late 15th century with sage and pupil (compare 1967) | 1,500 |

439

£

| | | |
|---|---|---|
| 1963 | S. Stumpy vase with petalled rim, 15th century | 3,400 |
| | Norton. S. 2nd sale. Ovoid jar, 15th century, 2¾ in. | 1,300 |
| | 15th century dish with fuzzy blue dragon, 8 in. diam. | 2,400 |
| | Conical bowl, Hsüan Tê mark (£870 in 1954), see also | |
| | 1964 | 2,000 |
| | Goris. S. Bowl with Ch'êng Hua mark (1465–87) and | |
| | stylized peonies (£112 in 1946), compare similar marked | |
| | bowls, 1967, 1968 | 4,800 |
| | Peter Boode. S. 15th century pilgrim bottle, 12¾ in. | 3,700 |
| | Countess of Rosse. S. Ewer, near Eastern shape, 15th | |
| | century | 1,200 |
| 1964 | S. Potiche jar with lion-dogs, Hsüan Tê mark, 7½ in. | 3,400 |
| | Conical bowl, lobed rim, Hsüan Tê mark (see 1963) | 2,400 |
| 1965 | Pollen. S. Platter, c. 1400, 7¾ in. diam. | 850 |
| | Fuller. C. 12 in. dice bowl, Hsüan Tê mark on rim | 1,995 |
| | Globular jar, early 15th century, 3¾ in. diam. | 1,785 |
| | Spencer Churchill. C. *Kende* or swallowing bottle, | |
| | c. 1600, English silver mounts, c. 1620 | 1,850 |
| 1966 | Stephens. S. Two platters, late 14th cent. 7¾ in. diam. | { 1,000 / 800 |
| | Williams. S. Stem cup with dragons, mark of Hsüan Tê, | |
| | 3½ in. (compare 1962) | 4,800 |
| | C. Early 15th century moon flask, white dragons on blue, | |
| | 17 in. high | 25,000 |
| 1967 | C. Early 15th century moon flask, blue dragons on white, | |
| | 18 in. high | 17,850 |
| | 14th century *mei p'ing* vase, 14 in. high | 3,360 |
| | S. Stem bowl, mark of Hsüan Tê, 4 in. high | 1,700 |
| | Wettering-Mulder. S. Cut down 14th century *kuan* jar | |
| | (£1,800 in 1970) | 1,900 |
| | S. Potiche jar, 10¼ in. high, 15th century | 6,500 |
| | Ewer, Portuguese emblems, before 1520, 10½ in. high | 5,000 |
| | Dish, arms of Portugal upside down, 12¼ in. diam. | |
| | c. 1520 | 4,200 |
| | Two *mei p'ing* vases, late 15th century, 11½ in. high | |
| | (compare 1963), sage and pupil motif | 1,600 and 2,000 |
| | Ovoid jar, 5¼ in. high, Hsüan Tê mark (£1,500 in 1963) | 3,200 |
| | Herschel Johnson. S. Bowl with irises, mark of Ch'êng | |
| | Hua (1465–87), now coll. David Rockefeller (£36 in 1940), | |
| | 6 in. diam. | 16,600 |
| | Bowl mark of Ch'êng Hua, fruiting melons on vine | |
| | (compare 1968) | 5,000 |
| | S. Melon-shaped vase, 14th century, 6½ in. high | 3,400 |
| | Oswald Lloyd. S. 'Kraakporzelan' bowl, c. 1600, 14½ in. | |

£

1967   diam., contemporary English parcelgilt mount    4,200
    C. 15th century water sprinkler, long spout (compare
    1963 and 1968)    4,200
    S. Damaged Hsüan Tê-marked stem cup with dragons,
    3½ in. high (compare perfect specimen, 1966)    950
    Chow. C. Globular bowl. Hsüan Tê mark, 3¾ in. high
    (see 1965)    2,100
      Dice bowl, 12 in. diam. (compare 1965), Hsüan Tê
      mark    4,200
1968   S. 14th century *Kuan* vase, 6¾ in. high    2,000
      Round-bellied tankard, 5 in. high, Hsüan Tê mark (in
      1935 similar tankard made £55)    6,500
    C. Stem-cup, dragons and waves, Hsüan Tê mark, 6 in.
    high    1,575
    Fairlough. S. Two conical bowls, 15th century, Ch'êng
    Hua style but unmarked, 8 in. diam.    3,200 and 3,500
      Dice-bowl, 12 in. diam. Hsüan Tê mark (compare
      1965). In 1937 three were sold for £146 in all    11,000
    Sedgwick. S. Dish, Chêng Té mark, Arabic inscription,
    16¼ in. diam. (Eumorphopoulos sale 1940, £24; 1962,
    £2,200)    20,000
      Blue-ground dish, stencilled white flowers and fruit,
      11½ in. diam. Hsüan Tê mark (£775 in 1954)    18,000
    Bowl, convolvulus meander, 6 in. diam., mark of Ch'êng
    Hua (£24 in 1940)    8,000
      14th century stepped stem-cup with dragon, 4½ in.
      high    1,500
      15th century potiche jar with Buddhist lions, 7½ in.
      high, Hsüan Tê mark (compare Shriro sale, 1963)    5,000
      Stem bowl and cover, Hsüan Tê mark, 15th century,
      5½ in. (similar piece without cover £1,700 in 1967)    3,600
      Jar with short neck, *ling chih* sprays, 5¼ in. high, Hsüan
      Tê mark    3,000
      Potiche jar with dragon, 3½ in. high, Ch'êng Hua
      mark    9,000
    Palmer. C. Water-sprinkler with long spout, early
    15th century (compare 1963, 1967)    3,360
    David Foundation. S. Bowl, fruiting melon, 6 in. diam.
    mark of Ch'êng Hua (compare 1967), £62 in 1935    6,500
    McKechnie Jarvis. S. *Kuan* or potiche jar, 11 in. high,
    end of the 14th century    8,400
1969   C. Ewer with bridged spout, high-looped handle, no
    mark, spout damaged, 15th century    2,520

£

| 1969 | Hobart. N.Y. 10-inch saucer, single peony design, Hsüan Tê mark, $40,000, J. D. Rockefeller III | 16,665 |
|---|---|---|
| | Tokyo. C. Massive 14th century *Kuan* jar, 14½ in. high (compare 1960), 22 million yen | 25,699 |
| | Hobart. N.Y. Bowl with fruit and flower sprays, zigzag border on inner rim, 7 in. diam., ascribed Yung Lo (1403–1424), $8,500 | 3,542 |
| | Standard *Lien Tzu* bowl, Hsüan Tê mark, 8 in. diam., $19,000 | 7,917 |
| | S. Statuette of Chung-li Ch'uan, the immortal, 10 in. high, late 16th century | 1,200 |
| | S. Massive bowl, stylized lotus meanders on both sides, *c.* 1400, 16 in. diam., broken in two | 4,200 |
| 1970 | C. (Tokyo) Pilgrim flask, Hsüan Tê mark, 12¼ in. high (compare 1963) 7 million yen | 8,101 |

### BLUE ON YELLOW GROUND
mostly early 16th century

| 1960 | Keastey. S. Chêng Té mark (1506–22), 8½ in. diam. | 750 |
|---|---|---|
| | S. Chêng Té mark, 11¾ in. diam. | 1,050 |
| 1961 | S. Chêng Té mark, 11¾ in. diam. | 1,070 |
| 1962 | Colin Smith. S. Hung Chih mark (1488–1505), 9 in. diam. | 1,600 |
| | Palmer. S. Chêng Té mark, 8 in. diam. | 1,800 |
| | Chêng Té mark, 11¼ in. diam., very strong blue | 5,500 |
| | Saucer dish, 6½ in. diam., blue dragons on yellow, mark of Chia Ching (1523–66) | 950 |
| 1965 | Evill. S. Chêng Té, 11½ in. diam., damaged | 800 |
| 1966 | S. Hung Chih mark, 11¼ in. diam. | 3,800 |
| | Marks ground off, 10¼ in. diam. | 860 |
| 1968 | S. The same dish | 680 |
| | David Foundation. S. Standard Hung Chih marked dish, 10¼ in. diam., no special merit | 5,700 |

### POLYCHROME WARES
late 15th–early 17th centuries

This is not a homogeneous group. The soft enamel or *T'ou Tsai* pieces of the late 15th century, being only 2 or 3 inches high and very slightly decorated, are about the dearest ceramics in the world for what they provide. Conversely the massive *fa-hua* jars in relief on background colour and only slightly later in date, are a declining market. Their apogee was in the 1920s before early Ming had been discovered, but they were no novelty. They are in decidedly late 19th century taste and had some influence on ceramics of that period. In 192. a double gourd vase of this type in meshed relief made £4,305 at the Rober

442

nson sale. The 1970 equivalent should be £21,500, but the real value of the
se in that year was probably under £3,000. To some extent the place of
-*hua* has been taken by three-colour or five-colour wares, enamelled on the
hite glaze in the manner that has been perpetuated into modern times. Four-
gure prices for 16th century examples of this type first appeared in 1953, but
e list is deceptive because the larger pieces tended to gravitate towards Japan—
d what they are worth there may be judged from the *kinrandé* vase, sold in
kyo in 1969. At £27,300 it was of no better quality than the example sold
London in 1963 for £1,700 and quite as hideous.

|  |  | £ |
|---|---|---|
| 60 Wannieck. Paris. Two *fa-hua* potiche jars | | 724 and 875 |
| 62 S. *Fa-hua* potiche jar, reticulated figures | | 580 |
| Palmer. S. Saucer, green dragons on white, mark of Hung Chih, 7 in. diam. (1488–1505) | | 1,700 |
| ditto bowl, mark of Chêng Té (1506–21), 7¾ in. (compare 1966) | | 1,900 |
| Three-colour ginger-jar, flying horses, 4½ in. high, mark of Chia Ching (1522–66) | | 1,900 |
| Palmer. S. Five-colour brush rest, mark of Wan Li (1572–1619) | | 1,500 |
| Oviform three-colour jar, mark of Chia Ching, fishes and waterplants, 9 in. high | | 4,200 |
| Five-colour saucer dish with birds, 9¼ in. diam., Wan Li mark | | 1,300 |
| Tonying. N.Y. 2 *fa-hua* vases, turquoise ground, elephant handles, 17 in. high, $4,500 | 2 for | 1,607 |
| 63 Norton. S. Saucer, green dragons on white, mark of Hung Chih (1488–1505), 6½in. diam (compare 1966) | | 1,400 |
| *Fa-hua* potiche jar, c. 1500, deep blue ground | | 2,000 |
| Double-gourd bottle, c. 1500, red on white, traces of gold so-called *Kinrandé* (compare 1969), 14 in. cut-down neck | | 1,700 |
| Norton. 2nd sale. Potiche jar, fishes in red and yellow, mid-16th century (another with lid, £1,900 in 1953) | | 1,300 |
| Bowl with incised green dragon, mark of Chêng Té, 8 in. | | 1,400 |
| 64 d'Ajeta. C. Very similar bowl | | 2,205 |
| Gilded *kinrandé* green bowl, late 16th century, 4½ in. diam. | | 1,155 |
| Sapsworth. S. *Fa-hua* jar with 8 immortals, 15½ in. high, c. 1500 | | 2,200 |
| Polychrome double-gourd vase, early 16th century | | 2,000 |
| 65 Evill. S. Potiche jar, c. 1550, with polychrome riders | | 1,200 |
| 66 Aykroyd. S. Cup in soft enamels under 2 in. high, mark of Ch'êng Hua (1466–87) (£170 in 1953) | | 6,000 |

443

1966  Rex Benson.  S.  Saucer with incised green dragon, 6¼ in.    £

diam., Hung Chih mark (compare 1962 and 1963)    1,800

1967  Chow.  C.  Fish-cistern, blue and white with green and
yellow enamels, 21 in. high, Chia Ching mark (1523–66).
Bought in    2,940

Paris.  Potiche jar, 5½ in. high, mark of Chia Ching (with
tax)    1,796

1968  C.  Saucer with incised green dragon, 9 in. diam. mark of
Chêng Té (1506–22)    1,029

Sedgwick.  S.  Stem cup, soft enamels, 3 in. high, mark
of Chê'ng Hua (£450 in 1954)    8,500

    'Chicken cup', 3¼ in. diam., Ch'êng Hua mark    3,500

    Stem cup, iron-red ground, dragon on inside bowl,
    unmarked, late 15th century, 4 in. high    5,000

    A somewhat rubbed and cracked companion    1,900

David Foundation.  Two tub-shaped bowls in soft enamel,
described as Ch'êng Hua period as marked, under 3 in.
diam.    850 and 820

1969  Ledebur.  S.  *Mei P'ing* vase of *fa-hua* ware, figures, blue
ground, 10¾ in. high    1,522 1C

S. (Tokyo).  Double-gourd vase, early 16th century,
3-colour enamels and gold, so called *Kinrandé*, 15½ in. high
(cut down) (compare 1963) 23 million yen    27,380

S.  Five-colour wall-vase, mark of Wan Li, 12¼ in. high    950

C.  Potiche jar, *fa-hua* ware, peacock in relief on dark
blue ground, 16 in. high    1,155

## CHINESE ART
### PORCELAIN, CH'ING DYNASTY, 1644–1912
#### PORCELAIN IN *famille verte* ENAMELS
late 17th and early 18th centuries. (*See also Figures*)

*Famille verte* in crowded export taste is less popular than formerly. Delicately modelled pieces, enamelled on the biscuit, have been an expensive market since the early years of the century, but have barely kept pace with inflation. The big rises have been reserved for dishes, painted with maidens or mythological subjects in more or less Chinese taste. A single very large dish made £2,540 in 1967, but, twenty years earlier, £100 would have bought anything of this kind. The list also includes two very infrequent visitors to the saleroom, examples of the big *famille noire* baluster vases which were capable of making £30,000 each (£240,000 in 1970 terms) at the time of the First World War.

|      |                                                                                                                        | £     |
|------|------------------------------------------------------------------------------------------------------------------------|-------|
| 1960 | S. Bowl K'ang Hsi mark (1661–1722) etched dragons, green, yellow and aubergine enamels, under 6 in. diam. (compare 1969) | 210   |
| 1961 | Wannieck, Paris. 2 octagonal vases and covers          2 for                                                           | 1,100 |
|      | S. 18-inch dish with imperial audience                                                                                  | 680   |
| 1962 | Tonying, N.Y. With black backgrounds (famille noire), Hawthorn pattern baluster vase, 19½ in. high, damaged             | 355   |
|      | Dragon pattern baluster vase, 19½ in. high, damaged                                                                     | 1,996 |
| 1964 | d'Ajeta. C. Two fluted saucer-dishes with bulbul birds, Chinese taste, 8¼ in. diam.          2 for                      | 630   |
| 1965 | Evill. S. Bowl, Chinese taste, ducks and reeds, (£330 in 1958)                                                          | 1,100 |
|      | Pair of 5-inch bowls with bulbul birds, one damaged 2 for                                                               | 800   |
| 1966 | Aykroyd. S. 2 yellow and aubergine biscuit houseboats, 6½×10½          2 for                                            | 2,600 |
|      | 2 dishes, yellow and aubergine peaches over incised dragons, K'ang Hsi (compare 1969), 10 in. diam. (£180 in 1953)          2 for | 1,500 |
|      | 2 rosewater sprinklers, export taste, 11½ in. high, 2 for                                                               | 1,750 |
| 1967 | Herschel Johnson. S. Bowl 5¾ in. diam., enamels on coral ground, mark of Yung Chêng (1723–36)                          | 950   |
|      | Winston Guest. N.Y. ($2·40 dollars to £)                                                                                |       |
|      | Flattened baluster vase, 21 in. high, biscuit enamels                                                                   | 3,940 |
|      | Rouleau vase, enamels on yellow ground, 17 in. high (£750 in 1956), $7,000                                              | 2,500 |

| | | | £ |
|---|---|---|---:|
| 1967 | Guest. N.Y. 2 pear-shaped bottles with *kylins*, 18½ in. high | | |
| | (£785 in 1956; £148 in 1939), $13,500 | 2 for | 5,625 |
| | Dish with figure of *mei jen*, Chinese taste, 21½ in. | | 2,540 |
| | Baluster vase, waterplants, 18 in. high (£643 in 1956) | | 3,020 |
| 1968 | S. 2 dishes illustrating abduction of Yang Kuei Fei, 15 in. diam. | 2 for | 2,400 |
| | Palmer. S. Set of '12 months of the year' cups, under 2 in. high, K'ang Hsi marks | 12 for | 4,200 |
| | Garniture, 5 coral-ground vases and urns, about 9½ in. high | 5 for | 2,300 |
| | David Foundation. S. Wine pot and cover in soft enamels 5½ in. high, mark of Yung Chêng, 1722–36 | | 1,650 |
| 1969 | S. Model of junk under sail enamelled *en biscuit*, 11½ × 11½ (compare 1966) | | 2,400 |
| | S. Single dish, 10 in. diam. Yellow and aubergine peaches over incised dragons, K'ang Hsi mark (compare 1960, 1966) | | 1,700 |
| | A second ditto, 9¾ in. diam. | | 2,200 |
| | Dish with palace courtyard scene, diaper border, 22 in. (1960, £210) | | 2,000 |

## FAMILLE ROSE ENAMELS, AFTER 1720
(excluding figures, services, tureens, mounted pieces and punchbowls)

Formerly the prizes in this market were the big chimneypiece garnitures in export taste, and the bigger the dearer. In 1913 there was an advertisement offering £3,000 for a rose-ground urn and cover to make up a pair. Since the price was equivalent to £24,000, it will be seen what has happened to rose-ground urns. 'Mandarins' or paired jars and covers, 4 to 5 feet high, were another mainstay of *famille rose*. Rare on the market of the 1960s, the highest price for a pair rose from 1,350 guineas in 1965 to £5,400 in 1969, but in 1916 Duveen had bid 5,400 guineas for a pair in real money. Call it £42,000. Delicacy and not size is the quality that is now wanted of *famille rose*. The 9-inch saucer dishes, known as *ruby backs*, fetch perhaps five or six times as much as in the 1930s, albeit only on paper. A much bigger advance was made by saucer dishes, painted after European engravings, with touches of the *famille rose* palette. Till the late 1940s almost any of them could be got for under £20, but in 1969 they could make as much as £800 apiece, while in 1970 a very common design achieved £2,800. Armorial porcelain, than which nothing could be less exciting, rose in about the same proportion. Bowls in pure Chinese taste, a fairly vexed subject, rose rather less.

| | | | £ |
|---|---|---|---:|
| 1962 | C. Pair of ruby-backed saucers (£157 in 1934) | 2 for | 682 10s. |
| | Palmer, S. Two dishes with birds etc. in Chinese taste, | 2 for | 2,100 |

| | | | £ |
|---|---|---|---|
| 1962 | Tonying. N.Y. Bottle, 21 in. high, with peach tree. Mark of Yung-Chêng, (1723–1736), ex Pierpont Morgan | | 1,338 |
| | Lord Bruce  C.  2 three-foot jars and covers | 2 for | 2,310 |
| 1963 | S.  Garniture, 3 covered urns, 24½ in. 2 beakers, 19 in. | 5 for | 1,850 |
| | Garniture, 3 covered urns, same size with figure subjects | 3 for | 2,800 |
| | Norton.  S.  *Mei p'ing* vase with peach tree etc. and very dubious mark of Yung Chêng (£20 in 1953) | | 1,700 |
| | Pair of oviform vases with varied enamels and a poem of T'ang Yin, age uncertain | 2 for | 2,800 |
| 1964 | Duits.  C.  Single ruby-backed saucer | | 924 |
| 1965 | Margadale of Islay.  2 ruby-ground urns and covers, 18 in. high | 2 for | 651 |
| | 2 urns and covers, 24 in. high, roosters (£7,500 in 1970) | 2 for | 2,310 |
| | 2 53-inch 'Mandarin' vases and covers, painted with phoenixes etc. | 2 for | 1,427 10s. |
| | Single urn and cover with roosters, 25 in. high | | 1,050 |
| 1966 | C.  2 bowls, painted with butterflies, Chinese taste, Yung Chêng marks, 5½ in. diam. | 2 for | 1,155 |
| | Pinson.  C.  Elaborate 9-inch armorial dish | | 609 |
| | C.  Ruby-back saucer with *Mei jen*, 8¼ in. diam. | | 630 |
| 1967 | Herschel Johnson.  S.  Ruby-back saucer with *Mei jen*, 9½ in. diam. | | 800 |
| | Winston Guest, N.Y.  20-inch dish with peach-bough, Chinese taste (£1,036 in 1957) $3,500 | | 1,460 |
| 1968 | S.  2 jars and covers, equestrian subjects, 35 in. | 2 for | 2,700 |
| | Export meat-dish, 20 in. long, arms of Mecklenburg | | 1,200 |
| | Sedgwick.  S.  Bowl with peony sprays inside and out, Chinese taste, 5¼ in. diam. (compare 1966) | | 3,000 |
| | S.  Ruby-back saucer with cockerels, 7¾ in. diam. | | 1,250 |
| 1969 | S.  Plaque *en grisaille*, European style, estuary scene after van Goyen, 10½ × 12¾ | | 1,300 |
| | Pair of 8½ in. saucers, quails *en grisaille*, export style borders | 2 for | 1,600 |
| | C.  Pair of oblong *plateaux*, imitating Rouen faience, famille rose colours, 17¾ in. wide | 2 for | 1,102 10s. |
| | Pair of wall-sconces with candle-mounts in shape of female arms, 6½ in. long | 2 for | 1,102 10s. |
| | Pair of wall-sconces, rococo shields in relief, 12½ in. | 2 for | 2,155 |
| | Pair of wall-sconces, matching but 15½ in. high | 2 for | 2,730 |
| | S.  Pair of 'Mandarin' jars and covers with bold *Mei jen* figures, 50½ in. high | 2 for | 5,400 |

447

| 1969 | S. | Wine cooler on feet, 'Monteith' shape, extensive bird and flower decoration, 21 in. long, 11½ in. high | £ 3,400 |
| 1970 | S. | Pair of urns and covers, painted with roosters, 25 in. high (see 1963) | 2 for 7,500 |
| | | Pair of apple-green urns and covers, imitating Sèvres, early 19th century | 2 for 4,500 |

### FIGURES IN THE ROUND
birds, animals and human beings, *Famille verte* and *Famille rose*

Chinese porcelain figures resolve themselves into two kinds. First there are the kind made more or less after European designs, the paired dogs or birds for instance which could be European but for the harshness of this late form of hard paste. Secondly there are the traditionally Chinese religious figures and symbolic beasts which the Chinese kilns were prepared to turn out endlessly, once European fashion had taken to their endearing hideousness. Both kinds belong to the same more expensive regions of unexacting taste to which Royalty have long been singularly attracted. The first kind were designed for the fashionable European drawing room from the beginning, whereas the second got acclimatized there. Since this happened mainly in the 19th century, it is probably that this was when many of them were made.

Paired dogs and birds are generally placed at the end of sale catalogues as the final and dearest *bonne bouche* of all. Dogs, puppies in particular, have become more popular than at any time in the two hundred years or so since Mme Pompadour established the aesthetics of the boudoir. In the 1960s puppies multiplied in value 5 to 10 times over, but birds much less. The dearest pair of crested birds on rocks in the 1960s made an optically impressive price of £12,175, but a pair, sold in 1918 for 1,600 guineas, were almost as dear in real money terms. Another pair exceeded £1,000 as far back as the Lelong sale of 1903.

| | | | £ |
| 1960 | S. | 2 pheasants on rocks, 24½ inches | 2 for 8,800 |
| 1961 | Wannieck. Paris. 2 parrots, *bleu celeste* monochrome, | | 2 for 1,450 |
| | S. | 2 parrots, aubergine and turquoise on biscuit | 2 for 4,800 |
| 1962 | S. | 2 cranes on rocks, 28 in. high | 2 for 5,000 |
| | C. | 2 *famille rose* cockerels | 2 for 1,260 |
| | Paris. 2 cockerels, 10½ in. high, FN40,500+tax | | 2 for 3,575 |
| | 2 falcons, 11 in. high | | 2 for 3,476 |
| | Ward. C. Boy and lady, 42 in. high, late 18th century | | 2 for 2,310 |
| | Mme I-min Chang. N.Y. *Famille verte* statue of Kuan-Yin 45 in. high with boy companion, 22 in. high, $85,000 | | 30,335 |

£

1963 Ionides. S. Pony, white figure, 15½ in. long     1,200

    2 figures, man and wife, European dress, 8¾ in.    2 for   1,500

    Stag, yellow and brown on biscuit, antlers restored, late 18th century, 22¼ in. long     2,400

    Fribourg. S. 2 hawks on rocks, rose enamels    2 for   3,600

1964 C. *Blanc de Chine* 'governor Duff' group with added rose enamels     1,102 5s.

    2 cranes on rocks, 17 in. high    2 for   3,150

1965 S. *Famille rose* figure of a Dutchwoman, damaged, 16¾ in. (compare 1968)     720

1966 Malone. S. 2 puppies in European style, 7 in. high,    2 for   1,050

    Jay Dorf. C. *Famille rose* figure, the Infant Christ, 11 in.   1,680

    C. Pair of *famille verte* laughing boys, 11 in. high    2 for   924

    Aykroyd. S. Pair of *famille verte* dogs of Fo on plinths 14 in. high    2 for   2,000

    Pair of biscuit equestrian figures, man and woman 6 in. high    2 for   2,100

    Biscuit figure of archer, 8¾ in. high    2 for   1,600

    S. *Blanc de Chine* figure of seated Kuan Yin, 8 in. high (£450 in 1958)     900

1967 S. Horse and groom, biscuit group, 6½ in. high, K'ang Hsi period (Similar groups £340 in 1925, £2,205 in 1956)     2,700

    Winston Guest. N.Y. Pair of *famille verte* biscuit lion-dogs, 7 in. high, $4,250    2 for   1,680

    Pair of *famille verte* biscuit lion-dogs on square pedestals, 17½ in. high, $19,000    2 for   7,916

    Ditto, brocaded plinths, 12½ in. high, $12,000    2 for   5,400

    Ditto, tall stands, 22 in. high, $28,000    2 for   11,665

    Cockerel, *famille verte* biscuit, 10¼ in. high     2,500

    2 brush-rests in form of cranes on plinths, 9½ in. $7,000    2 for   2,928

    Pacing wolf, 15 × 16, brown glaze on biscuit, $11,000   4,582

1968 Paris. 2 pecking cockerels, 10¼ in. high, FN35,000+tax    2 for   3,470

    C. 2 late 18th century figures of European puppies, 6½ in.    2 for   3,150

    2 *famille rose* pheasants on rocks, 27¾ in.    2 for   12,175

    Metcalfe. S. 2 *famille rose* cranes, 10½ in. high    2 for   1,800

    S. 2 mottled turquoise hounds, 8 in. high    2 for   5,500

    2 cranes on rocks, 20½ in. high    2 for   2,600

| | | |
|---|---|---|
| 1968 | Prince de Ligne. S. 2 hawks on rocks, 15 in. high | |
| | 2 for | 6,200 |
| | C. 2 hawks on rocks, 10½ in. high 2 for | 1,837 |
| | S. European lady and gentleman, *famille rose*, said to be imitated from Thuringian porcelain, late 18th century 7¼ in. | |
| | 2 for | 3,400 |
| | Czinner. S. Pair of puppies, European style, 7¼ in. high, one tail replaced (similar pair (£1,050 in 1966) 2 for | 5,800 |
| 1969 | S. Pair of pug dogs, European style, one damaged, 10¼ in. high (£500, 1958) 2 for | 4,500 |
| | Pair of dappled horses, European style, 10½ in. high | |
| | 2 for | 4,000 |
| | C. Cocker spaniel, glass eyes, 9¾ in. wide, European painted wooden stool | 1,680 |
| | Fribourg. N.Y. Pair of hawks on rocks, 11 in. high, $6,500 2 for | 2,712 |
| | S. Pair of flop-eared dogs in European style, one with a puppy on its back, mainly iron red, one damaged, 7 in. high 2 for | 2,200 |
| | Pair of seated *Lohans*, rose and other enamels, 17 in. high 2 for | 2,400 |
| | Pair of grotesque ponies in a drab mottled glaze, 10 in. high, 19th century 2 for | 3,400 |

## MONOCHROME WARES, UNMOUNTED

| | | |
|---|---|---|
| 1962 | Tonying. N.Y. Turquoise baluster vase in relief, 22½ in. high, $2,300 | 821 10s. |
| 1963 | Norton. S. *Sang de boeuf* vase, *Mei p'ing* shape, 5½ in. high | 820 |
| | C. Beehive-pot, peachbloom glaze, K'ang Hsi mark, 3½ × 5 | 819 |
| 1965 | Adda, Paris. Winepot, turquoise on biscuit, peach-shape | 1,500 |
| 1966 | S. *Mei P'ing* vase, underglaze red, white dragon | 950 |
| | Aykroyd. S. Another ditto, a month later | 1,850 |
| 1967 | Herschel Johnson. S. Beehive-pot, peach-bloom, 3½ × 5, K'ang Hsi mark (compare 1963) | 1,200 |
| | S. A second ditto | 1,100 |
| | Winston Guest, N.Y. White openwork cylindrical brush-pot, *c.* 1800, 3¾ in. high, $2,800 | 1,168 |
| 1968 | David Foundation. S. Yellow bowl, K'ang Hsi marked, 6½ in. diam. | 1,200 |
| | Wine cup and stand, K'ang Hsi marked, 3 in. high | 700 |
| | Yellow jar and cover, K'ang Hsi marked, 10¾ in. high | 3,400 |

| | | | £ |
|---|---|---|---|
| 1969 | N.Y. Violet-coloured baluster vase, moulded decoration, 24¼ in. high, \$3,250 | | 1,362 |
| | S. Pair of Yung Chêng-marked fluted yellow saucers, 5¾ in. wide | 2 for | 850 |
| | Yung Chêng-marked lemon-yellow bowl, 4½ in. diam. | | 640 |
| | Turquoise flared bowl, 18th century? no mark, 7½ in. diam. | | 660 |

### MONOCHROME AND OTHER WARES
#### mounted in Europe in the 18th century

Most of the Chinese porcelain, chosen for mounting in the rococo and, later, in the neo-classic style, was monochrome. The difficulty of obtaining even approximately paired pieces made the monochrome wares surprisingly expensive by 18th century standards. Thus, paradoxically, a high valuation was placed on the pure Chinese taste of these pieces only in order to destroy their intended aesthetic function. The high valuation continued far into the 19th century before a strictly temporary eclipse of the fashion for mounts caused the price of monochrome porcelain to decline. Comparison of the two lists will, however, show that in the 1960s monochromes could on occasion be just as dear without mounts, though porcelain of any kind in mounts, made before the end of the 18th century, had become scarce. The high cost of *monture* has never born much relation to the quality of the pieces or even to their suitability. Almost the dearest mounted piece of the 1960s was not even porcelain but provincial stoneware. One of the two pairs of monochromes which succeeded in making 14,000 guineas, was very far from being a perfect match for size. The list of mounted pieces in the section 'Porcelain, Meissen' should be compared. It will be found that Meissen groups and animals, mounted as candelabra, can be dearer than mounted Chinese monochromes—a complete reversal of the scale of valuation in 18th century Paris.

| | | | £ |
|---|---|---|---|
| 1960 | C. Pair of unusual rouleau vases on mirror-black grounds, Louis XV mounts, 36½ and 38 in. high | 2 for | 3,150 |
| | Miligan. C. 2 hawks on Louis XVI plinths | 2 for | 7,510 |
| 1962 | Powis. S. 2 celadon rouleau vases, Louis XVI mounts | 2 for | 6,000 |
| | N.Y. 2 cut-down powder-blue rouleau vases, mounted by Duplessis ainé | 2 for | 4,650 |
| 1963 | Fribourg. S. Fluted stoneware bowl, mounted as potpourri vase and cover, Louis XV | | 8,000 |
| | 2 celadon rouleau vases, Louis XVI mounts | 2 for | 5,200 |
| | Candelabrum, supported by *famille rose* parrot, Louis XV | | 3,400 |

| | | | £ |
|---|---|---|---|
| 1963 | Elaborate inkstand, based on *blanc de Chine* Kuan Yin figure | | 2,600 |
| | Fribourg. S. 2nd sale. 2 *clair de lune* oviform vases, Louis XVI mounts | 2 for | 2,900 |
| | 2 celadon vases, Louis XVI mounts (£215 in 1939) | 2 for | 8,300 |
| 1964 | Rosebery. S. Pair of leaping carp vases on gilt-bronze rockery (similar pair, 1942 £309 15s.) | 2 for | 4,200 |
| 1965 | Baroness Burton. C. 3 beakers, *clair de lune* and underglaze colours, heavy Louis XVI mounts | 3 for | 3,780 |
| | Earl of Harewood. C. 2 celadon beakers, not matching but in identical Louis XV mounts | 2 for | 14,700 |
| | 2 unusual blue and white beakers, Louis XV mounts | 2 for | 7,140 |
| | 2 celadon long-necked bottles, Louis XV mounts | 2 for | 6,825 |
| | 2 hexagonal 2-handled celadon vases, Louis XV | 2 for | 5,040 |
| | Other pairs at £2,940 and £2,730 | | |
| 1966 | James de Rothschild. Paris. Pair of turquoise parrots, converted into double candlesticks (with tax) | 2 for | 7,306 |
| | Pair of Ch'ien Lung falcons, rocaille vases | 2 for | 6,583 |
| | C. *Blanc de Chine* reticulated brush-holder, mounted with two Meissen swans as a *surtout de table* | | 5,040 |
| 1967 | Wallraf. S. Pair of celadon bowls, mounted as potpourri jars and covers, Louis XV, 15½ in. high | 2 for | 4,000 |
| | Winston Guest. N.Y. Pair of late Ming *fa hua* enamelled garden seats, Louis XVI stands, 19 in. high ($180 or £37 in 1939), $8,500 | 2 for | 3,042 |
| 1968 | S. Pair of cut-down *famille verte* vases, very elaborately mounted with Vincennes birds, *c.* 1740–50 | 2 for | 5,500 |
| | Pair of 4-light candelabra on Ch'ien Lung laughing boys, 19¼ in. high | 2 for | 3,400 |
| | Pair of 3-light candelabra, made entirely out of *blanc de Chine* elements, including figures mounted on lions | 2 for | 7,000 |
| | Pair of 3-light candelabra on biscuit stags | 2 for | 5,000 |
| | C. Powder-blue vase and cover, mounted as a table fountain with Meissen swans | | 5,040 |
| | Pair of celadon fishes, 12½ in. high, including Louis XV handle-mounts | 2 for | 9,450 |
| | Single rectangular pear-shaped celadon vase with Louis XV wing-handles, 15½ in. high | | 9,975 |
| | Four bowls, simulated *Kuan* ware, mounted as a pair of pot-pourri bowls and covers, Louis XV, 15 in. high | 2 for | 14,700 |

|  |  | £ |
|---|---|---|
| 968 | Pair of *famille rose* kneeling boys, mounted as 3-light candelabra      2 for | 5,460 |
|  | *Sang de boeuf* bottle, mounted in medieval style by William Burges, *c.* 1870 | 1,575 |
|  | S. Pair of K'ang Hsi stags, mounted with Vincennes flowers as 2-light candelabra      2 for | 5,000 |
|  | Pair of export-ware tureens, and covers, *famille rose* with fishes in panels, mounts in Régence style of uncertain date, height 8¾ in. overall      2 for | 2,700 |
| 969 | Fribourg. N.Y. Crackled lavender bulb bowl, richly mounted, *c.* 1750, 12½ in. wide, $8,000 | 3,335 |
|  | C. (Geneva). Horse and groom in *émail sur biscuit*, K'ang Hsi (compare 1967) on ormolu plinth supporting Japanese red lacquer bowl and cover with Chantilly flowers, 11 in. high, FS59,000+tax | 6,043 |

## PUNCH BOWLS

| 955 | C. Armorial, Mandarin style, 15¾ in. diam. | 141 15s. |
|---|---|---|
| 960 | S. With foxhunt after English painting or engraving | 350 |
| 964 | Knowlan Cooke. C. With foxhunt, 16 in. diam. | 609 |
| 966 | Jay Dorf. C. With foxhunt, 15 in. diam. | 861 |
|  | With view of Cantonese factories, 15½ in. diam. | 892 10s. |
| 967 | Steevens. S. 14¼ in. diam. view of European factories, Canton | 2,600 |
|  | Parsons. S. Pair of masonic punchbowls, 14¼ in. diam.      2 for | 1,850 |
|  | S. With foxhunt, 15½ in. diam. | 1,200 |
|  | C. With view of Cantonese factories, 13 in. diam. | 3,570 |
| 968 | Prince de Ligne. S. Ditto, 14½ in. diam. ormolu plinth | 3,000 |
|  | C. With foxhunt, 16 in. diam. | 1,995 |
|  | Vull. S. With crudely rendered foxhunt, 14¼ in. diam. | 1,000 |
| 969 | C. With European lovers in landscape etc., 16 in. wide | 1,365 |
|  | S. With view of the Cantonese factories, 14¼ in., damaged | 1,100 |
|  | Hunting scene, *rouge de fer* trellis ground, 16 in. | 1,500 |
|  | C. *En grisaille*, after an engraving of 'Wilkes and Liberty' 1770s., 14 in. diam. | 997 10s. |
| 970 | S. With animal fables *en grisaille* after Barlow, 11¾ in. diam. | 3,800 |
|  | With country horse and hunt, Mandarin palette, 19¾ in. diam. | 2,400 |
|  | With haymakers and haystack, European style, 11¼ in. diam. | 2,100 |

### SERVICES AND PART SERVICES

The two most expensive lots of porcelain of any kind in the salerooms of th 1960s were dinner services in the standard 'tobacco-leaf' pattern at 33,00 guineas each. The second service, which was extremely incomplete, worke out at over £375 a unit, though this garish and thoroughly un-Chinese desig had been mass-produced to a greater extent than any other. Not so long ag such a service could have been built up at the rate of £5 a plate, while £3 to £40 bought a tureen, complete with its stand and cover, such as mad £1,500 in 1969. Possibly this was the greatest advance for any kind of Chines porcelain on the market in the 1960s and it was achieved, not by museu rarities, but by something which the purchasers intended to use. It had bee unusual in the 1950s for Chinese dinner services to cost more than £15 a uni Embarassment at eating off someone's coat of arms and reluctance to subm very expensive china to the wear and tear of the kitchen sink still counted fc something. All such inhibitions have gone. A fraction of a service in the Do Quixote pattern was sold in 1968 at £500 a unit, but two plates in a less com monplace variation of this pattern cost £800 each, and would presumably hav been even dearer, had they been sold with a service.

Hardly anything in the following lists is older than the second half of th 18th century, or remotely comparable in beauty of paste with contemporar European porcelain. Certain tureens are based on a European *faience fine* model but are even more expensive than the original, one pair with covers havin, been sold in 1969 for £27,300. With singular appropriateness all these tureen are in the shape of geese.

|  |  | £ |
|---|---|---|
| 1962 | Northesk.   C.   Armorial service, arms of Carnegie, 110 pieces | 5,460 |
| 1965 | Frelinghausen.   N.Y.   *bianco sopra bianco*, 35 pieces | 3,650 |
|  | S.   *Compagnie des Indes* service, 301 pieces | 5,600 |
|  | Wenner Gren.   S.   *Famille rose*, 116 pieces | 2,600 |
|  | Margadale of Islay.   C.   40 dishes and plates in a pure Chinese design, Dresden Johanneum marks, 40 pieces | 2,730 |
|  | Peale-Brown.   S.   Armorial service of average quality, 40 pieces | 3,000 |
| 1966 | C.   *Famille rose*, 19 plates and dishes, 9 to 15¼ in. diam. | 2,520 |
|  | Tobacco leaf pattern (about 60 damaged or replaced with copies) 301 pieces | 34,650 |
|  | Lord Torpichen.   S.   Armorial service, 48 pieces | 4,300 |
|  | Eardley Knolles.   S.   Plain armorial service, 90 pieces | 1,550 |
|  | S.   *Famille verte* service, standard design, 29 pieces | 1,800 |
| 1967 | C.   Plates and dishes only, tobacco leaf pattern (compare 1966) 92 pieces | 34,650 |
|  | S.   Standard *famille rose*, 265 pieces | 13,200 |

£

| | | | |
|---|---|---|---|
| 1967 | Princess Guirey. C. Variation, tobacco leaf, 130 pieces | | 14,910 |
| | Steevens. S. Armorial, 29 pieces | | 2,300 |
| | S. Neo-classic armorial, *c.* 1780–90, 166 pieces | | 4,000 |
| 1968 | van Waay, Amsterdam. Dutch armorial, 322 pieces | | 21,500 |
| | S. So-called Don Quixote service, but in fact Chiang Kuo on his mule in landscape, plates and dishes, 22 pieces | | 10,500 |
| | Broadwood. S. Plain armorial, 104 pieces | | 5,000 |
| | Bremridge. S. Plain armorial, 34 pieces | | 3,200 |
| 1969 | Two more 9-inch plates from another Don Quixote service (see 1968) 2 pieces | | 1,600 |
| | C. Common tobacco-leaf service (compare 1966–7) 96 pieces | | 22,575 |
| | Plain neo-classic service, arms of MacGregor, *c.* 1800, 188 pieces | | 19,425 |
| | Common *famille rose* service, floral pattern, 76 pieces | | 4,200 |
| | S. Armorial part-service, 14 plates | 14 for | 1,900 |
| | Common 'Mandarin' service, 65 pieces | 65 for | 2,200 |
| | Kersabiec. C. Tobacco leaf part service, 56 pieces | | 7,560 |
| | C. Armorial service, European style sprigged ornament, 54 pieces | | 2,520 |
| 1970 | S. In Worcester style, early 19th century, arms of Hay within borders, 354 pieces | | 17,500 |
| | Single dinner-plate with well-known design of a Highland rifleman and piper, late 18th century, 9 in. diam. | | 2,800 |

### TUREENS WITH STANDS AND COVERS

| | | | |
|---|---|---|---|
| 1955 | Warwick Bryant. C. *Famille rose* tureens and covers in form of a goose, 15½ in. high (see 1963, 1966, 1967, 1968, 1969) | | 315 and 378 |
| 1961 | Wannieck. Paris. Two armorial 'compagnie des Indes' tureens | 2 for | 2,660 |
| 1963 | Fribourg. S. In form of a goose (Strasbourg model?) | | 11,000 |
| | Smaller goose | | 4,600 |
| 1965 | Lloyd Bowles. C. Armorial, 13 in. high | | 504 |
| 1966 | S. Tobacco leaf pattern, 15 in. long | | 640 |
| | C. Boar's head, 15 in. long | | 787 |
| | S. Pair in shape of a goose, 13½ in. high, 1 damaged | 2 for | 4,300 |
| | Jay Dorf. C. Pair with elephant and rider | 2 for | 2,310 |
| 1967 | Tureens in form of a goose: | | |
| | S. 13¾×16 | | 8,000 |
| | C. 13¾×14 | | 10,500 |
| | S. 13¾×16¼ | | 4,800 |

£

1967 C. Stand alone for a boar's head tureen, repeating the
motif, 20 in. long                                                1,785
1968 C. Tureen in form of a goose, 12½ × 15                        5,880
1969 C. Pair of goose tureens, 14½ in. high, 14 in. wide   2 for 27,300
Puttick and Simpson. Tureen, stand and cover from
standard tobacco leaf service (compare 1966)                       1,500
S. Pair of tureens on feet with covers, Jean Berain style,
said to be copied from Alcora faience, 11¾ in. long   2 for  4,500
Boar's head tureen, damaged and lacking stand, 15¼ in.
long, compare 1966                                            2,000
1970 S. Pair of boar's head tureens, 14½ in. long, lacking stands
2 for  4,200
C. Pair of goose tureens, one damaged, 13½ in. long
Bought in at 12,600

# CHINESE ART
## JADE CARVINGS (INCLUDING INDIAN JADE)

The Imperial Jade Mining Company of Minneapolis can provide a mausoleum of jade at prices ranging from $10,000 to $25 million. Presumably one would have to be cremated to fit inside the cheapest, but what better indication could one want that this toffee-like surface still enjoys the respect of extreme wealth? Even so, the universal spread of the concept, 'art as an investment', has not kept the price of intricately carved Chinese jade abreast of the latest plunges of inflation. A spinach-green cylindrical brush-washer, smothered in landscape relief, cost £900 in 1944, £3,400 in 1948, £6,000 in 1960, £7,600 in 1966, the dearest to date. One wonders whether excessive Chinese intricacy is less in demand—or has this appetite found its outlet in Fabergé and glass paper-weights? Very few jade objects bear dated inscriptions. It is generally assumed that intricately carved examples are 18th century, but many of them are certainly not older than the 19th. It is possibly this doubt that checks the pace. The squatting buffaloes which are not intricate but endearingly clumsy and reputed Ming, have fared rather better, but very tamely when compared with most of the Chinese market. The price of £3,900 was reached in 1946, £6,000 in 1960, £9,500 in 1962, and £13,214 in 1966.

|  |  | £ |
|---|---|---|
| 1960 | S. Squatting buffalo, Ming (£1,400 in 1949) | 6,000 |
| | Kitson. S. Spinach-green brushwasher | 5,000 |
| 1961 | N.Y. Blue jade vessel in form of duck, inlaid with precious stones and dated 1765, 10 in. high, $14,000 | 5,000 |
| | Kitson. S. Spinach-green bowl | 3,600 |
| | Brush holder, landscape in high relief | 5,800 |
| | Bowl with fishes in relief | 2,400 |
| | White pilgrim bottle, 12 in. high | 2,000 |
| | Mughal jade bowl and cover | 2,100 |
| | 'Sodden snow' vase, 15 in. high | 2,800 |
| | (three others at over £1,500) | |
| | S. Grey-green flat vase with reliefs, 16½ in. high | 2,300 |
| 1962 | Bought by Victoria and Albert Museum. Shell-shaped bowl with ibex handle, inscription of Shah Jehan, 1657 (Mughal?) | 8,650 |
| | Johnson. S. Squatting buffalo, grey, 13 in. long, Ming dynasty | 9,500 |
| | S. Elephant, grey jade, 18th century | 1,100 |
| 1963 | Cooper. C. Spinach-green bowl, bat-handles | 4,725 |
| | Pair of green incense cylinder-vases 2 for | 3,360 |
| | Bottle-vase with poem of Ch'ien Lung | 2,730 |
| | 40 lots made £41,853 | |
| | S. Ibex-head ewer, Mughal shape, mark of Chia-Ching II (1796–1821) | 1,400 |

457

| | | £ |
|---|---|---|
| 1963 | Louis von Cseh. C. Four spinach-green screens, depicting the seasons, perhaps 19th century, said to have been made from one piece of Siberian jade     4 for | 42,000 |
| 1964 | S. Squatting buffalo, 6¾ in. long, ascribed Ming | 2,600 |
| | Spinach-green brushwasher, highly undercut, dated 1795 | 3,600 |
| | Sapsworth. S. Spinach-green bowl, inturned rim, 7½ in. diam. | 2,600 |
| 1965 | Gladstone. S. Spinach-green bushwasher, 6½ in. diam. (see 1969) | 4,000 |
| | Spencer Churchill. C. Recumbent Mongolian pony, 2½ in. long | 2,310 |
| | C. Inturned bowl, spinach-green jade, 10½×9 | 4,620 |
| | Quadrangular ribbed vase and cover, 20 in. high | 2,730 |
| | 2-handled *Kuei*, 11 in. diam. | 2,205 |
| | Beattie. S. Oblong incense burner (*Ting*) and cover, 7½ in. | 2,300 |
| | Wells. S. Incense burner in form of a pagoda, 7 sections, 27½ in. high | 2,400 |
| | Janek Kahn. S. Recumbent horse, *c.* 1800, 10 in. long | 1,600 |
| 1966 | Gladwyn. S. Squatting buffalo, damaged after the loot of the Summer Palace. Bought in at | 8,000 |
| | Brenda Seligman. S. Squatting buffalo, only 8½ in. long | 1,250 |
| | De Kay. N.Y. Squatting buffalo, pale green, $37,000 | 13,214 |
| | Pair of spinach-green brushwashers, $42,500    2 for | 15,178 |
| | S. Jadite vase and cover, 18 in. high | 2,000 |
| | MacCracken. C. Pale celadon brushwasher, 6¾ in. | 3,800 |
| | Knight. C. Spinach-green brushwasher, 8 in. | 4,800 |
| 1967 | S. Squatting buffalo, 10½ in. | 1,500 |
| | Squatting buffalo, 9¾ in. | 3,000 |
| | 11 in. *koro* and cover on four lions | 2,500 |
| | Summers. S. Garniture of two beakers and a *koro* with covers, Ch'ien Lung marks | 3,000 |
| 1968 | Shaw Stewart. C. Spinach-green shallow bowl, Ch'ien Lung mark, 12 in. diam. | 1,600 |
| | S. Jadite figure of Kuan Yin, 18¼ in. | 1,500 |
| | Flat-sided moon flask and cover, 13 in., early 19th century | 2,100 |
| | Gamble-North. S. Boulder jade, 5¼×12×10¼, inscription of Ch'ien Lung, dated 1769 | 2,100 |
| | Dark green oval bowl, 11¾ in. long, with dragons | 2,900 |
| | S. Spinach-green brushpot with poem, 6 in. high (compare 1965) | 5,700 |
| | Spinach-green bowl, pendant rings, 13½ in. wide | 1,700 |

| | | £ |
|---|---|---|
| 1968 | Lord Allington. C. Spinach-green thin table screen, 13 × 8½ | 2,730 |
| 1969 | S. Spinach-green brushwasher, 6½ in. (see 1965) | 5,800 |
| | Seligman. S. Recumbent water buffalo, length 8½ in. | 1,200 |
| | S. Figure of Kuan Yin, 13 in. high | 1,900 |
| | Laidlaw-Smith. C. Double cylinder vase, pale celadon, 7¾ in. high, mask-handles | 2,415 |
| | C. Mongolian pony, spinach-green and black, 7½ in. | 2,310 |
| | Another Mongolian pony, celadon green, 6¼ in., called Sung | 4,830 |
| | S. Richly carved spinach-green brushwasher, 6 in. high | 6,200 |
| | Spinach-green bowl with cage-work, 7½ in. wide | 4,800 |
| | Sage green bowl with carved dragons, supposed K'ang Hsi period, 11¾ in. long by 9½ wide | 4,200 |
| | Flat flask (white) with cover, Ch'ien Lung mark, 12¾ in. high | 3,400 |
| | Emerald green bowl, lipped rim, ring-handles, 9½ in. wide | 2,800 |
| | Flat flask and cover, unmarked, 13¼ in. | 2,300 |
| | *Koro* and cover, white, 6¾ in. high | 2,600 |
| | Hobart, N.Y. Incense burner, meshed cover, 4 ring handles 8½ in. high, $10,500 | 4,375 |
| | Gadsby. S. Vase and cover, flattened baluster shape, pale spinach-green, 12½ in. high | 2,100 |
| | S. Group of *Kylin* and water buffalo, post-Ming, 7 in. wide | 2,100 |
| | Maynard. C. Spinach-green table screen, 12¾ × 10, carved wood stand | 5,145 |
| | Pale celadon bowl, ring-handles, Ch'ien Lung period, 10¼ in. diam. | 3,360 |
| | Compressed globular bowl, carved all over, dark green, 8¾ in. | 4,410 |
| | Sold by Spink and Sons to Somerset de Chair, Recumbent horse, datable *c.* 1520 | 27,000 |
| 1970 | Nicole. C. Recumbent Mongolian pony, 11½ in. long, ascribed Ming dynasty.                    Bought in at | 12,600 |

# CHINESE ART
## LACQUER (INCLUDING FURNITURE)

£

1962 David. S. Red lacquer bowl in relief, dated 1778     820
     15th century red lacquer dish     900
     16th century red lacquer dish     650
     Vase and cover with inscriptions and date, 1776     1,300
    S. Canton cabinet, Padouk wood, inlaid with 13 mirror-paintings, *c.* 1760     2,300
     Canton knee-hole lacquer dressing table     1,250

1963 Norton. S. Red lacquer box, 8½ in. diam. *c.* 1400 (see 1968)     5,200

1965 S. 14-in red lacquer dish, marks of Yung Lo and Hsüan Tê, but probably 17th century     1,900

1967 Norbury. C. Box and cover, cinnabar red lacquer, 8½ in. diam., mark of Hsüan Tê     1,317 10s.
    Winston Guest. N.Y. Pair of red lacquer tables, 33 × 50, wide, $9,750     2 for   3,482

1968 Sedgwick. S. Red lacquer box, 8½ in. diam., *c.* 1400 (see 1963)     2,300
     *Guri* lacquer box and cover signed P'ing Liang, *c.* 1490, 6½ × 12½ in.     9,500
     7-in. disc, cinnabar red lacquer relief, 15th century     1,600
     Box and cover, 5¾ in. diam., mark of Yung Lo, considered early 15th century     650
     Black lotus dish, same period with signature, 6¾ in.     420
     Black dish, flying ducks, 15th century, 11¾ in. diam.     400

1970 Krolik. S. Red lacquer dish, ascribed 15th century, 17½ in. diam. (David sale, 1962 £600)     1,900

# CHINESE ART
## METALWORK, ANCIENT AND MEDIEVAL

One of the least explicable falls from grace, now at an end, has been that of the ancient bronze vessels of China. In 1923 the British Museum paid the equivalent of £8,750 in 1970 terms for a Chou bronze. Even at the disastrous Eumorphopoulos sale of 1940 a most important bronze from Anyang made £1,400 (equivalent to £7,000). Yet between 1940 and 1955 it was barely possible for an ancient bronze vessel to reach £1,000. Very interesting pieces changed hands at £120 to £250. Till 1963 the most important bronzes stayed below £3,000. Then in 1965 the British Museum paid £28,000 for a famous dated bell, while in 1967 a frail and elegant ritual wine jar of the Shang dynasty was sold for £38,000. It was a dramatic change for a matter of four years, but revaluation had been long overdue. No other metal antiquities of the early bronze age have made as much as these, but then Chinese metal work of the early bronze age is in many respects more diversified than anything excavated in Europe or the Near East. And here again private wealth has followed the antiquarian tastes of museum directors. It could do a great deal worse. £38,000 will also buy a van Dongen, indistinguishable from a magazine advertisement or the bald silhouette of three jam-jars by Nicolas de Stäel.

| | | £ |
|---|---|---:|
| 960 | S. Two bronze shaft-finials in the shape of mules' heads, Chou dynasty (Eumorphopoulos sale, 1940, £820) 2 for | 4,800 |
| | Libation cup, Shang dynasty | 550 |
| 962 | C. *Kuei* or 2-handled food vessel and cover, Chou dynasty | 2,990 |
| | *T'ing* or tripod vessel, Shang dynasty, inscribed | 1,575 |
| | *Piao* bell, Han dynasty, with tiger handle | 500 |
| | S. Gilt-bronze tiger, Han period, fragment, 8½×3½ | 540 |
| 963 | S. Vessel, shaped as a goose, alleged Chou period. Aberdeen University | 1,200 |
| | Shriro. S. *Kuei* or 2-handled vessel, early Chou dynasty, 7 in. high | 10,000 |
| | S. Pear-shaped vase (*Yu*) Chou dynasty | 3,000 |
| | Toeg. S. Massive cauldron (*Kuei*) early Chou dynasty, (£4,200 in 1968) | 1,600 |
| | Shriro. S. Tripod cauldron, ascribed Shang dynasty. Aberdeen University | 1,900 |
| | N.Y. Pear-shaped vessel (*Yu*) Chou dynasty | 3,575 |
| | Another similar, 11½ in. high | 3,930 |
| 964 | C. Bronze damascened bowl, Han dynasty | 1,575 |
| | Plesch. S. *Chiao* or tripod vessel, Shang dynasty, 9¾ in. high, Aberdeen University | 1,300 |
| | Hauswedel, Hamburg. *T'ing*, vessel on three feet, Shang dynasty 6½ in. high, DM25,000+tax | 2,700 |

£

1965   S.  Silver-engraved wine cup, baluster-stand, 3 in. high,
T'ang dynasty                                         1,350
       S.  *Ku* or slender beaker, Shang dynasty, 11½ in.    1,400
      Minett.  S.  Another ditto, 12½ in.            3,600
      Spencer Churchill.  C.  Another ditto, 12¼ in.    2,940
      Stoclet.  S.  Bronze bell, associated with year 482 B.C.,
21¼ in. high, roughly cast.  British Museum      28,000
         6½-in. Plaque, bronze and turquoise mosaic, Shang
dynasty                                           1,600
         8-in. bronze and turquoise slender belt-hook, Warring
States period                              2,800
         7-in. axe-head, Chou period            2,800
         Square mirror-back, 3½ in. Chou period      1,900
      Randon Bennett.  S.  Beaker-shaped vessel (Tsun) Chou
dynasty, 10¾ in. high (1955 bought in at £170)     2,500
         Cauldron-shaped vessel (*Kuei*) Chou dynasty, 7½ in.
high (1955, bought in at £120)             2,700
1966  Lempertz, Cologne.  *Kuei*, early Chou dynasty, 5¾ in. high
11¾ in. wide DM30,000+tax               3,100
1967  Alexandrine de Rothschild.  S.  *Yu* or ritual 2-handled
wine jar, Shang dynasty, 11½ in. high        38,000
       S.  Flat-sided flask, Warring States period, 14½ in.    15,000
         *Kuei*, jar without handles, 10×7, Warring States
period                                     8,500
         Nine others exceeded £1,000
       C.  Shang dynasty tripod cauldron, 14¼ in. high    3,780
       S.  *Yu*, early Chou dynasty, 7¾ in. high       4,000
1968   S.  Shang dynasty *Ku*, very slender, 12¾ in.      5,000
         Early Chou *Kuei* or 2-handled cauldron with historic
inscription, 12×5¾ (£1,600 in 1963)         4,200
       C.  *Kuei* of similar size and age, no inscription    2,730
      Sedgwick.  S.  Gilt-bronze slieveweight in form of two
birds, T'ang dynasty, 2¾ in. long           5,500
         Silvergilt wine cup, 3½ in. diam., Sung dynasty    2,400
       C.  Cauldron without handles, Shang dynasty (*Lei*), 8¾ in.
diam.                                      2,730
      Van Steenwijk.  C.  Ceremonial axehead, Shang dynasty
from Anyang, excavated 1938, 8×5¼         4,200
       C.  Bronze knife, 2nd millenium B.C., 15 in. long    819
       S.  *Fang yi*, roofed rectangular vessel, 10 in. high, from
Anyang, Shang dynasty                22,000
      Furness.  S.  Very slender *Ku* vase, Shang dynasty, 13¾ in.   4,800
1969  van Steenwijk.  C.  *T'ing* on three legs, 8 in., Shang
dynasty                                 6,825

| | | | |
|---|---|---|---|
| 69 | N.Y. Tripod cauldron, *T'ing*, Shang dynasty, 10¼ in., $12,000 | | £ 5,000 |
| | C. Covered cauldron or *Yu*, rope-twist handle, 12½ in. high, called late Shang dynasty | | 3,315 |
| | S. Normal Shang dynasty *Ku* beaker, 10¼ in. high | | 2,000 |
| | C. Handleless cauldron or *Lei* with monster masks, 11 in. high, Shang dynasty | | 2,520 |
| | Cauldron and cover, *Kuei*, 11 in. high, Western Chou dynasty | | 2,415 |
| | S. Covered wine vessel with swing handle, *Yu*, 12½ in. high 11th–10th century B.C. (similar *Yu*, £3,000, 1963) | | 7,600 |
| | Trumpet necked wine vessel, *Tsun*, Shang dynasty, 9¾ in. | | 3,600 |
| | Tripod cooking bowl, *li-ting*, Shang dynasty, 8 in. high | | 3,200 |

## METALWORK WITH CLOISONNÉ ENAMELS, 15TH–19TH CENTURIES

essels of copper, smothered in cloisonné enamels, were mainly intended for ual use and were not exported in the 18th century to satisfy the European petite for *Chinoiserie*. They were rarely found in Europe before the 'opium ar' and they did not become a fashion till the sales of the loot of the Summer lace in the 1860s. In 1865 a huge basin, supported by kneeling figures, was d in Paris for £450, equivalent in 1970 to more than £4,000, which would quite a good price for a late imperial piece even on this monumental scale. e Japanese mania of the 1880s drove a taste which had been thoroughly con-nial to the mid-Victorian *Zeitgeist*, clean out of fashion. There was no revival the Duke of Gloucester's sale in 1954. The new level of prices was maintained the two Kitson sales, but there was no substantial rise in the market again 1969 when, at £14,175, a gigantic pair of cranes were shewn to have ultiplied in value nearly ten times over a period of nine years. On the other nd, the rare fifteenth century pieces had advanced continuously on account their close affinity with the designs on the fashionable contemporary blue d white porcelain.

| | | | £ |
|---|---|---|---|
| 60 | C. Pair of cranes under palm trees, 73 in. high (see 1969) | | 1,470 |
| | Pair of cranes, 18 in. high | 2 for | 1,522 10s. |
| | Kitson. S. Basin in shape of double peach | | 700 |
| | Pair of candlesticks borne by rams | 2 for | 1,550 |
| 61 | Kitson. S. Box and cover, late Ming | | 780 |
| | Pair of dwarf statues, over 2 ft high | 2 for | 1,500 |
| | Pair of pricket candlesticks, 8 in. high | 2 for | 750 |
| | S. 2 cranes standing on tortoises, 24 in. high | 2 for | 2,700 |
| | 2 vases carried on elephants, 13 in. high | 2 for | 950 |
| 62 | David. S. Ritual disc, early Ming (£24 in 1933) | | 1,400 |

| | | | |
|---|---|---|---|
| 1962 | S. Pair of cranes, 62 in. high, 19th century, restored | | |
| | | 2 for | 2,600 |
| 1964 | Sherwood. S. Miniature figure of a ram, 18th century | | 700 |
| 1965 | S. Pair of cranes, 16 in. high | 2 for | 660 |
| | Margadale of Islay. C. Jar and cover, 20 in. high, mark of Hsüan Tê (1423–1435), bought by British Museum | | 7,350 |
| | Evill. S. 8-in. saucer with three fruits, 16th century | | 620 |
| 1966 | S. Pair of green spotted cats of uncertain age | 2 for | 3,200 |
| 1968 | S. Pair of cranes, 18 in. high (compare 1960) | 2 for | 1,800 |
| | Oblong plaque, 24 in. long, story of the chequer players, 17th century | | 680 |
| | C. Pair of cranes, mounted on plinths as torchères, 7 ft high | 2 for | 2,415 |
| | Sedgwick. S. Oviform bottle, funnel neck, c. 1450, 10¼ in. | | 2,800 |
| | Cup-stand, 8½ in. diam., mark of Hsüan Tê, 15th century | | 2,000 |
| | C. Another similar, 7½ in. diam. | | 1,470 |
| | S. Cockerel, 7½ in. high, late 18th century | | 1,700 |
| | C. Pair of quails, 5½ in. high, late 18th century | 2 for | 924 |
| 1969 | C. Pair of cranes under palm trees, 73 in. high (£1,470 in 1960) | 2 for | 14,175 |
| | S. Pair of cranes, 23¼ in. high with plinths | 2 for | 3,200 |
| | Pair of elephants, supporting baluster vases, Ch'ien Lung marks, 10¼ in. high | 2 for | 2,600 |
| | C. Jardinière in form of two hollow peaches, 29 in. wide | | 1,890 |
| | Mello de Rego. S. Pair of cockerels, 14½ in. high, c. 1800 | | 2,800 |

# CHINESE ART
## PAINTINGS AND SCREENS

Most of the objects in this list are in export taste, painted on glass, inlaid on wood, enamelled on copper or designed as wall paper. Very few are painted in the pure Chinese tradition for Chinese collectors, and still fewer are signed old masters. Some by no means exciting landscape albums in the 2nd Hobart sale of 1969 fetched what appear to be very high prices, but it is certain that international competition between museums has created very much higher prices than these outside the saleroom. Chinese paintings only began to be taken seriously in the West within the past half century so that now there is a rush to make up for lost opportunities. But the subject is hideously bedevilled by the most unhelpful sort of Chinese book-learning and by still more unhelpful Western interpreters. Everything with a name tagged on it has been disputed, and there is singularly little that compels belief by the sheer force of its artistry. Whether it is too soon for reliable *expertise* or centuries too late is an open question.

|  |  |  | £ |
|---|---|---|---|
| 1960 | N.Y. 23 ft Coromandel screen, 12 leaves |  | 2,409 |
| 1961 | S. Scroll painting in European style, after Boucher |  | 320 |
|  | C. 12-leaf Coromandel screen |  | 1,312 |
| 1962 | S. Set of 9 panels, *papier peint chinois* | 9 for | 580 |
|  | Set of 4 glass paintings, 18th century | 4 for | 1,750 |
|  | Ward. C. Set of 16 panels, *papier peint chinois* | 16 for | 1,470 |
|  | Cantonese paintings on glass, 18th century, £1,575, £1,995 and |  | 2,520 |
| 1963 | N.Y. Late Ming landscape scroll, seals of Ming Shan T'ang and others |  | 645 |
|  | Ward. C. Two upright mirror paintings | 2 for | 1,575 |
|  | Another pair (bought in at £504 in 1962) | 2 for | 1,150 |
| 1964 | Rosebery. S. Coromandel screen after a Dutch view of Amsterdam |  | 2,400 |
|  | Butlar-Braunfels. S. 12-fold Coromandel screen, 8 ft 3 in. high |  | 1,250 |
| 1965 | Stoclet. S. Mongol horseman, painting on silk, alleged Yüan dynasty (£420 in 1930) |  | 2,800 |
|  | N.Y. 12-fold Coromandel screen, 17 ft long |  | 2,321 |
| 1966 | Kevorkian. N.Y. Fresco painting, early Ming, Kuan Yin and attendants, 6 ft 9 in. × 2 ft 6 in., $2,100 |  | 750 |
| 1967 | C. 10-fold Coromandel screen, 18 ft 4 in. long |  | 945 |
|  | Another, 12 panels, 9 ft high |  | 997 10s. |
|  | N.Y. 12-fold Coromandel screen, 9 ft high, $12,000 |  | 4,250 |
| 1968 | Neville Barry. S. Two panels, soapstone and pearwood, European architecture and figures, 44 × 35¾ | 2 for | 3,360 |

1968    S.   Suite of 22 panels, *papier peint chinois*, some over 10 ft    £

           high, restored                                                3,600

           Tayleur.   C.   Canton enamel wall-plaque in relief on

           copper after an 18th century French engraving, $27\frac{3}{4} \times 47\frac{1}{2}$    2,310

1969    Kemsley.   S. (at Dropmore).   12-fold Coromandel screen,

           $9\frac{1}{2}$ ft high                                                    1,650

           S.   12-fold Coromandel screen, $10\frac{1}{2}$ ft high, possibly before

           1700                                                          4,600

           C.   23 strips, *papier peint chinois*, 37 in. wide, apparently

           unused                                          23 for   2,730

           Hobart.   N.Y.   Album of 12 ink landscapes, signed Lan

           Ying and dated 1642, \$24,000                           12 for   10,000

                Album of colour-tinted landscapes signed Fan Ch'i,

                18th century, \$23,000.   Metropolitan Museum   8 for   9,600

# CHINESE ART
## SCULPTURE, STONE, WOOD, IVORY, BRONZE

|  |  | £ |
|---|---|---|
| '62 | Gilou. S. Gilt-bronze figure of Kuan Yin, 7 in. high, 13th century | 520 |
|  | d'Ajeta. C. Gilt-bronze figure of Matreya, dated A.D. 492 | 2,310 |
|  | Tonying, N.Y. Gilt-bronze Buddha 10 in. high with pedestal, dated A.D. 556 $2,800 | 1,000 |
| '64 | d'Ajeta. C. Gilt bronze Avalokitesvara, Northern Wei Dynasty, 4½ in. high | 1,890 |
| '65 | Stoclet. S. Gilt bronze Avalokitesvara, Northern Wei dynasty, 10½ in. high | 5,200 |
|  | Spencer Churchill. C. Ivory Buddha, 6½ in., fitted into a lump of unworked turquoise, Ming dynasty | 2,600 |
| '66 | Kevorkian. N.Y. Stone figure of Kuan Yin, T'ang dynasty, $40,000 | 14,285 |
|  | N.Y. Wooden Buddha, red and gold lacquer, 27½ in. high, $9,000 | 3,216 |
| '67 | S. Winged lion, stone, Liang dynasty, 23½ in. high | 2,200 |
|  | Chow. C. Gilt-bronze Avalokitesvara, 16¾ in., Sung dynasty | 1,512 10s. |
|  | Grey stone bear, 7 in. high, uncertain parentage | 1,123 10s. |
|  | Somerset Maugham. S. Wooden Kuan Yin, 46½ in. high, supposed Sung | 1,700 |
| '68 | Carpenter Denne. C. T'ang dynasty marble horse's head, 9½ in. high | 3,360 |
|  | C. Grey stone stele, Buddha etc., Northern Wei dynasty, 50 in. | 1,102 10s. |
|  | Sedgwick. S. Contemplative Lohan, gilt-bronze, 6 in. high, Yüan or early Ming | 2,600 |
| '69 | S. Ming wooden Bodhisatva riding on kylin, 38½ in. high | 850 |
|  | C. Squatting bear, black stone, 7¼ in. high, uncertain age | 2,205 |
|  | N.Y. Gilt-bronze figure of Kuan Yin, Sung dynasty, 18½ in. high, $10,500 | 4,375 |
|  | Hindson. S. Ivory group, ewe and lamb, mark of Ch'ien Lung, 3 in. high, late 18th century | 1,600 |
|  | C. Seated Kuan Yin, gilt-bronze, 29½ in. high, probably late Ming | 1,575 |
|  | N.Y. Stone figure of a groom, T'ang dynasty, 31½ in., $3,100 | 1,292 |
|  | Head of helmeted warrior, marble, T'ang dynasty, 10¾ in., $3,500 | 1,458 |

# CLASSICAL ART
## BRONZE

In 1928 two Hellenistic statuettes in bronze were sold in London and Paris f
about £4,000 each. The ensuing list suggests that in 1970 they will not ha
kept their true value, that is to say £20,000 each. But an even better illustrati
of the decline of the classical taste is the price in open saleroom competiti
which the British Museum paid in 1963 for the bronze head of the Emper
Claudius from Rendham, the most important Roman bronze to have be
found in Britain. It was £15,500, whereas five years later, a standard 9-in
collared bronze head from Benin, no rarity at all, made £21,000—and no o
even knows its age.

| | | | £ |
|---|---|---|---:|
| 1961 | S. | Etruscan lion, 2 in. high | 360 |
| 1962 | S. | Etruscan javelin thrower, 6¼ in. high, *c.* 480 B.C. | 980 |
| | C. | Male figure, possibly Adonis, Roman, 1st–2nd century A.D., 17 in. high | 6,825 |
| | S. | Etruscan figurine of a girl, *c.* 500 B.C. | 540 |
| | | Etruscan figurine of a girl, *c.* 460 B.C., 5½ in. high | 1,500 |
| | | Late Celtic buckle from Catterick | 400 |
| 1963 | S. | Late Celtic collar, British, 1st–2nd century A.D. | 2,300 |
| 1964 | S. | Corinthian helmet, 6th century B.C. | 400 |
| | C. | Greek figurine, 6 in. high, 6th century B.C. | 1,700 |
| | | Stoclet. S. Caucasian openwork plaque, called 4th century B.C. | 850 |
| 1965 | | Spencer Churchill. C. Deer, 13 in. long, Roman, 1st century B.C. | 6,615 |
| | | Winged victory, 8½ in. high, 1st century B.C. | 2,100 |
| | | Etruscan warrior, 7 in. high, 5th century B.C. | 2,520 |
| | | Late Etruscan cyst, 17 in. high, 5th century B.C. | 2,100 |
| | | South Italian figure, 7¾ in. high, 5th century B.C. | 4,410 |
| | | Two primitive Greek figures, 7th century B.C., 5 in. and 4½ in. high          Each | 2,100 |
| | | Hollond. S. Head of Claudius from Rendham, Suffolk, 13 in. high, British Museum | 15,500 |
| 1966 | S. | Sardinian figurine, 4 in. high, 8th century B.C. | 1,800 |
| | | Doublet. S. Etruscan mirror, 9½ in. high | 2,500 |
| | | Detroyat. S. Dancing figure of Lar, 8½ in. *c.* 100 A.D. | 2,600 |
| | | Gallatin. S. Bronze head of a Roman boy, silver inlaid eyes, 11½ in. high, 1st century, A.D., Metropolitan Museum | 24,500 |
| | S. | Incomplete figure of a youth, 4¾ in. high, Attic, *c.* 450 B.C. | 1,300 |
| | | Female portrait head, 3rd century A.D., 11¾ in. | 3,100 |
| | | Rothschild. S. Female castanet player, Etruscan, 6th century B.C., 4½ in. high | 980 |

| | | | £ |
|---|---|---|---|
| 1966 | Basel. Archaic horse, Peloponnese, 5½ in. high, c. 700 B.C., FS29,000+tax | | 2,710 |
| 1968 | S. Figure of Dionysus from Rumania, 8¾ in. high, 1st century A.D. | | 1,000 |
| | Russell. S. *Protome* from the lid of a cauldron in form of a griffin's head, 6 in. long, S. Greece early 6th century B.C. | | 3,300 |
| 1969 | S. Bronze *Oinochoe*, handle in form of a youth, 8½ in. high, restored, mid 6th century B.C. | | 4,100 |
| | Kouchakji. S. Bronze head of a 2nd century Roman matron, said to have been found in Chiavenna in 1879, 14 in., bought in | | 18,000 |
| | S. South Italian Greek helmet with plume-carrier, 11¼ in. high, 3rd century B.C. | | 2,600 |
| | Gladiator helmet. South Italian, 3rd century B.C., Boston Museum | | 550 |
| 1970 | C. Candelabrum on three lion's feet, from Pompeii before 79 A.D., lacks top, 58½ in. high | | 1,050 |

# GLASS
## (some post-classical)

This is the only kind of Graeco–Roman antiquity which shared in the higher range of price-rises of the 1950s and 1960s. The ancient glass-blowers were never able to achieve the devastating symmetry and formalism of classical pottery and metal. They produced a subtle asymetry which, combined with the adventitious effects of iridescence, pleases the modern palate. The Sidonian bottles, moulded as a double human face, can make £200. In the 1920s they were to be found at £5 and even less.

| | | £ |
|---|---|---|
| 1960 | Fischer, Lucerne. Syrian beaker *en cabouchon*, FS3,200+tax | 325 |
| 1962 | S. Sidonian bottle shaped as a double head | 200 |
| | Syrian green glass flask | 240 |
| | Judaean amber-coloured hexagonal flask, late Roman period | 480 |
| 1963 | S. Roman *millefiore* bowl, 2nd century A.D. | 380 |
| 1964 | Brummer. S. Coptic vase and cover *en cabouchon*, 5th century A.D. | 800 |
| 1966 | Lempertz, Cologne. Roman bottle, 3rd century A.D., relief snakes, 8 in. high, DM16,000+tax | 1,615 |
| | S. Anglo-Saxon cone-beaker, 7th century A.D. from Aclam, 9¼ in. | 1,450 |
| 1967 | S. Coptic glass amphora imitating agate, 5th century A.D., 9½ in. high, from the Fayyum | 1,000 |
| | Cooke. S. Romano–British beaker from Newport Pagnell, nearly 7 in. high, Ashmolean Museum | 650 |

## GOLD, SILVER AND HARD STONES
### (including Barbaric and pre-classical art)

£

| | | |
|---|---|---|
| 1961 | S.   Silver Roman statuette of Hercules | 340 |
| 1962 | Stuker, Berne.   Gold medallion, head of Olympias and sea nymph riding dolphin, 320 B.C., 2 in. diam., FS78,000+tax | 7,800 |
| 1964 | S.   Etruscan gold stands to support an amphora   2 for | 780 |
| | Scythian gold plaque, charging boar, 1st century B.C., length 3 in. | 800 |
| | Gold votive barley stalk, Attica, 5th century B.C. | 2,600 |
| 1965 | S.   Hellenistic gold bracelet, garnet medallion | 1,100 |
| | Harewood.   C.   Plain gold vase, 1st century B.C., 11 in. high, 55½ ounces | 11,000 |
| 1966 | C.   Silver conical beaker, embossed relief, 4½ in. Roman, 1st century B.C. | 1,217 10s. |

D. of Westminster.   S.   Two gold torques, bronze age ⎱ 16,500
from Holywell, Flintshire.   National Museum of Wales ⎰ 4,700

S.   Greek silver libation dish, semi-Persian style, 5th century, B.C., 7 in. diam.   1,300

2 Celto-Iberian penannular gold torques, 6¼ in. diam ⎱ 1,250
3rd century, B.C.   ⎰ 1,000

| | | |
|---|---|---|
| 1967 | Bachelor.   S.   Gold cross with garnets, 7th century A.D., lately found at Thurnham near Maidstone | 5,000 |
| | Clements.   S.   Excavated wooden cyst containing 5 gold ornaments, Irish bronze age, National Museum, Dublin | 10,000 |
| | Ashotis.   S.   Cypriot gold necklace with 12 pendant ornaments, 3rd century B.C. | 800 |
| | S.   Intricate gold necklace and earrings, 4th century B.C. | 3,100 |
| | Roman silver bowl, vertical sides, engraved vine leaves, 1st century A.D., 4½ in. diam. | 1,350 |
| | Williams-Wynn.   S.   Bronze age gold torque, 62¾ in. found in Merioneth, Wales | 6,000 |
| 1968 | D. of Northumberland.   S.   Silver roundel relief bust of Athene, 4½ in. diam., possibly 1st century B.C. | 1,700 |
| | S.   Gold necklace, Medusa-head medallion, 2nd century A.D. | 640 |
| 1969 | Silver alms-dish with dedication to Emperor Licinius for the *decenanalia* of A.D. 318, made at Naissus in Illyria, 8 in. diam. | 3,465 |
| | S.   Alleged Graeco-Scythian dish, silver with mythological figures in relief, 2nd century B.C., 8¼ in. diam. | 2,000 |
| | Gavin Astor.   C.   Oval onyx cameo, head of Augustus, ex. D. of Marlborough, 1899, modern mount, 3½ in. diam. | 2,940 |
| | N.Y.   Bronze boat figure-head, early imperial, $3,000 | 1,250 |

## MARBLE SCULPTURE AND FRAGMENTS

The fall of the patched-up Graeco–Roman statues, the essentials of every great country house, and the highest prizes of the auction rooms of the late 18th and early 19th centuries, has been fully dealt with in Volume Two. One more comparison may be added. Among the marbles at Wilton, sold in 1961, were two busts of the emperors Caracalla and Geta which made 850 and 650 guineas respectively. One may compare that with Christies in 1825 after the death of Nollekens, when a bust of Commodus which the deceased sculptor had doctored liberally according to his fashion, made 320 guineas. In 1961 this meant about 3,000 guineas, in 1970 nearer 4,000, yet there is no reason to suppose that it would have made any more than the two busts from Wilton even in 1970. So much for patched-up Roman emperors of the early third century. Copies of Greek sculpture, made at that time, did rather better in the 1960s, fetching up to £5,000 in the incomplete and un-restored state that was preferred, but the competition could hardly be called breathtaking.

| | | £ |
|---|---|---|
| 1961 | Earl of Pembroke.   C.   At Wilton. | |
| | Statue, Gallus, 2nd century B.C. | 1,155 |
| | Caracalla, imperial bust, 3rd century A.D. | 892 10s. |
| | Stele, Hellenistic Greek, 4th century B.C. | 1,050 |
| | Seated empress, 2nd century A.D. | 682 10s. |
| | Geta, imperial bust, end of 2nd century A.D. | 682 10s. |
| | Stuker, Berne.   Apollo, marble after Praxiteles, torso only, 34 in. high, FS24,000+tax | 2,300 |
| 1962 | S.   Venus, marble torso, 1st century A.D. | 2,300 |
| | Smiling faun, head from el Djem, Tunisia, 1st century B.C. | 680 |
| 1964 | S.   Marsyas, incomplete figures, 25 in. high | 700 |
| | Osgood.   S.   Portrait bust, clean-shaven man, early 2nd century A.D. | 2,900 |
| 1965 | Spencer Churchill.   C.   Gaius Caesar, basalt head, 1st century A.D., 13½ in. | 2,205 |
| | Hadrian, portrait head, 17½ in., 2nd century A.D. | 1,627 10s. |
| 1966 | S.   Torso fragment, Romano–Egyptian porphyry, 2nd–3rd century A.D., height 6¼ in. | 750 |
| 1967 | C.   Headless Apollo, 2nd–3rd century A.D., cut down, 65 in. high | 2,100 |
| | Aylward.   S.   Two alabaster heads in crude Palmyrenian style from Quataban, about 10 in. high, 2nd century A.D. | 850 and 1,100 |
| | Basel.   Cycladic idol, 3rd Milennium B.C., 8 in. high, FS17,500+tax | 1,678 |
| | Head of Antinous, mid-2nd century A.D., 9¾ in. high, FS27,000+tax | 2,620 |

|  |  | £ |
|---|---|---|
| 1967 | S.  Headless Aphrodite, Roman, 37 in. high | 1,000 |
| 1968 | D. of Northumberland.   S.   Aphrodite, torso, 2nd century A.D., 49½ in. high | 5,000 |
|  | S.   Celto-Ligurian stone relief of decapitated heads, 13 in. high, 2nd century B.C. | 2,800 |
|  | Kevorkian.   S.   Bust of a senator, *c.* 200 A.D., 25 in. high | 1,800 |
|  | S.   Two marble figures of Muses, part mutilated, about 38 in. high, 2nd century A.D., 2nd figure lacks arms.   Coll. Paul Getty | } 5,000<br>3,500 |
| 1969 | S.   Headless torso of Apollo, 13½ in. high, 1st century A.D. | 1,300 |
|  | Cypriot limestone head of a man, 6th century B.C., 10¾ in. | 800 |
|  | S.   Herm, boy in panther skin, 43 in. high, 1st century A.D. from Grottaferrata | 1,200 |
|  | Sarcophagus with bust and putti, emblematic of the seasons, 72 in. long, 3rd century A.D. | 1,800 |
|  | Lord Lonsdale.   S.   Roman–British redstone funereal stele from Old Penrith, end of 1st century, 87 in. high | 1,200 |
|  | Front of a 3rd century sarcophagus, Medusa heads and putti, 87 in. long | 1,300 |
|  | Christian arched relief with symbols, 66 in. high, *c.* 500 A.D. | 1,200 |
|  | C.   South Arabian alabaster stele in form of a bull from Timna, 1st century A.D. or earlier, 17¾ in. high | 1,207 |
|  | Kalebdjian.  N.Y.  Sarcophagus front with triumphal procession, 26 × 86½, $5,000 | 2,083 |
|  | Paris.  *Apollo Sauroctonos*, marble torso, 3rd century B.C. (£310 in 1928), FN44,000+tax | 4,150 |

### GREEK POTTERY AND CLAY FIGURES

Not such an impressive list as it looks. As long ago as 1884 the Louvre pai £1,000 for a three-handled hydria at the Castellani sale, the equivalent £9,000. On the other hand only five Greek vases exceeded £3,000 in the 1960 four of them sold in Switzerland. It is, however, probable that much highe prices were paid by American museums, particularly for archaic pieces.

|  |  | £ |
|---|---|---|
| 1960 | S.   Attic red figure *krater* | 1,000 |
| 1961 | British Museum buys *bell krater* by the Altamura painter, 18¼ in. high, *c.* 470 B.C. | 2,000 |
|  | S.   Attic black figure *amphora*, *c.* 600 B.C., Ashmolean Museum | 560 |

£

| | |
|---|---|
| 1962 S. Romano–British red vessel (Castor ware), 10 in. high. | |
| Hounds in relief (much repaired), British Museum | 1,050 |
| Red figure *dinos* by the Altamura painter. King's College, Newcastle | 600 |
| C. Black figure *amphora*, *c.* 500 B.C. | 782 10s. |
| S. Prehistoric clay figure of a goddess, Cyclades | 820 |
| Attic red figure *loutrophoros* | 800 |
| Fischer, Lucerne. Attic white ground *lekythos* by the Achilles painter, *c.* 440 B.C. With tax | 3,390 |
| *Oenochoe*, black ground, *c.* 520 B.C. With tax | 3,210 |
| 1963 Randolph Hearst. N.Y. | |
| Attic black figure *amphora* and cover, 18½ in., 6th century B.C. | 1,355 |
| Red figure *hydria*, *c.* 490 B.C., 14 in. | 1,397 |
| Black figure *amphora*, 540 B.C., 17 in. | 1,250 |
| Basel. *Oenochoe* by the Eritrea painter, *c.* 430 B.C., FS45,000+tax | 4,492 |
| 1964 S. Set of Phrygian terracotta revetment plaques in painted relief, 6th century B.C. 6 for | 2,720 |
| Attic black figure tazza. Heracles and the Nemean lion, 550–540 B.C. | 1,100 |
| C. Black figure *hydria*, 520–500 B.C., 18½ in. | 2,000 |
| 1965 S. Black figure amphora by Nikosthenes, *c.* 530 B.C., 12¼ in. | 1,600 |
| Tracagni. S. Attic black figure *hydria*, *c.* 510 B.C., 18 in. by the 'Rycroft painter' | 950 |
| Spencer Churchill. C. Attic black figure *kyathos* or libation bowl, 3 in. high, *c.* 500 B.C. | 819 10s. |
| A second attic black figure *kyathos* or libation bowl, 3 in. high, c. 500 B.C. | 735 |
| 1966 Bancroft. S. Laughing Silenus, painted terracotta figure, S. Italy, 1st century B.C. | 700 |
| 1967 Basel. Tanagra figure, seated Aphrodite and column, height 8 in., 3rd century B.C., FS11,000+tax | 1,052 |
| Black figure *amphora* by the 'S painter', *c.* 500 B.C., 24½ in. high, foot restored, FS39,500+tax | 3,782 |
| 968 S. Etruscan red pottery brazier, 22¾ diam., 7th century B.C. | 600 |
| Kevorkian. S. Attic black figure *amphora* by the Acheloos painter, *c.* 510 B.C., 17 n. high | 1,200 |
| Attic black figure *amphora* by the Swing Painter, *c.* 540 B.C., 15¾ in. high | 1,500 |
| *Oenochoe*, black figure, Nikosthenes workshop, dancing Maenads, 12½ in. high (£480 in 1949) | 2,500 |

1968 S. Black-figure *amphora*, signed Nikosthenes, *c.* 530 B.C.,
12¼ in.     1,500

1969 C. (Tokyo). Pear-shaped Proto-Corinthian jar, birds and
animals, 20¾ in. high, 950,000 yen     1,109

        Another 11¾ in. high, *c.* 600 B.C., 1,800,000 yen     2,102

   S. Attic red figure *column Krater* by the Eucharides painter,
*c.* 490 B.C. 17 in. high     3,400

        Attic black figure *amphora* (warriors), *c.* 440 B.C.,
14¼ in.     1,600

        Attic black figure *hydria*, *c.* 510 B.C., 14¾ in.     1,500

        Attic red figure *column krater* by the Boreas painter,
470–60 B.C., 18 in. high     1,350

# CLOCKS
## RENAISSANCE

It will be noticed that, apart from two historic pieces, the Electors' Emerald Clock and the Clock-salt of Charles 1st, the oldest portable clocks were not the dearest. In fact the relatively plain English clocks, made three or four generations later by Tompion and others, cost several times as much. But the market for Renaissance clocks was never built up in the same way. Even when wedding-cake taste was at its height, clocks were surprisingly unpopular. The largest collection of Renaissance clocks ever sold comprised 70 lots at the vast Spitzer sale of 1893. Among this formidable assembly five tabernacle clocks and one flat table clock made from £240 to £400 each, the equivalent of £2,150 to £3,600 in 1970, and that might conceivably be their worth.

| | | £ |
|---|---|---|
| 1961 | C. Silver hexagonal table clock by Hussermann. S. German 17th century | 441 |
| 1962 | Stukker. Berne. The 'emerald clock' of the Electors of Saxony, c. 1580, plated in gold, silver etc., FS480,000, Gulbenkian Foundation | 40,000 |
| | S. Table clock, Augsburg, c. 1585, Orpheus and Eurydice, 8¾ in. diam. | 5,200 |
| 1963 | Burns. S. Table clock, believed to have been made in 1547 for Diane de Poitiers, but largely a 19th century reconstruction | 1,550 |
| 1964 | S. Augsburg monstrance clock on Atlas support, c. 1580 | 1,300 |
| 1965 | Adda. Paris. Upright bronze table clock, surmounted by lions, 11¼ in. high, style of Metzger of Augsburg, c. 1600 | 1,565 |
| | Gilt-bronze horizontal table clock, 5½ in. diam. | 1,158 |
| | Another gilt-bronze horizontal table clock, 4¾ in. diam., both late 16th century About | 1,000 |
| | Gilt-metal table clock, Metzger of Augsburg, c. 1600 With tax | 1,778 |
| | Wenner Gren. S. Automaton table clock with animated lion, Dresden, c. 1520 | 5,800 |
| 1966 | van Waay. Amersterdam. Table clock by Jakob Gerker of Nuremberg, 1645. Hfl8,800+tax | 960 |
| | van Alfen. S. Dutch astrological striking clock, 17th century | 3,400 |
| | French circular table clock, silver case, 5¾ in. diam. Before 1582 | 2,100 |
| | C. Early 17th century tabernacle clock, Nicolas Plantart, Abbéville, 8 in. high | 1,312 10s. |
| | 30-hour crucifix clock by Jacob Mayr, Augsburg, late 17th century, 12¾ in. high | 1,417 10s. |
| | Another German crucifix clock with Virgin and St. John | 1,050 |

£

1967   C.   Monstrance clock by David Amstetter of Augsburg,
*c.* 1600, 13 in. high (Spitzer sale, 1893, £64)          1,470

        S.   Clock surmounting lavish cabinet of amber, tortoise-
shell and silver, 35 in. high, S. German, *c.* 1700. Possibly
by Ferdinand Plitzner                              4,100

        Stopford-Savile.   C.   Clock-salt, Nuremberg, *c.* 1540,
silver-gilt, cameos and enamels, globe-dial added later, in-
ventoried among Charles 1st's possessions, 1649 (resold in
U.S.A., 1968 for £28,000)                         7,350

        Koller, Zurich.   Night clock with projector lamp and
ebony case, Augsburg, 1630, FS13,800+tax     About   1,350

1968   Koller, Zurich.   Table clock by Conradus Rex, Dresden,
1589, gilt and engraved with story of Prodigal Son, 6½ in.
high, FS14,800+tax                              1,610

        Lempertz, Cologne.   Gilt-bronze hexagonal engraved
table clock by Plantart, Lyon, *c.* 1600, DM6,500+tax     854

1968   Chester Beatty.   S.   Table clock, Augsburg, 1592, 3¾ in.
high                                          720

              Table clock, French late 16th century, 4 in. high     950

        S.   Sundial-astronomical compendium of diptych form by
Ulrich Schniep of Munich, 1575, 5¼×7 in.           4,830

              Astronomical striking clock by Michael Schultz of
              Danzig, early 17th century, flat and hexagonal     2,520

        Travers.   S.   Tabernacle gilt-copper clock with auto-
mata, South German, *c.* 1600, 18¼ in. high          2,800

         S.   In the form of automaton lion-rampant, holding shield-
dial. S. German, *c.* 1600                          1,000

        Ketzebue.   S.   Elaborate astrolabic bracket clock by
Jeremias Metzger, Augsburg, 1570, highly chased gilt
copper                                     1,400

1969   Smith.   S.   Gilt metal crucifix clock with figures, 13½ in.
high, *c.* 1625                                  540

        Bull.   C.   Standing astrolabe clock, brass, *c.* 1600, with
modern movement by Louis Desoutter, 17¾ in. high    1,102 10s.

        Peyer.   S.   Astronomical sun-dial compendium in flat
octagonal gilt-metal case, 3½ in. diam. by Christopher
Schissler, Augsburg 1556                     11,000

        S.   Vertical table clock, steeple-shaped, 5½ in. Augsburg,
1625                                        700

              Vertical table clock, tabernacle-shaped, signed Adam
              Elyzovicz, Cracow, 1634, mounted on sphinxes, move-
              ment restored, 16¾ in. high                  750

              Striking bracket clock, 22 in. high, Christian Reynaert,
              Leyden, towards 1700                     1,300

£

1969  van Alfen.  S.  Gilt metal tabernacle clock with automaton lion and armillary sphere, 20¾ in. high, 17th century    4,000

Lord Rothschild.  S.  Silvergilt and rock crystal astronomical pillar-dial, Nuremberg, 1563, 4½ in. high    4,000

Koller, Zurich.  Gothic clock, Constanz region, *c.* 1500, uncased, 21½ in. high, FS16,000+tax    1,780

# CLOCKS
## ENGLISH (mainly late 17th and early 18th centuries)

The cult of the Tompion clock is by no means recent, but it was only in the 1950s that the general public was made aware that these square, somewhat puritanical objects had a mysterious financial quality like glass paperweights. It is a shame that such good honourable clocks should be degraded to a sort of stock exchange quotation. At the same time it is an interesting symptom of aesthetic change that the dearest clocks money can buy should be valued for their movement rather than their ornament. A hundred years ago, when the Marquess of Hertford was paying more for French clocks, smothered in ormolu, than they fetch today, a clock by Tompion or his disciples would have been worth only a few pounds. It is equally significant that the only clocks that approach them are Breguet clocks of the 19th century, bought not as works of art at all, but as precision-instruments.

| | | £ |
|---|---|---|
| 1949 | Eckstein. S. Bracket clock by Tompion and Banger, ebony case, 9½ in. high | 2,300 |
| 1959 | C. Miniature travelling clock by Thomas Tompion, 1680, 8¼ in. high | 4,117 10s. |
| 1960 | C. Long case by Daniel Quare, early 18th century | 997 10s. |
| | Chrysler. N.Y. Long case by Tompion, dated 1690 | 2,000 |
| | N.Y. Long case by Tompion, dated 1705 | 1,518 |
| 1961 | S. Bracket clock by Tompion, c. 1700 | 2,700 |
| 1962 | C. Brass and ormolu clock by Eardley Norton, c. 1750, 13½ in. high | 945 |
| 1963 | Prestige, 1st sale. S. Bracket clock by Tompion à grande sonnerie | 4,300 |
| | Parquetry long case by W. Clement before 1700 | 2,200 |
| | Burr-walnut long case by Tompion and Banger | 1,400 |
| | Long case by John Fromenteel, late 17th century | 1,700 |
| | Marquetry long case with calendar movement by Tompion | 1,600 |
| | Ionides. S. Late 18th century fantasy clock made for the Chinese court | 2,200 |
| | Morrison, McCleary, Glasgow. Table clock by Tompion, ebony and silver | 10,000 |
| | S. Ebonized bracket clock by Tompion, numbered 198 | 3,000 |
| 1965 | Phillips. S. Long case by Tompion | 4,800 |
| | Long case by John Knibb | 2,600 |
| | C. Ebonized bracket clock by Joseph Knibb | 3,780 |
| | S. Two long case clocks in Tompion style, parquetry of olive wood and walnut Each | 5,500 |
| 1966 | Millar. S. Ebony and gilt-bronze bracket clock by Tompion and Banger, 17½ in. high | 4,400 |

£

| | |
|---|---|
| 1966 S.  Tompion burr-walnut 'month-long' case, 7 ft high | 2,400 |
| Anderson.   S.   Bracket clock by George Graham, *c.* 1700, | |
| 10¼ in. high | 8,500 |
| 1967 S.  Tompion bracket clock, *c.* 1680, ebonized case, 12½ in. | 7,000 |
| Balfour.   C.   Repeater bracket clock, Joseph Knibb, *c.* | |
| 1690, burr-walnut, 12 in. high | 4,725 |
| Koller, Zurich.   Projector night-clock by William Barlow, | |
| King's Lynn, late 17th century, FS4,450+tax | 483 |
| S.  Ebonized bracket clock, Tompion no. 312, 14½ in. high | 5,500 |
| C.  Ebonized bracket clock, Tompion and Banger, 15 in. | 5,775 |
| S.  Bracket clock by Joseph Knibb, undated, 11 in. high | 3,100 |
| 1968 Prestige.   S.   25 late 17th or early 18th century English | |
| clocks, which made a total of £139,210. | |
| Ebony bracket clock by Thomas Tompion, only 10 in. | |
| high and numbered 285 | 15,500 |
| Long case, veneered ebony by John Fromenteel, *c.* 1660 | 15,000 |
| Olivewood longcase, signed by Tompion, very plain | 14,000 |
| Ebony bracket clock by G. Graham, *c.* 1718 | 9,000 |
| Joseph Knibb, burr walnut long case, signed | 9,000 |
| Ebony bracket repeater, signed Tompion, no. 108 | 8,500 |
| 14 others in same sale at £1,000 to £8,200 | |
| Brown.   S.   Tompion walnut long case, no. 28, 79 in. | |
| high | 4,800 |
| 12 in. bracket clock by Joseph Knibb | 6,825 |
| Lucas.   C.   Tortoiseshell and silver bracket clock, | |
| Nathaniel Barnes, 12¾ in. high, late 18th century | 3,360 |
| C.  Long case by Tompion, *c.* 1690 | 3,780 |
| Long case by Alfred East, 78 in., *c.* 1690 | 5,775 |
| S.  Pair of gilt-metal column clocks by Paul Rimbault, | |
| Soho, *c.* 1780, 27 in. high                             2 for | 5,200 |
| Burr-walnut long case, no. 778 by George Graham | |
| after 1713 | 2,600 |
| Dent & Co.   C.   'Rolling ball' clock, Congreve escape- | |
| ment in form of a Greek temple, early 19th century, by | |
| E. Dent, 13¾ in. high (for another, see 1969) | 2,625 |
| Half-second chronometer regulator by Arnold and | |
| Dent | 1,260 |
| Frere.   C.   Long case by Tompion, numbered 311, 94 in. | 4,200 |
| S.  Copper-gilt casket clock, heavily jewelled, 9 in. wide, | |
| style of James Cox, late 18th century | 2,200 |
| Oliver Hunter.   S.   Burr-walnut bracket-clock by Joseph | |
| Knibb, *grande sonnerie*, before 1700, 16½ in. high | 10,500 |
| Fortescue-Foulkes.   S.   Ebony bracket clock by John | |
| Knibb of Oxford after 1700, 12 in. high | 8,000 |

£

1968   S.  Ebony bracket clock by Daniel Quare, 13½ in., after
1700     3,800

Marquetry long case by Tompion, *c.* 1680, 73½ in. high   13,000

Prestige. S. Horizontal chronometer by Pennington Pendleton, numbered 26, 1798, 5·7 in. diam.   7,000

1969   S.  Bracket clock by Joseph Knibb, before 1700, 12½ in.   4,600

Bracket clock by George Graham, numbered 613, *c.* 1715, 14 in.   11,000

Barnett. S. Long case, star parquetry by Tompion, numbered 122, 80 in. high   7,800

Graves, Hove. Bracket clock by Henry Jones, early 18th century   4,200

Bracket clock by Jacob Massy, early 18th century   2,600

Fison. S. Veneered bracket clock, 5 in. dial, by Quare and Horseman, before 1724   2,200

S. Ebony bracket clock by Tompion, unnumbered, 6½ in. dial   7,500

Ebonized bracket clock, 13 in. high, by Daniel Quare   5,000

Richly silver-mounted bracket clock by Joseph Windmills, before 1700, 14½ in. high   3,600

Roman-striking long case by Joseph Knibb, 87½ in. high   7,800

Walnut long case by Joseph Knibb, 10 in. dial, 79½ in. high   9,000

Parquetry long case by Daniel Quare, 10 in. dial., 84 in. high   7,500

C. Tortoiseshell, mounted and jewelled, table clock by Eardley Norton, *c.* 1760–70, 16½ in. high   1,575

James. C. Mounted on miniature drawer-cabinet in jewelled and framed agate, style of James Cox, late 18th century, 9¼ in.   5,040

S. Musical architectural clock in Chinoiserie style, c. 1770, striped agate and jewelled ormolu mounts, 14½ in. high by James Cox (d. 1788)   3,200

Month regulator, plain long case, by George Graham, *c.* 1740, 74½ in. high   10,700

Star parquetry long case by Thomas Tompion, numbered 122, 80 in. high, 10-in. dial   4,000

Lord Kenyon. S. Rococo silver-mounted bracket clock by John Ellicott, *c.* 1755, 17½ in. high   4,800

Tennyson d'Eynecourt. Mounted bracket clock by Thomas Colley, before 1770, 16½ in. high   3,360

Bracket clock in Tompion style by Daniel Delander, before 1733, 17 in. high   3,150

£

1969  Derek Cooper. S. Quarter-striking bracket-clock by
    Joseph Knibb, 12¼ in. high                                7,200
        Walnut marquetry long-case by Joseph Knibb, 90½ in.
        high                        7,000
        Burr-walnut long-case by John Ellicott, _c._ 1730, 70 in.
        high                        3,400
    Fraser. S. Walnut marquetry long-case by Joseph Knibb,
    97 in.                                        4,200
    Lord Burnham. C. (at Hall Barn). Organ clock by
    Charles Clay, before 1740, 91 in. high, heavily mounted     4,200
    Leland Hayward. C. 'Rolling ball' clock without casing
    by G. H. Bell, Winchester, early 19th century (compare
    1968)                                      1,575
    S. Bracket clock, _grande sonnerie_, no. 169 by Thomas
    Tompion, more than usually ornate, 14½ in. high     12,000
        Plain walnut long case, signed by Tompion, 77 in. high    5,000
        Table night-clock of tabernacle form, painted dial,
        Charles II period, by John Fromenteel, 43½ in. high    2,200
    C. 'Universal Ring' for fixing solar time by dial and
    compass, brass, by Richard Glynne, London, early 18th
    century                                     8,400

# CLOCKS
## FRENCH
### 18th and early 19th centuries

The market for marble pedestals, gilt-bronze nymphs, Father Time and garlanded porcelain flowers—the most luscious clocks that were ever made. In the 1960s they cost between £1,350 and £7,500, but prices within that range had been paid now and again for the same sort of clock a good hundred years earlier. Therefore, a singularly flat and unresponsive market. Exceptionally a Louis XV cartel clock cost the Metropolitan Museum nearly £30,000 in 1966. One may compare this purchase with the £6,000 which the Marquess of Hertford paid for the Yverdon clock in 1866 (equivalent to £60,000) or the £4,040 which M. Camondo paid for the Three Graces clock of the Louvre in 1881 (equivalent to £36,350). But they were paying for a different commodity, virtually a work of sculpture, whereas in 1966 the Metropolitan Museum paid for what was supposed to be a unique combination, Chantilly figures and flowers on a Louis XV *monture*.

The passionate horologist is, however, more interested in the plainness and incredible precision of Breguet's little carriage clocks of the Bourbon restoration. His is a force to be reckoned with and the prices show it (see p. 484 and 695).

| | | £ |
|---|---|---|
| 1960 | Dusendschon. S. By Leroi, Louis XV, mounted with Kaendler's Meissen group, the Peasant Lovers | 3,200 |
| | By Benoist Gérard with lacquered bronze *magots* and Vincennes flowers, Louis XV | 2,310 |
| | Lord Hillingdon. C. By Baillou, on bronze elephant, Louis XV | 1,575 |
| | Dusendschon. S. By Leroi on Meissen figures of peasants | 3,200 |
| 1961 | C. By Herbault and Foullet before 1775 | 1,785 |
| | S. By Michel with Chinoiserie figures, Louis XV | 1,350 |
| | Topic. S. Louis XV, supported by a Meissen cockerel by Kaendler | 1,400 |
| 1962 | S. On bronze elephant by Delachaux, Louis XV | 1,650 |
| 1963 | S. On bronze elephant and porcelain mounts, Louis XV | 1,200 |
| | On bronze elephant and porcelain mounts, Caffieri style, Louis XV | 1,800 |
| | René Fribourg. 1st sale. S. | |
| | Louis XV cartel clock—thermometer by Lepauté | 2,300 |
| | Table clock by Lepauté and Vion, supported by the Three Graces, Louis XVI, 20½ in. high | 5,600 |
| | Mantel clock by Berthoud, Louis XVI, with lacquered bronze negro supporters | 2,900 |
| | René Fribourg, 2nd sale. | |
| | Ormolu clock *en rocaille* by Balthazar with three Kaendler figures, early Louis XV | 4,000 |

1963  S. Cartel clock Louis XV, by l'Espinasse, mounted in £
Caffieri style                                                3,600
1964  Paris. Musical temple-shaped clock, enamelled gold
mounts, presented to Marie Antoinette, FN110,000+tax          8,430
1965  S. Long case, marquetry, by Berthoud, c. 1730            2,200
1966  Vernon. S. Long case in Boulle style by Ourry, c. 1740  2,500
Fortescue. C. Cartel clock by Lenoir, elaborately
mounted with three Chantilly *magots*, c. 1740, and Vincennes
flowers of the 1750s. Metropolitan Museum                    29,400
1967  C. Mantel-clock, Louis XV, on ormolu palm trees and
*comedia* figures, unsigned                                   3,150
N.Y. Louis XV mantel clock on Meissen Chinoiserie
group by Fritsche. Vincennes flowers etc., $12,000           4,250
Winston Guest. N.Y. Cartel clock by Gourdain, c. 1740,
34½ × 22                                                      3,678
Barometer with thermometer to match by Caffieri,
Louis XV, 47 × 5 in.                                   2 for  4,640
Paris. Empire style, lapis and ormolu, 28 in. high, given
by Napoleon to Marshal Cambacères, FN45,000+tax              3,630
1968  S. Mantel-clock by Benoist Gérard, Meissen figures and
flowers                                                       2,400
Vanderbilt-Balsan. C. By Le Loutre, Vincennes flowers
and Kaendler white figures of Gods, Louis XV                 1,890
Elie de Rothschild. S. Marquetry long case by Voisin
and Lieutaud, Louis XV, 95 in. high                          7,500
S. Lyre-shaped clock by Collas, *bleu du ciel* Sévres borders,
4½ in. high, c. 1812                                          1,470
Paris. Louis XV mantel-clock, mounted with Vincennes
porcelain flowers, ormolu etc., FN52,000+tax                 4,855
Koller, Zurich. Mounted long case in rosewood and
palisander by David Roentgen, Neuwied, 1759, FS29,000+tax 3,140
1969  Hasson. C. Lyre-shaped miniature regulator by
Ridereau and Goyer, c. 1740, 27 in. high                     3,045
C. By Lenoir, c. 1740–50, mounted with Mennecy
coloured group, flowers and ormolu plinth, 11¾ in. high.
Bought in                                                     6,300
S. Louis XV mantel-clock by Ribaucourt, mounted with
Kaendler figures and Meissen flowers, 19 in. high            2,500
Fribourg. C. Tulipwood and amaranth regulator long
case, 7 ft 7 in. high, by Jean Goyer, end of the 18th century,
$7,750                                                        3,254
Villa Demidoff. S. (Florence). By Basile Leroy, set in
block of green porphyry surmounted by bronze bust of
lady in tiara, c. 1815, numbered 547, 22 in. high, 7 million
lire+10% tax                                                  5,132

| 1969 | Cartel clock by Baillou, Louis XV, 45 in. high, 6,200,000 lire+10% tax | £ 4,536 |
|------|-----|------|
| | S. Mantel-regulator by Papst and Robin, *c.* 1785 | 3,200 |
| | C. Cartel clock by Ageron, Louis XV, 32 in. high, white porcelain flowerheads | 4,200 |
| | Musical clock by Ageron on elaborate cagework plinth with ormolu nymph, Louis XV | 3,360 |
| | Paris. Louis XV musical clock, mounted lacquer, movement by Carte, Nevers, 33¼×20¾, FN80,000+tax | 7,460 |
| 1970 | S. Mounted regulator, long case with 8 subsidiary dials, adapted to the French Revolution calendar, by Antide Janvier, *c.* 1800, 110 in. high | 6,000 |

### Abraham Louis Breguet (1747–1823)

| 1963 | S. Precision timekeeper, bought by the Prince Regent in 1814 for £290 | 5,200 |
|------|-----|------|
| | Muir. Plain silver travelling clock (£230 in 1828) | 12,000 |
| 1964 | S. Carriage clock, 1815 | 4,200 |
| 1965 | S. Travelling clock, 5 in. high, £150 in 1826 | 5,000 |
| 1967 | C. Travelling clock, 1820s, 7¼ in. high, some decoration | 2,520 |
| 1968 | S. Mantel-regulator clock made by Breguet in 1822 for the Duchess de Ventimille | 7,800 |
| | Prestige. S. Carriage clock by Breuget, numbered 179, sold to King of Naples, 1804, £174 (4,000 francs) 5¾ in. high | 5,000 |
| 1969 | C. Marine chronometer no. 3057, before 1820 | 1,155 |

# CRYSTAL AND MOUNTED HARD STONE
## Renaissance and later (*see also* Fabergé)

Renaissance crystal is a very sparsely provided market. The little that reaches the salerooms fetches rather more than in the 1930s but on the whole less than in the early 1900s. For instance, the remarkable mounted *biberon* for which Baron Bruno Schroeder paid £20,000 in 1905, would certainly not be worth £160,000. This older taste of the Rothschild dynasty lacks support.

In his onslaught on the great collector, William Beckford in 1823, Hazlitt denounced his love of carved crystal as seeking 'the polished surface of art'. Those who seek it nowadays, go in for Chinese jade, Fabergé toys and French glass paperweights. In fact they don't want too much art history. Quite a number of items in this list—and not the cheapest either—are French or Viennese imitations of the mid-late 19th century.

| | | £ |
|---|---|---|
| 1960 | C. Imitation of a Renaissance *biberon*, rock crystal and enamel on gold, Vienna mid-19th century | 1,155 |
| | S. Crystal *bonbonnière* and cover, enamelled gold mounts, arms of Catherine de Medici, mid-16th century | 660 |
| | The Hope Family green jasper bowl, made in 1855 in heavily mounted and jewelled Renaissance style (£1,200 in 1937) | 5,500 |
| 1963 | Lord Astor. C. Engraved Italian crystal cup, 11¾ in. high, late 16th century | 840 |
| | Agate ewer, mounted in enamelled gold, French 19th century reproduction by Charles Duron | 787 10s. |
| | Mounted bloodstone tazza by Charles Duron, *c.* 1860 | 630 |
| | Fribourg. S. Carved crystal Chinese ewer in Louis XV ormolu mounts | 3,800 |
| | Paris. Onyx leopard, N. Italian, *c.* 1600 (with tax) | 4,818 |
| | C. Crystal ewer by the Saracchi family, Milan, *c.* 1580, in English silvergilt mounts, *c.* 1620 (bought recently for £200) | 2,100 |
| 1965 | Desmond Hurst. C. Serpentine vase and cover, mounts by Stoer, Nuremberg, *c.* 1600 (£63 in 1902, £273 in 1954) | 1,680 |
| | Adda, Paris. Crystal pyx, German silvergilt mounts, *c.* 1606 | 1,415 |
| | Crystal tazza, 7 in. high, mid-17th century, Italian stand | 1,200 |
| 1966 | James de Rothschild. Paris. Two-handled crystal tankard, mounted in gold and enamels, 17¼ in. high | 2,450 |
| 1967 | S. Agate ewer, richly mounted in form of a dwarf. S. German, *c.* 1750, 4½ in. high | 1,350 |
| 1968 | S. Quartzite bowl. S. German, silvergilt mounts, *c.* 1700, 12 in. diam. | 3,000 |

| | | £ |
|---|---|---|
| 1968 | Davies. S. Cross-legged jester in mock crown, brown jasper, jewelled and mounted, 3¾ in. high. By Johann Dinglinger, Dresden, *c.* 1700 | 3,800 |
| | C. Hispano-Mauresque casket, late 15th century, crystal plaques in parcelgilt frames, 7¾ in. long | 1,155 |
| 1969 | S. Pair of swans, lapis, silvergilt and jewels in S. German Renaissance style, Vienna, 1866, 18 in. high 2 for | 2,350 |
| | *Nef,* Agate, crystal, jasper and ormolu, Vienna, mid-19th century, 12 in. long | 3,100 |
| | Rock crystal elephant, supporting gold and lapis clock, Viennese, mid-19th century, 7½ in. high | 900 |
| | C. Serpentine tankard, silver mounts and cover, marked IPS (John Plummer, York) 1665, 6¾ in. high | 1,350 |
| | C. Silver and lapis inkstand in the shape of an obelisk and fountain with statues, 26¾ in. high, by Vincenzo Coaci, Rome, *c.* 1800 | 6,720 |
| | Melvin Gutman. N.Y. Standing cup, carved from a single piece of lapis, shell-shaped with mask finial and dolphin foot, 5 in. wide, Florence after 1570, $12,000 | 5,000 |
| | Tazza on tall stem, solid jasper, gold mounted, 6½ in. high, Italy after 1570, $17,000 (£74, 1931, £273 1939) | 7,084 |
| | Miniature rock crystal scent-bottle, jewelled and enamelled gold mounts, Italy towards 1600, 2¼ in. high, $3,750 | 1,562 |
| | Gavin Astor. C. Fluted bowl, mauve jasper, N. Italian, late 16th century, chased gold mounts to the foot, 9¾ in. wide | 2,310 |
| | Stuker, Berne. Engraved crystal ewer, tulip-shaped, made for Rudolf II in Prague or Milan, *c.* 1550, FS83,000+tax | 8,780 |

EGYPT AND THE ANCIENT NEAR EAST
(Antiquities of all kinds)

EGYPT

£

| | | |
|---|---|---|
| 1960 | Hirsch, Lucerne. Bronze pacing goose, c. 1200 B.C. | 2,570 |
| | S. Basalt figure of Osiris, 18 in. high | 980 |
| 1961 | Earl of Pembroke. C. (at Wilton). Bronze figurine, Hekatifnet, Saitic period | 992 10s. |
| | Red granite head of a king | 682 10s. |
| 1962 | Stheeman. S. Bronze Saitic cat, 13½ in. high | 9,500 |
| 1963 | Bought by Berlin Staatliches Museum in London. Akhenaton's court sculptor with his wife, 18th dynasty granite stele Reported price | 75,000 |
| | Bruce Ingram. S. Green glazed torso in Greek style of a Goddess, 4½ in. high | 450 |
| | S. Glazed turquoise jar, Romano–Egyptian | 240 |
| | Wooden Ushabti figure, 18th dynasty, 16 in. high | 520 |
| | Miniature bronze Saitic cat | 1,400 |
| 1964 | S. Diorite head, 8 in. high, 12th dynasty | 800 |
| | Brummer. S. Saitic glass figure, Maat, Goddess of truth, 6¼ in. | 1,000 |
| | Bronze falcon, 14th dynasty, 8½ in. | 1,400 |
| | A second bronze falcon, 14th dynasty, 8½ in. | 1,250 |
| | Gold and enamel scarab, Saitic, 6th century B.C. | 1,000 |
| | Saitic bronze cat, 4¾ in. high | 1,000 |
| | Fragmentary quartzite statue, 22 in. 19th dynasty | 1,600 |
| 1965 | Spencer Churchill. C. Blue faience cat, 2¼ in. high, 18th dynasty | 1,260 |
| 1966 | Gallatin. S. Fayyum mummy portrait painting, 2nd century A.D., 15 × 8 (compare 1969) | 1,650 |
| 1967 | Bauer. S. Bronze cat, Saitic period, 10½ in. | 2,600 |
| | C. 14 in. basalt figure, New Kingdom | 577 10s. |
| | Bellecombe. C. Granite Pharaoh head, 12 in. 18th dynasty | 1,260 |
| | Paris. Saitic ibis figure, wood and gilded stucco, 19 in. high, FN25,000+tax | 2,320 |
| 1968 | S. Steatite inscribed Ushabti figure, 18th dynasty, 7¾ in. | 1,250 |
| | Bronze cat, Saitic period, 7¼ in. high | 1,000 |
| | Bronze hawk of Horus, much restored, 26th dynasty, 11¼ in. high | 1,050 |
| | Bronze cat, Saitic period, 13 in. high | 2,800 |
| | Paris. Stone head of a dignitary, late Saitic, c. 700 B.C., FN102,000+tax | 9,553 |
| 1969 | Paris. Bronze Saitic cat, FN50,000+tax | 4,709 |

| | | |
|---|---|---:|
| 1969 | Paris. Headless torso, alabaster, Old Kingdom, FN 50,000+ tax | 4,709 |
| | S. Bronze Saitic cat, 7 in. high | 2,600 |
| | Bronze Saitic cat, 5½ in. high, with gold earring | 1,100 |
| | Mummy portrait, young girl, encaustic on wood, 10¼ × 4½, c. 200 A.D. | 2,600 |
| | Phillipps Library. S. Papyrus roll, spells for the scribe, Pa-Aa, 13th century B.C., Hieratic script, 60 × 7, unrolled and framed in 1958 | 4,000 |
| | N.Y. Stone half-length figure, the scribe Gurneh, 18th dynasty, 21 in. high, $18,000 | 7,500 |
| | Lapis lazuli figure of Horus, 26th dynasty, 7th–6th century B.C., $1,800 | 750 |

## ASSYRIA AND BABYLONIA ETC., STONE AND BRONZE SCULPTURE

The ancient kingdoms of Mesopotamia are represented in the salerooms only by stone fragments of fairly rare occurrence, and consequently more expensive than Egyptian antiquities of the same kind. The value of Akkadian and Sumerian sculpture which is subject to the competition of museums is quite unpredictable. On the other hand, Assyrian fragments from Nimrud and other sites, which have been in the country in some cases over a century, and which make a saleroom appearance most years, have gone up very little since the end of the war.

| | | |
|---|---|---:|
| 1960 | Ducane. S. Assyrian relief fragment from Niniveh, half figure, 21 × 10 in. Birmingham City Museum | £ 2,700 |
| | N.Y. Another smaller fragment from Niniveh | 1,607 |
| 1964 | Brummer. S. Bronze Akkadian figure from Lagash, 7¾ in. | 4,600 |
| | 18-in. Assyrian relief from Koyunjuk | 4,000 |
| | Pre-dynastic Sumerian seal cylinder from Warka, 3½ in., Ashmolean Museum | 1,000 |
| 1965 | Stoclet. S. Sumerian stone head of priest with lapis-in-laid eyes, 3½ in. high | 1,700 |
| | S. Akkadian diorite head of Gudea, King of Lagash, (Mesopotamia), c. 2100 B.C., National Gallery, Melbourne | 11,500 |
| 1966 | Gallatin. S. Black stone weight in the form of a duck, Akkadian, Lagash | 850 |
| | Recumbent limestone bull from Uruk, Mesopotamia, 7¼ in. high, 4th millenium B.C. | 10,200 |
| 1967 | S. Hittite bronze axe head, Anatolia, c. 1,000 B.C. | 1,400 |

£

| | | |
|---|---|---|
| 1968 | S. Assyrian bas-relief fragment from Nimrud, 26½×28¾ | 3,000 |
| | Another (headless figure) from Palace of Sennacherib, 39½×18 | 5,400 |
| | Complete Hittite stele, bas-relief figure from Arslan Tash, 8th century, B.C., 40½×50½ | 3,500 |
| 1969 | St Audries School. S. Assyrian relief fragment from Nimrud, kneeling winged figure, 33×25 in. | 10,500 |

## BABYLONIA AND PERSIA, SILVER
Mainly late Achaemenid, 5th–4th century, B.C.
or late Sassanid, after 6th century A.D.

Danger, men at work!

| | | |
|---|---|---|
| 1962 | S. Sassanid dish, 8⅛ in. diam., supposed 7th century A.D. | 1,500 |
| | Graeco-Bactrian bowl, c. 300–250 B.C., akin to the Oxus treasure | 900 |
| 1964 | S. Achaemenid silver *phiale*, 4th century B.C., 12 in. diam. | 3,000 |
| 1965 | S. Silver ewer, alleged late Sassanid, 6th–7th centuries A.D., Melbourne National Gallery | 3,000 |
| | Boat-shaped silver dish, alleged Sassanid | 800 |
| 1966 | S. Graeco-Achaemenid silver libation dish from Asia Minor, 7 in. diam., 5th century B.C., bought in at | 1,300 |
| 1967 | S. The same | 1,300 |
| | Solley. S. Achaemenid *phiale*, 5th century B.C., 8½ in. diam. | 900 |
| 1968 | C. Sassanid dish, part gilded, 8 in. diam. | 1,050 |
| | *Phiale*, Ionian-Achaemenid, 5th–4th century B.C. | 800 |
| | C. Beaker from Marlik, Babylonian style, 9th century B.C., 5½ in. | 1,680 |
| | Another, same dimensions. Bought in at | 735 |
| | Graeco-Achaemenid fluted jug, 8¼ in., 3rd century B.C., bought in | 787 10s. |

# FABERGÉ

Objects in gold, hard stones and enamel, made at the Karl Fabergé workshop, Petersburg, between the 1890s and the Russian revolution.

It will be gathered from some of the prices in this list that, among these very costly toys, anything with an imperial Russian monogram or with imperial insignia is likely to make several times as much as anything else. In this brave new world of ours there is nothing left to be snobbish about except the past, and even the most recent past will do, if it is a matter of extinct dynasties. Among other remarkable results of this situation, a timid pastiche of an oviform Louis XVI clock cost in 1964 four or five times as much as the original could possibly have made. Similarly, a gold and enamelled snuffbox with the monogram of Nicholas II cost almost as much as any 18th century snuffbox, sold in the 1960s. What else were the happy purchasers buying apart from Imperial associations? Fabergé and his team may have been competent jewellers, but artistically there was nothing very adventurous about them. There were two quite distinct styles. The quaint and folky Russian peasants and soldiers, as well as the comic animals in various hard stones, are in the Snow White and the Seven Dwarfs tradition, that facet of the Swiss genius which created all those bears and cuckoo-clocks and received the edge of Whistler's tongue. Almost everything else is in the style once known as Edwardian Adam or *early Wagon-Lit*, the international *table d'hôte* which the rich expected and the Petersburg court encouraged because it was not subversive. But I have already committed *lèse-majesté*, so I will hold my peace.

| | | |
|---|---|---|
| 1959 | S. Gold and enamel cigarette case, monogram Queen Marie of Rumania | £ 1,500 |
| | Marabu stork in agate, 7½ in. high | 2,200 |
| | Smoky crystal ape, 3½ in. high | 1,600 |
| | Dodds. C. Cat in purpurine | 1,732 10s. |
| | Eagle in chalcedony, 3 in. high | 1,680 |
| | Ibis, chalcedony | 1,207 10s. |
| 1960 | Duchess of Kent. S. Basket of flowers, gold and enamels, 3¾ in. high | 2,800 |
| | C. Gold and nephrite box, 3½ in. diam. | 1,029 |
| | S. Russian peasant and his wife, various stones, 5 in. high 2 for | 14,000 |
| | C. Opal parrot in gold cage, 3¾ in. high | 997 10s. |
| 1961 | C. Gold and pale blue enamel box with miniature portrait, 3½ in. wide | 4,200 |
| | Cigarette case, gold with blue enamel | 3,675 |
| | Gold and enamel frame, miniature of the Czarina | 2,625 |
| 1961 | Gold and pink enamel table clock, 4 in. high | 3,300 |

490

| | | |
|---|---|---|
| 1961 | Grand Duchess Xenia. S. Easter egg with imperial cross of St George, white enamel on gold, 3¼ in. high, 1916 | £ 11,000 |
| | Russian pie-pedlar, figure in various stones, 4¾ in. | 8,000 |
| 1963 | S. Gold and enamel Sedan chair, ivory shafts, 3½ in. long | 4,200 |
| 1964 | S. Russian peasant woman, hard stones, 7¼ in. high, 1915 | 2,600 |
| | Cavalry officer, 5¼ in. high, 1914–15 | 6,950 |
| | Clock, shaped as an enamelled fan | 900 |
| 1965 | de Courcy. C. Jewelled and gold mounted nephrite dish, 8½ in. long | 1,995 |
| | S. Cigarette case in two-colour gold | 780 |
| | Parrot on swing, various stones | 2,000 |
| | N.Y. Miniature folding screen in gold, portraits of Imperial family, 8 in. long, $18,000 | 6,430 |
| | C. Miniature vitrine, gold and enamels | 1,050 |
| | S. Set of desk fittings, nephrite and ormolu | 3,000 |
| | N.Y. Oviform clock, monogrammed plinth in Louis XVI style, 7 in. high, $50,000 | 17,855 |
| 1966 | Sykes. S. Walking-stick handle, serpent's head | 820 |
| | C. Miniature easter-egg *bonbonnière*, gold and enamel | 2,100 |
| | Agate toucan on perch, 3¼ in. high | 3,990 |
| 1967 | Astor. C. Circular snuffbox, gold and enamels, 2½ in. diam. | 1,365 |
| | Cole Porter. N.Y. Platinum square flat case with jewelled sunburst motif, $4,000 | 1,429 |
| | Grand Duchess Olga. N.Y. Smoke-crystal bowl in gold mount, height 2¼ in. $2,500 | 893 |
| | Donahue. N.Y. Frog, nephrite, $9,000 at 2·80 to £ | 3,215 |
| | Squatting chimpanzee, agate, $16,000 | 5,714 |
| | S. *Kovsh*, hard stone and gold, 1898, 4 in. wide | 1,100 |
| | Christie. N.Y. Miniature cabinet, gold and hard stones in Louis XVI style, 5¼ × 3½, $39,000 | 16,250 |
| | Gold and enamel snuffbox, monogram of Nicolas II, $40,000 | 16,666 |
| | Miniature table, Louis XVI style, 3¼ in. high, $20,000 | 8,333 |
| 1968 | Koller, Zurich. Cigarette case, gold and diamonds, portrait-miniature and Czarina's autograph, FS37,000+tax | 4,020 |
| | Fothergill-Byrne. S. Square gold and enamel desk-clock, sunray motif, 4 in. diam. | 1,400 |
| | Bekhor. C. Bowenite elephant, enamelled howdah, 8¾ in. high | 1,890 |
| | S. Beaker, silvergilt and enamels with photographic view of the Fabergé establishment, 4½ in. high | 1,200 |
| | Cigarbox, silver and cloisonné enamel, rubies, 8 in. | 1,900 |
| | Lamp in Art Nouveau style, green and gold opalescent glass, 11¼ in. high, ex the imperial yacht, *Standard* | 1,200 |

| | | |
|---|---|---:|
| 1968 | Stuker, Berne.   Figure of John Bull in hard stones FS72,000+tax | £ 8,038 |
| 1969 | S.   Sprig of forget-me-nots in glass, rock crystal, nephrite and jewels | 980 |
| | Pair of amazonite parrots in gold and enamel cage, 6½ in. | 4,800 |
| | Hirst-Broadhead.   S.   Triptych containing three imperial miniature portraits, 1913, by Karl Hahn, 7½ in. with gold easel support | 5,200 |
| | Smith.   S.   Imitation Louis XVI gold snuffbox with classical cameo, 2 in. diam. | 4,000 |
| | Byrne.   S.   Nephrite desk clock, Louis XVI style, gold, enamels and stones, 6½ in. high | 4,000 |
| | Hirst-Broadhead.   S.   Nephrite cigarette case, imperial eagle in diamonds, 4 in. | 4,400 |
| | Baroque pearl forming flamingo, 4¼ in. high | 3,200 |
| | Nephrite *Kovsh*, handle part gilded, 7 in. wide | 2,900 |
| | N.Y.   Enamel and gold goblet, *piqué à jour*, $21,000 | 8,750 |
| | Presentation snuffbox of Nicolas II, gold, enamel and diamonds, $12,500 | 5,282 |
| | Repeater table clock, silver and enamel, $10,250 | 4,271 |

# FURNITURE
## GOTHIC AND RENAISSANCE
### ITALIAN BEFORE 1700

For a brief period, just after the Napoleonic wars, when the neoclassicism o the Revolution and the Empire was unpopular and the Romantic movement was on the lookout for a congenial historic style, Italian furniture of the 16th–17th centuries became the most expensive on the market. Ebony cabinets, inlaid with all sorts of *pietre dure* fetched £367 10s. in 1819, £572 5s. in 1823 and £320 15s. in 1825, that is to say prices between £4,800 and £7,450 on the 1970 scale. They were linked with the names of Cellini and Michelangelo, though sometimes no older than the reign of Louis XIV. In reality this sort of furniture in 1970 is unlikely to pass the £1,000 mark unless it is mounted on English carved giltwood stands. True early Renaissance Italian furniture is on a different footing, painted *cassone* chests of the 15th century being valued as pictures by the primitive masters. But the elaborately carved *cassone* of the 16th century, even when at their best, tell the sad story of the decline in High Renaissance objects. Throughout the 1920s they were capable of making £1,500 to £2,500, that is to say £7,500 to £12,500 in 1970 terms. But there was little chance of such prices in the 1960s.

|  |  | £ |
|---|---|---|
| 1959 | Marlborough House. C. Cabinet, ivory and ebonized wood | 787 10s. |
| 1960 | Myron Taylor. N.Y. Sienese walnut armorial *credenza* | 393 |
|  | Tuscan octagonal table on dolphins | 286 |
|  | Florentine *credenza* | 321 10s. |
| 1961 | Shelley-Rolls. C. Florentine gilt *cassone*, c. 1500 with painted panels of a procession | 6,090 |
| 1963 | Berwind. N.Y. 16th century walnut *cassone*, carved with arms of Visconti, Rome | 536 |
| 1964 | S. Florentine painted *cassone* c. 1500 | 4,200 |
| 1965 | S. Writing table, ivory inlay on ebony, c. 1670 | 800 |
| 1966 | C. Florentine ebonized cabinet, *pietre dure* inlays, c. 1600 | 336 |
|  | Another ditto, giltwood baroque stand, 17th century | 735 |
|  | S. Venetian spinet, painted and figured lid, c. 1590 | 880 |
| 1967 | Watney. C. (at Cornbury Park). The throne of Giuliano de' Medici (sic), a *cassapanca*, inlaid woods, c. 1500 (Demidoff sale, 1880, £740), bought Paul Getty | 6,300 |
|  | Heber Percy. C. Florentine *stipo* cabinet, ebonized wood, crystal, ivory, etc., 17th century (Valued for D. of Northumberland, 1786, £6 6s.) | 1,102 10s. |
|  | Eckman. S. Miniature 17th century Florentine *stipo* in numerous marbles, 23 in. wide, in George II case and mahogany stand | 1,200 |

| | | £ |
|---|---|---|
| 1967 | Zuckerman. N.Y. Inlaid walnut arcaded cabinet, 5 ft. high, Venice, *c.* 1600 | 500 |
| | Feinberg. N.Y. Synagogue circumcision throne, walnut inlaid, late 17th century, $3,500 | 1,893 |
| | Finarte, Milan. Pair of 16th century walnut cupboards with inlaid portrait medallions, 1·6 million lire+tax    2 for | 1,040 |
| 1968 | Congreve. C. Walnut *credenza*, 17th century, 86 in. long | 1,470 |
| | Elaborately carved and gilded walnut *cassone*, *c.* 1560 | 3,675 |
| | Four walnut armchairs, 17th century, contemporary needlework    4 for | 1,155 |
| | Warwick Castle. C. Florentine *stipo* cabinet, *pietre dure* and ebony, towards 1700 | 840 |
| | ·S. Another, 4 ft 8 in. high with stand, includes coromandel wood and ivory | 1,000 |
| | Mason. S. Walnut *cassone*, Roman style reliefs, towards 1600, 71½ in. long | 787 10s. |
| 1969 | Villa Demidoff. S. (Florence). *Certosino* or ivory-inlaid walnut *cassone*, 71 in. long, late 16th century, 2·8 million lire+tax | 2,052 |
| | Evershed. C. Architectural cabinet, columns and central alcove in walnut, *c.* 1600, 75 in. high | 1,260 |
| | S. 17th century cabinet in *pietre dure*, George I giltwood stand in *Régence* style | 4,100 |
| | Villa la Ferdinanda, Florence. Sculptured nuptial bed of Francesco de' Medici, Milan, *c.* 1650, 3·7 million lire+tax | 2,713 |
| | Lord Burnham. C. (at Hall Barn). Highly sculptured upright secrétaire cabinet on lion feet, walnut, *c.* 1600, 44½ in. wide | 2,205 |

### OTHER CONTINENTAL COUNTRIES

| | | |
|---|---|---|
| 1960 | Weinmüller, Munich. 15th century S. German cabinet, flamboyant Gothic tracery in maple and larch | 6,600 |
| 1961 | Weinmüller, Munich. 13th century chest, 5 ft long | 618 |
| | Lempertz, Cologne. Four-door cabinet, Tyrolese, *c.* 1500, 7 ft 6 in. high | 2,260 |
| | Lyons walnut buffet, *c.* 1590, 5 ft. high | 722 |
| 1962 | S. Flemish painted cabinet, early 17th century | 1,500 |
| 1963 | Scarisbricke Hall. (Spencer, Retford.) A collection of Renaissance carvings, made into panels by Pugin *c.* 1840 | 2,100 |
| | Paris. Gothic coffer, arcaded front, 6 ft long, FN26,000+ tax | 2,250 |
| 1965 | Margand. S. French walnut *meuble à deux corps*, reliefs in style of Jean Goujon, late 16th century | 380 |

| | | | |
|---|---|---|---|
| 1966 | C. Spanish *Vargueno* cabinet, ivory, etc., inlaid on walnut, late 17th century | £ | 1,260 |
| | Ruef, Munich. Walnut tabernacle cupboard, 84 in. high, Frankfurt, late 17th century, DM18,000+tax | | 1,850 |
| 1967 | van Waay, Amsterdam. Flemish cabinet, *c.* 1600, 94½ in. high | | 1,035 |
| | C. Cabinet on stand, numerous drawers, coloured ivory inlays, Antwerp before 1650 and perhaps by Forchoudt | | 2,100 |
| | Ronald Tree. N.Y. Walnut writing table, Louis XIII | | 1,070 |
| 1968 | Howard. S. *Meuble à deux corps*, finely carved walnut, Henri IV, *c.* 1600 | | 900 |
| | Marshall Brookes. C. North German oak vestry cupboard, linenfold panelling, early 16th century | | 1,680 |
| | Antwerp cabinet and stand, *c.* 1660, ebony and tortoiseshell inlays, 45×65 | | 787 10s. |
| | S. Mid 17th century Dutch drawer-cabinet, ebony inlaid with chased silver, black painted stand, 4 ft 10 in. high | | 3,200 |
| | Warwick Castle. C. Two Spanish *varguenos*, 57 in. high | { | 1,365 / 1,260 |
| | N.Y. French walnut *meuble à deux corps*, 5 ft 9×4 ft 9 | | 1,240 |
| 1969 | Bryce. C. Spanish walnut *vargueno*, ivory inlays, 43 in. | | 1,050 |
| | Silberman. N.Y. French walnut *meuble à deux corps*, 2nd half 16th century, 7 ft high, $10,500 | | 4,410 |
| | Gatty. S. Three elaborately carved Dutch chairs of Padouk wood, early 17th century 3 for | | 920 |
| | Dutch centre-table, laburnum wood, same date, 39×29 in. | | 750 |
| | S. Dutch walnut display cabinet, 100 in. high, *c.* 1700 | | 2,250 |
| | Heber Percy. C. Louis XIII ebonized cabinet and stand, richly carved, *c.* 1640, 70×82 | | 1,890 |
| | Newton. S. Harpsichord, painted wood, by Jean Ruckers Antwerp, 1642, with painting by van der Werff, *c.* 1690, on inside lid, heavily restored and a new stand fitted, 1896, 8 ft long | | 9,500 |

## ENGLAND, BEFORE 1700
### (mainly oak)

In the 1920s there was a particularly popular style of interior decoration which extended from the Sussex stockbroker-belt via California to the Côte d'Azur. It comprised rough-hewn stucco walls, wrought iron, dripping sconces and oak furniture, stripped and pickled in a way that its makers never intended. Under its stimulus the price of an Elizabethan drawer-table rose to £1,000 and more, equivalent to £5,000 in 1970. English oak still has its devotees, but rarely at £5,000. A home-made peasant look is essential in the high-class market for English pottery and fervently prayed for in English porcelain but less desired in furniture. It wouldn't match the 'telly'.

| | | | £ | |
|---|---|---|---|---|
| 1964 | S. | Late 15th century oak armchair | 892 | 10s. |
| | | Oak dining table, Commonwealth period | 682 | 10s. |
| 1965 | S. | Oak drawer-refectory table, early Jacobean | 800 | |
| | | Plain refectory table, Charles I | 324 | |
| 1966 | C. | Early 16th century oak stool, 20×21 | 840 | |
| | | Early 16th century triangular envelope-table, 27 in. | 609 | |
| 1967 | Watney. C. | Walnut spinet by Hitchcock, London, 1625 | 892 | 10s. |
| | Micklem. S. | Elizabethan oak aumry, 50 in. wide | 850 | |

1968 Marshall Brooks. C. Late 17th century two-flap draw table, 82×80 in. extended — 735

Court cupboard, dated 1658, 64 in. high — 304 10s.

Three 17th century four-poster beds, oak, one dated 1670 — 682 10s. / 504 / 420

Lord Hanley. S. Early 16th century oak chest, 61½ in. long and very narrow — 1,200

1969 S. Oak marquetry four-poster bed, dated 1565 — 2,300

Oak dining table, triple plank top, 20 ft 1½ in.× 2 ft 8½ in. — 1,400

Kemsley. S. (at Dropmore). 10 ft. oak dining table, 'bobbin' legs double plank top, c. 1660 — 1,250

Hart. C. Press-cupboard, heavily carved oak, inlaid with holly and fruitwood, 48 in. wide, early 17th century — 787 10s.

Maxwell Joseph. S. 4-poster bed, elaborately carved columns etc., Henry VIII period with Victorian tester — 9,000

Oak aumry, slight Gothic tracery, early 16th century — 4,800

Elizabethan draw-leaf table on winged sphinxes and lions, exceptionally rich, 95 in. long — 3,800

James I court cupboard, fairly plain, 44 in. high — 2,800

1970 S. Armchair with seat-cupboard and two Italianate portrait roundels, c. 1520–30 — 3,000

Four-poster bed, carved oak canopy and baluster columns, Sydenham House, Devon, 62 in. wide, late 16th century — 2,730

# FURNITURE
## ENGLISH, LATE 17TH AND 18TH CENTURIES

*Pace* the £43,000 Harewood writing table, there was only a moderate advance in the price of English furniture in the 1960s, less than an adjustment to the 40 per cent devaluation of the pound in purchasing power. The advance of the entire art market after November, 1967, had an immediate effect only on certain types of English furniture which had attracted speculation. These included pieces in the rococo French style, red lacquer furniture of the beginning of the 18th century and Carlton House desks of the very end. The latter rose from an average £2,000 to as much as £8,200. The price of large desks certainly owed a great deal to the taxation allowance on office expenses. Plain partners' kneehole desks, made at any time between 1800 and 1830 can cost from £2,000 to £3,000. Before the war the largest were the least wanted and were worth no more than £20 to £30.

In the 1960s both inlaid satinwood furniture of the late 18th century and the walnut of the earlier part of the century advanced moderately, but carved mahogany in the Chippendale style, even sets of chairs which are always in demand, advanced a great deal less. Very exceptionally, an unusual set of four armchairs was sold in 1969 for £15,000, having multiplied in value six times since the Chrysler sale of 1960. The increased value of pieces out of the usual run was also reflected in the sum of £23,000, paid in 1968 for a peculiar pair of French-looking giltwood candle-stands by Matthias Lock. Another interesting price, paid in 1968, was £9,000 for a William and Mary red lacquer bureau-cabinet. A cabinet of this kind was sold for £2,047 10s. in 1928, the equivalent of £10,200, but in the 1930s and 1940s £200 would have been quite high. If one is to draw any inference from these prices, it is that the native quality of puritanism is less in demand in English furniture and that the greatest speculation is in colourful pieces.

### TABLES, DESKS, SIDEBOARDS, COMMODES, BOOKCASES ETC.

|  |  | £ |
|---|---|---:|
| 1960 | C.   George II walnut bookcase, 8 ft 10 in. high by 8 ft wide | 3,780 |
|  | Phillips, son and Neale.   Queen Anne bureau bookcase, walnut | 1,900 |
|  | Chrysler.   N.Y.   Lady's secrétaire, Hepplewhite | 575 |
|  | China cabinet, Chippendale | 2,320 |
|  | *Commode bombé*, ditto | 2,320 |
|  | Library table, style of William Kent | 2,140 |
| 1961 | Whitmarshe.   N.Y.   Documented Chippendale commode from Rainham, Norfolk (£3,900 in 1921), $70,000 | 25,000 |
|  | Commode, inlaid in French style, serpentine front | 3,572 |
|  | *Demi-lune* console table in Adam style | 1,964 |
|  | Countess of Craven.   S.   Chippendale kneehole desk from |  |

£

| | | |
|---|---|---|
| 1961 | Combe Abbey, documented | 13,000 |
| (*cont.*) | Chippendale mahogany writing table, under 4 ft wide | 2,700 |
| | Olaf Hambro. C. Marquetry commode, *c.* 1770 | 3,990 |
| | Chippendale black lacquer commode | 3,570 |
| | N.Y. Walnut secrétaire cabinet with mirror, *c.* 1720 | 4,820 |
| | Countess of Cadogan. C. Commode, *c.* 1780, inlaid in French style | 7,560 |
| | Duke of Norfolk. C. Two commodes, *c.* 1765   2 for | 3,570 |
| | Lady Hague. S. Round Chippendale stand, 15 in. diam. | 2,100 |
| | Hart. S. Queen Anne japanned cabinet and stand | 3,300 |
| 1962 | Knight, Frank. Mid-18th century partners' desk, 4 ft 6 in. | 2,500 |
| | C. Lacquer cabinet, late 17th century, on later stand | 1,995 |
| | Sheraton satinwood commode | 1,575 |
| 1963 | C. Marquetry commode by John Cobb, *c.* 1770, mounts in French style | 9,450 |
| | Harrington. S. Pair of red lacquer cabinets, *c.* 1700   2 for | 2,000 |
| | S. Pedestal writing desk, *c.* 1750, burr walnut | 4,600 |
| | N.Y. Pair of marquetry commodes, serpentine fronts and mounts in French style, Pierre Langlois, *c.* 1760, $20,000   2 for | 7,142 |
| | S. William and Mary red lacquered bureau-cabinet, elaborately crowned with urns.  8 ft 8 in. high | 9,000 |
| | Satinwood marquetry commode, semi-French style, 1960s | 7,500 |
| | Lady's secrétaire, satinwood marquetry, 34 in. wide | 3,350 |
| | C. Marquetry commode, French style of Pierre Langlois (compare 1966) | 5,040 |
| | Pair of six-foot sideboards in festooned Adam style   2 for | 4,410 |
| 1964 | Prestige. S. Double-ended walnut writing table, George II | 4,000 |
| | Breakfront mahogany bookcase, made by Chippendale for Nostell Priory | 4,000 |
| | S. Hepplewhite satinwood commode in French taste | 2,500 |
| | C. Pair of marquetry commodes, imitating Louis XV style   2 for | 5,040 |
| 1965 | Phillips. S. Norfolk House pedestal desk, richly mounted | 3,700 |
| | Kayser. C. Mahogany carved commode by Chippendale in French style, bought in at | 9,450 |
| | Harewood. C. Writing table by Chippendale after Robert Adam, tulipwood marquetry mounted, top 81 × 47½, *c.* 1770 | 43,050 |
| | Chinese mirror painting in Chippendale gilt frame | 10,500 |

498

£

| | | |
|---|---|---:|
| 1965 | C. Marquetry and giltwood side-table, Chippendale after Robert Adam | 6,800 |
| | Reece. S. Serpentine marquetry commode, French taste, *c.* 1765 | 4,200 |
| | Bearnes auctioneer, Torquay. Queen Anne walnut bureau-bookcase, 28½ in. wide | 3,300 |
| | Lord Craven. S. Two Chippendale French style commodes from Combe Abbey 2 for | 8,000 |
| | Small Chippendale mahogany commode from Combe Abbey | 4,800 |
| 1966 | Lord Torpichen. S. Giltwood overmantel mirror by Chippendale, incorporating a portrait by Alan Ramsay | 7,000 |
| | Lord Shaftsbury. C. Pair of William Kent giltwood side-tables 2 for | 5,775 |
| | Johnstone. S. Pair of mounted bureau-cabinets in early Sheraton style, 7 ft 6 in. high 2 for | 7,800 |
| | *Demi-lune* commode, satinwood marquetry, Adam style | 6,000 |
| | Young. C. Giltwood mirror, 5 ft 6 × 4 ft, with Chinese paintings | 3,360 |
| | Lord Carew. C. Pair of marquetry commodes, French style of Pierre Langlois, *c.* 1762 (compare 1963 and 1968) 2 for | 19,950 |
| | Baroness Zouche. C. Curved sideboard with pedestal urns and wine cooler, Adam style, white and gold | 6,825 |
| | C. Pair of Chippendale style giltwood side-tables with Italian painted tops 2 for | 6,510 |
| | Croome. C. Very plain mahogany commode, George III, with serpentine front | 4,410 |
| | Pair of lacquer cabinets in Chinese style on giltwood stands, *c.* 1680 2 for | 4,200 |
| | Summers. S. Chippendale yew-wood serpentine commode | 4,800 |
| | Macmillan. S. Serpentine commode in floral marquetry, George III | 3,900 |
| 1967 | C. Walnut Queen Anne cabinet desk, 80 in. high, 28 in. wide | 2,800 |
| | C. Satinwood *bonheur du jour*, Adam style, 38 in. wide | 3,360 |
| | Flat-sided commode, satinwood, Adam Style | 5,775 |
| | Lord Caledon. S. Pair of giltwood console tables with mirrors, Chinoiserie style, *c.* 1760 4 for | 7,200 |
| | C. Pair of marquetry serpentine commodes by John Cobb, mounted in French style towards 1770 2 for | 7,500 |
| | Phillips. S. Mounted marquetry commode by Chippen- | |

499

£

| 1967 (cont.) | dale in Adam style, matching the Harewood writing table (see 1965) | 4,000 |
|---|---|---|

<table>
<tr><td></td><td>S. Miniature Queen Anne bureau cabinet, japanned, round top, 5 ft high, 23 in. wide</td><td>2,100</td></tr>
<tr><td></td><td>William and Mary folding card table, 6 legs, walnut, 30 in. wide</td><td>2,400</td></tr>
<tr><td></td><td>Micklem. S. Two Queen Anne bachelor chests, burr walnut, extremely plain     Each</td><td>3,100</td></tr>
<tr><td></td><td>Burr-walnut bureau cabinet, only 24 in. wide, after 1714</td><td>3,600</td></tr>
<tr><td></td><td>C. Mahogany secrétaire bookcase, c. 1780</td><td>3,360</td></tr>
<tr><td></td><td>Heber Percy. C. Round torchère table, painted in Angelica Kaufmann style, 28½ in. high, 14½ in. diam.</td><td>3,570</td></tr>
<tr><td></td><td>Donahue. N.Y. Queen Anne walnut bureau-cabinet, 90 in. high, $11,000</td><td>3,920</td></tr>
<tr><td></td><td>C. Pair of satinwood round card-tables, marquetry c. 1780  2 for</td><td>6,300</td></tr>
<tr><td>1968</td><td>Tree. C. Oval library table, style of Robert Gillow, c. 1790, 74 in. wide</td><td>6,300</td></tr>
<tr><td></td><td>Two massive painted-wood and marble console tables, style of William Kent (bought in)  2 for</td><td>10,500</td></tr>
<tr><td></td><td>S. Pair of painted satinwood side-tables, c. 1780, 48 in. long, 18 in. deep  2 for</td><td>4,800</td></tr>
<tr><td></td><td>William and Mary red lacquer bureau-cabinet, 8 ft 2 × 3 ft 6</td><td>7,500</td></tr>
<tr><td></td><td>Wrottesley. S. Pair of 4 ft side-tables in Chippendale French style marquetry  2 for</td><td>7,000</td></tr>
<tr><td></td><td>Semi-circular marquetry commode in Adam style</td><td>6,500</td></tr>
<tr><td></td><td>Marquetry commode bombé in the French style of John Cobb, 4 ft 6 wide</td><td>7,500</td></tr>
<tr><td></td><td>Earl Poulett. S. Pair of painted and giltwood candle-stands in French style, 1744, by Matthias Lock, 5 ft 9 in. high  2 for</td><td>23,000</td></tr>
<tr><td></td><td>Giltwood and painted side-table en suite, 5 ft wide</td><td>7,400</td></tr>
<tr><td></td><td>Queen Anne black japanned side-table on V stretcher with river landscape, 44 in. wide</td><td>5,000</td></tr>
<tr><td></td><td>Pair of painted and giltwood candlestands, 5 ft high, by Benjamin Goodison, c. 1730 (Régence style)  2 for</td><td>3,600</td></tr>
<tr><td></td><td>Pair of matching side-tables by the same, 37 in. high, marble tops  2 for</td><td>5,600</td></tr>
<tr><td></td><td>Carved pinewood picture frame by Grinling Gibbons, c. 1690, 76 × 54 in. outside dimensions</td><td>3,200</td></tr>
<tr><td></td><td>Paravicini. C. Mahogany breakfront library bookcase, end 18th century, 68 × 88 in. high</td><td>5,460</td></tr>
</table>

£

| | |
|---|---|
| 1968 Paul. C. Pair of semi-circular side-cabinets, Sheraton style, satinwood, elaborately inlaid and with painted panels, 42 in. wide 2 for | 21,000 |
| S. Pair of *commodes bombés*, satinwood and harewood, style of Langlois, *c.* 1760, 54 in. wide 2 for | 11,000 |
| C. *Bonheur du jour*, Louis XVI style, 31¼ in. wide | 4,410 |
| 1969 S. Satinwood secrétaire bookcase, Sheraton style, 37 in. wide | 6,500 |
| Red japanned bureau-cabinet, William and Mary, 40 in. wide | 5,800 |
| C. Very elaborate Chippendale Gothic mahogany bureau-cabinet, 50×90 in. front, *c.* 1760–70 | 2,520 |
| Kemsley. S. (at Dropmore). Red japanned bureau cabinet, *c.* 1720, 7 ft 9 in. high by 3 ft 4 wide | 8,500 |
| Mahogany breakfront secrétaire-bookcase, *c.* 1760, 8 ft 4 high | 5,200 |
| Steel basket-grate, fender and accessories, Adam style | 2,800 |
| Pair of oval mirrors, rococo carving, giltwood, 64 in. high, *c.* 1760–70 2 for | 3,200 |
| Pair of red japanned cabinets on giltwood stands, 7 ft 6 high, 3 ft 11 in. wide 2 for | 8,000 |
| Villa Demidoff. S. (Florence). Giltwood centre table, malachite top, made for D. of Buccleuch, *c.* 1765, 26 million lire+tax | 19,066 |
| C. Pair of Hepplewhite marquetry card tables, 36 in. wide 2 for | 4,074 |
| International Publishing Corp. Pair of mounted kneehole writing desks in William Vile style, 63 in. wide (said to have cost £15,000), bought in at | 5,250 |
| C. Picture-marquetry *bureau de dame* in French style, 44¾ in. wide | 2,520 |
| Hague. C. Late 18th century mahogany partners' desk with light mounts, 72×42 | 10,500 |
| C. Late 18th century mahogany partners' desk with slight carving on the chamfered angles, 58½ in. | 3,780 |
| S. Late 18th century mahogany partners' desk, quite plain, 50 in. wide | 2,800 |
| Semi-circular side-table, late 18th century, 47 in. wide | 3,800 |
| Hart. C. Drawer-cabinet, elaborately lacquered on cream ground, George I with French giltwood stand in *Régence* style, 30½ in. wide | 6,825 |
| Queen Anne walnut bureau cabinet, 90 in. high | 3,990 |
| Pair of gilt gesso wall-sconces with embroidered silk panels, 28×10½, Queen Anne 2 for | 2,835 |

| 1969 | S. Pair of mahogany card tables, folding legs, *c.* 1760–80, 52 in. wide | £ 2 for 4,600 |

## CARLTON HOUSE DESKS
### (Made in 1790s and early 1800s)

| 1951 | Princess Royal.  C.  Nearly 6 ft wide | 1,942 10s. |
| 1960 | S.  65 in. wide | 2,500 |
| 1961 | Duke of Leeds.  S. | 1,500 |
|  | C.  Mahogany | 1,890 |
| 1962 | C.  Mahogany | 1,850 |
| 1965 | Motcomb's Rooms.  66 in. wide | 2,300 |
|  | S.  42 in. wide | 1,600 |
| 1966 | Wargrave Manor (Knight, Frank), Mahogany | 2,600 |
| 1967 | Eckman.  S.  60 in. wide | 1,900 |
| 1968 | Coulson.  S.  Mahogany, 63 in. wide | 3,600 |
|  | Pleydell-Bouverie.  S.  55 in. wide | 4,900 |
|  | C.  42 in. wide, satinwood and other veneers | 4,725 |
|  | Earl Poulett.  S.  64 in. wide, mahogany, fluted legs | 8,200 |
|  | Paul.  S.  Satinwood, 52 in. wide | 1,000 |
| 1969 | C.  Satinwood, Regency, 55 in. wide | 4,200 |

## CHAIRS AND SUITES OF CHAIRS

| 1960 | N.Y.  Single Chippendale armchair, Fulham tapestry, $5,000 | 1,786 |
| 1960 | C.  8 lyre-backed chairs, Thomas Chippendale Jnr., *c.* 1780 | 8 for 5,775 |
|  | Chrysler.  N.Y.  8 Queen Anne walnut chairs in petit-point embroidery from Maddingley Hall, $17,000 | 8 for 6,070 |
|  | Two oval-backed chairs, Chippendale style | 2 for 2,500 |
| 1961 | Whitmarshe.  N.Y.  Single George II wing armchair in grospoint embroidery, $4,250 | 1,517 |
|  | Lady Hague.  S.  Two mahogany library chairs, style of William Kent | 2 for 3,000 |
|  | S.  Set of 9 giltwood salon chairs in French style | 9 for 5,000 |
| 1962 | Lady Bailey.  S.  8 fauteuils in Louis XV style, painted wood | 8 for 1,400 |
|  | Ward.  C.  George II mahogany needlework suite, 8 chairs, 2 armchairs, settee and stool | 12 for 6,090 |
| 1963 | C.  Set of 10 Hepplewhite mahogany dining chairs, vase-shaped splats | 10 for 9,450 |
|  | Lord Harrington.  S.  Two giltwood 'French chairs', illustrated in Chippendale's directory, 1762 | 2 for 3,700 |

£

964 Earl of Yarborough. C. 18 mahogany chairs, *c.* 1760
(25 guineas in the Stowe sale, 1848)     18 for   3,780

965 S. Four Hepplewhite mahogany chairs, shield-backs and
reeded splats     4 for   2,600

966 Lord Shaftsbury. C. Four Chippendale mahogany armchairs, modern upholstery (4 from same suite, £1,995 in
1953)     4 for   9,022 10*s.*

S. Ten Chippendale dining chairs     10 for   5,200

Judah. S. Seven George II walnut chairs, petit-point
embroidery (Aubrey Fletcher sale, 1946, £3,800)     7 for   3,200

967 Lord Astor. C. Four beechwood chairs, painted and
gilded Chippendale style     4 for   4,730

Northey. S. Six walnut side-chairs and settee, 1740,
contemporary needlework     7 for   7,400

C. 12 open armchairs, 2 settees, mahogany in French style,
*c.* 1760     14 for   4,725

Eckman. S. Four open armchairs, contemporary needlework     4 for   3,400

Micklem. S. Single walnut Queen Anne chair, stuffed
violin back     1,600

Anderson. C. Set of very early walnut chairs, reign of
Charles II, red velvet upholstery     20 for   2,730

Heber Percy. C. Giltwood salon suite from Northumberland House in Adam style     15 for   3,360

Sandys-Lumsdaine. C. Painted suite, Hepplewhite
French style, settee, 8 open armchairs, 3 window seats
    12 for   5,775

968 Haskard. C. Eight painted open armchairs, similar style,
contemporary chintz     8 for   3,570

Freeman-Thomas. C. Four mahogany lyreback armchairs, brass strings, *c.* 1770     4 for   4,725

Warwick Castle. C. Suite of oval-backed giltwood open
armchairs, Hepplewhite, contemporary damask     8 for   5,775

Earl Poulett. S. Set of carved walnut dining chairs,
scallopshell backs, *c.* 1730     6 for   4,800

Set of 9 upholstered mahogany armchairs, *c.* 1730–40,
    9 for   4,800

969 S. Set of 12 mahogany armchairs, proto-Regency style,
    12 for   7,000

Kemsley. S. (at Dropmore). 18 armchairs, stool and
window seat giltwood, modern upholstery, *c.* 1770 20 for 11,500

S. Set of mahogany armchairs, fish-scale carving,
attributed John Gordon, *c.* 1756 (Others, Chrysler sale,
1960 $3,000 a pair)     4 for 15,000

1969 C. Set of Charles II walnut *farthingale* chairs, spirally £
turned legs, adapted tapestry covers 8 for 2,310
Clark. S. Set of burr-walnut chairs with vase-splat backs
and carved legs, sold in three lots (George I) 8 for 7,000
S. Set of Queen Anne armchairs, blue japanned, cane
panels, carved legs and top 4 for 4,200
Lord Burnham. C. (at Hall Barn). Pair of giltwood open
armchairs in French style, *c.* 1750 2 for 2,310
S. Set of George I walnut chairs, rectangular stuffed
backs, claw-and-ball feet 10 for 5,200
1970 Glemham Hall. S. 10 chairs, 2 stools, 2 settees, giltwood
in *Régence* style, *c.* 1720. Victoria and Albert Museum.
14 for 19,000

# FURNITURE
## ENGLISH, 'REGENCY' STYLE
### (anything from 1800 to 1830)

The fashion for English furniture of this period (or for Furniture made to look like it) was started by a few enthusiasts in the 1920s and is now so universal that a great deal is sold on the Continent. The ensuing lists show only very selective upward movements in the 1960s, such as in the case of secrétaires and dwarf cabinets, and also what may be termed board-room expense account furniture, partners' pedestal desks at up to 7,000 guineas and extension tables at over £6,000. Certain preferences were established in the 1950s. A round rosewood table may be worth only a few hundreds, but a drum-top table nearer £3,000. A card table is hard to sell at £250, but a sofa table of the same dimensions can make over a thousand. Sets of chairs, if painted or japanned, can make £100 to £200 a unit, but the dearest, which made £2,500 for a set of six, was quite different, being in the heavy French Empire style of Thomas Hope who published it in his *Household furniture* of 1807. At the sale of the Hope furniture in 1917 the same set made 23 guineas, but that was nothing out of the ordinary. Till well into the 1930s there was a pyramid of chairs in a yard in the Fulham Road, accompanied by the notice 'any chair, ten shillings'— and some of them were Regency chairs, painted or Japanned.

### DRUM-TOP TABLES AND RENT-TABLES

|  |  | £ |
|---|---|---:|
| 1961 | Duke of Leeds. S. Drum-top, 42 in. diam. | 1,800 |
| 1962 | Lady Bailey. S. Book-table 50 in. diam. | 1,400 |
| 1963 | Evill. S. Drum-top, pyramid pedestal, light mahogany | 1,250 |
| 1966 | Fletcher. S. Centre table, 42 in. diam. painted on red ground in Chinoiserie style | 3,000 |
|  | S. Another, same dimensions | 1,200 |
| 1967 | Eckman. S. Drum-top, 48 in. diam., rosewood | 2,500 |
| 1968 | Warwick Castle. C. Revolving rent table, mahogany, 48 in. | 2,310 |
| 1969 | C. Revolving 4-tier bookstand, 62 in. high, brass feet | 1,050 |
|  | Drum-top table, lettered drawers, 34½ in. diam. | 1,155 |
|  | Phillips, son and Neale. Drum-top library table | 1,050 |
|  | C. Revolving drum-top table in miniature, satinwood, 25½ in. | 1,785 |

### GAMES TABLES

| 1960 | Chrysler. N.Y. Sewing-table supported on Atlas figure | 321 |
|---|---|---:|
| 1963 | Evill. S. Games table, thin curved legs reinforced with iron | 2,500 |

17+E.O.T.

£

1967 Eckman. S. Satinwood, 32 in. wide      950
1968 Dashwood. C. Mahogany, 36 in. wide      1,050
     S. Inlaid mahogany, 48 in. wide      780
     C. Work and games table, tulipwood and brass, 27¾ in. wide      682 10s.
1969 C. *Tricoteuse* in red and gold pseudo lacquer in the style of Weisweiler, 24½ in. wide      945

### SOFA TABLES AND CARD TABLES

1961 C. Sofa table, 41 in. wide      357
1965 C. Two card-tables and matching sofa-table, inlaid satinwood      3 for   1,365
1966 S. Amboyna wood sofa table, 48 in. wide      880
     N.Y. Card-table, supported on winged sphinxes, by Honoré Lannuier, New York, *c.* 1810, 31 × 36, $3,700      1,321
1967 Astor. C. Sofa table, rosewood and satinwood, 57 in.      1,260
     C. Sofa table, amboyna and brass inlay      682 10s.
1969 C. Pair of rosewood card tables, on four legs      2 for   1,680
     Normal card table, painted gilt pedestal      420

### BOOKCASES

1960 C. Style of Thomas Hope, front 8 ft × 7      609
1961 Duke of Leeds. S. *Secrétaire* book cabinet, 32 in. wide      290
1963 Phillips, auctioneer. Mahogany and satinwood, stamped Bertram and Son      540
1965 Spencer Stanhope (at Banks Hall). Pair of small open stepped bookcases      2 for   1,250
1967 Astor. Phillips auctioneer (at Cliveden). Circular revolving bookcase, 97 in. high      1,300
1968 Countess of Munster. C. 86 × 58 front, rosewood and calamander      2,310
     C. *Secrétaire* bookcase, glazed doors, 88 in. high      1,470
     Dugan-Chapman. S. Ditto with ebonized tracery      2,700
1969 C. Breakfront glazed bookcase, 88 in. wide, 96 in. high      1,995

### CHAIRS

1960 Suite of green lacquer chairs from Brighton Pavilion      8 for   199 10s.
1962 S. Suite of japanned armchairs, X splats      8 for   650
1963 Ionides. S. Suite of japanned armchairs      8 for   2,100
     Japanned suite, 7 chairs, 2 armchairs      9 for   1,050

£

| 1963 | Evill. S. Suite of 6 armchairs in Empire style made by George Smith after Thomas Hope's design (Deepdene sale, 1917 £24 3s.) | 6 for | 2,500 |
|---|---|---|---|
| | Single armchair made for George IV's visit to Walmer Castle. Bought for Brighton Pavilion | | 520 |
| 1965 | C. Set of 10 painted chairs, X splats | 10 for | 945 |
| | S. Set of 9 armchairs, rosewood, brass inlay | 9 for | 1,100 |
| 1966 | S. Suite of 10 painted simulated-bamboo armchairs with lyre splats | 10 for | 2,200 |
| 1967 | S. Pair of hall-seats, 4 ft wide, in the form of sphinxes, painted gesso in the Thomas Hope style | 2 for | 600 |
| 1969 | C. Dining suite of ten, mahogany, hocked knees, claw-feet, style of George Smith | 10 for | 3,780 |
| | Hotham. C. Dining suite of 20, mahogany, reeded legs, | 20 for | 2,940 |

### REGENCY, OTHER ITEMS
### Including side-cabinets

| 1960 | Chrysler. N.Y. 4-poster bed, brass inlays, Brighton Pavilion style, c. 1810 | | 393 |
|---|---|---|---|
| 1961 | Duke of Leeds. Kneehole writing table | | 2,600 |
| | C. Chiffonier, 52 in. wide, rosewood, brass inlay | | 504 |
| 1962 | Lady Bailey. S. Lady's writing desk | | 460 |
| | S. Upright rosewood and satinwood secrétaire | | 420 |
| | Lady's writing desk, lacquer firescreen back | | 520 |
| | Pair of *torchères*, style of Thomas Hope | 2 for | 420 |
| | Extension dining table, pedestal-legs, 20 ft (compare 1968) | | 680 |
| 1963 | N.Y. Pair of bow-front dwarf cabinets, 47 in. wide, $2,400 | 2 for | 885 |
| | Phillips, son and Neale. Round table, brass inlaid rosewood | | 540 |
| | Ionides. S. Cabinet, concave front, pseudo-lacquer in Brighton Pavilion style | | 2,300 |
| | Evill. S. *Bonheur du jour*, calamander wood, lyre supports | | 1,300 |
| | Cabinet, Chinese lacquer | | 800 |
| 1965 | C. Curved buffet, open ends, lacquer front | | 1,050 |
| | S. Rosewood and brass inlay writing table | | 2,200 |
| 1966 | S. Pair of dwarf cupboards, amboyna wood, 3 ft high | | 1,050 |
| | Judah. S. Plain rosewood writing table, 4 ft long | | 1,750 |
| 1967 | Earl of Feversham. C. Pair of Red Indians, gilt mahogany, 30 in. high | 2 for | 577 10s. |

1967    Eckman.   S.   Occasional table, calamander wood, 25 in.     £
wide          1,700
       Hutchinson.   S.   Plain   satinwood   breakfront   cabinet,
34 in. wide      1,700
1968    Morter.   S.   Side-cabinet with tabernacle, style of George
Bullock, 4 ft 10 in. high      780
       Paul.   S.   Pair of dwarf side-cabinets, inlaid rosewood,
concave sides, 34 × 41 × 16 in.      2 for   4,400
       S.   Banquet table, 6 pedestals, 17 ft 9 in. extended (com-
pare 1962, 1969)      6,200
1969    S.   Rosewood side-cabinet, brass inlays, style of George
Bullock, *c.* 1819, 43 in. wide      920
       Kemsley.   S.   (at Dropmore).   Breakfront side-cabinet,
rosewood and satinwood, tapering legs, 65 in. wide      3,500
Burroughs.   S.   Banquet table, 8 pedestals, 20 ft 9 in. extended,
brass lion-claw feet (compare 1962, 1968)      6,500
       C.   Dwarf cabinet, sphinxes and japanned panels, 34¾ in.
wide      735
       C.   *Bonheur du jour*, Southill style, trelliced gallery, 42½ in.
high, 30 in. wide      2,520
             Another similar, 30¾ in. wide, 44½ in. high      3,570
             Pair of mahogany and rosewood secrétaire cabinets
with Gothic glazed doors and porcelain plaques 2 for   2,940
Duke of Newcastle.   S.   Pedestal desk, mahogany with
ormolu plaques, *c.* 1830, 73¾ × 47¾      2,730
Faber.   C.   Pair of satinwood *bonheurs du jour* after a late
Hepplewhite design, 25½ in. wide      2 for   3,360
             Satinwood *secrétaire* bookcase in a similar style, 30¾ in.
wide, 77 in. high, Gothic glazing bars      1,995
News of the World.   C.   Pedestal desk, light mahogany
with profuse mounts, 96 × 57 in., made for Hothfield Place   7,350

# FURNITURE
## AMERICAN COLONIAL, 18TH CENTURY

In general American colonial furniture is very much dearer than furniture of comparable quality, made in England. In the late 1920s, when English furniture became for a short period actually more sought after than French furniture on the millionaire market, the patriotic taste for colonial furniture received a tremendous stimulus. But the long aftermath of the great crash of 1929 dealt very severely with this exclusively domestic market. In 1944 an imposing 'shell-top highboy' was worth only $4,000 at the Lorimer sale, but recovery began towards 1954. Two of the most extraordinary prices of the 1960s for the English style of furniture, were paid for American walnut armchairs. Made in Philadelphia about 1760, these not particularly distinguished chairs in entirely modern upholstery fetched $18,000 and $27,500 in 1966, equivalent to £6,425 and £9,820—and this in a decade when not a single English chair made as much as £4,000. However, just as the dearest English chairs compared feebly with some of the prices of the past in terms of real money, so did these astonishing American chairs. At the Reifsnyder sale of 1929, on the eve of the great crash, a Philadelphia Queen Anne wing-armchair by Benjamin Randolph made $33,000 or £6,786. The 1970 equivalent would be $81,600 or £34,000. It seems something out of the realms of fantasy.

| | £ |
|---|---|
| 1963 Hallam-Kemp. N.Y. Block-front highboy, New England, early 18th century, $24,600 | 8,572 |
| Bonnet-topped highboy, Massachusetts, $8,500 | 3,037 |
| Philadelphia armchair, Chippendale style, $4,250 | 1,512 |
| Philadelphia wing armchair by William Savory, modern upholstery, $15,000 | 5,358 |
| New England settee, claw-and-ball feet, 90 in. long, $7,000 | 2,500 |
| Wing armchair, Massachusetts, mid 18th century, modern upholstery, $10,000 | 3,572 |
| N.Y. New England block-front lowboy, $24,000 | 8,350 |
| 1966 N.Y. Walnut armchair, vase-splats and cabriole legs, Philadelphia, c. 1760, $18,000 | 6,425 |
| A second ditto, $27,000 | 9,820 |
| Philadelphia scroll-top highboy, c. 1760, $23,000 | 7,857 |
| 1967 Podbereski. N.Y. Cherrywood lowboy, Philadelphia, Queen Anne period, 29½ × 36, $9,500 | 3,390 |
| Mahogany breakfront secrétaire bookcase, Philadelphia, c. 1790, 102 in. high, $25,000. Metropolitan Museum | 8,928 |
| 1969 N.Y. Philadelphia walnut highboy, c. 1750, richly carved, $60,000 | 25,000 |
| Pair of walnut side-chairs, high backs and claw-and-ball feet, mid 18th century, $13,000       2 for | 5,418 |
| Mahogany chest of drawers in Chippendale style, Philadelphia, serpentine front, bought by U.S. State Department, $55,000 | 22,917 |
| 1970 N.Y. Philadelphia walnut lowboy, Chippendale style, 29 in. high, $24,000 | 10,000 |

# FURNITURE
## FRENCH, 18TH CENTURY

Two items of French furniture, sold in the 1960s, were claimed as all-time saleroom records, not only for furniture but for *objets d'art* of any kind. In 1964 it was the Rosebery picture-marquetry commode by Roentgen at £63,000. In 1967 it was the Astor pair of matching *bonheurs du jour* by Martin Carlin at £86,100. Apart from the obsessive semi-lunatic imbecility which can talk about a record in terms of a currency which has lost seven-eighths of its purchasing power in 55 years, absolutely nothing could be less like a saleroom record than these two instances. The high-class French furniture market is essentially a market of the past. Such competition as there is today between rival museums or rival millionaires is dictated by the memory of what was paid in an age when French furniture was much more highly thought of. Thus at the Hamilton Palace sale of 1882 a commode and secrétaire in black and gold lacquer made 9,000 guineas each or close on £75,000 in the money of 1967. But saleroom prices are no more than the tip of the iceberg. Only a little is known of the private sales to the richest men of the late 19th and early 20th centuries. But that little reduces the Rosebery and Astor prices to a very modest status. For instance, a commode that had been made for Mme du Barry, cost Edmond de Rothschild in 1878 either £24,000 or £30,000— £216,000 to £270,000 in 1967 terms. Towards the year 1900 the same collector was believed to have paid £48,000 for the *bureau du Duc de Choiseul* possibly £335,000 in 1967 money. As late as 1915 Henry Clay Frick paid Duveen $250,000 or £51,650 for a commode and secrétaire by Riesener, and that on the scale of 1967 meant at least £390,000.

In those days the three main categories of millionaire extravagance in *objet d'art* were French royal furniture, tapestry-suites and very large Chinese porcelain vases, enamelled on coloured backgrounds. This kind of buying barely survived the First World War because the exaggerated worship of individual genius had already begun to undermine the market for skill and virtuosity. Even so, the 1920s honoured French 18th century furniture at least as much as the 1960s. At the Gary sale in New York in 1928 a writing table with the arms of Pompadour by Oeben and Lacroix made $70,000 (then worth £14,640). If this is to be equated with £73,200 in 1970, it is a higher price than anything paid in the past decade, for, having responded for a time to inflation, French furniture has failed to keep up with the pace of the art market. Yet the opening movement was pretty lively. In 1948 the first £4,000 price appeared in London since the outbreak of war, but, just ten years later, the table of the Llangattock sale had already made £35,700.

It is difficult to plot any price movements from the ensuing lists. French *ebenisterie* is a synthesis of so many different technical processes that any number of special factors may determine the value of a given piece. The *bureau plat*, a cross between a desk and a dining table and the most impractical object ever invented, does not normally display any special degree of variety either in richness· or dimensions, particularly when signed by Jacques Dubois. Yet *bureaux plats* with this signature varied from £5,000 to £10,500 at the end of the decade. Rather more elaborate examples by other makers cost from £20,000 to £38,300. A much more remarkable feature of the French furniture market in the 1960s was that the very highest prices suggested no preference for any particular style, nor even for furniture of any particular function. Prices exceeding £25,000 were paid impartially for bulbous and jazzy rococo, spindly elegance and slab-sided neo-classic severity. On a much cheaper level was the lacy richness of the Louis XIV Boulle style, yet this was the only section of the French furniture market which was quite demonstrably going up.

## COMMODES

| | | £ |
|---|---|---|
| 1960 | Penard y Fernandez. Paris. *Meuble d'appui*, Louis XVI, by Peridiez | 8,940 |
| | Mulligan. C. In green *vernis Martin*, Louis XV | 18,375 |
| | With Chinese black lacquer panels, by Dubois | 6,300 |
| | With picture marquetry, early Louis XVI, by David Roentgen | 9,975 |
| 1962 | Lady Powis. S. Ebony with Florentine marble picture inlays, by Beneman, *c.* 1780 | 33,000 |
| | Pair of marquetry commodes by Foullet, 1760s (see 1968) | 2 for 10,500 |
| | C. Pair of plain commodes, amboyna wood, by Weisweiler, towards 1790 | 2 for 9,450 |
| | Paris. With picture marquetry by Riesener, from Chanteloup, FN160,000+tax | 13,900 |
| | *Commode à ressaut*, stamped Riesener, FN156,500+tax | 13,590 |
| | Pecquignot. Lausanne. Coloured lacquer panels, signed BVRB, FS300,000+tax | 28,750 |
| 1963 | Fribourg. S. With Chinese lacquer panels, by Cramer, Louis XVI | 8,000 |
| | By Leclerc, Louis XV | 6,500 |
| | S. With marquetry by Boudin, Louis XV | 12,400 |
| | *Commode bombé* by Angot, Louis XV | 9,000 |
| 1964 | Rosebery. S. With elaborate picture marquetry by David Roentgen, *c.* 1780, royal cypher and Versailles stamp. Coll. Linsky | 63,000 |
| | Two pairs of thuya wood commodes by Weisweiler, Louis XVI | 2 for 11,000 |
| | | 2 for 13,000 |
| | Black and gold commode by Levasseur, Louis XVI | 16,000 |
| | Paris. Pair of *commodes bombés* with mounts by Cressent, Louis XV, FN340,000+tax | 2 for 27,280 |

| | | |
|---|---|---:|
| 1964 | Farquhar. S. Attributed Riesener, profuse mounts, Louis XVI | 9,000 |
| | S. Plain commodes signed Dester, towards 1790    2 for | 7,500 |
| | Mrs Gaby Solomon. S. Louis XVI mahogany commode by Beneman | 9,200 |
| | Louis XV *commode bombé* by Garnier | 9,500 |
| 1965 | Bensilium. S. Painted commode by Joubert and Martin, Louis XV, Versailles stamp | 20,000 |
| | Plain commode by Riesener, Fontainebleau stamp, *c.* 1780 | 5,000 |
| | Paris. With green porcelain plaques and floral marquetry signed Riesener, Louis XVI, FN168,000+tax | 13,500 |
| | Mrs Gaby Solomon. S. *Commode à portes* by Weisweiler, 6 ft wide, *c.* 1790 | 6,800 |
| 1966 | S. Black lacquer *commode bombé* by Félix, *c.* 1755 | 13,000 |
| | James de Rothschild, Paris. Régence period, mounts by Cressent. FN403,000+tax | 31,314 |
| | Pair of Boulle commodes by Levasseur, early Louis XVI    2 for | 20,875 |
| | C. Elaborate parquetry commode, late Louis XIV, Cresssent style mounts | 5,775 |
| | S. By Peridiez, elaborate Louis XV mounts | 6,000 |
| | Perhaps by Criaerd, black lacquer, Louis XV | 14,500 |
| | Goelet. N.Y. *Commode en tombeau*, Boulle style, Louis XV | 6,428 |
| | S. *Commode bombé* by Roussel, Louis XV, 44 in. wide | 7,900 |
| 1967 | Farrow. S. *Commode bombé* by Dubois, Louis XV | 8,200 |
| | *Commode bombé* by Roussel, Coromandel lacquer panels | 26,000 |
| | Pearson. S. *Commode bombé*, black lacquer, rich mounts, unsigned | 14,000 |
| | Earl of Mansfield. S. *Commode à portes* by Martin Carlin, mark of Poirier's shop, 1770s | 17,000 |
| | *Commode à encoignures* by Riesener, 1780s, mark of St Cloud | 18,000 |
| | N.Y. *Commode plat*, signed twice by Riesener, picture-marquetry, $30,000 | 10,714 |
| | Winston Guest. N.Y. By Doirat, mounted in Régence style, *c.* 1730, $42,500 | 15,180 |
| | *Commode en tombeau*, Boulle atelier, *c.* 1708, $50,000 at 2·80 to £ | 17,860 |
| 1968 | Paris. *Commode bombé*, perhaps by Gaudreau, Chinese lacquer panels, Louis XV, FN485,000+tax | 44,900 |
| | *Régence* commode in leaf marquetry, heavily mounted, 33½ in. wide, FN168,000+tax | 15,600 |

£

| 1968 | Paris. Commode by Criaerd, Louis XV, FN252,000+tax | 23,470 |
|---|---|---|
| | Rubin. S. Commode by Criaerd, polychrome lacquer | 17,000 |
| | Fairfax-Cartwright. C. Plain *commode plat* by Beneman, towards 1790 | 8,190 |
| | C. *Commode plat* in Riesener style by Pafrat, *c.* 1790 | 5,460 |
| | In black lacquer with Chinoiserie landscape, Louis XV | 5,775 |
| | De Trafford. S. Pair of *commodes plats* by Foullet, Louis XVI, rich mounts and picture inlays (see 1962)   2 for | 10,700 |
| | S. *Commode bombé* by Dubois, 54 in. wide, Chinoiserie, black lacquer, Louis XV | 15,000 |
| 1969 | Villa Demidoff. S. (Florence). *Commode bombé*, arms of Novgorod, cypher of Catherine the Great, marquetry and stag's horn inlay, silver mounts, 52 million lire+10% tax, 41½ in. wide | 38,132 |
| | Fribourg, N.Y. *Commode bombé*, Louis XV, floral marquetry, unsigned, width 52 in., $18,000 | 7,500 |
| | Paris. Commode with two matching *encoignures* black Chinese lacquer, Louis XV, heavily mounted, FN345,000+tax   3 for | 28,750 |
| | S. *Commode bombé*, Louis XV, 51 in. wide, attributed BVRB | 8,200 |
| | Another in tulipwood marquetry, signed Joubert and inventoried in the Royal *garde meuble* in 1753 | 9,500 |
| 1970 | Lord Wharton. C. *Commode à vantaux* by Weisweiler, *c.* 1780, 48¾ in. wide | 40,950 |

## WRITING TABLES OR BUREAUX-PLATS

| 1960 | Lady Foley. C. By Migeon, Louis XV | 8,400 |
|---|---|---|
| 1961 | Paris. *Régence* period, heavily inlaid, FN170,000+tax, About | 15,000 |
| | Reid. S. Riesener, 1780s, 55 in. long | 11,500 |
| | Louis XIV, Chinoiserie inlays | 8,000 |
| | Harcourt. C. Signed RVLC, Louis XVI | 6,510 |
| 1962 | Lord Leigh. C. By Dubois, kingwood, Louis XV | 6,300 |
| | Paris. Leaf marquetry by Montigny, Louis XVI, FN 160,000+tax | 12,790 |
| 1963 | Couturier, Paris. With lacquer panels by Baumhauer, Louis XV, FN315,000+tax | 25,220 |
| | Fribourg. S. In kingwood by Dubois, early Louis XV | 9,000 |
| | Kreisler. N.Y. In mounted mahogany, Louis XV | 9,285 |
| | Paris. With leaf marquetry and Japanese lacquer panels, stamped Joseph. FN378,000+tax | 30,250 |
| 1964 | Couturier. Paris. By Leleu, *c.* 1770, FN120,000+tax | 9,650 |

| 1965 | Fitzgerald. S. Miniature bureau-plat, 30 in. wide, Louis XV | £ 6,000 |
| | Miniature bureau-plat, 30 in. wide, Louis XVI | 5,700 |
| | Saumarez. S. Heavily mounted, early Louis XV | 24,000 |
| | Paris. With *cartonnier* in the 'bureau Choiseul' style, signed Dubut, Louis XV, FN480,000+tax | 38,300 |
| 1966 | James de Rothschild. Paris. *Régence* period, unsigned | 10,300 |
| | Vyner. C. In Boulle style, but Louis XVI period | 8,925 |
| | Hutton. S. Signed BVRB, kingwood marquetry, Louis XV, 54 in. | 20,500 |
| 1967 | Winston Guest. N.Y. Signed BVRB, Louis XV ($35,000 or £13,220 in 1957), $50,000 at 2·40 | 20,835 |
| | Boyle. S. By Dubois, Louis XV | 6,500 |
| | Earl of Mansfield. S. By Ellaume, Louis XV | 6,500 |
| 1968 | Seymour. C. By Nicolas Petit, late Louis XV, 78 in. wide | 6,300 |
| | Harewood. C. Louis XV, Compiègne inventory mark, 61 in. wide | 13,650 |
| | S. *Table à écrire* by BVRB, Louis XV, 27 in. wide | 7,500 |
| | Miniature bureau-plat by Riesener with Sèvres plaques, 1780s, 39 in. wide | 6,500 |
| 1969 | C. By Dubois, Louis XV, 72 in. wide | 10,500 |
| | Paris. By Saunier, 'Style Etrusque', Louis XVI, FN242,000+tax | 22,600 |
| | Lord Burnham. C. (at Hall Barn). By Dubois, with fitted *trictrac* table, 54½ in. wide | 5,040 |
| | Davis. S. By BVRB, though unsigned, assay marks 1745–9 | 16,000 |

## WRITING DESKS
### (secrétaires and bureaux)

| 1961 | S. Pair of *bureaux à dos d'âne*, Boulle workshop, Louis XIV | 2 for | 4,000 |
| | de Cruz. S. *Secrétaire en tombeau*, black lacquer, by Dubois, Louis XV, 25 in. wide, £18,500 in 1967 | | 11,000 |
| 1962 | C. *Secrétaire à abattant*, Louis XV, with stamp of royal *Ecuries* (Oppenheim sale, 1913, £367 10s.) | | 17,352 |
| | Paris. Two *secrétaires à abattant*, signed BVRB, Louis XV, FN275,000+tax | | 23,600 |
| | FN245,000+tax | | 21,015 |
| | *Secrétaire à abattant* by Garnier, 1742, FN160,000+tax | | 13,487 |
| | Pair of *secrétaires à doucine* by BVRB, floral marquetry, Louis XV, FN480,000+tax | 2 for | 42,500 |
| | *Secrétaire à hauteur d'appui* by Garnier, Louis XV | | 13,180 |

|      |                                                                                                                                                       | £      |
|------|-------------------------------------------------------------------------------------------------------------------------------------------------------|--------|
| 1963 | S. *Secrétaire* with inscription of Maria Theresa, 1761                                                                                                | 6,500  |
|      | Fribourg. S. *Cabinet-bureau* with *cartonnier*, style of BVRB, Louis XV                                                                               | 4,400  |
|      | Pair of pedestal-desks with Sèvres plaques by Martin Carlin, Louis XVI, 39 in. high, 18 in. wide                                                       | 6,800  |
|      | S. Marquetry bureau, Louis XV, by BVRB                                                                                                                 | 12,000 |
|      | Parquetry *secrétaire* by Oeben, Louis XV (£682 10s. in 1895, £4,200 in 1912)                                                                          | 8,500  |
|      | *Table-bureau*, Louis XVI in style of Riesener, 28 in. high                                                                                            | 20,000 |
|      | Soellner. N.Y. *Secrétaire à abattant* by Peridiez, c. 1760                                                                                            | 8,213  |
| 1964 | Mrs Gaby Solomon. S. Lacquer bureau, 20 in. wide, Louis XV, by Dubois                                                                                  | 7,700  |
|      | *Secrétaire à abattant* by Beneman, Louis XVI                                                                                                          | 9,200  |
| 1965 | Paris. Lacquered *secrétaire à abattant* by Rubestuck                                                                                                  | 14,380 |
|      | Thompson-Dodge. S. *Table à écrire* by Oeben, Louis XV, 25 in.                                                                                         | 6,800  |
| 1967 | Harth. Paris. *Bureau à cylindre* by Riesener, 4 ft wide FN170,000+tax                                                                                 | 15,125 |
|      | S. *Secrétaire à abattant* by Riesener, ultra plain, perhaps made after 1790                                                                           | 8,000  |
|      | *Secrétaire en tombeau* by Dubois, black lacquer, 25 in. wide, Louis XV (£11,000 in 1961)                                                              | 18,500 |
|      | Egerton. C. *Secrétaire à abattant* with grisaille panel by Dubois, late Louis XV                                                                      | 8,935  |
| 1968 | Montgomery. C. *Bureau de dame*, Louis XV, 27 in. wide                                                                                                 | 6,300  |
|      | Harth. Paris. *Bureau à cylindre*, Louis XV picture marquetry, FN150,000+tax                                                                           | 13,925 |
|      | *Table-bureau* by G. Feilt, Louis XV, FN138,000+tax                                                                                                    | 12,900 |
|      | *Petit-bureau cylindre* by David Roentgen, FN182,000+tax                                                                                               | 17,108 |
| 1969 | Lord Burnham. C. (at Hall Barn). *Bureau Mazarin* in Boulle style, 70½ in. long, Louis XIV                                                             | 2,730  |
|      | S. *Secrétaire à abattant*, Black Chinese lacquer by Christophe Wolff towards 1770, 58 in. high                                                        | 13,500 |
| 1970 | Lord Wharton. C. By RVLC, c. 1770, 41½ in. wide (£6500 in 1959)                                                                                        | 16,800 |

### OCCASIONAL TABLES
including *guéridons*, *bonheurs du jour* etc.

|      |                                                                                                                                                       | £      |
|------|-------------------------------------------------------------------------------------------------------------------------------------------------------|--------|
| 1960 | Jones. S. *Table de milieu*, mother of pearl and tortoiseshell inlays, Louis XIV, 27 in. high                                                         | 8,000  |
|      | Paris. *Guéridon*, Sèvres porcelain top, by Martin Carlin, FN150,000+tax                                                                              | 12,850 |

£

| | | |
|---|---|---|
| 1960 | Lady Foley (Hillingdon Collection). C. Round table by Martin Carlin in similar style | 19,950 |
| | 3-tier *Table à ouvrage*, Louis XV, by Oeben | 13,650 |
| | Round-top table, Sèvres plaque, by Weisweiler, bought in | 9,450 |
| 1961 | Paris. Oval table, 16 in. wide by Topino, *c.* 1780 | 8,610 |
| | *Guéridon*, late Louis XV, by Leleu | 9,200 |
| | Duke of Leeds. S. *Poudreuse*, or toilet table, 31 in. wide by Peridiez, Louis XVI | 8,610 |
| 1963 | Fribourg. S. *Secrétaire-poudreuse* by RVLC, top 21½ × 15½ in. with original toilet fittings and mirror | 28,000 |
| | Oval *guéridon*, style of Martin Carlin, Sèvres plaque and painted metal tray, 17 in. wide, 29 in. high | 18,800 |
| | *Table à ouvrage* by Martin Carlin, 28 in. high, 15 in. wide | 17,500 |
| | Guéridon in style of Riesener, Louis XVI, 33 in. high, 10½ in. wide | 11,000 |
| | Fribourg (2nd sale). S. *Poudreuse*, Louis XV, coloured marquetry, 29 in. high, 32 in. wide | 16,000 |
| | *Bonheur du jour* by Topino, late Louis XV, 2 ft wide, 3 ft high | 4,200 |
| | *Étagère-guéridon* by the same, 15 in. wide, 30 in. high | 4,200 |
| 1964 | S. Oval *guéridon*, signed RVLC, early Louis XVI, 20 in. wide | 12,500 |
| | *Bonheur du jour* by Charles Topino, early Louis XVI, picture inlays | 12,500 |
| | Gaby Solomon. S. *Guéridon* by Topino, early Louis XVI, 16½ in. | 5,700 |
| | *Serviteur fidèle* by Riesener, Sèvres porcelain top, 8½ in. | 4,400 |
| | Picture marquetry card-table by David Roentgen, late Louis XV, 34 in. wide | 8,200 |
| | Rosebery. S. Parquetry *guéridon*, attributed RVLC, late 1760s, 15½ in. diam. | 12,800 |
| | Oval parquetry *table de chevet* by Martin Carlin, Louis XV | 20,000 |
| | Guéridon in Riesener style with Sèvres plaque, 9½ in. diam. | 6,000 |
| 1966 | S. Marquetry *guéridon* by RVLC, late Louis XV, 17½ in. wide | 15,000 |
| | Paris. *Table mouvementée* by Carel, Louis XV About | 10,000 |
| | C. *Table ambulante*, Sèvres top 17½ in. diam., after Teniers, by Adam Weisweiler, *c.* 1780, bought in | 5,775 |
| | Paris. *Trictrac* table by Pioniez, made for Marie Antoinette FN206,000+tax | 14,850 |

£

| | | |
|---|---|---|
| 967 | Stern. S. *Guéridon* by Dubois in vernis Martin, 18 in. wide, Louis XV | 8,000 |
| | Lord Astor. C. Matching *pair of bonheurs du jour* by Martin Carlin, *c.* 1770, inlaid Sèvres plaques 2 for | 86,100 |
| | Harth. Paris. 2-tier table, 16½ in. wide, signed BVRB, FN220,000+tax | 20,380 |
| | Games table by Peridiez, 1753, 32 in. wide FN170,000 +tax | 15,810 |
| 968 | Bensilium. C. *Table d'accouchée* by Migeon in *vernis Martin* with painted picture lining, 26½ in. wide | 5,775 |
| 969 | S. Marquetry *petite commode*, 18 in. wide, signed RVLC, *c.* 1770–80 | 7,600 |
| | Paris. *Petite table* by Martin Carlin, Louis XVI, with Sèvres bouquet plaque, FN510,000+tax (Versailles stamp) | 47,162 |
| | du Chastel. C. *Bonheur du jour*, picture marquetry by M. B. Evalde, 1770s, 27 in. wide | 9,450 |

### OTHER ITEMS

| | | |
|---|---|---|
| 960 | C. Jewel cabinet by BVRB | 5,250 |
| | Lady Foley. C. Pair of pedestals by Charles Boulle, Louis XIV (Hamilton Palace sale, 1882, £1,575) 2 for | 1,155 |
| | Paris. Marie Antoinette's dog-kennel by Sené | 6,425 |
| 961 | Duke of Leeds. S. Pair of parquetry vitrines, Louis XV | 4,000 |
| 962 | Paris. *Armoire* by Charles Boulle, Louis XIV, inlaid inside and out. With tax | 7,455 |
| 963 | Fribourg. S. Marquetry *armoire* by Migeon, 1760s, 42 in. high | 9,000 |
| | *Console-desserte* by Pafrat towards 1790, 51½ in. long | 7,000 |
| | Fribourg (2nd sale). S. Marriage-bed of Napoleon and Marie Louis by Thomire and Desmalter, 1810 | 3,800 |
| 964 | Rosebery. S. Pair of *consoles-dessertes* by Saunier, *c.* 1780 | 12,800 |
| | Parquetry centre table by RVLC, Louis XVI | 12,800 |
| | Harrington. C. Pair of *consoles-dessertes* in Boulle style, Louis XIV 2 for | 7,400 |
| 965 | Fitzgerald. S. *Console-desserte*, Riesener style, Louis XVI | 10,500 |
| | Paris. *Armoire* by Charles Boulle with subjects from Ovid, Louis XIV (wrongly identified with the Hamilton Palace example) | 7,795 |
| 966 | Duke of Wellington. S. Pair of cabinets, simulated white ground lacquer, made by Mollitor for Versailles, *c.* 1790 2 for | 21,000 |
| | Lord Hillingdon. C. Pair of Louis XIV dwarf cupboards in Boulle style 2 for | 7,827 10s. |

| | | | £ |
|---|---|---|---|
| | Goelet. N.Y. Red lacquer and rosewood *armoire* by Delorme, Louis XV, $25,000 | | 8,929 |
| 1967 | Winston Guest. N.Y. Pair of giltwood console tables, Régence period, $35\frac{1}{2} \times 45\frac{1}{2}$ in. | 2 for | 12,860 |
| | Paris. Pair of *consoles-dessertes*, attributed Weisweiler | | 10,250 |
| | C. Four giltwood *torchères* after Blondel, *c.* 1737, 68 in. high | 4 for | 4,200 |
| 1968 | Warwick Castle. C. Set of *torchères* from the Boulle workshop, Louis XIV, 52 in. high | 4 for | 8,925 |
| | Pleydell Bouverie. S. Side-table, 46 in. wide by Adam Weisweiler with adapted Japanese lacquers, 1780s | | 17,500 |
| 1969 | Villa Demidoff. S. (Florence). Marquetry travelling coffer, made 1778 for Comte d'Artois by Jacob (original cost £68 5s.), 16 million lire+10% tax | | 11,732 |
| | Paris. *Commode-bureau* with cabinet top, Louis XV parquetry, FN230,000+tax | About | 19,000 |
| | Lord Hastings. S. Pair of vitrines imitating Louis XIV, Boulle style, *c.* 1800, over 6 ft high | 2 for | 4,200 |

### DRAWING ROOM SUITES AND INDIVIDUAL CHAIRS

On the surface at least, the recovery of the once famous market for the *Louis drawing room* has been impressive. In the 1940s the best sets did not work out at more than £150 to £400 for a *fauteuil*. In the 1950s there was no great advance, though exceptionally a pair of settees by Tilliard made £7,500 in 1955 and two *bergères* with the same signature £4,200 in 1956. Seldom did an assembled suite exceed £600 a chair, whereas in the 1960s they averaged well over £1,000 when stamped by good makers, an important suite very much more. Thus, the well known, extremely massive, suite from the Rothschild mansion in Piccadilly made £26,000 in 1967 for 4 *fauteuils*, 4 chairs and 2 settees. Very much bigger prices were paid for the remains of suites, bearing the inventory numbers of the French royal palaces. A pair of *pliants* made for Compiègne in 1786, reached £3,800 in 1965—a lot for these stools for the less than royal, but nothing to what happened in New York two years later when two *pliants* made for Versailles in 1730, achieved $45,000 or £18,750 between them. Compared with these, the price, paid by the French government for the three *fauteuils* and settee of the James de Rothschild sale, missing pieces which they needed to make up a Versailles suite, was quite modest. It was £32,117.

However, what appeared on the surface to be the threshold of a totally new range of prices for *ameublements de salon* was only the echo from a very old one. Before the First World War, suites which averaged £1,000 a chair, equivalent in 1970 to £8,000, were quite common. In 1913 a completely mixed suite, partly re-gilded and re-covered, made £16,500, equivalent to £132,000 for settee and six *fauteuils*. For a suite to make such a price in 1969 it would have to be not only royally stamped but fully documented and complete, unique in the world—with the Louvre and the Metropolitan in competition.

£

| | | | |
|---|---|---|---|
| 1960 | C. 6 painted and carved *fauteuils* by Lebas, Louis XV brocade covers | 6 for | 7,860 |
| 1961 | Whitmarshe. N.Y. Pair of Louis XV *bergères*, gold brocatelle covers (see 1963) | 2 for | 2,320 |
| | Taylor. N.Y. Gilt and painted *canapé* by Foliot, Louis XVI, yellow satin | 1 for | 3,748 |
| 1962 | Paris. 6 flat-backed *fauteuils* by Delanois, Louis XV, Aubusson tapestry, regilded | 6 for | 7,440 |
| 1963 | Paris. Settee and 6 *fauteuils*, *Régence*, damask covers | 7 for | 9,120 |
| | Pair of Louis XV giltwood *bergères*, modern upholstery, FN45,000+tax | 2 for | 3,800 |
| | Pecquignot, Lausanne. 2 settees, 4 *bergères*, 4 *tabourets*, *Régence* period, modern upholstery, FS120,000+tax | 10 for | 11,000 |
| | Fribourg. S. 1 settee, 6 *fauteuils*. Beauvais tapestry, Régence period | 7 for | 7,000 |
| | Pair of *Bergères*, early Louis XV (see 1961) | 2 for | 4,400 |
| | Pair of Consulate *fauteuils*, c. 1800, mahogany, style of Jacob fils | 2 for | 2,300 |
| | S. Pair of *marquises*, Louis XVI | 2 for | 3,100 |
| | Pair of settees to match | 2 for | 4,200 |
| | Pair of beechwood *fauteuils* by Michel Cresson, Louis XV | 2 for | 6,000 |
| 1964 | Paris. Régence suite, 8 *bergères*, 1 settee with *petit point* embroidery, FN100,000+tax | 9 for | 7,950 |
| | Single *marquise* by Jacob, 1780–90 | | 2,060 |
| | S. Set of 12 plainly upholstered *fauteuils*, signed Lebas, Louis XV | 12 for | 9,000 |
| | Beauvais tapestry suite, 4 *fauteuils* and a settee, Fables of Lafontaine | 5 for | 3,400 |
| 1965 | Mrs Derek Fitzgerald. S. 4 *fauteuils* and 1 settee, c. 1730–40, 19th century embroidery | 5 for | 7,000 |
| | Pair of giltwood *pliants*, made by Hauré and Sené 1786, for Compiègne palace, 19th century tapestry covers (Beauvais) | 2 for | 3,800 |
| 1966 | James de Rothschild. Paris. Settee and 3 *fauteuils*, part of a Versailles suite by Georges Jacob, 1785, modern damask. Acquired by the French government, FN440,000 | 4 for | 32,117 |
| | N.Y. Pair of giltwood *bergères*, Louis XV | 2 for | 5,178 |

| 1967 | Farrow. S. 6 *fauteuils* by Lebas, late Louis XV, polished beechwood and modern upholstery | 6 for | 4,100 |
|---|---|---|---|
| | James de Rothschild. S. 4 *fauteuils*, 4 chairs, 2 settees in massive Louis XV giltwood, attributed to Heurtaut, Modern upholstery (ex Victor Rothschild) | 10 for | 26,000 |
| | Paris. Settee and 6 *fauteuils* by Heurtaut, Louis XV, Gobelins tapestry | 7 for | 9,875 |
| | S. 4 *fauteuils*, 2 *bergères* and 1 settee by Pothier, early Louis XV | 7 for | 6,500 |
| 1967 | Winston Guest. N.Y. Single *Régence* giltwood *fauteuil* | | 3,035 |
| | Pair of *tabourets* en suite (at 2·40 to £) | 2 for | 2,588 |
| | Pair of *pliants* by Foliot, *c.* 1730, Versailles marks ($45,000 at 2·40 to the £) | 2 for | 18,750 |
| | Harth. Paris. *Marquise* in natural wood by Tilliard, *c.* 1730, modern upholstery | 1 for | 2,300 |
| 1968 | Astor. C. Louis XV Beauvais tapestry suite by Carpentier, 2 settees and 8 *fauteuils*, giltwood | 10 for | 12,600 |
| | Paris. Six *fauteuils*, later damask, by Michel Cresson, Louis XV, FN166,000+tax | 6 for | 15,385 |
| | Viguier. Paris. Pair of giltwood *tabourets*, Louis XIV (regilded), FN34,500+tax | 2 for | 3,358 |
| | Pair of *fauteuils à oreilles*, giltwood, Louis XIV, FN30,000+tax | 2 for | 2,820 |
| | Single *bergère*, Louis XV, FN38,000+tax | | 3,591 |
| 1969 | Kemsley. S. (at Dropmore). Pair of *marquises* by G. Jacob, 44 in. wide, Louis XVI | 2 for | 4,800 |
| | Lord Burnham. C. (at Hall Barn). Set of 27 in. giltwood *pliants* in *Régence* style | 4 for | 5,460 |
| 1970 | Lord Wharton. C. Single carved walnut *fauteuil*, green velvet, late Louis XIV. Musée de Versailles | | 4,200 |

## SMALLER OBJECTS IN GILTBRONZE

Mostly candelabra and wall-lights. *See also under clocks, Chinese porcelain, mounted,* and *Meissen porcelain, mounted*

| 1959 | Egerton. C. Pair of three-light candelabra, Louis XV, mounted on Mennecy figures | 2 for | 2,730 |
|---|---|---|---|
| | C. Pair of three-light candelabra mounted on Kaendler figures, etc. | 2 for | 3,150 |
| 1960 | C. Somewhat similar pair, mounted on Meissen cupids | 2 for | 1,575 |
| | Milligan. C. Pair of 4-light candelabra, mounted on Sèvres *jardinières* with wired flowers, Louis XV, 24 in. high | 2 for | 3,150 |
| | Pair of Louis XV wall lights, Vincennes flowers | 2 for | 2,835 |

£

| | | |
|---|---|---|
| 1962 | Motcombe's Rooms. Pair of Louis XV candelabra, 2 lights on single giltbronze figures, painted over in white  2 for | 5,100 |
| | S. Pair of Louis XV candelabra, Meissen plinths  2 for | 2,700 |
| | Pair of Russian malachite vases, mounted, early 19th century  2 for | 3,800 |
| | Pair of glass vases, Louis XVI mounts  2 for | 1,800 |
| | Paris. Pair of 2-light candelabra, Louis XV, with Meissen parrots, fitted to each arm, FN145,000+tax  2 for | 12,400 |
| | Pecquignot, Lausanne. Pair of 2-light wall brackets on blued metal urns, Louis XVI, FS66,000+tax  2 for | 5,500 |
| 1963 | René Fribourg. 1st sale. S. | |
| | Pair of 7½-inch candlesticks, mounted on Japanese lacquer figures  2 for | 6,400 |
| | Miniature bust of Louis XV on herm, 10½ in. high, Giltbronze, inscribed *donné par le roi, 1772* | 6,800 |
| | Two giltbronze firedogs in the form of lions at bay, style of Gouthière, late Louis XV  2 for | 3,200 |
| | Chinese rock-crystal ewer, mounted *en rocaille* | 3,800 |
| | Pair of 2-light candelabra *en rocaille* with a few Vincennes flowers  2 for | 3,100 |
| | Candle-holder mounted on a Japanese lacquer tray with Vincennes flowers etc. | 2,300 |
| | Fribourg. 2nd sale. S. | |
| | Surtout de table or *candelabrum-épergne* by Messonnier, 8 branches, elaborate Louis XV style | 2,000 |
| | Pair of *bleu du roi* urns, mounted in style of Thomire, *c.* 1790, *brûle-parfum* lids  2 for | 3,400 |
| | Pair of *bras appliqués* for 2-lights, early Louis XV | 2,800 |
| | Pair of *chenets*, modelled *en rocaille* with dressed monkeys, early Louis XV  2 for | 3,500 |
| | For other giltbronze items in the Fribourg sales see *Chinese porcelain mounted* and *Meissen porcelain mounted* | |
| | S. Pair of *bras-appliqués*, *Régence* period  2 for | 3,300 |
| 1964 | C. (ex Stroganoff collection, U.S.S.R.). Pair of 3-light candelabra, marble drum-plinths, Directoire or Consulate period (1794–1808)  2 for | 3,990 |
| | Earl of Rosebery. S. Four 3-light *bras-appliqués* by François Germain, 1756, inventory marks, Palais Luxembourg  4 for | 39,000 |
| | Pair of 3-light candelabra, Louis XVI, blued metal urns, 51 in. high, style of Gouthière  2 for | 6,200 |
| | Second pair to match (see 1967)  2 for | 5,000 |
| | Mrs Gaby Solomon. S. Pair of plain *bleu du roi* Sèvres urns in Gouthière style mounts  2 for | 3,500 |

£

1964   S. Pair of 54-inch lapis columns, encased in giltbronze, Louis XIV     2 for   5,300

1965   Goulandris. S. Pair of *chenets*, surmounted by monkeys and dragons, in giltbronze, Louis XV     2 for   3,000

Kerguelin. S. Pair of Louis XV wall-lights, 2 ft high     2 for   3,200

Hamilton Rice. Paris. Pair of Louis XV wall-lights supported by Chinoiserie figures, FN136,000+tax   2 for   10,815

1966   C. Table-fountain, Louis XV, formed from a *blanc de Chine* spill vase and 2 Meissen swans     5,040

S. Pair of 2-light *bras appliqués* with enamelled sockets and flowers, German or Austrian rococo   2 for   2,300

James de Rothschild. Paris. Pair of *chenets* with leaping horses, Régence period, FN34,000+tax   2 for   2,830

1967   Alexandre de Rothschild. S. Pair of ormolu-mounted bloodstone vases, 7¾ in. high, by Robert Auguste, dated 1755     2 for   8,500

S. Pair of late 18th century 3-light candelabra on blued metal urns (see 1964, £5,000)     2 for   3,400

Dice-roulette machine, kingwood and ormolu, 5 in. high by Gallond, *c.* 1735–40     10,000

Pellenc. S. Casquet-inkstand with statue, inlaid with malachite, etc. Made for Joseph Bonaparte by Biennais, *c.* 1808, 17×17½     2,000

1968   Paris. Pair of 3-light candelabra, supported by crouching *putti, c.* 1770, height 18¼ in., FN152,000+tax   2 for   4,820

Inkstand with biscuit figure of Li T'ai Po and Vincennes flowers     2,400

Prince de Ligne. C. Pair of candelabra, 35 in. high by Feuchères. On metal vases, *c.* 1780   2 for   6,090

C. Pair of 3-light candelabra, elaborately built up of *Blanc de Chine* figures and cups, Régence period, 15 in. high     2 for   7,000

Urn, formed of half a *famille verte* vase and 2 Vincennes bullfinches in elaborate Louis XV casing     5,500

1969   Fribourg. N.Y. Set of *bras appliqués* for three candles each, late Louis XV, 21 in. high, $15,000   4 for   6,350

Pair of ormolu icepails with mask handles in Régence style, 8 in. high, $14,000     2 for   5,800

C. Pair of bronze and ormolu candelabra with military trophies, 54 in. high, style of Thomire, *c.* 1810–15   2 for   3,150

Set of four 2-light *bras appliqués* with Doccia porcelain flower-heads, Louis XV, 26 in. high   4 for   7,825

## CHANDELIERS AND LUSTRES      £

| | | |
|---|---|---|
| 1960 | Chrysler. N.Y.   Cut-glass lustre, late George III | 1,165 |
| 1961 | D. of Leeds.   S.   8-light giltwood chandelier, George II, 4 ft high | 7,800 |
| | S.   Queen Anne brass chandelier, 12 lights, 3 ft 8 in. high | 1,450 |
| 1962 | Hambro.   C. (at Linton Park).   Pair of 16-light Regency lustres, cut glass        2 for | 1,995 |
| |    Somewhat larger ditto | 1,470 |
| | Benthall.   C.   English late 18th century cut-glass lustre with glass branches, 5 ft 6 in. high | 4,200 |
| 1963 | Ionides.   S.   Regency chandelier, 4 ft 8 in. high | 1,100 |
| | C.   Chandelier, Louis XV, 52 in. high | 3,150 |
| | Fribourg.   S.   6-light chandelier, Louis XIV, giltbronze | 4,900 |
| |    Chandelier, Louis XV, rock-crystal and gilt metal, 8 lights | 3,200 |
| |    Chandelier, 1780–90, 18 lights | 2,000 |
| |    Lustre, crystal, glass and ormolu, Louis XV, 10 lights | 2,900. |
| | Harrington.   S.   8-light giltbronze chandelier, Louis XV | 3,400 |
| | Paris.   Giltbronze foliate chandelier, 6 lights, Louis XV | 5,454 |
| | Rasmussen, Copenhagen.   Russian glass lustre (U.S.S.R. sale, Berlin, 1929) | 2,600 |
| | N.Y.   12-light lustre, Directoire period | 1,285 |
| 1965 | Stevens.   S.   Pair of carved and gilded wooden chandeliers, English, c. 1730      2 for | 4,200 |
| 1966 | Patrick Hall.   S.   English cut-glass lustre, Regency period, 30 lights, 6 ft × 3 ft 9 | 2,400 |
| 1967 | Kories.   N.Y.   14-light lustre, Scandinavian, c. 1790 | 2,321 |
| |    Another Scandinavian lustre, 12 lights, 59 × 30, c. 1800 | 2,240 |
| | Eckman.   S.   Cut-glass lustre, English late 18th century, 4 ft 3 × 2 ft 3 | 2,000 |
| | N.Y.   24-light giltbronze chandelier with putti, etc. Empire period, 3 ft 5 × 3 ft 10, $11,000 | 3,925 |
| | Winston Guest.   N.Y.   *Régence* period, giltbronze chandelier, 6 lights, 25 × 29 in., $133,000 at 2·80 to £ | 11,785 |
| | Paris.   20-light lustre, Louis XVI, FN78,000+tax | 6,260 |
| | Watney.   C. (at Cornbury Park).   Pair of cut-glass lustres, 16 lights each, 5 ft 6 high, late George III    2 for | 1,365 |
| 1968 | Paris.   *Grand lustre*, numerous lights, height 5 ft 4, c. 1800, FN65,000+tax | 6,060 |
| 1969 | Kemsley.   S. (at Dropmore).   Pair of late 18th century English glass chandeliers, 24 lights, 4 ft high   2 for | 4,800 |
| | Villa Demidoff.   S. (Florence).   Silver 8-light chandelier by J. C. Lefèvre, Berlin, c. 1730, perhaps made for George II, 15 million lire+10% tax | 10,266 |

# FURNITURE
## ITALIAN, 18TH CENTURY

Till late in the 1950s only French, English and American furniture was capable of reaching the four-figure class. All other 18th century furniture was regional or provincial and best sold in its country of origin. The sudden appearance of Italian furniture as an expensive item on the London market did not mean that this taste had become international. It meant simply that, having been exported in the past to a greater extent than most regional furniture, it was now being brought back to Italy. The same thing happened subsequently to Dutch, German, Austrian and Scandinavian furniture, though on a rather less impressive scale, since very few pieces from these countries cost as much as £3,000.

The most striking prices in this list were paid for Venetian furniture in the Rococo style. The Venetians aimed at the colourful French Louis XV taste, but they wanted it on the cheap. Paint took the place of lacquer or marquetry, gold-painted and moulded plaster took the place of giltbronze mounts. The result was pure theatre and not without a comic charm. The commodes with their dwarf cabinets *en suite*, absurdly pot-bellied and bandy-legged, look like caricatures of over-indulged gentlemen in contemporary dress. Suites of this kind were bought by English tourists as occasional novelties. Some may have served as summer-house or grotto furniture. Yet, astonishingly, a Venetian painted commode made nearly £10,000 at Christies—and as far back as 1961.

|      |                                                                                                   |         | £      |
|------|---------------------------------------------------------------------------------------------------|---------|--------|
| 1961 | C. Painted *commode bombé*, Venice                                                                 |         | 9,975  |
|      | Pair of dwarf cupboards *en suite*                                                                 | 2 for   | 5,040  |
|      | Venetian 7 foot mirror                                                                             |         | 2,520  |
|      | Anachorena. S. Pair of Venetian *torchères* in form of painted blackamoors, 80 in. high           | 2 for   | 1,700  |
|      | Pair of painted stools in form of acrobats, 23 in. high                                            | 2 for   | 750    |
| 1962 | C. Pair of small Venetian painted commodes                                                         | 2 for   | 6,300  |
|      | S. Pair of giltwood console tables, marble mosaic tops, by Andrea Brustolon, Venice, *c.* 1720     | 2 for   | 5,800  |
|      | Hambro. S. (at Linton Park). Pair of *torchères* in form of Blackamoors                            | 2 for   | 1,050  |
| 1963 | Kavanagh. S. Pair of Venetian console tables, on dolphins, scagliola tops                          | 2 for   | 7,000  |
| 1964 | C. Venetian painted *commode bombé*, 48 in. wide                                                   |         | 1,365  |
|      | Finarte, Venice. Painted and gilt suite of 6 *fauteuils* and 1 settee, Venice, *c.* 1750 with 6 matching reproduction *fauteuils* (18 million lire+tax) | 13 for  | 11,500 |
| 1965 | C. Venetian painted *commode bombé*, *c.* 1760, 51½ in. wide                                       |         | 5,460  |
|      | S. Another Venetian painted *commode bombé*, 48 in. wide                                           |         | 5,800  |

£

966  Wicklow.  C.  Pair of *scagliola* picture table-slabs, 54 × 57, by Belloni of Florence, *c.* 1750, George II giltwood stands  6,510

C.  *Scrivania* or folding combination-desk and chair in Empire style by Socchi of Florence, *c.* 1810, 65 in. wide  2,100

Painted Bureau-cabinet with double tabernacle  735

S.  Venetian *commode plat*, *c.* 1770, painted on pale green ground, marble top, 51 in. wide  3,600

Rubenstein.  N.Y.  Grotto furniture, short settee in form of two shells, $2,000  715

Pair of blackamoors, painted and gilded, 6 ft high  2 for  590

Finarte, Milan.  Walnut cabinet writing-desk, Lombardy early 18th century, 3 million lire+tax  1,920

Pair of carved walnut Venetian *bergères*, 4·2 million lire+tax  2 for  2,800

967  Finarte, Milan.  Bookcase, Venice, 97 in. high 108 in. long  1,040

Walnut inlaid oval table, N. Italian, 70 in long, 5 million lire  3,255

S.  Console table, supported on river god, gilt and painted, Mantua, *c.* 1690  3,900

Dewar.  C.  Pair of *Scagliola* picture table-tops with harbour scenes by L. C. Gori of Florence, late 18th century  2 for  1,680

Finarte, Milan.  Pair of painted Venetian dwarf cupboards, 32 in. high, 3·7 million lire+tax  2 for about  2,800

968  Finarte, Milan.  Venetian painted commode, 4·5 million lire+tax  3,450

Lempertz, Cologne.  Writing desk, Rome, *c.* 1715, entirely inlaid with gouache copies of paintings by Agostino Carracci, DM160,000+tax  19,165

Wallraf.  C.  Pair of painted *torchères* in form of blackamoors, 68 in. high  2 for  1,575

Warwick Castle.  C.  Another pair, of painted *torchères* in form of blackamoors, 54 in. high, before 1700  2 for  7,350

Venetian painted *commode bombé*, 58 in. wide  6,510

The two matching dwarf cupboards, 29½ in. wide  2 for  5,040

S.  Commode and two matching dwarf cupboards in same style, painted on pale green ground  3 for  5,000

C.  Walnut bureau-cabinet, elaborate giltwood finials, 98 in. high, Venice, *c.* 1750  2,100

969  Villa Demidoff.  S. (Florence).  Pair of *torchères* as seated blackamoors, *c.* 1700, 66 in. high, 5·4 million lire+tax  2 for  3,960

| | | |
|---|---|---|
| 1969 | Giltwood side-table by Andrea Brustolon, Venice, *c.* 1720, 4·5 million lire+tax | 3,372 |
| | Lord Burnham. C. (at Hall Barn). Pair of standing blackamoor *torchères*, mid 18th century, 88 in. high   2 for | 2.940 |
| | Set of four Venetian armchairs, *c.* 1720 with sculptured blackamoors, by Andrea Brustolon   4 for | 1,422 10s |
| 1970 | Lord Wharton. C.   Pair Venetian blackamoor *torchères*, 53¼ in. high, *c.* 1750   2 for | 3,675 |

# FURNITURE
## 19TH–20TH CENTURIES (after 1830)

The most expensive French furniture at the great Hamilton Palace sale of 1882 was less than a hundred years old, but at present there is little danger of a repeat-performance with furniture of the 1870s at £80,000. For one thing there was no French monarchy in the 1870s to furnish its many palaces with the inconceivable extravagance of Louis XVI and Marie Antoinette. Nor could the early years of the Third Republic provide any ingredients for that sort of romantic cult, though the period has become subject to romantic cults of far greater costliness. Furniture of the age of the young Impressionists seems particularly ill-suited for romance. My generation still locates the absolute nadir of the arts of design between the 1840s and 1880s. But of course younger generations, long taught to attach the deepest significance to hideous objects, are sure there must be something it it. To most people the situation is quite simply this. While older and better furniture has become too dear, a hundred years ago even the cheapest and nastiest furniture was at least hand-made up to a point. Furthermore what seemed hopelessly vulgar even 20 years ago begins to attract by the force of its own aberration. So there are the rudiments of a fashionable market for the frankly mid or late Victorian. The dearest items, however, are not in the style of their age, but close copies of famous 18th century pieces, an elaborate secrétaire at £8,925, a royal coin-cabinet at £3,600. The true fruity early Victorian style is represented by a mother-of-pearl inlaid drawing room suite of 1835 at £6,607 and by *papier-mâché* inlaid chairs at over £100 each. The much admired *art nouveau* of the 1880s, 1890s and early 1900s seems to be more popular in glass, metal and ceramics than in furniture, though an excessively uncomfortable armchair, designed by Mackintosh of Glasgow in 1900, has made £360.

## FURNITURE IN THE NORMAL ECLECTIC 'VICTORIAN' STYLES

|  |  | £ |
|---|---|---|
| 966 Rubinstein. N.Y. Pair of rosewood settees in Baroque style, made in the 1860s by H. H. Belter, New York, $1,000 | 2 for | 343 |
| Quilted sofa and 4 chairs by H. H. Belter, New York | 5 for | 554 |
| Mother of pearl-inlaid suite, made for the Duc de Montpensier in 1835, $18,500 | 12 for | 6,607 |
| Pair of mid-19th century Boulle console tables, length 32 in., $2,000 | 2 for | 715 |
| Margadale of Islay. C. Coin-cabinet of inlaid and enamelled steel, 41×28, by Placido Zuloaga, *c.* 1890 |  | 1,050 |
| Medal chest by the same, tortoiseshell and inlaid steel, 48½×30 in. |  | 1,260 |

£

1966   C.   Pair of watercarriers, bronze and hard stones by
Cordier, 1862, 74 in. high        2 for   1,575

1967   N.Y.   Monumental clock in rococo style, mid-19th
century (Viennese?) lapis, ivory and silver, 56×42 in.     1,518

Cliveden House (Phillips, son and Neale). Inlaid ivory
davenport, Madras, c. 1850     700

Paris. Suite of 6 *fauteuils* and one settee, unmounted
mahogany, 1830s., FN19,800+tax     7 for   1,870

1968   Digby Morton. C. Three *papier-mâché* inlaid chairs,
English, c. 1851       3 for   315

C.   French giltwood table, round porcelain top, 31½ in.
diam., late 19th century.

> French giltwood table, round porcelain top, 22 in.
> diam., depicting court of Louis XV.

Lord Leigh. C. Italian picture-marquetry oval table,
c. 1870, 62×38     399

C.   Bureau-cabinet, ebony and ivory, c. 1865, 108 in. high,
English     357

> Elaborate display cabinet, 90 in. high (£50 8s. new,
> 1891), English     336

> Kidney-shaped kneehole desk, walnut and sycamore,
> 48 in. wide, mid-Victorian English     682 10s.

N.Y.   *Torchère*, painted figure of Indian chief, 62 in. high,
on trolley, Baltimore, c. 1870–85, $4,100     1,708

1969   Phillips, son and Neale. Marquetry centre-table, 32×24,
Louis Philippe (1830–48)     750

C.   *Bonheur du jour*, burr-walnut and other inlaid woods,
34×56 in. high    English mid-19th century     945

> Library bookcase c. 1830, elaborate flamboyant Gothic
> tracery, 18½×11½ ft, English     2,940

## EXPERIMENTAL FURNITURE, INCLUDING ART NOUVEAU

1961   Order of Bethany. S. Cabinet by Norman Shaw, 1862,
Victoria and Albert Museum     500

1965   N.Y.   *Gueridon* table, encased in Sheffield plate by
Elkington, Birmingham, 1845, 29×17½ in., $800     286

1966   Versailles. Mounted and inlaid *buffet* in art nouveau style
by Majorelle, FN1,750+tax     147

S.   Workbox, inlaid woods by Gallé, art nouveau, 14 in.
wide     160

*Étagère* by Majorelle of Nancy, art nouveau, 56×29½     210

1967   Versailles. *Fauteuil* by Majorelle, art nouveau, c. 1906,
FN1,900+tax     160

|  |  | £ |
|---|---|---|
| 1967 | Alexandrine de Rothschild.  C.  Pair of enamelled candlesticks, silver-gilt mounts, *c.* 1860, 9½ in. high                2 for | 850 |
|  | Paris.  *Coiffeuse* in Macassar wood by Ruhlmann, *Art decor* style, *c.* 1925, FN5,500+tax | 462 |
|  | C.  Polished steel triptych casket with paintings in Rossettian style by Nelson and Edith Dawson, 1896, 16 in. wide | 525 |
|  | Busacre.  S.  Armchair by Mackintosh, Glasgow, *c.* 1900 | 360 |
|  | Ebonized drawer-table by the same, 29½ in. wide | 220 |
|  | N.Y.  Art nouveau sideboard by Louis Majorelle, 6 ft 6 in. ×7 ft 4 in., $1,150 | 470 |
| 1968 | S.  Pinewood Gothic dresser, painted panels in William Morris style, *c.* 1880, 76 in. high | 440 |
|  | C.  'The charm of Orpheus,' musical cabinet in mahogany and beech wood, *c.* 1890, front 76× 34 in., National Museum, Stockholm | 1,995 |

## CLOSE REPRODUCTIONS OF FRENCH 18TH CENTURY FURNITURE

|  |  |  |
|---|---|---|
| 1966 | C.  *Secrétaire à abattant,* tulipwood marquetry, Louis XVI style, original in Wallace collection | 8,925 |
| 1967 | N.Y.  *Bureau-plat,* Louis XV style, *c.* 1860, 30½ × 57 in. | 572 |
|  | Paris.  Vitrine, Louis XV style, 76 in. long, FN11,500+ tax | 952 |
|  | C.  Boulle *bureau-plat,* Louis XV style, by Befort jeune, *c.* 1860 | 1,150 |
| 968 | Paris.  *Bonheur du jour,* Louis XVI style, inlaid with porcelain plaques, 47 in. wide, *c.* 1860, FN25,000+tax | 2,362 |
|  | S.  Mahogany centre table, marble top and mounts in Louis XVI style, 33 in. wide, by Henri Dasson, 1880 | 900 |
|  | *Bureau-plat,* Louis XVI style, 54 in. long, by Gervais Durand, *c.* 1870 | 1,600 |
|  | C.  Occasional table, Louis XV style, 27½ in. wide, by Henri Dasson, d. 1896 | 462 |
| 969 | Cooper Renders.  S.  Copy of Louis XV's coin cabinet-commode, rococo style after Gaudreaux, 1739, 67 in. wide | 3,600 |
|  | S.  Mahogany and ormolu games-table, 34 in. wide, by Prosper Durand, before 1862 | 680 |
|  | Blake.  C.  Copy of commode by Cressent in Wallace Collection, 72 in. wide | 1,785 |
|  | C.  Copy of Boulle side-table by René Dubois in Wallace Collection, 54½ in. wide | 735 |
|  | Reproduction of a very lavish commode by Riesener, now in the Louvre, 54 in. wide, mid-19th century | 3,675 |

1969　C.　*Bonheur du jour* in Louis XV style with inlaid porcelain　£
　　　　　plaques, 28½ in. wide, stamped Mombro, mid-19th
　　　　　century　　　　　　　　　　　　　　　　　　　　　　2,100

　　　S.　*Bureau de dame bombé,* floral marquetry in Louis XV
　　　style, 32 in. wide, mid-19th century　　　　　　　　　1,600

　　　　　*Bonheur du jour,* Sèvres plaques, Louis XVI style, Louis
　　　　　Philippe, before 1848, 35 in. wide　　　　　　　　2,300

# GLASS, EUROPEAN

(for other glass *see* special sections under NEAR EASTERN ART and

CLASSICAL ART)

ENGLISH BEFORE 1700

*ce* Webb's Wonders of the late 19th century, this is the dearest European *ass* on the market. Should another complete Anglo-Venetian goblet of the *e* 16th century or an example of Ravenscroft's Henley glass of the late *th* century reach the salerooms, the price would be quite unpredictable.

| | | £ |
|---|---|---:|
| 60 | Dawson. S. The 'Wentworth' sealed posset-pot by Ravenscroft of Henley, *c.* 1670 (see 1967) | 1,250 |
| | S. The 'Goring brewery' tazza by Ravenscroft, *c.* 1675 (£300, 1947, see also 1967), 4½ in. high | 780 |
| 63 | S. Goblet with twisted stem containing 1686 shilling | 480 |
| | Whitefriars goblet by Jacob Verzelini, inscribed K.Y., 1583, 8¼ in. high (£1,400 in 1947), some gilding | 6,500 |
| | The two inscribed 'Butler Buggin' bowls by Ravenscroft of Henley, 1676, 5 in. diam. (bought at Tring in 1937 for 2*s.* 6*d.*). The first made | 3,200 |
| | The second acquired by Victoria and Albert Museum | 3,600 |
| 64 | Cunning. S. Ravenscroft decanter, *c.* 1676, engraved on the Continent | 580 |
| | Ravenscroft lead-glass goblet, *c.* 1685 | 620 |
| 66 | Stuart. S. Lead glass goblet in elaborate Venetian style, 8½ in. *c.* 1680 | 1,000 |
| | Nyburg. S. Carved rummer, lead glass, *c.* 1685 | 780 |
| | D. of Northumberland. S. Whitefriars gilt glass goblet, dated 1590 and inscribed *Wenifrid Geares*, 7¼ in. high. One of the eight known glasses by Verzelini (compare 1963) | 9,500 |
| 67 | Plesch. S. Cylindrical posset-pot by Ravenscroft, *c.* 1670, 3½×4¾ in. (see 1960) | 2,600 |
| | C. Punchbowl, lead-glass in Venetian style, *c.* 1690 | 441 |
| | Walter Smith. S. The 'Goring brewery tazza' by Ravenscroft, Henley, *c.* 1675 (£300 in 1947, £780 in 1960) | 2,100 |
| | Goblet containing fourpenny piece of 1689 | 520 |
| 68 | Walter Smith. S. Greenwich goblet, *c.* 1660, *crisselled* and studded in Venetian style, 5¾ in. high | 1,400 |
| | Plain goblet, *c.* 1700, 9½ in. high | 550 |
| | Ale glass, Venetian style, *c.* 1685, 5½ in. high (£26 in 1929, £80 in 1956) | 520 |
| | Wine glass, cylinder stem, *c.* 1700, 7¼ in. high | 560 |
| 69 | C. Candlestick, lead glass with convoluted stem in Silesian style, towards 1700, 10¼ in. high | 357 |

## ENGLISH, 18TH CENTURY

Enamelling on glass was not widely practised in 18th century England. At a
rate there are not many surviving examples. Very slight enamels on wh
opaque glass in the Chinese *famille rose* style are in the £1,000 region desp
their almost peasant quality. Beilby's armorial enamelled goblets are dea
still, while the addition of gilded birds from the Giles workshop can mak
pair of blue decanters worth £4,200. Anglo-Saxon snobbery was a strong fo
on both sides of the Atlantic in the 1960s, when Bohemian opaque white gl
tankards, enamelled in a far more accomplished style than anything produc
in Staffordshire, could make no more than £20 to £80 for examples in f
rate condition. But to the purist glass-collector all this is triviality. The pl
English wine glass with subtle variations in the stem is his chief quarry and i
remarkable how many inconspicuous rarities changed hands at £400 to £7

| | | £ |
|---|---|---|
| 1960 | Barton. S. South Staffordshire opaque white vase, en-amelled flowers, 6¾ in. high | 760 |
| | Dickson. S. Enamelled goblet, royal arms, 1760, by Beilby of Newcastle, 9¼ in. high (£220 in 1927) | 1,820 |
| 1962 | S. Wine glass, engraved by David Wolff in Holland, *c.* 1785, with royal portraits | 460 |
| 1963 | S. Decanter, Beilby, arms of George III, 9¼ in. high | 1,000 |
| | Goblet by Beilby with enamelled landscape, 7 in. high | 2,500 |
| | Another golbet by Beilby with enamelled landscape, 7 in. high | 900 |
| | Goblet with engraved portrait of Charles 1st, 8¾ in. (£160 in 1936) | 800 |
| | South Staffordshire white glass flask, enamelled in Chinese style by 'the finch painter,' 6¾ in. high | 830 |
| 1964 | Cunning. S. Punchbowl with engraved country house view, 1760 | 740 |
| 1965 | Fitzroy. C. South Staffordshire white oviform beaker, Chinoiserie enamels by 'the finch painter' (see 1968) | 945 |
| | S. Rummer, in German style, 10¼ in. high | 780 |
| 1966 | C. Baluster vase, enamels on white, S. Staffordshire, 7 in. | 966 |
| | S. Another, globular, 3 in. high, enamelled flowers | 360 |
| 1967 | S. Pair of tea caddies with ormolu lids, same school (compare 1969), with typical finches, 5¾ in. high, inscribed 'Green' 2 for | 1,000 |
| | Plesch. S. Wine-glass, engraved in Holland by David Wolff, end of 18th century | 520 |
| | Walter Smith. S. Engraved wine glass inscribed 'success to the Lion', with engraving of a privateer (£210 in 1960) | 500 |
| | Wine glass, yellow colour-twist stem, *c.* 1760, 6 in. | |

£

| | | | | |
|---|---|---|---|---|
| 1967 | high (£160 in 1960, £56 in 1952) (another at Christies, 1962, £44 2s.) | | | 420 |
| 1968 | C. Pair of blue decanters, finely gilded with birds in the style of James Giles's workshop, c. 1760–70 | 2 for | 4,200 | |
| | Walter Smith. S. Wine glass, 1705, with heart-shaped tear in the stem, 6¾ in. high (£42 in 1955) | | | 620 |
| | A similar glass, 6 in. high | | | 620 |
| | Colour-twist candlestick, c. 1760, 8 in. high (£110 in 1952) | | | 1,350 |
| | Wine glass, squared stem, 1715, 'God save King George' (£60, 1950) | | | 620 |
| | Ale glass, 1730, star-studded stem, 9 in. high (£10 10s. in 1930, £16 in 1953) | | | 460 |
| | Light green rummer in German style, 1760, 4¾ in. high | | | 470 |
| | C. Enamelled white oviform beaker, 7 in. high (see 1965) | | | 682 10s. |
| | S. Bowl on splayed foot by Beilby, Newcastle, with landscape enamelled in white, 6½ in. high (£21 in 1930) | | | 400 |
| 1969 | S. Opaque white Staffordshire teacaddy, enamelled by 'the Finch painter,' inscribed 'Bohea,' Coppergilt stopper (see 1967) | | | 550 |
| | Cyder glass, engraved with apple tree on the long bowl and inscribed, 8 in. high | | | 540 |
| | Opaque white beaker, gilded in Greek vase style allegedly in James Giles's workshop, c. 1775, 3¾ in. high | | | 400 |

## JACOBITE GLASSES

This is the revival of a cult dating from the end of the First World War. In 1935 a Jacobite 'Amen' goblet of the year 1720 made £448, equivalent to £2,240 in 1970, so there has been no real advance. Apart from the disillusionment created by numerous forgeries, the article is less rare than was thought. Jacobites were thick on the ground in the first two thirds of the 18th century, and their associations not very clandestine, despite the high conspiratorial air of all these engraved toasts and anagrams.

| | | £ |
|---|---|---|
| 1960 | Thomas. S. With etched portrait of Flora MacDonald, 6¼ in. | 800 |
| 1963 | S. With crowned cypher 'J.R. Send him soon home,' 9½ in. high | 880 |
| | The Henry Peach *Amen* goblet | 350 |
| 1964 | S. Another somewhat similar engraved *Amen* goblet | 600 |
| 1965 | S. *Amen* goblet, dated 1715 (£300 in 1924) | 1,300 |
| 1967 | Walter Smith. S. Another with J. R. cypher, c. 1750, 7 in. high | 1,800 |

1967 S. Young Pretender tumbler, *c.* 1750, 3 in. high (£77 in   £
1930, £160 in 1953)                                       600

C. Young Pretender wine glass, inscribed 'Britta's glory,
Britta's shame.'                                           420

1968 Walter Smith. S. Young Pretender goblet, finely gilt
and engraved, 'Audentior ibo,' *c.* 1750, 5¾ in. high      1,100

S. Wine glass, bowl engraved with badge of the Society of
Sea Serjeants, a Jacobite association, 6½ in. high (£49, 1946) 1,100

Paul-Huhne. S. Wine glass, bowl engraved with portrait of Young Pretender and device 'Audentior ibo,' 6¼ in.  1,700

S. Ale glass, 7½ in. Rose and two buds emblem, unin-
scribed                                           420

1969 Kilbracken. C. Set of four air-twist wine glasses with
rose and word *fiat*                              4 for  1,680

S. Trumpet-bowl glass with rose emblems, 'reddas in-
columem'                                          380

Fidler. C. Baluster air-twist wine glass, rose emblem
with device *Turno tempus erit,* 6½ in.            577 10*s.*

## CONTINENTAL (EXCLUDING VENICE)

On the whole the richer the dearer, and quite unlike the market for English glass which is essentially one of rarities, in themselves simple. There have nevertheless been considerable changes of emphasis since the High Renaissance reigned supreme. The Lords of this market used to be the huge enamelled *Humpen,* super-tankards smothered in armorial devices, one of which made £280 at the Spitzer sale of 1893, the equivalent of £2,500. In the 1960s only a very few of these managed to exceed the £400 mark. Diamond-engraved glass tended to be much dearer than enamelled glass, particularly the earliest Tyrolese and South German imitations of Venetian sophistication.

1960 S. Cut ruby-glass beaker and cover by Gottfried Spiller   £
Potsdam, early 18th century                             850

Dusendschon. S. 14-inch goblet and cover, Petersdorf,
*c.* 1720, Intaglio portrait of Augustus the Strong       900

1961 Weinmüller. Munich. *Reichsadelhumpe,* enamelled and
dated 1561, 11½ in. high, with tax                  437

1962 S. Potsdam goblet and cover, 1730 (£20 in 1936)      260

1963 S. Green rummer and cover, 17th century, Dutch      420

1964 Beck. S. Silesian covered goblet by Schaffgotsch, *c.*
1700                                           2,600

Goblet by Schwartz, Nuremberg, 1719, with intaglio
portrait of Prince Eugene                          1,900

Bohemian beaker and cover, 1791, enamelled with a
balloon ascent at Naples                          1,450

| | | £ |
|---|---|---|
| 1964 | S.  Bohemian ruby beaker, late 17th century (£380 in 1960) | 1,300 |
| | Rosse.  C.  *Krautstrunk* beaker, 16th century, 3 in. high | 630 |
| 1965 | S.  *Reichsadelhumpe*, late 16th century, 11 in. high | 400 |
| 1966 | S.  Potsdam beaker, *c.* 1800, with wheel-cut allegory | 350 |
| 1967 | S.  Engraved green bottle, 9 in. high, by W. van Heemskirk, Amsterdam, *c.* 1675 | 2,800 |
| | Beaufoy-Milton.  S.  7-inch dish, gilded and enamelled, semi-Moorish style, Barcelona, *c.* 1560 | 1,800 |
| | S.  Nuremberg ruby glass tankard, 6 in. high with parcel-gilt lid, *c.* 1700 | 750 |
| | Heavily mounted bowl, engraved by Killinger, Nuremberg, *c.* 1690 | 920 |
| | C.  Marriage *Humpe*, Saxony, 1696, figures in enamel, 7½ in. | 472 10s. |
| | Vienna, Dorotheum.  Gilded and enamelled beaker by Mildner, 1795, 4½ in. high Sch.60,000+tax | 1,112 |
| 1968 | Ditto.  Beaker with Cossack horsemen by Gottlob Mohn, *c.* 1812, Sch.20,000+tax | 350 |
| | Spik.  Berlin.  Pair of Kunkel ruby glass beakers in silver-gilt mounts, *c.* 1700, DM19,800+tax    2 for | 2,370 |
| | Cavender.  S.  Wine glass by David Wolff, Amsterdam, arms of William V of Holland, *c.* 1790 | 540 |
| | Walter Smith.  S. (4th sale).  Wine glass, 5½ in. high, enamelled by J. F. Meyer, Dresden, *c.* 1725 (£82 in 1957) | 850 |
| | Diamond engraved *Vasenpokal*, Innsbruck, *c.* 1580, some gilding, 12½ in. high | 4,400 |
| | Wavy goblet by Hochstetter, Hall im Tirol, *c.* 1550, 7½ in. high (£14 in 1947) | 1,650 |
| | Nuremberg goblet and cover, trees and buildings, engraved by Heramm Schwinger, 14½ in. high, late 17th century (£50 in 1953) | 1,900 |
| | Nuremberg goblet and cover, Perseus and Andromeda in relief, 17½ in. high, late 17th century | 850 |
| 1969 | Carlson.  S.  Nuremberg *Schwarzlot* beaker, dated 1667, 'mein Hertz gib ich den Freind', 4 in. high (£12 10s., 1939) | 2,300 |
| | Bohemian enamelled bottle with crucifixion, dated 1573, 6¾ in. high | 820 |
| | S.  Enamelled green *Roemer* and cover, 1677, 9½ in. high | 800 |
| | Christie Rae.  S.  Silver mounted Kunckel teapot, *c.* 1700, 4½ in. | 780 |
| | Pair of engraved armorial purple glass dishes (Saxony?) dated 1613, 9½ in. diam.    1,400 and | 1,300 |
| | Baker.  C.  *Reichsadelhumpe* with Habsburg double eagle, dated 1614, 14 in. high | 840 |

1969   C.   Goblet and cover, *Zwischengold*, figure of Judas
Thaddaeus, 10½ in.                                                        273
        Dutch engraved goblet, drinkers, inscribed *Vivad de
        Wynkooperey*                                                       315

## VENICE, 15TH–17TH CENTURIES

The Renaissance glass tradition was born in Venice which until well into the
16th century provided the fine glass that served all Europe. Northern regional
patriotism seems lately to have obscured this fact which was the basic premise
of Victorian collecting. Better prices were certainly paid before the First World
War and even in the late 19th century, when a polka-dot enamelled bowl could
make the present devaluation prices in real currency. The following prosaic list
would certainly have been enlivened, had something, painted with figures in
the quattrocento style, got into the salerooms in the 1960s. The last, the *Fairfax
Cup* made £4,600 in 1959, but in 1905 a figured blue ewer in a Paris sale made
£2,120, the equivalent in 1970 of £17,000.

| | | | £ |
|---|---|---|---|
| 1962 | C. | Bowl with enamelled arms of Medici, *c.* 1520. Cassel Museum | 315 |
| | | *Laticinio* vase and cover, 16th century | 294 |
| | S. | Enamelled tazza, *c.* 1500 (£52 8s. in 1893, £48 in 1940) | 380 |
| 1963 | Astor. C. | Goblet and cover in Saracenic style, 16th century | 462 |
| | | Late 15th century goblet with polka-dot enamels, 7½ in. | 1,260 |
| | | Pilgrim bottle with masks in relief | 472 10s. |
| 1964 | S. | Vase and cover, *Laticinio*, late 16th century | 367 10s. |
| 1966 | S. | Goblet, *c.* 1500, blue-spangled with gold, 8½ in. high | 380 |
| 1967 | S. | Tazza with polka-dot enamels, 10¼ in. high, 16th century | 273 |
| | C. | Goblet, late 15th century, polka-dot enamels, 7½ in. high | 525 |
| 1968 | S. | Cylindrical *Laticinio* beaker, 11 in. high, late 17th century | 680 |
| 1969 | Melvin Gutman. N.Y. | *Laticinio* goblet, enamelled silver rims, height 5 in. After 1600, $1,700 | 708 |

## 19TH AND 20TH CENTURY, ALL COUNTRIES

The following list includes some of the worst and the most expensive gla[
objects ever sold. No one, not even on the foggiest of nights and bereft of h
spectacles, could possibly mistake George Woodall's red cameo plaque, *Ven*
*and Cupid*, for a work of art. And as to the 'fairy nightlights' of 'Burme[
glass' produced by Webb of Stourbridge, I cannot conceive why the ve[
name is not accepted for the danger signal that it is. They are straight fro[

Mr Pooter's mantelpiece on Muswell Hill, the indoor companions of the plastic gnome. The shame of these prices should be placed squarely where it belongs— among the directors of up to date museums, obsessed like moles with technical means and gimmicks. Other items on the list are on a different footing. The engraved and enamelled glasses of Bimann and Kothgasser belong to the 'Biedermeyer' or early 19th century romantic taste of Central Europe, which has become expensively nostalgic and cosy after two bouts of total war, famine and inflation. A very different but even more expensive practictioner was Emile Gallé of *art nouveau* fame, the begetter of tortured elongated shapes in the colour and texture of old decayed bathroom sponges. There is nothing sweet and sugary here or quaint and gnomish, but it looks unintentional as well as sinister which is what intellectual taste needs most (or appears to think that it needs).

As to Tiffany's *favrille* glass, it succeeds somehow in combining the visceral *morbidezza* of *art nouveau* with the Mr Pooter affinities of Webb's fairy night-lights, an astonishing achievement and appropriately priced. Then there are the Tiffany reading lamps with their *art nouveau* glass domes which make anything up to $16,000 or £6,665 if sold in New York. And lastly a glass window panel suffusing a dim religious light through a Walt Disney landscape that only needs an electric cinema organ of the period, a small extra item on a bill that already approaches £9,000, as if the window had come out of Chartres Cathedral.

| | | £ |
|---|---|---|
| 1964 | Beck. S. Viennese goblet with engraved landscape by Samuel Mohr, 1816 | 270 |
| | Engraved portrait-medal plaque by Dominik Bimann, Prague, 1834 | 1,650 |
| 1965 | S. Red cameo plaque, Venus and cupid, by George Woodall for Thomas Webb of Stourbridge, 1890 (£140 in 1926), Corning Museum, U.S.A. | 7,600 |
| | Portrait-medal plaque, 1835, by Bimann of Prague | 700 |
| 1966 | Pearson. C. Cameo-glass roundel by Joseph Locke for Thomas Webb, c. 1890, 15½ in. diam. | 756 |
| | T. Wells & Sons. S. Double-handled cameo vase by George Woodall, c. 1890 | 3,500 |
| | Pair of portrait plaques of old worthies, cameo glass, by Woodall, 1885 2 for | 2,400 |
| | 'Fairy pyramid nightlight stand', by Samuel Clarke, Webb's Burmese glass, 1887, 8 in. high | 350 |
| | Mildmay. S. Viennese enamelled beaker with architectural view by Kothgasser, 4¾ in. high, c. 1820 | 380 |
| | Dorotheum. Vienna. Another Viennese enamelled beaker with architectural view by Kothgasser, 4¾ in. high, c. 1820, Sch.38,000+tax | 580 |
| | Coats. N.Y. Two paperweight vases in mottled colours by L. C. Tiffany, c. 1910, each $2,750 | 983 |

| | | | £ |
|---|---|---|---|
| 1966 | N.Y. Other paperweight vases at $2,100 and $1,870 £671 and | | 750 |
| | Meyran. N.Y. Two 'favrille' Tiffany glasses, *c.* 1910 ($25–$30 each in 1946), $3,500 and $3,250 £1,250 and | | 1,160 |
| | S. Ovoid flambé vase by Emile Gallé, 13½ in. Art nouveau | | 280 |
| | 'Verrière parlante', by Gallé, 1884, 8½ in. high | | 370 |
| | Filter flask by Gallé, *c.* 1900, 10¾ in. high | | 200 |
| | Set of Tiffany 'favrille' fingerbowls and stands | 6 for | 220 |
| | Paris. 'Volubilis' vase by Gallé, mauve and green, FN6,500+tax | | 558 |
| 1967 | Paris. Cup by Gallé in shape of shell with coral branches, FN14,900+tax | | 1,222 |
| | Flower vase, red and yellow, dancers in high relief FN18,000+tax. By Gilou and Dammousse | | 1,470 |
| | S. *Marqueterie de verre* vase by Gallé, *c.* 1900, 7½ in. high | | 300 |
| | *Verre-triple* table lamp by Gallé, 18½ in. high, 1904 | | 260 |
| | Miniature flambé vase by Tiffany, 4¼ in. high | | 370 |
| | *Marqueterie de verre* vase by Gallé, 13½ in. high, 1900 | | 320 |
| | Set of four 'Burmese ware' fairy nightlights by Webb of Stourbridge, 1880s, 6½ in. high | 6 for | 270 |
| | Weinmüller. Munich. Enamelled tumbler by Kothgasser with view of Schönbrunn towards 1830, DM2,800+tax | | 278 |
| | Dorotheum. Vienna. Kothgasser beaker with engraved view of Karlskirche, Vienna, *c.* 1825, 4½ in. high, Sch40,000 +tax | | 690 |
| | C. Oviform vase, Webb cameo glass, *c.* 1890, 13½ in. high | | 525 |
| | Kny. C. Cameo glass plaque with cupids by Ludwig Kny, *c.* 1910, 9½ in. diam. (Danish) | | 336 |
| 1968 | S. Tumbler by Kothgasser, enamelled view of Schönbrünn, early 19th century | | 340 |
| | Paperweight vase by Tiffany, *c.* 1910 | | 370 |
| | *Marqueterie de verre* vase by Gallé, 8 in. high | | 170 |
| | Williams. C. Pear-shaped bottle, Webb's cameo glass, yellow ground, 14¼ in. high | | 609 10s |
| | S. Tapering cylinder vase, acid-cut, by Maurice Marinot, Troyes, 1922, 9½ in. | | 600 |
| | N.Y. Tiffany 'favrille' lamp and domed shade 60 in. high, $2,500 | | 1,042 |
| | Square tapering glass, deep-engraved by Simon Gate, Orrefors, 1930, 9½ in. high | | 280 |
| | Pair of enamelled amethyst glass vases by Kolo Mooser, Art Nouveau, 23 in. high | 2 for | 670 |

| | | | £ |
|---|---|---|---|
| 1969 | S. | 'Ivory cameo' vase by Thomas Webb of Stourbridge, c. 1890, 12½ in. high | 300 |
| | | Enamelled glass bottle by Emile Gallé, Nancy, 1889, 6½ in. | 320 |
| | | Lithyalin beaker, imitating hardstone, by Eggermann of Blottendorf, 1840–50, 4¼ in. high | 360 |
| | | Another, 5¼ in. high | 400 |
| | | Tiffany 'dragonfly lamp', by Clara Driscoll, 1890s, 23½ in. | 1,600 |
| | Astor. C. | An almost identical object, 20½ in. high | 892 10s. |
| | N.Y. | Tiffany 'lava' vase, $3,500 | 1,458 |
| | | Tiffany 'bamboo' lamp and shade, $7,000 | 2,918 |
| | | Tiffany 'dragonfly' lamp and shade by Clara Driscoll, $4,000 | 1,566 |
| | | Tiffany stained glass window, landscape panel, $21,000 | 8,750 |
| | S. | Another Tiffany lamp, giltbronze stem, 22 in. | 700 |
| | C. | Oviform vase by Gallé with six elephants, overlaid and carved, 14½ in. high | 840 |
| | S. | Clichy scent bottle, the base and stopper in the paperweight style, c. 1860, 5 in. high | 800 |
| 1970 | N.Y. | Floor-lamp, Tiffany's favrille glass with bronze 'poppy' stand, 78 in. high, $8,500 | 3,542 |
| | | Tiffany wisteria lamp in favrille glass, 27 in. high, $16,000 | 6,665 |
| | | Another of this type, same size, $13,500 | 5,625 |
| | | Tiffany floor lamp, 'Laburnum' shade, 78 in. high, $16,500 | 6,875 |

### PAPERWEIGHTS, mainly French, c. 1845–1860

In the 1930s any serious collector who met a man, prepared to spend £25 apiece on such nursery trifles, would have shaken his head significantly. Yet in 1968 a single collection of 287 paperweights made £153,000. Thirty-four of them exceeded the price of £1,000 and one of them reached £6,000. They are no longer toys. Serious books are written about these paperweights, full of comparisons and cross-references, of technical rarities and enigmas. The sale catalogues look so purposeful that no one any longer dares to suggest that the aesthetic merits of the little imprisoned flowers and reptiles are nil. George III, it was believed, was much exercised to know how the apple got into the pudding. Like minds have been moved in the same way. How the coloured reeds of glass got inside their sealed dome is a mystery, that can easily become an obsession.

No other kind of glass, very few other kinds of *objet d'art*, can show such an impressive list of four-figure prices. Yet it would be an error to suppose that this was the first decade to spend money on anything so mindless. Even in 1952 a special *bonne bouche*, a weight containing a silkworm on a leaf, cost £1,200. In 1931 it had been exceptionally dear at £26. The £3,000 region was passed as early as 1954, when the Egyptian government sold the possessions of the ex-King Farouk. This was an enormous dispersal which temporarily depressed the market, but recovery was well on the way by 1957. It is still probably true that French paperweights are most cherished where the Arab tradition of taste is strong, that is to say in the Eastern Mediterranean and in Latin America. In defence of glass paperweights it can at least be said that their vulgarity is of a harmless kind, belonging as it does to the more domestic and simple-minded regions of taste of the Great Exhibition period—unlike the pretentious and truly excruciating vulgarity of Solon, working for Minton, and Woodall working for Webb of Stourbridge, a generation later.

Such things as these threaten to become dearer still, whereas French paperweights no longer move as fast as they did ten years ago, even though, early in 1970, there was a new record price of £8,500 for a single glass paperweight. In most sales the average price of a weight, 2 to 4 inches in diameter, is still under £50, while £10 or less will secure a passable modern imitation.

| | | £ |
|---|---|---|
| 1952 | Applewhaite-Abbot.  S.  St Louis weight with salamander | 1,300 |
| | St Louis, with silkworm on leaf (£26 in 1931) | 1,200 |
| 1957 | S.  St. Louis, encased yellow overlay | 2,700 |
| 1960 | S.  Baccaret, pink and blue | 750 |
| | Baccarat, snake weight, 3½ in. (£1,900 in 1968) | 460 |
| 1961 | S.  St Louis, green overlay with moulded salamander | 750 |
| | Guggenheim.  S.  Baccarat snake weight (see 1968) | 1,250 |
| | Clichy overlay weight | 700 |
| | S.  St Louis basket weight | 850 |
| 1963 | Jokelson.  S.  Baccarat with red snake | 1,800 |
| | *Laticinio* snake weight | 1,250 |
| | Maba.  S.  With liver-red salamander (see 1968) | 3,900 |
| | St Louis, with parrot (see 1968) | 2,500 |
| | Encased pink overlay weight (see 1968) | 1,000 |
| | With ducks on a pond | 2,000 |
| 1964 | S.  Flat Baccarat bouquet weight (see 1968) | 2,800 |
| | Baccarat triple-weight in gourd form | 2,100 |
| 1965 | S.  St Louis, encased pink inlay | 3,300 |
| | Clichy red overlay (see 1968) | 1,500 |
| | St Louis with parrot | 3,600 |
| | Baccarat with red snake | 1,350 |
| | Baccarat with green snake | 1,000 |
| 1966 | N.Y.  Turquoise blue overlay, *millefiore* (Clichy) | 2,500 |
| | St. Louis, enclosed pink overlay | 1,200 |
| | St Louis, butterfly and frog | 3,800 |
| | Baccarat, translucent overlay | 950 |
| | Baccarat, butterfly and pansy | 1,200 |
| | Clichy, convulvulus bouquet | 5,200 |

| | | £ |
|---|---|---|
| 1967 | de Cosio. S. Clichy, with dahlia | 1,750 |
| | St Louis, flowers | 1,250 |
| | St Louis, *marbrié* | 1,800 |
| | Clichy, opaque blue overlay | 1,200 |
| | St Louis, encased pink overlay | 3,400 |
| | St Louis, with dahlia | 1,300 |
| | N.Y. Tiffany weight with swimming goldfish, 5¼ in., $2,250 | 804 |
| | Another ditto, 5¼ in., $1,500 | 536 |
| 1968 | S. A collection of 287 weights which made £153,000 in two sales. There were 34 lots at £1,000 and over. | |
| | St Louis, liver-red salamander (£3,900 in 1963) | 6,000 |
| | Baccarat snake weight (£1,250 in 1961) | 3,200 |
| | Baccarat, flat bouquet | 2,800 |
| | Clichy, convulvulus (£480 in 1965, £90 in 1953) | 2,550 |
| | St Louis, facetted with snake | 2,200 |
| | (2nd sale). St Louis, flat bouquet | 3,600 |
| | St Louis, with parrot (see 1963) | 3,200 |
| | St Louis, encased pink overlay (see 1963) | 2,800 |
| | Clichy, red overlay (see 1965) | 2,400 |
| | S. Ormolu mounted snake weight, dated 1860, Baccarat | 2,100 |
| | Salamander, exceptional size, nearly 4½ in. diam. | 2,600 |
| | Dark blue, double overlay, Baccarat | 2,400 |
| | Camomile on *laticinio*, St Louis (1952, £9) | 820 |
| | Wilkinson. S. Baccarat snake weight, 3½ in. (£460 in 1960) | 1,900 |
| 1969 | S. Clichy 'carpet ground,' 2¼ in. diam. | 1,700 |
| | St Louis mushrooms weight, 3 in. | 1,100 |
| | Clichy turquoise overlay, 3 in. | 1,450 |
| | Baccarat with three swans swimming, 3¼ in. | 5,500 |
| | St Louis, double clematis bloom, 3¾ in. | 1,700 |
| | C. Baccarat flat bouquet with striped clematis, 3¾ in. | 2,415 |
| | St Louis, pink camomile and pansy, 3¼ in. | 1,995 |
| | Baccarat cruciform flat spray weight, two pansies | 3,045 |
| | S. Baccarat flower weight, clematis more or less, 3¼ in. | 3,800 |
| | Clichy turquoise double overlay, 3¼ in. | 1,750 |
| | S. Baccarat gilt turquoise overlay, 6 windows, 3¼ in. | 6,800 |
| | St. Louis encased overlay flower weight, 3¾ in. | 3,800 |
| | Baccarat, pink white and blue periwinkles (£540, 1966) | 1,800 |
| | St Louis facetted snake weight, 3 in. | 1,800 |
| | Seven others at £1,000 to £1,500 | |
| 1970 | S. Clichy, lilies of the valley, pink ground with windows | 8,500 |
| | St Louis encased blue and white overlay, running horse and fox | 3,800 |
| | N.Y. Baccarat triple weight, 2¾ in. $7,000 | 2,917 |

# HISPANO–MAURESQUE POTTERY
## Lustre ware, mainly 15th century

A hundred years ago, all this heraldic grandeur and glittering colour meant more to the collector than it does today. The great Alhambra vase of the Hermitage Museum was sold by the painter Fortuny to Count Basilewski for £1,200 as early as 1875. In the first decade of the present century standard lustre dishes were fetching as much as in the 1960s but in real money, while in 1912 an exceptional dish with Gothic figures was sold in Paris for 43,000 francs, equivalent with tax to £1,892 or in 1970 money to £15,135. Yet in 1961 the two finest dishes that had been seen in the salerooms for a whole generation barely exceeded £3,000 each, and there has been nothing comparable with them since.

There is something inexplicable about this. In the course of the 1960s the earlier lustre pottery of Persia multiplied in value perhaps ten times over. It is true that, compared with 13th century lustre pottery and its free organic brush-work, Hispano-Mauresque looks somewhat frozen and heraldic, but then so does 15th century Chinese blue and white porcelain and so does 16th century Turkish faience, both of which multiplied in value even more than ten times over, while Hispano-Mauresque stayed virtually static. All that, however, can change overnight.

|      |                                                                                              | £     |
|------|----------------------------------------------------------------------------------------------|-------|
| 1959 | 9½-in. bowl with rabbit on shield, late 15th century                                          | 650   |
| 1961 | S. Deep dish, baking-pan sides, badly damaged, about 19 in. diam., c. 1490–1500               | 600   |
|      | (ex Otto Beil coll.), 17-in. dish, arms of Crèvecoeur, eagle on the reverse, c. 1470          | 3,400 |
|      | 18-in. dish, arms of Gentili, Florence, c. 1450, Fitz-william Museum                          | 3,200 |
|      | Dish with close leaf design and armorial centre, 17 in.                                       | 3,100 |
|      | Dish with armorial design, c. 1460                                                            | 1,800 |
| 1962 | S. Briony pattern dish, IHS monogram, 18 in. diam.                                            | 660   |
|      | C. Gadrooned pair of dishes, close floral ornament, early 16th century            17½ in. diam. | 651   |
|      |                                                                              18½ in. diam.     | 462   |
| 1963 | C. (ex Randolph Hearst). Briony pattern dish, 17 in. diam., IHS monogram, broken in two and mended | 609   |
|      | Ditto. N.Y. Close patterned dish, crested leopard, c. 1490.                                   | 465   |
|      | Damaged 15th century dishes at £250 to £320.                                                  |       |
| 1965 | Adda. Paris. Early 15th century dish, bird with Gothic inscription                            | 1,375 |
|      | Armorial dish, grapes pattern, 18½ in. diam., c. 1470                                         | 1,596 |
|      | Armorial dish, briony pattern, 17 in. diam., c. 1470                                          | 1,050 |
|      | Early 15th century striped albarello jar, 14 in. high                                         | 950   |

£

1965  Adda.  Paris.  Single 11½ inch albarello, *c.* 1425      972
Pair of albarelli jars with grapes pattern, *c.* 1450, 11½ in.
high                                     2 for  3,272
Albarello jar, very bold foliage, *c.* 1460, 12 in. high   1,675
Others at £850 to £1,200.
     Bak.  S.  Briony dish, IHS monogram, 18 in. diam. (£700
in 1961)                                       1,100
1966  C.  Two albarelli, briony pattern, *c.* 1470, 11½ in. high,
Each    504
Small ewer, *c.* 1490, 8¼ in. high              714
Albarello, briony pattern, arms of Aragon, 12¼ in.
high, *c.* 1460                             1,029
1969  C.  Albarello, horizontal bands, *c.* 1500, 11½ in.    441

# ICONS
### RUSSIAN AND GREEK, 16TH–20TH CENTURIES

|  |  | £ |
|---|---|---|
| 1960 | C. The 12 feasts of the Greek Orthodox church in 4 panels, set in silver filigree frame, Stroganoff school, 16th century | 504 |
| 1964 | French. S. Our lady of Vladimir, unframed, Novgorod, c. 1500 | 580 |
| 1965 | C. Christ Emmanuel, the 'vigilant eye' depicted in Heaven, Moscow, c. 1650, 12 in. high | 241 10s. |
| 1966 | C. Veneration of the Icon of the Holy Root by numerous saints with silver Oklad, Moscow hall mark, 1788, 21 in. | 273 |
| 1967 | C. History of Job with saints, 12¼ in. high, Stroganoff school, c. 1600 | 462 |
|  | Presentation, silver-mounted triptych, Moscow, c. 1900, with various saints, 14¾ in. high | 262 10s. |
|  | Graeco-Venetian arched triptych, Holy Family with Italian saints, 8 in. high, 16th century | 630 |
|  | Modern Russian enamelled triptych with jewelled silver mounts, numerous saints, 7 in. high | 304 10s. |
|  | Presentation of the Virgin, Novgorod, 16th century, contemporary silver frame, 12¼ in. high | 1,050 |
| 1968 | C. Holy Family, Dalmatia, 18th century, 20¼ in. high | 735 |
|  | S. Baptism of Christ, Moscow, c. 1600, 13 × 11 | 280 |
|  | Transfiguration, silvergilt Oklad, Stroganoff school, c. 1600, 12½ × 10½ | 880 |
|  | St Demetrius of Salonika, Stroganoff school, 16th century, 12¼ × 10½ | 540 |
|  | Annunciation, Central Russian, 17th Century, 12 × 10 | 520 |
|  | The three angels at the oak of Mambre, 12¼ × 10¼, Russia c. 1600 | 390 |
|  | Panel in 4 compartments, Annunciation etc., Moscow, 17th century, 10 × 8¼ | 370 |
| 1969 | Redwood Anderson. S. Annunciation, Moscow, c. 1600, 11 × 9 | 1,600 |
|  | Mallen. C. Annunciation, Greece, 16th century, 19¾ in. high | 504 |
|  | S. Russian, Pantokrator, modern with Fabergé jewelled mount | 440 |
|  | C. Polyptych, 20 compartments in 4 arched panels, Stroganoff school, c. 1600, 12½ × 10½ | 1,260 |
|  | Holy Family, 21½ in. high, late 16th century, Moscow school | 1,260 |
|  | Cretan triptych, the Deisis, 9½ in. high, 16th century | 1,050 |
|  | S. Ascension of Elijah, N. Russian, 32½ × 27, early 17th century | 1,650 |

1969    S.   Modern enamel copy of the *Theotokos* of Smolensk    £
with jewelled frame by Fabergé      1,500

1970    C.   'Novoexport', Moscow.   God the Father and hierarchy, Stroganoff style, but Moscow, 18th century, 24½ in.
high      1,785

Society of St Francis.   C.   Life of St Eustaphius Placida,
Nicomedia, Asia Minor, dated 1750, 21 in. high      3,675

C.   Adorations of the Kings and Shepherds on one panel
called N. Italian 14th century, but more probably Cretan
16th century, arched top, 7½ in. high      2,100

S.   *Iconastasis*, with 14 side-panels, 20 × 53, 19th century      1,450
The angels under the oak of Mambre, Moscow 17th
century, 12 × 10¼      1,050
Virgin, Christ and St John, 3 panels forming a *Deisis*,
17th century Palekh school, each 13 × 11     3 for    1,100

Wehrlin.   S.   The Pentecost with the resurrected Christ
and 6 disciples, 12 × 16½, ascribed to the 15th century
Novgorod school      12,000

# ILLUMINATED MANUSCRIPTS
## 8TH–16TH CENTURIES

Since 1911 or thereabouts illuminated manuscripts of the best quality have been valued on the footing of old master paintings of the primitive schools. Thus we find that the Chester Beatty *Vincent of Beauvais* manuscript rose from £6,700 in 1920 to £88,000 in 1968. This would not be a very striking rise for an old master over that period. But then the manuscript is not quite first-rate. The value of illuminated manuscripts which occupy an important place in the history of art has become incalculable. In 1929 the British Museum had to raise £35,000 and £33,000 in order to get the *Luttrell Psalter* and the *Bedford Book of Hours*. Their value today would not be simply a matter of multiplying by 13. A million apiece might fail to rescue them from American competition.

It may be noticed, however, that one of the four dearest illuminated manuscripts, sold in the 1960s, did not owe its price to the illuminated miniatures which were few and perfunctory. The *Ovid* of the former Phillipps library, which made £90,000 in 1966, was bought as the lost portion of a translation which Caxton wrote but never printed. The price was, therefore, that of a unique Middle English text. Several other expensive manuscripts, sold in the 1960s, came into the same category, for instance an Icelandic text at £36,000, an early *Piers Ploughman* at £28,000, and an example of 8th century pre-Carolingian script at no less than £48,000. As illuminated books of fine quality disappear from the market, rare early texts are likely to take their place till the situation of the early 19th century is reached again, when the illuminations were of little consequence and the subject matter was everything.

The rise in value of individual medieval paintings can hardly be judged from the price of manuscripts which vary so much in wealth of content. But an excellent yardstick for the 1960s is provided by four illuminations of rather better than average quality in the Chester Beatty sale of 1968. Separated from an early 15th century French Book of Hours, they totalled £12,700. Four other illuminated leaves from the same manuscript were sold in 1962 for £1,400, but the value of miniatures of real importance in the history of art is incalculable. A missing leaf from Jean Foucquet's *Hours of Etienne Chevallier* cost £220 in 1922. A second leaf in 1946 cost £2,900, but should another appear in 1970, £30,000 can be considered only as a base-line.

| | |
|---|---:|
| 1960   3rd Dyson Perrins sale. S. (£464,350, making a total of more than a million since 1958). | £ |
|        Bavarian or Swiss psalter, 13th century, 17 full-page miniatures | 62,000 |
|        Poems of *Gilles le Muisis*, Tournai, 1351. Royal Library, Brussels | 25,000 |
|        Confessions of St Augustine, Bamburg 1169. Bamburg Stadtsbibliothek | 19,000 |
|        Fragments from a sacramentary, Beauvais, *c.* A.D. 1000 | 17,000 |

£

| | | |
|---|---|---:|
| 1960 (cont.) | Sachsenheim Hours, c. 1470–5. Württemburg State Library | 16,000 |
| | Hours, school of Simon Benninck, Bruges, 1500–1520 | 15,000 |
| 1961 | Cherry-Garrard. S. Missal, c. 1360, style of Jean Pucelle, Northern France | 22,000 |
| | Tollemache. S. The Helmingham Hall bestiary, English, late 15th century, 150 tinted drawings | 33,000 |
| | Chaucer, early 15th century, no miniatures | 12,000 |
| | French poems, illuminated, c. 1470 | 17,000 |
| | S. Hebrew bible with *Massorah*, N. French, dated 1260, decorated but not illuminated | 8,000 |
| | 14th century psalter, written at Laon | 3,800 |
| | Froissart's chronicle, N. French, c. 1410 | 3,400 |
| 1963 | S. Boccaccio, *Cas des nobles femmes* etc., 7 miniatures, 78 initials, style of Maître François, c. 1470 | 3,500 |
| 1965 | Spencer Churchill. C. Hours of Charles the Bold of Burgundy, 34 miniatures in the style of Vrelant | 28,000 |
| | Phillipps Library. S. Apocryphal Acts of the Apostles in Icelandic, slightly illuminated, mid 14th century | 36,000 |
| | Poems of Charles Duc d'Orleans, Blois, 1453, not illuminated. Bibliothèque Nationale | 15,000 |
| | Bede, commentary on St Mark, Lyons, 9th century, illuminated initials, Franco-Saxon style | 15,000 |
| | Byzantine gospels, 13th century, 4 frontispieces | 15,000 |
| | French illuminated Livy, c. 1410 | 8,000 |
| | Statius, *Thebaid*, with Italian Lombard initials, 11th century | 10,000 |
| | Newbery library. S. *Biblia Latina*, printed on vellum, 1476, 74 historiated initials, 2 vols. | 23,000 |
| 1966 | Adair. C. Flemish book of hours, c. 1500 | 7,100 |
| | Phillipps Library. S. Part of unique MS of Caxton's translation of Ovid's *Metamorphoses*, four small illuminations in half-grisaille. Now with remainder of MS at Magdalene College, Cambridge (Pepysian library) | 90,000 |
| | D. of Westminster. S. *Vision of Piers Ploughman*, un-illuminated, c. 1460 | 28,000 |
| | S. Bruges book of hours, c. 1500, made for a member of the Borgia family, full page miniatures | 10,000 |
| 1967 | S. Average French book of hours, c. 1480, 96 large and 24 small miniatures | 9,500 |
| | Cathedral Chapter, Portsmouth C. Hours of Charles V, school of Jean Pucelle, c. 1340, 50 small miniatures | 23,000 |

£

1967 Phillipps Library, third part. S. Fragments of Mero-
vingian codex, written on papyrus, Tours 7th century,
not illuminated     7,800

     Bede, *de natura rerum* etc., Tegernsee, 11th century,
     42 outline drawings     27,000

     Dante, *Divina Comedia*, written in Venice, 1363, no
     illuminations     20,000

     *The craft of Venery* etc., in English, *c.* 1450, a few draw-
     ings     11,000

     *Flores historiarum*, English, same date, a few initials     10,500

     Filippo di Vadi, *treatise on swordsmanship*, Urbino, c.
     1490, numerous drawings and illuminations     15,000

Eckman. S. Hours of Duchess of Clarence, English, *c.*
1420, 19 miniatures, numerous initials     6,000

Drayton. S. Paris book of hours, *c.* 1460, 20 small
miniatures and initials     6,800

1968 S. *Roman de la rose*, NE France, 1460–70, 1 large and
55 very small miniatures     25,000

Chester Beatty. S. *Speculum historiale* of Vincent of
Beauvais, 2 vols, Paris, *c.* 1380, 1 full page and 706 small
miniatures (Yates Thompson sale, 1920, £6,700)     88,000

     Breviary of Jean d'Armagnac, French, early 15th cen-
     tury, 2 vols., 10 miniatures, 37 historiated initials
     (£1,050 at Yates Thompson sale 1921)     30,000

     Breviary, Naples, *c.* 1360, 180 small initials and mini-
     atures     23,000

     *Livy's Second Punic War*, Ferrara, 1449, frontispiece,
     border and 19 initials in early Renaissance style     18,000

     *Bede's commentary on the Apocalypse*, pre-Carolingian
     script, Nonantola, *c.* 850, 12 rudimentary initials     17,000

     *Peter Lombard, commentary on Pauline epistles*, Spain,
     A.D. 1081, 10 large, 10 small Romanesque initials     17,000

     Book of hours, Paris, *c.* 1460, 16 large initials and other
     smaller miniatures, only average quality     17,000

Paris. Alexandrine de Rothschild, French Apocalypse,
*c.* 1290, 72 ¾-page miniatures, FN1,000,000+tax. Metropolitan Museum     93,220

     Hours, school of Jacquemard de Hesdin, Paris, *c.* 1350,
     FN600,000+tax     55,975

     *Commentaria*, English, early 13th century, about 250
     historiated initials, FN600,000+tax     55,975

     *Christine de Pisan*. Livre des trois vertus, 4 miniatures,
     school of Vrelant and Leydet, Flemish, *c.* 1470,
     FN360,000+tax     33,559

1969  Chester Beatty, 2nd sale, S.

St Augustine's sermons, pre-Carolingian minuscule script
without illumination, Nonantola, late 8th century       48,000
Canons of Council of Aachen, after A.D. 816, Carolingian
illuminated initials, one later drawing                 19,000
Capitularies, N. French, late 9th century, 11 Carolingian
decorated capitals and a later drawing                  24,000
Councils and decretals of the same age, Rhineland, without decorations or miniatures                           12,000
Part of a psalter, Saxony 1300, 2 full-page miniatures,
2 historiated initials                                  18,000
Hours of Charlotte of Savoy, Paris, c. 1420, 13 full
page and 33 smaller miniatures                          45,000
Quintilian, Lombardy, 1st half 15th century, 13 large
initials                                                12,000
N. Italian bible, 1428, 2 whole-page, 11 smaller miniatures, 81 historiated initials                         85,000
Hours in the style of Jean Bourdichon, c. 1490, $4\frac{1}{2} \times 3\frac{1}{2}$,
14 miniatures of which 6 full page, 10 historiated
initials, bought in                                      9,000
Hours, style of Geofroy Tory, c. 1520, $5\frac{3}{4} \times 3\frac{1}{2}$, 16 full
page miniatures, 34 smaller                             16,000
Part-bible, South French, towards 1150, 27 decorated
initials                                                12,000
Azzone's commentaries on Justinian, Bologna, c. 1300,
$17 \times 10\frac{3}{4}$, 12 historiated initials       9,500
Wildash.  S.  East Anglian psalter, c. 1350, 8 pages with
borders and historiated initials, $14\frac{3}{4}$ in. high, part mutilated   33,000
S. Psalms, Job and Prophets in Hebrew, Montalcino, near
Siena, 1467, 8 borders, 2 half-page miniatures, $4\frac{1}{2}$ in. by 3    22,000
Gavin Astor.  C.  Book of hours, Rouen, c. 1500, 22
miniatures by a 2nd rate painter in the manner of Bourdi-
chon, small figured borders on every page              32,550
Phillipps Library.  S.  Medieval MSS, 5th sale.

St Adhelm, de laude virginitatis, fragment, 28 leaves,
25 ornamented initials, early 9th century Anglo-Saxon
hand, $8 \times 5\frac{3}{4}$ (Heber sale, 1836, £20 9s. 6d.)       17,000
Passional and Homiliary, Nonantola, 10th century, no
illuminations, 182 leaves, $11\frac{3}{4} \times 8$. Italian Government                                                    22,000
Pierre de Beauvais, le Bestiaire, N. French, late 13th
century, 72 small miniatures on 51 leaves, $7\frac{3}{4} \times 5\frac{3}{4}$    23,000
Breviary of Ferdinand I, Naples, c. 1482, 16 miniatures,
25 historiated initals, 170 leaves, $14\frac{1}{2} \times 8\frac{3}{4}$.  Bought by
Italian Government                                      34,000

1969 Phillipps. S. *Pelérinage de la vie humaine*, 71 2½-inch
drawings washed with watercolour, bound with a
plain MS of William of Rubruc, provincial French,
late 14th century, 10¼ × 7½        14,000

    S. The mirror of life and other poems in English, 1st half
15th century, decorated initials but no miniatures    22,000

SINGLE ILLUMINATED MINIATURES
sold separately

1960 S. Leaf from 13th century Tuscan bible     4,200

    Christ in Glory, attributed Sano di Pietro, Sienese,
*c.* 1450, much cut     900

    6 small miniatures, Lorenzo Monaco school, mid 14th
century     6 for  1,200

    S. Entombment, Padua school, *c.* 1500    1,300

1961 14th century Italian initial     550

1962 Sir Kenneth Clark. S. 18 cut-out initials by Niccolo da
Bologna, late 14th century     18 for  3,000

    Springell. S. 4 small miniatures, average French book of
hours, *c.* 1420. For others, from same MS see Chester
Beatty, 1968     4 for  1,400

1963 Berwind. N.Y. Whole-page miniature from a Livy MS
style of Jean Colombe, late 15th century, $1,200     428

    Davy. S. Pair of 14th century historiated initials, close
clipped, from a Swiss antiphonal     2 for  800

1966 S. Nativity, 8¼ × 7¾, Umbrian school, *c.* 1500    3,200

    Philosopher with his pupils by Michele da Carrara,
*c.* 1460     2,100

    C. Collection of 83 English historiated initials, late 13th
and 14th centuries     83 for  8,000

1967 S. Initial with David and two prophets, N. Italian, *c.* 1480,    700

    Crucifixion, Sienese, *c.* 1300, 6¾ × 6½     550

    Last Supper, style of Simon Benninck, *c.* 1500, 5½ in.
high     280

1968 C. Pope Boniface VIII and the Sacred College, style of
Niccolo da Bologna, late 14th century, 7 × 6¾     420

    S. Calling of St Matthew, 11¼ × 10½, Perugia, *c.* 1400    950

    Chester Beatty. S. Virgin and child in garden, French,
*c.* 1410     3,200

        Crucifixion, ditto     1,500

        Christ in Majesty, ditto     4,000

        Office for the dead, ditto     2,200

        Resurrection, ditto. All these about 3½ × 3 (see also
1962)     1,800

1969   Chester Beatty.   S.   Eleven leaves with half-page minia-
tures, (page 7 × 5), from a book of hours, Paris, 1408, total
£17,700
The dearest were: David in prayer, $2\frac{3}{4} \times 2\frac{1}{2}$         2,400
Coronation of the Virgin, $2\frac{1}{3} \times 2\frac{1}{2}$             2,200
St Michael trampling on the Devil, $2\frac{3}{4} \times 2\frac{1}{2}$   2,000
Crucifixion, about $2\frac{1}{2}$ in. square                1,800

## INDIAN AND SOUTH EAST ASIAN SCULPTURE

This is a very recent market, but it would be incorrect to describe the Indian sculpture cult as a purely post-war symptom. To some extent all Buddhist sculpture was carried along by the changed allegiance of collectors of Chinese art, when they began to look for the Chinese Middle Ages rather than the 18th century. After a prickly encounter of some years with T'ang burial figures, it began to sink through that the Graeco-Bactrian inspiration of all Buddhist sculpture had achieved the best results outside the Chinese cultural sphere. A sign of this appreciation was the price of £1,400, paid in Paris in 1932 for a Mathura torso of the 3rd century A.D. This was equivalent to £7,000 in 1970. So the high prices of 1967 are nothing new. Even at the ill-starred Eumorphopoulos sale of 1940 a headless Khmer torso from Cambodia made £1,600.

The profuse and riotous medieval nude sculpture of Central and Southern India was much slower in finding favour. The market owes much to museum competition. High though the prices seem, American museums have certainly paid far more. At a single good sale in 1967 four medieval South Indian bronzes made from £6,000 to £10,000 each. Few Italian Renaissance and still fewer Graeco-Roman bronzes cost as much in the 1960s. For more serious rivals one must look to West Africa.

|  |  | £ |
|---|---|---|
| 1961 | Hauswedel, Hamburg. Damaged Gandhara stone head, over life-size, height 20¾ in., DM30,000+tax | 3,120 |
|  | South Indian stone Bodhisatva in relief, 31 in. high, 12th–13th century, DM16,000+tax | 1,650 |
| 1963 | S. Sandstone figure of a Yakshi, S. Indian, 5th century | 1,600 |
|  | C. Gandhara stone Buddha, 53 in. high | 810 18s. |
| 1965 | S. Schist head of Buddha, 10½ in. high, Gandhara 2nd century A.D. | 500 |
|  | Granite figure of Vishnu, 19 in. high, Khmer art of Indo-China, 11th century | 2,100 |
| 1966 | Kevorkian foundation. N.Y. Gandhara schist figure of Matreya, 49 in. high, $15,000 | 5,360 |
| 1967 | S. Indian sculpture sale: | |
|  | Red sandstone half-figure of Kugera, Gupta 7th century, 14½ in. Metropolitan museum | 1,050 |
|  | Fragmentary sandstone stele, Deccan, 9th century 34 in. | 1,000 |
|  | Bronze Vishnu, 12¾ in., Madras region, 11th century | 1,200 |
|  | S. Indian bronze Ganesa, 13th century, 25¼ in. | 10,000 |
|  | 19-in. bronze, the naked Tithankara, Jain 15th century | 2,500 |
|  | Bronze seated Parvati, S. Indian 15th century, 12 in. high | 1,800 |
|  | Aiyanar. S. Indian seated bronze, 15¼ in., 17th century | 2,100 |

£

1967   S.   Dancing Krishna, 15 in. bronze, Madras 13th century    1,600

Diva and Parvati, 13th century, South Indian bronze group, 27½ in.    8,500

12th century bronze Syudha-Prusha, South Indian, 23½ in.    2,200

13th century bronze Chandesvara, South Indian, 23¾ in.    6,600

Bronze Parvati, South Indian, 26¾ in. 11th century    6,000

1968   C.   Standing bronze Buddha, gilt Lacquered, Khmer, 4th(?) century    651

S.   Wooden Nepalese figure of Samvara and his Sakti, 8 in.    1,100

Sandstone stelle of upright *yali*, Eastern Punjab, 42 in. high, 13th century    1,200

Bust-portion of a goddess-figure in sandstone, Uttar-Pradesh, 11th century, 27 in. high    1,800

1969   Asking price for a Khmer relief of the reclining Vishnu in the Angkor style, *c,* 12th century    14,700

S.   Grey schist standing Buddha, 46¼ in. high, Gandhara, 3rd to 4th century A.D. Right hand missing (compare 1963)    3,600

Another, 38½ in. high, whole arm missing    2,400

Another, seated, 29¾ in. high, right arm missing    3,200

Two Gandhara schist figures of a squatting winged Atlas extremely Hellenistic, 16 in. high    £1,750 and 1,900

Bronze standing Parvati, South Indian, 39 in. 17th century    1,300

# IVORY, EUROPEAN
## 17th and 18th centuries (*see also* Medieval art, ivory)

The Baroque ivory tankard, whose ample Germanic curves were commonly enhanced by the protuberating bottoms of nymphs, remained a good seller throughout the 19th century, an exemplar of the Teutonization of taste which had begun during the Napoleonic wars. An ivory 'flagon' in the Duke of Norfolk's sale in 1816 made 165 guineas at Christies, the equivalent in 1970 of close on £2,250. Robert Napier's ivory tankard at 870 guineas in 1877 was equivalent to £8,200. But the most costly works in ivory were the hunting horns, now vanished from the market. For instance the Andrew Fountaine hunting horn made £4,450 (£40,000) in 1884, the hunting horn of the present Wallace collection £1,995 (£17,950) at the Hollingworth Magniac sale of 1892. There has probably never been a style to fall more out of fashion than Northern Baroque. The fall began in the 1890s, and thereafter it was barely possible for an ivory tankard in its parcelgilt mount to make more than £150 for another sixty years. The growing support for this market in the 1960s came largely from Scandinavia. Important examples were still in the £500 and £600 region in 1962, whereas a richly mounted specimen made £3,900 in 1968. Like the even more monstrous Victorian oddities which they inspired, the fact that they are truly hideous has given these tankards a new significance.

|      |                                                                                                 | £ |
|------|-------------------------------------------------------------------------------------------------|---|
| 1962 | S.  Pair of figurines, Venus and Paris, by Ignaz Elhafen, *c.* 1700 (£525 in 1925)  2 for       | 1,400 |
|      | C.  Tankard, mounted by Elias Adam, Augsburg, *c.* 1700, 9 in. high                              | 472 10s. |
|      | C.  Viennese casket, ivory and enamels, early 18th century                                       | 546 |
|      | S.  Mounted tankard by Thélot, *c.* 1690                                                         | 680 |
| 1963 | Mayer. S.  Ecce homo, German statuette, late 17th century                                        | 340 |
|      | S.  Medallion portrait, Isaac Newton, *c.* 1700, by David le Marchand                            | 1,250 |
| 1965 | S.  Newton and Locke, portrait busts by David le Marchand, early 18th century  2 for             | 2,200 |
|      | Spencer Churchill. C.  Descent from the Cross, numerous figures, S. German, *c.* 1600, 22×16 in. | 1,995 |
|      | St Martin, 5½ in. plaque, Spanish(?) 17th century                                                | 357 |
|      | Adda. Paris.  Mounted tankard, 8¾ in. high, Würzburg, *c.* 1680                                  | 950 |
|      | Another by Kunlin of Ulm                                                                         | 815 |
| 1966 | Fergus Graham. S.  Meleager, late 17th century Flemish figurine, 13½ in. high                    | 1,000 |
|      | C.  Eliptical relief plaque, 11½×7 in., Fall of the rebel angels by Jakob Suer, late 17th century | 840 |

| | | £ |
|---|---|---|
| 1966 | Neuburg. S. Ewer in relief, 13½ in. high, by Maucher, Gmund | 400 |
| | S. George II and Queen Caroline, oval relief portraits by van der Heyen after Rysbrack, 6½ in. high 2 for | 1,250 |
| 1967 | S. Mounted tankard, Küsel of Augsburg, late 17th century | 600 |
| 1968 | C. Crucifixion with attendant figures on tortoiseshell plinth, Flemish, late 17th century | 5,670 |
| | Travers. S. Tankard in the Elhafen style, mounted in parcelgilt by Schneeweiss, Augsburg, c. 1675, 11½ in. high | 3,900 |
| | Windischgraetz. S. Christ at the column, figurine by Adam Lenckhardt, 7½ in. high, c. 1650–70 | 900 |
| | S. Ebony house-altar crucifixion with numerous ivory attendants, Bavaria, c. 1650 | 2,600 |
| | Travers. S. Decapitation of John the Baptist, relief plaque, in style of Ignaz Elhafen, 12 × 6½, c. 1700 | 2,300 |
| 1969 | S. Pair of dismountable anatomical figures, 6½ in. long, Nuremberg, late 16th century 2 for | 700 |
| | Tankard, elaborate Augsburg mounts dated 1757, 12½ in. high | 1,150 |
| | Another, mounts undated but 18th century, 13¾ in. high | 1,050 |
| | Brandt, Amsterdam. Standing cup in relief, mounted on silvergilt column by Erhart, Strasbourg, c. 1640, 16 in. high Hfl26,000+tax | 3,400 |

# JAPANESE ART
## LACQUER

Under two groupings will be found the market movements of Japanese lacquer in the 1960s. During the second half of the 18th century the price of a miniature cabinet or writing-box with its fitted trays varied between £40 and £80 in London and Paris. One may equate that with £800 to £1,600 in 1970, but few such prices will be found in the ensuing list. Possibly these are the only *objets de vertu*, cultivated two hundred years ago, which have actually declined in real money terms. But it must be born in mind that in 1770 Japanese lacquer was still a miracle and a mystery of which the monopolist Dutch East India company could never find enough, whereas in 1970 it is the domain mainly of specialists, poring over signatures. The best known form of Japanese lacquer, the *Inro*, did not however, get to Europe at all in the 18th century. In fact very few *Inro* are as old. Of about the shape and dimensions of a pocket cigarette case, *Inro* are composed of a series of beautifully interlocking sections. Made to carry about, there is no satisfactory way of exhibiting them, but that was no obstacle at all to a single *Inro* costing £1,900 in 1969. *Inro* are indeed the highest achievement in sheer virtuosity, of which the Japanese lacquer artists, some of them alive within human memory, were capable. The archaeologically minded may prefer the black *Guri* Chinese lacquers of the 15th century, and sometimes they have paid much more for them, but aesthetically the best *Inro* cannot be faulted.

In 1945, at the time of the capitulation of Japan, an *Inro* costing more than £5 to £10 was almost unimaginable, whereas in 1969 a collection of 96 *Inro*, good, bad and indifferent, averaged over £300 apiece. Seven of them passed the thousand mark. *Inro* may have advanced faster than *Netsuke*, whose practical advantages they do not altogether share, since their extreme delicacy demands periodic attention.

### INRO OR POCKET MEDICINE CASES

|      |                                                              |        | £        |
|------|--------------------------------------------------------------|--------|----------|
| 1963 | Richards.  S.  By Ritsuo, depicting a Chinese junk           |        | 280      |
|      | Unsigned, 25 personages                                      |        | 230      |
| 1964 | Kalish.  S.  Fitted with a watch, Japanese numerals          |        | 200      |
|      | S.  Allegedly with Christian emblems                         |        | 230      |
| 1965 | Stocklet.  S.  Imitating round Chinese ink-cake              |        | 290      |
|      | Set of 12 by Kwansai in lacquer case                         | 12 for | 2,000    |
|      | S.  By Koma Kwansai, Toba on his mule (see 1968)             |        | 260      |
|      | Paris.  4-case *Inro* by Yoyusai, FN1,600+tax               |        | 134      |
| 1966 | An American Museum.  C.  4-case, gold lacquer                |        | 199 10s. |
| 1968 | S.  Toba on his mule by Koma Kwansai (see 1965)             |        | 315      |
| 1969 | Major Hall.  S.  With silver horses by Kwanshosai           |        | 540      |
|      | S.  By Kwansai, in form of picnic set                       |        | 340      |

£

| | | | |
|---|---|---|---|
| 1969 | Dodds. S. By Koma Yasunori, with Noh dancer etc. | 620 | |
| | Blad. S. By Ritsuo, depicting two ink cakes | 850 | |
| | By Gyokuzan, Ho birds and clouds on gold ground | 650 | |
| | By Tatsuki Yoshihide, the seven lucky Gods | 600 | |
| | By Tokoku, two doves, pearl inlay | 620 | |
| | By Tokoku, Samurai and attendant | 560 | |
| | By Masayoshi, circular, Daruma leaning on the cone of Fuji | 540 | |

C. With gold *kirimons* and some European emblems, ascribed without evidence of any kind to the late 16th century — 787 10s.

Three-case *Inro* by Zeshin Shibata with its *ojime* and *netsuke*, story of Momotaro — 735

C. (Tokyo). Ten-case by Koman Yasukuni with *netsuke* 450,000 yen — 526

C. Three-case with alighting geese by Kwanshosai, *ojime* and *netsuke* included — 840

Hindson, 8th sale. S. 96 Inro made £29,433

| | |
|---|---|
| 3-case with red lacquer head of Daruma by Gyokusan | 1,350 |
| 3-case in form of leather pouch by Ritsuo | 1,250 |
| 3-case with prancing horse by Jokasai and Yosei | 1,300 |
| 4-case, silver inner sheaf, by Shummei | 1,200 |
| 3-case with cockerel by Tatsuki Takamasu | 1,050 |
| 5-case by Yoyusai | 1,050 |
| 5-case by Shibata Zeshin (1807–1894) sold with another for £11, Bois sale, 1947 | 1,900 |

Petersen. S. 4-case with Ojimi by Kwanshosai — 800

4-case, unsigned with vase of flowers in Shibayama lacquer — 1,250

Houghton, S. Tsuishu 2-case, semi-European subject — 720

Budgitt. S. 5-case sheaf-Inro by Kajikawa with bamboos — 720

### OTHER LACQUER OBJECTS

| | | | |
|---|---|---|---|
| 1961 | Kitson. S. Flat writing box, 8 in. long | 220 | |
| | Gourd-shaped box for tea ceremony utensils | 190 | |
| 1964 | Luxmoore. S. Pearl and gold box, *c*. 1600 | 260 | |
| 1965 | Stoclet. S. 17th century box, European figures | 620 | |

1967 Alexandrine de Rothschild. S. Pair of plaques, *lac bargauté* on copper, bouquets of flowers in Chinese style, elaborate Louis XV frames — 2 for — 6,800

N.Y. Mask, part gilded, Fujiwara period, 9 in., $2,500 — 1,042

Lanckoronska. C. Plaque on copper, view of St Peters after Piranesi, $22 \times 15\frac{3}{4}$, towards 1800 — 1,155

1968 Buchanan-Jardine. C. Suit of lacquered armour by
Miochin Mineakiru, early 18th century. Tower armouries 1,365
C. Export chest, inlaid mother-of-pearl, 17×30, 17th
century 441
    Cabinet, 10 in. wide, 17th century 441
    Another export lacquer chest, 26×17 in., 17th century 735
    Two gold lacquer boxes, age not specified, 7×6 420
    Pair of boxes with fitted trays, 8½×8, 9½×7½ 682 10s.
    Five small boxes by Zeshin    from £315 to 420
S. *Bunko* or document-box, early 19th century, 16¾×13½ 320
*Shibuyama* miniature cabinet, 3¼ in. wide 480
*Shibuyama* two-fold screen, 8×8 390
*Shibuyama* inlaid lacquer box with three drawers,
5½×7¼ 720
1969 Lady Dodds. S. *Suzuribako* by Shunsho, gold swallows
in flight, 6¾×7 520
S. *Suzuribako* with a sampan, inscribed Kenzan, 8¾ in. 480
    Hexagonal box with landscape, 5 in. wide 480
    Miniature *Shibuyama* screen, 2 panels, each 4¾×8½ 450
C. (Tokyo). Pair of gold ground *Shibuyama* hexagon
vases, 12¾ in. high, 1,900,000 yen 2 for 2,254
C. Pair of *Shibuyama* vases, silver-mounted and pear-
shaped, ivory inlays, 12 in. high 2 for 651
    *Norimono* cabinet, black and gold with Tosa school
    paintings on inner doors 651
Hindson, 8th sale. S. Perfume box, gold lacquer, silver
mounts, 6¾ in. wide, signed Kajikawa 850

## NETSUKE: CLOAK TOGGLES IN IVORY, BONE OR WOOD

Sometimes on a very clear day one may discern with the naked eye in the
London salerooms a small table, surrounded by only a few people, themselves
apparently on a reduced scale and gazing intently on something absolutely
invisible which is presented them on a tray. These are the *afficionados* of the
*netsuke* cult. Frequently they will be found paying £300, on special occasions
nearly £3,000, for their morsel of bone-ivory or hardwood, barely bigger
than a button, and a button more or less is what they are buying.

They have been buying buttons for a long time. In 1875, in the early days of
the re-discovery of Japan, the *netsuke* was a romantic novelty, worthy of a long
catalogue-entry, describing each individual legend. And a single *netsuke*,
signed by Okotomo, made 19 guineas at Christies, the equivalent of £180 in
1970. After the First World War, when all Japanese art became outcast, *netsuke*
were practically worthless. They descended to the level of the anti-aesthetic
collector, the amasser of potlids and Baxter prints. This was unjust, for despite
repetitious whimsicality, *netsuke* are neither soulless nor vulgar, and they

entirely lack that chop-suey restaurant quality which is displayed by Chinese snuff bottles, the subject of one of the many mystical elevations of the 1960s. *Netsuke* remained in the wilderness for more than a generation. Then came 1945 and the capitulation of Japan which had the oddest results on the art market. More people took to *netsuke* collecting than ever before. *Netsuke* proved, and may possibly continue to prove a particularly choice target for the speculator. As one of many substitutes for spurious paper money and captive investments, the *netsuke* is both easily hidden and easily removed. And one does not have to be a millionaire to acquire a few. These several considerations having got as far as the daily press, it is not surprising that the spread of improving knowledge was followed by a burglary confined exclusively to *netsuke*. The new standards of appreciation, thus clearly demonstrated, were followed by a wonderful increase in the size of catalogues. From the modest two-penny-worth, which disposed of three or four objects in two lines of small print, they rose to fifteen-shilling affairs, in which every single object was illustrated. Then, in 1969, came a dramatic increase in value from the region of £500–£900 for the best signatures of all to that of £2,000 to £3,000. The seven dispersals of the Hindson collection showed that a few cabinets, filled with *netsuke*, could be worth near on a quarter million. That, however, meant no more than £30,000 at the beginning of the century. And this, as the price of well over 3,000 pieces, would not have been so remarkable at a time when *netsuke* had not begun to fall from grace.

| | | £ |
|---|---|---|
| 1961 | S.   Recumbent horse by Kweiguokusai | 165 |
| 1962 | Glendinning, auctioneers, by Hoshin | 145 |
| | S.   By Ittan, 5 horses, wood | 230 |
| | Hauswedel, Hamburg.   By Tomotada, baying *kirin* (see 1969), DM1,900+tax | 204 |
| | Sennin carrying a frog, DM1,700+tax | 182 |
| 1963 | Monteverde.   S.   Fishergirl and octopus | 290 |
| | Cicada on oak branch by Bunshojo | 390 |
| | Bushell.   S.   Goat, wood, by Soichi | 155 |
| 1964 | Luxmoore.   S.   Tiger and cub by Tomotada | 400 |
| | Dog by Tomotada | 310 |
| | Williams, Boon's Park (Brackett auctioneer).   Puppy playing with a bird, unsigned | 900 |
| 1965 | S.   Boar's tusk by Seiyodo | 360 |
| | Group of 11 cranes by Kagetoshi | 390 |
| | Boar by Ikkwan | 400 |
| | Dog by Okotomo | 340 |
| 966 | An American Museum.   C.   Recumbent goat, nearly 3 in. wide | 420 |
| | Ram by Okatori, 1½ in. wide | 199 10s. |
| | C.   Mythical beast by Masayoshi, 1½ in. | 472 10s. |

| | | £ |
|---|---|---|
| 1966 | C. By Hoshimbe Masanobu, group of three immortals, 7½ in. | 399 10s. |
| 1967 | Watney. C. By Mitsohiro, pigeon, inlaid mother-of-pearl | 441 |
| | Oppenheimer. S. Dog by Hidemasa | 520 |
| | Hindson. S. Horse by Muneharu | 500 |
| | Puppy by Kwaiguokusai | 380 |
| | Two hares by Ikkwan | 360 |
| 1968 | S. Tortoise by Ohara Mitsuhiro (£350 in 1963) | 600 |
| | Hindson. S. Carp by Masanao | 750 |
| | Reclining stallion by Ikkwan | 700 |
| | Grazing horse by Shigemasa | 680 |
| | Mythical beast, hard stone, by Yasuchika | 640 |
| | Bitch and puppy by Tomotada | 500 |
| 1969 | Luxmoore. S. Reclining deer by Okotomo | 320 |
| | S. Figure of Kwanyu, late 18th century | 320 |
| | Hindson. S. Ox by Tomotada | 1,650 |
| | Sleeping cat by Jugyoku I (Riokusai) | 1,700 |
| | Dried salmon by Ritsuo (fish-skin and wood lacquer, unsigned) | 1,400 |
| | Puppydog by Kwaigyoku Masatsugu | 1,050 |
| | Seven others exceeded £800 each, 181 netsuke made £46,340 | |
| | Hindson (7th sale). S. Reclining cat by Kwaigyoku Masatsugu | 2,800 |
| | Shishi and its cub by Gechu | 2,500 |
| | Coiled dragon by Hoshin | 2,300 |
| | Kirin, squatting and baying, by Tomotada (see 1962) | 1,800 |
| | Crayfish, carved from a sperm-whale tooth by Tomihara, dated 1788 | 2,300 |
| | Curled crayfish, lacquered ivory, by Chokusai | 1,600 |
| | Female ghost, painted wood, unsigned | 1,500 |
| | Manchurian crane by Mitsuhiro | 1,300 |
| | The bound Oni by Ikkosai, wood | 1,300 |
| | Standing tiger by Otoman Chikuzen | 1,300 |
| | and five others at over £1,000 each | 1,250 |

### SCREEN PAINTINGS ON PAPER

| | | |
|---|---|---|
| 1963 | C. Mountains and figures in Tosa style, cut down to 4 panels | 315 |
| 1965 | d'Ajeta. C. Momoyama period, early 17th century | 273 |
| | With phoenix, early 18th century | 315 |
| 1967 | Lanckoronska. C. Six screens, 17th–18th centuries, at upwards of £525 each. Archery contest, c. 1650 | 1,150 |

| | | |
|---|---|---:|
| 1968 | C. Two-panel screen with 17th century Dutch ship, but not contemporary | 1,312 10s. |
| | S. Crysanthema in Sotatsu style, cut down to 4 panels | 500 |
| 1969 | C. Magnolia tree and pines, gold ground, alleged Muromachi period | 630 |
| | Whisteria on gold ground, alleged Momoyama period | 682 10s. |
| | Bridge with weeping willows, gold ground | 504 |
| | Cherries and camelias, alleged Kano school, 2-panel | 504 |
| | Portuguese ship landing supplies, gold ground, the 6 leaves detached, much later in date than the style, 68 in. high | 1,250 |

## SWORDS AND SWORD-FITTINGS

| | | |
|---|---|---:|
| 1961 | S. dagger, blue-lacquered scabbard, 10 in. | 165 |
| 1966 | Harding. S. Sword guard (*tsuba*) by Natsuo | 530 |
| | by Tosnai | 320 |
| | by Umetada Mioshin | 170 |
| 1967 | C. Kutana Sword blade, 30 in. | 294 |
| | Sword blade by Kotetsu, 29 in., shortened 1865 | 241 10s. |
| | *Tsuba* my Natsuo | 252 |
| | Milward. S. Kutana blade | 280 |
| | Dagger, dated 1413 | 250 |
| | C. Two sword blades by the 13th century masters, Ichimonji and Masamune,         Each | 1,995 |
| 1968 | C. Mounted Kutana, 22 in. unsigned | 630 |
| 1969 | C. Kutana and scabbard, unsigned but attributed to Bizen Ichimonji workshop, 13th century | 1,575 |
| | S. Kutana, unmounted blade by Sukehiro, dated 1479 | 1,050 |
| | Katasa, mounted, length 28¼ in. by Wakizashi | 750 |
| | C. Unmounted blade, signed Bizen Kunikane, said to date from the Heian period, 30¼ in. long | 840 |
| | 19th century *tsuba* or sword guard enamelled in *kinko* work by Gyokuseido Haruo | 525 |
| | S. *Tachi* blade with certificates attributing to Bizen Ichimonji Norimune, early 13th century, 30 in. | 2,000 |
| | Petersen. S. *Tsuba*, signed Hamano Noriyuki, leather case | 460 |
| | Another by Ushiguro Masayoshi | 360 |
| 1970 | Mitsui. C. Katana blade ascribed to Kaneuji, early 14th century, the scabbard and fittings, late 18th | 5,400 |
| | Another, ascribed to Nobokuni, 14th century, heavily gilded scabbard and later fittings | 2,730 |
| | S. *Tsuba*, ascribed Umetada Mioku, 17th century | 1,250 |
| | *Tsuba* by Seiryoken Katsuhira, 19th century | 1,150 |

# JAPANESE ART
PORCELAIN
(mainly 17th–18th centuries)

The recovery of this market from its lowest depths to something fashionab and lively took place in the 1950s and can be followed in Volume Two. the 1960s history was reversed, for it was then that the Japanese came to Euro in order to get back their own antiquities in the teeth of the fiercest America competition. In the salerooms the outward signs were scarcely visible befo 1965 when Sothebys sold two almost identical early Arita jars from differer collections for £750 and £850. In 1955 the pair would not have been wort more than £60 to £70. The full effect of Japanese competition is best assesse in the cost of Arita figures of Geisha girls, so poor in modelling that they shou be classed as dolls rather than statues, despite brilliant and sensitively applie enamels. A pair at Christies seemed dear in 1964 at £273. In 1968, howeve a very similar pair was sold by Sothebys for £3,200, to be followed by a thir pair which Christies sold for £3,570. One figure from the last pair reappeare in Christies' first sale in Tokyo in May, 1969, when it made 2½ million ye equivalent to £2,920. It can be said that these figures have gone up more tha twenty times since 1964 and three hundred times since 1954. But even th prices at the Tokyo sale were probably nowhere near the prices which Japane collectors were prepared in the 1960s to pay for important early Arita piece There are rumours of 40,000 dollar prices which would put them in the highe Meissen class.

It must be added that the range of this competition is highly selective so th very fine things can still be relatively cheap. Apart from figures, the Japane prefer the shapes and sizes that suit the Tea Ceremony. Large jars are in deman but small bowls and saucers are useless unless in complete sets. Consequentl the smaller and more delicate wares of the Kakiemon and other Arita work shops are the least favoured, the competition for these being mainly Wester (and sometimes extremely indiscriminate). On the other hand, a class of war which was made exclusively for the 18th century European market and whic was highly unworthy of the true Japanese taste, tended in the 1960s to retur to Japan. These are the large and garish garniture-sets of covered urns an beakers, popularly named *Imari* from the former port of shipment, whic could once be found in every English country seat. Since 1967 standard ur and covers, 27 to 30 inches high, can be counted on to make from £500 £1,200 a pair. Till at least 1953 a pair could have been bought for £10. Sinc large jars and urns in true Japanese taste were never produced in commerci quantities, and are now almost impossible to find, the Japanese insistence o size may drive the demand for *Imari* still further.

| | | £ |
|---|---|---|
| 1960 C. | Early Arita figures of stag and doe (similar to the Burleigh House pair, sold in 1959 for £850) | 2 for 1,155 |

| | | | £ |
|---|---|---|---|
| 1962 | S. Pair of Hampton Court hexagonal jars, Kakiemon, c. 1690, modern lids (compare 1963, 1966) | 2 for | 230 |
| | Another pair with cranes, early 18th century 1 repaired | 2 for | 220 |
| | C. Pair of Arita figures of cross-legged boys, both damaged, late 17th century (compare 1965) | 2 for | 138 12s. |
| | Geisha figurine in Kakiemon style, bought by Fitzwilliam Museum (compare 1964 and 1968) | | 180 |
| | Kutani pear-shaped bottle, 19 in. high, c. 1670, bought by Freer Gallery, Washington (compare 1966) | | 800 |
| 1963 | S. Pair of Hexagonal bowls and covers in Kakiemon style, Louis XV mounts | 2 for | 1,350 |
| | Early Arita jar, described as Kutani | | 240 |
| | Ionides. S. Pair of Arita eagles, c. 1750, 21 in. high | 2 for | 1,800 |
| | Garner. S. 'Hampton Court' hexagonal jar and cover, Kakiemon (compare 1962 and 1966) | | 340 |
| 1964 | Cholmondeley. S. Pair of Arita leaping-carp vases, early 18th century, on ormolu rocks, 13 in. high | 2 for | 4,200 |
| | Earl of Dartmouth. S. Early Arita blue and white jar with added enamels, 22 in. high | | 290 |
| | C. Pair of Kakiemon Geisha figures (compare 1962, 1968) | 2 for | 273 |
| | Pair of Kakiemon bowls with horses, Directoire or Consulate mounts. Bought in | 2 for | 378 |
| 1965 | S. Arita jar in early Kakiemon style, 9¾ in. | | 750 |
| | Gandon. S. Approximate pair to the above | | 850 |
| | Puttick & Simpson. Pair of figures of cross-legged boys in kimonos (compare 1962) | 2 for | 780 |
| | Fitzgerald. S. Pair of Kakiemon bowls and covers in Louis XVI mounts, 26 in. high (resold to Japan without the mounts, £4,500) | 2 for | 3,800 |
| 1966 | C. Hampton Court hexagonal jar and cover, Kakiemon style (compare 1962, 1963) | | 651 |
| | Kakiemon figure of a Geisha, damaged | | 315 |
| | Bordewich (formerly at Clumber). S. Pair of plainly mounted early Arita jars, one damaged, 14½ in. high | 2 for | 1,310 |
| | Bought by David Rockefeller in U.S.A., Kutani pear-shaped bottle, 19 in. high (compare 1962) | | 4,000 |
| | C. Early Arita tureen and cover, strong colours | | 294 |
| 1967 | Garner. S. Geisha figure in early Kakiemon style, 13¼ in. high | | 550 |
| | Ailwyn. S. Kutani enamelled bottle with mounted neck, 16½ in. high | | 1,100 |
| | S. Double gourd bottle, Kutani style, 10¼ in. | | 1,600 |

563

|      |    |                                                                                                       | £          |
|------|----|-------------------------------------------------------------------------------------------------------|------------|
| 1967 | S. | Pair of Kakiemon 10-in. saucers, fruiting pomegranates                                                 | 340        |
|      |    | Standard Imari jar and cover, 26 in.                                                                   | 240        |
| 1968 | S. | Pair of Kakiemon figures of geishas, 15½ in. high, 2 for                                               | 3,200      |
|      | C. | A similar pair (compare 1962, 1964, 1966, 1967, and see 1969) 2 for                                    | 3,570      |
|      |    | Winepot and cover, overhead handle, Kakiemon style                                                     | 546        |
|      |    | Pair of Arita begging puppies, 10 in. high 2 for                                                       | 1,207 10s. |

Ex-King Umberto. C. (Geneva). 7½ in. saucer with rare design as copied in Meissen, Kakiemon style ........................ 252

Octagonal bowl, 8½ in. diam. Johanneum mark, Kakiemon style ........................ 945

S. Damaged Kutani enamelled potiche jar, 10½ in. ........................ 320

Poulett. S. A pair of absolutely commonplace Imari export jars and covers, 29¼ in. high 2 for 1,100

S. Pair of blue and white recumbent horses, copied from Delft prototypes, 7 in. long 2 for 540

1969 S. Pair of Imari jars and covers, 27 in. (one cover wrecked) 2 for 490

Puttick and Simpson. Pair of 'brocaded Satsuma' late 19th century pottery vases, 51 in. high 2 for 300

Burrows. S. Early Arita jar with continuous river scene in coarse enamels, 10½ in. high 1,300

C. (Tokyo). Winepot in Kakiemon style, overhead handle, 6½ in. high (£546 in London, 1968) 450,000 yen 479

Arita blue and white export ewer, 8¾ in., 250,000 yen 269

Geisha figure with Kakiemon enamels (about £1,600 in London, 1968), 2½ million yen 2,920

Pair of standard Imari jars and covers 27½ in. high, 850,000 yen 2 for 911

Pair of coarse Arita enamelled figures of actors, 12½ in. high, 700,000 yen 2 for 794

Pair of long oviform vases, export blue and white, c. 1700, 19¼ in. high, 800,000 yen 2 for 935

Set of three standard Imari urns, one lacking cover, mid-18th century, 18½ in. high, 880,000 yen 3 for 1,016

S. Slightly damaged Kutani globular jar, 11 in. high 350

Fortescue. C. Pair of early Arita oviform jars in Kakiemon style enamels, 10 in. high 2 for 4,830

S. Octagonal dish, Kakiemon style, the so-called *Hob in the Well* pattern, 9½ in. diam. (2 for £9 in 1947) 460

Imari garniture, 3 covered urns, 31 in. 2 beakers, 22 in. 5 for 850

C. Potiche jar, Arita enamels in Kutani style, 11½ in. 2,100

1970 C. (Tokyo). Geisha figure carrying vase, 17½ in. high, 3½ million yen 3,472

## JEWELRY BEFORE 1700
### enamelled on gold with pearls and other stones

: the beginning of the 16th century an entirely novel style of jewelry was
eated which basically remained the same for 200 years. These pendants,
t-badges, morses and pomanders seem the very summit of the jeweller's
aft. The incredible ingenuity with which Raphael's *grottesche* designs were
veloped in a new medium, the telling use of the white enamel and of the
tural shapes of uncultured pearls, these are all worthy of study and admira-
on. Examples are now very scarce outside museums and of course very dear,
at nothing like as dear as they have been in the past. René Gimpel records
at he sold Mortimer Schiff a 16th century jewel in 1911 for $41,000, the
uivalent in 1970 of £67,500. In the following year, bidding in London at
e Taylor sale, Duveen paid £4,305 (equivalent to £34,450) for the *Caradosso*
rse. Those were the days when the finest medieval and Renaissance *objets*
rt had to go to Pierpont Morgan, whatever the cost. But a generation earlier,
e Rothschild dynasty had not paid much less. The *Lyte jewel*, now in the
itish Museum, was bought by Ferdinand de Rothschild in 1881 for £2,340,
e equivalent of £21,000.

One may wonder that a quite incredible jewel which the astute Mr Melvin
utman could pick up for $500 in 1950, should multiply in value 46 times in
 years. The fact remains that Renaissance jewels are still undervalued. The
strated *Kitsch* of Karl Fabergé's Russo-Swiss peasants and the moronic de-
;hts of French glass paperweights are worth as much as the finest Renaissance
wels, and, on occasion, even Webb's cameo glass. And they say that this
all island alone supports 24,000 *art students*.

| | | £ |
|---|---|---:|
| 60 Desmoni. S. South German pendant in form of a merman (£200 in 1936) | | 3,450 |
| Gold and enamelled armlet, alleged Cellini workshop | | 4,000 |
| S. South German pendant, dated 1550 | | 5,800 |
| South German pendant, baroque pearl in form of pelican | | 2,400 |
| Venus and Cupid, late 17th century baroque pearl, style of Daniel Marot | | 2,000 |
| 61 Robert Horst. C. German 16th century pomander | | 8,190 |
| English 16th century pendant | | 8,190 |
| S. German pendant, 6 in. high, *c.* 1570 | | 5,880 |
| Smaller German pendant | | 3,570 |
| Italian hat-badge medallion, *c.* 1570 | | 2,100 |
| 62 C. Pendant, miniature of Queen Elizabeth by Simon Passe, enamel inscriptions | | 1,650 |
| 63 C. South German pendant, baroque pearl in form of a merman | | 2,730 |
| 65 Harmsworth. C. Pendant by Hans Maelich, *c.* 1550 | | 892 10s. |

£

1966  S.  English hat-badge, *c*. 1540, Nativity enamelled on gold
medallion, 1¾ in. diam.                                                    5,600
Stevens.  S.  White enamelled pendant in form of a swan,
1½ in. diam. with chain and catch, mid 15th century,
excavated at Dunstable, July 1965.  British Museum          4,800
S.  Italian brooch with baroque pearl forming a merman   6,000
South German pendant, *Annunciation* enamelled on
gold                                                                        5,000
South German baroque pearl pendant, formed as a
lion *couchant*                                                            4,400
Lee of Fareham.  C.  Lozenge-shaped pendant with
cameo, Prague, *c*. 1600                                               3,990
French pendant, *c*. 1600, miniature by Peter Oliver    3,990
German oval pendant with enamelled George and
dragon                                                                      4,410
C.  German pendant, *c*. 1670.  Baroque pearl in form of
a merman                                                                    7,140
1967  de Kay.  N.Y.  Enamelled and jewelled gold cup, Vienna,
1665, $50,000                                                          17,857
Real & Co.  N.Y.  The captain's whistle, from the sunken
Florida plate fleet, gold dragon and treble chain, late 17th
century Spanish, $50,900                                          17,857
S.  Baroque pearl in form of jester, *c*. 1700, 2½ in.       1,100
1968  Mdivani.  S.  Necklace, 13 scrolled gold links, pearls, etc.,
South German, late 16th century                                   8,500
1969  S.  Enamelled gold badge of a Nova Scotia baronet, 1629,
Scottish royal devices, said to be unique                      1,900
Enamelled gold badge, profile of Gustavus Adolphus,
King of Sweden, monogram GARS, 2½ in. high, *c*.
1635                                                                          980
Melvin Gutman.  N.Y.  English pendant with cameo
head of Queen Elizabeth                                             3,750
Enamelled gold pectoral cross, Flemish or German,
mid-16th century 3¼ in., $17,500 (Brummer sale, 1949,
$1,900)                                                                   7,292
South German pendant with mounted St George, late
16th century, 3½ in., $18,000                                      7,500
Spanish gold pendant, late 16th century, pelican
formed of baroque pearl, 3 in. high, $27,000               11,250
Oval bloodstone pendant with gemmed relief of
Neptune and Amphitrite, 3¾ in. diam., late 16th
century, $23,000 ($500 in 1950)                                  9,584
Ship-brooch with elaborate strapwork chain, Italy,
after 1550, 2¾ in., $16,000 (£115 in 1950)                   6,665

1969 (*cont.*) South German pendant, embossed group, Cimon and     £
         Pera, 3 in. high, end 16th century, $20,000       8,335
         Strapwork necklace, 17 in. long, S. German, after 1550,
         $17,500       7,292
         Scottish necklace, gold and enamelled entrelacs with
         rubies, 17½ in. long, before 1550, $32,000       13,335
         French pomander, opening into six inscribed com-
         partments, glass enamels on gold, *c.* 1600, $31,000
         ($1,800 in 1948)       12,916
N.Y.   'La Peregrina', Baroque pearl said to have been
given by Philip II to Mary I of England, $37,000       15,417

# LIMOGES ENAMELS

## on copper

### (late 15th to early 17th centuries)

The Limoges enamels were a peculiar regional product, technically very original, but artistically provincial and latterly copied from Italian engravings of the Mannerist school. But there was nothing quite like them even in Italy. So long as High Renaissance taste reigned supreme, they advanced steadily in value. Before the Strawberry Hill sale of 1842 nothing had made more than 40 guineas, but at the Andrew Fountaine sale of 1884, the *Feast of the Gods* dish cost 7,000 guineas. And at that time Count Basilevski had already refused £10,000 for a Limoges triptych by Nardon Penicaud. The 1970 equivalent would be £90,000.

More information concerning the long reign of the Limoges enamels in the saleroom will be found in Volume Two. A triptych by Nardon Penicaud was still worth over £3,000 during the First World War, but between 1933 and 1951 not even the earlier triptychs could make £1,000 and the later 16th century *tazze* and oval dishes, which had been so sought after in the 1880s, no more than £25 to £75. The recovery of the 1950s received a fresh momentum in 1969, though hardly sensational. This brief list of the highest prices of the 1960s reads very like the prices of the 1880s as given in Volume Two, except that money then was worth nine times as much.

|  |  | £ |
|---|---|---:|
| 1960 | S. Single plaque from a triptych, the Crucifixion, attributed to Monvaerni, before 1500 | 1,900 |
| 1965 | Birmingham and Midland Institute. S. 10-inch plaque by Susanne Court, c. 1590, the Pentecost | 1,400 |
|  | 9½-in. plaque, the family of St Anne, c. 1500 | 2,400 |
|  | 7-inch plaque, John the Baptist, attributed Jean Limousin | 800 |
|  | Diptych, 8¼ in. high, c. 1520, Sts Peter and Paul | 1,400 |
|  | Adda. Paris. Restored ewer by Pierre Reymond, c. 1560, 11 in. | 745 |
|  | Casket with amorini by Pierre Reymond, c. 1530 (£300 in 1951) | 2,335 |
| 1966 | James de Rothschild. Paris. Pair of *tazze* by Jean Court, late 16th century, 10¼ in. diam. 2 for | 1,450 |
|  | Candlestick by Pierre Nouailher, c. 1600 | 423 |
| 1967 | Gaussens. S. Pair of salts, under 4 in. high, *grisailles* by Pierre Reymond (£630 in 1892) 2 for | 1,500 |
|  | Leather casket with plaques by Couly Nouailher, 7½ in. | 1,700 |
|  | A second leather casket with plaques by Couly Nouailher 7½ in. | 1,150 |
|  | (53 lots of Limoges enamel made £14,432) |  |

568

| | | £ |
|---|---|---|
| 1968 | S. Basin, dated 1562, 18¼ in. diam. Numerous allegorical figures in style of Pierre Reymond (£76 8s. in 1846) | 1,200 |
| | Oval plaque, Susanna and the Elders, Pierre Courteys after René Boyvin, 1570–80, 10×8 in. | 1,200 |
| 1969 | S. Tazza and cover, signed Pierre Reymond, biblical scenes after Bernard Solomon, c. 1560, 7¼ in. diam. | 700 |
| | C. Casket on caryatid feet, 7½ in. wide, plaques of putti, possibly by Couly Nouailher, c. 1550 | 4,620 |

# MAJOLICA
## Italian faience, 15th and 16th centuries

Those who are appalled when a Faenza dish in a colour scheme far from enticing—and possibly patched up—makes the best part of £4,000, will be surprised to know that the same sort of thing could happen in 1910 when the pound was worth eight times as much. Like Limoges enamels, Majolica suffered a catastrophic decline between the early 1920s and the post-war period. Like Limoges enamels, it recovered to its previous levels, but only in terms of devalued pounds. In fact the value of Majolica, the mainstay of enlightened and scholarly 19th century collecting, is still less than an eighth what it was. The great Richard Wallace was believed to have paid in the 1880s no less than £12,000 for a vast Urbino basin. In the salerooms the highest prices are still those of the three Urbino vases in the Salomon sale in New York in 1923. These aggregated $101,000, the equivalent of £108,500 in 1970 money.

It should be noticed that both cases concerned the bulbous baroque style of the mid-16th century which became the most unpopular Majolica of all. At the Pringsheim sale of 1939 an important signed Urbino dish of 1540 made no more than £20 to rise to £1,785 in 1962. This was a year which saw a great deal of speculation by Italian business men who favoured the High Renaissance rather than the *Quattrocento*. But in the 1960s as a whole the tendency of the 1920s was resumed, that is to say a concentration on primitive pieces in an ascetic range of colours. As one instance, a Florentine 'oak leaf jar' was not worth more than £250 in 1919, when much later types of Majolica had several times reached the £3,000–4,000 range in the salerooms. Yet an oak leaf jar which was sold for £3,990 in 1967, was as dear as any piece of Majolica which had appeared in the salerooms during the past 44 years.

The indications are that there is very little fine Majolica which can still reach the market and not much of even average quality. At any rate, one is unlikely to see another such accumulation as the Adda collection which was sold in Paris in 1965. Four years passed before another sale was devoted entirely to one Majolica collection. The Hannaford sale of 1969 could hardly be compared with the Adda and Bak sales of 1965, yet even the few important items showed no apparent rise in value, despite the fall of the pound and the general boom of the art market, and the fact that the sale was held in the best place for the buyers. Less and less does Majolica appear to be in the smart international taste of the day.

|  |  |  | £ |
|---|---|---|---|
| 1961 | S. | Urbino dish, dated 1531, by Francesco Xanto (£380 in 1957) | 780 |
|  |  | Gubbio dish, 1526, arms of Vitelli | 980 |
|  |  | Faenza *albarello* jar, c. 1520, Cleopatra and the asp | 500 |
| 1962 | S. | A series sold with the Pringsheim collection in 1939. |  |
|  |  | Two-handled Florence *albarello*, c. 1480 (£38 in 1939) | 980 |

£

1962 S. Siena pitcher, *c.* 1500, arms of Piccolomini (£95 in 1939)

    1,400

Faenza *albarello*, *c.* 1470 (£37 in 1939)    750

Urbino dish, Francesco Xanto Avelli    1,000

Pair of Deruta lustre dishes, *c.* 1525    2 for  1,300

Faenza drug jar, Cleopatra and the asp, 1520    920

C. Urbino dish, History of Coriolanus by Guido Merlino, *c.* 1540 (Pringsheim sale, 1939, £20)    1,785

Armorial dish, 1532, by Francesco Xanto, Urbino    2,735

Armorial dish, Pesaro    1,050

Paris. Gubbio lustre dish, Maestro Giorgio    2,920

Faenza *albarello*, *c.* 1490    1,820

Two Casteldurante dishes, *c.* 1520    1,240 and 1,350

*Tondino*, depicting hand holding thunderbolt, Gubbio, *c.* 1520    3,295

1963 S. Siena jug, *c.* 1500, arms of Piccolomini, 14½ in.    1,400

Deutsch. S. Urbino dish, 1535, Horatius on the bridge, 18 in.    1,050

Casteldurante portrait dish, signed Astolfo Niccolo Pellipario, *c.* 1525    850

C. Gubbio lustre dish, 1532, Dares and Entellus after Dente    1,522 10*s.*

S. Faenza *albarello*, scrollwork, no figures, *c.* 1470, 13 in.    1,550

Deruta lustre dish, girl's head in profile, *c.* 1520    1,800

1964 Paris. Caffagiolo dish, *c.* 1500, paschal lamb, scollop border    1,360

Finarte, Milan. Jar with banded design, Florence, *c.* 1450, 3 million lire+tax    About  2,000

1965 C. Urbino dish, 1535, Victory of Octavian and Lepidus    1,890

Adda. Paris. Caffagiolo pitcher with monogram, *c.* 1525    2,735

Caffagiolo dish, 1510–15, scenes from the Passion, 19 in.    3,470

Trilobe *tazza*, Urbino, mid-16th century, height 3½ in.    2,025

Casteldurante dish, bust of Palamedes by Niccolo Pellipario, *c.* 1525, 8¾ in. diam.    3,990

Deruta lustre dish, *c.* 1520, with winged sphinx    2,490

Deruta lustre dish, *c.* 1510, with portrait, 16½ in. diam.    2,392

Deruta lustre dish, all-over decoration of rosettes    2,155

Deruta lustre dish, female portrait and armorial device    1,772

Deruta lustre dish, *c.* 1515, female portrait, 17 in.    2,794

Deruta lustre dish, same date, helmeted man, 16·8 in. diam.    3,375

Pair of Deruta portrait *albarelli*, *c.* 1500, 8¾ in.    2 for  4,064

Faenza dish, *c.* 1470, arms of Ranieri, 15½ in. diam.    2,872

£

1965 (*cont.*) Faenza dish, *c.* 1525–30, portrait inscribed 'Lucrezia bella' — 2,612

Gubbio lustre dish, Christ visited by Mary and Martha, 12½ in. — 2,470

Gubbio lustre dish, *c.* 1515, portrait of a girl, 9¼ in. diam. — 2,164

Bak. S. Early Florentine two-handled drug jar, *c.* 1425–50, 6½ in. — 1,600

Florentine oak leaf jar, *c.* 1450, winged harpy, 9½ in. high — 2,520

Faenza two-handled drug jar, *c.* 1470, 10 in. high — 2,100

Faenza portrait charger, 1470–80, 15¼ in. diam. — 2,300

Faenza dish, *c.* 1510, *putto* and swan, signed C.I., 9¾ in. diam. — 3,800

Deruta blue-ground dish with girl's portrait, *c.* 1530, 14 in. — 2,440

36 lots were sold for £1,000 or more out of 70 in all (£77,980)

1966 S. Urbino dish. Victory of Octavian and Lepidus, 16½ in. — 1,890

1967 S. *Tondino* by Pellipario, Casteldurante, *grottesche* painted *en grisaille* on blue, dated 1521, 10 in. diam. — 2,100

Dundas. C. Florentine oak leaf jar, *c.* 1450, 9½ in. diam. — 3,990

Its companion, damaged (compare 1949, 1959, 1965) — 472 10s

Adda. C. *Tazza* by Fra Xanto, Urbino, 1541, 11¼ in. diam. — 1,155

C. Urbino tazza after Parmigianino, *c.* 1540, 10¼ in. (£136, 10s., 1959) — 1,155

1968 C. Gold lustre portrait charger, Deruta, *c.* 1520, 16½ in. diam. (Walker sale, 1945, £220 10s.) — 1,890

Urbino *istoriato* dish in the Fontana style, illustrating the Punic wars, 14 in. diam., *c.* 1540 — 1,260

1969 C. Faenza drug jar with two portrait heads, *c.* 1530, 'Olem di cappario', 10 in. high — 1,050

S. Faenza drug bottle with portrait head, *c.* 1520, 'Aqua Buglosse', 16¾ in. — 1,200

C. Urbino tazza, Hector and Achilles by Fra Xanto Avelli, 1538, 10¼ in. diam. Damaged — 1,155

Oak leaf jar with leaping hounds, late 15th century, oviform, 10½ in. high — 1,050

Hannaford. S. (Florence). Oak leaf jar, leaping deer, *c.* 1450, 10 in. high, 1·6 million lire+tax — 1,188

Faenza 2-handled albarello, *c.* 1470, 8½ in., 2·2 million lire+tax — 1,628

| 1969 | Maestro Giorgio style lustre dish, Gubbio 1521, 10 in., 2·2 million lire+tax | £ 1,628 |
|---|---|---|
| | Faenza 2-handled drug-bottle with portrait, 14¼ in. high, *c.* 1520, 2·7 million lire+tax | 1,980 |
| | Faenza spirally fluted *crespina*, 10½ in. *c.* 1540, 2·5 million lire+tax | 1,815 |
| | 2nd ditto, 11¼ in. diam., 2·8 million lire+tax | 2,035 |
| | Another ditto, *istoriato*, Cadmus and Hermione, *c.* 1540–45, 10½ in. diam., 1·9 million lire+tax | 1,375 |
| | Casteldurante dish, ordeal of Moses, dated 1533, 10 in., 2·2 million lire+tax | 1,628 |
| | Casteldurante dish, gods of Parnassus after Raphael, portrait on the back, *c.* 1525–30, 16½ in. diam., 4 million lire+tax | 2,860 |
| | Casteldurante dish, Christ in the house of Simon the Pharisee, after Marcantonio Raimondi, *c.* 1545–50, 16 in. diam., 6 million lire+tax | 4,400 |
| | Urbino tazza, Hector and Achilles, signed by Xanto Avelli 1539, 10½ in., 1·7 million lire+tax | 1,606 |
| | 136 pieces of Majolica made about £69,300 with tax | |

# MEDIEVAL ART
## METALWORK AND ENAMELS

The Christian-Romantic concept of the Age of Faith is singularly dead among us. Those dreadful guides which tell you where canned Beaujolais can be ordered with dinner for 36 francs, seldom recommend the Romanesque carvings. No one paints the quest of the Holy Grail. Taking rubbings from brass effigies in churches is no longer an act of passionate devotion but a commercial racket, run by interior decorators. But objects of Western Medieval art on a portable or collectable scale are now very rare indeed, and those of this country almost non-existent outside museums. Hence a scramble among American museums to secure the remains at high cost. Hence efforts to impede their export at still higher cost. The resultant prices persuade one to forget the squalid and tendentious implications of the words, *the arts*, in all public pronouncements. In fact the high cost of the last surviving medieval relics almost tempts one to believe that it is truly love that makes it so, and not the dim confusions of purpose that accompany the saleroom interventions of governments on all occasions.

Particularly to be noticed are the £40,000 which were needed to rescue a scrap of English 12th century morse-ivory, scarcely bigger than a *netsuke*, and the £35,000 which were paid for a Dinant Romanesque enamelled plaque. It was the size of a cigarette case and strangely exciting to handle. The emphasis is of course on Romanesque rather than Gothic, but even so standardized an example of Gothic *Kleinkunst* as a 14th century *château d'amour* ivory mirror-case can go up enormously in a few years.

|  | | £ |
|---|---|---|
| 1960 | S. The Pershore Censer or Thurible of Goderic, Anglo–Saxon pierced bronze, 10th century. Victoria & Albert | 2,600 |
| 1961 | Robert Horst. C. Limoges 13th century chasse with crucifixion in high relief | 9,240 |
| | Two plaques from a chasse of the same type, £840 and | 861 |
| | Findlay. S. Brass astrolabe, 13th century, Hispano–Arab or S. Italian. British Museum | 2,800 |
| | Brass astrolabe, *c.* 1425 | 1,800 |
| 1962 | Gilou. S. *Appliqué* figure of Christ, crucified, from a 13th century Limoges chasse | 680 |
| 1963 | S. Aquamanile, incised bronze, Hildesheim, 13th century | 3,600 |
| | *Appliqué* figure, the crucified Christ, from an Irish bronze casket, 13th century | 700 |
| | Paris. Bookbinding plaque, 13th century Limoges enamel | 2,030 |
| 1965 | C. Limoges bookbinding plaque, the crucifixion, 13th century | 1,832 10s. |
| | Birmingham & Midland Institute. S. The Pentecost, *champlevé* enamel plaque, Dinant, *c.* 1160 | 35,000 |

| | | £ |
|---|---|---|
| 1965 | S. Eleven 38-inch panels of early 14th century stained glass, Lavantthal, Austria | 11 for 30,700 |
| | Stoclet. S. Byzantine enamelled clasp, 12th century | 6,500 |
| | Byzantine mosaic icon, 11 × 10 in. 14th century | 34,000 |
| | Limoges enamelled crucifix, 12½ in. high, c. 1200 | 3,600 |
| | S. Limoges chasse, 8¾ in. wide, vermiculated ground, c. 1200 | 32,000 |
| | Bronze 'Hansa dish', vices and virtues, c. 1200, 10 in. diam. | 2,600 |
| | Pomeroy. S. Limoges enamel crozier, 11¾ in., 13th century | 2,200 |
| | Craig de Cleves. S. Part of Limoges ciborium, 13th century | 2,600 |
| | Stoclet, 2nd sale. S. Limoges enamel burette, 5¾ in. high, 13th century | 2,000 |
| | Gilt-bronze Christ from a 12th century crucifix, 10¼ in. high | 21,000 |
| | Rhineland enamel crucifixion plaque, 12th century, 3¼ in. | 2,600 |
| | S. Irish silver annular brooch from Ballymoney, 10th century | 1,400 |
| 1966 | van Zuylen. S. Crozier-head, richly enamelled and gilded, Limoges, c. 1220, 11 in. high | 3,600 |
| | Chasse, 6¾ in. wide, appliqué figures, Christ, crowned, with saints, Limoges, 13th century | 6,800 |
| | C. Christ from a copper-gilt crucifix, German, 11th century, 7¾ in. high | 2,940 |
| | Enamelled gold crucifix, N. Italian, 15th century, 9¾ in. | 2,735 |
| | S. Chasse, Limoges, c. 1200, with martyrdom of Thomas à Becket, 6¼ in. long | 1,900 |
| 1967 | Paris. Enamelled bookbinding plaque, Limoges, c. 1340, 12 × 7½ in., FN40,000+tax | 3,232 |
| | Alexandrine de Rothschild. S. Bronze candlestick, monster supporting castle, Meuse school, 13th century, 6 in. high | 2,100 |
| | Bahssin. S. Gilt-bronze chef-réliquaire in the form of a bust of St Antigius, Bishop of Brescia, N. Italian, c. 1470, 18½ in. high | 1,050 |
| | Silvertop. S. 'Becket' chasse, Limoges, early 13th century, 4½ in. long, very rough | 1,900 |
| | Bernhardt. S. Limoges enamelled copper crucifix, 6¾ in. high, early 13th century | 2,600 |
| | N.Y. Limoges enamelled chasse with glass pastes, rough work, c. 1300, 6 × 6½ in. | 1,440 |

£

1968 Abbey. S. Four enamelled plaques with apostle symbols
from a gospel book-cover, Meuse school, c. 1150, each 1½ in.
square                                                    4 for    5,000
S. Gilt reliquary-casket, dated 1446, Florence, 7½×7½    4,600
Ushaw College. S. 11th century English bronze Virgin
in relief, 4¼ in. from a bookbinding                             4,300
C. Crozier-head, Limoges enamel, c. 1250, 13½ in.               2,730
Streitenberger. C. Spanish parcelgilt processional cross,
late Gothic, c. 1530, 45 in. high                               3,780
Bought from Oscott College by the Metropolitan Museum,
15th century brass lectern from Louvain of great elabora-
tion, supported on lions with candlesticks, etc.             105,000
1969 S. Limoges enamelled ciborium, 14th century 9½ in.        1,300
Limoges crucifix, *champlevé* enamel on tripod stand,
10¾ in. high, 13th century                                      2,000
S. Bronze mortar, clenched fist handles, English 15th
century, 8 in. high                                             1,300
Bonstetten. S. Limoges enamelled chasse with Christ
figure of exceptional quality, 6×3¼×7½, 13th century           8,000
Another Limoges chasse with Christ in plainer style
without enamels, 7×4×6                                          1,500
13th century Limoges book-cover with *appliqué*
figure of crucified Christ, 12½×7¾                             2,800
Miniature chasse, with apostle figures, 4 in. wide             2,100

## IVORY

1960 S. Norse reliquary cross, c. 1200                            680
1961 Robert Horst. C. 14th century French triptych              5,250
Two diptychs, ditto                            1,470 and 1,575
1962 Gilou. S. French 14th century statuette of the Virgin,
5½ in. high, traces of paint                                    3,600
2nd ditto, rather smaller                                       1,400
1964 Weinmüller, Munich. Lion's head, morse ivory, 2×4 in.
Found at Eichstadt, 1924, 10th century   with tax about        8,000
1965 Stoclet. S. Chessman (king), Cologne, 13th century,
morse ivory, 3 in. high                                        10,000
Paris. 14th century French mirror-case, 4·4 in. diam.
carved with *le château d'amour* (similar piece in 1950, £750,
see also 1968), FN80,000+tax                                    6,460
1966 S. Pectoral cross, morse ivory, Canterbury school, early
12th century. Victoria and Albert Museum, 4¾ in. long         40,000
Dreyfus. S. Casket, 5 in. long, Paris, early 14th century
(Spitzer sale, 1893, lot 115, with tax £165)                  11,000

| | | £ |
|---|---|---:|
| 1966 | McNulty. S. St Luke, plaque from a German 11th century bookbinding, under 2 in. square | 5,000 |
| | Incomplete Christ from French crucifix, painted, *c.* 1320, 7¾ in. high | 1,200 |
| 1967 | Alexandrine de Rothschild. S. Miniature mirror-case, just over an inch wide, French 14th century | 1,700 |
| | Chessman (queen) 2¼ in. high, French late 14th century | 1,700 |
| | C. Byzantine casket, neo-Pagan style of the 11th century (Veroli group), 9 in. wide (£110 5s. in 1936), Bought-in | 3,675 |
| 1968 | S. Mirror-case, French 14th century, *le château d'amour*, 6½ in. diam. (similar mirror-cases £430 5s. in 1901, £693 in 1936 £6,460 in 1965) | 13,500 |
| | Prince de Ligne. S. 15 plaques of the life of Christ from a French casket, *c.* 1350–1400 | 2,600 |
| | Foljambe. C. Comb with chess-playing scene, Rhineland, *c.* 1380 | 6,825 |
| | S. Single wing from a Parisian triptych, 6¼ × 3½ in. mid-14th century | 1,500 |
| 1969 | Reyne. S. Mirror-case, French 14th century, the lover crowned, 4 in. diam. | 7,200 |
| | Batthyany-Strattmann. S. Wooden German parade-saddle, covered with relief-plaques in painted deerhorn, *c.* 1400–50 (21 known. Similar saddle, Zschille sale 1897, £480. Another in true ivory, 13th century (Louvre), in Spitzer sale, 1893, £3,400) | 12,500 |
| | Bearns. Torquay. Single panel from French 14th century diptych, 8 × 4½ | 4,100 |
| | S. Figurine, Virgin and child, with massacre of innocents carved on the back, 10½ in., N. Italian, *c.* 1400 | 8,000 |
| | Rhineland diptych, life of Christ in 4 panels, 8½ in. high, *c.* 1350–75 | 5,200 |

## NEAR EASTERN ART
### (Glass, ivory, metal, miniatures, pottery)
#### GLASS

The 'St Hedwig's glasses' are dotted about in a number of church treasuries, some of them in medieval mounts. Brought back by pilgrims or Crusaders from the Near East, they were deemed of so rare and precious a material as to be worthy of the relics of saints, and this has been the cause of their preservation. They are quite the most romantic glasses in the world and the most expensive. Traditionally it is not this sort of glass, carved to stimulate rock crystal, that has dominated the Islamic market but the great enamelled mosque lamps of the 13th and 14th centuries which in the 1840s were believed to have been made in Venice. At the Hamilton Place sale of 1882 a round-bellied glass 13th century tankard with horsemen and a blazon, enamelled in the style of the mosque lamps but only 7 inches high, had cost the 11th Duke of Hamilton £70. It was bought by Alfred de Rothschild for £2,730 or £25,000 in 1970 money, but one wonders whether it could fetch as much. An exceptionally good example of an enamelled glass mosque lamp, full-size and made less than a century later, was sold in 1963 for £2,700, no more than the price of another with the same inscription which was sold in 1921. On the other hand, a much later example, seriously damaged, made £6,090 in 1970.

|  |  | £ |
|---|---|---:|
| 1959 | Bought by British Museum. Amber coloured cut-glass beaker, 3½ in. high, so called 'St Hedwig's glass' Syria, 12th century (compare 1967) | 16,000 |
| 1961 | S. Long-necked enamelled bottle, 14th century, sparse design | 320 |
| 1963 | Earl of Rosebery. S. Mosque lamp with enamelled titles of Sultan ibn Qalaun of Egypt, d. 1340 | 2,700 |
| 1964 | Hausweldel, Hamburg. Fragmentary green tumbler with yellow and brown enamels, Nishapur, 10th century, 4½ in. high | 683 |
| 1966 | de Salis. C. Miniature inscribed mosque lamp, 7¾ in. high | 945 |
| 1967 | Alexandrine de Rothschild. S. St Hedwig's glass (compare 1959), 12th century, 3½ in. high, Cleveland Museum | 19,000 |
| 1969 | C. Enamelled mosque lamp with dedications to Sultan Malik Zahir Barkuk (1382–99), base broken away, 14¼ in. high as cut down. Bought in at | 4,725 |
| 1970 | C. Another with the same inscription, base broken away, 13 in. high | 6,090 |

#### IVORY

| 1958 | S. Ivory cyst, Sicilian or Spanish, 10th century (£1,837 10s. in 1913), Victoria and Albert Museum | 5,700 |
|---|---|---:|

| | | £ |
|---|---|---|
| 1967 | Alexandrine de Rothschild. S. 10th century Hispano–Arab coffer, 6in. long, much repaired and lacking its inscription | |
| | | 8,000 |
| 1968 | Kevorkian. S. Siculo–Arab casket, *c.* 1200, incised decoration, $14\frac{1}{2}$ in. long | |
| | | 850 |
| 1969 | Bonstetten. S. Plain ditto, *c.* 1200, added French 14th and 15th century coppergilt fittings, Roman agate cameo, $7\frac{1}{2}\times4$ | |
| | | 650 |

## METALWORK (INCLUDING SILVER)

| | | £ |
|---|---|---|
| 1962 | Finlay. S. Brass astrolabe, possibly Persian, dated 1480, $3\frac{3}{4}$ in. diam. | |
| | | 3,600 |
| 1963 | Bobrinskoi. C. Pair of Persian silver inlaid candlestick-bases, 13th century. Bought in (see 1965)    2 for | 398 |
| | Kenney. S. Persian astrolabe, dated 1292 A.D. | 850 |
| 1964 | Brummer. S. Persian bronze relief mirror-back, *c.* 1200, 8 in. | |
| | | 720 |
| 1965 | Bobrinskoi. C. Pair of candlesticks (see 1963)    2 for | 651 |
| | Stoclet. S. Egyptian bronze figure of a hare, part of a basin, Fatimid, 11th century, $4\frac{3}{4}$ in. long | |
| | | 800 |
| 1966 | Storm-Rice. C. Persian sword-hilt, Saljuq period, 11th century, under 6 in. wide | 2,047 10s. |
| | Brass bowl, silver inlays, arms of Hugh IV, King of Cyprus (d. 1359), Egypt or Syria | 2,520 |
| 1967 | Alexandrine de Rothschild. S. Silver ewer, gold inlays, supposed Ommeyad in Sassanid style, 8th century, $5\frac{1}{2}$ in. | 1,250 |
| 1968 | Kevorkian. S. 16th century Mamluq helmet, silver-inlaid iron | |
| | | 2,100 |
| | Another helmet, same school, both with St Irene arsenal mark, Istanbul | |
| | | 850 |

## MINIATURES AND MANUSCRIPTS
### PERSIA, INDIA AND THE ARAB COUNTRIES

Persian illuminated manuscripts were already highly esteemed at the beginning of the century. Their subsequent market history compares closely with that of their European counterparts. Thus a well-known book of Persian romances, illuminated in the year 1410, which has been for some years in the British Museum, cost Dyson Perrins £5,000 at the Yates Thompson sale of 1919. A slightly later manuscript in this style, a *Shah Nameh* of about the same dimensions, went to the U.S.A. in 1968 at £50,000. It contained 58 miniatures as against 38 in the Yates Thompson manuscript, but the latter were rather better in quality. £5,000 had the purchasing power in 1919 of about £23,000 in 1968. The result of this comparison is to reduce the 1968 purchase, which left everyone gasping, to something quite rational.

As usual, it is the things which were considered trivial in the days when the market could afford to be critical that have advanced out of all measure. A large Persian miniature in the Europeanizing style of Muhammed Zaman, painted about the year 1700, made £3,000 in 1967. In the days when men like Goloubeff, Claude Anet, André Sambon and Coomaraswamy were still collecting, such an object would have been thought a waste of money at £15. On the other hand, in 1921, Alphonse Kann paid £935 for a rare and exciting illuminated page of the 13th century Baghdad school. This will have advanced only moderately, since almost comparable pages cost £1,220 in 1958, £1,800 in 1965 and £3,800 in 1967 and 1969. Clearly the worst has advanced the most, though this situation is not quite the same in the case of *Indian* miniatures. The English collecting tradition, which went right back to the 18th century, favoured royal and noble portraits. Thus the price which the British Museum had to pay in 1912 for its large miniature of the Princes of the House of Timur was as high as £350, the equivalent of £2,800 in 1970 money. As much as was paid in 1921 for a large miniature, portraying the court of Jehangir. But fine Mughal miniatures, when devoid of portrait interest, were much less esteemed than Persian miniatures and could be very cheap. In that same year, 1921, Sothebys sold a number of miniatures from a *Razam Nameh*, painted for Akbar himself in 1598, at an average of less than £3 each. One of them in 1966 made £750, but that price had come to look quite modest by 1970. It was in fact easier before the Kevorkian sale of December, 1969, for a Mughal miniature to make £3,000 to £5,000 than it was for a Persian miniature. The frenzied competition of American museums for Indian miniatures was enhanced by the belief that it was too late in the day to wait for Persian miniatures of really fine quality to turn up. Hence four-figure prices even for late 18th century miniatures, commissioned by Europeans at Lucknow or Calcutta. Hence prices of £400 to £500 for nineteenth century miniatures in the rather sugary style of the Kangra school.

The second Kevorkian sale restored the balance for Persian miniatures. In fact the leaf from the Demotte *Shah Nameh* at £30,000 (equivalent to £3,750 in 1914) was easily the costliest book painting ever sold. Representing a watershed between the half-Byzantine Baghdad school and the first symptoms of the Persian style, this manuscript has a similar importance to that of Giotto's Assisi frescoes. Yet, compared with the finest Western illuminations and even with later Persian and Indian painting, this particular specimen is neither very accomplished nor very inviting. But the finest Western illuminations no longer reach the market. If they did, they might fetch more than £30,000 which could be less than the value of the missing leaf from Jean Foucquet's *Hours of Etienne Chevallier* which Sothebys sold in 1946 for £2,900.

## ILLUMINATED MANUSCRIPTS
### PERSIAN AND NEAR EASTERN

£

1961  S.  Gulistan of Sa'adi, school of Bihzad, *c.* 1500, 8
miniatures                                       6,500

1963  Parvanta.  S.  The Language of Birds of Farid ed din
Attar, 8 miniatures by Sultan Ali of Herat, 1483, Metropolitan Museum            18,000

        14th century Egyptian Koran, contemporary binding   1,500

1967  Kevorkian.  S.  *Shah Nameh* of Firdawsi, dated 1539, 14
miniatures (£95 in 1935)         9,000

        *Shah Nameh*, Shiraz, *c.* 1550–60 (£150 in 1935), 16
miniatures         11,000

        Turkish scrap-book album, early 17th century, four
Persian miniatures and numerous European engravings   1,400

1968  Dufferin and Ava.  C.  *Shah Nameh*, Shiraz before 1450,
555 leaves, 58 miniatures, 10½ × 7 in.       50,000

      Vassib.  C.  *Nigaristan* of al Jaffari, Shiraz, 1573, 319
leaves, 41 miniatures, 14½ × 9¼.  Some damage    7,350

      Robinson Trust.  S. (Phillipps library). Half a *Shah Nemeh*,
dated 1654–7, 29 miniatures mainly by Muin Musawwir   34,000

        Turkish version of the *Shirin Khusraw* of Hatifi, 6
miniatures  dated  1498,  contemporary  binding.
Metropolitan Museum       7,000

1969  S.  Part of a Koran, written at Marrakesh by the Almohad
emir, Murtada, in 1256, script ornaments and contemporary
gilded leather binding       6,200

      Kevorkian.  S.  *Shah Nameh*, dated 1457, 52 miniatures
mainly in the Shiraz style, 13½ × 9¾       12,000

        Koran fragment, Egypt, 9th–10th century, 80 leaves,
7½ × 10½       4,000

        Jami, *Yusuf and Zuleika*, Istanbul, late 16th century, 5
miniatures, 7½ × 5½       4,200

1970  C.  *Khamsa* of Nizami with Baghdad colophons of years
1386–8, leaves 9¾ × 6¾, 23 miniatures remaining, mostly
half-page       45,000

### SINGLE MINIATURES

1962  S.  A poet, pen-drawing, signed Riza Abbasi, 1626     320

1965  S.  Page from the automata of al Jaziri, Egypt, 14th century
(compare 1963)       1,800

        Moses and the plague of serpents, European style, mid-
17th century, Persia       650

| | | £ |
|---|---|---|
| 1966 | Phillips. S. Majnun in the wilderness, semi-European style of Muhammad Zaman, 1675 (bought in India, 1917, £33 10s.) | 530 |
| 1967 | Lister. S. Portrait, seated youth, by Ali Riza, 1662 | 300 |
| | Kevorkian. S. Allegorical figure in European style by Ali Quli Jabbadar, Persia, c. 1700 | 3,000 |
| | Two pages from the automata of al Jaziri, Egypt, c. 1350 (compare 1965) Each | 3,800 |
| | Page with drawing of two lizards from the *Munafi al Hayawan*, Persian, c. 1300 (compare 1969) | 1,300 |
| | Page from a *Shah Nameh*, c. 1340, with small miniature at the bottom | 750 |
| | Sultan Bayazid at the battle of Ankara, 15th century, Shiraz school, 9 in. high | 1,400 |
| | Double-page miniature from a Shiraz MS of Sa'adi, c. 1580 | 1,700 |
| | Young prince, smelling a rose, by Muhammad Mu'min, c. 1600 | 1,500 |
| | Youth and old age, pen-drawing by Riza Abbasi, c. 1600, Metropolitan Museum | 1,300 |
| 1968 | S. Solomon and Queen of Sheba, *Shah Nameh* miniature, Shiraz, c. 1560 | 1,700 |
| | Cavalry engagement, Shiraz, c. 1570 | 520 |
| | Three pairs of lovers in Spring landscape, Shiraz, c. 1570 | 520 |
| | Composite Persian painting, Inju style, probably 16th century, 14½ × 10 | 1,100 |
| | S. Portrait miniature on vellum in European style, Istanbul, early 17th century, 10½ × 8¾ | 1,400 |
| 1969 | C. Standing girl with cup, Riza Abbasi school with portrait in European style on back, 17th century, 15 × 9¾ | 1,300 |
| | Meugens. S. Characters in Turkish dress watching holy man on a mule, Istanbul, c. 1600, 7 × 4½ | 1,400 |
| | Kevorkian. S. The execution of Mani, one of the 58 illuminated leaves of the *Demotte Shah Nameh*, mid-14th century Tabriz school, 11½ × 7¾ (another leaf, New York, 1943, $14,000 or £3,500) | 30,000 |
| | Afrasyab and Pashang, leaf from a *Shah Nameh*, c. 1570–80, signed Sadiqui, 12¼ × 7½ | 6,800 |
| | Posthumous portrait of Sultan Husayn Bayqara, Qazwin, c. 1580, 5¾ × 3¾ + text | 6,000 |
| | Two leaves from a treatise on automata of al Jaziri, Egypt 1315, 12½ × 8¾ (compare 1965, 1967) £3,600 and | 3,800 |
| | Another from a version dated 1354, 15¾ × 10¾ | 1,800 |
| | Leaf from the *Munafi al Hayawan* of Ibn Bakhtishu, the miniature 4¼ × 7¼, Persian, c. 1300 (compare 1967) | 3,000 |

£

| | | |
|---|---|---|
| 1969 | *Shah Nameh* leaf, Persian, *c.* 1350, the miniature 2×4¾ | 1,700 |
| | The poet Hatifi, portrait in Bihzad style, *c.* 1530, 2¾×2½ | 1,400 |
| | Page holding wine flask, signed Riza Abbasi, 1625 (£320 Homberg sale, Paris, 1931) | 4,400 |
| | Page holding a sheet of writing, signed Muhammad Qasim Musawwir, 7¾×4, after 1650 | 3,400 |
| | Unsigned miniature, Riza Abbasi style, two youths surprising a sleeping girl | 1,700 |
| | Two entwined dragons *en grisaille*, 4¾×2, called Turkish, late 16th century with caligraphy borders | 1,600 |
| | Leaf from Turkish MS of Al Celebi, *c.* 1600, 6¾×4, Ali enthroned as Caliph | 1,500 |
| | Turkish portrait of Sultan Selim II, late 16th century, 9×5¼ | 1,900 |
| | Sultan Muhammad I from the same series | 1,900 |

## ILLUMINATED MANUSCRIPTS, INDIAN

| | | |
|---|---|---|
| 1962 | S. *Shah Nameh* of Firdawsi, Mughal school, *c.* 1600, 17 miniatures | 3,900 |
| 1963 | Linnaean Society. S. Album of 64 natural history drawings, semi-European style, Calcutta, 1774–82 | 6,015 |
| 1969 | Kevorkian. S. *Zafar Nameh* of Hatifi, 10 miniatures Mughal school, early 17th century, 10½×6¼ | 3,200 |

### *Single miniatures, Indian, chiefly Mughal school*

| | | |
|---|---|---|
| 1961 | S. Page from *Razam Nameh*, 1598 (£3 in 1921, compare also 1966) | 320 |
| 1962 | S. Solomon and Queen of Sheba in European style, Shah Jehan period, *c.* 1630 | 580 |
| | Another in European style, *c.* 1600 | 360 |
| 1965 | Jehangir with falcon, *c.* 1630 | 1,200 |
| | Spencer Churchill. C. Demons in their mountain caves, *c.* 1600 | 945 |
| | Portrait of Asaf, brother in law of Shah Jehan, *c.* 1640 | 420 |
| 1966 | Phillips, son and Neale. Page from *Hamza Nameh* on cotton, 27×20, *c.* 1570, very rubbed (similar miniature, £300 in 1949). British Museum | 1,550 |
| | S. Page from *Razam Nameh*, 1598 (compare, 1961) | 750 |
| 1967 | S. Portrait of a ruler of Bijapur, early 17th century | 360 |
| | The cats arguing over the mice, Akbar period, *c.* 1600 | 300 |
| | A lady casts off her jewelry, Kangra school, *c.* 1810 | 300 |

£

| | | |
|---|---|---|
| 1967 | Kevorkian. S. A poet by Mir Sayyid Ali, Indo-Persian, *c.* 1556 | 4,000 |
| | Two leaves, *Babur Nameh*, before 1600. Metropolitan Museum 2 for | 1,500 |
| | A prince on a prancing horse; before 1600. Metropolitan Museum | 1,400 |
| | Reception scene from a *Babur Nameh* MS, *c.* 1600 | 900 |
| | Scene from the *Harivamsa*, Mughal miniature, *c.* 1600. Metropolitan Museum | 1,300 |
| | Gayumarth holding court, 12½-in. Mughal miniature, *c.* 1590 | 1,700 |
| | Ascetic walking by a stream, Mughal, early 17th century | 1,600 |
| | Hunting activities, *grisaille*, Jehangir period, *c.* 1620 | 900 |
| | Poet reading a book, Mughal, by Paimji, *c.* 1615 | 1,400 |
| | Portrait by Abdulrahim of Herat, Shah Jehan period, *c.* 1640 | 900 |
| | Captive dove, signed Mansur, same date | 800 |
| 1968 | S. Kangra school (Himalayan) miniature, early 19th century. Disconsolate lady on a terrace | 340 |
| | Portrait of Shah Jehan, *c.* 1650, 9 × 5¾ in. Mughal | 1,900 |
| | Palace with assembled women, Lucknow school, *c.* 1760, 16½ × 9¼, inner measurement | 1,000 |
| | Equestrian prince and bathing girls, 7½ × 10¾, Murshidabad, *c.* 1760 | 1,000 |
| | Two Lucknow paintings in European style, crested hawk and white vulture, late 18th century, 25¼ × 18½ 2 for | 1,400 |
| | Robinson Trust. S. (Phillipps Library.) A king watching a wrestling match, 11¾ × 7, from a Sa'adi MS, *c.* 1590 | 3,800 |
| | C. Jehangir hunting, signed Farukh Khurd, 10½ × 7¾, *c.* 1617–20 | 4,600 |
| | A prince visiting a hermit's cave, *c.* 1600, 13¾ × 9¼ | 3,200 |
| 1969 | C. Shah Jehan and attendants, after 1630, 14¾ × 9¾ with mounts | 4,200 |
| | Meugens. S. Two princes hawking in rocky landscape, Indo-Persian style, *c.* 1580, 8¾ × 5¼ | 2,600 |
| | A prince watching bathing girls in rocky pool, *c.* 1620, 8 × 4¼ | 3,000 |
| | S. Sixteen miniatures from the *Akhbar i Barmakiyan*, *c.* 1600, from 6¼ to 8¾ in. high. The whole suite of 16 made | 21,400 |
| | The dearest single miniatures were: Yahia with Isa ibn Bakhtishu, the Christian physician, depicted as a Jesuit father, 6¼ × 4½ | 2,800 |

|  |  | £ |
|---|---|---|
| 1969 | Yahia and Ja'far in a palace courtyard, 10¾ × 6 | 3,000 |
|  | Ja'far and Abdelmalik, 8¾ × 5 | 3,600 |

Clifton. S. Portrait, Shanawaz Khan, seven other portraits in border, Mughal, *c.* 1650, 8½ × 8¼ — 3,000

Kevorkian (2nd sale). S. Woman reclining on carpet and suckling child, European style but *not* the Virgin Mary, early 17th century, 8½ × 5½ — 8,500

A prince attacking a lion, Mughal towards 1600, 4¾ × 8½ — 2,800

Fat woman in Chagatai costume, Mughal, *c.* 1600, 9 × 5¼ — 1,700

Akbar watching a hunt with elephants, *c.* 1600, 8 × 5¾ — 3,000

Dervish reading with a cat, inscribed by Jehangir's son, Kurram, early 17th century — 3,200

Portrait head of European man, 3¾ × 3, same inscription — 2,200

Prince feeding a falcon, 5¾ × 3½, both *c.* 1620 — 2,000

The blind king Dhrita Rashtra from a *Razam Nameh* of 1616, 15 × 9½ — 2,000

Portrait, Rao Chattar Sal, figures in border, 14¾ × 12 — 2,000

Shah Jehan and a Holy Man, figures in border, *c.* 1645, 14¾ × 10½ — 1,700

9 others at £1,000 to £1,500

1970 C. Three women among trees, Deccani school, 16th century — 6,200

# NEAR EASTERN ART
POTTERY
## EXCAVATED GLAZED POTTERY, 9TH–14TH CENTURIES

In the first quarter of this century a very wealthy collector would scarcely avoid acquiring a few specimens of Islamic pottery, purchased perhaps from such legendary dealers as Kelekian or Parrish Watson at prices which were to seem formidable indeed in the second quarter-century. These lovely but terribly fragile things first came to Europe from Persia in the 1870s, almost invariably incomplete and made up with plaster and oil paint. They were not for orthodox collectors in the Renaissance tradition like Salting and Pierpont Morgan, but the next generation welcomed them. In 1909 Kelekian was believed to have paid $12,400 for a single large lustre dish, the equivalent of £20,000 in 1970. Prices exceeding £1,000 were quite common before 1930, the year of the great Persian exhibition at Burlington House. This attracted a great many new buyers. The older collectors, like those who had bought Greek vases in the past, were never much bothered by incompleteness and restoration. But to those accustomed to the standards of porcelain-collecting which condemned anything that had so much as a hair crack, the discovery that their treasures were more than a quarter paint and plaster, or even made of interpellated fragments from other pieces, was profoundly disillusioning. This, coupled with the impact of the Great Slump on the entire art market, drove down the price. By the outbreak of the Second World War £10 was the price of average quality, £40 the price of magnificence.

Recovery proved very slow. The value of the older collections was depressed by the importation since the 1940s of Persian 13th century lustre and monochrome pieces which had been excavated intact, though these were of very poor quality, compared with the earlier imports, and sometimes highly suspect as well. Pre-First World War prices were not reached again even on paper till the middle 1960s. The Kevorkian sales in New York and London in 1967–8 were a landmark. It must however, be borne in mind that these four-figure prices meant no more than £120 to £400 in pre-1914 money and that examples of this quality (or pretention) are not seen very often.

| | | £ |
|---|---|---|
| 1959 | Eldred Hiscock.   S.   Nishapur or Samarkand type bowl, 10th century | 420 |
| | Rayy bowl, turquoise ground and figures, 13th century | 280 |
| 1963 | S.   Blue Rayy bowl with multiple spouts and pierced rim, 13th century | 230 |
| 1964 | Olsen.   S.   Rayy *Minai* bowl, dated 1186 (£597, New York, 1936) | 700 |
| | Rayy *Minai* bowl dated 1187 (£513 in 1936) both Metropolitan Museum | 680 |
| 1965 | Hamilton Rice.   N.Y.   Three Rayy *Minai* tankards, 4½ in. high, *c.* 1220 (ex Parrish Watson)                    3 for | 1,340 |

| | | | £ |
|---|---|---|---|
| 1967 | Kevorkian. N.Y. Kashan *Mihrab* lustre tile in relief, *c.* 1260, 24 × 15¾, $2,400 | | 1,000 |
| | 11th century 'Lakkabi' dish, very heavily restored 7¾ in. diam., $1,700 | | 708 |
| | Standard 13th century Rayy *Minai* bowl, 8½ in. diam. | | 312 |
| 1968 | Jacks. C. Rayy lustre bottle with horsemen, *c.* 1200 | | 483 |
| | Kevorkian. S. Turquoise glazed lion, 7½ in., called 13th century | | 1,500 |
| | Kashan lustre basin with figures, 18 in. diam. | | 1,300 |
| | Rayy lustre ewer with upturned spout, 14 in. high | | 880 |
| | Kashan lustre bowl, two figures 6½ in. diam. | | 1,050 |
| | Kashan bottle, lustre with horsemen, 8¾ in. high | | 1,350 |
| | 2nd Kashan bottle, lustre with horsemen, 8½ in. high | | 1,600 |
| | Kashan bottle, Rayy, inscriptions only, 12½ in. high | | 950 |
| | Kashan flower-shaped lustre bowl with doves, intact, 10¾ in. | | 2,400 |
| | Kashan lustre beaker with doves, 7 in. high | | 1,300 |
| | Rayy bottle, polychrome *Minai* style, heavily restored, 10¾ in. high | | 1,050 |
| | Rayy *lajvardina* bowl, ivory ground, 7 in. diam. | | 1,600 |
| | Ditto bottle, blue ground, much refired, 13 in. high | | 3,300 |
| | Rakkah (Rusafa) red lustre dish, 13½ in. diam. | | 800 |
| | 36 pieces of pottery made £24,480 | | |
| | S. Kashan lustre tile, Nashqi inscription, *c.* 1220, 10¾ in | | 820 |
| | Rakkah *albarello* jar, brown lustre and blue, 10¼ in. | | 450 |
| 1969 | S. Rayy *Minai* bowl with camel frieze, 8¼ in. | | 650 |
| | Wide ivory coloured tankard, incised decoration, 5½ in. high, Kashan early 13th century, restored | | 1,200 |
| | C. Water-bottle, compressed sphere on foot-ring base, light red and white enamels on blue glaze, Rayy, *c.* 1200, 10 in. high, restored | | 1,050 |
| | Round-bellied bottle with long neck and tulip mouth turquoise relief, restored, *c.* 1200, 21 in. high, Rayy | | 725 |

## TURKISH AND LATER PERSIAN POTTERY, 16TH–18TH CENTURIES

The pottery of the Islamic Renaissance, particularly the Turkish faience, nowadays called Isnik, was known to collectors long before the earlier excavated Persian pottery reached Europe. A typical Isnik tankard in the Victoria and Albert Museum was acquired as long ago as the Bernal sale of 1855. Some thirty years later the Museum paid £450 (about £4,000 in 1970 money) for a famous Isnik mosque lamp. The rich geometrical formalism of the ware fitted in well with High Renaissance taste, but by the 1920s it had yielded ground to the growing preference for excavated pottery. Yet Isnik—or Rhodian as it was still called—put up a fight for a little longer so that a dish, sold at Sothebys in 1931, cost Kelekian £1,050, the equivalent of £5,250 in 1970 money. The apparently stupendous prices of the Adda sale of 1965, which began a new revival, should be seen in this light. They were in fact no more than an adjustment to inflation. After 1965 the acute shortage of Isnik pieces of any quality sent up the price of 17th century Persian wares and of the rather fussy Turkish pottery, produced at Kutahia in the 18th century. These had always been abundant and relatively cheap. The present market is nothing more than a substitution for that which can no longer be found.

| | | £ |
|---|---|---|
| (*Isnik* unless otherwise stated) | | |
| 1961 | S.   Dish with European ship, *c.* 1620 | 240 |
| | 16th century dish, 12½ in. diam. fair quality | 370 |
| 1963 | Paris.   16th century dish, normal palette | 1,465 |
| | 16th century tureen-shaped vase and cover | 1,640 |
| 1965 | Adda.  Paris.  Dish, *c.* 1540–50, in blue, turquoise and aubergine, 15½ in. (said to have been re-sold for £10,000) | 8,130 |
| | Platter-dish, *c.* 1580, prunus-blossoms on red ground, 10¼ in. | 1,990 |
| | Unique long-necked bottle, rosettes on turquoise ground, 1520–30, 11 in. high (ex Kelekian) | 4,790 |
| | 'Golden horn' blue and white ewer and cover, 10 in. high, badly damaged | 1,172 |
| | 'Golden horn' blue and white petalled dish, 12 in. | 1,214 |
| | Dish with normal ceiling-wax red palette, *c.* 1580, 12 in. | 1,676 |
| | Dish with lion and sun motif, normal palette, *c.* 1600 | 1,380 |
| | Dish with scale background, *c.* 1580, 11 in. | 1,020 |
| | 11½-in. tankard of extreme magnificence, *c.* 1570 | 4,314 |
| | Unique dish with horseman and fishes, *c.* 1600 | 1,728 |
| | A further 16 Isnik pieces made from £700 to £1,000 each. | |
| 1967 | Adda.  C.  Scale-pattern tankard (£480 in 1959) | 630 |
| | 37 lots of Kutahia pottery made about £6,700. | |
| | Bowl, cover and stand | 483 |
| | Canister, 9½ in. high | 840 |
| | Jug of European shape, 8½ in. high | 420 |
| | Blue and white bowl and cover, 7 in. high | 336 |
| | All these 18th century. | |
| | Kevorkian.  N.Y.  Isnik dish, blue and turquoise, *c.* 1540, 13 in. diam., $1,800 | 750 |
| | Kirman dish, mid-17th century with *Fo* dog, 16 in., $1,100 | 458 |
| | Kirman (Persian) water bottle, *c.* 1680, polychrome, 11¼ in., $1,100 | 458 |
| | Eight tiles, forming picnic scene, Shiraz, Persian late 18th century, 28¾ in. sq., $1,400 | 585 |

|  |  | £ |
|---|---|---|
| Paris. Isnik scale-pattern bottle, replaced neck (£350 in 1965), FN5,000+tax | | 490 |
| 1969 C. Kutahia bowl, cover and stand, 8½ in. high, 18th century | | 399 |
| Isnik dish, c. 1600, 10¾ in. | | 525 |
| Isnik dish, c. 1600, blue tulips etc., 12¼ in. wide | | 504 |
| S. Isnik dish, c. 1580, bunch of grapes, blue and green only, 10¾ in. | | 700 |
| Kirman polychrome bottle, 15¼ in., c. 1680 | | 700 |
| 1970 S. 'Golden horn' tankard c. 1530, repaired | | 1,000 |

# PORCELAIN, ENGLISH

The highlights of the European porcelain market are still figures and group which were never intended to be serious sculpture but were designed as dinin table ornaments. A Capo di Monte group can make £14,340, a Meissen harle quin group £13,000. While these sums of money, which still had some mean ing in the 1960s, appeared to buy little beyond affectation, inanity and a splas of vulgarity, the £7,000, paid for a Chelsea 'girl in a swing' figure, was th price of simpering gentility and cottage charm. The one market was exagger atedly German, the other exaggeratedly English, but both, it seemed, had th same appeal to the world of High Finance. Both are expected to keep their plac Chelsea must stick to its essentially English character. The worse falls since th attempts of the 1950s to make Chelsea an international market have been tho of imitations of continental models. An example of the *music lesson* after Bouch responded to the mood of 1944, the year of victories, by making 1,950 guinea but might not be worth any more in 1970 and certainly not its equity value £4,500. In 1951 *Isabella holding a masque* cost £2,050. In 1969 another examp was sold for no more than £1,150. In 1960 the Chelsea group, *The Tyrole dancers*, achieved £3,600, but the same example fell to £1,785 in 1963, while 1969 a Bow version made only £1,200. On the other hand, the earliest an simplest Chelsea figures have at least held their ground. A white owl whic rose astonishingly beyond its class in 1951 to make £3,400, might almost b expected to reach its 1970 equivalent, namely £7,000, inasmuch as an examp was sold in 1966, for £4,200.

Outside the domain of figures and groups, it is less clear how the price-rati for English porcelain is determined. Aesthetic considerations have even bee known to intrude. The not very numerous survivors from services, painte after Gay's fables by O'Neale, seem at least to have been priced for thei superior artistry. There are little teapots at £2,100 and £2,400, while the sam painting on Worcester blue-scale border plates is woth £2,700. But there ar other kinds of Chelsea and Worcester teapots of no very special distinctio which soar up to £3,800 on account of rarity alone. And again it is rarity alon which makes an inconspicuous 3-inch cup with the commonest of copie Kakiemon patterns, but the least common of factory marks, worth £1,05 But what is it that has raised the nisnamed Hans Sloane botanical dinner plate to the level of £800–£2,100? They are neither very rare nor specially we painted, nor even effectively designed. Still less are the Worcester plates from the Duke of Gloucester service which have reached £1,800. Other high price seem to be determined neither by quality nor by rarity but by quaintness an whimsicality, a Chelsea teapot in the form of a guineafowl on a rose-bush a £2,730, a pair of miniature Longton Hall tureens or covered sauce-bowls in th shape of lettuces at £2,800.

Sumptuousness as the highest selling qualification disappeared some tim after the Second World War. In 1956 a big Chelsea Gold Anchor period meat dish with claret and gold borders could still make 2,100 guineas, but woul have little chance of fetching an equivalent £3,450 in 1970. There was certainly some demand in the 1960s for Worcester hexagonal covered jars and Chelsea rococo urns, but this was only the ghost of one of the most famous mid and late Victorian markets. Two pairs of these Rococo urns made £1,500 and £3,600 in 1963, but nearly a hundred years earlier, the third Earl of Dudley had paid £10,000 for them, the equivalent in 1963 of more than £75,000.

What would Lord Dudley's 150 per cent virile taste for highly gilded curvaceousness have made of the costly scraps of whimsicality which appealed to the 1960s? In the 1870s it was left to the bargain-hunting Lady Charlotte Schreiber to pick up a rare Chelsea tureen and cover in the shape of a rabbit at £4 10s. Another rabbit tureen made £4,280 in 1967, still the highest price for any English tureen. But one does not have to go back to Lady Charlotte Schreiber's day for such bargains. The cult of whimsicalities and stamp-collectors' rarities is more recent than one would expect. An early Chelsea strawberry dish with the triangle mark was sold in 1962 for £1,150 and could be worth at least twice as much in 1970, but in 1951 it made no more than £7 10s. A tureen in the shape of a coiled eel which made £1,300 in 1962, cost 6 guineas shortly before the war.

As these earlier and simpler products of the English factories disappear to Australia or the U.S.A., one would naturally expect some promotion for the later wares in rococo taste, but the 1960s showed little trace of it. Early 19th century English porcelain seems to be moving much faster with a Worcester tureen of the late Napoleonic wars at 500 guineas and a set of desk-furniture in the same style at £2,350. And one must not overlook dinner services. Before the last war early 19th century services had no more than the value of second hand goods and could sometimes be bought for less than a shilling a unit. In the 1960s even early Victorian services by Flight, Barr and Barr of Worcester became worth at least £10 a unit and the better-painted sort of Crown Derby of the 1820s nearer £100 a unit.

## CHELSEA

(includes Bow, Longton Hall and Derby, *but to be read as Chelsea unless otherwise stated*)

*Figures and groups, including birds and animals*

| | | £ |
|---|---|---:|
| 1960 | Dusendschon. S. The Tyrolese dancers, group after Eberlein, Meissen (others, 1959, £273, 1968, £1,785, 1969, £1,200) | 3,600 |
| 1962 | S. Woodward, the actor, in *Lethe* (Bow) | 450 |
| | Hen-pheasant, under 5 in. high | 1,050 |
| | Shepherd and shepherdess, inscribed I.B. 1757, Bow (£290 in 1947) 2 for | 1,220 |
| | Three copies of white bust of a baby after Fiammingo, 4½ in. high (similar bust in 1949, £640 in 1941, £16) | 1,200 / 1,250 / 2,000 |

£

| 1963 | S. Pair of white groups, Rape of Europa and Rape of Ganymede, Gold Anchor period (£27 in 1941) 2 for | 1,120 |
|---|---|---|
| | Stewart Grainger. C. The Tyrolese dancers (see 1960) | 1,785 |
| | Lion and Lioness, Bow 2 for | 1,300 |
| 1964 | S. Kitty Clive and Woodward (£120 in 1937) 2 for | 320 |
| | Arnold. S. Pair of white-ware pheasants, Bow 2 for | 2,000 |
| | Pair of pheasants, raised anchor period 2 for | 1,850 |
| 1965 | S. Pair of white figures of owls, 8¼ in. high, triangle mark, c. 1746 2 for | 2,500 |
| | Tufnell. C. The Pietà, group by Willems after Vandyck, 10 in. | 4,410 |
| 1966 | McHarg. S. Longton Hall tiger, based on Arita model (£95 in 1949), 4 in. high | 1,500 |
| | C. White figure, barn owl, 8¾ in. high | 4,200 |
| | S. The doctor after Kaendler of Meissen, 8¼ in. | 3,500 |
| | Chinaman after Kaendler, 7 in. | 4,200 |
| | Beggar by Joseph Willems | 2,000 |
| 1967 | Olwen Davies. C. Barn owl, white ware, 8 in. | 1,785 |
| | Pearson. S. Derby figure, street cordial-seller | 1,950 |
| | C. Pair of figures from the Five Senses, Red anchor period, 11 in. high 2 for | 3,150 |
| | Scapin after Kaendler, Red Anchor period, 4½ in. | 2,940 |
| 1968 | Statham. S. Pair of cook-maids, Bow, 1756, 6¾ in. 2 for | 2,100 |
| | S. Woodward and Kitty Clive, Bow, white figures, 10½ in. (compare 1964) 2 for | 1,450 |
| | Derby group after Kaendler, lovers with clown, 12 in. | 1,550 |
| | Roper. S. Figure of a dancing girl from the conjectural 'girl in a swing' workshop, 6 in. high, one of four coloured examples known | 7,000 |
| 1969 | S. Pair of white busts of noble Chinese or Mongolians, Bow, c. 1750, 10½ in. high 2 for | 2,100 |
| | Pair of Bow pug dogs, 5 in. wide 2 for | 1,450 |
| | C. Chelsea white figure of a secretary bird, rocky base, 7¾ in. | 5,460 |
| | Hely-Hutchinson. S. Bow Harlequin and Columbine, group by 'the Muses modeller,' 6½ in. high | 3,400 |
| | Bow figure of waterman with Doggett's coat and badge, 8¾ in. | 1,800 |
| | Bow group, Scaramouche and Isabella after Watteau, 7½ in. | 1,400 |
| | Bow group, the Tyrolese dancers after Eberlein, 7½ in. (compare 1960, 1963) | 1,200 |

| | | £ |
|---|---|---|
| 1969 | Chelsea Italian Comedy figure, Isabella, 6 in. (similar figure, £2,050 in 1951) | 1,150 |
| | S. Derby figures of stag and doe, mounted with porcelain wired flowers perhaps by Duesbury, 1751–3, as 2-light candelabra     2 for | 2,000 |

*Tureens and urns*

| | | |
|---|---|---|
| 1956 | Mansel. S. Pineapple tureen, 7 in. high, red anchor mark (see 1969) | 800 |
| 1959 | MacTaggart. S. Asparagus tureen, 7½ in. wide (compare 1962, 1963, 1969) | 520 |
| 1962 | S. Asparagus tureen, 7½ in. wide (compare 1962, 1963, 1969) | 950 |
| | Longton Hall melon tureen and cover (£68 in 1947, see 1967) | 900 |
| | Tureen with eel modelled on the cover (£6 6s. in the 1930s) | 1,300 |
| 1963 | S. Asparagus tureen, the 30th sold since 1945 (see 1959, 1962, 1969) | 1,450 |
| | Pair of Gold Anchor vases, 24 in. high, known as the Foundling and Chesterfield vases     2 for | 1,500 |
| | Pair of companion vases (all four were bought-in at the Dudley sale, 1886, at £4,200 having cost £10,000). Victoria and Albert Museum     2 for | 3,600 |
| 1964 | de Trafford. C. Pineapple tureen, red anchor mark (compare 1956 and 1969) | 1,050 |
| | C. Pair of Gold Anchor pot-pourri vases and covers, claret ground     2 for | 1,102 10s. |
| | A second pair     2 for | 1,102 10s. |
| 1966 | Parkinson. S. Pair of oviform jars, Hans Sloane botanical subjects, 7½ in. high     2 for | 3,000 |
| | C. Tureen in form of coiled eel, 7½ in. high | 1,217 10s. |
| 1968 | Donohue. N.Y. Pair of miniature Longton Hall tureens in the form of lettuces, length 4½ in., $7,500     2 for | 2,800 |
| | Melon-shaped Longton Hall tureen, length 6½ in., $3,000 | 1,071 |
| | Miniature Chelsea lettuce tureen, length 4¾ in., $3,750 | 1,340 |
| | Chelsea, cauliflower tureen, length 5¼ in., $3,250 | 1,160 |
| 1969 | Cole. C. Chelsea pineapple tureen, 7 in. high, red anchor mark (£800, 1956). Others £1,050 in 1964, £32 in 1941 | 3,990 |
| | Cauliflower tureen, red anchor mark, 7 in. wide | 1,417 10s. |
| | C. Garniture of three Chelsea gold anchor urns and covers, c. 1780, Boucher subjects, Mazarine blue grounds, 12¼ in.     3 for | 1,365 |

1969  C.  Asparagus tureen and cover, 7 in. wide, red anchor    £,
       mark (compare 1959, 1962, 1963)        1,050
      S.  Pair of Derby covered sauceboats in the form of plaice,
       9½ in. wide (sold 1953 as Chelsea, £900)     2 for   4,200

### Dinner services

1960  C.  Crown Derby by Quaker Pegg after 1800, individual
       flower subjects        2,730
1968  S.  Gold Anchor, claret grounds, birds in style of James
       Giles, 27 pieces including two Derby icepails        3,300
       Kinnaird.  S.  Gold Anchor, claret grounds, flowers by
       James Giles, 32 plates and dishes        8,500
       Thompson.  C.  Crown Derby (rococo revival after
       1820), painted on turquoise ground by Richard Dodson
       with various birds     34 for   3,150

### Teapots and tea service items

1961  S.  Acanthus leaf cream-jug, crown and trident mark        1,050
       Octagonal teapot by O'Neale (£52 in 1946)        1,000
1962  S.  Teapot, raised anchor period (£17 in 1941, £85 in 1949)   1,550
       Milk jug, earliest period (£8 in 1866)        1,300
1963  S.  Hexagonal teapot by O'Neale after Oudry        2,400
       Teabowls and saucers with fable subjects by O'Neale
                  From £500 to    750
       Duncan.  S.  Tea and coffee service, purple grisaille
       landscapes, Chelsea-Derby, c. 1770     18 for   2,200
1964  Arnold.  S.  Cream jug, Vincennes motifs        1,050
       White Acanthus-leaf cream jug, triangle mark, 5 in.
       (see 1966)        820
1965  Last.  S.  White coffeepot and cover, 'tea plant' pattern in
       relief        1,450
      S.  Cream-jug, earliest blue and white, 4¾ in.        1,400
1966  McHarg.  S.  White acanthus leaf cream jug (see 1964)     520
       White beaker, 3¼ in. high, crown and trident mark     950
       Parkinson.  S.  Acanthus-moulded teapot, 4 in. high, with
       Kakiemon style tiger pattern        3,100
       Teapot, scolopendrium pattern, 5 in. high (£17 in
       1941)        3,800
       Teabowl and saucer to match the above (another in
       1969 made £480)        500
       Peach-shaped cup and saucer, 'lady in the pavilion'
       pattern after Kakiemon        1,600
1967  S.  Sucrier and cover, 'girl in the swing' workshop, 5¼ in.   1,300

| | | £ |
|---|---|---|
| 1967 | Carnegie. C. Teapot (at first called Longton Hall), octagonal with strawberry-leaf feet, 5¼ in. high | 2,940 |
| | Holmes. S. Beaker, Kakiemon style, crown and trident mark, under 3 in. high (Joshua Reynolds pattern) | 1,050 |
| | C. Eccentric teapot in form of guineafowl on a rosebush, white ware, triangle mark, 7 in. wide | 2,730 |
| | McHarg. S. Hexagonal fable teapot, painted by O'Neale, 5 in. high (compare 1963), £62 in 1946 | 2,100 |
| | Dalglish. S. White teapot, Chinaman and serpent in relief, triangle mark, 7 in. high, only three others known | 2,600 |
| | A second ditto, repaired | 1,200 |
| 1969 | S. Cream boat, 5 in. long, painted by O'Neale | 850 |
| | Statham. S. Longton Hall teapot in shape of a melon, coloured powder-blue, 4¼ in. high | 1,050 |
| | Ruck. C. Gold anchor tea-service, floral sprays and claret ground borders, 16 pieces including teapot, separate lots 16 for | 1,627 15s. |

## Plates and dishes

| | | £ |
|---|---|---|
| 1962 | S. Oblong fluted dish, painted by O'Neale | 620 |
| | Six 10-inch plates after Hans Sloane's botanical specimens, *raised anchor* period (single plate £360 in 1957) (compare 1967, 1968, 1969, 1970) 6 for | 2,740 |
| | Strawberry dish, triangle mark (£7 10s. in 1941), see 1966 | 1,150 |
| | Steele. S. Pair of Longton Hall plates, painted by James Giles 2 for | 680 |
| 1966 | McHarg. S. Strawberry dish, 4¾ in. diam. triangle mark | 950 |
| | Bauer. S. Octagonal saucer-dish, 4½ in. diam. blue and white with blue anchor mark, c. 1753 | 1,100 |
| | Parkinson. S. Pair of leaf-shaped dishes, 9 in. long, fables painted by O'Neale 2 for | 2,050 |
| | 8-inch fluted dish, fable by O'Neale | 1,300 |
| 1967 | S. Hans Sloane plate, petalled rim, 9½ in. diam. | 800 |
| | C. Ditto (compare 1957, 1962, 1968, 1969) | 997 10s. |
| 1968 | S. Ditto, wavy rim, 9 in. diam. | 1,700 |
| | ditto, with prickly pear, 9¼ in. diam. | 1,500 |
| 1969 | St. Aubyn. C. Ditto, pomegranates | 892 10s. |
| | Caldwell. S. 9-inch. blue and white plate, Chinese style, blue anchor mark | 480 |
| | C. Two botanical lobed plates, 9¾ and 10½ in. diam. Red Anchor period £735 and | 687 10s. |
| | Hely-Hutchinson. S. Hans Sloane botanical plate, wavy rim, 9¼ in. Beetroots etc. (compare 1962, 1967, 1968) | 1,200 |

£

| 1970 | Last. S. Hans Sloane plate, custard marrows and butter-flies, 11 in. diam. | 2,100 |
| | Last. S. Ditto, tigerlilies, 9 in. diam. | 1,600 |

*Miniature scent bottles, under 4 in. high*

| 1960 | S. Harlequin (see 1963) | 320 |
| | Pugdog (compare 1962) | 440 |
| 1962 | Blohm. S. Rooster | 2,200 |
| | Parrot and gamecock (see 1963) | 1,050 |
| | Pugdog (compare 1960) | 1,000 |
| | Harlequin (compare 1960) | 1,050 |
| 1963 | Stewart Grainger. C. Parrot and gamecock (see 1962) | 997 10s |
| | Harlequin (see 1960) | 892 10s |
| | Pugdog (combined patch-box) | 1,050 |
| 1965 | Fitzgerald. S. Parrot and gamecock (compare 1963) | 1,050 |
| | Of 65 scent bottles, aggregating £22,320, six exceeded £900 each. | |
| 1969 | Cole (ex Fitzgerald sale). S. Peacock (£765 in 1965) | 682 10s |
| | Two squirrels forming bottle (£920 in 1965) | 546 |
| | Fox and stork forming bottle (£550 in 1965) | 966 |
| | The highest price for Chelsea scent bottles was £60 18s. in 1923 and £220 in 1949. In 1772 eight were sold for 5 guineas. | |

## WORCESTER, BRISTOL AND OTHER FACTORIES
### (Worcester unless otherwise stated)

*Figures and groups*

| 1963 | S. Tureen in form of two billing doves (a Chelsea prototype was sold in 1957 for the same price) | | 3,800 |
| 1965 | Homewood. S. The Turk and his companion, pair by Tebo, c. 1768 | 2 for | 2,730 |
| 1966 | Parkinson. S. Pair of tureens in form of partridges, 6 in. high | 2 for | 1,600 |
| 1967 | Abbey. S. Set of Bristol figures of the Elements, signed by Tebo | 2 for | 1,550 |
| | S. Group of two canaries among apple blossom, c. 1770, 7×7 in. | | 4,800 |
| 1968 | S. The gardener's companion, c. 1760, 6½ in. high | | 1,700 |
| | Eccles. S. White figure, sportsman and gun, 7¼ in. high | | 2,000 |
| 1970 | S. Two canaries among apple blossoms (compare 1967) | | 2,600 |

*Services*                                                                                              £

1961 C. Part of the 'Mark Herford' Bristol tea and coffee service, sold in 14 lots (£75 16s., 1916)          1,683 10s.

1962 C. Dinner service, Dr Wall period, painted with views
                                                               50 for    2,625
        Dinner service with crest in border, Flight Barr and
        Barr, Worcester, 1813–40 (compare 1968) over 200 for    2,100

1963 Lord Swansea. S. Swansea dessert service, c. 1820 with
        floral spray pattern                        27 for    2,000
        Kingdon. S. Barr, Flight and Barr tea and coffee service,
        1810                                          23 for    1,800

1965 S. Botanical dessert service, Chamberlain's Worcester
        after 1783                                   30 for    1,800

1968 Minet. S. Barr, Flight and Barr dinner service, 1807–13,
        arms of Minet, 150 pieces                   150 for    3,200
        Lindsay of Downhill. S. Dinner service, Flight Barr and
        Barr, 1813–1840                            175 pieces   1,800
        Barber. S. Set of desk furniture, painted with feathers
        and shells, Barr, Flight and Barr, 1807–1813, 11 pieces   2,350
        S. Barber S. Dinner service, puce vine-leaves, 108 pieces   1,900

1969 Spurrier. S. Tea and coffee service, hop-trellis pattern,
        c. 1770                                    26 pieces   2,800
        Puttick and Simpson. Flight, Barr and Barr, 1813–40
                                                   175 for    1,700
        S. Chamberlain service, c. 1800, painted with sea shells etc.
        orange ground, gilt net pattern              38 for    4,500
        Blue ground tea and coffee service, exotic birds, first
        period Worcester                             36 for    2,300
        Earl of Caledon. C. Coalport Service, royal blue
        grounds, towards 1840                     118 pieces for   3,780
        S. Worcester tea and coffee service, hop trellis pattern
        first period, c. 1750–60                  36 pieces for   3,400
        Spode service, c. 1830, rich bouquets on gold ground
                                                    42 for    1,850
        Armorial service, coral ground gilt, Barr, Flight and
        Barr, 1807–13                            107 pieces   2,600
        C. Caughley-Coalport service, red ground, highly ornate,
        1830–40                                  109 pieces for   1,680

1970 S. Worcester first period tea and coffee service, sunflower pattern
                                                   47 pieces for   3,700

*All other types*

1960 S. Tankard with scratch-cross mark, dated 1754          720
        Apple-green sauce tureen                              540

£

| | | |
|---|---|---:|
| 1962 | S. Yellow mask-jug with coloured transfer decoration (compare 1969) | 700 |
| | Yellow ground jug, transfer decoration | 850 |
| 1963 | Pair of rococo vases, Sèvres style, wolf hunt and buck hunt by Giles after Oudry, royal blue ground 2 for | 3,900 |
| 1965 | Capell. S. Mug with transfer portrait of General Wolfe | 280 |
| | Saunders. S. Yellow ground coffeepot and cover (£150 in 1950) | 1,100 |
| | Teabowl and saucer (£130 in 1951) | 620 |
| | Dish, puce scale border (£195 in 1952) | 1,300 |
| | Apple-green ground coffeepot and cover | 2,200 |
| | Jug, apple-green ground, mask-spout | 1,300 |
| | Broth-bowl and cover, blue scale borders, 7½ in. wide (£780 in 1970) | 950 |
| | Yellow ground junket dish, 9 in. diam. (£1,550 in 1970, for another, see 1969) | 900 |
| | Dessert plate, D. of Gloucester service, 9 in. diam. (for another, see 1966 and 1970) | 780 |
| 1966 | Forbes-Wallace. S. Cauliflower-shaped tureen, transfer-printed 4 in. high | 850 |
| | First Parkinson sale, 111 lots £67,305 | |
| | 5-in. mug, exotic birds, apple-green ground | 1,800 |
| | Ditto, 3½ in. globular (similar mugs £1,500 in 1968, £1,155 in 1969) | 1,300 |
| | 'Wigornia' creamboat, 4½ in. (similar, £850 in 1970) | 1,500 |
| | Pair of partridge tureens, 6 in. high 2 for | 1,600 |
| | 9-inch standard floral dish. D. of Gloucester service, (£190 in 1954, resold 1970, £1,800) | 1,050 |
| | Cauliflower tureen (£400 in 1959) | 1,150 |
| | Richly gilt blue-scale teapot in James Giles style | 1,200 |
| | Pair of O'Neale fable plates, blue scale ground (Heathcote sale, 1947, £335) 2 for | 5,400 |
| | Pink scale teabowl and saucer, Giles after Teniers (£115 in 1949) | 1,500 |
| | Yellow scale teapot and stand (part of £700 service, Cochrane sale, 1949) | 3,800 |
| | S. Yellow ground teacup, coffee cup and saucer, blue flowers | 1,650 |
| | 23 lots exceeded £1,000 each | |
| | 2nd Parkinson sale, June, 113 lots £35,194 | |
| | Yellow scale spoon-tray, 6¾ in. | 2,800 |
| | Pegg. C. 5-inch mug, apple-green ground | 1,470 |
| 1967 | Lauderdale. C. Barr, Flight and Barr, tureen and stand, c. 1815 | 525 |

£

Benhall Lodge. S. Lowestoft blue and white mug, dated 1769, 4½ in. high                                                                            580

1967    S. Teapot, with birds, painted by Giles                                              1,100

Perrins. S. Tankard, lilac ground, 6 in. high                                        880

1968    Sidders. S. Pair of hexagonal jars and covers 'Jabberwocky' pattern, *c.* 1760, 11¾ in. (smaller pair in 1970, £2,200)                                                                  2 for  1,550

S. Pair of hexagonal vases and covers, perforated shoulders and mask-handles, 16 in. high                              2 for  2,400

Garniture of three vases, birds and insects, apple-green ground, 5¾ and 7¼ in.                                            3 for  3,400

S. Yellow ground jug, cabbage leaf pattern, 11½ in. high  3,000

A second jug almost identical, sold 3 months later        3,800

Fable dish, blue scale ground, by O'Neale, 9¾ in. diam. (in 1950 three of these dishes aggregated £195)           1,700

Gundry. C. Cream jug and cover, 5¼ in. high, figures in landscape by Giles                                                           2,940

969    S. Pair of baluster vases and covers, exotic birds, apple-green backgrounds, 6½ in. high                                           1,890

Tankard to match, 6¼ in. high (compare 1966)            1,155

Garniture in same style, 2 trumpet vases 4¾ in. high and one hopelessly smashed, 7¼ in. high                3 for  3,000

Yellow ground cream jug, botanical subjects, 6 in. high                                                                         2,300

Pair of square dishes, apple-green borders, 7½ in.  2 for  1,250

Neil Primrose. S. Baluster vase and cover, royal blue ground, exotic birds, 14½ in. high                                        1,000

S. Yellow ground mask-jug, transfer printed and enamelled, 8 in. high (another, 7 in. high, £950 in 1970)    1,900

Yellow ground junket dish, flowers in panels, 9 in. diam.                                                                       1,200

Simpson. C. Teapot, cover and stand, Chamberlain's Worcester, 1802-5, arms and orders of Lord Nelson        1,260

Caldwell. S. Worcester garniture, 3 oviform jars, 2 beakers blue and white, crescent mark                    5 for   580

Tennyson d'Eyncourt. C. Hot water jug, Dr Wall period, floral *Hausmalerei* in the Giles style, 9 in. high   892 10s.

Hely-Hutchinson. S. Another yellow-ground mask jug, transfer-printed and enamelled, 7 in. high (see also 1962)   945

C. Oval basket dish, Rockingham porcelain, griffin mark, *c.* 1830, with view of Wentworth House, 9 in. diam.    525

70    Patten. S. Plate from the D. of Gloucester service, 9 in. diam. (£190 in 1954, £1,050 in 1966)                         1,800

# PORCELAIN, CONTINENTAL
## MEISSEN

To the general public Meissen or Dresden porcelain means figures and grou
Possibly these names conjure up no other image, since the enormous diversific
tion of Meissen products even at a very early period is not generally appreciate
A 6½-inch figure of Harlequin has twice reached £9,000, while a single sm
group has made £13,000, prices that suggest the market supremacy of hum
figures, though in fact tureens, paired and mounted birds, and giant modell
animals have made as much. Since they are so expensive, Meissen figures hav
like the works of Picasso, soared beyond the range of criticism. It would be ve
modish to own both, though nothing could exceed the contempt which t
early admirers of Picasso bestowed on such figures. At that time they we
nearing the end of a long vogue which had been just as vulnerable to conserv
tive criticism. *Dresden shepherdesses* as an expression of contempt is decided
late Victorian and Edwardian, dating from a time when the first high prices
the saleroom were no protection against the attacks which Winckelmann, t
pontiff of neo-classicism, had launched against Meissen figures in the middle
the 18th century. So successful had these attacks been that in 1805 three Kaendl
figures were worth no more than 33 shillings between them. Even in 1876
Kaendler harlequin could still be bought for 14 guineas. But in the followi
year a famous crinoline group made 200 guineas at Christies. Thus was i
augurated a vogue which culminated in 1912 with the sale in Paris of *the mu
lesson* for 38,000 francs, plus tax, then equivalent to £1,640 and in 1970 to
least £13,000. So one may say that Kaendler groups have not gone up in near
sixty years, but in fact for a large part of that time all Meissen porcelain was
decline. The revulsion against Ritzy taste in the 1920s was augmented by t
financial depression of the 1930s. The recovery of Meissen only became serio
at the Fribourg sales of 1963, when *Harlequin with a tankard* made £9,000. Oth
copies had made £400 in 1948, and £1,575 in 1959. The dearest of the crinoli
groups at the Fribourg sale, *the duet*, cost £7,500 but as late as 1960 a crinoli
group had been exceptionally dear at £685. So it was in very much the sam
proportion that two specially splendid 'Augustus the Strong' vases reache
£16,000 in 1966, having made £1,505 at the famous Pannwitz sale in Colog
in 1905.

All these instances of 1963 show that, enormous as the prices then appeare
the rise had barely exceeded the decline in the purchasing power of money. B
items from services had been less highly esteemed at the beginning of the ce
tury, and these, particularly when they came from Count Brühl's Swan Servic
may have beaten inflation. And still more the early experimental pieces of t
Boettger period. Since it was then a scholar's market, the dearest figure
Boettger's red polished ware in the great Fischer sale of 1906 made only £17
A much less important Boettger figure reached £3,000 in 1960 and might hav
been worth double at the end of the decade.

The very high price of early Meissen tureens, two of them in the £12,0 region in 1968, has overtaken the traditional supremacy of mounted pieces. Even so, the Duke of Fife's pair of Kaendler swans, mounted as candelabra, which made £23,000 in 1967, were dearer than any mounted Chinese porcelain. It is possible that Meissen figures, tureens, vases, mounted birds and giant animals which make £11,000 to £13,500 apiece, are not really the top of the European porcelain market. A Sèvres *rose Pompadour* tureen made $29,000 or £10,360 in 1957. Since there has not been a comparable tureen in the salerooms for 13 years, its value in 1970 might well be £20,000 to £30,000.

£

*Earliest period*, Boettger's polished red stoneware and white porcelain, 1710–28

| | | |
|---|---|---|
| 1960 | Blohm. S. Plain apple-green jar and cover, *c.* 1720, 5¾ in. high | 2,400 |
| | Pantaloon after Callot, red polished ware, 7¾ in. | 3,000 |
| 1961 | C. Harlequin, white ware, *c.* 1720, decorated later at Augsburg, 6¾ in. high (compare 1967 and 1968) | 2,100 |
| 1962 | C. Tea service of white ware, Augsburg decoration 23 for | 1,890 |
| 1965 | S. Grotesque white-ware relief ewer by Kirchner after Jacques von Stella, 28½ in. high | 1,000 |
| 1966 | S. Red polished stoneware winepot and cover, 5¾ in. high | 1,000 |
| | Colling. S. Pair of white ware pilgrim bottles with stoppers and masks in relief, 8 in. high 2 for | 880 |
| 1967 | S. Dwarf after Callot, white ware figure with added gilding, 3¾ in. high (see 1968) | 2,300 |
| | Pearson. S. Gilded white ware figure of Harlequin by Kirchner (see 1961) | 1,600 |
| 1968 | S. Another example of the same | 3,400 |
| | Teapot in shape of an eagle, 4½ in. high with domed lid, red polished stoneware | 3,900 |
| | Ex King of Italy. C. (Geneva). Pair of octagonal polished stoneware bottles and covers, 5¼ in. high 2 for | 1,890 |
| | White vase and cover, 13¾ in. | 1,470 |
| | White beaker with relief masks, 7 in. | 1,050 |
| | Pair of white squatting *pagods*, 9¾ in. high 2 for | 4,200 |
| 1969 | C. Teapot with eagle spout and domed lid, polished red stoneware, *c.* 1715, 8 in. wide, light silvergilt mount | 2,730 |
| | White figure of Neptune by Kirchner, 1728, 13 in. high | 1,995 |
| | Fribourg. N.Y. *Pagod* in red ware, part gilded and enamelled, 3¾ in. high, $3,250 | 1,354 |
| 1970 | N.Y. 'Bearded man' white ware teapot, satyr handle and dolphin spout, Augsburg decorated *c.* 1725, 6½ in. high, $13,000 | 5,417 |

*White sculpture*

(Birds and animals of large size from the Japanese pavilion of Augustus the Strong of Saxony, 1730–34

|  |  |  | £ |
|---|---|---|---|
| 1959 | S. Pelican by Kaendler, 1732, 31 in. high | | 2,400 |
| 1961 | S. Goat and kid, 1732, 2 ft long, damaged, Ashmolean Museum | | 900 |
| | Weinmüller, Munich. Eagle, 22 in. high, by Kirchner, 1732 | | 3,000 |
| 1962 | S. A second ditto, less perfect | | 2,000 |
| 1963 | N.Y. Crane by Kaendler, 1730, 29 in. high, $8,000 | | 2,860 |
| | Goat and kid (see 1961), 20 in. high | | 3,395 |
| | C. Monkey by Kirchner | | 3,460 |
| 1964 | C. Recumbent goat, Kaendler, 1734, nearly 2 ft long | | 4,830 |
| 1966 | Aurora Trust. S. Lion by Kirchner, damaged, bought in | | 2,200 |
| 1967 | Winston Guest. N.Y. Peacock on tree stump by Kaendler, 45 in. high, the largest of the series, $32,000 | | 13,345 |
| | Maxwell McDonald. C. Parrot by Kaendler, 28 in. high (damaged) | | 1,995 |

*Figures and groups*

| 1960 | C. The harlequin family by Kaendler, *c.* 1740, 7¼ in. high (compare 1963, 1967, 1968) | | 1,417 10s |
|---|---|---|---|
| | Weinmüller, Munich. Countess of Kösel, crinoline group | | 685 |
| 1961 | S. Group of three miners | | 1,200 |
| 1962 | S. The scowling harlequin by Kaendler (see 1963, 1966), 7½ in. high | | 2,700 |
| 1963 | S. Countess of Kösel, crinoline group, Kaendler, 5¾ in. | | 2,700 |
| | Stewart Grainger. C. The Tyrolese dancers by Eberlein (£900 in 1960, others at £850, in 1964 and 1967) | | 1,155 |
| | The harlequin family by Kaendler, bought in | | 4,640 |
| | The indiscreet harlequin by Kaendler, bought in | | 3,675 |
| | Fribourg. S. Harlequin with a tankard, Kaendler, 6½ in. high (compare others, £480 in 1948, £9,000 in 1967) | | 9,000 |
| | Kaendler crinoline group, lady and black page, 1737 (see 1968) | | 4,800 |
| | Kaendler crinoline group, the Polish salutation (£375 in 1906) | | 5,000 |
| | Kaendler crinoline group, lady and gentleman playing duet | | 7,500 |
| | Chinaman in arbour by Fritsche, 9¾ in., *c.* 1728 | | 4,000 |
| | Harlequin with monocle by Kaendler (see 1967, 1968) | | 3,700 |
| | Scowling harlequin by Kaendler (see 1962, 1966), 7½ in. | | 3,000 |

| | | | £ |
|---|---|---|---|
| 1963 (*cont.*) Italian dancers by Kaendler | | | 3,200 |
| The indiscreet harlequin by Kaendler (see 1964, 1967) | | | 2,400 |
| Frohlich and Schmiedel, group by Kaendler, 1741, 9½ in. | | | 2,500 |
| Harlequin and Columbine, seated, by Kaendler (others, £260 in 1952, £850 in 1957) | | | 3,600 |
| Dancing Mezzetin by Kaendler | | | 3,400 |
| Greeting Harlequin by Kaendler (compare 1967) | | | 3,200 |
| The frightened harlequin (£580 in 1945, see 1966) | | | 3,600 |
| Stuker. Berne. Augustus III and consort, crinoline group | | | 5,500 |
| Lady taking chocolate, crinoline group | | | 3,000 |
| Hunter and greyhound by Kaendler | | | 3,600 |
| Two freemasons and globe by Kaendler | | | 2,850 |
| 1964 S. The Tyrolese dancers by Eberlein (see 1963) | | | 850 |
| The indiscreet harlequin (see 1963, 1967) | | | 700 |
| 1965 Hutton. S. Pair of bitterns on boughs by Kaendler, 1753, 14½ in. high | | 2 for | 7,500 |
| Harlequin carrying pugdog by Kaendler, 6¾ in. (compare 1966, 1968) | | | 2,300 |
| 1966 S. Pair of chained monkeys and their young by Kaendler, 6 in. high (compare 1966) | | 2 for | 4,000 |
| C. Another pair, same model | | 2 for | 3,150 |
| Langer. S. Crinoline group by Kaendler, Acis and Galatea, 9 in. | | | 3,400 |
| S. Frohlich, the court jester, by Kaendler, dated 1741, 9¼ in. | | | 1,700 |
| Schindler, the court jester, by Kaendler, 7 in. high | | | 2,100 |
| Aurora Trust. S. Lady, child and cavalier, Kaendler crinoline group, 7 in. high | | | 11,000 |
| The gout sufferer, Kaendler group, 5½ in. high (see 1969) | | | 6,500 |
| S. The frightened Harlequin, 6¾ in. high (compare 1963) | | | 4,800 |
| Harlequin playing with a pugdog (compare 1965, 1968) | | | 3,800 |
| The scowling harlequin (compare 1962, 1963, 1968) | | | 3,800 |
| 1967 S. Pair of pugdogs by Kaendler and Reinicke, 1744, 6 in. | | 2 for | 2,500 |
| Harlequin and the quack doctor by Kaendler, 8 × 7½ in. | | | 13,000 |
| Crinoline group, cavalier and lady, 8½ in. high | | | 3,900 |
| Alfred Pearson. S. Kaendler figures: | | | |
| Harlequin with monocle (similar 1963, 1968), 7¼ in. high | | | 5,000 |
| Masked Harlequin dancing, 7½ in. | | | 7,200 |
| Greeting harlequin (similar 1963, £3,200) | | | 2,100 |
| The wrestling harlequins 6½ in. (£950 in 1952, compare 1968) | | | 6,000 |

| | | |
|---|---|---:|
| | | £ |
| 1967 | Harlequin with a dated tankard (1738), 6½ in. (similar, 1963, £9,000) | 9,000 |
| | Columbine, one of five known | 7,000 |
| | Scowling harlequin (similar 1966, £3,800, 1963, £3,000, 1962, £2,700) | 3,600 |
| | The indiscreet harlequin (similar £3,675, 1963), see also 1968 | 2,000 |
| | Mezzetin (similar 1963, £3,400) | 3,200 |
| | The frightened harlequin (better version, 1966, £4,800) | 2,400 |
| | The harlequin family by Kaendler, 6¾ in. (compare 1968) | 3,600 |
| 1968 | Pearson. S. Harlequin carrying pugdog (compare 1965, 1966) | 1,800 |
| | S. The indiscreet harlequin (compare 1963, 1967) | 1,300 |
| | The greeting harlequin (compare 1963, 1967) | 1,400 |
| | The harlequin family (compare 1967) | 3,400 |
| | Harlequin with monocle (see 1963) | 1,100 |
| | Wade. C. The Tyrolese dancers by Eberlein (£900 in 1960, £1,155 in 1963) | 1,470 |
| | S. The wrestling harlequins by Kaendler, 6½ in. (see 1967) | 6,000 |
| 1969 | S. Amazon parrot by Kaendler, 6 in. high | 4,200 |
| | African parrot by Kaendler, 7½ in. high | 3,600 |
| | South American parrot by Kaendler, 6½ in. | 2,300 |
| | van Zuylen. C. Single Kaendler parrot, 5¾ in. | 2,000 |
| | Dreyfus. S. Kaendler group, the gout sufferer (compare 1966, £6,500) | 2,100 |
| | Kaendler group, Scaramouche and Columbine | 950 |
| | C. Geneva. Harlequin drinking from long glass by Kaendler, 6 in. high, FS.30,000+tax | 3,072 |
| | Thornhill. S. Group of two parrots on rockwork by Kaendler, c. 1745, 16¼ in. high, much repaired | 7,000 |
| | Best. S. Pair of pug dogs on cushions by Kaendler, 6 in. 2 for | 1,800 |
| | S. The mine-overseer or *Obersteiger* by Kaendler and Reinicke, 7¾ in. (another example £240 in 1964) | 1,950 |
| | Lovers with cupid and harlequin on rockwork by Kaendler, datable 1743, 6¾ in. high | 2,300 |
| | C. Another pair of pug dogs by Kaendler and Reinicke, 6¼ in. high 2 for | 2,100 |

*Tankards* (mostly mounted in Augsburg silver-gilt and painted in *Hausmalerei*)

| | | |
|---|---|---:|
| 1965 | S. With *Hausmalerei* by Bressler and silver lid, dated 1727 | 700 |
| | Princess Olga. S. Gold Chinoiserie painting by Höroldt, 6½ in. | 1,700 |

£

| | | |
|---|---|---|
| 1966 | S. By Höroldt, 6½ in. high | 3,500 |
| 1967 | S. The Chinese lady's toilette by Höroldt, 7¼ in. high | 3,500 |
| | By Höroldt, c. 1725, 6¼ in. high | 3,200 |
| | Weinmüller, Munich. Tankard, painted by Höroldt in *famille verte* style, silver lid with gold medallion. DM19,500+tax | 2,000 |
| 1969 | C. Four continents, displaying map to the Chinese Emperor, by Höroldt, silver-gilt lid dated Dresden 1729 | 3,570 |
| | C. Geneva. With Chinese seaport scene in Höroldt style and silver-gilt lid by Elias Adam, Augsburg. FS32,000+tax | 3,278 |
| 1970 | N.Y. With Chinese tea-party, style of Höroldt, silver-gilt lid, c. 1730, 7¾ in. high, $10,000 | 4,167 |

*Pieces mounted in ormolu*
(Including figures, paired birds and animals, vases fitted with porcelain flowers). See also Furniture, French, smaller objects

| | | |
|---|---|---|
| 1960 | Dusendschon. S. Sultan riding elephant, 12 in. high | 3,600 |
| 1961 | Whitmarsh. N.Y. Pair of blue vases, encrusted flowers, mounted, c. 1760 | 2 for 1,430 |
| 1962 | Pearson. C. The Tyrolese dancers by Eberlein (£409 10s. in 1955, £787 10s. 1966), ormolu base | 1,890 |
| 1963 | Fribourg. S. Pair of prancing horses with Turkish grooms, rococo plinths (£294, 1930; £480, 1958), compare 1969 | 2 for 20,000 |
| | Pair of Kaendler cockatoos, mounted as candelabra (compare 1968) | 2 for 19,000 |
| | Pair of monkey groups, later mounts, Vincennes flowers | 2 for 12,500 |
| | Pair of caparisoned camels under ormolu palm-trees (£420 in 1949, £476 in 1906) | 2 for 8,000 |
| | Pair of mounted squirrels by Kaendler (£2,860 in 1959) | 2 for 3,600 |
| | Pair of spaniels, mounted in Louis XVI style | 2 for 2,600 |
| | Group from Kaendler's Nine Muses, representing *poetry* in Louis XV style mount 9¼ in. (dropped to £400 in 1969) | 1,450 |
| | Pair of *Verrières* in the Kakiemon style, mounted with Vincennes flowers | 2 for 8,200 |
| | Fribourg. S. The Tyrolese dancers by Eberlein (other examples *in mounts*, £260 in 1952, £850 in 1957, £1,890 in 1962, £787 10s. in 1966) | 1,700 |
| | Pair of hunting figures by Kaendler, mounted as candlesticks with additional Vincennes flowers | 2 for 5,600 |

£

| | | |
|---|---|---|
| 1963 | C. Lemon-shaped tureen mounted with blue-tits as a pot-pourri vase | 2,730 |
| | S. Vase and two swans, ormolu base | 3,200 |
| | Basket-jardinière with Meissen and Vincennes flowers | 2,300 |
| 1964 | S. Pair of jays by Kaendler on Ormolu bases        2 for | 5,000 |
| | Chinaman with bird by Georg Fritsche on rough ormolu | 2,200 |
| | Three baluster vases, Watteau subjects, mounted with flowers by Klinger, 1750–60, 14 and 10 in. high   3 for | 5,200 |
| | Kaendler's *greeting harlequin* mounted with Louis XV clock (for unmounted example, see 1963) | 5,600 |
| 1965 | Coventry. C. Pair of cedar-waxwings by Kaendler, mounted with Vincennes flowers        2 for | 7,560 |
| 1966 | C. The Tyrolese dancers by Eberlein, Louis XV ormolu base (£1,890 in 1962) | 787 10s. |
| 1967 | Duke of Fife. S. Pair of swans by Kaendler and Reinicke, mounted as pair of 5 light candelabra, 19 × 13     2 for | 23,000 |
| | C. Pair of Kaendler monkeys, ormolu stands, 6 in. high        2 for | 3,150 |
| | Parker. S. Pair of 6-in. pug dogs by Kaendler and Reinicke, ormolu stands        2 for | 2,500 |
| | Dreyfus. S. Pair of 7-in. guinea fowls, mounted with basket salts in Kakiemon style, 7 in. high     2 for | 2,600 |
| 1968 | S. Pair of prancing horses with Turkish grooms, Louis XVI plinths (for example with Louis XV mounts, see 1963)        2 for | 2,100 |
| | C. Pair of terns by Kaendler, mounted as 3-light candelabra, 11¾ in. high        2 for | 10,500 |
| | Methuen-Campbell. S. Pair of cockatoos by Kaendler, mounted as candelabra, 14½ in. high (compare 1963)  2 for | 14,500 |
| | S. Dolphin and amorini, 16¼ in. high with mount (sold for £1,000 at the Fribourg sale, 1963 | 1,100 |
| 1969 | C. Harlequin, Columbine and birdcage with other Kaendler figures in Louis XV gilt-bronze arbour, 13 in. high | 4,200 |
| | Fribourg. N.Y. Pair of parrots by Kaendler, c. 1740, mounted as three-light candelabra, 15 in. high, between 1744 and 1749, $65,000        2 for | 27,084 |
| | Pair of courting figures, elaborately mounted as candelabra, c. 1750, 9¼ in. high, $7,500     2 for | 3,125 |
| | Pair of blue *mayflower* vases, Watteau subjects, Louis XV mounts, c. 1750, 12 in. high, $10,500     2 for | 4,375 |
| | S. Pair of ewers in form of hares, Louis XV candlestick mounts, porcelain flowers, 11 in. high, A.R. mark   2 for | 4,800 |

1969 S. *Surtout de table*, aviary of many elements mounted with branches, 11 in. wide £ 2,300

  C. (Geneva). Pair of prancing horses with Turkish grooms on Louis XV plinths, 12 in. high (compare 1963 on much inferior plinths), FS260,000+tax 2 for 26,633

   Mounted *Augustus Rex* vase and cover, Chinese scenes on yellow grounds, 21½ in. high FS72,000+tax 7,375

   Pair of may-blossom baluster vases, Louis XV mounts with wired flowers, 14 in. high, FS32,000+tax 3,277

   *Brûle-parfum* in form of magic lantern on a rockery with three Meissen figures, 12 in. wide, FS34,000+tax 3,481

  S. Pair of Kaendler parrots, mounted with flowers as 2 light candlesticks, 10 in. high 2 for 2,800

*Tureens, urns and other large pieces*

1960 S. Pair of hexagonal vases and covers in Kakiemon style (£97 10s. in 1906), ormolu stands 2 for 650

  Paris. Tureen, surmounted by figure of Amphitrite, arms of Count Brühl (Swan Service) with cover 2 for 3,530

1961 S. A second tureen from the Swan Service, Kaendler and Eberlein, 1738, with cover 2 for 3,800

   Two sauce-tureens and covers en suite with the above 2,950

   Two Monteith *verrières*, and covers en suite (compare 1966) 2 for 2,950

1962 S. *Augustus Rex* jar and cover, Löwenfinck panels on yellow ground 2,950

1963 Lempertz. Cologne. Tureen and cover, Count Brühl's Swan Service (compare 1960, 1961, 1968), with tax about 4,500

  C. *Augustus Rex* bottle-shaped vase by Löwenfinck 1,680

1966 S. *Verrière* from the Swan Service, 15 in. diam. (compare 1961) 1,800

  Aurora Trust. S. Pair of *Augustus Rex* vases, yellow ground, painted by Stadler, *c.* 1730, 18¾ in. high (£1,505 in 1905) 2 for 16,000

1967 C. Armorial *Augustus Rex* vase by Bonaventura Häurer, 11 in. high 1,575

  S. Pair of *Augustus Rex* vases, 20½ in. high, painted after Petrus Schenck (see 1969) 2 for 7,000

  Donahue. N.Y. Kaendler tureen and cover, forming a Paduan hen, 10½ in. high, $12,000 2 for 4,248

   Tureen, stand and cover from Count Brühl's Swan Service, repaired, 15 in. high (compare 1963), $32,500 3 for 11,900

  S. Circular tureen, cover and stand with parrot and yapping dog motif. 11¾ in. wide 3 for 1,800

1968    S.   Elaborate *surtout de table* from Count Brühl's Swan    £

Service by Kaendler, 22 × 15 × 13½                 3,570

Ex King of Italy.   C. (Geneva).   Pair of trumpet-necked
blue and white vases, elephant handles, unmarked, *c.* 1720–
25, 20½ in. high, FS80,000+5% tax          2 for   9,040

     Tureen, stand and cover, heavily gilded in Herold style,
     height 9¾ in. with stand 11¾ in., FS120,000+5% tax
                                     3 for   12,600

         Pair of blue and white double-gourd vases, *c.* 1720–5,
         Frankfurt style, 20½ in. high, FS54,000+5% tax   2 for   5,670

S.   *Augustus Rex* jar and cover, white ground, lacks knob    2,000

Whitfield.   S.   Pair *Augustus Rex* jars and cover, yellow
grounds, *Chinoiseries* in the Löwenfinck-Schenck style,
12¾ in.                                    2 for   16,000

Brooksbank.   S.   Pair of tureens, stands and covers, harbour scenes reserved on gold ground in style of Heintze,
14 in. wide                              6 for   8,000

     Tureen, stand and cover, yellow ground, seaport
     scenes after Höroldt, 9 in. wide         3 for   2,800

1969    C.   Urn and cover caryatid handles, gold arabesques and
two hunting scenes, 15 in. high          2 for   2,362 10s.

     Tureen, cover and stand, 10 in. high with *Fabeltiere* by
     Löwenfinck                     3 for   2,205

S.   Single *Augustus Rex* trumpet vase, yellow ground,
Chinoiserie panels in Schenck style, 18¾ in. (pair of companion vases, sold in 1967, £7,000)             5,500

C. (Geneva).   Tureen and cover with battle-scenes by
Häurer *c.* 1740, 13½ in. wide, FS32,000+tax    3 for   3,278

     Pair of vegetable-dishes with stands and covers,
     Munchhausen service, 1739–40, painted with *Fabeltiere*,
     11¾ in. wide, FS48,000+tax        6 for   4,916

Stuker.   Berne.   Pair of *Augustus Rex* vases, blue ground
Chinoiserie panels by Höroldt, with covers (one slightly
damaged), FS104,000+tax           2 for   11,000

S.   *Augustus Rex* vase and cover, Watteau subjects, yellow
ground, 13 in. high                     2,000

## *Services and part-services*

1961    Stuker.   Berne.   Cabaret by Höroldt, 1724, in its original
canteen, FS50,000+tax              11 for   4,590

1962    S.   Tea service, style of Löwenfinck, puce ground   18 for   2,500

     Tea service, painted by Seuter in Chinoiserie style at
     Augsburg (compare 1967)          18 for   1,890

   C.   Dinner service, 1770s, birds and flowers, about 100 for   4,200

| | | | | |
|---|---|---|---|---|
| 1962 | Lempertz. Cologne. Coffee service by Höroldt, *c.* 1725, with gold Chinoiseries | 15 for | £ 4,350 | |
| 1963 | Ionides. S. Pair of sugar castors from Count Brühl's *Plat de ménage* in form of Chinese lovers | 2 for | 2,700 | |
| | Fribourg. S. Dishes from the Count Brühl Swan Service (compare 1968), 12 to 15 in. diam. In three lots | 5 for | 2,250 | |
| 1965 | Wolff. S. Tea and coffee service by Höroldt, powdered puce ground, miniature paintings | 47 for | 5,000 | |
| 1966 | Davies. S. Set of ornithological plates, *c.* 1750–60, in French leather travelling case | 17 for | 3,500 | |
| | S. Teapot and cover by Kaendler in form of a monkey, 7¾ in | | 2,600 | |
| | Tea service by Höroldt with *Fabeltiere* on lilac ground | 31 for | 5,000 | |
| 1967 | S. Part of the Sulkowski armorial dinner service, 1735, 30 pieces in 17 lots made | | 21,935 | |
| | These included an 18-inch dish | | 2,600 | |
| | Also a pair of 9 in. table-candlesticks (compare 1968) | 2 for | 2,600 | |
| | C. Part of the Count Brühl Swan Service, 1732–5, viz., Bottle stand, 9½ in. high | | 1,627 | 10s. |
| | Five 21-inch dishes | 5 for | 4,525 | |
| | S. Domed dish-warmer from the same service, 11 in. diam. | | 800 | |
| | Coffee service with figures of miners by Häurer | 22 for | 3,300 | |
| | Puce-ground tea and coffee service by Höroldt | 29 for | 2,700 | |
| | Strickland. S. Tea and coffee service by Höroldt in Chinoiserie style | 21 for | 8,200 | |
| | C. Gold ground Meissen-Augsburg tea and coffee services | 17 for | 3,150 | |
| 1968 | Winston Guest. N.Y. Pair of pierced serpentine bottles from the Count Brühl Swan Service | 2 for | 3,125 | |
| | 6 plates and dishes from this service | 6 for | 5,600 | |
| | Harth. Paris. Tea and coffee service *en Chinoiserie* by Höroldt, FN110,000+tax | 20 for | 10,380 | |
| | S. Pair of 15-inch dishes from the Swan Service | 2 for | 1,600 | |
| | *Verrière* from same service, much damaged (compare 1961) | | 1,000 | |
| | S. From the Sulkowsky service (see 1967), pair of table-candelabra, porcelain throughout on female figures, 24 in. | 2 for | 3,000 | |
| | Ex. King of Italy. C. (Geneva). Pair of long coffee cups and saucers in gilded Höroldt style, FS29,000+5% tax | 2 for | 3,045 | |
| | Teapot with gold *Hausmalerei* by Seuter, KPM mark 4½ in. | | 2,310 | |

| | | | £ |
|---|---|---|---|
| 1968 | C.  Coffeepot and cover, silver-gilt hinge, 8¾ in., painted *en Chinoiserie* by Höroldt | | 1,890 |
| | Teapot in same style | | 1,575 |
| | Combined Meissen porcelain and silver tea and coffee service in travelling case | 42 for | 4,000 |
| | Three plates with Chinoiserie subjects by Löwenfinck, 8½ in. diam. | 3 for | 4,372 |
| | Sigmund Katz.  S.  Single dish, 15½ in. diam., from the Empress Elizabeth service, *c.* 1745 | | 1,600 |
| | C.  Cream pot and cover, 4½ in. high, *Hausmalerei* by Ignaz Preissler, Breslau, Abraham sacrificing Isaac | | 2,625 |
| 1969 | C.  Combined tea and chocolate service, lilac ground, mainly painted with harbour scenes by C. F. Höroldt, J mark, *c.* 1738 (sold in 19 lots including £1,417 10s. for 2 chocolate cups and saucers) | 38 for | 13,010 |
| | Part tea-service, painted with architectural subjects by C. F. Höroldt on yellow ground (8 lots) | 12 for | 3,948 |
| | Pair of 15-inch dishes from the Count Brühl Swan Service (compare 1967 and 1968) | 2 for | 2,730 |
| | Tea and coffee service, Chinoiserie subjects on white ground, sold in 9 lots (coffeepot and cover, 8¼ in. £1,627, 10s.) | 13 for | 8,694 |
| | Single coffeepot and cover, harbour scene and gold strapwork by Höroldt, 9½ in. high | | 3,360 |
| | Horowitz.  S.  Beaker and cover with gold strapwork and river landscape in Höroldt style, 8¼ in. high | | 2,500 |
| | Tea and coffee service, landscapes reserved on turquoise ground | 37 for | 5,000 |

*Miscellaneous*

| | | | |
|---|---|---|---|
| 1962 | Dusendschon.  S.  Snuff box in style of Höroldt | | 1,700 |
| 1963 | C.  The *Affenkapelle* or monkey orchestra, 19 small figures by Kaendler (£50 8s. in 1935), compare 1968 | 19 for | 3,150 |
| 1964 | Weiss.  S.  A more complete set of the same on rococo giltwood stand | 37 for | 4,200 |
| 1966 | S.  Pair of still-life pictures with simulated frames, inclusive size, 9¾ × 13 | 2 for | 3,000 |
| | Pair of candlesticks, copied from Kakiemon, ormolu nozzles, 12¼ in. high | 2 for | 1,700 |
| 1967 | Heber Percy.  C.  Ewer and basin, 8½ in. high, 12¼ in. wide, landscapes by Höroldt | 2 for | 2,205 |
| | S.  Red ground snuff box, Löwenfinck style, 3½ in. diam. | | 1,550 |
| | Pair of bowls and covers, turquoise ground, Kakiemon style | 2 for | 2,205 |

£

| 1968 | Donahue. N.Y. Covered box in form of a lemon, 3 in. high, $17,000 | | 6,710 |
| | S. Set of the monkey orchestra or *Affenkapelle* (compare 1963, 1964) | 30 for | 2,800 |
| | Ex King of Italy. C. Geneva. Decagonal bowl, Löwenfinck-Kakiemon, style, 8¾ in. diam., FS22,000+5% | | 2,310 |
| 1969 | C. Thimble ⅓in. high, minutely painted with harbour scene, Höroldt style | | 1,575 |
| | The *Affenkapelle*, part-set, 14 monkey-figures, 5½ in. high (compare 1963, 1964, 1968) | 14 for | 4,200 |
| | Stuker. Berne. Set of 24 miniature soldiers, made for Frederick the Great, 1750s, FS100,000+tax | 24 for | 10,780 |
| | Dreyfus. S. Teapot in shape of monkey with two young, datable to 1735, by Kaendler, 7 in. high | | 2,100 |
| | Ramsay. E. The *Affenkapelle*, another part-set of 16 figures (1947, with 5 other small figures, £315) | 16 for | 2,625 |

### OTHER FACTORIES

The lesser porcelain factories, maintained by the German kings and princes in the 18th century, seem timid and derivative after the earlier triumphs of Meissen. Hence there is nothing very sensational about the German items in the list apart from the cost of Nymphenburg figures. In the person of Franz Anton Bustelli the Nymphenburg factory had the services of an artist who could really model and who produced sculpture in the place of dolls. But the dolls have won. When Kaendler's harlequins reached the five-figure region, Bustelli's figures declined. In 1954 a pair, *Harlequin* and *Lalage*, made £11,130 at Christies, equivalent in 1970 to rather more than £18,000, but the best price in the 1960s was almost precisely the same, namely £11,400 for two figures in 1969. It may seem a lot of money nevertheless, but if anything could be more insipid than Kaendler's figures at their worst, it is those modelled by Giuseppe Gricci for the Capo di Monte factory near Naples. These can cost more than twice as much as anything by Bustelli, though in 1946 a Gricci figure, which made £6,800 in 1969, was sold for £52, then a fair average price. Competition became serious in 1960 with an example of *the spaghetti-eaters* at £2,000, and in the following year with *the rabbit-catchers* at £4,000. In 1968 another example of this group, much poorer in colour, achieved £9,450, and this also was the price in 1969 of *Isabella and the Doctor*. Later in the year, the *mice-catchers*, almost pathetic in their silliness, were sold by Christies in Geneva for a sum, equivalent with tax to £14,340. If one shares the apparent innocent belief of saleroom correspondents that a half-crown socialist paper pound is as good as a gold sovereign, this was a record price for a single piece of European porcelain. But even if one regards it as 1,800 gold pounds, the price was grotesque. No one can say that Italian collectors lack patriotism. Not even Chelsea and Worcester can boast a teapot which cost over £3,000 with a repaired spout, like the Vezzi example sold in 1968.

*Capo di Monte*

| | | £ |
|---|---|---|
| 1960 | Blohm. S. Group, the spaghetti eaters by Giuseppe Gricci | 2,000 |
| 1961 | Blohm (3rd sale). S. Another example of the same group | 3,400 |
| | Dancing harlequin, 6¾ in. high | 3,400 |
| | (2nd sale) group, the rabbit-catchers (see 1968) by Gricci | 4,000 |
| | Single figure the wounded soldier by Gricci | 1,900 |
| | C. Pair of candelsticks, 8 in. high, modelled as blacka-moors | 1,785 |
| 1962 | S. Single figure, the bird-catcher | 1,780 |
| 1963 | Earl of Buckinghamshire. S. Fisherman and girl, group in colours by Gricci (compare 1966 and 1970) | 1,200 |
| 1964 | C. The porcelain-seller, group by Gricci, coloured | 4,935 |
| 1965 | Fitzgerald. S. Scent-bottle with portrait, the Young Pretender | 750 |
| 1966 | Lord Cunliffe. S. Fisherman and girl by Gricci (com-pare 1963 and 1970) | 580 |
| | C. The lovers, coloured group by Gricci, 6½ in. high | 2,100 |
| 1967 | Dreyfus. S. Pair of 16 inch. dishes with harbour scenes 2 for | 2,600 |
| 1968 | Dreyfus. S. Mirror frame with painted panel after Watteau by Maria Caselli, 47 in. high | 5,800 |
| | Dolleymore. C. The rabbit-catchers, 6¾ in. high (for a better example see 1961) | 9,450 |
| | S. Fisherman and his companion, coloured group by Gricci, 8 in. high | 2,100 |
| | C. White *commedia* group, 5½ in. wide | 861 |
| | S. Ovoid vase lacking cover, flowers in Meissen style by Maria Caselli, 13½ in. high | 4,000 |
| 1969 | C. Group of three figures round a tree by Giuseppe Gricci, 10½ in. high | 4,410 |
| | The masked lovers by Giuseppe Gricci, 8 in. high | 9,450 |
| | Isabella and the doctor, by Giuseppe Gricci, 5¾ in. | 9,450 |
| | Pair of family groups, seated on benches, Ferdinand IV style, *c.* 1790–1800, 8 in. wide 2 for | 3,150 |
| | S. White ware figure, Turkish dwarf after Jacques Callot, 5¾ in. high | 2,415 |
| | S. White cane handle, 2¾ in. signature, Ambrogio di Giorgio | 900 |
| | S. The peasant and his companion by Gricci, 8 in. | 8,400 |

£

| | | | |
|---|---|---|---|
| 1969 | S. | A peasant girl by Gricci, 7¼ in. (Paget sale, 1946, £52) | 6,800 |
| | C. | (Geneva). The mice-catchers by Gricci, 7¼ in. high, FS.140,000+tax | 14,340 |
| | | A variant on the masked lovers (see above) by Gricci, 8 in. high, FS70,000+tax | 7,170 |
| | | Urn and cover with modelled flowers and mythological paintings, Charles III period, 10½ in. high FS22,000+tax | 2,253 |
| | S. | Snuffbox, shell-moulded, painted inside lid, gilt metal mounts, 3¾ in. diam. | 2,100 |
| 1970 | C. | Reclining fisherman and girl by Giuseppe Gricci, 6¾ in. wide (£1,200 in 1963) | 6,300 |

### Chantilly, Mennecy and St Cloud

| | | | | |
|---|---|---|---|---|
| 1960 | Paris. Pommade box *en camäieu bleu*, St Cloud | | | 1,090 |
| 1961 | Phillips. S. Pair, Chantilly enamelled *magots*, simple ormolu plinths, supporting jars | | 2 for | 3,600 |
| | Ryan. S. Pair of Mennecy coloured peacocks, 5 in. high | | 2 for | 1,800 |
| 1963 | Fribourg. S. Pair of Chantilly *Cachepots*, Kakiemon style enamels, 6¼ in. high | | 2 for | 1,200 |
| | Mennecy white figure of a satyr, lightly enamelled, 7 in. | | | 1,800 |
| | Pair of Mennecy groups of children, 6½ in. and 5¾ in. high | | 2 for | 1,700 |
| | C. Mounted Mennecy figure of a *magot* | | | 2,520 |
| | Pair of Mennecy figures of *pagods* | | 2 for | 1,680 |
| 1967 | Gilbert Levy. Paris. Chantilly *drageoir*, formed of two lemons, FN20,000+tax | | | 1,895 |
| | St Cloud, pot-pourri jar and cover, polychrome relief, 6¾ in., FN26,100+tax | | | 2,440 |
| | Mennecy ewer and basin, coloured and gilded relief, FN28,000+tax | | | 2,628 |
| | Pair of white squatting *pagods*, St Cloud, FN55,000+tax | | 2 for | 5,130 |
| 1968 | N.Y. Mounted Chantilly pot-pourri jar in form of melon and tiger, 6¼×7½, $4,500 | | | 1,875 |
| | Ex King of Italy. C. (Geneva). White St Cloud figure of a cross-legged *pagod*, 9¾ in. high, FS45,000+5% tax | | | 4,725 |
| | Price de Ligne. S. Chantilly figure, Chinese girl reclining | | | 900 |
| | S. Garniture, three white St Cloud pot-pourri vases, ormolu covers, 10¼, 5 and 5½ in. high | | 3 for | 3,400 |
| | Bayard Swope. S. Pair of white Chantilly parrots, 13 in. | | 2 for | 1,100 |

1969 S. Chantilly pot-pourri jar in form of a melon, licked by £
a puma, white on simple ormolu plinth, 6½ in. high 2,200
Mennecy *magot*, mounted as two-light, candelabrum,
6×8 3,000
Mennecy white figure, squatting Chinaman, 8¼ in. 1,100

### Frankenthal

1961 Blohm. S. Pair of figures of monkeys 2 for 2,700
Harlequin, single figure by Lanz, 6 in. high 2,300
1966 Aurora Trust. S. Group, *der Jagdfruhstuck* (see 1967),
7 in. 560
Pair of coloured groups by Lück, the merchant and his
wife, 6¾ in. 2 for 1,000
Pair of coloured hairdressing groups by Lück, 10 in.
2 for 3,200
S. Another example of the second of these groups 1,000
The flute lesson by Lück, 13 in. 2,000
1967 Beck. S. Hunting group by Lück, 11 in. (see 1966) 1,900
1968 Dreyfus. S. Dinner service, birds in Sèvres style, 1770–80,
123 for 8,600
1969 S. Coloured figure, Thetis in Louis XV costume by
Konrad Linck, 10½ in. high 3,400
Dreyfus. S. Peepshow group after Boucher and Falconet,
8½ in. 1,200

### Höchst (see also pottery and faience, Germany)

1963 Fribourg. S. The sportsman's repose, group 7½ in. high
on ormolu base, 1755 2,400
1965 Hutton. S. Pair of parrots, Louis XV ormolu bases,
2 for 8,500
1966 S. Two rococo arbour groups after Nilsen, 11½ in. high,
2 for 3,000
Amyntas and Silvia, group 11½ in. high 1,900
1967 S. A second example of the same group 1,000
1968 S. The print-seller, group 7½ in. high 1,200
1969 C. The dancing lesson, group 6¼ in. high 2,100
van Zuylen. S. Lovers by Melchior, 9 in. high 1,300
Group after the Nilsen engraving, *le songe pastoral*, by
Melchior or Russinger, 13 in. wide 1,350
Dreyfus. S. Chinese Empress with attendant, probably
by Russinger after Huquier, 8½ in. 2,200

### Nymphenburg

1961 Blohm. S. Columbine and harlequin, pair by Franz
Bustelli, ex Berlin Schloss Museum 2 for 7,000

614

|      |      |                                                                                                                           | £         |
|------|------|---------------------------------------------------------------------------------------------------------------------------|-----------|
| 1962 | S.   | Harlequin's companion by Bustelli, 8½ in. high                                                                             | 5,000     |
|      | C.   | Pantaloon, ditto (compare 1949, £720 and 1954, £1,622 5s.)                                                                 |           |
| 1967 |      | Maria zu Wied. S. Capitano Spavento by Bustelli (compare 1956, £2,100)                                                     | 3,150     |
|      |      |                                                                                                                           | 2,800     |
|      |      | Boyle. S. Leda by Bustelli, 7¾ in. high                                                                                    | 4,400     |
| 1969 |      | van Zuylen. S. (see also Vol. II, under 1954). The egg-seller, 5¾ in.                                                      | 5,800     |
|      |      | The fisherman, 6½ in.                                                                                                      | 5,400     |

## Vienna (Dupaquier)

|      |      |                                                                                                                           |                     |
|------|------|---------------------------------------------------------------------------------------------------------------------------|---------------------|
| 1960 | C.   | Pair of pilgrim-bottles and covers, c. 1730, 14 in. high, 2 for                                                           | 1,050               |
|      |      | Blohm. S. Two tureens, gold and grisaille painting, 9 in. high, 14 in. long, ex Hermitage, Leningrad                      | 1,700 and 1,800     |
| 1961 |      | Blohm. S. Another ditto                                                                                                    | 2,300               |
| 1962 |      | Phillips, son and Neale. Teapot and cover in same style                                                                    | 480                 |
| 1966 | C.   | Silvergilt mounted tankard, *Hausmalerei* by Dann-höfer                                                                    | 1,365               |
|      |      | Olio-pot and cover in form of a Kakiemon *Koro*, 6¾ in. diam.                                                              | 1,207               |
| 1968 | S.   | Tankard, 6½ in. high, painted *en grisaille* by Dannhöfer                                                                  | 1,000               |
|      | C.   | Garniture, 3 urns, covers and wide stands, Sorgenthal period 1803, 17½ in. high                                3 for       | 966                 |
| 1969 |      | Lever. S. Teabowl and saucer, Dupaquier period, *Hausmalerei* in style of Faber (*Schwartzlot*)                           | 1,750               |
| 1970 | S.   | Teapot, Dupaquier period, similar painting by Preissler or Bottengrüber                                                    | 2,600               |

## Various factories

|      |      |                                                                                                                           |            |
|------|------|---------------------------------------------------------------------------------------------------------------------------|------------|
| 1960 |      | Blohm. S. Fifteen Fürstenburg figures by Simon Feilner, sold in separate lots                             15 for           | 15,000     |
| 1961 |      | Blohm. S. Pair of Fürstenburg figures. Harlequin and Columbine                                            2 for            | 2,300      |
|      |      | Ditto, Pantaloon by Feilner, single figure (see 1967)                                                                      | 1,200      |
|      |      | Zurich figure, equestrian lady, 7 in. high                                                                                 | 1,550      |
| 1962 |      | Fribourg. S. Tournai white ware bust, Louis XV after Lemoyne, by Gillis, 12½ in. high                                      | 1,200      |
|      |      | Ditto, picnic group *en bosquet* by Nicolas Lecreux, 20 in.                                                                | 1,600      |
| 1965 | S.   | Pair of tall *campana* vases by Simon Golov, Petersburg 1836                                              2 for            | 2,600      |

| 1965 | Viva King.  S.  Buen Retiro Chinoiserie group, 12½ in. high | £ 1,150 |
|---|---|---|
| 1966 | S.  Ludwigsburg crinoline group by Haselmeyer, 6 in. high | 1,500 |
| | Nickstadt.  S.  Ditto, dinner service, floral sprays in Meissen Klinger style | 61 for 2,625 |
| | Princess Olga.  S.  Doccia armorial tureen, cover and stand | 1,600 |
| 1967 | Princess Maria zu Wied.  S.  Berlin service, 1822–5, floral borders on gold, some with views of Berlin, 458 for | 18,500 |
| | Pearson.  S.  Fürstenburg figure by Feilner, Captain Boloardo (£1,100 in 1961), 8½ in. high | 2,750 |
| | Doccia oval dish with figure of a Turk by Carlo Anreiter, 12 in. diam. | 2,000 |
| | Ahrens.  S.  Fulda figure, *Madonna Immaculata* by Wenzel Neu, 18 in. high.  Bought in | 2,000 |
| 1968 | C.  Zurich figure, woman street singer, *c.* 1770, 6½ in. | 2,520 |
| | Fairfax Cartright.  C.  Vezzi (Venice) teapot, Chinoiserie painting, spout repaired | 3,045 |
| | S.  Pair of Ludwigsburg tureens covers and stands, 11¼ in. wide | 6 for 1,400 |
| | Dreyfus.  S.  Buen Retiro coloured relief plaque, Christ and woman of Samaria, 13 in. diam. | 1,100 |
| | S.  Weesp (Holland).  Part coffee service, painted with birds, *c.* 1770–80 | 9 for 1,350 |
| 1969 | C.  Pair of Fulda gardening figures, 7½ in. high | 2 for 2,835 |
| | Zurich group by Sonnenschein, mother rocking child in cradle, 6½ in. high | 1,890 |
| | S.  Doccia dinner service, *c.* 1800, with blue enamels after engravings | 147 for 5,000 |
| | C.  Paris service, painted in Brussels with ornithological subjects by Louis Cretté, early 19th century | 162 for 3,150 |

## PORCELAIN, CONTINENTAL
### SÈVRES (INCLUDING VINCENNES)

Three porcelain bouquet-baskets with gilt metal foliage and wired porcelain flowers, characteristic products of the Vincennes factory and one of the 18th century's most detestable innovations, made £11,500 each in 1963-4. While this did not restore the great lead over all other European porcelain which Sèvres had possessed from the mid 18th century to the end of the First World War, it did at least make it level with the dearest Meissen. In 1929 at the very nadir of the dictatorial Parisian taste for those heavy gilded backgrounds and tiresome little painted vignettes, the famous Rohan dessert service was sold for about £7 a unit. In 1870 the service had cost the third Earl of Dudley ten times as much. One would in fact have had to travel back a hundred years to 1829 to get a Sèvres service so cheap. By 1963 a batch of 15 items from the Rohan service, some of them repaired, were worth nearly £800 a unit, to be resold privately at the rate of £1,300 for a dessert plate. In 1970 plates from the Rohan service might make considerably more than that in the saleroom.

This particular instance does not create a general rule for the recovery of the Sèvres market. Paired urns and garnitures were formerly many times more costly than items from services, and in their case there is no recovery at all. In 1886 the Earl of Dudley's garniture of three urns with panels, painted by Dodin after Wouverman and reserved on *bleu du Roi* grounds, made 1,550 guineas. At the Fribourg sale of 1963 they had to be bought in at £1,300, and two years later they were let go for £290. This, it may be argued, is the long-unpopular, hard paste neo-Classic style of the late 18th century, but, compared with mid-Victorian times, even the most sought-after Sèvres has fared little better. Thus in 1875 the same Earl of Dudley gave £6,825 for two very peculiar and very early pot-pourri jars. In the money of 1963 this meant about £48,000. But in 1963, having disappeared for three quarters of a century, these legendary objects were seen again in the saleroom, where the final bid, £5,800, was not even an eighth as much. In 1886 when the two pot-pourri jars had made their last saleroom appearance, George Redford compared them with the famous Bernal vases, which had astonished a market that reckoned in hundreds at the most, by making close on two thousand in 1855. He considered their value in 1886 to be 'not far short of 10,000 guineas which has become the standard for the very loveliest of the lovely Sèvres.' In 1970 terms Redford was thinking of £95,000. The beautiful coloured lithograph, published by Chavaignac, shows that the Bernal vases were a pair of *vases d'oreilles*, painted with cupids in panels, reserved on a *rose Pompadour* background. A closely similar pair in the Michelham sale of 1966 made not £95,000 but £7,500, and at that price they were surpassed by two other pairs of *rose Pompadour* vases, one of which made £11,500. These were the highest prices of the 1960s for what was still the most sought after kind of Sèvres and probably with very little to come. A *rose Pompadour* tureen, which reached £10,360 in 1957 may be the very last of its kind. And as to a *vaisseau à mats*, which was the crowning achievement of that style, there is not a hope of it.

Even though this is but the ghost of the mid-Victorian market, some astonishment remains that things which are so little in the current of modern taste, can make so much. But multi-millionaires or billionaires cannot be expected to eat their *mousse de framboises* off Benin bronze.

|      |                                                                                                                                                                     |        | £      |
|------|---------------------------------------------------------------------------------------------------------------------------------------------------------------------|--------|--------|
| 1960 | C.   Pair of *bleu du Roi* urns with shipping scenes by Morin, *c.* 1780                                                                                            | 2 for  | 1,102  |
|      | S.   Early Vincennes white group, *les mangeurs de raisins* after Boucher, 9½ in. high, 1750s (compare 1967)                                                        |        | 2,100  |
|      | Paris.   Tureen and cover, apple-green ground, panels of flowers by Aloncle                                                                                         |        | 4,870  |
|      | Pair of *cachepots* by Aloncle from the Buffon service                                                                                                              | 2 for  | 1,800  |
| 1961 | Strauss.   Paris.   Equestrian figure of Louis XV in *biscuit de Vincennes*, 14 in. high                                                                            |        | 2,280  |
| 1962 | S.   Pair of *gros bleu* urns, harbour scenes by Fabius after Joseph Vernet                                                                                         | 2 for  | 1,000  |
|      | Paris.   Covered *écuelle* and stand, Vincennes, turquoise ground, 1755, FN23,500+tax                                                                               |        | 2,058  |
|      | Tall cup and saucer, 1757, blue cameo on yellow by Vieillard, FN16,000+tax                                                                                          |        | 1,312  |
| 1963 | S.   Pair of *pot-pourri* jars by Dodin, 1757, 11¼ in. high, bought by Lord Dudley in 1875 for £6,825 (£2,625 in 1886)                                             | 2 for  | 5,800  |
|      | Fribourg.   S.   Pair of *Brûles-parfums, bleu celeste*, mounted *c.* 1770                                                                                          |        | 2,000  |
|      | Pair of plaques by Dodin, 1774–5, 8×5½, ormolu frames                                                                                                               | 2 for  | 3,500  |
|      | Vincennes dessert service, *en camaïeu rose*                                                                                                                        | 72 for | 3,800  |
|      | Gondola-shaped jardinière, *rose Pompadour*, 1757                                                                                                                   |        | 3,400  |
|      | Vincennes basket of flowers, gilt-metal stalks etc. 17½ in. high, *c.* 1750 (sold from Rosebery collection, 1939, £89 5s. see 1964)                                 |        | 11,500 |
|      | *Sucrier* stand and cover, *rose Pompadour*, 1757 (see 1969)                                                                                                        |        | 1,600  |
|      | Vincennes dessert service, flowers on white                                                                                                                         | 115 for| 4,400  |
|      | Two jardinières, metal-stemmed flowers, 1763                                                                                                                        | 2 for  | 3,700  |
|      | *Déjeuner* for four, apple-green ground, 1757                                                                                                                       |        | 2,300  |
|      | Garniture, three *bleu du Roi* urns, painted by Dodin after Wouverman (£1,627 10s. 1886, and see 1965) Bought in                                                    | 3 for  | 1,300  |
|      | Two *rose Pompadour* shell-dishes, painted by Tandart, 1757                                                                                                         | 2 for  | 5,000  |
|      | Two Vincennes square dishes, apple-green ground                                                                                                                     | 2 for  | 2,700  |

£

1963   Dunlap. N.Y. Part of the Rohan service, some pieces repaired (147 for £1,045 in 1929, 36 for £21,420 in 1959)

                                                 15 for  11,567

1964   Rosebery. S. Pair of Vincennes baskets of flowers, c. 1750 (compare Fribourg, 1963)      2 for  23,000

1965   Harewood. C. Pair of Vincennes *vases hollandais*, 7½ in.

                                               2 for   3,625

      Pair of Vincennes flower-shaped vases with cupid panels on *bleu celeste* grounds by Dodin, 1756   2 for   2,940

      Set of three bleu celeste *vases hollandais* by Vieillard, 1761                                     3 for   7,350

      Somewhat similar set by Vieillard with subjects after Teniers                                3 for  10,500

      Set of 3 *Fontenoy* vases by Dodin, 1763, apple-green ground, ormolu plinths (single vase 1905, £4,200)

                                             3 for   9,925

      Pair of elaborate *cassolettes*, 1770, *bleu du Roi* grounds, Bought by Louvre                        2 for   2,730

  Paris. Pair of dinner plates from Napoleon's *Quartiers generaux* service                     2 for   1,365

  Fitzgerald. S. Pair of *caisses à fleurs*, mounted with Vincennes flowers, blue ground         2 for   2,400

  Fribourg. S. Jardinière, *rose Pompadour*, 1757         2,600

      Garniture of three urns by Dodin after Lancret and Wouverman (£1,637 10s. in 1886, £1,300 in 1963)

                                             3 for     290

1966   Michelham. S. (July and November). Pair of rose ground *vases à oreilles*, 12¾ in. high      2 for   7,500

      Pair of *caisses à fleurs* by Vieillard, dated 1757, 5¾ in.

                                             2 for   9,500

      Pair of *vases hollandais, oeil de perdrix*, 8¾ in.   2 for   6,000

        Pair of ditto, rose ground, dated 1757

                                           2 for  11,500

      *Ecuelle*, cover and stand, 1760, rose ground       5,500

      Biscuit cupid after Falconet on rose plinth       5,200

      Ewer and basin, 11½ in. diam., Rose ground   2 for   3,800

  J. de Rothschild, Paris. Fluted vase and cover, called *vase Boileau*, green ground, 19 in. high, FN50,000+tax     4,390

1967   Galliers-Pratt. S. *Verseuse*, gold mounted lid, paintings on *rose marbré* ground, 1761, 3 in. high        2,600

  Sainsbury. S. Vincennes biscuit group, *les Mangeurs de Raisins* after Boucher, 9¼ in. high (glazed version, 1960, £2,100)                                       750

      Another Boucher biscuit group, *la leçon de flûte*, 8¾ in.   860

1967    Alfred Pearson. C. *Rose Pompadour* tray, medallion painting, 4¼ in. diam.       £ 1,600

Lindsay. S. *Caisse à fleurs*, mounted with Vincennes flowers 1758, 23 in. high, overall      1,300

Gilbert Levy. Paris. *Pot-pourri* vase *en camaïeu rouge*, Vincennes, FN24,500 (11·88 to £)+tax      2,390

     *Écuelle*, cover and stand by Taillandier, FN20,000+tax      1,892

     Vincennes tureen, 1750–3, apple-green ground, floral bouquets, etc., FN62,000+tax      5,780

1968    Kinnaird. C. Vincennes *jardinière à éventail* on white ground, 11½ in. wide      819

S. Dinner service, 1784, floral borders and centres      94 for   3,500

1969    S. *Sucrier*, cover and stand, *rose Pompadour*, date-letter 1757, 9¼ in. wide (Fribourg sale, 1963, £1,600)      1,200

Davis. S. Vincennes ewer and basin, floral panels on apple-green ground, silver-mounted lid, dated 1756, 10 in. wide and 7 in. high      2 for   1,350

# PORCELAIN AND POTTERY
## ALL COUNTRIES, LATE 19TH AND 20TH CENTURIES

The chief interest of this list is to be found in the truly astonishing fact that figures and groups, made in the past 35 years, can cost as much as the rarest and finest European 18th century porcelain. Yet neither Dorothy Doughty nor Edward Marshall Boehm show the least vestige of a personal style. While their basis is to be found in Audubon's coloured aquatints, the effect is that of stuffed birds, cast in another material of a most inadaptable texture and with all the vigour of inanimate death. At $50,000, a pair of such efforts can rival a pair of tureens from the Meissen Swan Service, an ormolu-mounted pair of Kaendler's cockatoos or parrots, a pair of Harlequin or Crinoline groups, or a pair of Augustus Rex vases. The porcelain models far surpassed the value of the original prints, though *the birds of America* were among the rarest of Americana. In 1969 the price of the complete edition of 1827–38 worked out at £206 for each of the 435 aquatints and considerably less for detached plates.

The price of $50,000 for a virtually new and wholly imitative product raises a question. Would those who buy the dearest 18th century porcelain, pay as much for new copies after that fast-approaching day when the originals will have vanished from the market? Of course, the Boehm and Doughty birds may be bought by a different sort of people with a different scale of values. Or are they?

Other items in this very odd list are in the idiom of their own time. A pair of Russian imperial dishes in Great Exhibition taste at its most *outré*, owes the price of £577 10s. to snobbery alone. Solon's masterpiece at £2,250 is a work of 1903, nothing so adventurous as *art nouveau*, but an example of the sentimentalized classicism of the school, encouraged by the Paris Salon, a bit of Bouguereau in pottery. The Martinware owls with detachable heads are in the material and, to some extent, in the form of German 16th century stoneware, and of course they are just as dear. As to Moonlight lustre and Fairyland lustre, the names alone tell you all you want to know.

£

| | | |
|---|---|---|
| 961 | Gavine. N.Y. Models made at the Worcester factory after Audubon's Birds of America by Dorothy Doughty, d. 1962 | |
| | Redstarts on hemlock, 1935, $10,500 — 2 for | 3,750 |
| | Goldfinches on thistles, 1936, $6,000 — 2 for | 2,148 |
| | Red cardinals with orange blossom, 1937 — 2 for | 1,575 |
| | Baltimore orioles on tulip trees — 2 for | 1,450 |
| 963 | S. Pair of Minton *pâte sûr pâte* vases by L. Solon, 1875 — 2 for | 1,250 |
| 965 | Murgatroyd. S. Minton *pâte sûr pâte* amphora by Solon, dated 1903 and considered his masterpiece | 2,250 |
| | N.Y. Pair of American quails by Dorothy Doughty, 1941, said to have been sold by Tiffany for $50,000 (one of 22 sets) — 2 for | 17,925 |

1967  N.Y.  Worcester bird-groups by Dorothy Doughty,     £

Kingfisher and autumn beech, 12 in.               750

    Pair of magnolia warblers on magnolias, 13½ and 14½

    in., $4,750                 2 for   1,696

    Pair of bluebirds, apple-blossom sprays, 1936   2 for    803

Kline.  N.Y.  Pair of bob-white quail, 1942, 4½ and 6½ in.

high, $30,000 (compare 1969)         2 for  10,712

Quintal.  N.Y.  Pair of Mexican Feijoa, 1950, 11 in. high,

$3,000                        2 for   1,071

    Other birds after Audubon by Edward Marshall

    Boehm; Pair of song sparrows on tulips, one of 50,

    14½ in. high, $18,000           2 for   6,430

    Pair of Eastern bluebirds and rhododendra, one of 100,

    12½ in.                     2 for   1,876

    Pair of cedar waxwings on blackberries, one of 100,

    11½ and 12¾              2 for   1,500

    Single biscuit American eagle, plain white, 1961, one

    of 64, 15¼ in. high, $3,000              1,072

U.S.S.R. government.  C.  Petersburg Imperial service,

made in the 1850s and later, excessively ornate.  There were

1,754 pieces in 28 lots which totalled £65,751, among them

a pair of 13-inch dishes             2 for   577 10s.

    C.  Wedgwood 'moonlight lustre' shell dessert service

20th century (compare 1968)        103 for  1,680

1968  S.  Equestrian figure, Princess Elizabeth at the trooping of

the colour, 1947, Worcester porcelain after Doris Linder,

12 in. high, one of 100                  1,800

Alcock.  S.  Pair of Minton *pâte sûr pâte* moon flasks by

L. Solon, 1881, 9½ in. high          2 for    400

Lancaster.  C.  20th century Wedgwood 'moonlight

lustre' shell-shaped dessert service (compare 1967)   50 for    504

McEachran.  C.  Baluster vase, Wedgwood 'fairyland

lustre', profusely decorated, 9 in. high, after 1915       189

    Bowl, ditto, 8 in. diam. (in 1969 a 10-inch example

    made £200)                         147

S.  Berlin porcelain plaque by Otto Dietrich after van der

Helst, 22½ × 29¼, late 19th century            1,700

Nicholson.  S.  Martinware jar and cover in form of a

barn owl, 1892, 9¼ in. high                350

    Grotesque bird with removable head, ditto 1888, 10¾ in.   200

1969  Monkhouse.  S.  Martinware plaque depicting a pottery,

1882, polychrome stoneware, 16¼ × 7            300

S.  Eggshell liqueur-bottle, *art nouveau*, Rozenburg 'blown

porcelain', the Hague, 1909, 8¼ in. high (a pair 7½ in., 1914

made £640)                         250

1969  Barratt. C. Pair of Sèvres baluster vases on tall pedestals,    £
Boucher subjects on *bleu du Roi* ground, 34 in. high, *c.*
1870                               2 for   2,415

C. Pair of late 19th century Dresden vases, covers and
stands, encrusted flowers, etc., 34 in. high       2 for     892 10*s.*

N.Y. By Edward Marshall Boehm, 1960. Pair of song
sparrows on tulips, 17 in. high, one of 38 pairs, $50,000,
Bought in                             2 for 20,835

Resold later in the year for $17,500 or £7,292

Birds by Edward Marshall Boehm;

         Pair of cedar-waxwings on blackberries, 12 in. high,
         one of 100 pairs, 1961 (compare 1967), $19,000    2 for   7,984

         Single group by ditto, sugar-birds, one of 100 sets,
         1966, 25½ in. high, $14,000                    5,840

         Pair of bob-white quails by Dorothy Doughty, 4½ and
         6 in. high, Worcester, 1942, $27,500 (see 1967)    2 for 11,550

         Dapple grey hunter by Boehm, one of 250, 14 in. high,
         $8,000                                          3,335

S. Minton copy of a Sèvres *vaisseau à mâts*, *bleu du roi*
ground, 17¾ in. high, 1881                     650

Egerton. Enamelled plaque of a nude by Alexander
Fisher, 1895, Sheffield plate frame and stand, 11¼ × 4¼    1,000

# POTTERY AND FAIENCE, EUROPEAN
(excluding Majolica and Hispano–Mauresque)
### ENGLISH

In the 1960s Staffordshire bragget pots and Wrotham tygs climbed gracefu
to the £2,000 region, showing what enthusiasts will put up with in order
buy an early dated inscription. Some of the tygs looked like the secret hob
of a village blacksmith, but the whole charm of English 17th century ceram
lies in their primitive innocence. No wonder Samuel Pepys was so shock
when he dined at the Guildhall banquet 'off earth'. In the case of the *Susan
and the Elders* charger, which made £2,500 in 1961 and was probably wo
double by 1970, one was prepared by the many examples of Jacobean stum
work embroidery, but was ever even stumpwork quite as crude as tha
Well, by 1709 Louis XIV too thought he might be setting a good example
eating 'off earth'. 'Le Roi s'agita de se mettre a la faïence.' Louis XIV cou
choose between Rouen, Nevers and Moustiers, but I think I would ha
preferred Pepy's kind.

The market for the commonest British dining ware of the late 17th a
18th centuries, tin-glazed with a pleasant modicum of decoration in cob
or two or three other simple pigments, has become largely an affair of payi
for dated inscriptions. One would not have called the year 1763 a very si
nificant date, for by that time the ware was being produced in half a doz
places at 2d. a plate. Yet it was sufficient to raise the price of a perfunctori
painted barber's bowl to £1,700. In fact the prettiest of English tinglaze,
*Delph* as it was once called, is seldom dated so that even in 1969 the very be
of undated punchbowls only just passed the hundred mark. It must be borne
mind that in the 1950s £10 would have bought as much. Before 1912, wh
innocence was not yet a costly luxury, ten shillings would have sufficed f
almost any English tin-glaze and half a crown for blue and white plates.

In 18th century Staffordshire the rural innocence of the tin-glaze traditio
became diluted with craftsmanship and the spirit of experiment. Most su
prisingly it was Marc Leon Solon, the begetter of all those cathartic came
vases in the style of the first Vienna–Orient sleeping cars, who perceived t
ingenuity of the old Staffordshire potters, when working for Minton in t
1870s. In his sale at Hanley in 1912 a salt-glaze pew group made £205. T
last group of this kind was sold in 1961 for £3,400, and if there is anything
good to come, one can expect it to make at least double. But as pew grou
vanish from the salerooms less estimable objects fill the void. The Lee
*pearlware* stallions, which commonly stood in saddler's shops in the age
Ferneley and Herring, reached the 4-figure level in 1967 and ended the deca
at £2,800. And from Wedgwood's Empress Catherine service, painted
engraving style on creamware in 1774, a dinner-plate made £900, a carving
dish £2,400, handmade jobs throughout, yet almost indistinguishable from t
finest mass production. Even a Meissen dish from the Empress Elizabeth servi
of 1745, which they sold in the following year, made only two thirds as muc

624

Yet this flourishing market for the ceramics of Staffordshire is still largely a regional and provincial affair. Only the Wedgwood jasper and basalt wares, the cold heart of pure neo-classicism, fail in real money terms to equal the triumphs of the late Victorian salerooms, in spite of a rapid advance since 1964.

### TINGLAZE AND SLIPWARE, 17TH CENTURY OR EARLIER

| | | £ |
|---|---|---|
| 1960 | S. Lambeth blue and white tankard, inscribed Thomas Ballard, 1644, 6½ in. high | 300 |
| | Lambeth pill-slab, arms of Apothecaries' Company (similar slabs, £4 15s. in 1915, £225 in 1953), compare 1969 | 580 |
| | Lambeth meat-dish in relief with *fecundity* figure after Bernard Pallissy, dated 1661 (similar dishes, £90 in 1924, £200 in 1959) | 480 |
| 961 | S. Lambeth polychrome charger, 1648, with painting of Susanna and the elders, 18¼ in. diam. | 2,500 |
| | Arbuthnot. S. Set of six Lambeth Delft 'merry man' plates dated 1693 6 for | 1,200 |
| 962 | S. Lambeth blue and white cup, head of William III | 290 |
| | Bright. S. Wrotham slipware tyg by John Livermore, 1631, 7⅛ in. high | 460 |
| 963 | S. Wrotham tyg by Thomas Ifield, 1649 (compare 1968) | 540 |
| | Lambeth blue and white cup, arms of Bakers' Company and date 1657 | 560 |
| 964 | Garner. S. Lambeth polychrome charger, mounted figure, Charles II | 280 |
| | Much damaged Lambeth blue and white harvest jug, 1659 | 380 |
| 965 | Garner. S. Barber's bowl, Lambeth blue and white, 1703 | 680 |
| | Lambeth polychrome urn, late 17th century | 460 |
| | Lambeth money box, double-gourd shape, 1692 | 540 |
| | 'Malling' blue round-bellied tankard, c. 1600, damaged | 540 |
| | Lambeth moulded charger, indistinct Commonwealth date | 460 |
| | Two miniature round-bellied stoneware tankards by John Dwight of Fulham, dated on the silver rims, 1681 and 1682 400 and | 370 |
| 66 | S. Slipware 'owl-jar' and cover, Staffordshire, c. 1700, 9¼ in. high | 1,050 |
| 67 | Williamson. S. Greenglaze pitcher, cockle shells in relief 14th century, 12 in. high (incomplete) | 420 |

1968 Lewis. S. Wrotham slipware tyg, signed Richardson, £
1652 (compare 1963), 4¾ in. high 1,500
    S. Staffordshire slipware jug, signed William Simpson
1691 1,700
Dickson. S. Lambeth blue-dash charger, 1658, with
loyalist figure of Charles I, 12½ in. diam. 950
    S. Another Lambeth blue dash charger with equestrian
figure of Charles I, 12¾ in. diam. 950
        Staffordshire slipware bragget-pot, inscribed 'the best
is not too good for you,' 1696 2,100
    C. Lambeth standing salt, blue and white, 5 in. diam.
inscribed AW 1675 735
Gollancz. S. 14th century green glazed 'bearded man'
jug, 7½ in. (£360 in 1961), London Museum 1,300
        Staffordshire slipware bragget-pot and cover, undated,
late 17th century, 10¾ in. high 1,800
        Wrotham tyg, signed George Richardson, 1654, 6 in. 1,600
        Wrotham tyg, signed Henry Ifield, 1660, 6 in. 1,200
        Staffordshire slipware posset-pot, dated 1688, 6¼ in. 1,600
    S. Staffordshire slipware bragget-pot, badly damaged,
'the best is not too good for you, 1697' (compare 1968) 480
        Wrotham tyg, signed I.E. 1701, only 4 in. high 750
        Liverpool Delft pill-slab, arms of Apothecaries' Com-
pany towards 1700, 10½ in. wide (compare 1960) 520
        Pair of Lambeth polychrome marriage plates, inscribed
and dated 1676, 8¾ in. diam. 2 for 800
        Unglazed late medieval jug on 3 feet, combed decora-
tion, repaired, 10¾ in. 250
        Lambeth white tin-glaze sack bottle with inscription,
*Whit 1650* in blue, 6 in. high 300
1970 S. Charger, Staffordshire slipware with 3 heads of Charles
II in the Toft style, attributed William Taylor, 16½ in. diam. 4,300

### ENGLISH, 18TH CENTURY
(Including saltglaze, creamware and pearlware etc.)

1960 S. Pair of crested birds, Whieldon's saltglaze, *c.* 1755,
8¾ in. high 2 for 1,500
1961 Fowler. S. Pair of saltglaze reclining horses, 8½ in. 2 for 1,450
        Staffordshire saltglaze arbour group, tea party, *c.* 1740 3,400
1962 S. Late 18th century saltglaze group, Polito's menagerie 520
1963 S. Pair of cockerels, *famille rose* saltglaze (£450 in 1945)
2 for 900
1965 Allman. S. Saltglaze crinoline figure in the pew group
style, very crude 1,650

| | | £ |
|---|---|---|
| 1966 | S. Whieldon coloured arbour group, 6¾×6 (Elkins sale, 1891 £9) | 1,900 |
| | Ralph Wood, coloured equestrian figure of the Duke of Cumberland as a Roman emperor, 15¼ in. high | 1,200 |
| | C. Ralph Wood, equestrian figure of Hudibras, 9 in. high (see 1969) | 945 |
| 1967 | S. Pair of saltglaze pierced baskets, 7½ in. diam.   2 for | 520 |
| | Prattware grotto group, 9¾ in. high | 300 |
| | Mackintosh. S. Toby jug, Admiral Rodney drawing his sword, 10½ in. high | 1,050 |
| | (69 lots of Toby jugs made over £15,000) | |
| | Sugden. C. Leeds pearlware figure of a stallion, lightly enamelled, 17 in. high (c. 1820–30) | 1,050 |
| | Walter Mills. C. Another ditto, 11 in. high | 1,785 |
| | Burr. C. Hexagonal saltglaze teapot, 8¼ in. wide | 1,102 |
| | Samson. C. Leeds creamware cockle-pot and cover, 21 in. | 315 |
| | S. Pair of Whieldon pigeons, 7½ in. high   2 for | 2,000 |
| | Viscount Eccles. S. Pair of Prattware hawks, 6½ in. high 2 for | 1,100 |
| 1968 | Donahue. N.Y. Pair of Whieldon parrots, 6½ in. high 2 for | 1,893 |
| | Towner. S. Elaborate centrepiece of Leeds creamware, 25½ in. | 480 |
| | Wallach. S. Two Leeds pearlware stallions, c. 1820, 14½×16½ (compare 1967). 4 others were withdrawn from sale     1,000 and | 1,500 |
| | Busfield. S. Another, same dimensions | 1,350 |
| | Gollancz. S. Another, 15½ in. high | 550 |
| | C. Saltglaze teapot, pink ground, 6½ in. wide | 399 |
| | Slater. S. Lambeth 'blue dash' charger, figure of Queen Ann, marked A. R., 14 in. diam. (similar dish £300, 1956) | 1,200 |
| | Dublin blue and white tinglaze bowl with basket-pierced rim, c. 1760, 9 in. diam. | 600 |
| | S. Bristol three-colour tinglaze dish, ship and estuary, c. 1740, 13 in. diam. | 310 |
| | Gollancz. S. Whieldon saltglaze teapot, pierced sides in the Chinese style (Lung ling) 6 in. high | 1,600 |
| | Whieldon hexagonal teapot, figures in relief, 6¼ in. | 920 |
| | S. Creamware dish with view of Richmond, Wedgwood's Empress Catherine service, 1774, 19½ in. wide (8 guineas in 1936) | 2,400 |
| | Alcock. S. Dinner plate, Wedgwood's painted creamware, with view of ruined castle; from the Empress Catherine service, 1774, 10 in. diam., numbered 30 | 900 |

627

1969  Carver.  S.  Leeds pearlware stallion, sponged with blue,
16 in. high (compare 1968)                                    2,800
Westley.  S.  Tinglaze dinner plate in manganese and
blue, 8¾ in. diam., inscribed Wincanton, 1738, with arms of
Apothecaries' Company                                        1,250
S.  Ralph Wood, giant teapot in shape of elephant and
howdah; base 11 in. long                                     1,300
Parker.  S.  Liverpool tinglaze 'privateer' bowl, inscribed
'Success to the Tyger', c. 1748, 9½ in. diam.                 600
Allman.  S.  Bristol tinglaze posset pot and cover, 10 in.
wide, c. 1720                                                 500
C.  Coloured saltglaze equestrian figure of Hudibras by
Ralph Wood, 9 in. (see 1966)                             1,942 10s.
S.  Another Leeds stallion, 14½ in. high, in a horrid colour
described as pale chestnut                                    800
C.  Whieldon tortoiseshell ware teapot with busts and
trophies of King of Prussia, 8 in. wide                       714
Group of two lovers, Whieldon's mottled glaze after
Kaendler, 4¾ in. high                                     787 10s.
S.  Whieldon figure of trotting horse, 7¼ in. high         1,000
Ditto, Chinese boy on a water buffalo, 8½ in. long           650
Ralph Wood plaque, the drinkers, 8 in. high                  650
Two saltglaze plates in Kakiemon style, 8 in. diam.
2 for       560
C.  Staffordshire coloured teaparty group by Obadiah
Sherratt, c, 1820, 7¾ in. wide                                315
Cooper.  S.  Lambeth tinglaze barber's bowl with em-
blems of the trade, inscribed BH 1763, 10¼ in. (compare
1965)                                                       1,700
Loufte.  S.  Leeds pearlware stallion, 15¾ in., dun coloured  1,900
S.  Ralph Wood green and brown teapot in form of a
monkey riding an elephant, 11 in. wide                      1,550
Saltglaze coffee pot, polychrome rose sprays, 9 in.          700
Astbury coffee pot, brown slip decoration on cream
body, crabstock spout, 9¾ in. high                           470


*Wedgwood jasper and basaltes wares*

1956  The Portland Vase, perfect copy from the first series, 1791
(one similar in 1902, £399) see 1964, 1970                    480
1963  C.  Another Portland Vase                           1,417 10s.
1964  S.  Bust of Francis Bacon, 18 in. high, black basaltes   400
Bust of Grotius, 20 in. high, black basaltes                 320
Coulburn.  S.  Bust of Dr Fothergill, 18 in. high, black
basaltes                                                     280

| | | | £ |
|---|---|---|---|
| 1964 | S. Set of basalt ware medals after Hellenistic prototypes (see 1969) | 102 for | 700 |
| | C. Portland vase, copy from the first series (compare, 1956, 1963, 1970) | | 3,045 |
| 1966 | C. Urn and cover, nearly 16 in. high, black basaltes | | 672 |
| 1967 | S. Agate ware, urn and cover, 19½ in. | | 440 |
| | Earl of Feversham. C. Urn and cover, jasper and cream-ware, 18½ in. | | 441 |
| | Eckman. S. Bust of Abraham Lincoln, 1860s, black basaltes, 16½ in. high with plinth | | 700 |
| | C. Two 10-inch basalt ware figures of the Seasons | 2 for | 399 |
| 1968 | Dearden. S. Set of 47 blue ground jasper ware wall-plaques, total length 82 ft, thought to be late 19th century | 47 for | 4,400 |
| 1969 | Drayton. S. The Neptune and Bacchus wine vases, black basaltes after Flaxman, 16 in. | 2 for | 430 |
| | C. Pair of two-handled urns with putti in relief, black basalt ware 9¾ in. high | 2 for | 1,155 |
| | Single two handled urn, creamware relief on marbled tortoiseshell ground 10¾ in. high | | 756 |
| | C. Set of basalt ware medallions after Hellenistic prototypes (£700 in 1964) | 102 for | 3,984 |
| | Portrait medallion, King of Sweden, blue and white jasper ware, 4 in. high | | 735 |
| | S. Graecian frieze-plaque in brown jasper cameo ware, Sacrifice to Love, 23¾ in. long | | 700 |
| | 'Sacred to Bacchus', wine vase in black basaltes after Flaxman, 16 in. high | | 280 |
| | Oblong blue jasper cameo plaque, the Birth of Bacchus, stamped Wedgwood and Bentley, 14¾ × 5¾ | | 780 |
| | Pair of Medici ewers, black basaltes, stamped Wedgwood and Bentley, 9½ in. high | 2 for | 680 |
| 1970 | C. Portland vase, unnumbered trial-piece on black ground (compare 1956, 1963, 1964) | | 2,940 |

# POTTERY AND FAIENCE, EUROPEAN
## FRANCE AND FLANDERS
(including Palissy and Henri Deux ware which were listed separately in vol. II)

*Faïence fine* which could reproduce all the beauty of a soft paste porcelain surface and which could be worked into the same intricate rococo contour even to the solid naturalistic flowers, was never achieved in 18th century England. Hence none of those big tureens which are the prizes of the faience market. In 1968 the ex King of Italy's truly regal Meissen porcelain tureen painted by Höroldt, achieved £12,600, but even a Brussels faience tureen in the less exalted form of a frog sitting on a cabbage was good for £8,214. There are consequently many tureens in this list of the most expensive French and Flemish faience objects which were sold in the 1960s. There are other objects which have fared less well. Examples of the once popular Palissy ware figure *la nourrice*, made no more than £440 and £260 in 1961 and 1963 and at that they are still the dearest Palissy since 1946. Apart from the decline in the taste for the fruity High Renaissance, Palissy ware was copied in the mid-19th century on such an enormous scale that everyone is scared of it, so that a good group, sold in 1967, made no more than in 1884. The standing salt of S Porchaire ware, sold in 1965, is a still more remarkable case, being the first example of this ware to appear in the saleroom in 13 years—and likely to be the last, since the 38 other known examples have all been frozen off the market. At £3,800 the price was less in true money terms than the £780, at which it had last changed hands in 1899. On paper it was almost the same price as that paid by Gustave de Rothschild for the magnificent *flambeau* of the 1884 Fountaine sale, which would be equivalent in 1967 to £27,000 at least. But bring on the Dorothy Doughty birds!

| | | £ |
|---|---|---|
| 1961 | S. Palissy ware figure, *la nourrice*, Avon period, early 17th century | 440 |
| | Paris. Large Rouen dish *en camaïeu bleu, c.* 1700, FN40,000 +tax | 3,630 |
| | Topic. S. Strasbourg (Hannong) polychrome figure of Harlequin, 14½ in. high, *c.* 1760 | 2,100 |
| 1962 | C. Pair of large faience lions, Lunéville, 18th century | 1,050 |
| | Igo Levy. Munich. Moustiers oval cistern, 32 in. wide, *c.* 1690 | 565 |
| 1963 | S. Palissy figure, *la nourrice* (compare 1961) | 260 |
| | Fribourg. S. Sceaux cabbage tureen, faience fine, *c.* 1750, 15 in. | 550 |
| | Niederviller tureen, cover and stand, *c.* 1755 | 1,155 |
| | Brussels tureen by Monbaers in form of a drake | 3,200 |
| | Pair of Strasbourg tureens with eagle handles 2 for | 2,400 |
| | Sceaux tureen and stand in Vincennes style | 2,800 |

1963 Fribourg. S. Pair of Marseilles tureens in form of pigeons £
1,200 and 1,000
Strasbourg tureen by Lanz in form of a duck with
stand 5,700

1964 S. Pair of Rouen armorial ewers, blue and white, 21½ in.,
c. 1720 2 for 1,150
Sceaux tureen in form of a duck, 12 × 15½ with stand 1,400
Rouen blue and white armorial dish, c. 1730, 18¾ in.
diam. 950

1965 Mme Ancel. S. Hexagonal salt, *Henri deux* or *St
Porchaire* ware, c. 1550 (£780 in 1899) 3,800
S. Strasbourg figure of Gilles after Watteau, coloured
*faïence fine*, 13 in. 3,600

1966 S. White ware version of the same, 13 in. damaged (a
third example, damaged, made £340 in 1968) 650
C. Pair of Lunéville lions, 18 in. wide (compare 1962) 787 10s.
Dinner service, unknown factory, late 18th century
52 for 2,730

1967 Mackintosh. S. Group, late 16th century Palissy ware.
Christ and the woman of Samaria (£105 in 1884, £24 in
1940) 115
Winston Guest. N.Y. Strasbourg tureen, 8¾ in. high, in
form of a woodcock, $15,000 at 2·40 6,250
Paris. Fish-dish, Veuve Perrin, Marseille, FN6,300+tax 612
Fischer, Lucerne. Rouen pitcher in Majolica style by
Abaquesnes Masseot, c. 1550, 8¼ in. high, FS16,500+tax 1,785

1968 Paris. Rouen polychrome dish, arms of St Evremond,
10 in. diam., FN29,000+tax 2,645
Rouen polychrome octagonal platter, 16 in. diam.,
FN25,000+tax 2,360
Rouen blue and ochre dish, 9¾ in. diam., FN42,000+
tax 3,932
Donahue. N.Y. Sinceny asparagus box, c. 1775, 11¾ in.
wide, $3,000 1,250
Sceaux tureen in form of a rooster, repaired, 17½ in.
long, $6,000 2,135
Sceaux tureen in form of a duck, repaired, 11½ in. long 4,643
Brussels tureen and stand in form of a cabbage and
frog, 15½ in. long, $23,000 8,214
White tureen in form of a duck, unknown French
factory, c. 1780, 16½ in. long, $6,500 2,321
Strasbourg tureen in form of a duck, repaired, 13 in.
long (compare 1963), $12,500 4,465
Vanderbilt-Balsan C. Another similar, 13½ in. long 2,520

| 1968 | Prince de Ligne.  S.  Brussels tureen in form of a turkey, 15½ in. long | £ 3,400 |
| | S.  Pair of Brussels (Monbaers) mottled duck tureens, 12¼ in. long | 2 for 1,250 |
| 1969 | C.  Marseilles tureen, Veuve Perrin, 14½ in. wide | 1,995 |
| | Brussels tortoise tureen, brown and yellow, 12½ in. wide | 1,470 |
| | Duck tureen, 12 in. wide, Brussels, Monbaers | 1,050 |
| | Nove (N. Italy) faience dinner service painted with fruit and flowers in French style | 74 for 3,400 |
| | C.  Sceaux duck tureen, 12 in. wide | 1,995 |
| | Marseille tureen and cover, Veuve Perrin, 17 in. wide | 1,995 |
| | Paris.  Moustiers water jug, FN22,000+tax | 2,053 |

# POTTERY AND FAIENCE, EUROPEAN
## GERMANY AND CENTRAL EUROPE

The saltglaze stoneware of the 16th and 17th centuries enjoyed a vogue by no means confined to Germany in the late 19th and early 20th century. Under the name of *grés de Flandre*, the earlier wares were patriotically adopted by Belgium and were not incompatible with Parisian taste. As early as 1886, a very rare Siegburg vase made £716, the equivalent of close on £6,000 in 1970 money. During the First World War German collectors were paying the present equivalent of £8,000 to £16,500 for specially important Raeren and Hafner ware specimens. But, very soon afterwards, distaste for the High Renaissance, particularly in its Germanic manifestations, made itself felt. Between the early 1920s and the late 1950s there was no market at all for German stoneware. Nor has a subsequent recovery gone very far. Good 16th century pieces are singularly shy of the saleroom. The best prices, such as they are, seem to be paid mainly for mounted 17th century Kreussen tankards in polychrome enamels.

German stoneware has in fact become a poor relation of German tinglaze faience of the 18th century, though the latter was produced at an immense number of factories, extending from Denmark to Rumania. Dutch and French styles were freely imitated, and attempts were made to rival the effects of porcelain. The *faience fine* of the Höchst factory is dearer than its porcelain, the prices of Zeschinger's paired birds in the Meissen and Chinese styles being particularly notable. The jugs and tankards of South Germany, painted in *Hausmalerei* by such excellent artists as Schaper, Helmhack and Seuter, probably multiplied their value three times in the course of the 1960s, but they are very seldom seen. The biggest advances were among the commonest wares, such as the blue and white Delft ware, made by immigrant Dutch potters at Frankfurt and Hanau from the 1660s onwards. Their general value may have multiplied more than ten times since the late 1950s.

*Stoneware* (for mounted pieces, see also Silver, English before 1660)

| | | | £ |
|---|---|---|---|
| 1962 | Igo Levi, Munich. Pair of Hafner ware stove tiles, forming niches with figures in high relief of the Duke and Duchess of Landshut, *c.* 1550, DM30,000+tax | 2 for | 3,256 |
| | Lempertz, Cologne. Kreussen apostle tankard, pewter mounts dated 1689; with tax | | 240 |
| | Siegburg *Schnelle* by Hans Hilgers, 1580, the sacrifice of Isaac; with tax | | 370 |
| | Siegburg armorial Schnelle, *c.* 1570, undated | | 103 |
| 1964 | Mrs. Maclean. S. Kreussen apostle tankard, 1662 | | 240 |
| | Kreussen 'planets' tankard, 1668 | | 160 |
| | Weinmüller, Munich. Kreussen apostle screw-flask, | | |

£

| | | |
|---|---|---|
| 1964 | pewter stopper dated 1670; with tax | 324 |
| | Hunting tankard, dated 1726 on the mount, 5 in. high | 165 |
| 1965 | S. Kreussen 'planets' tankard with parcelgilt mount, 7 in. | 320 |
| 1967 | Lord Wharton. C. Kreussen apostle tankard, 1662, silvergilt mounts made for D. of Sussex, 1838 (£15 4s. 6d. in 1843) | 441 |
| | Second Kreussen apostle tankard, mounted in 1831 £22 6s. 6d. in 1843), same date | 399 |
| | Cunningham. S. Kreussen tankard, no figures, Scandinavian silver lid, c. 1690 | 260 |
| | C. Raeren elector tankard, 11 in. high, undated but early 17th century | 210 |
| 1969 | S. Siegburg ewer, dated 1593, German silver lid and grip, 10¼ in. high (compare 2 Siegburg tankards with English mounts in section, *Silver, English, before 1660, mounted pieces*) | 360 |

*Tinglaze and Faïence fine*

| | | |
|---|---|---|
| 1961 | Blohm. S. Pair of Höchst *faïence fine* parrots by Zeschinger, 15 in. high    2 for | 3,000 |
| | Pair of Höchst *faïence fine* wall-sconces, 29 in. | 1,900 |
| 1962 | Igo Levy, Munich. Nuremburg tankard, *Hausmalerei* by Schmerzenreich, c. 1720, parcelgilt lid and mounts | 1,628 |
| | *Hausmalerei* tankard after Teniers | 748 |
| | Schrezheim épergne-candelabrum | 1,056 |
| | Schrezheim candlestick, supported by a Moor | 836 |
| | Ansbach dish, c. 1735, in *famille verte* style | 1,028 |
| | Bayreuth *Hausmalerei* tankard, hunting scene | 700 |
| | Nuremberg ewer by Helmhack, c. 1720, 13 in. high (see 1967) | 1,052 |
| | Nuremberg *Hausmalerei* tankard, painted by Schmerzenreich, 1715, 10 in. | 1,930 |
| | Globular vase, Höchst, by André Ludwig, 1749, 8¾ in. | 978 |
| | Nuremberg *Hausmalerei* tankard, signed MS, 1700 | 888 |
| | Höchst figure of a galloping hussar, 7 in. high | 892 |
| 1964 | Munich. Pair of Hollitsch tureens in shape of sitting hens    2 for | 1,670 |
| 1965 | Hutton. S. Höchst faience figure of a jay | 5,200 |
| | Höchst parrot group by Zeschinger | 4,600 |
| 1966 | Spencer, Retford. Pair of puce-coloured tankards, parcelgilt lids and mounts, factory unknown    2 for | 2,000 |
| | S. *Enghalskrug*, Nuremberg, with *Hausmalerei* by Bartolomaeus Seuter, c. 1720, 9¾ in. high | 1,700 |
| | Greenish-brown monkey ewer, Proskau, 10½ in. high (see 1967) | 380 |

| | | £ |
|---|---|---|
| 1966 | C. White figure, imitating *blanc de Chine* Kuan Yin, Ansbach | 399 |
| | Winterthur plaque by H. Pfauw, 11×9, dated 1675 | 546 |
| 1967 | Fischer, Lucerne. Hollitsch tureen in shape of a frog, 14×9×3¾, FS51,000+tax | 5,540 |
| | Stuker, Berne. Pair of Lenzburg arbour groups, 8 in. wide, FS18,000+tax 2 for | 1,960 |
| | Weinmüller, Munich. Nuremberg *Reformationsplatte*, depicting Luther and the Kurfurst of Saxony, *c.* 1730, 14 in. diam., DM12,000+tax | 1,265 |
| | *Enghalskrug*, Nuremberg with *Hausmalerei* painting by Abraham Helmhack, *c.* 1720 (see 1962), DM20,000+tax | 2,006 |
| | Buchanan. S. Proskau ewer in form of a monkey, 10 in. (see 1966) | 380 |
| | C. Blue and white armorial winecooler in form of a mitre, 13 in. high, Kiel or Schleswig | 1,785 |
| 1968 | Vanderbilt-Balsan. C. Höchst basket-shaped tureen, 13 in. long | 1,575 |
| 1969 | S. Stockelsdorf pot-pourri jar and cover, painted after Teniers, much damaged, 16¾ in. high | 360 |
| | Lord Chesham. C. Oviform vase in colours, Frankfurt or Hanau, *c.* 1670, 18½ in. high, damaged neck | 525 |
| | S. Nuremberg *Enghalskrug* with landscape *Hausmalerei* by Johann Schaper before 1670, 9 in. high | 3,200 |
| | C. Pair of Hollitsch duck-shaped ewers, 9¾ in. wide 2 for | 1,155 |
| | Höchst partridge tureen and cover, 12 in. wide | 945 |
| | van Zuylen. S. Called Netherlands but probably Nuremberg, Pewter-mounted pitcher in Majolica style, Sacrifice of Isaac, dated 1570, the mount 1571, 10 in. high | 3,800 |
| | S. Garniture of three urns, and covers, *faïence fine* in painted relief, attributed to Kiel, 17 and 14½ in. 3 for | 2,100 |

# POTTERY AND FAIENCE, EUROPEAN
## HOLLAND
### Tinglaze pottery, made mainly at Delft

The adaptation of the Chinese late Ming blue-and-white style in European tinglaze pottery has been attributed to Delft for so long a time that the name of this town has come to denote, not only all blue and white decoration, but virtually all European tinglaze outside Spain and Italy. In fact the influence of Chinese blue and white is to be found at Lambeth and Hamburg almost a generation before it reached the Delft potters. This legend of primacy may have helped in the early years of the century to give the wares, made at Delft, a much higher rating then they enjoy today. As one instance, a pair of Delft jars and covers, imitating Japanese export Imari porcelain in polychrome enamels, was sold in Paris in 1911 for 35,000 francs plus tax, the equivalent in 1970 of more than £12,000, an almost unthinkable price. Then in 1917 Duveen sold privately a remarkable pair of large polychrome dishes for £5,000, which with all allowance for wartime inflation should represent £25,000 at least. was always the polychrome wares, particularly *Delft doré*, which attracted the highest prices. As late as 1936, a rich garniture made £730 (£3,650) but the long market decline had begun. There was hardly any recovery before the 1960s. In spite of the great charm of the painting, the habitually lace-like effect of Delft designs was even then by no means popular, but there was some extremely patriotic Dutch buying in 1968.

|      |                                                                                                 | £      |
|------|-------------------------------------------------------------------------------------------------|--------|
| 1961 | N.Y. Fountain, early 18th century, drinker astride a barrel in colours                           | 536    |
|      | Double-gourd bottle, Aelbrecht de Keyser                                                         | 375    |
|      | Bough-vase, Cornelis de Keyser                                                                   | 321    |
|      | Pair of blue and white jugs in form of figures         2 for                                    | 536    |
|      | Pair of octagonal covered jars, 'Cachemire' decoration                                           | 429    |
| 1963 | S.  Pair of polychrome jugs in form of monkeys         2 for                                     | 320    |
|      | Oval polychrome tray, 22½ in. wide, Chinoiserie style, *Delft doré*                              | 250    |
| 1964 | S.  Pair of polychrome cockerels                       2 for                                     | 1,900  |
|      | Polychrome dish with Chinese procession in *Famille Verte* style                                | 1,200  |
|      | Two pairs of candlesticks, *Delft doré*, mark of Pieter Adriaenus Koeks, 2 for £650 and   2 for | 680    |
| 1967 | van Waay, Amsterdam. Four butter-boxes and covers, surmounted by figures of the Four Seasons, polychrome, mark of *de Porceleyne Bijl*, 6¾ in. high, Hfl 5,000+tax      4 for | 1,940  |
|      | Donahue. N.Y. Pair of rabbit-shaped tureens by Lambartus Sanderus, mark of *de Klauw*, c. 1760, 7 in. high, $1,700      2 for | 792    |

£

1968   van Waay, Amsterdam.   Garniture of five covered jars and beakers, 'Cachemire' pattern, 10½ and 8 in. high, Hfl13,000 + tax                                 1,680

      S.   Oval portrait-plaque after an engraving in blue and white, Queen Anne, 1704, wrongly attributed to Lambeth   1,000

             Tulip vase, blue and white, 13 in. high, AK mark       450

             Pair of oviform *Delft doré* jars and covers Pynaker mark, 14¼ in. high                            2 for   340

      Dormeuil.   Paris.   Ewer and basin, Delft doré, 'red A' mark, FN37,000 + tax                     2 for   3,497

             Pair of dishes with warriors in *famille verte* style, polychrome, by Rochus Hoppstein, FN37,000 + tax   2 for   4,989

1969   Bexfield.   S.   Inscribed dish, 'Sert God', Netherlands majolica, *c.* 1600–25, 12¾ in. diam.                    500

# PRIMITIVE ART
## AFRICA, AMERICA, OCEANIA

I do not know how many of those Benin bronze heads there are in the world, sitting-up in their simulated wicker collars. Since they never fail to make an appearance once or twice a year, their rarity is not exceptional. Variety is almost non-existent, and, as to antiquity, it is anyone's guess. With so many disadvantages, there remains their fascination. Few kinds of *objets d'art* in the more expensive class have advanced as fast. From the region of £400–£500 in 1930 they fell below £100 in the great slump. In 1952 a collared head was sold for £720, but the big movement began only in the 1960s, from £2,800 in 1961 to £4,300 in 1965 and £8,000 in 1968, then suddenly at the end of that year to £21,000. In about the same progression miniature bronze belt-masks rose from £180 in 1954 to £280 in 1962 and £4,000 in 1968.

With all that, Benin bronze represents the more conservative taste in African art and sells best in London. For those who want African art that approaches closer to classical serenity, there is the famous Benin bronze queen in the pointed head-dress which made £5,500 in 1954 and might be worth £40,000 or £50,000 in 1970. In a sense this is not the real *primitive* taste. In the more heady climate of New York the most savage-looking objects of wood, which make the bronze heads seem quite stodgy, can reach $30,000. Furthermore, while beauty and subtlety are to be found in many of the wooden figures and masks, the highest prices appear deliberately to avoid these qualities, as if the ambition of the buyers was chiefly to shock. Like all *avant-garde* manifestations which have met with universal and almost compulsory acceptance in the course of sixty years, the ambition to shock is already old-hat. In the first quarter of the century it was still possible to believe that the example of Africa might revitalize the moribund artistic traditions of Europe. No one can think so any longer. The tribal fetishes have in reality gone back to their old status of ethnographic exhibits—but very expensive ones. American pre-Columbian antiquities, the best of which are sold in New York, might be expected to inspire even wilder saleroom fantasies, but the build-up of this market is fairly recent. In the first quarter of this century they lacked the stimulus of the enthusiasm which African sculpture provoked among artists and their propagandists. There are, moreover, so few pre-Columbian objects, which are situated between the extremes of scraps of unglazed pottery and masses of monumental stone, as to restrict the demand mainly to museums with little competition from private collectors. Still more recent is the market for art of the Pacific, the wildest market of all. It would need something more than tolerance to find aesthetic merit in the images from New Ireland. One does not know whether these extraordinary prices express the belated *épatisme* of American collectors, or simply the high price of scarce *ethnographica* among competing museum directors. The former want to keep them with their Picassos, the latter with instructive maps and models of tribal settlements.

## AFRICA

|  |  | £ |
|---|---|---|
| 1960 | Hauswedel. Hamburg. Gold mask, Gold Coast | 340 |
|  | Kasai ivory mask (Congo) | 305 |
|  | Allman. S. Ivory mask, perfect condition, Benin, 10 in. high | 6,200 |
|  | Ivory standing figure, 21 in. Benin | 1,800 |
|  | Carved ivory tusk, Benin, 6 ft long | 950 |
|  | Another, 4 ft 4 in. long | 450 |
|  | S. Ijaw wood figure, Niger delta. Museum, Primitive Art, N.Y. | 640 |
|  | Ibibio wood figure, S. Nigeria. Museum, Primitive Art, N.Y. | 500 |
|  | Trustees of British Museum. S. Bronze Benin warrior plaque | 900 |
| 1961 | Searle. S. Benin bronze head of an Oba, 10 in. high | 2,800 |
|  | S. 18-inch female head of an Oba, 10 in. high | 1,900 |
|  | 14-inch bronze Benin plaque with executioner group | 1,300 |
|  | Two 16-inch figures of warriors, Benin bronze     each | 1,200 |
|  | 15-inch bronze Benin plaque, single figure | 1,400 |
|  | Pair of gold figurines of lions, Ashanti, 2 in. long (2) | 980 |
| 1962 | S. Benin bronze head in choker collar, 9 in. high | 3,000 |
|  | Another, 13½ in. high | 1,350 |
|  | Standard Benin bronze belt-mask, 7 in. high (compare 1968) | 280 |
| 1963 | S. Benin bronze head, 8½ in. high, lacks collar | 2,000 |
| 1964 | Paul Rose. S. 20-inch bronze Benin plaque, chief with two attendants | 5,000 |
|  | Another, same size | 3,000 |
| 1965 | Gaze. S. Ivory Benin leopard mask | 3,500 |
|  | Benin bronze head, choker collar | 4,300 |
|  | Stoclet. S. Ivory double figurine. N.W. Congo | 1,100 |
|  | S. 17-inch bronze Benin plaque, two warriors | 3,600 |
|  | Benin bronze figure, warrior with flintlock, 20 in. high | 4,200 |
|  | Benin female head, pointed head-dress, bronze | 4,000 |
|  | Benin bronze tortoise | 2,800 |
|  | Benin bronze female head, plaits and ringlets | 2,800 |
|  | Dogon wood figure, 6 ft high | 2,500 |
| 1966 | S. Benin bronze warrior plaque, 18¾ × 12 | 2,000 |
|  | Benin bronze warrior plaque, 17¼ × 11 | 2,600 |
|  | Mornington. S. Baluba wooden stool, 22½ in. | 1,020 |
|  | Helena Rubinstein. N.Y. Bambara dance head-dress, 57 in. | 8,570 |
|  | Fang wooden head from Oyen region, $24,000 | 8,570 |

£

| | |
|---|---|
| 1966   Bakongo figure, 11 in., $22,000 | 7,860 |
| Bangwa wooden figure of a woman, $33\frac{1}{2}$ in., $29,000 | 10,350 |
| Senufo wooden figure of a woman, 36 in., $27,000 | 9,640 |
| Dengese wooden figure of a king, $21\frac{1}{2}$ in., $14,500 | 5,180 |
| Bena-Lulua figure, 20 in., $10,000 | 3,570 |
| Paris.   Bakuba wooden dance-mask, Congo, FN36,000+ tax | 2,915 |
| 1967   Leff.   N.Y.   Benin bronze warrior-plaque, $21 \times 14\frac{1}{2}$ | 5,710 |
| Nelson Rockefeller.   N.Y.   Bambara wooden figure, nursing child, $46\frac{1}{2}$ in. high, $10,000 | 3,570 |
| Olmer.   S.   Bakota wooden figure, $22\frac{1}{2}$ in. | 1,900 |
| Walker.   S.   Fragmentary bronze warrior plaque, Benin, $18\frac{1}{2} \times 20\frac{3}{4}$ | 3,000 |
| Wilson.   S.   Mayumba wooden nail-fetish | 3,000 |
| Wooden shoulder mask, Baga tribes, Guinea | 2,800 |
| S.   Ashanti gold necklace, $4\frac{1}{2}$ oz. | 1,600 |
| Ashanti gold disc, fine relief, 7 oz. 12 dwt. | 2,600 |
| 1968   S.   Benin bronze warrior plaque with two bearded Europeans, $16 \times 14\frac{1}{2}$ | 11,000 |
| Benin bronze head in wicker collar, $10\frac{1}{2}$ in. high | 8,000 |
| Benin bronze head in wicker collar, $15\frac{3}{4}$ in. high | 7,000 |
| Baluba (Congo) wooden helmet-mask, with horns, $20\frac{3}{4}$ in. high | 8,000 |
| S.   Bambala (Congo) ivory staff finial, $8\frac{3}{4}$ in. | 3,500 |
| Two Bakongo wooden nail-fetishes, $31\frac{3}{4}$ and $29\frac{1}{2}$ in. high | 2,800 |
| Dan wooden mask and fibre wig, Ivory Coast, 18 in. high | 2,000 |
| Benin bronze plaque with single warrior, $18\frac{3}{4} \times 12\frac{1}{2}$ | 4,500 |
| Benin bronze belt-mask, 7 in. high (compare 1962) | 4,000 |
| Benin bronze plaque with two warriors, $19\frac{1}{2} \times 13\frac{1}{2}$ | 5,200 |
| Banks.   S.   Bakongo nail-fetish, upper half only, $19\frac{1}{4}$ in. | 1,900 |
| Hope.   C.   Benin bronze head, wicker collar, $9\frac{1}{4}$ in. high | 21,000 |
| 1969   C.   Benin bronze belt-mask, $7\frac{3}{4}$ in. high | 682 10s. |
| Fang wooden male 'Beiri' figure, 20 in. high | 1,365 |
| Pretty.   S.   Single warrior, fragment of Benin bronze plaque, 17 in. high | 2,000 |
| Christophe Tsara.   S.   Dogon wooden equestrian figure, incomplete, $16\frac{1}{2}$ in. high | 1,050 |
| Leather reliquary box, Fang tribes of Gaboon, $18\frac{1}{4}$ in. high | 1,000 |
| Snow.   C.   Kuba wooden male figure from the Kongolo region, 11 in. high | 1,575 |
| St Barbe Baker.   S.   Benin bronze figure with choker collar, clasping sword, 16 in. high | 7,200 |

|      |                                                                                                   | £     |
|------|---------------------------------------------------------------------------------------------------|-------|
| 1962 | S.   Aztec gold jaguar, 6 in. long                                                                | 720   |
|      | Aztec gold monkey, $3\frac{1}{2} \times 2\frac{1}{2}$                                              | 620   |
|      | Aztec double-idol pendant, $4\frac{1}{4} \times 6\frac{1}{4}$                                      | 580   |
| 1964 | S.   Gold seated figure, Quimbaya civilization, Colombia                                           | 1,500 |
| 1966 | Charles Laughton.   N.Y.   Tarascan clay head-jar, $9\frac{1}{2}$ in. high, $2,700                 | 960   |
|      | Tarascan pottery seated figure, 22 in. $2,800                                                      | 1,000 |
|      | Tarascan pottery figure, $15\frac{1}{2}$ in. high, $2,600                                          | 929   |
|      | Kwakiutl grave marker, British Columbia, $37\frac{3}{4}$ in. wide                                  | 786   |
|      | Mixtec onyx effigy bowl, 18 in. high $4,000                                                        | 1,429 |
|      | N.Y.   Chiapas (Maya) stele, $68\frac{1}{4}$ in., $4,500                                           | 1,605 |
|      | Hauswedel, Hamburg.   Quimbaya gold figure, Colombia, $2\frac{3}{4}$ in., DM6,800+tax              | 712   |
|      | S.   Tlingit chief's head-dress, British Columbia, $19\frac{1}{2}$ in.                             | 800   |
|      | N.Y.   Veraguas (Panama), spread-eagle gold pectoral ornament, $5\frac{1}{4}$ in. high, $5,500    | 1,980 |
| 1968 | Olsen.   N.Y.   Maya stone stele from Peten, 71 in.                                                | 3,750 |
|      | Maya stone bat-god from Copan, $24\frac{1}{2}$ in., $5,000                                         | 2,618 |
|      | Frumkin.   N.Y.   Kwakiutl *Potlatch* figure, Vancouver Island, 55 in., $6,500                     | 2,708 |
|      | Teotihuacan stone mask, under 5-in high, $3,000                                                    | 1,250 |
|      | Chimu gold beaker, 7-in. high                                                                      | 1,250 |
|      | Remojadas clay figure, 24-in. high, $3,100                                                         | 1,292 |
|      | C.   Chimu (Peruvian) gold necklace of 8 anthropor-morphic plaques                                 | 1,785 |
|      | S.   Tlingit wooden frontal plate.   Pacific North West                                            | 1,350 |
|      | Huaxtec stone figure of an old man                                                                 | 1,300 |
|      | Aztec squatting stone male deity, $25\frac{1}{2}$ in.                                              | 4,800 |
|      | Inca shroud or *manta* from Paracas, 93 in. long                                                   | 2,000 |
|      | Group of fragments, Inca shroud or *manta* from Paracas, 102 in. long                              | 1,800 |
|      | de Batz.   N.Y.   Mexican East coast clay figure, Maya period, 11 in. high, $2,500                 | 1,041 |
| 1969 | Kilroy.   C.   Haida (North West coast) wooden food dish, $13\frac{3}{4} \times 11\frac{1}{2}$     | 1,365 |
|      | Teed.   S.   Tlingit wood mask, $6\frac{1}{2}$ in., Pacific North West                             | 1,600 |
|      | N.Y.   Pottery male figure, 16 in high, East Coast of Mexico, $4,500                               | 1,875 |
|      | Pottery, standing priest, $17\frac{1}{4}$ in. $2,400                                               | 1,000 |
|      | Panamanian gold (Veraguas), spread eagle pectoral ornament, $6\frac{3}{4}$ in. high (compare 1967), $5,000 | 2,082 |

£

| | | |
|---|---|---|
| 1969 | N.Y.  Inca feather banner, time of the conquest, 30×75, $5,400 | 2,249 |
| | Mayan limestone stele, 72 in. high, $6,500 | 2,708 |
| | Mayan stucco head, 11 in. high, $3,750 | 1,562 |

### OCEANIA

| | | |
|---|---|---|
| 1960 | Archdale.  S.  New Zealand greenstone Tiki, 9½ in. high, the largest recorded | 850 |
| 1961 | S.  Hawaiian bone figure, 2 in. high | 780 |
| 1963 | S.  New Guinea coral-wood stool | 820 |
| | Easter Island amulet figure | 420 |
| 1964 | S.  New Zealand jade Heitiki | 620 |
| | Fish-mouth drum, Torres straits, New Guinea | 730 |
| 1966 | S.  Maori wooden house-post figure, dated 1869 | 640 |
| 1967 | S.  Another fish-mouth drum (see 1964) | 500 |
| | Bearnes auctioneers, Torquay.  Carved wooden Kava bowl on bearer figures, Hawaii, 17½ in. wide | 15,000 |
| | Heinrich.  N.Y.  Wooden figure, 54½ in., New Ireland | 4,647 |
| | Ditto, 60 in. | 2,500 |
| | Coloured and carved wood panels, New Ireland | { 2,680 / 2,590 |
| | Rockefeller.  N.Y.  New Ireland Uli figure, 63½ in. | 1,429 |
| 1968 | S.  Wooden totem pole from the Marquesas islands, 90¾ in. | 5,000 |
| | Easter Island wood male figure, 8 in. high | 2,000 |
| | Maori wooden head with spiral tattooing.  New Zealand, 6¼ in. | 1,700 |
| | Ditto, complete figure, 44½ in. high | 3,000 |
| | Roberts.  C.  Wooden *tiki* from Tahiti, 9 in. high | 682 10s. |
| 1969 | C.  Maori canoe figurehead, carved wood, 21×17 | 7,875 |
| | Astbury.  C.  Maori canoe stern-piece, pierced wood-work, 17 in. | 1,470 |
| | Warwick Castle.  S.  Wooden figure, Hawaii, fibre hair, 10¼ in. | 12,000 |
| | Olsen.  N.Y.  Tahitian wood fly-whisk handle, 7¾ in. | 1,354 |
| | New Ireland *totak* or fetish pole, 59 in., $7,500 | 3,125 |
| | S.  Hawaian stick-god on wooden spike, 23½ in. high | 6,200 |
| | Hawaian wooden weapon, armed with sharks' teeth, 30 in. | 1,300 |

# SILVER

Silver plate in the 1960s was one of the most publicized of markets and at the same time the least understood. Because at the height of each sales-season hardly a week went past without a 'record' price, blazoned in the press, silver was regarded as the best speculation of all. In reality there were many sorts of *objets d'art* that advanced more rapidly. Again silver was regarded as specially expensive, compared with craftsmanship in other materials. In fact gilt-bronze in the same styles could sometimes be quite as dear. Then too, because much of this expensive silver plate looked familiar, unexciting and even commonplace, it was believed that there was far too much of it about to justify the price. In 1969 there was even some recession in the duller sort of English 18th century domestic silver. But in fact there were cogent reasons why there should never be enough silver plate of respectable age to satisfy the demand, and why towards the end of the decade the silver of baser periods should prove so easy to promote in its place.

Silver and gold are the most durable of metals in domestic use, unsusceptible to the diseases and decay of iron and bronze. They are also the most convenient metals from which to eat and drink, so that silver as the lower priced metal, was used at table by all who could afford it, prior to the cheap manufacture of hard-wearing ceramics. If all this unbreakable and virtually undeteriorating plate had survived, there would be enough left of the 17th and 18th centuries to bring it within the reach of modest means even today. But at all times and even within human memory it has been the fate of most silver plate to pass into the melting pot. Formerly, when a piece of plate was ordered, that part of the price which was due to the workmanship or 'fashion' became as good as irrecoverable, once it had been delivered. No one, when forced to part with his plate, expected more than a melting-down price. Plate was melted down not only as a contribution to the cost of war, as in the ages of Charles I, Louis XIV, and the French Revolution; it was also melted down—and right into the present century—simply because the design was out of fashion: It is the fate of all work of human hands to provoke displeasure at one time or another. The aesthetic creed of the common man is as simple as this. 'Of course I know nothing about art, but I know what I dislike.'

The discovery of a style, the creation of a market boom, both these begin with the weakening of a prejudice. Early in the 19th century some of the older silver began to advance from second-hand or melting-down status to the mildly antiquarian. Not of course the most recent. At the Duke of York's sale in 1827 a vast ornate cistern which had lately been ordered for £1,500, was sold at 11s. an ounce and made £446 6s. 6d. Such monstrosities are now regarded with the tolerance of a permissive society and have been known to fetch as much as £20 an ounce. But fairly recently their fate was dismal indeed. In the 1930s, when the bullion-price of silver was the lowest since the Middle Ages, one of these huge early 19th century contraptions was about to be knocked down at 1s. 9d. an ounce. And there was the stranger who raised the bid to half-a-crown and who thought that he had bought a four-foot *surtout de table* for this price.

In the late 1960s there were the frailest snippets of silver which reached very high prices, for instance a plain wine cup of 1662, weighing only 2 oz. 14 dwt, at £2,100. Yet, even then, larger pieces most definitely cost more according to their size, a hangover from the custom of selling by the ounce which died in 1941, having lasted at least since the Roman Empire. Selling a work of art as if it were cheese was only rational so long as the bullion was at least as valuable as the workmanship, ludicrous when the bullion represented a minute fraction. The most expensive silver lot to be sold since the Second World War is still the Berkeley Castle dinner service at £207,000 in 1960. Yet the bullion value of that three-quarter ton of silver plate accounted for hardly more than 4 per cent of the price at the rate of the day. In the case of gold plate there is very little, older than the 19th century, which has avoided the melting pot, so the *mystique* of gold has created prices out of all proportion to the craftsmanship and still more out of proportion to the value of the bullion. In 1967 a bullet-shaped teapot of 1736 was sold for £40,000. At the official price before the November devaluation, the gold was worth no more than £263 16s., yet the same teapot, had it been made of silver, would have been worth less than £1,000. Similarly in December, 1969, a little porringer and cover of the year 1671 made £37,000. The gold was worth less than £325 but the value of the object had it been made of silver might have been £3,000 or £4,000 at the most.

## CONTINENTAL, BEFORE 1660

It may well be imagined that Augsburg and Nuremberg silver of the 16th and early 17th centuries, monumental, smothered with scrolls, caryatids and monsters, was the dream of the rich collector in the mid-Victorian period. In fact the Rothschild dynasty, whose first artistic acquisitions were of this kind, prolonged the tradition of collecting High Renaissance silver into the present century. The sums which they spent become incredible when translated into the paper currency of 1970. Perhaps one should discount the Wenzel Jamnitzer cup, for which in the year 1880 Meyer Rothschild gave the highest sum hitherto spent on *any* work of art. It was more a work of jewelry than a piece of plate (see Vol. II, page 116). But one should notice that, two years later at the Hamilton Palace sale, Charles de Rothschild bid 3,090 guineas for a by no means outstanding covered cup, for which William Beckford had paid 100 guineas sixty years earlier. The 1970 equivalent would be £29,200. At Carl Meyer Rothschild's decease-sale in 1911 a Nuremberg *bocale double* made £4,600 or the equivalent of £37,000. Prices for German Renaissance silver occasionally reached the levels of this great sale right down to the general slump of the early 1930s. The change could be observed at a very different Hamilton Palace sale in 1931 when early 16th century pieces such as the market never sees today were going for £200 to £400. The recovery that followed was short-lived. The year 1940, when France fell, was no time for German art, so, instead of £4,000, Anthony de Rothschild's majestic ewer and dish made no more than £245. By 1951 the prices of the 1920s were returning but in terms of a currency with barely two-fifths the purchasing power of 1940. Since 1961 there has been very little movement in this market. In the later 1960s up to £4,000 could be paid for a specially good standing cup, mounted nautilus shell or table statuette, but this meant at most £500 in pre-1914 money. Only two items in the list accord with the very high prices, paid at the end of the decade for English Elizabethan silver, and neither of these are German. The Adam Vianen ewer and basin could be counted a work of sculpture; the two Paris candlesticks were about the rarest things a silver collector could hope to get.

| *Standing cups, salts, nautilus-shell cups etc.* | £ |
|---|---|
| 1960 Rutschi. Berne. Columbine cup, Hans Petzolt, Nuremberg | 735 |
| Spik. Berlin. Columbine cup, Nuremberg | 420 |
| 1961 C. French silver-gilt tazza, *c.* 1563, 8½ in. high | 1,000 |
| 1962 Noble. C. Rosewater ewer and dish, Freiburg, *c.* 1560, 108 oz. | 4,000 |
| S. Norwegian peg tankard, Albertszenn of Bergen, 1625, engraved with animal figures | 2,100 |
| Paris. Parcelgilt chased ewer, Saragossa, *c.* 1590, FN24,000 +tax | 2,110 |
| 1963 Randolph Hearst. N.Y. Double pineapple cup, silver-gilt, 19½ in, high, very elaborate, Nuremberg 1519 | 430 |
| Dutch nautilus cup, 1610 | 428 |
| Pineapple cup by Hans Keller, Nuremberg, 1585, 13¼ in. | 680 |
| 1964 Weinmüller. Munich. Another pineapple cup by Hans Keller, 1590 | 1,650 |
| 1965 Janssen. S. Nautilus-shell *nef*, Torgau, 1610, 23½ in. high | 3,900 |
| Lord Bruce. C. Pair of plain candlesticks, the Hague 1653, 42¾ oz. 2 for | 4,800 |
| Matching écuelle, stand and cover, 34½ oz. | 2,300 |
| This small group of Dutch plate made £12,000 having cost £400 in 1895. | |
| Adda. Paris. Pair of tumbler cups, 3¾ in. high, 14 oz. by Buhel, Nuremberg, 1570 | 2,785 |
| Mounted nautilus, sculptures by Jeremias Michael, Augsburg, *c.* 1620, height 16½ in. | 3,200 |
| 1966 Berne. Nautilus, mounted by P.B. of Berne, 1633, 13½ in. high, FS40,000+tax | 3,830 |
| S. Dutch beaker with engravings after Jacques Callot, 1632, 18 oz. 12 dwt. | 3,000 |
| 21-inch covered standing cup by Michael Kabeas, Nuremberg, *c.* 1600 | 1,700 |
| Portuguese chased silver-gilt dish, *c.* 1525, 12½ in. | 1,550 |

£

| | | |
|---|---|---|
| 1966 | James de Rothschild. Paris. 9½-inch covered cup by Glaubrich, Augsburg | 2,360 |
| | Nautilus-shell, mounted as a swan, late 16th century | 1,560 |
| 1967 | St Monica's Priory, Louvain. S. Engraved octagonal platter, Antwerp 1616, 11 in. diam., 12 oz. 18 dwt. | 2,100 |
| | S. Nautilus, mounted as a statue of Neptune, Strasbourg, 1640, 8½ in. high | 4,200 |
| | C. South German engraved tankard, *c.* 1540, 4½ in. high, 16 oz. 3 dwt. | 3,000 |
| | Spanish mask-ewer, *c.* 1550, 6¼ in. high, 34 oz. | 1,300 |
| | Coxon. C. Portuguese silver-gilt dish with semi-Gothic reliefs, late 15th century, 10¾ in. diam., 14 oz. 18 dwt. | 2,200 |
| | C. Norwegian engraved tankard, dated 1610, 8 in., 20 oz. 5 dwt. | 1,800 |
| 1968 | Travers. S. Standing cup by David Laur, Nuremberg, 1590, arms of the *Schwartzfarber* guild, 21½ in. high, 38 oz. | 4,000 |
| | Nautilus, mounted by Hans Lind, Nuremberg, *c.* 1620, very elaborate, 13½ in. high | 2,800 |
| | S. Silver-gilt arm reliquary, 15 in. long, crowned M mark and Paris year-letter, 1540–41 | 1,650 |
| | N.Y. Jewish cylindrical *Kiddush* goblet in parcelgilt by Heinrich Hamma, Constanz, 1610, 9½ in. high, $3,200 | 1,333 |
| | Rasmussen, Copenhagen. Covered standing cup by Mads Claussen, Copenhagen, 1610, 8 in. high, 670 gr., Dkr.74,000 | 5,005 |
| 1969 | S. Mechanical silver-gilt windmill cup, Amsterdam, 1635, 8½ in. high, 6 oz. 7 dwt. | 1,800 |
| | South German chased silver-gilt tazza, arms of Sigismund Vasa, King of Sweden and Poland, dated 1600, 17 oz. 18 dwt. | 3,800 |
| | Boyle. S. South German standing cup after 1550, statue on lid, 15½ in. high, 30 oz. 19 dwt. | 1,550 |
| | S. South German standing cup and cover, high baroque, *c.* 1640, unmarked, 11¼ in., 22 oz. | 1,250 |
| | Bessborough. S. Chased ewer and basin by Adam Vianen, Utrecht, early 17th century, 12¾ × 17¾, 76 oz. 17 dwt. | 16,000 |
| | N.Y. Pair of pricket candlesticks, silver-gilt with rock-crystal stems and drum plinths, Paris 1583, $47,000 2 for | 19,582 |
| | Vernon. S. Silver-gilt monstrance, enclosing glass pyx by Ebbekin, Haarlem, 1626, 23¼ in. high, 52 oz. 1 dwt. | 1,900 |
| | S. Mechanical silver-gilt windmill cup, Amsterdam, 1643, 9 in. high, 7 oz. 15 dwt. | 1,700 |

*Figures and animals in the round*

|  |  | £ |
|---|---|---|
| 1961 | S. Pedlar with pack and dog by Joachim Hiller of Breslau, *c.* 1575 (£65 14*s.* in 1843) | 1,150 |
| 1962 | C. Augsburg squirrel, *c.* 1630, 10½ in. high (1961, bought in at £1,300) | 750 |
|  | S. Leaping stag by Biermann the elder, Basel, 1640, 23 oz. 15 dwt. | 550 |
| 1965 | Adda. Paris. Comfit box in form of a bear, Augsburg, mid-17th century, 10¾ in. high | 2,515 |
|  | Grape-gatherer and basket, Frankfurt, *c.* 1600, 12 in. high, 18 oz., FN50,000+tax | 4,055 |
| 1966 | James de Rothschild. Paris. Statuette, Gustavus Adolphus of Sweden, Hamburg, *c.* 1650, 16¾ in. high, FN118,000+tax | 9,474 |
|  | Silver-gilt salt in form of lion rampant by Ehrard of Augsburg, 1580 | 2,600 |
| 1967 | S. Huntsman, 10½ in. high, by David Lauer, Nuremburg, *c.* 1590, 19 oz. 10 dwt. | 800 |
|  | Weinmüller. Munich. Stag by master ML, Augsburg, 1576–83, DM25,500+tax | 3,335 |

# SILVER
## ENGLISH, BEFORE 1660

It will at once be noticed that English silver of the 16th century is much dearer than German silver, even several times dearer. Yet till well into the reign of James I, English silver had very little character of its own. Many of the unknown London monogrammists of the 16th century were probably immigrants from the Continent. As to quality, the Augsburg and Nuremberg silversmiths surpassed them in this overburdened style. The reason for the English preference lies in the fact that early in the century the Rothschild dynasty gave way to collectors in America, where Anglo-Saxon snobbery remains very strong, hence the high cost of keeping in the country the Leeds tankards and the Westwell Church livery-pots. They are, of course, true pairs than which nothing is rarer. Yet in shillings per ounce it seems that the most expensive silver plate on the market of the 1960s was not such ornate products as these, but the exceedingly plain small domestic pieces, attuned to the Puritan influence between the 1630s and 1660s. Such humble objects could not have been worth more than a matter of shillings before the late 19th century. The freak of chance that saved them from the melting pot has made them the most precious of collectors' pieces.

*Standing cups and salts; flagons* £

| | | £ |
|---|---|---|
| 1960 | S. Covered cup, dated 1590 (£1,080 in 1942), partly in mother-of-pearl, 7¾ in. high | 6,500 |
| | The Wilbraham cup (£3,275 5s. in 1930), gourd-shaped, 12 in. high and dated 1585 | 2,700 |
| | C. Standing salt, 1600, on five columns, 12 in. high | 3,400 |
| | Pilaton Hall. C. Patten and chalice, silvergilt, 1530, Victoria and Albert Museum | 5,350 |
| | Marquess of Ely. C. The Great Seal of Ireland cup, 1593 (£5,200 in 1902), Belfast City Gallery, 19½ in. high | 7,000 |
| 1961 | Makower. S. Six-sided cup and cover, 1650, 7 in. high, 48 oz. (£1,750 in 1948) | 6,500 |
| | Nicholson. S. Bell-salt, silvergilt, marked TS 1600, 8 in. high | 2,600 |
| 1962 | S. Steeple cup and cover, 1613, illustrating a hunt, Leicester Museum | 1,500 |
| 1963 | S. Rosewater ewer and dish, 1618  2 for | 2,100 |
| 1964 | Rex Beaumont. C. Bell salt, 1599, 8¾ in. (£900 in 1924, £346 in 1891) | 3,800 |
| | Steeple cup and cover, 15¾ in. high, 1604 (£1,600 in 1905, £1,000 in 1941) | 4,600 |
| | Steeple cup and cover, 15¾ in. high, dated 1615 | 2,600 |
| | Steeple cup and cover, 15¾ in. high, dated 1608 | 4,000 |

648

| | | | £ |
|---|---|---|---|
| 1964 | S. Beaker, 1586, 6¼ in., 90 oz. 8 dwt., later engraving (£480, 1943) | | 3,200 |
| 1967 | S. Scottish Nautilus cup, plain stem without supporting figures, unmarked, c. 1600 | | 1,300 |
| 1968 | C. Steeple cup, 1618, 12 in. high, 12 oz. 5 dwt. | | 1,800 |
| | Aked. C. Parcelgilt cup and cover, baluster stem, 1593, 7¾ in., 6 oz. 17 dwt. | | 4,200 |
| | Westwell Church. C. Pair of livery pots or Communion flagons, parcelgilt, by John Morley, 1594, 11¾ in. high, 72 oz. 9 dwt. | 2 for | 36,000 |
| | S. Standing salt, heavily chased with statue of warrior on cover, 1589 and 1591, 7¼ in. high, 7 oz. 6 dwt. | | 3,200 |
| 1969 | Bought for the Victoria and Albert Museum, standing salt in form of a crowing cock, the lower body a nautilus shell | | 6,250 |

*Wine cups, tumblers and tankards, porringers*

| | | | |
|---|---|---|---|
| 1961 | Makower. S. Tankard, James Plummer, York, 1649, 6 in. (£529, 1931) | | 3,200 |
| | Duke of Leeds. S. Pair of tankards, parcelgilt, London 1602, 33 oz., 8¾ in. high, mark I.B. (see 1966) | 2 for | 9,200 |
| 1962 | C. Plain wine cup, 1639, National Gallery, Melbourne | | 1,450 |
| | P. Plain beaker, 1579, 3¾ in. high | | 2,400 |
| 1964 | S. Heavily embossed tankard, parcelgilt, 1575 | | 4,000 |
| | Unmarked parcelgilt tankard, 16 oz. 16 dwt., late 16th century | | 4,100 |
| 1965 | Harewood. C. Pair of plain wine cups, 1640, baluster stems, 15½ oz. (6,400 shillings an ounce) | 2 for | 5,000 |
| | Single pair of plain wine cups, 1635, 3 oz. 7 dwt. (13,600 shillings per oz.) | | 2,300 |
| | Single pair of plain wine cups, 1631, 8 in. high, 9 oz. 8 dwt. | | 2,400 |
| | Rex Beaumont. C. Beaker, 1586, 6¾ in. high | | 3,200 |
| 1966 | Gilston and Eastwick Church. S. Tankard, 1639, 11 in., 37 oz. | | 2,200 |
| | Milner. C. Plain wine cup, 1657, 5 oz. 7 dwt. | | 1,600 |
| | Duke of Leeds. S. Pair of parcelgilt covered tankards, 1602, 33 oz. (see 1961) | 2 for | 17,000 |
| 1967 | Reif. S. Wine cup, trellis pattern, 1608, 6 oz. 16 dwt. | | 2,200 |
| | S. Plain tankard, marked RF 1658, 6 in., 21 oz. 5 dwt. | | 2,900 |
| | Wine taster, lightly chased, marked HB 1651, 3¼ in. high, 1 oz. 13 dwt (12,000 shillings an ounce) | | 1,000 |
| | N.Y. Plain covered tankard, 1656, $29,000 ($1,400 in 1939) | | 12,083 |

£

| | | |
|---|---|---|
| 1969 | Norman Hurst. C. 2-handled porringer, 4¾ in. high, marked FL 1658, 19 oz. 17 dwt. | 5,200 |
| | Harmsworth. S. Gadrooned bowl, punched and beaded sprays, by Thomas Maundy, 1640, 15 oz. 3 dwt. | 5,500 |
| | S. Wine cup, marked AD, 1657, 4½ in. high, 10 oz. 10 dwt. | 3,400 |
| | C. Chased porringer and cover, marked PD 1656 (Rothermere sale, 1941, £260), 16 oz. 3 dwt. | 5,000 |
| | Skillet and cover on conical feet, quite plain, 1653, 4 in. high, 10 oz. 13 dwt. (about 13,600 shillings an ounce) | 7,200 |
| | Morton. C. Plain tankard and cover with spread-foot, marked TB. 1636, 8 in. high, 31 oz. | 1,250 |
| | S. Wine cup on very long baluster stem, 1618, 6½ in., 6 oz. 9 dwt. | 1,800 |

*Dishes, tazzas and chargers*

| | | |
|---|---|---|
| 1961 | S. Salver on foot, signed AM 1657, 15¼ in. diam. | 3,200 |
| 1962 | C. Plain dish, 18 in. diam., 1631 | 2,800 |
| 1964 | Parcelgilt tazza, unmarked, late 16th century, 12 oz. 16 dwt. | 3,100 |
| | Tazza, 8½ in. diam., 10 oz. 4 dwt., marked WS 1627 | 3,200 |
| 1967 | Reif. S. Parcelgilt tazza, 1579, 12 oz. 17 dwt. (£920 in 1911, £1,050 in 1943), 5 in. diam. | 6,500 |
| 1968 | Dor. C. Charger with beaded spiral fluting by Thomas Maunday, 1638, 10 oz. 18 dwt. | 3,300 |
| | C. Plain dish with medallion centre, by AM, 1650, 13½ in. diam., 28 oz. | 2,300 |
| | Tazza with hexafoil bowl and tudor rose, marked FT 1622, 8¼ in. diam., 10 oz. 1 dwt. | 2,900 |
| 1969 | St Michael's Church, Southampton. S. Silver-gilt tazza, marked AW 1567, Isaac and Rebecca at the well in relief, 5¾ in. high, 23 oz. 1 dwt. (18,220 shillings an ounce) | 21,000 |

*Spice-boxes, inkstands*

| | | |
|---|---|---|
| 1960 | D'Estainville. S. Spice-box, scallop shell-shaped, 1599 | 3,100 |
| 1962 | Knight, Frank. Another spice-box, 1610 (£500 in 1941) | 3,000 |
| 1963 | Louis Taylor, Hanley. Another, same date | 1,700 |
| | C. Another, dated 1621, 8 oz. 10 dwt. | 2,600 |
| 1967 | Haddington. S. Casket-shaped standish inkstand by FS, 1652, lid added after 1700, 57 oz. 14 dwt. | 6,200 |
| 1969 | C. Spicebox, scallop-shaped, 6 in. long, marked IP 1627, with sugar spoon bearing matching initials, 10 oz. 4 dwt. | 1,680 |

*Mounted cocoanuts and ostrich eggs*

| | | |
|---|---|---|
| 1959 | Earl of Ducie. C. Ostrich egg, 1584 (see 1964), 14½ in. high | 4,400 |

£

| | | |
|---|---|---|
| 1960 | C.   Dried gourd, late 17th century mounts | 2,700 |
| 1964 | J. de Rothschild.   C.   Ostrich egg (see 1959), 1584 | 8,500 |
| 1966 | C.   Mounted cocoanut, *c.* 1600 | 650 |
| | J. de Rothschild, Paris.   Mounted coconut, 1620 | 1,040 |
| | Hamwee.   C.   Cocoanut in plain 2-handled Elizabethan mount | 680 |
| 1967 | C.   Cocoanut, elaborate mounts, Frankfurt, *c.* 1600 | 640 |
| 1968 | S.   Cocoanut as loving cup, John Plummer of York, 1667, 4¼ in. | 3,600 |

*Mounted stoneware jugs*, mainly Rhineland with English mounts

| | | |
|---|---|---|
| 1962 | ex Sir Andrew Noble.   S.   Raeren brown ewer with clenched fist spout; late 16th century mount, unmarked | 650 |
| 1963 | Randolph Hearst.   N.Y.   Tigerware jug, mount dated 1594 | 500 |
| 1965 | Adda Paris.   Cologne tankard, unmarked mount with inscription, *c.* 1590, FN18,000+tax | 1,492 |
| 1967 | S.   Tigerware tankard, finely chased lid, *c.* 1575 | 500 |
| 1968 | Tringham.   S.   Tigerware jug 12½ in. marked IB, 1607 | 1,050 |
| | Van den Berg.   S.   Tigerware jug, Exeter, *c.* 1570, no lid or year letter, 8¼ in. | 420 |
| 1969 | Norman Hurst.   C.   Tigerware jug, silver-gilt lid marked IC, 1565, 7½ in. | 2,500 |
| | Kenyon.   S.   Two round-bellied Siegburg tankards; unmarked silver-gilt mounts shortly after 1600, 8¾ and 8½ in. | 1,750 / 1,800 |
| | C.   Mounts *c.* 1620; a later faience ewer, called Venice, substituted for the original stoneware jug | 1,300 |

*Spoons and forks*

| | | | |
|---|---|---|---|
| 1957 | Harris.   C.   Henry VIII apostle spoon with finial, St James the Less | | 1,350 |
| | With alleged year-letter 1463 | | 1,600 |
| 1959 | C.   Early 15th century with gauntlet finial | | 1,800 |
| 1960 | C.   With mace finial, 1514 | | 1,050 |
| | S.   With diamond finial, *c.* 1350 | | 1,450 |
| 1961 | C.   Pair of apostle spoons, 1545 | 2 for | 2,700 |
| 1962 | Painter Stainers Company.   C.   Six spoons, 1560, with warriors as finials, bearing arms of the company | 6 for | 1,000 |
| 1966 | S.   The oldest silver toasting fork, 1560 | | 1,350 |
| 1968 | Aked.   C.   With diamond finial, leopard's head mark, *c.* 1450 | | 850 |
| 1969 | S.   Six two-pronged forks by William Scarlett, 1694, trifid handles, 8 oz. 10 dwt. | 6 for | 5,200 |

£

1969 Harrods. Pair of apostle spoons, 1580 (£580 in 1966)
2 for 1,400
Bowyer-Smith. C. Six 'Lion sejant' spoons, 1558–78,
6 for 1,100
1970 S. Single apostle spoon, mark attributed to 1490 1,350

# SILVER
## CONTINENTAL, 1660–1820

*France*

In spite of the destruction caused by the commissioners of the French Revolution, French plate of the 18th century is not as rare as one would expect. A great deal of plate had already been exported under the *ancien régime*. Even Louis XIV plate in small quantities has survived an earlier destruction. The great scarcity of still earlier French plate is due less to the offerings to the treasury in 1709 than to the change of style in the second half of the 17th century which had caused most pieces, which were thought old-fashioned, to be melted down. Under Louis XV a great deal of sumptuous Parisian plate was presented to foreign royal houses or ordered by them. The Russian revolution released some of it onto the open market, and these items from Imperial services are much dearer in relation to their size and merits than their English equivalents, none of which in the 1960s vied for instance with the Empress Elizabeth tureen at £45,000. But in general all kinds of 18th century French plate are dearer than their English equivalents and have been so for more than a century.

Thanks to his many lavish gifts, Napoleon's Imperial silver was also capable of a saleroom appearance in the 1960s, and here too personal association created prices which would scarcely be possible for contemporary English silver in spite of that exaggerated cult of Paul Storr, for instance a coffee pot of 1800 at £6,600 and a casket of 1810 at £7,500.

|  |  |  | £ |
|---|---|---|---|
| 1960 | Berkeley. S. The Berkeley Castle dinner service by Jean Roettiers, 1735–8, weighing ¾ of a ton. Metropolitan Museum (Louvre underbidding) | 168 for | 207,000 |
|  | Penard y Fernandez. Paris. Ewer and stand by Nicolas de Launay, 1704 | 2 for | 12,370 |
|  | Baluster ewer by Boursin, 1681 |  | 3,520 |
|  | Pair of candlesticks by Jacques Roettiers from the Orloff service, 1771 | 2 for | 3,400 |
| 1961 | Makower. S. Ecuelle and cover, Paris 1680, 7 in. diam. |  | 1,600 |
|  | Pair of tazzas by Tessier, 1688 | 2 for | 3,000 |
|  | S. Engraved casket, 11 in. long, by Besnier, 1714 |  | 2,900 |
| 1963 | S. Napoleon's parcelgilt tea and coffee service by Biennais, 1810, 128 oz. 7 dwt. |  | 10,200 |
|  | Lord Astor of Hever. C. Toilet set, partly glass and Sèvres porcelain, by François Riel, 1770–1 | 18 for | 14,500 |
|  | Morgan. C. Pair of candlesticks by Pierre Massé, 1675 (£114 in 1905) |  | 2,600 |
|  | Paris. Twelve plain dinner plates by Jacques Lamine, wavy gadrooned borders and English royal arms, 1789, 230 oz. | 12 for | 4,945 |

| | | £ |
|---|---|---|
| 1963 | Paris   Tureen, stand and cover by J. B. Cheret, 1784 and 1793, 125 oz. | 3 for 2,973 |
| | Helmet-ewer by Nicolas Mahon, Paris, 1722 | 3,750 |
| | Fribourg.   S.   Pair of Louis XV tureens, cover and liners by Simeon Gaucher, 280 oz. 15 dwt. | 6 for 7,000 |
| | 2 pairs, Louis XV table candlesticks by Lephendrick, 1753, 105 oz. 4 dwt. | 4 for 3,200 |
| | Kavanagh.   S.   Tureen with cover, liner and stand, François Papché, 1772–3, 387 oz. | 3 for 10,000 |
| | Stuker, Berne.   Silver-gilt coffee pot from Napoleon's travelling service by Biennais, 1800, with tax | 6,600 |
| 1964 | S.   Tureen, cover and stand by J. N. Roettiers, 1770, made for Empress Catherine, 443 oz. | 13,000 |
| | C.   Tureen, cover and stand by Cheret, 1780s (compare 1963) | 2,600 |
| 1965 | Clifford of Chudleigh.   C.   Parcelgilt mirror frame, 1685, 22 in. high | 3,800 |
| | C.   Silver-gilt soup tureen by François Germain, 1759, one of eight made for the 'Service de Paris' of the Empress Elizabeth of Russia (another sold by the Russian government to the Metropolitan Museum and two more to Calouste Gulbenkian in 1929–30), 600 oz.   Bought by Baron Thyssen Bornemisza | 45,000 |
| | Silver-gilt service, made for the Grand Duke Michael between 1793 and 1820 by Odiot, Cahier and Biennais, 4661 oz.   Bought in at | 56,000 |
| | Lord Ilchester.   C.   Two pairs of candlesticks by Nicolas Nolin, 1724, 102 oz. | 4 for 5,500 |
| | Adda.   Paris.   Two tumbler cups, Paris, 1713, 3½ in., 12 oz. | 2 for 2,000 |
| | Helmet-ewer, Louis XV, by Croze, Paris, 10 in. high, 24 oz. | 4,185 |
| | Tureen, cover and stand by Cheret, 1788, 64 oz. | 1,930 |
| | Stuker, Berne.   *Surtout de table* by Robert Joseph Auguste, 1783, with Sèvres porcelain fittings, 25 × 18 in. FS70,000+ tax | 6,680 |
| 1966 | S.   Pair of candelabra by Antoine Boulier, 1781 | 2 for 2,900 |
| 1967 | Earl of Kingston.   S.   Two pairs, table candlesticks by Gouel, 1719, 8¾ in. high | 4 for 4,300 |
| | Pellenc.   S.   Casket, 9¾ in. by Martin Biennais, made for Hortense Bonaparte, Queen of Holland, *c.* 1810, silver-gilt bees and classical relief panels | 7,500 |
| | Casterlé.   S.   Pair of Louis XV candlesticks, 4¾ in. 18 oz. 13 dwt., by Antoine Plot, Paris, 1756 | 2 for 2,400 |
| | Paris.   Ten candlesticks, 10¾ in. high, by Cauwenberg, | |

£

| | | |
|---|---|---|
| Paris, *c.* 1775, 196 oz., FN118,000+tax | 10 for | 10,960 |
| *Écuelle* and cover by Rey, Chambéry, *c.* 1730, modern stand, FN115,000+tax | 3 for | 10,285 |
| Dish and domed cover from the Orloff service, 1770, by J. N. Roettiers (see 1960), FN157,000+tax | 2 for | 12,563 |

68 Burns, S. Pair of table-candlesticks, marked SG 1740, 9 in., 47 oz. 2 dwt.     **2 for**   3,100

Holmes. S. Set of 24 silver-gilt dinner plates by Guilleaume Biennais, 1810, 444 oz. 13 dwt.   **24 for**   8,000

Viguier. Pairs. Set of 38 silver-gilt knives, forks and spoons by Imler and Alberti, Strasbourg, 1759 and 1783, FN160,000+tax     **38 for**  14,860

    12 plates by Guilleaume Pégeron 1773, 7,160 gr., F66,700+tax     6,195

    Silver-gilt beaker by P. L. Reynard, 1756, 4½ in. high, FN75,000+tax     8,380

    8 table-candlesticks by Robert Auguste, 1778, 11¼ in. high, FN120,000+tax   **8 for**  11,155

Paris. Single dinner plate, *service de l'Empereur*, by Biennais, FN25,000+tax, *c.* 1808     2,400

69 C. Pair of 2-handled sauceboats by Rigal, 1745, and Lescahudel, 1753, 35 oz.     **2 for**   4,400

    Ewer and basin, 9½ in. high, 13¼ in. wide, 1733 by Sebastien Igonet, 63 oz.     **2 for**   3,700

Combe-Rowe. C. Pair of table-candlesticks, Alexis Loir, 1740, 10½ in. high, 58 oz. 11 dwt.   **2 for**   2,800

C. Ewer and basin by Outrebon, Paris, 1765, 60 oz.   2,400

N.Y. Pair of 5-light candelabra, Paris, 1809–19, $7,750     **2 for**   3,230

de Vogué. C. (Geneva). Tureen, stand and cover, 14½ × 19, Antoine Boulier. Paris. 1781–2, FS145,000+tax     **3 for**  14,650

Paris. Pair of mixing bowls from the Empress Catherine service, 1778, by Robert Auguste, about 119 oz., FN149,000. Taken over by the Louvre     **2 for**  11,400

    Ewer and basin by Louis Regnard, 1787, FN178,770 incl.     15,150

    Tureen, cover and stand, *c.* 1780, Henri Auguste, FN227,070 inclusive     19,243

    Pair of powder-boxes, Jean-Baptiste Chevet, 1784, arms of Rohan-Montmorency, FN130,070 inclusive   11,023

## Netherlands and Flanders £

1963 Fribourg. S. Wine taster, Amsterdam, late 17th century
3 oz. 16 dwt., at 5,480 shillings an ounce 1,020

1965 de Thouars. S. Wine cistern, Brussels, *c.* 1690, 44½ in.
diam. 1,353 oz. 15,000

1966 N.Y. Dutch colonial two-handled cup by Jacob Boelen,
New Amsterdam (New York), before 1700, 16 oz. 6 dwt. 8,930
S. Pair of pillar candlesticks, the Hague, 1665, 35¼ oz. 4,000

1967 Lancaster. C. Mirror with 12 toilet accessories by van
Dyck, Delft, 1705, in Queen Anne style with English coats
of arms 13 for 8,400

1968 C. Silver-gilt porringer, cover and stand by Brechtel, the
Hague, 1680, arms of William and Mary, 76 oz. 3 dwt.
3 for 9,000

1969 C. Two-handled oval basket by Koolhaas, Utrecht, 1757,
11¼ in. wide, 38 oz. 1,650
de Fontanes. C. Pair of silver-gilt table candlesticks by
Brencke, Groningen, 1730, 7 in. high, 27 oz. 2 for 1,600

## Germany and Central Europe

1962 S. Pair of dishes and covers, Augsburg, 1718, and 1730,
4 for 2,600

1964 Weinmüller, Munich. Engraved coffee pot and cover,
Esaias Busch, Augsburg, *c.* 1725, DM33,500+tax 3,660

1967 S. Gold cup, Augsburg, inlaid with 26 coins and medals
and arms of Opalinski, 1712, 4½ in. high, 11 oz. 5 dwt. 1,700

1968 Chased and engraved standing cup, silver-gilt, depicting
relief of siege of Vienna, marked MS, Augsburg, 1683,
12 in. high, 20 oz. 10 dwt. 2,600

1969 S. Silver-gilt sideboard dish, Riga, *c.* 1700, 20½ in. diam.
157 oz. 12 dwt. 2,600
C. Oval soup tureen and cover by Bromm, Danzig, 1760,
12¾ in. wide, 123 oz. 2,000

## Scandinavia

There is little to distinguish Swedish silver from the more restrained sort
contemporary German silver, The only reason for a much higher level
prices is the small amount available in proportion to the great wealth of t
country. It is in fact a patriotic market, comparable with the market for silv
of the Colonial period in the U.S.A.

£

1957 S. *Kallskul*, Stockholm, 1715, monogram Charles XII,
86 oz. 8,300

1960 S. Swedish tankard on ball feet, 1691, 8½ in. high 1,150

£

1961  Hudson.  S.  Coffee pot, 1748, by Wittkop, Stockholm,
11¼ in.  1,400

1966  S.  *Kallskul*, Gothenburg 1725 (bowl and cover) with
pomegranate handles, 70 oz.  8,500

Plain beaker, Stockholm, 1796, 16½ oz.  3,400

C.  Peg tankard and cover, Trondheim, Norway, 1670,
55 oz.  3,200

1967  S.  Sugar box and cover, Gothenburg, 1759, 10 oz. 3 dwt.  3,200

Peg tankard, Gothenburg, 1727, 43 oz. very plain  2,450

S.  Oval sugar box by Lampe, Stockholm, 1765, 6½ in.
13 oz. 12 dwt.  4,000

Stadts Auktionverket, Stockholm.  Coffee pot by Peter
Zethelius, Stockholm, 1771, SKr44,000+tax (see 1969)  4,390

1968  Bukowski, Stockholm. Beaker by Johan Lund. Stockholm,
1699, inside gilt, 7¼ in. high, Skr. 40,500+tax  3,700

Tureen by Bergquist, Petersburg, 1768, 20 in. wide,
Skr35,500+tax  3,260

S.  Tureen and cover by Peter Lund, Stockholm, 1752,
13¾ in. wide, 82 oz. 8 dwt.  5,000

Oval sugar box by Jons Lund, Skara, 1765, 11 oz.
16 dwt.  2,100

Tankard on pomegranate feet, Ingemudessen of
Upsala, 1680, 20 oz. 18 dwt., 6 in. high  2,600

1969  S.  Pair of tureens and covers by Otersen, Hamburg, 1785,
16¾ in. wide, 221 oz. 17 dwt.  2 for  5,200

Zethelius.  S.  Coffee pot by Pieter Zethelius, Stockholm,
1771, 34 oz. 17 dwt. (see 1967)  5,000

S.  Winetaster by Mansson, Mariestad, c. 1660, 6¾ in. diam.  1,250

Tankard by Borg. Trondheim, c. 1715, 27 oz.  1,550

Bridgeman.  C.  Norwegian peg-tankard, 1690, 30 oz.  1,250

# SILVER
## ENGLISH, 1660–1820

*Restoration, 1660–1700*

Two very distinct styles belong to this period, first the old plain Common
wealth style, which was enriched with engraved designs of a slight and delica
kind. Secondly, towards the end of the reign of Charles II, the massive hig
relief Louis XIV style was introduced by refugee Huguenot silversmiths fro
France. The earlier kind of Restoration silver threatens to become the mc
sought-after style in the world, particularly when the engraving is in t
Chinoiserie manner of the Brownlow paired tankards which rose from £17,0
in 1963 to £56,000 in 1968. It is probable that the two much prettier ging
jars with their covers and stands, which made £18,000 in 1962, will ha
advanced as much, though not a perfectly matching pair, for at the end of t
1960s prices of 10,000 to 16,000 shillings an ounce for silver of the Restorati
period had become commonplace. It is worth recalling that in 1862 Christ
sold a flat-lidded tankard, dated 1661, at 9s. 10d. an ounce. After the passa
of 200 years this was less than Samuel Pepys had paid to have such a tanka
made.

|      |                                                                                 | £      |
|------|---------------------------------------------------------------------------------|--------|
| 1959 | C.  Quaich, Glasgow, 1698 (£200 in 1898)                                          | 1,700  |
| 1960 | S.  Casket, 10½×8 by Pierre Harrache, 1695 (part of a toilet service of 18 pieces, sold in 1888 for £1,215) | 8,000 |
|      | Two-handled cup and cover by James Chadwick, 1696, 7¾ in. high (£500 in 1942)    | 4,800  |
|      | Pair of tankards by James Cockburn, Edinburgh, 1685, 7 in. high (£1,800 in 1954)    2 for | 4,600 |
| 1961 | Makower.  S.  Taper-winder and jack, Charles II (£395 in 1937)                   | 3,600  |
|      | Cup-shaped ewer by Charles Shelley, 1666, 8½ in. high                            | 3,800  |
| 1962 | S.  Silvergilt ewer and salver, dated 1671, £3,200 and                           | 1,600  |
|      | C.  Monteith by Isaac Dighton, 1699, Temple Newsam Gallery                       | 1,250  |
|      | S.  Pair of Ginger jars and covers on octagonal stands, 7½ in. high and 8 in. wide respectively, Chinoiserie engraved designs, London, 1682 (about 5,000 shillings an ounce)    6 for | 18,000 |
|      | Candle-sconce, Chinoiserie figures, 1665, 12½ in. high, silvergilt, marked WG    | 3,000  |
| 1963 | S.  Hand-candlestick, 1686, 5 oz. 8 dwt.                                         | 2,200  |
|      | Combemarle.  C.  Peg-tankard by Plommer of York, 1678, 30 oz. 2 dwt. (£280 in 1953) | 2,100 |
|      | Lord Brownlow.  C.  Massive pair of tankards, 1686, Chinoiserie engraving on sides and lids, 123 oz. 5 dwt. (see 1968)    2 for | 17,000 |

| | | |
|---|---|---|
| 1963 | Pair of firedogs with royal cypher, 1670, 184 oz. (£360 in 1936) | £ |
| | 2 for | 8,800 |
| | Lord Astor of Hever. C. Pair of frosted tumblers, fitted together, 1672, 5 oz. 7 dwt. 2 for | 2,100 |
| | 18-piece toilet service in Chinoiserie style, 1683 (£922 in 1905) | |
| | 18 for | 12,000 |
| | Lord Rothschild. S. Saucepan, 1685, with spout and cover, 6¾ in. high, 36 oz. 1 dwt. | 2,900 |
| 964 | Rex Beaumont. C. Tea-urn, Thomas Bolton, Dublin, 1696, 15¾ in. 34 oz. 18 dwt. | 2,500 |
| | Armorial charger by Pierre Harrache, 1692, 21¾ in. diam. 114 oz. 7 dwt. (£430 in 1943, £163 in 1893) | 5,000 |
| | Pair of octagonal bowls and covers, 1683, 4 in. diam. 16 oz. 16 dwt.; mark, 3 storks 4 for | 3,600 |
| | Porringer and cover by Richard Smart, Cork, 1675, 9 in. high, 54 oz. 11 dwt. National Museum, Dublin | 5,600 |
| | S. Pair of table-candlesticks, spreading feet, 1675 2 for | 2,100 |
| | Silvergilt dinner plate by Francis Garthorne, 1690 | 3,400 |
| 965 | Lord Ilchester. C. Pair of 15-inch firedogs, 1695, by Philip Rollos 2 for | 3,000 |
| | S. Silvergilt wall-sconce with Chinoiserie backplate, 1665, 27 oz. 4 dwt. | 3,600 |
| 966 | S. Octagonal casket, Chinoiserie engraving 1683, 44 oz. | 3,200 |
| | Pair of partly chased tankards, 1681, 53 oz. 17 dwt. 2 for | 3,000 |
| | Tankard, 1678, dolphin thumb-piece (1921, £163 2s. 9d.) | 3,700 |
| | C. Plain tankard by Charles Shelley, 1685, 50 oz., 8¾ in. high (£253 in 1920) | 3,500 |
| | Similar plain tankard, 1677, 54 oz. (£321 in 1923) | 9,500 |
| | S. Salver by Edward Winslow, Boston, Mass., 1695, 11 oz. 16 dwt. | 2,500 |
| 67 | Bagot. S. Helmet-ewer, 1674, mark TK, 33 oz. 9 dwt. | 4,000 |
| | 2nd helmet-ewer by Thomas Issod, 1686, with its sideboard dish, 157 oz. 14 dwt. 2 for | 9,800 |
| | C. Pair of tankards with Chinoiserie engraving, 1685, 67 oz. (unequal sizes) 2 for | 4,800 |
| | Mdivani. S. Toilet service, 1691, by Anthony Nelme, including easel-mirror, 288 oz. 12 for | 13,500 |
| | Noble. C. Ewer and basin, Daniel Garnier, 1697, 43 oz. 2 for | 5,700 |
| | Écuelle and cover by the same, 1694, 23 oz. (£28 9s. 7d. in 1901) | 4,000 |
| | Pair of silvergilt cups, covers and stands by Anthony Nelme, 1692, 22 oz. (£360 in 1945) 6 for | 5,000 |

659

| | | £ |
|---|---|---|
| 1967 | Cotton. S. Two-handled beaker, 2½ in. high, 3 oz. 3 dwt., no year-letter, but a Leeds maker's mark, *c.* 1675 (14,000 shillings an ounce) | 2,100 |
| | Lewis, Toronto. S. Combined snuffer, stand and candle-stick, marked WB, *c.* 1685, 7 in. high, 10 oz. 3 dwt. | 3,000 |
| 1968 | Spencer, Retford. 2-handled porringer and cover, 12½ in. maker's mark S, 1680, 93 oz. 10 dwt. | 9,000 |
| | Morrison C. Cylindrical tankard by Marmaduke Best, York, 1664, arms of Mauleverer, 5½ in. high, 23 oz. | 2,900 |
| | S. Miniature tankard, Chinoiserie engraving, marked WA, 1683, 4 in. high, 9 oz. 4 dwt. | 5,200 |
| | Brocklehurst. C. Plain dish with deep well by Robert Cooper, 1692, 14 in. diam., 36 oz. | 7,400 |
| | C. Chased oval dish, Nessus and Deianeira in the Vianen of Utrecht style, 1665, 23 in. wide, 118 oz. | 4,400 |
| | Tringham. S. Porringer by John Segar, Dublin, 1685–7, Chinoiserie engraving, 20 oz. 12 dwt., 9¼ in. wide | 6,800 |
| | S. Charger in extreme baroque taste, 1673, 25 oz. 11 dwt., 14½ in. diam. | 2,200 |
| | Lady Wantage. S. Caudle-cup and cover in the repoussé style, I.R. 1672, 6¾ in. high, 33 oz. 1 dwt. | 2,300 |
| | C. Pair of tankards, 1686, Chinoiserie engraving on sides and lids, 123 oz. 5 dwt. (see 1963), 8½ in. high        2 for | 56,000 |
| | Hirsch. C. Porringer and cover, marked IN, 1674, en-graved inscription, 6 in. high, 34 oz. | 8,200 |
| | C. Pair of grooved column-candlesticks, marked TI 1686, 7¾ in., 25 oz. (for closely similar pair see 1969)      2 for | 7,000 |
| | St Mary's Church, Newington. S. Pair of plain cylin-drical cups, marked WG., 1675, domed covers by John Gammon, 1730, 44 oz. 2 dwt.        2 for | 11,000 |
| | Inscribed cylindrical tankard, TS, 1681, 13¾ in. high, 56 oz. 15 dwt. | 3,800 |
| | Miles. S. Wine cup, marked JS., 1662, virtually Charles I in style, 2 oz. 14 dwt. (15,600 shillings an ounce) | 2,100 |
| | Clarke Jervoise. C. Christening cup and cover, silver-gilt, given by Bishop Burnet to his godson; by Pierre Harrache II 1695, 5 in. diam., 16 oz. 2 dwt., 14,650 shillings an ounce | 11,800 |
| | Butlin. C. Four 3-light sconces, 1668, and 1670, 23¼ in. high, backplates added by Paul Storr, 1810 (£1,150 in 1947)        4 for | 8,500 |
| 1969 | S. Wine-taster by Pierre Harrache, 1684, 4 oz. 6 dwt. | 2,800 |
| | C. Porringer and cover, marked IM, 1681, 6¾ in. high, 28 oz., Chinoiserie engraving and arms of Selleck | 5,200 |
| | Norman Hurst. C. Snuffer-tray and snuffer-scissors by Francis Garthorne, 1678, 8¾ in. wide, 15 oz. 12 dwt. | 9,500 |

£

1969    Sevastopulo.   C.   Pair of plain fluted column candlesticks, mark 1683, 7¾ in. high, 27 oz. (for similar pair see 1968)

                                                2 for   6,800

Lord Hastings.   C.   Silvergilt monteith in French style by William Gamble, 1701, 13 in. diam., 85 oz.        4,800

S.   Pair of one-handled mugs in plain lobed relief with flared rims by John Borthwick, Edinburgh, 1693, 3¼ in. high, 13 oz. 4 dwt.            5,200

Denny.   S.   Two-handled cup, gadrooned foot and cover by Seth Lofthouse, 1697, 10½ in. high, 31 oz. 17 dwt.    2,600

S.   Pair of table-candlesticks by Alice Sheen, 1712, 7 in. high, 26 oz.                      2 for   4,000

Helmet ewer in Huguenot style by Thomas Boulton, Dublin, 1702, 10½ in. high, 47 oz. 6 dwt.      7,000

Plain tankard by Ralph Walley, Chester, 1686–90, 7½ in. high, 32 oz. 5 dwt.                 4,000

S.   Silvergilt toilet set and mirror, 9 items mainly by Robert Cooper, 1675–6, 144 oz. 13 dwt.       9 for   6,800

C.   Sideboard dish, Huguenot style, David Willaume, 1711, 28½ in. diam., 276 oz. 15 dwt.        4,200

St. Michael's Church, Lambourn.   Silvergilt plain tankard, marked HG, 1661, dedicated 1701, matted sides, 8 in. high, 62 oz.                               15,000

Richly chased monteith by Colin Mackenzie, Edinburgh, 1698, 13 in. wide, 70 oz.         5,500

Mirror by Anthony Nelme, 1681, lightly incised Chinoiserie borders, 22 in. high        4,500

Snuffer-stand and snuffers, marked BB 1688, 7¾ in., 12 oz. 17 dwt.                  4,000

S.   Porringer with Chinoiserie figures, 3½ in. high, 1690, 10 oz. 10 dwt.                   2,000

Caudle cup and cover, 1681, 7½ in. high, 44 oz. 14 dwt.   2,200

Pair of plain baluster wine cups, James Penman, Edinburgh, 1685, 8¾ in. 34 oz. 3 dwt.      2 for   1,900

S.   Monteith punchbowl in rich Louis XIV style by Robert Stokes, 1698, 13 in. diam, 81 oz. 16 dwt.     3,100

Waleran.   C.   *Gold* porringer and cover, 1671, 4¾ in. high, 21 oz. 16 dwt.                   37,000

Townshend.   C.   Silvergilt helmet-ewer and dish in French style by John Humphreys, Dublin, 1693–5, 350 oz.   12,000

Tankard, Chinoiserie engraving, marked IA 1684, 6½ in., 29 oz.                      5,500

Yates.   C.   Pair of column-candlesticks, marked TA 1684, 8 in., 26 oz. (Larger pair, 1970, £1,300)      3,200

£

| 1969 | Waleran. C. Pair of plain salvers, marked TH, 1670, feet added in 1687, 10¾ in. diam. 44 oz. | 2 for | 2,400 |
|---|---|---|---|
| | Unwin. C. 2-handled porringer and cover, Chinoiserie engraving, 1688, 6½ in. high, 23 oz. | | 3,500 |

## The plain 'Queen Anne' style, c. 1695–1735

The second phase of puritanically plain silver lasted at least forty years, beginning before the death of William III and extending almost a generation beyond the reign of Queen Anne, in which the best pieces were made. The price of Queen Anne silver has become such a legend that one scarcely perceives the loss of the absolute pre-eminence which this period enjoyed between the two world wars. In the 1960s Restoration silver was dearer and silver of the later Lamerie style just as dear after nearly a hundred years of the Queen Anne *mystique*. As a revolt against 'Great Exhibition' taste, the Queen Anne revival began to appear in architecture and interior decoration in the late 1860s. By 1875 a Queen Anne silver porringer and cover had achieved the revolutionary price of £165 in the Dasent sale. By the beginning of the present century Queen Anne silver was dearer than in 1970 in terms of real money, the £2,050 tankard by Garthorne in the Huth sale of 1905 being equivalent to £16,400. The Ashburnham toilet service, made by Benjamin Pyne in 1719 was sold for £6,100 in 1914. With some additional items it made £17,850 in New York in 1957, but the 1914 price was equivalent in 1970 to close on £50,000.

One of the last of these truly impressive prices was paid at the Brownlow sale of 1929 for a pair of table ewers, made in 1713 by Simon Pantin. They fetched £4,200, the equivalent of £21,000 in 1970 when they might not be worth nearly as much. In 1938 they were sold for only a third of the original price. In fact the prices of the 1920s for Queen Anne silver were not recovered even on paper till after 1950. In the 1960s it was the simplest pieces of all which tended to keep pace with the devaluation of money. In the 1920s, the Queen Anne coffeepot with its rounded or faceted tapering body, domed lid and wooden handle, cocked to one side, was not one of the dearer items. Prices ranged from £200 to £500, one example which reached £3,600 in 1966, making £320 as late as 1949. At that time bullet-shaped teapots were more popular, for one of them achieved £1,900 in 1951. The rage for coffeepots began in the 1960s. A Simon Pantin coffeepot was sold in 1962 for £2,800. By 1967 there were several by different makers selling at £5,000 to £6,000, while in 1969 the value of this Simon Pantin example had multiplied more than four times in the course of seven years since its price was now £11,500. But later in the year there were good Queen Anne coffeepots to be had again for £2,000 and less. Too much English 18th century silver had been bought as a short term speculation and the market began to show it.

£

| 1960 | S. Sugar-box and cover, James Fraillon 1716, 4¾ in. wide | 3,000 |
|---|---|---|
| | Sideboard dish by John Chartier, 1707, 24½ in. diam. (£450 in 1941) | 4,100 |

£

| | |
|---|---|
| 1960 S. Seven-sided teapot by Isaac Ribouleau, 4¾ in. high, 1724 (see 1966) | 2,500 |
| Cup and cover by John Clifton, 1709 | 2,500 |
| 1961 C. Sugar-box by John Coney of Boston, Mass., 16 oz., c. 1700 | 6,500 |
| O'Sullivan, S. Chocolate pot on lion's feet by Nathaniel Lock, 1708, 9½ in. high | 2,150 |
| S. Pair of sauceboats by Huddell, 1720, 8½ in. wide 2 for | 2,900 |
| Duke of Sutherland. C. Wine-cistern by Lamerie, 1719, arms of Gower, 38 in. wide, 700 oz. at 772s. an ounce | 27,000 |
| C. Two-handled cup and cover by Lamerie, 1728 | 2,800 |
| S. Shaving ewer and dish, Thomas Ker, Edinburgh, 1703, 7¾ in. high and 13½ in. diam. Museum Fine Arts, Boston 2 for | 2,650 |
| 1962 S. Monteith by Benjamin Pyne, 1715, 192 oz. (£530 in 1940) | 3,600 |
| Pratt. S. Octagonal coffeepot by Thomas Tearle, 1724, 10¼ in. high | 1,750 |
| Carlyon. S. Octagonal tea kettle and stand by Humphrey Payne, 1711–14, stand unmarked, 9 in. high, 270 oz. 8 dwt. | 3,100 |
| Octagonal milk-jug by Edward Barnett, 1717, 8 oz. 11 dwt. | 1,950 |
| C. Octagonal coffeepot by George Bayley, 1718, 24 oz. 5 dwt. | 1,600 |
| Set of silvergilt knives, forks, and spoons, one dozen of each, 1712 (£172 in 1910) 36 for | 4,000 |
| Octagonal castor by Lamerie, 1724 | 3,200 |
| Conical coffeepot by Simon Pantin, 1709 (see 1969) | 2,800 |
| Plain tankard by Lamerie, 1716, 28 oz. 11 dwt. (£80 in 1931) | 3,300 |
| de Kusel. C. Cream jug by David Willaume, 1718, 8 oz. 10 dwt. | 1,200 |
| S. Toilet service and mirror by Anthony Nelme, 1705 14 for | 5,200 |
| Oblong tray by Simon Pantin, 57 oz. 12 dwt. (£650 in 1942) | 2,200 |
| Coffeepot by Jacob Margas, 1710, 10 in. high, 34 oz. 3 dwt. | 2,400 |
| 1963 Hamwee. S. Pair of strawberry-dishes by David Willaume, 1729 (£2,600 in 1962) 2 for | 3,800 |
| Pair of sauceboats by Sarah Holidays, c. 1720, 27 oz. 16 dwt. (£720 in 1954) 2 for | 2,800 |
| Hot water jug by Gabriel Sleath, 1724, 25 oz. 9½ in. high | 3,300 |

£

| | | |
|---|---|---:|
| 1963 | Brownlow. C. Pair of wall-sconces by David Willaume, 1707, 110 oz. 6 dwt. Victoria and Albert Museum    2 for | 6,000 |
| | Charger by Mettayer, 1717, arms of George I, 2462 oz. | 5,600 |
| | Inkstand by Lamerie, 1726, 31 oz. 8 dwt. (£300 in 1931) | 4,000 |
| | Monteith by Lamerie 1725, 100 oz. 15 dwt. | 3,800 |
| | Lisburn. S. Toilet service by John Edwards, 1725, 344 oz. 8 dwt. | 9,700 |
| | S. Five lots which had been sealed-up in deposit since 1859: | |
| | Silvergilt ewer and dish, Philip Rollos, 1705, royal arms, 252 oz. 4 dwt. Victoria and Albert Museum   2 for | 11,000 |
| | two-handled cup and cover, Rollos, 1712, arms of Raby, 13½ in. high, silvergilt | 3,200 |
| | Pair of silvergilt salvers, 1715, 11½ in. diam.    2 for | 3,100 |
| | Helmet-ewer, David Willaume, 1702, 83 oz. 3 dwt., arms of Raby | 5,200 |
| | Silvergilt round salver, gadrooned rim, arms of Wentworth, by John Bache, 1713, 180 oz. 3 dwt. (see 1969) | 4,100 |
| | S. Bullet-shaped teapot by Bowles Nash, 1723, with stand by Edward Carnock, 1722 (£750 in 1948)    2 for | 1,800 |
| | Dunlap. N.Y. Silvergilt toilet set by John White, 1727 | 6,070 |
| 1964 | Tremayne. S. Beer jug by Thomas Bolton, Dublin, 1717 | 2,550 |
| | S. Octagonal tea set of three pieces by Richard Watts, 1710 (£2,900 in 1954)    3 for | 9,200 |
| | Earl of Kintore. S. Pair of square waiters by Edward Carnock, 1725    2 for | 4,000 |
| | S. Octagonal covered bowl by Tumbrell and Bentley, 1712 | 5,000 |
| | Pair of wine-coolers by Edward Farrer, 1727, 9 in. high, 164 oz. 2 dwt.    2 for | 3,200 |
| | C. Wine jug by Simon Pantin 1708, 12 in. high | 4,000 |
| | Inkstand by Benjamin Pyne, 1725 | 2,500 |
| | Mrs James de Rothschild. C. Helmet-ewer by Pierre Harrache, 1703, 12 in. high, 78 oz. 11 dwt. (£27 in 1920) | 4,000 |
| 1965 | C. Shaving jug by Fawdery, 1706 (£166 in 1940) | 3,400 |
| | Lord Cottisloe. S. Armorial salver, Robert Cooper, 1712, 62 oz. | 3,300 |
| | Norman Hurst. C. Snuffer-tray by Lamerie, 1728, 8½ oz. | 2,600 |
| | Clifford of Chudleigh. C. Oval sugar-box, Exeter, 1705, 17½ oz. | 3,300 |
| | Lord Bathurst. C. Pair of silvergilt salvers, engraved arms, by David Willaume, 1708, 136 oz.    2 for | 4,500 |

£

| | |
|---|---|
| Silvergilt charger by Pierre Harrache, 1700, 24 in. diam. 187 oz. | 5,200 |
| 1966 C. Covered punchbowl by James Fraillon, 1717, 232 oz. | 5,400 |
| Milner. C. Irish wine cistern, 1715, 315 oz. | 5,200 |
| Hamwee. C. Pair of covered water jugs, Robert Cooper, 1705, 66 oz. 2 for | 9,500 |
| Pair of double-ended sauceboats, Paul Crespin, 1723, 38 oz. 2 for | 3,800 |
| C. The Paul Methuen service, 144 silvergilt knives, forks and spoons, 1714 (original cost £175 11s. 6d.) 144 for | 12,500 |
| Four plain baluster candlesticks by Paul Lamerie, 1726, 7½ in. high, 89 oz. 4 for | 10,000 |
| Pair of salvers by Philip Rollos, 1705, 11¾ in. diam., 79 oz. 2 for | 6,000 |
| S. Pair of double-ended sauceboats by Louis Cuny, 1724, 42 oz. 2 for | 5,600 |
| Another pair by Anthony Nelme 1721, 35 oz. 3 dwt. 2 for | 2,350 |
| Seven-sided teapot, 1725, by Isaac Ribouleau (£2,500 in 1960), bought in at | 5,200 |
| 1967 Protheroe-Beynon. C. Two-handled cup and cover, oval in section, by Pierre Patel, 1707, 48 oz. | 3,500 |
| C. Octagonal box and cover, 1720, by Lamerie and Crispin | 6,000 |
| Lord Haddington. S. Chocolate pot with side-handle, 8 in. high, 21 oz. 11 dwt., by Pierre Harrache, 1703 | 4,700 |
| Pair of baluster jugs and covers by Seth Lofthouse, 1713, 9½ in. high, 61 oz. 11 dwt. 2 for | 5,800 |
| Two-handled cup and cover by Simpsone, Edinburgh, 1709, 10½ in. high, 59 oz. 11 dwt. | 4,000 |
| Octagonal coffeepot by Colin Mackenzie, Edinburgh, 1713, 35 oz. 15 dwt. (the first to achieve this price) | 6,000 |
| Hot-water jug matching the above, 7½ in. high, 15 oz. 3 dwt. | 3,800 |
| Two pairs of candlesticks by Pierre Patel, 1717 and 1724 adapted as candelabra, 139 oz. 5 dwt. 4 for | 8,200 |
| Michael Noble. C. *Gold* bullet-shaped teapot, a race prize, 1726, by James Ker, Edinburgh (£70 in 1847, £1,250 in 1940), 20 oz. 4 dwt. | 40,000 |
| *Gold* cup and cover by Pierre Harrache, race prize, 1705, 23 oz. 6 dwt. (£450 in 1898, £1,800 in 1911) | 31,000 |
| Fifteen-sided salver, 11¼ in. diam. 35 oz. by Augustine Courtauld, 1723 | 8,500 |
| Plain *gold* mug, Newcastle, 1722, 8 oz. 5 dwt. | 6,800 |

| | | | |
|---|---|---|---|
| 1967 | Lewis, Toronto. S. Four silvergilt candlesticks by Thomas Folkingham, 1725 | 4 for | 5,500 |
| 1968 | Phillips, Son and Neale. Two candlesticks by Nathaniel Locke, 1715, 36 oz. | 2 for | 4,000 |

Bearns, Torquay. Queen Anne teapot, undated, Pentecost Symonds, Exeter, 16¼ oz. 5,400

C. Octagonal coffeepot, ivory side-handle, 9¼ in. 28 oz. by Anthony Nelme, 1720 5,500

Cylindrical coffeepot by Johathan Rand, 1707, 9½ in., 19 oz. 1 dwt. (£320, 1949), compare 1969 3,600

McPherson-Grant. S. Chocolate pot, same design, 9¾ in. 27 oz. 8 dwt., by Gabriel Sleath, 1711 4,200

Milligan. S. Coffeepot by Semirot, Cork, c. 1715, 10½ in., 33 oz. 16 dwt. 5,000

Morrison. C. Covered jug by Alice Sheen, 1703, 11 in. high, 39 oz. 4,000

Bruegger. S. Octagonal teapot, 6¼ in. high, 17 oz. 5 dwt. by Richard Green, 1718 2,800

S. Snuffer-stand by Lewis Mettayer, 1708, 4¾ in. high, 10 oz. 18 dwt. 2,400

Colville. C. Round-bellied jug by John East, 1724, 7 in. high, 30 oz. 3,000

Fluted and scalloped armorial dish by David Willaume, 1715, 10 in. diam., 26 oz. 5,800

Mirror by Samuel Margas, 1725, gadrooned silver rim, 37 in. high, 113 oz. 4,800

Makins. S. Cylindrical coffeepot by Edward Feline, 1725, 8½ in. high, 24 oz. 3,800

C. Pair of castellated double-ended sauceboats by Abraham Buteaux, 1726, 41 oz 2 for 10,000

Octagonal coffeepot by Edward Yorke, 1719, Petley Ley, overstriking, 10 in. high, 33 oz. 5,800

Pear-shaped teapot by Thomas Farren, 1716, 11 oz. 19 dwt. 3,200

Octagonal teapot by William Fleming, 1714, 7½ in. high, 17 oz. 12 dwt. 2,800

Three cylindrical castors by William Gamble, 1700, 17 oz. 15 dwt. (£381 in 1929) 3 for 4,200

Pair of candlesticks, fluted columns, by Richard Syng, 1698, 9½ in. high, 31 oz. (£107 in 1937) 2 for 3,200

Gubbay. S. Salver by Francis Crump, 1758, on tripod by Ambrose Stephenson, 1715, 24½×21½, 364 oz. 3 dwt. 5,500

S. Octagonal coffeepot, 10 in., 28 oz. 14 dwt., by John Bache, 1718 5,500

1968  Johnston-Stewart. S. Plain bowl, 7½ in. diam. by Colin  £
Campbell, Edinburgh, 1718, 20 oz. 11 dwt.     4,200

Richmond. S. Pair of table candlesticks by Paul Lamerie,
1720, 6¾ in., 24 oz.        2 for   4,100

S. Coffeepot 1734, by Augustine Courtauld. 8 in.,
23¼ oz.             2,600

Hannam. S. Four candlesticks, 6¾ in. by John Diggle,
1725, with two fitting Louis XV branches, 86 oz. 14 dwt.
             2 for   6,800

Johnston-Stewart. S. Octagonal salver by W. Aytoun,
Edinburgh, 1731, 13¾ in. diam., 47 oz. 19 dwt.    3,400

Hartnoll. S. Cylindrical plain coffeepot, Gabriel Sleath,
1733, 9¾ in., 25 oz. 15 dwt.       2,700

Cameron. S. Two candlesticks, James Gould, 1732, 6¾ in.,
25 oz. 17 dwt.          2,000

S. Bullet teapot, Bowles Nash, 1723, 14 oz. 12 dwt. (compare 1963)            2,100

C. Cylindrical coffeepot, David King, Dublin, 1734,
8¼ in., 23 oz.          4,200

Carbery. C. Pear-shaped jug, harp-handle, Francis
Spilsbury, 1735, 8 in. high, 36 oz.      6,200

S. Cup, 1½ in. high, Colin Mackenzie, c. 1700, weighs
only 17 dwt.           580

Cylindrical coffeepot, Gabriel Sleath, 1733, 8¾ in.,
22 oz. 16 dwt.          3,200

C. Pair candlesticks, later nozzles, Simon Pantin, 1711,
30 oz.

1969  S. Silvergilt salver, Fleurant David, 1724, 54 oz. 4 dwt.,
13¾ in.            5,000

Cylindrical coffeepot, Edward Feline, 1733, 26 oz.   3,000

Cylindrical coffeepot, Joseph Saunders, 1738, 8¾ in.
high, 26 oz. 16 dwt.         2,700

C. Pair of exceptionally plain table candlesticks, octagonal
bases by Matthew Cooper, 1715, 8 in. high, 30 oz   2 for   5,000

Pair of covered water-jugs by Charles Kandler, 1733,
*Régence* style, 10¾ in. high, 105 oz.    2 for   9,500

Norman Hurst. C. Pair of very plain pear-shaped jugs
by David Willaume, 1730, 8 in. high, 73 oz.   2 for   16,500

Conical coffeepot by Simon Pantin, 1709, unusual
large knob to the domed lid, 9¾ in. 27 oz. (see 1962)   11,500

S. Baluster water-jug by Robert Cooper, 1708, 9¼ in. high,
29 oz. 3 dwt.          4,800

Bullet teapot, 5¼ in. high, by Richard Bayley, 1737,
21 oz. 2 dwt. (24.4.69. On 3.12.69 it was bought in at
Christies at £900)         3,200

1969 C. Cylindrical coffeepot. Simon Pantin 1723, 10 in., £
28 oz.                                                                    2,800
International Publishing Corp. C. Round silvergilt
salver, gadrooned rim, arms of Wentworth, by John Bache,
1713, 24 in. diam., 180 oz. 3 dwt. (£4,100 in 1963)       10,000
Barker. C. Octagonal teapot, wooden handle, Peter
Archambo, 1721, 22 oz.                                               6,800
C. Pear-shaped plain milk jug, wood handle, by William
Lukin, 1710, 6 in. high, 12 oz. 11 dwt.                        3,570
N.Y. Chocolate pot, 1702 by the same, $14,000       5,833
Tankard, Cornelius Kierstade, New York, 1710,
$16,500                                                                       6,875
Ketton-Cremer. C. Cylindrical coffeepot, · Anthony
Nelme, 1714, 10 in. high, 25 oz.                             1,732 10s.
C. Oblong inkstand, Benjamin Pyne, 1718, 12¾ in. long,
55 oz.                                                                           1,890
Gilmour. S. Octagonal coffeepot by Henry Jay, 1718,
19 oz. 18 dwt.                                                           1,900
C. Chamber-pot by Isaac Ligier, 1725, 7¼ in., 31 oz.   2,900
St Mary's Church, Twyford. C. Pear-shaped jug by
John Elston, Exeter, 1722, 9 in. high, 41 oz.            3,400
C. Bullet-shaped teapot by Lamerie, 1717, 12 oz. 18 dwt. 4,000
Gough. C. Octagonal coffeepot, William Paradise, 1726,
23 oz.                                                                          2,900
Octagonal pear-shaped teapot by Joseph Ward, 1717,
13 oz. 9 dwt.                                                            2,600
Octagonal pear-shaped milk pot, Richard Raine, 1713,
9 oz. 6 dwt.                                                              2,800
Octagonal kettle-stand and lamp, John Rand, 1713,
9½ in., 27 oz                                                           2,800
Lord Waleran. C. Set of 4 table candlesticks, Anthony
Tripe, Exeter, 1737, 6½ in. high, 49 oz.                  2,100
Denny. S. Cylindrical coffeepot, Jonathan Rand, 1705,
21 oz. 10 dwt. (compare 1968)                               2,200

*Rococo*, 1730–1770

The ponderous rococo revival of the early and middle 19th century should have favoured the collecting of silver in the rich French style, the later style of Paul Lamerie. In fact silver, later than the reign of Charles I, had scarcely any antiquarian value so that Lamerie's most important works were sold at not much over melting down price. Most of Horace Walpole's Lamerie salvers in 1842 and the Duke of Sussex's Lamerie tea urn in 1843 were sold for 8 shillings and even 5 shillings an ounce. Two big oval tureens in the Duke of Argyll's sale in 1858 made no more. It was only in the 1890s when rococo silver was less frequently a subject of emulation, that Lamerie made as much as 60 shillings an ounce. Yet by the year 1919 the Victoria and Albert had to pay £3,000 to secure a Lamerie *surtout de table*, dated 1743. Equivalent to £24,000 this meant that the level of 1970 had been equalled if not surpassed. Similarly, two Lamerie candelabra, made for Robert Walpole in 1731, cost £308 in 1893 at 40s. an ounce. Bought in 1924 at £3,003 they were worth more than the sum of £11,000 which they made in devalued money in 1966. The great slump and the fall in the world-price of bullion silver dealt particularly hard with Lamerie. At the Hillingdon sale in 1933 two of Horace Walpole's salvers, weighing nearly 53 ounces, were sold for £227, while a third and larger salver, which was to make £3,100 in 1965 was sold for £263. A recovery almost to the levels of the 1920s was followed by a second fall during the Second World War, almost as severe as the fall during the slump. The most important pieces could again be had for a few hundreds. English rococo silver was not well and truly in fashion again until the 1950s. Yet another of Horace Walpole's salvers had made over £100 in 1842 at 14s. 6d. an ounce on account of its special ornateness. The price of £7,800 which the Victoria and Albert Museum paid in 1955, was as good as £12,500 in the money of 1970 but it was equivalent to no more than £2,500 in the money of the 1920s, when this salver might have been in the £3,000 to £4,000 class. Not only has English rococo silver failed to recover its former position, but in the case of standard quality pieces of little varying appearance it has failed to retain the gains of the 1960s. The list shows that table-candlesticks which have survived in particular abundance, fell by a half or more in the course of the generally booming year 1969. Some sets of four may have dropped to a third of the value which they had reached in the summer of 1968, a matter which did not elude the eye of the Sunday press. But if the 1960s ended with a question mark, the run of prices for English rococo silver had been none the less impressive. It is certain that in the course of the decade at least 50 lots changed hands at £5,000 or more, 7 of them exceeding £15,000 each. Most of these costly pieces bore the mark of Paul Lamerie. Considering the enormous output of this workshop, output of a quality not above average by contemporary French standards, these prices are pretty remarkable.

| | | £ |
|---|---|---|
| 1960 S. Canteen and two caddies by Lamerie, 1737 (£1,500 in 1954) | 3 for | 6,600 |
| Fitted inkstand by Lamerie, 8½ in. long 1733 (£285, 1942) | | 3,600 |
| Covered cup by Lamerie, 1744 (£350 in 1941) | | 2,500 |
| Three scallop-shaped épergnes by Lamerie, 4½ in. wide (£225 in 1942) | 3 for | 3,200 |
| S. Pair of candlesticks by Lamerie, 1726, 7¾ in. high, 88 oz. (£780 in 1944) | 2 for | 5,600 |
| Fairfax of Cameron. S. Sideboard ewer by Lamerie, | | |

|  |  |  | £ |
|---|---|---|---|
| | 1736, 14 in. high, 79 oz. | | 4,200 |
| | Tureen and cover by Lamerie, 1734, 13½ in. wide | | 3,400 |
| | Pair of cake-baskets by Lamerie, 203 oz. | 2 for | 3,600 |
| 1961 | Whitmarshe. N.Y. Toilet service, 1761 | | 2,235 |
| | Duke of Leeds. S. Pair of covered bowls and stands by | | |
| | S. Herbert, 1752, 5¼ in. diam. | 2 for | 2,800 |
| | Pair of salvers by Lamerie | 2 for | 2,100 |
| | Klein. S. Chamber pot by Isaac Ligier, 1737, 29 oz. | | 2,600 |
| | S. Six salvers, silvergilt, by David Willaume, 1743 | 6 for | 6,800 |
| 1962 | S. Pair of tureens and covers by Lamerie, 1734–7, arms of | | |
| | Lord Chancellor Hardwicke, 359 oz. | 2 for | 6,300 |
| | C. Pair of beer-jugs by Aymé Videau, 1751 | 2 for | 2,300 |
| | de Kusel. C. Pair of candlesticks by Lamerie, 28 oz. | | |
| | 1 dwt. (£112 in 1924) | 2 for | 2,800 |
| | S. Elaborate épergne-centrepiece by David Willaume, | | |
| | 1732 | | 3,400 |
| | Hasell. S. Set of eight strawberry-dishes by Lamerie, | | |
| | 1730s, 83 oz. 4 dwt. | 8 for | 9,000 |
| | S. Oblong tea-tray by Lamerie, 28¾ in. wide, 182 oz. | | |
| | 13 dwt. | | 8,500 |
| | Pair of strawberry-dishes by Lamerie, 1736, 9¾ in. | | |
| | diam., 43 oz. | 2 for | 5,000 |
| 1963 | Lord Bury. C. The Young Pretender's silvergilt canteen | | |
| | and fittings by Oliphant, Edinburgh, 1740, captured at | | |
| | Culloden | | 7,200 |
| | Vivian. S. Service of 60 octagonal plates and dishes by | | |
| | Godfrey and le Sage, 1728, 1733 and 1742 | 60 for | 14,000 |
| | Hamwee. S. Pair of cake-baskets by Lamerie, 1734, | | |
| | height 5¼ in., 81 oz. 10 dwt. (recently acquired for £8,000) | | |
| | | 2 for | 15,500 |
| | Set of four strawberry-bowls and stands, c. 1750 | | |
| | (£5,200 in 1961) | 4 for | 6,500 |
| | Pair of strawberry-dishes by David Willaume, 1729 | | |
| | (£2,600 in 1962) | 2 for | 3,800 |
| | Lord Brownlow. C. Wine-cooler by Thomas Hem- | | |
| | ming, 1770, 1,460 oz. bought in at | | 15,000 |
| | Dinner service, 1761–8, various makers, 2,663 oz. | | |
| | | 94 for | 22,500 |
| | C. The Exeter toilet set, David Willaume the younger, | | |
| | 1734 (£5,200 in 1959), 332 oz. 5 dwt. | | 8,800 |
| 1964 | Rex Beaumont. C. Cake-basket by Lamerie, 1743, | | |
| | 14¼ in. wide, 62 oz. 15 dwt. (£270 in 1941) | | 3,200 |
| | Mrs James de Rothschild. C. Tureen, cover and stand by | | |
| | Paul Crespin, arms of Somerset, 1740 (£178 in 1888) | | 8,500 |

£

Phipps. S. Pair of salvers by Lamerie, 1736    2 for   10,500

1965   Harewood. C. Pair of candlesticks, Lamerie, 1739, 49 oz.
             2 for   4,000

Alexander. S. Two pairs, engraved beakers, 1¾ and 3¾ in. high, 14¼ oz. by Aimé Videau, 1743    4 for   3,800

Earl of Devon. S. 2-handled cup and cover, John le Sage, 1734, 100 oz.             2,800

Johnson. C. Pair of candlesticks, Lamerie, 1741, 8½ in.
             2 for   3,400

Bathurst. C. Pair of salvers by Edward Vincent, 1728, engraved in Hogarth's style, 13 in. diam.    2 for   6,500

Bryan Jenks. S. Pair of tureens and covers by Lamerie, 1758, 11 in. wide, 201 oz. (£357 in 1893, £382 in 1929)
             2 for   7,000

Two square waiters by Lamerie, 1747, 27 oz. 12 dwt.
             2 for   4,400

Inkstand, Lamerie, 1744, 81 oz. 16 dwt. (£500, 1946, see also 1967)              4,400

Four candlesticks, Lamerie, 1739, 96 oz. 13 dwt. (£1,650, 1958)    4 for   6,500

Tea-kettle, stand and lamp by Lamerie, 1736, 106 oz. 5 dwt.              6,000

1966   C. Pair of four-armed candelabra by Lamerie, 1731, arms of Robert Walpole, 154 oz. (£308 in 1893, £3,003 in 1924)
             2 for   11,000

S. Silvergilt toilet service by Isaac Ligier, 1728 (£1,050 in 1937)    23 for   14,500

Pair of covered water-jugs by Charles Kaendler, 1733
             2 for   4,800

Milner. C. Kettle-stand and lamp by Lamerie, 1732, 96 oz.              6,500

Adain. C. Ornate cup and cover by Lamerie, 1732, 99 oz.              6,500

1967   S. Inkstand by Lamerie, 1744, 81 oz. (£500 in 1946, £4,400, 1965)              4,000

Holman. S. Pair of wall-sconces in Régence style by Lamerie, 1725, 20½ in. high, 228 oz.    2 for   23,000

Lord Haddington. S. Pair of fruit-baskets by Lamerie, 1724, 10½ in, diam., 61 oz. 5 dwt.    2 for   6,000

1968   Breadalbane. C. The Cumberland tankard, 12¾ in. high, 114 oz. 10 dwt. by Gabriel Sleath, 1746, with engraving of the battle of Culloden (£114 10s. in 1843)              12,000

C. Pair of chased chargers by David Willaume, 1742, silvergilt, 24 in. diam., 398 oz.    2 for   5,400

1968    S.   Two strawberry-dishes by David Williams, 1742, 10 in. diam., 41 oz. 19 dwt.        2 for    4,800

C.   Pair of sauceboats by Lamerie, 1735, 31 oz.    2 for    6,000

Pair of parcelgilt caddies with matching sugar-box, Lamerie, 1747 and 1750, 52 oz. 11 dwt.    3 for    5,500

Irnham.    C.   Pair of tureens and covers by George Methuen, 1759, 11 in. wide, 164 oz.      2 for    5,000

Gundry.   C.   Cake-basket, 13½ in. wide, by John Luff, 1744, 71 oz.          3,800

Butlin.   C.   Tureen and cover, 12 in. wide, by Archambo and Meure, 1751, 112 oz.        2,100

Inkstand by John Edwards, 1744, 16½ in. wide, 116 oz.    6,000

C.   Set of four candlesticks by William Cripps, 1770, 9½ in. high, 91 oz. (for comparable sets, see 1969)    4 for    6,000

Earl of Rosse.   C.   Pair of salvers by Lamerie, 1749, arms of Hawke, 9 in. diam., 51 oz. (£26 5s. 7d. in 1751) 2 for   20,500

Pair of tea-caddies with matching sugar-box, highly chased by Lamerie, arms of Hawke, 1742–4, 5 in. high, 41 oz.          3 for    9,500

N.Y.   Tankard by Thauvet Besley, New York, 1740, $13,000          5,417

S.   Four table candlesticks, Lamerie, 1734, 7¾ in., 76 oz. 15 dwt. (4)        4 for    9,500

Poulett.   S.   Service, 102 dishes and plates, gadrooned borders, William Tuite, 1764, 2,179 oz. 13 dwt; in several lots        102 for   32,685

S.   Four table candlesticks, William Gould, 1768, 68 oz.        4 for    4,000

1969    S.   Four table candlesticks by William Cafe, 1757, 8¾ in. high, 70 oz. 11 dwt.       4 for    3,600

Four table candlesticks by John Cafe, 1765, 91 oz. 4 for    2,300

C.   Shell-shaped sugar bowl and cover, Christian Hillan, 1739, 9 oz. 2 dwt.        2,835

C.   Set of four table candlesticks in ornate French style by Peter Archambo, 1747, 12 in. high, 186 oz.    4 for    2,730

Norman Hurst.   C.   Exceptionally ornate tureen and cover by John Edwards, 1737, with crab lid and dolphin handles, 16¼ in. wide, 141 oz.        15,500

S.   Pair of baluster-shaped covered beer jugs in elaborate French taste by Phillips Garden, 1754, 13½ in. high, 175 oz. 12 dwt.        2 for    17,000

Two oval carving dishes with a fitted *Mazarin* or gravy-strainer by Paul Lamerie, 1744, 20½ in. wide, 203 oz.        3 for    5,800

| | | £ |
|---|---|---|
| 1969 Fausett-Osborne. S. Set of four table-candlesticks by John Cafe, 1755, 8¾ in., 76 oz. 3 dwt. (compare 1968) 4 for | | 1,900 |
| S. Square armorial salver by John Tuite, 1731, 12 in. sq., 33 oz. 17 dwt. (£1,300 in 1963) | | 2,200 |
| C. Set of table-candlesticks by John Edwards, 1749, 8¾ in. high, 85 oz. | 4 for | 2,835 |
| S. Another by William Cafe, 1762, 11 in. high, 102 oz. 17 dwt. | 4 for | 1,800 |
| Another by W. H. Dublin c. 1750, 100 oz. 7 dwt. | 4 for | 1,550 |
| C. Another set by Frederick Kandler, 1746–7, 9 in. 4 for | | 1,800 |
| S. Another by Paul Lamerie, 1733–4, 83 oz. 15 dwt., 8 in. high | 4 for | 5,000 |
| A pair ditto 1735, 6¼ in. high, 28 oz. 11 dwt. | 2 for | 2,800 |
| Also by Lamerie, tea kettle, lamp and stand, 1734, 69 oz., 9 dwt. | | 2,800 |

## Neo-classic, c. 1770–1815

In the earlier neo-classic period English silver adopted the suffocating symmetry of Greek vases, long attenuated handles which seem at odds with the solidity of the material, and a tiresome, lacy and repetitive style of engraved ornament. Among all the styles of pre-Victorian silver this is the least costly. As late as 1947 the sum of £400 bought a late 18th century wine-cistern, three feet wide, at about its melting down value. In the later 1960s the fact that late 18th century English silver was readily available made it a substitute for the improcurable and sent up the price of uninteresting items of no quality. About six months after the devaluation of the pound, this sort of silver, together with rococo English silver made after the time of Lamerie, showed signs of wilting. Particularly vulnerable were bulbous coffeepots and table candlesticks in the French manner. It was alleged that hall marks had been bought on the public advice of the tipster-pundits as if they were rare postage stamps. But I think the real reason was even sillier, namely a fall in the bullion-price of silver from the boom-price of 22s. 6d. an ounce to 14s. 1d.

The temporary recoil of some silver of the second half of the 18th century had little effect on the continuous rise of silver in the heavier, more ostentatious, neo-classic style, introduced from France after 1800. Simply because until recently it had offended against the canons of good taste, this silver could not be anything else than fashionable, particularly the work of Paul Storr, a man of no originality but a capable designer who could accommodate himself to the even more exuberant vulgarity of the 1830s as well as anybody. As late as the 1930s his work was entirely without friends. In 1930 the Earl of Balfour's dessert service, made by Storr and Mortimer between 1809 and 1829, was sold at 9s. 6d. an ounce. At £3,600 it was £520 cheaper than in 1861 when it was a

22*

secondhand service in an out-of-date style. With the price of this service which weighed a third of a ton, one may compare a mere 28 items from Paul Storr's Harewood service, which realized £44,300 in 1965.

Of the earlier neo-classic style—the Adam style as it were—very few single objects have made more than £3,000, but there is one notable exception. In 1968 Parke Bernet sold a typical teapot of 1793, straight sided, fluted with some prim engraving and a wooden handle. As an English teapot, it might have made well under a thousand pounds, but as the work of Paul Revere of Boston, it was thought worthy of $70,000 or £29,166, more than four times as much as any silver teapot sold in the inflated currency of the 1960s.

|      |                                                                                                      |         | £     |
|------|------------------------------------------------------------------------------------------------------|---------|-------|
| 1961 | Lady Craven.  S.  Pair of candelabra by Schofield, 1783, 145½ oz. (see 1967)                         | 2 for   | 3,600 |
|      | Toilet service by Smith and Sharp, 1783, 437 oz.                                                      | 12 for  | 9,600 |
| 1962 | Packe.  C.  Two-handled wine cistern by James and Eliza Bland, 1794, 35 in. wide, 1,150 oz. (£400 in 1947) |    | 3,400 |
|      | Rolt.  S.  Punchbowl by Hester Bateman, 1784, 12¾ in. diam., bought by Chester Corporation            |         | 1,500 |
| 1963 | S.  Set of wine-coolers by Paul Storr, 1807, arms of Hamilton, 686 oz.                               | 4 for   | 4,700 |
|      | C.  Jewish sabbath-lamp by Hester Bateman, 1781                                                       |         | 1,700 |
| 1964 | Tremayne.  S.  Pair of covered boxes on pedestals, inspired by Chinese lacquer, by Paul Storr, 1810, 15 in. high | 2 for | 2,800 |
|      | S.  Set of four candelabra with naturalistic lilies, 1794                                            | 4 for   | 4,700 |
| 1965 | Harewood.  C.  Set of four 2-light candelabra by Thomas Hemming, 1774, 17 in. high, 123 oz.          | 4 for   | 2,800 |
|      | Matching pair, 18½ in. high, 67 oz. 15 dwt., by John Schofield, 1794                                 | 2 for   | 2,200 |
|      | Silvergilt banquet service by Paul Storr, 1814–15, 28 pieces in 13 lots, £44,300 e.g.                |         |       |
|      | 2 pairs of oval dessert-baskets, 207 oz. 14 dwt.                                                     | 4 for   | 6,300 |
|      | 4 sugar-urns and covers, 8 in. high, 130 oz. 2 dwt. (see 1966)                                       | 4 for   | 4,000 |
|      | 12 dessert plates, 8½ in. diam., 206 oz.                                                             | 12 for  | 4,000 |
|      | Pair of 14-inch dessert stands, 266 oz. 18 dwt. (see 1966)                                           | 2 for   | 4,400 |
|      | Eight-light candelabrum, 43½ in. high, 1,019 oz.                                                     |         | 2,800 |
|      | Pair of six-light candelabra, 32 in. high, 1,027 oz.                                                 | 2 for   | 7,600 |
|      | Pair of 'Warwick vase' wine-coolers, 18 in. high, 672 oz. 10 dwt.                                    | 2 for   | 3,000 |
|      | Oval tray (part of the service, but by Scott and Smith, 1805), 25¾ in., 250 oz. 5dwt.               |         | 3,300 |
| 1966 | S.  Four wine-coolers by Benjamin Smith, 1806                                                        | 4 for   | 4,000 |

£

| | | |
|---|---|---|
| 1966 | S. Pair of matching tureens, stands and covers 2 for Killam. C. Seven lots from the Harewood sale, 1965, rose from £16,400 to £22,600 e.g. | 3,300 |
| | Four sugar urns by Paul Storr, 1814 (£4,000 in 1965) 4 for | 4,600 |
| | Pair of dessert stands by Paul Storr, 1814 (£4,400 in 1965) 2 for | 5,200 |
| 1967 | S. Pair of two-light candelabra, John Schofield, 1783 (see 1961) 2 for | 6,000 |
| | Silvergilt punchbowl by Thomas Hemming in Adam style, 1771, 195 oz. | 6,200 |
| | C. Pair of wine-coolers, arms of Lowther, 1807, by Benjamin Smith, 284 oz. (£390 in 1947) 2 for | 3,600 |
| | Feinberg. N.Y. Jewish sabbath lamp, 34½ in. high, by Samuel Hennell, 1813, $8,000 at 2·40 | 3,335 |
| 1968 | C. Complete cruet-frame by Rundell, Bridge and Rundell, 1804, 14 in. wide, 123 oz. (£58 3s. in 1827, £173 in 1914) | 4,800 |
| | Butlin. C. Set of 12 armorial dishes by Benjamin Smith, 1807, with four replacements by Garrard, 1862, 540 oz. (16) | 16,000 |
| | S. Pair of wine-coolers by Benjamin Smith, 1811, 11¼ in. high, 273 oz. 2 for | 7,200 |
| | Three tureens, covers and stands by Paul Storr in Adam style, 1792, 400 oz. 2 dwt. 3 for | 9,500 |
| | Spencer. Retford. Two wine-coolers in Egyptian style by Scott and Smith, 1805, 12 in. high, 399 oz. 2 for | 6,050 |
| | Butlin. C. Pair of wine-coolers and stands by B. & J. Smith, 1811, arms of Crawford, 14¼ in. high, 503 oz. 4 for | 9,000 |
| | C. Boat-shaped tureen, cover and stand by Robert Sharp, 1789, 19¼ in. wide, 177 oz. | 4,200 |
| | Four sauceboats, covers and stands of the same form by Robert Breading, Dublin, 1788, each 11¼ in. wide, 172 oz. 4 for | 5,200 |
| | Braybrooke. S. Pair of tureens and covers by Wakelin and Garrard, 1798, 16½ in. wide, 168 oz. 2 for | 3,600 |
| | C. Pair of 3-light candelabra by John Schofield, 1799, 17 in. high, 59 oz. 2 for | 4,000 |
| | Clarke-Jervoise. C. Pair of oval soup tureens and covers, 13½ in. wide, 235 oz., by J. Denzilow, 1779 2 for | 5,800 |
| | Christie. N.Y. Straight sided fluted teapot, wooden handle, Paul Revere, Boston, 1793, $70,000 | 29,166 |
| | Matching cream jug, height 5 in., $16,500 | 6,791 |
| | Tankard by the same with engraved ship, c. 1770, 8½ in., $14,500 | 6,417 |

1969 S. Set of four wine-coolers, silvergilt in ornate Grecian    £
style, 2 by Paul Storr, 1813, and 2 by Benjamin Smith, 1807,
11¾ in. high, 448 oz. 17 dwt.                4 for    8,000

     Oval engraved tea-caddy by Hester Bateman, 1782,
5½ in. high, 11 oz. (another dated 1785, 4½ in. 11 oz.
11 dwt., made £950)                              2,000

d'Arcy Sykes. S. Richmond race cup by Smith and
Sharp, 1768, with *appliqué* riding scene, 17½ in. high, 112 oz.
17 dwt.                                          1,850

C. Pair of 2-light candelabra in Adam style by William
Pitts, 1805, 18½ in. high, 175 oz.           2 for    2,500

S. Two-handled cup and cover in *gold* by Parker and
Wakelin, 1772, 9½ in. high, 40 oz. (commissioned at 78s. an
oz. plus £50, making £157 15s.)                 8,500

     Four-piece tea set by Paul Storr, 1815, 134 oz. 18 dwt.
                                         4 for    3,500

     Heavy six-light centrepiece, mounted on lions in
Empire style by Paul Storr, 1813, 394 oz. 1 dwt.
(£2,700 in following December)                  5,200

     Latticework *épergne* with 8 branches by Thomas
Powell, 1774, 14 in. high, 121 oz. 8 dwt.         1,950

C. Pair of entrée-dishes by Paul Storr, 1815, plain except
for the gadrooned edges, 12¼ in. wide, 223 oz.    2 for    2,800

S. Four salt cellars in form of tritons bearing shells, Paul
Storr after William Theed, 1811, 4¾ in. wide, 82 oz. 12 dwt.
                                         4 for    3,400

     Eight silvergilt toilet boxes with mythology scenes by
Smith and Sharp, 1783, 375 oz.           8 for    25,000

Grocers Company. C. Pair of tureens, stands and covers
by Parker and Wakelin, 1772 (semi-rococo), 14½ in. wide,
525 oz.                                    6 for    6,200

N.Y. Five-piece tea and coffee set by John David, Snr.
and Jnr., Philadelphia, c. 1790, $26,500      5 for   11,042

Reeve. C. Pair of very simple table-candlesticks, lightly
engraved by Hester Bateman, 1781, 11¾ in. high   2 for    2,625

C. Pair of 2-light candelabra by Ebenezer Coker, 1766–8,
13¾ in. high, 82 oz.                    2 for    2,205

     Three spherical sugar urns and covers, 5¾ and 7½ in.
high, 36 oz. by Paul Storr, 1800          3 for    2,000

C. Heavy six-light centrepiece, silvergilt, by Paul Storr,
1813, 23½ in. high (£5,200 in April, see *supra*) in December   2,700

     Plain coffeepot, Hester Bateman, 1781, 11½ in., 28 oz.    1,100

*Eclectic styles, 1815–1900*
(largely Renaissance and rococo styles)

Imitations of German baroque ivory tankards, of medieval objects and what was thought to be the Cellini style are to be found in English silver, made before the end of the Napoleonic wars. But that peculiar flyblown rococo style, which was to remain universal between the 1830s and 1880s, scarcely arrived before 1815 and was not widely used at first. Well into the 1820s rich plate tended to borrow French motives, derived from Roman silver, the source of all those tendrils and grape clusters, beloved of Paul Storr. The present list is mainly concerned with the rococo revival, though it includes excursions into the Renaissance throughout the century. Most of it is of a kind which made no more than melting-down prices until as late as the 1950s. In the 1920s, when few *Victoriana* had become expensively amusing, a lot of this silver lay hidden in attics. In the 1960s, when even late 19th century silver could make £7 an ounce at times, attics ceased to be what they were. *Lasciate ogni speranza voi ch'entrate!*

|      |                                                                                                                                              |        | £     |
|------|----------------------------------------------------------------------------------------------------------------------------------------------|--------|-------|
| 1958 | C.  Pair of tureens by Robert Garrard, 1829, 225 oz.                                                                                          | 2 for  | 680   |
| 1961 | Duke of Sutherland.  C.  Four wine-coolers by Philip Rundell, 1819 and 1822, 429 oz.                                                          | 4 for  | 1,700 |
|      | S.  Set of chessmen in medieval style by Edward Farrell, 1816 (£145 in 1937, £483 in 1956)                                                    |        | 2,250 |
| 1962 | C.  Pair of pilgrim-bottles by Edward Farrell, 1823, 225 oz. 15 dwt., Renaissance style                                                       | 2 for  | 1,550 |
| 1965 | Harewood.  C.  Nine-light candelabrum, silvergilt, supported on figures in rococo style, by Robert Garrard, 1844, 42 in. high, 785 oz.        |        | 1,250 |
| 1966 | Mitchell.  S.  Tankard by Paul Storr, 1835, with bacchanals in German 17th century style                                                      |        | 1,350 |
| 1967 | Milnes Coates.  C.  Hercules slaying the hydra, silvergilt sculpture group with candle-holders, by Edward Farrell, 1824, 1,144 oz. (£343 5s. 6d. in 1827) |        | 4,800 |
| 1967 | Feinberg.  N.Y.  Jewish Barmitzvah candelabrum by Robert Garrard, 1862, 43 in. high, $4,750 at 2·40                                           |        | 1,980 |
| 1968 | Bromage.  S.  Pair of wine-coolers by W. K. Reid, 1832, 270 oz. 13 dwt.                                                                       | 2 for  | 2,600 |
|      | Stephenson.  S.  The George Stephenson tankard, Newcastle, 1817, 9½ in. high, 83 oz. 15 dwt.                                                   |        | 1,750 |
|      | Spencer (Retford) auctioneers.  Pair of three-branch candelabra by Storr and Mortimer, 1836–8, 365 oz. 18 dwt., arms of Ashburham            | 2 for  | 2,500 |
|      | Salver, monogram of Queen Victoria, 1838, 114 oz.                                                                                             |        | 1,250 |
|      | von Essen.  C.  Pair of 7-light candelabra in Louis XV style by J. S. Hunt, 1848 and 1852, 30¾ in. high, 484 oz.                              | 2 for  | 2,625 |

| | | £ |
|---|---|---|
| 1968 | Butlin. C. Pair of double wine coaster-wagons, 20½ in. long, 403 oz. 1829 (original cost £187 19s. 10d.) 2 for | 5,800 |
| | Charger by Paul Storr, 1817, the Triumph of Bacchus after Stothard, 30¾ in. diam., 357 oz. (£250 in 1944) | 8,500 |
| | Cecil King. S. Presentation cup and cover in High Renaissance style, by Paul Storr, 1837, 13½ in. high, 53 oz. 15 dwt. | 1,350 |
| | Silvergilt *surtout de table* with 12 lights by Paul Storr, 1816, 36¾ in. high, 1,356 oz. 15 dwt. | 6,000 |
| | Similar pair with six lights each en suite, 24 in. high, 760 oz. 2 dwt. 2 for | 14,000 |
| | Cornell. S. Four sauceboats in elaborate baroque renaissance style by Paul Storr, 1812, and Robert Garrard, 1818, 10 in. wide, 163 oz. 2 dwt. 4 for | 5,500 |
| | S. Four table-candlesticks with two fitting three-light branches, by Paul Storr, 1816, 278 oz. 13 dwt. 4 for | 6,500 |
| | S. Soup-tureen, cover and stand by Robert Garrard, 1839, Renaissance style, 268 oz. 10 dwt. | 2,400 |
| | Phillips, son and Neale. Pair of Gothic claret jugs by George Angell after William Burges, 1864–5, 116 oz. 2 for | 1,800 |
| | Clarke. S. Rococo *épergne* with eight branches in the style of Lamerie by Martin Hall, 1878, 315 oz. 10 dwt. | 2,100 |
| | Butlin. C. 2-handled vase, heavily chased battle scene, by Paul Storr, 1834, 23 in. high, 250 oz. | 2,300 |
| | S. Pair of 3-light candelabra; stands, 1838, branches 1825, 18 in. high, 236 oz. 13 dwt. 2 for | 2,400 |
| | Pair of campana-shaped wine-coolers, Richard Sibley, 1828, 10½ in. high, 188 oz. 10 dwt. 2 for | 2,100 |
| 1969 | S. Mirror-plateau, silvergilt in Renaissance style by Benjamin Smith, 1828, 23¾ in. wide | 3,600 |
| | Arundell. C. Pseudo-medieval 'Glastonbury' tankard and cover by Philip Rundell, 1820, 8½ in., 101 oz. | 1,950 |
| | Modinos. S. Pair of pie-dishes, covers and stands by Barnard Bros., 1844, Renaissance style, 17 in. wide, 200 oz. 17 dwt. 2 for | 1,550 |
| | Zetland. S. Pair of frosted glass claret jugs, richly mounted with grape-vines etc., John Hunt, 1845, 14 in. high 2 for | 920 |
| | S. Presentation silvergilt, *surtout de table* in rococo style, Bernard Bros., 1844, 33½ in. high, 427 oz. 15 dwt. | 2,900 |
| | Tureen, rococo style, Sheffield, 1837, 140 oz. 17 dwt. | 1,200 |
| | C. King's pattern table service, 193 knifes, forks, spoons, etc., 1827–8, 370 oz. | 2,100 |
| | S. Pair of rococo tureens by Paul Storr, 1820, 287 oz. 17 dwt., 15¼ in. wide 2 for | 5,500 |

1969   S.   Pair of wine-coolers to match, 8¾ in. high, 269 oz. 13 dwt.   £ 4,000

Slaughter.   S.   4-piece tea set in high rococo style by Paul Storr, 1827, 94 oz. 9 dwt.   4 for   1,300

C.   Pair of entrée dishes with covers and stands in an unbelievably ornate German Renaissance style, by J. H. Hunt, 1846, 20 in. wide, 700 oz.   2 for   2,400

S.   Pair of wine-coolers, campana-shaped in baroque revival style, by Emes and Barnard, 1822, 3,400 oz.   2 for   4,500

Grocers' Company.   C.   Pair of 9-light candelabra, Robert Garrard, 1850 and 1853, 36¼ in., 1,158 oz.   2 for   3,465

Pair of 9-light candelabra, Robert Garrard, dated 1836 and 1842, 42 in. high, rococo style, 1574 oz.   2 for   5,880

S.   Caviar pail in form of conch, supported by tritons, arms of Worontsov Dashkov. Mortimer & Hunt, 1841, 187 oz. 8 dwt.   2,200

N.Y.   Ewer and cover in Baroque revival style by Paul Storr, 1827, $3,500   1,459

C.   4 table candlesticks, Craddock and Reid, 1819–20 in high rococo style, 11¾ in. high, 150 oz.   4 for   1,260

Marsden.   S.   Pair of 5-light centrepieces, elaborately sculptured by Barnard Bros., 1849, 33 in. 634 oz.   2 for   1,600

S.   An inconceivable tankard by Sasikov, Petersburg, 1855, 10 in. high, 46 oz. 18 dwt.   700

Pair of twist-stem candlesticks in the Lamerie style by Paul Storr, 1832, 11¾ in., 63 oz. 6 dwt.   2 for   900

Armorial salver in rich rococo style by Richard Sibley, 1833, 346 oz., 31 in. diam.   850

Jowett.   S.   2-handled cup and cover in sculptured Renaissance style by Frederick Courthope, 1886, 179 oz. 16 dwt.   500

# SNUFFBOXES
## Gold, enamel and hard stones

Basically made of gold, smothered in diamonds and the most delicate of enamels, it is the highest triumph of the jeweller's art, so a royal snuffbox of the reign of Louis XV cannot be anything else than extremely expensive. Two of them have cost over £20,000 apiece, but there is no reason why a snuffbox should not cost £50,000. In fact they have gone up less than almost any kind of *objet d'art*. A thousand pounds for a snuffbox was first reached in Paris in 1872 at the Allègre sale. The precise sum, 27,000 francs or £1,088, was equivalent to £9,800, more or less, in 1970. At the second of the famous Hawkins sales in 1904 a box by Hamelin was bought on behalf of Pierpont Morgan for £6,400. Since this was equivalent to £51,200 in 1970 money, the price may well have been the double of its present value, and the same can be said of a considerable number of snuffboxes which were in the £2,000 to £4,000 class before the First World War. Even as late as 1928, a snuffbox, portraying the less than breathtaking charms of Mme Pompadour, made £3,360 which was equivalent to £16,800. But another twenty years were to pass before a snuffbox could again reach £1,000 in the saleroom. At the beginning of the Second World War a chased gold snuffbox by one of the best goldsmiths of the reign of Louis XV made no more than £78. It was only in 1954 at the King Farouk sale in Cairo that record prices for snuffboxes began to be mentioned again. Yet the £12,000 Frederick the Great snuffbox meant no more than £2,300 in pre-1914 money while the £23,000 snuffbox of 1968 meant less than £3,000.

This is not an unusual market performance. Snuffboxes have shared the vicissitudes of French 18th century works of art in general. Two factors have been at work. Firstly the tradition that skill, particularly when allied with precious materials, should rate higher than genius, came under severe attack after the First World War. Secondly the more recent concept of works of art as an escape from bad money favours rarities that are dear to specialists and museum-directors. Such rarities take rank next to alleged works of genius. Objects with a more obvious appeal to wealth retain that appeal, but occupy only the third place.

## ENGLAND
### (including other sorts of enamelled box)

| | | £ |
|---|---|---:|
| 1960 | S. Oblong box, gold, 14½ oz., Edinburgh | 2,450 |
| 1961 | Chester Beatty. S. By Wirgman and Moser, London, 1772 (£350 in 1942) | 4,000 |
| 1963 | Brownlow. C. Patchbox of Mary II, 1690, diamonds on enamelled gold, 2¼ in. diam. | 8,500 |
| | Ionides. S. Battersea enamelled casket after Lancret | 3,300 |
| | Koller, Zurich. Gold enamelled oval box with mechanical bird, London, 1784, FS34,000+tax | 3,300 |

| | | |
|---|---|---|
| 1963 | S. *Nécessaire* in chalcedone and jewelled gold, style of James Cox (£400 in 1950) | £ 2,600 |
| 1967 | S. Round gold box, 2¾ in. diam., David King, Dublin, 1733 | 1,550 |
| 1968 | Ward. C. By Rouw and Barker, 1815, portrait of George IV as Prince Regent | 1,512 |
| | S. Gold and enamel oblong, trellis work, late 18th century | 2,700 |
| 1969 | Henriques. S. Casket, Birmingham enamel, 8 in. wide with *grisaille* subject after Watteau | 3,200 |
| | Pair of Birmingham or Sheffield enamel tea-caddies, 7½ in. with matching spoon and fitted case    2 for | 3,000 |
| | C. *Nécessaire* in form of casket, panels of various stones, mounted on gold stand, late 18th century, style of James Cox, bought in at | 5,250 |
| | Ex King Leopold. S. Freedom box, presented to Prince Leopold of Saxe-Coburg, by John Bridge, 1816, 4½ in. | 3,000 |
| | S. Oblong box, gold and enamel in rococo taste, by Strachan, London, 1835 | 2,800 |

## FRANCE
### (mainly Paris)

| | | |
|---|---|---|
| 1960 | S. Gold and lacquer box, 1752 | 2,150 |
| | Gold, enamelled with brilliants, 1760 | 2,800 |
| | Chiselled gold, 1746 | 3,200 |
| | Gold box, painted *en plein* by Blarenberghe, Louis XVI | 2,500 |
| 1961 | S. By Vachette, 1789, black lacquer and gold | 2,200 |
| | Chester Beatty. S. With buildings in relief in 4-colour gold, *c.* 1735 | 8,500 |
| | By de Mailly, 1787, enamels on gold | 6,200 |
| | By Ducrollay after Teniers, 1759, enamels on gold | 5,400 |
| | By Blarenberghe, 1767 enamelled *en plein* | 5,800 |
| 1963 | Fribourg, 1st sale. S. 109 boxes made £142,187 | |
| | In bloodstone with diamonds, portraits of Louis XV by Mlle Brisson, 1760 | 7,800 |
| | With rhinoceros; lacquer, picqué and gold, by Roucel, 1768 | 4,600 |
| | Strawberry-enamel and diamonds, by Blerzy, 1775 | 2,900 |
| | Enamelled *en grisaille* on gold by Roger and de Gault, 1775 | 6,500 |
| | Oval box, 1795, numerous miniature scenes on gold | 3,000 |
| | Oval box, Venus and loves by Charlier, 1784 | 7,200 |
| | *Grisaille* enamels by Barrière, 1771 | 5,000 |

| | | £ |
|---|---|---|
| 1963 | Oblong box, enamel flowers, picked out on chased gold by Moynat, 1749 | 14,000 |
| | By Poitreau, Cameo reliefs after Teniers on chased gold | 7,800 |
| | S. In enamelled gold by Louis Gallois, 1767 | 5,550 |
| 1964 | Paris. By Drais with insert gouache paintings, FN100,000 +tax | 8,030 |
| 1965 | S. Gold lacquered mother of pearl, Paris, 1757 | 5,200 |
| | Gold, miniature enamel portrait by Tiron, 1768 | 2,800 |
| | Gold, with miniature, by Mothet, 1766 | 3,600 |
| | C. Enamelled on gold-mounted natural shells by Sageret, 1746 | 13,650 |
| 1966 | Vyner. C. Gold mounts, mother of pearl lacquer in Chinese style, by Hardivillers, 1787 | 2,735 |
| | Ward. C. Gold with enamelled portrait miniature by Louis Ray, 1776 | 2,100 |
| | S. Four-colour gold by Ducrollet, 1761 | 3,100 |
| | S. Enamelled with flowers on gold by Moynat, 1748 | 10,500 |
| | Another in similar technique, dated 1752 | 6,200 |
| | Smaller oval box in same style by Delobel, 1752 | 4,000 |
| 1967 | Alfred Pearson. S. By Croissant, 1744, with oval Vincennes porcelain plaques on green ground | 6,000 |
| | S. By Jean Frémin, 1756, gold and mother of pearl, Chinese astrologers (£1,800 in 1948) | 21,000 |
| | Astor. C. Oval portrait-box by Marguerite, 1815, miniature of Napoleon, Empress and Prince Imperial, by Menuisier | 4,620 |
| 1968 | C. By Barrière, Paris, 1768, oval, gold and enamel, 2¾ in. | 3,045 |
| | Prestige. S. In gold mounted Japanese lacquer by Ducrollay, 1750, 3 in. diam. | 5,200 |
| | Rendlesham. S. Gold and tortoiseshell oblong, 3¼ in. with French royal portraits, 1729, by Lemaire and Massé | 23,000 |
| | Another ditto by Govaers, 1726, with portraits of Louis XV and Marie Leczinska (valued at 4,440 livres or £202 in 1743) | 8,500 |
| | S. Gold and mother of pearl box, 3¼ in. by Antoine Filassier, 1746 | 11,000 |
| | Two-colour gold, Roman scenes in high relief by Gabriel Morel, c. 1800, 3½ in. | 5,000 |
| 1969 | Sheffield. C. Two-colour gold with mother of pearl inlays and portrait by Zincke, possibly by Joubert, 1744 | 16,800 |
| | Oval gold box with enamel picture by Blerzy, 1776, 3¼ in. | 5,250 |
| | C. Rectangular chased gold box, Tiron after Oudry, 1756 | 8,925 |
| | Fockema. C. Gold and *verre églomisé*, by Vachette after | |

£

1969   Domenichino and others, 1789, 4 in. oblong    6,090
      With staghunt, chased in gold on mother of pearl,
      *c.* 1730, cartouche form, 3¼ in. wide    2,730
      With cameo-portrait of Eugène de Beauharnais, cir-
      cular crystal and gold, 2½ in. diam., by Beltrami,
      *c.* 1815    2,625
1970   Hutchinson   S.   Chinoiserie in mother-of-pearl on gold
      by Jean Gaillard, 1745, 3¼ in. wide    15,000

### GERMANY, AUSTRIA, SWITZERLAND ETC.

1960   Weinmüller, Munich.   Chased gold box by Neuber of
      Dresden with *pietre dure* portrait of Gustavus Adolphus    1,280
      Dusendschon.   S.   With Meissen plaques and gold borders    1,700
1961   Blohm.   S.   By Helcher, Vienna, with du Paquier porce-
      lain plaques, *c.* 1750    1,000
      Chester Beatty.   S.   German box with landscape in gold
      and mother of pearl    5,500
1966   Berne.   By Neuber, Dresden, 1786, with 112 stones and
      descriptive tablet, FS40,000+tax    3,830
1967   Astor.   C.   Swiss musical automata snuffbox, 1815    4,410
1968   C.   Swiss oval box, gold and enamel, *c.* 1800    997 10s.
      Perkins.   S.   Swiss automaton box by Royard, *c.* 1820,
      3¾ in.    5,500
1969   Cromartie.   S.   Jewelled gold portrait-box, presented by
      King of Sweden to Marshal Count MacLeod in the 1760s,
      3 in. diam.   Believed Swedish    3,100
      Gavin Astor.   C.   Gold cagework on amethyst, Dresden,
      *c.* 1750    2,310
      Fockema.   C.   Russian oval box, enamelled on gold,
      made for Anna Pavlovna, sister of Alexander I, late 18th
      century    2,520
      C.   Viennese gold and diamond box with miniature por-
      trait of Franz Josef II, *c.* 1900, 4½ in. diam.    2,100
      S.   Mother of pearl on bloodstone, imitating *Shibayama*
      lacquer, Berlin, 3 in. diam.    3,300
      Austin.   S.   Oval box, composed of numerous hard stones
      with cornelian cameo in lid by Neuber, Dresden, *c.* 1770    5,600

# TAPESTRY
## LATE GOTHIC AND RENAISSANCE, BEFORE 1550

In common with other *objets d'art* of this period, such as Majolica and Limoges enamels, the rise in value of 15th–16th century tapestries in the 1960s was not on a level with their scarcity. In the first quarter of the century they had been very much to the taste of the richest men in the world. It can hardly be pretended that they are so today. The competition is mainly between museums and apparently not always lively. The Victoria and Albert Museum surely obtained their dated fragment of the year 1455 at a bargain price. A Tournai panel at £35,280 seemed to set a new price-scale at the Cornbury Park sale of 1967, yet it was not dear in terms of the heyday of this sort of collecting. The almost identical panel which was in the great Taylor sale of 1912, made the equivalent of £57,000 in 1967 money. So too, the Hamilton Rice Tournai panel from Knole, which fetched £15,140 in 1965, must have cost James Pierpont Morgan in 1911 the equivalent of at least £60,000. It had then formed part of a suite of eight which had reputedly cost him £67,100 in the money of the day. On Morgan's death in 1913 the suite was valued at £115,000 and it is probable that Widener got the Hamilton Rice panel on this basis, not £15,140 but £95,000 in 1965 money. A reference to Volume Two will show that Joseph Widener was capable of paying even more for some of Morgan's acquisitions from Knole.

|  |  |  | £ |
|---|---|---|---:|
| 1959 | S. | Brussels suite, *c.* 1530, Prudence in search of Divine Wisdom, each about 15×20 ft (one bought for Burrell Gallery Glasgow at £7,400) | 4 for 12,250 |
| 1960 | N.Y. | *Mille Fleurs* armorial panel, *c.* 1500, Tournai, $32,500, Metropolitan Museum | 11,607 |
|  |  | The Triumph of Knowledge, Tournai square panel, *c.* 1520, $16,000 | 5,715 |
| 1962 | S. | The Battle of Roncesvaux from a *Chanson de Roland* suite, fragment dated 1455, 85×74 in. Victoria and Albert Museum | 2,300 |
|  |  | Tournai panel, illustrating Book of Revelations, 1525 | 3,200 |
|  |  | Tournai *mille fleurs* panel, 10×9 ft, the Lady and the Falconer, *c.* 1510 | 2,200 |
| 1963 | Paris. | Single Brussels panel, early 16th century, FN75,000 +tax About | 6,000 |
|  | Lord Astor. C. | Part of the suite, Miracles of Our Lady of Sablons, Brussels, 1518 (Spitzer sale, 1893, £1,320) 3 for | 5,250 |
|  |  | Roland at Roncesvaux, upright panel, French, *c.* 1470 | 3,780 |
|  | Paris. | *Mille fleurs* panel, *c.* 1500–20, Princess and attendants, 8½×13 ft, FN140,000+tax | 11,200 |
|  | Bader. N.Y. | The Sibyls of Tibur and Delphi, Brussels, garden panel, *c.* 1530, 10 ft 8×13 ft | 3,567 |

| | | £ |
|---|---|---|
| 1964 | Weinmüller, Munich. The Court of Love, Burgundian panel dated 1527 | 4,960 |
| | Sold by French & Co., New York, four panels of moral allegories, Tournai, *c.* 1510 | 4 for 90,000 |
| | Finarte, Venice (ex Palazzo Labia). Suite of six, the Triumph of Scipio after Giulio Romano, made for Francis I. Brussels, *c.* 1530 | 6 for 22,000 |
| 1965 | Kent. S. *Le jardin privé*, Tournai panel with gold threads *c.* 1500, 10 ft × 13 (see 1966) | 6,000 |
| | Hamilton Rice. N.Y. Tournai panel depicting a tournament, *c.* 1520, 14 ft × 22; one of a suite of eight for which Pierpont Morgan paid £67,100 in 1911 (from Knole Park), $42,500 | 15,140 |
| 1966 | Lorimer. S. *Le chasse au faucon*, Tournai, *c.* 1500, 9½ × 12½ ft exceptional preservation | 8,000 |
| | S. *Le jardin privé* (see 1965), 10 × 13 ft | 7,000 |
| | J. de Rothschild. Paris. *Mille fleurs* panel, Oudenarde, *c.* 1530, 11 ft 4 × 13, FN50,000+tax | 3,972 |
| 1967 | Watney. C. (at Cornbury Park). *Riposo*, Tournai gold and silver thread panel, *c.* 1500, 7 ft 8 × 7 ft 3, said to be identical with the panel which made £2,800 in the Spitzer sale, 1893, and £8,190 in 1912) | 35,280 |
| | S. *Le jardin secret* Tournai, *c.* 1520, figures with inscriptions, 10 × 13 ft. (£2,440 in 1902) | 4,600 |
| | Paris. The Four Apostles, Tournai, *c.* 1500, FN47,000+tax | 4,460 |
| | Moorehead Patterson. N.Y. Court scene, numerous figures, Tournai, *c.* 1520, 10 ft 10 × 9 ft 8 | 2,232 |
| | N.Y. Altar-cloth, Resurrected Christ and Saints, 66 × 35 in., South German, late 15th century, $9,300 | 3,250 |
| | Adoration, Nuremberg Altar cloth, 15th century, 50 × 34 in., $4,700 | 1,678 |
| | Court scene, Tournai panel, 1500–20, 8 ft 9 × 17 ft 6, $7,000 | 2,928 |
| 1968 | Ogilvie. S. *Le cerf fragile*, Tournai hunting panel, *c.* 1520, 81 × 77 in. | 2,600 |
| 1969 | Paris. Tournai panel, attributed Jean Grenier, *c.* 1520, *l'arrivée de bonne compagnie*, FN110,000+tax | 10,250 |
| | En suite with the same, *le saccage du festin*, FN181,000+tax | About 17,000 |

## LATE RENAISSANCE, 1550–1660

There are no spectacular falls here from the triumphs of the past, because at no period during the hundred years or so in which tapestries were thought worth collecting has this singularly prolific age been popular. Rare oddities like the maps of the Sheldon weavers can be dear enough, but the very best Brussels panels of the early 17th century have made no more than £3,000 to £4,000. They will hardly have kept level with inflation since 1939. Designed by Flemish imitators of the Italian Mannerist style, they are at times dismally hideous—a virtue which will no doubt be discovered.

£

| | | |
|---|---|---|
| 1960 | Yorkshire Philosophical Society. S. Map of Warwickshire, 1647, woven at Sheldon, one of five bought by Horace Walpole in 1781 for 30 guineas (this panel made £1,010 in 1921). Victoria and Albert Museum | 6,000 |
| 1961 | C. Fontainebleau panel, c. 1600, the Bath of Diana after Toussaint Dubreuil, 12 × 20 ft, Victoria and Albert Museum | 1,522 |
| | Norwegian 17th century armorial tapestry | 1,470 |
| 1962 | C. Pair of Brussels panels, 11 × 16½ ft, Roman battle scenes, early 17th century      2 for | 1,785 |
| 1963 | S. Brussels panel, Story of Perseus, 13 ft 6 × 15 ft 4, mid-17th century | 1,800 |
| | Lord Astor. C. Enghien panel, c. 1550, fruit and flowers, 13½ × 15½ ft | 4,725 |
| | Two Flemish panels, same age      2 for | 2,730 |
| | N.Y. The feast of Esther, Brussels panel, c. 1650, 10½ × 15 ft | 1,428 |
| 1964 | Paris. Figures in a park, Brussels, c. 1620, 17 × 10 ft., FN40,000+tax | 3,213 |
| 1965 | S. Single Brussels panel from the history of Mark Anthony, c. 1640, 13¼ × 11¼ ft | 1,500 |
| | Two panels from the Barberini factory, Rome, c. 1635, both 15 ft 10 × 18 ft 7, Apollo and Daphne | 2,700 |
| | Latona and the frogs | 3,000 |
| | C. The Calvary, Brussels panel after Raphael, late 16th century, 6 ft × 4¾ ft, ex Balbi collection | 3,780 |
| | Oudenarde *verdure* panel, late 16th century, 8¾ × 10½ ft | 2,310 |
| | S. Santa Barbara (Spain) floral panel, mid 17th century | 2,600 |
| 1966 | Brussels. Marriage procession, Brussels, c. 1600, FB700,000 +tax      About | 6,000 |
| 1967 | S. Hunting suite, Brussels, c. 1630, by Frans Raes, each 12¾ × 11¾ ft      4 for | 4,250 |
| | Late 16th century Florentine *groettsche* panel, 11 ft 4 × 10 ft 6 | 2,400 |
| | C. Daniel and Nebuchadnezzar's envoy, Brussels panel, mid 16th century, after a lost Raphael cartoon of 1504, 10 ft 6 × 13 ft. | 2,520 |
| | Watney. C. (at Cornbury Park). Brussels hunting suite, early 17th century, 11½ ft high, various lengths      4 for | 3,780 |

£

| | | £ |
|---|---|---|
| 1967 | C. Brussels *verdure* panel, 9½ × 14 ft mid 16th century | 1,995 |
| | Eckman. S. Dutch panel, the woman taken in adultery, medallion composition, 8 ft 10 × 6 ft 7, after 1600 | 2,700 |
| | N.Y. Brussels arabesque tapestry, *c.* 1600, 10 ft × 12 ft 4 | 2,225 |
| | Paris. Aubusson armorial tapestry, *c.* 1650, 10 ft 11 × 10 ft 6 | 2,275 |
| | Henri IV (Paris) panel, *c.* 1600, bear hunt, 128 × 124 in., FN38,000+tax | 3,532 |
| 1968 | Ogilvy. S. Felletin marriage panel, *c.* 1600, 8 ft 11 × 8 ft 8 | 2,000 |
| | S. Siege of a city, Brussels, *c.* 1600, 11 ft 1 × 14 ft 10 | 2,200 |
| | Armorial panel, very rich, signed Albert Auverox, late 17th century, 10 ft 5 × 8 ft 6 | 2,700 |
| | Iveagh. C. (at Pyrford Court). Story of Scipio and Hannibal by Leefdael and Stricker, Brussels, *c.* 1650, various sizes 3 for | 8,925 |
| | Colville Barclay. S. Three panels from a hunting suite by Cornelius Tseraets, *c.* 1600, 11 ft 4 high, separate lots 3 for | 6,900 |
| | S. Brussels suite of eight, Story of Cyrus by Willem Segers, late 16th century, various sizes but mostly about 14 ft high, separate lots, 8 for | 11,600 |
| | Foerderer. N.Y. Scandinavian panel, *c.* 1600, scenes in life of John the Baptist, 9 ft 5 × 6 ft 10, $10,500 | 4,333 |
| 1969 | Greenwich Foundation, Connecticut. Suite of 8 hunting-panels, Brussels, style of Jan Raes, early 17th century. Mostly about 11 ft high, 15 ft wide 8 for | 8,925 |
| | S. Brussels panel with battle scene from the Story of Hannibal, 11 ft 3 × 17, towards 1600 | 4,200 |
| | Maxwell Joseph. S. Months of the year, set of 5 Mortlake panels, mid 17th century, each about 11 ft × 7 ft 6, 5 for | 5,800 |

## LOUIS XIV TO LOUIS XVI
### (after 1660)

ɪn what may be called the Pierpont Morgan age the alternative to a gold-thread Tournai tapestry of the beginning of the 16th century was a silk Beauvais tapestry, woven after the designs of Boucher in the reign of Louis XV. No other tapestries were in quite such an exalted class. In the 1960s several of these favourites of the early 20th century returned to the saleroom, and in 1963 there was that rarest of events, the sale of an entire suite of eight—but at the not very remarkable price of £36,780. It was therefore a considerable advance in 1968 when Boucher's *toilet of Psyche*, one of a particularly luscious series, made £18,900 at the Pyrford Court sale. Yet five panels from the series had cost Mrs Hamilton Rice at the end of the First World War no less than $750,000 or £154,300 at the normal rate of exchange before the fall of the pound. In the money of 1968 it meant £689,400 or £137,900 for a single panel. It may be argued that this was a purchase from Duveen by a daughter of Joseph Widener, whose grandiose scale of collecting was far above the market. But was that altogether true? At the Polovtseff sale in Paris in 1909 a single panel from Boucher's *loves of the Gods* made 435,000 francs in an open bid, the equivalent with 10 per cent tax of £19,140. Since this was pre-1914 money, the price has to be multiplied by 7·6 to get the 1968 equivalent, which is nearly £146,000 for a single panel.

However, the alleged return of the French 18th century tapestry market is based on something more striking, the sale at Sothebys in 1967 of four Gobelin panels from a Don Quixote suite after Charles Coypel for £200,000. On paper this was an absolutely unprecedented price, and it was paid for a former Austrian imperial possession in incredibly fine preservation. Yet even this does not stand up to the sales of the past. The Don Quixote suite, consisting originally of 28 episodes, was re-issued with modifications several times during the 18th century. The panels, sold in 1967, came from the last and finest edition, redesigned early in the reign of Louis XVI on specially rich backgrounds for presenting to fellow-monarchs. Four panels belonging to the King of Spain, were bought by Duveen in 1910 for £64,000 and sold to Pierpont Morgan for £80,000. The latter was almost certainly the price at which they were taken over by Messrs French after Morgan's death (see Volume Two, pp. 180–1). The equivalent in 1967 money would be £580,000 for four panels, which may not have been as fine as the four which Sothebys sold for £200,000.

|      |                                                                                                                   | £            |
|------|-------------------------------------------------------------------------------------------------------------------|--------------|
| 1960 | C.  Gobelins panel, *c.* 1720, after Teniers                                                                        | 2,205        |
| 1961 | S.  Beauvais panel, Boucher style, nearly 16 ft long, The Polish village                                           | 3,000        |
|      | Hambro.  S. (at Linton Park).  Lille panel, *c.* 1700, 17 ft long                                                  | 2,100        |
|      | The Arts of War, Gobelins panel after Audran, *c.* 1730                                                             | 5,370        |
| 1962 | Lady Bailey.  S.  Two Gobelins panels after Audran, the Loves of the Gods, Gobelins, *c.* 1700                     | 1,450 and 1,750 |
|      | C.  Brussels panel, the Fish Quay after Teniers, *c.* 1700 (£378 in 1952)                                          | 2,100        |
|      | Paris.  Two Don Quixote panels *en medaillon*, the 1771–3 series, altered from Audran's designs after Coypel (see 1967) | 2 for 7,125 |
|      | Paris.  Two panels about 10½ ft square, Gobelins, from *les Metamorphoses*, FN48,000+tax                            | 2 for 4,160 |
| 1963 | Paris.  *Le concert du Sultan* from *la Tenture chinoise* after Boucher, Beauvais, 9½ ft × 18 ft, FN48,000+tax    | 4,160        |

£

1963  Fitzgerald.  S.  The Maypole dancers, Brussels, *c.* 1720   1,150
Paris.  Beauvais suite.  *La Tenture chinoise*, Besnier and
Oudry after Boucher (single panel, 1911, £5,680)  8 for  36,780
Fribourg.  S.  The worship of Demeter, Gobelins, from
Triumphs of the Gods after Joseph Vien, 10 ft × 10 ft 4,
bought by Rijksmuseum, Amsterdam  2,100
*Concert champêtre* after Oudry, Beauvais, Louis XV,  10 ×
13 ft  2,900
S.  The Tamers by Behagle after Jules Berain, from *les*
*Grotesques chinoises*, Beauvais, *c.* 1710, 10 ft × 15½ ft  3,700
C.  Neptune and Diana, 2 Gobelins panels after Claude
Audran, 1699, 11 ft 8 × 8 ft 8  2 for  3,780
1964  Paris.  Napoleon crossing the St Bernard after David,
Gobelins, 1810, 8 ft × 7 ft 8 in.  2,000
C.  Audience with the Emperor from *les tentures chinoises*,
Beauvais after 1742 (in 1959 four panels made £21,400)  3,675
Finarte, Venice.  Three panels from *les tentures chinoises*,
Gobelins, by Behagle, 1711–34, ex. Palazzo Labia,
3 for about  16,000
S.  Soho Chinoiserie panel by Vanderbanck, 1720  1,800
1965  C.  Single panel, 10½ ft × 9¼ from *les grotesques italiennes*,
Behagle after Berain, Beauvais, *c.* 1700  3,360
Stephens.  C.  6-fold screen, Savonnerie tapestry  3,200
Paris.  A second screen of the same type, both Louis XV  11,095
S.  Daphnis and Chloe, four panels woven at Gobelins for
the Regent Duke of Orleans, *c.* 1720, 10 ft 7 × 8 ft 7  4 for  16,000
Hamilton Rice.  N.Y.  Beauvais panel, *c.* 1740, two
nymphs supporting the royal arms of France, 11 ft 4 ×
14 ft 8  12,500
Europa and the bull, Brussels, *c.* 1700, 10 ft 9 × 16 ft 7  3,212
Soho arabesque panel by Joshua Morris, *c.* 1730,
8 ft 10 × 15 ft 3,  Metropolitan Museum  5,357
Gobelins panel, Diana and attributes, 10 ft 5 × 7 ft, 1730  2,607
1966  Mrs Gaby Salomon.  S.  Beauvais panel after Huet, the
Farmer's Wife from *les pastorales à draperie rouge* by Menou,
*c.* 1780, 8 ft 7 × 11 ft 1  3,800
Paris.  Set of four Chinoiserie panels after Boucher,
Aubusson, late 18th century, FN170,000+tax  4 for  13,651
Sanchez-Elia.  S.  *Le cheval fendu* from the suite, *les*
*amusements champêtres* after Oudry, dated Beauvais 1730,
11 ft 4 × 12 ft 6 (in 1928 a set of four was sold for £22,400)  4,600
J. de Rothschild.  Paris.  Single panel from *la tenture*
*chinoise* by Veransal and others, Beauvais, *c.* 1740, 11 ft 8 ×
13 ft 8, FN70,000+tax  5,625

| | | | £ |
|---|---|---|---|
| 1966 | Paris. Three panels from the Metamorphoses of the Gods, Behagle after Berain, Beauvais, *c.* 1750, each about 10½× 8½ ft, FN142,000+tax | 3 for | 11,250 |
| | N.Y. Single Aubusson panel with *Comedia* figures, 1725, 10 ft 10×7 ft 3, $8,500 | | 3,040 |
| 1967 | Watney. C. (at Cornbury Park). Beauvais panel, Behagle after Teniers, peasants bowling, *c.* 1690, 8 ft 6× 9 ft 4 | | 2,730 |
| | Bonde. C. Diana and attendants, Gobelins panel before 1750, 9½×13½ ft | | 3,150 |
| | S. Four panels from the Don Quixote suite, altered from the designs of Charles Coypel by Audran and Cozette, Gobelins, 1771–3 (compare 1962), ex Austrian imperial household, each about 12×15 ft | 4 for | 200,000 |
| | N.Y. Narrow panel, 9 ft×5 ft 2, from *La Comédie Italienne* Philippe Behagle, Beauvais, *c.* 1700, $6,000 | | 2,140 |
| | Cut-down panel, the flute lesson from *la Noble Pastorale* after Boucher (complete panel, 1927, £11,200), $8,000 | | 2,768 |
| | Harth. Paris. Africa, from the Four Continents by van der Borght, Brussels, *c.* 1720, 122×124 in., FN57,000+tax | | 5,325 |
| 1968 | Paris. Rinaldo and Armida, Gobelins panel after Louis de Boulogne, 10 ft×7, FN48,500+tax | | 4,527 |
| | Iveagh. C. (at Pyrford Court). The toilet of Psyche from the Story of Psyche, suite by Oudry and Besnier after Boucher, Beauvais, 1741, 9 ft×13 ft 5 (in 1919, Mrs Hamilton Rice paid $750,000 for a set of 5. In 1925 a much restored version of the present panel made £8,300) | | 18,900 |
| | The battle of Solebay, suite of three Mortlake panels by Francis Poyntz, late 17th century, arms of Walpole | 3 for | 13,650 |
| | Headfort. C. Aubusson garden suite, various widths, height 9 ft 9, arms of Taylour, *c.* 1750 | 5 for | 12,600 |
| | Ruef. Munich. Repose of Diana, Brussels, by V. Legniers, *c.* 1720, 140×200 in., DM71,000+tax | | 9,300 |
| 1969 | C. Pair of Lille panels, Guillaume Werniers after Teniers, early 18th century, 13×16 ft and 12×13 ft 8 | 2 for | 6,500 |
| | S. *Rétour des chasses de Diane*, Gobelins panel by de la Fosse and de la Fraye, *c.* 1720, 9½×12½ ft | | 5,200 |
| | de Viron. C. Jaguar attacking zebra from the *Nouvelles Indes* suite, Neilson after Desportes, *c.* 1760, Gobelins, 11½×13½ ft | | 3,360 |
| | C. Louis XIV and court at St Germain from the Gobelins suite, Months of the Royal Residences, Lefebvre after Lebrun, late 17th century, 10 ft by 13 | | 2,730 |

1969  Fitzwilliams.  S.  The history of Cyrus, Brussels suite of £
four, woven by the van der Borghts for Maria Theresa,
1730–40, condition exceptional, 13 ft 6 high        4 for  12,700
   The dearest, the Emancipation of the Jews by Cyrus,
   was bought by the Victoria and Albert Museum for        3,600
S.  Soho panel in 'Indian' style probably by Vanderbank,
c. 1715, 7 ft 10 × 13 ft 9                                 8,000
Norris.  S.  Brussels panel, early 18th century, the
Triumph of Diana, 10 ft 5 × 16 ft 9                       2,800
Lord Waleran.  C.  Pair of Soho panels by John Vander-
bank, after Teniers, 8 ft × 7 ft 5 and 8 ft 6 × 11 ft 10    2 for 3,045

# WATCHES

(including those in snuff-box and other fanciful mountings)

| | | | £ | |
|---|---|---|---|---|
| 1959 | C. | Swiss pistol scent-spray watch in gold and enamels, 4¼ in. long (see also, 1966) | 1,207 | 10s. |
| 1960 | C. | Gold and enamel case by Tompion, end 17th century, numbered 2982 | 756 | |
| | | Enamel-cased, by Berronneau, c. 1690 | 399 | |
| | | Quarter-repeating enamel cased verge by Thuret | 430 | 10s. |
| 1961 | C. | Swiss oval enamelled gold snuffbox watch, c. 1770 | 1,207 | 10s. |
| | | Swiss gold musical verge watch | 525 | |
| | | Wheeler. S. Swiss gold and jewelled heart-shaped watch, c. 1820 | 2,000 | |
| | | Swiss quarter-repeater, shaped and enamelled as a rose | 800 | |
| | | English verge watch by Fromenteel, picture enamel case, late 17th century | 700 | |
| 1962 | C. | Verge watch, gold and enamel case, by Huaud frères | 714 | |
| | | Swiss quarter-repeating watch with automata | 1,522 | 10s. |
| | | Astronomical carriage verge watch, Samuel Michelin, Langres, c. 1680 | 756 | |
| | | Timex. S. Singing-bird musical box watch by Jacob Frisard | 3,000 | |
| | | S. Swiss gold and enamelled automaton snuffbox watch | 2,000 | |
| 1963 | | Chester Beatty. S. Elaborate gold and enamelled watch and châtelaine, John Scott, London, 1820 (see 1968) | 1,250 | |
| | | Quarter-repeating cylinder watch, George Graham, 1733, elaborately chased gold case | 540 | |
| | | Flat cylinder watch, portrait miniature, Barrauds, Cornhill | 560 | |
| 1964 | | Inchbald. S. French verge watch, Théodore Girard, 1830 | 880 | |
| | | Kalish. S. With diamond-shaped hard stone case by Ilbery, London, said to have been ordered in China | 1,250 | |
| | | Bruce Ingram. S. Gold case with enamelled barking dog | 750 | |
| | | S. Gold case with diamonds and châtelaine by Abraham Colomby | 880 | |
| | | Automaton watch, set in gold and enamel telescope, length unextended, 3½ in. | 2,000 | |
| | C. | Swiss gold and enamel musical box watch, c. 1800, 3½ in. wide | 1,207 | |
| 1965 | | S. 17th century picture enamel by Henry Grendon, London | 900 | |
| | | 17th century square gold and enamelled watch by Paul Bizot, St Germain | 1,850 | |
| | | Turkish astrolabe watch, made at Galata, c. 1740 | 1,100 | |

| | | £ |
|---|---|---|
| 1965 | C. Swiss gold and enamelled watch with kitchen scene automata | |
| | | 1,470 |
| 1966 | Montgomery. C. Musical watch with automata | 892 |
| | C. Gold and enamelled pistol scent-sprayer watch (see 1959) | |
| | | 2,205 |
| | S. Gold and enamelled quarter-repeater by Piguet and Meyland, Geneva | |
| | | 2,000 |
| 1967 | C. Gold enamelled verge by Maupas, Blois, before 1650 | 725 |
| | Craven. C. 17th century verge calendar watch | 714 |
| | Dubois. C. Swiss gold enamel repeater in shape of mandolin, 5 in. long | |
| | | 1,417 |
| | Agate table-watch, urn shaped case, $3\frac{3}{4}$ in. | 840 |
| | Gold enamelled verge watch and châtelaine by Grignion, London, paintings by Huaud Frères, c. 1725–50 | |
| | | 1,260 |
| | S. In shape of perfume flask, $4\frac{1}{2}$ in. high, gold and enamel, c. 1780 | |
| | | 3,000 |
| | S. Automaton repeater gold case, c. 1840 | 520 |
| | Hubbard. S. Plain lever watch, Robert Pendleton, London, 1797, no. 175 | |
| | | 1,300 |
| | de Kay. N.Y. In giltbronze pierced and engraved case by Pierre Norry, Gisors, 1645, 5 in. diam., $5,000 | |
| | | 1,785 |
| 1968 | S. Gold and enamelled trefoil-shaped case with automata, $1\frac{2}{3}$ in. diam., c. 1820 | |
| | | 2,600 |
| | Gem-set gold watch and châtelaine by Arned, London | 1,600 |
| | Gold and agate watch and châtelaine, David Hubert, London, c. 1720 | |
| | | 980 |
| | Gold case, enamelled on back, shaped as a peony, c. 1770, $2\frac{3}{4}$ in. | |
| | | 880 |
| | Enamelled snuff-box watch in form of a butterfly, with musical box in base, nearly 3 in. wide | |
| | | 1,050 |
| | Another, closely similar | 1,500 |
| | Verge watch and châtelaine, highly enamelled, John Scott, 1820 | |
| | | 920 |
| | Chester Beatty. S. Quarter repeating verge by Thomas Tompion, numbered 144 and dated 1697, $2\frac{1}{8}$ in. diam. | |
| | | 4,400 |
| | Silver-cased chaise-watch by Peder Nottestad, Kristiania, late 18th century $4\frac{1}{8}$ in. diam. | |
| | | 950 |
| | Evans. C. Swiss lyre-shaped watch with automata, 3 in. | 2,520 |
| | S. Dutch 'stackfreed' clock-watch, c. 1570, $3\frac{1}{4}$ in. diam. giltmetal case | |
| | | 900 |
| | Combined watch and powder horn, antler shaped, heavily chased after Jan Stradanus, late 16th century, height 8 in. | |
| | | 6,200 |

| | | £. |
|---|---|---|
| 1968 | Prestige. S. Plain lever watch by Josiah Emery, no. 939, 1792 | 2,100 |
| 1969 | Winthrop Edey. S. Stackfreed clockwatch-alarum by Michael Bumel of Nuremberg, early 17th century, 2⅞ in. diam. | 2,100 |
| | Verge watch no. 902 by Broekhuysen, 1735, with enamel miniature of 'charity', 2¼ in. | 1,900 |
| | With matching fob in relief, enamels by Baillon, Paris, towards 1840, 5¼ in. overall, numbered 972 | 1,700 |
| | Baring. S. Crystal-cased verge watch by Estienne Hubert, Rouen, 1⅜ in. diam., c. 1520 | 1,300 |
| | C. Gold and enamel in shape of mandolin with royal portraits, Louis XVI | 1,417 10s. |
| | Enamelled on gold in shape of a rose, 5 in. long | 819 |
| | Melvin Gutman. N.Y. Lozenge-shaped, landscape-enamelled dial, by Michel Cuper, Blois, before 1634, 2¾ in. diam., $10,000 | 4,168 |
| | S. Gold hunting-cased free-sprung keyless lever tourbillon, Northern Goldsmiths' Co., 1919 | 1,600 |
| | Gold enamelled verge by Boisaumoyne, Paris, c. 1750, enamel pictures on case, face and both sides of lid, 2½ in. | 4,200 |
| | Fockema. C. Compass watch, set in scent-flask encased in gold by James Cox, c. 1760, 5 in. high | 1,995 |
| | C. Gold and agate cased duplex by Ilbery, early 19th century, 4½ in. | 6,050 |
| | Gold and enamel musical watch-key, 19th century, 1¼ in. diam. (Farouk sale, Cairo, 1954, £500) | 4,400 |
| | S. Gold pair-cased with châtelaine, elaborately chased, George Graham, no. 5838, 1738–9 | 1,650 |
| | Dumb quarter-repeating chronometer, plain gold, by Louis Berthoud, no. 2521, Paris, c. 1790 | 3,600 |
| | Gold verge with automaton procession of figures, c. 1820 | 2,300 |
| | 'Bras en l'air' with coloured gold statuette, Robert and Courvoisier, c. 1800, 2¼ in. | 4,200 |
| | Pair-cased repeating cylinder, Ellicott, London, no.5685, 1782, with enamelled conversation-piece, 2 in. diam. | 2,100 |
| | Centre-seconds duplex watch, enamelled miniature, the Blind Homer, set with pearls, by Ilbery, no. 1774, c. 1820 | 6,500 |
| | Musical automaton with miniature enamelled on gold, perhaps by Piguet et Meylan, Geneva, c. 1820 | 4,400 |
| | Gold and agate-cased duplex in form of a seal by Ilbery, no. 6139, early 19th century | 2,050 |

### BY ABRAHAM LOUIS BREGUET, 1747–1823
Mainly plain silver

| | | £ |
|---|---|---:|
| 1959 | C. Tourbillon repeater, no. 2555 | 546 |
| 1960 | C. Blind man's watch, cylinder escapements and parachute | 357 |
| 1961 | C. Quarter repeater | 441 |
| 1962 | S. Pocket chronometer, no. 374 | 2,200 |
| | *Montre à tact*, no. 960, 1798 | 1,050 |
| | Percival David. S. Gold, pedometer-movement, no. 164 | 2,400 |
| | Hill. S. Mouvement perpetuelle, no. 5, 1791 | 2,100 |
| 1963 | Prestige. S. No. 2522, pocket chronometer, independent centre seconds dial | 4,600 |
| | Dumb minute-repeating pedometer watch, no. 28 (£182 in 1791) | 3,400 |
| | Quarter-repeating self winding lever watch, no. 217 with devices for equation of time, 1791 | 8,500 |
| | Self winding *montre à tact*, no. 4548 (£305, paid by George IV in 1827) | 3,100 |
| 1964 | Duke of Wellington. S. No. 1226, double dial, with time equation (1807, £235; 1816, £208) | 27,500 |
| | Inchbald. S. *Montre à tact*, no. 887, gold and enamel | 1,050 |
| | Double cased, no 3008, 1817 | 1,000 |
| 1965 | Sir David Salomons. C. (102 Breguet watches, £79,342) | |
| | Movement perpetuelle, 1792, no. 64 | 8,925 |
| | Repeater, no. 3917 (£250 in 1803) | 2,415 |
| | Tourbillon regulator, no. 2520 (£95 in 1818) | 3,675 |
| | Perpetuelle, no. 574, 1807 (£185 in 1807) | 2,100 |
| | *Montre souscription-equation*, no. 444 | 2,310 |
| | Tourbillon regulator, no. 2568, 1818 | 6,510 |
| 1966 | C. *Montre à grande sonnerie*, no. 4270 (£140 in 1825) | 997 |
| 1967 | Quill. C. Tourbillon regulator, no. 3204 (£120 in 1822) | 3,570 |
| 1968 | C. Gold and enamel *montre à tact*, no. 1099 | 787 |
| | S. Gold cased quarter repeater, no. 164, 1797 | 6,900 |
| 1969 | S. Tourbillon regulator, no. 2569, 1812 (Fr.1,700=£75) | 2,100 |